MW00993316

AMERICAN HISTORY

To start, download the free BouncePages app on your smartphone or tablet. Simply search for the BouncePages app in your mobile app store. The app is available for Android and IOS (iPhone®/iPad®).

Activate your digital course videos directly from the page.

To launch the videos look for this icon.

1. AIM the camera so that the page is easily viewable on your screen.
2. TAP the screen to scan the page.
3. BOUNCE the page to life by clicking the Bounce icon.

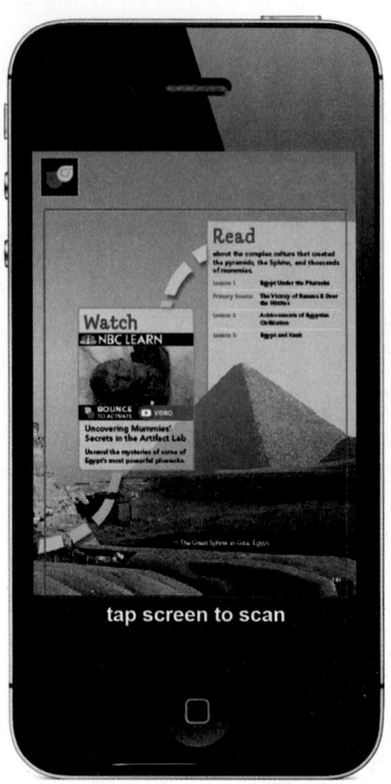

Savvas Learning Company LLC, 15 East Midland Avenue, Paramus, NJ 07652

Cover: Thomas Jefferson Memorial - DEA/G. MERMET/Getty Images

Attributions of third party content appear on pages 1149–1154, which constitute an extension of this copyright page.

ISBN-13: 978-0-32-896022-4
ISBN-10: 0-32-896022-5
13 23

AUTHORS

Program Authors

James West Davidson

Dr. James Davidson is coauthor of *After the Fact: The Art of Historical Detection* and *Nation of Nations: A Narrative History of the American Republic*. Dr. Davidson has taught at both the college and high school levels. He has also consulted on curriculum design for American history courses. Dr. Davidson is an avid canoeist and hiker. His published works on these subjects include *Great Heart*, the true story of a 1903 canoe trip in the Canadian wilderness.

Michael B. Stoff

Dr. Michael Stoff received his Ph.D. from Yale University and teaches history at the University of Texas at Austin. He is the author of *Oil, War, and American Security: The Search for a National Policy on Foreign Oil, 1941–1947*, coauthor of *Nation of Nations: A Narrative History of the American Republic*, and coeditor of the *Manhattan Project: A Documentary Introduction to the Atomic Age*. Dr. Stoff has won numerous grants, fellowships, and teaching awards.

Contributing Author

Jennifer L. Bertolet

Jennifer Bertolet is a Professional Lecturer at George Washington University where she teaches American History courses, among them Introduction to American History. She received her Ph.D. from George Washington University. In addition to teaching, she has served as an education consultant, a subject matter expert for online teaching and learning, and as a historian and policy consultant specializing in Indian policy and environmental issues.

TEACHER REVIEWERS

Ruth Castro
Inglewood USD
Inglewood, California

Colleen Eccles
Instructional Coach and PDLT
Samuel Ogle Middle School
Bowie, Maryland

Piper Hudmon
Content Specialist/Secondary Social Studies
Muscogee County School District
Columbus, Georgia

Dana L. Roberts, Ed. S
Academic Coach and Gifted Lead Coordinator
Lindley Middle School
Mableton, Georgia

Anthony Zambelli
San Diego Center for Economic Education
San Diego, California

PROGRAM CONSULTANTS

ELL Consultant
Jim Cummins Ph.D.
Professor Emeritus, Department of Curriculum, Teaching, and Learning
University of Toronto
Toronto, Canada

Differentiated Instruction Consultant
Marianne Sender
In-Class Resource Teacher
Renaissance @ Rand Middle School
Montclair, New Jersey

Reading Consultant
Elfrieda H. Hiebert Ph.D.
Founder, President and CEO of TextProject, Inc.
University of California, Santa Cruz

Inquiry and C3 Consultant
Dr. Kathy Swan
Professor of Curriculum and Instruction
University of Kentucky
Lexington, Kentucky

PROGRAM PARTNERS

NBC Learn, the educational arm of NBC News, develops original stories for use in the classroom and makes archival NBC news stories, images, and primary source documents available on demand to teachers, students, and parents. NBC Learn partnered with Savvas to produce the topic opening videos that support this program.

Campaign for the Civic Mission of Schools is a coalition of over 70 national civic learning, education, civic engagement, and business groups committed to improving the quality and quantity of civic learning in American schools.

Constitutional Rights Foundation is a nonprofit, nonpartisan, community-based organization focused on educating students about the importance of civic participation in a democratic society. The Constitutional Rights Foundation is the lead contributor to the development of the Civic Discussion Quests for this program.

CONTENTS

TOPIC 1
The Early Americas and European Exploration (Prehistory–1700)

TOPIC 2
European Colonization of North America (1500–1750)

TOPIC 3
The Revolutionary Era (1750–1783)

TOPIC 4
A Constitution for the United States (1776–Present)

CONTENTS

TOPIC 5
The Early Republic (1789–1825)

ACCESS MORE ONLINE
videos, audio, etext, interactivities, games, worksheets, and more!

TOPIC 6
The Age of Jackson and Westward Expansion (1824–1860)

TOPIC 7
Society and Culture Before the Civil War (1820–1860)

CONTENTS

TOPIC 8
Sectionalism and Civil War (1820–1865)

ACCESS MORE ONLINE
videos, audio, etext, interactivities, games, worksheets, and more!

TOPIC 9
The Reconstruction Era (1865–1877)

TOPIC 10
Industrial and Economic Growth (1865–1914)

TOPIC 11
The Progressive Era (1865–1920)

TOPIC 12
Imperialism and World War I (1853–1919)

TOPIC 13
Prosperity and Depression (1919–1939)

CONTENTS

TOPIC 14
World War II (1935–1945)

TOPIC 15
Postwar America (1945–1975)

TOPIC 16
A Global Superpower Facing Change
(1975–2000)

TOPIC 17
Meeting New Challenges (1975–Present)

CONTENTS

DIGITAL RESOURCES

Core Concepts

These digital lessons introduce key concepts for all of the social sciences and personal finance.

Culture
Economics
Geography
Government and Civics
History
Personal Finance

Landmark Supreme Court Cases

How has the Supreme Court interpreted the law of the land? Find out in these online multimedia lessons.

TOPIC 5
Lesson 4 *Marbury* v. *Madison*
Lesson 6 *McCulloch* v. *Maryland*
Lesson 6 *Gibbons* v. *Ogden*

TOPIC 6
Lesson 3 *Worcester* v. *Georgia*

TOPIC 8
Lesson 2 *Dred Scott* v. *Sandford*

TOPIC 9
Lesson 4 *Plessy* v. *Ferguson*

TOPIC 12
Lesson 5 *Schenck* v. *United States*

TOPIC 14
Lesson 3 *Korematsu* v. *United States*

TOPIC 15
Lesson 4 *Brown* v. *Board of Education*

TOPIC 17
Lesson 5 *National Federation* v. *Sebelius*

Topic Videos NBC LEARN

Begin each topic with a front seat view of history.

TOPIC 1
Austin Celebrates His Heritage

TOPIC 2
John Smith, Jamestown and the Roots of America

TOPIC 3
Benjamin Franklin and the Fight for Independence

TOPIC 4
James Madison, The Federalist Papers

TOPIC 5
William Clark, Mapping the American Frontier

TOPIC 6
Narcissa Whitman and the Journey West

TOPIC 7
Lucy Larcom, Weaving Opportunity

TOPIC 8
Robert E. Lee, The Marble Man

TOPIC 9
Born into Slavery

TOPIC 10
The McCormicks, Strike and Violence in Chicago

TOPIC 11
Max Marcus's Lower East Side

TOPIC 12
Theodore Roosevelt Pushes for Expansion

TOPIC 13
Billie Holiday, Lady Day

TOPIC 14
A Liberation Encounter

TOPIC 15
Minnijean Brown-Trickey, A Sojourn to the Past

TOPIC 16
Irene Zoppi, Gulf War Veteran

TOPIC 17
Steve Jobs, Innovation for a New Generation

Lesson Videos

Preview key ideas from the lesson in these videos.

TOPIC 1
Lesson 1 Maya and Aztec Civilizations
Lesson 2 Native American Culture Regions of North America
Lesson 3 New Technologies and Exploration
Lesson 4 The Columbian Exchange

TOPIC 2
Lesson 1 Northern Borderlands of New Spain
Lesson 2 France, the Netherlands and the Fur Trade
Lesson 3 Religious Freedom in New England
Lesson 4 The Middle Colonies
Lesson 5 The Southern Colonies
Lesson 6 Colonial Cultural Achievements
Lesson 7 Colonial Government

TOPIC 3
Lesson 1 Causes and Results of the French and Indian War
Lesson 2 Taxation and Mercantilism
Lesson 3 The Boston Tea Party
Lesson 4 The Declaration of Independence
Lesson 5 Winning Independence

TOPIC 4
Lesson 1 The Articles of Confederation
Lesson 2 The Constitutional Convention
Lesson 3 Roman and Enlightenment Influences on the Constitution
Lesson 4 The Bill of Rights
Lesson 5 The Three Branches of Government
Lesson 6 Amending the Constitution
Lesson 7 Responsibilities of Citizenship

TOPIC 5
Lesson 1 Securing the New Government
Lesson 2 The Origin of Political Parties
Lesson 3 John Adams's Presidency
Lesson 4 Jefferson's Presidency
Lesson 5 The War of 1812
Lesson 6 Strength After the War

TOPIC 6
Lesson 1 Jackson as President
Lesson 2 North vs South in the Age of Jackson
Lesson 3 The Trail of Tears
Lesson 4 The Journey West
Lesson 5 Why Oregon Country?
Lesson 6 The Mexican-American War
Lesson 7 Manifest Destiny

TOPIC 7
Lesson 1 The Spread of Industrialization
Lesson 2 Cotton Shapes the South
Lesson 3 The Second Great Revival
Lesson 4 Abolitionism
Lesson 5 The Seneca Falls Convention
Lesson 6 American Artists, American Themes

TOPIC 8
Lesson 1 Compromise
Lesson 2 Bleeding Kansas
Lesson 3 Southern States React
Lesson 4 Strategies for War
Lesson 5 The Emancipation Proclamation
Lesson 6 The Civil War Ends

TOPIC 9
Lesson 1 Lincoln's Reconstruction Plan
Lesson 2 Radical Reconstruction
Lesson 3 New Forces in Southern Politics
Lesson 4 Reconstruction Ends

TOPIC 10
Lesson 1 Mining, Expansion and Growth
Lesson 2 The Cattle Boom and the Homestead Act
Lesson 3 A Way of Life Ends
Lesson 4 Big Business
Lesson 5 The Labor Movement
Lesson 6 A Surge of Invention

TOPIC 11
Lesson 1 An Immigrant Story
Lesson 2 Life in Cities
Lesson 3 Rise of the Progressive Movement
Lesson 4 Progressives in the White House
Lesson 5 Victories and Setbacks
Lesson 6 Entertainment and the Arts

TOPIC 12
Lesson 1 Expansion in the Pacific
Lesson 2 The Spanish-American War
Lesson 3 The "Big Stick" in Latin America
Lesson 4 The Causes of World War I
Lesson 5 The U.S. Enters the War
Lesson 6 The Tide Turns
Lesson 7 Before and After: Europe Before and After World War I

TOPIC 13
Lesson 1 Calvin Coolidge's Presidency
Lesson 2 New Ways of Life

Interactive Primary Sources

Go to the original sources to hear voices from the time.

Biographies

Read about the people who made history.

TOPIC 3
Lesson 2 King George III
Lesson 2 Abigail Adams
Lesson 2 John Adams
Lesson 2 Samuel Adams
Lesson 2 Mercy Otis Warren
Lesson 2 Patrick Henry
Lesson 2 George Washington
Lesson 2 Crispus Attucks
Lesson 3 Thomas Jefferson
Lesson 4 Patrick Henry
Lesson 4 Benjamin Franklin
Lesson 5 Haym Salomon
Lesson 5 Marquis de Lafayette
Lesson 5 Wentworth Cheswell
Lesson 5 Bernardo de Galvez

TOPIC 4
Lesson 2 Gouverneur Morris
Lesson 2 James Wilson
Lesson 4 Alexander Hamilton
Lesson 4 James Madison
Lesson 4 George Mason

TOPIC 5
Lesson 1 Alexander Hamilton
Lesson 3 John Marshall
Lesson 5 Henry Clay
Lesson 6 James Monroe
Lesson 6 Daniel Webster

TOPIC 6
Lesson 1 John Quincy Adams
Lesson 1 Andrew Jackson
Lesson 1 Alexis de Tocqueville
Lesson 2 John C. Calhoun
Lesson 2 Daniel Webster

TOPIC 7
Lesson 4 Charles Finney
Lesson 4 Theodore Weld
Lesson 4 William Lloyd Farrison
Lesson 4 Frederick Douglass
Lesson 4 Charles Remond
Lesson 4 Sojourner Truth
Lesson 4 Harriet Tubman
Lesson 4 Robert Purvis
Lesson 5 Susan B. Anthony
Lesson 5 Elizabeth Cady Stanton
Lesson 5 Margaret Fuller
Lesson 5 Lucretia Mott
Lesson 5 Charley Parkhurst

TOPIC 8
Lesson 2 Abraham Lincoln
Lesson 2 John Brown
Lesson 3 Jefferson Davis
Lesson 3 Robert E. Lee
Lesson 4 Ulysses S. Grant

TOPIC 9
Lesson 3 Hiram Rhodes Revels

TOPIC 10
Lesson 4 Andrew Carnegie
Lesson 4 John D. Rockefeller

TOPIC 12
Lesson 3 Theodore Roosevelt
Lesson 6 John J. Pershing
Lesson 7 Woodrow Wilson

TOPIC 13
Lesson 6 Franklin D. Roosevelt

TOPIC 14
Lesson 4 Chester W. Nimitz
Lesson 4 George Patton

TOPIC 15
Lesson 2 Harry Truman
Lesson 2 Dwight Eisenhower
Lesson 6 John F. Kennedy
Lesson 7 Richard M. Nixon

TOPIC 16
Lesson 1 Ronald Reagan
Lesson 1 Bill Clinton
Lesson 1 Sandra Day O'Connor
Lesson 2 Mikhail Gorbachev

TOPIC 17
Lesson 5 Barack Obama
Lesson 5 Donald J. Trump

21st Century Skills

Learn, practice, and apply important skills using these online tutorials.

Analyze Cause and Effect
Analyze Data and Models
Analyze Images
Analyze Media Content
Analyze Political Cartoons
Analyze Primary and Secondary Sources
Ask Questions
Avoid Plagiarism
Being an Informed Citizen
Categorize
Compare and Contrast
Compare Viewpoints
Compromise
Consider and Counter Opposing Arguments
Create Charts and Maps
Create Databases
Create a Research Hypothesis
Develop a Clear Thesis
Develop Cultural Awareness
Distinguish Between Fact and Opinion
Draw Conclusions
Draw Inferences
Evaluate Existing Arguments
Evaluate Web Sites
Generalize
Generate New Ideas
Give an Effective Presentation
Identify Bias
Identify Evidence
Identify Main Ideas and Details
Identify Trends
Innovate
Interpret Sources
Make Decisions
Make a Difference
Make Predictions
Organize Your Ideas
Participate in a Discussion or Debate
Paying Taxes
Political Participation
Publish Your Work
Read Charts, Graphs, and Tables
Read Physical Maps
Read Special Purpose Maps
Search for Information on the Internet
Serving on a Jury Sequence
Set a Purpose for Reading
Share Responsibility
Solve Problems
Summarize
Support Ideas With Evidence
Synthesize
Take Effective Notes
Use Content Clues
Use Parts of a Map
Voting
Work in Teams
Write an Essay
Write a Journal Entry

Interactivities

Explore maps one layer at a time to see how events unfolded over time, go on a gallery walk to examine artifacts and primary sources, analyze data, and explore key historical sites and objects in 3-D!

INTERACTIVE MAPS

North American Geographic Regions Topic 1
Native American Culture Regions of North America Topic 1 Lesson 2
Routes of Exploration and Trade Topic 1 Lesson 3
The Columbian Exchange Topic 1 Lesson 4
European Settlements in North America, 1750 Topic 2
Spanish Explorers and Settlements in North America Topic 2 Lesson 1
Lands Controlled by Colonial Powers, 1660 Topic 2 Lesson 2
The New England Colonies Topic 2 Lesson 3
Comparing the Thirteen Colonies Topic 2 Lesson 5
The Triangular Trade Topic 2 Lesson 7
Key British Colonies, 1775 Topic 3
Major Battles of the French and Indian War Topic 3 Lesson 1
Opinions of Delegates to the Constitutional Convention Topic 4
Ratification of the Constitution Topic 4 Lesson 4
U.S. Expansion During the Early Republic Topic 5
Foreign Affairs Under Washington Topic 5 Lesson 1
Expansion and Exploration Topic 5 Lesson 4
Indian Lands Lost by 1810 Topic 5 Lesson 5
The War of 1812 Topic 5 Lesson 5
Westward Expansion of the United States Topic 6
Tariffs and Trade Topic 6 Lesson 2
Selected Native American Groups, 1820 Topic 6 Lesson 3
Southern Native Americans on the Trail of Tears Topic 6 Lesson 3
The Erie Canal Topic 6 Lesson 4
The Oregon Trail Topic 6 Lesson 5
The Settlement of Texas Topic 6 Lesson 6
The Growth of the West to 1860 Topic 6 Lesson 7
Two Different Economies Topic 7
The Underground Railroad Topic 7 Lesson 4
Early American Music and Literature Topic 7 Lesson 6
Two Different Economies Topic 5

Interactivities (continued)

States in the Civil War Topic 8
The Union's Strategies to Win the Civil War Topic 8 Lesson 4
The Battle of Vicksburg Topic 8 Lesson 6
Key Battles of the Civil War Topic 8 Lesson 6
Reconstruction Topic 9
Change in Southern Industry Topic 9 Lesson 4
New States in the West Topic 10
The Transcontinental Railroad Topic 10 Lesson 1
Cattle Trails Topic 10 Lesson 2
Native American Losses, 1850–1890 Topic 10 Lesson 3
Railroads and Industry Topic 10 Lesson 4
Changes in Immigration, 1870 and 1910 Topic 11
Era of Imperialism Topic 12
U.S. Expansion in the Pacific, 1867–1899 Topic 12 Lesson 1
Spanish-American War Topic 12 Lesson 2
Key Battles Fought by Americans in World War I Topic 12 Lesson 6
The Great Depression in the United States Topic 13
New Deal Programs Topic 13 Lesson 6
German and Japanese Conquests Topic 14
Axis and Allied Nations in Europe, 1939–1942 Topic 14 Lesson 2
Surprise Attack on Pearl Harbor Topic 14 Lesson 2
Civil Rights in the Postwar Years Topic 15
Early Cold War Alliances Topic 15 Lesson 1
Phases of the Korean War Topic 15 Lesson 2
The Break Up of the Soviet Empire Topic 16
Shifting Alliances in Europe Topic 16 Lesson 2
Smartphones–A Global Product Topic 17

INTERACTIVE CHARTS

Reasons to Explore Topic 1 Lesson 4
Social Classes in New Spain Topic 2 Lesson 1
Thomas Hooker Topic 2 Lesson 3
Education in the Colonies Topic 2 Lesson 6
Influences on Colonial Government Topic 2 Lesson 7
Effects of the French and Indian War Topic 3 Lesson 1
Crisis on the Frontier Topic 3 Lesson 2
Advantages & Disadvantages of the British and Colonists Topic 3 Lesson 3
The Great Compromise Topic 4 Lesson 2
Federalists Versus Antifederalists Topic 4 Lesson 4
Methods of Amending the Constitution Topic 4 Lesson 6
A Controversial Tax Topic 5 Lesson 1
Jefferson's Goals and Policies Topic 5 Lesson 3
Political Parties in the Age of Jackson Topic 6 Lesson 1
Disagreements Over the Bank Topic 6 Lesson 2
Different Ways of Life in the South Topic 7 Lesson 3
Lives of Free and Enslaved African Americans Topic 7 Lesson 3
Opposing Views on Slavery Topic 7 Lesson 4
Resources in the North and the South, 1860 Topic 8 Lesson 3
Abraham Lincoln and Jefferson Davis Topic 8 Lesson 3
The Cycle of Poverty Topic 9 Lesson 3
Advantages and Disadvantages of Big Business Topic 10 Lesson 4
Inventions Improve Daily Life Topic 10 Lesson 6
Immigration, 1870–1910 Topic 11 Lesson 1
Issues Facing Immigrants Topic 11 Lesson 1
Progressive Political Reforms Topic 11 Lesson 3
Three Presidents' Accomplishments Topic 11 Lesson 4
U.S. Influence in Foreign Nations Topic 12 Lesson 1
Causes and Effects of the Spanish-American War Topic 12 Lesson 2
Chain of Events, 1914 Topic 12 Lesson 4
Economic Expansion in the 1920s Topic 13 Lesson 1
Points of View on Foreign Affairs in the 1920s Topic 13 Lesson 1
The Great Depression–Causes and Effects Topic 13 Lesson 5
The Great Depression's Impact Topic 13 Lesson 7
United States Debates Going to War Topic 14 Lesson 2
Cold War–Cause and Effect Topic 15 Lesson 1
Cold War Actions–The United States and the Soviet Union Topic 15 Lesson 2
Hawks and Doves Topic 15 Lesson 6
Compare Four Presidents Topic 16 Lesson 1
U.S. Engagement Around the World Topic 16 Lesson 3
Economic Challenges in the 2000s–Causes and Effects Topic 17 Lesson 2
Turning Points in U.S. History Topic 17 Lesson 4

INTERACTIVE GALLERIES

Housing and the Environment Topic 1 Lesson 2
The Economy of the Middle Colonies Topic 2 Lesson 4
The Arts in Colonial America Topic 2 Lesson 6
Important People of the American Revolution Topic 3 Lesson 2
Thomas Paine's *Common Sense* Topic 3 Lesson 4
Interactive Declaration of Independence Topic 3 Lesson 4

Notable People of the American Revolution Topic 3 Lesson 5
Delegates to the Constitutional Convention Topic 4 Lesson 2
The First Amendment Topic 4 Lesson 6
Early American Leaders Topic 5 Lesson 2
Expansion of Federal Powers Topic 5 Lesson 6
New Transportation Methods Topic 6 Lesson 4
New Technology: The Steamboat Topic 6 Lesson 4
Oregon Country Topic 6 Lesson 5
The Defenders of the Alamo Topic 6 Lesson 6
The People of California Topic 6 Lesson 7
The Steam Locomotive Topic 7 Lesson 2
Changes in American Schools Topic 7 Lesson 5
Painting America Topic 7 Lesson 6
Uncle Tom's Cabin Topic 8 Lesson 1
The Effects of The Kansas-Nebraska Act Topic 8 Lesson 2
The Dred Scott Case Topic 8 Lesson 2
The Hardships of Soldiers Topic 8 Lesson 5
Photography and the Civil War Topic 8 Lesson 5
Lincoln and Reconstruction Topic 9 Lesson 1
Reconstruction-Era Political Groups Topic 9 Lesson 3
Boomtowns and Ghost Towns Topic 10 Lesson 1
Cowhands and Their Gear Topic 10 Lesson 2
Urban Problems Topic 11 Lesson 2
National Land Conservation Topic 11 Lesson 4
New Opportunities for Women Topic 11 Lesson 5
Leisure Activities at the Turn of the Century Topic 11 Lesson 6
American Realist Artists Topic 11 Lesson 6
The Panama Canal Topic 12 Lesson 3
World War I Technology Topic 12 Lesson 4
World War I Homefront Topic 12 Lesson 5
Life of American Soldiers in World War I Topic 12 Lesson 6
Woodrow Wilson Topic 12 Lesson 7
Changes in American Life in the 1920s Topic 13 Lesson 2
The Prohibition Era Topic 13 Lesson 2
American Culture in the 1920s Topic 13 Lesson 3
Key Figures in the Harlem Renaissance Topic 13 Lesson 3
Contrasts in American Society Topic 13 Lesson 4
The Impact of the Great Depression Topic 13 Lesson 5
The Dust Bowl Topic 13 Lesson 7
Characteristics of Totalitarianism Topic 14 Lesson 1
Life on the Home Front During World War II Topic 14 Lesson 3
The Experience of Japanese Internment Topic 14 Lesson 3
Holocaust Aftermath and Remembrance Topic 14 Lesson 4
Life in the 1950s Topic 15 Lesson 3
Nonviolent Strategies in the Civil Rights Movement Topic 15 Lesson 4
Leaders for Change Topic 15 Lesson 5
Apollo 11 Topic 15 Lesson 7
September 11, 2001 Topic 17 Lesson 1
Pivot to Asia Topic 17 Lesson 2
Technology in the 21st Century Topic 17 Lesson 3
Advances in Technology Topic 17 Lesson 4

INTERACTIVE GRAPHS

The Downfall of the Southern Economy Topic 9 Lesson 1
New York City Changes, 1840 to 1900 Topic 11 Lesson 2
Limiting Immigration Topic 13 Lesson 4
America's Changing Demographics Topic 17 Lesson 4

INTERACTIVE TIMELINES

Foreign Aid Plays a Role Topic 3 Lesson 5
Influences on the Constitution Topic 4 Lesson 3
Changing Voting Rights in Early America Topic 6 Lesson 1
Choosing a Presidential Candidate Topic 6 Lesson 2
Texas: From Settlement to Statehood Topic 6 Lesson 6
New Inventions Improve Life Topic 7 Lesson 1
The Early Women's Rights Movement Topic 7 Lesson 5
Early Battles of the Civil War Topic 8 Lesson 4
Oppression of African Americans Topic 9 Lesson 4
American Inventors That Changed Society Topic 10 Lesson 6
Government Reforms in the Progressive Era Topic 11 Lesson 3
African American Reform Movement, 1895–1915 Topic 11 Lesson 5
Build Up to War Topic 12 Lesson 5
Confronting Cuba Topic 15 Lesson 6
Watergate Topic 15 Lesson 7
War in Iraq, 2003–2011 Topic 17 Lesson 1

INTERACTIVE ILLUSTRATIONS

How an Astrolabe Works Topic 1 Lesson 3
A Southern Colonial Plantation Topic 2 Lesson 5

INTERACTIVE CARTOONS

The Fugitive Slave Act Topic 8 Lesson 1
The Massacre of New Orleans Topic 9 Lesson 2
Roosevelt's Big Stick Diplomacy Topic 12 Lesson 3
The New Deal Political Cartoon Topic 13 Lesson 6
Reacting to Crises Under Carter Topic 16 Lesson 1
The U.S. Role in the Middle East Topic 17 Lesson 2

Interactivities (continued)

INTERACTIVE 3D MODELS
Aztec Temple Topic 1 Lesson 1
Plymouth Plantation Topic 2 Lesson 3
The Covered Wagon Topic 6 Lesson 5
Early Textile Mill Topic 7 Lesson 1
The Cotton Gin Topic 7 Lesson 3
The Battle at Gettysburg Topic 8 Lesson 6
Nineteenth-Century Sod House Topic 10 Lesson 2
Living in a Tenement Topic 11 Lesson 2
Trench Warfare Topic 12 Lesson 4
The B-24 Liberator Topic 14 Lesson 4
The World Today Topic 17 Lesson 3

Maps

The World: Political
The World: Physical
The United States: Political
The United States: Physical
North and South America: Political
North and South America: Physical
Europe: Political
Europe: Physical
Africa: Political
Africa: Physical
Asia: Political
Asia: Physical
Australia, New Zealand, and Oceania: Political-Physical
The Arctic: Physical
Antarctica: Physical

SPECIAL FEATURES

All of these resources are found right here in your student textbook.

Ask questions, explore sources, and cite evidence to support your view!

Primary Sources

Excerpts from original sources allow you to witness history.

SPECIAL FEATURES

All of these resources are found right here in your student textbook.

Primary Sources (continued)

Primary Source Quotations

Quotations in the text bring history to life.

Primary Source Quotations (continued)

Analysis Skills

Practice key skills.

SPECIAL FEATURES

All of these resources are found right here in your student textbook.

Biographies

Read about the people who made history.

Charts, Graphs, Tables, and Infographics

Find these charts, graphs, and tables in your text. It's all about the data!

Charts, Graphs, Tables, and Infographics (continued)

Timelines

Maps

Where did this happen? Find out with these maps.

Maps (continued)

TOPIC 12

TOPIC 13

TOPIC 14

TOPIC 15

TOPIC 16

TOPIC 17

ATLAS

ENGLISH-LANGUAGE ARTS HANDBOOK

As you explore United States history in this course, you will read informational texts and primary sources. For this course and in other courses and beyond, you will need to think critically about the texts you read to absorb information and be able to express your thoughts about world events, past and present. You will need to communicate your ideas through writing (summaries, arguments, informative essays, and narratives), speaking (debates and one-on-one and small group discussions), and by giving presentations.

This Handbook will give you some tools for reading critically and expressing your ideas. The Quests and other activities in this program give you opportunities to write and speak about your ideas and create projects that will help you practice these skills.

INTERACTIVE

The 21st Century Skills Tutorials, found online, support many of the skills discussed here. Go online to find a Quick Reference, video of the skill being modeled, and more.

READING

Analyze Informational Text

Reading nonfiction texts, like a magazine article or your textbook, is not the same as reading a fictional story or novel. The purpose of reading nonfiction is to acquire new information. It's something that you, and the adults around you, do all of the time.

Process What You Read When you read informational text, it helps to know what to look for and what questions to ask yourself as you read. Use the chart below as a guide when you read.

	Look for	Questions to Ask	For More Help
Central Ideas and Details	• Central ideas or claims • Supporting details or evidence	• What is the subject or main point of this text? • What details support the main point? • What inferences do you need to make? • How does the author develop a few central ideas throughout a text?	**Skills Tutorial** • Identify Main Ideas and Details • Draw Inferences • Summarize **Analysis Skill** Identify Central Issues and Problems
Word Choice	• Unfamiliar words and phrases • Words and phrases that produce a certain effect on a reader	• What inferences about word meaning can you make from the context? • What tone and mood are created by word choice? • What alternate word choices might the author have made?	**Skills Tutorial** • Draw Inferences
Text Structure	• Ways the author has organized the text • Ways sentences and paragraphs work together to build ideas • Clue words signaling a particular structure	• Does the text have a specific structure? • For instance, is it structured by sequence or chronology? By comparisons and contrasts? By causes and effects?	**Skills Tutorial** • Identify Evidence • Analyze Cause and Effect • Sequence • Compare and Contrast

Evaluate Arguments

One important reason to read and understand informational text is so you can recognize and evaluate written arguments. When you think of an argument, you might think of a disagreement between two people, but the word has another meaning, too. An argument is a logical way of presenting a belief, conclusion, or stance. A good argument is supported with reasoning and evidence and will often address opposing claims. Study the model below to see how the writer developed an argument about restrictions against African Americans after the Civil War.

These two sentences express the conclusion that Conservative Democrats in the South tried to restrict the rights of African Americans, including their right to vote.

This paragraph offers evidence for the conclusion by describing one way southern states restricted African American voting rights.

These sentences explain how literacy tests were used to keep African Americans from voting.

This paragraph explains how southern states let poor and illiterate white people vote while using poll taxes and literacy tests to stop African Americans.

New Legislation Restricts African American Rights

As federal troops withdrew from southern states, Conservative Democrats found new ways to keep African Americans from exercising their rights. Many of these were laws specifically intended to prevent African Americans from voting.

Over time, many southern states passed poll taxes, requiring voters to pay a fee each time they voted. As a result, poor freedmen could rarely afford to vote.

States also imposed literacy tests that required voters to read and explain a section of the United States Constitution. Since most freedmen had little education, such tests kept them away from the polls. Election officials also applied different standards to Black and white voters. African Americans who were able to read often had to answer more difficult questions than white people on literacy tests.

Still, many poor white people could not have passed any literacy test. To increase the number of white voters, states passed grandfather clauses. These laws stated that if a voter's father or grandfather had been eligible to vote on January 1, 1867, the voter did not have to take a literacy test. No African Americans in the South could vote before 1868, so the only effect of the grandfather clauses was to ensure that white men could vote.

INTERACTIVE

Go online for these interactive skills tutorials:

- Evaluate Arguments
- Consider and Counter Opposing Arguments
- Support Ideas With Evidence

Analyze Visuals

Another key component of understanding informational texts is being able to understand visuals like the maps, graphs, charts, and photos in your student text. Study the chart and the example to help you analyze some common types of visuals in your social studies text.

	Look for	For More Help
Maps	• Read the title. • Read the key. • Study the locator globe, scale bar, and compass rose. • Apply the key and labels to the map.	**Skills Tutorial** • Use Parts of a Map • Read Physical Maps • Read Political Maps • Read Special-Purpose Maps
Graphs and Tables	• Read the title. • Use labels and key. • Look for patterns or changes over time.	**Skills Tutorial** • Read Charts, Graphs, and Tables • Create Charts and Maps
Photographs	• Identify the content. • Note emotions. • Read captions or credits. • Study the image's purpose. • Consider context. • Respond.	**Skills Tutorial** • Analyze Images • Analyze Political Cartoons

Example

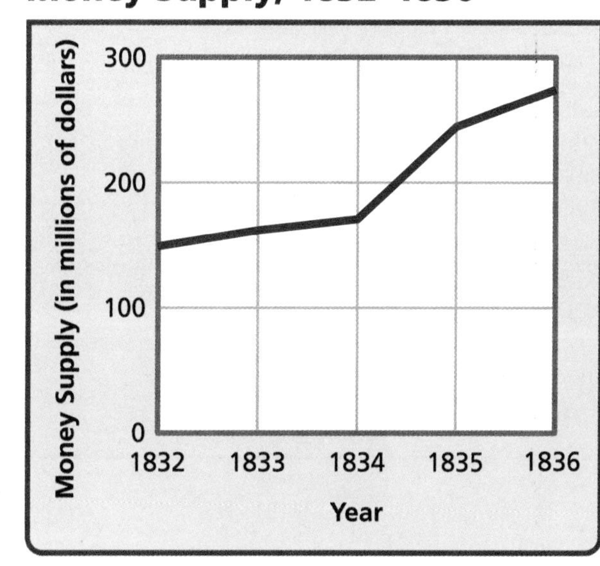

1. What is the title of the graph?
2. Read the labels. What does the x-axis, or the horizontal edge of the graph, show? What does the y-axis, or the vertical side of the graph, show?
3. How much did the money supply increase between 1832 and 1836?
4. What is a likely cause for this change?

Analyze Primary and Secondary Sources

A primary source is an account or a document from someone who saw or was part of what is being described. A secondary source is information recorded later by someone who was not part of it. You will encounter many primary and secondary sources throughout your textbook and in Quests and other activities. Study these questions and the model primary sources that follow to help you unlock the meaning of these sources.

	Questions to Ask	For More Help
Determine the Author's Purpose	• Is the source written mainly to convey information, like a textbook? • Or is its purpose to persuade you to think a certain way, like an opinion piece in a newspaper?	**Skills Tutorial** • Analyze Primary and Secondary Sources • Analyze Media Content • Draw Inferences
Determine the Author's Point of View	• What is the author's point of view? • Is the author's point of view shaped by subjective influences such as feelings, prejudices, or experiences? • Is the author's point of view shaped by his or her field of study?	**Skills Tutorial** • Analyze Primary and Secondary Sources • Compare Viewpoints
Compare Viewpoints	• How is the author's point of view different from that of other authors' writing on the same subject? • Does the author avoid including certain facts that would change his or her point of view?	**Skills Tutorial** • Compare Viewpoints
Analyze Word Choice	• Does the author use words in a neutral, factual way? • Does the author use loaded words that try to persuade the reader to think a certain way?	**Skills Tutorial** • Identify Bias
Analyze Interactions	• How have individuals, events, and ideas influenced each other? • What connecting words signal these interactions (next, for example, consequently, however, etc.)?	**Skills Tutorial** • Analyze Cause and Effect

Primary Sources Models As white settlers moved west into the interior of North America, they settled in lands that American Indian groups had settled for centuries. American Indians reacted in different ways to this new threat. The Cherokee Nation hoped to use the courts to stay on their land. They also rejected a treaty signed by several Cherokees giving up Cherokee land.

Study the excerpts and call-outs to help you better understand each author's purpose, word choices, and point of view.

The "we" is Ross and other Cherokee leaders.

Redress means to set something right. The Cherokee hoped that President Van Buren would set things right between the United States and the Cherokee Nation.

The author is choosing words with negative meanings to describe the treaty.

The author is a chief of the Cherokee Nation who was present at the negotiations between the United States and Cherokee governments.

Van Buren became President after Jackson. The event described in the primary source took place at the beginning of the Van Buren administration.

Forced infers that the Cherokee did not leave their land willingly.

Meeting with President Van Buren

On the 4th of March (1837), Mr. Van Buren assumed the presidential chair. On the 16th of March, we addressed the new president, stating to him fully our position and wishes, reviewing the circumstances which had occurred, and the hopes we entertained of receiving redress at his hands. We entreated the president to examine for himself into the grounds upon which we rested our charge, that the document called a treaty was fraudulent and equally an imposition upon the United States and upon ourselves.

—Letter from John Ross, the principal chief of the Cherokee nation, to a gentleman of Philadelphia

The Cherokee

The Cherokee also tried to hold out. They were still on their land in 1836 when Jackson left office. A small group of Cherokee agreed to become citizens of North Carolina. As a result, they were allowed to stay. Other Cherokee hid in remote mountain camps.

Finally, in 1838, President Martin Van Buren forced the Cherokee, who had not made agreements with North Carolina and those who were not in hiding, to move. The United States Army forced more than 15,000 Cherokee to march westward.

Support Your Analyses with Evidence

Historians and other writers make assertions, or claims, about events. Before accepting a claim as fact, however, look carefully at the evidence the author provides. Study the chart and the model secondary source to learn more about how to use evidence to support your ideas.

	Look for	Questions to Ask	For More Help
Support Your Analyses With Evidence	• The subject of the passage • Any assertion or claim that something is true • Appropriate evidence to support the claim • How well the evidence supports the claim, either explicitly or by inference	• What is the passage about? • Are there claims that something is true? • If so, what language supports the claim? • Does the evidence support the claim? • Did the author convince you that the claim was correct?	**Skills Tutorial** • Identify Evidence • Support Ideas With Evidence

Model Secondary Source Look for evidence in this model passage. Do you think the main point is supported by the evidence?

The writer claims that Vanderbilt used ruthless tactics.

The writer offers evidence of what Vanderbilt did when the owners of one railroad refused to sell to him.

The writer shows that Vanderbilt was able to accomplish his objectives by using these ruthless tactics.

Vanderbilt sometimes used ruthless tactics to force smaller owners to sell to him. In the early 1860s, he decided to buy the New York Central Railroad. The owners refused to sell. Vanderbilt then announced that the New York Central passengers would not be allowed to transfer to his trains. With their passengers stranded and business dropping sharply, the New York Central owners gave in and sold their line to Vanderbilt.

WRITING

Using the Writing Process

Writing is one of the most powerful communication tools you will use for the rest of your life. A systematic approach to writing—including planning, drafting, revising, editing, rewriting, and proofreading—will help you strengthen your writing.

Prewriting: Plan Your Essay

1. **Choose a topic.** Often your teacher will provide you with a topic. Sometimes, you will be able to choose your own topic. In that case, select a topic that you care about and that you think will be interesting.

2. **Narrow your focus.** Most writers begin with too broad a topic and need to narrow their focus. For example, you might start off knowing you want to write about the Civil War. You will need to narrow your focus to a single battle or a cause of the war in order to write a meaningful essay.

3. **Gather information.** Collect facts and details to write your essay. Research any points you want to include that you are unsure about.

4. **Organize your ideas.** Writers often find it useful to create an outline to help them plan their essay. You need not create a formal outline, but you'll at least want to jot down your main ideas, the details that support them, and the order in which you will present your ideas. A graphic organizer, such as a Venn diagram or concept web, can help you organize your ideas. Here is a graphic organizer for a paper on the causes of the Civil War:

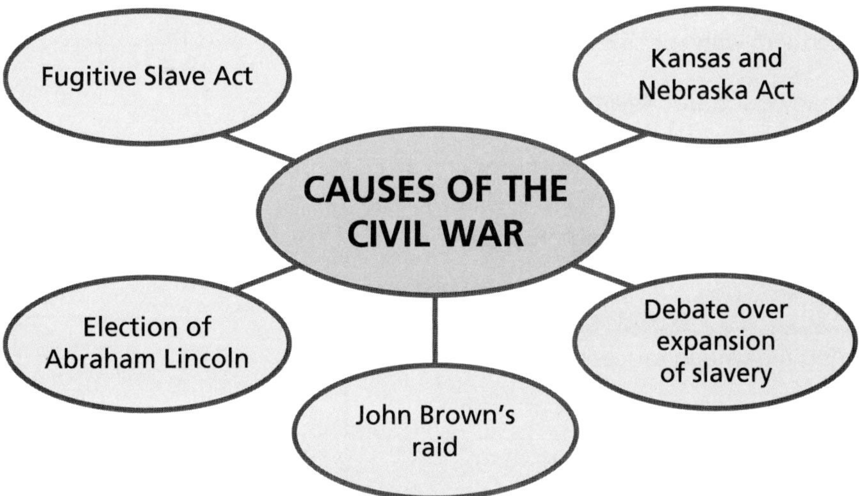

5. **Write a thesis statement.** A thesis statement focuses your ideas into a single sentence or two. Your thesis statement should tell your reader what the essay is about.

Drafting

1. **Maintain a clear focus.** If you find that your writing is starting to get off track, go back to your thesis statement.
2. **Elaborate for interest and emphasis.** Give details about each point in your essay. For instance, if you are writing an essay about the causes of the War of 1812, give details and specific examples.
3. **Provide evidence.** Evidence is key to convincing an audience. Provide factual, concrete evidence to back up your ideas and assertions.

INTERACTIVE

Go online for these interactive skills tutorials:

- Identify Main Ideas and Details
- Organize Your Ideas
- Write an Essay

Revising, Editing, and Rewriting

1. **Add transition words.** Clarify cause-and-effect relationships with words such as *because* and *as a result*. To compare or contrast ideas, use linking words, such as *similarly, both,* and *in contrast* and *yet*. Use words such as *first, next,* and *finally* to help readers follow a sequence.
2. **Focus on addressing your purpose.** Be sure that your essay addresses your purpose for writing. For a problem-solution essay, that means anticipating and responding to opposing arguments. For a cause-and-effect essay, stress the way one event leads to the next.
3. **Focus on your audience.** Check that you have not left out any steps in your essay and that your audience can follow your thinking. Make sure that your writing will hold your audience's interest.
4. **Review organization.** Confirm that your ideas flow in a logical order. Write your main points on sticky notes. Reorganize these until you are satisfied that the order best strengthens your essay.
5. **Revise sentences and words.** Look at your sentence length. Vary it to include both short and long sentences. Then scan for vague words, such as *good* or *nice*. Replace them with specific and vibrant words.
6. **Peer review.** Ask a peer to read your draft. Revise areas of confusion.

Proofread Always proofread your writing for spelling and grammar errors. Do not simply rely on spell check. There are many spelling errors that slip by even when you use the best spell checking programs.

Use Technology
Technology has many uses during the writing process: ✓ Use a word processing program to plan and write your essay.
✓ Use the Internet for research.
✓ Use email and other online tools to collaborate with classmates.
✓ Create slides, charts, graphs, and diagrams for presentations.
✓ Share you writing with others through a blog or website.

Write an Argument

In addition to evaluating other writers' arguments, you also need to be able to express arguments of your own, in writing and speaking. An argumentative, or persuasive, essay sets forth a belief or stand on an issue. A well-written argument may convince the reader, change the reader's mind, or motivate the reader to take a certain action.

In this program, you'll practice writing arguments in some Document-Based Inquiry Quests and Writing Workshops, with support in your **Active Journal**. Use the checklist to help you write a convincing argument.

An Effective Argument Includes
✓ a precise claim
✓ consideration of alternate claims, or opposing positions, and a discussion of their strengths and weaknesses
✓ logical organization that makes clear connections among claim, reasons, and evidence
✓ valid reasoning and evidence, using credible sources and accurate data
✓ a concluding statement or section that follows from and supports the argument
✓ formal and objective language and tone
✓ error-free grammar, including accurate use of transitions

INTERACTIVE

Go online for these interactive skills tutorials:

- Evaluate Arguments
- Consider and Counter Opposing Arguments
- Support Ideas With Evidence

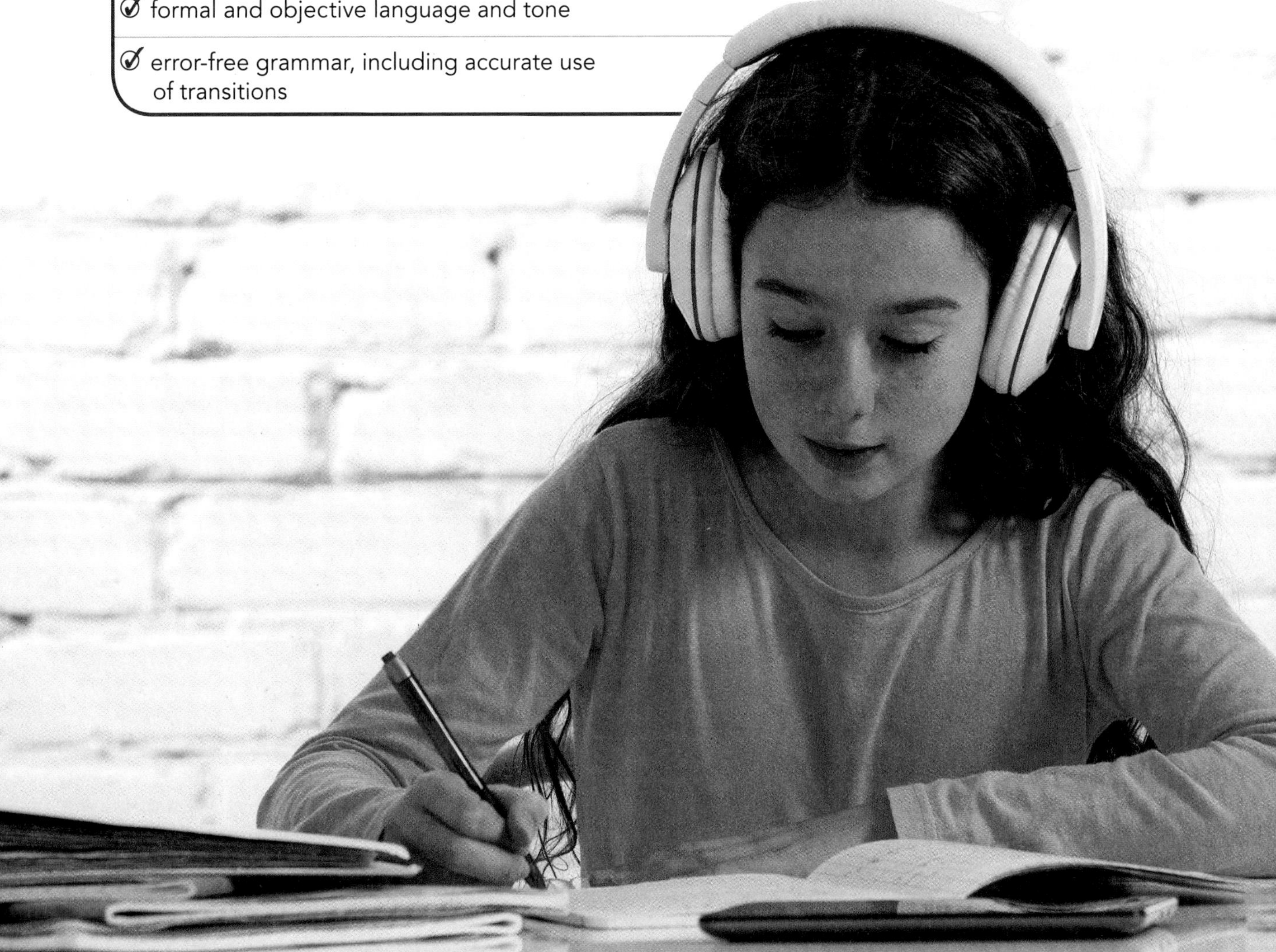

Write Informative or Explanatory Essays

Informative/explanatory texts present facts, data, and other evidence to give information about a topic. Readers turn to these texts when they wish to learn about a specific idea, concept, or subject area, or if they want to learn how to do something.

An Effective Informative/Explanatory Essay Includes
✓ a topic sentence or thesis statement that introduces the concept or subject
✓ an organization (such as definition, classification, comparison/ contrast, cause/effect) that presents information in a clear manner
✓ headings (if desired) to separate sections of the essay
✓ definitions, quotations, and/or graphics that support the thesis
✓ relevant facts, examples, and details that expand upon a topic
✓ clear transitions that link sections of the essay
✓ precise words and technical vocabulary where appropriate
✓ formal and objective language and tone
✓ a conclusion that supports the information given and provides fresh insights

INTERACTIVE

Go online for these interactive skills tutorials:

- Organize Your Ideas
- Compare and Contrast
- Analyze Cause and Effect
- Develop a Clear Thesis
- Draw Conclusions
- Support Ideas With Evidence

Suppose you are writing an essay comparing and contrasting the beliefs of Thomas Jefferson and Alexander Hamilton. You might start by creating a Venn diagram like this one to help you organize your ideas. You would then fill it in with facts, descriptions, and examples.

Jefferson and Hamilton

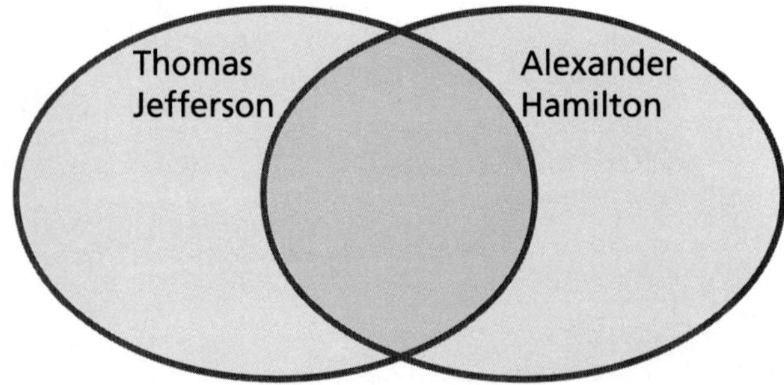

Write Narrative Essays

A narrative is any type of writing that tells a story. Narrative writing conveys an experience, either real or imaginary, and uses time order to provide structure. Usually its purpose is to entertain, but it can also instruct, persuade, or inform.

An Effective Narrative Includes
✓ an engaging beginning in which characters and setting are established
✓ a well-structured, logical sequence of events
✓ narrative techniques, such as dialogue and description
✓ a variety of transition words and phrases to convey sequence and signal shifts from one time frame or setting to another
✓ precise words and phrases, relevant descriptive details, and sensory language that brings the characters and setting to life
✓ a conclusion that follows naturally from the story's experiences or events

Model Narrative This passage is the beginning of a story by Edgar Allan Poe, a famous American author in the mid-1800s. Notice how it begins by grabbing the reader's attention with an assertion that the speaker is not mad. Notice how the author uses exclamation points to draw attention to his words

> True!—Nervous—very, very dreadfully nervous I had been and am; but why will you say that I am mad! The disease had sharpened my senses, not dulled them. Above all was the sense of hearing acute . . . How then, am I mad! Hearken! and observe how healthily—how calmly I can tell you the whole story.
>
> —*The Tell-Tale Heart*, Edgar Allan Poe

INTERACTIVE

Go online for these interactive skills tutorials:

- Sequence
- Draw Conclusions
- Write an Essay
- Write a Journal Entry

Find and Use Credible Sources

You will often need to conduct research using library and media sources to gain more knowledge about a topic. Not all of the information that you find, however, will be useful—or reliable. Strong research skills will help you find accurate information about your topic.

Using Print and Digital Sources An effective research project combines information from multiple sources. Plan to include a variety of these resources:

- **Primary and Secondary Sources:** Use both primary sources (such as interviews or newspaper articles) and secondary sources (such as encyclopedia entries or historians' accounts).
- **Print and Digital Resources:** The Internet allows fast access to data, but print resources are often edited more carefully. Plan to include both print and digital resources in order to guarantee that your work is accurate.
- **Media Resources:** You can find valuable information in media resources such as documentaries, television programs, podcasts, and museum exhibitions.
- **Original Research:** Depending on your topic, you may wish to conduct original research, such as interviews or surveys of people in your community.

Evaluating Sources It is important to evaluate the credibility and accuracy of any information you find. Ask yourself questions such as these to evaluate sources:

- **Authority:** Is the author well known? What are the author's credentials? Does the source include references to other reliable sources? Does the author's tone win your confidence? Why or why not?
- **Bias:** Does the author have any obvious biases? What is the author's purpose for writing? Who is the target audience?
- **Currency:** When was the work created? Has it been revised? Is there more current information available?

Did you know?

Beware of online encyclopedias. They can be a good starting place for information, but their contributors are not required to fact-check their submissions.

Using Search Terms Finding information on the Internet is easy, but it can be a challenge to find facts that are useful and trustworthy. If you type a word or phrase into a search engine, you will probably get hundreds of results.

However, those results are not guaranteed to be relevant or accurate. These strategies can help:

- ✓ Create a list of keywords before you begin using a search engine.
- ✓ Enter six to eight keywords.
- ✓ Choose unique nouns. Most search engines ignore articles and prepositions.
- ✓ Use adjectives to specify a category. For example, you might enter "ancient Rome" instead of "Rome."
- ✓ Use quotation marks to focus a search. Place a phrase in quotation marks to find pages that include exactly that phrase.
- ✓ Spell carefully. Many search engines correct spelling automatically, but they cannot catch every spelling error.
- ✓ Scan search results before you click them. The first result isn't always the most useful. Read the text before making a choice.

Avoiding Plagiarism When you conduct research, you must give credit for any ideas or opinions that are not your own. Presenting someone else's ideas, research, or opinion as your own—even if you have phrased it in different words—is plagiarism. Plagiarism is the equivalent of stealing. Be sure to record your sources accurately so you can identify them later. When photocopying from a source, include the copyright information. Include the web addresses from online sources.

Quoting and Paraphrasing When including ideas from research into your writing, you will need to decide whether to quote directly or paraphrase. You must cite your sources for both quotations and paraphrases. **A direct quotation** uses the author's exact words when they are particularly well-chosen. Include complete quotations, without deleting or changing words. Enclose direct quotations in quotation marks. **A paraphrase** restates an author's ideas in your own words. Be careful to paraphrase accurately. A good paraphrase does more than simply rearrange an author's phrases, or replace a few words with synonyms.

Formats for Citing Sources When you cite a source, you acknowledge where you found your information and give readers the details necessary for locating the source themselves. Always prepare a reference list at the end of a research paper to provide full information on your sources in a list of sources called a bibliography.

INTERACTIVE

For more help, find these interactive skills tutorials on your Realize course:

- Search for Information on the Internet
- Evaluate Web Sites
- Take Effective Notes
- Avoid Plagiarism

Did you know?

A citation for a book should look like this: Pyles, Thomas. *The Origins and Development of the English Language*. 2nd ed. New York: Harcourt, 1971. Print.

A citation for a website should include this information:

Romey, Kristin. "Face of 9,500-Year-Old Man Revealed for First Time." *National Geographic*, Jan. 2017. *news.nationalgeographic.com* Web. 20 Jan. 2017.

Write Research Papers

You will often need to conduct research in the library or on the Internet for a project or essay. In this program, you will conduct research for Quest projects and some Writing Workshop assignments. Before you begin, review the information in Using Writing Process as well as in Find and Use Credible Sources. Then follow these additional tips to help you make the most of your research.

1. Narrow or Broaden Your Topic Choose a topic that is narrow enough to cover completely. If you can name your topic in just one or two words, it is probably too broad. Topics such as The Progressive Era are too broad to cover in a single report. When you begin to research, pay attention to the amount of information available. If there is way too much information, narrow your focus.

You might need to broaden a topic if there is not enough information available. A topic is too narrow when it can be thoroughly presented in less space than the required size of your assignment. It might also be too narrow if you can find little or no information in library and media sources. Broaden your topic by including other related ideas.

2. Generate Research Questions Use research questions to focus your inquiry. For example, instead of hunting for information about the Revolutionary War, you might ask, "How did France influence the outcome of the Revolutionary War?" or "What events marked turning points in the Revolutionary War?" As you research your topic, continue to ask yourself questions. Follow your new questions to explore your topic further. Refocus your research questions as you learn more about your topic.

INTERACTIVE

Go online for these interactive skills tutorials:

- Ask Questions
- Create a Research Hypothesis
- Synthesize

3. Synthesize Your Sources Effective research writing is more than just a list of facts and details. Good research synthesizes—gathers, orders, and interprets—those elements. These strategies will help you synthesize effectively:

- ✓ Review your notes. Look for connections and patterns among the details you have collected.
- ✓ Organize notes or notecards to help you plan how you will combine details.
- ✓ Pay close attention to details that emphasize the same main idea.
- ✓ Also, look for details that challenge each other. For many topics, there is no single correct opinion. You might decide to conduct additional research to help you decide which side of the issue has more support.

SPEAKING AND LISTENING

Discuss Your Ideas

A group discussion is an informal meeting of people that is used to openly discuss ideas, readings, and issues. You can express your views and hear those of others. In this program, you'll participate in Discussion Inquiry Quests and many one-to-one, group, and teacher-led discussions. You'll work with different partners on many topics and issues. Use Keys to Effective Discussions to help you be an active participant.

Keys to Effective Discussions
✓ Come to discussions prepared, having studied the required material and/or read relevant background information.
✓ Build on others' ideas and express your own ideas clearly.
✓ Be sure that your comments directly contribute to the topic, text, or issue under discussion.
✓ Give specific evidence for the points you wish to make.
✓ Follow rules for civic discussions, including letting everyone have a chance to speak and listening carefully to others' points of view.
✓ Pose and respond to specific questions and issues with elaboration and details.
✓ Be prepared to demonstrate your understanding of the different perspectives people have put forth during the discussion.
✓ Acknowledge the views of others respectfully, but ask questions that challenge the accuracy, logic, or relevance of those views.

INTERACTIVE

Go online for these interactive skills tutorials:

- Participate in a Discussion or Debate
- Support Ideas With Evidence
- Work in Teams

Give an Effective Presentation

Many of the Quests in this program will require you to give a presentation to your teacher and classmates, and sometimes even to a wider audience. These presentations will be good practice for the presentations you will need to give in school and in professional settings. You can speak confidently if you prepare carefully and follow this checklist.

Keys to Effective Presentations
✓ Prepare your presentation in advance and practice it to gain comfort and confidence.
✓ Present your claims and findings in a logical sequence so that your audience can easily follow your train of thought.
✓ Use relevant descriptions, facts, and specific details.
✓ Consider using nonverbal elements like hand gestures and pauses to emphasize main ideas or themes.
✓ Use appropriate eye contact, adequate volume, and clear pronunciation.
✓ Use appropriate transitions (for example, *first, second, third*) to clarify relationships.
✓ Use precise language and vocabulary that is specific to your topic.
✓ Provide a strong conclusion.
✓ Adapt your wording to your purpose and audience. Use formal English for most presentations, but try to sound natural and relaxed.
✓ Include multimedia components such as you see in this chart to clarify information.

INTERACTIVE

Go online for these interactive skills tutorials:

- Give an Effective Presentation
- Create Charts and Maps
- Support Ideas With Evidence

Maps	Graphs/Charts/ Diagrams	Illustrations/Photos	Audio/Video
Clarify historical or geographical information	Show complex information and data in an easy-to-understand format	Illustrate objects, scenes, or other details	Bring the subject to life and engage audiences

Effective Listening

Active listening is a key component of the communication process. Like all communication, it requires your engaged participation. Follow the Keys to Effective Listening to get the most out of discussions, presentations by others, lectures by your teacher, and any time you engage in listening.

Keys to Effective Listening
✓ Look at and listen to the speaker. Think about what you hear and see. Which ideas are emphasized or repeated? What gestures or expressions suggest strong feelings?
✓ Listen carefully to information presented in different media and formats—including videos, lectures, speeches, and discussions—so you can explain how the information you learn contributes to the topic or issue you are studying.
✓ Listen for the speaker's argument and specific claims so that you can distinguish claims that are supported by reasons and evidence from claims that are not.
✓ Listen to fit the situation. Active listening involves matching your listening to the situation. Listen critically to a speech given by a candidate for office. Listen with kindness to the feelings of a friend. Listen appreciatively to a musical performance.

INTERACTIVE

Go online for these interactive skills tutorials:
- Identify Bias
- Identify Evidence
- Distinguish Between Fact and Opinion
- Evaluate Existing Arguments

TOPIC 1

The Early Americas and European Exploration

(Prehistory–1600)

GO ONLINE to access your digital course

- VIDEO
- AUDIO
- ETEXT
- INTERACTIVE
- WRITING
- GAMES
- WORKSHEET
- ASSESSMENT

Go back over 10,000 years

to **PRESENT-DAY ALASKA**. The first people to live in North America are arriving from Asia. Over time, American Indians spread across North and South America and learned how to use the environment to make their lives easier.

Explore The Essential Question

How much does geography affect people's lives?

Throughout history people have been affected by the geography that surrounds them. How did early American Indians and people around the world use the land on which they lived?

Unlock the Essential Question in your Active Journal.

Read

about the different civilizations that lived in the Americas, about the Middle Ages, and European exploration.

Watch

NBC LEARN

BOUNCE TO ACTIVATE VIDEO

Austin Celebrates His Heritage.

Learn how one boy investigates who he is.

The Pyramid of the Sun is in an ancient city called Teotihuacan in modern day Mexico.

TOPIC 1

The Early Americas and European Exploration

(Prehistory–1600)

Learn more about the early Americas and European exploration of the world by making your own map and timeline in your Active Journal.

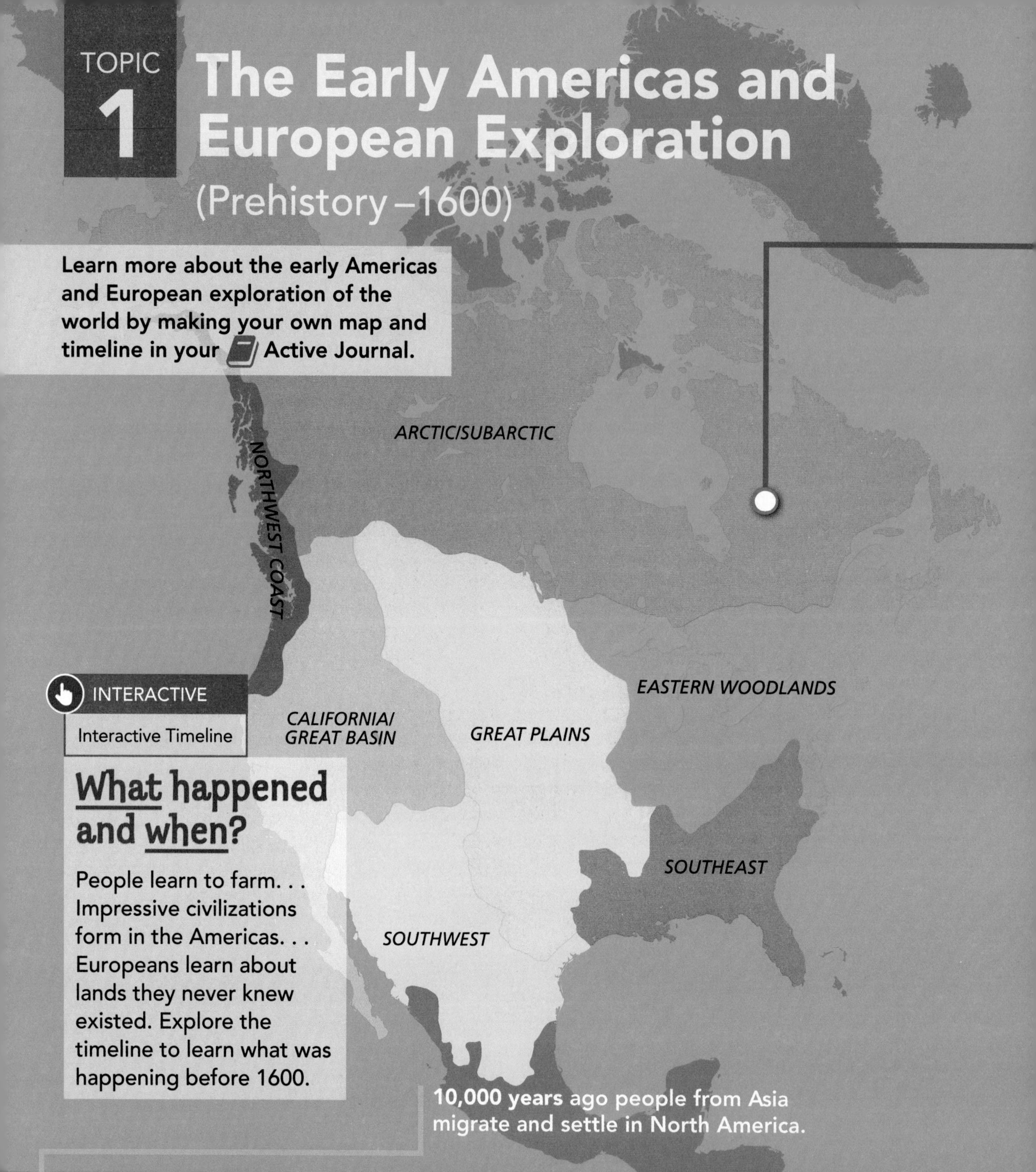

Interactive Timeline

What happened and when?

People learn to farm. . . Impressive civilizations form in the Americas. . . Europeans learn about lands they never knew existed. Explore the timeline to learn what was happening before 1600.

10,000 years ago people from Asia migrate and settle in North America.

TOPIC EVENTS

500

700

WORLD EVENTS

c. 600
Islam is founded.

1095
The First Crusade begins.

INTERACTIVE

Interactive Map

Where did some early American Indians live?

Before European explorers arrived in the Americas, many different cultures thrived in the Western Hemisphere. Locate the regions on the map where the Eastern Woodlands and Great Plains cultures existed.

1492
Christopher Columbus arrives in the Americas.

900
The Maya abandon their cities.

c.1300
The Aztec create a civilization in central Mexico.

900 | 1100 | 1300 | 1500

1307
Emperor Mansa Musa strengthens the empire of Mali.

c. 1430
Gutenberg uses movable type.

1520
Magellan crosses Pacific Ocean.

Who will you meet?

Hiawatha, who helped organize an alliance of the Iroquois nations

Christopher Columbus, who led Europeans to the Americas in the 1400s

Ferdinand Magellan, a Portuguese explorer whose crew sailed around the world

Document-Based Writing Inquiry

The Easter Mutiny

Quest KICK OFF

The year is **1520**, and Ferdinand Magellan is trying to sail around the world. During the journey, members of his crew revolt against Magellan and lead a mutiny on Easter Sunday.

How reliable is Antonio Pigafetta's account of the Easter Mutiny?

How do the different accounts of the Easter Mutiny differ? Find out as you explore how point of view can affect our understanding of a person or event.

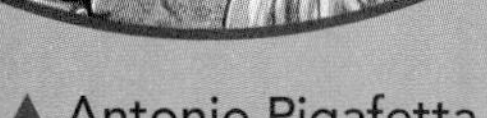

▲ Antonio Pigafetta

1 Ask Questions

Start by considering the language Pigafetta used in his account. Get started by making a list of questions you would want to ask about how to judge word choices and tone. Write the questions in your Active Journal.

2 Investigate

As you read the lessons in this topic, look for Quest CONNECTIONS that provide information on how different points of view can affect how we evaluate information. Capture notes in your Active Journal.

3 Examine Primary Sources

Next explore primary sources about the Easter Mutiny. They will help you learn about the different ways people remembered the events. Make notes about the sources in your Active Journal.

Quest FINDINGS

4 Write Your Essay

At the end of this topic, you will write an essay in which you examine the reliability of Pigafetta's account. In your essay, be sure to clearly state your view in a strong topic sentence, use logical organization, and support your conclusion with evidence and relevant facts.

LESSON 1

The Early Americas

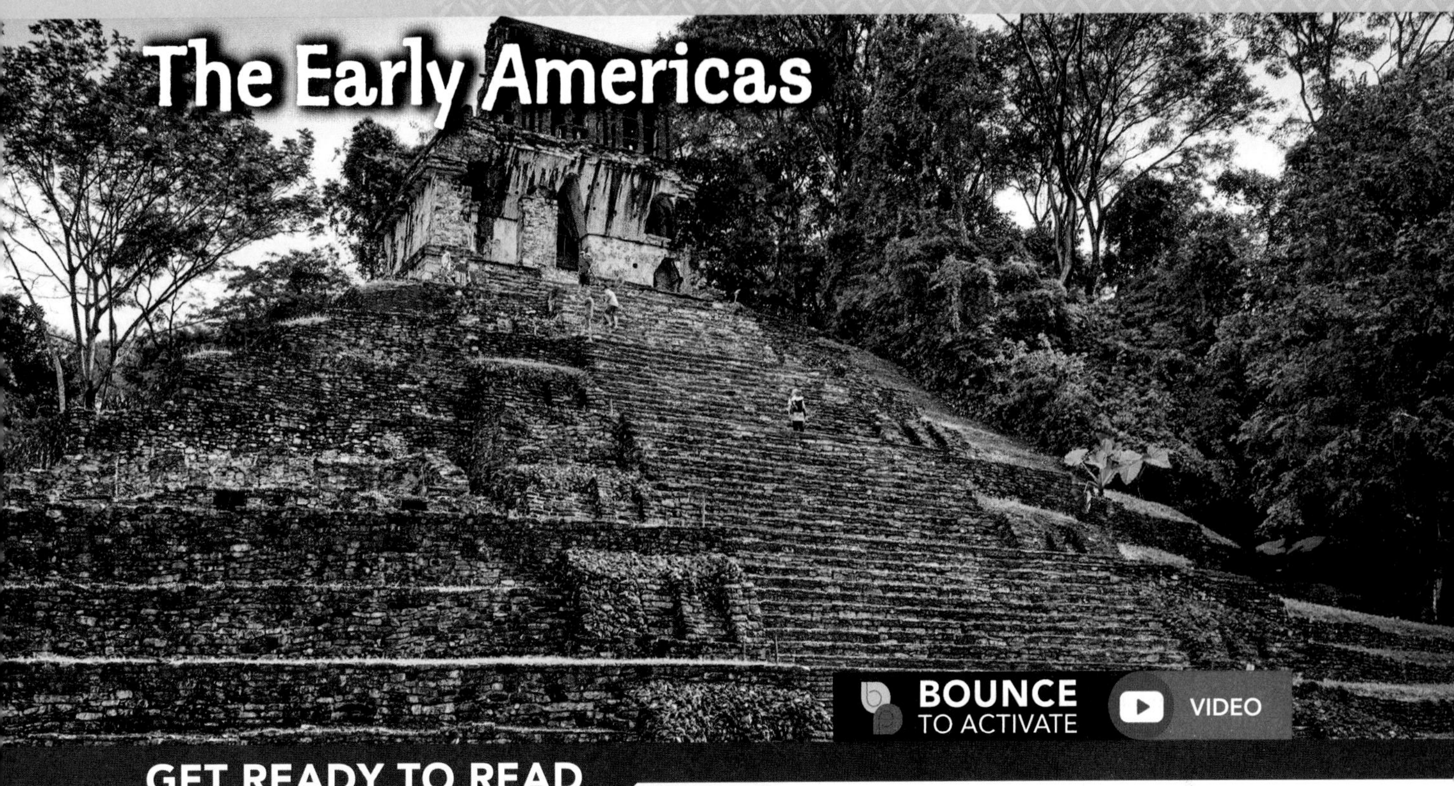

GET READY TO READ

START UP

Examine the photo of the Maya temple. What does this pyramid tell you about Maya society?

GUIDING QUESTIONS

- How did people first reach the Americas?
- How would you describe the early civilizations and cultures of the Americas?
- What are some of the greatest achievements of early civilizations in the Americas?

TAKE NOTES

Literacy Skills: Summarize

Use the graphic organizer in your Active Journal to take notes as you read the lesson.

PRACTICE VOCABULARY

Use the vocabulary activity in your Active Journal to practice the vocabulary words.

Vocabulary		Academic Vocabulary
glacier	city-state	according to
settlement	causeway	complex
surplus	quipu	
civilization	terrace	

Like other early people around the world, the first Americans left no written records to tell us where they came from or when they arrived. However, scientists have found evidence to suggest that the first people reached the Americas sometime during the last ice age.

Who Were the First Americans?

According to geologists, the Earth has gone through several ice ages. The last ice age occurred between 100,000 and 10,000 years ago. During that time, thick sheets of ice, called **glaciers**, covered almost one third of the Earth. In North America, glaciers stretched across Canada and reached as far south as present-day Kentucky.

Early Peoples Spread Across a Continent Glaciers locked up water from the oceans, causing sea levels to fall and uncovering land that had been under water. In the far north, a land bridge joined Siberia in northeastern Asia to present-day Alaska.

Most scientists think that bands of hunters, tracking herds of grazing animals, reached North America by way of this land bridge.

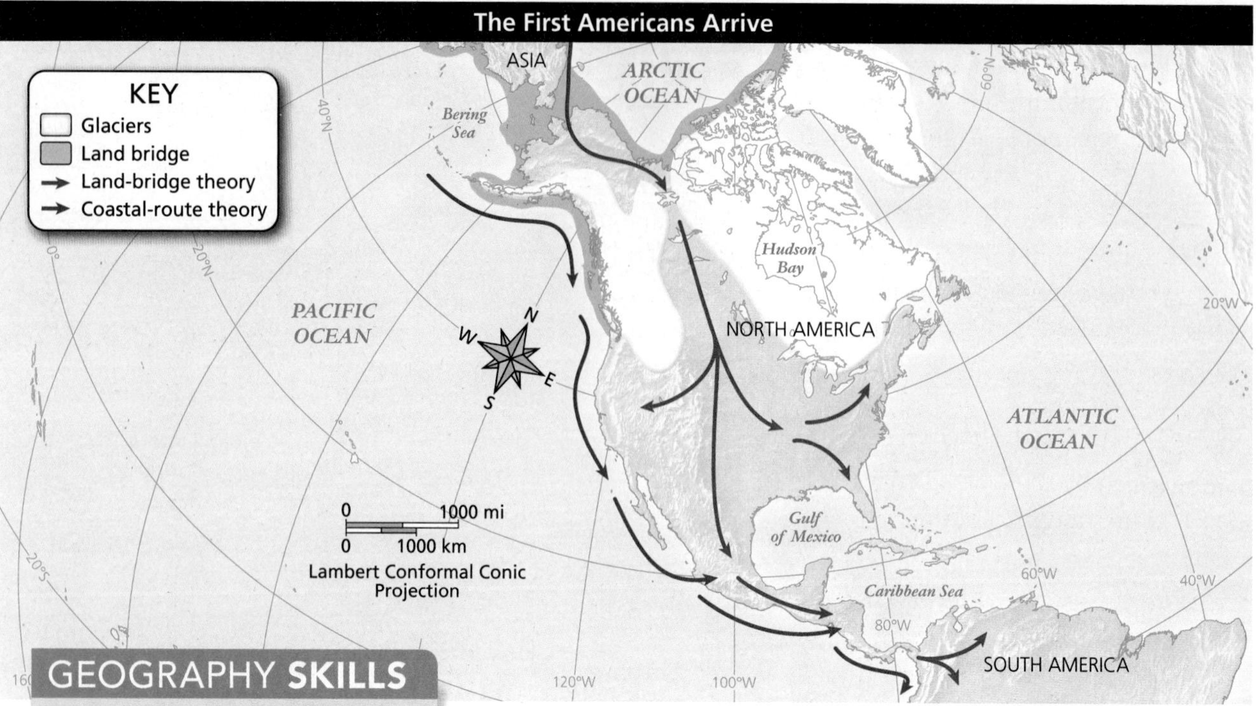

GEOGRAPHY SKILLS

This map depicts both the land-bridge and coastal-route theories of North American migration.

1. **Movement** What were the two ways the first Americans may have arrived from Asia?
2. **Identify Supporting Details** What route do scientists who disagree with the land-bridge migration theory believe early Americans followed?

Other scientists disagree. They think that the first Americans crossed the icy Arctic waters by boat, reaching North America by sea.

Once these early hunters reached the Americas, they had to keep moving in search of food. Slowly, over thousands of years, they spread across North America, Central America, and South America. The physical environments where they settled varied widely. American Indians adapted to the physical environments of mountain plateaus, dry deserts, fertile plains, lush woodlands, and thick rain forests. In adapting to these varied environments, American Indian groups developed many different customs.

Adapting to and Modifying Environments About 12,000 years ago, the last ice age ended. Glaciers melted. The land bridge between Siberia and Alaska disappeared.

About the same time, some kinds of large animals died out. This forced hunting bands to adapt to new conditions. Smaller animals, wild berries, nuts, grains, and fish became a larger part of their diets.

About 5,000 years ago, people in the Americas learned to grow crops such as corn, beans, and squash. Farming modified the environment and brought great changes to those who practiced it. Farmers no longer had to keep moving to find food. Instead, they stayed in one place and began to build permanent **settlements**, or small communities. As farming methods improved, people produced more food, which in turn allowed the population to grow.

Academic Vocabulary
according to • *prep.*, as stated by

READING CHECK **Understand Effects** How did farming affect communities in the Americas?

The Olmec

Farming was a key advance for early societies in the Americas. In time, some farming communities in the Americas grew enough **surplus**, or extra, food to support large populations, and the first cities emerged.

Cities marked the rise of the first civilization in the Americas. A **civilization** is a society—or a people sharing a language, territory, and economy—that has certain basic features. Among these are cities, an organized government, different social classes, a **complex** religion, and some method of record keeping.

Academic Vocabulary
complex • *adj.*, composed of two or more parts

The earliest known civilization in the Americas was that of the Olmec in present-day Mexico. The Olmec lived in the lowlands along the Gulf of Mexico about 3,500 years ago. Scientists have found huge stone heads carved by the Olmec. Some were 10 feet tall and weighed several tons. Smaller figures showed creatures that were part human and part animal.

Olmec farmers supplied nearby cities with food. There, powerful leaders built stone temples. The Olmec left few written records, but they did make many advances. They studied the stars and developed a calendar to predict the change of seasons and mark the passage of time.

READING CHECK **Identify Supporting Details** What features of Olmec society indicate that it was a civilization?

The Maya

The Olmec influenced many later peoples, including the Maya. The early Maya lived in the rain forests of what are today Honduras, Belize, Guatemala, and southern Mexico. About 3,000 years ago, they began clearing the rain forest and draining swamps to create farmland.

Maya farmers were able to produce great harvests of corn, enough to feed large cities. As the Maya population grew, city-states began to spring up from Central America to southern Mexico. A **city-state** is a political unit that controls a city and its surrounding land. Trade flowed along a network of roads that linked inland city-states and the coast. City-states often waged war with one another for land, riches, and access to trade routes.

Maya Social Classes Nobles also held great power in Maya society. The most powerful nobles were the kings, who also served as high priests.

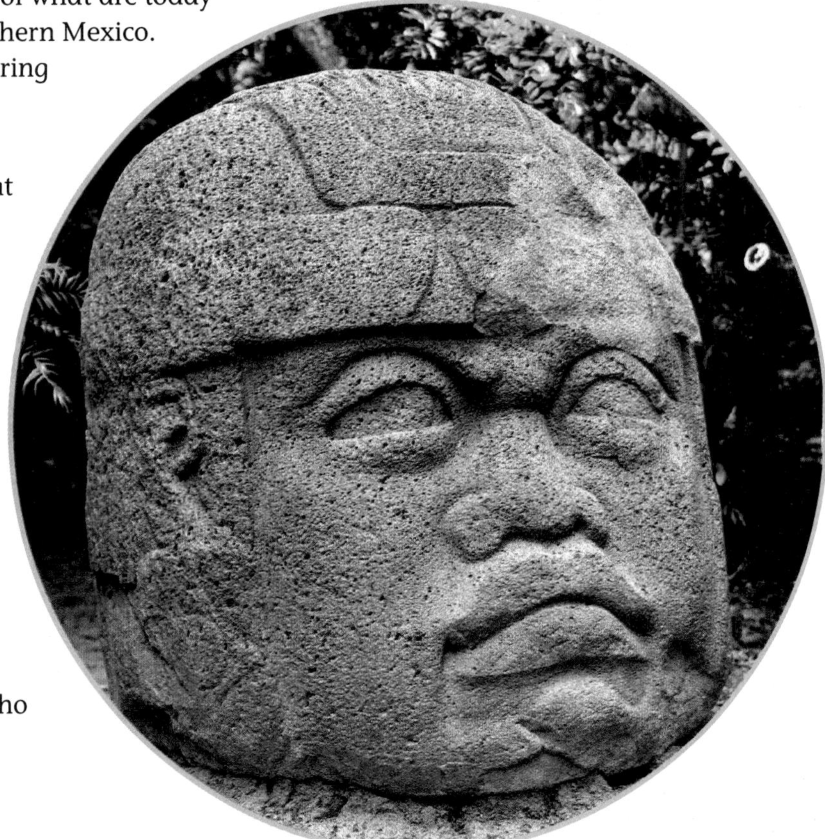

Analyze Images The Olmec, a tropical civilization, left behind many carvings of giant stone heads. They are generally thought to be portraits of Olmec rulers. **Use Visual Information** How can you tell that this object is made of stone?

Analyze Images Like the Maya, the Aztec also built temples and palaces atop huge stone pyramids. **Infer** What position in society might the person at the top of the pyramid hold?

Other nobles also became priests. Priests held great power in Maya society. Only priests, the Maya believed, could perform the ceremonies needed to bring good harvests or victory in battle. Priests conducted these ceremonies in temples built on top of huge pyramids.

Still other nobles served as warriors and government officials. Near the bottom of Maya society were laborers and farmers, who grew corn, squash, and many other crops. Below them were slaves, most of whom were prisoners of war or criminals.

Achievements in Mathematics and Astronomy Maya priests had to know exactly when to honor the many gods who were thought to control the natural world. Every day, priests anxiously studied the sun, moon, and stars. They learned much about the movement of these bodies.

Based on their observations, priests made great advances in astronomy and mathematics. They learned to predict eclipses and created a relatively accurate, 365-day calendar. They also developed a system of numbers that included the new concept of zero.

Then, around 900 CE, the Maya abandoned their cities. Historians are not sure why. Perhaps they did so because of warfare, a drought—or both. The rain forests swallowed up the great Maya temples and palaces. Although Maya cities decayed, the Maya people survived. Today, more than 2 million people in Guatemala and southern Mexico speak Mayan languages.

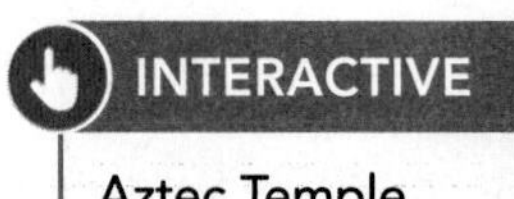

READING CHECK **Infer** Why did city-states form as the Maya population grew?

The Aztec

▲ The Aztec used astronomy to develop a calendar. This calendar is carved from stone.

Long after the Maya cities were abandoned, a new civilization arose to the northwest. Its builders were the Aztec. The early Aztec were nomads, people who moved from place to place in search of food. In the 1300s, the Aztec settled around Lake Texcoco (tays KOH koh) in central Mexico. From there, they built a powerful empire.

Tenochtitlán On an island in the middle of the lake, the Aztec built their capital, Tenochtitlán (tay nawch tee TLAHN). They constructed a system of **causeways**, or raised roads made of packed earth. The causeways linked the capital to the mainland.

The Aztec learned to farm the shallow swamps of Lake Texcoco. In some places, they dug canals, using the mud they removed to fill in parts of the lake. In other places, they attached floating reed mats to the lake bottom with long stakes. Then, they piled mud onto the mats to create farmland. Aztec farmers harvested several crops a year on these *chinampas*, or floating gardens.

With riches from trade and conquest, Tenochtitlán prospered. Its markets offered a wide variety of goods. "There are daily more than 60,000 people bartering and selling," wrote a Spanish visitor in the 1500s.

Religion Like the Maya, Aztec priests studied the heavens and developed complex calendars. Such calendars gave them the ability to tell their people when to plant or harvest.

The Aztec paid special attention to the god who controlled the sun. They believed that each day the sun battled its way across the heavens.

Analyze Charts Aztec society was hierarchical, meaning some groups have more power than those below them. **Draw Conclusions** What does the organization of Aztec society tell us about Aztec values?

Aztec Society

Level	Group	Description
1	**Emperor**	Chosen by nobles and priests to lead in war
2	**Priests**	Performed rituals, gave advice, and ran schools
2	**Nobles**	Served as officials, judges, and governors
3	**Warriors**	Could become nobles by killing or capturing enemies
4	**Merchants**	Often acted as spies for the empire
4	**Artisans**	Passed skills on to their children
5	**Farmers**	Made up most of population
6	**Serfs**	Worked land owned by nobles
6	**Servants**	Worked for those in the higher classes
6	**Slaves**	Were mostly prisoners or criminals

Did you know?

At its height, the Aztec empire is thought to have been made up of more than 400 small states and some 5 to 6 million people. It covered a territory of more than 80,000 square miles.

They compared the sun's battle to their own, calling themselves "warriors of the sun." They believed that the sun required human sacrifices in order to rise each day. The Aztec therefore killed thousands of prisoners each year to please this powerful god.

A Powerful Empire By 1500, the Aztec ruled a huge empire. It stretched from the Gulf of Mexico to the Pacific Ocean and included millions of people. The Aztec took great pride in their empire and their capital. "Who could conquer Tenochtitlán?" boasted an Aztec poet. "Who could shake the foundation of heaven?"

The Aztec world was far from peaceful, however. Heavy taxes and the sacrifice of huge numbers of prisoners of war sparked many revolts. The Aztec waged war in part to capture more prisoners for sacrifice. Across the empire, people conquered by the Aztec were eager for revenge. Enemies of the Aztec would eventually help outsiders from distant lands destroy the Aztec empire.

READING CHECK **Summarize** How did the Aztec benefit from digging canals?

The Inca

Far to the south of the Aztec, the Inca built one of the largest empires in the Americas. By 1500, their empire stretched for almost 2,500 miles along the west coast of South America.

An Impressive Capital The center of the Incan empire was the magnificent capital at Cuzco (KOOS koh), located high in the Andes in present-day Peru. Cuzco was a holy city to the Inca. All nobles in the empire tried to visit it at least once in their lifetimes. The city had massive palaces and temples made of stone and decorated with gold.

Analyze Images The remains of the ancient city of Machu Picchu show evidence of the incredible engineering capabilities of the Inca. **Infer** How might the buildings at Machu Picchu have looked when the Inca lived there?

At the center was the palace of the emperor, who was known as the Sapa Inca. The emperor was regarded as a god descended from the sun god.

From Cuzco, the emperor ruled more than 10 million people. They lived in varied environments, from coastal deserts to lowland jungles to the highlands of the Andes. The Inca had conquered the land through warfare.

The Incan empire was very well organized. The emperor was kept well informed about affairs in all parts of his empire. He sent high officials out to act as governors of his domain. The governors made sure that every person worked at least part of the time on projects for the state, such as road building, mining, and farming.

Analyze Images The Inca created a water system for the city of Machu Picchu using the natural stone from the mountains. **Use Visual Information** Why do you think the Inca designed the system in this way?

Incan Achievements To unite their empire, the Inca maintained a system of roads that covered more than 10,000 miles. Builders carved roads in rock cliffs and stretched rope bridges across deep gorges. Runners spread royal orders using the roads.

The runners carried with them a **quipu** (KEE poo). This was a cord or string with knots that stood for numbers or categories. The numbers might represent bags of goods that the government ordered from different parts of the empire. The quipu was also used by officials to keep records.

The Inca were skilled engineers. They built massive stone temples and forts. With only human labor, ropes, and wooden rollers, they moved stones weighing up to 200 tons. They also used their engineering skills to farm the dry, rugged mountain lands. They became experts at creating **terraces**—or wide, flat steps of land—out of the steep mountainsides. Sturdy stone walls kept rain from washing away the soil.

READING CHECK **Identify Main Ideas** Why was a system of roads so important to the Inca?

Lesson Check

Practice Vocabulary

1. How did a **surplus** of food lead to the first **civilizations**?
2. Why did the Aztec construct **causeways**?

Critical Thinking and Writing

3. **Identify Cause and Effect** How might the last ice age have helped hunters reach North America?
4. **Identify Supporting Details** What major impact did the development of farming have on the early settlers of the Americas?
5. **Understand Effects** How did the Aztecs' religious beliefs weaken their empire?
6. **Writing Workshop: Generate Questions to Focus Research** At the end of this topic, you will write a research paper on the question: How did a travel-related invention or improvement in one of the societies covered impact people's lives? Make a list of questions for this lesson that would need to be answered in order to write the paper. Record your questions in your Active Journal

LESSON 2

Cultures of North America

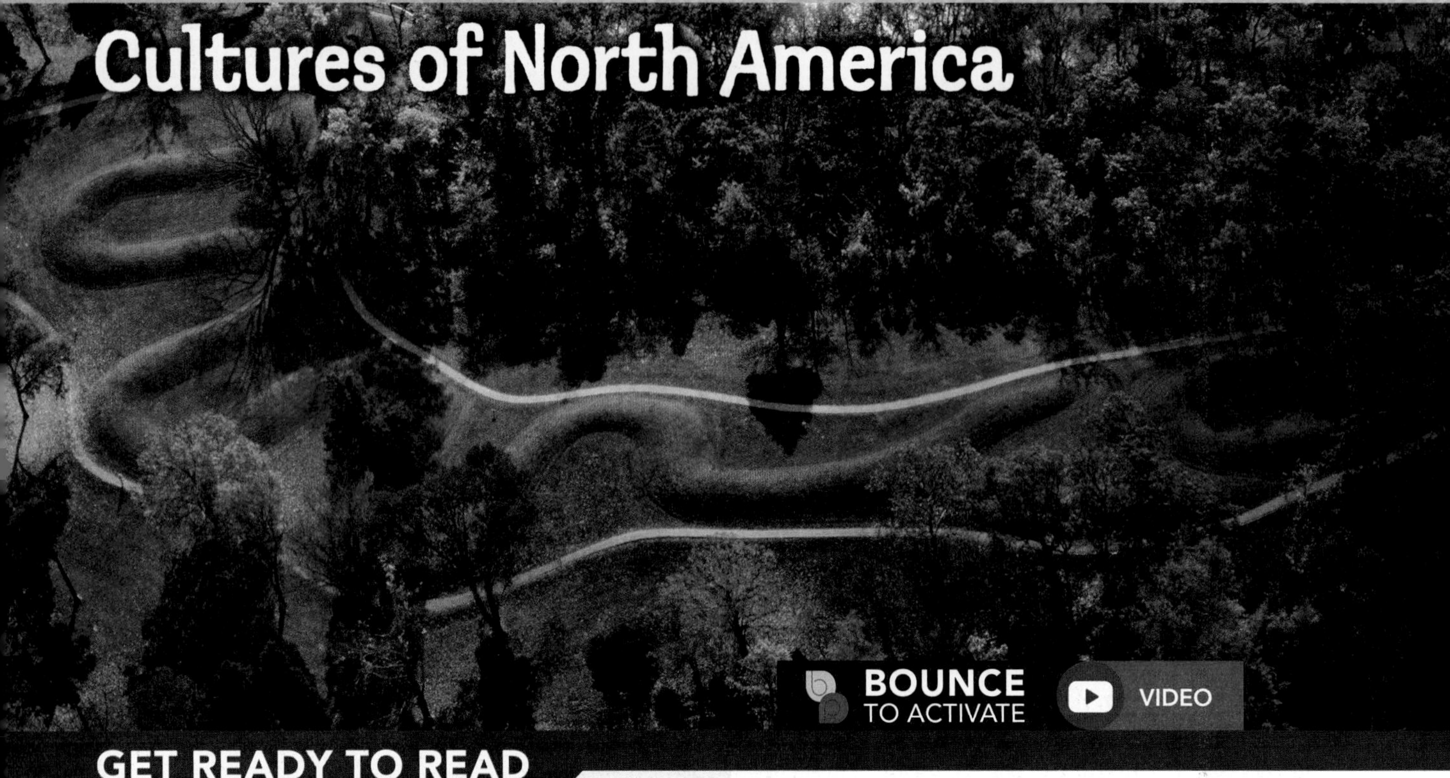

GET READY TO READ

START UP

Examine the photo of the Serpent Mound found in present-day Ohio. Why do you think the American Indians of the region constructed such a mound?

GUIDING QUESTIONS

- What early societies formed in North America?
- What are the human and physical characteristics of different regions of North America?
- What were the religious beliefs of American Indian groups in North America?

TAKE NOTES

Literacy Skills: Classify and Categorize Use the graphic organizer and your Active Journal to take notes as you read the lesson.

PRACTICE VOCABULARY

Use the vocabulary activity in your Active Journal to practice the vocabulary words.

Vocabulary		Academic Vocabulary
culture	diffusion	characteristic
adobe	potlatch	maintain
pueblo	clan	
culture region	Iroquois League	
tribe		

Scholars have found evidence of complex societies in North America. Traders and migrating people carried foods, goods, arts, and beliefs from Central America and Mexico to the early peoples of North America.

Early North American Societies

These peoples developed many distinct cultures in North America. A **culture** is the entire way of life of a people. It includes their homes, clothing, economy, arts, and government.

Land and People of the Southwest At least 3,000 years ago, knowledge of farming spread northward. Gradually, farming societies emerged in what is today the American Southwest. Much of this region is desert, with little rainfall and hot summers. The early societies in this region included the Hohokam (hoh HOH kum) and Ancestral Puebloans (PWEB loh unz).

The Hohokam lived in present-day southern Arizona. About 2,000 years ago, they dug networks of irrigation ditches for farming.

The ditches carried water from nearby rivers to fields in the desert land, allowing farmers to grow corn, squash, and beans.

The Ancestral Puebloans lived in the Four Corners region, where modern-day Colorado, Utah, New Mexico, and Arizona meet. Like the Hohokam, the Ancestral Puebloans irrigated the desert in order to farm. They also created a network of roads to link dozens of towns. Traders traveled these roads, carrying cotton, sandals, and blankets woven from turkey feathers.

Ancestral Puebloan Houses The Ancestral Puebloans built large buildings with walls of stone and **adobe**, or sundried brick. When the Spanish later saw similar buildings in the early 1500s, they called them **pueblos** (PWEHB lohz), the Spanish word for "villages." (They also called the descendants of the Ancestral Puebloans the Pueblo Indians.) About 1,000 years ago, some Ancestral Puebloan villages faced attacks from warlike neighbors. To escape that threat, they built new homes along steep cliffs. Toeholds cut into the rock let people climb the cliff walls. Farmers planted their crops on land above the cliffs.

Mound Builders Far to the east, other farming cultures flourished in North America. Among them were the Mound Builders, various cultures that built large earth mounds beginning about 3,000 years ago. Thousands of these mounds dot the landscape from the Appalachian Mountains to the Mississippi Valley and from Wisconsin to Florida. What is now the eastern half of the United States had a wetter climate than the Southwest, and the Mound Builders were able to farm without irrigation.

The first mounds were used for burials. Later mounds were used for religious ceremonies. They were similar in function to the pyramid temples of the Maya.

The best-known groups of Mound Builders were the Hopewell and the Mississippians. The Mississippians took advantage of their moist climate to grow enough crops to feed large towns. Between 700 CE and 1500, the Mississippians built a city at Cahokia (kah HOH kee ah) in present-day Illinois. As many as 30,000 people may have lived there at one time.

READING CHECK **Identify Supporting Details** How did the Hohokam adapt to living in a desert region?

Analyze Images The Ancestral Puebloans used stone and adobe to build this settlement in modern New Mexico.
Infer Much of this settlement still stands, even though it was built more than 900 years ago. What does that tell you about Ancestral Puebloan construction skills?

American Indian Culture Regions

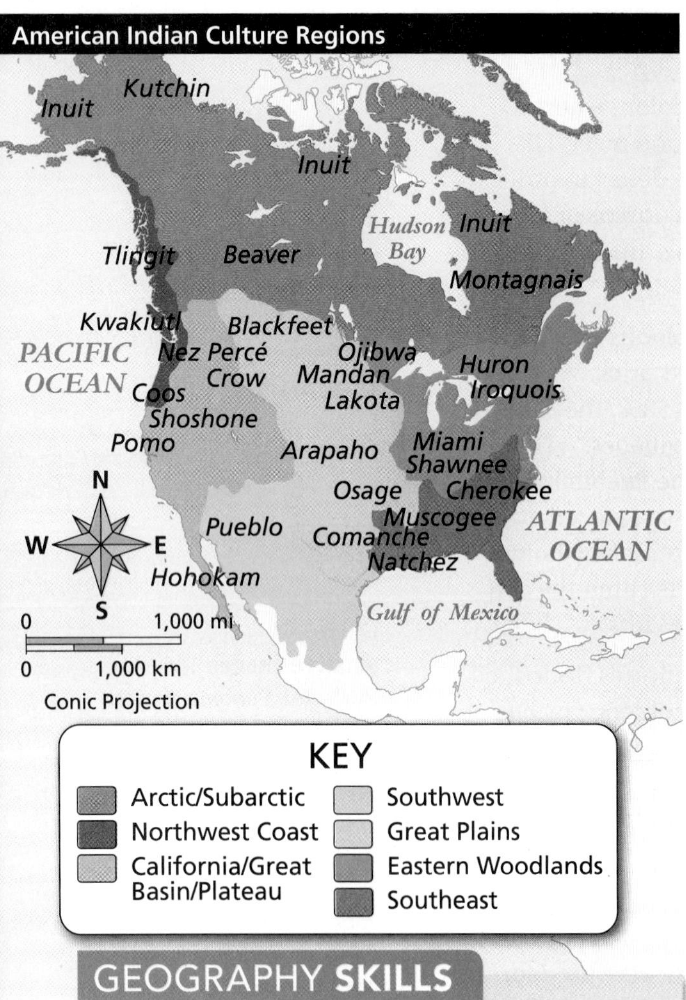

GEOGRAPHY **SKILLS**

Groups of American Indians formed shared cultures in different geographic regions.

1. **Place** In what culture region did the Miami live?
2. **Infer** Why do you think few tribes lived in the Arctic/Subarctic region?

What Were the Cultural and Physical Characteristics of North America?

Like American Indian groups today, early American Indians included many different people with many distinct cultures. In North America alone, there were hundreds of American Indian languages spoken. American Indian cultures, too, varied greatly, much like the cultures of the people of Europe.

American Indian cultures were adapted to the many different physical environments of North America. The physical **characteristics** of the environment in each region influenced population distribution and settlement patterns, or where American Indians lived, right up to modern times.

A **culture region** is a region in which people share a similar way of life. Most culture regions shared similar physical environments. Each culture region was home to many different tribes. A **tribe** is a community of people who share common customs, language, and rituals. Members of a tribe saw themselves as a distinct people who shared a common origin. Tribal leaders often made decisions for the group.

Hunting, Gathering, and Fishing

American Indians developed a variety of ways to meet their basic needs for food, clothing, and shelter. In some culture regions, tribes hunted animals and gathered nuts, fruits, and vegetables that grew in the wild. Other tribes depended on the sea for food. They made boats out of animal skins or carved canoes out of trees. From their boats and canoes, they speared or netted fish or hunted marine animals such as seals, walrus, and whales.

Farming Other tribes lived mostly by farming, planting corn, beans, and squash. American Indian tribes farmed in many parts of North America, from the American Southwest to the Eastern Woodlands. Over time, farmers improved their crops. For example, more than 5,000 years ago, wild corn was tiny, about the size of a human finger. Indian farmers developed dozens of varieties of corn, including ones with larger ears.

Academic Vocabulary
characteristic • *n.*, a distinguishing trait, quality, or property

Trade American Indians traded with one another for goods not found within their own region. Trade networks linked people across large distances. Goods sometimes traveled more than 1,000 miles from where they were made.

In the Northwest, traders met near the Dalles on the Columbia River. Local Indians caught and dried salmon, which they exchanged for goods and produce from other places. More than goods were exchanged by the different groups. New ideas and skills also spread.

This process of spreading ideas from one culture to another is known as **diffusion**. Through diffusion, skills such as farming spread from one American Indian group to another.

Adapting to and Modifying Environments American Indian cultures adapted to the physical features of different regions. These features influenced the kinds of food people raised, collected, or caught. Climate determined people's needs for clothing and shelter. Resources provided the materials they were able to use.

Climate and resources also affected organization. Where climates were harsh and resources limited, people struggled to find enough food and shelter. In such regions, people were often nomadic. They lived in small hunting bands. Each band included a number of families. In regions with more favorable climates and plentiful resources, people tended to live in larger groups and stay in one place for longer periods.

Cultures of the Arctic and Subarctic Regions
Frozen seas and icy, treeless plains made up the world of the Inuit, who lived in the Arctic region. The Inuit used all the limited resources of their environment. In the short summer season, they collected driftwood along the ocean shore, using it for tools and shelters.

INTERACTIVE

Native American Culture Regions of North America

Analyze Charts American Indians supported themselves by being resourceful. **Draw Conclusions** How did the foods American Indians ate influence their way of life?

Ways American Indians Supported Themselves

	FORAGING	FARMING	HUNTING
FOOD SOURCE	Fruits, nuts, seeds, roots, stems, and leaves from wild plants	Cultivated plants such as maize, beans, and squash	Wild game and fish
TOOLS AND TECHNOLOGY	Grinding tools for crushing seeds	Tools for clearing and cultivating: axes; hoes made with bone, shells, or stone	Tools such as spears and sharp points; trapping and netting food
INNOVATIONS	Baskets for storage	Methods for storing and preserving foods over winter months; irrigation methods	Techniques for drying meat and fish to balance the food supply over the winter
CULTURAL CHANGES	Mobility needed to find new food sources	Cultivating land required more labor but also created settlements and communities	Mobility needed when food resources became depleted
ADVANTAGES	No need to work in fields and risk fatal encounters with wild animals	Control over the food supply when growing conditions were favorable	Hunted animals provided clothing and shelter in addition to food
DISADVANTAGES	Poor weather could lead to shortages	Poor weather conditions could wipe out a harvest	Required a plentiful supply of wild game

Analyze Images The Inuit used caribou and seal fur to make warm clothing that would offer protection against extreme Arctic weather. **Infer** How might clothing worn by groups to the south have been different?

For most of the year, the Inuit lived in pit houses, houses dug into the ground and covered with wood and skins. Lamps filled with seal oil kept their homes warm even in the bitter cold. Women made warm clothing out of furs and waterproof boots out of seal skins.

The Subarctic culture region consisted of a belt of forest stretching across North America south of the Arctic. This forest is made up mainly of conifers, or cone-bearing trees such as hemlock and spruce. People in the Subarctic lived where they could find food. Groups like the Chipewyan (chip uh WY un) were nomads, following large game like caribou. Physical characteristics of the environment influenced their settlement patterns. The Carrier, for example, settled near salmon streams, although they sometimes moved to other hunting sites.

Cultures of the California, Great Basin, and Plateau Regions The California region offers more forgiving climates, with mainly hot, dry summers and mild, wet winters. The physical features included mountains, coastal lowland, and interior valleys and deserts.

Over 200 different tribes called this region home. Along the Colorado River, land was irrigated to grow corn, pumpkin, and beans. In the Northwest, the Yoruk (YAWR uk) used redwood trees to build houses and canoes and caught the plentiful fish of that region. In central California, salmon and acorns were plentiful. People there hunted and gathered plant products instead of farming. With enough food nearby, people could spend time producing crafts. The Pomo wove watertight baskets out of grasses and reeds.

The Great Basin culture region consisted of mountains and valleys with a dry climate, with hot summers and cold winters. Many of the bands that lived here, like the Bannock, were small and nomadic. They traveled to find seeds, nuts, roots, and bulbs. The Northern Paiute (PY yoot) lived near lakes and marshes. Hunting, fishing, and farming often provided enough food for them to stay in one place.

The Plateau region, centered on the Columbia Plateau, has a cool and dry environment, but winter snows feed rivers flowing through the region. Surprisingly, numbers of hardy plants and animals thrive in the region. Among the people of the Plateau region were the Ute (YOOT) and Shoshone (shah SHOH nee). The American Indians of the region had few possessions beyond digging sticks, baskets, and tools and weapons needed for hunting.

Cultures of the Northwest Coastal Region Elsewhere in North America the climate was kinder, which helped more complex cultures emerge. The people of the mountainous Northwest Coast enjoyed milder temperatures and abundant rainfall and food supplies. They gathered rich harvests of fish from the sea.

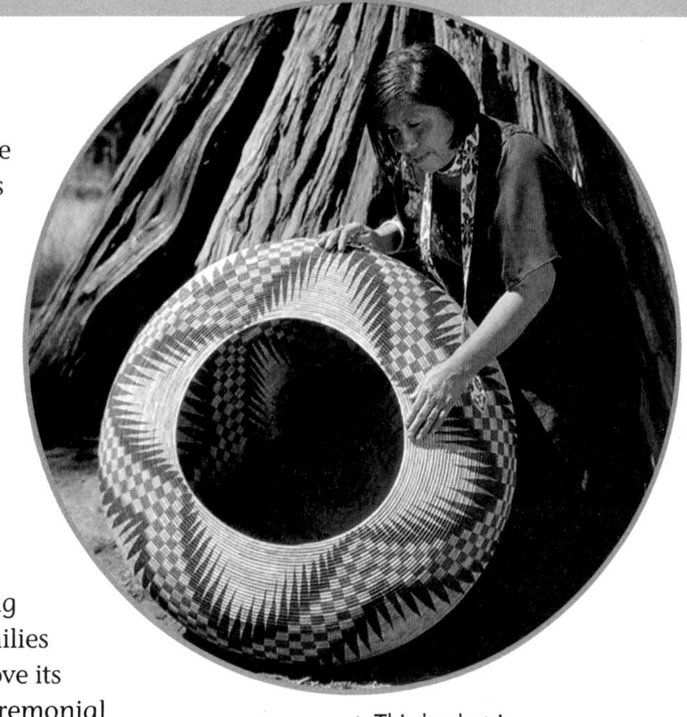

▲ This basket is representative of Great Basin American Indian artwork. It is made of grass roots, fern roots, and redbud roots.

From nearby forests, they cut down tall cedar trees and split the trunks into planks for houses and canoes. With plenty of food, the people of the Pacific Northwest stayed in one place. They built permanent villages and prospered from trade with nearby groups.

Within a village, a family gained status according to how much it owned and could give away. Families sometimes competed with one another. To improve its standing, a family might hold a **potlatch**, or ceremonial dinner, to show off its wealth. The potlatch could last for many days. The family invited many guests and gave everyone gifts. The more goods a family gave away, the more respect it earned. However, people who received gifts at a potlatch were then expected to hold their own potlatches.

Analyze Images The abundant forests of the Pacific Northwest provided the trees American Indians used to carve totem poles. The images on the poles often told stories from Indian creation stories. **Use Visual Information** Do you think the images symbolize animals or people?

▲ This stone head was made by a Mississippian artist. It dates to between 1200 and 1500 CE.

Cultures of the Southwest Region

The Southwest is a hot and dry region consisting of deserts, the southern Rocky Mountains, and the Colorado Plateau. People could survive only if they found water.

The Pueblo people used irrigation methods such as building dams and tanks to store water. They were able to grow corn and cotton on small farms. However, it wasn't all work in the desert. The Hohokam played games on ballcourts and made beautiful art with acid-etchings on shells.

Cultures of the Southeast Region

Many tribes lived in southeastern North America. This region is made up of coastal plains, the southern Appalachian Mountains, and rolling hills and valleys. It has hot summers, mild winters, and plenty of rainfall. Among the people of this region were the Natchez (NACH ihz). They benefited from the region's warm, moist climate. They hunted, fished, and farmed in the fertile Mississippi Valley.

The Natchez calendar divided the year into 13 months. Each month was named after a food or an animal that the Natchez harvested or hunted. Their months included Strawberry, Little Corn, Mulberry, Deer, Turkey, and Bear.

The ruler of the Natchez was known as the Great Sun and was worshipped as a god. The Great Sun's feet never touched the ground. Either he was carried on a litter or he walked on mats. Below the Great Sun were members of his family, called Little Suns.

Analyze Images The Nachez built ceremonial mounds to bury their dead and for other religious events. **Synthesize Visual Information** What do you think the Nachez may have done with the smaller mound atop the large mound?

Analyze Images Before Europeans brought horses to the Americas, Great Plains tribes hunted buffalo on foot, dressed as wolves. **Use Visual Information** How did horses make it easier for American Indians to hunt buffalo?

Next came Nobles, then Honored People, and finally Stinkards, or commoners, who made up the majority of the people.

By law, Nobles had to marry Stinkards. Even the Great Sun chose a Stinkard as a wife. In this way, no one family could hold the position of Great Sun forever. In time, even descendants of a Great Sun became Stinkards.

Cultures of the Great Plains Region The Great Plains were dry, open grasslands in the center of North America with very few trees, hot summers, and cold winters. Tribes like the Sioux (SOO) hunted wild animals to survive. The Sioux were nomads who followed the buffalo. They ate buffalo meat and used the hide to build tents. These tents were easy to carry when they were on the move. No part of the buffalo was wasted. They made spoons and cups out of the horns and weapons from the bones.

Cultures of the Eastern Woodlands Region Like the peoples of the Southwest and Southeast, the peoples of the Eastern Woodlands were not nomads. Their culture region spanned what is today much of the Midwest and Northeast. This region includes coastal plains, the northern Appalachian Mountains, the Great Lakes region, and interior rolling hills and plains. The region receives plenty of rainfall, with warm summers and snowy winters.

The Iroquois (IHR uh kwoi) lived near lakes and streams. They cleared land for farming, which was mostly done by women. Their diet was based on the "Three Sisters": corn, squash, and beans. Algonquian (al GAHN kwee un) tribes lived near the ocean and along the Great Lakes. Many of them farmed as well. In some places the soil was too poor to farm. Instead, the Algonquian built boats for fishing. Like the Iroquois, they also used trees from the forests to make houses and tools.

READING CHECK **Identify Cause and Effect** Why did the tribes who lived in the Southwest region irrigate the land?

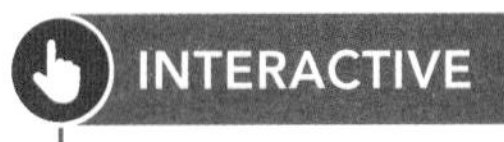
INTERACTIVE

Housing and the Environment

Religious Beliefs

The many American Indian groups held a wide variety of beliefs. Yet, they shared some basic ideas.

Close Ties to Nature Whether hunting, fishing, farming, or gathering wild plants, many American Indians felt a close connection to the physical environment. Their prayers and ceremonies were designed to **maintain** a balance between people and the forces of nature. They believed that they must adapt their ways to the natural world in order to survive and prosper.

Academic Vocabulary
maintain • *v.*, to keep in an existing state

Many American Indians believed that the world was full of powerful, unseen forces and spirits. They honored those spirits, which were thought to act and feel like humans.

In the Pacific Northwest, many tribes relied on fishing. One such group was the Kwakiutl (kwah kee OOT ul). Each year when they caught their first fish of the season, they chanted this prayer:

Primary Source

"We have come to meet alive, Swimmer, do not feel wrong about what I have done to you, friend Swimmer, for that is the reason why you came, that I may spear you, that I may eat you, Supernatural One, you, Long-Life-Giver, you Swimmer. Now protect us, me and my wife."

—Kwakiutl Prayer of Thanks

Analyze Images American Indians, such as the Kwakiutl, still fish for salmon using traditional methods. **Infer** Why are these people fishing from a plank instead of from the shore?

Analyze Images Pueblo Indians perform a dance in New Mexico. **Use Visual Information** What is the woman second from the right in this picture holding in her hands? Why might this be the case?

Special Ceremonies Kachinas were spirits represented by masked Indian dancers. The Pueblo believed kachinas could bring good harvests. At Pueblo festivals, the kachinas danced. Religious leaders prayed to the spirits and gave them gifts.

In the Southwest and the Southeast, many tribes held a Green Corn Ceremony when the corn ripened in the fall. The ceremony lasted for several days. It marked the end of the old year and the beginning of a new one. On the last day, a sacred fire was lit. Dancers circled the flames, and the people enjoyed a great feast. Women used coals from the fire to make new fires in their houses.

READING CHECK **Draw Conclusions** What do you think American Indians might have assumed if there was a lack of rain?

The Iroquois League

The Iroquois (IHR uh kwoi) people of present-day New York State called themselves the People of the Long House. They took great pride in their sturdy dwellings, called long houses. A typical long house was about 150 feet long and 20 feet wide. Twelve or more families lived in a long house.

Women had a special place in Iroquois society. They owned all the household property and were in charge of planting and harvesting. When a man married, he moved in with his wife's family.

Women also had political power. They chose clan leaders. A **clan** is a group of related families. If a clan leader did not do his job well, the women could remove him from his position.

Quick Activity

Create a matching game. Match characteristics of different American Indian cultures to facts about their climate, resources, and lifestyles.

Analyze Images The Iroquois lived in wooden long houses that were built clustered together. The long houses were built of posts and poles covered with tree bark. **Draw Conclusions** Why would the cultures of the Great Plains have been unable to build long houses covered with tree bark?

The Iroquois included five nations that spoke similar languages: the Mohawk, Seneca, Onondaga (ahn un DAW guh), Oneida (oh NY duh), and Cayuga (kay YOO guh). Each nation had its own ruling council. Until the 1500s, the five nations were frequently at war.

Then, in the 1500s, the five Iroquois nations formed an alliance to end the fighting. According to legend, a religious leader named Dekanawida (deh kan ah WEE dah) inspired Hiawatha (hy ah WAH thah) to organize the alliance. It became the **Iroquois League**.

A council of 50 specially chosen tribal leaders, called sachems, met once a year. The council made decisions for the League. Here, too, women had a political role because they chose the sachems and watched over their actions.

The Iroquois alliance did not end the fighting. The Iroquois spoke a different language from the Algonquian tribes, their neighbors to the east and west. The two groups fought many wars over land and trade.

READING CHECK **Identify Supporting Details** What role did women play in Iroquois culture?

Lesson Check

Practice Vocabulary

1. What were the buildings in Ancestral Puebloan **culture** made from, and what did the Spanish call them?
2. What role did women play in the **clans** of the **Iroquois League**?

Critical Thinking and Writing

3. **Compare and Contrast** What did the Ancestral Puebloans and Hohokam do to adapt to their environments?
4. **Identify Main Ideas** How did harsh climates and warmer climates affect American Indian cultures differently?
5. **Writing Workshop: Support Ideas with Evidence** In your Active Journal, record details about the impact of trade networks on the peoples of North America.

Primary Sources

Constitution of the Iroquois Nations: The Great Binding Law

In the 1500s, the five Iroquois nations formed an alliance to end the frequent wars among them. A council of 50 tribal leaders met once a year to resolve issues. Women chose the leaders and monitored their actions. The oral constitution of the Iroquois Confederacy was called the Great Binding Law.

▶ Hiawatha speaks to members of the council at the creation of the Iroquois League.

When a leader or lord was selected to represent his tribe, the constitution required that this pledge be recited.

"We now do crown you with the sacred emblem of the deer's antlers, the emblem of your Lordship. You shall now become a mentor of the people of the Five Nations. The thickness of your skin shall be seven spans—which is to say that you shall be proof against ① anger, offensive actions and criticism. Your heart shall be filled with peace and good will and your mind filled with a yearning [longing] for the welfare of the people of the Confederacy. With endless patience you shall carry out your duty and your firmness shall be tempered [lessened] with tenderness for your people. Neither anger nor fury shall find lodgement ② in your mind and all your words and actions shall be marked with calm deliberation. In all of your deliberations in the Confederate Council, in your efforts at law making, in all your official acts, self interest shall be cast into oblivion. ③ Cast not over your shoulder behind you the warnings of the nephews and nieces should they chide you for any error or wrong you may do, but return to the way of the Great Law which is just and right. Look and listen for the welfare of the whole people and have always in view not only the present but also the coming generations, even those whose faces are yet beneath the surface of the ground—the unborn of the future Nation."

—Constitution of the Iroquois Nations: The Great Binding Law, Gayanashagowa

Reading and Vocabulary Support

① "Be proof against" means that these behaviors should not occur.

② "Lodgement" means to reside.

③ What does it mean to "cast into oblivion"?

Analyzing Primary Sources

Cite specific evidence from the source to support your answers.

1. **Cite Evidence** What behavior was a tribal leader told to avoid?
2. **Identify Supporting Details** According to the pledge, what were two things that the leaders were expected to focus on?

Be an Informed Citizen

Follow these steps to become an informed citizen.

INTERACTIVE

Being an Informed Citizen

1 **Learn the issues.** A great way to begin to understand the responsibilities of citizenship is to first find topics of interest to you. Next, become well informed about civic affairs in your town, city, or country. Read newspapers, magazines, and articles you find online about events happening in your area or around the world. Analyze the information you read to come to your own conclusions. Radio programs, podcasts, and social media are also great ways to keep up with current events and interact with others about issues.

2 **Get involved.** Attend community events to speak with others who know the issues. Become well informed about how policies are made and changed. Find out who to speak to if you would like to take part in civic affairs and policy creation. There are government websites that can help direct you to the right person. These websites will also provide his or her contact details.

3 **Take a stand and reach out.** Write, call, or meet with your elected officials to become a better informed, more responsible citizen. To be an informed voter, do research about candidates who are running for office. Start your own blog or website to explore issues, interact with others, and be part of the community or national dialogue.

Complete the graphic organizer below to help you become an informed citizen.

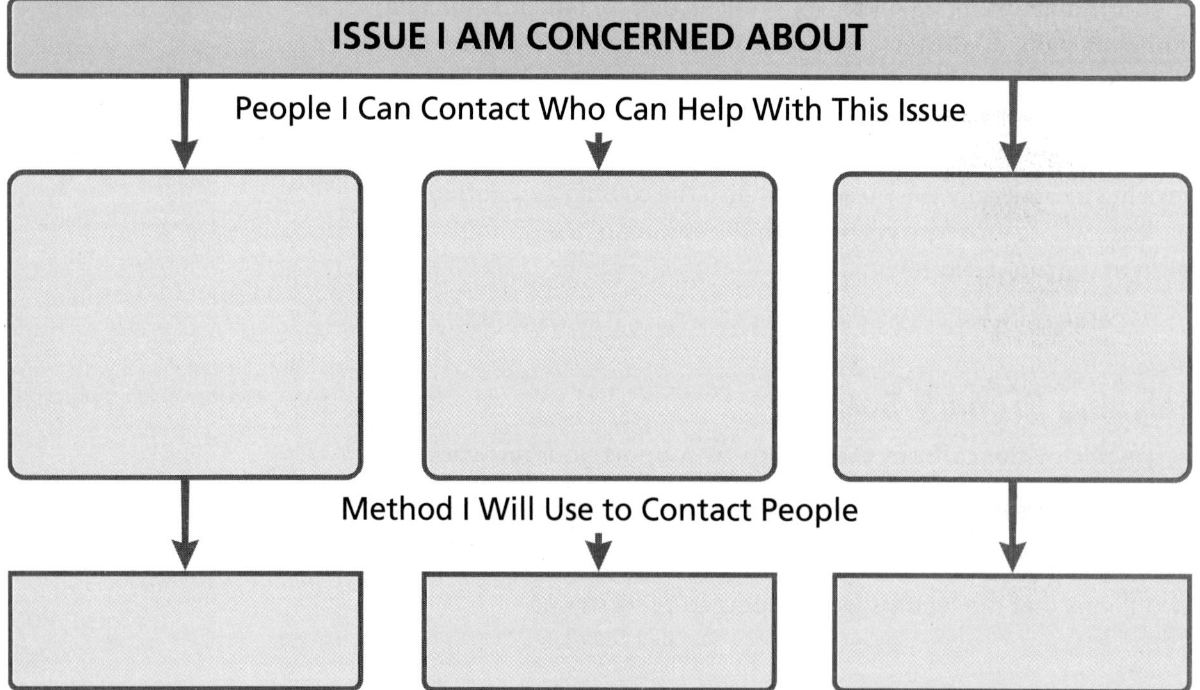

LESSON 3

Early Europe, Africa, and Asia

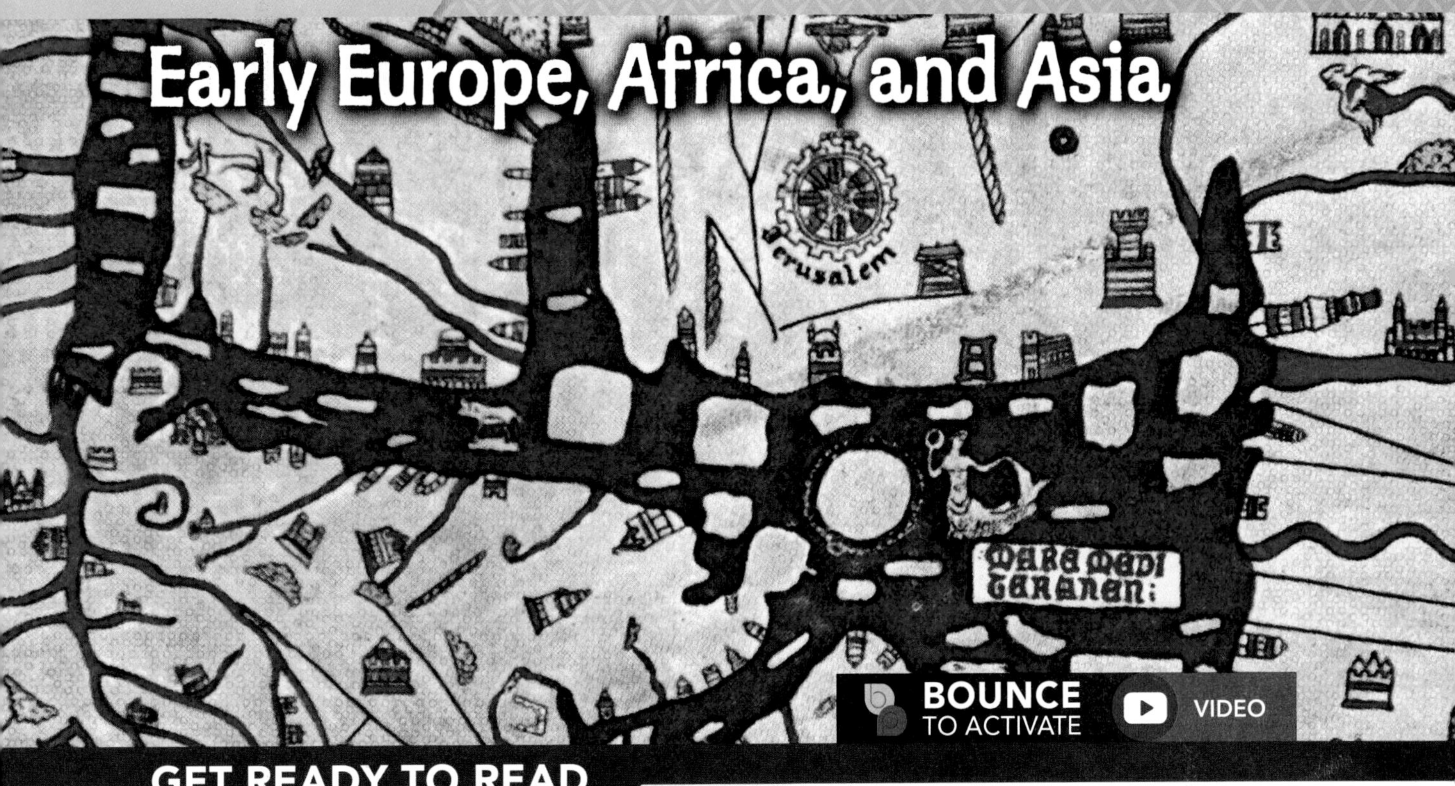

GET READY TO READ

START UP

Examine the map of the world from 1280. How does it differ from modern maps?

GUIDING QUESTIONS

- How did Europe change during the Middle Ages?
- Describe trade and technological innovations in the Muslim world, Africa, and East Asia.
- What was the impact of technological innovations on the Renaissance?

TAKE NOTES

Literacy Skills: Summarize

Use the graphic organizer in your Active Journal to take notes as you read the lesson.

PRACTICE VOCABULARY

Use the vocabulary activity in your Active Journal to practice the vocabulary words.

Vocabulary		Academic Vocabulary
feudalism	caravan	decline
manor	kinship	innovation
Crusades	Renaissance	
astrolabe		
Silk Road		

The period from about 500 to around 1500 is known as the Middle Ages. Many wars were fought, but the world also became more interconnected as trade grew and explorers traveled widely.

What Was Europe Like in the Middle Ages?

During the early Middle Ages, invasion and war were common. People in Europe had to find new means of defending themselves.

Feudalism A new kind of government evolved during the Middle Ages. Kings and queens divided their lands among warrior nobles. In return, nobles promised to fight for the ruler when asked. This system of rule by lords who ruled their lands but owed loyalty and military service to a monarch is called **feudalism** (FYOOD ul iz um).

At the top of feudal society stood the king and the most powerful lords. Next came the lesser nobles. Most people in feudal society were peasants who farmed the lord's lands and could not leave the land without the lord's permission.

Analyze Images A typical medieval manor included a castle, a church, fields for agriculture and livestock, and dwellings for serfs. ❶ Castle ❷ Church ❸ Serf home ❹ Fields ❺ Mill
Identify Cause and Effect Why was the mill placed along the river?

Feudal Life Feudal life revolved around the **manor**, which included the lord's castle and the lands around it. Manor lands might include several villages. Each manor was self-sufficient. That is, people made almost everything they needed. Life for peasants was hard. Peasants were farmers who worked mostly by hand on small plots. They struggled to produce enough food just to survive.

By about 900, life began to change. Peasants used new methods of farming to produce more food. Warfare **declined** and trade began to grow. Slowly, people began to look beyond their isolated villages.

Religion in Medieval Europe The most powerful force in medieval western Europe was the Roman Catholic Church. The Roman Catholic Church was the main branch of Christianity in western Europe. Like other branches of Christianity, it was based on the teachings of Jesus, who had lived centuries earlier. During ancient and early medieval times, the religion spread across Europe.

The Church ruled more than religious life. It owned large amounts of land and offered the only source of education. The clergy were often the only people who could read and write. Because of their efforts, much of the learning from the ancient world was preserved.

While Christianity was the main religion in western Europe, the region also had a strong Jewish community. The Jewish people's religion was Judaism, a religion centuries older than Christianity. It, too, had spread across Europe in ancient and early medieval times. While Jewish people played an important role in medieval Europe, they often faced persecution, or attacks because of their beliefs.

Academic Vocabulary
decline • *v.*, to draw to a close

The Crusades The pace of change in Europe increased between 1100 and 1300. This was in part because of the Crusades.

The **Crusades** were a series of wars fought by Christians to control the region then known as the Holy Land or Palestine, much of which is now Israel. This region included Jerusalem and the other places where Jesus had lived and taught. Muslims had controlled this region for centuries.

INTERACTIVE

How an Astrolabe Works

During the Crusades, tens of thousands of Christians journeyed to the Middle East. Fighting between Christians and Muslims continued for almost 200 years. Christians won some victories, and they ruled kingdoms in the region for more than 100 years. But in the end, they failed to keep control of the Holy Land.

Trade Grows The Crusades had important effects on Europe, however. Crusaders traveled beyond their villages and came into contact with other civilizations. In the Middle East, they tasted new foods, such as rice, oranges, dates, and new spices. They saw beautiful silks and woven rugs.

Europe had traded with the Middle East before the Crusades. However, returning Crusaders demanded more Asian foods, spices, and silks. Italian merchants could get high prices for such goods. They outfitted ships and increased trade with the Muslim world.

Academic Vocabulary
innovation • *n.,* a new method or idea

Technological Innovations in Navigation Trade brought new knowledge and with it, new technological **innovations**. From the Muslim world, Europeans acquired sailing skills and the magnetic compass. Muslims had adopted the magnetic compass from the Chinese. The magnetic needle of the compass always pointed north, which helped ships stay on course.

Another useful instrument was the **astrolabe** (AS troh layb), which helped sailors determine their latitude while at sea. These new instruments let Europeans sail far out to sea, beyond sight of land. By 1500, Portugal had taken the lead in this new overseas travel.

READING CHECK **Identify Main Ideas** How did the Crusades affect trade in the Middle Ages?

Analyze Images Many medieval Christians joined the Crusades to fight for control of territory in the Middle East. **Identify Supporting Details** What item hanging from the horse suggests a battle will occur?

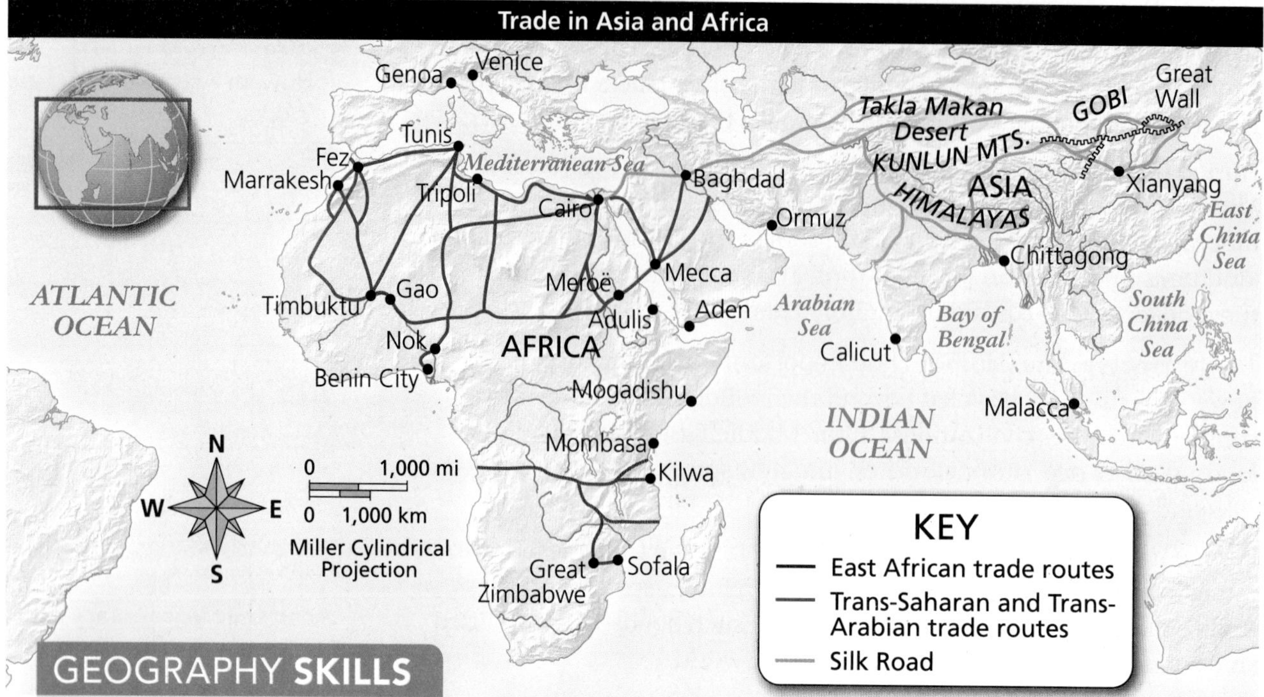

GEOGRAPHY **SKILLS**

Traders used routes such as the Trans-Saharan route and the Silk Road to transport goods to different places.

1. **Location** Which cities on the Trans-Saharan and Trans-Arabian trade routes were located on or near the Mediterranean Sea?
2. **Draw Conclusions** Which of the three routes probably had the least amount of trading? Why?

How Was the Middle East a Crossroads of the World?

Middle Eastern merchants played a large role in this growing trade. Linking Europe, Africa, and Asia, the Middle East was a major crossroads of the world.

Muslim Conquests and Inventions The growth of trade was also linked to the spread of a new religion. In the early 600s, a new religion, Islam, emerged in Arabia. A people called the Arabs lived in Arabia, in the southern Middle East.

Islam won many followers among the Arabs. Beginning in the 600s, Islam spread rapidly. Devout followers conquered North Africa and much of Spain. They conquered lands to the east, too, from Persia to India and beyond. Eventually, the Muslim world spread from South Asia to what is now Portugal and Spain. In many countries ruled by Muslims, however, there were also communities of Christians and Jewish people.

Islam expanded through trade and conquest. While some remained faithful to Christianity, Judaism, and other religions, many people in conquered lands chose to convert to the new religion.

Others were converted by force, or under the threat of crippling taxes. Elsewhere, Muslim merchants carried the new faith to people living along the trade routes of Asia and Africa.

Islam united Muslims from many lands and fostered the growth of trade. Muslims had a basic duty to make a pilgrimage, or journey, to the holy city of Mecca at least once in their lives. Every year, people from across the Muslim world traveled to Mecca.

INTERACTIVE

Routes of Exploration and Trade

Muslims from North Africa, Persia, Afghanistan, India, Spain, and West Africa crowded Mecca's dusty streets. They prayed in Arabic, the language of Islam. This regular travel encouraged trade among the Muslim lands.

People in the mainly Muslim Middle East developed many of the technologies we use today. Experiments with how light enters the eye led 10th century Muslim mathematician Ibn al-Haitham to invent the first pin-hole camera. A Muslim engineer invented the crankshaft, a key device in modern machinery, and the windmill was invented in Persia in the 600s to grind corn.

▲ The astrolabe helped sea captains determine the latitude of their ships.

Navigating the Seas Middle Eastern merchants traded across a vast area. They sailed to ports around the Indian Ocean. Their ships used large, triangular sails that allowed captains to sail close to the direction the wind was blowing from.

Middle Eastern sailors had knowledge of wind and weather conditions in the Indian Ocean. As a result, merchants in ports around the region knew when the trading ships had to sail and when they would return. Middle Easterners made important technological innovations in the astrolabe, which, as you have learned, helped sailors find their way far from shore.

Middle Eastern merchants sold porcelains, perfumes, and fabrics from China. Jade and tea were popular, too.

The Spice Islands of Indonesia offered nutmeg, clove, and mace. Cloth, indigo, and sugar came from East Africa, as well as spices and salt. Enslaved people were also traded. Goods like textiles and spices traveled well. They quickly spread across the globe.

Analyze Charts Trade routes made it possible for people in Africa and Eurasia to exchange goods with one another. **Identify Main Ideas** How did the exchange of goods and information between Africa and Eurasia benefit both regions?

Trade in Africa and Eurasia

AFRICA		EURASIA	
Domesticated camels enabled North African merchants to cross the Sahara. Caravans could include merchants, missionaries, pilgrims, and scholars.		Improvements in land and sea travel enabled goods and ideas to travel between East Asia, South Asia, the Middle East, and Europe.	
RESOURCES AND GOODS	**TECHNOLOGY AND EDUCATION**	**RESOURCES AND GOODS**	**TECHNOLOGY AND EDUCATION**
• Gold, copper, and salt • Ivory for artistic carving • Kola nuts for medicine; coffee beans prized as a stimulant	• Advanced metal forging techniques for toolmaking • Weaving techniques for patterned textiles • Education in mathematics, medicine, law, geography, history, and art at universities • Training in carpentry, fishing, and tailoring	• Spices for flavorings, perfumes, and medicines as well as European wines • Textiles including silk and wool • Copper, iron, and silver	• Techniques for making pottery, ceramics, glazes, glass, and lacquerware • Study in mathematics, medicine, and engineering; advances in agricultural and irrigation techniques • Architectural domes and arches in mosques, temples, and churches • Surgical instruments and techniques

Trade Along the Silk Road Some Middle Eastern traders traveled the overland routes that crossed the grasslands, mountains, and deserts of Central Asia and linked China and the Middle East. These routes had become known as the **Silk Road** because prized Chinese silks had been carried westward along them for more than 1,000 years.

Travel on the Silk Road was dangerous. Desert storms, hunger, and bandits were a constant threat. Traders formed **caravans**, or groups of people who traveled together for safety. Despite the dangers, trade along the Silk Road prospered.

By the 1400s, trade goods were flowing across a huge area. More than just silk was traded on the Silk Road. Everything from horses to spices and gems traveled along the route.

READING CHECK **Identify Cause and Effect** What impact did the Silk Road have on trade?

African Trade and Cultures

Trade routes played a large role in Africa, too. Long-distance trade routes crossed the vast Sahara, the desert linking West Africa and North Africa.

A peaceful afternoon in a West African village might be pierced by sounds of a horn. Children would shout, "Batafo! Batafo!" Traders! Soon, a long line of porters and camels arrived. Villagers watched as the tired travelers unloaded sacks of salt or dried fish. Gold, fabrics, jewelry, and enslaved people were also part of the caravan.

Sea traders also spread navigation technologies throughout Africa and eventually to Europe. The lateen sail was a triangular sail that allowed ships to travel toward the wind.

Although historians cannot be certain, it is likely that North Africans adapted the astrolabe for sea travel, too. It was used by African, Arab, and Indian sailors and then adopted by Europeans.

BIOGRAPHY 5 Things to Know About

MANSA MUSA

Emperor of Mali c. 1280 -c. 1337

- He built an empire in West Africa that was known far and wide for its wealth.
- On his journey to Mecca, his caravan had more than 70,000 men and 80 camels, which carried 300 pounds of gold each.

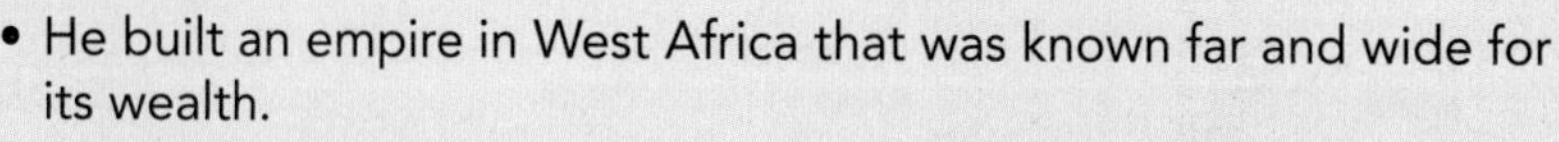

- Historians say he might have been the wealthiest person to have ever lived.
- His empire was one of the largest in the world at that time.
- He built the Great Mosque in the city of Timbuktu, which still stands.

Critical Thinking What information indicates that Mansa Musa was rich and powerful?

Analyze Images This medieval map shows Mansa Musa on his throne. **Use Visual Information** What information does the image of Mansa Musa on his throne, holding a golden object, add to the map?

East African City-States Trade had long flowed up and down the coast of East Africa. Small villages that had good natural harbors grew into busy trading centers.

Gold from Zimbabwe (zim BAH bweh), a powerful inland state, was carried to coastal cities such as Kilwa and Sofala. From there, ships carried the gold, and prized goods such as hardwoods and ivory, across the Indian Ocean to Arabia, India, and China.

Wealth from trade helped local East African rulers build strong city-states. East African city-states gained wealth and power by trading people as well as goods. They traded enslaved people from the interior of East Africa to Arabs and other groups across the Indian Ocean.

Many rulers of these city-states became Muslims. In time, Muslim culture influenced East African traditions. The blend of cultures led to the rise of a new language, Swahili, which blended Arabic words and local African languages.

West African Trading Kingdoms A region of grasslands, called the savanna, covers much of West Africa. Several rich trading kingdoms emerged there. Among the best known were Mali and Songhai (SAWNG hy). The city of Timbuktu was the major trading center for both kingdoms. These West African empires gained power through warfare. They conquered neighboring peoples and took control of surrounding lands.

The kingdom of Mali rose in about 1200 and flourished for about 200 years. Like the rulers of East Africa's city-states, many rulers in West African kingdoms adopted the religion of Islam.

Mali's most famous ruler, Mansa Musa, was a Muslim. In 1324, the emperor made a pilgrimage to Mecca. On the way, he and his caravan stopped in Cairo, Egypt. His wealth in gold amazed the Egyptians.

Analyze Images African villages included huts with roofs made from grass. **Infer** What other material from the environment did Africans use?

In time, stories of Mansa Musa's immense wealth reached Europe. A Spanish map from that time shows Mansa Musa on his throne, holding a golden object:

Primary Source

"So abundant is the gold in his country that this lord is the richest and most noble king in all the land."

—*Catalan Atlas*, 1375

In the 1400s, Songhai emerged as the most powerful empire in West Africa. Muslim emperors extended Songhai's power and made Timbuktu into a thriving city.

Ways of Life in Africa Ways of life varied greatly across the huge continent of Africa. While powerful trading states flourished in some regions, most people lived outside these kingdoms. Many lived in small villages. They made a living by herding, fishing, or farming.

Family relationships were important in African cultures. Although family patterns varied across Africa, many people lived within an extended family.

In an extended family, several generations live in one household. An extended family usually included grandparents, parents, children, and sometimes aunts, uncles, and cousins. The grandparents, or elders, received special respect for their wisdom and knowledge.

Ties of **kinship**, or sharing a common ancestor, linked families. People related by kinship owed loyalty to one another. Kinship ties encouraged a strong sense of community and cooperation.

Religious beliefs varied widely across Africa. Yet, African beliefs reflected some common threads. Links among family members lasted after death.

Read the quote. Does the quote verify the information in Mansa Musa's biography? Record your findings in your Active Journal.

In their rituals and ceremonies, many Africans honored the spirits of their ancestors as well as the forces of nature. Powerful spirits, they believed, could harm or could help the living.

READING CHECK **Summarize** How would you explain what an extended family is to a friend?

Chinese Trade and Technology

Africa had many different cultures and kingdoms. By contrast, in China, power was centered on one emperor. Chinese rulers were often suspicious of outsiders. Long distances and physical barriers separated China from Egypt, the Middle East, and India. This isolation contributed to the Chinese belief that China was the center of the Earth and the sole source of civilization. The ancient Chinese looked down on outsiders.

China Uses Technology to Increase Trade Chinese inventions changed shipbuilding around the globe. The Chinese invented the rudder, which made it easier to steer large ships. They created watertight compartments that went in the ship's hull to reduce the risk of sinking. They also probably invented the magnetic compass, which decreased the likelihood of getting lost on the open seas.

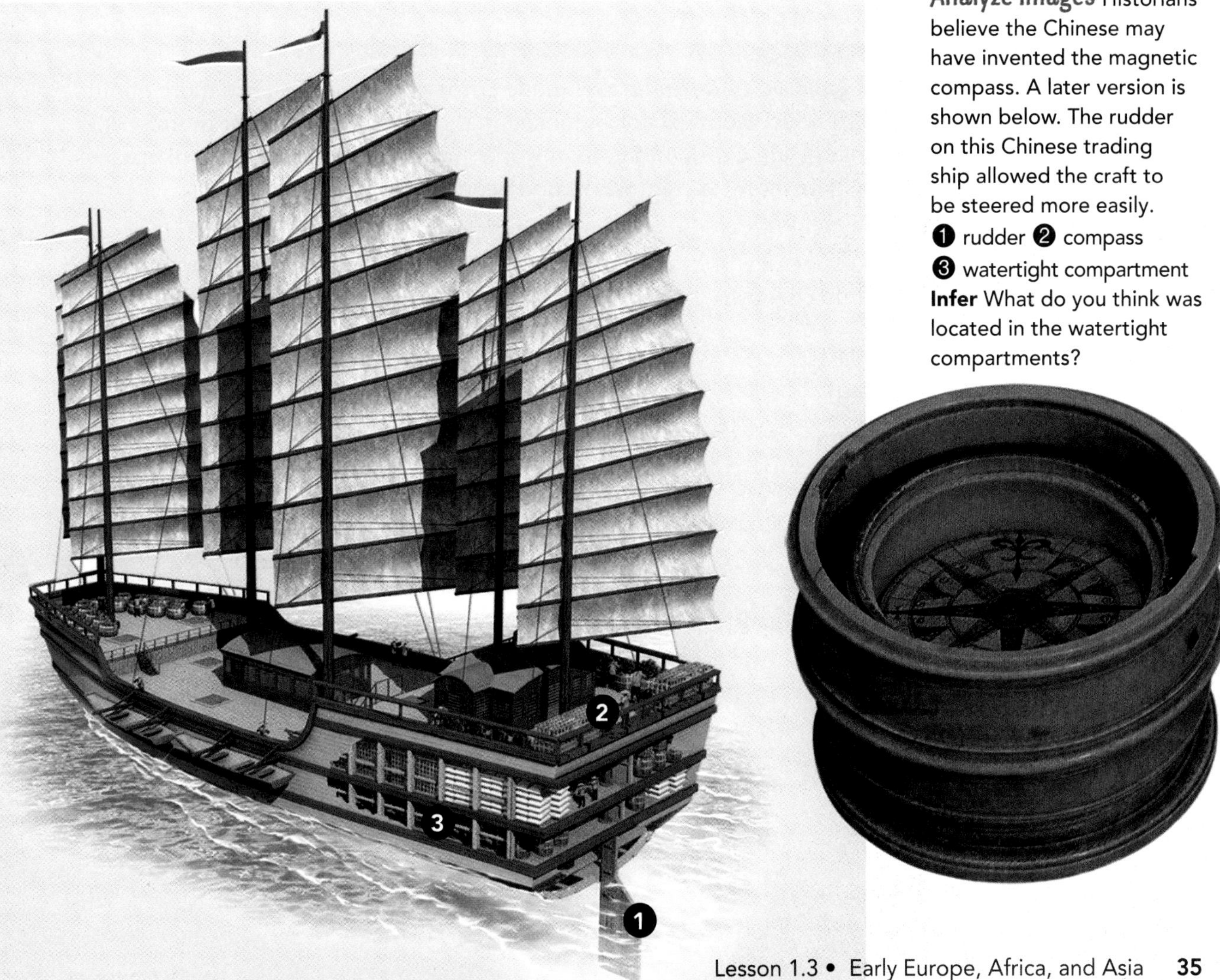

Analyze Images Historians believe the Chinese may have invented the magnetic compass. A later version is shown below. The rudder on this Chinese trading ship allowed the craft to be steered more easily. ❶ rudder ❷ compass ❸ watertight compartment **Infer** What do you think was located in the watertight compartments?

A young emperor who came to power in 1402 was eager to use these new technologies to increase trade. He ordered a huge fleet to be built and named Zheng He (JUNG HUH) to command it. Zheng He's fleet numbered more than 300 ships. It carried tons of trade goods. The largest ships were more than 400 feet long.

Zheng's fleet traded at ports in Southeast Asia, India, Arabia, and East Africa. At every port, Chinese traders carried on a brisk business. They expanded Chinese trade and influence across a wide region.

The Voyages End Zheng He's great fleet returned home with exotic goods and animals, such as giraffes, that the Chinese had never seen. However, China's overseas voyages soon ended. A new emperor decided that China had nothing to learn from the outside world. He outlawed most foreign trade. However, traders like Zheng He had spread Chinese technological innovations around the world.

The Chinese first invented paper in 105 CE. They also developed a printing press with movable type. The Chinese made advancements in timekeeping, developing several different kinds of clocks. They also invented gunpowder. Europeans later used gunpowder in handguns and cannons, which were based on Chinese designs.

READING CHECK **Identify Supporting Details** How did new technologies improve Chinese ships?

European Renaissance and Exploration

Increased trade and travel made Europeans eager to learn more about the wider world. Scholars looked in monastery libraries for manuscripts of ancient Greek and Roman works. Some traveled to the Middle East, where many ancient works had been preserved.

As scholars studied ancient learning, they began to make their own discoveries. They produced new books on art, medicine, astronomy, and chemistry.

Analyze Images Nobles benefited from the trade with Asia and Africa. They wore clothes made from silk and ate food flavored with spices from East Asia. **Infer** Why do you think nobles chose expensive fabrics for their clothes?

This great burst of learning and technological innovation was called the **Renaissance** (REN uh sahns). It is a French word meaning rebirth. The Renaissance lasted from the late 1300s until the 1600s.

The Chinese had invented the printing press and movable type, or block letters that could be used to print paper. However, the Chinese language required thousands of different letters, and movable type had little impact.

During the 1430s, a German printer named Johannes Gutenberg (GOOT un burg) is believed to have invented movable type without knowing that it had existed in China. Movable type was much more useful for printing in European languages, which used only 26 letters. Together, movable type and the printing press helped to spread Renaissance learning. Before movable type and the printing press, books were scarce and costly because each was copied by hand. With these technological innovations, large numbers of books could be produced quickly and at a low cost. Soon more people began to read, and learning spread more quickly.

▲ Moveable type made printed books available to many people and spread the knowledge of Renaissance thinkers and explorers.

A Search for New Trade Routes

During the Renaissance, trade brought new prosperity. European rulers began to increase their power. In England and France, kings and queens worked to bring powerful feudal lords under their control. In Spain and Portugal, Christian monarchs drove out Muslim rulers, who had governed there for centuries.

Rulers in England, France, Spain, and Portugal were eager to increase their wealth. They saw the great profits that could be made through trade. However, Middle Eastern and Italian merchants controlled the trade routes across the Mediterranean Sea. So, western Europe's leaders began hunting for other routes to Asia. European rulers also looked to Africa as a source of riches. Tales of Mansa Musa's wealth had created a stir in Europe, but no one knew the source of African gold.

Portuguese Voyages Portugal was an early leader in the search for a new trade route to Asia and for the source of African gold. In the early 1400s, Prince Henry, known as Henry the Navigator, encouraged sea captains to sail south along the coast of West Africa. Realizing that Portugal needed better navigators to accomplish the task, he set up an informal school to teach sailors techniques of navigation and the art of shipbuilding.

Under Henry's guidance, the Portuguese designed a new type of ship. The caravel (KAR uh vel) had triangular sails and a steering rudder. Caravels could be sailed closer to the direction from which the wind was blowing. Portuguese caravels stopped at many places along the coast of West Africa.

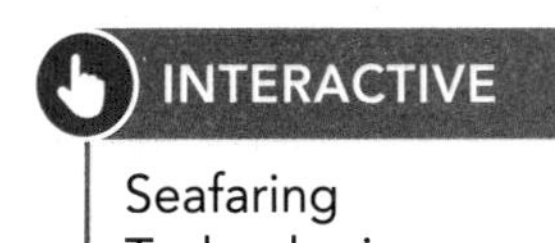

GEOGRAPHY SKILLS

This map shows the sea routes taken by Bartolomeu Dias and Vasco da Gama.

1. **Movement** Which Portuguese explorer stayed closer to land?
2. **Infer** Why do you think Vasco da Gama chose a route that did not follow the west coast of Africa?

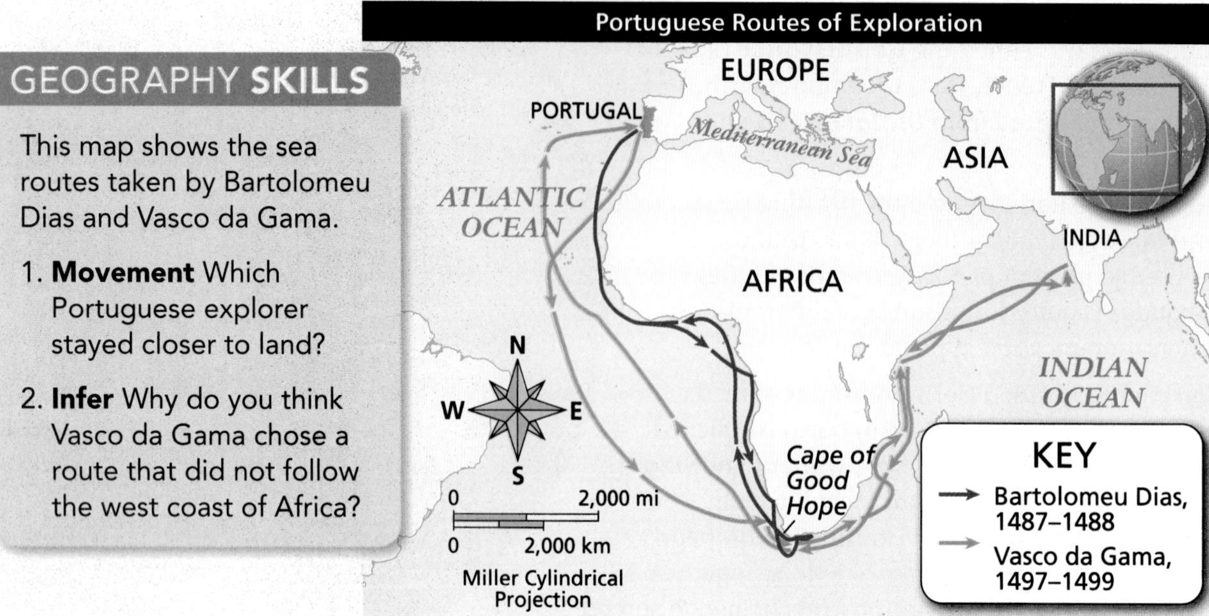

They traded cloth, silver, textiles, and grain for gold and ivory. They also bought Africans who had been forced into slavery and sold them in Europe and elsewhere.

Further Exploration Slowly, Portuguese explorers ventured farther south, hoping to find a sea route around Africa to the rich spice trade of Asia. In 1488, Bartolomeu Dias reached the southern tip of Africa. The Portuguese pushed on to the East Indies, the islands of Southeast Asia and the source of valuable spices.

READING CHECK **Understand Effects** What effect did movable type and the printing press have on learning?

Lesson Check

Practice Vocabulary

1. Describe life on the **manor** in **feudal** Europe.
2. How did innovations such as the compass and **astrolabe** help sailors?
3. What happened in Europe during the **Renaissance**?

Critical Thinking and Writing

4. **Identify Supporting Details** What was the impact of the Roman Catholic Church in medieval western Europe?
5. **Identify Cause and Effect** What encouraged Muslims from different lands to trade with one another?
6. **Identify Cause and Effect** What advantages did Middle Eastern merchants possess that allowed them to take such a central role in the expansion of trade?
7. **Draw Conclusions** In what ways did trade between China and other civilizations have long-term effects worldwide?
8. **Writing Workshop: Find and Use Credible Sources** You will need more information to write your paper. List three credible sources of information you could use to write a research paper about improved technology for travel, such as the astrolabe.

LESSON 4

European Exploration in the Americas

GET READY TO READ

START UP

Study the replica of one of the ships Christopher Columbus used to reach North America. Write three questions you have about sea travel during that time.

GUIDING QUESTIONS

- Why did Europeans explore the Americas?
- What was the impact of European exploration of the Americas?
- How did European and American Indian interactions affect both cultures?

TAKE NOTES

Literacy Skills: Identify Cause and Effect

Use the graphic organizer in your Active Journal to take notes as you read the lesson.

PRACTICE VOCABULARY

Use the vocabulary activity in your Active Journal to practice the vocabulary words.

Vocabulary	Academic Vocabulary
colony	modification
turning point	despite
circumnavigate	
Columbian Exchange	

Many stories exist about early people from Europe or Asia sailing to the Americas. Yet, real evidence has been hard to find. Most experts agree that such voyages were rare, if they occurred at all. Unlike other possible early voyagers to the Americas, the Vikings left behind a detailed record of their voyages.

Contact with the Americas

In 1001, Viking sailors led by Leif Erikson reached the eastern tip of North America. Archaeologists have found evidence of the Viking settlement of Vinland in present-day Newfoundland, Canada. The Vikings did not stay in Vinland long and no one is sure why they left. However, Viking stories describe fierce battles with Skraelings, the Viking name for the Inuit.

Evidence suggests that Asians continued to cross the Bering Sea into North America after the last ice age ended. Some scholars believe that ancient seafarers from Polynesia may have traveled to the Americas using their knowledge of the stars and winds.

Analyze Images The Vikings were one of the first groups to travel from Europe to the Americas. Their boats were powered by sail and oars. **Draw Conclusions** What disadvantages do you see in using this type of boat for travel in the ocean?

Modern Polynesians have sailed canoes thousands of miles in this way. Still others think that fishing boats from China and Japan blew off course and landed on the western coast of North or South America.

Perhaps such voyages occurred. If so, they were long forgotten. Before 1492, the peoples of Asia and Europe had no knowledge of the Americas and their remarkable civilizations.

READING CHECK **Identify Supporting Details** Why are we uncertain whether early people from Europe or Asia, other than the Vikings, sailed to America?

The Voyages of Columbus

Portuguese sailors had pioneered new routes around Africa toward Asia in the late 1400s. Spain, too, wanted a share of the riches. King Ferdinand and Queen Isabella hoped to keep their rival, Portugal, from controlling trade with India, China, and Japan. They agreed to finance a voyage of exploration by Christopher Columbus. Columbus, an Italian sea captain, planned to reach the East Indies by sailing west across the Atlantic. Finding a sea route straight to Asia would give the Spanish direct access to the silks, spices, and precious metals of Asia. The spice trade was a major cause for European exploration and a reason the Spanish rulers supported Columbus's voyage. They also wanted wealth from any source. "Get gold," King Ferdinand said to Columbus. "Humanely if possible, but at all hazards—get gold."

Crossing the Atlantic In August 1492, Columbus set out with three ships and about 90 sailors. As captain, he commanded the largest vessel, the *Santa María*. The other ships were the *Niña* and the *Pinta*.

After a brief stop at the Canary Islands, the little fleet continued west into unknown seas. Fair winds sped them along, but a month passed without the sight of land. Some sailors began to grumble. They had never been away from land for so long and feared being lost at sea. Still, Columbus sailed on.

Did you know?

Many streets in the United States have been named in honor of Christopher Columbus, such as this one in New York City.

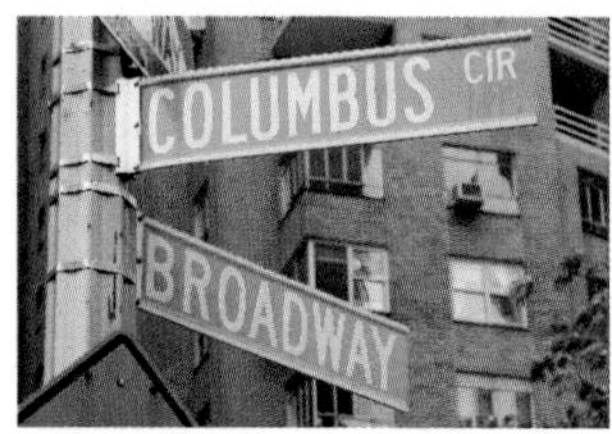

On October 7, sailors saw flocks of birds flying southwest. Columbus changed course to follow the birds. A few days later, crew members spotted tree branches and flowers floating in the water. At 2 A.M. on October 12, the lookout on the *Pinta* spotted white cliffs shining in the moonlight. *"Tierra! Tierra!"* he shouted. "Land! Land!"

At dawn, Columbus rowed ashore and planted the banner of Spain. He was convinced that he had reached the East Indies in Asia. He called the people he found there "Indians." In fact, he had reached islands off the coasts of North America and South America in the Caribbean Sea. These islands later became known as the West Indies. For three months, Columbus explored the West Indies. To his delight, he found signs of gold on the islands. Eager to report his success, he returned to Spain.

Columbus Claims Lands for Spain In Spain, Columbus presented Queen Isabella and King Ferdinand with gifts of pink pearls and brilliantly colored parrots. Columbus brought with him many things that Europeans had never seen before: tobacco, pineapples, and hammocks used for sleeping. Columbus also described the "Indians" he had met, the Taino (TY noh). The Taino, he promised, could easily be converted to Christianity and could also be used as slaves.

The Spanish monarchs were impressed. They gave Columbus the title Admiral of the Ocean Sea. They also agreed to finance future voyages. The promise of great wealth, and the chance to spread Christianity, gave them a reason to explore further.

Columbus made three more voyages across the Atlantic. In 1493, he founded the first Spanish colony in the Americas, Santo Domingo, on an island he called Hispaniola (present-day Haiti and the Dominican Republic). A **colony** is an area settled and ruled by the government of a distant land. Columbus also explored present-day Cuba and Jamaica. He sailed along the coasts of Central America and northern South America. He claimed all of these lands for Queen Isabella of Spain.

Columbus proved to be a better explorer than governor. During his third expedition, settlers on Hispaniola complained of his harsh rule. Queen Isabella appointed an investigator, who sent Columbus back to Spain in chains.

Analyze Images This illustration shows Columbus meeting the Taino of the West Indies. His voyages benefited Spain but brought much misery to the world of the Taino. **Infer** How do you think the Taino might have reacted to Columbus's arrival?

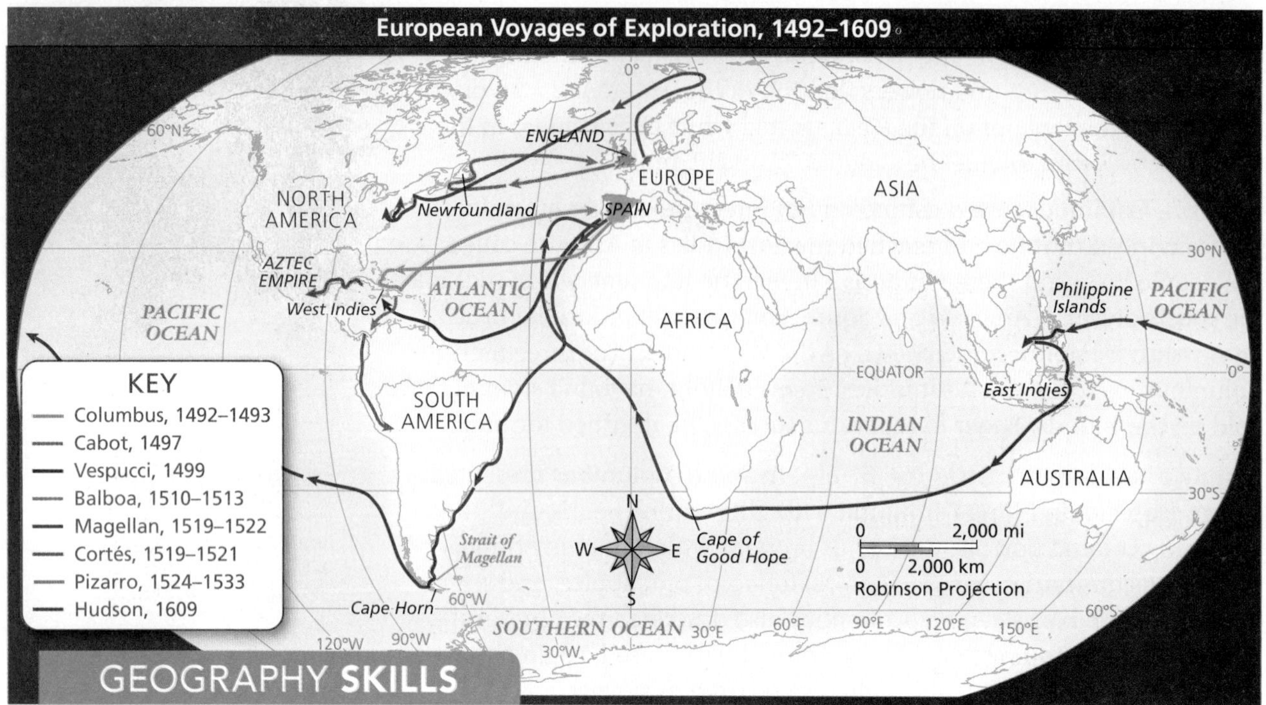

GEOGRAPHY SKILLS

Many Europeans went on voyages of exploration in the 1400s, 1500s, and 1600s.

1. **Location** From which European country did most voyages of exploration originate?
2. **Infer** Why do you think Magellan was the only explorer to sail around the world?

In the end, the queen pardoned Columbus, but he never regained the honors he had won earlier. He died in 1506, still convinced that he had reached Asia.

The Impact of Columbus's Voyages Columbus has long been honored as the bold sea captain who "discovered America." Today, we recognize that American Indians had discovered and settled these lands long before 1492. We also recognize that Columbus and the Europeans who followed him treated the ancient inhabitants of the Americas brutally. Still, Columbus's voyages did change history. They marked the beginning of lasting contact among the peoples of Europe, Africa, and the Americas.

For a great many American Indians, contact had tragic results. Columbus and those who followed were convinced that European culture was superior to that of the Indians. The Spanish claimed Taino lands and forced the Taino to work in gold mines, on ranches, or in Spanish households. Many Taino died from harsh conditions or European diseases. The Taino population was wiped out.

Still, the voyages of Columbus signaled a turning point for the Americas. A **turning point** is a moment in history that marks a decisive change. Curious Europeans saw the new lands as a place where they could settle, trade, and grow rich.

READING CHECK **Identify Main Ideas** What reasons did Spain have for sending Columbus on his voyages?

Spanish Exploration Continues

After the voyages of Columbus, the Spanish explored and settled other Caribbean islands that Columbus had found. They sought gold, land for crops, people to enslave, and converts to Christianity for the Spanish crown. By 1511, they had conquered Puerto Rico, Jamaica, and Cuba. They also explored the eastern coasts of North America and South America in search of a western route to Asia.

In 1513, Vasco Núñez de Balboa (bal BOH uh) crossed the Isthmus of Panama. American Indians had told him that a large body of water lay to the west. With a party of Spanish soldiers and Indians, Balboa reached the Pacific Ocean and claimed the ocean for Spain.

The Spanish had no idea how wide the Pacific was until a sea captain named Ferdinand Magellan (muh JEL un) sailed across it. The expedition—made up of five ships and about 250 crew members—left Spain in 1519. Fifteen months later, it cut through the stormy southern tip of South America by way of what is now known as the Strait of Magellan and entered the Pacific Ocean. Crossing the vast Pacific, the sailors ran out of food:

Quest CONNECTIONS

What fact from Magellan's biography helps you to verify the facts in Pigafetta's account? Record your ideas in your Active Journal.

Primary Source

"We remained 3 months and 20 days without taking in provisions or other refreshments and ate only old biscuit reduced to powder, full of grubs and stinking from the dirt which rats had made on it. We drank water that was yellow and stinking."

—Antonio Pigafetta, *The Diary of Antonio Pigafetta*

INTERACTIVE

Reasons to Explore

BIOGRAPHY 5 Things to Know About

FERDINAND MAGELLAN

Portuguese Explorer 1480–1521

- He sailed around South America and spent 99 days crossing the Pacific Ocean.
- He became interested in sea exploration as a boy, when he worked for the family of Portugal's queen.
- He launched his journey because he was looking for the Spice Islands, which are off the coast of Indonesia.
- During the journey, members of his crew rebelled against him and tried to take over the fleet, but Magellan stopped them.
- Magellan died in battle before he reached the Spice Islands.

Critical Thinking Why do you think Magellan's crew rebelled against him?

INTERACTIVE

The Columbian Exchange

Magellan himself was killed in a battle with the local people of the Philippine Islands off the coast of Asia.

In 1522, only one ship and 18 sailors returned to Spain. They were the first people to **circumnavigate**, or sail completely around, the world. In doing so, they had found an all-water western route to Asia. Europeans became aware of the true size of the Earth.

READING CHECK **Understand Effects** Explain the significance of Magellan's voyage.

How Did the Columbian Exchange Affect the Rest of the World?

Academic Vocabulary
modification • *n.*, a change

The encounter between the peoples of the Eastern and Western Hemispheres sparked a global exchange of goods and ideas. Because it started with the voyages of Columbus, this transfer is known as the **Columbian Exchange**. The Columbian Exchange refers to a biological and cultural exchange of animals, plants, human populations, diseases, food, government, technology, the arts, and languages.

The exchange went in both directions. Europeans learned much from American Indians. At the same time, Europeans contributed in many ways to the culture of the Americas. This exchange also brought about many **modifications**, or changes, to the physical environment of the Americas, with both positive and negative results.

Changing Environments Europeans introduced domestic animals such as chickens from Europe and Africa. European pigs, cattle, and horses often escaped into the wild and multiplied rapidly. Forests and grasslands were converted to pastures. As horses spread through what would become the United States, Indians learned to ride them and used them to carry heavy loads.

Analyze Images Horses and other domesticated animals were introduced to the Americas by Europeans. Horses soon became part of American Indians' way of life. **Understand Effects** In what ways do you think horses helped American Indians?

THE COLUMBIAN EXCHANGE

Famines and starvation were common events in Europe during the Middle Ages. Famine affected native peoples of the Americas as well. As a result of the Columbian Exchange, newly arrived species made the food supply more abundant and diverse on both sides of the ocean.

CORN OR MAIZE

Previously unknown, corn became a dietary staple in Mediterranean, African, and Asian countries.

WHEAT AND RICE

Brought by Spaniards, wheat and rice grew well in the Americas. Rice was sometimes used as a substitute for corn.

FROM THE AMERICAS TO EUROPE, AFRICA, AND ASIA

- maize
- potatoes
- sweet potatoes
- beans
- peanuts
- squash
- pumpkins
- peppers
- pineapples
- tomatoes
- cocoa

FROM EUROPE, AFRICA, AND ASIA TO THE AMERICAS

- wheat
- sugar
- bananas
- rice
- grapes
- olive oil
- dandelions
- horses
- pigs
- cows
- goats
- chickens

SUGAR

Europeans brought both sugar cane and enslaved Africans to grow it to the Americas.

COWS AND PIGS

Cows and pigs were unknown in the Americas before Europeans brought them. Over time, American Indians added beef and pork to their diets.

Analyze Graphs The Columbian Exchange affected people all over the world. **Identify Main Ideas** What were some positive consequences of the Columbian Exchange?

Plants from Europe and Africa changed the way American Indians lived. The first bananas came from the Canary Islands. By 1520, one Spaniard reported that banana trees had spread "so greatly that it is marvelous to see the great abundance of them." Oranges, lemons, and figs were also new to the Americas. In North America, explorers also brought such plants as bluegrass, the daisy, and the dandelion. These plants spread quickly in American soil and modified American grasslands.

Tragically, Europeans also brought new diseases, such as smallpox and influenza. American Indians had no resistance to these diseases. Historians estimate that within 75 years, diseases from Europe had killed almost 90 percent of the people in the Caribbean Islands and in Mexico.

American Indian Influences on Europe, Africa, and Asia For their part, American Indians introduced Europeans, Africans, and Asians to new foods, customs, and ideas. After 1492, elements of American Indian ways of life gradually spread around the world. Sadly, disease also spread from the Americas to Europe and other parts of the world.

American Indians introduced Europeans to valuable food crops such as corn, potatoes, sweet potatoes, beans, tomatoes, manioc, squash, peanuts, pineapples, and blueberries. Today, almost half the world's food crops come from plants that were first grown in the Americas.

Europeans carried the new foods with them as they sailed around the world. Everywhere, people's diets changed and populations increased. In South Asia, people used American hot peppers and chilies to spice stews. Chinese peasants began growing corn and sweet potatoes. Italians made sauces from tomatoes. People in West Africa grew manioc and corn.

Quick Activity

Plan a dinner party using food from the Columbian Exchange. Record your plan in your Active Journal.

Analyze Images In the 1600s, European settlers traveled along the Mississippi River in canoes. **Synthesize Visual Information** What is one difference between this canoe and the boats the Vikings used?

European settlers often adopted American Indian skills. In the North, Indians showed Europeans how to use snowshoes and trap beavers and other fur-bearing animals. European explorers learned how to paddle Indian canoes. Some leaders studied American Indian political structures. In the 1700s, Benjamin Franklin admired the Iroquois League and urged American colonists to unite in a similar way.

Positive and Negative Consequences

Through the Columbian Exchange, Europeans and American Indians modified their environments and gained new resources and skills. At the same time, warfare and disease killed many on both sides. Europeans viewed expansion positively. They gained great wealth, explored trade routes, and spread Christianity. Yet their farming, mining, and diseases took a toll on the physical environment and left many American Indians dead. **Despite** these negatives, the Columbian Exchange shaped the modern world, including what would become the United States.

Academic Vocabulary
despite • *prep.*, in spite of; notwithstanding

READING CHECK **Summarize** How would you define the Columbian Exchange?

Lesson Check

Practice Vocabulary

1. What was the first Spanish **colony** in the Americas?
2. How did the **Columbian Exchange** affect Europe and the Americas?

Critical Thinking and Writing

3. **Use Evidence** How did European expansion in the Americas affect American Indians?
4. **Compare and Contrast** How did the expeditions of Vasco Nuñez de Balboa and Ferdinand Magellan differ?
5. **Summarize** the career of Christopher Columbus.
6. **Draw Conclusions** Why were American Indians so susceptible to European diseases, such as influenza?
7. **Writing Workshop: Develop a Clear Thesis** You should now choose the invention or improvement for your paper. Write a thesis in your Active Journal in which you address the question: How did a travel-related invention or improvement in one of the societies covered in this topic impact people's lives?

Primary Sources

Christopher Columbus, Diary

During his voyage across the Atlantic Ocean, Christopher Columbus recorded his thoughts. In these excerpts, you will see that Columbus was concerned about his crew.

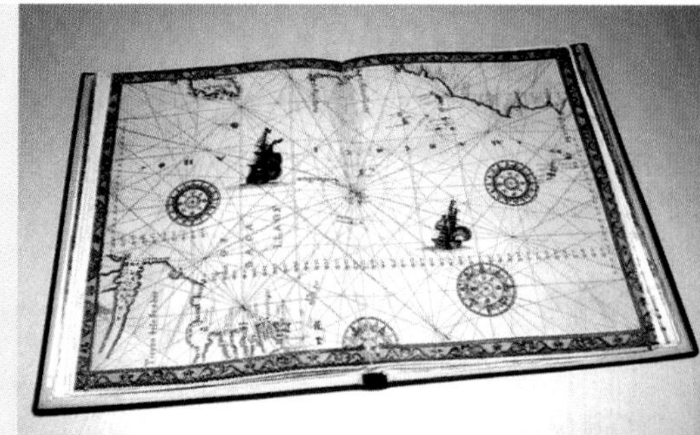

▶ When Columbus returned to Europe from his first voyage, he gave his journal, written during the expedition, to Queen Isabella.

Sunday, 9 September. Sailed this day nineteen leagues ①, and determined to count less than the true number, that the crew might not be dismayed if the voyage should prove long. ② In the night sailed one hundred and twenty miles, at the rate of ten miles an hour, which make thirty leagues. The sailors steered badly, causing the vessels to fall to leeward toward the northeast, for which the Admiral reprimanded them repeatedly.

Monday, 10 September. This day and night sailed sixty leagues ③, at the rate of ten miles an hour, which are two leagues and a half. Reckoned only forty-eight leagues, that the men might not be terrified if they should be long upon the voyage. . . .

Thursday, 11 October. Steered west-southwest; and encountered a heavier sea than they had met with before in the whole voyage. Saw pardelas ④ and a green rush near the vessel. The crew of the Pinta saw a cane and a log; they also picked up a stick which appeared to have been carved with an iron tool, a piece of cane, a plant which grows on land, and a board. The crew of the Nina saw other signs of land, and a stalk loaded with rose berries. These signs encouraged them, and they all grew cheerful. ⑤

After sunset steered their original course west and sailed twelve miles an hour till two hours after midnight, going ninety miles, which are twenty-two leagues and a half; and as the Pinta was the swiftest sailer, and kept ahead of the Admiral, she discovered land and made the signals which had been ordered.

Reading and Vocabulary Support

① A *league* is a unit of measurement equal to about four miles.

② Why do you think Columbus wanted his crew to believe they had traveled fewer miles than they had?

③ How many miles is 60 leagues?

④ A *pardela* is a type of bird.

⑤ Why do you think the crew was encouraged by all the signs of land they had seen?

Analyzing Primary Sources

Cite specific evidence from the document to support your answers.

1. Why was it a problem that the sailors accidentally steered the ship toward the northeast?
2. How do you think Columbus's crew felt when they saw land, after more than two months at sea? Explain.

Do you believe Columbus's account of his journey? Do the details he provides give credibility to his account?

TOPIC 1

Review and Assessment

VISUAL REVIEW

Life in the Northwest and Eastern Woodlands Regions

Trade in Africa and Eurasia

TRADE, TECHNOLOGY, AND EDUCATION IN AFRICA, EUROPE, AND ASIA

Technology	Education
• Advanced metal-forging techniques for toolmaking • Weaving techniques for patterned textiles • Teaching in mathematics, medicine, law, geography, history, and art at universities • Training in carpentry, fishing, and tailoring	• Techniques for making pottery, ceramics, glazes, glass, and lacquerware • Study in mathematics, medicine, and engineering; advances in irrigation techniques • Architectural domes and arches in buildings • Surgical instruments and techniques

READING REVIEW

Use the Take Notes and Practice Vocabulary activities in your Active Journal to review the topic.

INTERACTIVE

Practice Vocabulary using the Topic Mini-Games.

Write Your Essay

Get help for writing your essay in your Active Journal.

ASSESSMENT

Vocabulary and Key Ideas

1. **List** What were the early **civilizations** of Central and South America?
2. **Define** What is a **city-state**?
3. **Describe** What are some ways that American Indian **tribes** interacted with one another?
4. **Describe** life for most people living under **feudalism**.
5. **Check Understanding** What happened during the **Renaissance**?
6. **Identify** Who founded the first Spanish **colony** in the Americas?
7. **Explain** How did the **Columbian Exchange** change the relationship between the Eastern and Western Hemispheres?

Critical Thinking and Writing

8. **Identify Supporting Details** How did the Maya and Aztec civilizations use science and math?
9. **Compare and Contrast** How did the physical environment of the Chipewyan and Carrier affect settlement patterns?
10. **Identify Cause and Effect** What was the impact of the Crusades on the trading relationship between Europe and the Middle East?
11. **Identify Main Ideas** What were the political, religious, and economic reasons for Spanish exploration of North America?
12. **Revisit the Essential Question** How much did geography affect the lives of American Indians and European explorers?
13. **Writer's Workshop: Write a Research Paper** Using the notes you made in your Active Journal, answer the following question in a research paper: How did a travel-related invention or improvement in one of the societies covered in this topic impact people's lives?

Analyze Primary Sources

14. How would you describe the people who Christopher Columbus met?
    A. suspicious
    B. friendly
    C. angry
    D. religious

"As I saw that they were very friendly to us, and perceived that they could be much more easily converted to our holy faith by gentle means than by force, I presented them with some red caps, and strings of beads to wear upon the neck, and many other trifles of small value, wherewith they were much delighted . . . Afterwards they came swimming to the boats, bringing parrots, balls of cotton thread, javelins, and many other things which they exchanged for articles we gave them, such as glass beads, and hawk's bells; which trade was carried on with the utmost good will."

—from the diary of Christopher Columbus

Analyze Maps

15. Which letter represents the route of Bartolomeu Dias?
16. Which letter represents the route of Vasco da Gama? How did it differ from that of Dias?
17. What was the easternmost point of da Gama's sea route?

▼ **Voyages of da Gama and Dias**

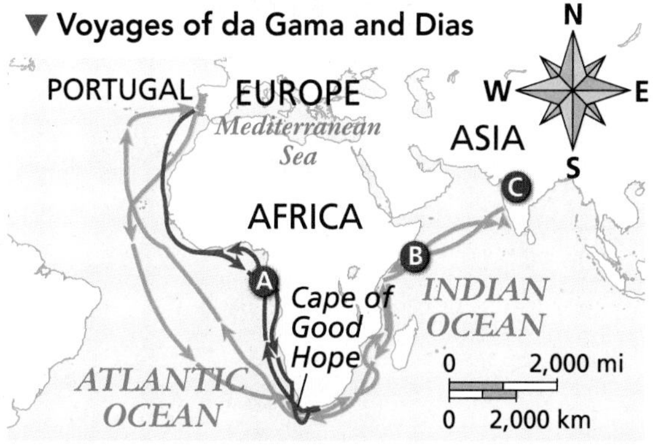

TOPIC 2

European Colonization of North America (1500–1750)

GO ONLINE to access your digital course

- VIDEO
- AUDIO
- ETEXT
- INTERACTIVE
- WRITING
- GAMES
- WORKSHEET
- ASSESSMENT

Go back five centuries

to the time of the EUROPEAN COLONIZATION OF NORTH AMERICA. Colonists from England came to North America for many reasons. Some wanted to practice their religions freely, while others were looking for economic opportunities or to start a new life.

Explore The Essential Question

Why do people move?

North America is far from Europe. Despite this, about 400 years ago many people began to emigrate to the land that would one day become the United States of America. Why?

Unlock the Essential Question in your Active Journal.

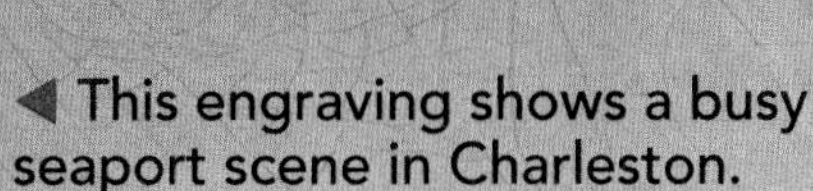

◀ This engraving shows a busy seaport scene in Charleston.

Read

about the North American colonies and the people who lived and worked there.

Lesson 1	**Spanish Colonization and New Spain**
Primary Sources	**Bartolomé de Las Casas, *Historia Apologética***
Lesson 2	**The First French, Dutch, and English Colonies**
Lesson 3	**The New England Colonies**
Primary Sources	**William Bradford, *Of Plymouth Plantation***
Lesson 4	**The Middle Colonies**
Lesson 5	**The Southern Colonies**
Lesson 6	**Colonial Society**
Lesson 7	**Colonial Trade and Government**

Watch

NBC LEARN

BOUNCE TO ACTIVATE

VIDEO

Watch a video about the exploits of John Smith in North America.

TOPIC 2 European Colonization of North America (1500–1750)

Learn more about the British colonies in North America by making your own map and timeline in your Active Journal.

INTERACTIVE

Topic Timeline

What happened and when?

Explorers reach North America . . . colonists make new homes. . . . Explore the timeline to see some of what was happening in North America.

1519 Hernando Cortés marches into Tenochtitlán.

1609 Henry Hudson sails up the river that later bore his name.

1607 Jamestown colony is settled.

TOPIC EVENTS

1500 | 1550 | 1600

WORLD EVENTS

1602 Dutch merchants form the Dutch East India Company.

Where were the original British colonies?

These colonies, which later became the United States of America, were located on the East Coast of North America, along the Atlantic Ocean. Locate the British settlements on the map.

1620
The Pilgrims settle Plymouth colony.

1664
New Amsterdam is taken over by England and renamed New York.

1673
Father Jacques Marquette sails up the Mississippi River.

1681
William Penn founds Pennsylvania.

1712
The Carolinas split into North and South Carolina.

1650 **1700** **1750**

1652
Dutch immigrants arrive in southern Africa.

1700
The French establish a fort in present-day Senegal.

1740
The population of China reaches 140 million.

Who will you meet?

Anne Hutchinson, an outspoken believer in religious freedom

William Penn, who believed everybody was equal in God's sight

Benjamin Franklin, who used reason to improve the world around him

Project-Based Learning Inquiry

Examining the Colonial Environment

Quest KICK OFF

The year is 1700. You've just moved to one of the British colonies that would later become the United States and need to make a living. There are many choices! How do you decide what to do?

How did the environment influence the economy and population of the British colonies?

What impact did the environment have on the colonists who lived there? Explore the Essential Question "Why do people move?" in this Quest.

▲ Colonial silversmiths at work.

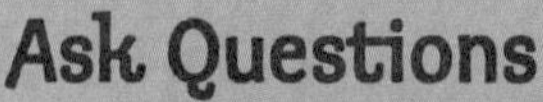

1 Ask Questions

The British colonies were very diverse and had many different environments and natural resources. Get started by making a list of questions you'd like to ask to learn about the environments and natural resources of the colonies. Write the questions in your Active Journal.

2 Investigate

As you read the lessons in this topic, look for Quest CONNECTIONS that provide information on how the British colonists made a living. Capture notes in your Active Journal.

3 Conduct Research

Next explore primary sources from the colonial period. They'll help you learn more about how the colonists in North America lived. Capture notes in your Active Journal.

Quest FINDINGS

4 Create an ePortfolio

Assemble a digital portfolio with maps, graphs, charts, and/or models that describe how the physical environment of the colonies influenced economic activities and population distribution. This will help you determine what type of work you should do!

LESSON 1

Spanish Colonization and New Spain

GET READY TO READ

START UP

Examine the image of Europeans meeting the Native American emperor Moctezuma. Why do you think they are wearing armor?

GUIDING QUESTIONS

- How did Spanish conquistadors defeat two American Indian empires?
- Why did Spain settle its colonies?
- What were the causes and effects of the transatlantic slave trade?

TAKE NOTES

Literacy Skills: Summarize

Use the graphic organizer in your Active Journal to take notes as you read the lesson.

PRACTICE VOCABULARY

Use the vocabulary activity in your Active Journal to practice the vocabulary words.

Vocabulary		Academic Vocabulary
conquistador	peninsular	shrewd
pueblo	creole	hesitate
presidio	mestizo	
mission		

"What a troublesome thing it is to discover new lands. The risks we took, it is hardly possible to exaggerate." Thus spoke Bernal Díaz del Castillo, one of the many Spanish **conquistadors** (kahn KEES tuh dorz), or conquerors, who marched into the Americas in the 1500s. When asked why they traveled to the Americas, Díaz responded, "We came here to serve God and the king and also to get rich."

Who Were the Conquistadors?

In their search for glory and gold, the conquistadors made Spain one of the richest nations in Europe. Spanish colonists followed the conquistadors and created a vast new empire in the Americas.

The rulers of Spain gave conquistadors permission to establish settlements. In return, conquistadors agreed to give Spain one fifth of any gold or treasure they captured.

Like other conquistadors, Hernando Cortés was eager to win riches and glory. He had heard rumors of a fabulously wealthy American Indian empire in Mexico. With only about 600 soldiers and 16 horses, Cortés set sail for Mexico in 1519 in search of gold.

Analyze Images Hernando Cortés kneels before the Aztec emperor Moctezuma. **Infer** What is the artist suggesting about this interaction between Moctezuma and Cortés?

The Spanish Destroy an Empire Moctezuma (mok tuh ZOO muh), the Aztec emperor who ruled over much of Mexico, heard disturbing reports of a large house floating on the sea. It was filled with white men with long, thick beards. Aztec sacred writings predicted that a powerful white-skinned god would come from the east to rule the Aztec. The strangers were approaching Tenochtitlán (tay nawch teet LAHN), the Aztec capital, which is now Mexico City. Moctezuma decided to welcome them as his guests.

Cortés took advantage of Moctezuma's invitation. **Shrewdly**, Cortés had already begun to win the support of other Indians who resented Aztec rule.

One of his trusted advisers was an Indian woman the Spanish called Doña Marina. She gave Cortés valuable information about the Aztec and acted as a translator and negotiator. On November 8, 1519, Cortés marched into Tenochtitlán. The city was much larger than any Spanish city at that time. Thousands upon thousands of Aztecs turned out to see the astonishing newcomers riding horses. Díaz recalled:

Primary Source

"Who could count the multitude of men, women and children which had come out on the roofs, in their boats on the canals, or in the streets, to see us?"

—Bernal Díaz del Castillo, *True History of the Conquest of New Spain*

At first, Cortés was friendly to Moctezuma. Soon, however, he made the emperor a prisoner in his own city. Tensions mounted in Tenochtitlán over the next half year.

Finally, the Aztec drove out the Spanish. Their victory, however, was brief. Aided by people whom the Aztec had conquered, Cortés recaptured the city. In the end, the Spanish destroyed Tenochtitlán, and Moctezuma was killed. The Aztec empire had fallen.

Academic Vocabulary
shrewd • *adj.,* clever

The Inca Empire Falls Another conquistador, Francisco Pizarro (pee SAHR oh), set his sights on the Incan empire. Pizarro sailed down the Pacific coast of South America with fewer than 200 Spanish soldiers.

In 1532, he captured the Incan emperor Atahualpa (ah tuh WAHL puh) and later executed him. Without the leadership of Atahualpa, Incan resistance collapsed. By 1535, Pizarro controlled much of the Incan empire.

Why the Spanish Won How were the Spanish able to conquer two great empires with only a handful of soldiers? First, the Spanish had superior military equipment. They were protected by steel armor and had guns. The Aztec and Inca relied on clubs, bows and arrows, and spears. Also, the Indians had never seen horses. They were frightened by mounted Spanish soldiers.

In addition, the American Indians did not fight as hard as they might have. The Aztec **hesitated** to attack at first because they thought the Spanish might be gods. Also, the Inca were weakened from fighting among themselves over control of their government.

Academic Vocabulary
hesitate • *v.,* to stop briefly because of nervousness

Finally, many Indians died from European diseases, such as smallpox, measles, and influenza. Some historians believe that disease alone would have ensured Spanish victory over the Indians.

From the Spanish perspective, their interaction with the Aztec and the Inca resulted in great victories that brought wealth and power. The Spanish also saw the conquests as further proof of their natural superiority. The Aztec and Inca, of course, had a much different view of the same events. From their perspectives, the Spanish conquests were disasters that devastated their civilizations.

READING CHECK **Identify Supporting Details** What reasons can you identify that help explain why the Spanish conquered the Aztec and the Inca so easily?

Analyze Images This 19th-century painting shows Pizarro capturing Atahualpa and slaughtering his followers. **Infer** Why did the artist include a Catholic friar in the scene?

INTERACTIVE

Spanish Explorers and Settlements in North America

Why Did the Spanish Explore Lands to the North?

The Spanish search for treasure reached beyond the lands of the Aztec and Inca. Moving north, conquistadors explored the Spanish borderlands. The borderlands spanned the present-day southern United States from Florida to California.

Juan Ponce de León (PAWN say day lay OHN) traveled through parts of Florida in 1513, looking for a legendary fountain of youth. Indians claimed that anyone who bathed in its magical water would remain young forever. Ponce de León found no such fountain.

An Expedition Proves Difficult Another explorer, Pánfilo Narváez (nahr VAH es), led an expedition that ended in disaster. In 1528, a storm struck his fleet in the Gulf of Mexico. Narváez and many others were lost at sea. The rest landed on an island in present-day Texas. Indians captured the few survivors and held them prisoner. Álvar Núñez Cabeza de Vaca (kah VAY suh day VAH kuh) assumed leadership of the small group.

Cabeza de Vaca, an enslaved African named Estevanico, and two others finally escaped their captors in 1533. The four walked across the plains of Texas, searching for a Spanish settlement. Finally, in 1536, they reached a town in Mexico. They had traveled by foot more than 1,000 miles through the Southwest.

The Search for Gold Continues From 1539 to 1542, Hernando de Soto explored Florida and other parts of the Southeast. In his search for gold, he reached the Mississippi River. De Soto died along the riverbank, without finding the riches he sought.

GEOGRAPHY **SKILLS**

Spanish explorers took several different routes through North America.

1. **Place** What impact might exploration of the Spanish borderlands have on the present-day United States?
2. **Use Visual Information** Which Spanish settlements on the map are still cities in the United States today?

Spanish Explorers and Settlements in North America

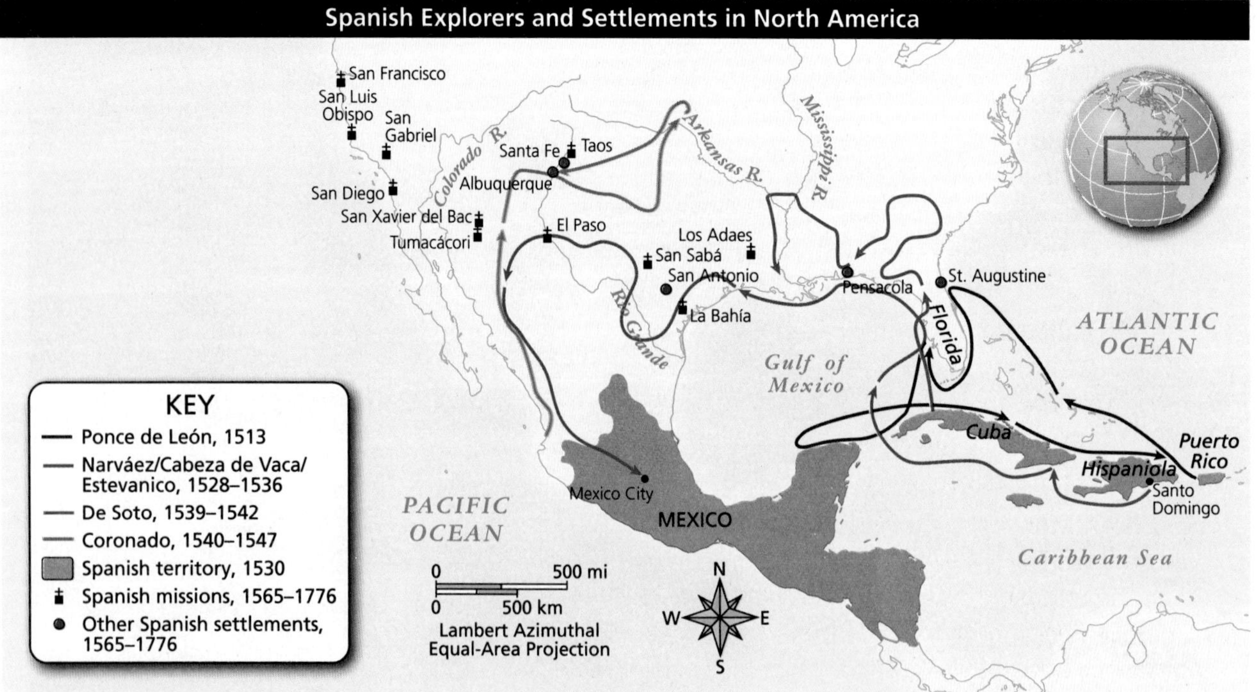

The conquistador Francisco Coronado (koh roh NAH doh) heard legends about "seven cities of gold." In 1540, he led an expedition into the southwestern borderlands. He traveled to present-day Arizona and New Mexico. Some of his party went as far as the Grand Canyon. Still, the Zuni (ZOO nee) villages he visited had no golden streets.

The Spanish expeditions into the borderlands met with little success. Faced with strong Indian resistance in the north, Spain focused instead on bringing order to its empire in the south.

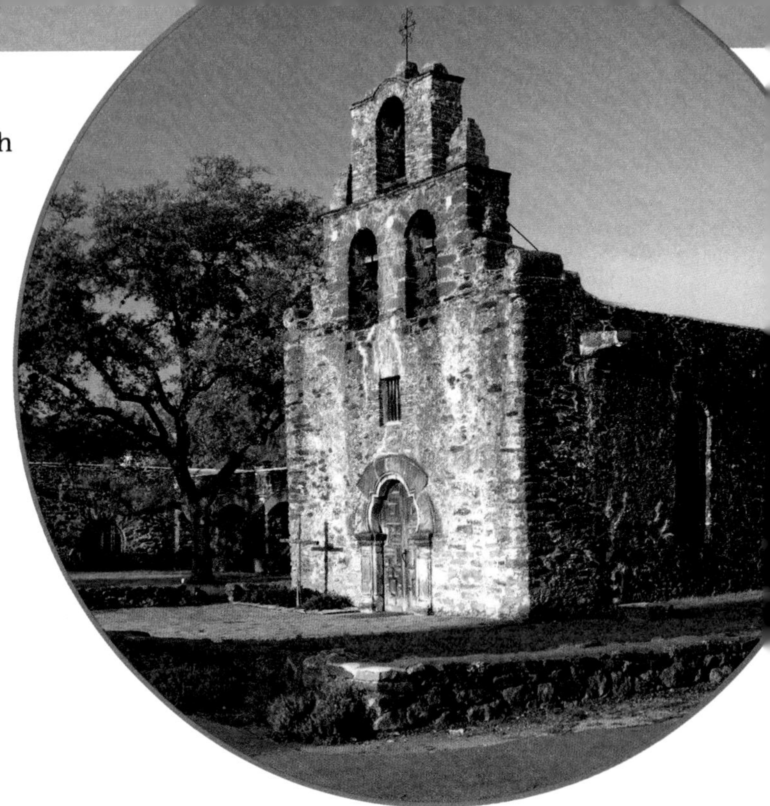

▲ Mission San Francisco de la Espada in San Antonio, Texas, was one of Spain's many religious settlements in the Americas. **Use Visual Information** What features do you see that distinguish this mission from a pueblo and a presidio?

READING CHECK **Identify Cause and Effect** What reasons did explorers have for traveling north?

Colonizing New Spain

The conquistadors set up colonies in many parts of the Americas. Spain had many reasons for colonization, or setting up colonies. One was the search for wealth. Settlements provided bases from which expeditions could set out in search of gold. Settlements could also create wealth through farming and trade. A second important reason for settlement was to spread Christianity by converting native peoples. A third reason was to satisfy a thirst for adventure and exploration. Sometimes, historians summarize the Spanish exploration and settlement of the Americas as motivated by "Gold, God, and Glory." Thousands of Spanish immigrants moved to Spanish settlements looking for opportunities the colonies offered, especially farming.

At first, Spain let the conquistadors govern the lands they conquered. When the conquistadors proved to be poor rulers, the Spanish king took away their authority. He then set up a strong system of government to rule his growing empire. In 1535, he divided his American lands into New Spain and Peru. The northern borderlands were part of New Spain. The king put a viceroy in charge of each region to rule in his name.

A set of laws called the Laws of the Indies stated how the colonies should be organized and ruled. The laws provided for three kinds of settlements in New Spain: pueblos, presidios (prih SID ee ohz), and missions. Some large communities included all three.

Spanish Settlements Spain established many settlements in the Americas. Many of these Spanish settlements were built in a similar pattern. The **pueblos**, or towns, were centers of farming and trade. In the middle of the town was a plaza, or public square. Here, townspeople and farmers came to do business or worship at the church. Shops and homes lined the four sides of the plaza.

Spanish Territories in the Americas

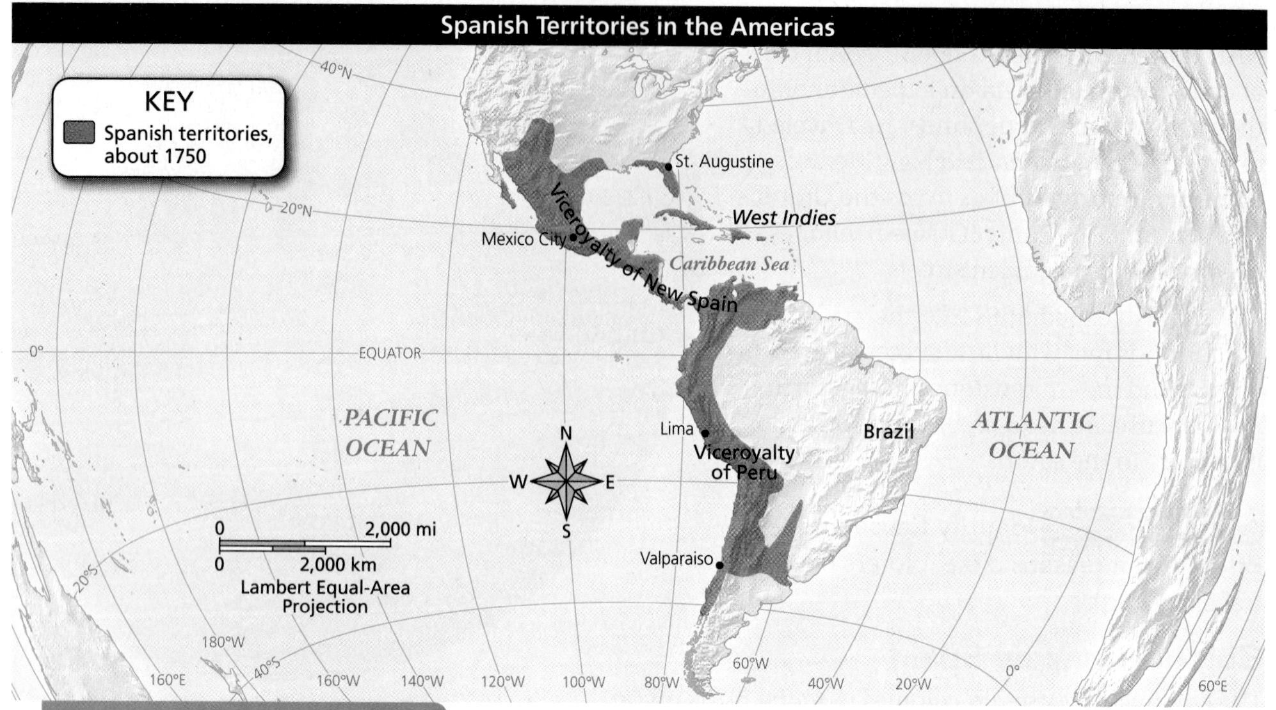

GEOGRAPHY SKILLS

Spanish territory covered Central America, part of North America, and much of the Caribbean islands and South America.

1. **Region** Into what two regions did Spain divide the lands it claimed in the western hemisphere?
2. **Infer** What language do you think is still spoken today in many of the countries that were claimed by Spain from the 1500s to 1750?

The Spanish took control of Indian pueblos and built new towns as well. In 1598, Juan de Oñate (oh NYAH tay) founded the colony of New Mexico among the adobe villages of the Pueblo Indians. He used brutal force to conquer the American Indians of the region. Don Pedro de Peralta later founded Santa Fe as the Spanish capital of New Mexico.

Presidios were forts where soldiers lived. Inside the high, thick walls were shops, stables, and storehouses for food. Soldiers protected the farmers who settled nearby. The first presidio in the borderlands was built in 1565 at St. Augustine, Florida. St. Augustine was the first permanent European settlement in what would become the United States. Its founding marked the beginning of the era of colonization in the future territory of the United States, which would continue until the United States declared independence in 1776.

The Legacy of Missions Like other Europeans in the Americas, the Spanish believed they had a duty to convert Indians to Christianity. They set up **missions**, settlements run by Catholic priests and friars whose goal was to convert Indians to Christianity. They often forced Indians to live and work on the missions.

In New Mexico, the Spanish tried to destroy any trace of traditional Pueblo Indians' religious practices and subjected them to severe punishments. This resulted in the Pueblo Revolt of 1680. The Pueblo Indians rose up against Spanish rule. They killed about 400 Spaniards and drove the others out of the region. The Spanish recaptured the region in the mid-1690s.

Missions gradually spread across the Spanish borderlands. The first mission in Texas was founded in 1659 at El Paso.

In 1691, Father Eusebio Francisco Kino (KEE noh) crossed into present-day Arizona. He eventually set up 24 missions in the area. The missions were a direct result of early Spanish colonization efforts. Over time, they had a significant impact in the Americas. By the late 1700s, a string of missions dotted the California coast from San Diego to San Francisco, and Spanish language and culture gradually spread with them.

INTERACTIVE

Social Classes in New Spain

READING CHECK **Understand Effects** What do you think the long-term impact of Spanish colonization has been on the religion and language of Central and South America?

How Was Society Organized in New Spain?

The Laws of the Indies also set up a strict social system. People in Spanish colonies were divided into four social classes: peninsulares (puh NIN suh LAH rayz), creoles (KREE ohlz), mestizos (mes TEE sohz), and Indians.

Different Social Classes At the top of the social scale were the **peninsulares**. Born in Spain, peninsulares held the highest jobs in government and the Church. They also owned large tracts of land as well as rich gold and silver mines.

Below the peninsulares were the **creoles**, people born in the Americas to parents of Spanish origin. Many creoles were wealthy and well educated. They owned farms and ranches, taught at universities, and practiced law. However, they could not hold the jobs that were reserved for peninsulares.

Below the creoles were people of mixed Spanish and Indian background, known as **mestizos**. Mestizos worked on farms and ranches owned by peninsulares and creoles. In the cities, they worked as carpenters, shoemakers, tailors, and bakers. Over the course of Spanish colonization, mestizos came to be the largest class of people.

The lowest class in the colonies was the Indians. In the early years of Spanish colonization, Indians were the largest class. The Spanish treated them as a conquered people. Under New Spain's strict social system, Indians were kept in poverty for hundreds of years.

A Blend of Spanish and Indian Cultures The effects of colonization can be seen in the new way of life in New Spain that blended Spanish and Indian ways. Spanish settlers brought their own culture to the colonies. They introduced their language, laws, religion, and learning. In 1551, the Spanish founded the University of Mexico.

▼ Penisulares and their children, called creoles, occupied a higher position in society than Indians.

▲ The Spanish made beautiful jewelry and objects, such as this crucifix, out of the gold they mined in the Americas.

American Indians also influenced the culture of New Spain. Colonists adopted Indian foods, such as corn, tomatoes, potatoes, and squash. Indian workers used materials they knew well, such as adobe bricks, to build fine libraries, theaters, and churches. Sometimes, Indian artists decorated church walls with paintings of local traditions.

Harsh Treatment of American Indians Spanish colonists needed workers for their ranches, farms, and mines. To help them, the Spanish government gave settlers encomiendas (en koh mee EN dahz), land grants that included the right to demand labor or taxes from American Indians.

Mines in Mexico, Peru, and other parts of the Americas made Spain rich. Treasure ships laden with thousands of tons of gold and silver sailed regularly across the Atlantic.

The Spanish forced American Indians to work in the gold and silver mines. In flickering light, Indians hacked out rich ores in narrow, dark tunnels. Many died when tunnels caved in.

These harsh conditions led one priest, Bartolomé de Las Casas (day lahs KAH sahs), to seek reform. Traveling through New Spain, Las Casas witnessed firsthand the deaths of Indians due to hunger, disease, and mistreatment. What he saw horrified him:

Primary Source

"The Indians were totally deprived of their freedom. . . . Even beasts enjoy more freedom when they are allowed to graze in the field."

—Bartolomé de Las Casas, *Tears of the Indians*

Many Spanish in New Spain did not share Las Casas's view or his values. So, he journeyed to Europe and asked the king of Spain to protect the Indians' civil rights. In the 1540s, the royal government passed laws prohibiting the enslavement of American Indians. The laws also allowed Indians to own cattle and grow crops. However, few officials in New Spain enforced the new laws or took the time to think about Indians' basic human needs.

READING CHECK **Identify Supporting Details** What were some ways in which peninsulares were powerful?

The Transatlantic Slave Trade

The death toll among American Indians continued to rise. Faced with a severe shortage of workers, Spanish colonists looked across the Atlantic Ocean for a new source of labor.

Reasons for the Slave Trade Still seeking to protect American Indians, Bartolomé de Las Casas made a suggestion that had a lasting, tragic impact. His idea was that Africans be brought as slaves to replace forced Indian laborers. Las Casas argued that Africans were less likely to die from European diseases. He also claimed that Africans would suffer less because they were used to doing hard farm work in their homelands.

Las Casas's arguments encouraged the Atlantic slave trade, or the trade of enslaved Africans across the Atlantic to the Americas. In many parts of Africa, slavery had existed for centuries. Often, war prisoners were enslaved. Eventually, these enslaved people or their children might gain freedom. After the Americas were colonized, though, some Africans began to capture and enslave people and sell them to European traders. The traders then shipped the enslaved men, women, and children to the Americas. Most Africans who settled in the Americas did so against their will.

By the time he died, Las Casas had come to regret his suggestion. He saw that enslaved Africans suffered as much as the Indians. By that time, however, it was too late to undo the damage. Slavery had become a key part of the colonial economy.

Slave Trade Expansion Demand for African labor grew rapidly, mainly in the West Indies—including what are now Cuba, the Dominican Republic, and Puerto Rico—and in other parts of the Americas.

Analyze Charts Enslaved Africans were shipped to destinations in Europe, Asia, and the Americas. **Use Visual Information** Which region received the fewest enslaved Africans? Which received the most?

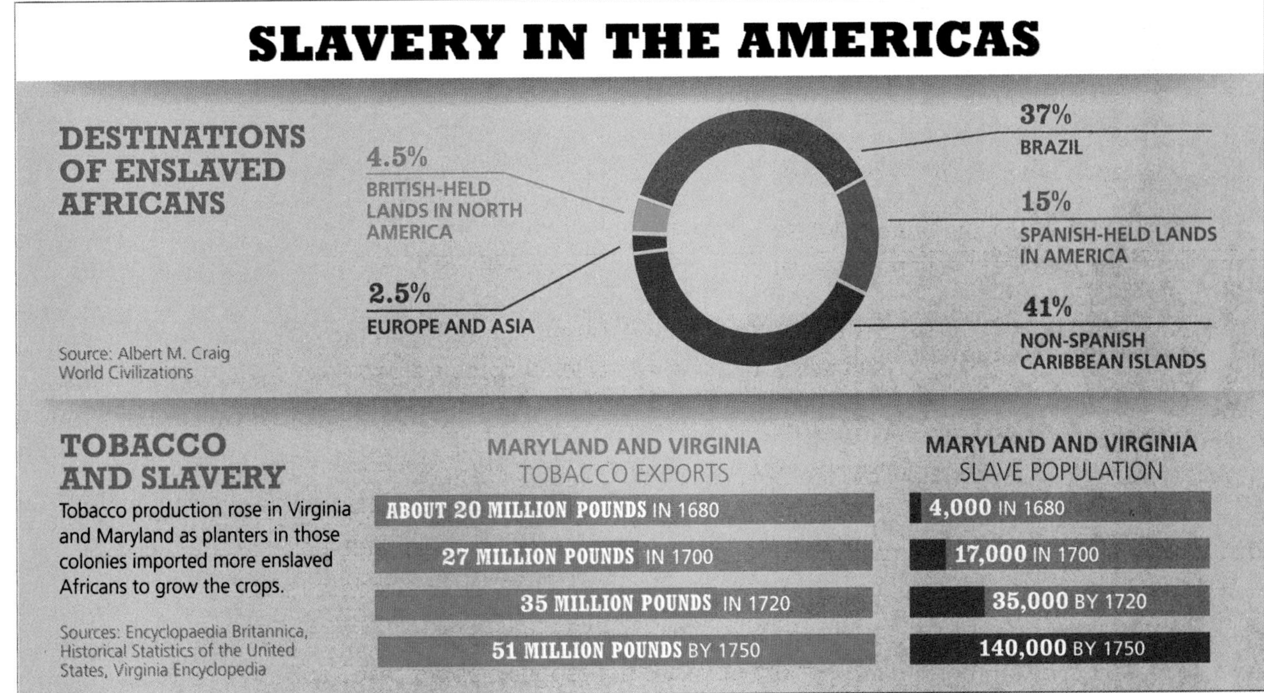

▲ Europeans brought enslaved Africans from gold mining regions of Africa to Brazil where they were forced to use their skills to mine gold.

Enslaved Africans were especially valued on sugar plantations in the West Indies and in the Portuguese colony of Brazil. A plantation is a large estate farmed by many workers. Sugar could not be grown on small estates because it required too much land and labor. Enslaved Africans often worked all through the night cutting sugar, which was then sold in Europe for a large profit.

Some scholars estimate that Europeans transported more than 10 million enslaved Africans across the Atlantic Ocean to the Americas between the 1500s and the 1800s. The vast majority came from West Africa.

READING CHECK **Draw Conclusions** Why did Bartolomé de Las Casas's idea to use enslaved Africans to work on farms backfire?

Lesson Check

Practice Vocabulary

1. What impact did the **conquistadors** have on the Aztec and Incan empires?
2. Why did the Spanish set up **missions**, **presidios**, and **pueblos**?

Critical Thinking and Writing

3. **Understand Effects** How did the Spanish search for gold impact the Aztec and Inca who were living in the Americas at the time?
4. **Identify Main Ideas** What two reasons did the Spanish have for deciding not to focus on their northern borderlands?
5. **Identify Implied Main Ideas** What makes St. Augustine a particularly notable Spanish settlement?
6. **Identify Cause and Effect** What did the Spanish government's land grants include that caused hardship for American Indians, and what hardship did it cause?
7. **Writing Workshop: Introduce Characters** Imagine you are a colonist living in North America. Write a few sentences in your Active Journal that describe who you are and what your role is in society. You will use this information for a narrative essay you will write at the end of this topic.

Bartolomé de Las Casas, *Historia Apologética*

Bartolomé de Las Casas was a Spanish historian and writer who traveled to the island of Hispaniola 10 years after Christopher Columbus discovered it. He spent much of the next 20 years there, and in 1527 he wrote the *Historia Apologética*, or Apologetic History. At the time, many Europeans felt the people of the Indies were not advanced. Las Casas disagreed.

▶ *Historia Apologética* was one of many books Bartolomé de Las Casas wrote about the Indians.

The ultimate cause for writing this work was to gain knowledge of all the many nations of this vast new world. They had been defamed by persons who feared neither God nor the charge, so grievous before divine judgment, of defaming even a single man and causing him to lose his esteem and honor. ① From such slander can come great harm and terrible calamity, particularly when large numbers of men are concerned and, even more so, a whole new world. ② It has been written that these peoples of the Indies, lacking human governance and ordered nations, did not have the power of reason to govern themselves. . . . From this it follows that they have all proven themselves unsocial and therefore monstrous, contrary to the natural bent of all peoples of the world; and that He did not allow any other species of corruptible creature to err in this way, excepting a strange and occasional case. . . . ③

Not only have [the Indians] shown themselves to be very wise peoples and possessed of lively and marked understanding, prudently governing and providing for their nations (as much as they can be nations, without faith in or knowledge of the true God) and making them prosper in justice; but they have equalled many diverse nations of the world, past and present, that have been praised for their governance, politics and customs; and exceed by no small measure the wisest of all these, such as the Greeks and Romans, in adherence to the rules of natural reason. ④ This advantage and superiority, along with everything said above, will appear quite clearly when, if it please God, the peoples are compared one with another.

Reading and Vocabulary Support

① Las Casas says that the Spaniards had damaged the reputation of the Indians, ignoring God's wishes.

② What calamity do you think Las Casas might have been writing about?

③ Las Casas is summarizing the argument that Indians were monstrous and that God didn't usually allow this to happen to people.

④ Las Casas argues that Indians follow the laws of reason as much as any civilization has.

Analyzing Primary Sources

Cite specific evidence from the document to support your answers.

1. **Infer** What is Bartolomé de Las Casas's overall opinion of the people of the Indies?

2. **Draw Conclusions** What reason does Bartolomé de Las Casas give to suggest that the people of the Indies might not have a true nation?

LESSON 2

The First French, Dutch, and English Colonies

GET READY TO READ

START UP

Study the engraving. How was shipping important for European colonization?

GUIDING QUESTIONS

- Why did Europeans explore North America's coast?
- Why did the French, Dutch, and English colonize North America?
- How did Virginia begin a tradition of representative government?
- In what ways did different groups in Jamestown interact with the environment?

TAKE NOTES

Literacy Skills: Sequence

Use the graphic organizer in your Active Journal to take notes as you read the lesson.

PRACTICE VOCABULARY

Use the vocabulary words in your Active Journal to practice the vocabulary words.

Vocabulary

northwest passage
coureurs de bois
alliance
charter
burgess
representative government
Bacon's Rebellion

Academic Vocabulary

pioneer
signify

European nations began to compete for riches around the world. Religious differences heightened their rivalry. Soon, there were competing religious views.

How Did European Rivalries Affect Exploration?

Until the 1500s, the Roman Catholic Church was the only church in Western Europe. That unity ended when a major religious reform movement sharply divided Christians.

Religious Reform In 1517, a German monk named Martin Luther publicly challenged many practices of the Catholic Church. Soon after, he split with the Church entirely. Luther believed that the Church had become too worldly. He opposed the power of popes. He also objected to the idea that believers could gain eternal life by performing good works. He said people were saved by faith in God.

Because of their protests against the Church, Luther's supporters became known as Protestants. The Protestant Reformation divided Europe. Soon, the Protestants themselves split, forming many different churches.

By the late 1500s, religion divided the states of Western Europe. Roman Catholic monarchs ruled Spain and France. A Protestant queen, Elizabeth I, ruled England. In the Netherlands, the Dutch people were mostly Protestant.

Religious Difference Leads to Rivalries As Europeans settled in the Americas, they brought their religious conflicts with them. Queen Elizabeth encouraged English adventurers to raid Spanish colonies and capture Spanish treasure fleets. Protestant England also competed with Catholic France for lands in North America.

Not all rivalries were religious. Both the Netherlands and England were Protestant. Still, they competed for control of land in North America and for economic markets all over the world, including Asia.

Reasons for the Exploration of North America Like Columbus, other Europeans continued during the 1500s to look for new ways to reach the riches of Asia. Magellan's route around South America seemed long and difficult. Europeans wanted to discover a shorter **northwest passage**, or waterway through or around North America.

Giovanni Caboto, an Italian sea captain whom the English called John Cabot, set out to find a northwest passage for the English. He was confident he had found such a passage, but he was mistaken. The "new-found land" that he thought he had discovered off the Asian coast in fact lay off the coast of North America. Today, Newfoundland is part of the easternmost province of Canada.

French Exploration The French sent another Italian captain, Giovanni da Verrazano (vehr rah TSAH noh), in search of a northwest passage. Verrazano journeyed along the North American coast from the present-day Carolinas to Canada. During the 1530s, Jacques Cartier (kar tee YAY), also sailing for the French, traveled more than halfway up the St. Lawrence River.

Mapping New Regions None of these explorers found a northwest passage to Asia. However, they did map and explore many parts of North America. The rulers of Western Europe began thinking about how to profit from the region's rich resources through colonization.

READING CHECK **Use Evidence** What factors contributed to rivalries between English and Spanish explorers?

Analyze Images In his *Ninety-five Theses*, Martin Luther listed disagreements he had with the Catholic Church. **Identify Main Ideas** What was the political significance of the Protestant Reformation?

How Did New France Develop?

Samuel de Champlain (sham PLAYN) founded Port Royal, the first permanent French settlement in North America, in 1605. Three years later, he led another group of settlers along the route Cartier had **pioneered**. On a rocky cliff high above the St. Lawrence River, Champlain built a trading post known as Quebec (kwih BEK). The opportunity to create wealth through trade was one of the main reasons for French colonization in America. The French also wanted to surpass their rivals, the English. Many French settlers were looking for adventure and hoped to find their fortune in the New World.

Academic Vocabulary
pioneer • *v.*, to develop or to be the first to do something

Economic Activity in New France Unlike Spain's American empire, New France had little gold or silver. Instead, the French profited from fishing, trapping, and trading.

French colonists who lived and worked in American Indian lands beyond the French settlements became known as ***coureurs de bois*** (koo RUHR duh BWAH), or "runners of the woods." The French brought knives, kettles, cloth, and other items for trade with American Indians. In return, the Indians gave them beaver skins and other furs that sold for high prices in Europe.

Coureurs de bois established friendly relations with American Indian groups. Unlike the Spanish, the French did not attempt to conquer the Indians. Also, because *coureurs de bois* did not establish farms, they did not interfere with Indian lands. Indians taught the French trapping and survival skills, such as how to make snowshoes and canoes. Many *coureurs* married Indian women.

GEOGRAPHY SKILLS

Explorers from Europe took different routes to North America.

1. **Interaction** Why might you expect conflict to develop between the French and the English in North America?
2. **Infer** What might have motivated French explorers to search the interior of North America as they looked for a northwest passage?

Exploring North America

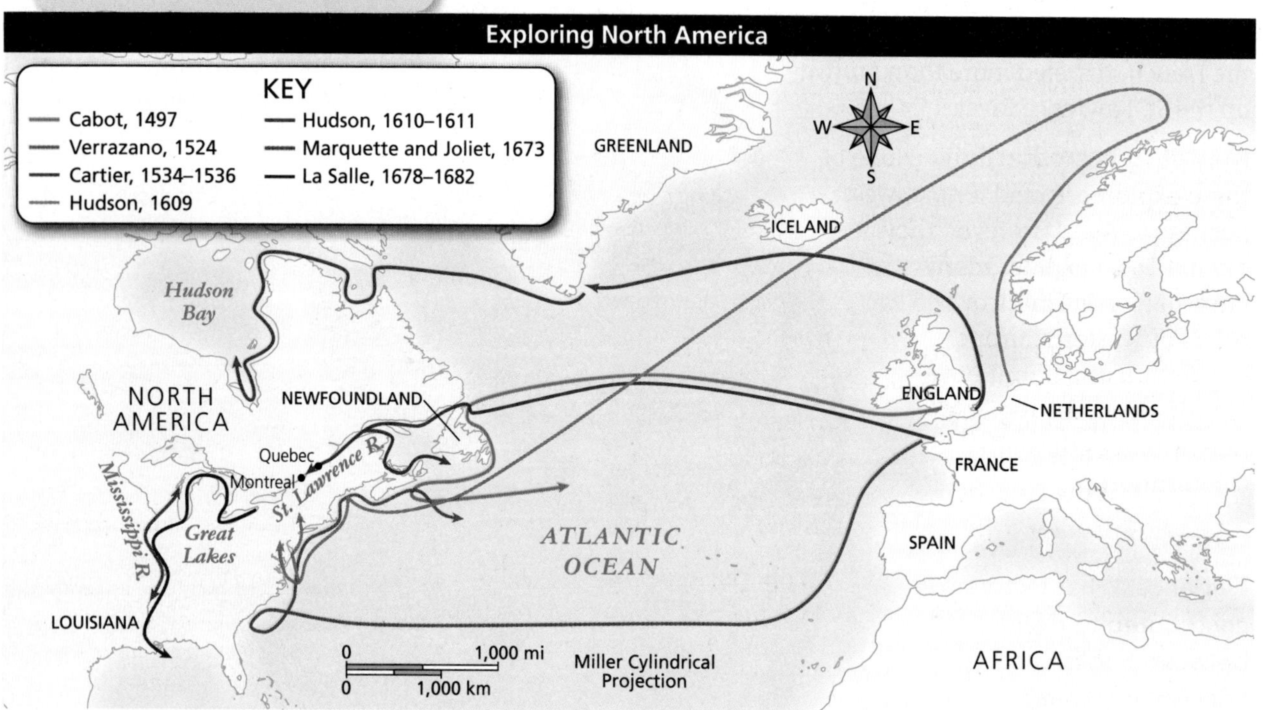

Analyze Images American Indians brought furs to trappers in exchange for goods like knives, kettles, and cloth. **Infer** Why did Indians buy knives and kettles from Europeans?

Missionary Work Continues Catholic missionaries often traveled with fur traders. A missionary is a person who goes to another land to win converts for a religion. French missionaries tried to convert American Indians to Christianity. They also drew maps and wrote about the lands they explored.

Life was difficult, especially in winter. One French priest recalled traveling on foot through deep snow:

Primary Source

"If a thaw came, dear Lord, what pain! . . . I was marching on an icy path that broke with every step I took; as the snow softened . . . we often sunk [sank] in it up to our . . . waist."

—Paul Le Jeune, quoted in *The Jesuits in North America*

Colonization Along the Mississippi River French trappers followed the St. Lawrence deep into the heart of North America. Led by Indian guides, they reached the Great Lakes. Here, Indians spoke of a mighty river, which they called Mississippi, or "Father of the Waters."

A French missionary, Father Jacques Marquette (mar KET), and a fur trader, Louis Joliet (joh lee ET), set out to reach the Mississippi in 1673. Led by Indian guides, they followed the river for more than 700 miles before turning back. Nine years later, Robert de La Salle completed the journey to the Gulf of Mexico. La Salle named the region Louisiana in honor of the French king, Louis XIV.

To keep Spain and England out of Louisiana, the French built forts in the north along the Great Lakes. Among them was Fort Detroit, built by Antoine de la Mothe Cadillac near Lake Erie. The French also built New Orleans, a fort near the mouth of the river. New Orleans grew into a busy trading center. French control of the network of waterways at the heart of North America gave the French a strategic advantage over the Spanish and the English.

French colonists imported thousands of Africans to work as slaves on plantations around New Orleans. Some enslaved Africans, however, joined with the Natchez Indians in a revolt against the French. The French put down the Natchez Revolt in 1729. Some enslaved Africans who fought on the side of the French received their freedom. In Louisiana, free and enslaved Africans together made up the majority of settlers.

Government in New France New France was governed much like New Spain. The French king controlled the government directly, and people had little freedom. A council appointed by the king made all decisions.

Did you know?

The Cadillac automobile, which was first built in Detroit, Michigan, is named in honor of Antoine de la Mothe Cadillac, explorer, trapper, and trader.

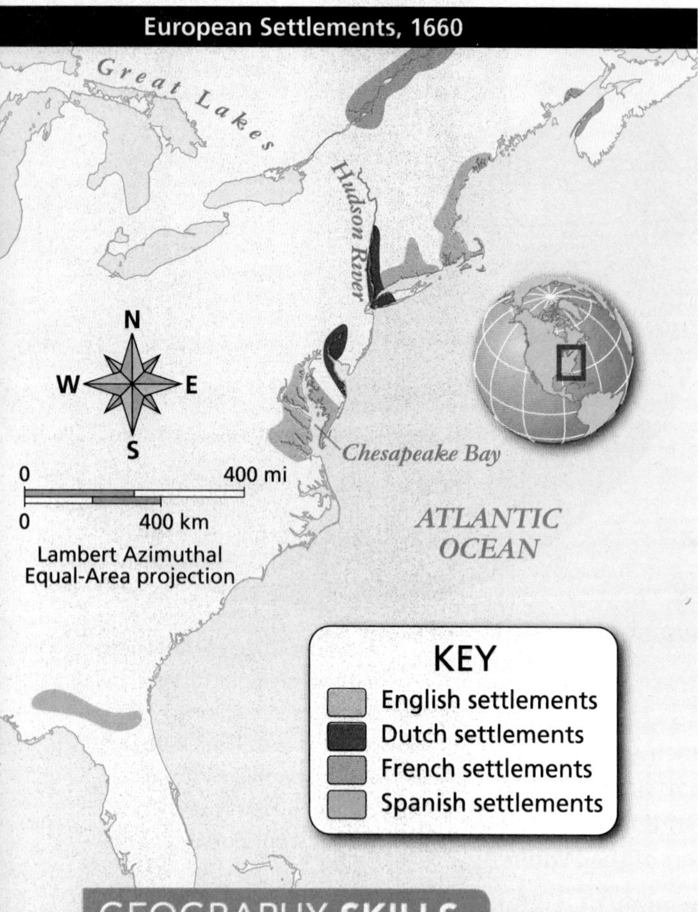

GEOGRAPHY SKILLS

Four European colonial powers planted settlements in eastern North America.

1. **Movement** What form of transport does the map suggest the settlers relied on?
2. **Draw Conclusions** Based on the map, where would you expect each country's settlements to expand next? Why?

Louis XIV worried that too few French were moving to New France. In the 1660s, he sent about a thousand people to the colony, including many young women. New France still grew slowly. Winters were harsh, and the short growing season made farming difficult. Only about 10,000 settlers lived in the colony by 1680. Some lived on farms, while others chose to become *coureurs de bois*, living largely free of government control.

READING CHECK **Summarize** How did both the French and American Indians benefit from one another?

Where Did the Dutch Establish New Netherland?

Like the French, the Dutch hoped to profit from their discoveries in the Americas by colonizing. In 1626, Peter Minuit (MIN yoo wit) led a group of Dutch settlers to the mouth of the Hudson River. Other Dutch colonists had already settled on Manhattan Island and farther up the Hudson River. Minuit bought Manhattan Island from local Indians. Minuit called his settlement New Amsterdam. The entire colony was known as New Netherland (now known as New York).

New Netherland was privately funded by the Dutch West India Company. Many colonists immigrated to New Netherland hoping to profit from the region's active fur trade.

From a tiny group of 30 houses, New Amsterdam grew into a busy port. The Dutch welcomed people of many nations, ethnic groups, and religions to their colony. A Roman Catholic priest who visited New Netherland in 1643 reported:

Primary Source

"On the island of Manhattan, and in its environs, there may well be four or five hundred men of different sects and nations: the Director General told me that there were men of eighteen different languages; they are scattered here and there on the river, above and below, as the beauty and convenience of the spot has invited each to settle."

—Father Isaac Jogues, quoted in *Narratives of New Netherland, 1609–1664*

The Dutch also built trading posts along the Hudson River. The most important one was Fort Orange, today known as Albany. Dutch merchants became known for their good business sense.

The Dutch enlarged New Netherland in 1655 by taking over the colony of New Sweden. The Swedes had established New Sweden along the Delaware River some 15 years earlier.

INTERACTIVE

Lands Controlled by Colonial Powers, 1660

Trade Rivalries in the Region Dutch traders sent furs to the Netherlands. The packing list for the first shipment included "the skins of 7,246 beaver, 853 otter, 81 mink, 36 cat lynx, and 34 small rats."

The Dutch and French became rivals in the fur trade. Both sought alliances with American Indians. An **alliance** is an agreement between nations to aid and protect one another. The Dutch made friends with the Iroquois. The Huron (HYOO rahn) helped the French. Fighting raged for years among the rival Europeans and their American Indian allies.

Interaction With American Indians and the Environment Dutch and French settlement on the east coast of North America brought major changes to American Indians and the environment. As in New Spain, European diseases killed thousands of Indians, and rivalry over the fur trade increased among different European countries' American Indian allies. The scramble for furs also led to overtrapping. By 1640, trappers had almost wiped out the beavers on Iroquois lands in upstate New York.

The arrival of Europeans affected American Indians in other ways. Missionaries tried to convert Indians to Christianity. Indians eagerly adopted European trade goods, such as copper kettles and knives. They also bought muskets and gunpowder for hunting and warfare. Alcohol sold by European traders had a harsh effect on American Indian life.

▼ The island of Manhattan, which Peter Minuit purchased from local Indians, eventually became one of the most valuable pieces of land in the United States.

Europeans all waged warfare to seize Indian lands. As American Indians were forced off their lands, they moved westward onto lands of other Indians, which sometimes led to violence between Indian groups. The conflicts between American Indians and Europeans would continue for many years.

READING CHECK **Recognize Multiple Causes** What were some results of the Dutch fur trade?

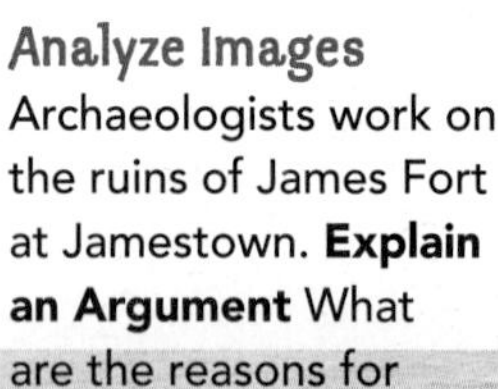

INTERACTIVE

The Early Years at Jamestown

Roanoke and Jamestown

England watched with envy as other European countries gained riches from their colonies in the Americas. Several ambitious English gentlemen proposed that England settle the Americas as well. With Queen Elizabeth's permission, Sir Walter Raleigh raised money to establish a colony in North America. In 1585, about 100 men set sail across the Atlantic. The colonists landed on Roanoke (ROH uh nohk), an island off the coast of present-day North Carolina. Within a year, however, the colonists had run short of food and were quarreling with neighboring American Indians. When an English ship stopped in the harbor, the weary settlers sailed home.

In 1587, Raleigh sent John White, one of the original colonists, back to Roanoke with a new group of settlers that included women and children. When supplies ran low, White returned to England, leaving behind 117 colonists. He planned to return in a few months. When he got back to England, however, he found the country was preparing for war with Spain. It was three years before he sailed back to Roanoke.

When White arrived, he found the settlement strangely quiet. Houses stood empty. Vines wound through the windows, and pumpkins sprouted from the earthen floors. On a tree, someone had carved the word CROATOAN, the name of a nearby island. No other trace of the colonists remained. White was eager to investigate, but a storm was blowing up and his crew refused to make the trip. To this day, the fate of the "Lost Colony" remains a mystery.

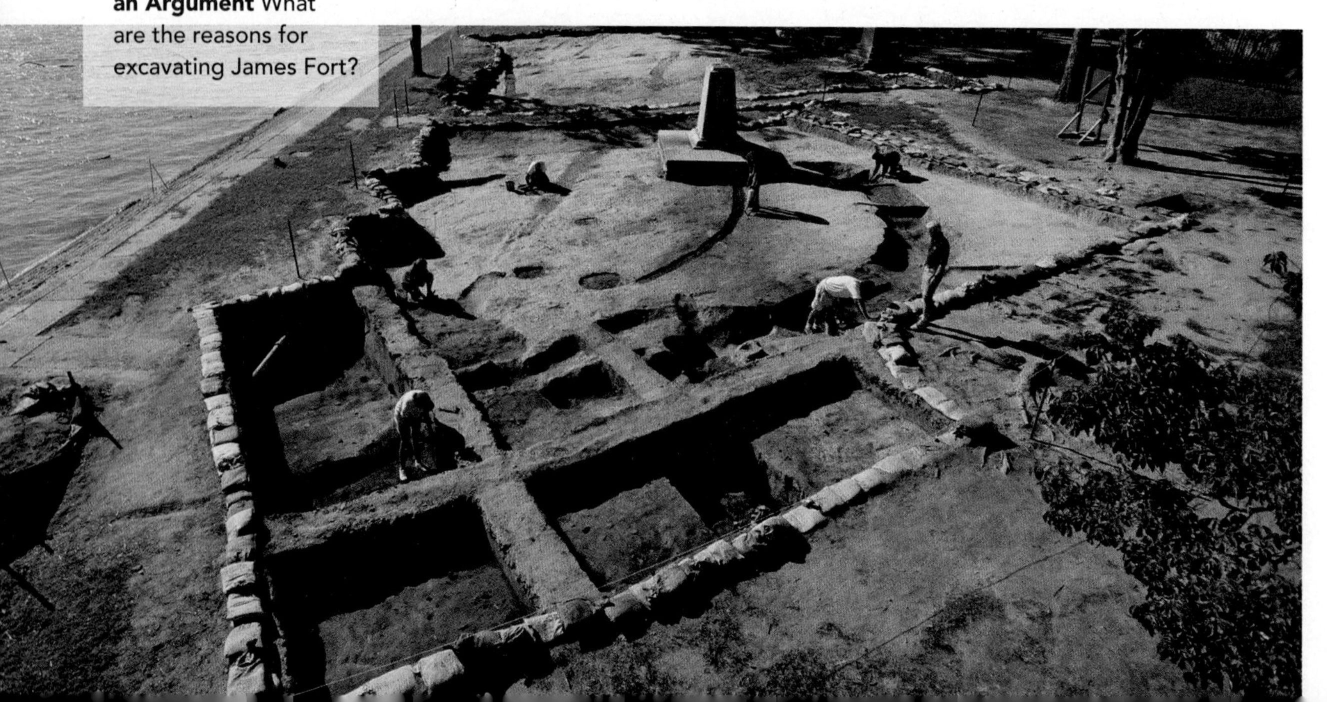

Analyze Images
Archaeologists work on the ruins of James Fort at Jamestown. **Explain an Argument** What are the reasons for excavating James Fort?

The Location of Jamestown

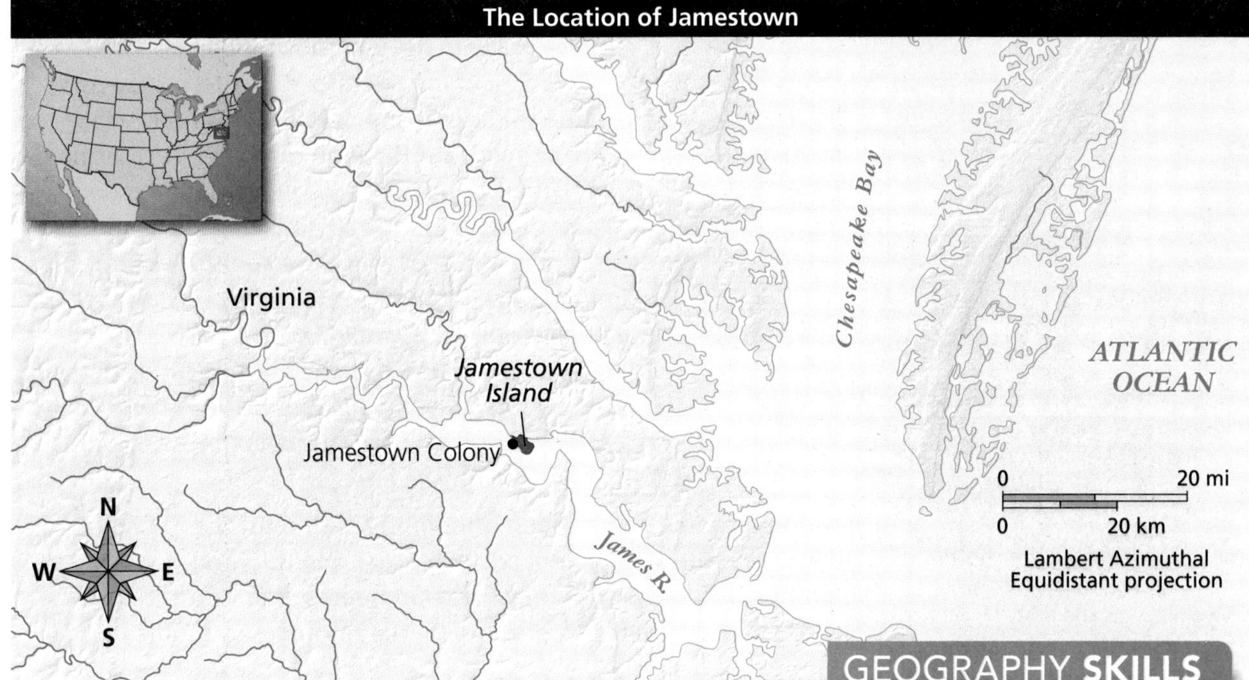

GEOGRAPHY SKILLS

The Jamestown colonists first settled upriver from the Chesapeake Bay.

1. **Location** Why might the colonists of Jamestown have chosen the location they did?
2. **Explain an Argument** What advantages and disadvantages are there to building a settlement near a river?

The Founding of Jamestown After the failure of Roanoke, nearly 20 years passed before England again tried to establish a colony in North America. In 1606, the Virginia Company of London, a private company, received a charter from King James I. A **charter** is a legal document giving certain rights to a person or company.

The royal charter gave the Virginia Company the right to settle lands along the eastern coast of North America. The charter also guaranteed that colonists of this land, called Virginia, would have the same rights as English citizens.

In the spring of 1607, a group of 105 colonists, funded by the Virginia Company, arrived in Virginia. They sailed into Chesapeake Bay and began building houses along the James River. They named their tiny outpost Jamestown after their king. Jamestown was the first permanent English settlement in what is now the United States.

Reasons for Colonization The settlers of Jamestown hoped to make a profit by finding gold or other riches. They also hoped to discover a water route to Asia. Furthermore, they wanted to claim the region for England.

One of the reasons they chose this particular location was security: they located their settlement in a place where Spanish ships would be unlikely to find them. If the Spanish did discover Jamestown, its location would make it more easily defensible against Spanish ships.

Governing the colony proved difficult. The Virginia Company had chosen a council of 13 men to rule the settlement. Members of the council quarreled with one another and did little to plan for the colony's future. By the summer of 1608, the colony was near failure.

Analyze Images The House of Burgesses in Jamestown, Virginia, was the first elected legislative assembly in the English colonies. **Infer** How was government in the English colonies different from that in the Spanish or French colonies?

The Colonists Face Difficulties Another major problem the Jamestown colonists faced was starvation. Many colonists were not used to living in the wilderness and did not know how to take advantage of the plentiful resources. Furthermore, the colonists did not spend enough time producing food. Captain John Smith, a young soldier and explorer, observed that the colonists were not planting enough crops. He complained that people wanted only to "dig gold, wash gold, refine gold, load gold." As they searched in vain for gold, the colony ran out of food. Smith helped to save the colony. He set up stern rules that forced colonists to work if they wished to eat.

However, problems arose soon after John Smith returned to England in 1609. Desperate settlers cooked "dogs, cats, snakes, [and] toadstools" to survive. To keep warm, they broke up houses to burn as firewood. The colonists gradually learned to use the resources available in their environment to survive.

Tobacco Crops Help Jamestown's economy finally improved after 1612, when colonists began growing tobacco. Europeans had learned about tobacco from American Indians.

King James called pipe smoking "a vile custom." Still, the new fad caught on quickly. By 1620, England was importing more than 30,000 pounds of tobacco a year. At last, Virginians had found a way to make their colony succeed.

English immigrants to Virginia interacted with their environment by cutting down forests and planting the land with tobacco. Their interaction with the environment was different from that of other groups of immigrants to North America, such as the Dutch and the French, whose trading activity led to the near elimination of beaver populations in some areas.

READING CHECK **Draw Conclusions** What do you think could have happened to the Jamestown colonists had John Smith not forced them to work if they wished to eat?

How Did Colonists Improve Government?

For a time, the governors sent by the Virginia Company ran the colony like a military outpost. Each morning, a drumbeat summoned settlers to work at assigned tasks. Harsh laws imposed the death penalty even for small offenses, like stealing an ear of corn. Such conditions were unlikely to attract new colonists. As John Smith commented after his return to England, "No Man will go . . . to have less freedom there than here."

The House of Burgesses To attract more settlers, the Virginia Company took steps to establish a more stable government. In 1619, it sent a new governor with orders to consult settlers on all important matters. Male settlers were allowed to elect **burgesses**, or representatives to the government.

The burgesses met in an assembly called the House of Burgesses. Together with the governor and his council, they made laws for the colony. The first session met in July and August 1619.

The House of Burgesses **signifies** the beginning of representative government in the English colonies. In a **representative government**, voters elect representatives to make laws for them.

Academic Vocabulary
signify • *v.*, to indicate or be a sign of

Political Rights and Responsibilities The idea that people had political rights was deeply rooted in English history. In 1215, English nobles had forced King John to sign the Magna Carta, or the Great Charter. This document said that the king could not raise taxes without first consulting a Great Council of nobles and church leaders. Over time, the rights won by nobles were extended to other people.

The Great Council grew into a representative assembly called Parliament. Parliament was divided into the House of Lords, made up of nobles, and an elected House of Commons. Only rich men had the right to vote, but now even monarchs had to obey the law.

Some Virginia Settlers Can Vote At first, free Virginians had even greater rights than citizens in England. They did not have to own property in order to vote. In 1670, however, the colony restricted the vote to free, white, male property owners.

Despite these limits, representative government remained important. The idea took root that settlers should have a say in the affairs of the colony. Colonists came to refer to the Virginia Company's 1619 frame of government as their own "Great Charter."

READING CHECK **Identify Main Ideas** Why was the House of Burgesses created in Virginia?

Analyze Charts The population of the English colonies in America included a variety of ethnic groups. **Draw Conclusions** What might account for the dramatic increase in the African American population of the Southern Colonies between 1700 and 1775?

COLONIAL SETTLERS' ORIGINS

ESTIMATED ETHNICITY OF AMERICAN COLONIES

- 1 IN 2 ENGLISH
- 1 IN 5 AFRICAN
- 1 IN 10 SCOTCH-IRISH
- 1 IN 10 GERMAN
- 1 IN 25 DUTCH

Sources: James T. Lemon, *Colonial America in the Eighteenth Century; Historical Statistics of the United States*

■ NEW ENGLAND
■ MIDDLE
■ SOUTHERN

ESTIMATED POPULATION IN 1700
89% WHITE 11% BLACK

	SOUTHERN	MIDDLE	NEW ENGLAND
White	81%	93%	98%
Black	11%	7%	2%

ESTIMATED POPULATION IN 1770
78% WHITE 21% BLACK

	SOUTHERN	MIDDLE	NEW ENGLAND
White	59%	94%	97%
Black	41%	6%	3%

Growth of the Jamestown Colony

During the early years of the Jamestown colony, only a few women chose to make the journey from England. Nor did enough workers come to raise tobacco and other crops.

Women in Jamestown The colony's first women arrived in 1608—a "Mistress Forrest" and her maid, Anne Burras. Few others followed until 1619, when the Virginia Company sent about 100 women to help "make the men more settled." This shipload of women quickly found husbands. The Virginia Company profited from the marriages because it charged each man who found a wife 150 pounds of tobacco.

Life for women was a daily struggle. Women had to make everything from scratch—food, clothing, even medicines. Many died young from hard work or childbirth. By 1624, there were still fewer than 300 women in the Jamestown colony, compared to more than 1,000 men.

Africans Arrive in Virginia Enslaved Africans were brought to Virginia early on. Records show that at least 15 Black men and 17 Black women were already living there by 1619.

Analyze Images A Dutch ship lands at Jamestown in 1619 with 20 African captives. **Analyze Visuals** How does the artist show the harsh conditions of the enslaved Africans?

That same year, a Dutch ship arrived with about 20 Africans. The Dutch sold the enslaved Africans to Virginians who needed laborers to grow tobacco. The colonists valued the agricultural skills that the Africans brought with them. From the enslaved Africans' perspective, this was a journey into a brutal life of forced labor.

About 300 Africans lived in Virginia by 1644. Some were enslaved for life. Others worked as indentured servants, or people who were pledged to work for a master for a period until they paid off the cost of their voyage, and expected one day to own their own farms.

Some Africans did become free planters. Anthony Johnson owned 250 acres of land and employed five servants to help him work it. For a time, free Africans in Virginia also had the right to vote. These newcomers from Africa helped to transform the environment of Virginia by cutting down forests and planting tobacco fields.

Bacon's Rebellion Meanwhile, English settlers continued to arrive in Virginia, attracted by the promise of profits from tobacco. Wealthy planters, however, controlled the best lands near the coast. Many newcomers were indentured servants.

When they finished their period of service, they looked for farmland, often on Indian lands.

Conflicts over land led to fighting. After several bloody clashes, settlers called on the governor to take action against American Indians. The governor refused, in part because he profited from the fur trade with Indians. Frontier settlers were furious.

Finally, in 1676, Nathaniel Bacon, a young planter, organized angry men and women on the frontier, including Black and white indentured servants. He raided American Indian villages, including peaceful ones. Then, he led his followers to Jamestown and burned the capital.

The uprising, known as **Bacon's Rebellion**, lasted only a short time. When Bacon died suddenly, the revolt fell apart. The governor hanged 23 of Bacon's followers. Still, he could not stop English settlers from moving onto Indian lands along the frontier, or the edge of the settlement.

▲ Governor Berkeley faces angry colonists during Bacon's Rebellion in Jamestown.

Wealthy Virginians generally supported Governor Berkeley. They were alarmed that Black and white indentured servants had joined together in a rebellion. In response, Virginia set up a system of laws defining people from Africa as a separate race. The laws replaced indentured servitude for Africans with a condition of lifelong slavery that would be passed on to enslaved Africans' children. The laws gave white settlers privileges denied to Africans so that white settlers would have an interest in the racist system. Free African Americans also lost rights. By the early 1700s, free African American property owners could no longer vote.

READING CHECK **Identify Supporting Details** How did Virginia come to have a large African population?

Lesson Check

Practice Vocabulary

1. What was the impact of the **Protestant Reformation** in Europe?
2. Why did the French and Dutch seek **alliances** with American Indians?

Critical Thinking and Writing

3. **Summarize** What did John Cabot, Giovanni da Verrazano, and Jacques Cartier all have in common?
4. **Use Evidence** What examples can you give to show that contacts between European colonists and American Indians had negative consequences?
5. **Infer** What do you think happened after Virginia law established lifelong enslavement for people of African origin?
6. **Writing Workshop: Introduce Characters** In your Active Journal, identify other people from colonial society that your character would interact with. Explain what these other characters do and how they know your character.

LESSON 3

The New England Colonies

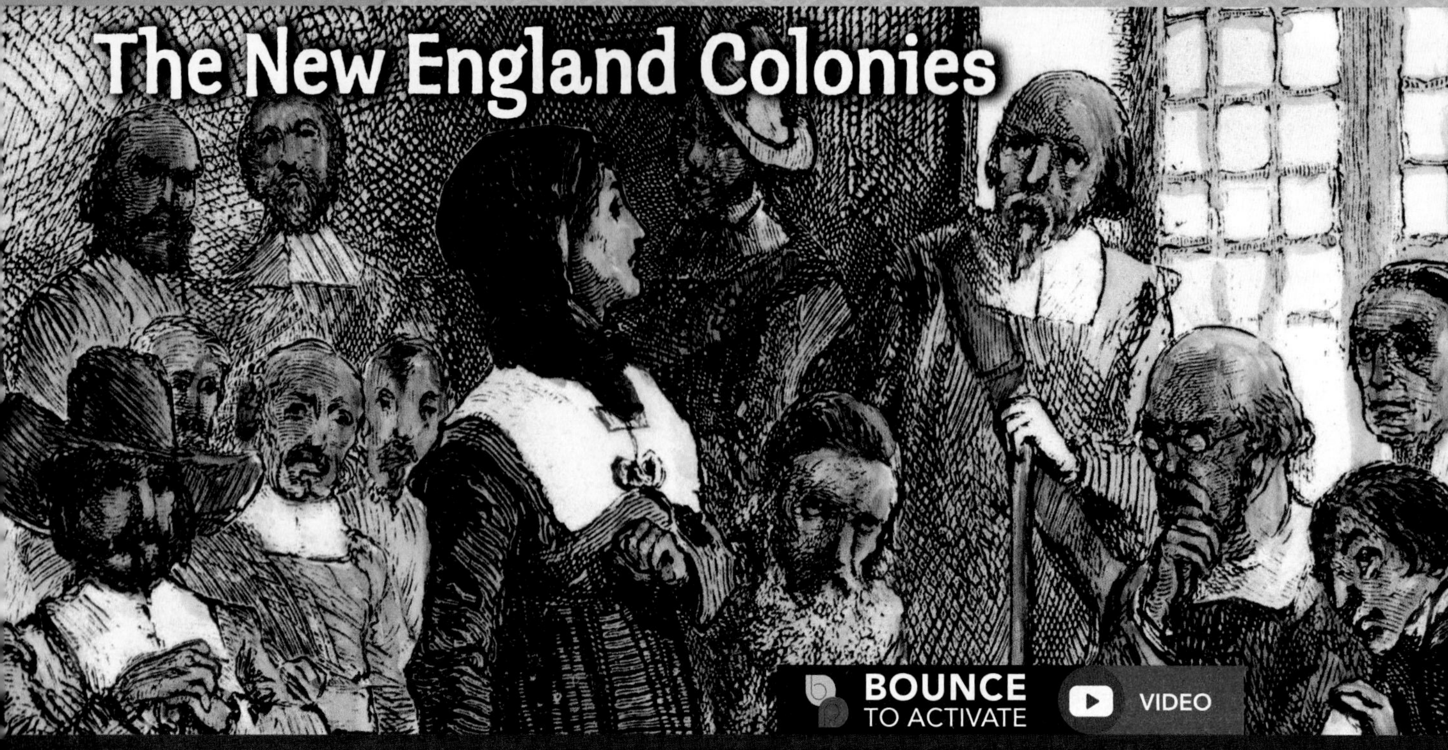

GET READY TO READ

START UP

Study the painting of a trial in the New England colonies. How do you think the men are reacting to the woman's words?

GUIDING QUESTIONS

- How did the desire for religious freedom lead to the settlement of the New England Colonies?
- Why was the Mayflower Compact significant?
- How were conflicts over religion and politics resolved in colonial New England?
- What were the reasons American Indians and settlers engaged in conflicts?
- How did the settlers of New England live?

TAKE NOTES

Literacy Skills: Compare and Contrast

Use the graphic organizer in your Active Journal to take notes as you read the lesson.

PRACTICE VOCABULARY

Use the vocabulary activity in your Active Journal to practice the vocabulary words.

Vocabulary		Academic Vocabulary
Pilgrim	Puritan	resolve
persecution	General Court	virtue
Mayflower Compact	religious tolerance	
	town meeting	

After two hard months at sea, the colonists on board the small sailing ship were relieved to see the shores of New England. Still, there were no European colonies for hundreds of miles.

Colonists Seek Religious Freedom

One of the voyagers, William Bradford, vividly remembered the situation:

Primary Source

"Being thus passed the vast ocean . . . they had now no friends to welcome them nor inns to entertain or refresh their weather-beaten bodies; no houses or much less towns to repair to. . . . And for the season it was winter, and they that know the winters of that country know them to be sharp and violent."

—William Bradford, *Of Plymouth Plantation*

Unlike the Jamestown colonists or the Spanish, these newcomers sought neither gold nor silver nor great riches. What they wanted most was to practice their religion freely. Years later, the founders of Plymouth became known to history as the **Pilgrims**, because they were religious people who traveled long distances to find a place where they could live and worship as they wanted.

Religion in Europe It was not easy for people to practice religion freely in Europe during the 1500s. As you have read, after the Protestant Reformation, Christians in western Europe were divided into Protestants and Roman Catholics. This division led to fierce religious wars. In France, for example, Protestants and Catholics fought each other for nearly 40 years. Thousands upon thousands of people were killed because of their religious beliefs.

Most European rulers believed that they could not maintain order unless everyone followed the ruler's religion. The religion chosen by the ruler was known as the established church. In England, for example, the established church was the Anglican church, or Church of England. In the 1530s, Parliament passed laws making the English monarch the head of the Church of England.

In England and other nations, people who did not follow the established religion were often persecuted. **Persecution** is the mistreatment or punishment of certain people because of their beliefs. Sometimes, members of persecuted groups had to worship secretly. If they were discovered, they might be imprisoned or even executed by being burned at the stake.

The Pilgrims One religious group in England that faced persecution were the people we now call the Pilgrims. At the time, they were known as Separatists. They were called that because, although they were Protestant, they wanted to separate from the Church of England.

The English government bitterly opposed the Separatists. William Bradford remembered what some Separatists had suffered.

Primary Source

"They . . . were hunted and persecuted on every side. . . . For some were taken and clapped up in prison, others had their houses beset and watched night and day . . . and the most were [glad] to flee and leave their houses."

—William Bradford, *Of Plymouth Plantation*

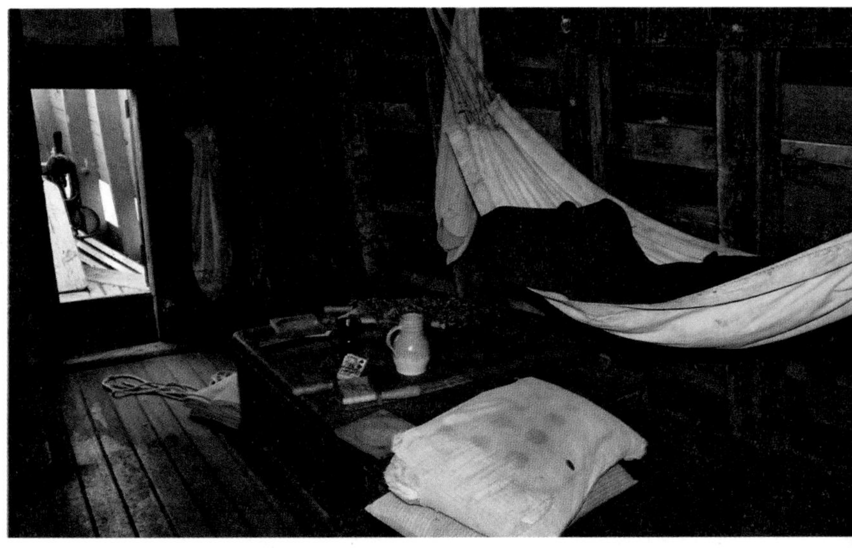

▼ This replica of the *Mayflower* in Plymouth, Massachusetts, was a gift from Great Britain. British and U.S. sailors sailed it across the Atlantic in 1957.

Quick Activity

In your Active Journal, write a letter from Pilgrims persuading other Separatists to join them on their journey across the Atlantic Ocean.

In the early 1600s, a group of Separatists left England for Leyden, a city in the Netherlands. The Dutch allowed the newcomers to worship freely. Still, the Pilgrims missed their English way of life. They were also worried that their children were growing up more Dutch than English.

READING CHECK **Identify Main Ideas** Why did the Pilgrims want to escape England and establish their own colony?

Founding the Plymouth Colony

A group of Separatists decided to leave the Netherlands. Along with some other English people who were not Separatists, they won a charter to set up a colony in the northern part of Virginia. Like the colonists who followed them, the Pilgrims' enterprise was started and funded privately in the hopes that it would earn a profit. In September 1620, more than 100 men, women, and children set sail aboard a small ship called the *Mayflower*. The journey was long and difficult.

Academic Vocabulary

resolve • *v.*, to come to a firm decision

At last, in November 1620, the *Mayflower* landed on the cold, bleak shore of Cape Cod, in present-day Massachusetts. The passengers had **resolved** to settle farther south along the Hudson River, but the difficult sea voyage exhausted them. The colonists decided to travel no farther. They called their new settlement Plimoth, or Plymouth, because the *Mayflower* had sailed from the port of Plymouth, England.

A New Pledge to Govern the Colony Before going ashore, the Pilgrims realized that they would not be settling within the boundaries of Virginia. As a result, the terms of their charter would not apply to their new colony. In that case, who would govern them? The question was especially important because not all colonists on the *Mayflower* were Pilgrims. Some of these "strangers," as the Pilgrims called them, said they were not bound to obey the Pilgrims, "for none had power to command them."

▼ The *Mayflower* reached the coast of modern-day Massachusetts after a difficult journey across the Atlantic Ocean.

In response, the Pilgrims joined together to write a framework for governing their colony. On November 11, 1620, the 41 adult male passengers—both Pilgrims and non-Pilgrims—signed the **Mayflower Compact**. They pledged themselves to unite into a "civil body politic," or government. They agreed to make and abide by laws that ensured "the general Good of the Colony."

The Mayflower Compact established an important tradition of self-government. When the Pilgrims found themselves without a government, they banded together themselves to make laws. In time, they set up a government in which adult male colonists elected a governor and council.

Analyze Images Male passengers on the *Mayflower* sign the Mayflower Compact, which established a government for the colony at Plymouth. **Synthesize Visual Information** What do you think the artist was trying to show about the Pilgrims?

Thus, like Virginia's Great Charter, the Mayflower Compact strengthened the English tradition of governing through elected representatives. These representatives were expected to show the religious **virtues** that the Pilgrims valued and to make decisions for the common good. The colony at Plymouth thought that this type of government, rather than the monarchy that they knew in England, would best protect their religious freedom.

Religious Motivation and Creating a Tradition of Religious Freedom The Pilgrims were the first of many immigrants who came to North America in order to worship as they pleased. That did not mean that religious freedom spread quickly through England's colonies. Many settlers who wished to worship as they pleased still believed that only their own religious beliefs should be observed. Most of the English colonies set up their own established churches.

Still, the Pilgrims' desire to worship freely set an important precedent, or example for others to follow in the future. In time, the idea of religious freedom for all would become a cornerstone of American democracy.

Academic Vocabulary
virtue • *n.*, morally good behavior or character

READING CHECK **Draw Conclusions** Why did the colonists at Plymouth believe that representative government would be the best way to protect their religious freedom?

▲ The Wampanoag taught the Pilgrims to plant native crops at Plymouth. Here, re-enactors work the fields at Plimouth Plantation.

What Hardships Did Colonists Face in Plymouth?

The Pilgrims built their settlement on the site of an American Indian village that had been abandoned because of disease. The colonists even found baskets filled with corn that they were able to eat.

A Cold Winter in Plymouth However, the corn was not enough to get the Pilgrims through their first winter. The Pilgrims had failed to bring enough food with them, and it was too late in the season to plant new crops.

The harsh season was also difficult to survive because the Pilgrims had not had enough time to build proper shelters. During the winter days, the men worked to build houses onshore, while most spent nights aboard the *Mayflower*. Half the settlers had perished of disease or starvation by spring.

American Indians Offer Assistance In the spring, the Pilgrims began to clear land and plant crops. They also received help from neighboring American Indians. A Pemaquid Indian, Samoset, had learned English from earlier explorers sailing along the coast. He introduced the Pilgrims to Massasoit (MAS uh soit), chief of the local Wampanoag (wahm puh NOH ahg) Indians.

The Wampanoag who helped the Pilgrims most was named Squanto. As a young man, Squanto had been captured by an English expedition led by John Smith. Squanto lived for a time in England, where he learned to speak the language. As a result, he could communicate easily with the Pilgrims.

Squanto brought the Pilgrims seeds of native plants—corn, beans, and pumpkins—and showed them how to plant them. He also taught the settlers how to catch eels from nearby rivers. By treading water, he stirred up eels from the mud at the river bottom and then snatched them up with his hands. The grateful Pilgrims called Squanto "a special instrument sent of God."

In the fall, the Pilgrims had a very good harvest. Because they believed that God had given them this harvest, they set aside a day for giving thanks.

More than 200 years after the Pilgrims' first successful harvest, President Abraham Lincoln proclaimed a national day of thanksgiving. Americans today celebrate Thanksgiving as a national holiday.

READING CHECK **Identify Supporting Details** How did American Indians help the Pilgrims?

Did you know?

Massachusetts was named for the Massachuset Indians.

Forming Massachusetts Bay Colony

The migration to Massachusetts Bay during the 1630s was led by a religious group known as the **Puritans**. Unlike the Pilgrims, the Puritans did not want to separate entirely from the Church of England. They wanted to simplify forms of worship. They wanted to do away with many practices inherited from the Roman Catholic Church. These included organ music, finely decorated houses of worship, and special clothing for priests.

Reasons for Immigration to Massachusetts The Puritans were a powerful group in England. Although some were small farmers, many were well educated and successful merchants or landowners.

Charles I, who became king in 1625, disapproved of the Puritans and their ideas. He canceled Puritan business charters and even had a few Puritans jailed.

By 1629, some Puritan leaders were convinced that England had fallen on "evil and declining times." They persuaded royal officials to grant them a charter to form the Massachusetts Bay Company. The company's bold plan was to build a new society based on biblical laws and teachings. John Winthrop, a lawyer and a devout Puritan, believed that the new colony would set an example to the world.

Some settlers joined the Massachusetts colonists for economic rather than religious reasons. In wealthy English families, the oldest son usually inherited his father's estate. With little hope of owning land, younger sons sought opportunity elsewhere. They were attracted to Massachusetts Bay because it offered cheap land or a chance to start a business.

Analyze Images John Winthrop said his colony would be a "shining city upon a hill." **Draw Conclusions** How was John Winthrop important in the development of the United States?

A Greater Say in Government In 1629, the Puritans sent a small advance party to North America. John Winthrop and a party of more than 1,000 arrived the following year. Winthrop was chosen as the first governor of the Massachusetts Bay Colony.

Once ashore, Winthrop set an example for others. Although he was governor, he worked hard to build a home, clear land, and plant crops. There was discontent among some colonists, though. Under the charter, only stockholders who had invested money in the Massachusetts Bay Company had the right to vote. Most settlers, however, were not stockholders. They resented taxes and laws that were passed by a government in which they had no voice.

Winthrop and other stockholders saw that the colony would run more smoothly if a greater number of settlers could take part. At the same time, Puritan leaders wished to keep non-Puritans out of the government.

Analyze Images Thomas Hooker led a group of settlers to set up a colony in Connecticut. **Identify Supporting Details** How did Hooker increase voting rights?

As a result, the colony granted the right to vote for governor to all men who were church members. Later, male church members also elected representatives to an assembly called the **General Court**.

READING CHECK **Identify Cause and Effect** Why was the right to vote expanded in the Massachusetts Bay Colony?

Which New Colonies Formed Over Religious Differences?

The Puritan leaders of the Massachusetts Bay Colony did not like anyone to question their religious beliefs or the way the colony was governed. Usually, discontented colonists were forced to leave. Some colonists who left Massachusetts founded other colonies in New England.

A New Colony with Limited Government In May 1636, a Puritan minister named Thomas Hooker led about 100 settlers out of Massachusetts Bay. Pushing west, they drove their cattle, goats, and pigs along American Indian trails that cut through the forests. When they reached the Connecticut River, they built a town, which they called Hartford.

Hooker left Massachusetts Bay because he believed that the governor and other officials had too much power. He wanted to set up a colony in Connecticut with strict limits on government.

The settlers wrote a plan of government called the Fundamental Orders of Connecticut in 1639. It created a government much like that of Massachusetts, which relied on people to obey the law and seek the common good. There were, however, two important differences. First, the Fundamental Orders gave the vote to all male property owners. This included those who were not church members. Second, the Fundamental Orders limited the governor's power. In this way, the Fundamental Orders expanded the idea of representative government in the English colonies.

A New Relationship Between Religion and Government Another Puritan who challenged the leaders of Massachusetts Bay was Roger Williams. A young minister in the village of Salem, Williams was gentle and good-natured. William Bradford described him as "zealous but very unsettled in judgment." Some Puritan leaders probably agreed with this. Most people, including Governor Winthrop, liked him.

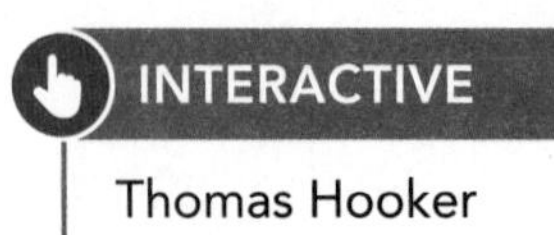

Williams's ideas, however, alarmed Puritan leaders. Williams believed that the Puritan church had too much power. In his view, the business of church and state should be completely separate, since concern with political affairs would corrupt the church. The role of the state, he said, was to maintain order and peace. It should not support a particular church. Finally, Williams did not believe that the Puritan leaders had the right to force people to attend religious services. Because of these political reasons, Williams sought to establish a new colony.

Williams also believed in religious tolerance. **Religious tolerance** means a willingness to let others practice their own beliefs. In Puritan Massachusetts, non-Puritans were not allowed to worship freely.

Puritan leaders viewed Williams as a dangerous troublemaker. In 1635, the General Court ordered him to leave Massachusetts. Fearing that the court would send him back to England, Williams fled to Narragansett Bay, where he spent the winter with Indians. In the spring of 1636, the Indians sold him land for a settlement. After a few years, the settlement became the English colony of Rhode Island.

In Rhode Island, Williams put into practice his ideas about tolerance. He allowed complete freedom of religion for all Protestants, Jews, and Catholics. He did not set up a state church or require settlers to attend church services. He also gave all white men the right to vote.

A Woman's Voice Calls for Religious Freedom Among those who fled to Rhode Island was Anne Hutchinson. A devout Puritan, Hutchinson regularly attended church services in Boston, where she first lived. After church, she and her friends gathered at her home to discuss the minister's sermon. Often, she seemed to question some of the minister's teachings.

Analyze Graphs This chart offers a snapshot of the people and economy of the New England Colonies. **Draw Conclusions** What does the graph of imports and exports tell you about the economy of the New England Colonies during the 1700s?

THE NEW ENGLAND COLONIES

TIMELINE OF SETTLEMENT

1620 Plymouth Colony was settled by Pilgrims wishing to escape religious persecution in England.

1630 Massachusetts Bay Colony was settled by Puritans wishing to escape religious persecution in England.

1623 New Hampshire began as a group of coastal settlements.

1636 Connecticut was founded as a colony with strict limits on government power.

1636 Rhode Island was founded as a colony where church and state were separated.

PEOPLE

First settled by about 50 Pilgrims. Thousands came later.
Most were Puritans who wanted to reform the Church of England.
Persecution by King Charles I in the 1600s caused many to leave England.

ECONOMY

AGRICULTURE
80% OF POPULATION INVOLVED IN SUBSISTENCE FARMING

— NEW ENGLAND —
EXPORTS & IMPORTS

Pounds Sterling (thousands)
400
300
200
100
0
1710
1730
1750
1770
Year
Imports
Exports

BIOGRAPHY
5 Things to Know About
ANNE HUTCHINSON
Religious Leader (1591–1643)

- Hutchinson was born in England and moved to the American colonies in her early forties.
- She was one of many women of the time who was active in religious life.
- Hutchinson's understanding of how to use herbal remedies attracted neighbors to her home, where she spoke of her views.
- She was banished from Massachusetts for her beliefs, which were condemned by the Puritans.
- Hutchinson moved to New York after her husband died, and she was killed in an Indian raid a few years later.

Critical Thinking Why do we still remember Anne Hutchinson and what she did?

Hutchinson was very persuasive, and neighbors flocked to hear her. Her teachings and her popularity angered the Puritan leaders. They believed that Hutchinson's opinions were full of religious errors. Even worse, they said, a woman did not have the right to explain God's law. In November 1637, Hutchinson was ordered to appear before the Massachusetts General Court.

At her trial, Hutchinson answered the questions put to her by Governor Winthrop and other members of the court. Each time, her answers revealed weaknesses in their arguments. They could not prove that she had broken any Puritan laws or that she had disobeyed any religious teachings.

Then, after two long days of hostile questioning, Hutchinson made a serious mistake. She told the court that God spoke directly to her, "By the voice of His own spirit to my soul." Members of the court were shocked. Puritans believed that God spoke only through the Bible, not directly to individuals. The court ordered her out of the colony.

In 1638, Hutchinson, along with her family and some friends, went to Rhode Island. The Puritan leaders had won their case. For later Americans, however, Hutchinson became an important symbol of the struggle for religious freedom.

READING CHECK **Identify Implied Main Ideas** What relationship did Roger Williams want to see between government and religion?

War Erupts Between Settlers and American Indians

From Massachusetts Bay, settlers fanned out across New England. Some built trading and fishing villages along the coast north of Boston. Port towns with good harbors were ideal for the fishing industry and also lured trading ships, building the area's economy. In 1680, the king would make some of these coastal settlements into a separate colony called New Hampshire.

Conflict Develops The first meetings between English settlers and American Indians did not foreshadow their future conflict. Some colonial leaders such as Roger Williams tried to treat American Indians fairly.

As more colonists settled in New England, they began to take over more American Indian lands. By 1670, nearly 45,000 English settlers were living in the towns in New England. Land was a resource, but as more people lived in the region, it became increasingly scarce. Fighting soon broke out between white settlers and Indian nations of the region.

King Phillip's War The largest conflict came in 1675. Metacom, also known by his English name, King Phillip, was chief of the Wampanoag. He watched for years as English towns were built on Wampanoag lands. "I am resolved not to see the day when I have no country," he told an English friend. Metacom's people attacked villages throughout New England.

Other Indian groups, from Rhode Island to Maine, soon allied themselves with the Wampanoag. They were determined to drive the English settlers off their land. Metacom and his allies destroyed 12 towns and killed more than 600 European settlers.

After more than a year of fighting, however, Metacom was captured and killed. The English sold his family and about 1,000 other Indians into slavery in the West Indies. Other Indians were forced from their homelands.

The pattern of English expansion followed by war between colonists and Indians was repeated throughout the colonies. It would continue for many years to come.

READING CHECK **Identify Cause and Effect** What was a significant cause of King Phillip's War?

The New England Colonies

GEOGRAPHY SKILLS

Most of New England's major towns were located on harbors along the coast.

1. **Location** On what body of water was Hartford located?
2. **Infer** What do the locations of New England towns suggest about their economies?

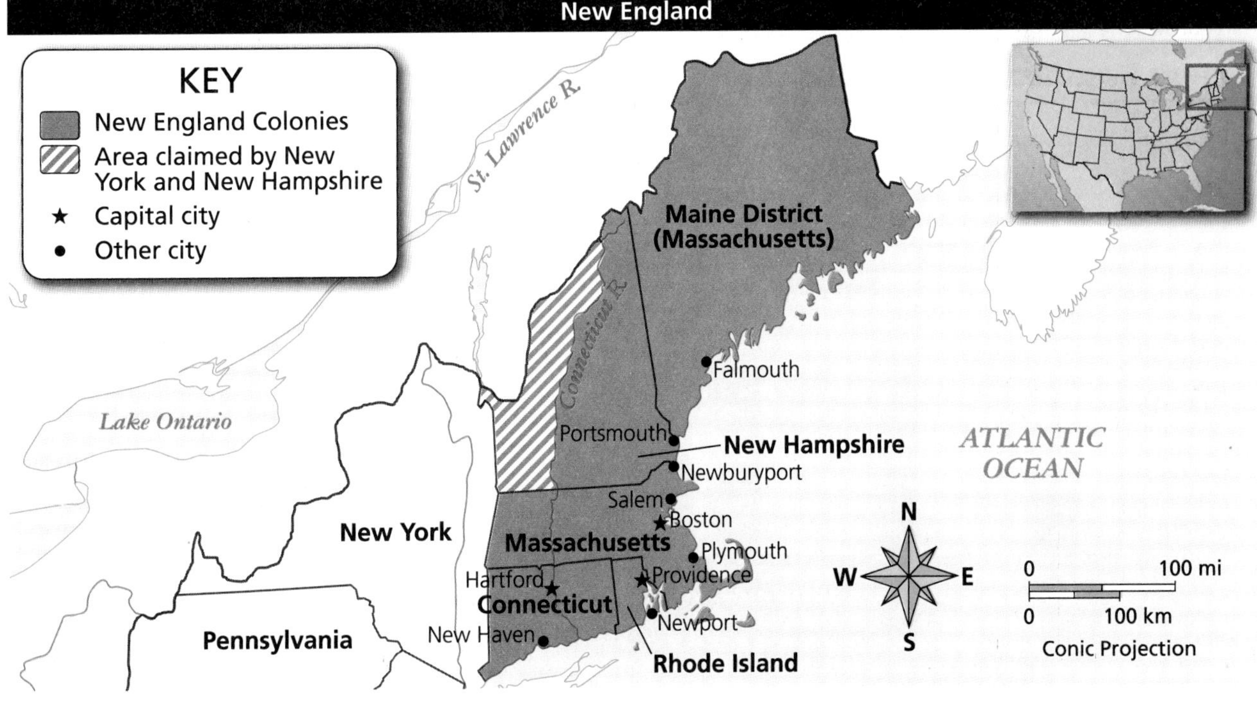

Quest CONNECTIONS

Read the section called "The Environment Influences Economic Activity." In what ways was the environment helpful to people looking to make a living? In what way was it unhelpful? Record your findings in your Active Journal.

How Did People Live in the Towns of New England?

Puritans believed that people should worship and tend to local matters as a community. As a result, New England became a land of tightly knit towns.

At the center of many towns was the common, an open field where cattle grazed. Nearby stood the meetinghouse, where Puritans worshiped and held town meetings.

Religious Practice The Puritans took their Sabbath, or holy day of religious observance and rest, very seriously. On Sundays, no one was allowed to play games or visit taverns. The law required all citizens to attend Sunday church services, which would last all day.

During the 1600s, women sat on one side of the church and men on the other. African Americans and American Indians stood in a balcony at the back. Children had separate pews, where an adult watched over them.

The Importance of Local Government At **town meetings**, which were normally held in the meeting houses, settlers discussed and voted on local and church issues. They also chose ministers. Town meetings gave New Englanders a chance to speak their minds.

These early experiences encouraged the growth of democratic ideas in New England. Values such as self-government, individual choice, and the common good took root and thrived.

Still, Puritan laws were strict. About 15 crimes carried the death penalty. One crime punishable by death was witchcraft. In 1692, Puritans in Salem Village executed 20 innocent men and women as witches.

The Environment Influences Economic Activity New England was a difficult land for colonists. The rocky soil was poor for farming and required much labor. After a time, however, American Indians taught English settlers how to grow many crops, such as Indian corn, pumpkins, squash, and beans. Still, some communities relocated to take advantage of better lands. In the mid-1630s, cattle and dairy farmers who had settled in Dorchester, Massachusetts, moved to the Connecticut River Valley. The rich river valley at Windsor, Connecticut, provided lush meadows and pastures better suited to their cattle than the sandy soils and rocky hills of Dorchester.

Although much of the soil was poor, the forests were full of riches. Settlers hunted wild turkey and deer. Settlers also cut down trees, floating them down rivers to sawmills near seaports such as Boston, Massachusetts, or Portsmouth, New Hampshire.

Analyze Graphs Fishing helped support the New England economy throughout the 1700s. **Synthesize Visual Information** Approximately how many fish were caught in 1731? Approximately how much did the catch that year weigh?

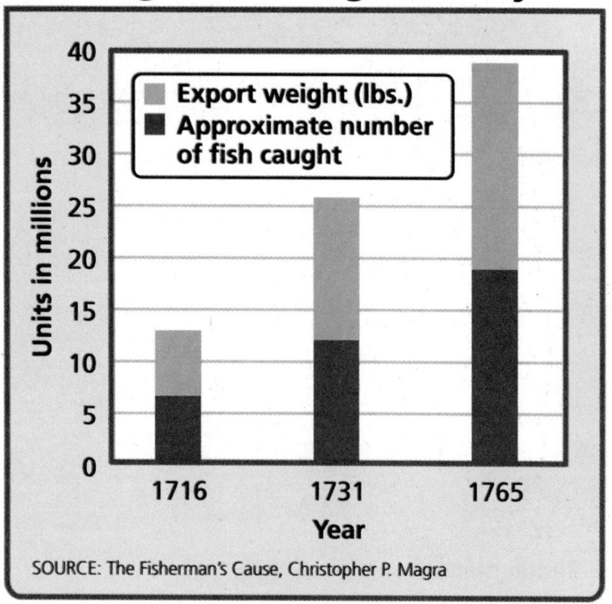

▲ English settlers learned how to grow many crops, such as Indian corn, pumpkins, squash, and beans, from American Indians.

With miles of coastline and nearby raw materials, these and other New England towns grew into major shipbuilding centers. Because abundant timber meant that ships could be built more cheaply in New England than in England, New England sold many ships to English buyers.

New Englanders fished for cod and halibut. In the 1600s, people began to hunt whales. Whales supplied oil for lamps and other products. In the 1700s and 1800s, whaling grew into a big business.

The Puritans Leave a Lasting Legacy During the 1700s, the Puritan tradition declined. Fewer families left England for religious reasons. Ministers had less influence on the way colonies were governed. Nevertheless, the Puritans had stamped New England with their distinctive customs and their ideal of a religious society. The ideas of Pilgrims and Puritans, their virtues of hard work and thrift, their high regard for education, and their contributions to democratic thought still influence American values and American identity today.

READING CHECK **Identify Supporting Details** What values did Puritans associate with town meetings?

Lesson Check

Practice Vocabulary

1. Why did many Europeans face **persecution** in the 16th century?
2. In what way were the **Puritans** different from the **Pilgrims**?

Critical Thinking and Writing

3. **Identify Main Ideas** Why did settling in Plymouth late in the year of 1620 pose significant problems for the Pilgrims?
4. **Identify Cause and Effect** What effect did population growth have on the conflict between colonists and American Indians?
5. **Cite Evidence** to support the claim that the New England Colonies promoted the ideals of democracy and self-government.
6. **Writing Workshop: Establish Setting** Write a few sentences in your Active Journal to describe the setting where your character lives in the colonies. You will use them in your topic narrative essay.

William Bradford, *Of Plymouth Plantation*

William Bradford was one of the Pilgrims who sailed on the *Mayflower* and landed in Plymouth. He became one of the leaders of the colony, helping to write the Mayflower Compact and serving as governor. He wrote a journal called *Of Plymouth Plantation* in which he describes the story of the Pilgrims from 1608 to 1647. In this excerpt, he discusses the decision to move to North America.

◀ The signing of the Mayflower Compact

Reading and Vocabulary Support

① *Ye* was an early modern English word that means "the."

② How did Bradford describe the challenges he expected to face on the journey across the Atlantic Ocean?

③ *Providente* is a reference to God.

④ How does Bradford describe the thought process that went into the decision to move to North America?

All great & honourable actions are accompanied with great difficulties, and must be both enterprised [undertaken] and overcome with answerable courages. It was granted ye ① dangers were great, but not desperate; the difficulties were many, but not invincible [too powerful] ②. For though there were many of them likely, yet they were not cartaine [certain]; it might be sundrie [several] of ye things feared might never befale [take place]; others by providente ③ care & ye use of good means, might in a great measure be prevented; and all of them, through ye help of God, by fortitude [bravery] and patience, might either be borne, or overcome.

True it was, that such atempts were not to be made and undertaken without good ground & reason; not rashly or lightly as many have done for curiositie or hope of gaine, &c. But their condition was not ordinarie; their ends were good & honourable; their calling lawfull, & urgente; and therfore they might expecte ye blessing of god in their proceding. Yea, though they should loose their lives in this action, yet might they have comforte in the same, and their endeavors would be honourable. ④

Analyzing Primary Sources

Cite specific evidence from the document to support your answers.

1. **Draw Conclusions** According to Bradford, what would the reward be for those who did not survive the journey to North America?
2. **Analyze Style and Rhetoric** How would you describe the tone of Bradford's journal entry?

LESSON 4

The Middle Colonies

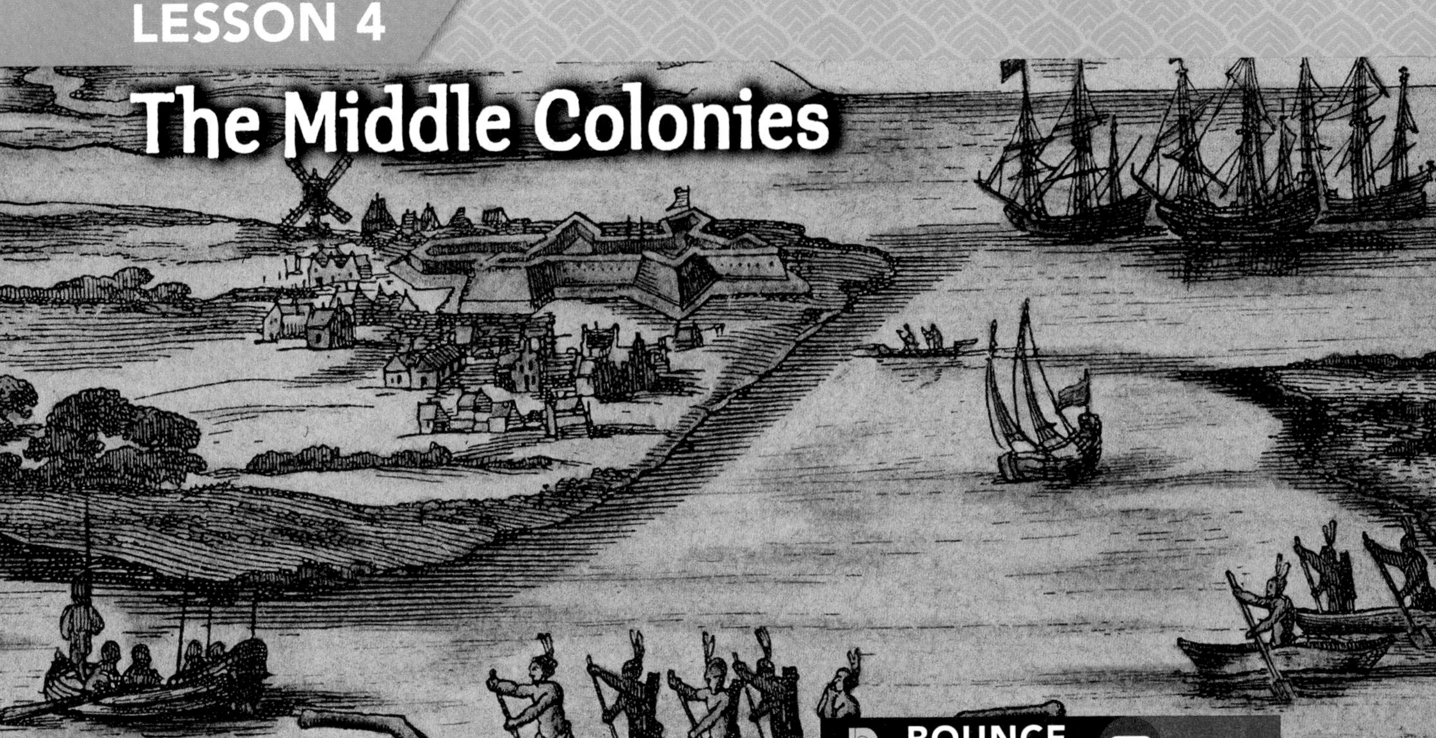

GET READY TO READ

START UP

This engraving shows New Amsterdam in the 1660s, which later became New York City. What would a picture of the same area look like today?

GUIDING QUESTIONS

- What were the reasons the colonies of New York and New Jersey were established?
- Why were the colonies of Pennsylvania and Delaware established?
- How would you describe the economy of the Middle Colonies, and what was the relationship between the economy and the physical environment?

TAKE NOTES

Literacy Skills: Analyze Text Structure

Use the graphic organizer in your Active Journal to take notes as you read the lesson.

PRACTICE VOCABULARY

Use the vocabulary activity in your Active Journal to practice the vocabulary words.

Vocabulary		Academic Vocabulary
proprietary colony	Quaker	haven
royal colony	Pennsylvania Dutch	commoner
	cash crop	

By 1700, England had four colonies in the region just south of New England. These colonies became known as the Middle Colonies because they were located between New England and the Southern Colonies. The Middle Colonies had a greater mix of people than either New England or the Southern Colonies.

Why Did the Dutch Colony Become English?

Each of the colonies along the Atlantic coast had been established by different people for different purposes. Sometimes colonies were formed to escape political oppression or social tensions back home in Europe.

In the case of New Netherland, however, the conditions back home for the Dutch were stable and fairly prosperous. New Netherland was founded simply to take advantage of economic opportunities in North America.

INTERACTIVE

The Middle Colonies

New Amsterdam The Dutch set up the colony of New Netherland along the Hudson River. They developed the fur trade and built settlements where fur-bearing animals were abundant. In the colony's early years, settlers traded with Indians and built the settlement of New Amsterdam into a thriving port. Located near good farmland and with a safe harbor for ships, New Amsterdam quickly became a center for commerce and trading valuable beaver skins.

Dutch officials also promoted agriculture. They granted large parcels of land to a few rich families. A single grant could stretch for miles. Owners of these huge estates were called patroons. In return for the grant, each patroon promised to settle at least 50 European farm families on the land. Patroons had great power and could charge whatever rents they pleased.

GEOGRAPHY SKILLS

The Middle Colonies lay between the New England Colonies and the Southern Colonies.

1. **Place** What colonies bordered New Jersey?
2. **Draw Conclusions** What geographic features of the Middle Colonies suggest that they were well placed for trade?

England Gains Control Many settlers lived in the trading center of New Amsterdam, which by 1664 had a population of about 1,500 people. They came from all over Europe. Most of them came for the economic opportunities, working as merchants or farmers, or in trades and crafts. Many were also attracted by the chance to practice their religion freely. African slaves were in demand as well. In the early years, they made up more than a quarter of the population of the town.

Dutch colonists were mainly Protestants who belonged to the Dutch Reformed Church. Still, they permitted members of other religions and ethnic groups—including Roman Catholics, French Protestants, and Jews—to buy land. "People do not seem concerned what religion their neighbor is" wrote a shocked visitor from Virginia. "Indeed, they do not seem to care if he has any religion at all."

Middle Colonies

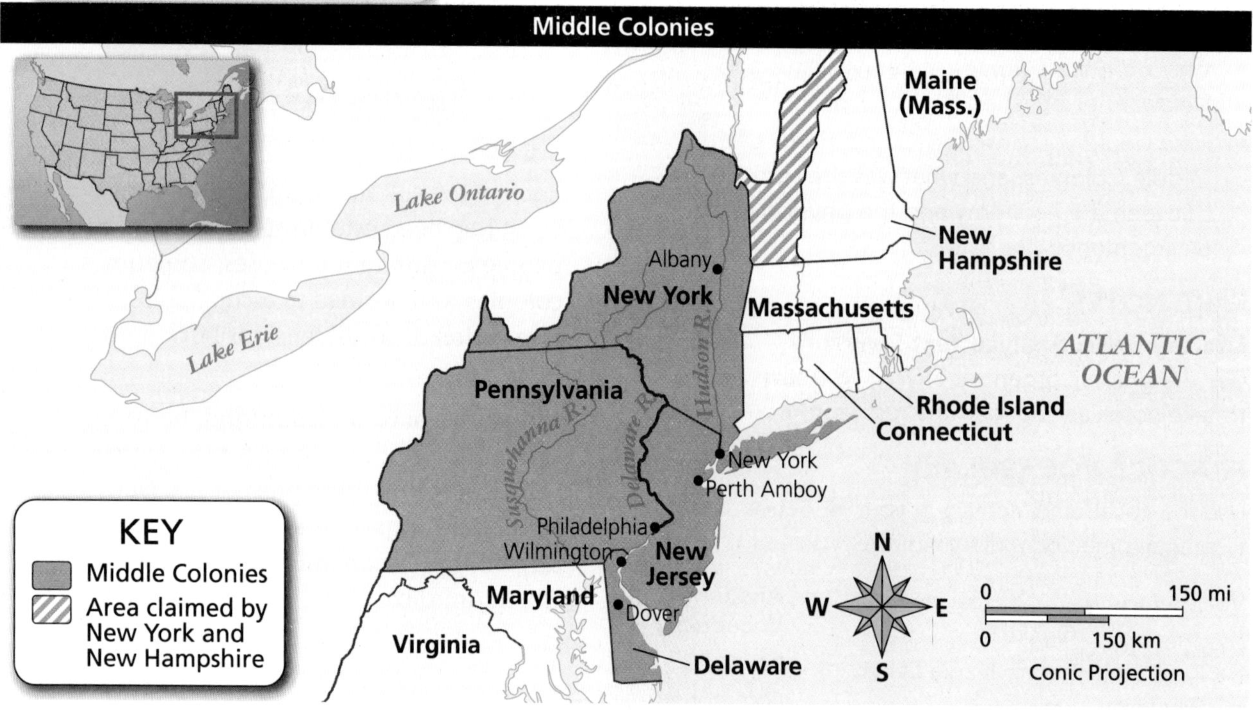

In fact, Peter Stuyvesant (STY vuh sunt), the governor of New Netherland, had been ordered not to interfere with other religions as long as they did not disturb the peace or restrict commerce.

The relationship between the English and the Dutch was complicated by their common interest in creating new colonies and expanding trade. In North America, the Dutch wanted to continue benefiting from New Amsterdam's economic growth. However, the English wanted New Amsterdam for themselves.

By 1664, the rivalry between England and the Netherlands for trade and colonies was at its height. In August of that year, English warships entered New Amsterdam's harbor. Governor Stuyvesant swore to defend the city. However, he had few weapons and little gunpowder. Also, Stuyvesant had made himself so unpopular with his harsh rule and heavy taxes that the colonists refused to help him. In the end, he surrendered without firing a shot.

King Charles II of England then gave New Netherland to his brother, the Duke of York. He renamed the colony New York in the duke's honor.

READING CHECK **Identify Cause and Effect** Why did many people come to New Amsterdam?

Analyze Images This statue of Peter Stuyvesant stands in Stuyvesant Park in Manhattan. **Identify Implied Main Ideas** Why was Stuyvesant ordered to observe a policy of religious tolerance?

New Jersey Forms Out of New York

At the time of the English takeover, New York stretched as far south as the Delaware Bay. The Duke of York decided that the colony was too big to govern easily. He gave some of the land to friends, Lord Berkeley and Sir George Carteret. They set up a proprietary (proh PRY uh tehr ee) colony, which they called New Jersey, in 1664.

A Proprietary Colony and a Market Economy In setting up a **proprietary colony**, the king gave land to one or more people in return for a yearly payment. These proprietors were free to divide the land and rent it to others. They made laws for the colony, but had to respect the rights of colonists under English law. This new system of colonization was different from most that had come before. Proprietary colonies placed vast lands and power in the hands of a few men loyal to the monarch. Earlier colonies had been financed by stock companies made up of a number of investors.

Like New York, New Jersey had fertile farmland and other resources that attracted people from many lands. Thousands of European settlers immigrated to New Jersey as a **haven** from war and poverty. Settlers came from Finland, Ireland, Scotland, Germany, and Sweden. English and Dutch settlers also moved there from New York.

Academic Vocabulary
haven • *n.*, a place where people are protected from danger and trouble

Analyze Images New Jersey's fertile farmland attracted many colonists. **Compare and Contrast** How was farming in New Jersey different from farming in New England?

In addition, some New England colonists, hoping to find better farmland, chose to relocate to New Jersey.

The proprietors of New Jersey encouraged the free enterprise system, which meant that government played a limited role in the economy. The free enterprise system benefited colonists. They could farm or run businesses without much control by the local government. Facing financial losses themselves, however, the proprietors eventually returned the colony of New Jersey to the English crown.

A Royal Colony In 1702, New Jersey became a **royal colony**, which is a colony under the direct control of the English king or queen. The colony's royal charter protected religious freedom and the rights of an assembly that voted on local matters. This charter could be viewed as a legal agreement between the monarch and settlers, binding to both.

Despite these moves toward democracy, direct English rule tended to be harsh toward colonists. New Jersey's independent-minded settlers struggled to gain more influence over decisions that affected them.

READING CHECK **Draw Conclusions** Why do you think the system in which government stays out of the way to let people run business with little control is called the free enterprise system?

How Did Pennsylvania Become a Colony?

West of New Jersey, William Penn founded the colony of Pennsylvania in 1681. Penn came from a wealthy English family and was a personal friend of King Charles II. At age 22, however, Penn shocked family and friends by joining the **Quakers**, one of the most despised religious groups in England.

The Quakers Seek Religious Freedom Like Pilgrims and Puritans, Quakers were Protestant reformers. Their reforms went further than those of other groups, however.

Academic Vocabulary
commoner • *n.*, a regular or average person

Quakers believed that all people—men and women, nobles and **commoners**—were equal in God's sight. They allowed women to preach in public and refused to bow or remove their hats in the presence of nobles. Quakers spoke out against all war and refused to serve in the army.

To most English people, Quaker beliefs seemed wicked. In both England and New England, Quakers were arrested, fined, or even hanged for their ideas. Penn became convinced that the Quakers must leave England. He took steps to found a new colony. Together with others, Penn purchased parts of New Jersey from their proprietors. Then he turned to the king for help.

Charles II issued a royal charter naming Penn proprietor of a large tract of land in North America. The king named the new colony Pennsylvania, or Penn's woodlands. During his time as proprietor, Penn took steps that aided the development of self-government in Pennsylvania. He proposed a constitution and a General Assembly. Later, he agreed to changes in the constitution and greater powers for the colonial assembly.

Showing Fairness to All Penn thought of his colony as a "holy experiment." He wanted it to be a model of religious freedom, peace, and Christian living. Protestants, Catholics, and Jews went to Pennsylvania to escape persecution. Later, English officials forced Penn to turn away Catholic and Jewish settlers.

Penn's Quaker beliefs led him to speak out for fair treatment of American Indians. Penn believed that the land in North America belonged to the Indians. He insisted that settlers should pay for the land. American Indians respected him for this policy. As a result, Pennsylvania colonists enjoyed many years of peace with their Indian neighbors. One settler remarked that, as Penn "treated the Indians with extraordinary humanity, they became civil and loving to us."

Analyze Images Painter Benjamin West imagined this scene of Penn signing the treaty with the American Indians. **Use Visual Information** How does the artist show peaceful relations among Penn, merchants, and Indians?

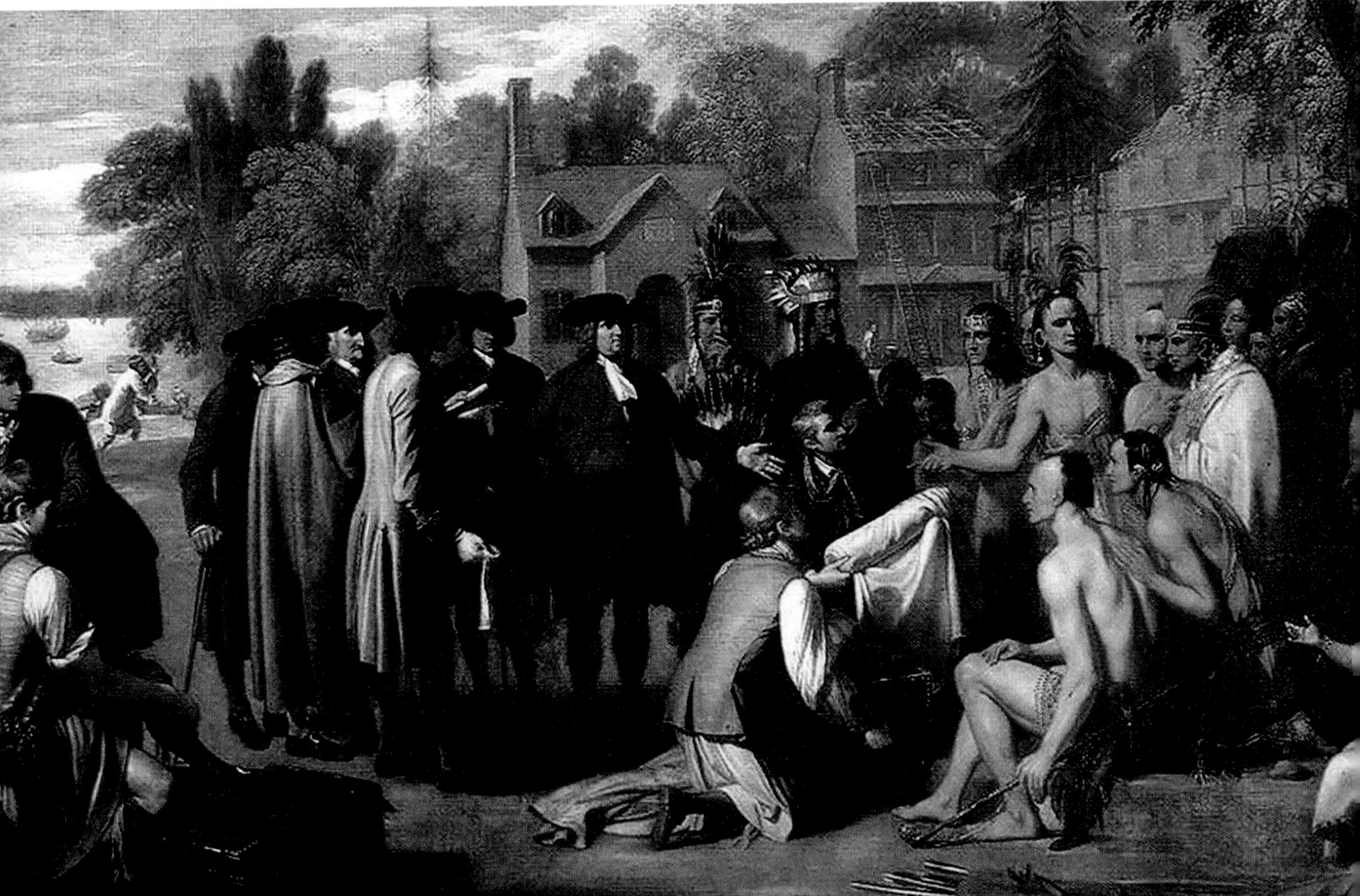

Quest CONNECTIONS

How was the environment of the Middle Colonies more favorable to workers than the New England colonies? Record your findings in your Active Journal.

Pennsylvania Expands Penn sent pamphlets describing his colony all over Europe. Soon, settlers from England, Scotland, Wales, the Netherlands, France, and Germany began to cross the Atlantic Ocean to Pennsylvania.

Among the new arrivals were large numbers of German-speaking Protestants. They became known as **Pennsylvania Dutch** because people could not pronounce the word Deutsch (doich), which means German. Many Pennsylvania Dutch had faced religious persecution in Europe, including the Amish and Mennonites. Because of their experiences in Europe, these German-speaking people were naturally attracted to the ideals of Penn's colony, in which people of different ethnicities and religions could live peaceably together. The ethnic diversity of Pennsylvania contributed to a developing American identity based on ethnic diversity.

▼ A statue of William Penn stands atop Philadelphia's City Hall today.

Pennsylvania, like most other colonies, was created for a mix of political, economic, religious, and social reasons. Pennsylvania was like the New England colonies in the religious reasons for its creation. Like New York, its political roots lay in a proprietor's ties to the king. Pennsylvania's social goals of harmony among different groups were similar to those of Rhode Island. Like most proprietors, Penn hoped to profit from his colony.

Enslaved Africans were also brought to the growing Pennsylvania colony. They made up about one third of all new arrivals between 1730 and 1750. Enslaved Africans were present in New York, New Jersey, and the New England Colonies as well, but in smaller numbers than in the Southern Colonies. Because of Philadelphia's location along the Delaware River, many worked as laborers in manufacturing and shipbuilding.

Delaware Is Born For a time, Pennsylvania included some lands along the lower Delaware River. The region was known as Pennsylvania's Lower Counties. Later, in 1704, the Lower Counties would break away to form the colony of Delaware.

READING CHECK **Identify Main Ideas** Why did Quakers want to establish their own colony?

Daily Life in the Middle Colonies

The majority of colonists made their living by farming. Farmers found more favorable conditions in the Middle Colonies than in New England. The broad Hudson and Delaware river valleys were rich and fertile. Winters were milder than in New England, and the growing season lasted longer.

A Thriving Economy On such promising land, farmers in the eastern counties of the Middle Colonies cleared their fields. They mostly chose to raise wheat, barley, and rye as a way to earn money. Wheat, barley, and rye were **cash crops**, or crops that were sold for money on the market and not consumed by the farmer's family. In fact, the Middle Colonies exported so much grain that they became known as the Breadbasket Colonies.

The Pennsylvania Dutch tended to settle the fertile interior lands. They altered the environment by clearing land and starting farms, turning these regions into rich fields that are still productive today.

▲ Farmers took advantage of the fertile land of the Middle Colonies by growing crops to sell at market.

Farmers of the Middle Colonies also raised herds of cattle and pigs. Every year, they sent tons of beef, pork, and butter to the ports of New York and Philadelphia. From there, the goods went by ship to New England and the South or to the West Indies, England, and other parts of Europe.

Farms in the Middle Colonies were generally larger than those in New England. Landowners hired workers to help with the planting, harvesting, and other tasks. Enslaved African Americans worked on a few large farms. However, most workers were farmhands who worked alongside the families that owned the land.

Aside from farmers, there were also skilled artisans in the Middle Colonies. Encouraged by William Penn, skilled German craftspersons set up shop in Pennsylvania. In time, the colony became a center of manufacturing and crafts. One visitor reported that workshops turned out "hardware, clocks, watches, locks, guns, flints, glass, stoneware, nails, [and] paper."

Settlers in the Delaware River valley profited from the region's rich deposits of iron ore. Heating the ore in furnaces, they purified it and then hammered it into nails, tools, and parts for guns.

The Economy of the Middle Colonies

Home Life Because houses tended to be far apart in the Middle Colonies, towns were less important than in New England. Counties, rather than villages, became centers of local government.

The different groups who settled the Middle Colonies had their own favorite ways of building. Swedish settlers introduced log cabins to the Americas. The Dutch used red bricks to build narrow, high-walled houses. German settlers developed a wood-burning stove that heated a home better than a fireplace, which sent heat up the chimney and pulled cold air in through cracks in the walls.

Everyone in a household had a job to do. Households were largely self-sufficient, which meant that most things needed for survival—food, clothing, soap, candles, and many other goods—were made at home. As one farmer said, "Nothing to wear, eat, or drink was purchased, as my farm provided all."

Expanding Beyond Philadelphia In the 1700s, thousands of German and Scotch-Irish settlers arrived in Philadelphia. From there, many traveled west into the back country, the area of land along the eastern slopes of the Appalachian Mountains. Settlers followed an old Indian trail that became known as the Great Wagon Road.

Although settlers planned to follow farming methods they had used in Europe, they found the challenge of farming the back country more difficult than they had thought it would be. To farm the back country, settlers had to clear thick forests. From Indians, settlers learned how to use knots from pine trees as candles to light their homes. They made wooden dishes from logs, gathered honey from hollows in trees, and hunted wild animals for food. German gunsmiths developed a lightweight rifle for use in forests. Sharpshooters boasted that the "Pennsylvania rifle" could hit a rattlesnake between the eyes at 100 yards.

Analyze Charts Religious, economic, geographic, and ethnic differences distinguished the Middle Colonies from New England. **Use Evidence** Which colonial region would you rather live in? Why?

Comparing the New England and Middle Colonies

	NEW ENGLAND	MIDDLE COLONIES
MAIN REASON FOR SETTLEMENT	Avoid religious persecution	Economic gain
BUSINESS AND TRADE	Shipbuilding, shipping, fishing, forestry	Agriculture, skilled trades, shipping
AGRICULTURE	Mostly limited to the needs of the colonies	Fertile farmland produced export crops
ETHNIC DIVERSITY	Mainly English	English, Dutch, German, and Scotch-Irish
SETTLEMENT STRUCTURE	Close-knit towns	More scattered settlements
CULTURE AND SOCIETY	Religious uniformity; small family farms and businesses with few servants or slaves	Ethnic and religious diversity; larger farms and businesses need indentured servants

Many of the settlers who arrived in the back country moved onto Indian lands. "The Indians . . . are alarmed at the swarm of strangers," one Pennsylvania official reported. "We are afraid of a [fight] between them for the [colonists] are very rough to them." However, officials did not step in to protect Indian rights. On more than one occasion, disputes between settlers and Indians resulted in violence.

Analyze Images Members of a Dutch colonial family sit around their tea table in New York in the 1700s. **Synthesize Visual Information** How does this image show differences in colonial men's and women's roles?

READING CHECK **Identify Main Ideas** Why was so much of the Middle Colonies' economy based on farming?

Lesson Check

Practice Vocabulary

1. What were the differences between a **proprietary colony** and a **royal colony**?
2. What were the **Quakers**' beliefs regarding equality?

Critical Thinking and Writing

3. **Identify Supporting Details** What did the term "free enterprise system" mean in New Jersey while it was a proprietary colony?
4. **Summarize** What did William Penn do to reflect the values of the Quaker religion in his colony?
5. **Draw Conclusions** How did the free enterprise system encourage the cultivation of cash crops in the Middle Colonies?
6. **Writing Workshop: Organize Sequence of Events** Make an ordered list of events in your Active Journal to show what happens to your character in your narrative essay. You will use this sequence of events when you write your narrative essay at the end of this topic.

LESSON 5

The Southern Colonies

GET READY TO READ

START UP

Examine the image of the ships sailing in Charleston Harbor. What do the number of ships tell you about the city during the colonial era?

GUIDING QUESTIONS

- Why was Maryland was established?
- What were the reasons the Carolinas and Georgia were established?
- How would you describe the relationship between environments, settlement patterns, and economic systems in the Southern Colonies?
- How did slavery spread in the Southern Colonies?

TAKE NOTES

Literacy Skills: Classify and Categorize

Use the graphic organizer in your Active Journal to take notes as you read the lesson.

PRACTICE VOCABULARY

Use the vocabulary activity in your Active Journal to practice the vocabulary words.

Vocabulary

Act of Toleration
indigo
debtor
slave code
racism

Academic Vocabulary

deprive
quarters

In 1632, Sir George Calvert persuaded King Charles I to grant him land for a colony in the Americas. Calvert had ruined his career in Protestant England by becoming a Roman Catholic. Now, he planned to build a colony where Catholics could practice their religion freely.

Why Did Lord Baltimore Start a Colony?

Calvert named his colony Maryland in honor of Queen Henrietta Maria, the king's wife. Calvert died before the colony could get underway. His son Cecil, Lord Baltimore, pushed on with the project.

Settlers Come to Maryland In the spring of 1634, about 200 colonists landed along the upper Chesapeake Bay, across the Potomac River from England's first southern colony, Virginia. Maryland was truly a land of plenty. Chesapeake Bay was full of fish, oysters, and crabs. Virginians were already enslaving Africans to grow tobacco for profit. Maryland's new settlers hoped to do the same.

Remembering the early problems at Jamestown, the newcomers avoided the swampy lowlands. They built their first town, St. Mary's, in a drier location.

As proprietor of the colony, Lord Baltimore owned Maryland. It was his personal responsibility, not that of a company, to start the colony. He used private funds to do it. He appointed a governor and a council of advisers. He gave colonists a role in government by creating an elected assembly.

At first, settlers had to pay rent to Lord Baltimore. Few settlers came to Maryland, because most wanted to own their land. Eager to attract settlers, Lord Baltimore decided to make generous land grants to anyone who brought over servants, women, and children. Later he offered smaller farms, as well as great estates, to attract more settlers.

A few women took advantage of Lord Baltimore's offer of land. Two sisters, Margaret and Mary Brent, arrived in Maryland in 1638 with nine male servants. In time, they set up two plantations of about 1,000 acres each. Later, Margaret Brent helped prevent a rebellion among the governor's soldiers. The Maryland assembly praised her efforts, saying that "the colony's safety at any time [was better] in her hands than in any man's."

Acceptance of Other Religions To make sure Maryland continued to grow, Lord Baltimore welcomed Protestants as well as Catholics to the colony. Later, Lord Baltimore came to fear that Protestants might try to **deprive** Catholics of their right to worship freely. In 1649, he asked the assembly to pass an **Act of Toleration**. The law provided religious freedom for all Christians. As in many colonies, this freedom did not extend to Jews.

Southern Colonies

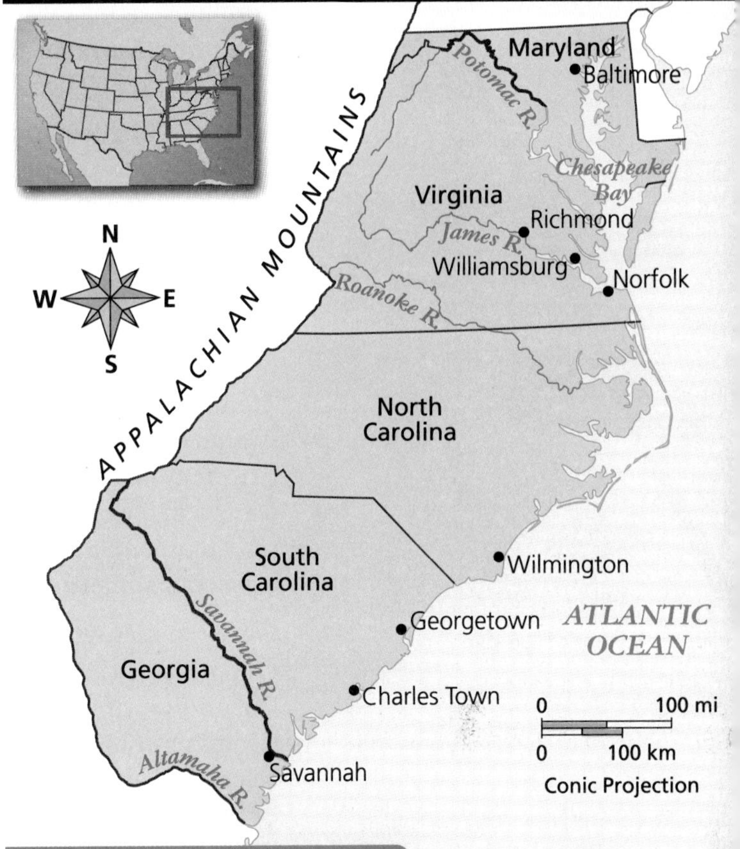

GEOGRAPHY SKILLS

The Southern Colonies were bordered on the west by the Appalachian Mountains and on the east by the Atlantic Ocean.

1. **Location** Which of the Southern Colonies was the southernmost?
2. **Draw Conclusions** Why do you think the Southern Colonies did not extend past the Appalachian Mountains?

READING CHECK **Identify Supporting Details** How did Lord Baltimore found the Maryland colony?

Who Settled the Carolinas and Georgia?

South of Virginia and Maryland, English colonists settled in a region that they called the Carolinas. In 1663, a group of eight English nobles received a grant of land from King Charles II. Settlement took place in two separate areas, one in the north and the other in the south.

Academic Vocabulary
deprive • *v.*, to take something away from

▲ The indigo plant is used to make blue dye.

The Carolinas Develop Differently In the northern part of the Carolinas, settlers were mostly poor tobacco farmers who had spread south from Virginia. They tended to have small farms. Eventually, in 1712, the colony became known as North Carolina.

Farther south, the proprietors set up a larger colony, Charles Town, where the Ashley and Cooper rivers met the ocean. The colony became known as South Carolina in 1719. Eventually, Charles Town's name was shortened to Charleston.

Most early settlers in Charleston were English people who had been living in Barbados, a British colony in the Caribbean. Later, other immigrants arrived, including Germans, Swiss, French Protestants, and Spanish Jews.

Around 1685, a few planters discovered that rice grew well in the swampy lowlands along the coast. However, they were unable to grow rich crops until enslaved Africans from rice-growing areas of Africa arrived in the colony. Before long, Carolina rice was a profitable crop traded around the world. Settlers farther inland in South Carolina later learned to raise **indigo**, a plant used to make a valuable blue dye.

Georgia Offers a Second Chance The last of England's Southern Colonies was carved out of the southern part of South Carolina. James Oglethorpe, an English soldier and social reformer, helped to found Georgia in 1732. He and the other trustees started and funded the colony privately. They wanted the new colony to be a place where **debtors**, or people who owed money they could not pay back, could make a fresh start. They also wanted to protect the colonies to the north from Spanish Florida. Like Penn, who had established Pennsylvania as a refuge for people of different religions, Oglethorpe established Georgia mainly for social reasons, as a refuge for debtors.

Analyze Images This 1782 map shows a plan for Savannah, the first settlement of the Georgia colony. **Use Visual Information** What elements of the planned settlement can you identify?

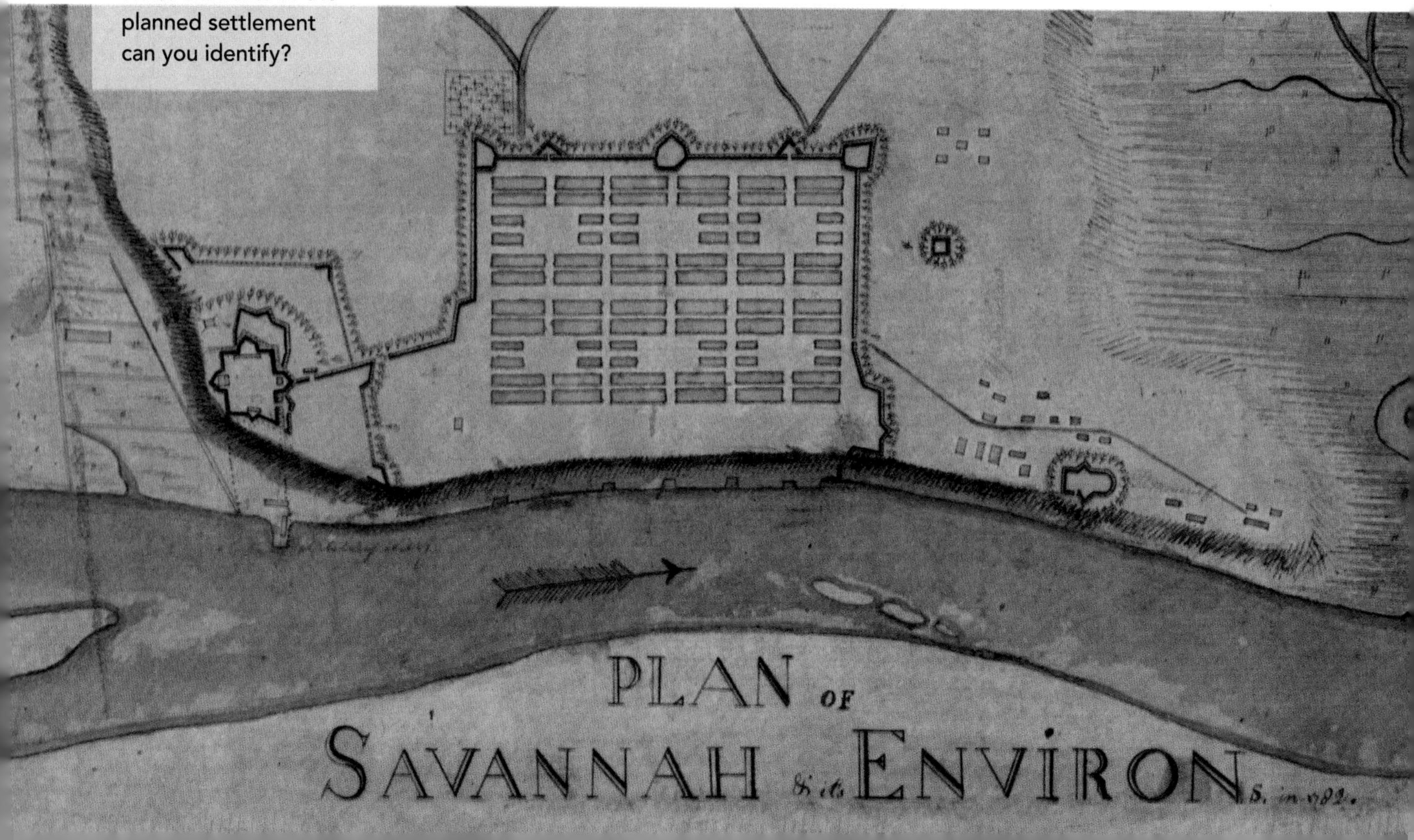

PLAN OF SAVANNAH & its ENVIRONS

Under English law, the government could imprison debtors until they paid what they owed. If they ever got out of jail, debtors often had no money and no place to live. Oglethorpe offered to pay for debtors and other poor people to travel to Georgia. "In America," he said, "there are enough fertile lands to feed all the poor of England."

In 1733, Oglethorpe and 120 colonists built the colony's first settlement at Savannah, along the Savannah River. Oglethorpe set strict rules for the colony. Farms could be no bigger than 500 acres, and slavery was forbidden.

At first, Georgia grew slowly. Later, however, Oglethorpe changed the rules to allow large plantations and slave labor. After that, the colony grew more quickly.

Analyze Images James Oglethorpe founded Georgia in 1732. **Use Visual Information** How does the image portray Oglethorpe's arrival in America?

READING CHECK **Understand Effects** Why did South Carolina's economy come to depend on rice crops?

How Did Two Regions Develop Differently?

The plantation system developed in the Southern Colonies because of the headright. The headright was a grant of land for each settler who came to a colony, or for the person who paid to bring a settler. Wealthy settlers saw a chance to gain even more wealth by paying for farm workers and thus gaining ownership of large amounts of fertile, coastal farmland.

Although the plantation system developed first in Virginia, South Carolina planters turned to it as well. They wanted large numbers of workers for rice plantations. Few white settlers were willing to work in rice paddies. As in Virginia, planters turned to Africa for slave labor.

By 1700, most people coming to Charleston were African men and women brought against their will. Each time a planter bought an enslaved African, the planter gained more land. This system led to the expansion of slavery across the South.

Tidewater Plantations on the Coast The Southern Colonies enjoyed warmer weather and a longer growing season than the colonies to the north. Parts of Virginia, Maryland, and North Carolina near the coast all became major tobacco-growing areas. Settlers in lowland South Carolina and Georgia raised rice, indigo, and cotton. In these regions, physical characteristics of the environment, such as flat landscapes and fertile soils, resulted in a relatively dense population during the 1600s and 1700s.

Comparing the Thirteen Colonies

▲ Most enslaved Africans worked on large plantations with rich farmland where they grew crops of rice, indigo, tobacco, and cotton.

Colonists soon found that it was most profitable to raise tobacco and rice on large plantations. As you may recall, a plantation is a large estate farmed by many workers. The earliest planters settled along rivers and creeks of the coastal plain. Because these rivers and creeks rose and fell with ocean tides, the region was known as the Tidewater. The Tidewater's gentle slopes and rivers offered rich farmland for plantations.

Farther inland, planters settled along rivers. Rivers provided an easy way to move goods to market. Planters loaded crops onto ships bound for the West Indies and Europe. On the return trip, the ships carried English manufactured goods and other luxuries for planters and their families.

Most Tidewater plantations had their own docks along the river, and merchant ships picked up crops and delivered goods directly to them. For this reason, few large seaport cities developed in the Southern Colonies.

Academic Vocabulary

quarters • *n.*, living accommodations

Large Tidewater plantations often consisted of brick or framed mansions with nearby storehouses and **quarters** for enslaved workers. The mansions overlooked fields or paddies, and often, the nearest river. On these southern plantations, anywhere from 20 to 100 enslaved Africans and African Americans did most of the work. Most of these enslaved workers worked in the fields. Others were skilled workers, such as carpenters, barrel makers, or blacksmiths. Still other enslaved Africans and African Americans worked in the main house as cooks, servants, or housekeepers.

Only a small percentage of white southerners owned large plantations, yet planters set the style of southern living. Life centered around the planter's house, or the Great House. There, the planter's family lived in elegant quarters, including a parlor for visitors, a dining room, and guest bedrooms.

A Southern Colonial Plantation

During the growing season, planters decided which fields to plant, what crops to grow, and when to harvest the crops. Planters' wives kept the household running smoothly. They directed enslaved cooks, maids, and butlers in the house and made sure daily tasks were done, such as milking cows.

In contrast to the lives of the planters, enslaved workers faced daily hardship. They were impoverished and denied basic rights. Their diets were often inadequate for the work they did. Their dwellings were rough and open to the weather. They faced diseases and other dangers.

Yet enslaved Africans played a crucial role on plantations. They used farming skills they had brought from West Africa. With their help, English settlers learned how to grow rice. Africans also knew how to use wild plants unfamiliar to the English. They made water buckets out of gourds, and they used palmetto leaves to make fans, brooms, and baskets.

The Backcountry Farther Inland West of the Tidewater, life and the local economy were very different. Here, at the base of the Appalachians, rolling hills and thick forests covered the land. These physical characteristics of the environment would in turn influence where people lived and how they made a living in the region during the 1600s and 1700s. As in the Middle Colonies, this inland area was called the backcountry. Attracted by rich soil, settlers followed the Great Wagon Road into the backcountry of Maryland, Virginia, and the Carolinas.

Among the settlers who moved into the backcountry were Scotch-Irish and Germans, including German Moravians. The Scotch-Irish tended to be Presbyterian farmers and craftspeople. Many were escaping famine and harsh treatment under English rule in Northern Ireland, or were the children of such immigrants.

▼ Planters' wives kept the household running smoothly and directed the enslaved workers.

Quest CONNECTIONS

How would a worker benefit from living in the Tidewater? How would a worker benefit from living in the backcountry? Record your findings in your Active Journal.

They built churches and started schools in their backcountry settlements. These immigrant groups transformed the environment by clearing the forests and creating fields where they grew crops such as wheat and building pens where they raised cattle and pigs.

The German immigrants to the backcountry, mostly Lutherans, sought good land at low cost. They often settled together in the same areas, speaking German and retaining German culture. The German Moravians were members of a Protestant group that sought to convert Indians to Christianity. They allowed women to preach and were pacifists. The Moravians kept careful records of backcountry life—including everything from the weather to fashions—that historians still use today.

The backcountry was more democratic than the Tidewater. Settlers there were more likely to treat one another as equals. Men tended smaller fields of tobacco or garden crops such as beans, corn, or peas. They also hunted game.

The distance of the backcountry from the coastline made trade difficult and prevented the development of a plantation economy. Instead of relying on income from cash crops, backcountry farmers had to be mostly self-sufficient. Surplus goods were sold or traded at local markets. Women cooked meals and fashioned simple, rugged clothing out of wool or deerskins. Another major difference between the backcountry and the Tidewater was slavery. Farms were smaller in the backcountry in part because of the hills and thick forests. Fewer enslaved Africans worked on these smaller farms, and most people were of European descent.

The hardships of backcountry life brought settlers closer together. Families gathered to husk corn or help one another build barns. Clustered in fertile valleys along the edge of the Appalachians, these hardy settlers felled trees and grew crops. By changing the environment, they in turn encouraged further economic development in the region.

READING CHECK **Identify Supporting Details** Why was there less slavery in the backcountry than in the Tidewater region?

Analyze Charts The Tidewater and the backcountry differed greatly in terms of physical environment, population, government, economy, and culture. **Understand Effects** How did the environment affect farming in each region?

Life in the Colonial Tidewater and Backcountry

	TIDEWATER	BACKCOUNTRY
LOCATION	Coastal plains	Appalachian Mountains and their foothills
TERRAIN	Flat plain	Hilly, mountainous
POPULATION	Early English settlers and enslaved Africans	Scotch-Irish, poorer English migrants, Germans
ECONOMY	Large-scale plantation farming of cash crops for export	Small-scale subsistence farming, fur trade

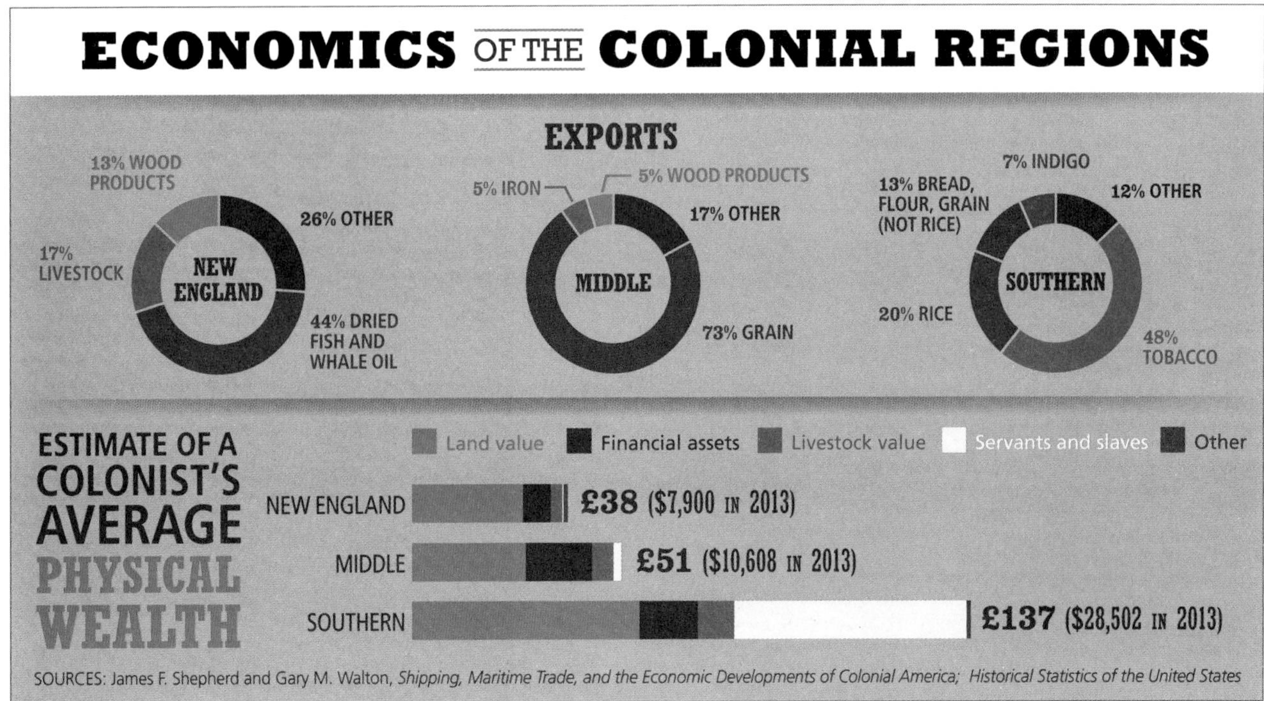

Analyze Charts The economies of the three colonial regions depended on different resources. **Synthesize Visual Information** What two resources did the Southern Colonies possess in great abundance that increased their wealth over that of the New England and Middle Colonies?

The Business of Enslavement

In the early years, Africans in the English colonies included free people and indentured servants as well as enslaved persons. At first, during the early 1600s, even Africans who were enslaved enjoyed some privileges. Before the 1670s, the status of Africans in the colony was not clearly established. Some enslaved Africans purchased their freedom. Several Africans during the 1600s, such as Anthony Johnson, became successful property owners. In South Carolina, some enslaved Africans worked without supervision as cowboys, herding cattle to market.

By 1700, plantations in the Southern Colonies had come to rely heavily on enslaved workers. Eventually, enslaved Africans made up the majority of the population in South Carolina and Georgia. They cleared the land, worked the crops, and tended the livestock. In order to maintain the supply of enslaved Africans, southern planters relied on a business of enslavement that stretched halfway across the globe.

Enslavement in Africa As you have learned, in parts of Africa and elsewhere around the world, forms of slavery had existed since ancient times. Prisoners taken during warfare often were enslaved. For many years, merchants had brought enslaved Africans and enslaved Europeans to the Middle East. In neither Africa nor the Middle East, though, was slavery based on race or automatically inherited.

For about 300 years, as demand for enslaved workers in the Americas grew, traders enslaved millions of Africans. Enslaving merchants from European nations set up posts along the West African coast. They offered guns and other goods in exchange for enslaved Africans.

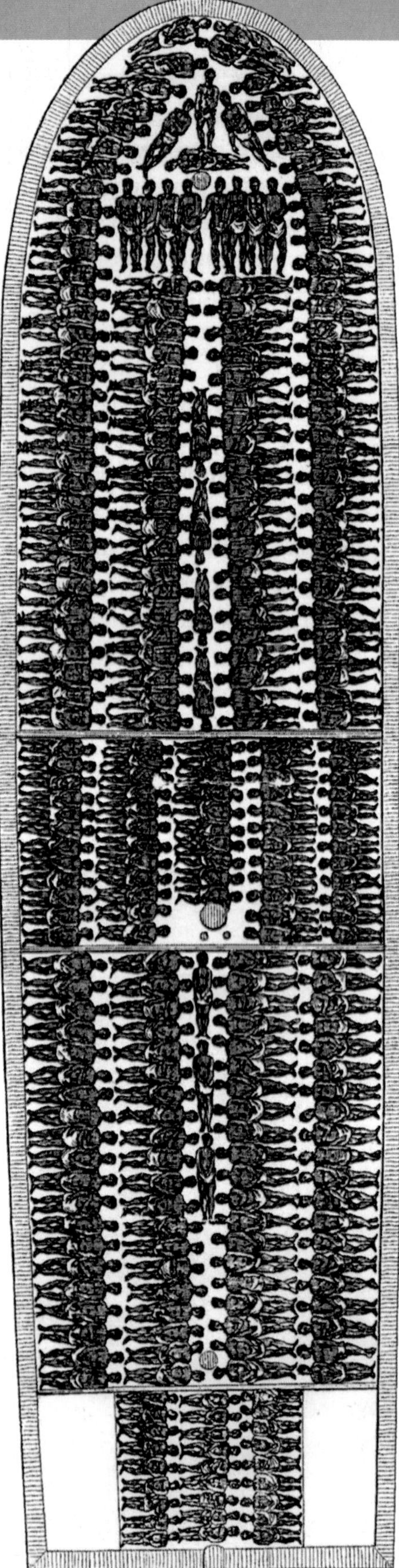

▲ Slave traders forced enslaved Africans to endure horrific conditions on ships during the Middle Passage, as shown in this illustration.

As the demand for cheap labor increased, Africans who lived along the coast made raids into the interior, seeking captives to sell to the Europeans. They marched their captives to the coast. There, the Africans were loaded aboard European ships headed for forced immigration to the Americas.

Sailing Across the Middle Passage In the 1700s, English sailors began referring to the passage of slave-trading ships west across the Atlantic Ocean as the Middle Passage. Below the decks of these ships, enslaved Africans were often crammed tightly together on shelves. One observer noted that they were "chained to each other hand and foot, and stowed so close, that they were not allowed above a foot and a half for each in breadth." The captives were allowed above deck to eat and exercise in the fresh air only once or twice a day.

Many enslaved Africans resisted, but only a few escaped. Some fought for their freedom during the trip. They would stage a mutiny or revolt. The slave traders lived in fear of this and were heavily armed. Other slaves resisted by refusing to eat or by committing suicide by jumping overboard to avoid a life of enslavement.

Records of slave-trading ships show that about 10 percent of Africans loaded aboard a ship for passage to the Americas died during the voyage. Many died of illnesses that spread rapidly in the filthy, crowded conditions inside a ship's hold. Others died of mistreatment. This slave trade lasted about 300 years. During that time, it may have caused the deaths of as many as 2 to 3 million Africans.

Human Rights Are Often Ignored As the importance of slavery increased during the 1600s, and particularly after Bacon's Rebellion in Virginia, greater limits were placed on the rights of enslaved Africans and African Americans. Colonists passed laws that set out rules for slaves' behavior and denied enslaved people basic human rights. These **slave codes** treated enslaved Africans and African Americans not as human beings but as property.

Analyze Images Some slave ships carried as many as 700 prisoners. **Use Visual Information** How does this image reflect the details described in the text?

Most English colonists did not question the justice of owning enslaved Africans. They believed that Black Africans were a racial group inferior to white Europeans. The belief that people are grouped into ranked races is called **racism**. Some colonists believed that they were helping enslaved Africans by teaching them Christianity.

A handful of colonists spoke out against the evils of slavery. In 1688, Quakers in Germantown, Pennsylvania, became the first group of colonists to call for an end to slavery.

READING CHECK **Draw Conclusions** Why did many colonists believe there was nothing wrong with slavery?

Lesson Check

Practice Vocabulary

1. Which colony was set up as a refuge for **debtors?**
2. What is **racism**?

Critical Thinking and Writing

3. **Cite Evidence** What evidence supports the claim that the planters in the southern part of the Carolinas could not make rice a profitable crop on their own?
4. **Summarize** What was the Middle Passage like for most enslaved Africans?
5. **Understand Effects** Why was South Carolina the only English colony in 1700 where the majority of the population was made up of enslaved Africans?
6. **Writing Workshop: Organize Sequence of Events** Continue adding to your ordered list of events in your Active Journal to show what happens to your character in your narrative essay. You will use this sequence of events when you write your narrative essay at the end of the Topic.

LESSON 6

Colonial Society

GET READY TO READ

START UP

Examine the image of colonial men and women dancing. What does it tell you about colonial society?

GUIDING QUESTIONS

- How was colonial society structured?
- What impact did the Great Awakening have on colonial society?
- How would you describe education in the colonies?
- How did art, music, literature, and ideas have an impact on colonial society?

TAKE NOTES

Literacy Skills: Summarize

Use the graphic organizer in your Active Journal to take notes as you read the lesson.

PRACTICE VOCABULARY

Use the vocabulary activity in your Active Journal to practice the vocabulary words.

Vocabulary		Academic Vocabulary
gentry	apprentice	tolerant
middle class	dame school	assumption
Gullah	Enlightenment	
Great Awakening	libel	

For the most part, colonists enjoyed more social equality than people in England, where a person's opportunities in life were largely determined by birth. Still, class differences existed.

Colonial Social Classes

Like Europeans, colonial Americans thought it was only natural that some people rank more highly than others. A person's birth and wealth still determined his or her social status.

The Upper and Middle Social Classes At the top of society stood the **gentry**. The gentry included wealthy planters, merchants, ministers, successful lawyers, and royal officials. They could afford to dress in the latest fashions from London.

Below the gentry were the **middle class**. The middle class included farmers who worked their own land, skilled craft workers, and some tradespeople. Nearly three quarters of all white colonists belonged to the middle class.

They prospered because land in the colonies was plentiful and easy to buy. In addition, skilled work was in high demand and paid relatively well.

The Lower Social Classes The lower social classes included hired farmhands and indentured servants. Far below them in status were enslaved Africans and African Americans.

Indentured servants signed contracts to work without wages for a period of four to seven years for anyone who would pay their ocean passage to the Americas. When their term of service was completed, indentured servants received "freedom dues": a set of clothes, tools, and 50 acres of land. Because there were so few European women in the colonies, female indentured servants often shortened their terms of service by marrying. Thousands of men, women, and children came to North America as indentured servants. After completing their terms, some became successful and rose into the middle class.

Working Life in the Countryside From New Hampshire to Georgia, most colonists survived by farming. Men worked long hours planting crops, tending the fields, and raising livestock—pigs, cows, and other farm animals. Anything beyond what the family needed to live was taken to markets to sell. Families also traded crops and livestock with their neighbors for additional goods.

While men typically did much of the agricultural work, women often worked within the home. They worked hard taking care of the household and the family. By the kitchen fire, they cooked the family's meals. They milked cows, tended chickens and a vegetable garden, watched the children, cleaned, did laundry by hand, and made candles, cheese, and clothes.

Life was different in the backcountry, out beyond more settled lands. Wives and husbands often worked side by side in the fields at harvest time. No one worried whether harvesting was proper "woman's work."

Analyze Images Many middle-class colonists worked in small cottage industries such as silk making. **Synthesize Visual Information** What was life like for children in this household?

One surprised visitor described a typical backcountry woman's activities: "She will carry a gunn in the woods and kill deer, turkeys &c., shoot down wild cattle, catch and tye hoggs, knock down [cattle] with an ax, and perform the most manfull Exercises as well as most men."

Working Life in Cities In cities, women sometimes worked outside the home. A young single woman from a poorer family might work for one of the gentry as a maid, a cook, or a nurse. Other women were midwives, who delivered babies. Still others sewed fine hats or dresses to be sold to women who could afford them. Learning such skills often required years of training. Some women learned trades from their fathers, brothers, or husbands. They worked as printers, butchers, shoemakers, and silversmiths. A woman might take over her husband's business when he died.

▲ A basket maker keeps Gullah traditions alive in Charleston, South Carolina.

Men often worked in trades, for example as coopers (who made and repaired wooden barrels), blacksmiths, and silversmiths. Most large towns in the colonies were seaports, where merchants and traders brought goods to and from Europe. As this trade grew, more white men also took on jobs as bankers, lawyers, and businessmen.

Some educated white men in the colonies became politicians. Others were pamphleteers, who wrote and distributed small booklets informing people on a subject. There were many doctors in the colonies, where illness was common. However, medical training varied. A surgeon might be a barber with little real medical training.

African Influences in the Colonies By the mid-1700s, the culture of Africans and African Americans in the colonies varied greatly. On rice plantations in South Carolina, enslaved Africans used methods from West Africa for growing and harvesting rice. For example, flat baskets holding the grains were shaken in the wind to separate the grains from leaves and other particles. Then a wooden mortar and pestle were used to clean the grains.

Language is another area where African influences were strong. In some coastal areas, enslaved Africans spoke a distinctive combination of English and West African languages known as **Gullah** (GUH luh). Parents often chose African names for their children, such as Quosh or Juba or Cuff.

In Charleston and other South Carolina port towns, some Africans worked along the dock, making rope or barrels or helping to build ships. Skilled craftworkers made fine wooden cabinets or silver plates and utensils. Many of their designs reflected African artistic styles. Although most Africans in these towns were enslaved, many opened their own shops or stalls in the market. Some used their earnings to buy their own and their family's freedom.

In the Middle Colonies and New England, the African and African American population increased during the 1700s. Africans and African Americans in the northern colonies included both free and enslaved people. Their numbers were much lower than in the Southern Colonies. However, they were still an important part of the population.

In some of the Middle Colonies, such as New York, there were even plantations that relied on slave labor. Often, these plantations produced grains and meat for sale to feed enslaved workers in the Southern Colonies or the West Indies.

The Arts in Colonial America

READING CHECK **Compare and Contrast** How was working life in the countryside similar to working life elsewhere? How was it different?

How Did Colonial Art, Literature, and Music Affect Society?

Colonists brought with them the artistic traditions of their homelands. New artistic styles also developed that reflected colonial society. Wealthy gentry decorated their homes with paintings of landscapes and religious art. Furniture, houses, and clothing were often decorated with intricate carvings or designs.

Art Reflects Colonial Society Paintings that celebrated important people of the time were especially popular works of art. Those who could afford it hired artists to paint portraits of their family members. These portraits showed off the family's importance and provided a valuable keepsake to be passed on for generations to come. Portraits also honored famous individuals and key events. One of the oldest surviving colonial portraits is of New Netherland Governor Peter Stuyvesant, painted in the 1660s.

Analyze Images This portrait of Peter Stuyvesant is one of the few colonial portraits that have survived. **Synthesize Visual Information** How did the painter try to please Stuyvesant?

Prints were also popular. Prints were made from engravings scratched into metal or carved into wood. Printmakers used the metal or wood with ink, paper, and a press to make a picture that could be easily reproduced. Many people had prints of famous figures, such as politicians or clergymen.

Many artists were self-taught. Few became wealthy from their work. They often traveled from town to town in search of people who wanted portraits done. The paintings they left behind are like time capsules. Much like photographs do today, they show how people dressed, what their tastes were like, and how their families lived.

American Literature Emerges Literature also developed in the colonies. The first colonial printing press was built in Massachusetts in 1640. It printed religious books and books for Harvard College. With the spread of printing, more colonists began to read.

Analyze Images A colonist plays the harpsichord, an instrument commonly featured in classical pieces of the period. **Infer** How many colonial homes do you think had a harpsichord? Why?

Colonists read reprints of European books and books by American writers. One of the most popular—and particularly American—types of stories was the captivity tale. In these stories, a white settler was captured by American Indians and had to overcome hardships in order to escape.

Colonial Music Music was another popular art form in the colonies. Colonists brought popular folk music from Europe. They sang and danced at weddings and other celebrations. Enslaved Africans brought musical traditions with them from Africa. These traditions combined with European traditions in musical forms such as work songs and spirituals, or religious songs.

Music was closely tied to religious life for many colonists. New organs appeared in churches. The hymns people sang grew especially popular during the Great Awakening.

READING CHECK **Identify Supporting Details** What clues can we find about colonial lives in artwork such as paintings?

What Was the Impact of a New Religious Movement?

In the 1730s and 1740s, a religious revival, or movement, known as the **Great Awakening** swept through the colonies. Its drama and emotion touched women and men of all races, ethnic backgrounds, and classes.

Enthusiastic Preachers A New England preacher, Jonathan Edwards, helped set off the Great Awakening. In powerful sermons, Edwards called on colonists, especially young people, to examine their lives.

He preached of the sweetness and beauty of God. At the same time, he warned listeners to heed the Bible's teachings. Otherwise, they would be "sinners in the hands of an angry God," headed for the fiery torments of hell. The powerful sermons of preachers such as Edwards were one of the main causes of the Great Awakening.

In 1739, when an English minister named George Whitefield arrived in the colonies, the movement spread like wildfire. Whitefield drew huge crowds to outdoor meetings. An enthusiastic and energetic preacher, his voice would ring with feeling as he called on sinners to repent.

Quick Activity

Imagine three events that show important aspects of colonial life, and write newspaper headlines about these events in your Active Journal.

After hearing Whitefield speak, Jonathan Edwards's wife reported, "I have seen upwards of a thousand people hang on his words with breathless silence, broken only by an occasional half-suppressed sob."

Academic Vocabulary
tolerant • *adj.*, willing to accept beliefs that are different from your own

The Great Awakening's Impact The colonies were made up of many different religious groups. There were Quakers, Puritans, Catholics, Presbyterians, and more. Each group had its own ideas about the proper relationship with God.

Some groups, like the Anglicans, disagreed strongly with Whitefield. Others, like the Baptists and Methodists, found new opportunities to expand during the Great Awakening as people revisited their faith.

The Great Awakening aroused bitter debate. People who supported the movement often split away from their old churches to form new ones. Opponents warned that the movement was too emotional. Still, the growth of so many new churches forced colonists to become more **tolerant** of people with different beliefs. Also, because the Great Awakening appealed to people in all of the colonies, from different classes and ethnic backgrounds, it brought colonists together for the first time. Ties formed during the Great Awakening helped establish the groundwork for future bonds among the colonies.

In the colonies, members of most churches controlled their parishes. The role parishes played in local communities made people think about the importance of self-rule—a key factor in the development of American democracy.

Analyze Visuals Crowds of people gathered to hear sermons by English minister George Whitefield. **Infer** What does the artist suggest about the attitude of Whitefield's audience?

The Great Awakening contributed in another way to the spread of democratic feelings in the colonies. Many of the new preachers were not as well educated as most ministers. They argued that formal training was less important than a heart filled with the Holy Spirit. Such teachings encouraged a spirit of independence. White colonists began to think differently about their political rights and their governments. They felt if they could figure out how to worship on their own and how to run their own churches, then they could govern themselves with those same virtues. Eventually, many colonists challenged the authority of colonial governors and the king.

READING CHECK **Identify Main Ideas** How did the Great Awakening change white colonists' thinking about their political rights?

Education in the Colonies

Among the colonists, New Englanders were the most concerned about education. Puritans taught that all people had a duty to study the Bible. If colonists did not learn to read, how would they study the Bible?

Public Schools in New England In 1642, the Massachusetts assembly passed a law ordering all parents to teach their children "to read and understand the principles of religion." They also required all towns with 50 or more families to hire a schoolteacher. Towns with 100 or more families also had to set up a grammar school to prepare boys for college.

In this way, Massachusetts set up the first public schools, or schools supported by taxes. Public schools allowed both rich and poor children to receive an education.

The first New England schools had only one room for students of all ages. Parents paid the schoolteacher with food. Each child was expected to bring a share of wood for the stove.

▼ In colonial New England, instructors taught students of all ages in a single classroom.

Private Education In the Middle Colonies, churches and individual families set up private schools. Because pupils paid to attend, only wealthy families could afford to educate their children.

In the Southern Colonies, people often lived too far from one another to bring children together in one school building. Some planters hired tutors, or private teachers. The wealthiest planters sent their sons to school in England. As a rule, enslaved African Americans were denied education of any kind.

Apprenticeships and Dame Schools Boys whose parents wished them to learn a trade or craft served as **apprentices** (uh PREN tis ez). An apprentice worked for a master to learn a trade or a craft. For example, when a boy reached the age of 12 or 13, his parents might apprentice him to a master glassmaker.

▲ Initially, colleges like Yale, shown here in a late-1700s engraving, were created to educate the clergy. Later, Yale expanded its offerings to other students.

The young apprentice lived in the glassmaker's home for six or seven years while learning the craft. The glassmaker gave the boy food and clothing and taught him how to read and write. He also provided him with religious training.

In return, the apprentice worked as a helper in the glassmaker's shop and learned needed skills. Boys were apprenticed in many trades, including papermaking, printing, and tanning (making leather).

In New England, most schools accepted only boys. However, some girls attended **dame schools**, or private schools run by women in their own homes. Other girls, though, usually learned skills from their mothers, who taught them to cook, make soap and candles, spin wool, weave, sew, and embroider. A few learned to read and write.

The Growth of Colleges In 1633, Puritan John Eliot spoke of the need for Massachusetts to establish an official college. Institutions of higher learning were held up as a way to promote European culture in the Americas. As Eliot cautioned, "if we no[u]rish not L[e]arning both church & common wealth will sinke."

Harvard College, the first college in the colonies, opened in 1638 with ten students. The goal of the college was to educate future ministers. It was modeled after English schools, where students studied six days a week in Latin and Greek. It was open only to men.

By the late 1600s, however, Harvard graduates were moving away from the ministry. Some became physicians, public servants, or teachers. The College of William and Mary opened in Virginia to prepare men for the Anglican ministry. Yale College in Connecticut aimed to educate clergymen. Gradually, nine colleges opened over the following century and expanded their areas of study.

INTERACTIVE

Education in the Colonies

READING CHECK **Draw Conclusions** Do you think children were better educated in New England than they were in the other colonies? Why or why not?

Analyze Images Isaac Newton proved that white light is made up of all the visible colors. **Draw Conclusions** Why is observation crucial for science?

How Did New Ideas Influence the Colonies?

Academic Vocabulary
assumption • *n.,* a belief held without proof

In the 1600s, European thinkers tried to question common **assumptions** and to base their understanding of the world on reason and logic. They developed theories and performed experiments to test them. In doing so, they discovered many of the laws of nature. The English scientist Isaac Newton, for example, explained the law of gravity.

The Ideas of the Enlightenment European thinkers of the late 1600s and 1700s also believed that reason and scientific methods could be applied to the study of society. They tried to discover the natural laws that governed human behavior. Because these thinkers believed in the light of human reason, the movement that they started is known as the **Enlightenment**. John Locke, an English philosopher, wrote works that were widely read in the colonies. He said people could gain knowledge of the world by observing and experimenting.

In the English colonies, the Enlightenment spread among better-educated colonists. They included wealthy merchants, lawyers, ministers, and others who had the leisure to read the latest books from Europe. Urban craftsmen also heard and discussed these ideas.

Benjamin Franklin's Thought and Inventions The best example of the Enlightenment spirit in the English colonies was Benjamin Franklin. Franklin was born in 1706, the son of a poor Boston soap and candle maker. Although young Ben had only two years of formal schooling, he used his spare time to study literature, mathematics, and foreign languages.

At age 17, Franklin made his way to Philadelphia. There, he built up a successful printing business. His most popular publication was *Poor Richard's Almanack*. Published yearly, it contained useful information and clever proverbs, such as "Early to bed, early to rise, makes a man healthy, wealthy, and wise."

Like other Enlightenment thinkers, Franklin wanted to use reason to improve the world around him. He invented practical devices that helped improve daily life. For example, Franklin suffered from poor eyesight, so he invented bifocal glasses to help himself—and countless others—see better. Franklin also invented a new kind of iron stove. It was set in the middle of a room instead of in a wall, and it kept houses warmer without filling them with smoke. Another one of Franklin's inventions, the lightning rod, protected buildings from catching fire in a storm because of lightning strikes. As a community leader, Franklin persuaded Philadelphia officials to pave streets, organize a fire company, and set up the first lending library in the Americas. Franklin's inventions and his public service earned him worldwide fame.

The Influence of Colonial Cities and Towns While most colonists lived on farms, towns and cities strongly influenced colonial life. Through the great ports of Philadelphia, New York, Boston, and Charleston, merchants shipped products overseas. Towns and cities also served as centers of a busy trade between the coast and the growing backcountry.

Culture flourished in the towns. By the mid-1700s, many colonial towns had their own theaters. Town dwellers found entertainment at singing societies, traveling circuses, carnivals, and horse races.

BIOGRAPHY 5 Things to Know About

Benjamin Franklin

Writer, Scientist, and Statesman (1706–1790)

- Franklin was born in Boston in 1706 and was one of the founding fathers of the United States.
- Even though he stopped going to school when he was 10 years old, he continued to educate himself and became a writer, scientist, inventor, and statesman.
- He moved to Philadelphia when he was 17 years old and later became a successful printer and publisher.
- Franklin helped create the city's first library, fire company, and police force. He also helped establish a postal service in the colonies.
- He famously (and dangerously) flew a kite in a lightning storm to show that lightning is electricity.

Critical Thinking Why do you think the creation of a library, fire company, and police force in Philadelphia was significant?

Analyze Images John Peter Zenger celebrates after a jury found that he had not committed libel. **Identify Implied Main Ideas** What important tradition did Zenger help establish?

In 1704, John Campbell founded the *Boston News-Letter*, the first regular weekly newspaper in the English colonies. Within 50 years, each of the colonies, except New Jersey and Delaware, had at least one weekly paper.

John Peter Zenger's Libel Trial The growth of colonial newspapers led to a dispute over freedom of the press. John Peter Zenger published the *Weekly Journal* in New York City. In 1734, he was arrested for publishing stories that criticized the governor. Zenger was put on trial for **libel**—the act of publishing a statement that may unjustly damage a person's reputation. Zenger's lawyer argued that, since the stories were true, his client had not committed libel. The jury agreed and freed Zenger. At the time, the case did not attract a great deal of attention. However, freedom of the press would become recognized as a basic American right.

READING CHECK **Understand Effects** How did Franklin's inventions influence the daily lives of colonists?

Lesson Check

Practice Vocabulary

1. Who were some of the people who were included in the **gentry**?
2. Why was John Peter Zenger found not guilty of **libel**?

Critical Thinking and Writing

3. **Infer** Women did not have access to certain jobs in the colonies. How was access to employment restricted for women?
4. **Understand Effects** How did the Great Awakening lead to greater religious tolerance?
5. **Draw Conclusions** Why do you think enslaved Africans were generally denied an education?
6. **Writing Workshop: Use Narrative Techniques** In your Active Journal, identify and record some narrative techniques you can use to tell your story. You will use these techniques when you write your narrative at the end of the topic.

LESSON 7

Colonial Trade and Government

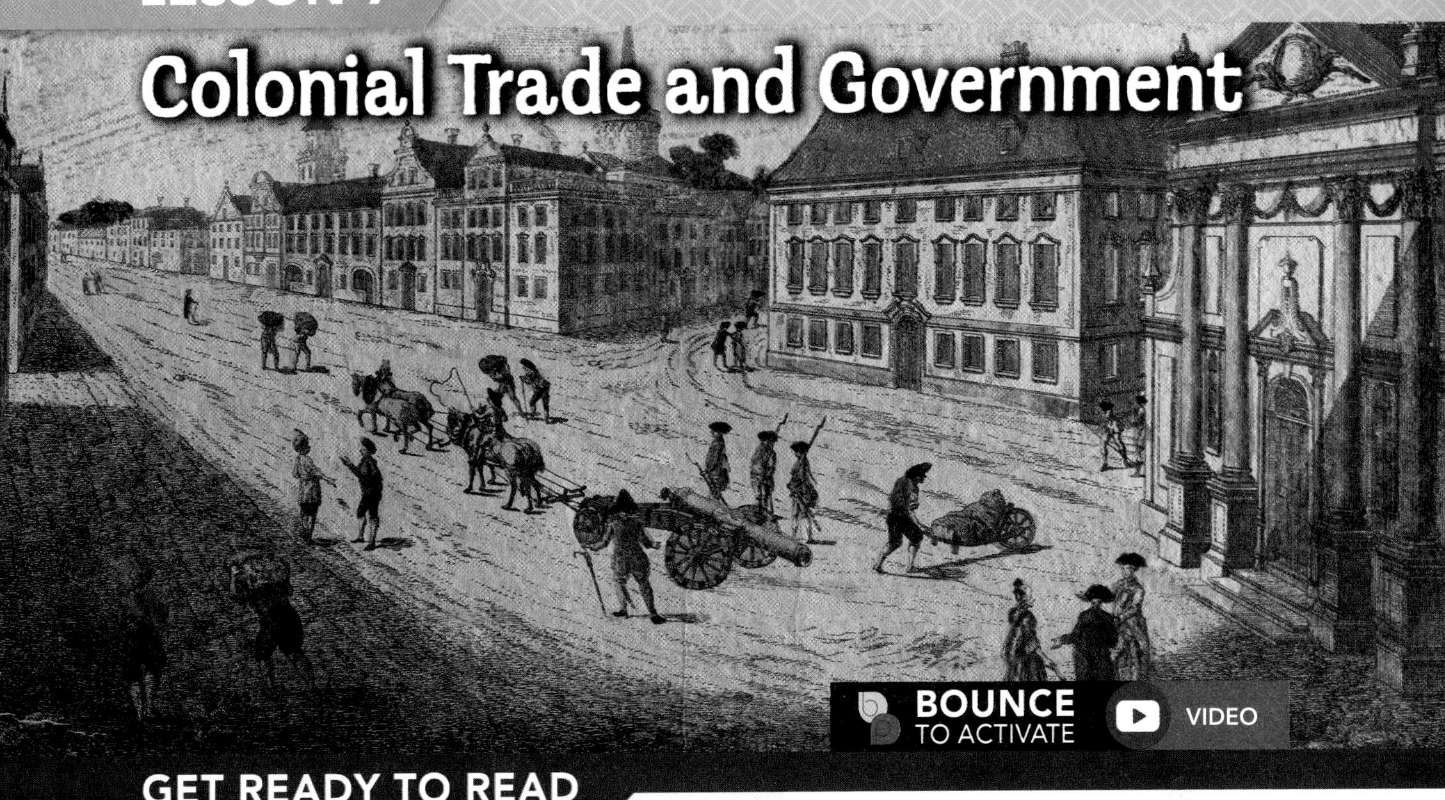

GET READY TO READ

START UP

Examine the image of a busy street in Boston. What does it tell you about daily life in the British colonies?

GUIDING QUESTIONS

- How did mercantilism develop?
- What is the relationship between the slave trade and other forms of trade?
- How did governments and legal systems in the colonies develop?

TAKE NOTES

Literacy Skills: Draw Conclusions

Use the graphic organizer in your Active Journal to take notes as you read the lesson.

PRACTICE VOCABULARY

Use the vocabulary activity in your Active Journal to practice the vocabulary words.

Vocabulary

mercantilism
export
import
Navigation Acts
Yankee
triangular trade
legislature
Glorious Revolution
bill of rights
English Bill of Rights

Academic Vocabulary

prosperous
bribe

Like other European nations at the time, England believed that its colonies should benefit the home country. This belief was part of an economic theory known as **mercantilism** (MUR kun til iz um).

Mercantilism and the English Colonies

According to the theory of mercantilism, a nation could become strong by keeping strict control over its trade. As one English gentleman put it, "Whosoever commands the trade of the world commands the riches of the world."

Imports and Exports Mercantilists thought that a country should export more than it imported. **Exports** are goods sent to markets outside a country.

Imports are goods brought into a country. If England sold more goods than it bought abroad, gold would flow into the home country as payment for those exports.

The Navigation Acts Beginning in the 1650s, the English Parliament passed a series of laws governing colonial trade.

The **Navigation Acts** regulated trade between England and its colonies in order to ensure that only England benefited from trade with its colonies.

Under the new laws, only colonial or English ships could carry goods to and from the colonies. Colonists were banned from trading directly with other European nations or their colonies. The Navigation Acts also listed certain products, such as tobacco and cotton, that colonial merchants could ship only to England. In this way, Parliament created jobs for English workers who cut and rolled tobacco or spun cotton into cloth.

The Navigation Acts helped the colonies as well as England. For example, the law encouraged colonists to build ships for their own use and for sale to England. As a result, New England became a **prosperous** shipbuilding center. Also, colonial merchants did not have to compete with foreign merchants because they were sure of having a market for their goods in England.

Academic Vocabulary
prosperous • *adj.*, having success, usually by making a lot of money

Still, many colonists resented the Navigation Acts. In their view, the laws favored English merchants. Colonial merchants often ignored the Navigation Acts or found ways to get around them.

READING CHECK **Identify Main Ideas** Why did England pass the Navigation Acts?

Trading Across the Atlantic

The colonies produced a wide variety of goods, and merchant ships sailed up and down the Atlantic coast. Merchants from New England dominated colonial trade.

GEOGRAPHY **SKILLS**

The trade in manufactured goods and rum, sugar and molasses, and enslaved people took a triangular route.

1. **Movement** Which region was the first destination for many enslaved Africans?
2. **Infer** Why did ships travel west from Africa?

The Triangular Trade

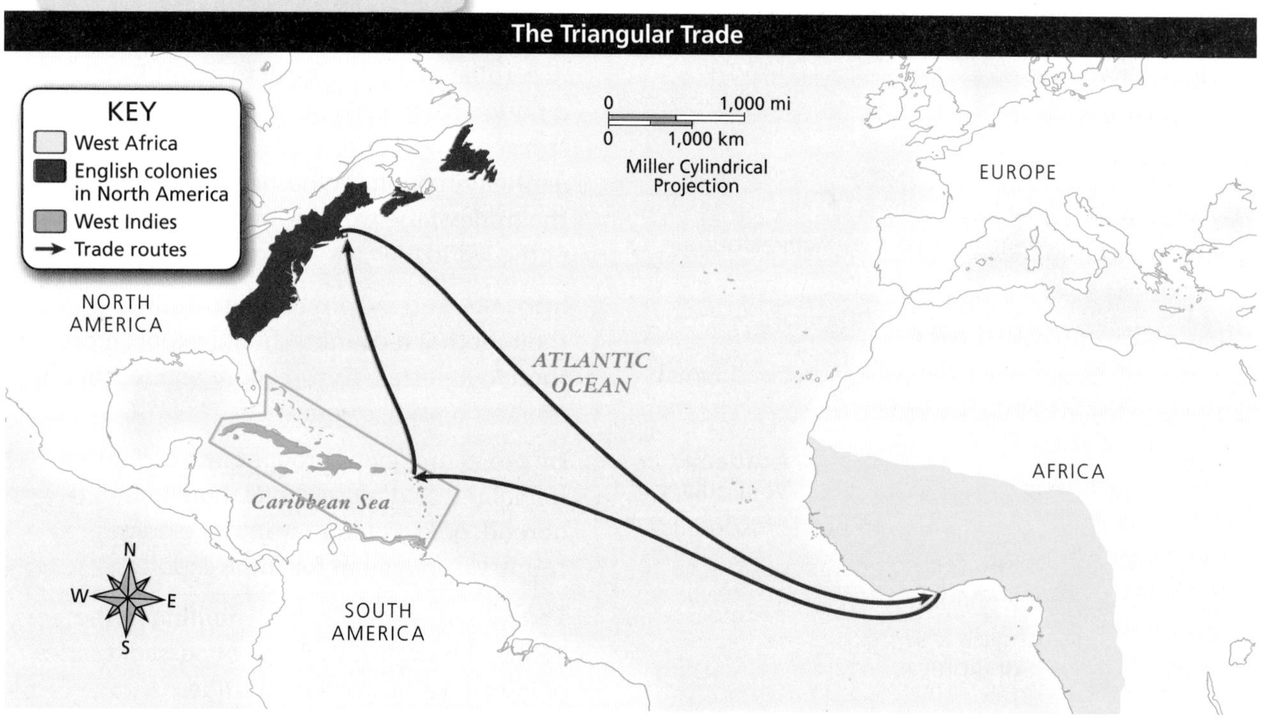

They were known by the nickname **Yankees** and had a reputation for being clever and hardworking. Yankee traders earned a reputation for profiting from any deal.

The Triangular Trade One colonial trade route was known as the **triangular trade** because the three legs of the route formed a triangle. On the first leg, ships from New England carried rum, guns, gunpowder, cloth, and tools from New England to West Africa. In Africa, Yankee merchants traded these goods for slaves.

On the second leg of the journey, ships carried enslaved Africans to the West Indies. This second leg of the voyage was known as the Middle Passage. With the profits from selling enslaved Africans, Yankee traders bought molasses—a dark-brown syrup made from sugar cane—and sugar. Ships then sailed back to New England, where colonists used the molasses and sugar to make rum for sale in Africa or Europe.

Merchants Disregard the Law Many New England merchants disobeyed the Navigation Acts and grew wealthy as a result. Traders were supposed to buy sugar and molasses only from English colonies in the West Indies. However, the demand for molasses was so high that New Englanders smuggled in cargoes from the Dutch, French, and Spanish West Indies, too. **Bribes** made customs officials look the other way.

▼ Ships leaving ports such as this one in Philadelphia were forced to sail to England because of the Navigation Acts.

READING CHECK **Identify Cause and Effect** Why did many traders ignore the Navigation Acts?

What Were the Foundations of Representative Government?

Although each colony developed its own government, the governments had much in common. A governor directed the colony's affairs and enforced the laws. Most governors were appointed, either by the king or by the colony's proprietor. In Rhode Island and Connecticut, however, colonists elected their own governors. Representative government and institutions spread in the colonies for several reasons.

Academic Vocabulary
bribe • *n.*, something valuable that is given in order to get someone to do something

Elected Assemblies As you learned, the Virginia Company established an elected assembly, the House of Burgesses, to attract more settlers. This example, as well as the tradition of representative government established in the Magna Carta, led the colonies to create a **legislature** soon after founding. A legislature is a group of people, usually elected, that has the power to make laws. In most colonies, the legislature had an upper house and a lower house.

The Triangular Trade

The upper house was made up of advisers appointed by the governor. The lower house was an elected assembly. It approved laws and protected the rights of citizens. It also had the right to approve or reject any taxes or budget items the governor asked for. This "power of the purse," or right to raise or spend money, was an important check on the governor's power.

As colonial settlers founded new cities and towns, representative government and institutions grew. Most colonial cities and towns had their own city and town councils.

The Right to Vote Each colony had its own rules about who could vote. By the 1720s, however, all of the colonies had laws that restricted the right to vote to white Christian men over the age of 21.

In some colonies, only Protestants or members of a particular church could vote. All colonies restricted the vote to men who owned a certain amount of property. Colonial leaders believed that only property owners knew what was best for a colony.

Common Law The colonies followed English common law, or case law. Under common law, laws develop from the past rulings of judges. In applying laws, courts follow the idea that "like cases should be tried alike."

In the 1760s, William Blackstone published a book, *Commentaries on the Laws of England*. In it, Blackstone reviewed the entire history of English law. As a member of Parliament and a judge in England, he believed common law was the highest and best form of law.

Blackstone's ideas about common law took hold in the colonies. Common law was a body of laws that was valid independent of Parliament's acts. As such, it provided a basis for self-rule and an independent legal system once the colonies began to move toward independence.

Analyze Charts Colonial government in the English colonies was influenced by three important documents. **Identify Main Ideas** How did these documents influence the state and federal constitutions of the United States?

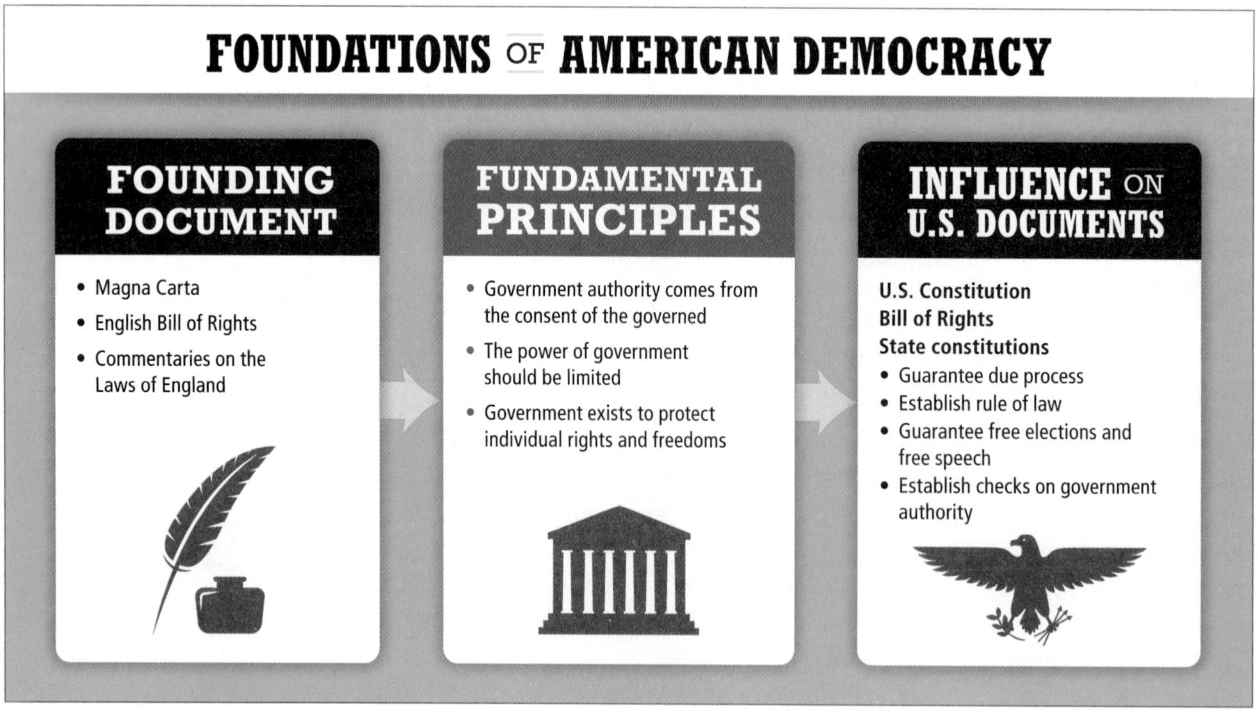

FOUNDATIONS OF AMERICAN DEMOCRACY

FOUNDING DOCUMENT

- Magna Carta
- English Bill of Rights
- Commentaries on the Laws of England

FUNDAMENTAL PRINCIPLES

- Government authority comes from the consent of the governed
- The power of government should be limited
- Government exists to protect individual rights and freedoms

INFLUENCE ON U.S. DOCUMENTS

U.S. Constitution
Bill of Rights
State constitutions

- Guarantee due process
- Establish rule of law
- Guarantee free elections and free speech
- Establish checks on government authority

▲ In most of the English colonies, women had the right to file suit in court.

The English Bill of Rights Colonists took great pride in their elected assemblies. They also valued the rights that the Magna Carta gave them as English subjects.

American colonists won still more rights due to the **Glorious Revolution** of 1688, when the English Parliament removed King James II from the throne and asked William and Mary of the Netherlands to rule. In return, William and Mary signed the English Bill of Rights in 1689. A **bill of rights** is a written list of freedoms the government promises to protect.

The **English Bill of Rights** protected the rights of individuals and gave anyone accused of a crime the right to a trial by jury. The English Bill of Rights also said that a ruler could not raise taxes or an army without the approval of Parliament. In addition, it strengthened the position of representative government and institutions in the colonies.

Liberties Are Restricted English colonists in the Americas often enjoyed more freedoms than did the English themselves. However, the rights of English citizens did not extend to all colonists. Women had more rights in the colonies than in England, but women colonists had far fewer rights than did free, white males.

In most colonies, unmarried women and widows had more rights than married women. They could make contracts and sue in court. In Maryland and the Carolinas, women settlers who headed families could buy land on the same terms as men.

African Americans and American Indians in the colonies had almost no rights. While so many colonists enjoyed English liberties, most African Americans were bound in slavery. The conflict between liberty and slavery would not be resolved until the 1860s.

INTERACTIVE

Influences on Colonial Government

READING CHECK **Understand Effects** How did the English Bill of Rights promote freedom?

Lesson Check

Practice Vocabulary

1. What are **exports** and **imports**?
2. What did the **English Bill of Rights** do?

Critical Thinking and Writing

3. **Cite Evidence** What evidence in the reading suggests that molasses was critical to the success of the triangular trade?
4. **Draw Conclusions** How do you think colonial traders might have responded if England started to strictly enforce the Navigation Acts?
5. **Summarize** How did English laws contribute to the development of freedom and self-government in the American colonies?
6. **Writing Workshop: Use Descriptive Details and Sensory Language** Write notes in your Active Journal about descriptive details and sensory language that you can use in the narrative essay you will write at the end of the topic.

TOPIC 2

Review and Assessment

VISUAL REVIEW

North American Colonial Powers

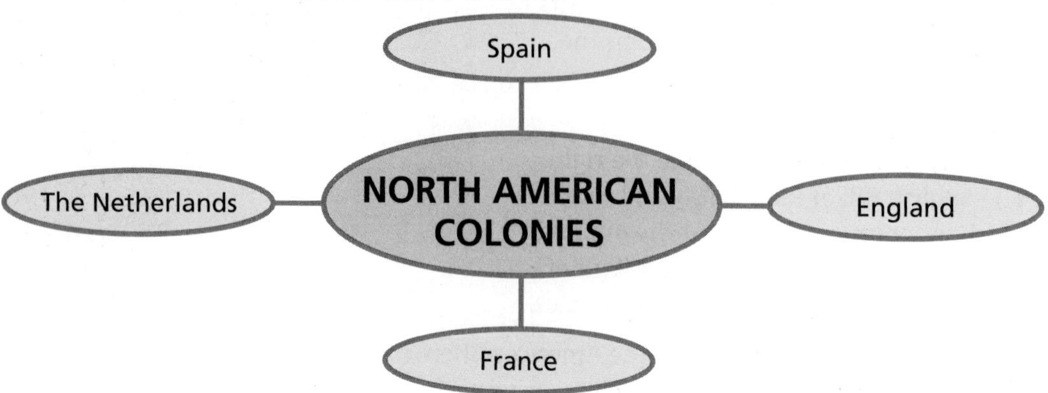

NORTH AMERICAN ENGLISH COLONIES

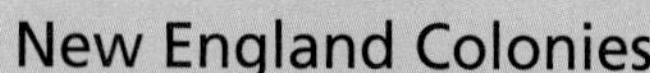

New England Colonies

- Settlers sought religious freedom.
- First settlements were at Plymouth and Massachusetts Bay.
- New colonies formed over religious differences.
- Fishing industry developed.

Middle Colonies

- First settlers were Dutch, but English took over.
- First colony was New York; New Jersey, Pennsylvania, and Delaware formed later.
- Land was fertile and had many natural resources.

Southern Colonies

- First settlement was Jamestown; settlers later arrived in Maryland, Carolinas, and Georgia.
- Life was different on the Tidewater and in the backcountry.
- The economy relied upon enslaved labor.

READING REVIEW

Use the Take Notes and Practice Vocabulary activities in your Active Journal to review the topic.

INTERACTIVE

Practice vocabulary using the Topic Mini-Games

Quest FINDINGS

Create Your ePortfolio

Get help for creating your digital portfolio in your Active Journal.

ASSESSMENT

Vocabulary and Key Ideas

1. **Describe** What did the **conquistadors** in the Americas do?
2. **Define** Who were the **Pilgrims**?
3. **Describe** How did **racism** affect English colonists' attitude toward the enslavement of Africans?
4. **Identify Main Ideas** What was the significance of the **Great Awakening**?
5. **Recall** What set Pennsylvania apart from the other colonies?
6. **Explain** How did southern agriculture cause an increase in the number of enslaved Africans brought to America?
7. **Identify Supporting Details** What impact did religion have on the Puritans' approach to education?

Critical Thinking and Writing

8. **Use Evidence** Why were Cortés and his soldiers able to conquer the Aztec?
9. **Draw Conclusions** Why did the growth in the number of settlers in New England lead to war between the colonists and the Wampanoag-led alliance?
10. **Identify Cause and Effect** How did enslaved Africans boost the economy of South Carolina?
11. **Identify Main Ideas** Why did the Pilgrims form a government in which they governed themselves?
12. **Revisit the Essential Question** Why do people move? Explain using evidence from the topic.
13. **Writing Workshop: Write a Narrative Essay** Use the notes you made in your Active Journal to write a narrative essay in which you are a colonist describing daily life.

Analyze Primary Sources

14. The excerpt below is from a speech given during the Great Awakening. What do you think Edwards was trying to encourage people to do?
    - A. Edwards wanted people to go to church more often.
    - B. Edwards wanted people to convert to a new religion.
    - C. Edwards wanted people to make sacrifices for God.
    - D. Edwards wanted people to worship God to avoid his wrath.

"The wrath of God is like great waters that are dammed for the present; they increase more and more, and rise higher and higher, till an outlet is given; and the longer the stream is stopped, the more rapid and mighty is its course, when once it is let loose."
—Jonathan Edwards, "Sinners in the Hands of an Angry God."

Analyze Maps

15. Which letter represents Pennsylvania? Who founded the colony?
16. Which letter represents New Jersey? Which colony was to its south?
17. Which letter represents New York? Which colonies bordered it to the east?

▼ The Middle Colonies

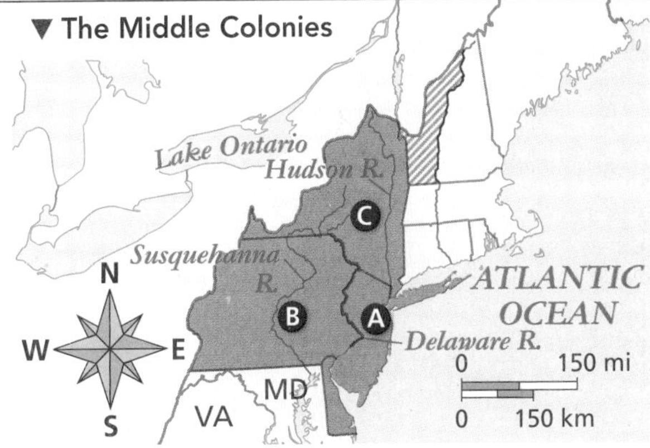

TOPIC 3

The Revolutionary Era (1750–1783)

GO ONLINE to access your digital course

- VIDEO
- AUDIO
- ETEXT
- INTERACTIVE
- WRITING
- GAMES
- WORKSHEET
- ASSESSMENT

Go back over 250 years

to **AMERICA IN THE LATE 1700s**. Why? Because you will see the birth of a new nation, get to know some of its greatest leaders, and learn how an upstart group of colonists took on one of the most powerful empires in the world.

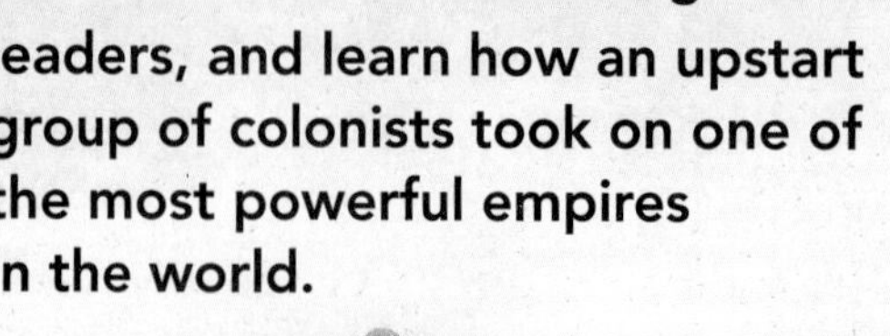

Explore The Essential Question

When is war justified?

In the late 1700s one war, called the French and Indian War, led to another war, the American Revolution. What were the causes of these wars?

Unlock the Essential Question in your Active Journal.

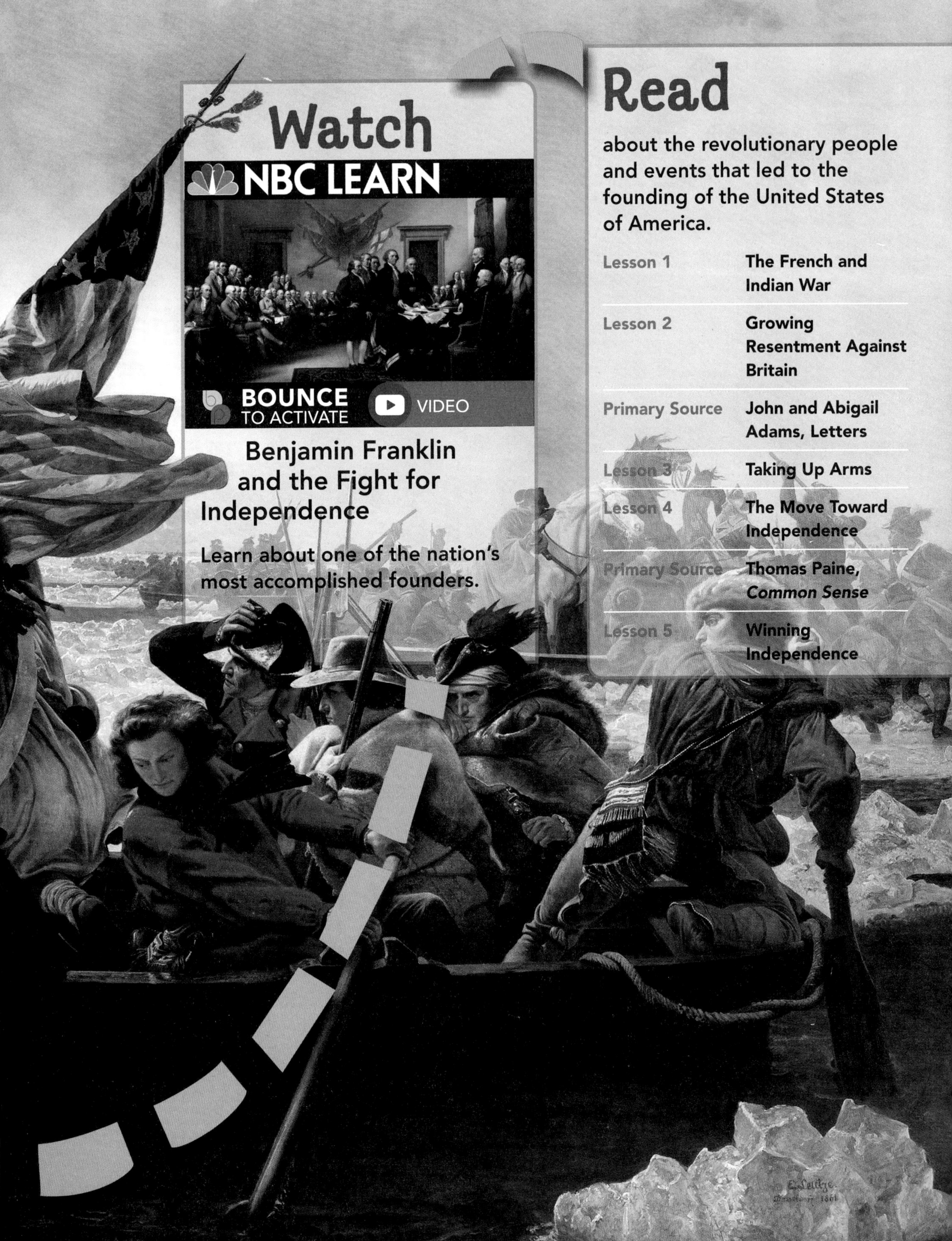

Watch

NBC LEARN

BOUNCE TO ACTIVATE

VIDEO

Benjamin Franklin and the Fight for Independence

Learn about one of the nation's most accomplished founders.

Read

about the revolutionary people and events that led to the founding of the United States of America.

TOPIC 3

The Revolutionary Era (1750–1783)

Learn more about the Revolutionary Era by making your own map and timeline in your Active Journal.

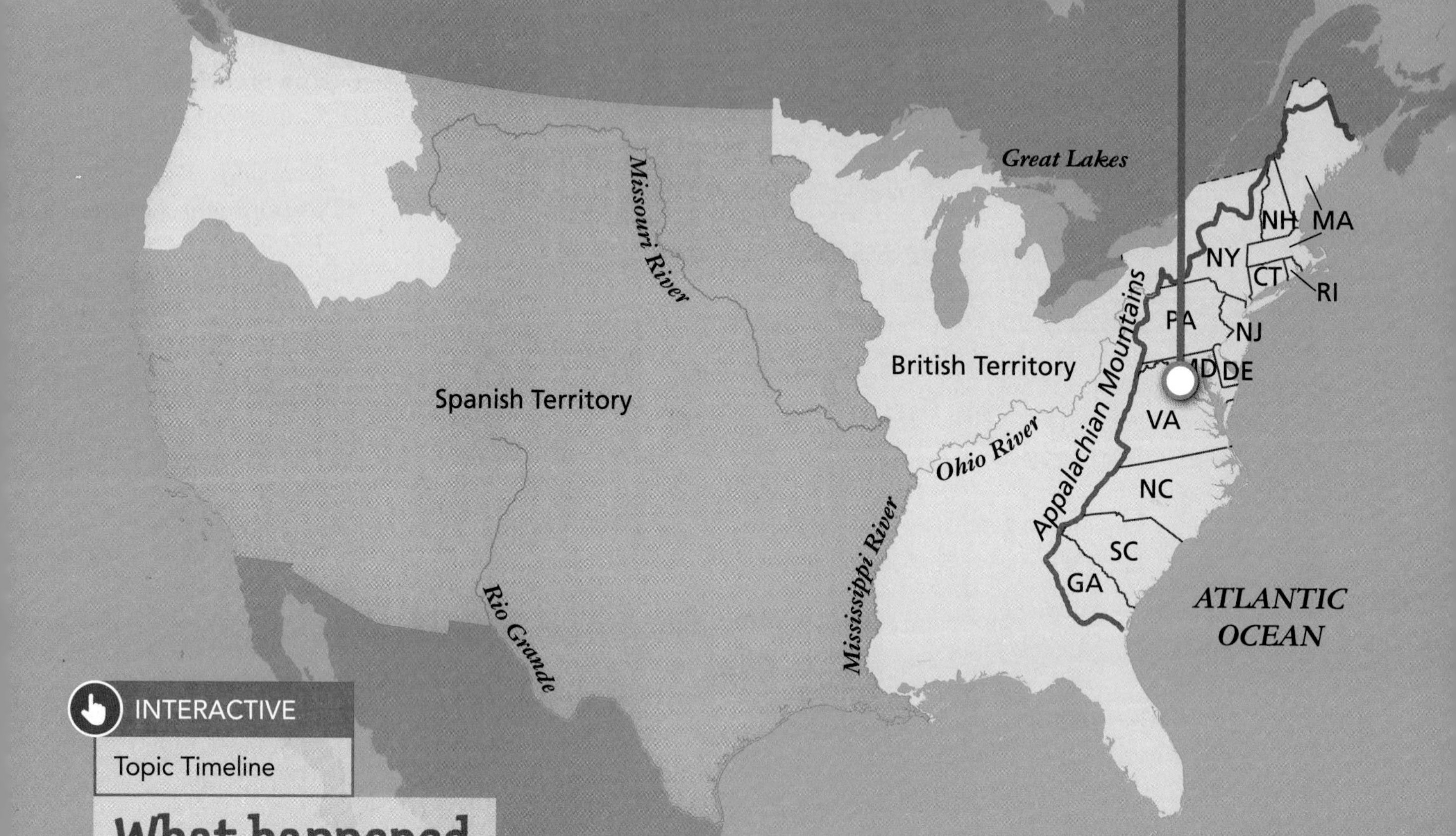

Great Lakes
Missouri River
NH
MA
NY
CT
RI
PA
NJ
MD
DE
British Territory
Spanish Territory
Appalachian Mountains
VA
Ohio River
NC
SC
GA
Mississippi River
Rio Grande
ATLANTIC OCEAN

INTERACTIVE

Topic Timeline

What happened and when?

Colonists resented the British presence in their lives during the last half of the 1700s. Explore the timeline to find out why.

TOPIC EVENTS

1754
The French and Indian War breaks out in North America.

1765
Parliament passes the Stamp Act, sparking protests by colonists.

1770
British troops fire on crowd in the Boston Massacre.

1773
British Parliament passes the Tea Act.

1750 **1760** **1770**

WORLD EVENTS

1762
Catherine the Great begins reign in Russia.

INTERACTIVE

Topic Map

Where was the American Revolution fought?

The British colonies stretched along the Atlantic seaboard. What were the names of the colonies?

1775
British soldiers and colonial minutemen fight at Lexington and Concord.

1777
The American victory at Saratoga is a turning point in the war.

1781
The British surrender to the Americans at Yorktown.

1783
Britain recognizes U.S. independence.

1780

1790

1778
Captain James Cook explores the Hawaiian island of Kaua'i.

1783
Ludwig van Beethoven has his first composition published.

Who will you meet?

Thomas Jefferson, writer of the Declaration of Independence

George Washington, General of the Continental Army

King George III of Britain

Project-Based Learning Inquiry

Choosing Sides

Quest KICK OFF

In **1776** the colonists were divided over a very important question: Should the colonies break away from Britain or stay loyal to the king? What would you have chosen? You may wonder . . .

How did colonists decide which side to support in the Revolutionary War?

Imagine you are living in the Chesapeake Bay region in 1776. You must decide whether to become a Patriot, become a Loyalist, or stay neutral. You will then write a blog documenting your decision-making process. Explore the Essential Question "When is war justified?" in this Quest.

1 Ask Questions

To make an important decision, you need to find reasons and facts that support one side or the other. Make a list of questions whose answers would provide reasons to help you decide. Write your questions in your Active Journal.

2 Investigate

As you read the lessons in the Topic, look for Quest CONNECTIONS about events and other facts that might be reasons for supporting one side or the other. Record notes in your Active Journal.

3 Conduct Research

Next begin your research by exploring primary sources from the Revolutionary Era. Capture notes in your Active Journal.

Quest FINDINGS

4 Write Your Blog

Now use your research and notes to decide whether to be a Patriot, a Loyalist, or a neutral colonist. Then write and produce your blog. Get help for writing your blog in your Active Journal.

LESSON 1

The French and Indian War

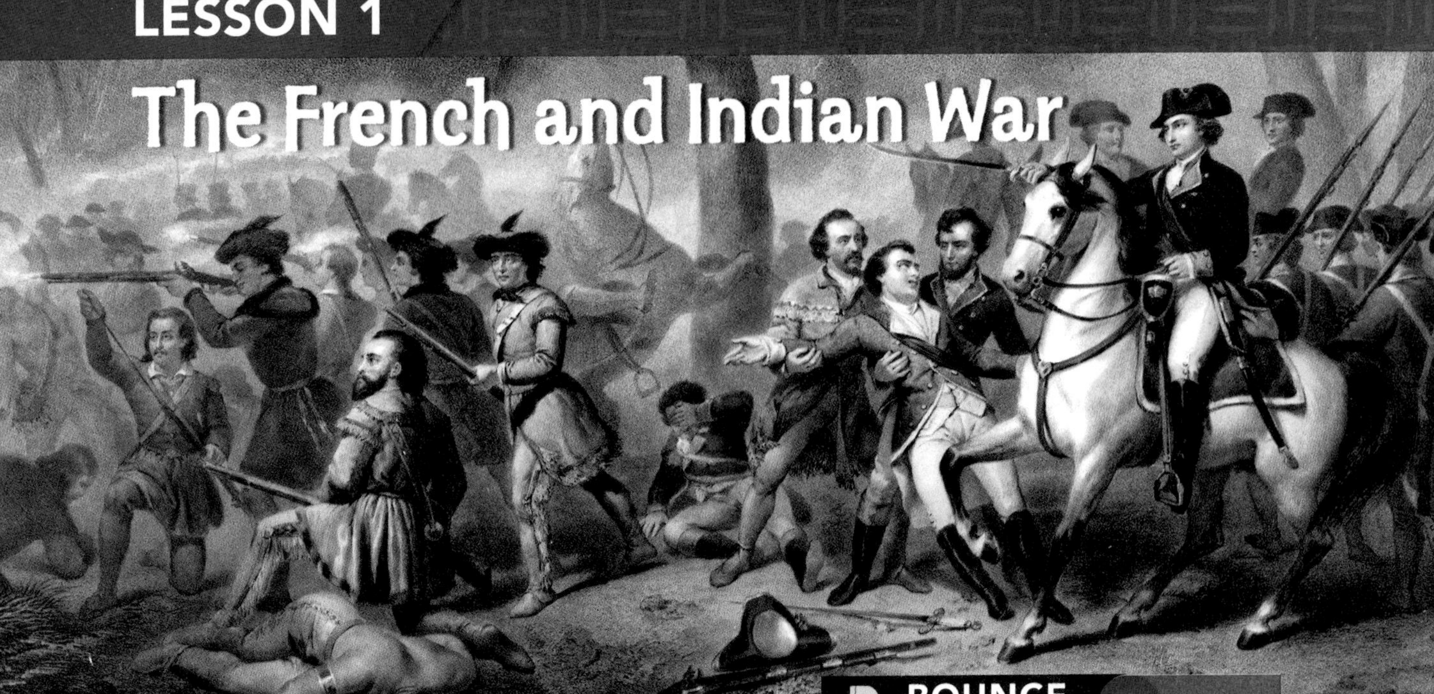

GET READY TO READ

START UP

Examine the illustration of George Washington at the Battle of Monongahela during the French and Indian War. Write what you would like to learn about his role in the war.

GUIDING QUESTIONS

- Why were Britain and France rivals in the mid-1700s?
- What role did American Indians play in the British-French rivalry?
- How did power in North America shift after the French and Indian War?

TAKE NOTES

Literacy Skills: Sequence

Use the graphic organizer in your Active Journal to take notes as you read the lesson.

PRACTICE VOCABULARY

Use the vocabulary activity in your Active Journal to practice the vocabulary words.

Vocabulary	Academic Vocabulary
ally	extensive
French and Indian War	devise
Albany Plan of Union	
Treaty of Paris	

By the mid-1700s, the major powers of Europe were locked in a worldwide struggle for empire. Britain, France, Spain, and the Netherlands competed for trade and colonies in far-flung corners of the globe. The British colonies in North America soon became caught up in the contest.

Why Did Europeans Fight Over North American Land?

The most serious threat came from France. It claimed a vast area that circled the English colonies from the St. Lawrence River west to the Great Lakes and south to the Gulf of Mexico. To protect their land claims, the French built an **extensive** system of forts. These forts blocked the British colonies from expanding to the west.

The Importance of the Ohio River Valley At first, most settlers in the British colonies were content to remain along the Atlantic coast. By the 1740s, however, traders were crossing the Appalachian Mountains in search of furs. Traders pushed into the forests of the Ohio Valley.

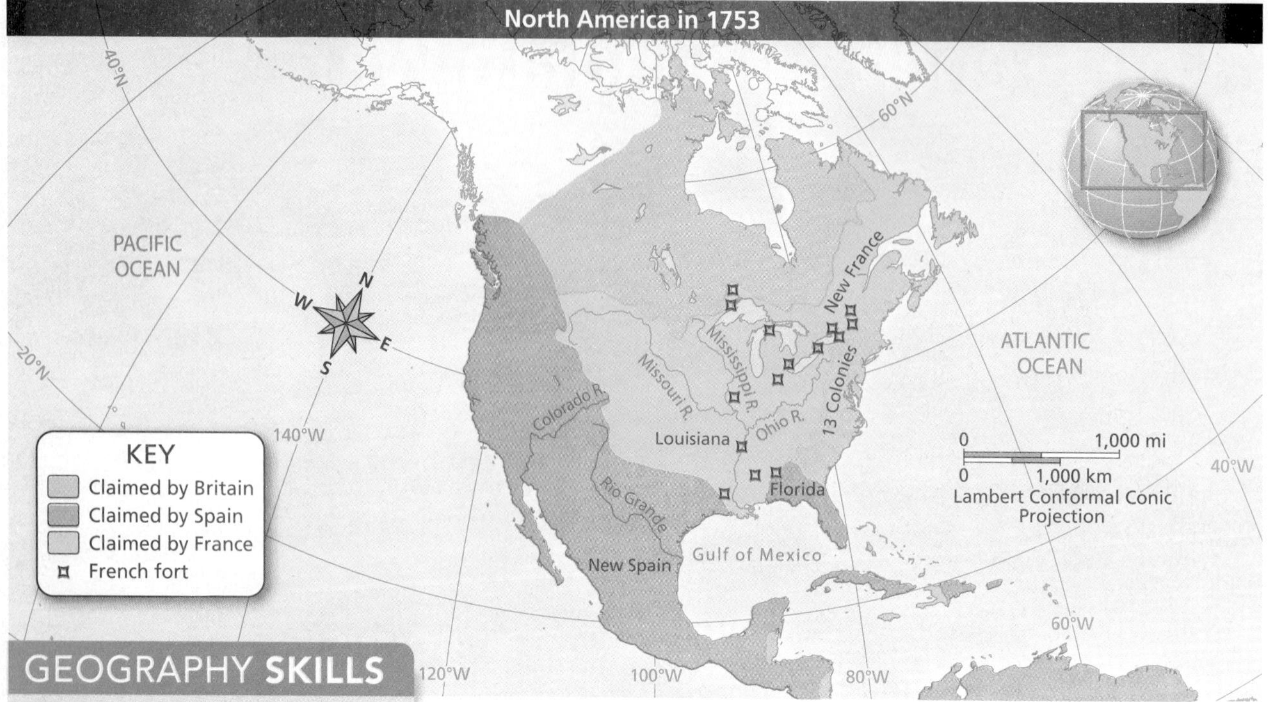

GEOGRAPHY SKILLS

By 1753, the French had claimed a vast area of North America.

1. **Location** Why do you think the French built forts along rivers and lakes?
2. **Infer** Why were the French determined to prevent British colonists from moving westward?

Because of the abundance of wildlife, settlers tried to take over the profitable French trade with the Indians.

France was determined to stop the British from expanding westward. The Ohio River was especially important to the French because it provided a vital link between their claims along the Great Lakes and their settlements along the Mississippi River.

Ohio Valley American Indians Choose Sides American Indians had hunted animals and grown crops in the Ohio Valley for centuries. They did not want to give up the land to settlers, French or British. One American Indian protested to a British trader, "You and the French are like the two edges of a pair of shears. And we are the cloth which is to be cut to pieces between them."

Academic Vocabulary
extensive • *adj.*, covering a large area

Still, the growing conflict between Britain and France was too dangerous to ignore. Some American Indians decided that the only way to protect their way of life was to take sides in the struggle, or to become an ally with the British or the French. An **ally** is a nation that works with another nation for a common purpose.

The French expected the Indians to side with them. Most French in North America were trappers and traders. Generally, they did not destroy Indian hunting grounds by clearing forests for farms. Also, many French trappers married American Indian women and adopted their ways. As a result, France had built strong alliances with such American Indian groups as the Algonquins and the Hurons.

Most British settlers were farmers. These settlers usually ignored American Indian rights by felling trees and clearing land for crops. However, an English trader and official, William Johnson, helped gain Iroquois support for Britain. The Iroquois respected Johnson. He was one of the few British settlers who had an Indian wife, Molly Brant. She was the sister of the Mohawk chief Thayendanegea, known to the British as Joseph Brant. Both Joseph and Molly Brant became valuable allies for the British.

In the end, Britain managed to convince the powerful Iroquois nations to join with them. The British alliance was attractive to the Iroquois because they were old enemies of the Algonquin and the Huron. The war reignited old conflicts in the Ohio Valley between the Iroquois and the Algonquins and Hurons. Some groups, like the Shawnees, Delawares, and Mingos, formed alliances to push Europeans off their lands. More often, however, the alliances formed with the British and the French pitted Indian groups against each other in the fighting to come.

READING CHECK **Identify Supporting Details** Which American Indian groups sided with the British and which sided with the French as the war began?

Where Did the French and Indian War Begin?

Three times between 1689 and 1748, France and Great Britain fought for power in Europe and North America. Each war ended with an uneasy peace.

In 1754, fighting broke out for a fourth time. British settlers called the conflict the **French and Indian War** because it pitted them against France and its American Indian allies. The French and Indian War was part of a larger war called the Seven Years' War that involved conflicts not just in North America but also in Europe and Asia. In North America, the Ohio River Valley was at the center of the dispute. There, the opening shots of the war were fired by soldiers led by George Washington.

▼ Many French living in North America were fur trappers who traded with American Indians for furs.

Washington Heads to Ohio

When Washington took part in the Ohio Valley conflict he was only 22 years old. He had grown up on a plantation in Virginia, the son of wealthy parents.

Gifted at mathematics, he began working as a land surveyor. His job took him to frontier lands in western Virginia.

In 1753, the governor of Virginia sent Washington to deliver a letter to the French asking them to withdraw from the Ohio Valley. The French refused. After Washington returned from this mission, the governor of Virginia sent him west again. This time Washington's assignment was to build a fort where the Monongahela and Allegheny rivers meet to form the Ohio River (present-day Pittsburgh, Pennsylvania).

Washington led 150 men into the Ohio country in April 1754. Along the way, he heard that the French had just completed Fort Duquesne (doo KAYN) at the very spot where Washington hoped to build his fort.

Defeat at Fort Necessity Determined to carry out his orders, Washington hurried on. Indian allies revealed that French scouts were camped in the woods ahead. Marching quietly through the night, Washington launched a surprise attack and scattered the French. The Iroquois helped the British fight against the French, as well as the French allies, the Algonquins.

Washington's success was brief. Hearing that the French were about to counterattack, he and his men quickly built a makeshift stockade. They named it Fort Necessity. A force of 700 French and Indians surrounded the fort. Badly outnumbered, the Virginians surrendered. The French then released Washington, and he returned home.

British officials recognized the significance of Washington's skirmish. "The volley fired by this young Virginian in the forests of America," a British writer noted, "has set the world in flames."

READING CHECK **Summarize** Why did Washington and his men fight the French?

Analyze Images George Washington and his soldiers quickly built the makeshift Fort Necessity in the Ohio Valley to help defend themselves from the French. Shown here is a replica of the fort. **Cite Evidence** What clues in the photo show that Washington's troops built this fort quickly?

The Colonies Meet in Albany

While Washington was fighting the French, delegates from seven colonies gathered in Albany, New York. One purpose of the meeting was to cement the alliance with the Iroquois, who were willing to defend the British claim to the Ohio Valley. This alliance would help the British fight the French and their American Indian allies. Another goal of the meeting was to plan a united colonial defense.

The delegates in Albany knew that the colonists had to work together to defeat the French. Benjamin Franklin, the delegate from Pennsylvania, proposed the **Albany Plan of Union**. The plan was an attempt to create "one general government" for the British colonies.

Albany Plan of Union, 1754

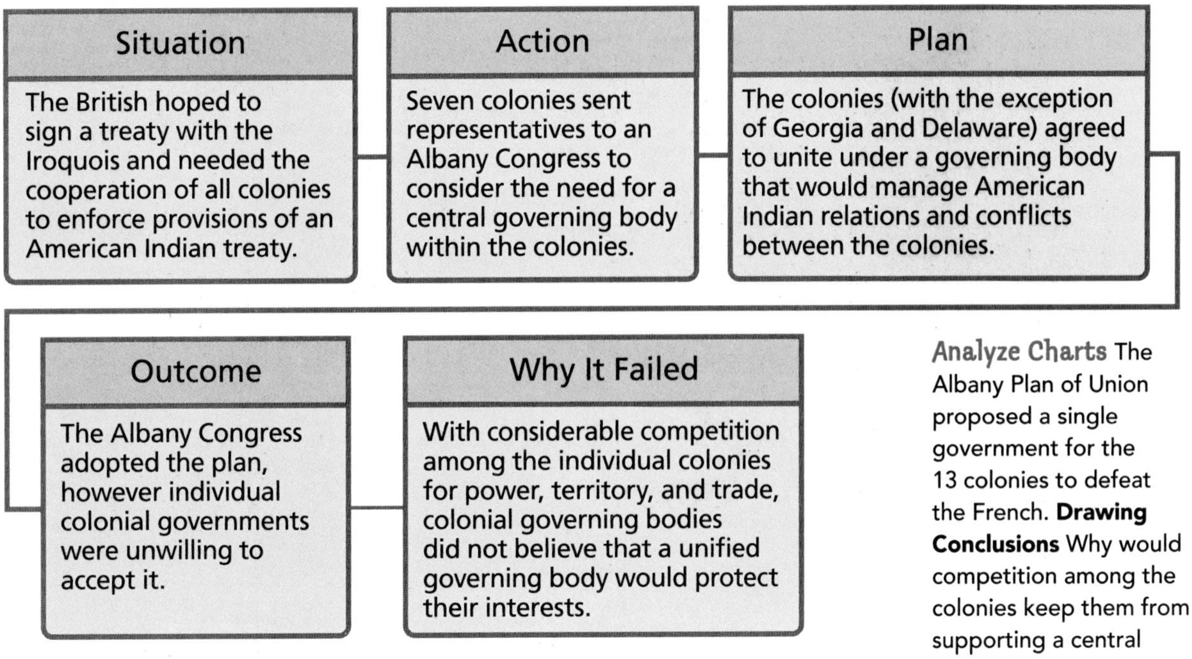

Situation	Action	Plan
The British hoped to sign a treaty with the Iroquois and needed the cooperation of all colonies to enforce provisions of an American Indian treaty.	Seven colonies sent representatives to an Albany Congress to consider the need for a central governing body within the colonies.	The colonies (with the exception of Georgia and Delaware) agreed to unite under a governing body that would manage American Indian relations and conflicts between the colonies.

Outcome	Why It Failed
The Albany Congress adopted the plan, however individual colonial governments were unwilling to accept it.	With considerable competition among the individual colonies for power, territory, and trade, colonial governing bodies did not believe that a unified governing body would protect their interests.

Analyze Charts The Albany Plan of Union proposed a single government for the 13 colonies to defeat the French. **Drawing Conclusions** Why would competition among the colonies keep them from supporting a central governing body?

It called for a Grand Council made up of representatives from each colony. The council would make laws, raise taxes, and set up the defense of the colonies.

The delegates voted to accept the Plan of Union. However, when the plan was submitted to the colonial assemblies, not one approved it.

None of the colonies wanted to give up any of its powers to a central council. A disappointed Benjamin Franklin expressed his frustration at the failure of his plan:

Primary Source

"Everyone cries a union is necessary. But when they come to the manner and form of the union, their weak noodles are perfectly distracted."

—Benjamin Franklin, in a letter to Massachusetts Governor William Shirley, 1755

READING CHECK **Identify Main Ideas** Why did the delegates from the colonies want to form a union?

British Defeats in the Ohio Valley

In 1755, General Edward Braddock led British and colonial troops in an attack against Fort Duquesne. Braddock was a stubborn man who had little experience at fighting in the forests of North America. Still, the general boasted that he would sweep the French from the Ohio Valley.

Surprise Attacks in the Forests Braddock's men moved slowly and noisily through the forests. Although warned of danger by Washington and by Indian scouts, Braddock pushed ahead.

As the British neared Fort Duquesne, the French and their Indian allies launched a surprise attack. Sharpshooters hid in the forest and picked off British soldiers, whose bright red uniforms made easy targets.

Braddock himself had five horses shot out from under him before he fell, fatally wounded. Almost half the British were killed or wounded. Washington, too, was nearly killed.

Analyze Images The French and their American Indian allies ambushed General Braddock's forces in the forests as the soldiers made their way to Fort Duquesne in 1755. **Infer** What advantages did the American Indians and French have fighting in forests that Braddock's soldiers did not have?

British Setbacks at Lake Ontario and Lake George During the next two years, the war continued to go badly for the British. British attacks against several French forts failed. Meanwhile, the French won important victories, capturing Fort Oswego on Lake Ontario and Fort William Henry on Lake George. (Both forts occupied land that is now part of New York state.) All these defeats put a serious strain on the alliances with the Iroquois, who had been counting on the British to protect them from the French. The Iroquois faced increasing danger from enemy American Indian groups, who fought them for prisoners and goods.

READING CHECK **Identify Supporting Details** Why were French attacks in the forests successful?

Quebec and New France Fall

In 1757, William Pitt became prime minister, meaning he was the new head of the British government. Pitt made it his first job to win the war in North America. Once that goal was achieved, he argued, the British would be free to focus on victory in other parts of the world. So Pitt sent Britain's best generals to North America. To encourage the colonists to support the war, he promised large payments for military services and supplies.

INTERACTIVE

Major Battles of the French and Indian War

Under Pitt's leadership, the tide of battle turned. In 1758, Major General Jeffrey Amherst captured Louisbourg, the most important fort in French Canada. That year, the British also seized Fort Duquesne, which they renamed Fort Pitt after the British leader. The city of Pittsburgh later grew up on the site of Fort Pitt.

The War Turns in Favor of the British The British enjoyed even greater success in 1759. By summer, they had pushed the French from Fort Niagara, Crown Point, and Fort Ticonderoga (ty kahn duh ROH guh). Next, Pitt sent General James Wolfe to take Quebec, capital of New France.

Climbing Cliffs to Attack Quebec Quebec was vital to the defense of New France. Without Quebec, the French could not supply their forts farther up the St. Lawrence River. Quebec was well defended, though. The city sat on the edge of the Plains of Abraham, on top of a steep cliff high above the St. Lawrence. An able French general, the Marquis de Montcalm, was prepared to fight off any British attack.

General Wolfe **devised** a bold plan to capture Quebec. He knew that Montcalm had only a few soldiers guarding the cliff because the French thought that it was too steep to climb. Late at night, Wolfe ordered British troops to row quietly in small boats to the foot of the cliff. In the dark, the soldiers climbed up the cliff and assembled at the top.

Academic Vocabulary
devised • *v.,* planned or invented a method of doing something

The next morning, Montcalm awakened to a surprise. A force of 4,000 British troops was drawn up and ready for battle.

Quickly, Montcalm marched his own troops out to join in battle. By the time the fierce fighting was over, both Montcalm and Wolfe lay dead. Moments before Wolfe died, a soldier gave him the news that the British had won. Wolfe is said to have whispered, "Now, God be praised, I will die in peace." On September 18, 1759, Quebec surrendered to the British.

INTERACTIVE
Effects of the French and Indian War

The British Make Huge Gains The fall of Quebec sealed the fate of New France, though fighting dragged on in Europe for several more years. Finally, in 1763, Britain and France signed the **Treaty of Paris**, bringing the long conflict to an end.

The Treaty of Paris marked the end of French power in North America. By its terms, Britain gained Canada and all French lands east of the Mississippi River except New Orleans. France was allowed to keep only two islands in the Gulf of St. Lawrence and its prosperous sugar-growing islands in the West Indies. Spain, which had entered the war on the French side in 1762, gave up Florida to Britain.

In return, Spain received all French land west of the Mississippi. In addition, Spain gained the vital port city of New Orleans. Spain retained control of its vast empire in Central America and South America.

Analyze Images After sneaking up a steep cliff under the cover of darkness, the British defeated the French on the Plains of Abraham the next morning and captured the capital city of Quebec. **Use Visual Clues** Why is the bird's-eye-view perspective helpful to understanding the action?

North America in 1763

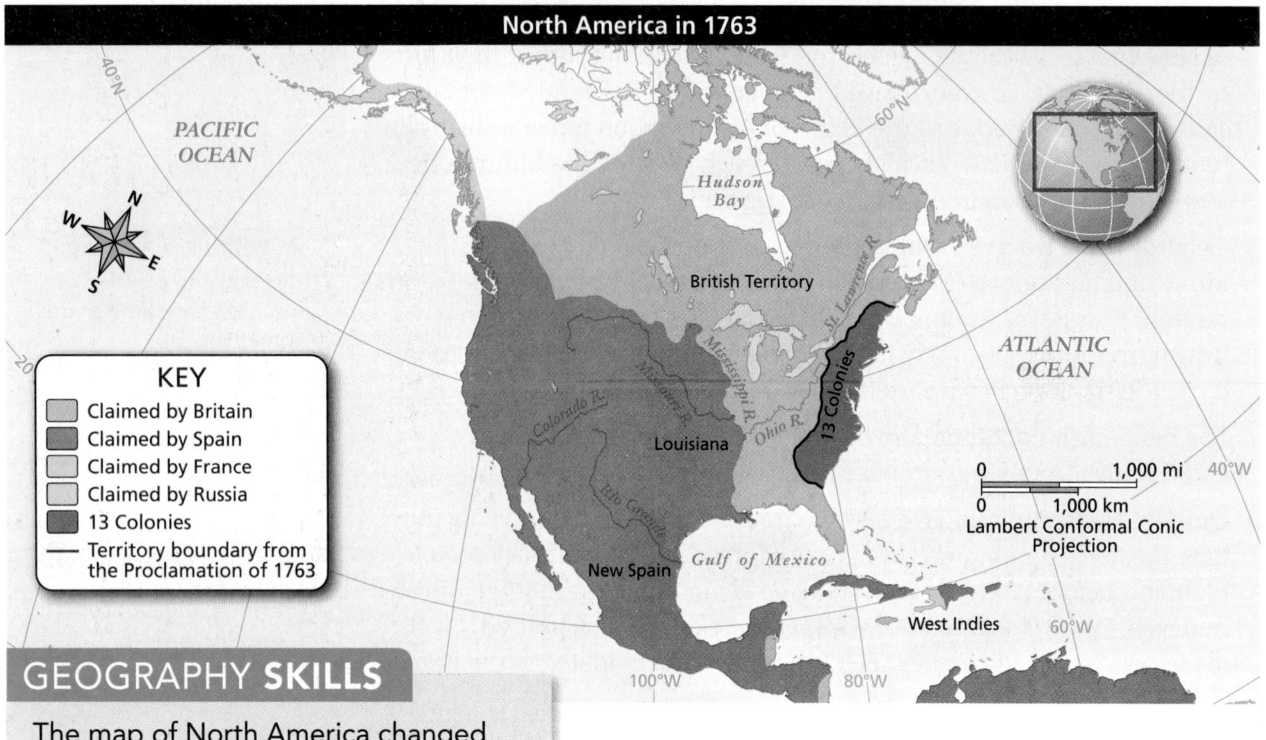

GEOGRAPHY SKILLS

The map of North America changed between 1753 and 1763, after the Treaty of Paris.

1. **Region** What caused the 13 colonies region to remain together after the French and Indian War?
2. **Draw Conclusions** What effect did the Treaty of Paris have on New Spain?

After years of fighting, peace returned to North America. Yet, in a few short years, a new conflict would break out. This time, the struggle would pit Britain against its own 13 colonies.

READING CHECK **Recognize Multiple Causes** In what ways did Pitt help Britain win the war?

Lesson Check

Practice Vocabulary

1. How did the **Albany Plan of Union** seek to involve the colonists in the **French and Indian War**?
2. Give two results of the **Treaty of Paris**.

Critical Thinking and Writing

3. **Summarize** Who fought the French and Indian War, and for what reason?
4. **Identify Supporting Details** What role did George Washington play in the French and Indian War?
5. **Revisit the Essential Question** When is war justified? Do you think the French and Indian War was justified? Why or why not?
6. **Writing Workshop: Consider Your Purpose and Audience** At the end of this Topic, you will write an essay to answer the question "Why was there an American Revolution?" Write a sentence in your Active Journal that tells what your purpose for writing will be and who you are writing for.

Identify Physical and Cultural Features

Follow these steps to identify physical and cultural features.

INTERACTIVE

Read Physical Maps

1 **Identify physical features.** Physical features include bodies of water, coastlines, mountains, valleys, and deserts. What are the main physical features shown on the map below?

2 **Identify cultural features.** Cultural features are features created by people, such as cities and towns, borders, buildings, roads, railroads, or canals. What is the main cultural feature on the western frontier shown on the map and mentioned in George Washington's report?

3 **Relate physical and cultural features.** Cultural features are often related to physical features. For example, a river (physical feature) can form a border between two countries (cultural feature). The natural landscape may determine where a city is built. People need water for drinking, cooking, and bathing. That is why so many early settlements were built near rivers or lakes. Bodies of water are a natural resource and a physical feature. People use that natural resource to meet their needs for living. Based on the map and the primary source, why was the fort George Washington built called Fort Necessity?

Secondary Source

Western Frontier, 1754

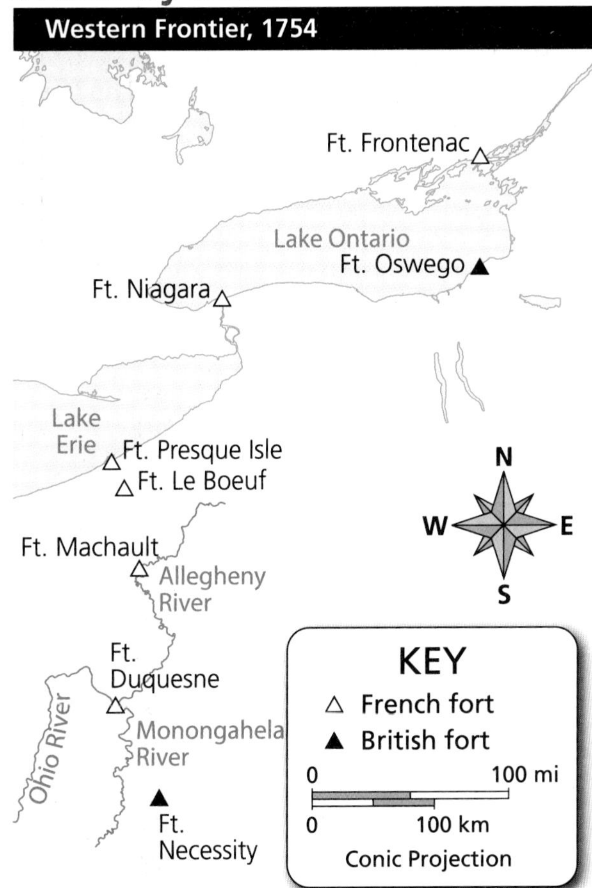

Primary Source

. . .we received Intelligence that the French, having been reinforced with 700 Recruits, had left Monongehela, . . . Upon this, as our Numbers were so unequal, . . . (not exceeding 300) we prepared for our Defence in the best Manner we could, by throwing up a small Intrenchment, which we had not Time to perfect . . .

—George Washington and James Mackay of the Capitulation of Fort Necessity Williamsburg 19 July 1754

LESSON 2

Growing Resentment Against Britain

GET READY TO READ

START UP

The illustration shows British troops searching a colonist's home. Explain in writing how colonists likely felt about such actions.

GUIDING QUESTIONS

- Why did the colonists oppose new taxes and feel that British law was increasingly oppressive?
- Who were the colonial leaders that emerged as tensions with Britain increased?

TAKE NOTES

Literacy Skills: Identify Cause and Effect

Use the graphic organizer in your Active Journal to take notes as you read the lesson.

PRACTICE VOCABULARY

Use the vocabulary activity in your Active Journal to practice the vocabulary words.

Vocabulary

petition
boycott
repeal
writ of assistance
committee of correspondence

Academic Vocabulary

prohibit
influential

By 1760, the British and their Indian allies had driven France from the Ohio Valley. Their troubles in the region were not over, however. For many years, fur traders had sent back glowing reports of the land beyond the Appalachian Mountains. The dense forests of the Ohio Valley offered new resources that were in short supply in the East, and with the French gone, British colonists wanted to head west to claim the lands for themselves.

Conflict Over Land

Many American Indian nations lived in the Ohio Valley. They included the Senecas, Delawares, Shawnees, Ottawas, Miamis, and Hurons. As British settlers moved into the valley, they often clashed with these Indians.

The British and American Indians Fight

In 1760, Britain made Lord Jeffrey Amherst military commander and governor general of its North American colonies. The British sent Amherst to the frontier to keep order. French traders had always treated American Indians as friends, holding feasts for them and giving them presents.

Amherst refused to do this. Instead, he raised the price of goods traded to Indians. Also, unlike the French, Amherst allowed settlers to build farms and forts on Indian lands.

Angry American Indians found a leader in Pontiac, an Ottawa chief who had fought on the French side during the French and Indian War. An English trader remarked that Pontiac "commands more respect amongst these nations than any Indian I ever saw." In April 1763, Pontiac spoke out against the British, calling them "dogs dressed in red, who have come to rob [us] of [our] hunting grounds and drive away the game." Pontiac led violent raids against British forts. Hundreds of British were tortured and killed, leading some officials to fear for the safety of colonists near American Indian land.

The British Secure the Frontier Later that year, Pontiac led an attack on British troops at Fort Detroit. A number of other Indian nations joined him. In a few short months, they captured most British forts in the Ohio country. British and colonial troops then struck back and regained much of what they had lost.

Pontiac's War, as it came to be called, did not last long. In October 1763, the French told Pontiac that they had signed the Treaty of Paris. Because the treaty marked the end of French power in North America, the Indians could no longer hope for French aid against the British. One by one, the Indian nations stopped fighting and returned home.

READING CHECK **Identify Supporting Details** What arguments did Pontiac have against the British and settlers?

How Did the Proclamation of 1763 Fuel Resentment?

Pontiac's violent raids against British troops convinced officials that they should **prohibit** British subjects from settling beyond the western frontier for their own safety. To do this, the government issued the Proclamation of 1763. The proclamation drew an imaginary line along the crest of the Appalachian Mountains. Colonists were forbidden to settle west of the line. All settlers already west of the line were "to remove themselves" at once.

The Purposes of the Proclamation The proclamation was meant to protect British settlers in the western lands. To enforce it, Britain sent 10,000 troops to the colonies. Few went to the frontier, however. Most stayed along the Atlantic coast.

The proclamation also created four new places where colonists could settle. French Canada became part of the province of Quebec. Florida, once a Spanish colony, was divided into East and West Florida. In the West Indies, the British also had gained control of a number of islands.

Quick Activity

Begin an online timeline of major events and ideas that led to the American Revolution. Add to it as you read. Explain each event and its significance.

INTERACTIVE

Crisis on the Frontier

Academic Vocabulary

prohibit • *v.*, to refuse to allow; to forbid

▼ Chief Pontiac of the Ottawa incited other American Indian groups to fight the British and led an attack on British troops at Fort Detroit.

Colonists Disagree with the Proclamation The proclamation angered many colonists. They thought it was unnecessary and unjust. They did not think the British government had the right to limit where they could settle. Nor were they concerned with the rights of American Indians. After winning the French and Indian War, many colonists felt they had rights to the land.

Also, colonists now had to pay for the additional British troops that had been sent to enforce the proclamation. In the end, many settlers simply ignored the proclamation and moved west anyway. The proclamation remained most controversial in the west, where colonists clashed with American Indians. Some colonies, including New York, Pennsylvania, and Virginia, claimed lands in the west. The Proclamation would continue to cause problems up to the American Revolution from the tension it caused between the colonists and Britain.

READING CHECK **Identify Cause and Effect** What was the reasoning behind the Proclamation of 1763?

How Did Mercantilism Affect Taxation and Cause Resentment?

The Seven Years' War, which included the French and Indian War, plunged Britain deeply into debt. As a result, the taxes paid by citizens in Britain rose sharply. The British prime minister, George Grenville, decided that colonists in North America should help share the burden. In a mercantilist system, colonies were expected to serve the colonial power. Grenville reasoned that the colonists would not oppose small tax increases.

GEOGRAPHY **SKILLS**

The Proclamation of 1763 prohibited colonial settlement west of the red line shown on the map.

1. **Location** Why would settlers resent the Proclamation border?
2. **Infer** How would people living in the Indian Reserve be affected if settlers ignored the Proclamation's border?

Westward Movement in Defiance of the Proclamation of 1763

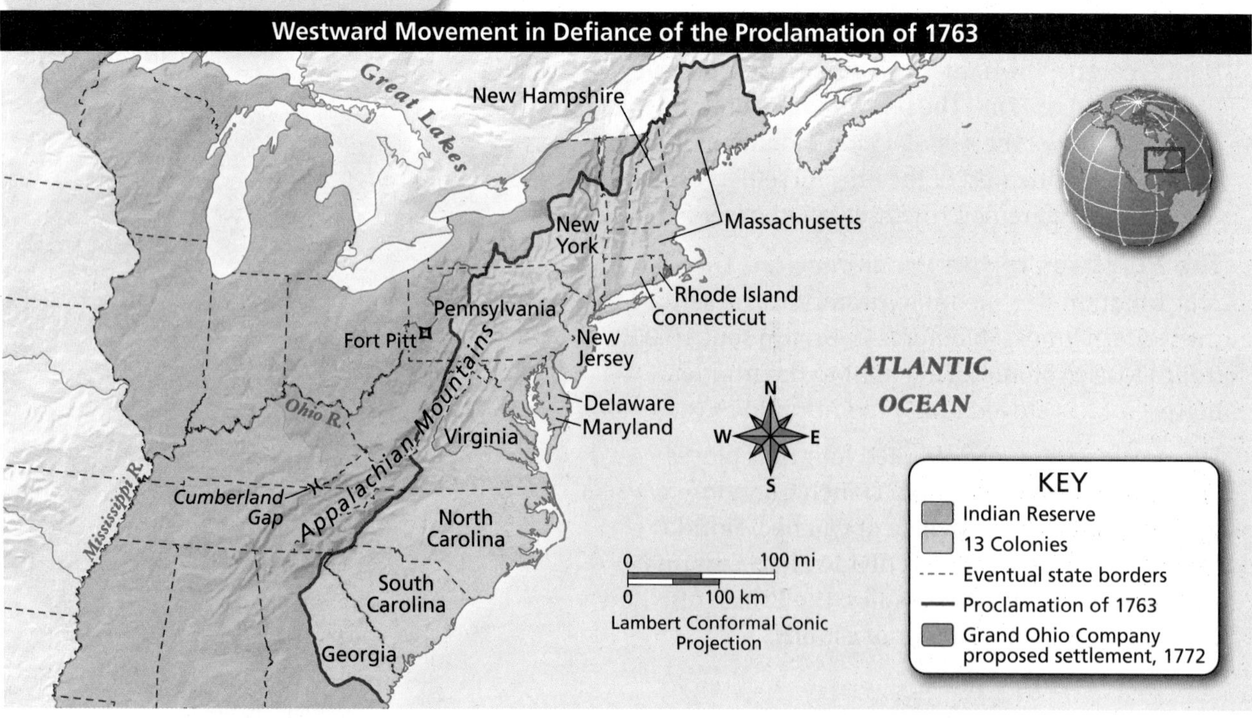

The colonists, however, strongly resented these taxes. They argued that mercantilism was unfair because it limited trade and made goods more expensive. Many colonists also objected that the power to raise these new taxes was not granted by the English constitution. Grenville's policy led to the political and economic conflicts that would divide the colonies and England.

Analyze Images British Prime Minister George Grenville wanted colonists to help share the burden of debt that Britain had incurred from the Seven Years' War. **Infer** How do you think colonists would react to sharing the expense of the Seven Years' War?

The Sugar Act Taxes the Colonies In 1764, Grenville asked Parliament to approve the Sugar Act, which put a new tax on molasses. The Sugar Act replaced an earlier tax, which had been so high that any merchant who paid it would have been driven out of business. As a result, most colonial merchants simply avoided the tax by smuggling molasses into the colonies. Often, they bribed tax collectors to look the other way.

The Sugar Act of 1764 lowered the tax. At the same time, the law made it easier for British officials to bring colonial smugglers to trial. Grenville made it clear that he expected the new tax to be paid.

READING CHECK **Identify Main Ideas** What arguments did the colonists have against more British taxes?

Why Did the Stamp Act Anger Colonists?

Grenville also persuaded Parliament to pass the Stamp Act of 1765. The act placed new duties (taxes) on legal documents such as wills, diplomas, and marriage papers. It also taxed newspapers, almanacs, playing cards, and even dice.

All items named in the law had to carry a stamp showing that the tax had been paid. Stamp taxes were used in Britain and other countries to raise money. However, Britain had never required American colonists to pay such a tax.

Resistance to the Stamp Act When British officials tried to enforce the Stamp Act, they met with stormy protests from colonists. Lieutenant Governor Hutchinson's house in Massachusetts was looted by a mob. He was not the only official to feel the mob's anger. Some colonists threw rocks at agents trying to collect the unpopular tax.

In addition to riots in Boston, other disturbances broke out in New York City, Newport, and Charleston. In New York City, rioters destroyed the home of a British official who had said he would "cram the stamps down American throats" at the point of his sword.

The fury of the colonists shocked the British. After all, Britain had spent a lot of money to protect the colonies against the French. The British at home were paying much higher taxes than the colonists. Why, British officials asked, were colonists so angry about the Stamp Act?

Quest CONNECTIONS

Look at the map. How would a disruption of trade with Britain affect colonists living in the Chesapeake Bay region? Record your findings in your Active Journal.

As one English letter-writer commented,

Primary Source

"Our Colonies must be the biggest Beggars in the World, if such small Duties appear to be intolerable Burdens in their Eyes."

—"Pacificus," *Maryland Gazette*, March 20, 1766

Lack of Representation in Parliament Colonists replied that the Stamp Act taxes were unjust and unnecessary. "No taxation without representation!" they cried. That principle was rooted in English traditions dating back to the Magna Carta.

Colonists insisted that only they or their elected representatives had the right to pass taxes. Since the colonists did not elect representatives to Parliament, Parliament had no right to tax them. Colonists were willing to pay taxes—but only if they were passed by their own legislatures. The colonists also felt that mercantilist policies like the Navigation Acts were unfair because they restricted their trade, which reduced colonists' income.

Peaceful Protests Lead Toward Revolution The Stamp Act crisis united colonists from New Hampshire to Georgia. Critics of the law called for delegates from every colony to meet in New York City. There, a congress would form to consider actions against the hated Stamp Act.

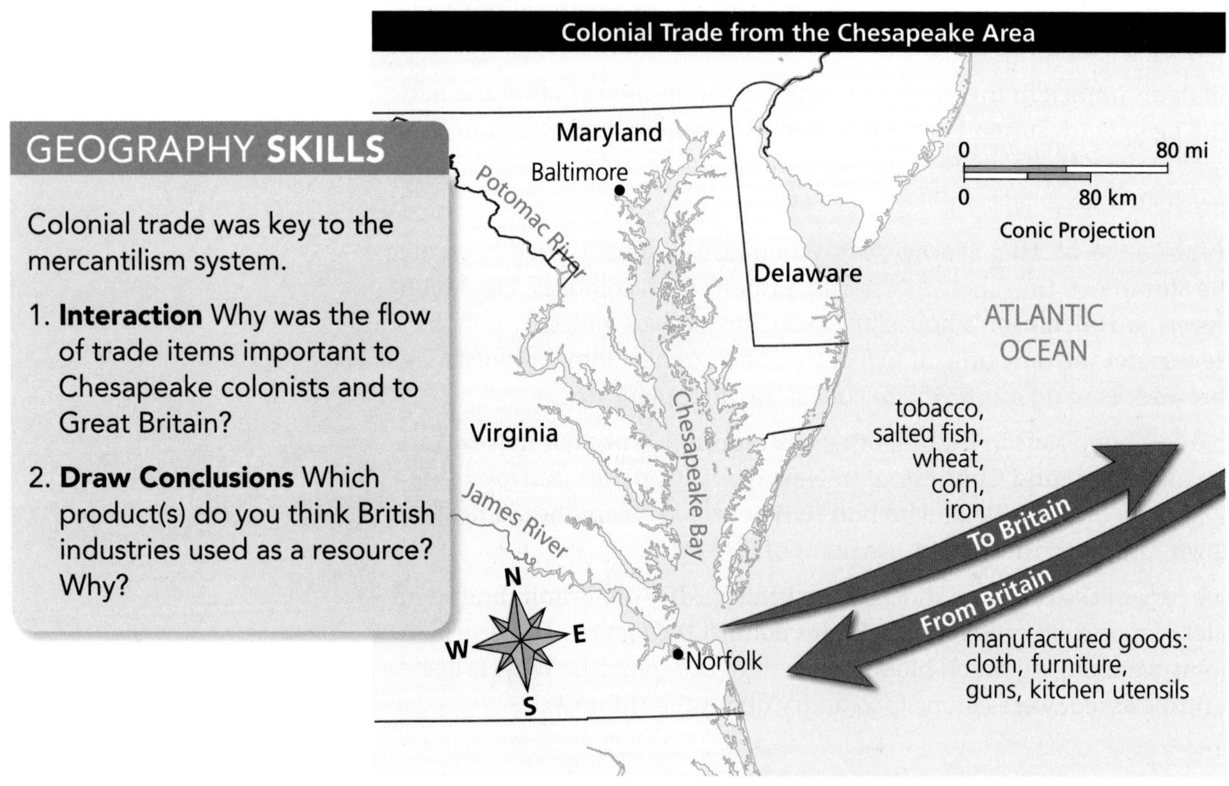

GEOGRAPHY **SKILLS**

Colonial trade was key to the mercantilism system.

1. **Interaction** Why was the flow of trade items important to Chesapeake colonists and to Great Britain?
2. **Draw Conclusions** Which product(s) do you think British industries used as a resource? Why?

Analyze Political Cartoons British officials held a "funeral" for the Stamp Act, which Parliament repealed in 1766. **Cite Evidence** What does this cartoon say about the artist's opinion of the Stamp Act?

In October 1765, nine colonies sent delegates to what became known as the Stamp Act Congress. The delegates drew up petitions to King George III, the British king, and to Parliament. A **petition** is a formal written request to someone in authority, signed by a group of people. In these petitions, the delegates rejected the Stamp Act and asserted that Parliament had no right to tax the colonies. Parliament paid little attention.

The colonists took other steps to change the law. They joined together to boycott British goods. To **boycott** means to refuse to buy certain goods and services. The boycott of British goods took its toll. Trade fell off by 14 percent. British merchants complained that they were facing ruin. So, too, did British workers who made goods for the colonies.

The colonists wanted the government to have less of a say over businesses and trade. They wanted a free-enterprise system, in which the market, rather than the government, determines what goods and services cost. British taxes, the colonists argued, unfairly restricted economic growth.

Finally, in 1766, Parliament **repealed**, or canceled, the Stamp Act. At the same time, however, it passed a law asserting that Parliament had the right to raise taxes in "all cases whatsoever."

READING CHECK **Recognize Multiple Causes** What events led to the repeal of the Stamp Act in 1766?

How Did Colonists React to the Townshend Acts?

In May 1767, Parliament reopened the debate over taxing the colonies. George Grenville, now a member of Parliament, clashed with Charles Townshend, the official in charge of the British treasury.

"You are cowards, you are afraid of the Americans, you dare not tax America!" Grenville shouted.

"Fear? Cowards?" Townshend snapped back. "I dare tax America!"

The next month, Parliament passed the Townshend Acts, which taxed goods such as glass, paper, paint, lead, and tea. The taxes were low, but colonists still objected. The principle was the same: Parliament did not have the right to tax them without their consent.

Searches Without Reason Cause Unrest The Townshend Acts also set up new ways to collect taxes. Customs officials were sent to American ports with orders to stop smuggling. Using legal documents known as **writs of assistance**, the officers would be allowed to inspect a ship's cargo without giving a reason.

Colonists protested that the writs of assistance violated their rights as British citizens. Under British law, a government official could not search a person's property without a good reason for suspecting that the person had committed a crime. Yet the writs of assistance allowed persons and their property to be searched and even seized without reason in the colonies. Colonists angrily cited the words of James Otis of Massachusetts. Arguing against a British attempt to impose writs of assistance six years earlier, he had said:

Analyze Political Cartoons In this cartoon, colonists imagined punishing tax collectors by tarring and feathering them. **Draw Conclusions** What might the caption for this cartoon say?

Primary Source

"Now, one of the most essential branches of English liberty is the freedom of one's house. A man's house is his castle; and while he is quiet, he is as well guarded as a prince in his castle. This writ, if it should be declared legal, would totally destroy this privilege. Customhouse officers may enter our houses when they please . . . break locks, bars, and everything in their way. . . ."

—James Otis, February 24, 1761

Colonists Rebel Against British Economic Policies Colonists responded swiftly and strongly to the Townshend Acts. From north to south, colonial merchants and planters signed agreements promising to stop importing goods taxed by the Townshend Acts. The colonists hoped that the new boycott would win repeal of the Townshend Acts.

The colonists began to view Britain's treatment of them as increasingly oppressive, or severe. To protest British policies, some angry colonists formed the Sons of Liberty. From Boston to Charleston, Sons of Liberty staged mock hangings of cloth or straw effigies, or likenesses, dressed as British officials. The hangings were meant to show tax collectors what might happen to them if they collected the unpopular taxes.

Some women joined the Daughters of Liberty. They paraded, signed petitions, and organized a boycott of fine British cloth. They urged colonial women to raise more sheep, prepare more wool, and spin and weave their own cloth. A slogan of the Daughters of Liberty declared, "It is better to wear a Homespun coat than to lose our Liberty."

Some Sons and Daughters of Liberty also used other methods to support their cause. They visited merchants and urged them to boycott British imports. A few even threatened people who continued to buy British goods.

▲ Mercy Otis Warren's popular plays making fun of British officials motivated colonists to take action against Britain.

READING CHECK **Summarize** How did many colonists respond to the Townshend Acts?

Leaders Emerge in the Struggle with Britain

As the struggle over taxes continued, new leaders emerged in all the colonies. Men and women in New England and Virginia were especially active and **influential** in the colonial cause.

Academic Vocabulary
influential • *adj.*, having great influence or power; effective

Massachusetts Citizens Fight for Their Beliefs Samuel Adams of Boston stood firmly against Britain. Adams seemed an unlikely leader. He was a failure in business and a poor public speaker. Often, he wore a red suit and a cheap gray wig for which people poked fun at him. Still, Adams loved politics. He always attended Boston town meetings and Sons of Liberty rallies. Adams's real talent was organizing people. He worked behind the scenes, arranging protests and stirring public support.

Sam's cousin John was another important Massachusetts leader. John Adams had been a schoolteacher before becoming a skilled lawyer. Adams longed for fame and could often be difficult. Still, he was more cautious than his cousin Sam. He weighed evidence carefully before taking any actions. His knowledge of British law earned him much respect.

Mercy Otis Warren also aided the colonial cause. Warren wrote plays that made fun of British officials. The plays were published in newspapers and widely read in the colonies. Warren formed a close friendship with Abigail Adams, the wife of John Adams. The two women used their pens to spur the colonists to action. They also called for greater rights for women in the colonies.

Important People of the American Revolution

Virginians Join the Cause Virginia contributed many leaders to the struggle against taxes. In the House of Burgesses, George Washington joined other Virginians to protest the Townshend Acts.

A young lawyer, Patrick Henry, became well known as a vocal critic of British policies. His speeches in the House of Burgesses moved listeners to both tears and anger. Once, Henry attacked Britain with such fury that some listeners cried out, "Treason!" Henry boldly replied, "If this be treason, make the most of it!" Henry's words moved a young listener, Thomas Jefferson. At the time, Jefferson was a 22-year-old law student.

READING CHECK **Use Evidence** How did some colonists show their strengths as leaders?

The Boston Massacre

Port cities such as Boston and New York were centers of protest. In New York, a dispute arose over the Quartering Act. Under that law, colonists had to provide housing, candles, bedding, and beverages to soldiers stationed in the colonies. The colonists did not want to house the soldiers. Many, including Sam Adams, did not think the soldiers should be stationed in the colonies at all during peacetime. When the New York Assembly refused to obey the Quartering Act, Britain dismissed the assembly in 1767.

Britain also sent two regiments to Boston to protect customs officers from local citizens. To many Bostonians, the soldiers were a daily reminder that Britain was trying to bully them into paying unjust taxes. When British soldiers walked along the streets of Boston, they risked insults or even beatings. A serious clash was not long in coming.

A Crowd Challenges British Soldiers On March 5, 1770, a crowd gathered outside the Boston customs house. Colonists shouted insults at the "lobsterbacks," as they called the red-coated soldiers.

Analyze Images This engraving of the Boston Massacre by Paul Revere helped spread anti-British feeling among the colonists. **Synthesize Visual Information** In what way could you say the image is inflammatory, or able to arouse anger in those who saw it?

5 BIOGRAPHY Things to Know About

PATRICK HENRY
Patriot Leader (1736–1799)

- Favored independence from Britain
- Known for the famous words, "Give me liberty or give me death!"
- Known for his wit and oratorical skills
- Was first governor of Virginia after independence was declared
- Succeeded as a criminal lawyer before the Revolutionary War

Critical Thinking Why would speaking skills be an advantage to a colonial leader?

Then the Boston crowd began to throw snowballs, oyster shells, and chunks of ice at the soldiers.

The crowd grew larger and rowdier. Suddenly, the soldiers panicked. They fired into the crowd. When the smoke from the musket volley cleared, five people lay dead or dying. Among the first to die were Samuel Maverick, a 17-year-old white youth, and Crispus Attucks, a free Black sailor.

Colonists React to the Massacre Colonists were quick to protest the incident, which they called the Boston Massacre. A Boston silversmith named Paul Revere fanned anti-British feeling with an engraving that showed British soldiers firing on unarmed colonists. Sam Adams wrote letters to other colonists to build outrage about the shooting.

The soldiers were arrested and tried in court. John Adams agreed to defend them, saying that they deserved a fair trial. He wanted to show the world that the colonists believed in justice, even if the British government did not. At the trial, Adams argued that the crowd had provoked the soldiers. His arguments convinced the jury. In the end, the heaviest punishment any soldier received was a branding on the hand.

Samuel Adams later expanded on the idea of a letter-writing campaign by forming a **committee of correspondence**. Members of the committee regularly wrote letters and pamphlets reporting to other colonies on events in Massachusetts. Within three months, there were 80 committees organized in Massachusetts. Before long, committees of correspondence became a major tool of protest in every colony.

The King Repeals Most Colonial Taxes By chance, on the very day of the Boston Massacre, a bill was introduced into Parliament to repeal most of the Townshend Acts. British merchants, harmed by the American boycott of British goods, had again pressured Parliament to end the taxes. The Quartering Act was repealed and most of the taxes that had angered the Americans were ended. However, King George III asked Parliament to retain the tax on tea.

▼ Crispus Attucks was one of five colonists killed at the Boston Massacre.

Growth of Colonial Cities

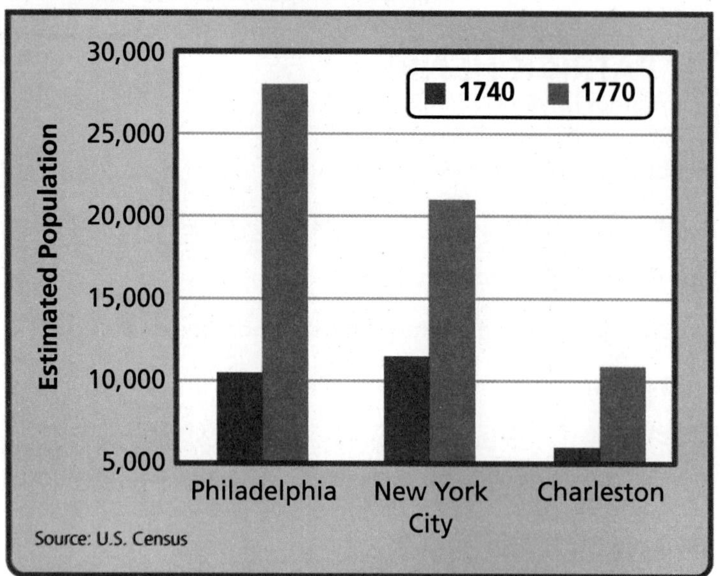

Analyze Charts Colonial cities grew both in size and density. **Use Visual Information** Which city was the largest in 1740? In 1770?

News of the repeal delighted the colonists. Most people dismissed the remaining tax on tea as unimportant and ended their boycott of British goods. For a few years, calm returned. Yet the angry debate over taxes had forced the colonists to begin thinking more carefully about their political rights.

READING CHECK **Identify Supporting Details** Why did John Adams choose to defend the British soldiers after the Boston Massacre?

An American Identity Develops

Before the French and Indian War, the colonists had lived mostly apart from British troops and were mainly content to be British subjects. After the war and with the debate over taxes, they grew to resent the British presence. The colonists had begun to see themselves as Americans, and the troops represented the British crown in their homeland.

The committees of correspondence and newspapers in New York, Boston, and Philadelphia kept people connected to what was happening in their cities and the British reactions to colonial unrest. Colonists felt more economically, politically, and socially tied to each other than to Britain.

READING CHECK **Recognize Multiple Causes** What caused the colonists to develop an identity as Americans?

Lesson Check

Practice Vocabulary

1. How did the colonists **boycott** and use **petitions** to get British tax laws **repealed**?
2. What role did the **committees of correspondence** play?

Critical Thinking and Writing

3. **Identify Supporting Details** What details about the colonists' response to the Stamp Act tell you that it was one cause of the American Revolution?
4. **Infer** Based on James Otis's response to British writs of assistance, what concerns did the colonists have about British searches?
5. **Understand Effects** How did the Boston Massacre influence the colonists' feelings toward Britain?
6. **Writing Workshop: Develop a Clear Thesis** Write a sentence in your Active Journal that explains why there was an American Revolution. This sentence will become the thesis statement for the essay you will write at the end of the Topic.

Primary Sources

John and Abigail Adams, Letters

Husband and wife John and Abigail Adams were key figures in the American Revolution and did much to further the Patriot cause. Below are excerpts from two of their letters to each other about the Declaration of Independence.

▶ Abigail Adams was an educated woman for her time. Her letters say much about her ideas about independence.

"Time has been given for the whole People, maturely to consider the great Question of Independence, and to ripen their judgment, ① dissipate their Fears, and allure their Hopes, by discussing it in Newspapers and Pamphlets, by debating it in Assemblies, Conventions, Committees of Safety and Inspection, in Town and County Meetings, as well as in private Conversations, ② so that the whole People, in every Colony of the thirteen, have now adopted it as their own Act. This will cement the Union . . . ."

—John Adams, Philadelphia, 3 July 1776

"I long to hear that you have declared an independency—and by the way in the new Code of Laws which I suppose it will be necessary for you to make I desire you would Remember the Ladies, and be more generous and ③ favourable to them than your ancestors. Do not put such unlimited power into the hands of the Husbands. Remember all Men would be tyrants if they could. If [particular] care and attention is not paid to the [Ladies] we are determined to foment a [Rebellion], and ④ will not hold ourselves bound by any Laws in which we have no voice, or Representation."

—Abigail Adams, Braintree, 31 March, 1776

Reading and Vocabulary Support

① *Dissipate* means "to make disappear."

② Who is John Adams including in his opinion that independence should be considered and accepted?

③ Some spellings in Abigail's letter are British spellings, and others may be spellings used at the time.

④ What phrase in Abigail's letter compares women's views on laws to the colonists' view on British laws?

Analyzing Primary Sources

Cite specific evidence from the letters to support your answers.

1. **Determine Author's Point of View** How does John Adams think that the colonists can form a unified opinion on the question of declaring independence from Britain?
2. **Determine Author's Purpose** What was Abigail's purpose in writing to her husband while he was a member of the Continental Congress?
3. **Draw Conclusions** What happened in 1776 that may have sparked Abigail's interest in women's rights?

LESSON 3

Taking Up Arms

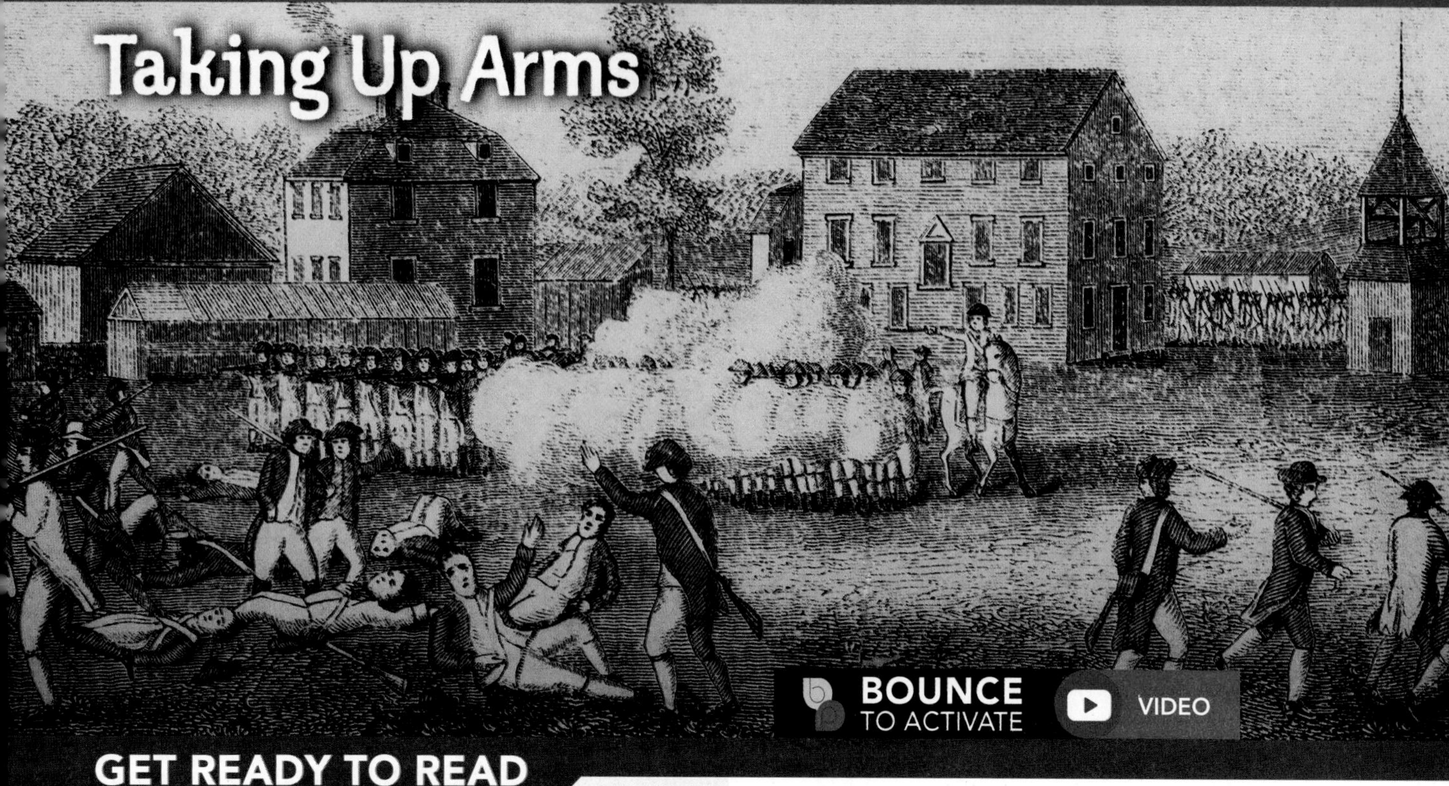

GET READY TO READ

START UP

Examine the illustration. Write a sentence contrasting the colonists with the British troops at Lexington.

GUIDING QUESTIONS

- What was the Boston Tea Party, and how did later British actions heighten tensions among the colonists?
- What actions were taken at the First and Second Continental Congresses?
- What advantages and disadvantages did each side have as the Revolutionary War began?

TAKE NOTES

Literacy Skills: Summarize

Use the graphic organizer in your Active Journal to take notes as you read the lesson.

PRACTICE VOCABULARY

Use the graphic organizer in your Active Journal to practice the vocabulary words.

Vocabulary		Academic Vocabulary
civil disobedience	Patriot	consequently
militia	Loyalist	approach
minutemen		

The calm between the colonies and England did not last long. Economic and political disputes continued, this time over a simple drink. Tea was tremendously popular in the colonies. By 1770, at least one million Americans brewed tea twice a day. People "would rather go without their dinners than without a dish of tea," a visitor to the colonies noted.

The Boston Tea Party

Since the 1720s, Parliament had given the British East India Company exclusive rights to sell tea to the American colonies. Parliament protected this by mandating that tea sold to the colonies had to be shipped to England first so taxes could be paid. Then the tea was shipped to colonial tea merchants for sale in the American colonies.

Mercantilist System This system met resistance due to the taxation of tea in the American colonies. Remember, to maintain its authority over the colonies, Parliament had kept a tax on tea when repealing the Townshend Acts. The tax was a small one, but colonists resented it.

As a result, many colonists refused to buy British tea. Also, the colonists were able to get cheaper tea directly from Dutch and French traders who smuggled it to American merchants.

Did you know?

The tea that the East India Company ships delivered to Boston Harbor came from China. There were five varieties and 340 chests of tea on board the ships *Beaver* and *Dartmouth*.

Mercantilist Policies Lead to the Tea Act In the 1770s, the British East India Company found itself in deep financial trouble, due in part to dwindling tea sales in the American colonies. As a result, more than 15 million pounds of tea sat unsold in British warehouses.

Parliament tried to help the British East India Company by passing the Tea Act of 1773. The act let the company bypass colonial tea merchants and sell directly to colonists.

The Tea Act also gave the British East India Company a rebate on tea taxes. Although colonists would still have to pay the tea tax, they would not have to pay the higher price charged by colonial tea merchants. As a result, the tea itself would cost less than ever before. Parliament hoped this would encourage Americans to buy more British tea.

To the surprise of Parliament, colonists protested the Tea Act. Many colonists were opposed to British mercantilist policies that were supposed to generate wealth for England by taxing the colonies. However, American tea merchants were especially angry because they had been cut out of the tea trade. They believed that allowing the government-sponsored British East India Company to sell tea to Americans violated their right to conduct free enterprise.

Even tea drinkers, who would have benefited from the law, scorned the Tea Act. They believed that it was a British trick to make them accept Parliament's right to tax the colonies.

A Boycott Against Tea Once again, colonists responded to the new law with a boycott. A Philadelphia poet, Hannah Griffitts, urged American women to:

Primary Source

"Stand firmly resolved and bid Grenville to see That rather than freedom we part with our tea, And well as we love the dear drink when a-dry, As American patriots our taste we deny."

—Hannah Griffitts in Milcah Martha Moore's *Commonplace Book*, 1773

Daughters of Liberty and women like Griffitts led the boycott. They served coffee or made "liberty tea" from raspberry leaves. At some ports, Sons of Liberty enforced the boycott by keeping the British East India Company from unloading cargoes of tea.

An Act of Civil Disobedience Three ships loaded with tea reached Boston Harbor in late November 1773. The colonial governor of Massachusetts, Thomas Hutchinson, insisted that they unload their cargo as usual.

Analyze Images The colonists loved tea but were prepared to give it up rather than pay British taxes on it. **Use Visual Information** What details about this tea cup from the 1700s lead you to believe that tea was important to the colonists?

Analyze Images On December 16, 1773, a group of colonists emptied hundreds of tea chests into Boston Harbor to protest British taxation. **Infer** Why might this act of civil disobedience mark a turning point?

Sam Adams and the Sons of Liberty had other plans. On the night of December 16, they met in Old South Meeting House. They sent a message to the governor, demanding that the ships leave the harbor. When the governor rejected the demand, Adams stood up and declared, "This meeting can do nothing further to save the country."

Adams's words seemed to be a signal. As if on cue, a group of men in American Indian disguises burst into the meetinghouse. From the gallery above, voices cried, "Boston harbor a teapot tonight! The Mohawks are come!"

The disguised colonists left the meetinghouse and headed for the harbor. Others joined them along the way. Under a nearly full moon, the men boarded the ships, split open the tea chests, and dumped the tea into the harbor.

By 10 P.M., the Boston Tea Party, as it was later called, was over. The contents of 342 chests of tea floated in Boston Harbor. The next day, John Adams wrote about the event in his diary.

Primary Source

"This destruction of the tea is so bold, so daring, so firm . . . it must have such important and lasting results that I can't help considering it a turning point in history."

—Diary of John Adams, December 17, 1773

The Boston Tea Party was an important act of **civil disobedience**. Civil disobedience is the nonviolent refusal to obey laws that one considers unjust. The colonists had many reasons for this act of civil disobedience. They wanted to voice their discontent to the British without hurting anyone. They also wanted to stop the tea from entering Boston. The impact of their civil disobedience was perhaps greater than they had expected. Harsh punishment would come from Britain.

READING CHECK **Identify Supporting Details** Why were many colonists dissatisfied with the Tea Act?

How Did King George III Strike Back at Boston?

Colonists had mixed reactions to the Boston Tea Party. Some cheered it as a firm protest against unfair British laws. Others worried that it would encourage lawlessness in the colonies. Even those who condemned the Boston Tea Party, though, were shocked at Britain's harsh response to it. The unrest in Boston and the British reaction to the Tea Party would be yet another cause of the Revolution.

The Intolerable Acts Anger Massachusetts The British were outraged by what they saw as Boston's lawless behavior. In 1774, Parliament, encouraged by King George III, acted to punish Massachusetts.

Colonists called the four laws they passed the Intolerable Acts because they were so harsh. These Acts pushed the colonists closer to revolution.

First, Parliament shut down the port of Boston. No ship could enter or leave the harbor—not even a small boat. The harbor would remain closed until the colonists paid for the tea they had destroyed in the Boston Tea Party and repaid British officials, such as Thomas Hutchinson, for damage to personal property. Boston's harbor was central to the life of the city. With the closing of the port, merchants could not sell their goods, and **consequently**, the colony's economy suffered.

Academic Vocabulary
consequently • *adv.*, as a result

Second, Parliament forbade Massachusetts colonists to hold town meetings more than once a year without the governor's permission. In the past, colonists had called town meetings whenever they wished. Public officials would now be selected by the king's governor rather than be elected by citizens.

Third, Parliament allowed customs officers and other officials who might be charged with major crimes to be tried in Britain or Canada instead of in Massachusetts. Colonists protested. They argued that a dishonest official could break the law in the colonies and avoid punishment by being tried before a sympathetic jury.

Fourth, Parliament passed a new Quartering Act. No longer would redcoats camp in tents on Boston Common. Instead, colonists would have to house British soldiers in their homes when no other housing was available. Colonists viewed this act as yet another tax, because they had to house and feed the soldiers. Many objected to having the British army stationed in the colonies at all.

▼ Following the Boston Tea Party, British warships closed the port of Boston. Parliament demanded that colonists repay the damages from the loss of tea before they would reopen the port.

▲ The First Continental Congress met in September 1774, at Carpenters' Hall in Philadelphia. The delegates resolved to suspend trade with Britain and encouraged the colonies to form small armies of citizens called militias.

Benjamin Franklin's sister, Jane Mecum, wrote to her brother complaining of the British troops and their behavior in Boston:

Primary Source

"... But at present we have a m[e]lancholy Prospect for this winter at Least the towns being so full of Profl[i]gate [soldiers] and many such officers there is hardly four and twenty hours Pas[s]es without some fray amongst them and [one] can walk but a lit[t]le way in the street without hearing th[eir] Profane language."

—Letter from Jane Franklin Mecum to Benjamin Franklin, November 21, 1774

The Quebec Act Redraws Borders Parliament also passed the Quebec Act. It set up a government for Canada and gave complete religious freedom to French Catholics. The Quebec Act also extended the borders of Quebec to include the land between the Ohio and Mississippi rivers. The act pleased French Canadians. American colonists were angry, however, because some of the colonies claimed these lands.

The Intolerable Acts Draw Other Colonies Into the Struggle The committees of correspondence spread news of the Intolerable Acts to other colonies. They warned that the people of Boston faced hunger while their port was closed. People from other colonies responded by sending rice from South Carolina, corn from Virginia, and flour from Pennsylvania.

In the Virginia Assembly, Thomas Jefferson suggested that a day be set aside to mark the shame of the Intolerable Acts. The royal governor of Virginia rejected the idea. However, on June 1, 1774, church bells tolled slowly. Merchants closed their shops. Many colonists prayed and fasted all day.

In September 1774, colonial leaders called a meeting in Philadelphia. Delegates from 12 colonies gathered in what became known as the First Continental Congress. Only Georgia did not send delegates.

After much debate, the delegates passed a resolution backing Massachusetts in its struggle. They agreed to boycott all British goods and to stop exporting goods to Britain until the Intolerable Acts were repealed. The delegates also urged each colony to set up and train its own militia (mih LISH uh). A **militia** is an army of citizens who serve as soldiers during an emergency.

Before leaving Philadelphia, the delegates agreed to meet again in May 1775. Little did they suspect that before then, an incident in Massachusetts would change the fate of the colonies forever.

READING CHECK **Identify Main Ideas** How did other colonies respond to the Intolerable Acts?

The Battles of Lexington and Concord

In Massachusetts, colonists were already preparing to resist. Newspapers called on citizens to prevent what they called "the Massacre of American Liberty." Volunteers known as **minutemen** trained regularly. Minutemen got their name because they kept their muskets at hand and were prepared to fight at a minute's notice. In towns near Boston, minutemen collected weapons and gunpowder. Meanwhile, Britain built up its forces. More troops arrived in Boston, bringing the total number of British soldiers in that city to 4,000.

Early in 1775, General Thomas Gage, the British commander, sent scouts to towns near Boston. They reported that minutemen had a large store of arms in Concord, a village about 18 miles from Boston. Gage planned a surprise march to Concord to seize the arms.

The Redcoats Cross the Charles River On April 18, about 700 British troops quietly left Boston in the darkness. Their goal was to seize the colonial arms. The Sons of Liberty were watching. As soon as the British set out, the Americans hung two lamps from the Old North Church in Boston. This signal meant that the redcoats were crossing the Charles River. The British had decided to cross the river rather than take a much longer route toward Concord by land.

Colonists who were waiting across the Charles River saw the signal. Messengers mounted their horses and galloped through the night toward Concord. One midnight rider was Paul Revere. "The redcoats are coming! The redcoats are coming!" shouted Revere as he passed through each sleepy village along the way.

▼ This statue honors Paul Revere and his ride to warn the colonists.

Fighting in Lexington and Concord At daybreak on April 19, the redcoats reached Lexington, a town near Concord. On the village green, some 70 minutemen were waiting, commanded by Captain John Parker. The British ordered the minutemen to go home. Outnumbered, the colonists began to leave the village green.

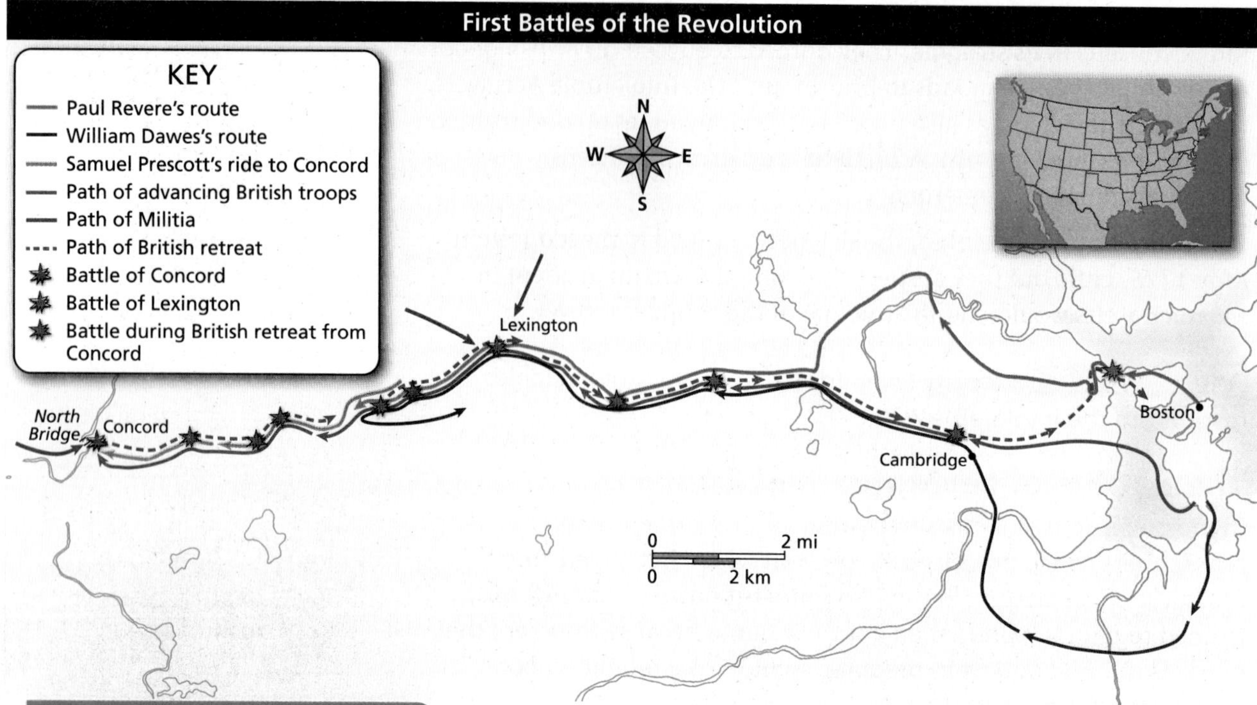

GEOGRAPHY SKILLS

The first battles the colonists fought were in Lexington and Concord, Massachusetts.

1. **Place** What geographic feature did the British encounter on their advance route but not on their retreat?
2. **Summarize** Why were the minutemen so prepared for the arrival of the British troops in Concord?

Suddenly, a shot rang out. No one knows who fired it. In the brief struggle that followed, eight colonists were killed.

The British pushed on to Concord. Finding no arms in the village, they turned back to Boston. On a bridge outside Concord, they met approximately 300 minutemen. Again, fighting broke out. This time, the British were forced to retreat because the minutemen used the geography of the region to their advantage. As the redcoats withdrew, colonial sharpshooters took deadly aim at them from the woods, making it difficult for the British soldiers to fire back. Local women also fired at the British from the windows of their homes. By the time they reached Boston, the redcoats had lost 73 men. Another 200 British soldiers were wounded or missing.

News of the battles of Lexington and Concord spread swiftly. To many colonists, the fighting ended all hope of a peaceful settlement. Only war would decide the future of the 13 colonies.

More than 60 years after the battles of Lexington and Concord, a well-known New England writer, Ralph Waldo Emerson, wrote a poem honoring the minutemen. Emerson's "Concord Hymn" created a vivid picture of the clash at Concord. It begins:

Primary Source

"By the rude bridge that arched the flood,
Their flag to April's breeze unfurled,
Here once the embattled farmers stood,
And fired the shot heard round the world."

—Ralph Waldo Emerson, "Concord Hymn," 1837

The "embattled farmers" would have years of difficult fighting in front of them. Lexington and Concord marked the beginning of the Revolutionary War.

The war and disagreements between the American colonists and the British prior to the war represent the era called the American Revolution. This period of struggle led to independence from Britain.

READING CHECK **Identify Cause and Effect** How were the minutemen able to defeat the British at Concord?

The Fighting Continues

Just a few weeks after the battles at Lexington and Concord, on May 10, 1775, colonial delegates met at the Second Continental Congress in Philadelphia. The delegates represented the 13 British colonies from New Hampshire to Georgia. Most of the delegates still hoped to avoid a final break with Britain. However, while the delegates were meeting, the fighting spread.

Quest CONNECTIONS

An olive branch is a symbol of peace. How might the colonists react to George III's response to their petition? Record your findings in your Active Journal.

King George III Rejects Peace After much debate, the delegates sent a petition to King George. In the Olive Branch Petition, they declared their loyalty to the king and asked him to repeal the Intolerable Acts.

George III was furious when he heard about the petition. The colonists, he raged, were trying to begin a war "for the purpose of establishing an independent empire!" The king vowed to bring the rebels to justice. He ordered 20,000 more troops to the colonies to crush the revolt.

Congress did not learn of the king's response until months later. But even before the petition was sent, leaders like John and Sam Adams were convinced that war could not be avoided.

Vermont Rebels Gain a Route to Canada Ethan Allen, a Vermont blacksmith, did not wait for Congress to act. Allen decided to lead a band of Vermonters, known as the Green Mountain Boys, in a surprise attack on Fort Ticonderoga, located at the southern tip of Lake Champlain. Allen knew that the fort held cannons that the colonists could use, and its strategic location would help colonists control the region.

In early May, the Green Mountain Boys crept quietly through the morning mists to Fort Ticonderoga. They quickly overpowered the guard on duty and entered the fort. Allen rushed to the room where the British commander slept. "Come out, you old rat!" he shouted. The commander demanded to know by whose authority Allen acted. "In the name of the Great Jehovah and the Continental Congress!" Allen replied.

The British commander surrendered Ticonderoga. By capturing the fort, the Green Mountain Boys won a valuable supply of cannons and gunpowder. Allen's success also gave Americans control of a key route into Canada.

Analyze Images When King George III, seen here, read the Olive Branch Petition from the colonists, he was so angered by the colonists' actions that he sent even more troops to North America. **Infer** How do you think the colonists will react to more troops coming to their cities and towns?

Advantages & Disadvantages of the British and Colonists

George Washington Takes Command In the meantime, the Second Continental Congress had to decide what to do about the makeshift army gathering around Boston. In June, delegates took the bold step of setting up the Continental Army. They appointed George Washington of Virginia as commander.

READING CHECK **Identify Supporting Details** Why was Fort Ticonderoga important to the colonists?

Opposing Sides at War

The colonists who favored war against Britain called themselves **Patriots**. They thought British rule was harsh and unjust. About one third of the colonists were Patriots, one third sided with the British, and one third did not take sides.

Academic Vocabulary
approach • *v.*, to come near

Washington Leads the Patriots The Patriots entered the war with many disadvantages. Colonial forces were poorly organized and untrained. They had few cannons, little gunpowder, and no navy. Also, few colonists wanted to enlist in the Continental Army for long terms of service. They preferred to fight near home with a local militia.

Yet, the Patriots also had advantages. Many Patriots owned rifles and were good shots. Their leader, George Washington, had experience and developed into an able commander. Furthermore, Patriots were determined to fight to defend their homes and property. Reuben Stebbins of Massachusetts was typical of many patriotic farmers. When the British **approached**, he rode off to battle. "We'll see who's going t'own this farm!" he cried.

Analyze Charts The Revolutionary War was largely a fight between the colonists and the British. **Draw Conclusions** Why was it also a fight between the colonists themselves?

★ AMERICANS IN CONFLICT ★

The **Revolutionary War** was also a conflict between groups living in the colonies. During the Revolution, families fought each other. Communities were split apart.

1775-1783
80,000 to 100,000 **Loyalists** left the colonies during the war.

1760
Everyone is a Tory and supports the King.

1775
The War begins . . . relatives, friends, and neighbors take sides.

1776
Population of the United States is 2.5 million.

Source: United States Census Bureau

★★★★★ PATRIOTS ★★★★★

- Called **Rebels** by the Loyalists
- Felt oppressed by British rule and taxation
- Led by well-educated and wealthy individuals
- Supported Declaration of Independence and freedom from British rule

★★★★★ LOYALISTS ★★★★★

- Called **Tories** by the Patriots
- Mostly government officials, merchants, bankers, and tradesmen who had financial interests in maintaining British rule
- Felt it was morally wrong to oppose the King
- Started their own fighting regiments that were not part of the British Army

British Advantages and Disadvantages The British were a powerful foe. They had highly trained, experienced troops. Their navy was the best in the world. Also, many colonists supported them.

Still, Britain faced problems. Its armies were 3,000 miles from home. News and supplies took months to travel from Britain to North America. Also, British soldiers risked attacks by colonial militias once they marched out of the cities into the countryside.

Loyalists Favor the King American colonists who remained loyal to Britain were known as **Loyalists**. They included wealthy merchants and former officials of the royal government. However, some farmers and craftsworkers were also Loyalists. There were more Loyalists in the Middle Colonies and the South than in New England.

Loyalists faced hard times during the war. Patriots tarred and feathered people known to favor the British. Many Loyalists fled to England or Canada. Others found shelter in cities controlled by the British. Those who fled lost their homes, stores, and farms.

▲ As commander of the Continental Army, Washington knew that he would be fighting against one of the world's toughest armies. He set off at once to take charge of the forces around Boston.

READING CHECK **Identify Main Ideas** What positions did colonists take in regard to the war as it began?

Lesson Check

Practice Vocabulary

1. Contrast the **Patriots** and the **Loyalists**.
2. Explain how **militia** and **minutemen** played a role in the fighting between colonists and the British.

Critical Thinking and Writing

3. **Recognize Multiple Causes** Why did the colonists choose to throw British tea into Boston Harbor?
4. **Infer** Why did Ralph Waldo Emerson call the first shot fired in Lexington "the shot heard round the world"?
5. **Summarize** How did King George react to the Olive Branch Petition?
6. **Writing Workshop: Support Thesis with Details** Think of details—facts, events, ideas—that support the thesis statement you wrote about why there was an American Revolution. Write down as many solid details as you can in your Active Journal.

Compare Different Points of View

Follow these steps to compare different points of view.

Compare Viewpoints

1 **Identify the event and the different points of view.** What is the issue that these points of view are addressing? Use what you know about Thomas Paine to assess his motivation for writing *Common Sense*.

2 **Identify the facts in each point of view.** Facts are statements that can be proved to be true. When both points of view agree about something, it is probably a fact. Does either point of view contain a fact or facts? If so, what are they?

3 **Identify the opinions in each point of view.** What is Inglis's opinion? Paine's? What words does Paine use to persuade the reader to adopt Paine's point of view?

4 **Develop your own opinion about the event.** Your opinion should be based on the facts and what you know about the people giving the opinions.

Primary Source

By a declaration for independency, every avenue to an accommodation with Great Britain would be closed. The sword only could then decide the quarrel, and the sword would not be sheathed till one had conquered the other. Besides the unsuitableness of the republican form to the genius of the people, America is too extensive for it. That form may do well enough for a single city, or small territory; but would be utterly improper for such a continent as this. America is too unwieldy for the feeble, dilatory [unhurried] administration of democracy.

—Charles Inglis, *The Deceiver Unmasked*, 1776

Primary Source

I challenge the warmest advocate for reconciliation to show a single advantage that this continent can reap by being connected with Great Britain. I repeat the challenge; not a single advantage is derived. ... Everything that is right or reasonable pleads for separation. The blood of the slain, the weeping voice of nature cries: 'TIS TIME TO PART.

—Thomas Paine, *Common Sense*, 1776

LESSON 4

The Move Toward Independence

GET READY TO READ

START UP

Examine the illustration of crowds celebrating the reading of the Declaration of Independence. Write a question you have about the Declaration.

GUIDING QUESTIONS

- What are the main ideas of the Declaration of Independence?
- What challenges faced the Continental Army at the beginning of the war?
- What helped turn the tide of the war?

TAKE NOTES

Literacy Skills: Use Evidence

Use the graphic organizer in your Active Journal to take notes as you read the lesson.

PRACTICE VOCABULARY

Use the vocabulary activity in your Active Journal to practice the vocabulary words.

Vocabulary		Academic Vocabulary
blockade	natural rights	evident
mercenary	unalienable rights	ensure
traitor		
preamble		

Lexington and Concord marked the start of armed conflict between colonists and the British—the beginning of the American Revolution. As the fighting spread, many colonists came to believe that Parliament did not have the right to make any laws for the 13 colonies. After all, they argued, the colonies had their own elected legislatures. Many felt it was time for the colonies to become completely independent from Britain.

The War Comes to Boston

During the first year of conflict, much of the fighting centered around Boston. About 6,000 British troops were stationed there. Colonial militia surrounded the city and prevented the British from marching out.

War Breaks Out Near Boston Harbor

Even before Washington reached Boston, the Patriots took action. On June 16, 1775, Colonel William Prescott led 1,200 minutemen up Bunker Hill, across the Charles River from Boston. From there, they could fire on British ships in Boston Harbor. Prescott, however, noticed that nearby Breed's Hill was an even better place.

Analyze Images In this illustration, British military forces clash with colonial militia atop Breed's Hill during the Battle of Bunker Hill on June 17, 1775. **Synthesize Visual Information** Which forces did the artist want the viewer to believe were winning this battle? State visual clues that support your answer.

He could use the local geography to his advantage. A hilltop would be easier to defend, so he ordered his men to move there.

At sunrise, the British general, William Howe, spotted the Americans. He ferried about 2,400 redcoats across the river to attack the rebels' position. As the British approached, the Patriots held their fire.

When the Americans finally fired, the British were forced to retreat. A second British attack was also turned back. On the third try, the British pushed over the top. They took both Bunker Hill and Breed's Hill, but they paid a high price for their victory. More than 1,000 redcoats lay dead or wounded. American losses numbered only about 400.

The Battle of Bunker Hill was the first major battle of the Revolution. It proved that the Americans could fight bravely. It also showed that the British would not be easy to defeat. Furthermore, it hinted that one effect of the Revolution would be continued bloodshed from a long and bitter war.

Washington Forces the British out of Boston When Washington reached Boston a few weeks after the Battle of Bunker Hill, he found about 16,000 troops camped in huts and tents around the city.

Thomas Paine's *Common Sense*

General Washington quickly began to turn raw recruits into a trained army. His job was especially difficult because soldiers from different colonies mistrusted one another. He wrote about their behavior.

"Connecticut wants no Massachusetts men in her corps." And "Massachusetts thinks there is no necessity for a Rhode Islander to be introduced into her [ranks]." However, Washington won the loyalty of his troops. They, in turn, learned to take orders and work together.

In January 1776, Washington had a stroke of good fortune. The cannons that the Green Mountain Boys had captured at Fort Ticonderoga arrived in Boston. Soldiers had dragged them across the mountains from Fort Ticonderoga. Washington had the cannons placed in a strategic location on Dorchester Heights, overlooking the harbor.

Once General Howe saw the American cannons in place, he knew that he could not hold Boston. In March 1776, he and his troops sailed from Boston to Halifax, Canada. About 1,000 American Loyalists went with them.

Although the British left New England, they did not give up. King George III ordered a blockade of all colonial ports. A **blockade** is the shutting of a port to keep people or supplies from moving in or out. The king also used **mercenaries**, or troops for hire, from Germany to help fight the colonists.

READING CHECK **Identify Supporting Details** How did the colonists use the physical geography of Boston to their advantage?

What Did Thomas Paine Say in *Common Sense*?

Thomas Paine was a British writer and editor who moved to Philadelphia in 1774. After Lexington and Concord, Paine wrote the pamphlet *Common Sense*, in which he set out to change the colonists' attitudes toward Britain and the king. Colonists, he said, did not owe loyalty to George III or any other monarch. The very idea of having kings and queens was wrong, he said.

Primary Source

"In England a King hath little more to do than to make war and give away [jobs]; which in plain terms, is to impoverish the nation. . . . Of more worth is one honest man to society and in the sight of God, than all the crowned ruffians that ever lived."

—Thomas Paine, *Common Sense*, 1776

▼ Thomas Paine's criticism of British rule in *Common Sense* prompted many colonists to consider the option of declaring full independence from Britain.

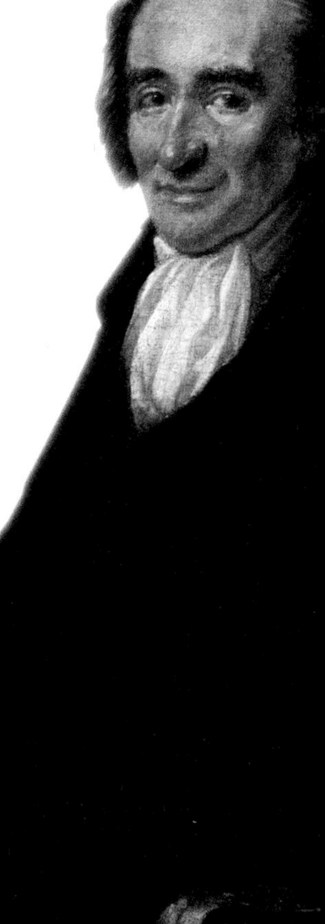

The colonists did not owe anything to Britain, either, Paine went on. If the British had helped the colonists, they had done so for their own profit. It could only hurt the colonists to remain under British rule. "Everything that is right or reasonable pleads for separation," he concluded. " 'Tis time to part." *Common Sense* was a great success, selling over 500,000 copies in six months. Paine's writing played an important role in moving toward revolution.

READING CHECK **Identify Main Ideas** What was the main idea of *Common Sense*?

What Steps Did Colonial Leaders Take Toward Independence?

Common Sense caused many colonial leaders to move toward declaring independence from Britain. It also deeply impressed many members of the Continental Congress. Richard Henry Lee of Virginia wrote to Washington, "I am now convinced . . . of the necessity for separation." In June 1776, Lee rose to his feet in Congress to introduce a resolution in favor of independence:

Primary Source

"*Resolved,* That these United Colonies are and of right ought to be, free and independent States, that they are absolved from all allegiance to the British Crown, and that all political connection between them and the State of Great Britain is, and ought to be, totally dissolved."

—Richard Henry Lee, Resolution at the Second Continental Congress, June 7, 1776

Analyze Images Thomas Jefferson labored several days writing the Declaration of Independence. In this painting, Jefferson and other committee members present the Declaration to the Continental Congress. **Infer** Why do you think a painting was made of this particular event?

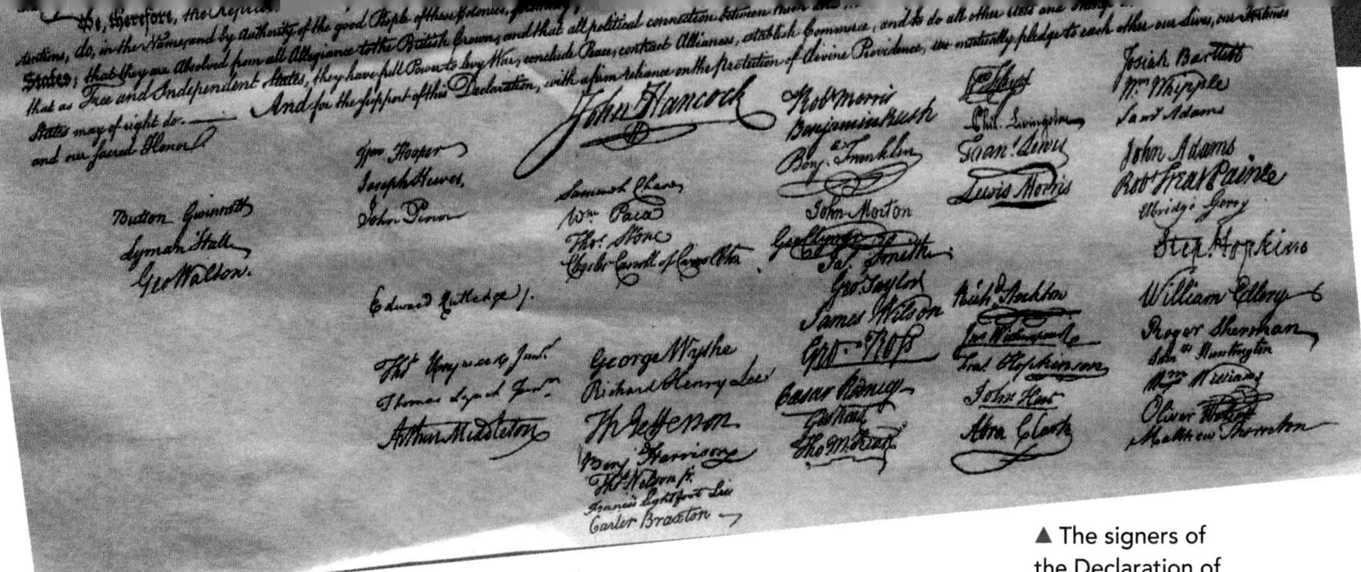

▲ The signers of the Declaration of Independence

Drafting the Declaration of Independence The delegates faced a difficult decision. There could be no turning back once they declared independence. If they fell into British hands, they would be hanged as traitors. A **traitor** is a person who betrays his or her country.

After long debate, the Congress took a fateful step. It appointed a committee to draft a formal declaration of independence. The committee included John Adams, Benjamin Franklin, Thomas Jefferson, Robert Livingston, and Roger Sherman. Their job was to tell the world why the colonies were breaking away from Britain.

The committee asked Thomas Jefferson to write the document. Jefferson was one of the youngest delegates. He was a quiet man who spoke little at formal meetings.

Among friends, however, he liked to sprawl in a chair with his long legs stretched out and talk for hours. His ability to write clearly and gracefully had earned him great respect.

Quick Activity

See how the delegates edited Jefferson's language to the preamble in your Active Journal.

Adopting the Declaration of Independence In late June, Jefferson completed the Declaration, and it was read to the Congress. On July 2, the Continental Congress voted that the 13 colonies were "free and independent States." After polishing Jefferson's language, the delegates adopted the document on the night of July 4, 1776. They then ordered the Declaration of Independence to be printed.

 **INTERACTIVE**

Interactive Declaration of Independence

John Hancock, president of the Continental Congress, signed the Declaration first. He penned his signature boldly, in large, clear letters. "There," he said, "I guess King George will be able to read that."

Copies of the Declaration were distributed throughout the colonies. Patriots greeted the news of independence with joyous—and sometimes rowdy—celebrations.

In New York, colonists tore down a statue of King George III. In Boston, the sound of cannons could be heard for hours.

Did you know?

The Declaration of Independence was not actually signed on July 4, but on August 2.

READING CHECK **Understand Effects** What were the potential consequences for the delegates who chose to declare independence?

▲ Bells such as these were rung at the reading of the Declaration of Independence.

The Declaration of Independence

The Declaration of Independence consists of a **preamble**, or introduction, followed by three main parts.

Unalienable Human Rights The first section of the Declaration stresses the idea of **natural rights**, or rights that belong to all people from birth. In bold, ringing words, Jefferson wrote:

Primary Source

"We hold these truths to be self-evident, that all men are created equal; that they are endowed by their Creator with certain unalienable rights; that among these are life, liberty, and the pursuit of happiness."

—The Declaration of Independence

According to the Declaration of Independence, people form governments in order to protect their natural rights and liberties. Some of these principles were also part of the Magna Carta, a document that challenged the power of King John of England 500 years before the writing of the Declaration.

These **unalienable rights**—including the rights to be free and to choose how to live—cannot be taken away by governments, for governments can exist only if they have the "consent of the governed." If a government fails to protect the rights of its citizens, then it is the people's "right [and] duty, to throw off such government, and to provide new guards for their future security." Ideas such as unalienable rights, adopted by the Founding Fathers (men such as George Washington, John Adams, Benjamin Franklin, and Thomas Jefferson), are good examples of the civic virtues that have since become the cornerstone of American government. These values continue to **ensure** that human rights are protected and human needs are met in our nation.

Academic Vocabulary

evident • *adj.*, obvious, apparent

ensure • *v.*, to make certain, to secure

Colonial Grievances The second part of the Declaration lists the wrongs, or grievances, that led the Americans to break away from Britain. Jefferson condemned King George III for disbanding colonial legislatures and for sending troops to the colonies in peacetime. He complained about limits on trade and about taxes imposed without the consent of the people.

Jefferson listed many other grievances to show why the colonists had the right to rebel. He also pointed out that the colonies had petitioned the king to correct these injustices. Yet, the injustices remained. A ruler who treated his subjects in this manner, he boldly concluded, is a tyrant and not fit to rule:

Primary Source

"In every state of these oppressions, we have petitioned for redress [remedy] in the most humble terms; our repeated petitions have been answered only by repeated injury. A prince whose character is thus marked by every act which may define a tyrant is unfit to be the ruler of a free people."

—The Declaration of Independence

Independence The last part of the Declaration announces that the colonies are the United States of America. All political ties with Britain have been cut.

As a free and independent nation, the United States has the full power to "levy war, conclude peace, contract alliances, establish commerce, and to do all other acts and things which independent states may of right do."

The signers closed the declaration with a solemn pledge: "And, for the support of this declaration, with a firm reliance on the protection of Divine Providence, we mutually pledge to each other our lives, our fortunes, and our sacred honor."

READING CHECK **Identify Main Ideas** What are some of the grievances Jefferson included in the Declaration?

Analyze Images Benjamin Franklin created this illustration encouraging colonists to band together in 1754 during the French and Indian War. It was later used for the same purpose during the American Revolution. **Draw Conclusions** What about this image made it appropriate and popular during the Revolutionary War era?

Analyze Images The British hired Hessian mercenaries to compensate for a shortage of British troops. At the time, British troops were fighting in other wars. **Identify Cause and Effect** What would be the effect of Britain hiring mercenaries to fight in North America?

What Challenges Faced the Continental Army?

Through an odd coincidence, the British began landing troops in New York in the same month that the Continental Congress voted for independence, July 1776. General George Washington, expecting the attack, had led his forces south from Boston to New York City. His army, however, was no match for the British under the command of General Howe. Howe had about 34,000 troops and 10,000 sailors. He also had ships to ferry them ashore. Washington had fewer than 20,000 poorly trained troops, which he spread in various locations to defend New York. Worse, he had no navy.

An Early Defeat In August, Howe's army landed on Long Island. In the Battle of Long Island, more than 1,400 Americans were killed, wounded, or captured. The rest retreated to Manhattan. The British pursued. To avoid capture, Washington hurried north.

Throughout the autumn, Washington fought a series of battles with Howe's army. In November, he crossed the Hudson River into New Jersey. Chased by the British, the Americans retreated across the Delaware River into Pennsylvania.

Early Heroes During the campaign for New York, Washington needed information about Howe's forces. Nathan Hale, a young Connecticut officer, volunteered to go behind British lines. On his way back with the information, Hale was seized by the British and searched. Hidden in the soles of his shoes was information about British troop movements.

There was no trial. Howe ordered Hale to be hanged the next morning. As Hale walked to the gallows, he is said to have declared: "I only regret that I have but one life to lose for my country."

Even as Washington's army retreated and the British took New York City, many people there remained as loyal to the American cause as Hale. Haym Salomon (HY um SAL uh mun), was a Jewish immigrant.

He came from Poland, was arrested by the British in September 1776 and thrown into prison. Salomon had supported the American cause from the start, helping the new government get loans. Salomon even gave his own money to soldiers for equipment. He managed to escape to Philadelphia and continued to aid the fight.

▲ Haym Salomon helped the Patriots' cause and was imprisoned by the British for it.

READING CHECK **Identify Main Ideas** What advantage did the British have in the Battle of Long Island?

A Surprise Attack Leads to Victory

Months of hard campaigning took a toll on the Continental Army. In December 1776, Washington described his troops as sick, dirty, and "so thinly clad as to be unfit for service." Every day, soldiers deserted. Washington wrote to his brother: "I am wearied to death."

Washington then decided on a bold move: a surprise attack on Trenton, New Jersey. The Delaware River separated the British in Trenton and the Americans, and the soldiers guarding Trenton would not expect American troops to cross it. On Christmas night, Washington secretly led his troops across the icy river. Soldiers shivered as spray from the river froze on their faces. Once ashore, they marched through swirling snow. Some had no shoes. They tied rags around their feet. "Soldiers, keep by your officers," Washington urged.

Early on December 26, the Americans surprised the Hessian troops guarding Trenton and took most of them prisoner. The Hessians were soldiers from Germany. An American summed up the Battle of Trenton: "Hessian population of Trenton at 8 A.M.—1,408 men and 39 officers; Hessian population at 9 A.M.—0."

Continental vs. British Forces

	CONTINENTAL	BRITISH
TOTAL FORCES	about 90,000 as a peak estimate	more than 70,000
COMPOSITION OF FORCES	Continental Army, State Militias	Army, Navy, hired mercenaries
ALLIES	France, Spain	Native Americans, Loyalists
QUALITY OF FORCES	untrained, unconventional	trained, disciplined
MOTIVATION	freedom from British control	regain British control
SUPPLIES	very limited weapons, food, and clothing	better availability of weapons, food, and clothing, but moving supplies was difficult

Analyze Charts Study the chart. **Summarize** Which forces, the Continental or the British, appear to be better prepared for battle? Why?

▲ At the Battle of Bennington in August 1777, the Continental Army defeated part of John Burgoyne's army.

British General Charles Cornwallis set out at once to retake Trenton and to capture Washington. Late on January 2, 1777, he saw the lights of Washington's campfires. "At last we have run down the old fox," he said, "and we will bag him in the morning."

Washington fooled Cornwallis. He left the fires burning and slipped behind British lines to attack a British force that was marching toward Princeton. There, the Continental Army won another victory. From Princeton, Washington moved to Morristown, where the army would spend the winter. The victories at Trenton and Princeton gave the Americans new hope.

READING CHECK **Identify Supporting Details** What advantages did Washington have in the Battle of Trenton?

▼ General John Burgoyne surrenders to General Horatio Gates after the British defeat at Saratoga.

How Did the Tide Turn for the Americans?

In London, British officials were dismayed by the army's failure to crush the rebels. Early in 1777, General John Burgoyne (bur GOIN) presented a new plan for victory. If British troops cut off New England from the other colonies, he argued, the war would soon be over.

The New England Strategy Burgoyne wanted three British armies to march on Albany, New York, from different directions to crush American forces there. Once they controlled the Hudson River, the British could stop the flow of soldiers and supplies from New England to Washington's army.

Burgoyne's plan called for General Howe to march on Albany from New York City. George III, however, wanted Howe to capture Philadelphia first.

In July 1777, Howe sailed from New York to the Chesapeake Bay, where he began his march on Philadelphia. Howe captured Philadelphia, defeating the Americans at the battles of Brandywine and Germantown. But instead of moving toward Albany to meet Burgoyne as planned, he retired to comfortable quarters in Philadelphia for the winter. For his part, Washington retreated to Valley Forge, Pennsylvania.

Meanwhile, British armies under Burgoyne and Barry St. Leger (lay ZHAIR) marched from Canada toward Albany. St. Leger tried to take Fort Stanwix. However, a strong American army, led by Benedict Arnold, drove him back.

American Troops Prevail at Saratoga Only Burgoyne was left to march on Albany. His army moved slowly because it had many heavy baggage carts to drag through the woods. To slow Burgoyne further, Patriots cut down trees and dammed up streams to block the route.

Despite these obstacles, Burgoyne recaptured Fort Ticonderoga, shocking Americans. However, he delayed at the fort, giving American forces time to regroup. He also sent troops into Vermont to find food and horses. There, Patriots attacked the redcoats. At the Battle of Bennington, they wounded or captured nearly 1,000 British.

GEOGRAPHY **SKILLS**

The battles of the American Revolution took place in every region of the 13 colonies.

1. **Region** During the early years of the war, in what region did the fighting mostly take place?
2. **Summarize** What were the results of the battles of 1777 that were part of General Burgoyne's plan?

Key Battles of the Revolutionary War

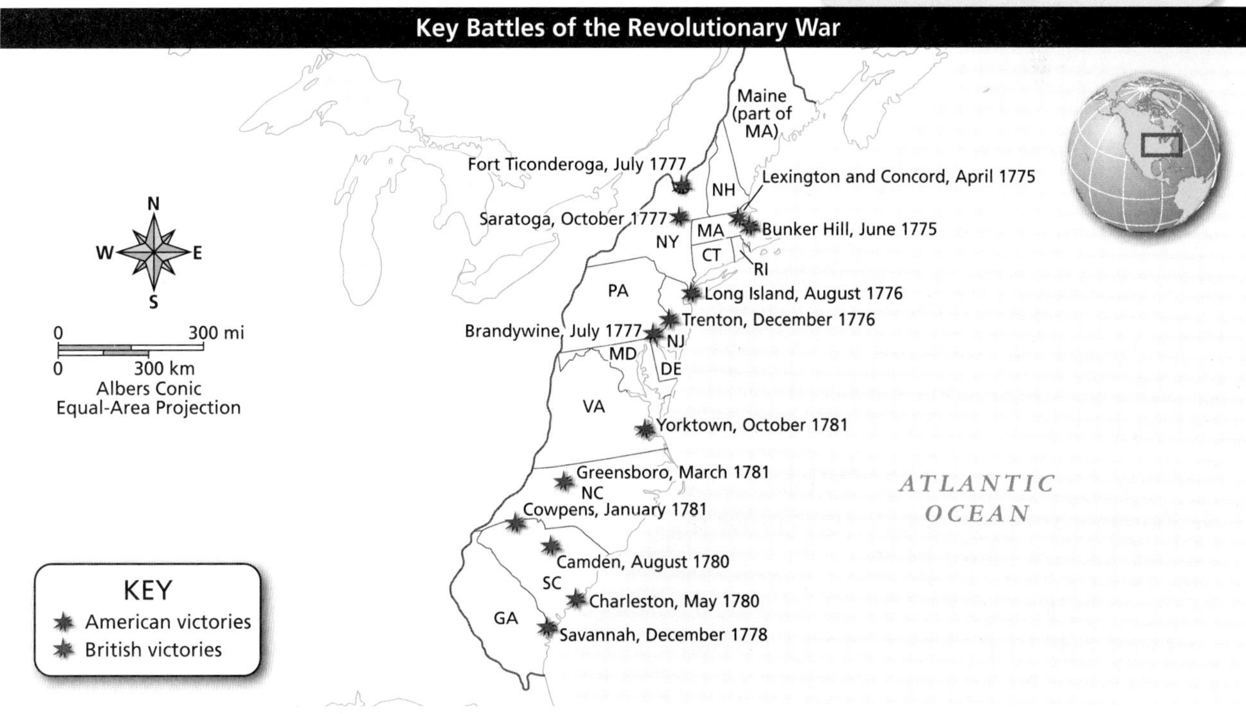

▲ King Louis XVI of France aided the American Revolution, but he would later face revolution in his own country.

Burgoyne's troubles grew. The Green Mountain Boys hurried into New York to help American forces there. At the village of Saratoga, the Americans surrounded the British. When Burgoyne tried to break free, the Americans beat him back. Realizing that he was trapped, Burgoyne surrendered his entire army to the Americans on October 17, 1777.

The American victory at the Battle of Saratoga was a major turning point in the war. It ended the British threat to New England. It boosted American spirits at a time when Washington's army was suffering defeats. Most importantly, it convinced France to become an ally of the United States. Nations that are allies work together to achieve a common goal.

France Aids the American Cause The Continental Congress had long hoped for French aid. In 1776, the Congress had sent Benjamin Franklin to Paris to persuade Louis XVI, the French king, to give the Americans weapons and other badly needed supplies. In addition, the Congress wanted France to declare war on Britain.

The French were eager to defeat Britain, but they were also cautious. Louis XVI did not want to help the Americans openly unless he was sure that they could win. The American victory at Saratoga convinced France that the United States could stand up to Britain. In February 1778, France became the first nation to sign a treaty with the United States. It recognized the new nation and agreed to provide military aid.

READING CHECK **Identify Cause and Effect** Why was the American victory at Saratoga significant to the Patriots?

Lesson Check

Practice Vocabulary

1. What role did the concept of **natural rights** play in the American Revolution and the Declaration of Independence?
2. What are **unalienable rights**?

Critical Thinking and Writing

3. **Summarize** What was the significance of the Battle of Bunker Hill?
4. **Identify Main Ideas** What was the main point of Thomas Paine's *Common Sense*, and how did he support this idea?
5. **Explain an Argument** What justifications for separation were included in the Declaration of Independence?
6. **Summarize** What advantages and disadvantages did the Continental Army have at the beginning of the war?
7. **Writing Workshop: Pick an Organizing Strategy** Decide on the best way to organize the supporting details you have listed to explain why there was an American Revolution. Note this organization in your Active Journal.

Primary Sources

Thomas Paine, *Common Sense*

Thomas Paine's pamphlet *Common Sense* stirred the emotions of colonists and rallied many to the Patriot cause.

▶ Thomas Paine is called one of the Founding Fathers of the United States.

I have heard it asserted by some, that as America hath flourished under her former connection with Great Britain, that the same connection is necessary towards her future happiness, and will always have the same effect. Nothing can be more ① fallacious than this kind of argument. ② We may as well assert that because a child has thrived upon milk, that it is never to have meat, or that the first twenty years of our lives is to become a precedent for the next twenty. But even this is admitting more than is true; for I answer roundly, that America would have flourished as much, and probably much more, had no European power had any thing to do with her. ③ The commerce, by which she hath enriched herself, are the necessaries of life, and will always have a market while eating is the custom of Europe.

But she has protected us, say some. That she has engrossed us is true, and defended the continent at our expense as well as her own, is admitted; and she would have defended Turkey from the same motive, ④ viz. the sake of trade and dominion. ⑤

Alas! we have been long led away by ancient prejudices, and made large sacrifices to superstition. We have boasted the protection of Great Britain, without considering, that her motive was INTEREST not ATTACHMENT; that she did not protect us from OUR ENEMIES on OUR ACCOUNT, but from HER ENEMIES on HER OWN ACCOUNT, from those who had no quarrel with us on any OTHER ACCOUNT, and who will always be our enemies on the SAME ACCOUNT. Let Britain wave her pretensions to the Continent, or the Continent throw off the dependence, and we should be at peace with France and Spain, were they at war with Britain.

Reading and Vocabulary Support

① *Fallacious* means "false."

② To what is Paine comparing the colonies?

③ What argument against independence does Paine refute in the first paragraph?

④ *Viz.* means "namely."

⑤ What argument against independence does Paine refute in the second paragraph?

Analyzing Primary Sources

Cite specific evidence from the document to support your answers.

1. **Analyze Style and Rhetoric** In the first paragraph, how does Paine paint a picture that everyday people could understand?
2. **Analyze Style and Rhetoric** Why does Paine capitalize words in the last paragraph?

Quest CONNECTIONS

Thomas Paine makes an argument for separating from Britain. Which argument might convince you to join the Patriot cause? Record your findings in your Active Journal.

LESSON 5

Winning Independence

GET READY TO READ

START UP

Examine the painting of George Washington and Martha Washington with troops at Valley Forge. Write a sentence telling what being a soldier in the war may have been like.

GUIDING QUESTIONS

- What roles did women and African Americans have in the war?
- How did the war progress until it ended at Yorktown?
- What did American colonists gain from winning the war?

TAKE NOTES

Literacy Skills: Sequence

Use the graphic organizer in your Active Journal to take notes as you read the lesson.

PRACTICE VOCABULARY

Use the vocabulary activity in your Active Journal to practice the vocabulary words.

Vocabulary		Academic Vocabulary
cavalry	siege	cease
guerrilla	ratify	sustain

Once France had agreed to support the Americans, the Netherlands and Spain also joined in the war against Britain. France, the Netherlands, and Spain all provided loans to the United States.

Europeans Aid the Colonies

On the southwestern frontier, Americans received help from New Spain. In the early years of the war, Bernardo de Gálvez (bayr NARDO day GOLL vess), governor of Spanish Louisiana, favored the Patriots. He secretly supplied medicine, cloth, muskets, and gunpowder to the Americans.

When Spain entered the war against Britain in 1779, Gálvez took a more active role. He seized British forts along the Mississippi River and the Gulf of Mexico. He also drove the British out of West Florida. Galveston, Texas, is named after this leader.

Foreign Individuals Contribute After France began to aid the United States, even before other European nations agreed to help the United States, individual volunteers had been coming from Europe.

They wanted to join the American cause. Some became leading officers in the American army.

Foreign Aid Plays a Role

The Marquis de Lafayette (mar KEE dah lah fay ET), a young French noble, convinced France to send several thousand trained soldiers to help the Patriot cause. Lafayette, who fought at Brandywine, became one of Washington's most trusted friends.

From the German state of Prussia came Friedrich von Steuben (STOO bun), who helped train Washington's troops to march and drill. Von Steuben had served in the Prussian army, which was considered the best in Europe.

Two Polish officers also joined the Americans. Thaddeus Kosciuszko (kosh CHUSH ko), an engineer, helped build forts and other defenses. Casimir Pulaski trained **cavalry**, or troops on horseback.

READING CHECK **Identify Main Ideas** In what ways did Europeans help the American war effort?

Winter at Valley Forge

The victory at Saratoga and the promise of help from Europe boosted American morale. Washington's Continental Army began preparing for the winter of 1777–1778 by building a makeshift camp at Valley Forge.

Conditions at Valley Forge were difficult, but the soldiers endured. About 2,000 huts were built as shelter. Several soldiers were improperly dressed, although many did have proper uniforms. As the winter wore on, soldiers also suffered from disease, a common problem in military camps. An army surgeon from Connecticut wrote about his hardships:

Primary Source

"I am sick—discontented—and out of humor. Poor food—hard lodging—cold weather—fatigue—nasty clothes—nasty cookery. . . . There comes a bowl of beef soup, full of burnt leaves and dirt. . . . "

—Albigence Waldo, *Diary*, December 14, 1777

As news of the hardships at Valley Forge spread, Patriots from around the nation sent help. Women collected food, medicine, warm clothes, and ammunition for the army. Some women, like Martha Washington, wife of the commander, went to Valley Forge to help the sick and wounded.

Analyze Images The winter at Valley Forge was hard on Washington's soldiers. **Classify and Categorize** Which details in the illustration show the cause of hardships soldiers suffered?

Analyze Images The Marquis de Lafayette, George Washington, and their troops spent the winter at Valley Forge training for upcoming battles. **Draw Conclusions** Do you think the winter experienced by the Continental Army at Valley Forge weakened or strengthened it? Why?

INTERACTIVE

Notable People of the American Revolution

The arrival of desperately needed supplies was soon followed by warmer weather. The drills of Friedrich von Steuben helped the Continentals to march and fight with new skill. By the spring of 1778, the army at Valley Forge was more hopeful. Washington could not know it at the time, but the Patriots' bleakest hour had passed.

READING CHECK **Identify Supporting Details** How did people help the soldiers at Valley Forge?

How Did Women Contribute to the War Effort?

When men went off to fight in the Revolution, women took on added work at home. Some planted and harvested the crops. Others made shoes and wove cloth for blankets and uniforms. One woman, Betsy Hagar, worked with blacksmith Samuel Leverett repairing cannons and guns for Patriot soldiers after the Battle of Concord.

Supporting the Army Many women joined their husbands at the front. They cared for the wounded, washed clothes, and cooked. Martha Washington joined her husband whenever she could. Some women achieved lasting fame for their wartime service.

Betsy Ross of Philadelphia sewed flags for Washington's army. Legend claims that she made the first American flag of stars and stripes.

A few women even took part in battle. During the Battle of Monmouth in 1778, Mary Ludwig Hays carried water to her husband and other soldiers. The soldiers called her Molly Pitcher. When her husband was wounded, she took his place, loading and firing the cannon.

Women's Rights and the Revolution As women participated in the war, they began to think differently about their rights. Those women who had taken charge of farms or their husbands' businesses became more confident and willing to speak out. The Revolution established important ideals of liberty and equality. In later years, these ideals would help encourage women to campaign for equal treatment—and eventually to win it.

READING CHECK **Identify Supporting Details** How did many women assist the Revolutionary War effort?

▲ Mary Ludwig Hays, known as Molly Pitcher for carrying water to soldiers during battle, helped fight for independence.

How Did African Americans Serve in the War?

By 1776, more than a half million African Americans lived in the colonies. This large group proved itself an important part of the American people due to African American contributions during the Revolution. At first, the Continental Congress refused to let African Americans, whether free or enslaved, join the army. Some members doubted the loyalty of armed African Americans. The British, however, offered freedom to some enslaved men who would serve the king. Washington feared that this would greatly increase the ranks of the British army. In response, Washington changed his policy and asked Congress to allow free African Americans to enlist.

Deciding to Fight About 5,000 African Americans, from all the colonies except South Carolina, served in the army. Another 2,000 served in the navy which, from the start, allowed African Americans to join. At least nine African-American minutemen saw action at Lexington and Concord.

Some African Americans formed special regiments. Others served in white regiments as drummers, fifers, spies, and guides.

BIOGRAPHY 5 Things to Know About

PHILLIS WHEATLEY
Poet 1753–1784

- Was first published African American female poet
- Born in West Africa; kidnapped and sold into slavery in Boston at age 7
- Mastered English, Greek, and Latin
- Wrote famous poem, "To His Excellency General Washington"
- Became a social success on London trip and later was freed

Critical Thinking What events during the war may have moved Wheatley to write a poem to General George Washington?

African Americans and the Revolution

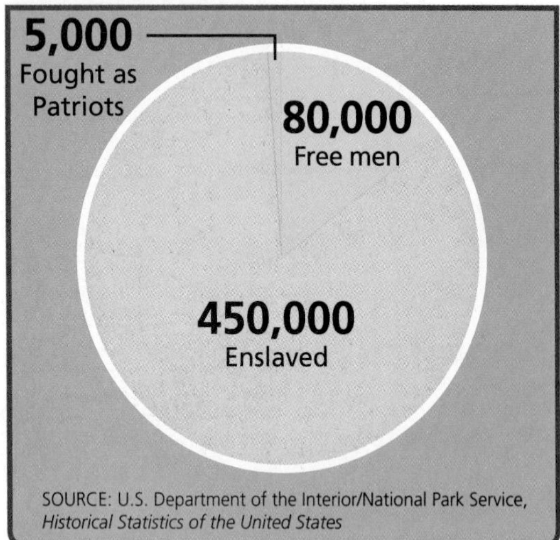

Analyze Graphs This circle graph shows the African American population engaged in the Patriot cause. **Draw Conclusions** What does this data tell you about the status of African Americans during the Revolution?

African Americans like Wentworth Cheswell served the Patriot cause from the start. A New Hampshire schoolmaster, Cheswell was a free African-American man who, like Paul Revere, rode all night from Boston to warn his community that the British were on the march. He later enlisted in the army to help fight at Saratoga.

Enslaved African Americans faced more difficult choices. If they joined the American army or continued to work on Patriot plantations, the British might capture and sell them. If they tried to flee to the British army to gain freedom, they risked being hanged by angry Patriots.

Belief in Freedom Yet, many slaves did flee their masters, especially those who lived near the coast. The British navy patrolled the coast. One British captain reported that "near 500" runaway slaves offered their services to him. Toward the end of the war, several thousand enslaved people sought freedom by following British troops through the Carolinas.

African-American Patriots hoped that the Revolution would bring an end to slavery. After all, the Declaration of Independence proclaimed that "all men are created equal." The promise of the natural rights professed in the Declaration motivated African Americans to try to secure these rights.

▲ At the Battle of Wyoming in 1778, Loyalists and American Indians, allied with the British, killed 360 colonial settlers in the Wyoming Valley of Pennsylvania.

Some white leaders also hoped the war would end slavery. James Otis wrote that "the colonists are by the law of nature free born, as indeed all men are, white or Black." Quakers in particular spoke out strongly against slavery.

During the American Revolution, several states moved to make slavery illegal, including Massachusetts, New Hampshire, and Pennsylvania. Other states also began to debate the slavery issue.

READING CHECK **Identify Main Ideas** What difficult consequences did many enslaved African Americans face when choosing sides in the American Revolution?

Analyze Images Captain John Paul Jones shouts orders to his crew during battle aboard his ship *Bonhomme Richard.* Jones and his crew captured the British warship *Serapis.* **Infer** What can you infer about the character of John Paul Jones from the caption and the illustration?

American Indians Choose Sides

At first, both sides tried to persuade American Indians to stay out of the conflict. However, as the war spread to American Indian lands in the West, the Americans and British both tried to win the support of American Indian groups. In the end, the British were more successful in creating alliances. They convinced many American Indians that a Patriot victory would mean more white settlers crossing the Appalachians and taking their lands.

In the South, the Cherokee, Creek, Choctaw, and Chickasaw supported the British. The British encouraged the Cherokee to attack dozens of settlements. Only after hard fighting were Patriot militia able to drive the Cherokee back into the mountains.

Fighting was equally fierce on the northern frontier. In 1778, Iroquois forces led by the Mohawk leader Joseph Brant joined with Loyalists in raiding settlements in Pennsylvania and New York. The next year, Patriots struck back by destroying dozens of Iroquois villages.

Farther west, in 1778, George Rogers Clark led Virginia frontier fighters against the British in the Ohio Valley. With help from Miami Indians, Clark captured the British forts at Kaskaskia and Cahokia near the Mississippi River.

He then plotted a surprise attack on the British fort at Vincennes. Clark's small force spread out through the woods to make their numbers appear greater than they really were. The British commander surrendered Vincennes in February 1779.

READING CHECK **Identify Main Ideas** Why were the British generally more successful at becoming allies with American Indian groups?

Fighting for Independence at Sea and in the South

At sea, the Americans could do little against the powerful British navy. British ships blockaded American ports, which were oftentimes important supply routes for Patriot troops and towns. From time to time, however, a bold American captain captured a British ship.

Analyze Images Benedict Arnold, although a traitor, was an able general for the Continental Army. **Identify Cause and Effect** What effect did Arnold's treason have on the British army that welcomed him?

The greatest American sea victory took place in September 1779 in Britain's backyard, on the North Sea. After a hard-fought battle, Captain John Paul Jones captured the powerful British warship *Serapis*. Jones was one of many important military leaders who contributed to the American cause during the war.

Battles in the South The South became the main battleground of the war in 1778. Sir Henry Clinton, the new British commander-in-chief, knew that many Loyalists lived in the southern backcountry. He hoped that Loyalists would join the British troops.

At first, Clinton's plan seemed to work. In short order, beginning in December 1778, the British seized Savannah in Georgia and Charleston and Camden in South Carolina. "I have almost **ceased** to hope," wrote Washington when he learned of the defeats.

Patriots and Loyalists Clash In the Carolina backcountry, Patriots and Loyalists launched violent raids against one another. Both sides burned farms and killed civilians.

After 1780, attacks by British troops and Loyalist militia became especially cruel. As a result, more settlers began to side with the Patriots. As one Loyalist admitted, "Great Britain has now a hundred enemies, where it had one before."

Momentum Shifts Toward the Patriots Two able American generals helped turn the tide against the redcoats. The main British army was led by General Charles Cornwallis.

In 1780, General Nathanael Greene took command of the Continental Army in the South. Using his knowledge of local geography, Greene engaged the British only on ground that put them at a disadvantage.

In January 1781, General Daniel Morgan won an important victory at Cowpens, South Carolina. Morgan divided his soldiers into a front line and a rear line. He ordered the front line to retreat after firing just two volleys. The British, thinking the Americans were retreating, charged. They moved into the fire of Morgan's second rank. In this way, the Americans won the Battle of Cowpens.

Greene and Morgan combined their armies when they fought Cornwallis at Guilford Courthouse, near present-day Greensboro, North Carolina. The battle was one of the bloodiest of the war. Although the Americans retreated, the British **sustained** great losses.

Adapting Tactics to Geography Known as the Swamp Fox, Francis Marion of South Carolina led a small band of militia that used **guerrilla**, or hit-and-run, tactics to harass the British. Marion's band took advantage of the region's environment, appearing suddenly out of the swamps, attacking quickly, and retreating swiftly back into the swamps.

READING CHECK **Identify Supporting Details** What did a superior navy allow the British to do?

Academic Vocabulary

cease • *v.*, to stop or end

sustain • *v.*, to undergo

A Decisive Win Brings the War to a Close

Cornwallis abandoned his plan to take the Carolinas. In the spring of 1781, he moved his troops north into Virginia. He planned to conquer Virginia and cut off the Americans' supply routes to the South.

Benedict Arnold's Betrayal The British had achieved some success in Virginia, even before the arrival of Cornwallis. Benedict Arnold was now leading British troops. Arnold captured and burned the capital city of Richmond and other towns.

Arnold had turned traitor to the American cause in September 1780, while commanding West Point, a key fort in New York. The ambitious general was angry because he felt that he had not received enough credit for his victories. He also needed money. Arnold secretly agreed to turn over West Point to the British. The plot was uncovered by a Patriot patrol, but Arnold escaped to join the British.

Arnold's treason and his raids on towns in Connecticut and Virginia enraged the Patriots. Washington ordered Arnold to be hanged. However, he was never captured.

The British Are Trapped at Yorktown Cornwallis hoped to meet with the same kind of success in Virginia that Arnold had achieved. At first, things went well. Cornwallis sent Loyalist troops to attack Charlottesville, where the Virginia legislature was meeting. Governor Thomas Jefferson and other officials had to flee.

American troops under Lafayette fought back by staging raids against the British. Lafayette did not have enough troops to fight a major battle. Still, his strategy kept Cornwallis at bay.

GEOGRAPHY SKILLS

The last battle of the war was fought in the Chesapeake Bay region.

1. **Location** Why was Cornwallis's position a problem for his troops?
2. **Summarize** What role did the French and American navies play in the Battle of Yorktown?

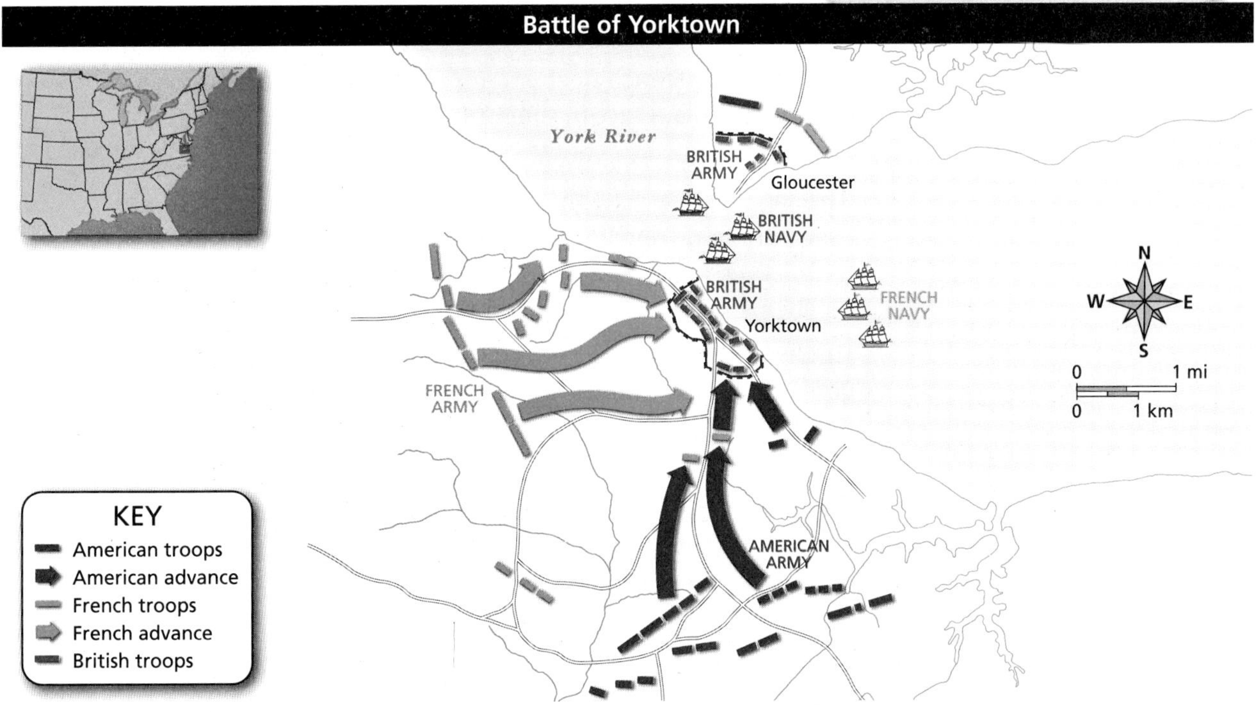

▲ Yorktown was a stunning victory for the American and French armies. As troops gathered to accept the formal British surrender, Cornwallis, claiming illness, did not attend the ceremony.

Then, Cornwallis made a mistake. He disregarded an order from Sir Henry Clinton to send part of his army to New York. Instead, he retreated to Yorktown peninsula, a strip of land jutting into the Chesapeake Bay. He felt confident that British ships could supply his army from the sea.

Washington saw an opportunity to trap Cornwallis on the Yorktown peninsula. He marched his Continental troops south from New York. With the Americans were French soldiers under the Comte de Rochambeau (roh shahm BOH). The combined army rushed to join Lafayette in Virginia.

Meanwhile, a French fleet under Admiral de Grasse was also heading toward Virginia. Once in Chesapeake Bay, de Grasse's fleet closed the trap. Cornwallis was cut off. He could not escape by land or by sea.

The War Is Won By the end of September, more than 16,000 American and French troops laid siege to Cornwallis's army of fewer than 8,000. A **siege** occurs when an army surrounds and blockades an enemy position in an attempt to capture it.

Finally, with casualties mounting and his supplies running low, the general decided that the situation was hopeless. The British had lost the Battle of Yorktown.

On October 19, 1781, the British surrendered. The French and the Americans lined up in facing columns. As the defeated redcoats marched between the victorious troops, a British army band played the tune "The World Turned Upside Down."

The talks began in Paris in 1782. Congress sent Benjamin Franklin and John Adams, along with John Jay of New York and Henry Laurens of South Carolina, to work out a treaty.

Because Britain was eager to end the war, the Americans got most of what they wanted.

Under the Treaty of Paris, the British recognized the United States as an independent nation. It extended from the Atlantic Ocean to the Mississippi River. The northern border of the United States stopped at the Great Lakes. The southern border stopped at Florida, which was returned to Spain.

For their part, the Americans agreed to ask the state legislatures to pay Loyalists for property they had lost in the war. In the end, most states ignored Loyalist claims.

On April 15, 1783, Congress **ratified**, or approved, the Treaty of Paris. It was almost eight years to the day since the battles of Lexington and Concord.

READING CHECK **Identify Cause and Effect** What were the results of the Treaty of Paris?

Explaining the American Victory

Geography played an important role in the American victory. The British had to send soldiers and supplies several thousand miles from home. They also had to fight an enemy that was spread over a wide area. The Americans also were familiar with the local geography.

Help from other nations was crucial to the American cause. Spanish forces attacked the British along the Gulf of Mexico and in the Mississippi Valley. French money helped pay for supplies, and French military aid supported American troops.

Did you know?

On losing the war, King George III said, "America is lost! . . . it is to be hoped we shall reap more advantages from their trade as friends than ever we could derive from them as Colonies."

GEOGRAPHY SKILLS

After the Treaty of Paris in 1783, the new United States gained some territory.

1. **Movement** In what direction do you think new U.S. immigrants would move when they looked for land to farm?
2. **Cite Evidence** How did the Treaty of Paris of 1783 change the balance of power in North America?

Treaty of Paris, 1783

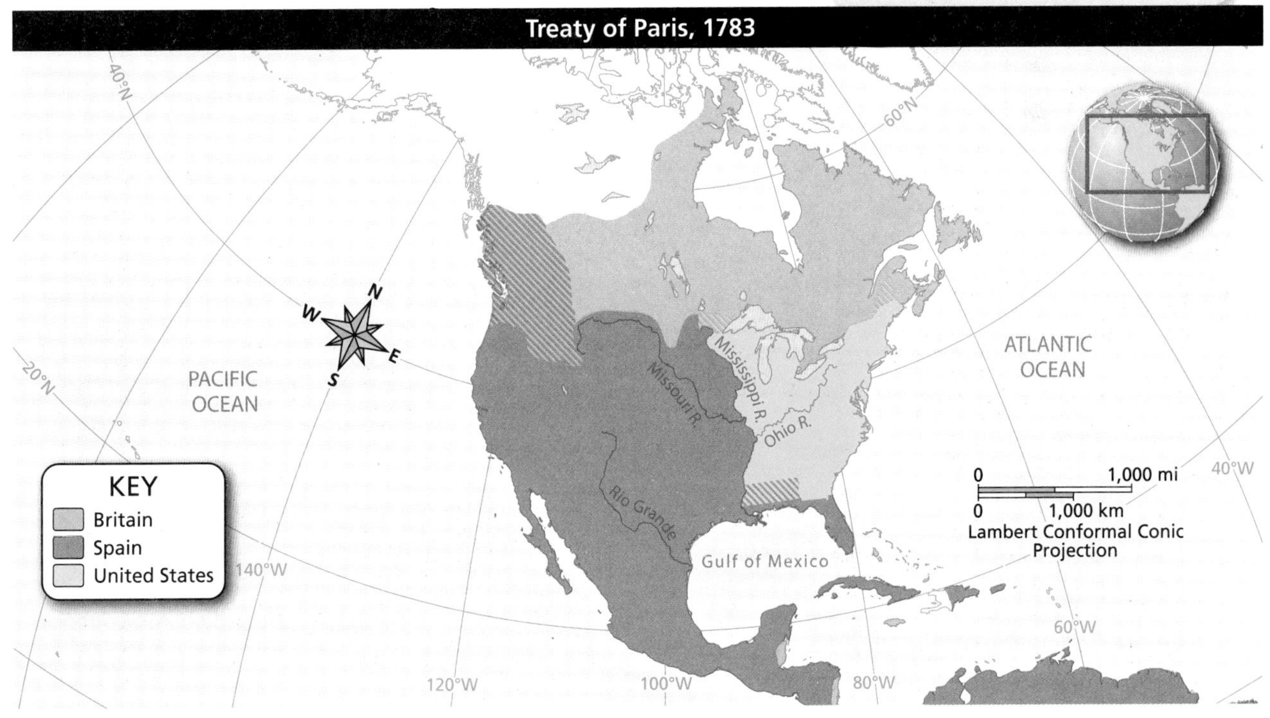

Analyze Images Here, Washington rides in triumph through the streets of New York City. **Identify Supporting Details** What details in the image help to show George Washington as an important military figure?

Throughout the war the colonists benefited from their ability to unify for a shared American cause. The American Revolution inspired people of many different ethnic groups as well as social classes to fight for the same American ideals of freedom and rights. Ideals from the Revolution would help define the American identity. Patriotism was another important factor in the American victory. Soldiers were fighting for their homes and their beliefs.

Gradually, Washington's inexperienced troops learned how to drill, how to march, and how to fight the British. Perhaps most important was Washington himself. By the end of the war, the general's leadership and military skills were respected by Americans and British alike. In December 1783, General Washington, before resigning, bid farewell to his officers at Fraunces Tavern in New York City. Colonel Benjamin Tallmadge recalled the event:

Primary Source

"Such a scene of sorrow and weeping I had never before witnessed. . . . We were then about to part from the man who had conducted us through a long and bloody war . . ."

—Benjamin Tallmadge, Memoir

READING CHECK **Summarize** What were the main reasons for the American victory?

Lesson Check

Practice Vocabulary

1. How did allies benefit the Americans?
2. How did **guerrilla** tactics benefit the Americans?

Critical Thinking and Writing

3. **Understand Effects** How did Europeans aid the American cause?
4. **Draw Conclusions** Why did many people believe that the Declaration of Independence justified an end to slavery?
5. **Summarize** How was General Cornwallis defeated at Yorktown?
6. **Identify Cause and Effect** How did the American Revolution develop the concept of natural rights?
7. **Writing Workshop: Write an Introduction** Write a short paragraph in your Active Journal that introduces the thesis of your essay about the American Revolution.

Relate Events in Time

Follow these steps to relate events in time.

1 **Identify key events and topics** Note the time period, people, and events you are focusing on. For example, where were Revolutionary battles fought? Who were some of the leaders in those battles?

2 **Look for clues about time** Important clues include information about dates and times of key events. For example, which battles took place in 1776? Is there action in two different regions in the same year? What can you infer about the war by relating the dates of battles in the different regions?

3 **Look for clues about relationships** Besides dates, a variety of words can signal how key events are related in time. Examples include words such as *before* and *after, meanwhile, several months ago,* and *in the winter* or other season. For example, what battle happened directly after Lexington and Concord? When did Washington retreat from New York?

REVOLUTIONARY BATTLES BY REGION

North	West	South
• **June 17, 1775** After the skirmish at Lexington and Concord, the British and Americans fight again at Bunker Hill in Massachusetts. • **August 27, 1776** General George Washington retreats from New York after losing the Battle of Long Island. • **December 26, 1776** After crossing the Delaware River, Washington surprises the British and wins the Battle of Trenton, New Jersey.	• **July 3, 1778** Loyalist officer Colonel John Butler leads British and American Indian militia against a Patriot militia at Battle of Wyoming in Pennsylvania. • **February 1779** George Rogers Clark and a small Patriot force take British fort in surprise attack in Battle of Vincennes.	• **December 1778** The British seize Savannah, Georgia. • **January 17, 1781** General Daniel Morgan leads continental soldiers and backwoodsmen against British officer Banastre Tarleton in Battle of Cowpens, South Carolina. • **October 19, 1781** British General Lord Cornwallis surrenders to American General George Washington at Yorktown, Virginia.

TOPIC 3

Review and Assessment

VISUAL REVIEW

Major Events Leading to the Declaration of Independence

British Action	Mercantilism and Taxation Without Representation	British Actions
• Proclamation of 1763: restricted colonists' movement west	• Sugar Act 1764: taxed molasses • Stamp Act 1765: taxed documents and other papers	• Quartering Act 1765: required colonists to house British troops • Townshend Acts 1767: assessed more taxes

Events	British Action	Battles
• Boston Massacre 1770 • Tea Act 1773 • Boston Tea Party 1773	• Intolerable Acts 1774	• Lexington and Concord 1775 • Battle of Bunker Hill 1775

MAJOR FIGURES OF THE REVOLUTIONARY ERA

Soldiers	Political Leaders	Patriots
• George Washington • John Paul Jones • Green Mountain Boys and Ethan Allen	• King George III • Thomas Jefferson • Benjamin Franklin • John Adams • Patrick Henry • John Hancock	• Abigail Adams • Samuel Adams • Nathan Hale • Thomas Paine

READING REVIEW

Use the Take Notes and Practice Vocabulary activities in your Active Journal to help you review the topic.

INTERACTIVE

Practice Vocabulary using Topic Mini-Games.

Quest FINDINGS

Write your blog

Get help for writing your blog in your Active Journal.

ASSESSMENT

Vocabulary and Key Ideas

1. **Describe** What is the difference between **natural rights** and **unalienable rights**?
2. **Identify** Name two allies of the United States during the American Revolution. Why were they considered allies?
3. **Check Understanding** Why was the Boston Tea Party considered an example of **civil disobedience**?
4. **Recall** How did **Patriots** and **Loyalists** differ?
5. **Identify** After the **preamble**, what are the three parts of the Declaration of Independence, and what is the purpose of each?
6. **Check Understanding** Why was the Battle of Saratoga important?
7. **Identify Main Ideas** How did the Stamp Act help fuel the Boston Massacre?

Critical Thinking and Writing

8. **Summarize** List three factors that contributed to the colonies winning the American Revolution.
9. **Identify Cause and Effect** What motivated African American soldiers to fight with the Patriots during the Revolution?
10. **Compare and Contrast** Compare and contrast the Treaty of Paris signed in 1763 and the Treaty of Paris signed in 1783.
11. **Summarize** What was the relationship of American Indians to Europeans and to the colonists during the Revolutionary Era?
12. **Revisit the Essential Question** Was the American Revolution justified? Explain your answer in one or two paragraphs.
13. **Writing Workshop: Write an Explanatory Essay** Using the notes you created in your Active Journal, answer the following question in a three-paragraph essay: Why was there an American Revolution?

Analyze Primary Sources

14. Who is most likely to have made the following statement?
    A. a Patriot
    B. a Loyalist
    C. a British citizen
    D. a mercenary

"Our Colonies must be the biggest Beggars in the World, if such small Duties appear to be intolerable in their Eyes."

Analyze Maps

Use the map to answer the following questions.

15. Which letters represent Lexington, Concord, and Saratoga? In which region of the colonies did these battles take place?
16. Which letter represents the Battle of Trenton? From which colony did Washington cross over the Delaware River to fight this battle?
17. Which letter represents the Battle of Yorktown? How did the geography of this location help lead to Cornwallis's defeat?

▼ Battles of the Revolution

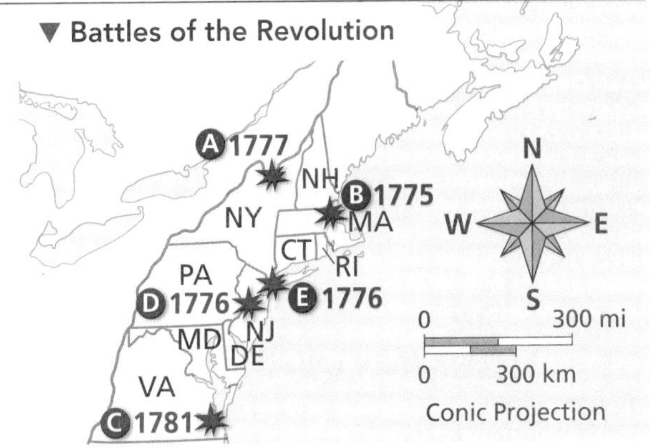

TOPIC 4

A Constitution for the United States

(1776–Present)

GO ONLINE to access your digital course

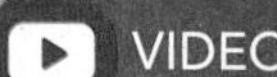

- VIDEO
- AUDIO
- ETEXT
- INTERACTIVE
- WRITING
- GAMES
- WORKSHEET
- ASSESSMENT

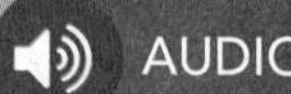

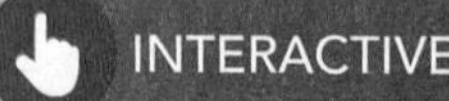

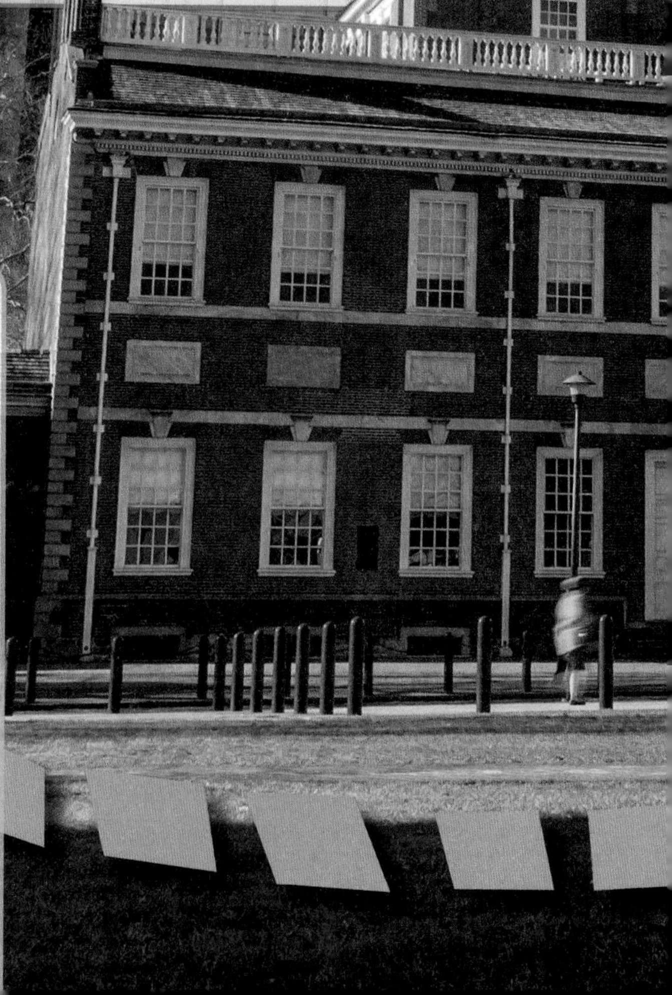

Go back to the late 1700s,

when the **NATION'S FOUNDERS PRODUCED A CONSTITUTION FOR THE UNITED STATES.** See how these leaders applied the ideals of the Declaration of Independence to create a government that has served Americans well for more than 200 years.

Explore The Essential Question

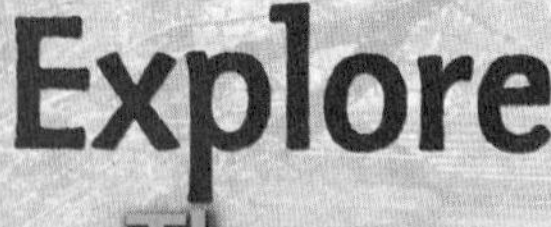

How much power should the government have?

The nation's founders debated this question. What did they decide?

Unlock the Essential Question in your Active Journal.

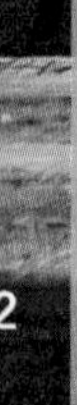

Watch

James Madison

Learn how a quiet man had a tremendous impact.

Read

about how the Constitution was written.

Independence Hall, Philadelphia, PA

TOPIC 4

A Constitution for the United States (1776–Present)

Learn more about the early United States by making your own map and timeline in your Active Journal.

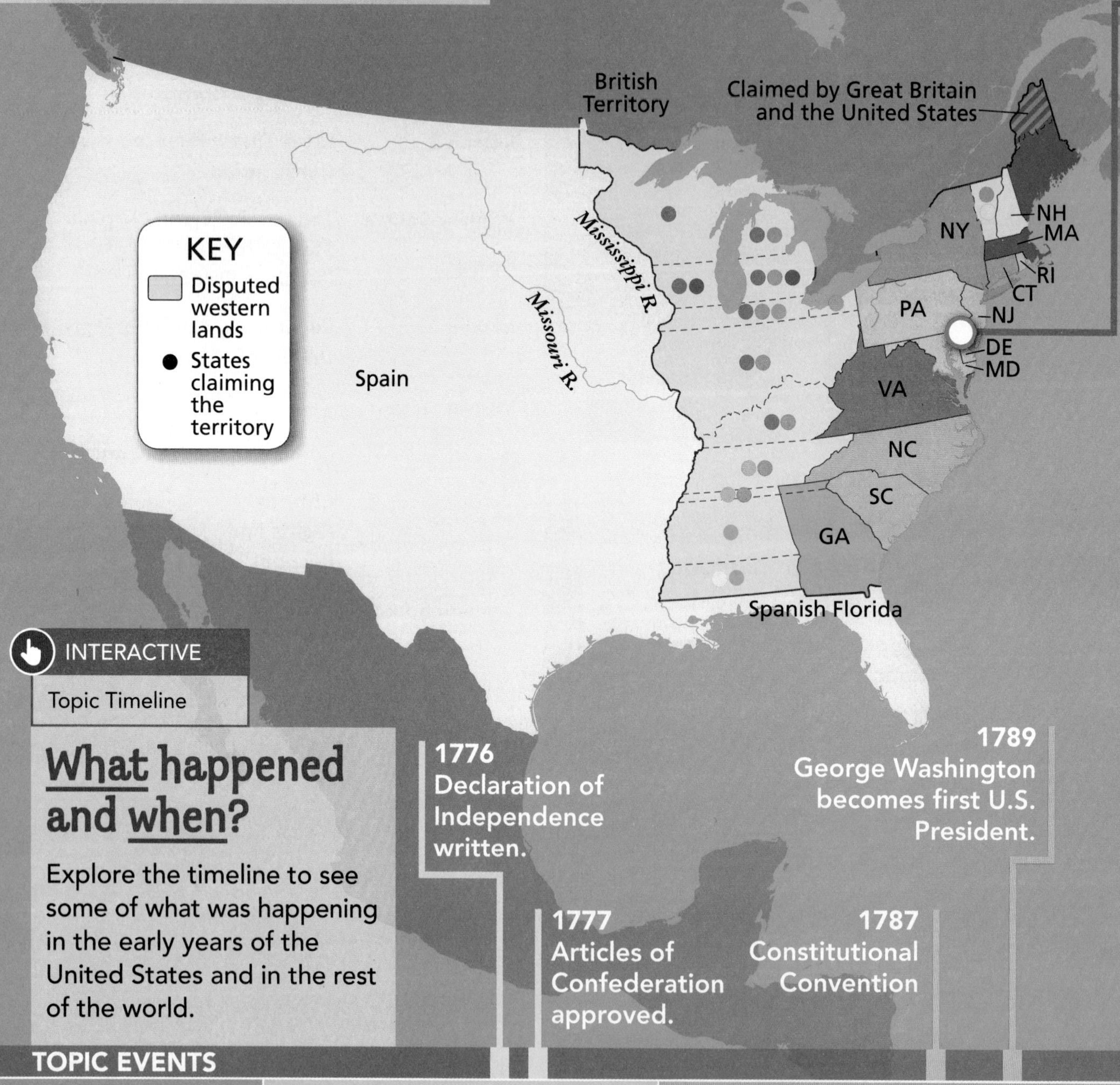

INTERACTIVE

Topic Timeline

What happened and when?

Explore the timeline to see some of what was happening in the early years of the United States and in the rest of the world.

TOPIC EVENTS

1776 Declaration of Independence written.

1777 Articles of Confederation approved.

1787 Constitutional Convention

1789 George Washington becomes first U.S. President.

1770 **1780**

WORLD EVENTS

1789 French Revolution begins.

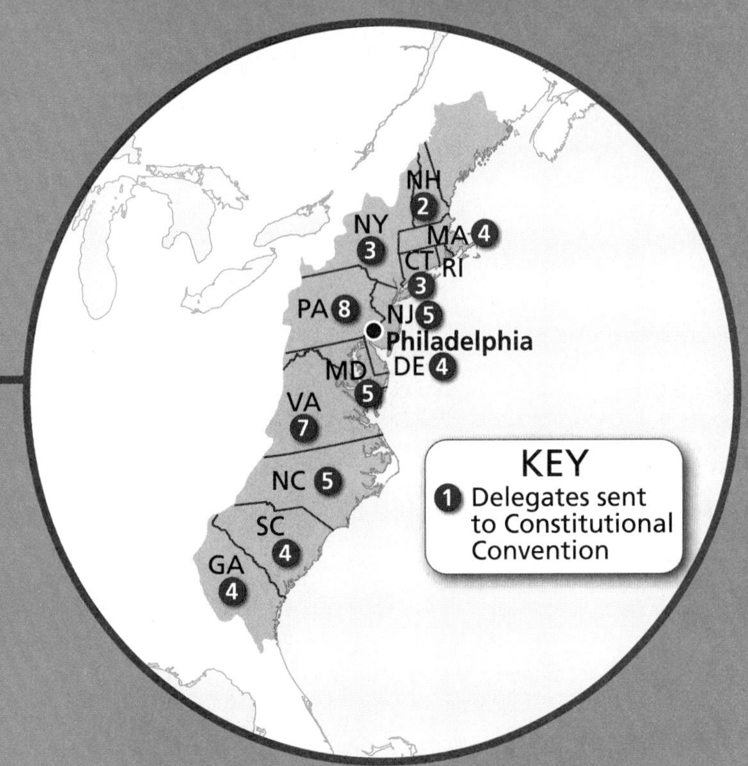

INTERACTIVE

Topic Map

Why did leaders from throughout the United States travel to Philadelphia in 1787?

These leaders were determined to make the existing constitution—and the government—stronger.

1791
Bill of Rights ratified.

1799
Rosetta Stone discovered.

1800
Federal government moves to Washington, D.C.

1803
Louisiana Purchase completed.

1806
Holy Roman Empire ends.

1790 | 1800 | 1810

Who will you meet?

James Madison, the "Father of the Constitution"

Roger Sherman, who masterminded the Great Compromise

Alexander Hamilton, who pushed for a stronger national government

Senate Representation

Quest KICK OFF

You are a member of the U.S. House of Representatives. Another representative has proposed an amendment to the Constitution. It would change the number of senators from each state so that the number is based on each state's population. Help decide the answer to this question:

Should representation in the Senate be based on population?

Be ready! Other representatives will challenge your arguments.

1 Ask Questions

You are determined to know the best answer to the Guiding Question. Get started by making a list of questions about the major debates in the Constitutional Convention. Write questions in your Active Journal.

2 Investigate

As you read the lessons in this Topic, look for Quest CONNECTIONS that provide information about the structure of the U.S. Congress. Collect examples in your Active Journal.

3 Examine Sources

Next, explore sources that support differing viewpoints about Senate representation based on population. Collect examples in your Active Journal.

Quest FINDINGS

4 Discuss!

After you collect clues and examine sources, prepare to discuss this question: Should representation in the Senate be based on population? Use your knowledge of the Constitutional Convention and your sources to answer YES or NO to the question.

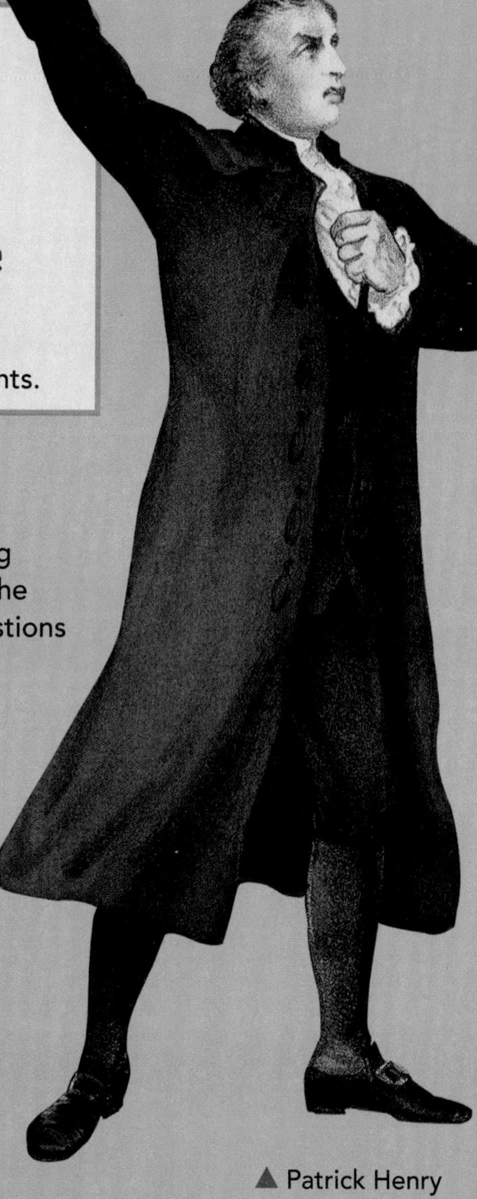

▲ Patrick Henry

LESSON 1

A Weak Confederation

GET READY TO READ

START UP

Look at the image of the Second Continental Congress. What principles did these men support?

GUIDING QUESTIONS

- What were the strengths and weaknesses of the Articles of Confederation?
- How did Congress plan for governing the Northwest Territory and opening it to settlers?
- How did Shays' Rebellion influence leaders to revise the Articles of Confederation?

TAKE NOTES

Literacy Skills Summarize

Use the graphic organizer in your Active Journal to take notes as you read the lesson.

PRACTICE VOCABULARY

Use the vocabulary activity in your Active Journal to practice the vocabulary words.

Vocabulary		Academic Vocabulary
constitution	cede	privatize
bill of rights	currency	depression
Articles of Confederation	Northwest Ordinance	
	Shays' Rebellion	

When Americans declared their independence in 1776, they also assumed the right to govern themselves. The next year, the Continental Congress drew up plans for a national government. By that time, several states had already begun to create their own governments.

How Were State Constitutions Similar?

Americans fought the Revolution to uphold the principles and ideas set forth in the Declaration of Independence. These include freedom, liberty, equality, democracy, and the concept that people have natural rights. States sought to reflect those principles in their **constitutions**, the documents that set out the basic laws, principles, organization, and processes of a government. They wanted to spell out the rights of all citizens and limit the power of government.

People valued the rights that state governments protected. Virginia's constitution included a **bill of rights**, or list of freedoms that the government promises to protect.

State of Maſſachuſetts-Bay.

In CONVENTION, June 16, 1780.

▲ The constitution of the state of Massachusetts declared that the primary purpose of the Massachusetts state government is to protect the natural rights of its inhabitants.

Virginia's bill of rights guaranteed trial by jury, freedom of religion, and freedom of the press. Several other states followed Virginia's lead. For example, the Massachusetts state constitution guaranteed people:

Primary Source

> ". . . the right of enjoying and defending their lives and liberties; that of acquiring, possessing, and protecting property; in [short], that of seeking and obtaining their safety and happiness."
>
> —Massachusetts Constitution of 1780

The new state governments were structured somewhat like the colonial governments had been. The states divided power between an executive and a legislature. Voters elected members of the legislature, who passed laws. Every state but Pennsylvania had a governor to execute, or carry out, the laws.

Under the state constitutions, more people had the right to vote than in colonial times. To vote, a citizen had to be white, male, and over age 21. He had to own a certain amount of property or pay a certain amount of taxes. For a time, some women in New Jersey could vote. In a few states, free African American men who owned property could vote.

READING CHECK **Identify Main Ideas** What freedoms did many states agree to protect?

The Articles of Confederation

As citizens formed state governments, the Continental Congress was drafting a plan for the nation as a whole. The delegates agreed on the principles for which the Revolution was being fought. But incorporating those principles into a plan of government was a struggle. Although they used state constitutions as guides, the delegates found it hard to write a constitution that all states would approve.

States did not want to give up power to a central government. Few Americans saw themselves as citizens of one nation. Instead, they felt loyal to their own states. Also, people feared replacing the "tyranny" of British rule with another strong government. After much debate, the Continental Congress approved the first American constitution in 1777. The **Articles of Confederation** created a loose alliance of 13 independent states.

Strengths and Weaknesses Under the Articles of Confederation, the United States became a union of states that were linked by a weak central government.

In a sense, the Articles simply put into law the existing reality of government in the colonies—a Congress with delegates acting on behalf of states that retained most of the power.

The new nation was still at war, its revolution not yet won. It was not the time to discuss the political relationship between the states and Congress. The Articles of Confederation represented an effective compromise during a difficult time.

As a plan of government, the Articles of Confederation had strengths. It left states free to make decisions for themselves. It prevented the federal government from gaining too much power.

Under the Articles, each state sent one delegate to Congress. Thus each state, no matter its size or population, had one vote. Congress did have the power to declare war. It could appoint military officers, coin money, and operate post offices. It also could conduct foreign affairs and sign treaties.

However, the Articles of Confederation had weaknesses as well. Compared to the states, Congress had very limited powers. Congress could pass laws, but nine states had to approve a law before it could go into effect. Even then it was up to the states to enforce the laws passed by Congress. The Articles included no president to execute laws.

Congress could not regulate trade between states or between states and foreign countries. Nor did it have the power to tax. To raise money, Congress had to ask the states for funds or borrow them. No state could be forced to contribute funds to the national treasury. There was also no system of courts to settle conflicts between states.

Dispute Over Western Lands One major dispute arose before the Articles of Confederation went into effect. Maryland refused to ratify the Articles unless Virginia and other states **ceded**, or gave up, their claims to lands west of the Appalachians.

GEOGRAPHY **SKILLS**

This map shows the states that disputed western areas, and the dates each state ceded its claim to the federal government.

1. **Interaction** What impact would disputed claims have had on the relationships among the states?
2. **Infer** What factors would have caused states to cede their claims?

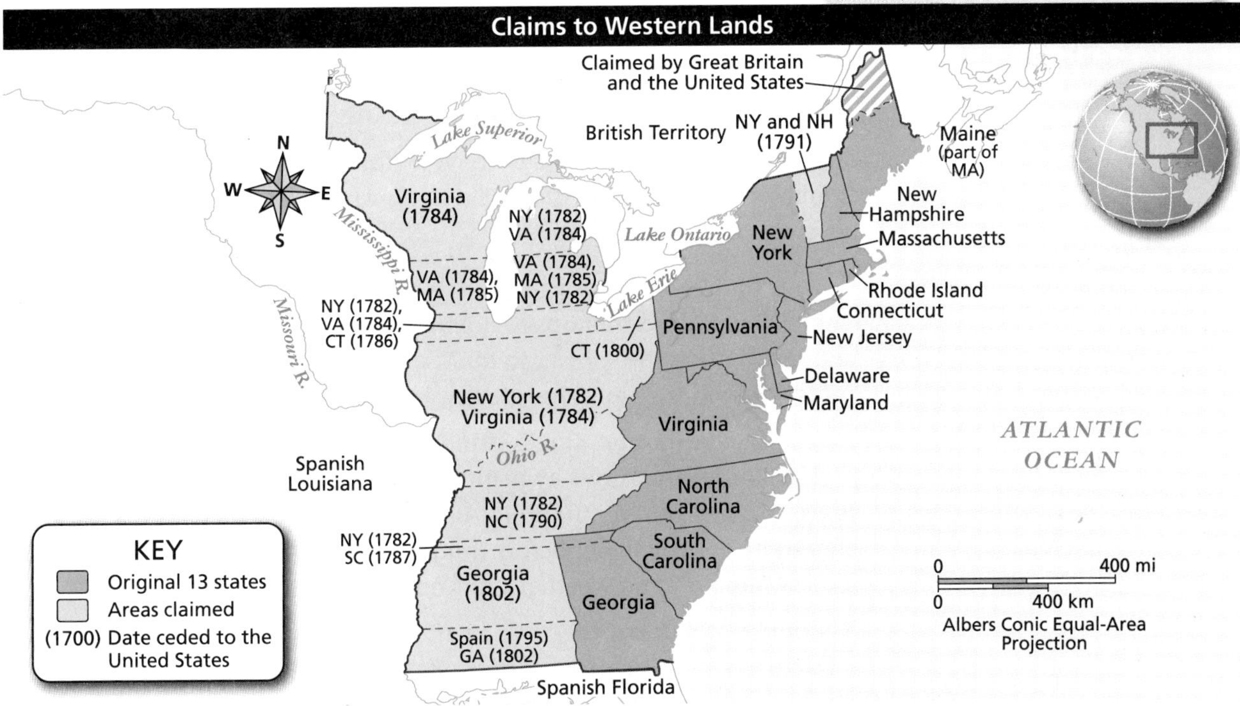

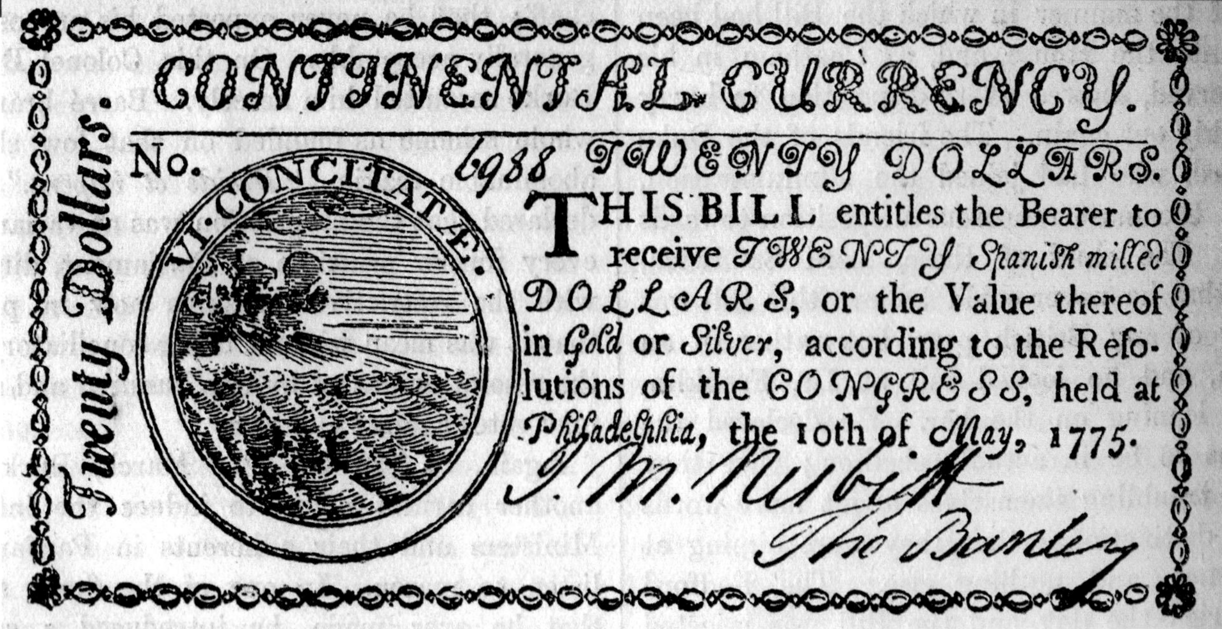

Analyze Images This $20 Continental bill was worth little in the eyes of the states. **Infer** If Congress had no power to raise money, how did that affect the value of the currency it issued?

Like other small states, Maryland feared that "landed" states would become too powerful. One by one, the states agreed to cede their western claims to Congress. Finally, only Virginia held out. However, Thomas Jefferson and other leading Virginians recognized the great need to form a central government. They persuaded state lawmakers to give up Virginia's claims in the West.

With its demands met, Maryland ratified the Articles of Confederation in 1781. The new American government could at last go into effect.

READING CHECK **Identify Supporting Details** What were the functions of Congress under the Articles of Confederation?

INTERACTIVE

Problems and Effects of the Articles of Confederation

Weaknesses of the Confederation

By 1783, the United States had won its independence. Yet, the end of the American Revolution did not solve the confederation's troubles. Americans doubted whether "these United States" could survive.

Many States Have Disagreements Disputes continued to arise among states. For example, both New Hampshire and New York claimed Vermont. The Articles did not give the central government power to resolve such conflicts.

Concerns Over Debt and Currency After the Revolution, the United States owed millions of dollars to individuals and foreign nations. Without the power to tax, Congress had no way to repay these debts. It asked the states for money, but the states often refused.

During the Revolution, the Continental Congress had solved the problem of raising funds by printing paper **currency**, or money. However, the Continental dollar had little value because it was not backed by gold or silver. Before long, Americans began to describe any useless thing as "not worth a Continental."

As Continental dollars became nearly worthless, states printed their own currency. This caused confusion. Most states refused to accept the money of other states. As a result, trade became very difficult.

Foreign Countries Promote Their Own Interests Foreign countries took advantage of the confederation's weakness. Ignoring the Treaty of Paris, Britain refused to withdraw its troops from American territory on the Great Lakes. Spain closed its port in New Orleans to American shipping. This was a serious blow to western farmers, who depended on the port to ship their products to the East.

READING CHECK **Understand Effects** Why did trade between states become increasingly difficult?

An Orderly Expansion

Despite its troubles, Congress did pass important laws about how to govern the Northwest Territory. This was the U.S. territory west of Pennsylvania, north of the Ohio River, south of the Great Lakes, and east of the Mississippi. The laws established how territories would be governed and how they could become states.

The Land Ordinance of 1785 set up a system for white Americans to settle in the Northwest Territory. The ordinance called for the territory to be surveyed and divided into townships. Each township would then be further divided into 36 sections of one square mile each (640 acres).

Congress planned to sell sections to white settlers for a minimum of $640 apiece. In this way, much of this federally owned land was **privatized**, or moved from public to private ownership. One section in every township was set aside for public schools. Selling the land provided income for the government.

In 1787, Congress passed the **Northwest Ordinance**. The law set up a government for the Northwest Territory, guaranteed basic rights to white settlers, and outlawed slavery there.

Academic Vocabulary
privatize • *v.*, to put private individuals or companies in charge of something

Analyze Images This infographic summarizes the changes that occurred after the Northwest Ordinance passed. **Infer** How did the ordinance reduce conflict among the states?

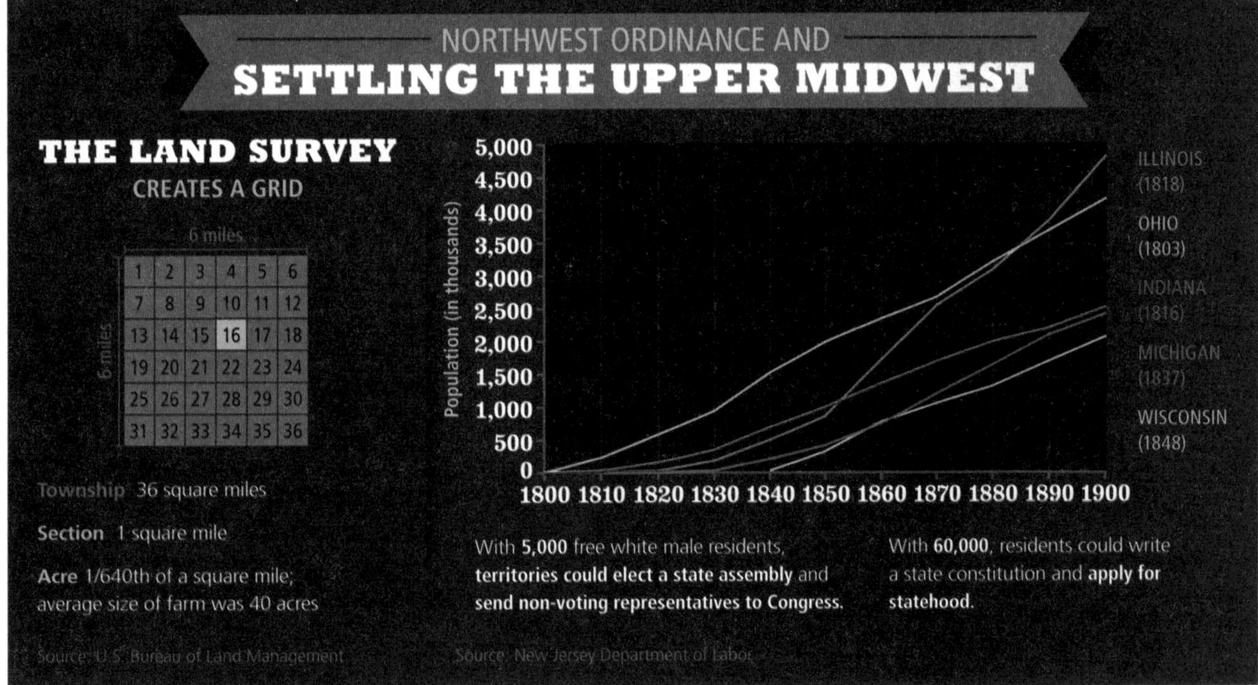

Academic Vocabulary
depression • *n.*, a period when business activity slows, prices and wages fall, and unemployment rises

It encouraged public education and said the vast region could be divided into separate territories in the future.

The Northwest Ordinance stated that new territories should be admitted as new states, rather than become part of existing ones. It provided a process, to admit new states to the nation. Once a territory had a population of 60,000 free white settlers, it could ask Congress to be admitted as a new state. Ohio, Indiana, Illinois, Michigan, and Wisconsin were created from the Northwest Territory.

However, the lands in this area were already home to American Indian nations. Although the Ordinance stated "the utmost good shall always be observed" toward these nations, white settlers' disregard for Indians' rights or interests often led to conflict.

Despite the drawbacks of the Articles of Confederation, the laws Congress created relating to the Northwest Territory proved to be a major success. These laws defined the basic rights of white settlers and established federal support for education.

READING CHECK **Identify Main Ideas** What was the purpose of the Northwest Ordinance?

How Did Economic Problems Lead to Change?

The Northwest Ordinance was the finest achievement of the national government under the Articles. Still, the government was unable to solve its economic problems. After the Revolution, the nation suffered an economic depression. A **depression** is a period when business activity slows, prices and wages fall, and unemployment rises.

Analyze Images Some Americans moved west after the Revolution, seeking new opportunities. **Infer** What do you think people were seeking?

Farmers Demand Fair Treatment The depression hit farmers hard. The war had created a high demand for farm products. Farmers borrowed money for land, seed, animals, and tools. However, when the Revolution ended, demand for farm goods went down. As prices fell, many farmers could not repay their loans.

In Massachusetts, matters worsened when the state raised taxes. The courts seized the farms of those who could not pay their taxes or loans. Angry farmers felt they were being treated unfairly.

Daniel Shays, a Massachusetts farmer who had fought at Bunker Hill and Saratoga, organized an uprising in 1786. More than 1,000 farmers took part in **Shays' Rebellion**. They attacked courthouses and prevented the state from seizing farms when farmers could not pay their debts. Finally, the Massachusetts legislature sent the militia to drive them off.

Analyze Images Shays' Rebellion resulted in bloodshed when state militia attacked angry rioters led by Daniel Shays. **Draw Conclusions** How did Shays' Rebellion test the strength of the new federal government?

A Call For Revision Many Americans saw Shays' Rebellion as a sign that the Articles of Confederation did not work.

To avert a crisis, leaders from several states called for a convention to revise the Articles of Confederation. They met in Philadelphia in May 1787. In the end, this convention would create an entirely new framework of government.

READING CHECK **Identify Implied Main Ideas** What did Shays' Rebellion show to many people?

Lesson Check

Practice Vocabulary

1. How did the Land Ordinance of 1785 and the **Northwest Ordinance** of 1787 **privatize** national resources?
2. Why did **currency** issues and **Shays' Rebellion** cause some leaders to decide that the **Articles of Confederation** should be revised?

Critical Thinking and Writing

3. **Identify Supporting Details** What were three weaknesses of the central government under the Articles of Confederation?
4. **Draw Conclusions** Why do you think slavery was outlawed in the Northwest Territory?
5. **Evaluate Explanations** Many American leaders, pointed to Shays' Rebellion as proof that the Articles of Confederation. were weak. Does this explanation for revising the Articles make sense to you? Why or why not?
6. **Revisit the Essential Question** How much power should the government have? Restrict your answer to what you have learned in this lesson.
7. **Writing Workshop: Introduce Claims** Write a brief paragraph in your Active Journal introducing two sides of the argument about how much power the government should have. This paragraph will get you started on an essay you will write at the end of the Topic.

LESSON 2

Drafting a Constitution

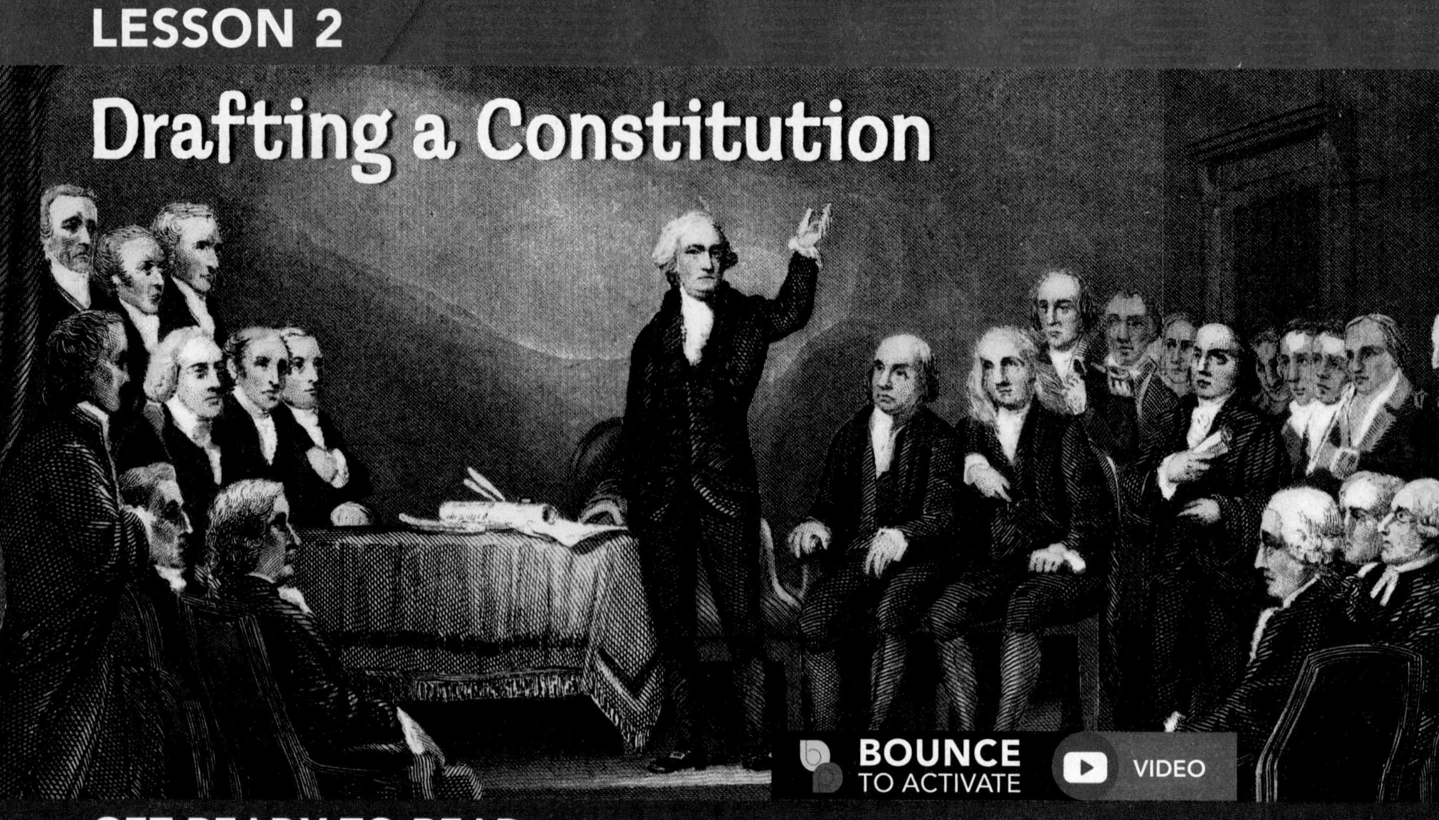

GET READY TO READ

START UP

Look at the image of the delegates. What issues are these men going to face?

GUIDING QUESTIONS

- What was the Revolution's legacy?
- Who led the Constitutional Convention?
- What were the main differences between the two rival plans for the new Constitution?
- How much power should the federal government have, and what should it do?

TAKE NOTES

Literacy Skills Compare and Contrast

Use the graphic organizer in your Active Journal to take notes as you read the lesson.

PRACTICE VOCABULARY

Use the vocabulary activity in your Active Journal to practice the vocabulary words.

Vocabulary

- Constitutional Convention
- Virginia Plan
- New Jersey Plan
- compromise
- Great Compromise
- Three-Fifths Compromise

Academic Vocabulary

- legacy
- ethical

The **Constitutional Convention** opened on May 25, 1787, in Philadelphia, Pennsylvania. Its purpose was to revise the Articles of Confederation. Every state except Rhode Island sent representatives. All of them wanted to honor the **legacy** of the Revolution and the principles for which they had fought. Yet not all delegates would agree on how to achieve that goal.

Who Led the Convention?

The convention would prove historic because it did not revise the Articles of Confederation. Instead, its delegates produced a new United States Constitution. That document established a government that has survived more than 200 years.

A Remarkable Group The convention's 55 delegates were a remarkable group. Eight of them had signed the Declaration of Independence, including the oldest, Benjamin Franklin. At age 81, Franklin was wise in the ways of government and human nature.

George Washington, age 55, represented Virginia. He was so well respected that the delegates at once elected him president of the Convention. Washington had long called for a stronger central government. Yet his role in the debates would be limited. It was his presence at the Convention that was important.

Academic Vocabulary
legacy • *n.*, something received by a predecessor or from the past

Most of the delegates belonged to a new generation of American leaders. Nearly half were young men in their thirties, including Alexander Hamilton of New York. During the Revolution, Hamilton had served for a time as Washington's private secretary. Hamilton despised the Articles of Confederation. "The nation," he wrote, "is sick and wants powerful remedies." The powerful remedy he prescribed was a strong central government.

INTERACTIVE

Delegates to the Constitutional Convention

Another of the younger delegates was Gouverneur Morris of Pennsylvania. Like Hamilton, he favored a strong central government. He would make his opinion known through many speeches at the Convention. Morris would also polish the final draft of the Constitution.

James Wilson, too, represented Pennsylvania at the Convention. Other delegates admired Wilson's political knowledge, which he would use to help clarify the issues facing the Convention.

A Student of History and Politics Perhaps the best-prepared delegate was 36-year-old James Madison of Virginia. For months, the quiet, shy Madison had been reading books on history, politics, and commerce.

His intelligence and his ideas about how to structure a democratic government strongly influenced the other delegates. Today, Madison is often called the "Father of the Constitution."

Keeping Conversations Among Themselves When the Convention began, the delegates decided to keep their talks private. They wanted to speak their minds freely in front of other delegates and be able to explore issues without pressures from outside.

Most of them thought the Articles of Confederation had made the central government too weak. They agreed that the government must be stronger, but not too strong. They did not want anything resembling the British monarchy.

READING CHECK **Compare and Contrast** How were the delegates to the Convention alike and different?

Analyze Images George Washington (in black, at right) was chosen by his fellow delegates to lead the Constitutional Convention in 1787. **Infer** Why do you think the delegates chose Washington to lead the proceedings?

INTERACTIVE

The Great Compromise

Disagreements Over a New Government

Soon after the meeting began, the delegates realized they would have to do more than simply revise the Articles of Confederation. They chose instead to write an entirely new constitution for the nation. They disagreed, however, about the form the new national government should take.

Virginia Proposes a Plan Edmund Randolph and James Madison, both from Virginia, proposed a plan for the new government. This **Virginia Plan** called for a strong national government with three branches that would be responsible for different tasks. Each would keep the others from growing too powerful.

Quest CONNECTIONS

How did states respond to these plans? Record your findings in your Active Journal.

Under the Virginia Plan, the legislature would consist of two houses. The number of representatives would be based on population. Thus, in both houses, larger states would have more representatives than smaller ones. Small states opposed the Virginia Plan. They feared that the large states could easily outvote them in Congress. Supporters of the Virginia Plan replied that it was only fair for a state with more people to have more representatives.

New Jersey's Proposal After two weeks of debate, William Paterson of New Jersey presented a plan that had the support of the small states. Like the Virginia Plan, the **New Jersey Plan** called for three branches of government. However, it provided for a legislature that had only one house. Each state, regardless of its population, would have one vote in the legislature, just as it had under the Articles of Confederation.

READING CHECK **Identify Main Ideas** What was the essential difference between the Virginia Plan and the New Jersey Plan?

Analyze Images Oliver Ellsworth and Roger Sherman, delegates from Connecticut, devised a solution to the problem of representation. **Summarize** Explain what their solution was.

The Great Compromise

For a while, no agreement could be reached. Tempers flared. The Convention seemed ready to fall apart. Finally, Roger Sherman of Connecticut worked out a **compromise**. A compromise, a solution in which each side gives up some of its demands to reach an agreement.

Sherman's compromise called for the creation of a two-house legislature. Members of the lower house, the House of Representatives, would be elected by popular vote. As the larger states wished, seats would be awarded to each state based on population. Members of the upper house, called the Senate, would be chosen by state legislatures. Each state, no matter what its size, would have two senators. Small states particularly liked this part of Sherman's compromise.

Virginia and New Jersey Plans

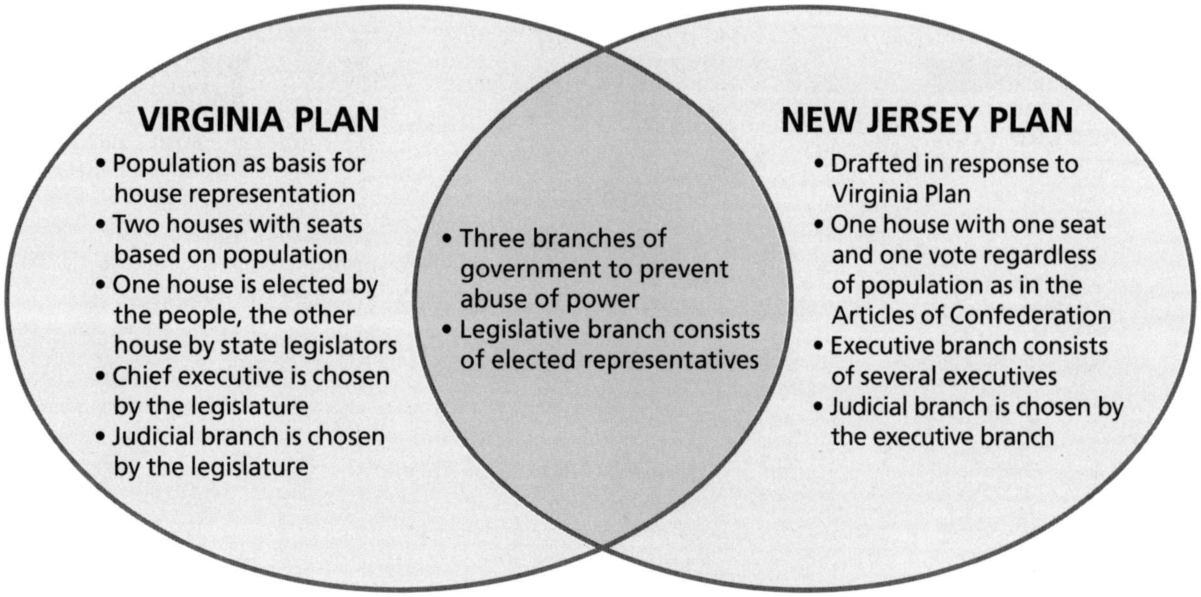

VIRGINIA PLAN	Both	NEW JERSEY PLAN
• Population as basis for house representation • Two houses with seats based on population • One house is elected by the people, the other house by state legislators • Chief executive is chosen by the legislature • Judicial branch is chosen by the legislature	• Three branches of government to prevent abuse of power • Legislative branch consists of elected representatives	• Drafted in response to Virginia Plan • One house with one seat and one vote regardless of population as in the Articles of Confederation • Executive branch consists of several executives • Judicial branch is chosen by the executive branch

Analyze Images This diagram summarizes the two plans presented for the new federal government. **Use Visual Information** How did the New Jersey Plan and Virginia Plan differ in their approach to the executive branch of government?

On July 16, the delegates narrowly approved Sherman's plan. It became known as the **Great Compromise**. Each side, in an admirable show of civic virtue, gave up some demands to achieve unity. With a margin of just one vote, the delegates had found a peaceful solution to a problem that had threatened to bring the convention to a halt.

READING CHECK **Identify Supporting Details** How did the Great Compromise address the concerns of small and large states?

The Three-Fifths Compromise

Just as there were disagreements between large states and small states, there were also disagreements between northern states and southern states. The most serious disagreements concerned slavery. Would enslaved people be counted as part of a state's population? Would the slave trade continue to bring enslaved Africans into the United States?

The States Reach an Agreement Southerners wanted to include enslaved people in their states' population counts because that would give southern states more representatives in the House of Representatives. Southern states stood to gain greatly if enslaved people were counted. Extra representatives meant additional influence.

Northerners objected. They argued that since enslaved people could not vote, they should not be counted when assigning representatives.

Once again, the delegates compromised. They agreed that three-fifths of the enslaved people in any state would be counted.

In other words, if a state had 5,000 enslaved residents, 3,000 of them would be included in the state's population count. This agreement became known as the **Three-Fifths Compromise**.

Quick Activity

Study the biographies and writings of delegates and draw conclusions about the relationships between their backgrounds and points of view.

THE THREE-FIFTHS COMPROMISE

ISSUE AND COMPROMISE

THE NORTHERN VIEW
We'll be outvoted if we let them count slaves, and slaves are unable to vote.

THE COMPROMISE
Each slave counts as $\frac{3}{5}$ of a person.

THE SOUTHERN VIEW
Our slaves should be counted as part of our population and representation.

ESTIMATING THE EFFECT OF COMPROMISE

REPRESENTATION FOR VIRGINIA 1790

POPULATION: **442,177** FREE WHITES; **292,627** ENSLAVED

STEP 1: $\frac{3}{5}$ OF **292,627** ENSLAVED POPULATION = **175,576**

STEP 2: **175,576** ENSLAVED + **442,177** FREE = **617,753** TOTAL

STEP 3: Counting only the free population, Virginia would have **15 representatives.**
Counting the free + enslaved populations, Virginia would have **25 representatives.**
Counting free + $\frac{3}{5}$ enslaved populations, Virginia would have **20 representatives.**

Source: University of Delaware

EFFECT ON SOUTHERN REPRESENTATION

SOUTHERN REPRESENTATION IN THE HOUSE 1790

NOT COUNTING THREE-FIFTHS OF SLAVES: 31%

COUNTING THREE-FIFTHS OF SLAVES: 43%

Analyze Images The Three-Fifths Compromise balanced regional concerns. **Use Visual Information** How did southern states benefit from the Three-Fifths Compromise?

The fraction in the Three-Fifths Compromise had come from a rule about taxes in the Articles of Confederation. The new compromise balanced the concerns of northerners and southerners.

Further Disagreement Over Slavery By 1787, some northern states had banned the sale of enslaved people within their borders. Delegates from these states wanted to ban the importation of enslaved Africans for the entire nation. Southerners argued that such a ban would ruin their economy.

In a second compromise, Northerners agreed that Congress could not ban imports of enslaved Africans for at least 20 years. After that, Congress could regulate or ban imports of enslaved people if it wished. Northerners also agreed that no state could stop a person fleeing slavery from being returned to an owner. This clause in the Constitution became a powerful tool for enslavers.

Academic Vocabulary
ethical • *adj.,* following accepted standards for conduct or behavior

The compromises, however, also brought up an **ethical** question. How could the nation's ideals of freedom, liberty, and democracy be adopted alongside slavery?

READING CHECK **Identify Main Ideas** Why did many of the northern states object to including enslaved people in population counts?

The Convention Comes to a Conclusion

After a long summer full of struggle and argument, the Constitution was ready to be signed on September 17, 1787. Its opening lines, or Preamble, expressed the goals of the Framers: "We the People of the United States, in order to form a more perfect union . . . " Had they succeeded in meeting the goals that brought them together? History's judgment has largely agreed that they had.

As the delegates gathered for the last time, Benjamin Franklin rose and said:

Primary Source

> "I cannot help expressing a wish, that every member of the Convention who may still have objections to it, would with me, on this occasion, doubt a little of his own infallibility, and . . . put his name to this instrument."
>
> —Benjamin Franklin, *Records of the Federal Convention of 1787*

Three delegates refused to sign. Edmund Randolph and George Mason of Virginia, along with Elbridge Gerry of Massachusetts, feared that the new Constitution handed over too much power to the national government.

The Constitution's creation began a process in which states had to decide whether to approve the Constitution. Each state would hold a convention to approve or reject the plan for the new government. Once nine states endorsed it, the Constitution would become law.

READING CHECK Identify Supporting Details Why did some delegates choose not to sign the Constitution?

Analyze Images Although some northern states wanted to ban slavery, the Constitutional Convention did not end slavery or the slave trade. **Summarize** Explain why the delegates decided to compromise on this issue.

Lesson Check

Practice Vocabulary

1. How did the legislative branch of government differ under the **Virginia Plan** and the **New Jersey Plan**?
2. What role did **compromise** play at the **Constitutional Convention**?

Critical Thinking and Writing

3. **Draw Conclusions** Could the Constitution have been produced if George Washington had not attended the Convention? Explain.
4. **Infer** What is so significant about the Preamble's opening words, "We the People of the United States . . ."?
5. **Writing Workshop: Support Claims** Write a few sentences in your Active Journal that support claims concerning how much power the government should have. These sentences will help you develop the essay that you will write at the end of the Topic.

LESSON 3

Ideas That Influenced the Constitution

GET READY TO READ

START UP

Look at the image of the signing of the Mayflower Compact. How did that document influence the Constitution?

GUIDING QUESTIONS

- What did American leaders learn about government from studying ancient Rome?
- How did ideas and traditions from Europe and the colonial past shape the Constitution?

TAKE NOTES

Literacy Skills Classify and Categorize

Use the graphic organizer in your Active Journal to take notes as you read the lesson.

PRACTICE VOCABULARY

Use the vocabulary activity in your Active Journal to practice the vocabulary words.

Vocabulary	Academic Vocabulary
republic	civic
dictatorship	free enterprise
Magna Carta	
English Bill of Rights	
separation of powers	

Long before the Revolution, John Adams called on Americans to investigate how governments worked. He urged them to "search into the spirit of the British constitution" and study the great examples of ancient Greece and Rome. Adams knew the new nation could learn much from the past.

The delegates to the Constitutional Convention followed his advice.

What Did Americans Learn from the Roman Republic?

The delegates wanted to create a **republic**, a government in which citizens rule themselves through elected representatives. Few republics in the history of the world survived very long. To create one that would last, American leaders looked to the ancient examples of Greece and Rome.

What Was Civic Republicanism?

Americans greatly admired the Roman Republic. Independence and public service were virtues that the founders saw in the citizens of Rome.

Roman citizens were willing to serve in public office because they were devoted to their republic. The tradition of encouraging citizen participation to promote the common good, or the well-being of the community, became known as **civic** republicanism. The founders kept this in mind as they worked.

Academic Vocabulary
civic • *adj.,* having to do with being a citizen

A Belief in Independent Citizens At the same time, the Founding Fathers saw the collapse of Rome's republic as a warning to the United States. No republic could survive unless its citizens remained independent and devoted to public service without the desire for personal or financial gains. Under the ruler Caesar Augustus, Rome eventually became a **dictatorship**, a government in which one person or a small group holds complete authority. The leaders of the American Revolution believed that Romans stumbled once they allowed corruption to take over.

Historians today admit that the Founding Fathers somewhat exaggerated the virtues of Rome's republic. Yet the lessons they learned still have force. Republics do not always die because they are invaded from outside. They can decay from within unless their citizens put the nation's needs above their own. Achieving this republican ideal takes dedication and also education, as American leaders knew. They had encouraged education in the Northwest Ordinance. Thomas Jefferson later wrote, "If a nation expects to be ignorant and free, in a state of civilization, it expects what never was and never will be."

READING CHECK **Identify Supporting Details** What qualities of citizens in the Roman Republic did many of the founders admire?

Analyze Images The Roman Republic inspired the founders because it was a long-lasting representative government. **Infer** Based on the image, who among the Roman population were citizens?

INTERACTIVE

Influences on the Constitution

How Did English Documents Influence the Framers?

Greece and Rome were not the only examples of democratic government. Despite their quarrel with Britain, leaders of the Revolution valued British traditions of freedom.

The Magna Carta King John of England signed the **Magna Carta** in 1215. The Magna Carta contained two basic ideas that helped to shape both British and American government. First, it made it clear that English monarchs themselves had to obey the law.

King John agreed not to raise taxes without first consulting the Great Council of nobles and church officials. Eventually, the Great Council grew into the British Parliament.

Just as important, the Magna Carta stated that English nobles had certain rights—rights that were later extended to other classes of people as well. These included rights to trial by jury and the right to private property. The idea of private property rights strongly influenced the beliefs of early Americans, which partly explains the development of a **free enterprise** system throughout the nation.

Academic Vocabulary

free enterprise • *n.*, an economic system in which businesses compete freely with little government control

The English Bill of Rights In 1689, the **English Bill of Rights** went further in protecting the rights of citizens. The document said that parliamentary elections should be held regularly.

It upheld the right to trial by jury and allowed some citizens to bear arms. It also affirmed the right of habeas corpus, the idea that no one could be held in prison without first being charged with a specific crime.

READING CHECK **Identify Central Issues** What are some of the significant ideas found in the Magna Carta?

Analyze Images This illustration shows King John of England signing the Magna Carta in 1215. **Identify Main Ideas** How might the Magna Carta have influenced the ideas of the Framers of the United States Constitution?

What American Traditions Did the Framers Draw On?

Americans enjoyed a long tradition of representative government. The Virginia colonists set up the House of Burgesses. Eventually, each colony elected its own legislature.

Analyze Images In this engraving, William and Mary receive the English Bill of Rights. **Cite Evidence** How did the English Bill of Rights expand the rights given to citizens in the Magna Carta?

Self-Government Americans were used to governing themselves, sometimes without representatives. In New England, the male residents of the town took a direct and active role in making their town's laws at an annual Town Meeting.

Americans were also used to relying on written documents that clearly identified the powers and limits of government. The Mayflower Compact, written in 1620, was the first document of self-government in North America. Each of the colonies had a written charter granted by the monarch or by Parliament.

Answerable to the People The Framers of the Constitution also drew on their own experiences. They bitterly remembered their grievances against the English king. In writing the Constitution, they sought to prevent such abuses.

For example, the Declaration of Independence accused the king of placing military power above civilian authority. The Constitution made the elected President "Commander in Chief of the Army and Navy . . . and of the militia of the several states." The Declaration protested that the king had made judges "dependent on his will alone." The Constitution set up a court system independent of the President and legislature.

The Framers were very familiar with the workings of the Second Continental Congress, the Articles of Confederation, and their own state governments. Much that went into the Constitution came either from the Articles or from the state constitutions.

Limits to Democratic Rights Not all Americans enjoyed the same democratic rights during this period. State voting laws generally reflected colonial ideas about race, gender, and wealth. Only white male adults who owned property could vote or hold office in much of the country.

This left out the vast majority of women, African Americans, and Native Americans. A few states, mostly in New England, did allow free Black men to vote if they met property qualifications, but the number who met those qualifications was very small. Unmarried women were allowed to own property and live independently and even enter into contracts. Married women were not so fortunate. Everything they owned before marriage or earned during it became their husbands' property. In either case, women had no political rights.

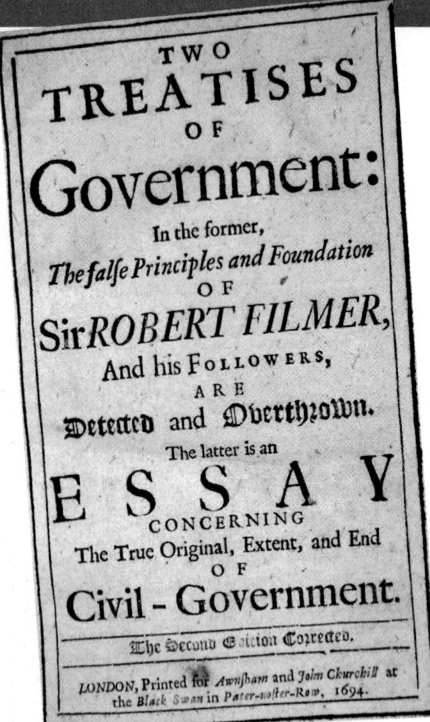

TWO
TREATISES
OF
Government:
In the former,
The false Principles and Foundation
OF
Sir ROBERT FILMER,
And his FOLLOWERS,
ARE
Detected and Overthrown.
The latter is an
ESSAY
CONCERNING
The True Original, Extent, and End
OF
Civil-Government.
The Second Edition Corrected.
LONDON, Printed for *Awnsham* and *John Churchill* at the *Black Swan* in *Pater-noster-Row*, 1694.

▲ John Locke's writings suggested the idea that governments exist to secure and protect the rights of their citizens.

INTERACTIVE

Two Treatises of Government

The Influence of the Enlightenment

The Constitution was also based on the ideas of the European Enlightenment. Enlightenment thinkers believed that people could improve society through the use of reason. Many of the Constitution's Framers had read the works of Enlightenment thinkers.

John Locke The English writer John Locke published *Two Treatises of Government* in 1690. In it, he stated two important ideas. First, Locke declared that all people had natural rights to life, liberty, and property.

Second, he suggested that government is an agreement between the ruler and the ruled. The ruler must enforce the laws and protect the people. If a ruler violates the people's natural rights, the people have a right to rebel.

Locke's ideas were popular among Americans. The Framers of the Constitution wanted to protect people's natural rights and limit the power of government. They saw the Constitution as a contract between the people and their government.

Locke's principle of a natural right to property was established in the Constitution. Certain guarantees in the Constitution protect the rights of people to own private property, enforce contracts, and engage freely in business activities. These freedoms are essential to a free enterprise system. Article I of the Constitution also gave Congress the power to regulate commerce and encourage the free flow of goods between states. This created an environment in which business could thrive.

Some Grievances Against the King

GRIEVANCE IN DECLARATION OF INDEPENDENCE	MODERN INTERPRETATION
He has forbidden his governors to pass laws of immediate and pressing importance, unless suspended in their operation till his assent should be obtained; and, when so suspended, he has utterly neglected to attend to them.	Colonial government in the colonies cannot function with the king's interference.
He has dissolved representative houses, repeatedly, for opposing, with manly firmness, his invasions on the rights of the people.	Colonial governments are not free to speak out against royal policies without fear of retribution.
He has kept among us, in time of peace, standing armies, without the consent of our legislatures.	The colonies have no representation in the British Parliament.
He has excited domestic insurrections amongst us and has endeavored to bring on the inhabitants of our frontiers, the merciless Indian savages, whose known rule of warfare is an undistinguished destruction of all ages, sexes, and conditions.	The king's actions are causing conflicts between Loyalists and Patriots. He is also attempting to pit the Native Americans against the colonists by appearing as if he is protecting Native American lands from further western settlement.

Analyze Images This lists some of the colonists' complaints. **Summarize** What role did American Indians play in the colonists' grievances?

Charles-Louis Montesquieu The French Enlightenment thinker Charles-Louis Baron de Montesquieu (MAHN tus kyoo) influenced American ideas of how a government should be constructed.

In his 1748 book *The Spirit of the Laws,* Montesquieu stressed the importance of the rule of law. The powers of government, he said, should be clearly defined and divided up.

He suggested that three separate branches be created. The legislative branch would pass the laws. The executive branch would carry out the laws. The judicial branch, or system of courts, would decide whether laws or the Constitution were violated. This idea, known as the **separation of powers**, was designed to keep any person or group from gaining too much power.

Analyze Images Baron de Montesquieu was a French Enlightenment thinker. **Summarize** How did Montesquieu's idea of the separation of powers affect the structure of the United States Constitution?

A New Tradition Emerges The founders drew on many traditions. In the end, though, the new system of government was not quite like anything that came before it.

When John Adams received the news from Philadelphia while serving as an ambassador to Great Britain, he wrote, "As we say at sea, huzza for the new world and farewell to the old one!" He called the Constitution "the greatest single effort of national deliberation that the world has ever seen."

READING CHECK **Identify Supporting Details** What idea from Baron de Montesquieu influenced American government?

Lesson Check

Practice Vocabulary

1. How did the **Magna Carta** and **the English Bill of Rights** influence the Framers' ideas about the structure of the United States government?
2. Why do you think the founders were drawn to Montesquieu's ideas about rule of law and **separation of powers**?

Critical Thinking and Writing

3. **Draw Conclusions** The British constitution is unwritten. Why do you think the Framers insisted on a written Constitution?
4. **Understand Effects** Why do you think English political traditions had such a strong influence on the founders?
5. **Writing Workshop: Distinguish Claims from Opposing Claims** Think about the claims that you have introduced and supported concerning how much power the government should have. For each claim, write an opposing claim in your Active Journal. This will help you write the essay at the end of the Topic.

Primary Sources

Thomas Jefferson, Virginia Statute for Religious Freedom

The Virginia Statute for Religious Freedom, drafted by Thomas Jefferson, was a forerunner of the First Amendment, which guarantees the free exercise of religion.

◀ Jefferson first drafted this document in 1777, and the Virginia legislature passed it in 1786.

Reading and Vocabulary Support

① Something that is temporal has to do with earthly life.

② Civil incapacitations are disadvantages a citizen might face.

③ To be compelled is to be forced.

④ Civil capacities refer to the ability of a citizen to participate in the political process. See the related phrase in Item 2, *civil incapacitations*.

Whereas, Almighty God hath created the mind free; that all attempts to influence it by temporal ① punishments or burthens [burdens], or by civil incapacitations ② tend only to beget habits of hypocrisy and meanness, and are a departure from the plan of the holy author of our religion, . . . Be it enacted by General Assembly that no man shall be compelled ③ to frequent or support any religious worship, place, or ministry whatsoever, nor shall be enforced, restrained, molested, or burthened in his body or goods, nor shall otherwise suffer on account of his religious opinions or belief, but that all men shall be free to profess, and by argument to maintain, their opinions in matters of Religion, and that the same shall in no wise diminish, enlarge or affect their civil capacities. ④ And though we well know that this Assembly elected by the people for the ordinary purposes of Legislation only, have no power to restrain the acts of succeeding Assemblies constituted with powers equal to our own, and that therefore to declare this act irrevocable would be of no effect in law; yet we are free to declare, and do declare that the rights hereby asserted, are of the natural rights of mankind, and that if any act shall be hereafter passed to repeal the present or to narrow its operation, such act will be an infringement of natural right.

Analyzing Primary Sources

Cite specific evidence from the document to support your answers.

1. **Vocabulary: Determine Meaning** What phrase in this document means that no one should be forced to attend a church?
2. **Compare and Contrast** Jefferson also drafted the Declaration of Independence. What principle, or "truth," that appears in the Declaration can also be found in this Statute of Religious Freedom?

LESSON 4

Federalists, Antifederalists, and the Bill of Rights

GET READY TO READ

START UP

Study the image of Patrick Henry. Write a sentence about something you feel strongly about.

GUIDING QUESTIONS

- What were the main arguments for and against ratifying the Constitution?
- Why did Antifederalists insist on adding a bill of rights to the Constitution?
- What difficulties were encountered during the process of ratification?

TAKE NOTES

Literacy Skills Sequence

Use the graphic organizer in your Active Journal to take notes as you read the lesson.

PRACTICE VOCABULARY

Use the vocabulary activity in your Active Journal to practice the vocabulary words.

Vocabulary	Academic Vocabulary
ratify	statute
Federalist	compel
Antifederalist	
Federalist Papers	
amend	

The Framers of the Constitution sent the document to Congress, along with a letter from George Washington. Washington warmly approved the document. He predicted that the Constitution would "promote the lasting welfare of that country so dear to us all."

The Federalists and the Antifederalists Debate

The Framers had set up a process for the states to approve, or **ratify**, the new government. The Constitution would go into effect when at least 9 of the 13 states had ratified it. In 1787 and 1788, voters in each state elected delegates to special state conventions. These delegates would decide whether to ratify the Constitution.

For Ratification: The Arguments of the Federalists In every state, heated debates took place. Supporters of the Constitution called themselves **Federalists** because they favored a strong federal, or national, government. They called people who opposed the Constitution **Antifederalists**.

Did you know?

When he was just 14, Alexander Hamilton was helping run a business on St. Croix, managing men much older than himself.

Federalists argued that the Articles of Confederation left too much power with the individual states. This imbalance produced a dangerously weak central government. Disputes among the states, Federalists said, made it too difficult for the government to function.

Federalists believed that the Constitution gave the national government the authority it needed to function effectively. At the same time, they said, the Constitution still protected the rights and powers of the individual states.

Federalists James Madison, Alexander Hamilton, and John Jay wrote a series of essays, known today as the ***Federalist Papers***. Their purpose was to explain and defend the Constitution. They used pen names, but most people knew who they were. Today, the Federalist Papers remain among the best discussions of the political theory behind the American system of government.

Courts still refer to the *Federalist Papers* in making decisions about the principles and role of government. In this way, they have had a lasting influence on the U.S. system of government.

Against Ratification: The Arguments of the Antifederalists

Antifederalists felt that the Constitution made the national government too strong and left the states too weak. They also thought that the Constitution gave the President too much power. Patrick Henry of Virginia protested:

Primary Source

"This Constitution is said to have beautiful features, but . . . they appear to me horribly frightful. . . . Your President may become king."

—Patrick Henry, Speech to the Virginia Convention, June 1788

5 BIOGRAPHY Things to Know About ALEXANDER HAMILTON

First U.S. secretary of the treasury 1755–1804

- Hamilton was born on the British island of Nevis in the West Indies.
- He represented New York State at the Constitutional Convention.
- He wrote more than 50 of the 85 Federalist Papers, in which he argued forcefully for a strong central government.
- He was killed in a duel with rival Aaron Burr.
- He was the subject of an award-winning musical that opened on Broadway in 2015.

Critical Thinking If he had not been killed in a duel, do you think Hamilton would have become President? Why or why not?

Most people expected George Washington to be elected President. Antifederalists admired Washington, but they warned that future Presidents might lack Washington's honor and skill. For this reason, they said, the office should not be too powerful.

READING CHECK **Identify Main Ideas** What issues of power led Antifederalists to oppose the Constitution?

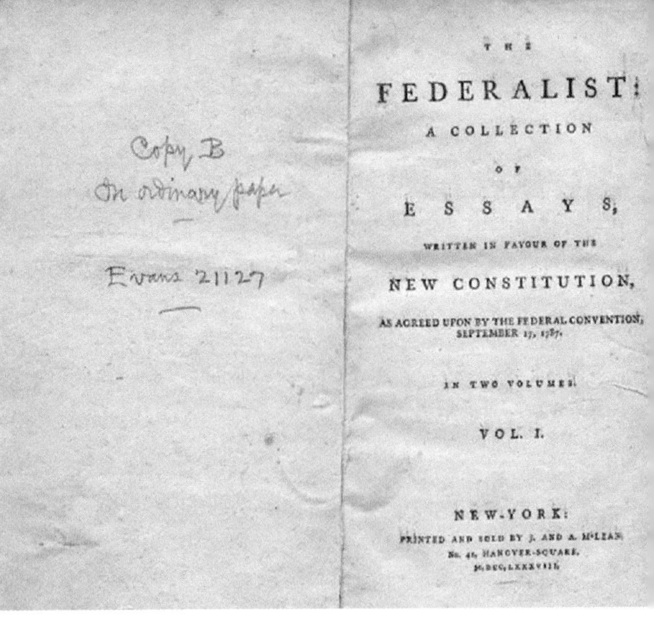

Copy B
On ordinary paper
Evans 21127

THE
FEDERALIST:
A COLLECTION
OF
ESSAYS,
WRITTEN IN FAVOUR OF THE
NEW CONSTITUTION,
AS AGREED UPON BY THE FEDERAL CONVENTION,
SEPTEMBER 17, 1787.
IN TWO VOLUMES.
VOL. I.
NEW-YORK:
PRINTED AND SOLD BY J. AND A. M'LEAN,
No. 41, HANOVER-SQUARE,
M,DCC,LXXXVIII.

Analyze Images The *Federalist essays* presented the argument for a strong central government. **Infer** What might have happened if *these essays* had not been written?

Why Did Antifederalists Demand a Bill of Rights?

The chief objection of Antifederalists was that the Constitution did not have a specific bill, or list, of guaranteed protections of individual rights. Federalists held that it was impossible to list all the natural rights of people. Besides, they said, the Constitution protected citizens well enough as it was.

Antifederalists responded that a bill of rights was needed to protect such basic liberties as freedom of speech and religion. Unless these rights were spelled out, they could be too easily ignored or denied by the government. Americans, after all, had just fought a revolution to protect their freedoms against a too-powerful government. Violations of those freedoms were the main grievances cited in the Declaration of Independence. Antifederalists argued that a bill of rights was needed to address those grievances.

Under the new Constitution, the President would have veto power over Congress—the people's representatives. Surely placing so much power in one man's hands, the Antifederalists argued, likewise demanded the protection of a bill of rights.

One of the strongest supporters of a bill of rights was George Mason of Virginia. In 1776, Mason had written the bill of rights for Virginia's constitution. After the Constitutional Convention refused to include a bill of rights, Mason joined the Antifederalists. He wrote a pamphlet opposing the ratification of the Constitution. The pamphlet was titled, simply, "Objections to This Constitution of Government." Its opening words were equally direct: "There is no Declaration of Rights."

INTERACTIVE

Federalists versus Antifederalists

READING CHECK **Identify Supporting Details** What was the purpose of George Mason's pamphlet?

The Ratification Process

One by one, the states voted. Delaware led the way, ratifying on December 7, 1787. Five days later, with the strong support of James Wilson, Pennsylvania ratified the Constitution. New Jersey soon followed. In these states, as in the states that ratified later, the main cause behind ratification was that Federalists were able to convince a majority of delegates that the Constitution would bring an improved system of government.

Ratification of the Constitution

The Debate in New England Massachusetts was the first key battleground. There, the old patriots Sam Adams and John Hancock held back their support. The delay seemed "very ominous," wrote Madison. Finally, Adams and Hancock convinced the state convention to recommend adding a bill of rights to the Constitution.

Still the debate continued. "Some gentlemen say, don't be in a hurry . . . don't take a leap in the dark," a Federalist farmer told his fellow delegates. "I say . . . gather fruit when it is ripe." In February 1788, Massachusetts became the sixth state to ratify.

In June, New Hampshire joined ranks as the ninth state. The new government could now go into effect. Still, the nation's unity remained in doubt. New York and Virginia, two of the largest states, had not yet ratified the plan. In both states, Federalists and Antifederalists were closely matched.

A Vote to Ratify After Long Debates In Virginia, Patrick Henry, George Mason, and Governor Edmund Randolph led the opposition. Still a spellbinding speaker, Henry at one point spoke for seven hours. Soft-spoken James Madison could not match Henry's dramatic style. Yet his arguments in favor of the Constitution were always clear, patient, and to the point.

The tide finally turned when Governor Randolph changed his mind. He gave his support only when the Federalists promised to support a bill of rights. Virginia voted to ratify in late June.

In New York, the struggle went on for another month. In July 1788, the state convention voted to ratify. North Carolina followed in November 1789. Only Rhode Island, which had refused to send delegates to the Constitutional Convention, remained. On May 29, 1790, Rhode Island

Analyze Timelines
Ratifying the Constitution was a long process, taking a year and a half. **Sequence** Which was the first state to vote for ratification? Which was the last?

Voting for Ratification

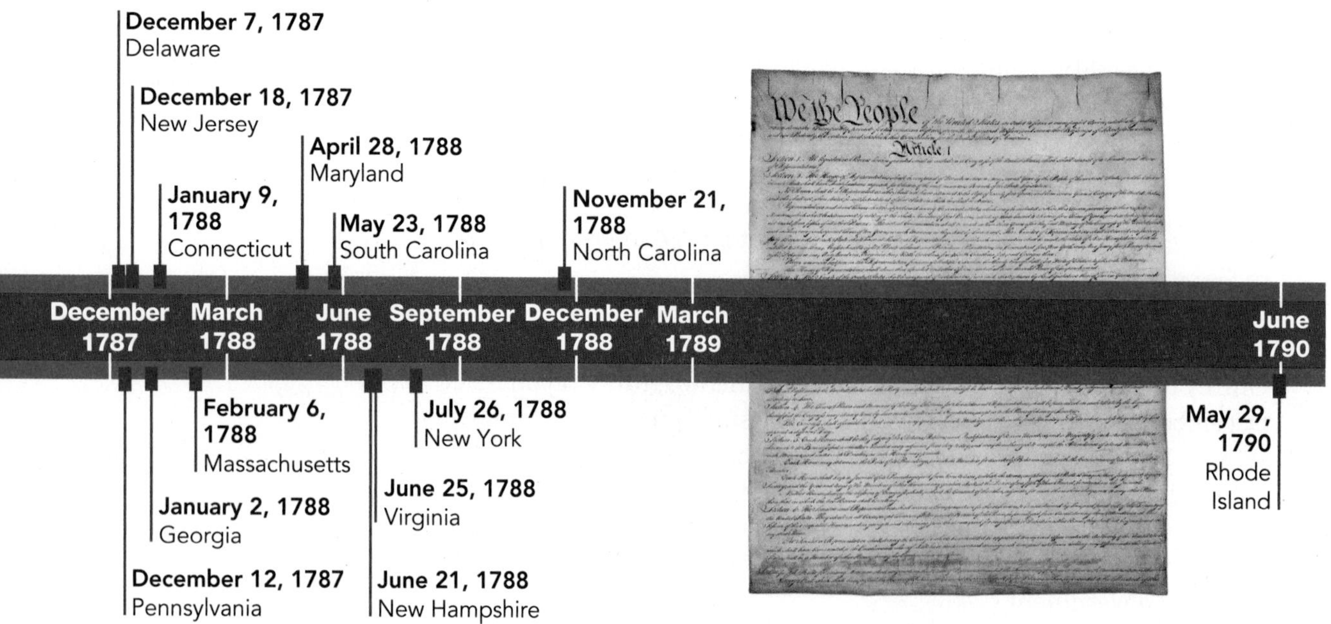

became the last state to ratify the Constitution. The effect of ratification was to create a new system of government for the United States, the same basic system that remains in effect today.

Celebration of a New Constitution Throughout the land, Americans celebrated the news that the Constitution was ratified. The city of Philadelphia set its festival for July 4, 1788.

A festive parade filed along Market Street, led by soldiers who had fought in the Revolution. Thousands cheered as six colorfully outfitted horses pulled a blue carriage shaped like an eagle. Thirteen stars and stripes were painted on the front, and the Constitution was raised proudly above it. Benjamin Rush, a Philadelphia doctor and strong supporter of the Constitution, wrote to a friend, "Tis done. We have become a nation."

Analyze Images A parade in New York celebrates the Constitution's ratification. **Infer** Why do you think people dedicated a float to Alexander Hamilton?

READING CHECK **Identify Cause and Effect** What factor encouraged many states to vote for ratification?

New Amendments

Americans voted in the first election under the Constitution in January 1789. As expected, George Washington was elected President, while John Adams was elected Vice President.

After the election the Congress met in New York City, which was chosen as the nation's capital. Congress quickly turned its attention to adding a bill of rights to the Constitution. Several states had agreed to ratify the Constitution only on the condition that a bill of rights be added.

Amending the Constitution The Framers had established a way to **amend**, or change, the Constitution to modify the rules for the national government. They did not want people to make changes lightly, however. Thus, they made the process of amending the Constitution fairly difficult. In 1789, the first Congress proposed a set of 12 amendments, written by James Madison. As required by the Constitution, the amendments then went for ratification by the states, three fourths of which had to ratify an amendment for it to take effect. By December 1791, three fourths of the states had ratified 10 of the 12 amendments. Together, these 10 amendments became known as the Bill of Rights.

The Bill of Rights James Madison insisted that the Bill of Rights does not *give* Americans any rights. The rights listed, he said, are natural rights that belong to all human beings. The Bill of Rights simply prevents the government from taking these rights away.

Some of the first 10 amendments were intended to prevent the kind of abuse Americans had suffered under British rule.

Analyze Images James Madison supported the separation of church and state. **Compare and Contrast** How did Madison's stance differ from Patrick Henry's?

For example, the Declaration of Independence had condemned the king for forcing colonists to quarter, or house, troops in their homes and for suspending trial by jury. The Third Amendment forbids the government to quarter troops in citizens' homes without their consent. The Sixth and Seventh Amendments guarantee the right to trial by jury.

Religious Freedom Other amendments protected individual rights, as many states had already done. A forerunner of the First Amendment was the Virginia Statute for Religious Freedom, written by Thomas Jefferson and made a state law in 1786. The **statute** said that "No man shall be **compelled** to frequent or support any religious worship . . . or otherwise suffer, on account of his religious opinions or belief."

Religious freedom became the very first right listed in the First Amendment. Jefferson later wrote that the First Amendment built "a wall of separation between Church & State." James Madison supported Jefferson's belief that the state, or government, should not promote religion. But not all founders agreed. Patrick Henry wanted Virginia to establish Christianity as the state religion. Others insisted that only Christians should be allowed to hold office. Still, the First Amendment made it clear that "Congress shall make no law respecting an establishment of religion." The First Amendment also emphasized a key element of the republic: freedom of speech, or people's right to express their point of view without fear of government punishment.

With the Bill of Rights in place, the new framework of government was complete. Over time, the Constitution would grow and change along with the nation.

Academic Vocabulary

statute • *n.*, a law or rule

compel • *v.*, to force

READING CHECK **Identify Supporting Details** What amendments make up the Bill of Rights in the Constitution?

Lesson Check

Practice Vocabulary

1. What was the key argument that the **Federalists** made to persuade states to **ratify** the Constitution?
2. Why did **Antifederalists** insist on a **bill of rights?**

Critical Thinking and Writing

3. **Summarize** the procedure for ratifying the Constitution.
4. **Express Problems Clearly** In June 1788, when nine states had approved the Constitution, it was officially ratified. Why did the issue of ratification still seem unsettled?
5. **Writing Workshop: Use Credible Sources** In your Active Journal, make a list of sources you might use to support or oppose claims regarding this question: How much power should the federal government have, and what should its responsibilities include?

Primary Sources

Federalist and Antifederalist Writings

Federalists John Jay, James Madison, and Alexander Hamilton wrote anonymous essays arguing that states should ratify the Constitution. Antifederalists responded with their own writings identifying problems with the Constitution.

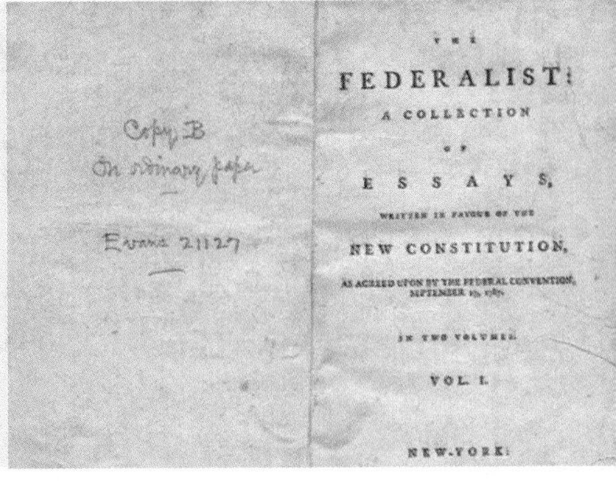

▶ Title page from *The Federalist: A Collection of Essays.*

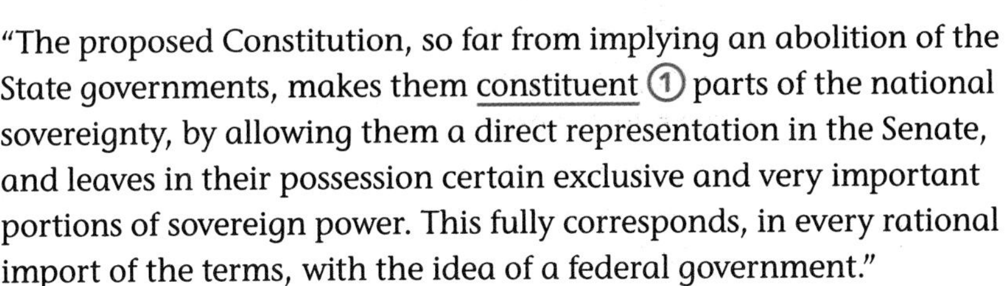

"The proposed Constitution, so far from implying an abolition of the State governments, makes them constituent ① parts of the national sovereignty, by allowing them a direct representation in the Senate, and leaves in their possession certain exclusive and very important portions of sovereign power. This fully corresponds, in every rational import of the terms, with the idea of a federal government."

—Alexander Hamilton, *Federalist* No. 9

"There is no Declaration of Rights, and the laws of the general government being paramount ② to the laws and constitution of the several States, the Declarations of Rights in the separate States are no security ③. . . . There is no declaration of any kind, for preserving the liberty of the press, or the trial by jury in civil causes; nor against the danger of standing armies in times of peace."

—George Mason, "Objections to the Constitution"

Reading and Vocabulary Support

① *Constituent* parts together make up the whole. In this case, what is the whole and what are the constituent parts?

② *Paramount* means "dominant" or "supreme."

③ Summarize how Hamilton's statement answers this antifederalist objection to the Constitution.

Analyzing Primary Sources

Cite specific evidence from these documents to support your answers.

1. **Compare Authors' Treatment of Similar Topics** Which of these statements most directly tries to address people's concerns about federalism? Explain your answer.
2. **Cite Evidence** How were George Mason's main objections to the Constitution later resolved?
3. **Write a Summary** Provide a brief summary of both excerpts. Take care to be objective, not introducing your own opinion into the summaries.

Distinguish Cause and Effect

Follow these steps to distinguish cause and effect.

INTERACTIVE

Analyze Cause and Effect

1 **Identify the key event.** Choose one event or condition as a starting point. Once you know the starting point, you can look for possible causes and effects of that event. What is the key event shown in the chart?

2 **Study earlier events or conditions as possible causes.** A cause of the key event must happen before the key event. Look for earlier events by asking, "Why did the key event happen?" or "What led to the key event?" You may also find such clue words as *because* and *reason* that suggest that one thing caused another. Look at the causes listed in the chart. How did each event or action help lead to the later creation of the Bill of Rights?

3 **Study later events or conditions as possible effects.** Effects must follow the key event. They may include short-term effects or longer-lasting ones. To find later events, ask, "What did the key event lead to?" or "What was a result of the key event?" You may also find clue words or phrases, such as *brought about, led to, as a result*, or *therefore*. Why might we call each of the effects in the chart both a short-term and a long-term effect of adding the Bill of Rights to the Constitution?

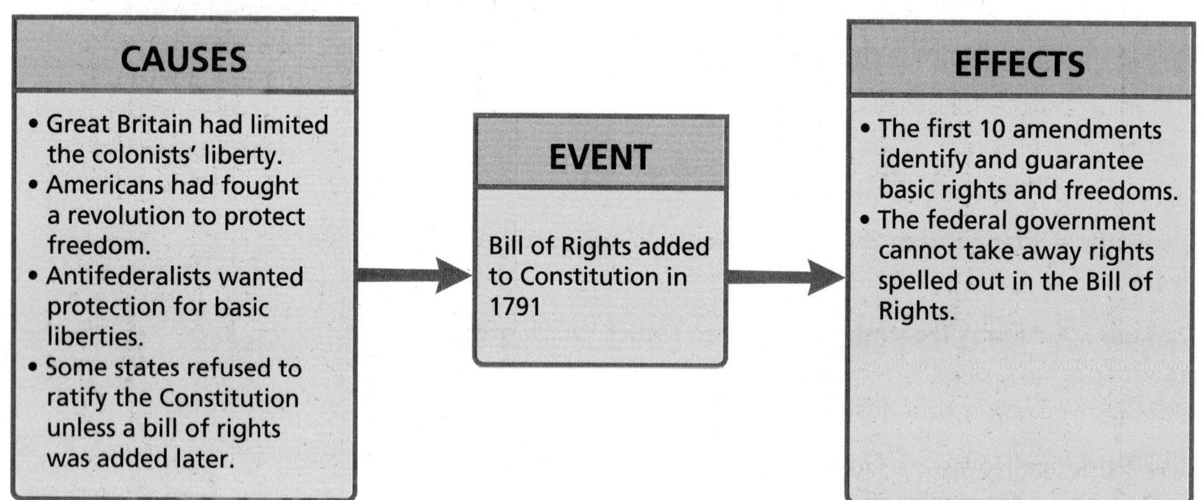

LESSON 5

Understanding the Constitution

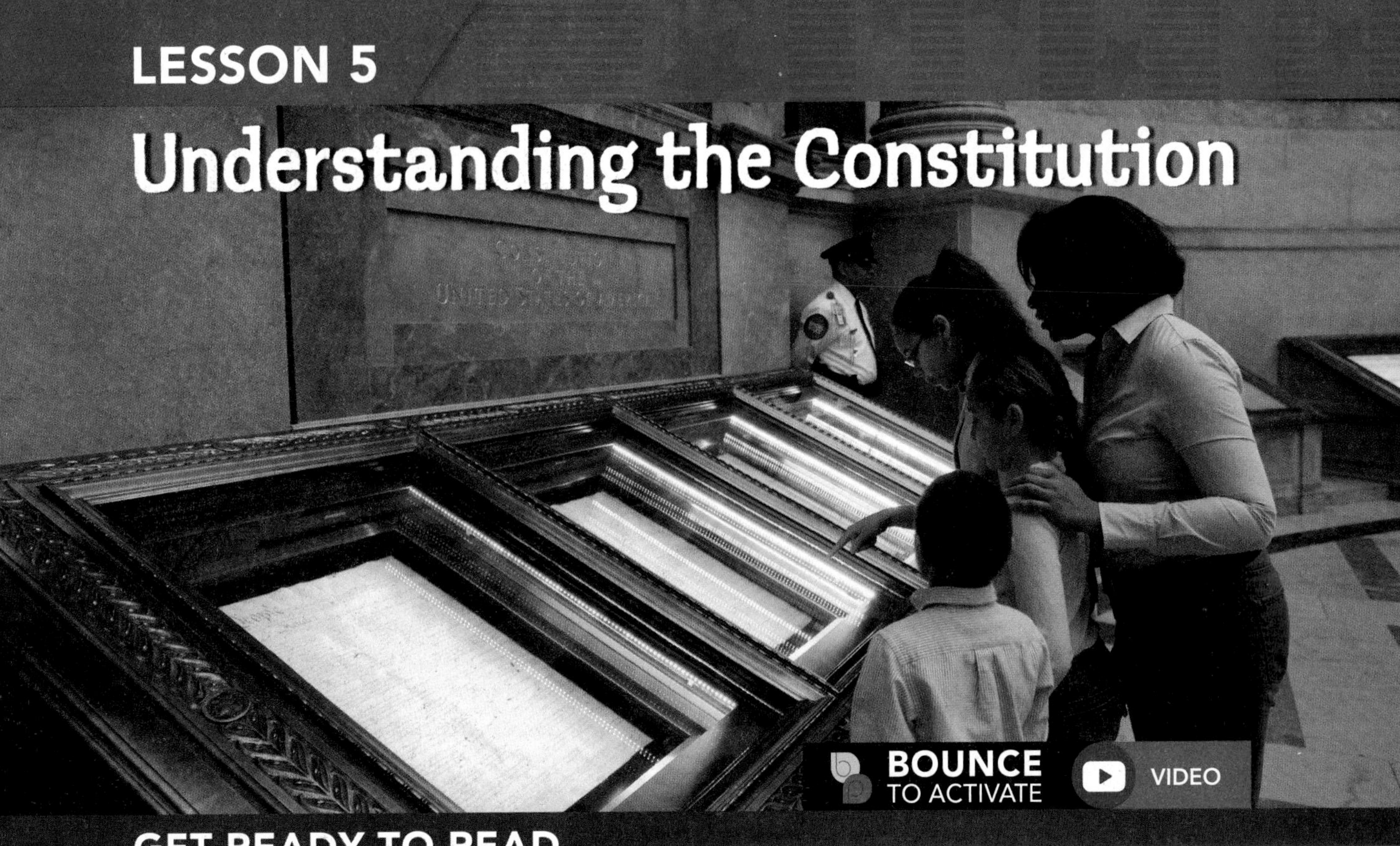

GET READY TO READ

START UP

Look at the photograph of people examining an original copy of the Constitution. Has the Constitution changed?

GUIDING QUESTIONS

- What are the basic goals of the Constitution, as defined in its Preamble?
- What are the powers and duties of each branch of government, as set forth by the Constitution?

TAKE NOTES

Literacy Skills Classify and Categorize

Use the graphic organizer in your Active Journal to take notes as you read the lesson.

PRACTICE VOCABULARY

Use the vocabulary activity in your Active Journal to practice the vocabulary words.

Vocabulary	Academic Vocabulary
popular sovereignty	civilian
bill	liberty
veto	
override	
impeach	

By December 1791, the Constitution had been ratified and the Bill of Rights added. Americans could now familiarize themselves with the new structure of their government.

First Comes the Preamble

The Constitution consists of the Preamble, articles, and amendments. The Preamble states the Constitution's six goals. They are:

To Form a More Perfect Union When the Constitution was written, the states saw themselves almost as separate nations. The Framers wanted to work together as a unified nation. Fortunately for us, they achieved this goal. Think of what it would be like if you had to exchange your money every time you visited another state!

To Establish Justice The Framers knew the nation needed a uniform system to settle legal disputes. Today, the American justice system requires that the law be applied fairly to every American, regardless of his or her race, religion, gender, or country of origin.

Analyze Images A National Guardsman helps a family. **Use Evidence** How does helping the public during times of emergency ensure domestic tranquillity?

To Ensure Domestic Tranquillity Under the Constitution, the national government has the power to ensure domestic tranquillity, or peace and order within our nation's borders. Have you seen reports of the National Guard providing assistance in a disaster area? That is one way that the government works to ensure domestic tranquillity.

To Provide for the Common Defense Every country has a duty to protect its citizens against foreign attack. The Framers of the Constitution gave the national government the power to raise armies and navies. At the same time, they placed the military under **civilian**, or nonmilitary, control.

To Promote the General Welfare The Constitution set out to give the national government the means to promote the general welfare, or the well-being of all its citizens. For example, today the National Institutes of Health leads the fight against many diseases.

To Secure the Blessings of Liberty During the Revolution, the colonists fought and died for **liberty**, or freedom. It is no surprise that the Framers made liberty a major goal of the Constitution. Over the years, amendments to the Constitution have extended the "blessings of liberty" to all Americans.

The Articles and the Amendments The main body of the Constitution is a short document, divided into seven parts called articles. Together, they establish the framework for our government.

Seven Articles The first three articles describe the three branches of the national government: legislative, executive, and judicial. Article 1 establishes the powers of and limits on Congress. Articles 2 and 3 do the same for the President and the courts.

Article 4 deals with relations among the states. It requires states to honor one another's laws and legal decisions. It also sets out a system for admitting new states. Article 5 provides a process to amend the Constitution.

Article 6 states that the Constitution is the "supreme law of the land." This means that states may not make laws that violate the Constitution. If a state law conflicts with a federal law, the federal law prevails.

Academic Vocabulary
civilian • *adj.*, nonmilitary
liberty • *n.*, freedom

The final article, Article 7, sets up a procedure for the states to ratify the Constitution.

Twenty-Seven Amendments In more than 200 years, only 27 formal changes have been made to the Constitution. The first 10 amendments, known as the Bill of Rights, were added in 1791.

READING CHECK **Identify Supporting Details** What is each of the seven main parts of the Constitution called?

Seven Basic Principles

The Constitution reflects seven basic principles. They are popular sovereignty, limited government, separation of powers, checks and balances, federalism, republicanism, and individual rights.

Popular Sovereignty The Framers of the Constitution lived at a time when monarchs claimed that their power came from God. The Preamble, with its phrase "We the people," reflects a revolutionary new idea: that a government gets its authority from the people. This principle, known as **popular sovereignty**, states that the people have the right to alter or abolish their government. Why? Because the people have supreme power, or sovereignty, over the government. No one rules because of divine right.

Analyze Images The first woman elected to Congress was Jeannette Rankin of Montana in 1916. **Infer** Why is it important for Congress to include men and women?

INTERACTIVE

The Federal System

Limited Government The colonists had lived under a British government with nearly unlimited powers. To avoid giving too much power to their new government, the Framers made limited government a principle of the Constitution. In a limited government, the government has only the powers that the Constitution gives it. Just as important, everyone from you to the President must obey the law.

Separation of Powers To further limit government power, the Framers provided for separation of powers. The Constitution separates the government into three branches. The legislative branch, or Congress, makes the laws. The executive branch, headed by the President, carries out the laws. The judicial branch, or courts, determines whether actions violate laws and whether laws violate the Constitution.

Checks and Balances A system of checks and balances safeguards against abuse of power. Each branch of government has the power to check, or limit, the actions of the other two. The separation of powers allows for this system of checks and balances. One reason the government has survived for more than 200 years is because of this system.

Federalism The Constitution also reflects the principle of federalism, or the division of power between the federal government and the states. Among the powers the Constitution gives the federal government are the power to coin money, declare war, and regulate trade between the states. States regulate trade within their own borders, make rules for state elections, and establish schools. Powers not clearly given to the federal government belong to the states.

Analyze Charts The graphic explains the separation of powers. **Use Visual Information** How is the power to make and enforce laws divided among the three branches of government?

Separation of Powers

Legislative Branch

(Congress)

Passes Laws

- Can override President's veto
- Approves treaties and presidential appointments
- Can impeach and remove President and other high officials
- Creates lower federal courts
- Appropriates money
- Prints and coins money
- Raises and supports armed forces
- Can declare war
- Regulates foreign and interstate trade

Executive Branch

(President)

Carries Out Laws

- Proposes laws
- Can veto laws
- Negotiates foreign treaties
- Serves as commander in chief of the armed forces
- Appoints federal judges, ambassadors, and other high officials
- Can grant pardons to federal offenders

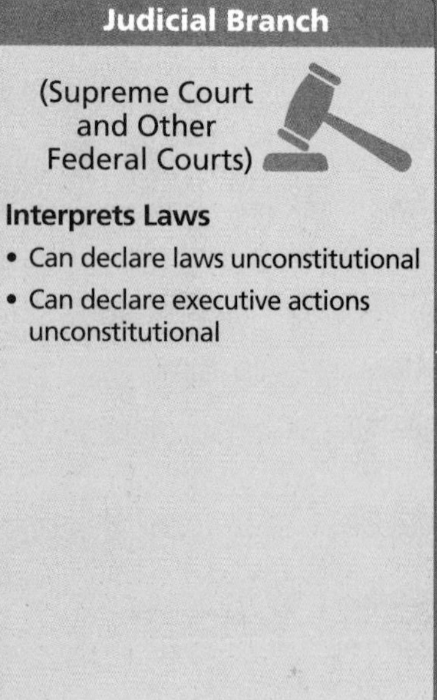

Some powers are shared between the federal government and the states. Thus, federalism results in dual sovereignty. That is, the federal government and the states both exercise authority over the same territory and people.

Republicanism The Constitution provides for a republican form of government. The United States is a constitutional republic. This means that the Constitution provides the basis for its republican form of government. Instead of taking part directly in government, citizens elect representatives to carry out their will. Once in office, representatives vote according to their own judgment. However, they must remain open to the opinions of the people they represent. For that reason, members of Congress maintain Web sites and offices in their home districts.

Individual Rights The final principle the U.S. Constitution reflects is individual rights, such as freedom of speech, freedom of religion, and the right to trial by jury. You will read more about the rights protected by the Constitution later.

Analyze Images The U.S. Capitol building is home to the House and Senate, as well as many offices. **Infer** Why does Congress have such an impressive building?

READING CHECK **Identify Supporting Details** Which of these principles restrict government power?

The Legislative Branch—Congress

The first and longest article of the Constitution deals with the legislative, or lawmaking, branch. Article I sets up Congress to make the nation's laws. Congress is made up of two bodies: the House of Representatives and the Senate.

INTERACTIVE

The U.S. Congress

The House of Representatives The larger of the two bodies is the House of Representatives, which currently has 435 members. Representation in the House is based on population, with larger states having more representatives than smaller states. Every state has at least one representative.

Quest CONNECTIONS

Which states have the largest and smallest numbers of representatives? Record your findings in your Active Journal.

Representatives are elected by the people of their district for two-year terms. As a result, the entire House is up for election every other year. Representatives may run for reelection as many times as they want.

The leader of the House is called the Speaker. The Speaker of the House is one of the most powerful people in the federal government. The Speaker regulates debates and controls the agenda. If the President dies or leaves office, the Speaker of the House is next in line after the Vice President to become President.

The Senate Unlike the House, the Senate is based on equal representation of the states, with two senators for each state. Senators are elected to six-year terms. Their terms overlap, however, so that one third of the members come up for election every two years.

This way, there is always a majority of experienced senators.

Not all of the founders trusted the judgment of the common people. As a result, they called for senators to be chosen by state legislatures. Over the years, the nation slowly became more democratic. The Seventeenth Amendment, ratified in 1913, provided that senators be directly elected by the people of each state, like members of the House.

The Vice President of the United States is president of the Senate. The Vice President presides over the Senate and casts a vote when there is a tie. The Vice President cannot, however, take part in Senate debates. When the Vice President is absent, the Senate's president pro tempore, or temporary president, presides over the proceedings.

Analyze Images Sixty members of the House of Representatives, including John Lewis of Georgia, Nancy Pelosi of California, and Charles Rangel of New York, held a sit-in during a Congressional session to demand action on gun safety in June 2016. **Infer** Why do you think these representatives took such an extreme action?

Powers of Congress The most important power of Congress is the power to make the nation's laws. All laws start as proposals called **bills**. A new bill may be introduced in either the House or the Senate. However, an appropriations bill, which is a bill that sets aside money for government programs or operations, must be introduced in the House. After a bill is introduced, it is debated. If both houses vote to approve the bill, it is then sent to the President. If the President signs the bill, it becomes a law.

The Constitution gives Congress many other powers besides lawmaking. Article I, Section 8, lists most of the powers of Congress. They include the power to borrow money and the power to levy, or require people to pay, taxes. Congress also has the power to coin money, to establish post offices, to fix standard weights and measures, and to declare war.

A clause in Article I, Section 8, also gives Congress the power to regulate commerce between states, with foreign nations, "and with the Indian tribes." When the Constitution was written, Native American nations were considered fully independent. Over time, Congress has used this commerce clause to assume complete authority over the affairs of those nations.

The Elastic Clause Not all the powers of Congress are specifically listed. Article I, Section 8, Clause 18, states that Congress can "make all laws which shall be necessary and proper" for carrying out its specific duties. This clause is known as the elastic clause because it enables Congress to stretch its powers to deal with the changing needs of the nation.

Americans have long debated the true meaning of the elastic clause. What did the Framers mean by the words *necessary* and *proper*? For example, early leaders debated whether the elastic clause gave Congress the right to set up a national bank, even though the Constitution does not specifically give Congress that power.

Today, political parties still have different points of view on how the elastic clause should be used. Some Americans continue to worry that Congress might use the elastic clause to abuse its powers. Sometimes, the terms *strict constructionists* and *loose constructionists* are used to refer to people with different views of the clause.

Strict constructionists think that Congress (and the courts that interpret laws) should strictly construe, or narrowly interpret, the elastic clause. They believe the elastic clause should be used to stretch the powers of government rarely, and only to a small degree. Partly because many members of the Republican Party today are strict constructionists, that party particularly believes in reducing or eliminating some government programs.

In contrast, loose constructionists think that Congress (and the courts that interpret laws) should loosely construe, or broadly interpret, the elastic clause. They think the elastic clause should be used to stretch the powers of government as often as needed, and to a greater degree. Many members of the Democratic Party today are loose constructionists. Because they believe that the role of the federal government can and should expand as needed, they may support government programs opposed by members of the Republican Party.

The Committee System

The First Congress, meeting from 1789 to 1791, considered a total of 31 new bills. Today, more than 10,000 bills are introduced in Congress each year. Clearly, it would be impossible for every member of Congress to give each new bill careful study. To deal with this problem, Congress relies on committees.

Both the House and the Senate have permanent, or standing, committees. Each committee deals with a specific topic, such as agriculture, banking, business, defense, education, science, or transportation. Members who have served longest are usually appointed to the most important committees.

Did you know?

Besides formal committees, members of Congress who have common interests and concerns can form unofficial groups called caucuses.

Analyze Images When a member of the federal government speaks up, is that person expressing an opinion or trying to exert influence? **Analyze Political Cartoons** How do you think the cartoonist would answer that question?

"Ruth Bader Ginsburg was just plain wrong trying to influence the Presidential election. That'd be just like if the Senate tried to influence the Supreme Court by refusing to vote on a President's nominee."

Congress may sometimes create joint committees made up of both Senate and House members. One of the most important kinds of joint committees is the conference committee. Its task is to settle differences between House and Senate versions of the same bill.

READING CHECK **Identify Supporting Details** How does a bill become a law?

The Executive Branch—The President

Article II of the Constitution sets up an executive branch to carry out the laws and run the affairs of the national government. The President is the head of the executive branch. Other members include the Vice President and the executive departments. The heads of the executive departments, who advise the President, are called the Cabinet.

Analyze Images Although Republican candidate Donald J. Trump lost the popular vote to Democrat Hillary Clinton, he won the electoral college vote and so became President in 2017. **Cite Evidence** Should the Electoral College still be used to elect the President? Support your opinion with evidence.

The Many Roles of the President You are probably more familiar with the President than with any other government leader. You see him on television climbing in and out of airplanes, greeting foreign leaders, or making speeches. Yet, many Americans do not know exactly what the President does.

The Framers thought that Congress would be the most important branch of government. Thus, while the Constitution is very specific about the role of the legislature, it offers fewer details about the powers of the President. Beginning with George Washington, Presidents have often taken those actions they thought necessary to carry out the job. In this way, they have shaped the job of President to meet the nation's changing needs.

The President is our highest elected official and, along with the Vice President, the only one who represents all Americans. As head of the executive branch, the President has the duty to carry out the nation's laws. The President directs foreign policy and has the power to make treaties with other nations and to appoint ambassadors.

The President is commander in chief of the armed forces. (Only Congress, however, has the power to declare war.) As the nation's chief legislator, the President suggests new laws and works for their passage.

The President can grant pardons and call special sessions of Congress. The President is also the living symbol of the nation. Presidents welcome foreign leaders, make speeches to commemorate national holidays, and give medals to national heroes.

The Electoral College The President is elected for a four-year term. As a result of the Twenty-second Amendment, adopted in 1951, no President may be elected to more than two complete terms.

The Framers set up a complex system for electing the President, known as the electoral college. When Americans vote for President, they do not vote directly for the candidate of their choice. Rather, they vote for a group of electors who are pledged to the candidate. The number of a state's electors equals the number of its Senators and representatives. No state has fewer than three electors.

A few weeks after Election Day, the electors meet in each state to cast their votes for President. In most states, the candidate with the majority of the popular vote in that state receives all that state's electoral votes. The candidate who receives a majority of the electoral votes nationwide becomes President. This is part of another key principle in the United States: majority rule. Whether passing a bill in a legislature or electing an official, a majority of the votes—more than 50 percent—is usually needed.

Because of the "winner-take-all" nature of the electoral college, a candidate can lose the popular vote nationwide but still be elected President. This has happened five times. Today, some people favor replacing the electoral college with a system that directly elects the President by popular vote. Others oppose any change, pointing out that the electoral college has served the nation well for more than 200 years.

READING CHECK **Draw Conclusions** Why is it said that the President represents all Americans?

The Judicial Branch—The Supreme Court

Article III of the Constitution establishes a Supreme Court and authorizes Congress to establish any other courts that are needed. Under the Judiciary Act of 1789, Congress set up the system of federal courts that is still in place today.

GEOGRAPHY SKILLS

A state's number of electors is based on the combined total of its Senators and representatives.

1. **Movement** As the population shifts, how would the number of electors change?
2. **Infer** What can you infer about a state's population from the number of electors it has?

Electoral College Votes, 2012–2020

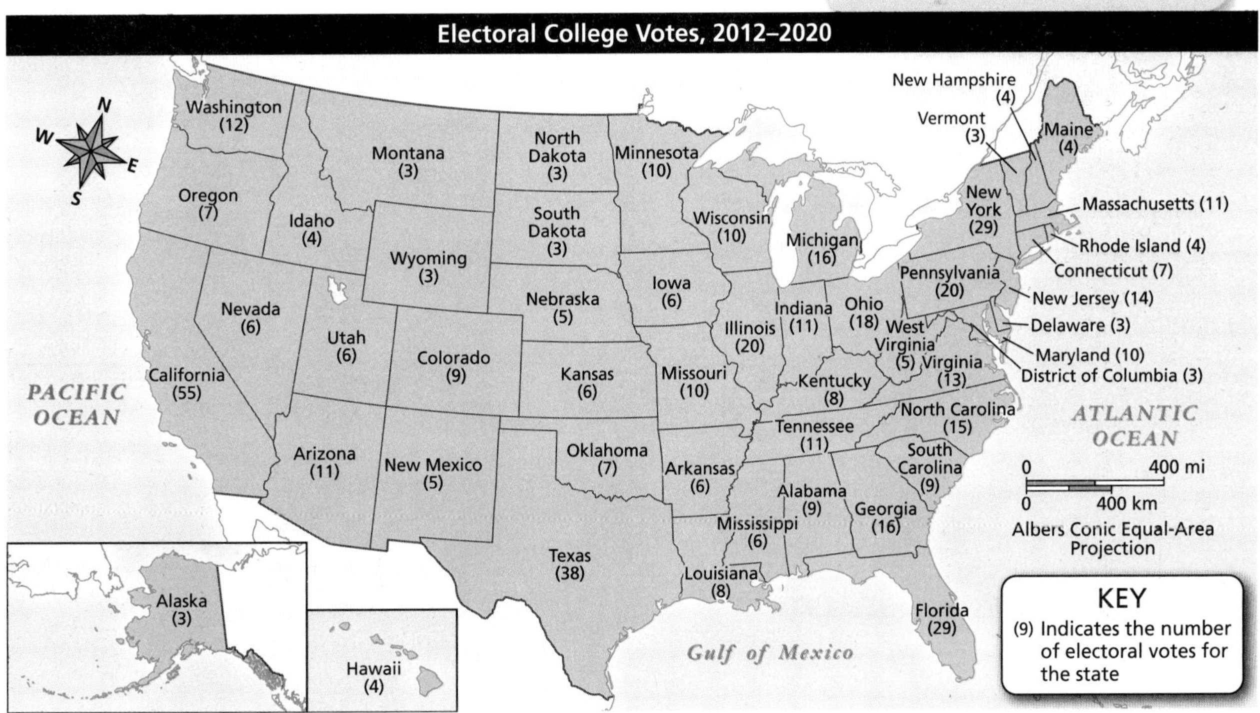

Lower Courts Most federal cases begin in district courts. Evidence is presented during trials, and a jury or a judge decides the facts of the case. A party that disagrees with the decision of the judge or jury may appeal it, that is, ask that the decision be reviewed by a higher court. The next level of courts is the appellate courts, or courts of appeal.

Appellate court judges review decisions of district courts to decide whether the lower court judges interpreted and applied the law correctly.

Supreme Court At the top of the American judicial system is the Supreme Court. The Court is made up of a Chief Justice and eight Associate Justices. The President appoints the Justices, but Congress must approve the appointments. Justices serve for life.

The main job of the Supreme Court is to serve as the nation's final court of appeals. It hears cases that have been tried and appealed in lower courts. Because its decisions are final, the Supreme Court is called "the court of last resort."

The Supreme Court hears and decides fewer than 100 cases each year. Most of the cases are appeals from lower courts that involve federal laws. After hearing oral arguments, the Justices vote. Decisions require a majority vote of at least five Justices.

Early on, the Court asserted the right to declare whether acts of the President or laws passed by Congress are unconstitutional, that is, not allowed under the Constitution. This power is called judicial review. The need for judicial review was first discussed in the *Federalist Papers*,

Analyze Images Members of the Supreme Court hear cases from lower courts and address the constitutionality of laws. **Identify Main Ideas** How does the work of the Supreme Court support the system of checks and balances?

UNITED STATES SUPREME COURT		
Reviews more than 7,000 petitions a year and selects 100–150 cases based on:	• National importance of the case • Need to eliminate conflicting court opinions related to a case	• Opportunity to set a precedent • Agreement among 4 of 9 Justices to accept a case

Original Jurisdiction	State Route	Federal Route
• Disputes between states or between a state and citizens of another state • Actions involving ambassadors or vice consuls of foreign nations • Actions between the U.S. and a state	State Supreme Court • Appeals of appellate court cases Appellate Court • Appeals of trial court cases Trial Court • Civil and criminal cases • Juries render verdicts • Judges enforce procedures	Court of Appeals • Appeals of cases originating in U.S. district courts • Reviews decisions by federal agencies District Court • Civil and criminal cases • Juries render verdicts • Judges ensure fair trial

Analyze Images A case can reach the Supreme Court through several paths. **Draw Conclusions** Why do you think so few cases reach the Supreme Court?

and the Supreme Court has argued that the power is implicit in the Constitution, but it was not established until the 1803 case *Marbury* v. *Madison,* which gave the Supreme Court the power of judicial review.

Although powerful, the Supreme Court is limited by the system of checks and balances. One check on its power is that Congress can, in certain circumstances, remove Supreme Court Justices from office. Also, the Supreme Court does not have the power to pass or enforce laws. It can only provide judicial review of laws.

READING CHECK **Check Understanding** What was significant about the Supreme Court decision in the case *Marbury* v. *Madison* (1803)?

What System Exists to Prevent the Abuse of Power?

The Framers hoped that the separation of powers among three branches would prevent the rise of an all-powerful leader who would rob the people of their liberty. But how could they prevent one of the branches from abusing its power? To answer this problem, they set up a system of checks and balances.

The system of checks and balances allows each of the three branches of government to check, or limit, the power of the other two. The President, for example, can check the actions of Congress by **vetoing**, or rejecting, bills that Congress has passed. Congress can check the President by **overriding**, or overruling, the veto, with a two-thirds vote in both houses. Congress must also approve presidential appointments and ratify treaties made by the President. The Supreme Court can check both the President and Congress by declaring laws unconstitutional through its power of judicial review.

Analyze Images Here, each tree branch represents a branch of government—executive, legislative, and judicial. **Analyze Political Cartoons** How does the cartoon show that each branch can limit the power of the other two?

Congress's most extreme check on the President is its power to remove the President from office. To do this, the House of Representatives must **impeach**, or bring charges of serious wrongdoing against, the President. The Senate then conducts a trial. If two thirds of the senators vote to convict, the President must leave office. Throughout our history, only two Presidents—Andrew Johnson and Bill Clinton—have been impeached by the House. Neither was convicted by the Senate.

The principle of checks and balances is based on the principle of separation of powers. Because the powers of government are separated into three branches, each branch can check the power of the other two. Like many principles in the Constitution, separation of powers and the system of checks and balances came from European philosophers of the Enlightenment.

READING CHECK **Identify Supporting Details** What checks does Congress have over the President?

Lesson Check

Practice Vocabulary

1. What words in the Preamble to the Constitution reflect the principle of **popular sovereignty**?
2. What roles do **vetoing** and **overriding** play in the process of turning a **bill** into a law?

Critical Thinking and Writing

3. **Draw Conclusions** Why is Article 6, which declares that the Constitution is the "supreme law of the land," so important?
4. **Draw Conclusions** Why do you think the Constitution deals with the legislative branch in its very first—and longest—article?
5. **Writing Workshop: Clarify Relationships with Transition Words** In your argument concerning how much power the federal government should have and what it should do, you can clarify relationships between ideas by using transition words and phrases. They can help compare ideas (*similarly*) or contrast them (*but, on the contrary*). They can also simply make an idea clearer (*to put it another way*). Think of more possible transition words and phrases and write them in your Active Journal.

LESSON 6

Federalism and Amendments

GET READY TO READ

START UP

Look at the photograph. Write a few sentences to identify the First Amendment freedoms you see.

GUIDING QUESTIONS

- How can the Constitution be amended?
- What rights does the Bill of Rights protect?
- Why have additional amendments to the Constitution been needed?
- How can state constitutions be amended?

TAKE NOTES

Literacy Skills Summarize

Use the graphic organizer in your Active Journal to take notes as you read the lesson.

PRACTICE VOCABULARY

Use the vocabulary activity in your Active Journal to practice the vocabulary words.

Vocabulary

Bill of Rights
civil
constitutional initiative
infrastructure
local government

Academic Vocabulary

infringe
incriminate

The Constitution of the United States spells out the powers of government. Its first 10 Amendments, or Bill of Rights, ensure the fundamental liberties of the American people. Although created more than 200 years ago, the Constitution is a living document that can be changed as the world changes.

Constitutional Amendment

The Framers foresaw that Americans might need to change the Constitution to address flaws or changed circumstances. However, they did not want to make it too easy to change the Constitution. As a result, they created a complex amendment process. The process may take months, or even years, to complete.

Article 5 outlines two ways to propose an amendment. An amendment may be proposed by two thirds of both the House and the Senate, or by a national convention called by Congress at the request of two thirds of the state legislatures. The second method has never been used.

An amendment may also be ratified in one of two ways. An amendment may be approved by the legislatures of three fourths of the states. Every amendment but the Twenty-first was ratified using this method. In the second method, an amendment may be approved by special conventions in three fourths of the states.

Not all amendments proposed by Congress have been ratified. In fact, Congress has proposed six amendments that the states refused to ratify.

READING CHECK **Identify** Which article of the Constitution outlines the amendment process?

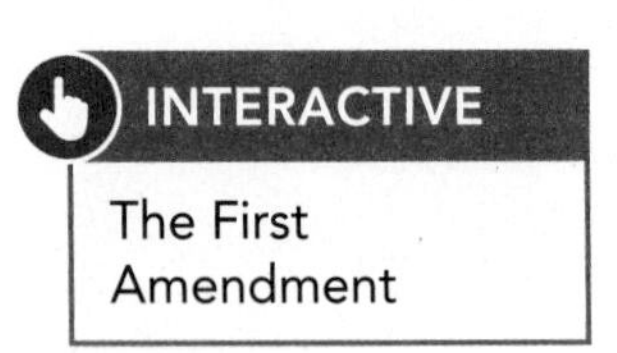

What Fundamental Liberties Does the Bill of Rights Ensure?

As one of its first acts, the new Congress drafted a series of amendments in 1789 and sent them to the states for approval. In 1791, the **Bill of Rights**, the first ten amendments, became part of the Constitution.

Free Speech, Press, and Religious Freedom The First Amendment safeguards basic individual liberties. It protects freedom of religion, speech, and the press. It also guarantees the right to assemble peacefully and to petition the government to change its policies.

The First Amendment's guarantee of freedom of religion allows Americans to practice religion as they please, or not at all, without fear of government interference. This guarantee has encouraged the religious diversity that is part of the American way of life.

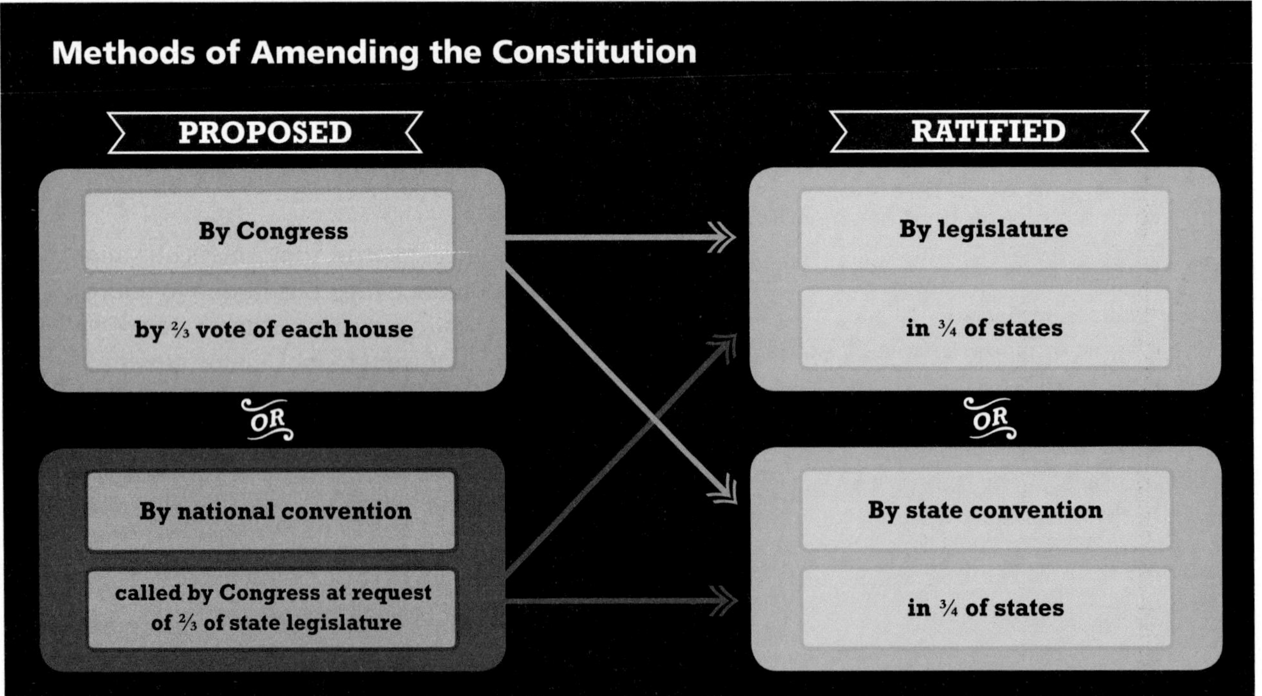

Analyze Images This graphic shows the process for amending the Constitution. **Use Visual Information** After an amendment to the Constitution has been proposed by both the Senate and the House of Representatives, what two options exist for the states to ratify the amendment?

Analyze Images Minutemen armed themselves before leaving for the Battle of Concord. **Draw Conclusions** In what ways did the Framers' recent experience with revolution affect what they included in the Constitution and Bill of Rights?

Because of the First Amendment's guarantee of free speech, you cannot be arrested for criticizing a government official. Still, there are limits on the First Amendment. For example, the government can limit free speech if there is "a clear and present danger," such as in time of war.

Freedom of the press means that you can read newspapers that do not support the views of the government. A free press is independent and is responsible only to its readers. It functions as a "watchdog," keeping an eye on the government.

These freedoms are important in a constitutional republic. They allow citizens to make informed decisions and participate freely in the political process.

Protection Against Abuse of Power The Second Amendment states, "A well-regulated militia being necessary to the security of a free state, the right of the people to keep and bear arms shall not be **infringed**." This and other amendments reflect the colonists' experiences under British rule. The Third Amendment says that Congress may not force citizens to put up troops in their homes. The Fourth Amendment protects Americans from unlawful searches of home or property.

Academic Vocabulary
infringe • *v.*, to restrict or put limits on

Methods of Amending the Constitution

Quick Activity

Discuss with a small group if there are ever times when speech should not be protected.

Academic Vocabulary
incriminate • *v.*, to give evidence against

Since early times, Americans have debated the exact meaning of the Second Amendment. Some believe that it guarantees individuals a basic right to bear arms. Others argue that it simply guarantees the individual states the right to maintain militias. The question of limits to gun ownership is one of the most complex and controversial constitutional issues facing Americans today.

Protecting the Rights of the Accused The Fifth through Eighth amendments deal with the rights of people accused of crimes. The Fifth Amendment states that people cannot be forced to **incriminate**, or give evidence against, themselves. The Sixth Amendment guarantees the right to a speedy and public trial by an impartial, or fair, jury. It also states that people accused of crimes have the right to know the charges against them, as well as the right to confront the person making the charges. The Seventh Amendment provides for juries for **civil** trials. The Eighth Amendment forbids excessive bail or fines or "cruel and unusual punishments."

Upholding Individual Rights Some Americans had opposed adding a Bill of Rights. They argued that if specific rights were listed in the Constitution, Americans might lose other rights that were not listed. The Ninth Amendment makes clear that a citizen's individual rights are not limited to those listed in the Constitution.

The Tenth Amendment reaffirmed the Framers' plan to create a limited federal government. It states that all powers not given to the national government or denied to the states belong to, or are reserved for, for the states or the people.

READING CHECK **Draw Conclusions** Why do you think the Framers devoted four amendments to protecting the rights of the accused?

Analyze Diagrams
Many amendments were suggested when the Constitution was being considered. **Use Visual Information** Approximately what percentage of the more than 200 amendments proposed by the states' ratifying conventions finally made it into the Bill of Rights?

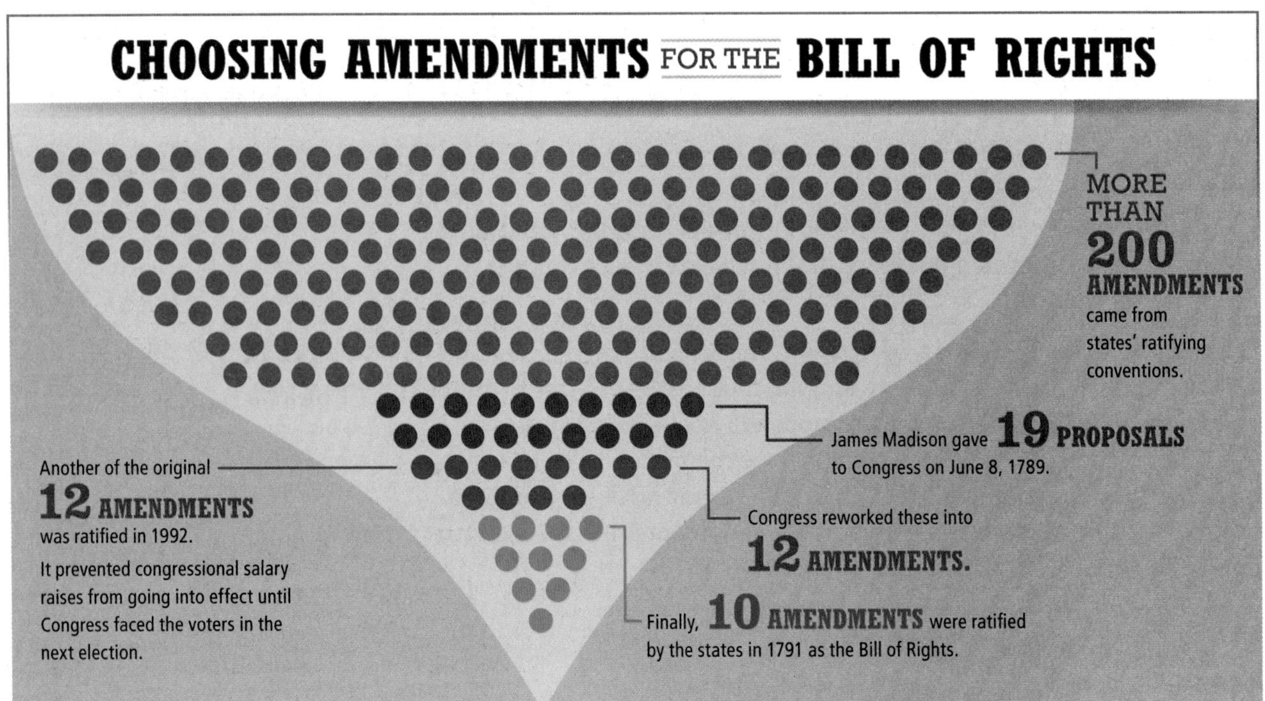

Analyze Images The members of both houses of the California legislature, as well as the governor, carry out their duties at the state capitol in Sacramento.
Infer Do you think having the legislative and executive branches in one building fosters cooperation? Why or why not?

Why Have Additional Amendments Been Created?

Since the addition of the Bill of Rights, the Constitution has been amended only 17 times. Additional amendments have adapted the Constitution to the needs of a changing society. Many later amendments reflect evolving attitudes about equality and the expansion of democracy.

The Thirteenth, Fourteenth, and Fifteenth amendments are known as the Civil War Amendments. The Thirteenth Amendment abolished slavery. The Fourteenth Amendment guaranteed citizenship to former slaves. The Fifteenth Amendment declared that states may not deny the vote to any citizen on the basis of "race, color, or previous condition of servitude." This guaranteed African American men the right to vote.

Other amendments further expanded voting rights. The Nineteenth Amendment, ratified in 1920, gave women the right to vote.

Women achieved this victory after more than 70 years of struggle. In 1971, changing attitudes toward the rights and responsibilities of young people led to the Twenty-sixth Amendment. It lowered the minimum voting age from 21 to 18.

READING CHECK **Understand Effects** How did the Fifteenth and Nineteenth amendments reflect changing attitudes about equality?

State Government

One principle of the Constitution is federalism, or the division of powers between the federal and state governments. The federal government deals with national issues. The states have the power to meet more local needs. There are also some powers that are shared. State governments provide many basic services that Americans use each day.

The Question of States' Rights Many Americans originally opposed the Constitution because they thought it gave too much power to the federal government at the expense of the state governments. The Tenth Amendment was written to help ensure that the states keep powers not granted the federal government:

Primary Source

"The powers not delegated to the United States by the Constitution, nor prohibited by it to the states, are reserved to the states respectively, or to the people."

—Tenth Amendment to the Constitution

Some Americans point to the Tenth Amendment as support for what is often called states' rights, or the idea that the federal government should not infringe on states' powers. A similar idea is that of state sovereignty, or the idea that, within a state, the state government is supreme.

Analyze Images In 2016, members of the Standing Rock Sioux protested plans to build an oil pipeline that would cross the river that provides their water. Thousands of other people joined their protest, and the planned route was denied. **Draw Conclusions** What role might social media have played in the success of the protest?

Analyze Images State and local governments provide infrastructure, such as this bridge in California. **Infer** If a city gets most of its revenue from property taxes and property values decline sharply, will there be enough money for large projects? Why or why not?

The federal government has used the elastic clause to assume powers that some believe belong to the states. The debate over how power should be shared between the federal and state governments has been a matter of controversy through most of American history.

State Constitutions Each of the 50 states has a constitution that sets forth the principles and framework of its government. Although constitutions vary from state to state, they must all conform to the Constitution of the United States. If a conflict arises, the national Constitution—the "supreme law of the land"—prevails.

Most state constitutions resemble the national Constitution in form. They start with a preamble stating their goals and include a bill of rights guaranteeing individual liberties. State constitutions tend to be longer and more detailed than the national Constitution. Many include provisions on finance, education, and other matters.

State constitutions set up a government with three branches. The powers of the legislative, executive, and judicial branches on the state level are similar to those of the national government.

Changing State Constitutions State constitutions can be changed in several ways. In the most common method, amendments are proposed by the state legislature and approved by the people in an election.

In almost one half of the states, citizens can act directly to change the constitution. In a process known as the **constitutional initiative**, sponsors of an amendment gather signatures on a petition. When the required number of signatures is attained, the petition goes to the legislature or to the voters for approval.

Finally, a state can rewrite its constitution. With the approval of the legislature or the people, the state may call a constitutional convention. The new constitution is then submitted to the people for approval.

The States' Obligations to Citizens State governments provide a wide range of services. They maintain law and order, enforce criminal law, protect property, and regulate business. They also supervise public education, provide public health and welfare programs, build and maintain highways, operate state parks and forests, and regulate use of state-owned land.

The states, not the federal government, have the main responsibility for public education in the United States. Most students attend schools paid for and managed by the state. The state sets general standards for schools and establishes a recommended course of study. It also sets requirements for promotion and graduation.

Each state must build and maintain its own **infrastructure**, or system of transit lines, roads, bridges, and tunnels. State departments or agencies manage more than 6,000 state parks and recreation areas. To help maintain high standards, state governments license professionals, such as doctors, lawyers, and teachers.

Analyze Images Locally supported public education is important not only to the states but also to the nation. **Cite Evidence** How are a community's property values related to the quality of education its children receive?

When you are old enough to drive, the state will test you and, if you pass, give you a license. State police keep highways safe and protect us against criminal acts.

READING CHECK **Classify and Categorize** What are some examples of services that states provide to their citizens?

What Responsibilities Do Local Governments Have?

The Constitution defines the powers of the federal and state governments. But it does not mention **local government**.

Local governments have perhaps the greatest impact on our daily lives. At the same time, it is on the local level that citizens have the greatest opportunity to influence government.

Public Education The service that local governments spend the most money on is education. While state governments set standards for schools, it is the cities, towns, or school districts that actually run them. Local school boards build schools and hire teachers and staff. They also have a strong say in which courses will be taught. However, school officials must make all decisions within the guidelines set by state law.

Education is one area of local government where citizens exert a great deal of control. Local residents may give up part of their time to serve on local school boards. In most communities, voters have the right to approve or turn down the annual school budget.

Many Other Services Local governments provide a variety of other services, including public safety, trash collection, public works, and library services. Many towns and cities also provide recreational facilities, such as parks.

Analyze Images Local governments take responsibility for providing citizens with public services, such as firefighters and police as well as trash and snow removal. **Infer** Describe how a winter where there is more snowfall than normal would affect a city's budget.

READING CHECK **Identify Supporting Details** On what service for citizens do local governments spend the most money?

Lesson Check

Practice Vocabulary

1. Which amendment in the **Bill of Rights** do you think meant more to Antifederalists, the First Amendment or the Second Amendment? Explain.
2. What is **constitutional initiative**?

Critical Thinking and Writing

3. Why do you think the Framers thought it was important to be able to amend the Constitution, but then made it difficult to do so?
4. **Use Evidence** How would you use the Tenth Amendment of the Constitution to support the idea that the federal government should not assume more power than it already has?
5. **Writing Workshop: Shape Tone** Think about the tone you want to take in your essay. To help shape your tone, write a few sentences in your Active Journal that reflect your personality and your feelings about the subject matter, while maintaining the formal style and informative approach required in presenting an argument.

Identify Sources of Continuity

INTERACTIVE

Identify Trends

Follow these steps to learn to identify sources of continuity in American society.

1 **Gather information about the society.** Look at a variety of resources to learn about life in the society that you are studying. What resources might help you learn about life in early America?

2 **Identify possible sources of continuity in the society.** Look for information about the society's government, values, economy, history, language, and culture. Imagine you are looking for information about these aspects of U.S. society. Would the source give you a complete picture? Which aspects would it help you with?

3 **Choose the important sources of continuity.** You may want to list the sources of continuity and take notes about each one. Why are legal documents so important to establishing continuity in a society?

4 **Summarize what you discover.** Use the information you have learned to make a general statement. Study the information in the source. What does it reveal about continuity in the political history of the United States?

Secondary Sources

Magna Carta: In 1215, King John of England signed the Magna Carta. This document limited the king's power, ensuring that even the king had to obey the law. It protected certain individual rights, including the right to trial and the right to private property. It also forced the king to consult with his nobles. Over time, this led to the establishment of a two-house Parliament.

English Bill of Rights: A revolution in 1689 increased Parliament's power and decreased the power of the king. The resulting English Bill of Rights restated many of the rights listed in the Magna Carta. It added the right of habeas corpus, the idea that no person could be held in prison without first being charged with a specific crime. It gave citizens the right to bear arms and also called for regular parliamentary elections.

State Constitutions: Colonies established representative governments, based in part on ideas developed in England. Eventually, each colony elected its own legislature.

U.S. Constitution and Bill of Rights: In 1787, the Framers of the Constitution called upon their knowledge of English political history and existing state constitutions to establish a new national government. They sought to prevent abuse of power by dividing the government into a legislative branch with two houses, an executive branch and a judicial branch. The Constitution called for regular elections of members of Congress and the President. A Bill of Rights, aimed at protecting individual rights, followed.

LESSON 7

Citizens' Rights and Responsibilities

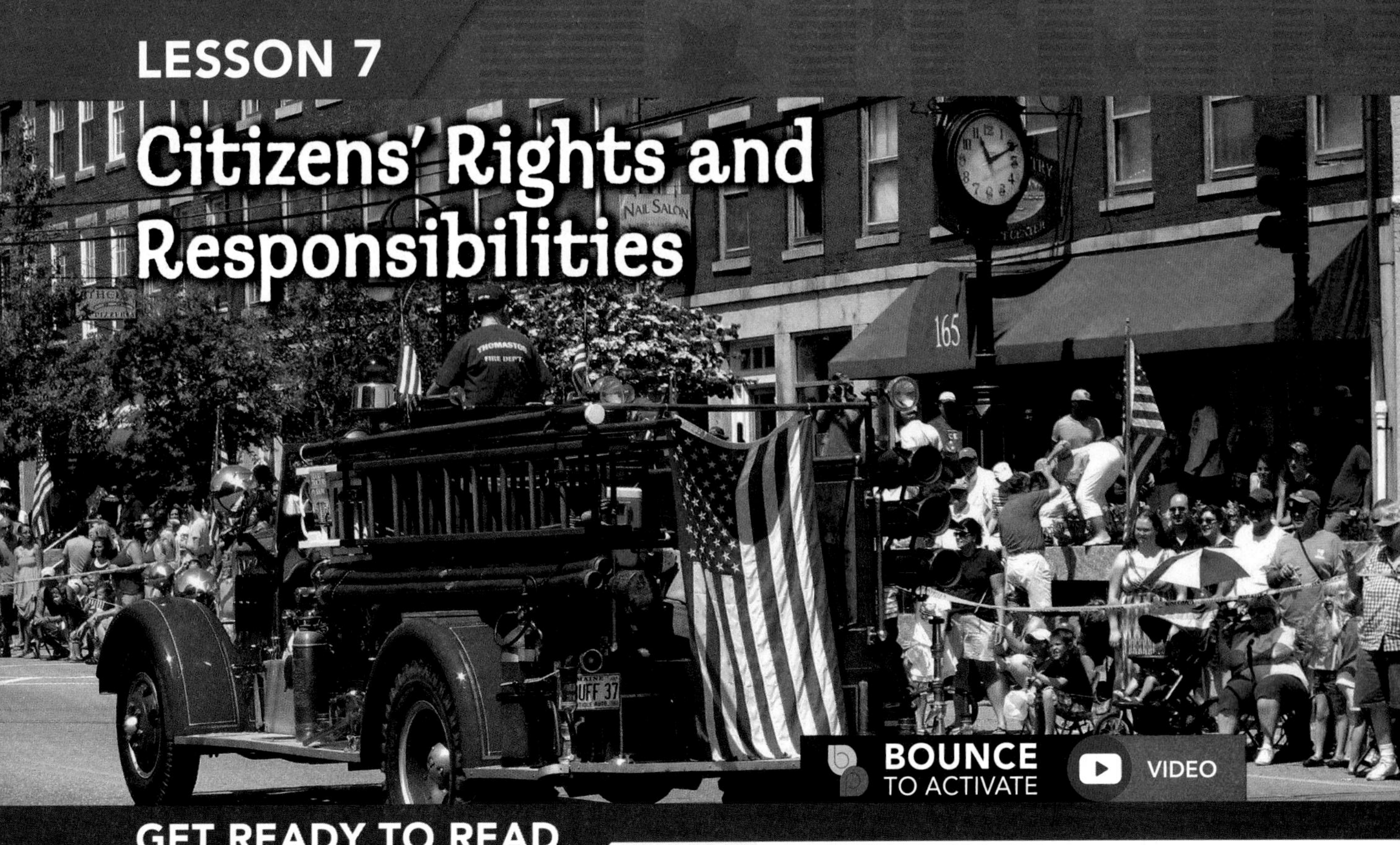

GET READY TO READ

START UP

Look at the photograph of people enjoying a Fourth of July parade. What does it mean to be an American citizen?

GUIDING QUESTIONS

- What makes a person a citizen of the United States?
- How can Americans develop democratic values?
- What responsibilities do citizens have?

TAKE NOTES

Literacy Skills Use Evidence

Use the graphic organizer in your Active Journal to take notes as you read the lesson.

PRACTICE VOCABULARY

Use the vocabulary activity in your Active Journal to practice the vocabulary words.

Vocabulary

citizen
naturalized
immigrant
resident alien
civic virtue
patriotism
jury duty

Academic Vocabulary

responsibility
respect

The nation provides its people with many rights, including freedom to speak our minds and the knowledge that we are being protected. However, citizens also owe a debt to the nation.

American Citizenship

A **citizen** is a person who owes loyalty to a particular nation and is entitled to all its rights and protections.

To be a citizen of the United States, you must have fulfilled one of three requirements:

- You were born in the United States, or at least one parent is a citizen of the United States.
- You were **naturalized**, that is, you have completed the official legal process for becoming a citizen if you were born outside the United States.
- You were 18 or younger when your parents were naturalized.

Becoming a Citizen Many millions of immigrants have become naturalized citizens of the United States.

Analyze Images A group of immigrants celebrate after being sworn in as new United States citizens. **Use Visual Information** Are there any generalizations you can make about immigrants?

An **immigrant** is a person who enters another country in order to settle there. To illustrate the naturalization process, we will look at one immigrant's story.

At age 15, Carla Rojas came to the United States from Argentina. Her mother returned home two years later, but Rojas decided to remain. After submitting numerous documents and photographs and attending several interviews, she received permission to remain in the country as a **resident alien**, or noncitizen living in the country.

After a required five-year waiting period, Rojas submitted an application for citizenship. She had to take a test to show that she was comfortable with the English language and that she was familiar with American history and government. She also had to show that she was of "good moral character." Then, a naturalization examiner interviewed her about her reasons for becoming a citizen.

At last, Rojas stood before a judge and took the oath that confirmed her as an American citizen:

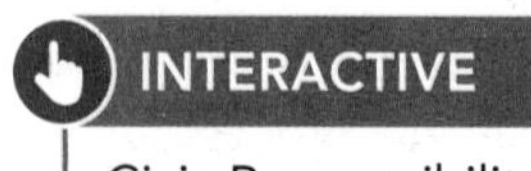

INTERACTIVE

Civic Responsibility

Primary Source

"I hereby declare, on oath, that . . . I will support and defend the Constitution and laws of the United States against all enemies . . . that I will bear true faith and allegiance to the same . . . so help me God."

—Oath of Allegiance to the United States

A naturalized citizen enjoys every right of a natural-born citizen except one. Only natural-born American citizens may serve as President or Vice President.

The Rights and Responsibilities of Citizens All American citizens have equal rights under the law. Americans have the right to speak freely, to worship as they choose, to vote, and to serve on juries. These rights are not based on inherited wealth or family connections. They are the rights of American citizens.

Still, nothing is free. As you will see, if we want to enjoy the rights of citizenship, we must also accept its **responsibilities**.

These rights and responsibilities reflect America's national identity—the common set of values that unite Americans. For example, citizens have both the right and the responsibility to vote. This reflects the principles of independence, liberty, and self-governance upheld in the Constitution and valued by the American people.

Academic Vocabulary

responsibility • *n.*, a duty or task one is expected to carry out

respect • *n.*, understanding when something is serious and acting appropriately

READING CHECK **Define** What is a citizen?

Civic Virtue, Citizenship, and Democratic Values

The founders of our country admired **civic virtue**, that is, the willingness to work for the good of the nation or community even at great sacrifice. They looked to Roman models such as Cincinnatus, who, it was said, gave up a peaceful life on his farm when called upon to lead Rome. Again and again, leaders such as George Washington, Thomas Jefferson, and John Adams put the common good ahead of their own wishes. These three presidents maintained that democracy requires virtuous behavior by citizens. Citizens must put the greater good ahead of their own desires when they follow the law, serve on juries, and make informed decisions about voting.

The leaders feared that without this responsible behavior, American liberty would be at risk. How can a democracy run if individuals do not think about what is best for society and not just for themselves?

You do not have to go to great lengths to be a good citizen. At home, at school, and in the community, you can work to develop the values that are the foundation of our democratic system. Among these basic values are honesty and compassion. Others include patriotism, **respect**, responsibility, and courage.

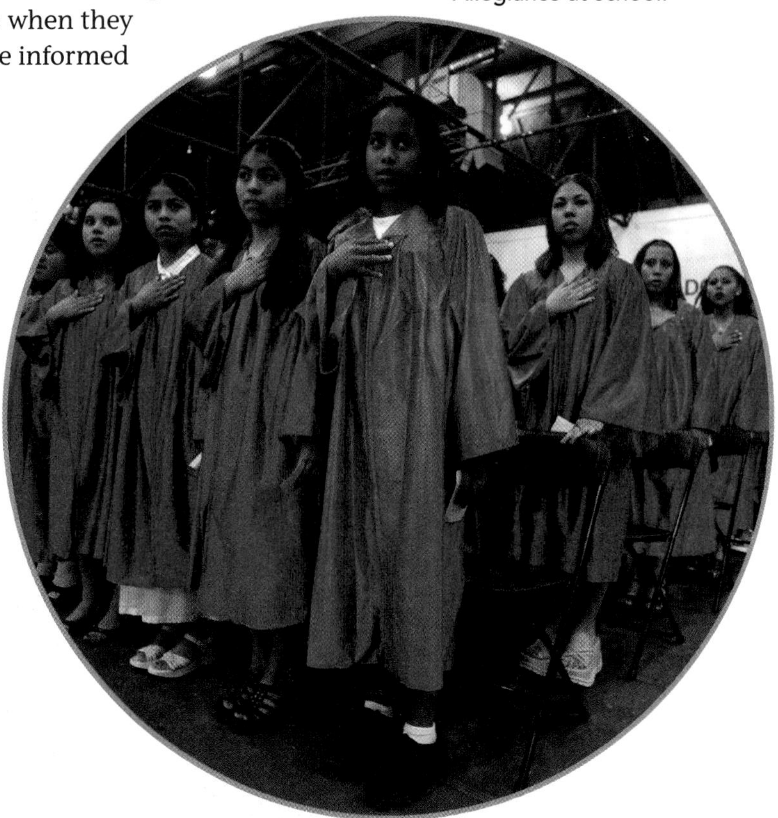

▼ One way students can express their civic virtue is by reciting the Pledge of Allegiance at school.

A key democratic value is **patriotism**, or a feeling of love and devotion toward one's country. A sense of patriotism inspires Americans to serve their nation. It also encourages us to fulfill the ideals set forth in the Declaration of Independence, the Constitution, and the Bill of Rights.

As citizens, we must respect ourselves, our families, our neighbors, and the other members of our community. Respect may also involve objects or ideas. For example, a good citizen respects the property of others.

Responsibility may be both personal and public. We must accept responsibility for ourselves and the consequences of our actions and behaviors. In a democracy, individuals are expected to look out for themselves and for one another. For example, parents have a duty to support their families and teach their children. This is important because children depend on parents and families depend on one another. As a student, you have a responsibility to learn.

Courage may be either physical or moral. Soldiers, police, or firefighters display physical courage when they risk their lives for the good of others. Moral courage enables us to do the right thing even when it is unpopular, difficult, or dangerous. Americans such as Abraham Lincoln, Susan B. Anthony, and Martin Luther King, Jr., showed their courage when they faced risks to defend democratic values.

READING CHECK **Define** What is civic virtue?

Analyze Images Taking part in beach and park clean-ups is a common way for students to get involved. **Infer** In what ways does a beach clean-up show responsible citizenship?

Voter Turnout, 1900–2000

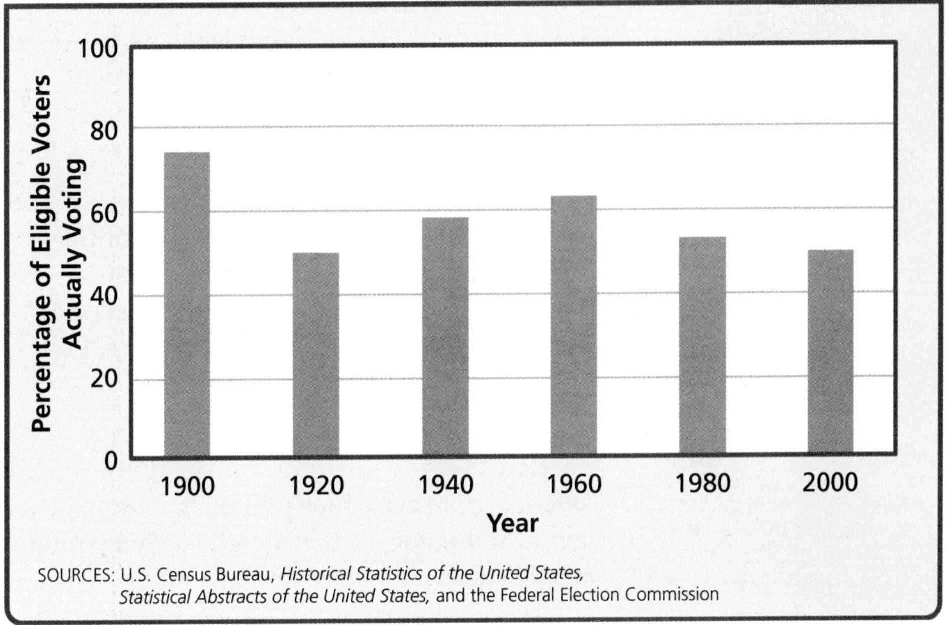

Analyze Data The chart shows how many people voted in elections between 1900 and 2000. **Infer** Based on the information in the chart, what trend can you identify in the percentage of the population actually voting from 1960 to 2000?

Responsible Citizenship

As citizens, we must accept our own civic responsibilities. Only if government and citizens work together can we meet our needs as a democratic society. Here are some important responsibilities.

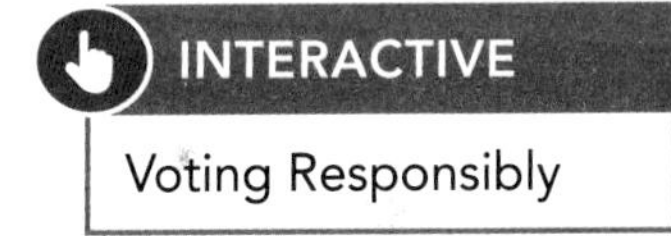

Vote As citizens of a republic, we have the right to select the people who will represent us in government. But if that right is to have any meaning, then we must fulfill our responsibility to vote. A good citizen studies the candidates and the issues before casting a vote in order to make responsible choices.

Obey Laws and Rules In the Constitution, "we the people" give the government the power to make laws for us. Thus, we have a duty to obey the nation's laws. We have thousands of laws that keep us from hurting one another, regulate contracts, and protect citizens' rights. No one can know them all, but you must know and obey the laws that affect your life and actions.

You also have a responsibility to obey rules. You already have rules at home and rules at school—even rules to games you play. These rules are not enforced by the government as laws are. Like laws, however, they keep us safe, help us live together, and teach us to be accountable for our behavior. By learning to obey rules such as not to hit or cheat when we are young, we learn about responsible citizenship.

Analyze Images
As citizens, it is our responsibility to stay informed on current events. **Use Evidence** Share examples of how citizens have used knowledge to be free and exercise their rights.

Defend the Nation Americans have the duty to help defend the nation against threats to its peace or security. At age 18, all men must register for the draft. In time of war, the government may call them to serve in the armed forces. Many young citizens feel the duty to enlist in the military without being called.

Serve on Juries The Bill of Rights guarantees the right to trial by jury. In turn, every citizen has the responsibility to serve on a jury when called. **Jury duty** is a serious matter. Jurors must take time out from their work and personal lives to decide the fate of others.

Participate in the Community Many Americans use their time and skills to improve their communities or to help others. Many young people participate in marathons, walk-a-thons, or bike-a-thons for charity. Others volunteer in hospitals or fire departments. When serious natural disasters damage cities and regions, millions of citizens aid in rescue efforts, donate blood, or contribute money and supplies.

Stay Informed on Public Issues Thomas Jefferson observed, "If a nation expects to be ignorant and free . . . it expects what never was and never will be." You cannot protect your rights as a citizen unless you know what they are. You cannot choose elected officials who will make good decisions unless you know where they stand on the issues. It is your responsibility to be informed. You can watch television news programs and read newspapers, magazines, or government pamphlets. Your work in school will help you become educated about our history, our government, and the workings of our society.

READING CHECK **Identify Supporting Details** What are some ways a citizen can stay informed about public issues?

Lesson Check

Practice Vocabulary

1. Explain how an **immigrant** can become a **naturalized citizen**.
2. Does a **resident alien** have the right to vote?

Critical Thinking and Writing

3. **Summarize** What are the main responsibilities of United States citizens?
4. **Infer** What might be the reason behind the declining number of citizens who vote?
5. **Writing Workshop: Write a Conclusion** Think about the argument that you have been working on about how much power the government should have. Now, write a conclusion for your argument in your Active Journal.

Hamilton and Madison Disagree

Alexander Hamilton and James Madison were both federalists, but they had differing views about government "by the people." Read the excerpts from the writings of each man.

▶ Alexander Hamilton believed that the people were the power behind government.

1) Alexander Hamilton expressed his faith in the people when he wrote the following:

"The fabric of American empire ① ought to rest on the solid basis of THE CONSENT OF THE PEOPLE. The streams of national power ought to flow from that pure, original fountain of all legitimate authority." ②

—Alexander Hamilton, *Federalist* No. 22

2) Madison expressed his fear of majority tyranny in an October 17, 1788, letter to Thomas Jefferson:

"Wherever the real power in a Government lies, there is the danger of oppression. In our Governments, the real power lies in the majority of the Community, and the invasion of private rights is chiefly to be apprehended, not from acts of Government contrary to the sense of its constituents, but from acts in which the Government is the mere instrument of the major number of the constituents. ③ This is a truth of great importance, but not yet sufficiently attended to. ... Whenever there is an interest and power to do wrong, wrong will generally be done, and not less readily by [a majority of the people] than by a ... prince."

—James Madison, Letter to Thomas Jefferson (1788), *Letters and Other Writings of James Madison*,Volume 3

Reading and Vocabulary Support

① Hamilton did not literally mean an empire.

② The consent of the governed was one of the ideas the founders took from the work of John Locke.

③ What do you think Madison means by this statement?

Analyzing Primary Sources

Cite specific evidence from the documents to support your answers.

1. What common ground did Hamilton and Madison share in their points of view?
2. Do you think Madison had faith in people? Why or why not?

TOPIC 4

Review and Assessment

VISUAL REVIEW

Comparing the Articles of Confederation and the Constitution

THE ARTICLES OF CONFEDERATION

- Weak central government
- No President
- No court system
- One-part Congress
- One Congressional delegate per state
- States free to make decisions for themselves
- Congress cannot enforce laws, regulate trade, levy taxes, resolve conflicts between states

BOTH

- A union of states
- A national legislature
- Congress can declare war, enter into treaties, coin money, operate post offices

THE CONSTITUTION

- Strong central government
- Separation of powers among legislative, executive, and judicial branches
- President leads the executive branch
- Two-part Congress
- In Senate, two senators per state
- In House, a number of representatives based on population
- Congress can levy taxes, regulate trade
- Federal laws supreme over state laws

Federalism

Federal Government	State Governments
• Administers delegated powers—those assigned to it in the Constitution • Deals with national issues • Makes and enforces laws for the country • Coins money • Declares war • Regulates trade between the states	• Administer reserved powers—those not given to the federal government • Deal with state and local issues • Make and enforce laws for the state • Maintain law and order • Protect property • Regulate business and trade within their borders • Make rules for state elections • Supervise public education • Provide public health and welfare programs • Build and maintain infrastructure

READING REVIEW

Use the Take Notes and Practice Vocabulary activities in your Active Journal to review the topic.

INTERACTIVE

Practice Vocabulary Using the Topic Mini-Games

Write Your Opinion

Get help for writing your response in your Active Journal.

ASSESSMENT

Vocabulary and Key Ideas

1. **Recall** How did the **Northwest Ordinance** address the slavery issue?
2. **Identify Main Ideas** What role did **compromise** play at the **Constitutional Convention** in 1787?
3. **Define** What is **popular sovereignty**?
4. **Identify Main Ideas** What protections in the **English Bill of Rights** can be found in the Constitution?
5. **Identify** What key ideals from the Declaration of Independence did the Framers include in the Constitution?
6. **Check Understanding** How does the power of the veto reflect the system of checks and balances?
7. **Identify Main Ideas** Why is jury duty considered an important responsibility of citizenship?

Critical Thinking and Writing

8. **Draw Conclusions** Why do you think the central government did not respond to Shays' Rebellion by sending in troops?
9. **Infer** Why was it important for the Framers to include, in the Constitution, key ideals from the Declaration of Independence?
10. **Identify Cause and Effect** What prevented many state convention delegates from voting to ratify the Constitution?
11. **Classify and Categorize** What branch of government is a Supreme Court justice part of? The President? A senator?
12. **Revisit the Essential Question** Does the federal government have enough power to carry out its constitutional responsibilities? Explain.
13. **Writing Workshop: Write an Argumentative Essay** Using the outline you created in your Active Journal, answer the following question in a three-paragraph argumentative essay: How much power should the federal government have, and what should its responsibilities be?

Analyze Primary Sources

14. Who most likely wrote this source?
    A. George Washington
    B. James Madison
    C. Benjamin Franklin
    D. Thomas Jefferson

"In the compound republic of America, the power surrendered by the people is first divided between two distinct governments, and then the portion allotted to each subdivided among distinct and separate departments. Hence a double security arises to the rights of the people. The different governments will control each other, at the same time that each will be controlled by itself."

—*from* Federalist *No. 51*

Analyze Maps

Use the map at right to answer the following questions:

15. Which state did not send a delegate?
16. How many states sent four delegates?
17. How many delegates did Georgia send?
18. Which state sent the most delegates?

▼ Convention Delegates

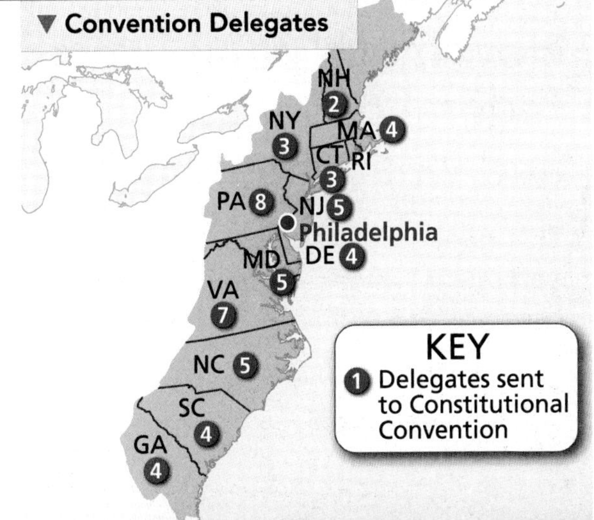

TOPIC 5 The Early Republic, 1789–1825

GO ONLINE to access your digital course

VIDEO

AUDIO

ETEXT

INTERACTIVE

WRITING

GAMES

WORKSHEET

ASSESSMENT

Go back in time

to **WHEN THE NATION WAS YOUNG.** You'll meet our first five Presidents, as well as explorers and leaders who shaped the country. You'll also find out how "everyday" people lived in the early republic.

▲ Meriwether Lewis and William Clark greet a group of American Indians known to their guide, Sacajawea.

Explore The Essential Question

How much power should the federal government have, and what should it do?

This question was debated strongly in the early years of the republic, and it is still being asked today.

Unlock the Essential Question in your Active Journal.

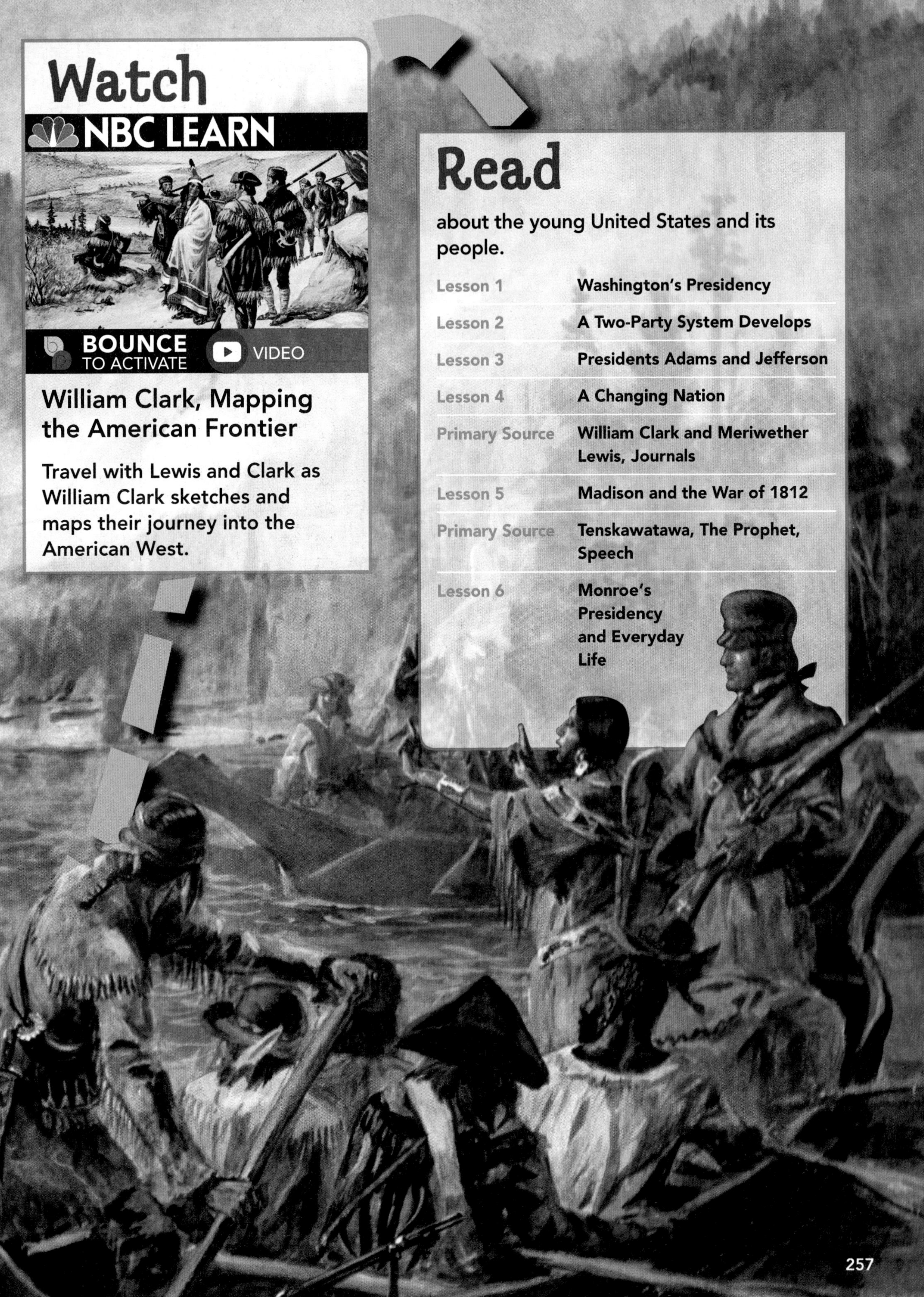

Watch

NBC LEARN

BOUNCE TO ACTIVATE VIDEO

William Clark, Mapping the American Frontier

Travel with Lewis and Clark as William Clark sketches and maps their journey into the American West.

Read

about the young United States and its people.

TOPIC 5 The Early Republic

1789–1825

Learn more about the early republic by making your own map and timeline in your Active Journal.

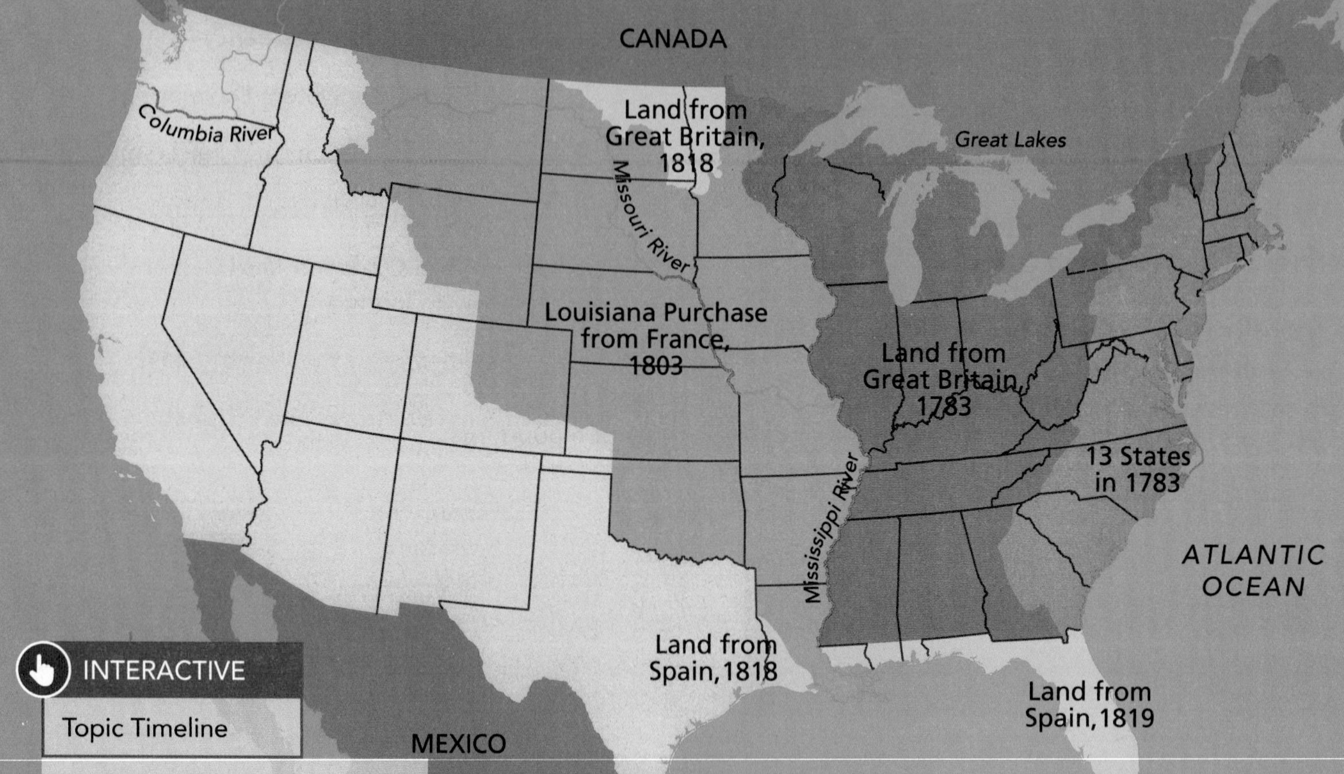

INTERACTIVE

Topic Timeline

What happened and when?

The United States grew in size but split politically and fought another war with Britain. Explore the timeline to see some events from 1789 to 1837.

TOPIC EVENTS

1789 George Washington is inaugurated as first President of the United States.

1797 John Adams becomes President; Thomas Jefferson becomes Vice President.

1803 United States purchases Louisiana territory.

1780 | **1790** | **1800**

WORLD EVENTS

1792 Mary Wollstonecraft publishes *Vindication of the Rights of Women.*

1804 Haiti declares independence from France.

INTERACTIVE

Topic Map

Where did the nation expand?

From 13 states hugging the Atlantic coast, the nation expanded westward. On the map, locate the acquisitions of land that made this expansion possible.

1812
War of 1812 begins.

1819
Supreme Court rules in *McCulloch* v. *Maryland*.

1823
President Monroe creates Monroe Doctrine.

1810 | **1820** | **1830** | **1840**

1810
Argentina declares its independence from Spanish royalist leaders.

1837
Louis Daguerre experiments with photography.

Who will you meet?

Alexander Hamilton, the man who stabilized the economy but lost a duel

James Monroe, the fifth President, who told Europe to stay out of America's business

John Marshall, Supreme Court Justice who expanded the powers of the Court

Stay Out? Or Get Involved?

Quest KICK OFF

You are working for a member of President Jefferson's Cabinet and must decide how to respond to war between Britain and France. Consider this question:

How do we determine which actions are in the best interest of the United States when other nations go to war?

What events will help you decide on the best course of action? Explore the Essential Question "How much power should the federal government have, and what should it do?" in this Quest.

▲ This photograph shows a modern Cabinet meeting with President Obama presiding.

1 Ask Questions

Think of questions you would ask about factors such as events and their outcomes that would help you decide on the best course of action when other nations go to war. Write your questions in your Active Journal.

2 Investigate

As you read the lessons in this Topic, look for Quest CONNECTIONS that provide information on events and issues that affected the U.S. response to war between other nations. Take notes in your Active Journal.

3 Conduct Research

Next explore primary sources from the period of the early republic. They'll help you decide on the best course of action to take. Record notes in your Active Journal.

Quest FINDINGS

4 Write a Position Paper

Hold a mock Cabinet meeting to review your notes, decide on the best course of action, and document this problem-solving process. In a small group, write a position paper summarizing the chosen solution. Get help for writing the paper in your Active Journal.

LESSON 1

Washington's Presidency

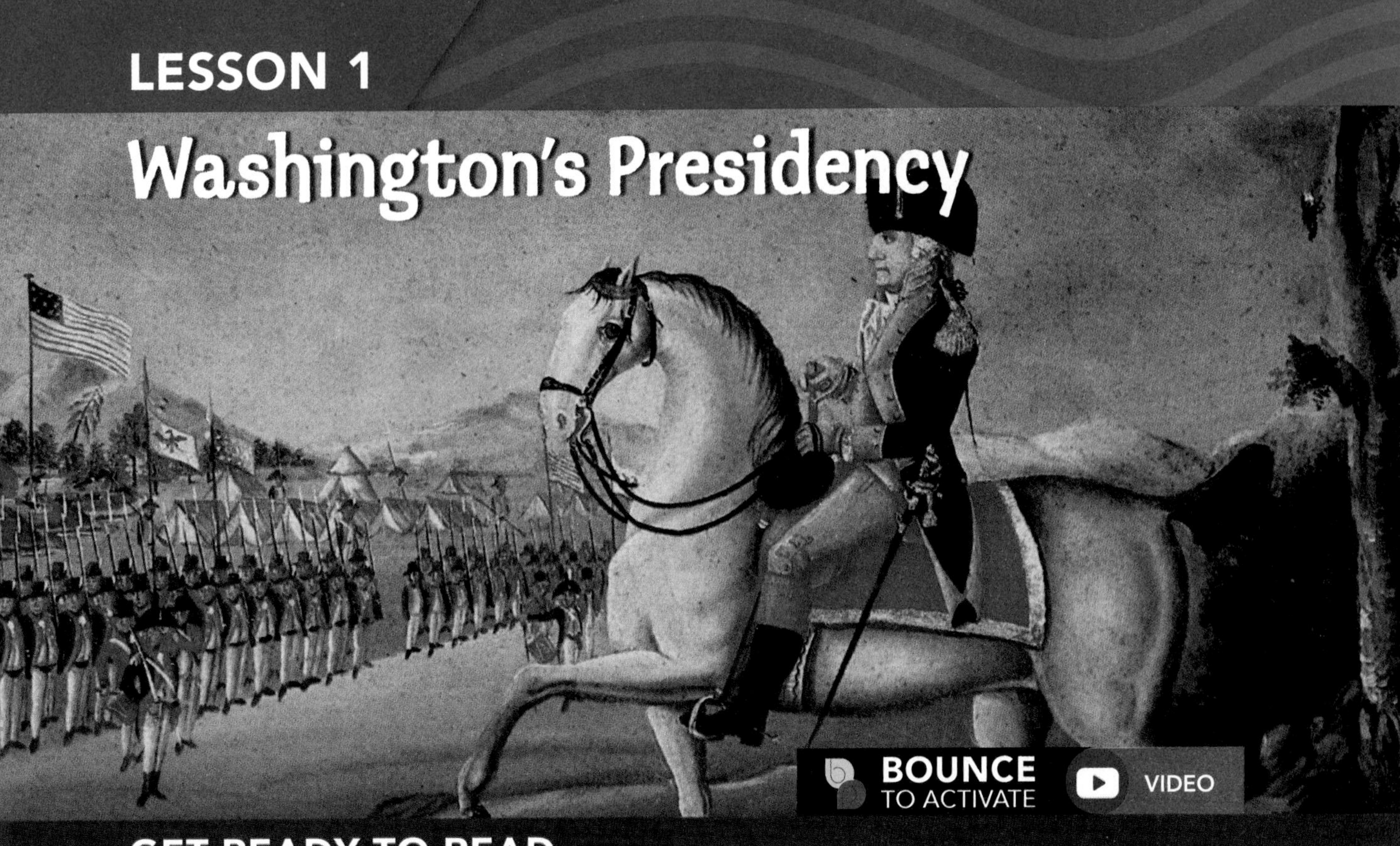

GET READY TO READ

START UP

President Washington reviews his troops before the Whiskey Rebellion. Write a prediction about events during Washington's presidency.

GUIDING QUESTIONS

- What steps did President Washington take to set up the government of the new republic?
- What were the causes and effects of the Whiskey Rebellion?
- What was the impact of Washington's foreign policy outlined in his Farewell Address?

TAKE NOTES

Literacy Skills: Summarize

Use the graphic organizer in your Active Journal to take notes as you read the lesson.

PRACTICE VOCABULARY

Use the vocabulary activity in your Active Journal to practice the vocabulary words.

Vocabulary		Academic Vocabulary
inauguration	tariff	accordingly
precedent	speculator	invoke
Cabinet	neutral	
bond		

George Washington was inaugurated in New York City on April 30, 1789. A presidential **inauguration** is the ceremony in which the President officially takes the oath of office. A witness reported that the new President looked "grave, almost to sadness." Washington, no doubt, felt a great burden. He knew that Americans were looking to him to make the new government work.

How Did Washington Shape the American Presidency?

Washington's presidency marked the beginning of what historians call the early republic. This period, between 1789 and about 1825, began when the first U.S. government was formed under the Constitution. Decisions made during the early republic had a lasting impact on the institutions and culture of the United States. As the first President, Washington showed his strong leadership and set an example for future generations.

The Constitution provided a framework for the new government of the United States.

Analyze Images John Jay led the new nation's judicial branch when he became the first Chief Justice of the United States Supreme Court in 1789. **Use Visual Information** On what kind of a book do you think the Chief Justice lays his hand? Hint: The Supreme Court is the highest court, making decisions about U.S. laws.

It did not explain how the President should govern from day to day. "There is scarcely any part of my conduct," he said, "which may not hereafter be drawn into precedent." A **precedent** (PRES uh dent) is an act or a decision that sets an example for others to follow.

Washington set an important precedent at the end of his second term. In 1796, he decided not to run for a third term. Not until 1940 did any President seek a third term.

The First Cabinet The Constitution says little about how the executive branch should be organized. It was clear, however, that the President needed talented people to help him carry out his duties.

In 1789, the first Congress created five executive departments. They were the departments of State, Treasury, and War and the offices of Attorney General and Postmaster General. The heads of these departments made up the President's **Cabinet**. Members of the Cabinet gave Washington advice and were responsible for directing their departments.

As a proven leader himself, Washington knew he needed to appoint others with similar qualities to his Cabinet. He needed effective leaders who had the ability to persuade others to adopt new proposals and implement his ideas.

Washington set a precedent by choosing well-known leaders to serve in his Cabinet. The two most influential Cabinet members were the Secretary of State, Thomas Jefferson, and the Secretary of the Treasury, Alexander Hamilton.

Establishing a Court System The Constitution calls for a Supreme Court. Congress, however, had to set up the federal court system. As one of its first actions, Congress passed the Judiciary Act of 1789. It called for the Supreme Court to consist of one Chief Justice and five Associate Justices. Today, the Supreme Court has eight Associate Justices because Congress later amended the Judiciary Act. Washington named John Jay the first Chief Justice of the United States.

The Judiciary Act also set up a system of district courts and circuit courts across the nation. Decisions made in these lower courts could be appealed to the Supreme Court, the highest court in the land.

READING CHECK **Identify Main Ideas** Why was the Cabinet created?

How Did Alexander Hamilton Deal with the National Debt?

As Secretary of the Treasury, Alexander Hamilton faced many problems. Among the most pressing was the large national debt. This is the total amount of money that a government owes to others.

During the Revolution, both the national government and individual states had desperately needed money. They had borrowed heavily from foreign countries and ordinary citizens to pay soldiers and buy supplies. Then, as now, governments borrowed money by issuing bonds. A **bond** is a certificate that promises to repay the money loaned, plus interest, on a certain date. For example, if a person pays $100 for a bond, the government agrees to pay back $100 plus interest (an additional sum of money) by a certain time.

A Plan to Reduce the Debt Hamilton wanted to pay off the government's debts and create a stable economic system for the United States. The plan he proposed showed that Cabinet members could provide strong leadership.

Hamilton called for the government to repay both federal and state debts. His first act in government was to ask Congress to pass a **tariff**, or tax on imports, to pay for the government. Congress passed this tariff in 1789. Hamilton wanted the government to buy up all the bonds issued by both the national and state governments before 1789. He then planned to issue new bonds to pay off the old debts. As the economy improved and income from the tariff increased, the government would then be able to pay off the new bonds. Many people, including bankers and investors, welcomed Hamilton's plan. Others attacked it.

Analyze Graphs This graph shows U.S. financial problems after the Revolutionary War. **Infer** Based on the information in the graph, what can you conclude about the economic situation of the federal government when Washington took office?

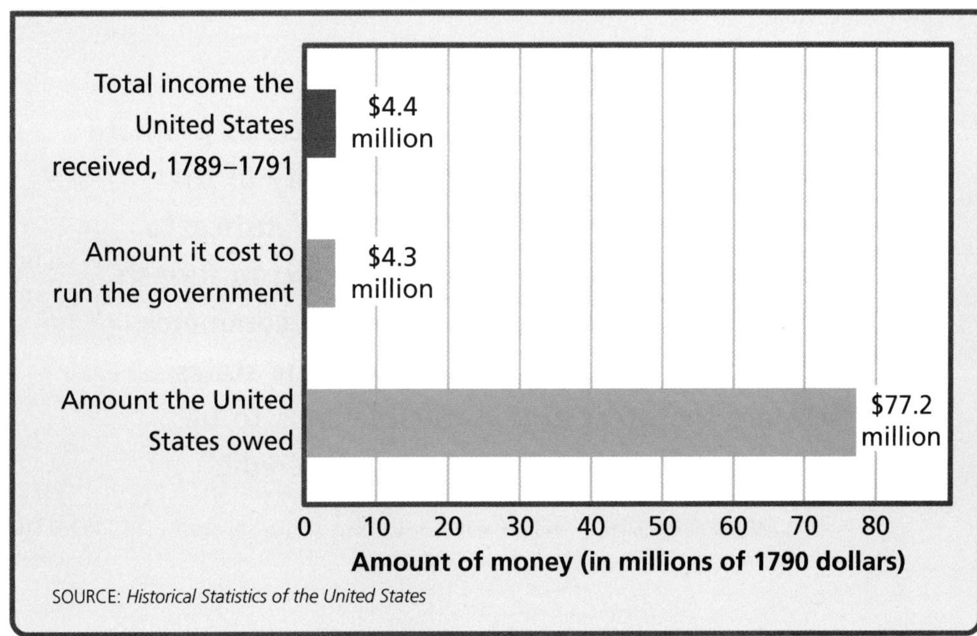

State Debt Assumed by the New Federal Government, 1790

STATE	ASSUMED DEBT (IN DOLLARS)	STATE	ASSUMED DEBT (IN DOLLARS)
New Hampshire	300,000	Delaware	200,000
Massachusetts	4,000,000	Maryland	800,000
Rhode Island	200,000	Virginia	3,500,000
Connecticut	1,600,000	North Carolina	2,400,000
New York	1,200,000	South Carolina	4,000,000
New Jersey	800,000	Georgia	300,000
Pennsylvania	2,200,000		

SOURCE: Library of Congress

Analyze Charts In the Funding Act of 1790, Hamilton adjusted the amount of debt that the federal government would take over from each state to make repaying state debt more acceptable to southern states.
Draw Conclusions Which states had the largest amount of debt? What region were the majority of those states in?

Hamilton's Plan James Madison led the opposition. Madison argued that Hamilton's plan rewarded speculators. A **speculator** is someone who invests in a risky venture in the hope of making a large profit.

During the Revolution, the government had issued bonds to soldiers and citizens who supplied goods. Many of these bondholders needed cash to survive and sold their bonds to speculators. Speculators bought bonds worth one dollar for only 10 or 15 cents. If the government paid off the old bonds in full, speculators stood to make fortunes. Madison thought that speculators did not deserve to profit.

Hamilton replied that the United States must repay its debts in full. The support of investors, he argued, was crucial to building the new nation's economy:

Primary Source

"To justify and preserve their confidence; to promote the encreasing [increasing] respectability of the American name; to answer the calls of justice; to restore landed property to its due value; to furnish new resources both to agriculture and commerce; to cement more closely the union of the states; . . . These are the great and invaluable ends to be secured, . . . for the support of public credit."

—Alexander Hamilton, "Report on Public Credit," January 9, 1790

After much debate, Congress approved full repayment of the national debt.

As a southerner, Madison also led the fight against the other part of Hamilton's plan, the repaying of state debts. By 1789, most southern states had paid off their debts from the Revolution. They thought that other states should do the same. The New England states, for example, still owed a lot. Thus, some northern states stood to gain more than others from the plan. As a result, the southern states bitterly opposed Hamilton's plan.

This fight over how to use scarce resources was only one of many in the early republic. To make government work, there were compromises.

Reaching a Compromise In the end, Hamilton proposed a compromise. Many southerners wanted the nation's capital to be located in the South. Hamilton offered to support that goal if southerners agreed to his plan to repay state debts.

Madison and others accepted the compromise. In July 1790, Congress voted to repay state debts and to build a new capital city. The new capital would not be part of any state. Instead, it would be built along the Potomac River on land given up by two southern states, Virginia and Maryland. Congress called the area the District of Columbia. Washington, the new capital, would be located in the District. Today, it is known as Washington, D.C., with *D.C.* standing for *District of Columbia.* Plans called for the new capital to be ready by 1800. Meanwhile, the nation's capital was moved from New York to Philadelphia.

READING CHECK **Identify Cause and Effect** Why were federal and state debts so high?

Analyze Images Locating the nation's capital in what is now Washington, D.C., was the result of a compromise in which southern states agreed that the federal government would take over state debts, mainly helping northern states. **Infer** What about Washington's location helped southern states accept the compromise?

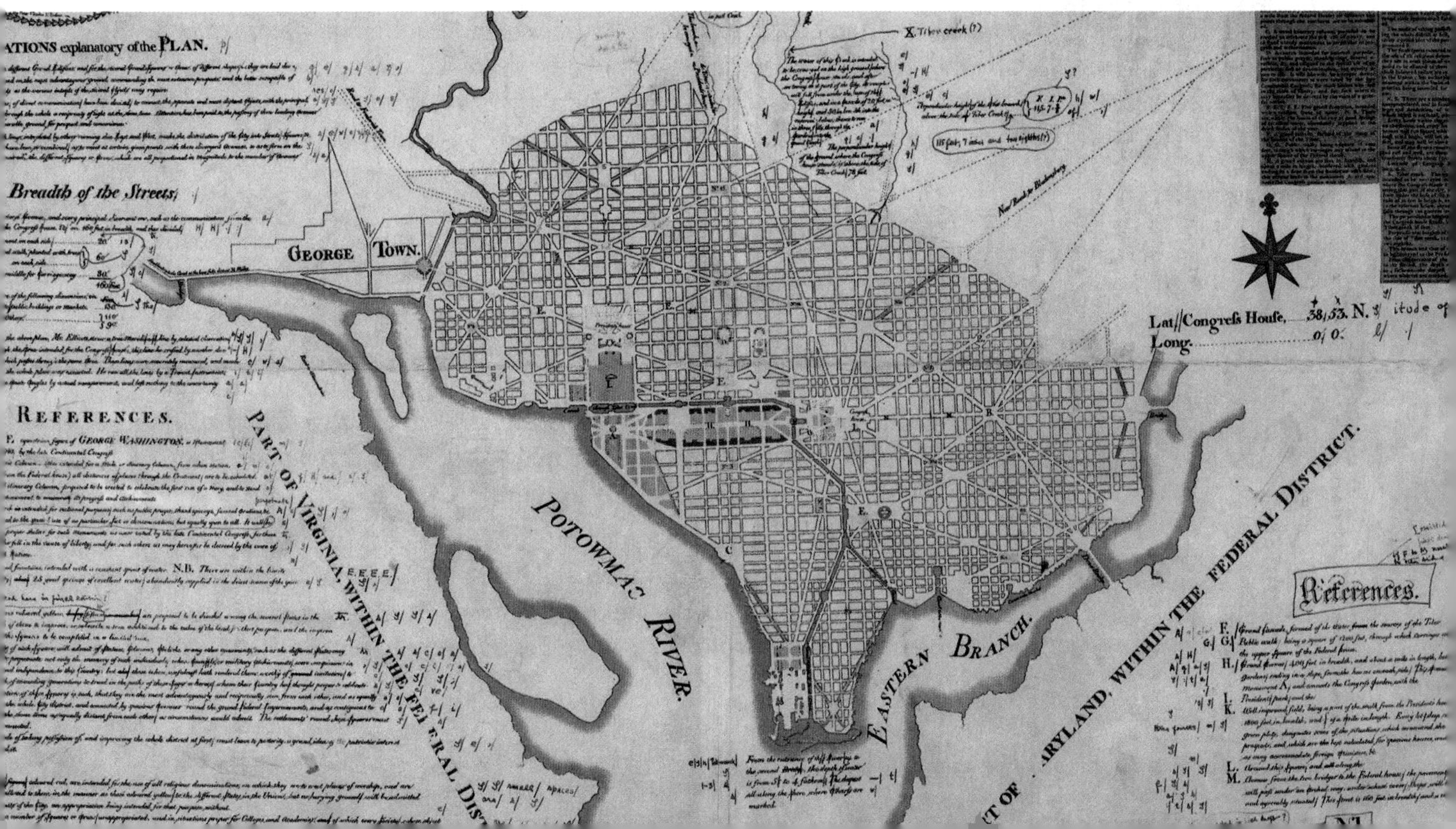

Analyze Images This building in Philadelphia was the headquarters of the first Bank of the United States. The Bank was founded in 1791. **Sequence** Why do you think the founding of the first bank came after the Revolution?

How Did Hamilton Create a Stable Economy?

Hamilton's next challenge was to strengthen the faltering national economy. **Accordingly**, his economic plan was designed to help both agriculture and industry.

Hamilton called on Congress to set up a national bank. In 1791, Congress created the first Bank of the United States. The government deposited money from taxes in the Bank. In turn, the Bank issued paper money to pay the government's bills and to make loans to farmers and businesses. Through these loans, the Bank encouraged economic growth and the development of a free-enterprise economic system.

To help American manufacturers, Hamilton asked Congress to pass a new tariff on foreign goods brought into the country. He wanted a high tariff to make imported goods more expensive than American-made goods. A tariff meant to protect local industry from foreign competition is called a protective tariff.

Hamilton's plan sparked arguments over taxation. In the North, where there were more and more factories, many people supported Hamilton's plan. Southern farmers, however, bought many imported goods. They opposed a protective tariff that would make imports more expensive.

In the end, Congress did pass a tariff, but it was much lower than the protective tariff Hamilton wanted. The tariff was also lower than American manufacturers would have liked in order to protect them from foreign competition. However, the tariff did help to pay off government debt, a central point in Hamilton's economic plan. The government needed to find a form of taxation that allowed it to pay off lenders because attracting lenders is key to financing government in a free market economy.

READING CHECK **Identify Supporting Details** What is the purpose of a protective tariff?

A New Tax Leads to Rebellion

To help reduce the national debt, Congress approved a tax on all liquor made and sold in the United States. Hamilton wanted this tax to raise money for the treasury. Instead, the new tax sparked a rebellion that tested the strength of the new government.

This tax was the first implemented by Congress under its new constitutional authority. Hamilton believed that reasonable taxes on alcohol would help to moderate consumption. He also hoped to gain a rich source of revenue for the federal government to pay its debts.

Academic Vocabulary
accordingly • *adv.*, in a fitting or appropriate way

However, the new law varied the tax rate and often left smaller liquor manufacturers paying more than larger ones. Furthermore, the tax had to be paid in cash. This was often difficult for small distilleries. Large liquor enterprises in the East had less trouble with the tax than those on the frontier or in small towns.

A Controversial Tax

Hamilton, though himself a man of humble origins, did not fully appreciate the economic concerns of Americans who lived on farms or in small towns. A large number of them opposed the new tax.

The Whiskey Rebellion Like many Americans, backcountry farmers grew corn. However, corn was bulky and expensive to haul long distances over rough roads. The cost of transport made western corn too expensive to sell in the East. Instead, farmers converted their corn into whiskey. Barrels of whiskey were worth much more and could be sold for a profit in the East, despite the cost of transport.

Back country farmers hated the tax on whiskey because it sharply reduced their income. Many refused to pay it. They compared it to the taxes Britain had forced on the colonies.

In 1794, when officials in western Pennsylvania tried to collect the tax, farmers rebelled. During the Whiskey Rebellion thousands marched in protest through the streets of Pittsburgh. They sang revolutionary songs and tarred and feathered the tax collectors.

Washington Shows Leadership President Washington responded quickly. He showed his abilities as a military leader once again.

Analyze Images Frontiersmen tar and feather a government tax collector during the Whiskey Rebellion to protest a tax on liquor. **Classify and Categorize** How would you describe the behavior of the crowd in the picture?

Analyze Images In this image showing the French Revolution, a mob in Paris burns symbols of the monarchy. **Understand Effects** What do you think some Americans thought about the increasing violence of the French Revolution?

He called up the militia and dispatched them to Pennsylvania. When the rebels heard that thousands of troops were marching against them, they fled back to their farms. Hamilton wanted the leaders of the rebellion executed, but Washington disagreed and pardoned them. He believed that the government had shown its strength to all. Now, it was time to show mercy.

The Whiskey Rebellion tested the will of the new government. Washington's quick response proved to Americans that their new government would act firmly in times of crisis. The President also showed those who disagreed with the government that violence would not be tolerated.

READING CHECK **Identify Cause and Effect** What was the main cause of the Whiskey Rebellion?

How Did Americans React to the French Revolution?

Late in 1789, French ships arrived in American ports with startling news. On July 14, an angry mob in Paris, France, had destroyed the Bastille (bahs TEEL), an ancient fort that was used as a prison. The attack on the Bastille was an early event in the French Revolution. Before long, the revolution would topple the monarch and lead to the execution of thousands of ordinary French citizens.

The French Revolution broke out a few years after Americans had won their independence. Like Americans, the French fought for liberty and equality. As the French Revolution grew more violent, however, it deepened political divisions within the United States.

Foreign Affairs Under Washington

The French had many reasons to rebel against their king, Louis XVI. The peasants and the middle class paid heavy taxes, while nobles paid none. Reformers wanted a constitution to limit the king's power and protect basic rights, as the American Constitution did.

Supporting Liberty in France At first, most Americans supported the French Revolution. Americans knew what it meant to struggle for liberty. Also, during the American Revolution, France had been an ally. Many Americans admired the Marquis de Lafayette, a leading French reformer who had fought with them in the American Revolution.

However, the French Revolution frightened most European rulers and nobles. They wanted to prevent revolutionary ideas from spreading to their lands. When two European countries, Austria and Prussia, **invoked** other rulers to help the French king regain his throne in 1792, France declared war.

Academic Vocabulary
invoke • *v.*, to call on; to appeal to

By 1793, the French Revolution was turning more and more violent. Radical reformers gained power. They beheaded the king and later the queen. During the Reign of Terror, tens of thousands of ordinary French citizens were executed.

Differing Opinions Violence in France divided Americans. Some, like Thomas Jefferson, continued to support the French revolutionaries. He felt that the French had the right to use violence to win freedom, although he condemned the executions of the king and queen.

Analyze Diagrams The information in the chart reflects Washington's foreign policy. **Identify Main Ideas** Based on the chart, how did Washington deal with European powers? How did his actions reflect his foreign policy preferences?

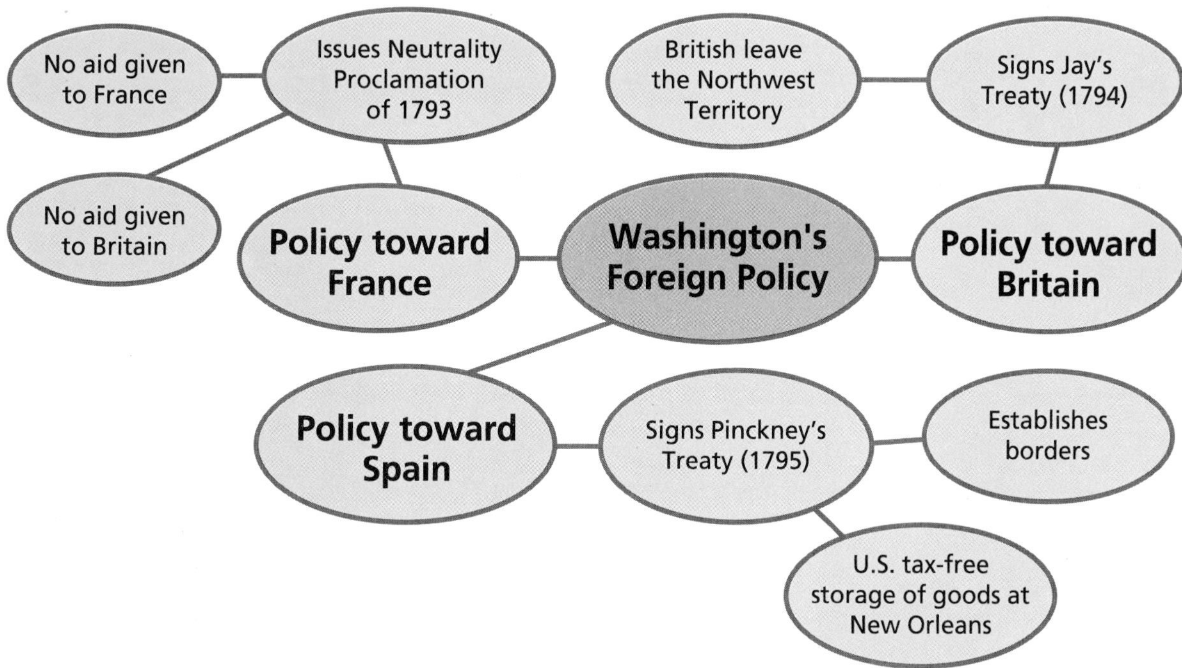

Quest CONNECTIONS

What was Washington's foreign policy? Why did he form this policy? Record your findings in your Active Journal.

Alexander Hamilton, John Adams, and others strongly disagreed about the use of violence. One could no more create democracy through widespread violence, claimed Adams, "than a snowball can exist in the streets of Philadelphia under a burning sun."

President Washington's Foreign Policy The French armies' attack on Austria led Britain to declare war on France. Europe was soon plunged into a string of wars that lasted on and off for more than 20 years. The fight between France and Britain, Europe's two leading powers, threatened the economy of the United States. These countries were America's main trading partners.

GEOGRAPHY SKILLS

Paris was the site of the violent French Revolution. The map also identifies places where the United States faced British hostility or outright aggression.

1. **Location** Near what bodies of water did the United States face British aggression in America?
2. **Draw Conclusions** Which nation—Britain or France—appeared to pose a more serious threat to the United States? Why?

Faced with war in Europe, President Washington had to decide on a foreign policy. Foreign policy is a nation's plan of action toward other nations. During the American Revolution, the United States and France had signed a treaty that made the two countries allies. Now, France wanted to use American ports to supply its ships and launch attacks on British ships. Allowing France to use American ports would expose the United States, still recovering from the Revolutionary War, to new British attacks. Washington worried that the United States could not honor its treaty with France and still remain neutral in the European conflict. Remaining **neutral** means not taking sides in a conflict.

Washington also hoped to protect the American economy from the conflict between Britain and France. Merchants and farmers in the United States depended on American ports to maintain overseas trade with Britain and other countries. The British navy ensured the safety of American trading ships.

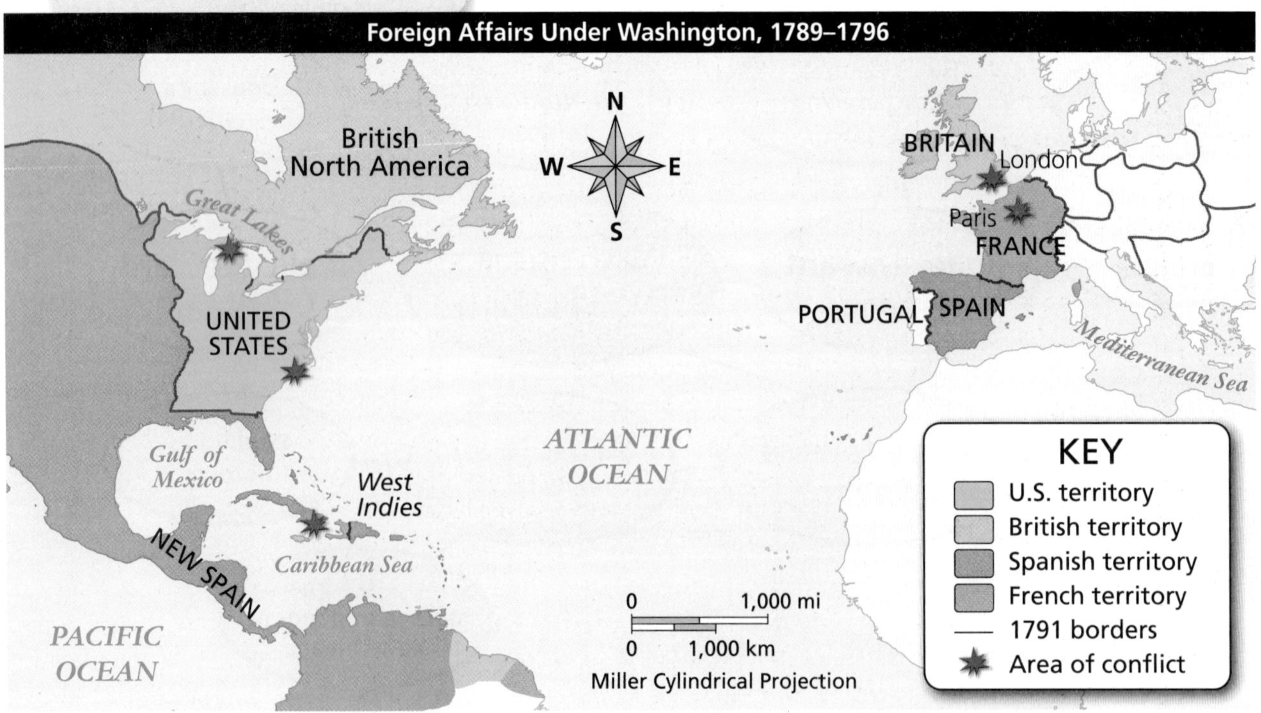

Still, many Americans favored France. Staying neutral appeared to be Washington's best option.

Protecting American Interests The issue of the treaty deepened the divisions within Washington's Cabinet. Hamilton pointed out that the United States had signed the treaty with Louis XVI. With the king dead, he argued, the treaty was no longer valid. Jefferson, a supporter of France, urged strict acceptance of the treaty.

After much debate, Washington issued the Neutrality Proclamation in April 1793. It stated that the United States would not support either side in the war. Further, it forbade Americans from aiding either Britain or France. The Neutrality Proclamation was a defeat for Jefferson. This and other defeats eventually led Jefferson to leave the Cabinet.

READING CHECK Identify Main Ideas Why did Washington decide on neutrality as his foreign policy?

Analyze Political Cartoons In this political cartoon, citizens burn an effigy of John Jay to protest Jay's Treaty, which they believed favored Britain. **Use Visual Information** How does the burning of the stuffed figure of John Jay make the image more powerful than if the mob did not burn the figure?

Washington Defends Neutrality

Declaring neutrality was easier than enforcing it. Americans wanted to trade with both Britain and France. However, those warring nations seized American cargoes headed for each other's ports.

Jay's Treaty In 1793, the British captured more than 250 American ships trading in the French West Indies. Some Americans called for war. Washington, however, knew that the United States was too weak to fight. He sent Chief Justice John Jay to Britain for talks.

Jay negotiated an agreement that called for Britain to pay damages for the seized American ships. Britain also agreed to give up the forts it still held in the West. Meanwhile, Americans had to pay debts long owed to British merchants.

Jay's Treaty sparked loud protests because it did nothing to protect the rights of neutral American ships. After furious debate, the Senate finally approved the treaty in 1795.

The Impact of Washington's Farewell Address After serving two terms as President, George Washington refused to serve a third.

Analyze Images In his Farewell Address, Washington gave clear warnings about the dangers of political entanglement with other nations. **Identify Main Ideas** Why did Washington fear such entanglements?

Before retiring in 1796, Washington published his Farewell Address. In it, he advised Americans against becoming involved in European affairs:

Primary Source

"Tis our true policy to steer clear of permanent Alliances, with any portion of the foreign World. . . . The great rule of conduct for us, in regard to foreign nations is . . . to have with them as little political connection as possible."

—George Washington, Farewell Address, 1796

Washington did not oppose foreign trade, but he did reject alliances that could drag the country into war. His advice guided American foreign policy for many years.

READING CHECK **Identify Main Ideas** What advice did Washington give in his final address?

Lesson Check

Practice Vocabulary

1. Why were many of President George Washington's actions considered **precedents**?
2. How were **bonds** and **speculators** related in the early republic?

Critical Thinking and Writing

3. **Identify Main Ideas** Explain Hamilton's argument in favor of paying the nation's debts in full.
4. **Identify Cause and Effect** Why was the nation's capital built as a new city in the South?
5. **Summarize** What was George Washington's response to the Whiskey Rebellion, and what effect did his response have on the nation?
6. **Writing Workshop: Generate Questions to Focus Research** In your Active Journal, write at least three questions about the country's physical landscapes, political divisions, and territorial expansion during the early republic. These questions will help focus your research and help you to write a research paper at the end of the Topic.

LESSON 2

A Two-Party System Develops

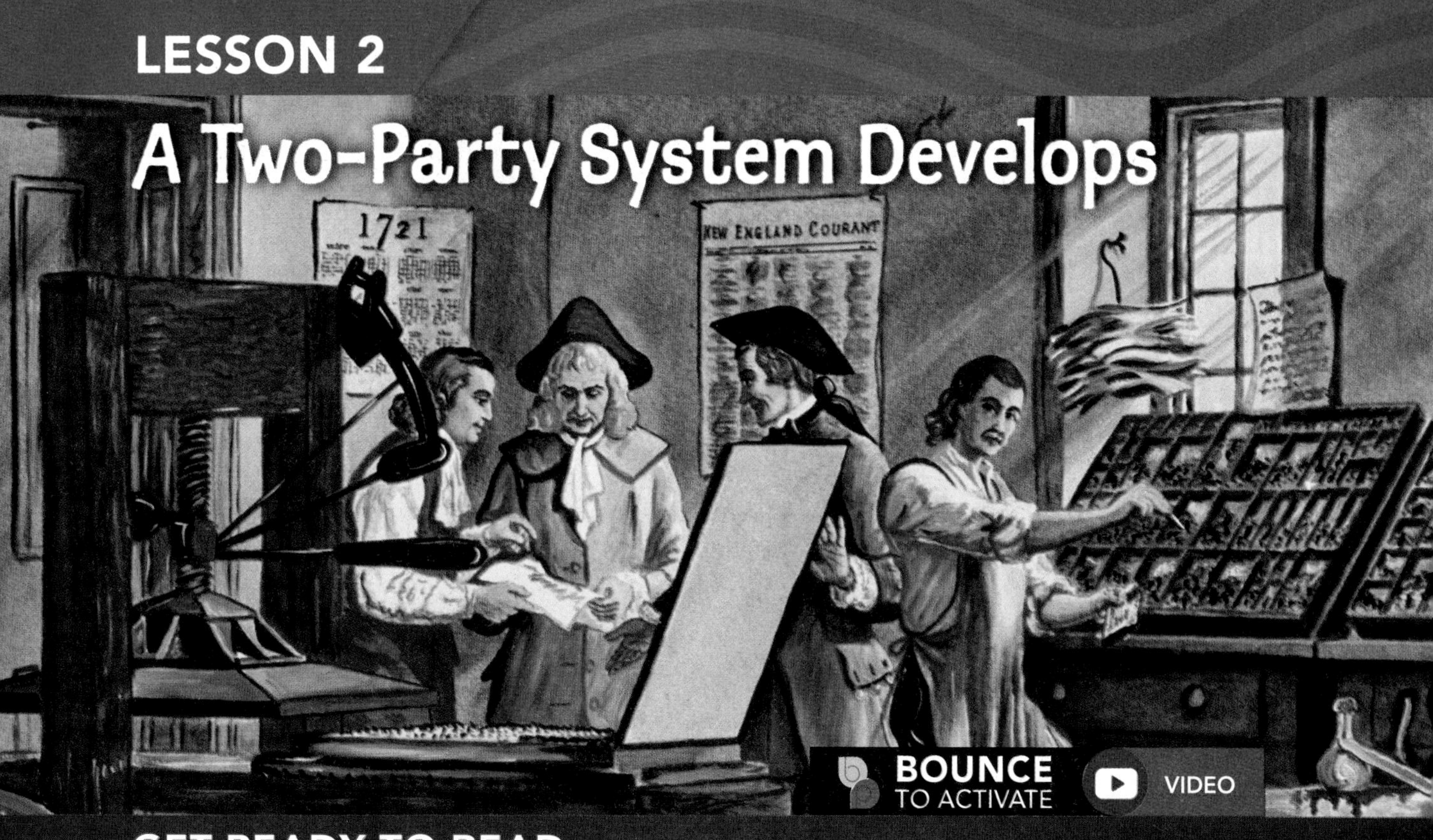

GET READY TO READ

START UP

Study the illustration. What do you think people were reading about in newspapers in the 1790s? Write your thoughts in your Active Journal.

GUIDING QUESTIONS

- How did the government change during the early republic?
- In what ways did Hamilton's and Jefferson's views of government differ?
- How did political parties develop?
- What political tensions appeared during the election of 1796?

TAKE NOTES

Literacy Skills: Compare and Contrast

Use the graphic organizer in your Active Journal to take notes as you read the lesson.

PRACTICE VOCABULARY

Use the vocabulary activity in your Active Journal to practice the vocabulary words.

Vocabulary

faction
unconstitutional
Democratic Republicans
Federalists

Academic Vocabulary

unify
subsidize

Political disagreements divided Americans early on. "Men who have been [friends] all their lives," noted Jefferson, "cross streets to avoid meeting, and turn their heads another way, lest they should be obliged to touch their hats." Washington was able to **unify** Americans with different political beliefs. He opposed political parties. Before he left office in 1797, however, two rival parties had emerged.

How Did Politics Divide Americans?

Americans saw political parties as a threat to national unity. They agreed with George Washington, who warned that parties would lead to "jealousies and false alarms."

Opposing Factions Grow in the Cabinet Despite the President's warning, **factions**, or opposing groups, grew up around two members of his Cabinet, Alexander Hamilton and Thomas Jefferson. The two men differed in both background and politics. Born in the West Indies, Hamilton had worked his way up from

Differing Views: Jefferson vs. Hamilton

JEFFERSON	HAMILTON
• Wanted strong state governments	• Wanted a strong central government
• Sympathetic to France	• Sympathetic to England
• Opposed a national bank	• Favored a national bank
• Thought the government should be controlled by ordinary Americans	• Thought the government should be controlled by the elite of society
• Wanted liberties to be protected by law	• Opposed to protecting individual liberties by law
• Believed the American government should not be modeled on the English government	• Wanted to model the American government after the English government

Analyze Charts Thomas Jefferson and Alexander Hamilton held opposing views on many issues. **Compare and Contrast** How did Jefferson's views on civil liberties differ from Hamilton's?

poverty. Hamilton believed that the wealthy and educated should control the government. He thought that supporting business and trade was the best way to improve the nation's economy. Hamilton also favored Britain over France.

Unlike Hamilton, Jefferson came from a wealthy family of Virginia planters. He owned large plantations and enslaved African Americans. Despite his wealth, Jefferson believed that the government should represent ordinary white people, not just the wealthy and educated. Jefferson strongly believed that public education was necessary for a free republican society. Jefferson supported policies that favored small farmers rather than businessmen. He also favored France over Britain.

READING CHECK **Identify Main Ideas** Why did many Americans distrust political parties?

What Issues Divided Hamilton and Jefferson?

The disagreements between Hamilton and Jefferson were not just differences of opinion. Their quarrels were rooted in their different views about what was best for the new nation.

Foundations of the American Economy The two leaders differed on economic policy. Hamilton wanted the United States to model itself on Britain. The government, he thought, should encourage manufacturing and trade. He believed the government should **subsidize** the building of roads and canals to encourage commerce. He also favored the growth of cities and the merchant class.

Jefferson thought that farmers were the backbone of the new nation. "Cultivators of the earth," he wrote, "are the most valuable citizens."

Academic Vocabulary

unify • *v.*, to bring together as one; to unite; to combine

subsidize • *v.*, to help pay for the cost of something

He feared that a manufacturing economy would corrupt the United States by concentrating power in the hands of wealthy Americans.

Federalism Hamilton and Jefferson also disagreed about the power of the federal government. Hamilton wanted the federal government to have greater power than state governments. A strong federal government, he argued, was needed to increase commerce. It would also be able to restrain mob violence like that of the Whiskey Rebellion. Earlier, he had written in his notes for a speech:

INTERACTIVE

Early American Leaders

Primary Source

"The general government must, in this case, not only have a strong soul, but strong organs by which that soul is to operate."

—Alexander Hamilton, Notes, June 18, 1787

In contrast, Jefferson wanted as small a federal government as possible, in order to protect individual freedom. He feared that a strong federal government might take over powers that the Constitution gave to the states.

Interpreting the Constitution Jefferson and Hamilton also clashed over the Bank of the United States. Jefferson worried that a national bank would give too much power to the government and to wealthy investors who would help run the bank.

Jefferson opposed the law setting up the bank. He claimed that it was **unconstitutional**, or not permitted by the Constitution. Nowhere did the Constitution give Congress the power to create a Bank, he argued. For Jefferson, any power not specifically given to the federal government belonged to the states.

Analyze Images Jefferson believed that farmers were the backbone of the nation. Hamilton believed in supporting manufacturing and trade in cities such as Boston and New York. **Recognize Multiple Causes** How do you think these two views resulted in these men having different points of view on how to run the U.S. government?

Hamilton did not agree with Jefferson's strict interpretation of the Constitution. He preferred a loose interpretation of the Constitution. The Constitution gave Congress the power to make all laws "necessary and proper" to carry out its duties. Hamilton argued that the Bank was necessary for the government to collect taxes and pay its bills.

Britain or France? Finally, the two leaders disagreed over foreign policy. Hamilton wanted close ties with Britain, because it was a major trading partner. Jefferson favored France, the first ally of the United States.

READING CHECK **Identify Supporting Details** How did Hamilton feel about division of power between the U.S. government and the states?

Political Parties Take Shape

At first, Hamilton and Jefferson clashed in private. Then Congress began to pass many of Hamilton's programs. James Madison shared many of Jefferson's views, and the two men decided to organize supporters of their views.

Analyze Political Cartoons In this cartoon, Congressman Matthew Lyon, a Democratic Republican, defends himself from Roger Griswold, a Federalist. **Infer** What does this cartoon suggest about the conflict between the parties?

Functions and Responsibilities of a Free Press

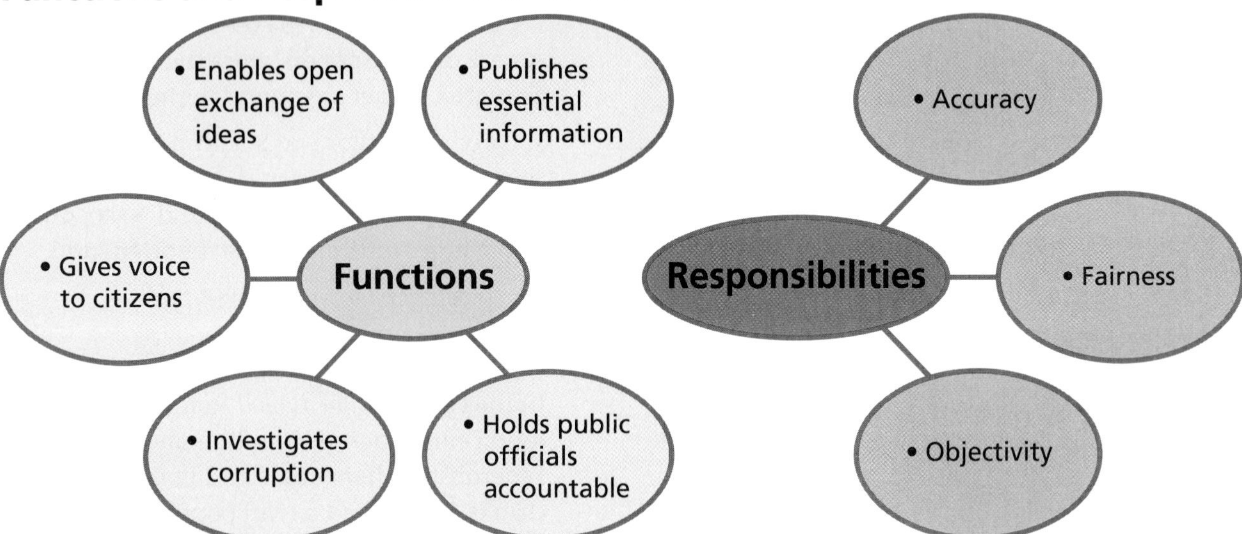

Analyze Charts A free press is essential to people living under a democratic form of government. **Identify Cause and Effect** What would be the effect if any of the functions or responsibilities of a free press were abandoned? Explain the consequences.

Jefferson and Madison moved cautiously at first. In 1791, they went to New York, telling people that they wanted to study its wildlife. In fact, Jefferson was interested in nature. Their main goal, though, was to meet with leading New York politicians such as Governor George Clinton and Aaron Burr, a fierce critic of Hamilton. Jefferson asked them to help defeat Hamilton's program by convincing New Yorkers to vote for Jefferson's supporters.

Republicans and Federalists Soon, leaders in other states were organizing to support either Hamilton or Jefferson. Jefferson's supporters called themselves **Democratic Republicans**, often shortened to Republicans. Today's Republican Party is not related to Jefferson's party. The Jeffersonian Republicans included small farmers, artisans, and some wealthy planters in the South.

Hamilton and his supporters were called **Federalists** because they wanted a strong federal government. In fact, Jefferson wrote a letter to President Washington calling Hamilton and his supporters a "corrupt squadron" whose

Primary Source

"ultimate object . . . is to prepare the way for a change, from the present republican form of government, to that of a monarchy, of which the English constitution is to be the model."

—Thomas Jefferson to George Washington, May 23, 1792

Federalists drew support mainly from merchants and manufacturers in such cities as Boston and New York. They also had the backing of some southern planters.

Quick Activity

Take sides. Tell whether you would support Hamilton's or Jefferson's views on the role of government. Write your ideas in your Active Journal.

Newspapers Influence Public Opinion In the late 1700s, the number of American newspapers more than doubled. This growth met a demand for information.

A European visitor was surprised that so many Americans could read. "The common people . . . all read and write, and understand arithmetic," he reported, and "almost every little town now furnishes a circulating library."

As party rivalry grew, newspapers took sides. In the *Gazette of the United States,* publisher John Fenno backed Hamilton and the Federalists. Jefferson's friend Philip Freneau (frih NOH) started a rival paper, the *National Gazette,* which supported Republicans.

Newspapers had great influence on public opinion. In stinging language, they raged against political opponents. Often, articles mixed rumor and opinion with facts. Emotional attacks and counterattacks fanned the flames of party rivalry.

▲ Philip Freneau's newspaper *the National Gazette* presented a counterpart to John Fenno's Federalist newspaper.

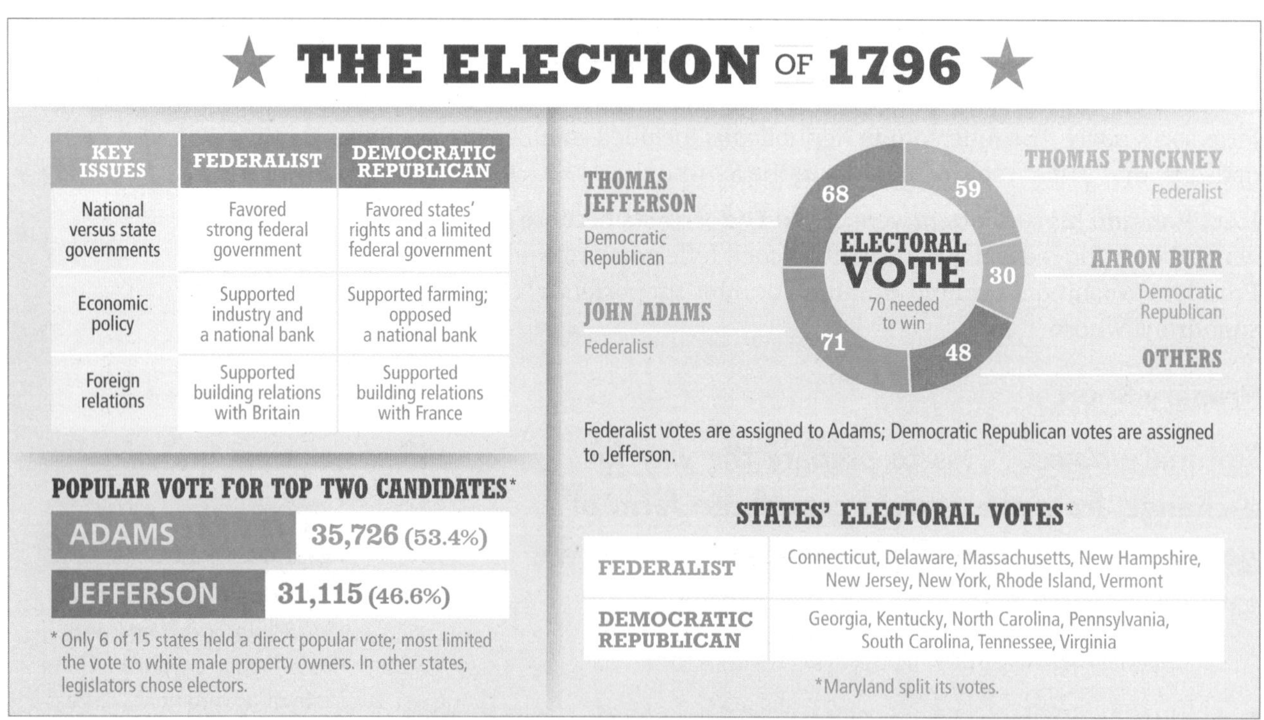

★ THE ELECTION OF 1796 ★

KEY ISSUES	FEDERALIST	DEMOCRATIC REPUBLICAN
National versus state governments	Favored strong federal government	Favored states' rights and a limited federal government
Economic policy	Supported industry and a national bank	Supported farming; opposed a national bank
Foreign relations	Supported building relations with Britain	Supported building relations with France

POPULAR VOTE FOR TOP TWO CANDIDATES*

ADAMS	35,726 (53.4%)
JEFFERSON	31,115 (46.6%)

* Only 6 of 15 states held a direct popular vote; most limited the vote to white male property owners. In other states, legislators chose electors.

Federalist votes are assigned to Adams; Democratic Republican votes are assigned to Jefferson.

STATES' ELECTORAL VOTES*

FEDERALIST	Connecticut, Delaware, Massachusetts, New Hampshire, New Jersey, New York, Rhode Island, Vermont
DEMOCRATIC REPUBLICAN	Georgia, Kentucky, North Carolina, Pennsylvania, South Carolina, Tennessee, Virginia

*Maryland split its votes.

Analyze Charts Study the chart. **Identify Main Ideas** Which political party championed agriculture and campaigned against the establishment of a national bank? Which candidate finished third in the electoral vote tally?

Choosing Washington's Successor Political parties played a large role in the election of George Washington's successor. In 1796, Democratic Republicans backed Thomas Jefferson for President and Aaron Burr for Vice President. Federalists supported John Adams for President and Thomas Pinckney for Vice President. The election had an unexpected outcome.

Under the Constitution, the person with the most electoral votes becomes President. At that time, the candidate with the next highest total was made Vice President. John Adams, a Federalist, won office as President. The leader of the Democratic Republicans, Thomas Jefferson, became Vice President.

Having the President and Vice President from opposing parties further increased political tensions. John Adams took office in March 1797 as the nation's second President. Events soon deepened the distrust between him and Jefferson.

▲ John Adams succeeded George Washington and became the second President of the United States in the election of 1796.

READING CHECK **Summarize** How did political parties begin in the United States?

Lesson Check

Practice Vocabulary

1. What **factions** developed despite Washington's warnings?
2. What makes a law **unconstitutional**?

Critical Thinking and Writing

3. **Compare and Contrast** What were Hamilton's and Jefferson's views on the power of the federal government?
4. **Draw Conclusions** Why did Thomas Jefferson, who claimed to dislike political parties, lead the way in founding a party?
5. **Summarize** In the late 1700s, the number of newspapers in the United States increased greatly. What are the functions and responsibilities of a free press in a democracy?
6. **Writing Workshop: Find and Use Credible Sources** Choose reliable print and Internet sources that you will use for your research paper at the end of this Topic. List them in your Active Journal. Take careful notes from your sources.

Distinguish Fact From Opinion

Follow these steps to distinguish fact from opinion.

INTERACTIVE
Distinguish Between Fact and Opinion

1 **Decide which statements are facts.** Facts are based on evidence and can be proved true. Find two facts in the diary entry. How could you prove each statement is a fact? What questions will you ask as you examine each bit of information?

2 **Decide which statements are opinions.** An opinion is a personal interpretation of an event. It reflects feelings, judgments, or beliefs. Find two opinions in the diary entry. How can you tell that each is an opinion? What questions will you ask as you examine whether a piece of information is an opinion?

3 **Recognize how the author mixes fact and opinion.** Find a sentence that includes both a fact and an opinion. What is the fact? What is the opinion? Why do you think the author mixed facts and opinions? Who do you think the writer is addressing, and does that make a difference in the way the writer expresses his or her ideas?

Diary Entry

February 28

After dinner tonight, I finished reading today's edition of the *Gazette of the United States*. The publisher of the newspaper is John Fenno. In my opinion, he is right to favor the Federalist leader, Alexander Hamilton. Of course, I am a merchant, and I agree with Hamilton's support of trade and manufacturing. To me, it is a more worthwhile policy than Mr. Jefferson's support of farmers.

I believe that I have Hamilton alone to thank for the National Bank. This Bank, established by Congress in 1791, has the power to make loans to businesses, such as my dry goods store. Of course, the federal bank is opposed by that friend of the states, Thomas Jefferson, who isn't thinking of our country's future. I only hope that Mr. Hamilton's party wins the next election. Isaac Smith

—*A fictional diary entry of a merchant living in colonial Philadelphia in the 1790s*

LESSON 3

Presidents Adams and Jefferson

GET READY TO READ

START UP

Examine this picture of the new capital of Washington, D.C. Make a prediction about events in the new capital in your Active Journal.

GUIDING QUESTIONS

- How did John Adams's foreign policy compare with Washington's foreign policy?
- What was the controversy over the Alien and Sedition Acts?
- What is the significance of the Supreme Court case *Marbury* v. *Madison*?

TAKE NOTES

Literacy Skills: Identify Main Ideas

Use the graphic organizer in your Active Journal to take notes as you read this lesson.

PRACTICE VOCABULARY

Use the vocabulary activity in your Active Journal to practice the vocabulary words.

Vocabulary		Academic Vocabulary
tribute	laissez faire	expel
sedition	judicial review	constitute
nullify		
states' rights		

No sooner had John Adams taken office than he faced a crisis with France. The French objected to Jay's Treaty because they felt that it put the United States on the side of Britain. In 1797, French ships began to seize American ships in the West Indies, as the British had done.

Conflict With France

As the conflict between the two nations escalated, Americans once again called for war, this time against France. To avoid war, Adams sent diplomats to Paris to discuss the rights of neutral nations.

The XYZ Affair The French foreign minister, Charles Maurice de Talleyrand, did not deal directly with the Americans. Instead, he sent three agents to offer the Americans a deal. Before Talleyrand would even begin talks, the agents said, he wanted $250,000 for himself and a $10 million loan to France. "Not a sixpence!" replied one of the Americans, angrily. (A sixpence was a British coin worth six pennies.)

Quest CONNECTIONS

Think about the XYZ Affair and Adams's response to French attacks on ships. What do these events suggest about dealing with conflicts? Record your ideas in your Active Journal.

The diplomats informed Adams about the offer. He then told Congress. Adams referred to the agents only as X, Y, and Z.

Many Americans were outraged when news reached them about the XYZ Affair in 1798. (The affair had taken place in 1797, but it took time for news to cross the ocean by ship.) They took up the slogan, "Millions for defense, but not one cent for **tribute**!" They were willing to spend money to defend their country, but they would not pay a bribe to another nation.

The XYZ Affair ignited war fever in the United States. Despite strong pressure, Adams refused to ask Congress to declare war on France. Like Washington, he wanted to keep the country out of European affairs. However, he could not ignore French attacks on American ships, so he strengthened the navy by building frigates, fast-sailing ships with many guns. That move convinced France to stop attacking American ships.

Adams's Foreign Policy Divides the Federalists Led by Hamilton, many Federalists criticized Adams. They hoped a war would weaken the Democratic Republicans, who supported France. War would also force the nation to build its military forces.

A strong military would increase federal power, a key Federalist goal. Many Federalists also favored Britain in its war against France.

Although Adams was a Federalist, he resisted Hamilton's pressure for war. Their disagreement created a split in the Federalist party.

Analyze Political Cartoons In this cartoon depicting the XYZ Affair, a five-headed monster demands a bribe from three Americans. **Use Evidence** What details in the cartoon reflect the cartoonist's attitude toward the French?

Over Hamilton's opposition, Adams again sent diplomats to France. When they arrived, they found an ambitious young army officer, Napoleon Bonaparte, in charge. Napoleon was planning for war against several European powers. Thus, he had no time for a war with the United States. He signed an agreement to stop seizing American ships.

Like Washington, Adams kept the nation out of war. His actions showed his qualities of leadership and courage. His success, however, cost him the support of many Federalists and weakened the party for the election of 1800.

▲ Representative Albert Gallatin opposed Federalists in their attempts to fund the fighting with France. Some believed that the Alien and Sedition Acts were written to remove Gallatin from power.

READING CHECK **Summarize** Why did many Federalists support a war with France?

What Were the Alien and Sedition Acts?

In 1798, during the crisis with France, Federalists pushed several laws through Congress. These laws were known as the Alien and Sedition Acts.

Under the Alien Act, the President could **expel** any alien, or foreigner, thought to be dangerous to the country. Another law made it harder for immigrants to become citizens. Before 1798, white immigrants could become citizens after living in the United States for five years. The new law made immigrants wait 14 years. The Federalists passed this act because many recent immigrants supported Jefferson and the Democratic Republicans. The act would keep these immigrants from voting for years.

INTERACTIVE

Relations With France

The Democratic Republicans grew even angrier when Congress passed the Sedition Act. **Sedition** means stirring up rebellion against a government. Under this law, citizens could be fined or jailed if they criticized the government or its officials. In fact, several Democratic Republican newspaper editors, and even members of Congress, were fined and jailed for expressing their opinions.

Democratic Republicans protested that the Sedition Act violated the Constitution. The First Amendment, they argued, protected freedom of speech and of the press. Jefferson warned that the new laws threatened American liberties:

Academic Vocabulary

expel • *v.*, to push or force out

Primary Source

"They have brought into the lower house a sedition bill, which . . . undertakes to make printing certain matters criminal . . . Indeed this bill & the alien bill both are so [against] the Constitution as to show they mean to pay no respect to it."

—Thomas Jefferson, *The Writings of Thomas Jefferson*, 1798

KENTUCKY LEGISLATURE.

In the Houſe of Repreſentatives,

NOVEMBER 10th, 1798.

THE HOUSE according to the ſtanding Order of the Day, reſolved itſelf into a Committee of the Whole on the ſtate of the Commonwealth,

Mr. CALDWELL in the Chair,

And after ſometime ſpent therein the Speaker reſumed the Chair, and Mr. Caldwell reported, that the Committee had according to order had under conſideration the Governor's Addreſs, and had come to the following RESOLUTIONS thereupon, which he delivered in at the Clerk's table, where they were twice read and agreed to by the Houſe.

I. RESOLVED, that the ſeveral ſtates compoſing the United States of America, are not united on the principle of unlimited ſubmiſſion to their General Government; but that by compact under the ſtyle and title of a Conſtitution for the United States and of amendments thereto, they conſtituted a General Government for ſpecial purpoſes, delegated to that Government certain definite powers, reſerving each ſtate to itſelf, the reſiduary maſs of right to their own ſelf Government; and that whenſoever the General Government aſſumes undelegated powers, its acts are unauthoritative, void, and of no force: That to this compact each ſtate acceded as a ſtate, and is an integral party, its co-ſtates forming as to itſelf, the other party: That the Government created by this compact was not made the excluſive or final *judge* of the extent of the powers delegated to itſelf; ſince that would have made its diſcretion, and not the conſtitution, the meaſure of its powers; but that as in all other caſes of compact among parties having no common Judge, each party has an equal right to judge for itſelf, as well of infractions as of the mode and meaſure of redreſs.

II. Reſolved, that the Conſtitution of the United States having delegated to Corgreſs a power to puniſh treaſon, counterfeiting the ſecurities and current coin of the United States, piracies and felonies committed on the High Seas, and offences againſt the laws of nations, and no other crimes whatever, and it being true as a general principle, and one of the amendments to the Conſtitution having alſo declared, "that the powers not delegated to the United States by the Conſtitution, nor prohibited by it to the ſtates, are reſerved to the ſtates reſpectively, or to the people," therefore alſo the ſame act of Congreſs paſſed on the 14th day of July, 1798, and entitled "An act in addition to the act entitled an act for the puniſhment of certain crimes againſt the United States;" as alſo the act paſſed by them on the 27th day of June, 1798, entitled "An act to puniſh frauds committed on the Bank of the United States" (and all other their acts which aſſume to create, define, or puniſh crimes other than thoſe enumerated in the conſtitution) are altogether void and of no force, and that the power to create, define, and puniſh ſuch other crimes is reſerved, and of right appertains ſolely and excluſively to the reſpective ſtates, each within its own Territory.

III. Reſolved, that it is true as a general principle, and is alſo expreſsly declared by one of the amendments to the Conſtitution that "the powers not delegated to the United States by the Conſtitution, nor prohibited by it to the ſtates, are reſerved to the ſtates reſpectively or to the people;" and that no power over the freedom of religion, freedom of ſpeech, or freedom of the preſs being delegated to the United States by the Conſtitution, nor prohibited by it to the ſtates, all lawful powers reſpecting the ſame did of right remain, and were reſerved to the ſtates, or to the people: That thus was manifeſted their determination to retain to themſelves the right of judging how far the licentiouſneſs of ſpeech and of the preſs may be abridged without leſſening their uſeful freedom, and how far thoſe abuſes which cannot be ſeparated from

Analyze Images The Kentucky Resolution declared that a state could nullify federal laws it deemed unconstitutional. **Identify Cause and Effect** Why did Jefferson and Madison urge states to pass such resolutions?

Academic Vocabulary

constitute • *v.*, to set up; to establish

States Challenge the Federal Government Vice President Jefferson bitterly opposed the Alien and Sedition Acts. He could not ask the courts for help because the Federalists controlled them. So, he urged the states to take strong action against the acts. He argued that the states had the right to **nullify**, or cancel, a law passed by the federal government. In this way, states could resist the power of the federal government.

With help from Jefferson and Madison, Kentucky and Virginia passed resolutions in 1798 and 1799. The Kentucky and Virginia resolutions claimed that each state "has an equal right to judge for itself" whether a law is constitutional. If a state decides a law is unconstitutional, said the resolutions, it has the power to nullify that law within its borders. Jefferson wrote:

Primary Source

"Resolved, that the several states composing the United States of America, are not united on the principle of unlimited submission to their General Government; but that by compact under the style and title of a Constitution for the United States and of amendments thereto, they constituted a General Government for special purposes, delegated to that Government certain definite powers, reserving each state to itself, the residuary [remaining] mass of right to their own self Government; and that whensoever the General Government assumes undelegated powers, its acts are unauthoritative, void, and of no force. . . ."

—Thomas Jefferson, November 10, 1798

The Kentucky and Virginia resolutions raised the issue of **states' rights**. Did the federal government have only those powers that were listed in the Constitution? If so, did the states possess all other powers?

For example, could a state declare a federal law unconstitutional? Soon the Alien and Sedition Acts were changed or dropped.

READING CHECK **Identify Main Ideas** What did some states argue after the Alien and Sedition Acts became law?

Why Was the Presidential Election of 1800 Important?

By 1800, the war cry against France was fading. As the election neared, Democratic Republicans focused on two issues. First, they attacked the Federalists for raising taxes to prepare for war. Second, they opposed the unpopular Alien and Sedition Acts.

Democratic Republicans backed Thomas Jefferson for President and Aaron Burr for Vice President. Despite the bitter split in the Federalist party, John Adams was again named its candidate.

Political Power Goes to a Different Party In the race for the presidency, Democratic Republicans won the popular vote. The electoral college was also dominated by Democratic Republicans. When the electoral college voted, Jefferson and Burr each received 73 votes. At the time, the electoral college did not vote separately for President and Vice President. Instead, the college voted for two candidates. The candidate winning the most votes became President, and the runner-up became Vice President. Because each Democratic Republican elector cast one vote for Jefferson and one vote for Burr, there was no clear winner.

Under the Constitution, if no candidate wins the electoral vote, the House of Representatives decides the election. After four days and 36 votes, the tie was broken. The House chose Jefferson as President.

Analyze Graphs Study the data shown. **Draw Conclusions** What explains the controversy over the electoral system that erupted after the 1800 presidential election?

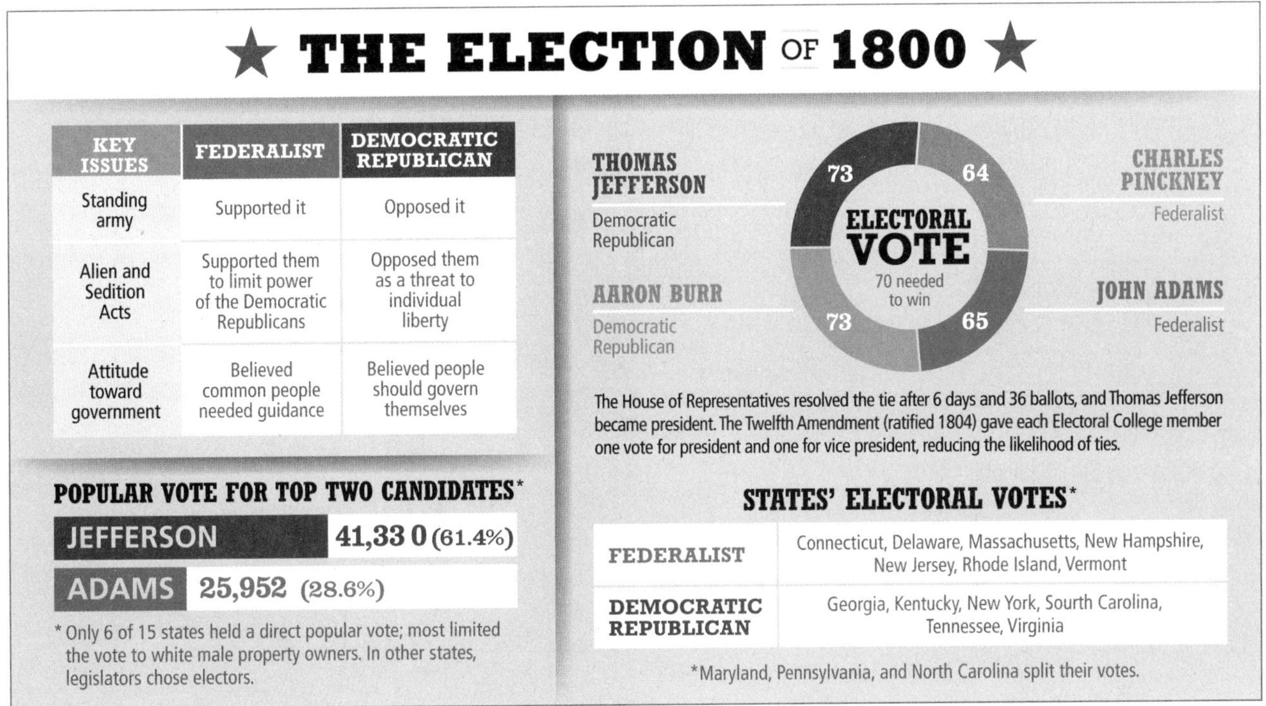

Did you know?

Alexander Hamilton was against dueling. Three years earlier his own son had been killed in a duel on the same spot as the Hamilton-Burr duel.

Burr became Vice President. The election of 1800 set an important precedent. It established the principle that power should pass peacefully from one party to another.

Soon after, Congress passed the Twelfth Amendment. It required electors to hold separate votes for President and Vice President. The states ratified the amendment in 1804.

The Federalist Era Comes to a Close After 1800, the Federalist party slowly declined. Federalists won fewer seats in Congress. In 1804, the party was greatly weakened after its leader, Alexander Hamilton, was killed in a duel with Aaron Burr. Despite its early decline, the Federalist party did help shape the new nation. Even Democratic Republican Presidents kept most of Hamilton's economic programs.

READING CHECK **Identify Supporting Details** Why did the House of Representatives have to decide the 1800 election?

How Did President Jefferson Redefine Government?

When Thomas Jefferson took office as the third President, some Federalists were worried about his political beliefs. They knew that he supported the French Revolution, and they feared that he might bring revolutionary change to the United States. They were also afraid that he might punish Federalists who had used the Alien and Sedition Acts to jail Democratic Republicans.

In his inaugural address, Jefferson tried to calm Federalists' fears. He promised that, although the Democratic Republicans were in the majority, he would not treat the Federalists harshly. "The minority possess their equal rights, which equal laws must protect," he said.

Analyze Images This painting shows Alexander Hamilton, at the right, about to lose his life in a duel with Aaron Burr in 1804. **Infer** What can you infer about the custom of dueling at this time, and why do you think it is an illegal act today?

Analyze Images Thomas Jefferson rode a white horse into Washington, D.C., for his inauguration. Unlike Presidents before him, he walked from his hotel to his inauguration ceremony on March 4, 1801. **Draw Conclusions** Why do you think riding a horse instead of taking a horse-drawn carriage was in keeping with Jefferson's ideas about government?

He called for an end to the political disputes of the past few years. "We are all Republicans, we are all Federalists," the President stated conclusively.

Jefferson had no plan to punish Federalists. He did, however, want to change their policies. In his view, the Federalists had made the national government too large and too powerful.

Promoting a Free Market Economy One way Jefferson wanted to lessen government power was by reducing the federal budget. Such budget cuts would also keep the federal debt low. His Secretary of the Treasury, Albert Gallatin (GAL uh tin), helped him achieve this goal. A financial wizard, Gallatin reduced government spending through careful management.

Jefferson believed in an economic idea known as **laissez faire** (les ay FAYR), a French term for "let do," meaning letting people do as they please. The idea of laissez faire was promoted by the Scottish economist Adam Smith.

▲ Adam Smith, in his 1776 book, *The Wealth of Nations,* described details of a free enterprise economy.

In his book *The Wealth of Nations,* Smith argued in favor of a system of free markets, where goods and services are exchanged between buyers and sellers with as little government interference as possible. Free competition, Smith said, would benefit everyone, not just the wealthy.

Laissez-faire economists believed that government should play as small a role as possible in economic affairs. Laissez faire was very different from the Federalist idea of government. Alexander Hamilton, you recall, wanted government to promote trade and manufacturing.

Jefferson Scales Back Government Jefferson believed that the government should protect citizens' rights. Beyond that, he wanted the federal government to take a less active role. He cut the federal budget and decreased the size of government departments.

With the approval of Congress, he reduced the size of the army and navy. He also asked Congress to repeal the unpopular whiskey tax.

The Sedition Act expired the day before Jefferson took office. Jefferson hated the law, and he pardoned those who were in jail because of it. He also asked Congress to restore the law allowing foreign-born white people to become citizens after only a five-year waiting period.

Some Federalist Economic Policies Remain Jefferson did not discard all Federalist programs. On the advice of Albert Gallatin, he kept the Bank of the United States. The federal government also continued to pay off state debts, which it had taken over while Washington was President. In addition, Jefferson let many Federalists keep their government jobs.

READING CHECK **Summarize** How would you define Jefferson's idea of government?

▲ Chief Justice John Marshall, a Federalist, helped to strengthen the U.S. Supreme Court by establishing its power to declare laws unconstitutional.

Landmark Supreme Court Cases

The election of 1800 gave Democratic Republicans control of Congress. Federalists, however, remained powerful in the courts.

Several months passed between Jefferson's election and his inauguration. In that time, Federalists in the old Congress passed the Judiciary Act of 1801, increasing the number of federal judges. President Adams then appointed Federalists to fill these new judicial positions. When Jefferson took office, Jeffersonians repealed this part of the act, firing 16 Federalist judges.

One of the judges that Adams appointed was John Marshall, the Chief Justice of the United States. Like Jefferson, Marshall was a rich Virginia planter with a brilliant mind. Unlike Jefferson, however, Marshall was a staunch Federalist. He wanted to make the federal government stronger.

The framers of the Constitution expected the courts to balance the powers of the President and Congress. However, John Marshall found the courts to be much weaker than the other branches of government. In his view, it was not clear what powers the federal courts had.

The Issues Behind *Marbury* v. *Madison*

In 1803, John Marshall showed courage and leadership by deciding a case that increased the power of the Supreme Court. The case involved William Marbury, one of the judges appointed by Adams. Adams made the appointment on his last night as President. The Republicans refused to accept this "midnight judge." They accused Federalists of using unfair tactics to keep control of the courts. Jefferson ordered Secretary of State James Madison not to deliver the official papers confirming Marbury's appointment.

Jefferson's Goals and Policies

Marbury sued Madison. According to the Judiciary Act of 1789, only the Supreme Court could decide a case that was brought against a federal official. Therefore, the case of *Marbury* v. *Madison* was tried before the Supreme Court.

The Significance of the *Marbury* v. *Madison* Decision The Supreme Court ruled against Marbury. Chief Justice Marshall wrote the decision, stating that the Judiciary Act was unconstitutional. The Constitution, Marshall argued, did not give the Supreme Court the right to decide cases brought against federal officials. Therefore, Congress could not give the Court that power simply by passing the Judiciary Act.

As a result of *Marbury* v. *Madison,* Congress had to amend, or change, the Judiciary Act to respond to the Supreme Court's objections. The part of the Judiciary Act of 1789 that the Supreme Court rejected could no longer be law.

The Supreme Court's decision in *Marbury* v. *Madison* set an important precedent. It gave the Supreme Court the power to decide whether laws passed by Congress were constitutional and to reject laws that it considered to be unconstitutional. This power of the Court is called **judicial review**.

The Reactions of Jefferson and Congress Jefferson was displeased with the decision. True, Marshall had ruled against Marbury, the Federalist judge.

But Marshall's decision gave more power to the Supreme Court, where Federalists were still strong. Jefferson also argued that the decision upset the balance of power among the three branches of government.

Primary Source

"The opinion which gives to the judges the right to decide what laws are constitutional and what not, not only for themselves . . . but for the Legislature and Executive also . . . would make the Judiciary a [tyrannical] branch."

—Thomas Jefferson, letter to Abigail Adams, 1804

Analyze Images These bronze doors lead into the Supreme Court chambers. The carved panels show important moments in legal history—including John Marshall discussing *Marbury* v. *Madison.* **Draw Conclusions** In what way do you think these bronze doors could be a symbol of rule of law in the United States?

▲ This is the original Supreme Court chambers where Supreme Court cases were heard between 1810 and 1860.

Jefferson did not want the judiciary to gain power over the executive branch. He refused the Court's order to testify at an important trial, saying it would upset the equality of the branches. He also used executive privilege to decide which government papers to show the Court and which to withhold.

In 1810, a year after Jefferson left office, Marshall's Supreme Court decided another landmark case involving judicial review. In *Fletcher* v. *Peck*, the Court ruled that the state of Georgia could not revoke a corrupt land sale. It was the first time the Court ruled a state law unconstitutional. By doing so, the Court also reinforced the idea that contracts cannot be broken.

In the end, the President and Congress accepted the right of the Court to overturn laws. Today, judicial review remains one of the most important powers of the Supreme Court.

READING CHECK **Identify Main Ideas** Why is the Supreme Court case *Marbury* v. *Madison* significant?

Lesson Check

Practice Vocabulary

1. What is a **laissez-faire** economy?
2. How did **judicial review** increase the power of the Supreme Court?

Critical Thinking and Writing

3. **Understand Effects** How did the Federalists contribute to shaping the United States as we know it today?
4. **Identify Cause and Effect** What was the important change in the Constitution that was prompted by the results of the election of 1800?
5. **Summarize** What were President Jefferson's economic policies?
6. **Writing Workshop: Pick an Organizing Strategy** Decide on an effective method of organizing the information you have gathered. Note this strategy in your Active Journal.

Detect Historical Points of View

Follow these steps to detect historical points of view.

INTERACTIVE

Compare Viewpoints

1 **Identify the context.** If you know the history of the period when a document was written, you can better understand the writer's point of view.

a. Why was this letter written?

b. How did the Bill of Rights settle the issue of an American national church?

2 **Identify the author's main idea.** Ask yourself what main point the author is making. What is the main idea of Jefferson's letter?

3 **Look for key words and phrases.** The writer may use words or phrases that strongly indicate the point of view being expressed. What is an example of a key word or phrase that sums up Jefferson's point of view?

4 **Identify the author's point of view.** Ask how the writer feels about the subject. How does Jefferson feel about establishing a national day of fasting and thanksgiving?

5 **Relate the point of view to the context.** Ask how the point of view was affected by historical context.

a. Jefferson's presidency began in 1801. What actions did he take that give clues to his point of view about the government's role?

b. How was Jefferson's point of view influenced by the events of the time?

Primary Source

The Danbury Baptist Association wrote to President Jefferson, asking why he would not establish national days of fasting and thanksgiving, as previous presidents had done. Jefferson answered the letter in 1802. His carefully worded reply reflects his opinion about the separation of government and religion in the new nation.

"Believing with you that religion is a matter which lies solely between man & his god, that he owes account to none other for his faith or his worship, that the legitimate powers of government reach actions only, and not opinions, I contemplate with sovereign reverence that act of the whole American people which declared that their legislature should make no law respecting an establishment of religion, or prohibiting the free exercise thereof, thus building a wall of separation between church and state."

—Thomas Jefferson, Jan. 1, 1802

LESSON 4

A Changing Nation

GET READY TO READ

START UP

Study the illustration of the Lewis and Clark expedition. Predict the significance of the expedition to the country in your Active Journal.

GUIDING QUESTIONS

- What was the reason for the Louisiana Purchase, and what were the results of it?
- Was the Louisiana Purchase constitutional?
- How did major western rivers play a role in the discoveries made by Lewis and Clark and Pike?

TAKE NOTES

Literacy Skills: Analyze Text Structure

Use the graphic organizer in your Active Journal to take notes as you read the lesson.

PRACTICE VOCABULARY

Use the vocabulary activity in your Active Journal to practice the vocabulary words.

Vocabulary	Academic Vocabulary
expedition	vital
continental divide	exceed
impressment	
embargo	
smuggling	

The United States overcame a number of challenges in its early years, including creating a stable economic system, setting up the courts, and defining the authority of the central government. As the economy continued to grow, Americans needed to protect their economic interests. The Louisiana Territory became a key part of this effort to expand the physical reach of the nation.

The Louisiana Purchase

The town of New Orleans was founded by the French. It lies at the mouth of the Mississippi River, where it empties into the Gulf of Mexico. By the early 1800s, it was the largest port in the South. President Jefferson feared that France would limit American access to New Orleans and the Mississippi River. To gain control of this important area, he decided to purchase it from the French.

Geography Shapes Domestic and Foreign Policy By 1800, almost one million Americans lived between the Appalachian Mountains and the Mississippi River. Most were farmers.

With few roads west of the Appalachians, western farmers relied on the Mississippi River to ship their wheat and corn. First, they sent their produce down the river to the city of New Orleans. From there, oceangoing ships carried the produce across the Gulf of Mexico, around Florida, and up to ports along the Atlantic coast.

Spain, which controlled New Orleans, sometimes threatened to close the port to Americans. In 1795, President Washington sent Thomas Pinckney to find a way to keep the **vital** port open. In the Pinckney Treaty Spain agreed to let Americans ship their goods down the Mississippi and store them in New Orleans.

Academic Vocabulary

vital • *adj.,* extremely important

exceed • *v.,* to go above and beyond

For a time, Americans shipped their goods through New Orleans peacefully. In 1800, however, Spain signed a new treaty giving Louisiana back to the French. President Jefferson was alarmed. He knew that the French ruler, Napoleon Bonaparte, had already set out to conquer Europe. Would he now try to build an empire in North America?

Jefferson had reason to worry. Napoleon wanted to grow food in Louisiana and ship it to French islands in the West Indies. However, events in Haiti, a French colony in the Caribbean, soon ruined Napoleon's plan. Inspired by the French Revolution, which in turn had been inspired by the American Revolution, enslaved Africans in Haiti decided to fight for their liberty. Toussaint L'Ouverture (too SAN loo vehr TYOOR) led the revolt. By 1801, L'Ouverture and his followers had nearly forced the French out of Haiti.

Napoleon sent troops to retake Haiti. Although the French captured L'Ouverture, they did not regain control of the island. In 1804, Haitians declared their independence.

▼ Toussaint L'Ouverture led a revolt by enslaved Africans to win independence from France for Haiti.

Negotiations for Louisiana Jefferson sent Robert Livingston and James Monroe to buy New Orleans and West Florida from Napoleon. Jefferson said they could offer as much as $10 million. Livingston and Monroe negotiated with Charles Maurice de Talleyrand, the French foreign minister. At first, Talleyrand showed little interest in their offer. However, losing Haiti caused Napoleon to give up his plan for an empire in the Americas. He also needed money to pay for his costly wars in Europe. Suddenly, Talleyrand asked Livingston if the United States wanted to buy all of Louisiana, not just New Orleans.

The question surprised Livingston. He offered $4 million. "Too low," replied Talleyrand. "Reflect and see me tomorrow."

Livingston and Monroe carefully debated the matter. They had no authority to buy all of Louisiana or to **exceed** $10 million. However, they knew that Jefferson wanted control of the Mississippi.

They agreed to pay the French $15 million for Louisiana. "This is the noblest work of our whole lives," declared Livingston when he signed the treaty. "From this day the United States take their place among the powers of the first rank."

Analyze Images This painting of New Orleans was made to celebrate the Louisiana Purchase in 1803. Read the banner. **Identify Supporting Details** Why do you think the city of New Orleans was hopeful it would prosper under the U.S. government?

Does the President Have the Power to Buy Land? Jefferson hailed the news from France. Still, he was not sure whether the President of the United States had the power to purchase Louisiana. He had always insisted that the federal government had only those powers spelled out in the Constitution. The document said nothing about a President having the power to buy land. Jefferson wrote:

Primary Source

"The General Government has no powers but such as the Constitution has given it; and it has not given it a power of holding foreign territory, & still less of incorporating it into the Union. An amendment of the Constitution seems necessary for this."

—Thomas Jefferson to John Dickinson, August 9, 1803

In the end, Jefferson decided that he did have the authority to buy Louisiana. The Constitution, he reasoned, allowed the President to make treaties, and buying the Louisiana territory was part of a treaty. Federalists opposed the purchase as unconstitutional and feared it would weaken the other states. But the Democratic Republicans supported it, and the Senate approved the treaty. The Louisiana Purchase went into effect. In 1803, the United States took control of the vast lands west of the Mississippi. With one stroke, the size of the nation had almost doubled.

Quick Activity

Explore the importance of the western rivers in your Active Journal.

READING CHECK **Identify Cause and Effect** Why did Jefferson want to gain control of New Orleans?

How Did Americans Explore These New Lands?

Few Americans knew anything about the Louisiana territory. In 1803, Congress provided money for a team of explorers to study the new lands. Jefferson chose Meriwether Lewis, his private secretary, to head the **expedition**, or long voyage of exploration. Lewis asked William Clark to go with him. Jefferson asked Lewis and Clark to map a route to the Pacific Ocean. He also told them to study the geography of the territory, including the rivers:

INTERACTIVE

Expansion and Exploration

Primary Source

"The object of your mission is to explore the Missouri river, & such principal stream of it as by [its] course and communication with the waters of the Pacific ocean whether the Columbia, Oregon, Colorado or any other river may offer the most direct & practicable water communication across this continent for the purposes of commerce."

—Thomas Jefferson, letter to Meriwether Lewis, 1803

Jefferson also instructed Lewis and Clark to learn about the American Indian nations who lived in the Louisiana Purchase. These American Indians carried on a busy trade with English, French, and Spanish merchants. Jefferson hoped that the Indians might trade with American merchants instead. He urged Lewis and Clark to tell the Indians of "our wish to be neighborly, friendly, and useful to them."

GEOGRAPHY **SKILLS**

For $15 million, Jefferson added the Louisiana Purchase to land owned by the United States.

1. **Location** What foreign territories bordered the Louisiana Purchase?
2. **Synthesize Visual Information** How did the Louisiana Purchase change the territory of the United States?

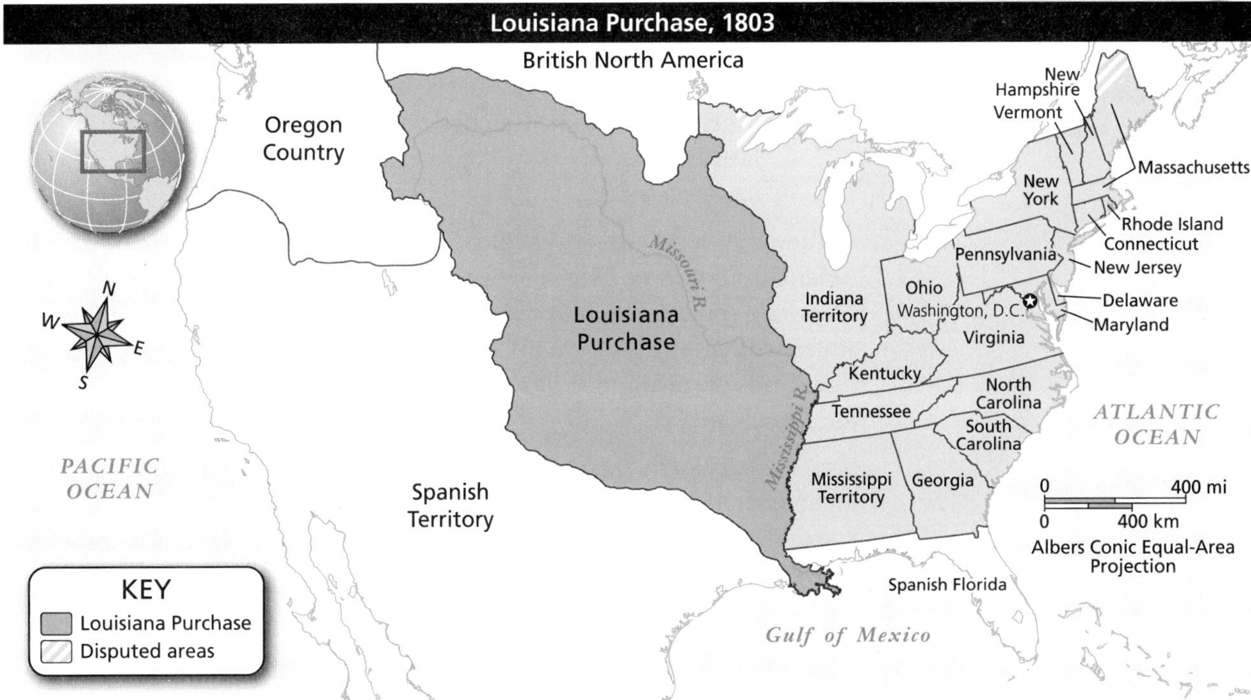

GEOGRAPHY SKILLS

The Lewis and Clark expedition helped Americans learn more about western lands.

1. **Interaction** What natural feature did Lewis and Clark use to help them travel through the Louisiana Purchase and Oregon Country?
2. **Draw Conclusions** How might westward expansion lead to conflict with other nations?

The Expedition Begins Dozens of adventurous young men eagerly competed to join the expedition. Lewis and Clark judged volunteers on the basis of their character, strength, hunting skills, and ability to survive in the wilderness. In the end, about 50 men made up the "Corps of Discovery."

In May 1804, Lewis and Clark started up the Missouri River from St. Louis. At first, the expedition's boats made slow progress against the Missouri's swift current. One night, the current tore away the riverbank where they were camping. The party had to scramble into the boats to avoid being swept downstream.

Exploring the Plains Eventually the expedition reached the plains of the Midwest. Lewis and Clark marveled at the broad, grassy plains that stretched "as far as the eye can reach." Everywhere, they saw "immense herds of buffalo, deer, elk, and antelope."

As they traveled across the plains, the expedition met people of various American Indian nations. Lewis and Clark had brought many gifts for American Indians, such as "peace medals" stamped with the United States seal. They also brought mirrors, beads, knives, blankets, and thousands of sewing needles and fishhooks.

During the first winter, Lewis and Clark stayed with the Mandans in present-day North Dakota. The explorers planned to continue up the Missouri in the spring. The members of the expedition built a fort to live in over the winter. They took the opportunity to repair equipment in preparation for spring's new challenges.

The Mandans lived along the upper Missouri River. They grew corn, beans, and squash, and hunted buffalo. During the winter, they helped the explorers find food and hunt buffalo. They also traded with the expedition members.

Staying with the Mandans was a woman named Sacajawea (sak uh juh WEE uh). Sacajawea belonged to the Shoshone (shoh SHOH nee) people, who lived in the Rockies. She and her French Canadian husband agreed to accompany Lewis and Clark as translators. Sacajawea carried her baby with her on the journey.

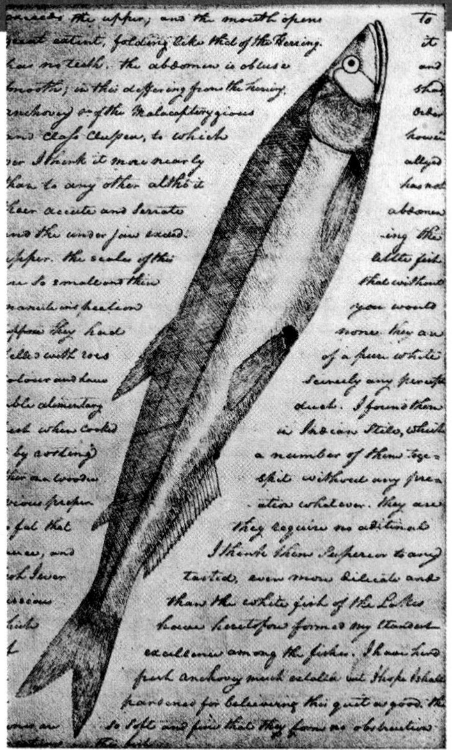

▲ On his expedition, William Clark encountered new people, animals, and land features. He drew this illustration of a trout.

Crossing the Rocky Mountains In early spring, the party set out again. In the foothills of the Rockies, the landscape and wildlife changed. Bighorn sheep ran along the high hills. The thorns of prickly pear cactus jabbed the explorers' moccasins. Once, a grizzly bear chased Lewis while he was exploring alone.

Crossing the Rocky Mountains meant crossing the Continental Divide. A **continental divide** is a ridge that separates river systems flowing toward opposite sides of a continent. In North America, some rivers flow east from the crest of the Rockies into the Mississippi, which drains into the Gulf of Mexico. Other rivers flow west from the Rockies and empty into the Pacific Ocean.

Past the Rockies, Lewis and Clark would be able to travel by river toward the Pacific. But to cross the Continental Divide, they needed horses. They began looking for the Shoshone, who had been using horses since Europeans had brought them to the Americas.

Finally, Lewis and Clark met some Shoshones. One of them was Sacajawea's brother, whom she had not seen for many years. Upon seeing her own people, wrote Clark, she began to "dance and show every mark of the most extravagant joy." The Shoshones supplied the expedition with the food and horses Lewis and Clark needed. They also advised the explorers about the best route to take over the Rockies.

BIOGRAPHY 5 Things to Know About

SACAJAWEA

Shoshone Guide (1786?–1812)

- She was a teenager when she guided Lewis and Clark.
- Finding edible plants, Sacajawea helped feed the members of the expedition.
- Through quick action, she saved valuable supplies from floating downstream when a boat capsized.
- After the expedition, she moved to St. Louis, but then returned to live in the West.
- Her children were adopted by William Clark when she died.

Critical Thinking What words describe the help Sacajawea gave to the Lewis and Clark expedition?

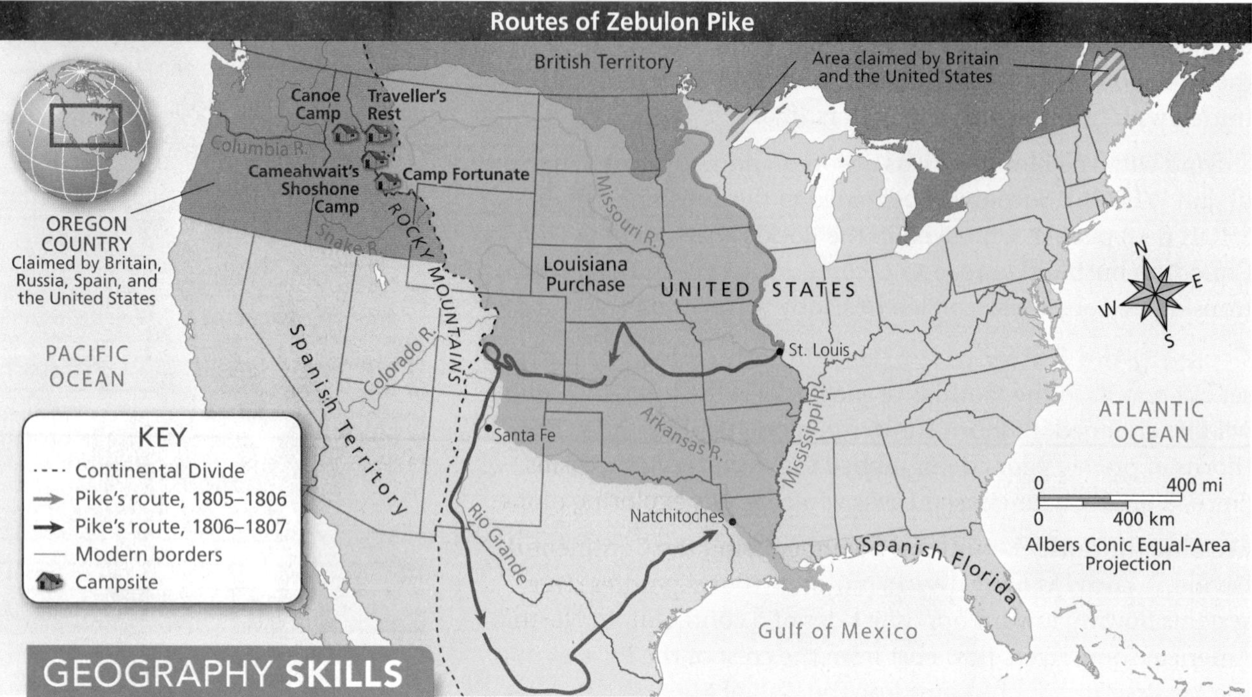

GEOGRAPHY SKILLS

Lewis and Clark's expedition took them into the northwest, where they established campsites. Zebulon Pike also explored the Louisiana Purchase, as well as Spanish territory.

1. **Interaction** What prominent geographic feature may have influenced Pike's route?
2. **Summarize** Summarize Pike's expeditions.

Reaching the Pacific After building canoes, Lewis and Clark's party floated toward the Columbia River into the Pacific Northwest. Finally, on November 7, 1805, Clark wrote in his journal, "Great joy in camp. We are in view of the ocean, this great Pacific Ocean which we have been so long anxious to see." Viewing the Pacific from present-day Oregon, Lewis and Clark claimed the region for the United States, though it had belonged to American Indian peoples for centuries.

The return trip to St. Louis took another year. In 1806, Americans celebrated the return of Lewis and Clark. The explorers brought back much useful information about the land and major rivers now part of the United States. The Mississippi, Missouri, Columbia, and Rio Grande rivers would provide settlers routes and a great natural resource as they moved west in later years.

Pike's Expedition Before Lewis and Clark returned, Jefferson sent another explorer, Zebulon Pike, to explore the southwestern part of the Louisiana Purchase. Pike set out from St. Louis. From 1805 to 1807, he explored the upper Mississippi River, the Arkansas River, and parts of present-day Colorado and New Mexico. In November 1806, Pike viewed a mountain peak rising above the Colorado plains. Today, this mountain is known as Pikes Peak.

Continuing southward, Pike entered Spanish territory. Spanish troops soon arrested Pike and his men and took them into present-day Mexico. The Americans were later escorted through Texas back into the United States. The Spanish took Pike's maps and journals, but he was able to hide one map in the barrel of his gun. His report on the expedition greatly expanded Americans' knowledge about the Southwest.

The journeys of Pike and Lewis and Clark excited Americans. However, settlers did not move into the rugged western lands for a number of years. As you will read, they first settled the region closest to the Mississippi River. Soon, the territory around New Orleans had a large enough population of American citizens for the settlers to apply for statehood. In 1812, this territory entered the Union as the state of Louisiana.

READING CHECK **Identify Supporting Details** Why did President Jefferson want Lewis and Clark to treat American Indians fairly on their journey?

Challenges to American Shipping

After the Revolution, American overseas trade grew rapidly. Ships sailed from New England on voyages that sometimes lasted three years. President Jefferson's foreign policy during this time centered around protecting American shipping.

An Era of Trade Wherever they went, Yankee captains kept a sharp lookout for new goods and new markets. Clever traders sawed winter ice from New England ponds into blocks, packed it in sawdust, and carried it to India. There, they traded the ice for silk and spices. In 1784, the *Empress of China* became the first American ship to trade with China. New England merchants quickly built up a profitable China trade.

More than ten years before Lewis and Clark, Yankee merchants sailed up the Pacific coast of North America. So many traders from Boston visited the Pacific Northwest that American Indians there called every white man "Boston." Traders bought furs from American Indians and sold them for large profits in China.

Analyze Images American trading ships in the late 1700s and early 1800s began trading with China. One route took them around the tip of South America. Another took them around Africa. **Synthesize Visual Information** What details in the picture indicate that China traded with more than one country?

Analyze Images This illustration shows American sailors being impressed, or taken by force, into the British navy. **Use Evidence** How do you think American sailors who were impressed on British ships were treated?

Jefferson Protects U.S. Ships Traders ran great risks, especially in the Mediterranean Sea. Pirates from the Barbary States, countries along the coast of North Africa, attacked passing vessels. To protect American ships, the United States paid a yearly tribute to rulers of the Barbary States such as Tripoli.

In 1801, Tripoli increased its demands for tribute. When Jefferson refused to pay, Tripoli declared war on the United States. Jefferson then ordered the navy to blockade the port of Tripoli, a city in northern Africa.

During the blockade, the American ship *Philadelphia* ran aground near Tripoli. Pirates boarded the ship and hauled the crew off to prison. The pirates planned to use the *Philadelphia* to attack other ships.

To prevent this, American naval officer Stephen Decatur and his crew quietly sailed into Tripoli harbor by night. They then set the captured American ship on fire.

In the meantime, American marines landed on the coast of North Africa, marched 500 miles, and, with the help of allies, successfully captured, the port of Derna. However, during the fight, the ruler of Tripoli signed a treaty promising not to interfere with American ships.

Caught Between France and Britain American ships faced another problem. Britain and France went to war again in 1803. At first, Americans profited from the conflict. British and French ships were too busy fighting to engage in trade. American merchants eagerly traded with both sides. As profits increased, Americans hurried to build new ships.

Neither Britain nor France wanted the United States to sell supplies to its enemy. As in the 1790s, they ignored American claims of neutrality. Napoleon seized American ships bound for England. At the same time, the British stopped Yankee traders on their way to France. Between 1805 and 1807, hundreds of American ships were captured.

Needing more sailors, the British navy stepped up **impressment**, the practice of forcing people into service. In Britain, impressment gangs raided English villages and took young men to serve in the navy. On the seas, British ships stopped American vessels, seizing any British sailors serving on American ships. Many American-born sailors were also impressed. Furious Americans clamored for war.

READING CHECK **Identify Cause and Effect** Why were Britain and France seizing American ships?

A Ban on Trade

Jefferson knew that the small American fleet was no match for the powerful British navy. Like Washington and Adams, he sought a foreign policy that would avoid war.

An Embargo on Foreign Trade Jefferson hoped that an American **embargo**, or ban on trade, would hurt France and Britain by cutting off needed supplies. "Our trade is the most powerful weapon we can use in our defense," one Democratic-Republican newspaper wrote. In 1807, Jefferson persuaded Congress to impose a total embargo on foreign trade. This meant that American traders could not receive goods from European traders, and American traders could not ship their goods to Europe.

The Embargo Act did hurt Britain and France. But it hurt Americans even more. Supplies of imports such as sugar, tea, and molasses were cut off. Exports dropped by more than $80 million in one year. Docks in the South were piled high with cotton and tobacco. The Embargo Act hurt New England merchants most of all.

Merchants protested loudly against the embargo. Some turned to **smuggling**, importing or exporting goods in violation of trade laws. Jefferson began using the navy and federal troops to enforce the embargo. On the border between New York and Canada, some smugglers engaged in skirmishes with federal troops.

The two political parties had different points of view on the embargo. Democratic Republicans mostly supported the embargo as a way to protect the country and punish France and Britain. Most Federalists opposed the embargo as damaging to the economy.

Quest CONNECTIONS

Think about the pros and cons of Jefferson's decision to place an embargo on French and British goods. Then write in your Active Journal whether his actions could start a war.

Analyze Graphs Study the data in the chart. **Identify Cause and Effect** Which data explain why Congress canceled Jefferson's Embargo Act in 1809?

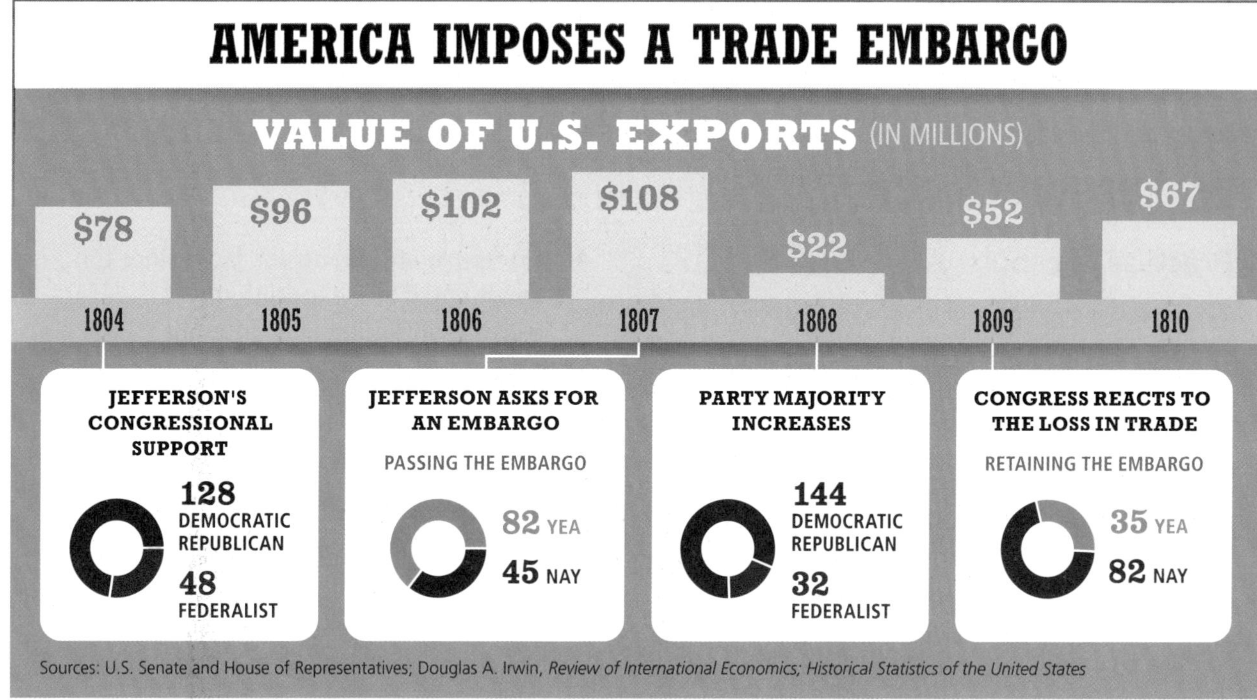

Analyze Images Trade with China introduced Americans to fine porcelain, silks, and silver made by Chinese craftspeople for the Western market. **Draw Conclusions** What effect do you think the China trade had on people living in the United States?

Congress Replaces the Embargo In 1809, Jefferson admitted that the Embargo Act had failed. Congress replaced it with the milder Nonintercourse Act. It allowed Americans to carry on trade with all nations except Britain and France. The Embargo Act had decreased support for the Democratic Republican party, as Americans hurt by the policy turned to the Federalists instead. Federalists favored maintaining closer relations with Britain.

They wanted to build ties with Britain because Britain was the main trading partner of the United States, and the powerful British navy could protect American merchants.

Although the embargo was the most unpopular measure of Jefferson's presidency, the Democratic Republicans still remained strong. Following President Washington's precedent, Jefferson refused to run for a third term. Democratic Republican James Madison easily won the 1808 presidential election. Madison hoped that Britain and France would soon agree to respect American neutrality.

READING CHECK **Understand Effects** Why did Americans turn against the Embargo Act?

Lesson Check

Practice Vocabulary

1. How is a **continental divide** related to rivers?
2. Why did **impressment** make Americans angry?

Critical Thinking and Writing

3. **Explain an Argument** Why did Jefferson, who believed in a strict interpretation of the Constitution, decide that the President had the power to buy land when that was not mentioned in the Constitution?
4. **Compare and Contrast** How were the Lewis and Clark expedition and the Pike expedition similar and different?
5. **Understand Effects** Why was the Embargo Act so unpopular?
6. **Writing Workshop: Support Thesis with Details** Gather and include specific details in your Active Journal to use in the research paper you write at the end of this Topic.

Primary Sources

William Clark and Meriwether Lewis, Journals

As Lewis and Clark traveled through the American West on their expedition, each took notes about what they observed and explored.

▶ William Clark drew this bird and many other animals and plants in the expedition diary.

William Clark, August the 1st 1804
a fair morning Despatched [Dispatched] two men after the horses lost yesterday, . . . The Prarie [prairie] which is Situated below our Camp is above the ① high water leavel [level] and rich Covered with Grass from 5 to 8 feet high intersperced [interspersed] with Copse of Hazel, Plumbs, Currents [currants] (like those of the U.S.) Rasberries [raspberries] & Grapes of Dift.[different] Kinds. also produceing [producing] a Variety of Plants and flowers not Common in the United States ②

Meriwether Lewis, May 1st 1806
the courses and distances of this day are ③ N. 45 E. 9 M. and N. 75 E. 17 M. along the Northern side of this creek to our encampment. some time after we had encamped three young men arrived from the ④ Wallahwollah village bringing with them a steel trap belonging to one of our party which had been negligently left behind; . . . during our stay with them they several times found the knives of the men which had been carelessly lossed [lost] by them and returned them. ⑤ I think we can justly affirm to the honor of these people that they are the most hospitable, honest, and sincere people that we have met with in our voyage.

Reading and Vocabulary Support

① What does "high water level" tell you about where Lewis and Clark are traveling?

② How might the information in Clark's journal interest possible settlers?

③ Lewis is giving the geographic coordinates that tell where they are and how far they have traveled.

④ The Wallahwollahs were an American Indian group.

⑤ What is Lewis complimenting the Wallahwollahs for?

Analyzing Primary Sources

Cite specific evidence from the documents to support your answers.

1. **Cite Evidence** Recall what Jefferson asked Lewis and Clark to do regarding the American Indians they met. Did they fulfill that request? Support your answer.
2. **Analyze Style and Rhetoric** What words does Lewis use to describe the behavior of the members of the expedition?

LESSON 5

Madison and the War of 1812

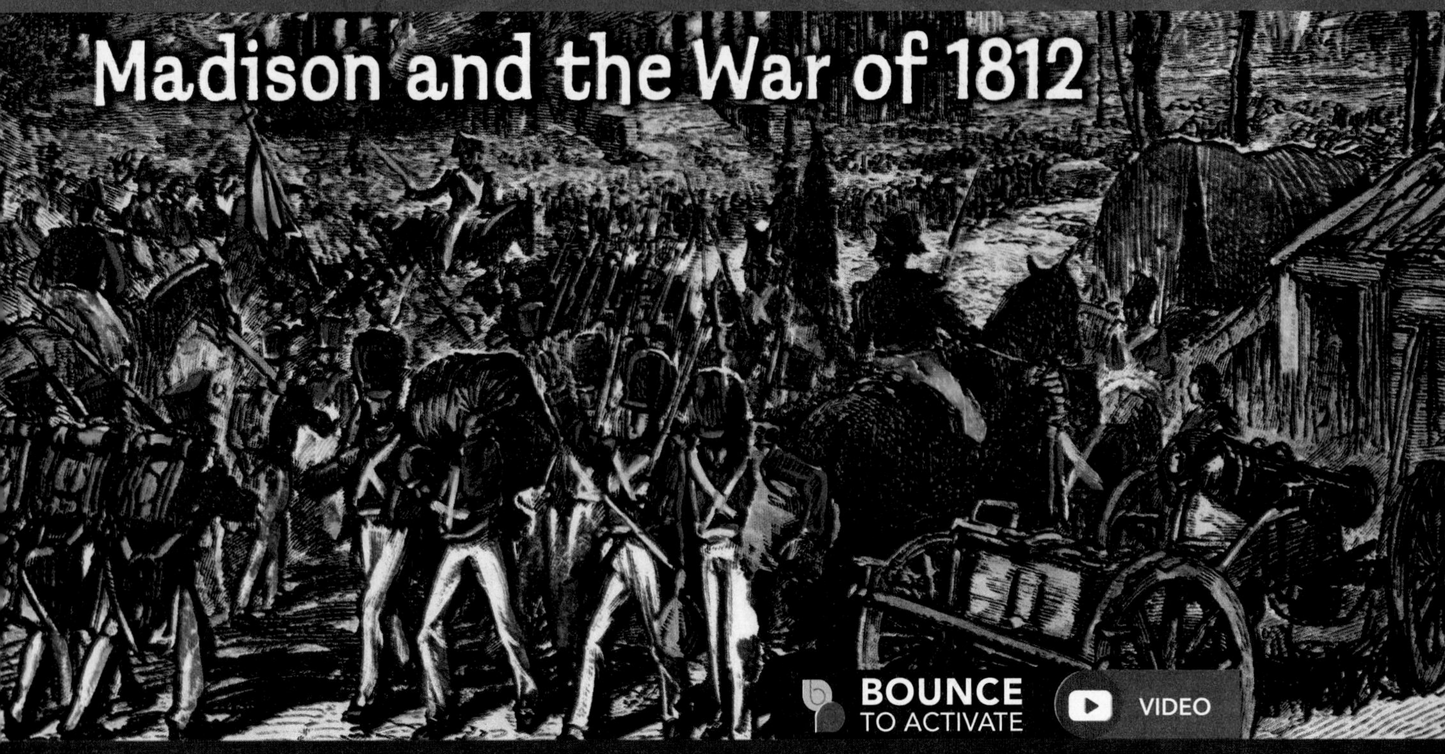

GET READY TO READ

START UP

Study the illustration of the British burning Washington, D.C., during the War of 1812. Scan the lesson images and captions, then write in your Active Journal a reason why the United States went to war.

GUIDING QUESTIONS

- Why was there conflict between white settlers and American Indians during the early 1800s?
- What were the causes of the War of 1812?
- What were the key events and consequences of the War of 1812?

TAKE NOTES

Literacy Skills: Sequence

Use the graphic organizer in your Active Journal to take notes as you read the lesson.

PRACTICE VOCABULARY

Use the vocabulary activity in your Active Journal to practice the vocabulary words.

Vocabulary	Academic Vocabulary
confederation	decisive
War Hawks	commence
nationalism	

About 900,000 white settlers moved west of the Appalachians between 1790 and 1810. These newcomers harmed American Indians by building farms on Indian lands and hunting the animals Indians needed for food. The settlers ignored treaties that the United States had signed with American Indian nations of the region.

What Caused Conflict in Ohio?

Fighting often broke out between these American Indian groups and the settlers. Isolated acts of violence led to larger acts of revenge. As both sides killed innocent people, warfare spread. In Ohio, Little Turtle of the Miamis and Blue Jacket of the Shawnees organized a resistance movement in 1791. Armed with British muskets and gunpowder, the Miamis and Shawnees drove white settlers from the area.

President Washington had sent General Anthony Wayne into Ohio in 1794. Forces from the Delaware, Miami, Iroquois, Wabash, and others gathered at a place called Fallen Timbers.

They thought that Wayne would have trouble fighting there because fallen trees covered the land. But Wayne's well-trained army pushed through the tangle of logs and defeated the American Indians.

Treaties Are Made In 1795, leaders of the Miami and other American Indian nations signed the Treaty of Greenville. They gave up land that would later become part of Ohio. In return, they received $20,000 and the promise of more money if they kept the peace.

The Treaty of Greenville was one of more than 300 treaties made between the U.S. government and American Indians during the early republic. The treaties were one method that the U.S. government used to gain land from Native Americans for whites to settle on. In return for American Indian acceptance of the treaty's terms, the government gave American Indian nations a sum of money and, in some instances, equipment. In return for American Indian acceptance of the treaty's terms, the government gave Native American nations a sum of money and, in some instances, equipment. The treaties' terms almost always involved Native Americans giving up claims to the land on which they depended for survival. Also, the U.S. government often violated treaties by not stopping citizens from settling beyond treaty lands.

Tecumseh's Confederation Confronts the New Republic Ohio joined the Union in 1803. By then, white settlers were pushing beyond Ohio into the Indiana Territory. Angry Shawnees, Kickapoos, and Ottawas vowed to keep settlers from taking more American Indian land. They included two Shawnee leaders: Tecumseh and his brother Tenskwatawa (ten SKWAH tuh wuh), a religious leader also called the Prophet. The Kickapoo, Ottawa, Chippewa, and Piankashaw joined with the Shawnee leaders. The Miami initially remained neutral.

The Wyandot, Seneca, and Delaware stayed allied with the United States. So did the Choctaw, Cherokee, Chickasaw, and some groups of Creek.

The U.S. government had treaties with several of these American Indian groups that said both sides would cease fighting. The treaties kept these groups from rallying together against the United States.

A New Settlement in Indiana Territory The Prophet and Tecumseh taught that white customs corrupted the American Indian way of life. They said that many American Indians depended too much on white trade goods.

GEOGRAPHY SKILLS

American Indians lost their lands through "sales," treaties, and force.

1. **Movement** In which direction were American Indians pushed because of the loss of their land?
2. **Infer** Why do you think American Indians gave up these lands?

American Indian Lands

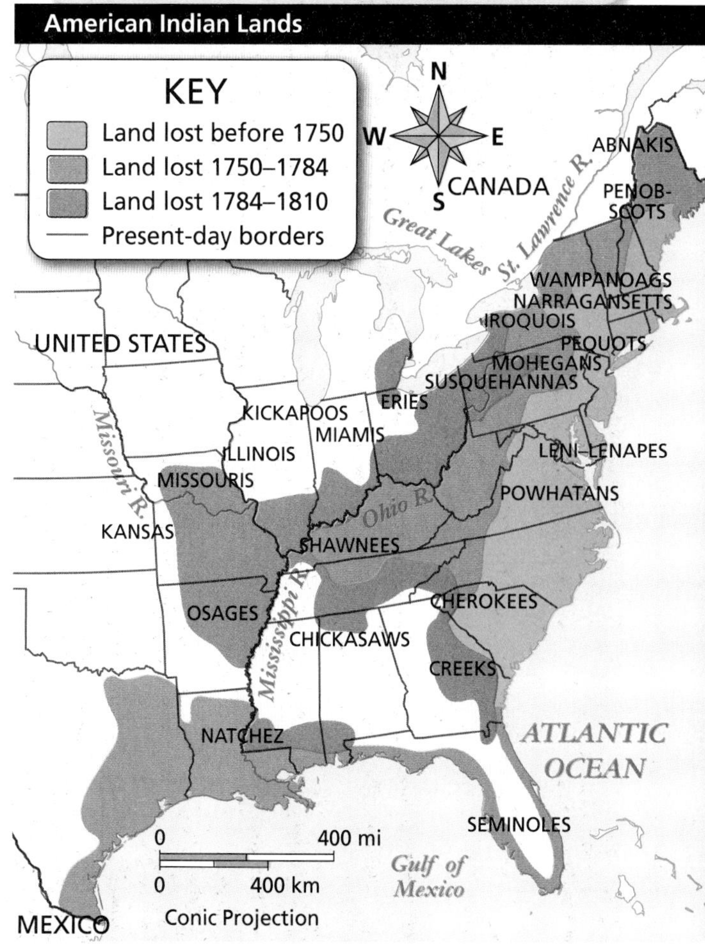

These included muskets, cloth, cooking pots, and whiskey. They believed that by returning to their old ways, American Indians could gain the power to resist the white invaders.

In 1808, the Prophet built a village for his followers along Tippecanoe Creek in Indiana Territory. American Indians from lands as far away as present-day Missouri, Iowa, and Minnesota traveled to Prophetstown to hear his message.

Tecumseh worked to organize the groups of the Northwest into a **confederation**, or alliance with a shared military command. He called for unity against settlers:

Primary Source

"The whites have driven us from the great salt water, forced us over the mountains. . . . The way, the only way, to check and stop this evil is for all red men to unite in claiming a common equal right in the land."

—Tecumseh, quoted in *Tecumseh: Vision of Glory* (Tucker)

Tecumseh impressed white leaders. Governor William Henry Harrison grudgingly admitted, "He is one of those uncommon geniuses which spring up occasionally to produce revolutions and overturn the established order of things."

A Major Battle at Tippecanoe Rivalries among American Indian nations kept Tecumseh from uniting all Indians east of the Mississippi River. Still, white settlers were alarmed at his success.

BIOGRAPHY 5 Things to Know About

TECUMSEH
Shawnee Leader and Orator (1768–1813)

- He led American Indian resistance to white settlement in the Ohio River Valley.
- At age 15, he attended a conference of American Indian nations after the American Revolution.
- By supporting a confederation of American Indian groups, he strengthened their forces to fight the U.S. military.
- His outstanding speaking skills were admired by American Indians and whites.
- He spoke out against cruelty on both sides of conflicts between American Indians and the U.S. government.

Critical Thinking Of people living today or in the recent past, who could you say has leadership skills similar to those of Tecumseh? Explain your reasoning.

Analyze Images Both sides suffered heavy losses, but General Henry Harrison's troops were able to destroy Prophetstown during the Battle of Tippecanoe in 1811. **Summarize** How does the image confirm or refute that there were heavy losses on both sides in this battle?

In 1811, Harrison marched 1,000 soldiers against Prophetstown on the Tippecanoe Creek. The Prophet was in charge. Tecumseh was away trying to organize Indians in the South. The Prophet led a surprise night attack on Harrison's troops. Both sides suffered heavy losses in the Battle of Tippecanoe.

In the end, Harrison's troops defeated the Prophet's forces and destroyed Prophetstown. Whites celebrated the battle as a major victory. Still, Tecumseh and his followers continued to resist white settlement.

READING CHECK **Identify Supporting Details** Why did Tecumseh advise many American Indians to stop trading with the settlers?

What Were the Causes of the War of 1812?

INTERACTIVE

Indian Lands Lost by 1810

Fighting with American Indians hurt relations between the United States and Britain. The British were supplying guns and ammunition to the American Indians on the frontier. They also encouraged Indians to attack U.S. settlements.

Meanwhile, the ban on trade with Britain and France expired. Congress then authorized President Madison to make a tantalizing offer. If either the British or French stopped seizing American ships, the United States would reopen trade with that nation. Napoleon quickly announced that France would respect American neutrality. Britain did not respond to the offer. As promised, the United States resumed trade with France, but continued to ban all shipments to or from Britain.

A Push for War While Madison did not want war, other Americans were not as cautious. In New England, antiwar feelings ran strong. However, members of Congress from the South and the West called for war. They were known as **War Hawks**.

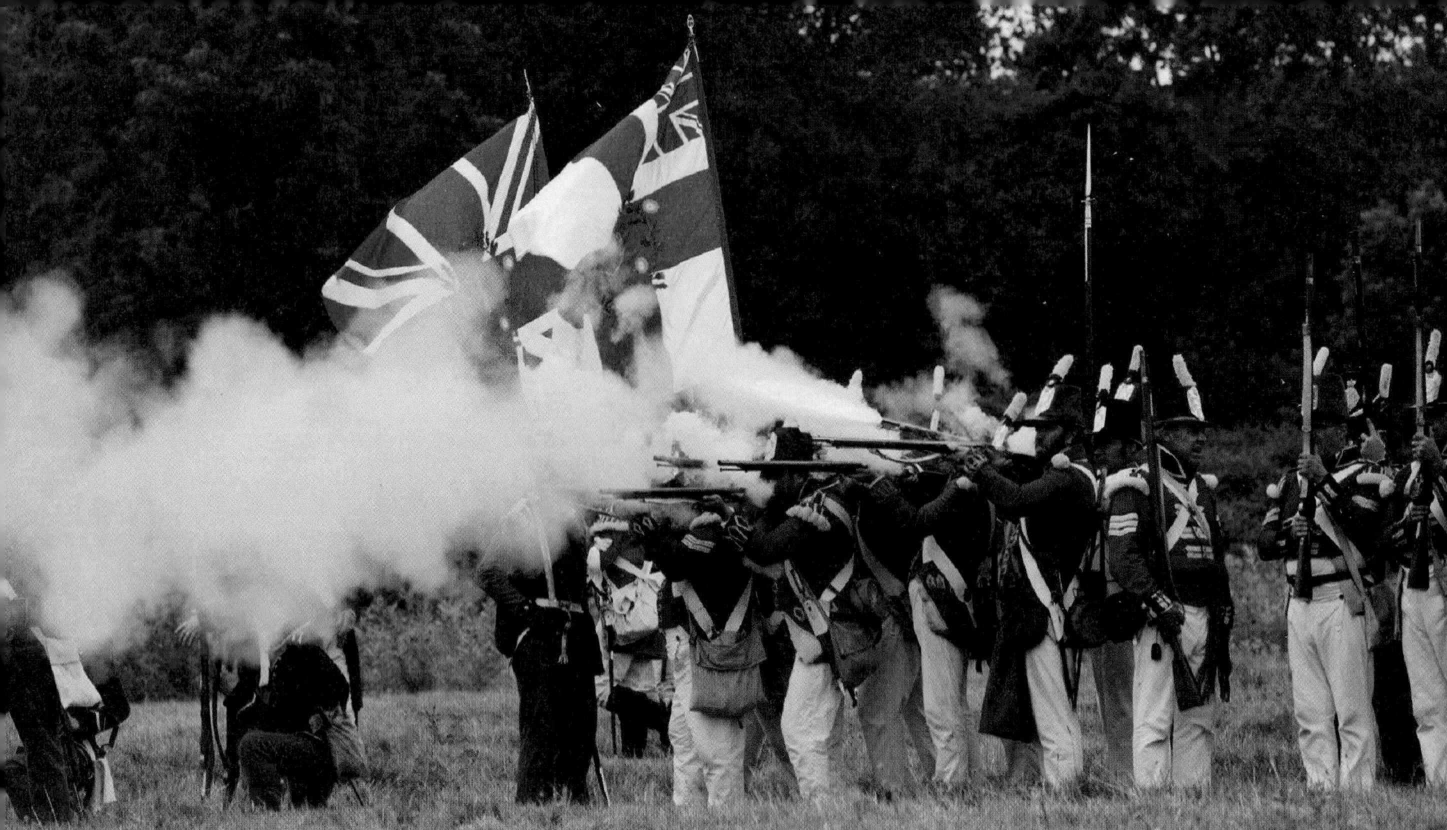

Analyze Images British soldiers like these reenactors fought side-by-side with their allies, American Indians living on the frontier. **Identify Implied Main Ideas** What did American Indian allies stand to gain by fighting with the British against the Americans?

War Hawks were stirred by a strong sense of **nationalism**, or devotion to one's country. War Hawks felt that Britain was treating the United States as if it were still a British colony. They were willing to fight a war to defend American rights.

The most outspoken War Hawk was Henry Clay of Kentucky. Clay wanted to punish Britain for seizing American ships. He also hoped to conquer Canada. "The militia of Kentucky are alone [able] to place Montreal and Upper Canada at your feet," Clay boasted to Congress.

War Hawks saw other advantages of war with Britain. If Americans went to war with Britain, War Hawks said, the United States could seize Florida from Britain's ally, Spain. They also pointed out that Britain was arming American Indians on the frontier and encouraging them to attack settlers. The War Hawks felt that winning a war against Britain would bring lasting safety to settlers on the frontier.

War Is Declared The United States and Britain drifted closer to war as the security of American ships remained an issue. The British continued to board American ships and impress American seamen. To cut off American trade with France, British warships blockaded some American ports. In May 1811, near New York Harbor, a battle broke out between an American frigate and a British ship. The Americans crippled the British ship and left 32 British sailors dead or wounded.

War Hawks urged Congress to prepare for war. Other members of Congress disagreed. John Randolph of Virginia warned that the people of the United States would "not submit to be taxed for this war of conquest and dominion." Representatives of New England were especially concerned. They feared that the British navy would attack New England seaports.

At last, President Madison gave in to war fever. In June 1812, he asked Congress to declare war on Britain. The House and Senate both voted in favor of war. Americans would soon learn, though, that declaring war was easier than winning.

READING CHECK **Identify Supporting Details** Who were the War Hawks?

Early Events in the War of 1812

The American declaration of war took the British by surprise. They were locked in a bitter struggle with Napoleon and could not spare troops to fight the United States. As the war **commenced**, however, the United States faced difficulties of its own.

The Difficulties of Building a Military The United States was not ready for war. Because Jefferson had reduced spending on defense, the navy had only 17 ships to meet the huge British fleet. The army was small and ill equipped, and many of the officers knew little about warfare. "The state of the army," said a member of Congress, "is enough to make any man who has the smallest love of country wish to get rid of it." These problems made it difficult to maintain national security.

Since there were few regular troops, the government relied on volunteers. Congress voted to give them a bounty of cash and land.

▲ As a War Hawk, Henry Clay seized the conflict with Britain as an opportunity to push his plan to conquer Canada from the British.

Academic Vocabulary
commence • *v.*, to begin

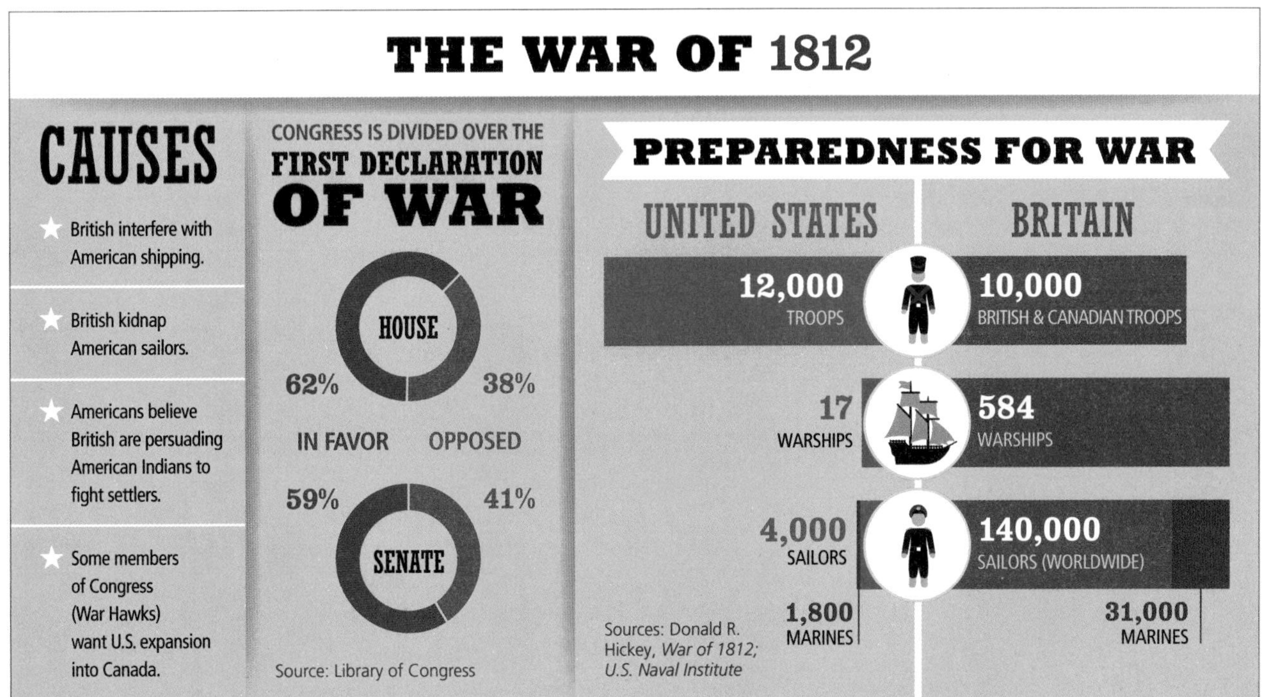

Analyze Charts The United States faced the world's greatest power in the War of 1812. **Infer** What information above helps explain the percentage of people opposed to war in Congress?

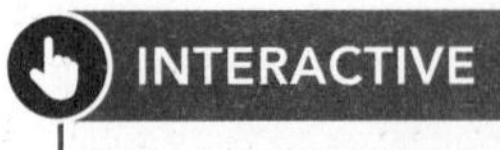
INTERACTIVE
The War of 1812

The money was equal to about a year's salary for most workers. Attracted by the high pay and the chance to own their own farms, young men eagerly enlisted. They were poorly trained, however, with little experience in battle. Many deserted after a few months.

Surprising Victories at Sea The British navy blockaded American ports to stop American trade. Though unable to break the blockade, several American sea captains won stunning victories.

One famous battle took place early in the war, in August 1812. As he was sailing near Newfoundland, Isaac Hull, captain of the U.S.S. *Constitution,* spotted the British ship HMS *Guerrière* (geh ree AIR). For nearly an hour, the two ships jockeyed for position. At last, the guns of the *Constitution* roared into action. They tore holes in the sides of the *Guerrière* and shot off both masts. Stunned, the British captain had no choice but to surrender.

American sea captains won other victories at sea. These victories cheered Americans but did little to win the war.

READING CHECK **Identify Supporting Details** What problems did the U.S. military face?

How Did the War Affect Canada?

One goal of the War Hawks was to conquer Canada. They were convinced that Canadians would welcome the chance to throw off British rule and join the United States.

An Untested Force General William Hull moved American troops into Canada from Detroit. The Canadians had only a few untrained troops to ward off the invasion. However, they were led by a clever British general, Isaac Brock.

Analyze Images The U.S. Navy surprised British naval forces early in the war when the U.S.S. *Constitution* defeated Britain's HMS *Guerriere* near Newfoundland. **Identify Supporting Details** What details in the image give strength to the U.S.S. *Constitution's* nickname, "Old Ironsides"?

Brock paraded his soldiers in red coats to make it appear that experienced British troops were helping the Canadians. He also led Americans to think that a large number of American Indians were fighting alongside the Canadians. Brock's scare tactics worked. Hull retreated from Canada. Other attempts to invade Canada also failed.

However, on April 27, 1813, U.S. soldiers crossed Lake Ontario and successfully captured York, present-day Toronto. The Americans seized British guns and supplies, and they set fire to public buildings.

American Victory on Lake Erie In 1813, the Americans, armed with the guns and supplies they had seized at York, set out to win control of Lake Erie. Captain Oliver Hazard Perry had no fleet, so he designed and built his own ships. In September 1813, he sailed his tiny fleet against the British.

During the Battle of Lake Erie, the British battered Perry's own ship and left it helpless. Perry rowed over to another American ship and continued to fight. Finally, the Americans won the battle. Captain Perry wrote his message of victory on the back of an envelope: "We have met the enemy and they are ours."

American Indian Losses After losing control of Lake Erie, the British and their ally Tecumseh retreated from Detroit into Canada. General William Henry Harrison, veteran of Tippecanoe, pursued them. The Americans won a **decisive** victory at the Battle of the Thames (temz). Tecumseh died in the fighting. Without Tecumseh's leadership, the Indian confederation soon fell apart.

Analyze Images After the British destroyed his flagship, the *Lawrence*, Captain Oliver Perry escaped to another American ship. Perry's fleet would regroup and eventually win the Battle of Lake Erie. **Classify and Categorize** How would you compare and contrast the actions of Perry to those of revolutionary naval hero John Paul Jones?

READING CHECK **Summarize** What became of the War Hawks' plan to conquer Canada?

The End of the War

While Tecumseh was defeated in Canada, some sections of the Creek continued their fight against U.S. settlers in the South. Andrew Jackson, a Tennessee officer, took command of American troops in the Creek War. In March 1814, with the help of Cherokee, Choctaw, and friendly Creek, Jackson won a crushing victory at the Battle of Horseshoe Bend. The leader of the enemy Creek walked alone into Jackson's camp to surrender. "Your people have destroyed my nation," he said.

Washington, D.C., Burns In the spring of 1814, Britain and its allies defeated France. With the war in Europe over, Britain could send more troops and ships to fight the United States.

In August 1814, British ships sailed into Chesapeake Bay and landed an invasion force about 30 miles from Washington, D.C. American troops met the British at Bladensburg, Maryland. As President Madison watched, the British quickly scattered the untrained Americans. The British met little further resistance on their march to the capital.

In the White House, First Lady Dolley Madison waited for her husband to return. Hastily, she scrawled a note to her sister about the attack.

Academic Vocabulary
decisive • *adj.* clearly settling a dispute or question

Analyze Images This painting shows the American artillery aimed at the British fleet at Fort McHenry in Baltimore Harbor. **Use Visual Information** Why do you think the painter has placed the American flag flying above the action of the soldiers?

Primary Source

"Will you believe it, my sister? We have had a battle or skirmish near Bladensburg and here I am still within sound of the cannon! Mr. Madison comes not. May God protect us. Two messengers covered with dust come bid me fly. But here I mean to wait for him."

—Dolley Madison, *Memoirs and Letters of Dolley Madison*

Soon after, British troops marched into the capital. Dolley Madison gathered up important papers of the President and a portrait of George Washington. Then, she fled south. She was not there to see the British set fire to the White House and other buildings. The British considered this an act of revenge for the burning of York.

From Washington, the British marched north toward the city of Baltimore. The key to Baltimore's defense was Fort McHenry on Baltimore Harbor. From the evening of September 13 until dawn on September 14 during the Battle of Baltimore, British rockets bombarded the harbor.

When the early morning fog lifted, the "broad stripes and bright stars" of the American flag still waved over Fort McHenry. American forces had won the Battle of Baltimore. The British withdrew, and the threat to the nation's capital ended. Francis Scott Key, a young American lawyer who witnessed the battle, wrote a poem about it. Soon, his poem, "The Star-Spangled Banner," was published and set to music. Today, it is the national anthem of the United States.

Did you know?

When Dolley Madison fled the White House, she left dinner on the table for her husband and his aides. The British ate the meal before burning the building down.

Jackson Becomes a Hero in the Battle of New Orleans In late 1814, the British prepared to attack New Orleans. From there, they hoped to sail up the Mississippi. However, Andrew Jackson was waiting. Jackson had turned his frontier fighters into a strong army.

He took Pensacola in Spanish Florida to keep the British from using it as a base. He then marched through Mobile and set up camp in New Orleans.

Jackson's force included both white settlers and Choctaw fighters. The Choctaw were longtime rivals of the Indian nations who had been allied with the British. Many of Jackson's troops were expert riflemen. Citizens of New Orleans also joined the army to defend their city from the British. Among the volunteers were hundreds of African Americans.

The American soldiers dug trenches to defend themselves. On January 8, 1815, the British attacked. Again and again, British soldiers marched toward the American trenches. More than 2,000 British fell under the deadly fire of American sharpshooters and, especially, American cannons. Only seven Americans died.

Americans cheered the victory at the Battle of New Orleans. Many hailed Andrew Jackson as a hero. His fame did not dim even when Americans learned that the battle had taken place two weeks after the war had ended. The United States and Britain had already signed a treaty in Europe, but news took two months to cross the ocean by sailing ship.

African Americans in the War The Battle of New Orleans was not the only place where Black and white soldiers fought together. Throughout the War of 1812, African Americans joined in defending the nation against the British.

After the British attacks on Washington and Baltimore, African American volunteers helped defend Philadelphia against a possible attack. Bishop Richard Allen and the Reverend Absalom Jones recruited some 2,000 men to build Philadelphia's fortifications.

GEOGRAPHY **SKILLS**

Both sides won battles in the War of 1812, with no clear overall winner. The inset map shows the movement of Andrew Jackson's forces.

1. **Movement** From where and which direction did American forces move to fight the British in Frenchtown?
2. **Use Visual Information** How is the role of the British navy reflected on the map?

The War of 1812

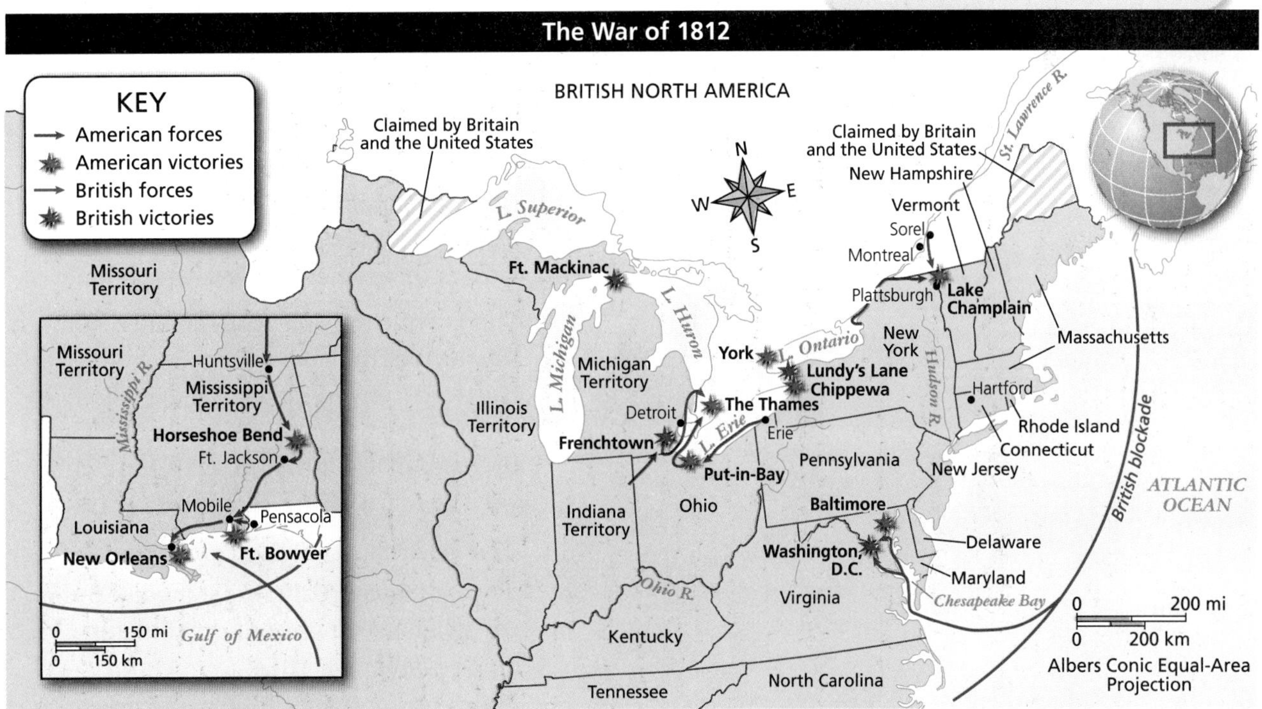

The state of New York organized two regiments of Black volunteers to serve in the army.

African Americans also served with distinction in the U.S. Navy. They helped win the Battle of Lake Erie as well as other naval battles. Commander Nathaniel Shaler praised one particular Black sailor who was wounded in battle:

Primary Source

> "He fell near me, and several times requested to be thrown overboard, saying he was only in the way of others. When America has such [sailors], she has little to fear from the tyrants of the ocean."
>
> —Nathaniel Shaler, letter to his agent, January 1, 1813

READING CHECK **Identify Main Ideas** What achievement made Andrew Jackson well known throughout the country?

What Were the Consequences of the War of 1812?

By late 1814, Americans knew that peace talks had commenced, but they did not know if they would succeed or how long they would last. As Jackson was preparing to fight the British at New Orleans, New Englanders were meeting to protest "Mr. Madison's War."

New Englanders Protest the War The British blockade had hurt New England's sea trade. Also, many New Englanders feared that the United States might win land in Florida and Canada. If new states were carved out of these lands, the South and the West would become more influential than New England.

Delegates from around New England met in Hartford, Connecticut, in December 1814. Most were Federalists. They disliked the Democratic Republican President and the war.

Analyze Images Cyrus Tiffany, an African American sailor shown here with his hand on the coat of Captain Oliver H. Perry, helped save the captain's life at the Battle of Lake Erie. **Compare and Contrast** How are the actions of Tiffany and the man described in the Primary Source quote on this page similar?

Some delegates to the Hartford Convention threatened to nullify, or cancel, the state of war in their states if the war continued. Others threatened to leave the Union.

Then, while the delegates debated what to do, news of the peace treaty arrived. The Hartford Convention ended quickly. With the war over, the protest was meaningless. In the end, the threat of secession further weakened the dying Federalist party.

The Indecisive Results of the War A peace treaty was signed in the city of Ghent, in present-day Belgium, on December 24, 1814. John Quincy Adams, son of John Adams and one of the

▲ General Andrew Jackson's victory at the Battle of New Orleans, shown here, made him a military hero to many. His fame would later help him become President.

American delegates, summed up the Treaty of Ghent in one sentence: "Nothing was adjusted, nothing was settled."

Britain and the United States agreed to restore prewar conditions. The treaty said nothing about impressment or neutrality. These issues had faded due to the end of the wars in Europe. Other issues were settled later. In 1818, for example, the two nations settled a dispute over the border between Canada and the United States.

Looking back, some Americans felt that the War of 1812 had been a mistake. Others argued that Europe would now treat the young republic with more respect. The victories of men like Oliver Hazard Perry, William Henry Harrison, and Andrew Jackson gave some Americans new pride in their country. As one Democratic Republican leader remarked, "The people are now more American. They feel and act more as a nation."

READING CHECK **Identify Supporting Details** What was the purpose of the Hartford Convention?

Lesson Check

Practice Vocabulary

1. What was the relationship between **War Hawks** and **nationalism**?
2. Why would Tecumseh work for a **confederation**?

Critical Thinking and Writing

3. **Draw Conclusions** Why were American Indian groups resistant to white settlement west of the Appalachians?
4. **Summarize** What did Andrew Jackson do that won him fame and popularity?
5. **Compare and Contrast** U.S. military strength before and after the War of 1812.
6. **Writing Workshop: Clarify Relationships with Transition Words** Be sure to consider transition words that you can use to show the relationships between facts in your research paper. List some in your Active Journal.

Tenskwatawa, The Prophet, Speech

Tenskwatawa, a Shawnee religious leader called The Prophet, warned that American Indians suffered harm when they turned from their traditional cultures to goods and practices brought by white settlers.

◀ Tenskwatawa, a Shawnee religious leader, was the brother of Tecumseh.

For many years we traded furs to the English or the French, for wool blankets and guns and iron things, for steel ① awls and needles and axes, for mirrors, for pretty things made of beads and silver. And for liquor. This was foolish, but we did not know it. ② We shut our ears to the Great Good Spirit. We did not want to hear that we were being ③ foolish.

But now those things of the white men have ④ corrupted us, and made us weak and needful. Our men forgot how to hunt without noisy guns. Our women dont want to make fire without steel, or cook without iron, or sew without metal awls and needles, or fish without steel hooks. Some look in those mirrors all the time, and no longer teach their daughters to make leather or render bear oil. ⑤ We learned to need the white men's goods, and so now a People who never had to beg for anything must beg for everything!

— Tenskwatawa, The Prophet, ca. 1804

Reading and Vocabulary Support

① An *awl* is a small metal tool used to punch holes into leather or heavy cloth.

② What does Tenskwatawa mean when he says, "We shut our ears to The Great Good Spirit"?

③ Why do you think people do not want to hear that they have been foolish?

④ One meaning of the word *corrupt* is to bribe. Why does The Prophet use the word *corrupted*?

⑤ What does Tenskwatawa say has caused his people to "beg for everything"?

Analyzing Primary Sources

Cite specific evidence from the document to support your answers.

1. **Cite Evidence** How does Tenskwatawa say that white settlers "corrupted" American Indians?
2. **Analyze Style and Rhetoric** Which words does Tenskwatawa use that may have raised the emotions of his American Indian audience?

LESSON 6

Monroe's Presidency and Everyday Life

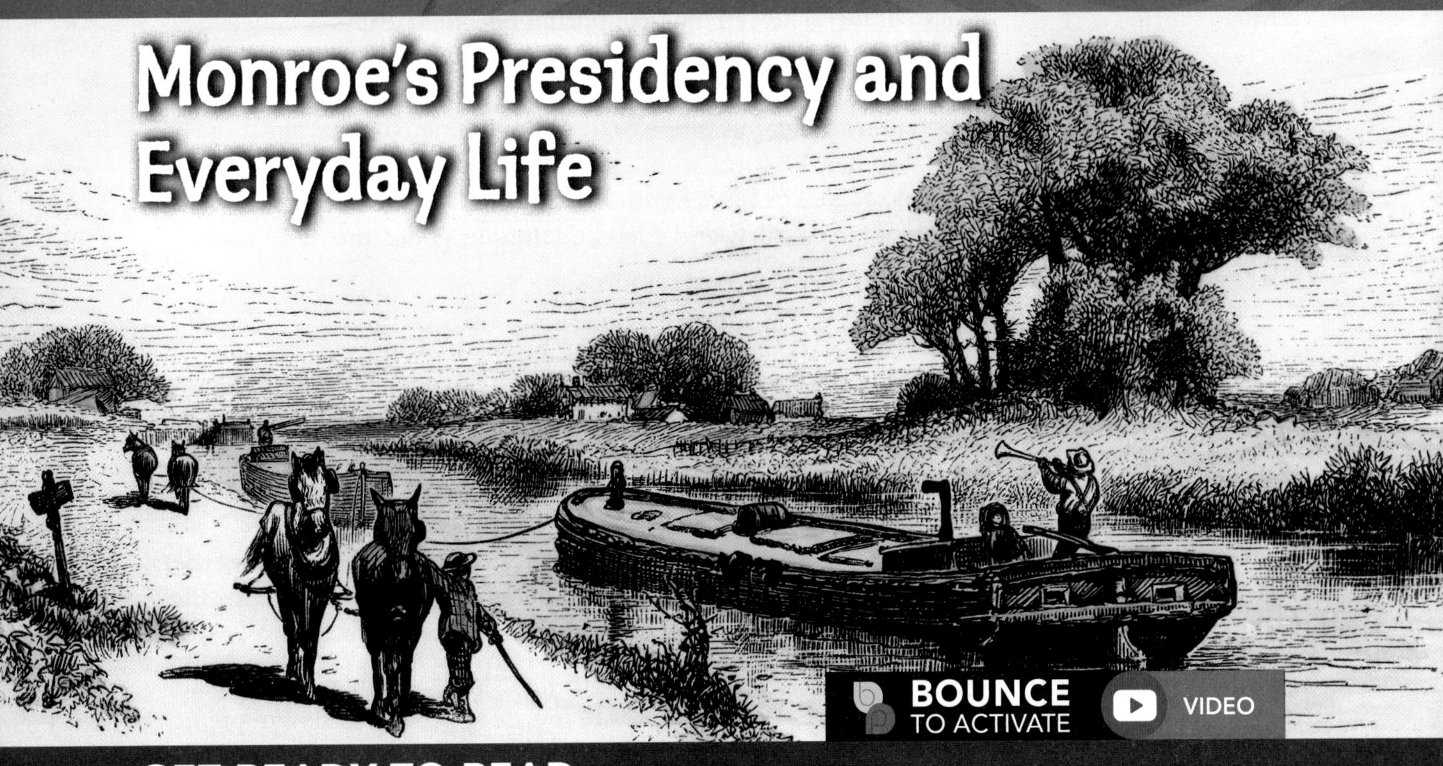

GET READY TO READ

START UP

Study the illustration of the Erie Canal, which was built between 1817 and 1825 to connect the Hudson River with Lake Erie. In your Active Journal write about what you think daily life was like in the early 1800s.

GUIDING QUESTIONS

- What role did regional differences begin to play in the early republic?
- How did John Marshall's Supreme Court expand the power of the federal government?
- What was President Monroe's foreign policy?
- What was life like in the early republic?

TAKE NOTES

Literacy Skills: Draw Conclusions

Use the graphic organizer in your Active Journal to take notes as you read the lesson.

PRACTICE VOCABULARY

Use the vocabulary activity in your Active Journal to practice the vocabulary words.

Vocabulary		Academic Vocabulary
sectionalism	interstate commerce	advocate
American System	Monroe Doctrine	regulate
	intervention	

In 1816, the Democratic Republican candidate for President, James Monroe, easily defeated Federalist Senator Rufus King of New York. The election showed how seriously the Federalists had declined in popularity. Many had voted for Monroe.

How Did Sectionalism Affect the Early Republic?

Monroe was the last Revolutionary War officer to become President. He was almost 60 years old when he took office. Americans were fond of his old-fashioned ways. In 1817, he made a goodwill tour of the country. In Boston, crowds cheered. Boston newspapers expressed surprise at this warm welcome for a Democratic Republican from Virginia. Boston had long been a Federalist stronghold.

An Era of Good Feelings Monroe hoped to create a new sense of national unity. One newspaper wrote that the United States was entering an "era of good feelings." By the time Monroe ran for a second term in 1820, no candidate opposed him. The Federalist Party had disappeared.

While conflict between political parties declined, disputes between different sections of the nation sharpened. These disputes were a result of **sectionalism**, or loyalty to one's state or section rather than to the nation as a whole. In Congress, three young men took center stage in these disputes. All three would play key roles in Congress for more than 30 years, as well as serve in other offices. Each represented a different section of the country, and each had unique leadership qualities.

Calhoun Opposes Federal Power John C. Calhoun spoke for white people in the South. He had grown up on a frontier farm in South Carolina. Calhoun's immense energy and striking features earned him the nickname "young Hercules."

He was slim and handsome, with deep-set eyes and a high forehead. His way of speaking was so intense that it sometimes made people uncomfortable to be in his presence.

Academic Vocabulary
advocate • *n.,* a person who argues for or supports

Calhoun had supported the War of 1812. Like many white southerners, he was a firm defender of slavery. In general, he opposed policies that would strengthen the power of the federal government.

Webster Stands Against Slavery and War Daniel Webster of New Hampshire was an **advocate** for the North and a skillful public speaker. With eyes flashing and shoulders thrown back, Webster was an impressive sight when he stood up to speak in Congress. An observer described him as a "great cannon loaded to the lips."

Analyze Charts Three leaders emerged as regional differences developed in the early republic. **Compare and Contrast** Who supported the War of 1812 and the idea of a strong federal government?

Like many New Englanders, Webster had opposed the War of 1812. He even refused to vote for taxes to pay for the war effort. After the war, he wanted the federal government to take a larger role in building the economy. Unlike Calhoun, Webster thought that slavery was evil.

Sectional Leaders: Calhoun, Webster, and Clay

JOHN C. CALHOUN	DANIEL WEBSTER	HENRY CLAY
• From South Carolina • Skilled orator, lawyer, and senator • Sectional leader and spokesman for his region (South) • Supported the War of 1812 • Opposed the idea of a strong federal government • Strong supporter of slavery • Showed a concern for the country's economy • Opposed the Compromise of 1850	• From New Hampshire • Skilled orator, lawyer, and senator • Sectional leader and spokesman for his region (North) • Against the War of 1812 • Supported the idea of a strong federal government • Wanted slavery abolished • Showed a concern for the country's economy • Defended the Compromise of 1850	• From Kentucky • Skilled orator, lawyer, and senator • Sectional leader and spokesman for his region (West) • Supported the War of 1812 • Supported the idea of a strong federal government • Supported compromise over slavery • Showed a concern for the country's economy • Defended the Compromise of 1850

Clay Supports Active Government Henry Clay spoke for the West. You have already met Clay as a leader of the War Hawks, who pushed for war against Britain in 1812.

Clay was born in Virginia but moved to Kentucky when he was 20. As a young lawyer, he was once fined for brawling with an opponent. Usually, however, he charmed both friends and rivals. Supporters called him "Gallant Harry of the West." Like Webster, Clay strongly favored a more active role for the central government in promoting the country's growth.

READING CHECK **Compare and Contrast** Which position did Webster share with Clay?

Analyze Images When the charter for the first Bank of the United States expired, state banks like this one in North Carolina began to make loans and print too much money, which caused prices to rise rapidly. **Infer** How do people usually react to higher prices?

How Was a Stable Economy Created After the War?

After the War of 1812, leaders such as Calhoun, Webster, and Clay had to deal with serious economic issues. Despite the nation's great physical growth and the soaring spirits of its people, the economy faced severe problems. This was due in part to the lack of a national bank.

The charter that had set up the first Bank of the United States ran out in 1811. Without the Bank to lend money and **regulate** the nation's money supply, the economy suffered. State banks made loans and issued money. However, they often put too much money into circulation. With so much money available to spend, prices rose rapidly.

Academic Vocabulary

regulate • *v.*, to make or use laws that control something

In the nation's early years, Democratic Republicans such as Jefferson and Madison had opposed a national bank because they saw it as unconstitutional. They thought that the Constitution did not give the federal government the right to charter corporations. By 1816, however, many Democratic Republicans believed that a bank was needed. They supported a law to charter the second Bank of the United States. By lending money and restoring order to the nation's money supply, the Bank helped American businesses grow.

Protection Against Foreign Competition Another economic problem was foreign competition from Britain. In the early 1800s, the Embargo Act and then the War of 1812 kept most British goods out of the United States. In response, American business leaders such as Francis Cabot Lowell established their own mills and factories. As a result, American industry grew quickly until 1815.

Foreign Goods Cause Domestic Problems With the end of the War of 1812, British goods again poured into the United States. Because the British had a head start in industrializing, they could make and sell goods more cheaply than Americans could. Most British factory buildings and machines were older and had already been paid for. In contrast, Americans still had to pay for their new factory buildings.

Sometimes, British manufacturers sold cloth in the United States for less than it cost to make so that they could capture the market.

Analyze Images
Inventions, such as the power loom shown here, helped propel American industry forward. **Identify Supporting Details** Who are the workers in the mill, and how do you think the work affected their lives?

British manufacturers hoped to put American rivals out of business. Then, the British planned to raise prices.

The Regional Impacts of Tariffs This British strategy caused dozens of New England businesses to fail. Angry owners asked Congress to place a protective tariff on all goods imported from Europe. As you have read, the purpose of a protective tariff is to protect a country's industries from foreign competition.

Congress responded by passing the Tariff of 1816. It greatly raised tariffs on imports. This increase made imported goods far more expensive than similar American-made goods.

The Tariff of 1816 impacted the North, West, and South differently because each region had a different economy. The North was the base of America's manufacturing. It therefore benefited the most. Higher prices on foreign goods made American goods more competitive. American factories sold more products, and businesses grew.

The economies of the South and West relied heavily on farming. They were not as financially invested in manufacturing and therefore did not experience the same benefits as the North. Goods like cloth and iron became more expensive to southern and western consumers. Northerners gained income as a result.

Higher tariffs led to angry protests. Lacking factories, southerners did not benefit from the tariff. Also, southerners bought many British goods. The new tariff drove up the price of British-made goods. Southerners complained that the tariff made northern manufacturers rich at the expense of the South.

Henry Clay Fights Sectionalism The bitter dispute over tariffs contributed to the growth of sectionalism. Americans identified themselves as southerners, northerners, or westerners. In Congress, representatives from different sections often clashed.

Henry Clay wanted to promote economic growth for all sections. His program, known as the **American System**, called for high tariffs on imports, which would help northern factories. With wealth from industry, Clay believed, northerners would have the money to buy farm products from the West and the South.

This exchange would strengthen a common market among the states, which the Constitution supported and protected in the clause on interstate commerce. High tariffs would also reduce American dependence on foreign goods.

Clay also urged Congress to use money from tariffs to build roads, bridges, and canals. A better transportation system, he believed, would make it easier and cheaper for farmers in the West and the South to ship goods to city markets.

Clay's American System never fully went into effect. While tariffs remained high, Congress spent little on internal improvements such as new roads, bridges, and canals. Southerners in particular disliked Clay's plan. The South had many fine rivers on which to transport goods. Many southerners opposed paying for roads and canals that brought them no direct benefits.

Some Americans also thought Clay's plan for developing transportation with federal support was unconstitutional. They did not believe the federal government had the authority to build such projects. They believed that by regulating industry and building roads and canals, the federal government would gain too much power.

READING CHECK **Identify Main Ideas** Why did many states in the South and West oppose the Tariff of 1816?

How Did Supreme Court Decisions Expand Federal Power?

Under Chief Justice John Marshall, the Supreme Court strengthened the power of the federal government. The Court gave the federal government the power to regulate the economy.

Analyze Graphs Cotton played a key role in the early U.S. economy, especially in the South. **Identify Cause and Effect** As cotton production soared, what other features of the American economy also grew?

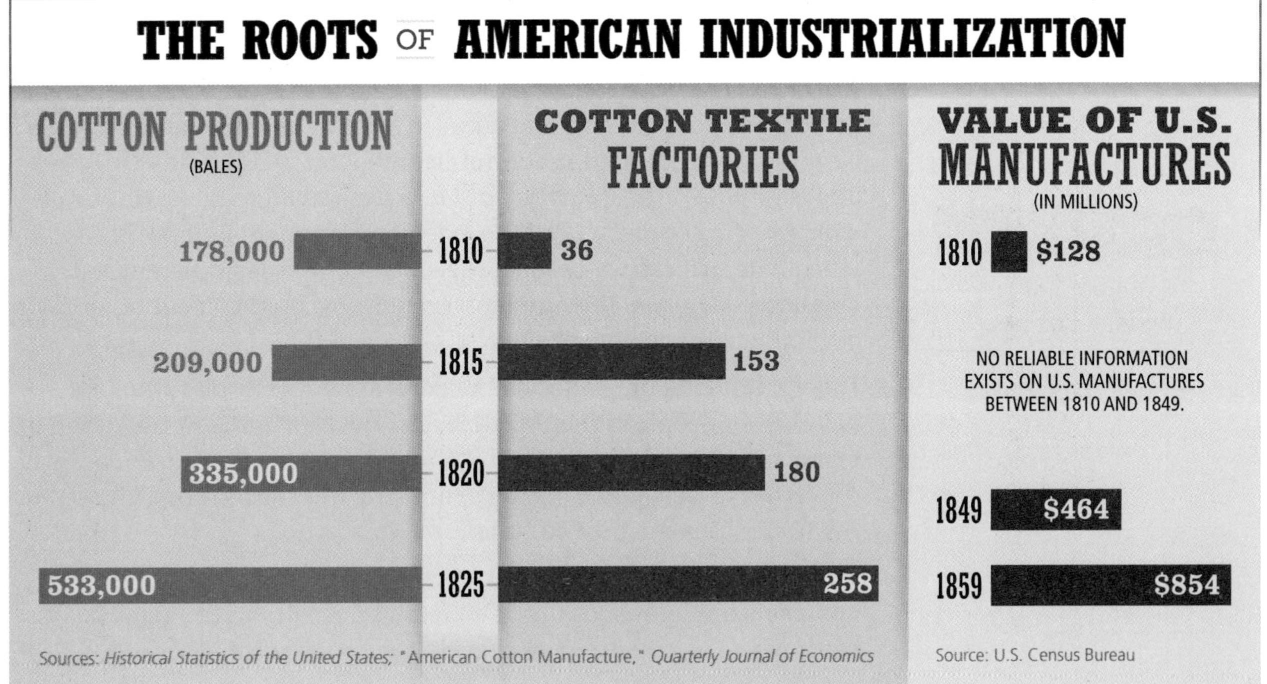

Analyze Images Robert Fulton built the first successful steamboats, shown here, and ran them as ferries from New York to New Jersey. **Synthesize Visual Information** What details in this image show how technology was changing American society?

A Broad Definition of "Necessary and Proper"

After Congress chartered the second Bank of the United States, Maryland tried to tax the Bank in order to drive it out of the state. James McCulloch, the Bank cashier, refused to pay the tax.

In the case of *McCulloch* v. *Maryland* (1819), the Court ruled that states had no right to interfere with federal institutions within their borders. The ruling strengthened federal power. It also allowed the Bank of the United States to continue, which helped the U.S. economy expand.

The Court decision addressed the issue of the meaning of the "necessary and proper" clause of the U.S. Constitution. It ruled that the federal government had the power to charter the Bank of the United States under the clause. This clause states that "The Congress shall have Power . . . To make all Laws which shall be necessary and proper" for carrying out functions outlined elsewhere in the Constitution. Since the Constitution gave the federal government the power to tax and borrow money and to regulate business, the Court stated that creating a bank could be considered "necessary and proper" to carrying out these powers.

The Supreme Court took a "loose constructionist" view of the Constitution, believing that the "necessary and proper" clause should be interpreted loosely as circumstances changed. Many Americans disagreed with the Court. Those who disagreed took a "strict constructionist" view that the "necessary and proper" clause permitted only actions absolutely necessary for performing the government's constitutional duties. Strict constructionists mostly agreed that the Bank of the United States was not necessary for the government to function.

Broad Powers Over Interstate Trade

In another case, *Gibbons* v. *Ogden* (1824), the Supreme Court upheld the power of the federal government to regulate trade between states. The Court struck down a New York law that tried to control steamboat travel between New York and New Jersey. The Court ruled that a state could regulate trade only within its own borders. Only the federal government had the power to regulate **interstate commerce**, or trade between different states. This decision helped the national economy by making it easier for the government to regulate trade.

INTERACTIVE

Expansion of Federal Powers

These rulings not only affected the government. They also changed daily life for people in the United States. The New York law had given a monopoly, or exclusive rights, to Robert Fulton's steamboat company to run ferries to New Jersey. Fulton's company was the only one allowed to run ferries between the two states.

When the Supreme Court struck down this New York law, Fulton's monopoly on steamboat traffic ended. As a result, his company could not compete with companies that charged a lower fare.

People working for Fulton lost their jobs. However, the increased competition was good for consumers because it led to lower fares.

This ruling helped create a single common market among the states for goods and services, regulated by the federal government. Having clear national laws to follow made it easier for people to do business nationwide. The Constitution's clauses on common coinage and full faith and credit also protect a common market. In these clauses, the Constitution gives only the federal government the power to coin money, and it requires that states recognize the laws and court decisions of other states.

Decisions About Contracts and Corporations Remember that in 1810, the Supreme Court ruled in a case where the state of Georgia tried to revoke a land sale. Its decision in *Fletcher* v. *Peck* upheld the idea that a contract cannot be broken.

In 1819 *Trustees of Dartmouth College* v. *Woodward*, another Supreme Court case, encouraged the growth of private businesses. When the president of private Dartmouth College was removed by its board of trustees, the state of New Hampshire tried to force the college to become a public state school. This would allow the governor to appoint the trustees.

The Supreme Court ruled that the contract clause of the Constitution applied to private corporations like Dartmouth. This landmark decision helped to encourage the growth of American businesses because it kept states from interfering with private corporations.

In the Supreme Court case, *Fletcher* v. *Peck*, the court declared as unconstitutional Georgia's repeal of a law that had allowed the state to purchase a land grant and sell off properties to speculators. The Supreme Court ruled that the state could not violate contracts made during the sale of properties, even if the contracts were illegal. This case further reinforced the idea that contracts need to be protected.

READING CHECK **Identify Cause and Effect** How did the decision in *McCulloch* v. *Maryland* increase federal power?

Independence in Latin America

By 1810, many people in Spain's colonies in the Americas were eager for independence. They had many reasons to be unhappy. Most people, even wealthy creoles, had little or no say in government. In Latin America, the term *creole* described people born to Spanish parents there. They demanded a role in government. Opposition to Spain was also growing among American Indians. Harsh rules kept American Indians forever in debt. All over Latin America, people were eager to be free of the Spanish.

Independence A Mexican priest named Miguel Hidalgo (mee GEL ee DAHL goh) called on Mexicans to fight for independence from Spain in 1810.

▼ Mexican freedom fighter Miguel Hidalgo declares Mexico's independence from Spain.

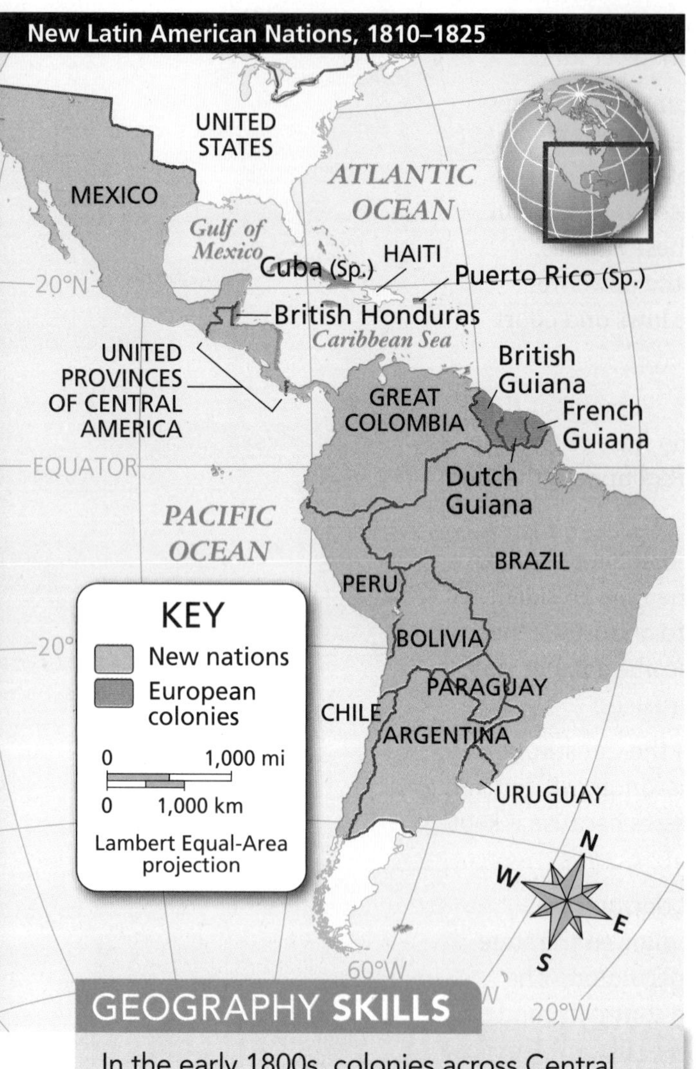

GEOGRAPHY SKILLS

In the early 1800s, colonies across Central and South America became free from Spanish rule as a result of revolution.

1. **Location** Which European countries continued to exercise control in South America?
2. **Use Visual Information** Which colonies remained under the control of Spain?

Many Mexicans answered his call. Rebel forces won control of several provinces before Father Hidalgo was captured. In 1811, Hidalgo was executed.

Another priest, José Morelos (hoh SAY moh RAY lohs), took up the fight. Because he called for a program to give land to peasants, wealthy creoles opposed him. Before long, Morelos, too, was captured and killed by the Spanish.

Slowly, though, creoles began to join the revolutionary movement. In 1821, revolutionary forces led by creoles won control of Mexico. A few years later, Mexico became a republic with its own constitution.

South America Frees Itself From Spanish Rule In South America, too, a series of revolutions freed colonies from Spanish rule. The best-known revolutionary leader was Simón Bolívar (see MOHN boh LEE vahr). He became known as the Liberator for his role in the Latin American wars of independence.

In a bold move, Bolívar led an army of rebel forces from Venezuela over the high Andes Mountains into Colombia. There, Bolívar defeated Spanish forces in 1819.

Soon after, Bolívar became President of the independent Republic of Great Colombia. It included the present-day nations of Venezuela, Colombia, Ecuador, and Panama.

Independence Movements Spread Other independent nations emerged in Latin America. José de San Martín (sahn mahr TEEN) led Argentina to freedom in 1816. He then helped the people of Chile and Peru win independence.

In 1821, the peoples of Central America declared independence from Spain. By 1825, Spain had lost all its colonies in Latin America except Puerto Rico and Cuba.

The New Republics Spain's former colonies formed several separate republics and modeled their constitutions on that of the United States. However, the new republics had a hard time setting up stable governments.

Under Spanish rule, the colonists had gained little or no experience in self-government. Powerful leaders took advantage of the turmoil to seize control. As a result, the new nations were often unable to achieve democratic rule.

READING CHECK **Compare and Contrast** In what ways was the achievement of independence for the Spanish colonies and the establishment of republics in Latin America similar to that which occurred in the British colonies that became the United States?

How Did the United States Gain Florida?

Spain lost another one of its colonies, Florida—not to independence, but to the United States. Many Americans wanted to gain possession of Florida. White southerners were especially worried about disturbances across the border. Creek and Seminole Indians in Florida sometimes raided settlements in Georgia. Also, Florida was a refuge for many Africans and African Americans who escaped slavery.

Jackson Invades Spanish Florida Since the 1700s, Spanish officials had protected enslaved Africans who had fled from plantations in Georgia and South Carolina. The Seminole allowed Africans to live near their villages. In return, these "Black Seminole" gave the Seminole a share of the crops they raised. The Black Seminoles adopted many Seminole customs.

One settlement on the Apalachicola River, known as the Negro Fort, contained about 1,000 Black Seminole. General Andrew Jackson demanded that Spain demolish the Negro Fort. When the Spanish governor refused, the United States invaded Florida and destroyed the fort.

Adams Buys Florida In 1818, Jackson again headed to Florida with a force of more than 3,000 soldiers. Spain protested but did little else. It was busy fighting rebels in Latin America and could not risk war with the United States.

In the end, Spain agreed to peace talks. Secretary of State John Quincy Adams worked out a treaty with Spain's foreign minister, Luis de Onís (LOO ess day oh NEES). In it, Spain agreed to give Florida to the United States in exchange for $5 million. The Adams-Onís Treaty took effect in 1821.

READING CHECK **Identify Cause and Effect** What was the result of the Adams-Onís Treaty?

What Did the Monroe Doctrine State?

Americans cheered as Latin America won independence. The actions of European powers, however, worried Secretary of State Adams and President Monroe.

▼ Black Seminole were African Americans who had escaped slavery and lived peacefully alongside Seminole Indians in Florida.

In 1815, Prussia, France, Russia, and Austria formed an alliance aimed at crushing any revolution that sprang up in Europe. They seemed ready to help Spain regain its colonies in Latin America. In addition, Russia claimed lands on the Pacific coast of North America.

The British, too, worried about other European nations meddling in the Western Hemisphere. They feared that their profitable trade with the newly independent countries would be hurt if Spain regained control of its former colonies. Thus, they suggested that the United States and Britain issue a joint statement guaranteeing the freedom of the new nations of Latin America.

Monroe decided to act independently of Britain. In a message to Congress in 1823, he made a bold foreign policy statement known as the **Monroe Doctrine**. Monroe declared that the United States would not interfere in the affairs of European nations or existing colonies of the European nations. At the same time, he warned European nations not to attempt to regain control of the newly independent nations of Latin America.

The Monroe Doctrine stated that the United States would oppose any attempt to reclaim old colonies or build new colonies in the Americas. Monroe's message showed that the United States was determined to keep European powers out of the Western Hemisphere.

Analyze Political Cartoons In this political cartoon, Uncle Sam brandishes a big stick, labeled "Monroe Doctrine," as a warning to European nations not to attempt to re-colonize territory in the Americas. **Identify Cause and Effect** How do you think other nations reacted to this new U.S. foreign policy?

EXPANSION!
The western patrol's long stretch.

The United States did not have the military power to enforce the Monroe Doctrine. Britain, however, supported the statement. With its strong navy, it could stop Europeans from building new colonies in the Americas.

As the United States became stronger, the Monroe Doctrine grew in importance. On several occasions, the United States successfully challenged European **intervention**, or direct involvement, in Latin America. In the 1900s, Presidents also used the Monroe Doctrine to justify sending troops to Caribbean nations. Thus, Monroe's bold statement helped shape United States foreign policy for more than 100 years.

READING CHECK **Identify Main Ideas** What was the purpose of the Monroe Doctrine?

What Was Daily Life Like in the Early Republic?

The government changed during the early years of the nation, and so did the daily lives of many Americans. The growth of industry was one reason. The country was still largely rural.

Many Americans worked on farms. But by the end of the period, factories had begun to sprout up. Many young women from farms in New England began to move to cities to work in textile factories.

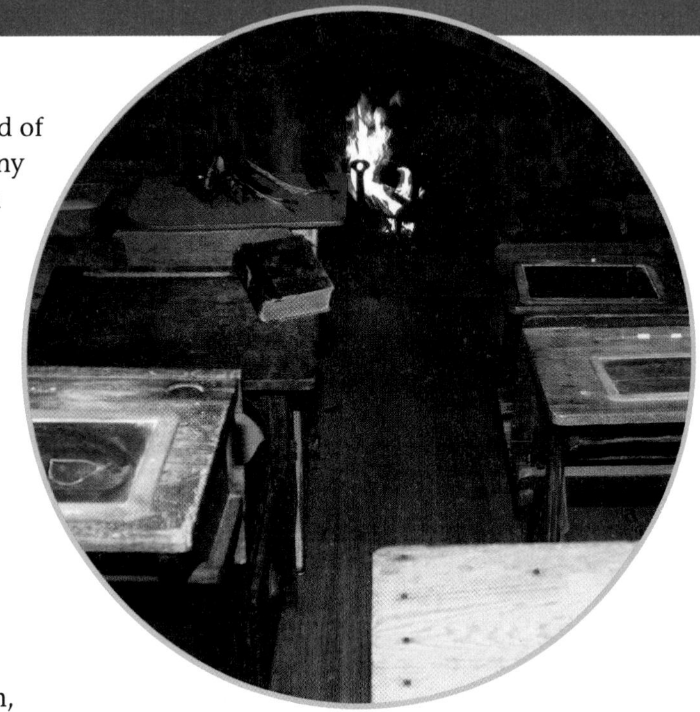

Analyze Images One-room schools such as this were common in rural areas in the early republic. **Compare and Contrast** What is the same and different about this classroom and those you use today?

Churches were centers of social life throughout the country. Protestant churches were most common, but Jews and Catholics were allowed to practice their religions under new state constitutions that required separation of church and state.

Free African Americans sometimes started their own churches, but they also formed many other organizations. These groups provided mutual aid and relief for those in need, such as widows and orphans.

Enslaved African Americans generally lived harsh, controlled lives. Families were broken up when members were sold. Many enslaved people turned to their own faith and customs for a sense of community.

Education Jefferson and others stressed the importance of education in a republican democracy. However, schools were mostly private. Americans received their education in different ways.

For example, a dame school was a small school run by a woman in her own home. She would teach young children the alphabet and numbers, as well as some reading and writing. Other Americans were educated in their own homes by family members or at church schools. The Bible was often used as a teaching tool for learning to read.

Wealthy Americans could subscribe to private membership libraries. Benjamin Franklin was an advocate for public libraries. In 1790 he donated books to a Massachusetts town that named itself Franklin after him. The residents voted for the books to be freely available for town members, forming a public library. As the number of public libraries increased, more and more Americans had access to books.

Art Wealthy, prominent Americans had their portraits painted. Gilbert Stuart's painting of George Washington is famous, as is Rembrandt Peale's portrait of Thomas Jefferson. Folk painters traveled around to paint portraits for less prominent rural Americans. However, formal painters and sculptors still looked to Europe, especially Britain, for training, style, and themes.

Useful household objects were often created with a sense of design. Furniture made in a style called Federal became popular. Newly wealthy merchants bought from the workshops of skilled craftspeople in New York or Philadelphia.

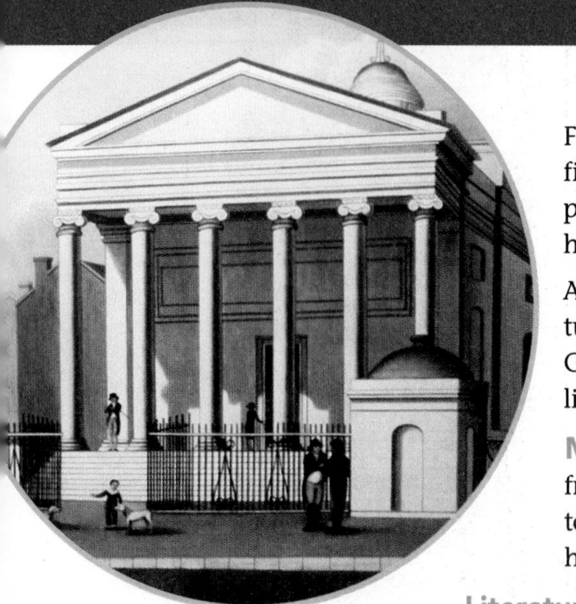

Analyze Images Federal-style architecture for public buildings in the early 1800s resembled Greek temples in order to suggest the democratic ideals begun in ancient Greece. **Infer** How does this architecture reflect ancient Greek ideals of balance and harmony?

Folk artists created samplers, weather vanes, ship's figureheads, and tavern and shop signs. They used many patriotic images in their craft, including likenesses of American hero George Washington.

Architecture also followed a style called Federal. Architects turned away from Britain and looked to the temples of ancient Greece for style. They used domes, pillars, and triangular roof lines for civic buildings.

Music People performed music in their homes for family and friends. British music was still enjoyed, and British entertainers toured the country. African Americans sang spirituals in their homes and churches, broadening American musical styles.

Literature The first American novel, *The Power of Sympathy*, was written by William Hill Brown in 1789. An original American voice in literature soon developed. Washington Irving's *The Sketch Book* included "The Legend of Sleepy Hollow" and "Rip Van Winkle," which was the first work by an American that won international popularity. James Fenimore Cooper wrote the extremely popular Leatherstocking Tales. The five novels tell of the wilderness adventures of a scout named Natty Bumppo.

READING CHECK **Draw Conclusions** Why do you think folk art of the early republic used patriotic images?

Lesson Check

Practice Vocabulary

1. How did **sectionalism** affect the country in Monroe's term?
2. What was the **Monroe Doctrine**, and what was its purpose?

Critical Thinking and Writing

3. **Recognize Multiple Causes** After the War of 1812, British goods were again available in the United States. Why were these imported British goods less expensive than similar American goods?
4. **Generate Explanations** What was the principal reason the South rejected the American System, Henry Clay's plan to promote economic growth in all regions of the United States?
5. **Compare and Contrast** In what ways were the outcomes in *McCulloch* v. *Maryland* and *Gibbons* v. *Ogden* similar?
6. **Writing Workshop: Include Formatting and Graphics** Decide what graphics you can use to illustrate your information in the research paper you will write. What formatting will make your paper easy and interesting to read? Note these ideas in your Active Journal.

Construct a Timeline

Follow these steps to construct a timeline.

Sequence

1 **Select key events of a time period and note the date of each.** The time period for this activity covers the first five presidencies. Some key events and their dates are noted below.

2 **Determine the beginning and ending dates of the period.** The timeline will span 1785 to 1825, a period of 40 years.

3 **Decide on how to break the line into time intervals. The intervals should be even.** Break your timeline into intervals of five years each. Draw a line on a piece of paper that can be broken evenly into eight sections of five years each. Mark the five-year intervals, beginning with 1785 and ending with 1825.

4 **Place a mark at the appropriate spot for each event and identify the year and the event.** Place the key events on the timeline. Then determine the dates of these events below and enter them on the timeline:

a. *Marbury* v. *Madison*

b. Burning of Washington, D.C., by the British

c. Washington's Farewell Address

Key Events of the First Five Presidencies

1789 Washington's inauguration

1794 Whiskey Rebellion

1797 Adams's inauguration

1798 Alien and Sedition Acts

1801 Jefferson's inauguration

1803 Louisiana Purchase

1809 Madison's inauguration

1812 Beginning of War of 1812

1817 Monroe's inauguration

1823 Monroe Doctrine

TOPIC 5

Review and Assessment

VISUAL REVIEW

A Two-Party System

Federalists	Democratic Republicans
• Wanted a strong central government	• Wanted strong state governments
• Sympathetic to England	• Sympathetic to France
• Favored a national bank	• Opposed a national bank
• Thought the elite of society should control government	• Thought ordinary white men should control the government
• Opposed to protection of individual liberties by law	• Wanted individual liberties to be protected by law
• Wanted an economy based on manufacturing and trade	• Wanted an economy based on agriculture

Five Presidencies

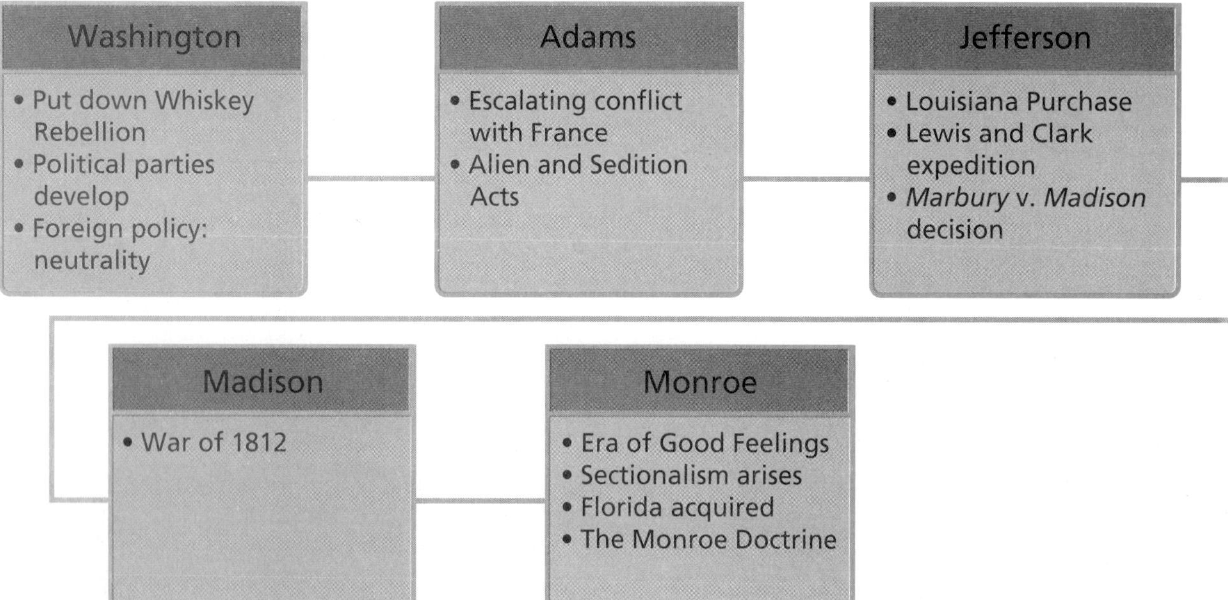

READING REVIEW

Use the Take Notes and Practice Vocabulary activities in your Active Journal to review the topic.

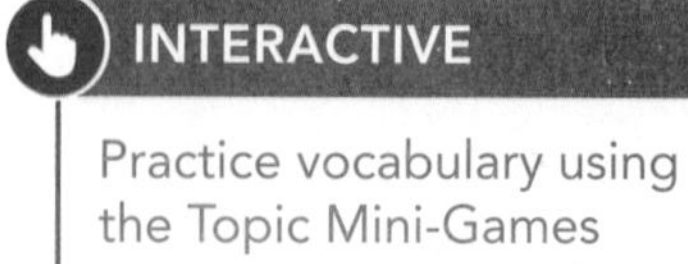

Quest FINDINGS

Write your position paper, summarizing your chosen solution. Get help for writing your position paper in your Active Journal.

ASSESSMENT

Vocabulary and Key Ideas

1. **Define** What is **judicial review**?
2. **Describe** What is **sedition**, and what did the Alien and Sedition Acts do?
3. **Check Understanding** What role did **tariffs** play in early economic policy?
4. **Use** Use **interstate commerce** in a sentence about the Supreme Court.
5. **Identify Main Ideas** What were the causes of the War of 1812?
6. **Describe** How did the Louisiana Purchase change the boundaries of the United States?
7. **Check Understanding** Explain the Monroe Doctrine.

Critical Thinking and Writing

8. **Synthesize** How did the question of neutrality influence the early republic?
9. **Identify Cause and Effect** How did the conflict between Jefferson and Hamilton result in the development of two political parties?
10. **Evaluate** Was the Louisiana Purchase constitutional? Support your answer.
11. **Analyze** Why was education considered important in the early republic?
12. **Analyze** How did the government change during the early republic?
13. **Revisit the Essential Question** How was the question "How much power should the federal government have, and what should it do?" reflected in actions taken in the early republic?
14. **Writer's Workshop: Write a Research Paper** Using your notes in your Active Journal, write a paper describing the country's physical geography, political divisions, and expansion during the terms of its first four Presidents.

Analyze Primary Sources

15. Who is most likely the source of the quote?
    A. Alexander Hamilton
    B. John Marshall
    C. John Adams
    D. Thomas Jefferson

"It is emphatically the province and duty of the judicial department to say what the law is. Those who apply the rule to particular cases, must of necessity expound and interpret that rule. If two laws conflict with each other, the courts must decide on the operation of each."

Analyze Maps

16. What body of water made New Orleans important during the war?
17. Based on the blue lines, which show American troop movement, which was likely the first battle to have occurred?
18. The red lines and arrows show British movements. The blue bursts show American victories. Based on this information, which side was more successful during this part of the war?

▼ The Battle of New Orleans

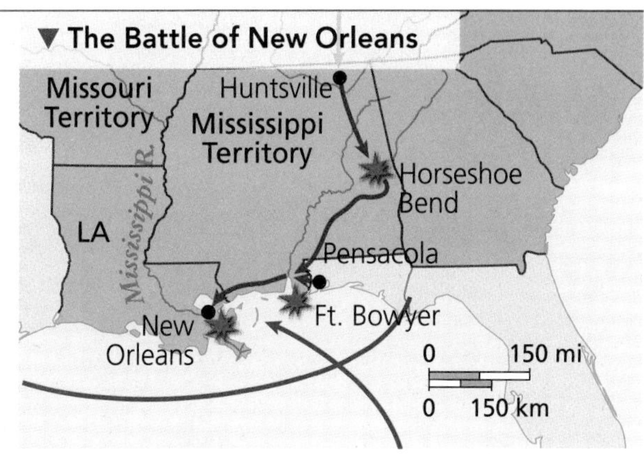

TOPIC 6

The Age of Jackson and Westward Expansion (1824–1860)

GO ONLINE to access your digital course

VIDEO

AUDIO

ETEXT

INTERACTIVE

WRITING

GAMES

WORKSHEET

ASSESSMENT

Go back to the early 1800s

and the AGE OF JACKSON AND WESTWARD EXPANSION. Why? Because it was the time when white American settlers moved west, expanding the country—and forcing American Indians to leave their lands.

Explore The Essential Question

Why do people move?

In the early 1800s, most Americans lived east of the Appalachian Mountains. What led people to leave their homes and risk moving to the untamed West?

Unlock the Essential Question in your Active Journal.

Watch

Narcissa Whitman and the Journey West

Learn what it was really like to be a pioneer moving west.

Read

about westward expansion and its impact on American Indians, the landscape, and American history.

Pioneers heading West on the Oregon Trail

TOPIC 6

The Age of Jackson and Westward Expansion (1824–1860)

Learn more about The Age of Jackson and Westward Expansion by making your own map and timeline in your Active Journal.

INTERACTIVE

Topic Timeline

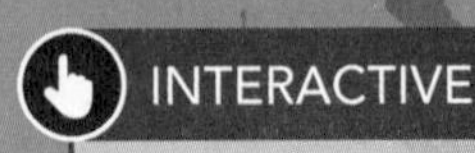

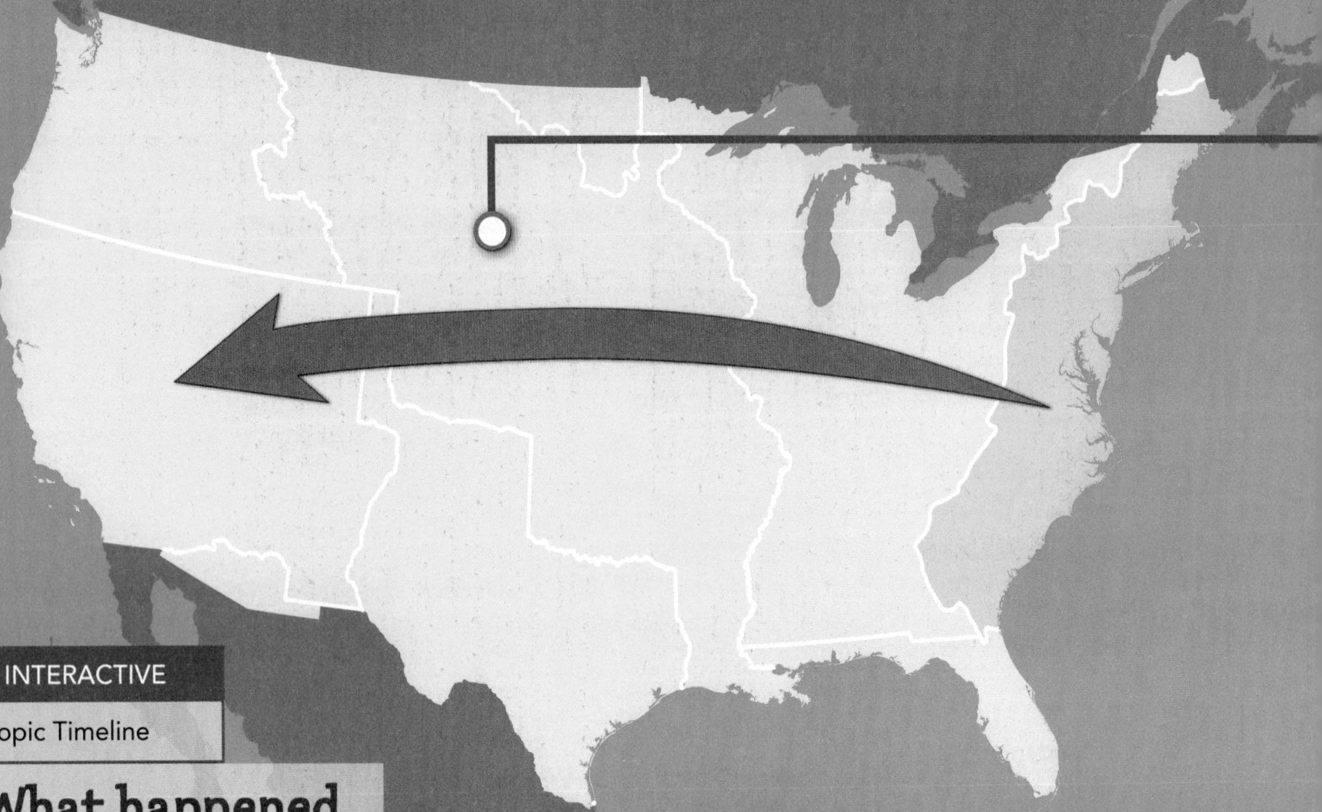

What happened and when?

Growing democracy in America...settlers moving west...Explore the timeline to see some of what was happening during the Age of Jackson and westward expansion.

TOPIC EVENTS

1828 Andrew Jackson elected president

1830 Indian Removal Act leads to forced migration of American Indians

1832 South Carolina passes Nullification Act

1837 Economic panic leads to depression

1820 | **1830**

WORLD EVENTS

1826 Friction match invented

1831 France invades and colonizes Algeria

INTERACTIVE

Topic Map

How did the United States expand westward?

By the middle of the 1800s, the United States extended far to the west from the original 13 colonies on the East Coast, reaching from the Atlantic to the Pacific. As new lands were acquired, explorers paved the way for settlers from the East.

Who will you meet?

Andrew Jackson, champion of the common people

James Beckwourth, mountain man freed from slavery

John Ross, leader of the Cherokee people

1848 Mexican-American War ends, United States takes control of California and New Mexico

1849 Gold discovered in California

1840 | 1850 | 1860

1848 Marx and Engels publish *The Communist Manifesto*

1850 Taiping Rebellion begins in China

Civic Discussion Inquiry

The Mexican-American War

▼ American soldiers raise the flag during the Battle of Chapultepec.

Quest KICK OFF

You are the leading historian on the topic of U.S. westward expansion. You're beginning the research for your next book on the Mexican-American War. One of the chapters in your book will focus on this question:

Was the Mexican-American War justified?

Be ready! Other historians will challenge your arguments. It's time to prepare!

1 Ask Questions

You are determined to know the best answer to the Guiding Question. Get started by making a list of questions about the Mexican-American War. Write the questions in your Active Journal.

2 Investigate

As you read the lessons in this Topic, look for Quest CONNECTIONS that provide information about the Mexican-American War. Collect examples in your Active Journal.

3 Examine Sources

Next, research primary sources about the Mexican-American War. Look for information that supports differing viewpoints about whether the war was justified. Capture notes in your Active Journal.

Quest FINDINGS

4 Discuss!

After you collect your clues and examine the sources, you will prepare to discuss this question: Was the Mexican-American War justified? You will use your knowledge as well as evidence from sources to make convincing arguments to answer YES or NO to the question. You may also come up with answers of your own.

LESSON 1

Jackson Wins the Presidency

GET READY TO READ

START UP

Look at the image of Jackson's 1828 inauguration celebration. What can you conclude about the kind of people who supported Jackson? Write a few sentences summarizing your ideas.

GUIDING QUESTIONS

- How did changes in suffrage affect political parties and elections?
- How did individual regions of the United States become both more similar and more different?
- What were the causes and effects of Jacksonian democracy?

TAKE NOTES

Literacy Skills: Identify Cause and Effect

Use the graphic organizer in your Active Journal to take notes as you read the lesson.

PRACTICE VOCABULARY

Use the Vocabulary Builder activity in your Active Journal to practice the vocabulary words.

Vocabulary

suffrage
majority
Whig Party
Democratic Party
spoils system

Academic Vocabulary

perceive
consequently

During the early 1800s, a growing spirit of democracy changed the political system and affected American ideas about social classes. The main cause stemmed from the influence of Andrew Jackson. He was an American politician during this time who supported expanding democratic rights. From the time of his first campaign for president in 1824 until his death in 1845, he dominated American politics. Jackson's policies had a significant effect on issues such as voting rights and the ways in which government functions. This period is often known as the Age of Jackson.

Democracy Expands

In the early 1800s, American democracy was a social outlook as well as a political system. Most Americans did not feel that the rich deserved special respect. Wealthy European visitors to the United States were surprised that servants in American households expected to be treated as equals. Others were amazed that butlers and maids refused to be summoned with bells, as in Europe.

Quick Activity

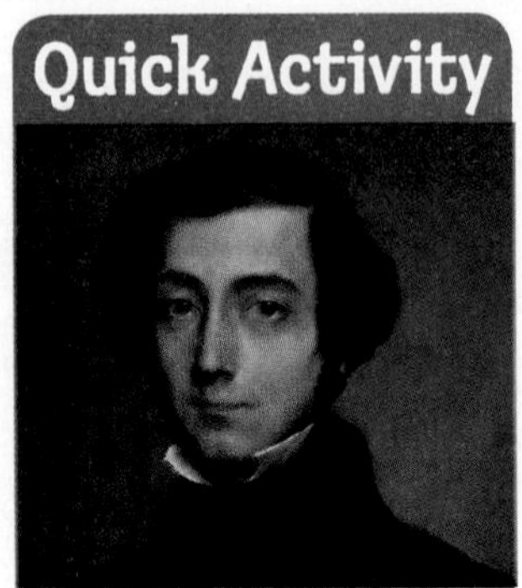

In your Active Journal, compare Tocqueville's description of American life with American life at another time.

Alexis de Tocqueville A visitor from France, Alexis de Tocqueville, became especially well known for his observations on American democracy. He came to the United States in 1831 to study the American prison system. For several months, Tocqueville toured the United States. However, he observed much more than prisons. He observed a society that was becoming more and more democratic.

After his return to France, Tocqueville recorded his experiences and observations in a book titled *Democracy in America*. In it, he admired the American democratic spirit and the American goals of equality and freedom. He also observed that, while Americans expected to be treated as equals, equality only went so far. But overall, he found that the results of the social "revolution taking place" in America, while "still far from coming to an end," were "already incomparably greater than anything which has taken place in the world before."

Increased Suffrage During the 1820s, or the early years of the Age of Jackson, more Americans gained **suffrage**, or the right to vote. Others, however, were denied full participation in the growing democracy.

The United States was growing rapidly. New states were joining the Union. This growth fed some of the sectional divisions among states over taxes, trade, and other interests. People in the North, South, and West differed in their views on these issues.

Despite these disagreements, the regions grew more alike in their eagerness to expand voting rights to nearly all white men and to strengthen democracy. There were many citizens eager to participate in elections. Some of the first states to give voting privileges to white males who did not own property were in the West. In these states, any white man over age 21 could vote.

Class in America in 1830

Voting and Jury Rights	• White men
Unable to Vote, Unable to Serve on Juries	• All women • Enslaved African American men • Most free African American men • American Indian men
Property Rights	• White men • Some free African Americans • Single white women • American Indians
Unable to Own Land	• Married women • Enslaved African Americans • Some free African Americans

Analyze Images Class differences in the 1800s were reflected in unequal voting and property rights. **Draw Conclusions** Based on this chart, who ranked in the highest class in American society?

Changing Voting Rights in Early America

Reformers in the East worked to expand suffrage in that region. By the 1830s, most eastern states had dropped the requirement that voters had to own land. In this way, laborers, artisans and craft workers, and shopkeepers gained the right to vote.

Throughout the country, growing numbers of Americans exercised their newly acquired right to vote. Before 1828, the turnout of eligible voters was never more than 27 percent. That low percentage rose to nearly 58 percent in the election of 1828. By 1840, voter turnout was nearly 80 percent.

Analyze Images Nearly all white men gained the right to vote during the Age of Jackson, but still, most adults, including the enslaved African American men shown here, were not allowed to vote. **Infer** Why might people who were able to vote be reluctant to extend the vote to others?

Limits on Suffrage Despite the nation's growing democratic spirit, a great many Americans did not have the right to vote. These included women, Native Americans, and the vast majority of African Americans. Meanwhile, even through Jackson's presidency, a few states kept the requirement that only white male property owners were eligible to vote.

Although most white men had won suffrage, free African Americans had lost it. In the early years of the nation, most northern states and a few southern states allowed free African American men to vote. By the 1820s, however, many of these states had taken away that right. By 1830, only a few New England states permitted free African American men to vote on equal terms with white men. In New York, African American men had to own property in order to vote while white men did not. No state allowed enslaved African Americans to vote.

READING CHECK **Summarize** How did democracy expand during the Age of Jackson?

The Election of 1824 Leads to a "Bargain"

There were four candidates for president in 1824. All four were members of the old Republican Party. However, each had support in different parts of the country. John Quincy Adams was strong in New England. Henry Clay and Andrew Jackson had support in the West. William H. Crawford was favored in the South, but became too ill to campaign.

The Candidates John Quincy Adams of Massachusetts was the son of Abigail and John Adams, the second President. A graduate of Harvard University, the younger Adams had served as Secretary of State and helped end the War of 1812. People admired Adams for his intelligence and high morals. In 1821 as Secretary of State, he gave a Fourth of July speech before Congress. It set the tone for American foreign policy for decades to come. Adams, however, was uncomfortable campaigning among the common people. In fact, to most people he seemed hard and cold.

The Election of 1824

CANDIDATE	Andrew Jackson	John Quincy Adams	William Crawford	Henry Clay
HOME STATE	Tennessee	Massachusetts	Georgia	Kentucky
MAIN POSITIONS	Presents himself as the champion of the common man	Supports tariffs and spending on roads and canals to promote business	Supports states' rights	Supports tariffs and spending on roads and canals to promote business, compromise between North and South
POPULAR VOTE*	151,271	113,122	40,856	47,531
ELECTORAL VOTE	99	84	41	37
HOUSE VOTE BY STATE	7	13	4	Not on ballot

*The popular vote does not accurately measure candidates' popular support, because in several states there was no popular vote, and electors were chosen by state legislatures.

Analyze Images This chart shows information about the four candidates in the presidential election of 1824. **Compare** Which two candidates' positions were most similar, and how were they similar?

Henry Clay, a Kentuckian, was Speaker of the House of Representatives. He was a skillful negotiator and a shrewd politician. Despite his abilities, Clay was less popular than the other candidate from the West, Andrew Jackson.

William H. Crawford had served as treasury secretary, war secretary, and ambassador to France after the War of 1812, and as a senator from Georgia. Crawford's support was concentrated in the Southeast.

To many Americans, especially on the western frontier, Andrew Jackson was a hero. A general during the War of 1812, he had defeated the British and a group of Creek Indians who were allied with the British. He had gone on to defeat the Seminoles and the Spanish in Florida, gaining that territory for the United States. He was known as the "Hero of New Orleans" for his victory in the War of 1812. He also earned the nickname "Old Hickory" after a soldier said he was "tough as hickory." Jackson's fame as a general helped him launch a political career. Although he was a landowner and a slave owner, many saw him as a man of the people. Jackson had been born in a log cabin, and his parents had been poor farmers. He was admired by small farmers and others who felt left out of the growing economy in the United States. The expansion of the vote to white men without property helped account for Jackson's political popularity.

The "Corrupt Bargain" No clear winner emerged from the election of 1824. Jackson won the popular vote, but no candidate won a **majority**, or more than half, of the electoral votes. As a result, under the provisions of the Constitution, the House of Representatives had to choose the President from among the top three candidates. Because he had finished fourth, Clay was out of the running.

As Speaker of the House, though, Clay played an important role in influencing the results. He urged members of the House to vote for Adams. After Adams won the vote in the House and became President, he named Clay his secretary of state. In the past, secretaries of state had often gone on to become President.

Although the election was decided properly according to the Constitution, Jackson and his backers were furious. They accused Adams and Clay of making a "corrupt bargain" and stealing the election from Jackson. The anger of Jackson and his supporters seriously hampered President Adams's efforts to unify the nation.

READING CHECK **Draw Conclusions** Why did some people refer to the 1824 election result as a "corrupt bargain"?

Academic Vocabulary
perceive • *v.*, notice or become aware of

The Presidency of John Quincy Adams

Adams **perceived** that the outcome of the election had angered many Americans. To "bring the whole people together," he pushed for a program of economic growth through internal improvements. His plan backfired, however, and opposition to him grew.

Promoting Economic Growth Like Alexander Hamilton and Henry Clay, Adams thought that the federal government should promote economic growth. He called for the government to pay for new roads and canals. These internal improvements would help farmers to transport goods to market.

Adams also favored projects to promote the arts and the sciences. He suggested building a national university and an observatory from which astronomers could study the stars. Most Americans objected to spending money on such programs. They feared that the federal government would become too powerful. Congress approved money for a national road and some canals but turned down most of Adams's other spending programs.

Analyze Images John Quincy Adams, the sixth President of the United States, thought that the federal government should adopt policies and pay for projects that would help the economy. **Identify Main Ideas** How would building roads and canals help the economy?

Origin of New Political Parties During the 1820s, nearly all politicians were members of Jefferson's Democratic-Republican Party. In the 1830s, however, new political parties took shape. These parties grew out of the conflict between John Quincy Adams and Andrew Jackson.

The Whig Party Democratic-Republicans who supported Adams and his programs for national growth called themselves National Republicans. In 1834, many of them joined a new party, organized by Henry Clay and known as the **Whig Party**.

Analyze Images Jackson drew wide support from small business people, farmers, laborers, and others. **Infer** Why do you think these people voted for Jackson?

Whigs wanted the government to act to help the economy. They wanted the federal government to promote business by paying for roads and canals. They also wanted the federal government to oversee banks. They believed that a stable banking system would encourage business. Whigs also wanted higher tariffs.

Tariffs are taxes or fees placed on imported goods. Because tariffs make imports more expensive, they help domestic producers. However, they may prompt foreign governments to counter with their own tariffs. This can harm exporters.

The Democratic Party Jackson and other Democratic-Republicans who supported him began to call themselves the **Democratic Party**. Today's Democratic Party traces its roots to Andrew Jackson's time. Like the Whig Party, Democrats also had a point of view. They called for more political power for ordinary white men and opposed privileges for the wealthy or educated. Democrats were opposed to a federal government role in the economy and to tariffs.

Democrats opposed high tariffs because farmers counted on being able to sell their goods overseas and did not want to risk retaliatory tariffs. Tariffs also protected American manufacturers from foreign competition. The result was higher prices for all kinds of goods that ordinary people needed. Democrats supported westward expansion to open up more land for frontier settlers.

Democrats were generally more tightly organized than Whigs. Members usually followed the direction set by party leaders.

INTERACTIVE

Political Parties in the Age of Jackson

Who Supported the Whigs and Democrats? The Whigs had their strongest support in the Northeast, with some support in cities and towns in the South and West. People from these places backed the Whigs because these places relied on manufacturing and commerce, and Whig policies aimed to help those parts of the economy.

Whig supporters included eastern factory owners and other businessmen, some southern planters, and many former Federalists. Whigs were often divided into factions, and not all of the party's members always followed the party's direction.

Democrats had strong support in the South and West, especially among laborers, artisans, and small farmers. These groups also supported Democrats in some parts of the Northeast. Small farmers and workers supported the Democrats because Democrats spoke up for them against bankers and Northeastern businessmen. While big business favored the Whigs, middle-class businesspeople and merchants lined up behind Jackson.

A Bitter Campaign In 1828, Adams faced an uphill battle for reelection. This time, Andrew Jackson was Adams's only opponent. The campaign was a bitter contest. Jackson supporters renewed charges that Adams had made a "corrupt bargain" after the 1824 election. They also attacked Adams as an aristocrat, or member of the upper class.

Adams supporters replied with similar attacks. They called Jackson a dangerous "military chieftain." If Jackson became president, they warned, he could become a dictator like Napoleon Bonaparte of France.

Jackson won the election easily. His supporters cheered the outcome as a victory for the common people. By common people, they meant white people who worked for a living, including farmers and city workers. For the first time since the Revolution, the politics of the common people were important.

READING CHECK **Summarize** Why did Andrew Jackson win the election of 1828?

Did you know?

After he lost the presidency, Adams was elected to the House of Representatives, where he served until he died in office 18 years later.

GEOGRAPHY SKILLS

This map shows the results of the 1828 presidential election.

1. **Movement** In which region of the country did most people vote for Jackson? Which region voted mostly for Adams?
2. **Use Visual Information** Which states were divided in their support of Jackson and Adams? Explain.

Election of 1828

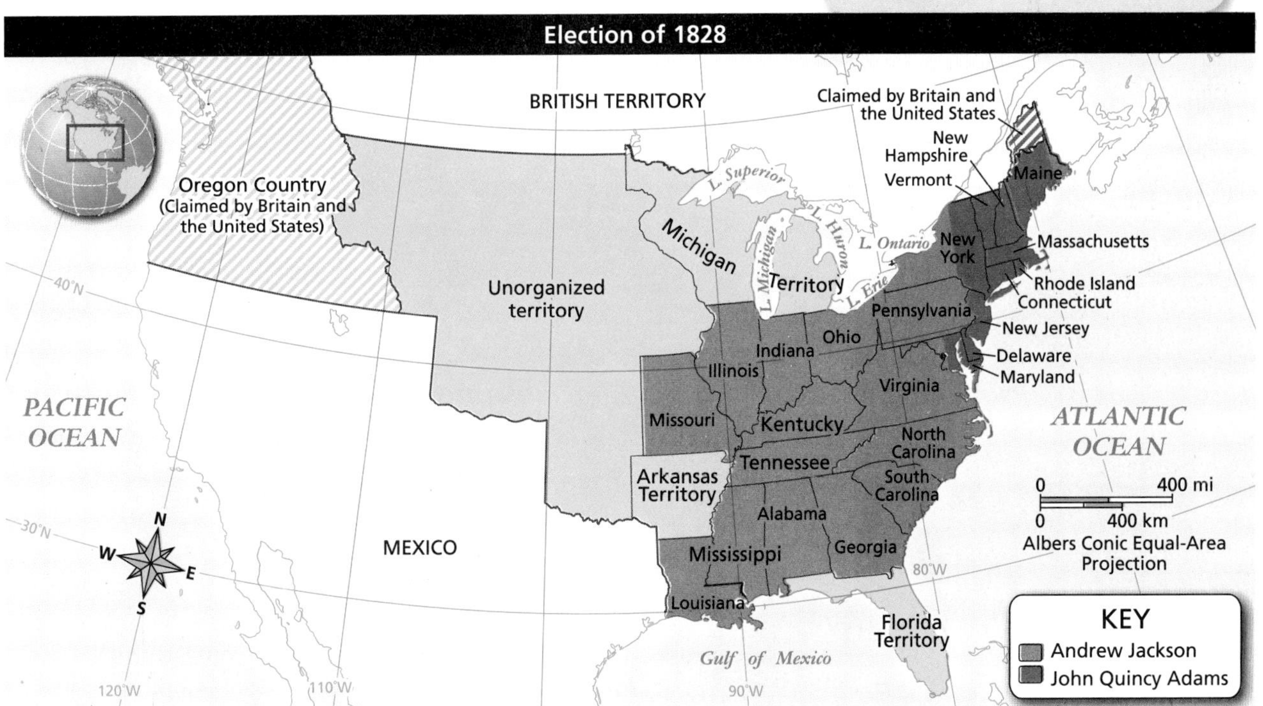

Jacksonian Democracy

Jackson was a new kind of American politician. Unlike the polished, aristocratic easterners who preceded him, Jackson was a plainspoken frontiersman. His personality and point of view would influence American politics for years to come.

Andrew Jackson Growing Up Like many who admired him, Andrew Jackson was born in a log cabin on the frontier. His parents had left Ireland to settle in the Carolinas. Both died before Jackson was 15. **Consequently,** Jackson had to grow up quickly.

Academic Vocabulary
consequently • *adv.,* as a result

Although he was lean, he was a strong fighter. A friend who wrestled with him recalled, "I could throw him three times out of four, but he would never stay throwed."

Always determined, Jackson showed his toughness at 13 when he joined the American Revolution. He was captured by the British while carrying messages for the Patriots.

Jackson Prepares to Be President After the Revolution, Jackson studied law in North Carolina. He later moved to Tennessee and set up a successful law practice. Over time he became very wealthy by buying and selling land in Georgia and Alabama. While still in his twenties, he was elected to Congress. He served for just a few years before becoming a judge and a major general in the Tennessee militia.

Analyze Images Taken prisoner by the British at age 13, Andrew Jackson refused to clean a British officer's boots. The officer slashed Jackson with his sword, scarring him for life. **Draw Conclusions** What does this experience tell you about Andrew Jackson's character?

Jackson won national fame for his achievements during the War of 1812. He led American forces to a major victory over the British at the Battle of New Orleans. He was also known for his leadership during the Creek War. A group of Creeks, angered in part by white settlers moving onto their land, began to attack settlers. These Creeks massacred at least 250 people, including soldiers and their families, at Fort Mims, in present-day Alabama. Jackson led an army to stop the attacks. His victory at Horseshoe Bend forced the Creeks to give up vast amounts of land in what are now Georgia and Alabama.

Analyze Images An artist drew this cartoon to criticize what he saw as Andrew Jackson's hunger for power. **Cite Evidence** What features of this cartoon suggest that Jackson was hungry for power?

Andrew Jackson was a complex person. He had led a violent and adventurous life. He was quick to lose his temper, and he dealt with his enemies harshly. When he became president, his opponents sarcastically called him "King Andrew." Jackson intended to be a strong president by expanding the powers of the presidency. At the same time, Jackson's supporters admired his ability to inspire and lead others. They considered him a man of his word and a champion of the common people.

Jackson's Inauguration As Jackson traveled to Washington to be inaugurated, large crowds cheered him along the way. For the first time, thousands of ordinary people flooded the capital to watch the President take the oath of office. After Jackson was sworn in, the crowd followed the new President to a reception at the White House. One onlooker described the scene with amazement:

Primary Source

"Country men, farmers, gentlemen, mounted and dismounted, boys, women and children, black and white. Carriages, wagons, and carts all pursuing [Jackson] to the President's house."

—Margaret Bayard Smith, *The First Forty Years of Washington Society*

The crowds were so huge, the observer continued, that the President was "almost suffocated and torn to pieces by the people in their eagerness to shake hands." Jackson's critics said the scene showed that "King Mob" was ruling the nation. Amos Kendall, a loyal Jackson supporter, saw the celebration in a more positive way: "It was a proud day for the people. General Jackson is their own President."

Causes of Jacksonian Democracy Andrew Jackson was elected in 1828 largely because white men without property could now vote. He drew much of his support from small farmers, laborers, artisans, and middle-class businessmen on the western frontier. The spread of political power to more people was part of what became known as Jacksonian democracy.

However, Jacksonian democracy was limited to select groups. In particular, Jackson owned slaves at his estate, The Hermitage, and opposed the antislavery movement.

Effects of Jacksonian Democracy Jackson was the first westerner to occupy the White House. His election marked a shift of political power to the West. He was seen as a daring individualist. His image helped shape an American consciousness focused on individual freedom and daring.

Another effect of Jacksonian democracy was the growth in political parties and in citizen participation in the political process. It was one thing to make it legal for nearly all white men to vote. It was another thing to convince them to vote.

Jackson's Democratic Party introduced political campaigns that appealed to common people and their concerns. These campaigns motivated white men to cast their vote for the Democrats.

READING CHECK **Draw Conclusions** Why was Andrew Jackson seen as a champion of the common people?

Analyze Images Jackson lived in this home he called The Hermitage from 1804 until his death in 1845. **Infer** Consider the kind of house Jackson lived in. Why do you think his supporters considered him a common man like themselves?

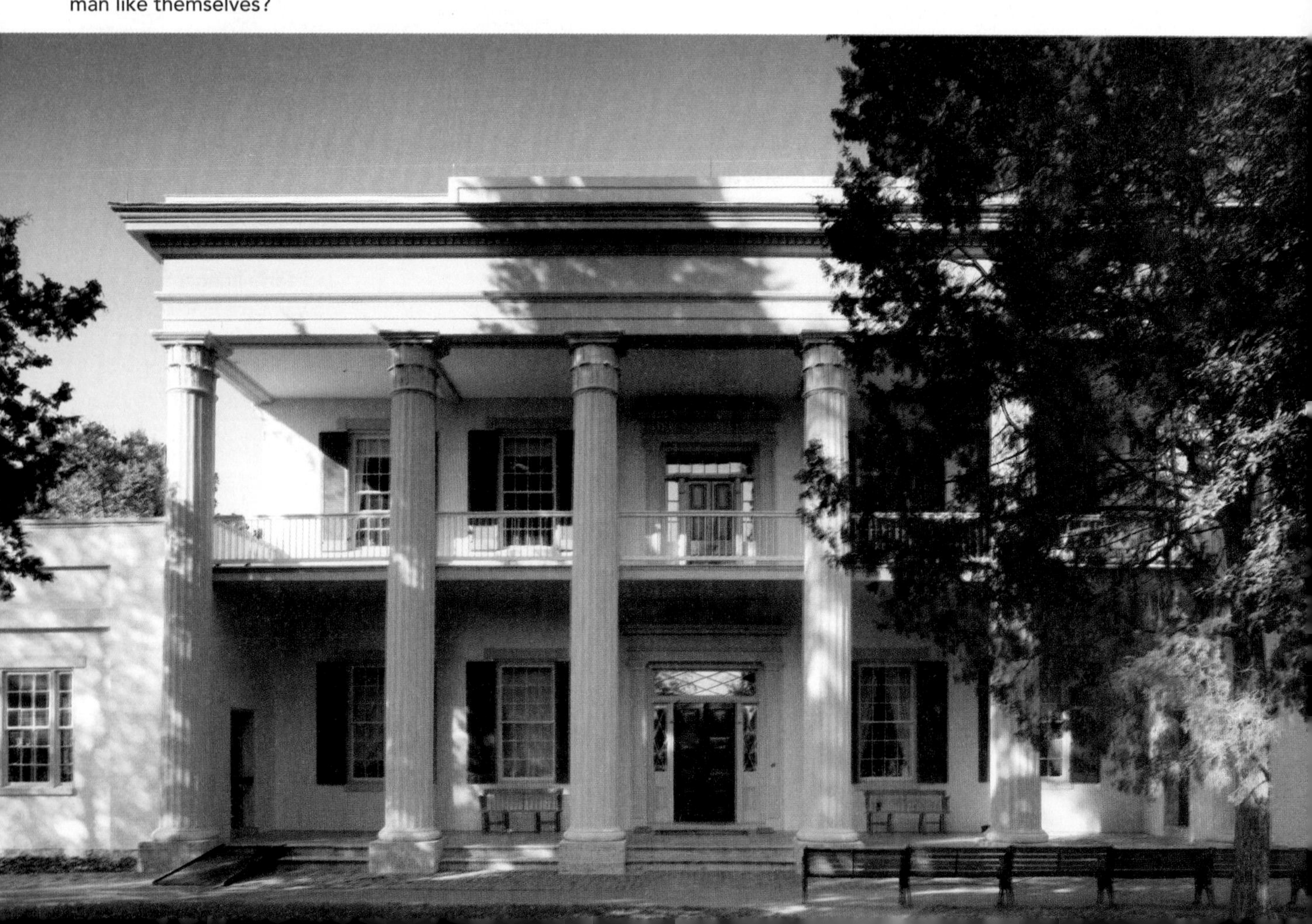

The Spoils System

One of the biggest effects of Jacksonian politics was the development of the **spoils system**. Spoils are loot or plunder. The spoils system was the practice of awarding government jobs to friends and supporters. As one Jackson supporter explained the system: "To the victor belong the spoils."

After taking office, Jackson fired many government employees. He replaced those employees with his supporters. Most other presidents had done the same, but Jackson did it on a much larger scale.

Critics said the spoils system was corrupt and unethical. They accused Jackson of rewarding his supporters instead of choosing qualified men. Jackson replied that giving government jobs to ordinary men would prevent a small group of wealthy men from controlling the government. He felt that most Americans could fill government jobs. "The duties of all public officers are . . . so plain and simple that men of intelligence may readily qualify themselves for their performance," he said.

READING CHECK **Draw Conclusions** Why did Jackson adopt the spoils system?

Analyze Images A cartoonist drew this cartoon in 1877 to criticize the spoils system, which survived long after Jackson introduced it. **Analyze Political Cartoons** How does the cartoon criticize the spoils system?

Lesson Check

Practice Vocabulary

1. How did changes in **suffrage** affect the election of Andrew Jackson as President?
2. According to critics, what was wrong with the **spoils system** during Jackson's presidency?
3. Why did Jackson not win the 1824 presidential election even though he won the **majority** of the popular vote?

Critical Thinking and Writing

4. Compare and Contrast How did Andrew Jackson represent what Alexis de Tocqueville recognized as the American character?
5. Explain an Argument Why would Jackson's supporters oppose the economic programs proposed by Adams during his presidency?
6. Writing Workshop: Introduce Characters Write a short paragraph in your Active Journal from the point of view of a person who is moving westward during this time period. Tell your name, age, and where you come from, tell about your family and your life, and explain why you are moving west. You will use these details in an essay you will write at the end of the Topic.

John Quincy Adams, Speech on Independence Day

On July 4, 1821, U.S. Secretary of State John Quincy Adams gave a speech stating his view of the United States' role in the world. His ideas influenced American foreign policy for decades to come.

◀ John Quincy Adams, Secretary of State 1817–1825

Reading and Vocabulary Support

① What do you think Adams means by "modifications of internal government"?

② *Vicissitudes* means "unexpected changes."

③ *Consecrated* means made sacred or very special.

④ What does "abstained from interference" mean?

⑤ What do you think the word *dominion* means?

In the progress of forty years since the acknowledgement of our Independence, we have gone through many modifications of internal government ①, and through all the vicissitudes ② of peace and war, with other powerful nations. But never, never for a moment have the great principles consecrated ③ by the Declaration of this day been renounced or abandoned.

And . . . what has America done for the benefit of mankind? . . . America [has] proclaimed to mankind the inextinguishable rights of human nature and the only lawful foundations of government. America, in the assembly of nations, . . . has uniformly spoken among them, though often to heedless and often to disdainful ears, the language of equal liberty, of equal justice, and of equal rights. She has . . . respected the independence of other nations while asserting and maintaining her own. She has abstained from interference ④ in the concerns of others. . . . Wherever the standard of freedom and Independence has been or shall be unfurled, there will her heart . . . and her prayers be. But she goes not abroad in search of monsters to destroy. . . . She well knows that by once enlisting under other banners than her own, were they even the banners of foreign Independence, . . . [s]he might become the dictatress of the world, [but s]he would be no longer the ruler of her own spirit. . . . [America's] glory is not dominion ⑤, but liberty. Her march is the march of mind. She has a spear and a shield, but the motto upon her shield is, Freedom, Independence, Peace.

Analyzing Primary Sources

Cite specific evidence from the document to support your answers.

1. **Determine Author's Point of View** According to Adams, what should the United States do if other countries go to war?
2. **Analyze Information** What does Adams mean in saying that by "enlisting under other banners than her own . . . [s]he would be no longer the ruler of her own spirit"?

LESSON 2

Political Conflict and Economic Crisis

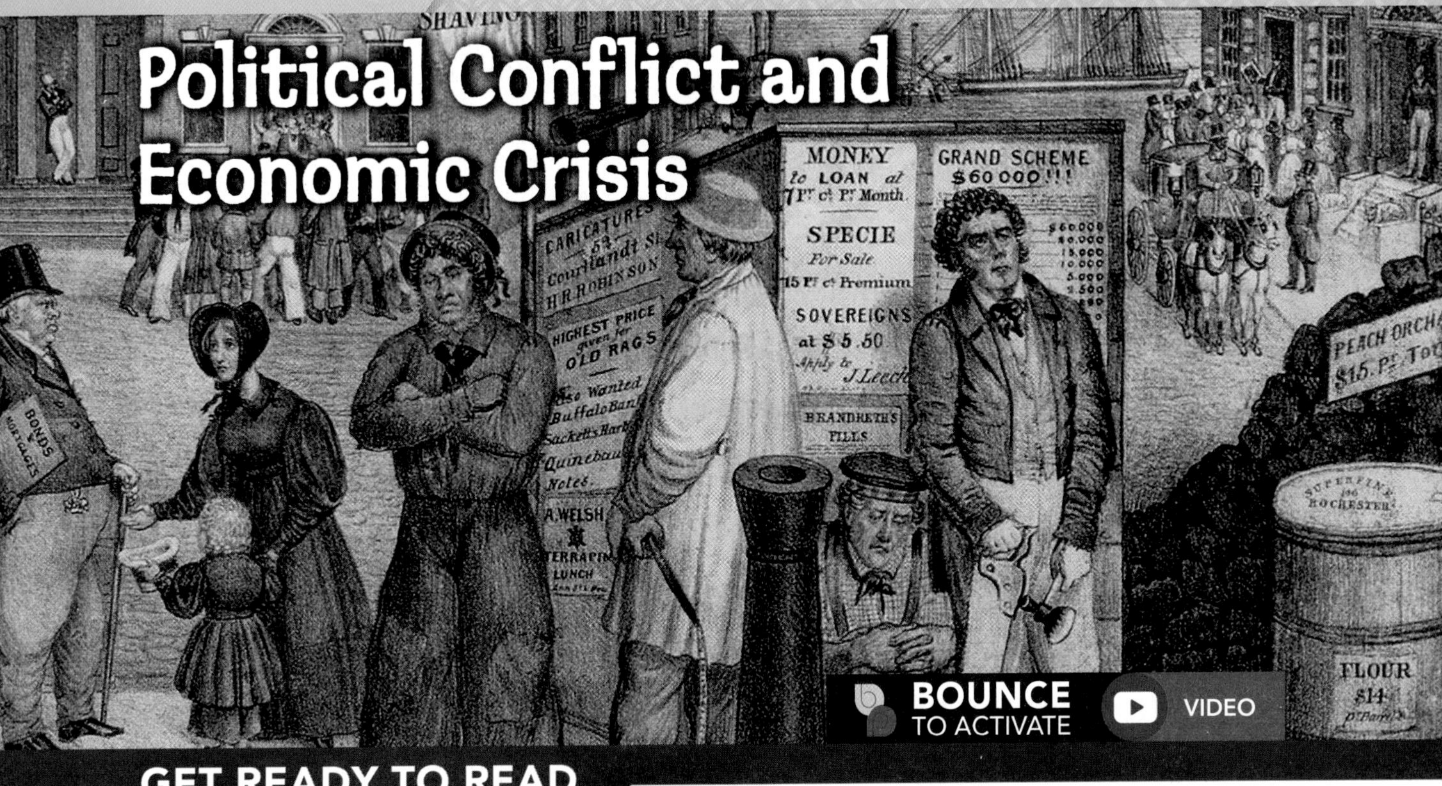

GET READY TO READ

START UP

This illustration shows people suffering from a nationwide economic downturn. How would you respond to an economic panic?

GUIDING QUESTIONS

- How did Andrew Jackson change the country?
- How did Jackson and his opponents clash over the issues of nullification and states' rights?
- Why did Americans disagree about the banking system?
- How did economic issues impact the election of 1840?

TAKE NOTES

Literacy Skills: Compare and Contrast

Use the Graphic Organizer in your Active Journal to take notes as you read the lesson.

PRACTICE VOCABULARY

Use the Vocabulary Builder activity Active Journal in your Journal to practice the vocabulary words.

Vocabulary		Academic Vocabulary
states' rights	caucus	implicit
Nullification Act	nominating convention	speculation
depression		

During Jackson's two terms as President, conflicts and crises shook the nation. Some were thrust upon Jackson by the grinding of sectional rivalries. Others were events of his own making. The effects of his responses to these crises were felt throughout the nation for decades to come.

A Conflict Over States' Rights

The first crisis Jackson faced arose almost immediately after he entered office. It was an intense quarrel over **states' rights**, or the rights of states to exercise power independent of the federal government.

Regional Differences on the States' Rights Issue The conflict over states' rights divided the country along regional lines. The United States at the time was made up of three regions.

The North included the New England and Middle Atlantic states. Manufacturing and trade were very important to the economy of the North.

Analyze Images The ❶ North, ❷ South, and ❸ West had economies based in different kinds of work and businesses. **Identify Supporting Details** How did the different regional economies depend on each other?

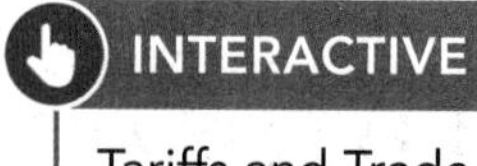

INTERACTIVE

Tariffs and Trade

The West was the region we now know as the Midwest. Its economy was based mainly on raising of livestock and farming food crops.

Finally, the South consisted of today's Southeast and South Central states. The South's people relied heavily on farming cash crops for export, such as cotton and tobacco.

Politically, northerners generally favored a strong federal government, which they saw as necessary to promote manufacturing and trade. Because white southerners feared the domination of the North and national policies that could hurt their interests, they tended to support stronger states' rights. These differences often made it hard for people from the North and South to agree on political issues.

Westerners sometimes sided with the North and sometimes with the South. For example, westerners wanted internal improvements for transportation, which most northerners supported. Westerners also wanted to be free to move into new territories, which white southerners also wanted. Some westerners supported slavery, while others did not. In general, westerners agreed with northerners about tariffs.

Anger Over Tariffs In 1828, before Jackson took office, Congress passed the highest tariff in the history of the nation. Manufacturers, most of whom lived in the North, were helped by the tariff. It protected them from foreign competition.

Southern planters, however, called it the Tariff of Abominations. An abomination is something that is wrong and evil. These planters sold much of their cotton to Britain and bought British manufactured goods in return. A high tariff would mean that Americans had to pay more for those British goods. Worse still, planters feared that if the United States imposed a tariff on British manufactures, Britain would respond by imposing a tariff on American cotton. Many southerners thought the tariff was unconstitutional.

Debate Over Nullification A leader in the South's fight against the tariff was Vice President John Calhoun of South Carolina. He claimed that a state had the right to nullify, or cancel, a federal law that the state considered to be unconstitutional. This idea is called nullification. Calhoun believed that the states could nullify federal laws, because the states had joined together to form the federal government based on their understanding of the Constitution.

Daniel Webster, a senator from Massachusetts, disagreed. He made a speech in 1830 to the Senate attacking the idea of nullification. The Constitution, he said, united the American people, not just the states, as a nation. If states had the right to nullify federal laws, the nation would fall apart. The U.S. Supreme Court had also ruled against earlier attempts at nullification. The justices said that the provisions of Article III of the U.S. Constitution gave federal courts, not states, the right to decide on the constitutionality of federal laws. President Jackson agreed with the views of Webster and the Supreme Court. Because Calhoun strongly disagreed with Jackson, he resigned from the office of vice president. He was then elected senator from South Carolina. The debate over nullification would continue for years.

▲ John Caldwell Calhoun of South Carolina served as representative, senator, secretary of war, secretary of state, and vice president twice.

The Nullification Act Leads to Crisis Anger against the tariff increased in the South. Congress passed a new law in 1832 that lowered the tariff slightly. South Carolina was not satisfied. It passed the **Nullification Act**, declaring the new tariff illegal. It also threatened to secede, or withdraw, from the Union if challenged. Jackson was furious. He knew that nullification could lead to civil war.

Milestones in the States' Rights Debate

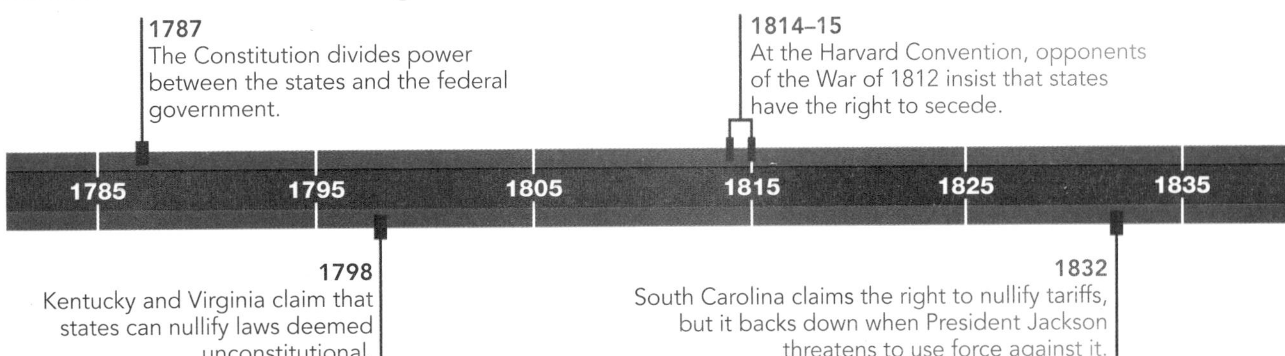

Analyze Timelines As the timeline shows, the states' rights conflict began early in the nation's history. **Identify** an instance on the timeline of tension between a specific state and the federal government. How might sectionalism have contributed to this tension?

To defuse the crisis, Henry Clay, now a senator from Kentucky, proposed a lower, compromise tariff, which President Jackson supported. Jackson also asked Congress to pass the Force bill, which would allow the President to use the army, if necessary, to enforce the tariff. Daniel Webster sided with Jackson on the Force bill but opposed Clay's compromise tariff. However, Congress passed both the compromise tariff and the Force bill.

Faced with Jackson's firm stand, no other state chose to support South Carolina. When Calhoun supported the compromise tariff, South Carolina repealed its Nullification Act, and the Nullification Crisis passed. National identity had proven stronger than a state's claim to sovereignty.

While Jackson's actions kept South Carolina in the union and reinforced federal authority, they did not bring the quarrel to a close. In the years ahead, tensions between the North and South would lead to increased sectionalism.

READING CHECK **Summarize** Why did Webster and Jackson oppose nullification?

The Bank War

In another political battle that had a long-term effect on the country, Jackson waged war against the Second Bank of the United States. Like many westerners, Jackson thought that the Bank was too powerful and needed to be eliminated. Jackson's Democratic Party opposed the Bank. The Whig Party, however, supported the Bank. Whigs believed that the Bank was needed to regulate lending by state banks to arrest the growth of debts that could not be repaid.

Analyze Images Senator Daniel Webster defended the interests of his home state of Massachusetts by arguing that states could not nullify the Tariff of 1828. **Explain an Argument** Why is it important for representatives to support their positions with good reasons?

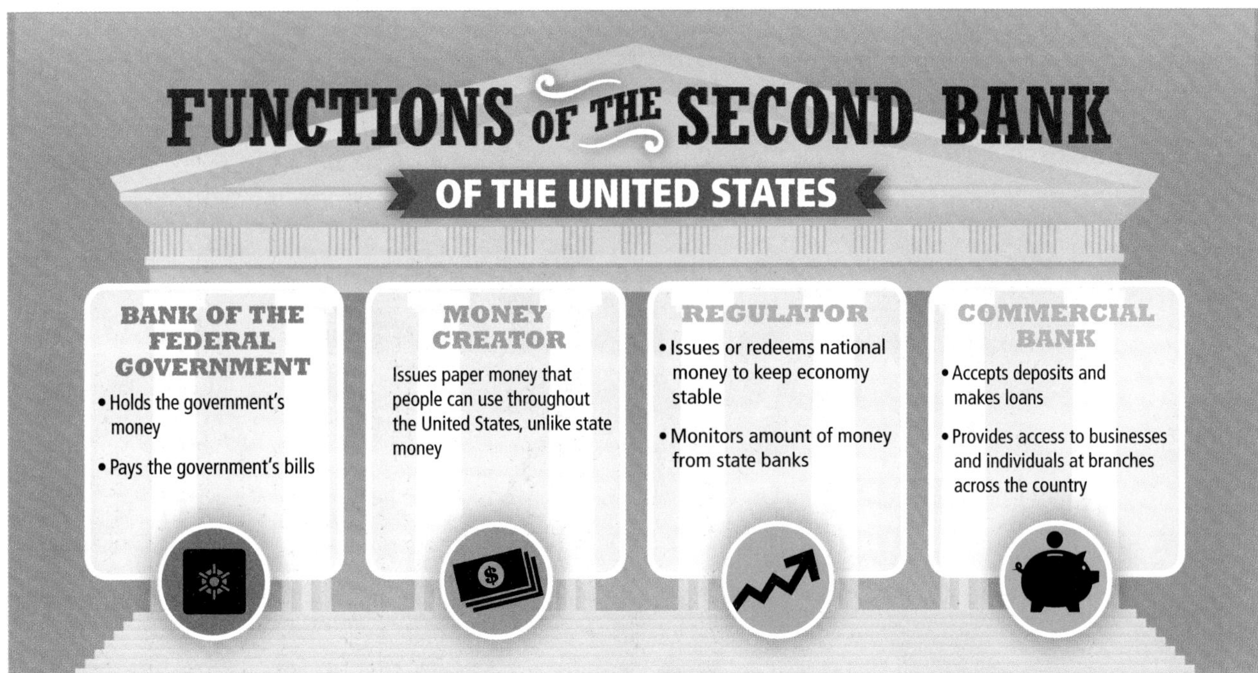

Analyze Charts The Second Bank of the United States was founded to help the federal government manage its income and expenses. **Classify and Categorize** How was the Bank involved in the nation's economy?

A Controversial Bank The Second Bank of the United States had been a subject of dispute since its early days. The Bank had great power because it controlled loans made by state banks. When the Bank's directors thought that state banks were owed too much money, they limited the amount these banks could lend. The cutbacks angered farmers and merchants, who often needed to borrow money to buy land or finance new businesses.

President Jackson and other leading Democrats saw the Bank as undemocratic. Although Congress created the Bank, it was run by private bankers. Jackson condemned these men as agents of "special privilege" who grew rich with public funds. He especially disliked Nicholas Biddle, president of the Bank since 1823.

With Biddle running the Bank, the U.S. economy had experienced stability and prosperity. However, Biddle was known to make loans to friends while turning down loans to people who opposed the Bank. Among these were many of Jackson's strongest supporters. Jackson felt that Biddle used the Bank to benefit the rich. He also resented Biddle's influence over certain members of Congress.

The Bank Applies for Renewal Biddle and other Whigs worried that the President might try to destroy the Bank. Two Whig senators, Henry Clay and Daniel Webster, thought of a way they might save the Bank and defeat Jackson in the upcoming election at the same time.

The Bank's charter was not due for renewal by Congress until 1836. However, Clay and Webster wanted to make the Bank an issue in the 1832 election. They persuaded Biddle to apply for renewal early. The Whigs believed that most Americans appreciated the role of the Bank in the nation's prosperity. If Jackson vetoed the bill to renew the charter, they felt sure that he would anger voters and lose the election.

Analyze Images In this cartoon, President Jackson fights a snake representing the Bank and its branches. The largest head is Nicholas Biddle's. **Analyze Cartoons** How is Jackson trying to destroy the Bank?

Clay was able to push the charter renewal bill through Congress in 1832. Jackson was sick in bed when he heard that Congress had renewed the Bank's charter. "The Bank . . . is trying to kill me," Jackson fumed, "but I will kill it!"

Jackson Cuts Off the Bank In an angry message to Congress, Jackson vetoed the Bank bill. He gave two reasons for his veto. For one, he believed that the Bank helped aristocrats at the expense of the common people. He warned:

Primary Source

> "When the laws undertake . . . to make the rich richer and the potent more powerful, the humble members of the society—the farmers, mechanics, and laborers—who have neither the time nor the means of [getting] like favors for themselves . . . have a right to complain of the injustices of their government."
>
> —Andrew Jackson, Veto Message, July 10, 1832

Jackson's other reason for vetoing the bank bill was his belief that the Bank was unconstitutional. Like other Democrats, Jackson believed that the federal government could not charter a bank because the Constitution did not explicitly give it the power to do so.

Jackson had already lost this argument. In *McCulloch* v. *Maryland*, the Supreme Court had ruled that the "necessary and proper clause" of the

Constitution **implicitly** gave the federal government the right to create a bank. This clause states that the federal government has the power "To make all Laws which shall be necessary and proper for carrying into Execution the . . . Powers [already described], and all other Powers vested by this Constitution." However, Jackson did not accept the court's ruling. He continued to believe that only states had the right to charter banks.

Academic Vocabulary
implicit • *adv.*, not expressed directly but able to be understood or inferred

As they had planned, the Whigs made the Bank a major issue in the election of 1832. They chose Henry Clay as their candidate to run against Andrew Jackson.

When the votes were counted, however, Jackson had won a stunning election victory. The common people had surprised the Whigs by supporting Jackson and rejecting the Bank of the United States.

The Bank Loses Its National Role Without a new charter, the Bank would have to close in 1836. Jackson refused to wait. He ordered Secretary of the Treasury Roger Taney to stop putting government money in the Bank. Instead, Taney deposited federal money in state banks. They became known as pet banks because Taney and his friends controlled many of them.

The loss of its federal deposits crippled the Second Bank of the United States. Its elimination as a national bank was another effect of Jackson's presidency—one that would have lasting impact. The end of the Bank contributed to an economic crisis that would have to be faced by the next President of the United States.

Without a national bank, responsibility for regulating banks fell to individual states. The period from the late 1830s until the 1860s is known as the state banking era. During this time, each state set its own rules for banks. Lax state regulations allowed banks to take risks.

READING CHECK **Identify Supporting Details** What did Jackson do with the government's money after he ordered that it should no longer be deposited in the Second National Bank?

Analyze Images During the state banking era, Americans relied on currency issued by state or private banks like that shown. Money from banks with poor reputations might not be accepted by other banks or merchants. **Infer** How might a person judge whether a bank's currency is trustworthy?

Academic Vocabulary
speculation • *n.*, risky buying in hope of a large profit

Economic Crisis and Political Changes

Following tradition, Andrew Jackson left office after two terms. Americans elected Martin Van Buren to succeed him as President. Although Van Buren did not have Jackson's popularity, he was clever and intelligent. As President, however, Van Buren needed more than sharp political instincts.

The Panic of 1837 Before leaving office, Jackson had been alarmed at wild **speculation**, or risky investment, in land. Since the Bank of the United States had closed, state banks were printing and lending money without limit. Speculators were borrowing more and more money to buy land and driving land prices up.

To slow this process, Jackson had ordered that anyone buying public land had to pay for it with gold or silver. This sent speculators and others rushing to state banks to exchange their paper money for gold and silver. However, many banks had loaned too much money. If a bank did not have enough gold and silver to buy back the notes it had issued, it could go broke and be forced to close.

Analyze Images A debtor negotiates with a merchant (left), a customer wonders how he can pay his bill (center), and a man warms himself at a stove (right). **Draw Conclusions** How did the Panic of 1837 affect people differently?

When Van Buren took office, the situation had only worsened. As more and more banks failed, the nation fell into a deep economic **depression**, a period when the economy shrinks and many people lose their jobs. This depression, known as The Panic of 1837, was the worst economic crisis the nation had yet known. It lasted five years. During the worst period, 90 percent of the nation's factories were closed. Unemployment was widespread. Hundreds of thousands of people were out of work.

Although many Americans blamed Van Buren and his policies for the economic depression, the roots of the problem lay in Jackson's administration. His closure of the Bank and his efforts to rein in land speculation both contributed to the crisis. Van Buren was not without fault, however. He believed in laissez-faire economics—the idea that government should play as small a role as possible in the economy. As the depression wore on, Van Buren became increasingly unpopular. His opponents called him "Martin Van Ruin."

▲ A national nominating convention

Party Caucuses and Conventions By the time of the next presidential election in 1840, Whigs and Democrats had developed more democratic ways to choose candidates for President. In the past, powerful members of each party had held a **caucus**, or private meeting, to choose their candidate. Critics called the caucus system undemocratic because only a few powerful people were able to take part in it.

In the 1830s, each party began to hold a national **nominating convention**, where delegates from all the states met to choose the party's candidate for President. Party leaders might still dominate a particular convention, but the people could now have some influence in the nominating process. Also, state nominating conventions encouraged citizen participation in elections. Once citizens learned about the events of the convention, they would work for their party's choices. Today, the major political parties still hold state and national conventions.

Democrats Lose the Election of 1840 Although Van Buren had lost support, the Democrats chose him to run for reelection in 1840. The Whigs chose William Henry Harrison of Ohio as their presidential candidate and John Tyler of Virginia as their vice presidential candidate. Their policies included creating a new Bank of the United States, improving roads and canals, and demanding a high tariff.

Choosing a Presidential Candidate

Analyze Images In 1840, just as in the present time, political parties distributed campaign buttons, posters, flags, and other items to promote their party's candidate. **Synthesize Visual Evidence** What ideas from Harrison's campaign did these buttons represent?

Harrison was known as the hero of the Battle of Tippecanoe, which was fought between the American military and a Shawnee-led alliance in 1811. To appeal to voters, the Whigs focused on Harrison's war record. "Tippecanoe and Tyler too" became their campaign slogan. The Whigs created an image of Harrison as a "man of the people" from the western frontier. They presented him as a humble farmer and boasted that he had been born in a log cabin. In fact, Harrison was a wealthy, educated man who, at the time of the campaign, lived in a large mansion.

Harrison won the election. However, Whig hopes were dashed when, soon after taking office, President Harrison died of pneumonia. John Tyler then became President. President Tyler failed to live up to Whig expectations and opposed many Whig policies. In response, the Whigs threw Tyler out of their party just months after he took office.

READING CHECK **Identify Supporting Details** How did President Jackson attempt to slow the land speculation that led to the Panic of 1837?

Lesson Check

Practice Vocabulary

1. How was the **Nullification Act** justified by those who believed in **states' rights**?
2. How does an economic **depression** affect employment?
3. How is a **caucus** different from a **nominating convention**?

Critical Thinking and Writing

4. **Infer** Why do you suppose Andrew Jackson supported Henry Clay's proposed compromise over nullification even though they had been enemies previously?
5. **Understand Effects** Why was it such a disaster for the nation when Andrew Jackson crippled the Second National Bank?
6. **Writing Workshop: Establish Setting** Write three or four sentences in your Active Journal describing what you see, hear, feel, and smell on a journey west during this time period. You will use these details in the narrative you will write at the end of the Topic. These details will make your narrative vivid and real for your readers.

Interpret Economic Performance

Follow these steps to help you interpret economic performance.

INTERACTIVE
Analyze Data and Models

1 Identify the type of statistics being presented Economists use statistics called economic indicators. These statistics help them to determine if the economy is improving or declining. They include

- **Money supply:** total amount of money that a country has in circulation
- **GDP:** total market value of all goods and services produced by a country
- **Current Employment Statistics, or CES:** information on rates of employment, unemployment, and wages and earnings
- **Housing Starts:** number of new private homes and housing units being built
- **Consumer Price Index, or CPI:** measures changes in retail prices
- **Producer Price Index, or PPI:** measures the average selling price of goods and services that are produced in a country
- **Consumer Confidence Index, or CCI:** tracks how consumers feel about the state of the economy
- **Retail Numbers:** statistics measuring sales in retail and food service industries
- **Manufacturing Trade Inventories and Sales:** tracks production, trade sales, and shipments by manufacturers
- **Standard & Poor's 500 Stock Index, or S&P 500:** a list of 500 stocks that help economists and the financial industry measure how companies are performing

2 Determine how the information is being presented Is the information displayed in a line graph, a bar graph, a circle graph, or in some other type of figure?

3 Evaluate what the graph or figure is displaying Does the information show the relationship between two different economic factors? Is it showing an increase or a decrease?

Money Supply, 1832–1836

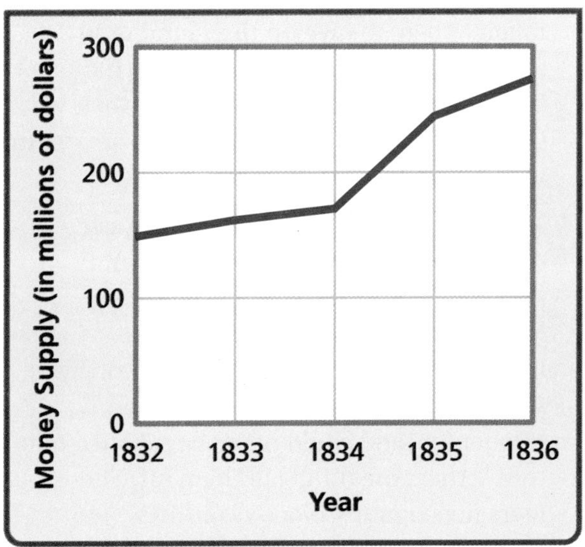

Price Levels, 1832–1836

Year	Index of Prices (year-to-year percentage change)	Total Value of Gold and Silver Coins (in millions of dollars)
1832	–	31
1833	4	41
1834	5	51
1835	20	65
1836	13	73

LESSON 3

Conflict with American Indians

GET READY TO READ

START UP

The U.S. Army captured these Seminole chiefs in 1824. Why did white Americans oust American Indians from their homes?

GUIDING QUESTIONS

- How did Indian removal change the country?
- What did the frontier mean to the nation in the first half of the nineteenth century?
- Describe the cultures of the American Indians living west of the Appalachians.

TAKE NOTES

Literacy Skills: Cite Evidence

Use the Graphic Organizer in your Active Journal to take notes as you read the lesson.

PRACTICE VOCABULARY

Use the Vocabulary Builder activity in your Active Journal to practice the vocabulary words.

Vocabulary		Academic Vocabulary
frontier	Indian Territory	acquire
Worcester v. *Georgia*	Trail of Tears	exceedingly
Indian Removal Act		

When the first Europeans arrived in North America, they settled on lands that had belonged to American Indians. Although the two groups made attempts to cooperate, repeated conflicts brought tension, mistrust, and sometimes violence.

American Indians and the Frontier

As American settlers moved West in the early 1800s, they often attacked American Indians to force them to give up their land or in response to hostile raids. American Indians, in turn, attacked settlers to protect their way of life. Oftentimes the settlers were greater in number and better armed.

A History of Conflict and Prejudice

On both sides, biases, stereotypes, and prejudices led to mistrust and hostility. Most white settlers saw American Indians as dangerous and untrustworthy. American Indians feared that settlers' hunger for land could never be satisfied and that settlers meant to kill them off. These fears fueled many bloody conflicts.

As you have learned, before the Revolution, the British had made peace with American Indian groups by drawing the Proclamation Line of 1763 through the Appalachian Mountains. This line marked roughly the **frontier**, or edge, of white settlement. The frontier separated white settlers from the lands beyond, which they regarded as free and open to them.

The 1763 Proclamation forbade whites to settle west of the line. This gave American Indians some protection from settlers who wanted to take over their lands. Seeing the British as protectors, many American Indians had sided with them during the Revolutionary War.

After the war, Congress passed the Northwest Ordinance to bring order to white settlement of the Northwest Territory. One part of the ordinance provided a method for settlers to **acquire** land and eventually achieve statehood. The Ordinance fueled even more movement of people into the territory.

Believing their land and culture were at stake, American Indians attacked white settlements in the new Northwest Territory. The Battle of Tippecanoe, in Indiana in 1811, was a major defeat for Shawnee leader Tecumseh and his forces during this time of unrest.

When conflict between the United Kingdom and the United States broke out again in the War of 1812, many, but not all, American Indian groups again sided with the British. A group of Creek in present-day Georgia and Alabama formed an alliance with both Tecumseh and the British. Meanwhile, other Creeks and the neighboring Choctaw sided with the United States. As you have learned, forces led by Andrew Jackson defeated the Creeks allied with the British.

Academic Vocabulary

acquire • *v.*, to get (something)

Selected Native American Groups, 1820

GEOGRAPHY SKILLS

This map shows the territories of several American Indian groups in 1820.

1. **Location** With a partner, take turns describing the location of each group on the map.
2. **Draw Conclusions** Considering where these American Indian groups lived, what would happen to them as settlers continued to move west?

Analyze Images Sequoyah, a Cherokee leader, developed and taught his people a new writing system for the sounds of the Cherokee language. **Draw Conclusions** Do you think Sequoyah's writing system helped ease conflicts with white settlers? Why, or why not?

The conflicts usually ended badly for the American Indians. They either lost in battle or signed treaties with the government that were soon broken. The first treaty between the U.S. government and American Indians was signed in 1778. Few promises made in that treaty with the Delaware were kept. Likewise, in 1794, the Pickering Treaty between the United States and the Iroquois was also broken. The treaty returned over a million acres to the Iroquois, but much of the land was taken again. American Indians were **exceedingly** distrustful of their white neighbors.

Efforts to Make Peace The Chickasaw, Choctaw, Creek, Seminole, and Cherokee nations lived in parts of what are now Mississippi, Alabama, Florida, Georgia, North Carolina, and Tennessee. The Shawnee, Potawatomi, Sauk, and Fox nations lived in parts of present-day Michigan, Ohio, Indiana, Illinois, and Wisconsin. Many hoped to live in peace with their white neighbors on the frontier.

The Choctaw believed they would be allowed to keep their land because they had sided with the United States during the War of 1812. Other tribes, like the Cherokee nation, adopted European customs, hoping this would help them to preserve their land. The Cherokee created a legal system and government that blended European and Cherokee traditions. In 1821, Sequoyah (suh KWOH yuh), a Cherokee man, created a writing system for his people. Using Sequoyah's letters, Cherokee children learned to read and write. The Cherokees also published a newspaper.

The efforts of American Indians to adopt European ways failed to end the conflict with white settlers. The American Indians' fertile land remained attractive to white settlers, and white settlers feared more violent conflict with American Indians.

READING CHECK **Generate Explanations** Why did tensions exist between American Indian groups and white settlers?

American Indian Removal

In the eyes of state and federal officials, American Indians east of the Mississippi River stood in the way of westward expansion of the United States. At first, they aimed to convince American Indians to rely less on hunting. They wanted them to start farming cash crops such as tobacco and cotton in addition to food crops. These government leaders thought that American Indians would then sell any land that they weren't farming to white settlers. While many American Indians in the South did adopt cash-crop farming, they were not willing to sell their land. Meanwhile, prejudices on both sides stood in the way of white settlers and American Indians living side by side.

Academic Vocabulary

exceedingly • *adv.*, to a very great degree; extremely

Pressure on American Indians Increases In 1825, President James Monroe had suggested moving all American Indians living east of the Mississippi to land west of the river. At that time, nothing came of the plan. Yet, year by year, the pressure on the American Indians living along the frontier grew. Those in the North occupied land good for growing corn and wheat and raising livestock. The Northwest Ordinance had already marked this land for white settlers.

In the South, American Indians occupied land that was good for growing cotton. Around them, more and more white settlers arrived, many with enslaved African Americans, seeking to acquire land to grow cotton. Many white southerners were demanding that American Indians be removed by force.

In 1825 and 1827, the state of Georgia passed laws forcing the Creeks to give up most of their land. Laws such as these had previously been struck down by the Supreme Court in *Johnson* v. *M'Intosh* (1823). The ruling in this case stated that only the federal government could acquire land from American Indians, not individuals or state governments.

Worcester* v. *Georgia* Decision Is Ignored** Georgia's actions were challenged in two suits that reached the Supreme Court. The decision in the first suit went against the Cherokees. In *Cherokee Nation* v. *Georgia* (1831), the Court decided that American Indian groups were not independent nations and so could not sue Georgia in court. The ruling meant the Cherokee could not stop Georgia from enforcing its law. But in ***Worcester* v. *Georgia (1832), the Court ruled that no state had the authority to enforce its laws within Indian territory. Only the federal government had authority over American Indian lands. Therefore, Georgia could not remove the Cherokee.

Analyze Images Traditional Cherokee homes were made with woven twigs—seen here in the home's window—and daub plaster over a pole frame. **Summarize** Why were the Cherokee forced to leave their homes?

▲ John Ross was the principal chief, or highest leader, of the Cherokee people when they challenged Georgia in the Supreme Court and later when they were forced to move west.

President Jackson disagreed with the ruling in *Worcester* v. *Georgia*. In the Nullification Crisis, Jackson had defended federal power. In the Cherokee case, however, he backed states' rights. Demonstrating that he was only willing to uphold the law when it suited his purpose, Jackson is reported to have said: "John Marshall has made his decision; now let him enforce it!" Instead, Jackson continued to displace American Indians from their homelands.

The Indian Removal Act At Jackson's urging, in 1830 Congress passed the **Indian Removal Act**. This law let the government take land from American Indians in exchange for land west of the Mississippi River. At the time, more than 100,000 American Indians still lived in the East.

Most white Americans, especially those in the South, supported the removal. They wanted the land for farming and new settlements. Some supported removal to protect the American Indians from conflicts with settlers. They assumed that the United States would never expand past the Mississippi, so American Indians could live there in peace. Some Americans believed the removal was cruel and unfair, but their protests were ignored.

The Indian Removal Act resulted in the expulsion of thousands of American Indians from their homes. In the North, the Ottawa, Potawatomi, Sauk, and Fox peoples all signed treaties to move west to Indian Territories in what are now Kansas and Oklahoma. While most members of these groups left, a few stayed behind in what are now Michigan and Wisconsin.

Numbers Affected by American Indian Removal

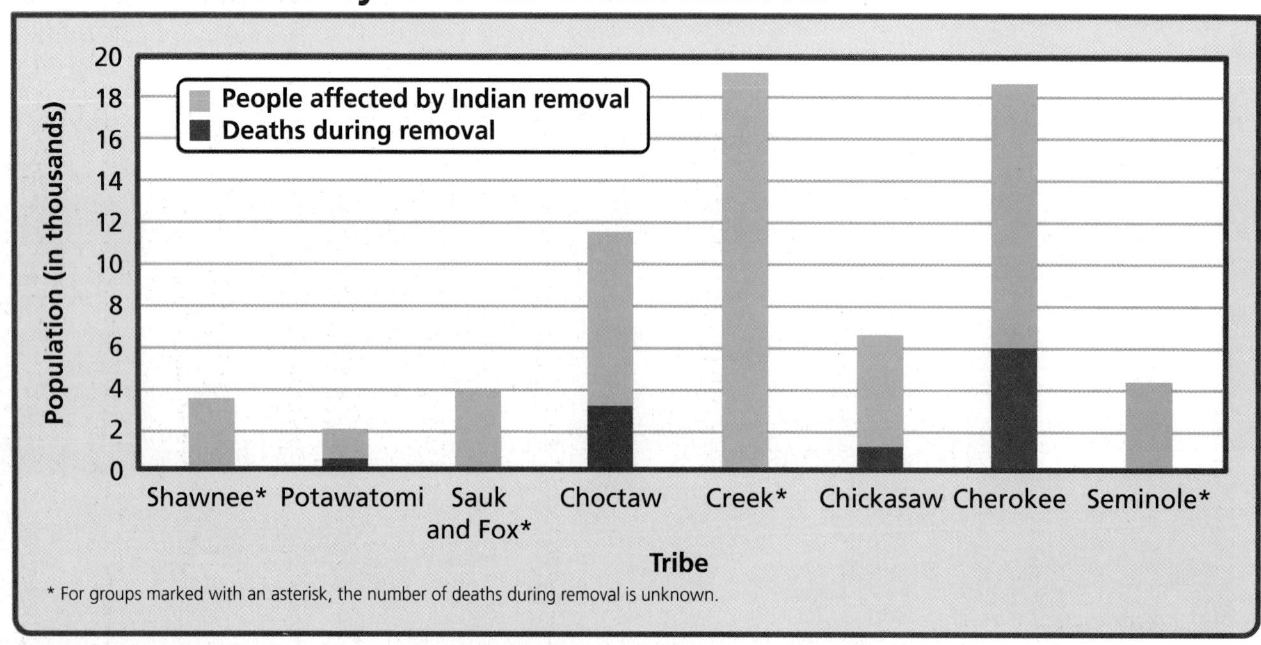

Analyze Images Several groups affected by American Indian removal are shown here. **Identify Patterns** Look at the groups whose number of deaths is known. About what proportion of those groups died during removal?

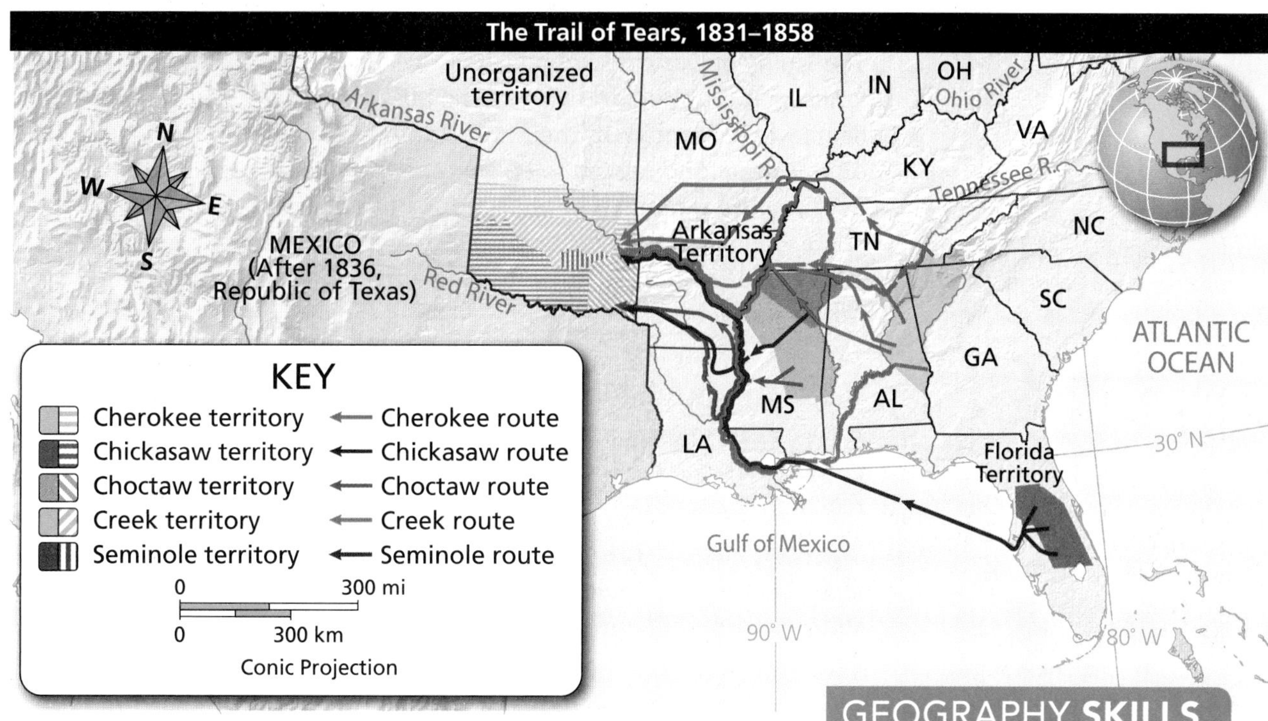

GEOGRAPHY SKILLS

This map shows the routes and destinations of the American Indians forced from their homes in the East.

1. **Movement** With a partner, use the scale to estimate how far the Cherokee walked on the Trail of Tears.
2. **Identify Cause and Effect** How might the distance the Cherokee walked help explain why so many died on the journey?

Among the groups who tried to refuse to sign treaties were the Choctaw, Chickasaw, Cherokee, and Seminole. Ultimately, they were forced to sign and forced from their homelands.

Jackson's American Indian removal policy changed the country in several ways. First, it opened up vast areas of the South to white settlers. Many brought slaves with them. So by removing the American Indians, slavery expanded to new places and more states and became more entrenched.

Also because of Jackson's policy, few American Indians today live east of the Mississippi. As a result, most events in the contemporary United States involving American Indians take place in the West.

As well, the policy of taking rich, fertile, forested land from American Indians and restricting them to semi-arid areas in the far West had enormous consequences for American Indians. It impoverished them for generations, separated them from their ancestors' burial grounds, and all but ended their traditional ways of life.

READING CHECK **Explain** Why did Congress pass the Indian Removal Act?

Southern American Indians on the Trail of Tears

Faced with threats of military action, most American Indian leaders in the South saw no choice but to sign new treaties giving up their lands. They agreed to move to what was called the **Indian Territory**. Today, most of that area is in the state of Oklahoma.

Southern Native Americans on the Trail of Tears

The Choctaw The Choctaw signed the first removal treaty in 1830. The Treaty of Dancing Rabbit Creek exchanged the Choctaw's tribal lands for a grant of land west of the Mississippi River. The people would be allowed to remain in their homeland if they gave up their tribal organization and agreed to be governed as citizens of Mississippi. A few Choctaw remained in Mississippi, but upwards of 15,000 people chose to leave so as to preserve some aspects of their culture. Between 1831 and 1833 the Choctaw made their way west, closely guarded by American soldiers.

The federal government, however, did not provide enough tents, food, blankets, shoes, winter clothes, or other supplies. Heavy rain and snow caused enormous suffering. An army lieutenant wrote that one group "walked for 24 hours barefoot through the snow and ice" before reaching shelter.

The Chickasaw The Chickasaw people held out for payment for their lands before they would agree to move. Finally, in 1837, the United States government agreed to pay them $3 million.

Expecting to receive this money, the Chickasaw spent $500,000 to purchase land from the Choctaw in what is now Oklahoma. The U.S. government, though, failed to pay the agreed amount for 30 years. As the Chickasaw trekked to their new land, many became ill and died.

Analyze Images The path of the Trail of Tears has been preserved as a National Historic Trail. It crosses through nine states, from Georgia to Oklahoma. **Synthesize Visual Information** What do you think you might learn from walking the actual route of the Trail of Tears?

The Cherokee The Cherokee also tried to hold out. They were still on their land in 1836 when Jackson left office. A small group of Cherokee agreed to become citizens of North Carolina, and so were allowed to stay. Other Cherokee hid in remote mountain camps.

Finally, President Van Buren forced those Cherokee who had not made agreements and those who were not in hiding from their homes. In the winter of 1838–1839, the U.S. Army marched more than 15,000 Cherokee westward. They trekked hundreds of miles over a period of several months to reach Indian Territory. Thousands perished during the march, mostly children and the elderly.

The Cherokee's long, sorrowful journey west became known as the **Trail of Tears**. A soldier's description helps explain why:

Primary Source

"On the morning of November 17th, we encountered a terrific sleet and snow storm with freezing temperatures, and from that day until we reached the end of the fateful journey on March the 27th, 1839, the sufferings of the Cherokee were awful. The trail of the exiles was a trail of death."

—Memoirs of Private John G. Burnett, December 1890

Analyze Images Seminoles began building chickee-style homes using palmetto thatch and a cypress log frame. **Use Visual Information** How did chickee-style homes help Seminoles to flee from the pursuing U.S. Army?

The Seminole Resist In Florida, people of the Seminole nation also resisted removal. Led by Chief Osceola (ah see OH luh), they began fighting the United States Army in 1835. This conflict, known as the Second Seminole War, was the costliest war ever waged to gain Indian lands. Although most of the Seminole people were forced to leave Florida, starting in 1855, the United States waged a Third Seminole War to hunt down Seminoles who still resisted relocation.

While Jackson's Indian removal cleared the area east of the Mississippi River for white settlement, settlers already had their eyes on lands west of the Mississippi, too. These lands represented the new frontier. Although occupied by American Indians who had their own cultures and civilization, to white settlers, the term *frontier* meant wild and uncivilized. In their minds, it was free and theirs for the taking. In a few years more, settlers would be streaming into these new lands as they had recently streamed into the Northwest Territory and the South.

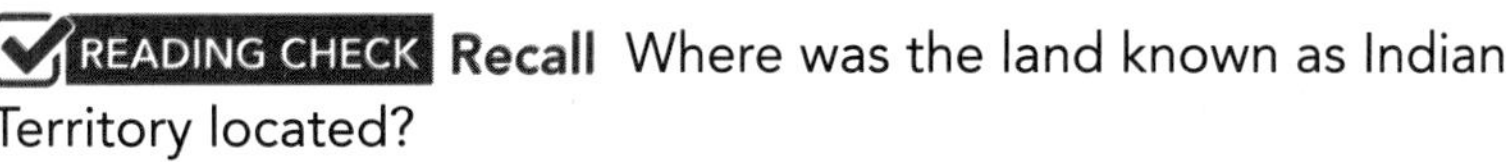

READING CHECK **Recall** Where was the land known as Indian Territory located?

Lesson Check

Practice Vocabulary

1. How did the **frontier** differ from the settled areas along the east coast?
2. How did the **Indian Removal Act** lead to the **Trail of Tears**?
3. What and where was the **Indian Territory**?

Critical Thinking and Writing

4. **Summarize** Why were white settlers and American Indians typically unable to live peacefully in neighboring areas?
5. **Draw Conclusions** What does *Worcester* v. *Georgia* demonstrate about the power of the judiciary?
6. **Writing Workshop: Organize Sequence of Events** In your Active Journal, list the main events you will tell about that take place on your journey west. Number them in the order you will write about them. You will follow this sequence of events in the narrative you will write at the end of the Topic.

LESSON 4
Westward Movement

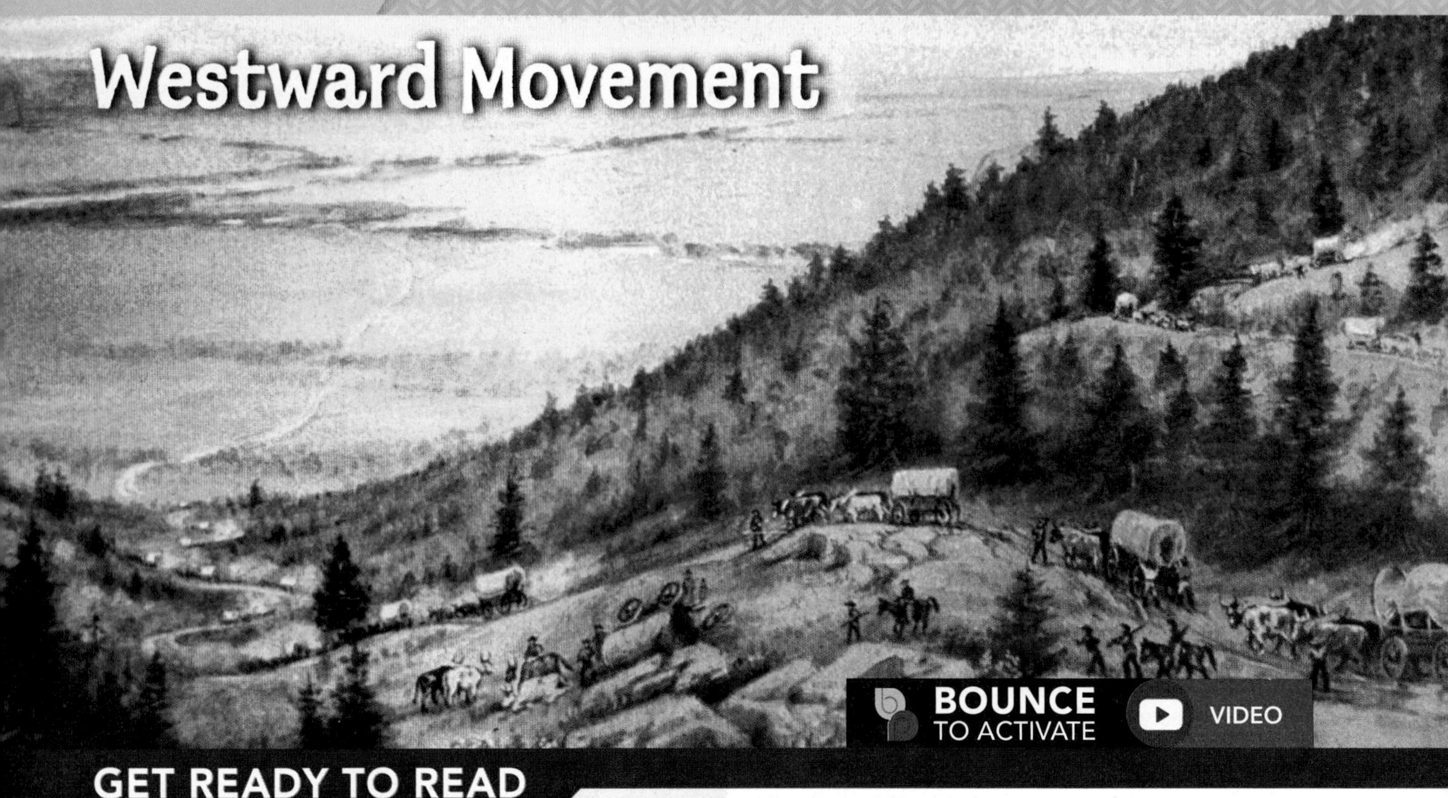

GET READY TO READ

START UP

Examine this painting of wagons heading west. What might people have thought as they looked across the vast expanse ahead of them?

GUIDING QUESTIONS

- What did the frontier mean to the nation in the first half of the nineteenth century?
- How did the Westward movement change family life?
- How did geography affect life in the West?

TAKE NOTES

Literacy Notes: Classify and Categorize

Use the Graphic Organizer in your Active Journal to take notes as you read the lesson.

PRACTICE VOCABULARY

Use the Vocabulary Builder activity in your Active Journal to practice the vocabulary words.

Vocabulary	Academic Vocabulary
revenue	extend
flatboat	despite
Clermont	
Erie Canal	
National Road	

English colonists began moving west almost as soon as they arrived in America in the 1600s. Westward expansion quickly became a tradition that helped define the nation.

Why Did Americans Move West?

As the population of the United States grew, land became more expensive, and some Americans began to feel crowded. By the early 1800s, the promise of new farmland and other work opportunities brought a flood of new emigrants from settled areas in the East to the lands west of the Appalachian Mountains.

Northwest Ordinance The Northwest Territory was the area north of the Ohio River and east of the Mississippi. Colonists had been moving into this area since before the American Revolution. When the United States acquired this land from the United Kingdom, the flow of settlers increased.

One of the first tasks of the new federal government was to organize how the territory was to be settled. In a series of three acts, passed between 1784 and 1787, Congress created the Northwest Ordinance. It applied specifically to the Northwest Territory at first. Later, the principles of the Ordinance were **extended** to other territories.

Academic Vocabulary
extend • *v.*, to expand or apply further

The Ordinance allowed individuals to buy land in 640-acre tracts. That much acreage was too expensive for most settlers. Soon, developers were buying land and dividing it into smaller parcels that were more affordable and more manageable.

New Transportation Methods

The sale of land attracted settlers, but it also provided needed **revenue**, or income, for the U.S. government. The money was needed to pay off debt from the American Revolution.

In the past, people thought of territories as colonies. The Ordinance changed that. Settlers in these territories could now organize into states that would have all the rights of the original thirteen states. People moving into the territories were not leaving the United States, they were expanding it.

Another part of the Ordinance outlawed slavery in the territories. This provision would cause many sectional disputes.

Opportunities and Challenges Americans moved west for many reasons, but mostly they wanted the opportunity to own land, start businesses, and build new lives. Some people, like the Mormons, moved west to find religious freedom.

In 1803, President Jefferson made the Louisiana Purchase from France, doubling the size of the country. The Louisiana Purchase opened up a vast new territory with many valuable natural resources.

GEOGRAPHY **SKILLS**

By 1819, the United States had grown to 23 states.

1 **Movement** What can the dates of statehood of the new states tell us about how settlers migrated into the western territories?

2 **Draw Conclusions** Based on this pattern of settlement, where will settlers move next?

New States, 1792–1819

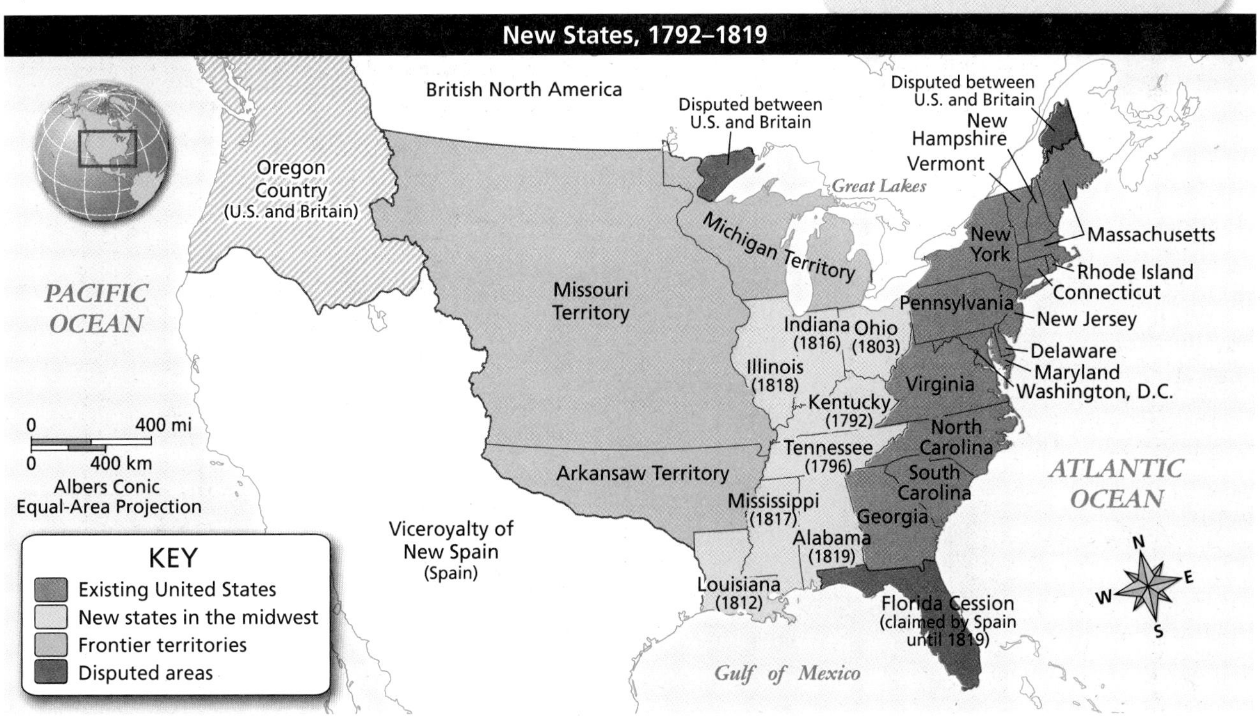

INTERACTIVE

New Technology: The Steamboat

Some of the first people moving into the new territories were fur trappers. Beaver fur, in particular, was in high demand in the east and in Europe. Many of the trails forged by trappers were later used by settlers moving west.

READING CHECK **Summarize** In what ways did the Northwest Ordinance encourage settlement of the West?

Heading Into the West

When the United States formed its first government, it already controlled most of the land east of the Mississippi River. There was ample land for settlers. Very quickly though, the United States acquired more territory and expanded westward.

Expanded Territories Not all the new territories were gained by treaty. In 1818, the U.S. Army, led by General Andrew Jackson, invaded Florida. His action led to Spain's surrender of that territory. In the 1840s, the United States acquired the Oregon territory in a settlement with Britain that narrowly avoided a war. Victory in the Mexican-American war added lands in the Southwest and California. In less than 50 years, the United States expanded all the way to the Pacific Ocean.

Following the Rivers People wanted to settle these territories, but few easy routes led west. The best routes were often rivers.

Many people moving to the Northwest Territory traveled west along the Mohawk River and then sailed across Lake Erie. Others crossed the Appalachians to Pittsburgh. There, they loaded their animals and wagons onto **flatboats**, or flat-bottomed boats, and floated down the Ohio River.

GEOGRAPHY **SKILLS**

This map shows how roads and canals crisscrossed the United States.

1 **Movement** What routes could one take from Albany to Columbus?

2 **Draw Conclusions** Why might a traveler take the Great Valley Road from Lancaster to Louisville instead of traveling in more of a straight line?

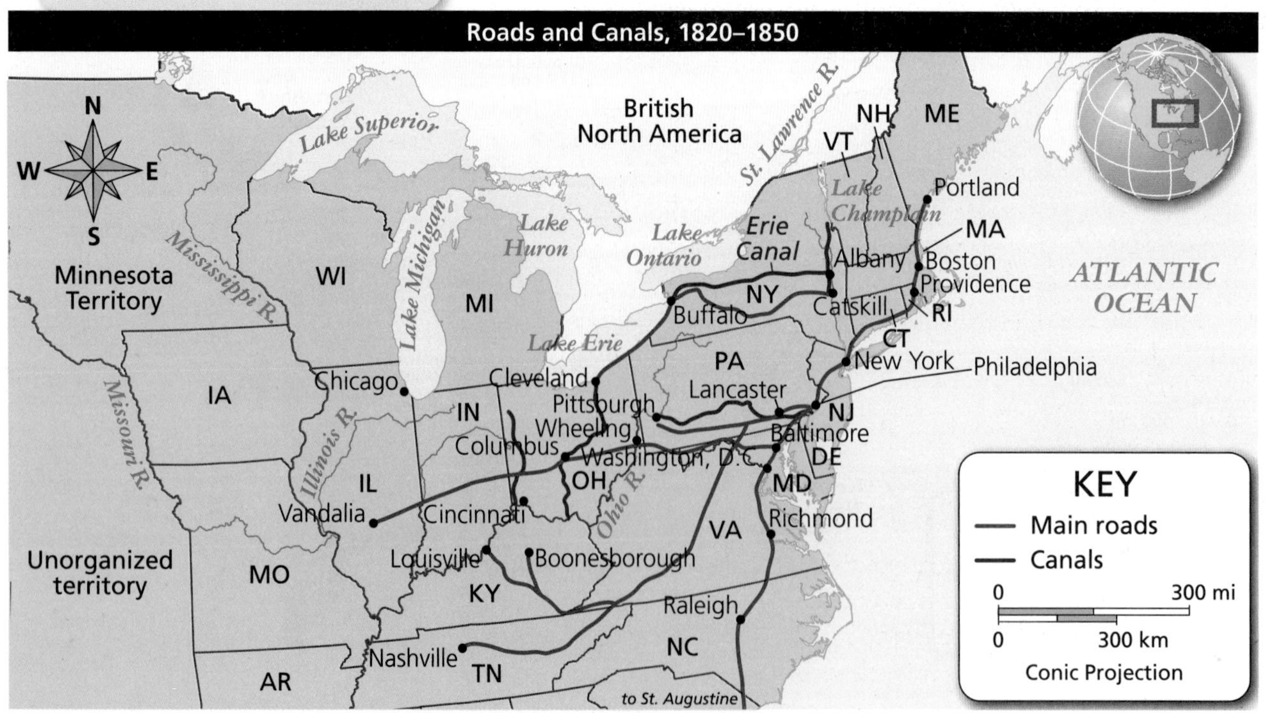

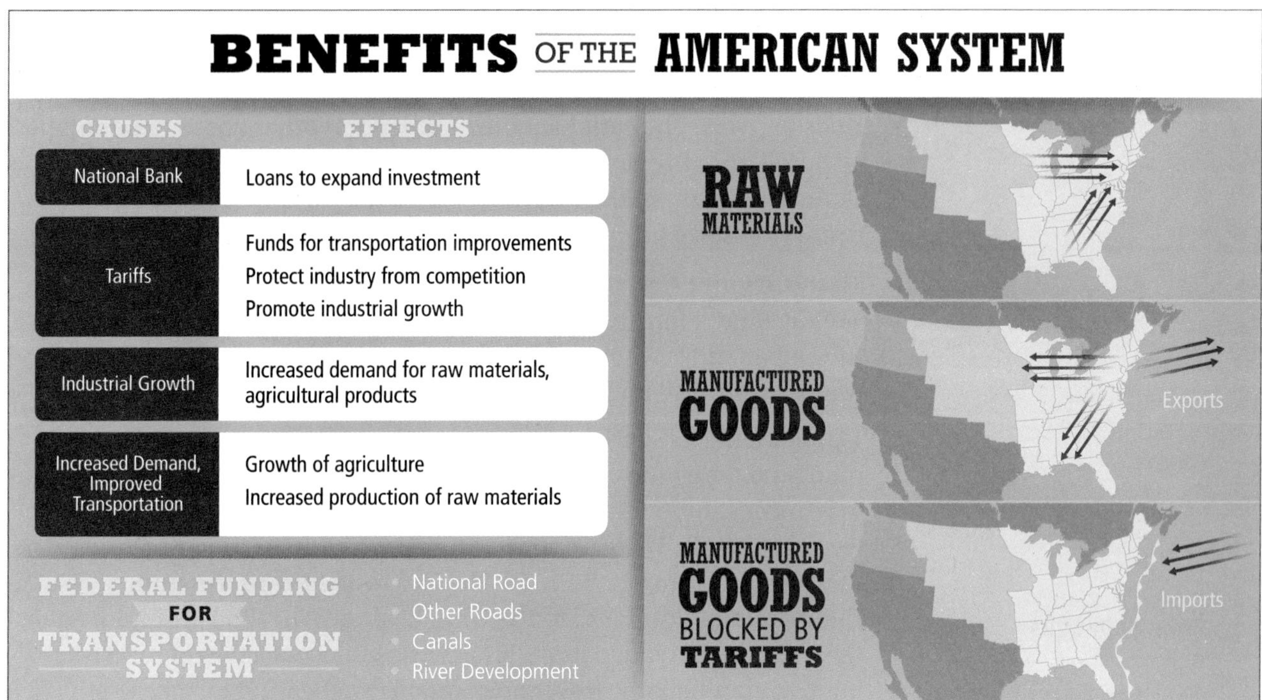

Analyze Charts The American System aimed to take advantage of regional differences. **Use Evidence** Which region benefited most from tariffs?

As settlers journeyed west of the Mississippi, the rivers continued to play a key role. Lewis and Clark followed the Missouri River as they explored the Louisiana Purchase. Long sections of the Missouri are fast and unpredictable, so few settlers used it for transportation.

The Platte River, in Nebraska, was too shallow for shipping, but it was a reliable source of water in a dry region. Traders, settlers, and the U.S. Army built forts and settlements along the river. Settlers stocked up on supplies at these outposts as they traveled across the West.

The American System As the country expanded, Americans sought ways to develop the economy. Henry Clay promoted a plan known as the "American System." It was a government policy to benefit agriculture, merchants, and industry.

The American system had three main parts. First, tariffs would protect industry. Second, a national bank would make loans to promote business growth. Third, the tariffs and the sale of public lands would provide funds for the building of roads, canals, and other improvements. These transportation improvements would help farmers and manufacturers get their products to market. Finally, money from the payment of tariffs plus money from selling public lands would help pay for improvements.

Technology Speeds Transportation **Despite** its advantages, river travel presented problems. Moving upstream, for instance, was difficult. Technology, however, soon made travel faster and cheaper.

Academic Vocabulary
despite • *prep.,* in spite of; notwithstanding

In 1807, Robert Fulton launched a steamboat, the ***Clermont***, on the Hudson River. Soon steamboats plied the Ohio, Mississippi, and Missouri rivers. They carried passengers and gave farmers and merchants a cheap way to move goods.

INTERACTIVE

The Erie Canal

Another improvement was the **Erie Canal**. New York Governor DeWitt Clinton pushed for approval of this project. The legislature approved $7 million for the canal to link the Great Lakes to the Mohawk and Hudson rivers. The canal enabled timber and other goods to be shipped by barge from the Northwest Territory to New York Harbor. Soon other states as well as private investors were building canals that helped connect western farms and eastern cities.

The National Road Settlers faced difficult journeys when traveling west by land. Many roads were narrow dirt trails. They often plunged through muddy swamps. Tree stumps stuck up in the roads and broke wagon axles. The nation badly needed better roads.

Thomas Jefferson and others supported construction of a national road paid for by the government. Critics argued that the project was unconstitutional, as road-building is not an expressed power. Nevertheless, in 1806, Congress approved funds for the first national road-building project. By 1818, the **National Road** ran from Cumberland, Maryland, to the Ohio River at Wheeling, Virginia. Later, the road was extended into Illinois. As each new section of road was built, settlers eagerly drove their wagons farther and farther west.

READING CHECK **Compare and Contrast** How was the landscape both an advantage and a disadvantage to settlers moving west?

Analyze Images Although the Erie Canal no longer bustles with traffic as it once did, it is still in use today. **Cite Evidence** What in the picture shows that constructing the Erie Canal was a major undertaking?

State Populations, 1810–1840

STATE	POPULATION, 1810	POPULATION, 1840
New York	959,049	2,428,921
Ohio	230,760	1,519,467
Illinois	12,282	476,183
Louisiana	76,556	352,411
Tennessee	261,727	829,210

Source: U.S. Censuses of Population and Housing

Analyze Images Over 30 years, many state populations exploded in size. **Analyze Charts** What caused each of these five states to grow so quickly in such a short time?

Movement Changes the West and the Nation

Moving west was a challenge for even the hardiest people. Settlers traveled long distances over rugged land for weeks or months. They lived outdoors in all kinds of weather. Sickness, hunger, and thirst were common. They risked confrontations with American Indians unhappy over white settlement, although few armed conflicts occurred.

Settlers Build New Lives When settlers finally arrived at their destination, the real work began. They found land that had never been plowed and was grown thick with trees, bushes, and dense grasses. The land was rich in natural resources, but it required extensive labor to use and develop them. Settlers created farms and built businesses and towns from the ground up.

Life in the West changed traditional roles for white men and women. Women's roles were as necessary as those of men, and the two often overlapped. Few farms were run by a single man. It took two people to succeed, usually a husband and wife. Wives didn't just run the household as they had back east, they worked alongside their husbands at all sorts of jobs. They helped plant and harvest crops and care for livestock, as well as making clothing and household tools and furnishings. Children had chores, too. Everyone had to work hard to make and maintain a home on this new land.

It is not surprising that the lifestyle that developed in the West was somewhat different from that of the East. Women enjoyed greater equality in the West and, overall, there were fewer class distinctions. Most people were respected for their actions and their character rather than for who they were or how much money they had. Westerners also had a high regard for democracy.

Changing the Country By the early 1800s, white Americans, some bringing enslaved African Americans, occupied many of the lands east of the Mississippi. By 1830, almost as many people lived west of the Appalachians as had lived in all of the United States in 1783. Settlers kept moving still farther west to such places as Oregon, Texas, and California. The result was a rapid shift in population westward.

Analyze Images Starting from a young age, white women in the West often took on jobs once regarded as work that only men did. **Synthesize Visual Information** What details in the illustration indicate how daily life in the West differed from daily life in an Eastern city?

As white settlers moved westward, so did the frontier. As the frontier moved, so did the line between lands controlled by white people and those controlled by American Indians. At each stage in westward movement, settlers learned how to survive in their new environment and how to use the available natural resources. They learned how to trade and cooperate with American Indians, and how to exploit and overcome them. They formed governments and disputed the slavery question. In these processes, they remade the United States.

While settlers were moving into the West, the rest of the country was still dealing with economic challenges and political disagreements. As you will read, sectional conflicts brewed through the first half of the 19th century as differences grew between the North and the South.

READING CHECK **Draw Conclusions** Why did white women experience greater equality in the West than in the East?

Lesson Check

Practice Vocabulary

1. How did the United States government get **revenue** from the Northwest Ordinance?
2. How did settlers use **flatboats** on their journey's west?
3. How did the ***Clermont*** and the **Erie Canal** help unite the country?

Critical Thinking and Writing

4. **Revisit the Essential Question** Why do people move?
5. **Infer** How did technology help unify the nation?
6. **Writing Workshop: Use Narrative Techniques** In your Active Journal, write a brief description of your first day on your journey west. Use narrative techniques, such as dialogue, description, and similes. You will use this narration in the narrative you will write at the end of the Topic.

LESSON 5

Settling Oregon Country

GET READY TO READ

START UP

This modern photograph of Oregon shows how the region might have appeared to settlers. In a few sentences tell what a landscape like this would have meant for the new arrivals.

GUIDING QUESTIONS

- What did the frontier mean to the nation in the first half of the nineteenth century?
- What challenges did the Oregon Trail present?
- How did mountain men lead the way for white settlement in the Far West?
- What role did missionaries play in Oregon Country?

TAKE NOTES

Literacy Skills: Summarize

Use the Graphic Organizer in your Active Journal to take notes as you read the lesson.

PRACTICE VOCABULARY

Use the Vocabulary Builder in your Active Journal to practice the vocabulary words.

Vocabulary		Academic Vocabulary
Oregon Country	rugged individualist	varied
mountain man	Oregon Trail	determination

By the 1820s, white settlers occupied much of the land between the Appalachians and the Mississippi River. Until this time, those lands were considered "the West." However, families searching for good farmland continued to move even farther west. In front of them were the Great Plains that stretched to the Rockies. Few settlers stopped on the plains, which were considered too dry for farming. Instead, most settlers headed to lands in the Far West. The movement to this distant region changed the meaning of the West for Americans. Now, it stretched all the way to the Pacific coast.

In Search of New Territory

Americans first learned about Oregon Country after Lewis and Clark explored the region in the early 1800s. **Oregon Country** was a huge area west of the Rocky Mountains. Today it includes the states of Oregon, Washington, Idaho, and parts of Wyoming, Montana, and western Canada.

Academic Vocabulary
varied • *adj.*, having many forms or types

INTERACTIVE

Oregon Country

Wild Country The geography of Oregon Country is **varied**. Along the Pacific coast, the soil is fertile. Temperatures are mild year round, and rainfall is plentiful.

Dense forest covered the Coastal Ranges and Cascade Mountains, which surrounded these lowlands. Beavers and other fur-bearing animals roamed these forests and the Rocky Mountains to the east. Between the Cascade Mountains and the Rockies is a dry plateau.

Guides to the West Fur trappers searching for beaver and other fur-bearing animals were the first outsiders to enter Oregon Country. They followed American Indian trails through passes in the Rocky Mountains. Later, they used these trails and the knowledge of the land they had gained from American Indians to guide settlers heading west. These men became known as **mountain men**.

Not all the mountain men were white. Manuel Lisa, a Latino fur trader, founded Fort Manuel, the first outpost on the upper Missouri. James Beckwourth, an African American freed from slavery, was a fur trader and lived among the Crow Indians. Beckwourth learned of a mountain pass that became a major route to California.

The U.S. government also sent expeditions to map and explore the new territories of the West. John C. Frémont (FREE mont), a young military officer, was commissioned to lead expeditions through many areas across the West, from Wyoming to California. The trapper and explorer "Kit" Carson served as a guide to Frémont. Later, Carson guided General Kearny on his campaign to take California from Mexico. Carson became a popular and legendary adventure hero.

BIOGRAPHY 5 Things to Know About JOHN C. FRÉMONT

American Explorer (1813–1890)

- As a U.S. Army officer, he led three expeditions to explore the West, mapping much of the land between the Mississippi River and the West Coast.
- On his third expedition, Frémont helped capture California for the United States during the Mexican-American War.
- Frémont accepted the Mexican surrender and then declared himself governor of California. For these acts he was accused of mutiny and court-martialed, but the ruling was later dismissed.
- He became a multimillionaire when gold was discovered on land he had bought in California.
- He ran for President in 1856, but lost to James Buchanan.

Critical Thinking How was Frémont important to the development of California?

Explorers of the Far West, 1807–1850

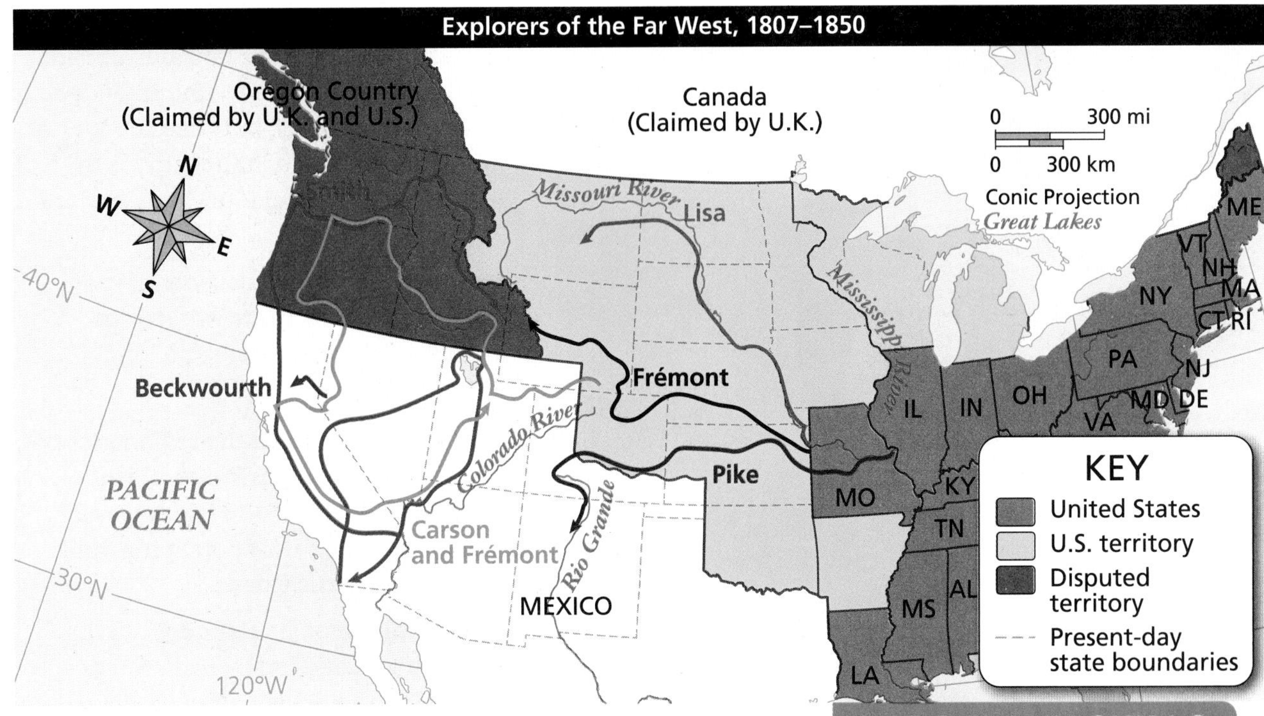

GEOGRAPHY SKILLS

Scouts and explorers traveled throughout the West before white settlers arrived from the East.

1. **Interaction** How were explorers important for westward movement?
2. **Infer** Why do you think some exploration routes were thousands of miles while others were much shorter?

Nations Compete In the early 1800s, four countries claimed Oregon Country: the United States, Great Britain, Spain, and Russia. Of course, American Indian groups had lived there for centuries. However, the United States and European nations gave little thought to their rights.

In 1818, the United States and Britain agreed to occupy Oregon Country jointly. Citizens of each nation would have equal rights. Spain and Russia had few settlers there, so they withdrew their claims.

READING CHECK **Predict Consequences** How might the arrival of many U.S. settlers affect the agreement between Britain and the United States about Oregon Country?

The Far West Fur Trade

The first Europeans and white Americans who traveled to Oregon Country were fur traders. Fur was so valuable that it was sometimes referred to as "soft gold."

Trade in Sea Otter Fur John Jacob Astor was one of the most successful American traders. Astor started his first fur business in St. Louis, selling pelts collected in the American West and Canada to cities in the Northeast and Europe. But the most valuable furs came from sea otters that were hunted off the coast of the Oregon Country.

Analyze Images James Beckwourth was a freed slave who became a fur trader and explorer. Later, he worked for the army and ran his own hotel and store. **Identify Main Ideas** What was the importance of the mountain men for the development of the nation?

Merchants came all the way from New England for the otters. Then, they crossed the Pacific and sold the furs in China for huge profits. Astor's ships regularly sailed to China loaded down with fur. He became very wealthy, but then the War of 1812 interrupted business. For a time, he made up for the loss by buying opium in Turkey and shipping it to China aboard his ships.

The fur trade flourished through the first decades of the century, but by the late 1830s, the fur trade was dying. Beaver hats, which had fueled the trade, were no longer fashionable. The sea otter trade continued, but it, too, slowed.

Mountain Men Mountain men roamed the region's forests, trapping animals and living off the land. Their colorful appearance set them apart. Their shirts and trousers were made of animal hides and decorated with porcupine quills. Pistols and tomahawks hung from their belts.

Many people admired mountain men as **rugged individualists**. Mountain men lived lonely lives. Many did not have families. Those that did were often separated from them for long periods of time. Based in part on the solitary lives of mountain men, a folklore of rugged American individualism developed. Today, it still influences our ideas of what America is and what makes an American.

Mountain men could make fine profits selling their furs, but their lives were hard and dangerous. Injuries, illness, and dangerous animals were a constant threat. Surviving alone, especially through the long, cold winters in the mountains, demanded special skills. "I have held my hands in an anthill until they were covered with ants, then greedily licked them off," one mountain man recalled.

READING CHECK **Interpret** How did mountain men come to know so much about the Oregon Country?

The Oregon Trail

The first white Americans to settle permanently in Oregon Country were missionaries who began arriving in the 1830s. Among the first of these were Marcus and Narcissa Whitman. In 1836, they set out from their home in New York for Oregon Country, where they planned to convert American Indians to Christianity.

Missionaries Bring Settlers The Whitmans built their mission near the Columbia River and began to work with the Cayuse (kay-YOOS), setting up a mission school and a clinic. Soon, other missionaries and settlers arrived.

Eager for others to join them, the missionaries sent back glowing reports about the Oregon Country. By 1840, more Americans were making the journey west.

As settlers spread onto Cayuse lands, conflicts arose. Worse, the newcomers carried diseases that proved deadly for the Cayuse. In 1847, a measles outbreak killed many Cayuse children. Blaming the settlers, a band of angry Cayuse attacked the mission, killing the Whitmans and 12 others.

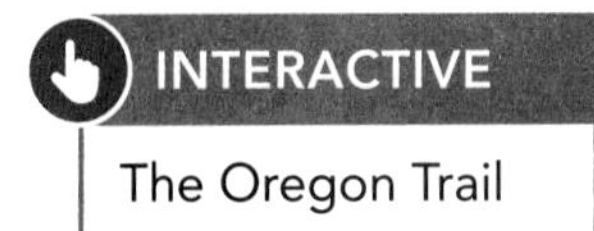

Wagons Ho! Despite such incidents, pioneers still set out for Oregon Country. Tales of wheat that grew taller than a person and turnips five feet around touched off a race to the territory. Americans called it "Oregon fever." Soon, pioneers clogged the trails west.

Beginning in 1843, wagon trains left every spring for Oregon Country. They followed a route called the **Oregon Trail**. Families heading west would gather at Independence, Missouri, in the early spring. There, they formed wagon trains and hurried to start west by May. Along the way, travelers stopped near settlements where they might buy supplies or get care for the sick or injured.

Timing was important. Travelers had to reach the Oregon lowlands by early October, before the snow fell in the mountains. This meant they had to cover 2,000 miles in five months. In the 1840s, traveling 15 miles a day was making good time.

Life in a Wagon Train On the trail, families woke at dawn to a bugle blast. Breakfast was prepared and eaten. Horses and oxen were hitched to the wagons. By 6 A.M., the cry of "Wagons Ho!" rang across the plains.

At noon the wagon train stopped for a brief meal and then continued on until 6 or 7 P.M.

GEOGRAPHY SKILLS

By 1830, the United States had a claim to part of the Pacific Coast.

1. **Movement** Work with a partner to estimate the distance from the Oregon Country to the nearest state.
2. **Express Problems Clearly** Considering the distance of states and organized territories from Oregon Country, why might it have been difficult for the United States to control that region?

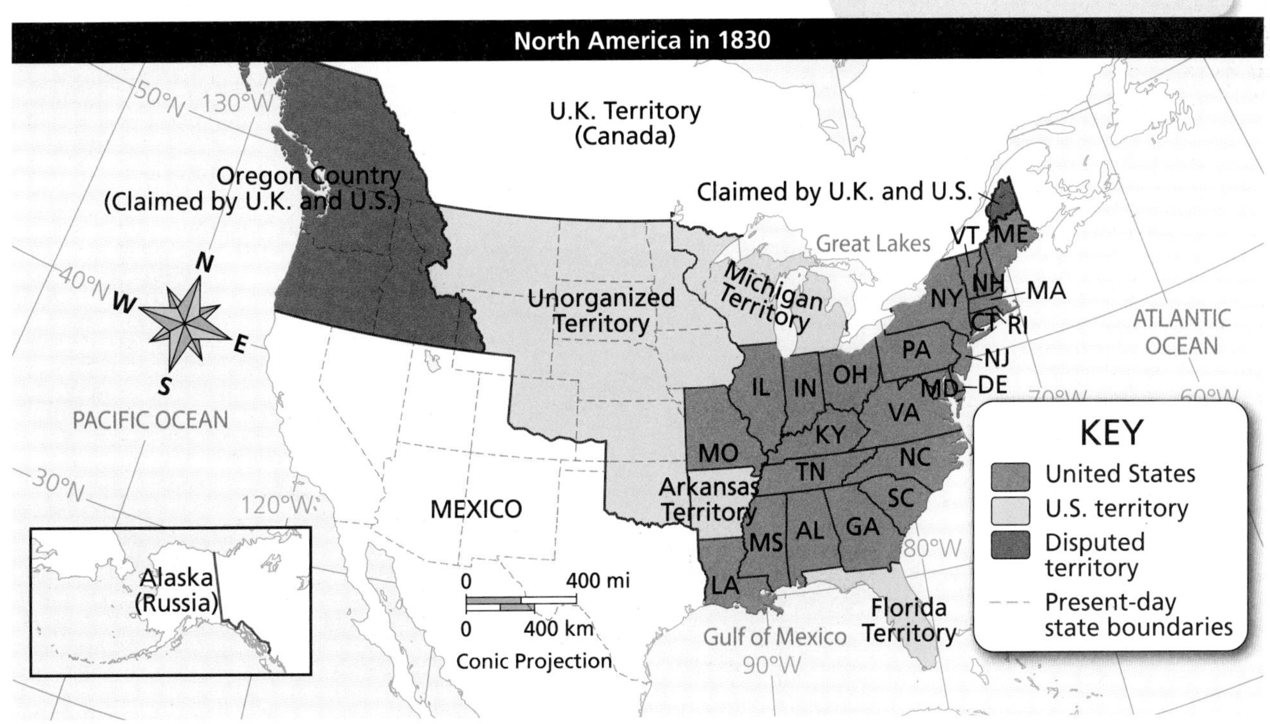

INTERACTIVE

The Covered Wagon

Men and women took on their usual roles when a wagon train first began its journey. Men managed the teams and hunted. Women cooked, washed, and collected fire wood.

As time passed, though, women began driving wagons, hitching up teams, and loading wagons. Men occasionally even cooked and did other "women's work." People did what was needed to get to Oregon.

Daily life was not easy. Meals were cooked over open fires. Fuel for the fires was often scarce and took time to gather. Wind blew sand into people's food as they ate. At night, most people wrapped themselves in blankets and slept on the ground. If it rained, they got soaked, and the wagons might get stuck in the mud.

The trail west held many dangers. During the spring, travelers risked drowning as they crossed rain-swollen rivers. In summer, water sources dried up. People went thirsty, and livestock might die. The biggest threat was sickness. Cholera and other diseases could wipe out entire wagon trains.

Despite the many hardships, more than 50,000 Americans reached Oregon between 1840 and 1860.

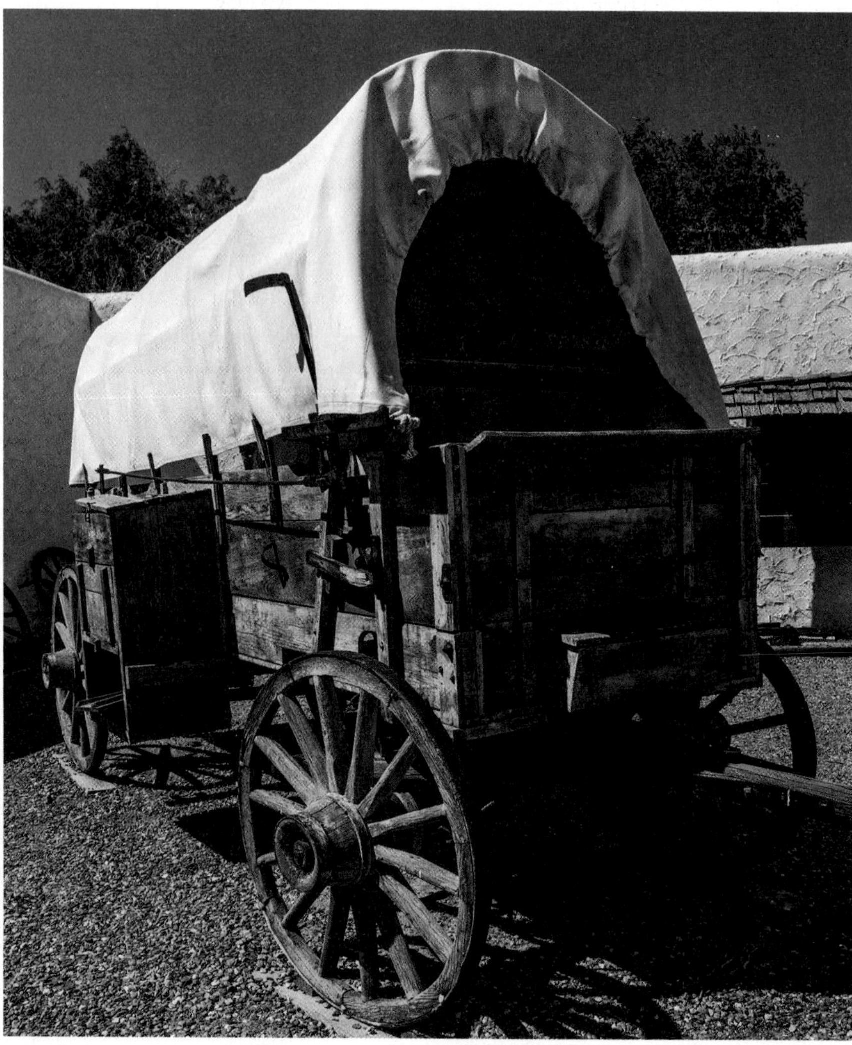

Analyze Images Settlers traveled in wagon trains for mutual assistance on their journey westward. **Use Visual Information** What features of the wagon can you identify that would be useful for settlers traveling to Oregon Country?

Meeting the Locals As they moved west, pioneers met and often traded with American Indians. Hungry pioneers were grateful for the food that the locals supplied in return for clothing and tools. A traveler noted:

Primary Source

"Whenever we camp near any Indian village, we are no sooner stopped than a whole crowd may be seen coming galloping into our camp. The [women] do all the swapping."

—John S. Unruh, quoted in *The Plains Across: The Overland Emigrants and the Trans-Mississippi West, 1840–1860*

▲ Settlers encountered many American Indians, such as the Klikitat, Chinook, and others who fished on the Columbia River in Oregon Country. **Identify Supporting Details** How did American Indians influence the life of settlers on the frontier?

Journey's End By the 1840s, Americans outnumbered the British in Oregon Country. Many Americans wanted Oregon Country for the United States alone. After a long negotiation, the United States and United Kingdom signed a treaty dividing up the Oregon Country. Two years later, in 1848, Congress organized the Oregon Territory.

Eastern merchants found new markets in Oregon Country as its population grew. But the territory's significance was not only economic. The Oregon Trail helped form America's national identify. It took courage and **determination** to complete the journey across the continent. The trail inspired Americans' faith that their nation can achieve anything.

Academic Vocabulary
determination • *n.,* personal drive to continue trying to achieve one's goal

READING CHECK **Identify Cause and Effect** How did missionaries attract settlers?

Lesson Check

Practice Vocabulary

1. Why did people go to **Oregon Country**?
2. In what way could **mountain men** be described as **rugged individualists**?

Critical Thinking and Writing

3. **Compare and Contrast** the lives of missionaries and mountain men in Oregon Country.
4. **Identify Main Ideas** Describe how settlers moving to Oregon Country made the trip from Independence, Missouri.
5. **Writing Workshop: Use Narrative Techniques** In your Active Journal, write about an important or unusual event that takes place during your journey west. Use narrative techniques, such as dialogue, flashback, or figurative language. You will use what you write here in the narrative you will write at the end of the Topic.

Distinguish Verifiable from Unverifiable Information

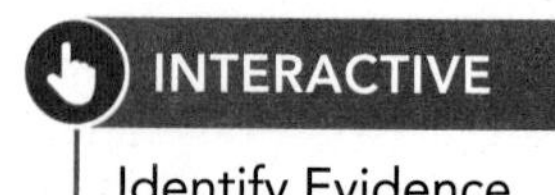

Follow these steps to distinguish verifiable from unverifiable information.

1 **Identify statements that could be verified** Historical sources may contain facts, or statements that can be proved true. What facts does the writer give you about the Red Buttes?

2 **Determine how you might verify these statements** Find ways to verify each statement. For example, you could compare a statement to an encyclopedia entry. How can you prove the statements about the Red Buttes are facts?

3 **Identify statements that cannot be verified** It is not possible to verify something like a person's opinion. Remember, though, that statements can be valuable even though they are not verifiable. Which statements in the journal entry for August 3 cannot be verified?

Primary Source

"July 25.— Since last date we camped at the ford where emigrants cross from the south to the north side of the Platte. . . . We stopped near the Red Buttes, where the hills are of a red color, nearly square and have the appearance of houses with flat roofs. . . . We also passed Independence Rock and the Devil's Gate, which is high enough to make one's head swim, and the posts reach an altitude of some 4 or 500 feet."

"Oregon, August 3. . . . Here the roads were so bad, as we went over the steep hills and clambered over the rocks, I could hardly hold myself in the wagon. Sometimes the dust is so great that the drivers cannot see their teams at all though the sun is shining brightly, and it a great relief to the way-worn traveler to meet with some mountain stream, meandering through a valley. . . . One day we only made seven miles through a very deep sand. . . ."

"Monday, September 15th. . . . Mount St. Elias is in the distance, and is covered with snow, so you can imagine somewhat the beauty and grandeur of the scene. We are now among the tribe of Wallawalla Indians."

—Journal of a Trip to Oregon, Elizabeth Wood

LESSON 6

New Spain and Independence for Texas

GET READY TO READ

START UP

The men in this painting were skilled with horses, roping, and caring for cattle. How are they similar to the American cowboy?

GUIDING QUESTIONS

- What were the causes and consequences of Texas independence?
- How did Mexican and American settlements affect the development of the Southwest?
- What was life like for the Spanish and American Indians who lived in California and New Mexico?

TAKE NOTES

Literacy Skills: Sequence

Use the Graphic Organizer in your Active Journal to take notes as you read the lesson.

PRACTICE VOCABULARY

Use the Vocabulary Builder in your Active Journal to practice the vocabulary words.

Vocabulary		Academic Vocabulary
Puebloan	vaquero	specify
Santa Fe Trail	dictator	generally
mission	Alamo	
self-sufficient	siege	

In the 1840s, New Mexico Territory included present-day Arizona, New Mexico, Nevada, and Utah, and parts of Colorado. California lay to the west. This huge region, ruled by Mexico, was southwest of the unorganized territory that the United States acquired through the Louisiana Purchase.

New Mexico Territory and California

The physical characteristics of the New Mexico Territory vary depending on location. Much of this region is hot and dry desert. There are also forested mountains. In some areas, thick grasses grow. Before the Spanish arrived, **Puebloans** (pweb LOH anz) farmed here using irrigation. Puebloans are American Indians who live in permanent towns made of mud, rock, and other materials. Other American Indians lived mainly by hunting and gathering.

Spain and New Mexico Territory The Spanish explorer Juan de Oñate (ohn YAH tay) claimed the region for Spain in 1598.

In the early 1600s, the Spanish founded the town of Santa Fe and made it the capital of the territory. With a bustling trade in horses, fur, and wool, Santa Fe grew into a busy trading center.

Some Americans were eager to settle in New Mexico. It was thinly populated but had good physical characteristics, including many natural resources. Spain, however, would not let Americans settle in Santa Fe or anywhere else in the territory. Only after Mexico became independent in 1821 were Americans welcome there.

William Becknell, a merchant and adventurer, was the first American to head for Santa Fe. In 1822, he led some traders from Franklin, Missouri, up the Arkansas River and across the plains to the New Mexico town. Other Americans soon followed Becknell's route, which became known as the **Santa Fe Trail**.

Spanish Settlements in California California, too, was ruled first by Spain and then by Mexico. In 1769, Captain Gaspar de Portolá led an expedition up the Pacific coast. With him was Father Junípero Serra (hoo NEE peh roh SEHR rah). Father Serra built his first mission at San Diego. He and other missionaries set up a string of 21 **missions** along the California coast. The Spanish built forts nearby.

Each mission complex included a church and the surrounding land. Each became **self-sufficient**, or able to produce enough for their needs. The missions had large herds of cattle and sheep as well as gardens and orchards. They produced enough food for their own needs and sometimes enough to supply neighboring forts and pueblos.

GEOGRAPHY SKILLS

Spain set up a series of missions, forts, and towns north of their earlier settlements in Mexico.

1. **Place** What common geographic feature do most of the Spanish settlements share?
2. **Draw Conclusions** Why do you think Spain built these settlements in these locations?

Spanish Territory in North America, 1820

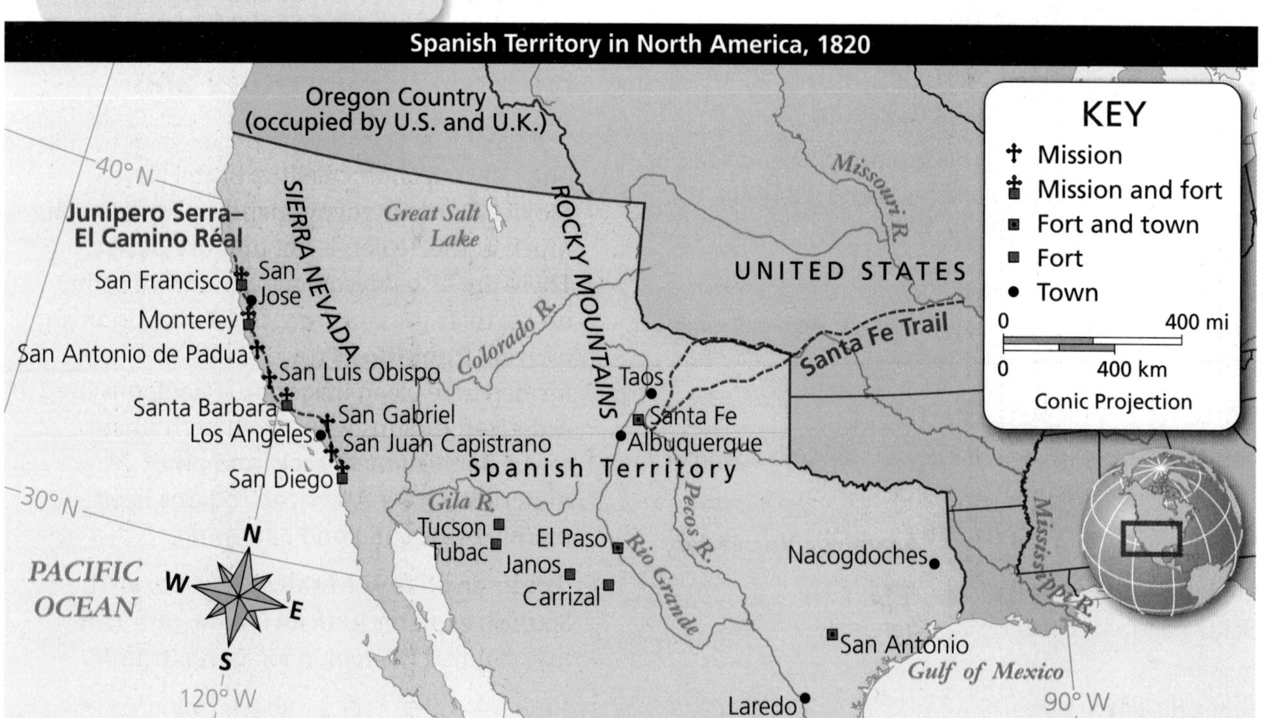

Analyze Images Many of the missions built by the Spanish remain and can still be visited, like the Mission San Carlos Borromeo del Rio Carmelo in Carmel, California. **Identify Main Ideas** Why did the Spanish build missions in California?

Before the Spanish arrived, American Indians in California lived in small, scattered groups. As a result, they had little success resisting the Spanish soldiers who made them work on mission lands. They were forced to herd sheep and cattle and raise crops for the missions. In exchange they received no pay, only food and clothing. Many were forced to live at the missions and practice the Roman Catholic faith.

Mission life was harsh for the American Indians. They were forced to give up their culture. Families were often separated, and thousands of American Indians died from overwork and disease.

Culture and Tradition on Mexican Ranches In the 1820s, newly independent Mexico decided that California's economy was growing too slowly. Hoping to speed up growth, the government took land from the missions and gave it to individuals. These land grants were usually given to wealthy people. The landowners set up huge cattle ranches, called ranchos, and became rancheros, or ranch operators.

A new culture began to develop among the rancheros. Their lives centered on cattle raising and the selling of beef and hides. Cattle ranching grew to become the principal business in California. Rancheros gained great wealth and occupied a high social class. They married and socialized with other rancheros and with wealthy merchants.

A new culture also developed among some workers on the ranches—the culture of the **vaqueros**. Vaqueros were the Indian and Mexican cowhands who tended the cattle and other animals. They were excellent riders and ropers, and their traditions strongly influenced later cowhands throughout the West.

READING CHECK **Summarize** Who were the vaqueros?

Analyze Images Vaqueros were skilled with horses and managing livestock. **Synthesize Visual Information** How do this vaquero's clothing and equipment help him do his work?

Americans Colonize Mexican Texas

In the early 1800s, Texas was part of a Spanish province in the colony of New Spain, or Mexico. At that time, Texas had only about 4,000 Mexican settlers. As a result, Spain had difficulty keeping order, and settlers faced frequent raids by American Indian groups, such as the Comanche.

Spain Authorizes a Colony in Texas In 1820, Spain gave Moses Austin a land grant and permission to colonize Texas with 300 Catholic families. Although Austin died before he could set up a colony, his son, Stephen, took over the grant. Also around this time, in 1821, Mexico gained its independence from Spain.

Stephen Austin had no trouble finding settlers. By the 1820s, most of the land in the United States that was arable, or suitable for farming, was already occupied. There was a scarcity, or short supply, of affordable, fertile land, or land that is good for growing crops. When it was available, good farmland was expensive.

In Texas, by contrast, there was a large supply of fertile land that settlers could buy cheaply. Many Americans were eager to buy this land and settle in Texas.

Austin Founds a Colony Austin gathered the 300 families, and in late 1821, they began settling the colony. Many settlers came from the cotton country of the Southeast. Some built large cotton plantations and brought in enslaved African Americans to work the land.

Quest CONNECTIONS

How did the United States' relationship with Mexico develop after Mexican independence from Spain? Note your findings in your Active Journal.

As Austin's colony grew, Mexico gave Austin several more land grants. Grants were also given to other entrepreneurs like Austin to attract settlers to Texas. Some of these settlers were from Mexico, but the largest number came from the United States. By 1830, about 20,000 Americans had moved to Texas.

The Settlement of Texas

READING CHECK **Identify Cause and Effect** Why were American settlers eager to move to Texas?

Conflict With the Mexican Government

In return for their land, the Mexican government **specified** that Austin and the original American settlers must become Mexican citizens and worship in the Roman Catholic Church. Later American settlers, however, felt no loyalty to Mexico. They spoke little or no Spanish, and most were Protestant. These and other differences led to conflicts between the settlers and the Mexican government.

Academic Vocabulary
specify • *v.*, to name something exactly and in detail

Mexico Tightens Its Grip on Texas In 1830, Mexico barred any more Americans from settling in Texas. Mexico feared that the Americans would try to make Texas a part of the United States. The United States had already tried twice to buy Texas from Mexico.

To assert its authority, Mexico sent troops to enforce laws requiring Texans to worship in the Catholic Church and banning slavery. White American settlers opposed these laws. The law against slavery was a serious problem for them. Many had brought enslaved people with them and relied on enslaved workers to grow cotton.

Analyze Images
Stephen F. Austin rallies Texas colonists to fight Karankawa Indians. Richmond, a man enslaved by Austin, looks in through the window. **Identify Main Ideas** What role did slavery play in the conflict between Texas settlers and Mexico?

In 1833, General Antonio López de Santa Anna gained power in Mexico. He rejected the Mexican constitution and attempted to govern the nation as dictator. A **dictator** is a ruler with absolute power and authority.

Texans Rebel By October 1835, Americans in Texas decided that the time had come for action. They had the support of many Tejanos (teh HAH nohs), people of Mexican descent born in Texas. Tejanos did not necessarily want independence from Mexico. However, they did want to be rid of the dictator, Santa Anna.

In October 1835, Texan settlers in the town of Gonzales (gahn ZAH les) clashed with Mexican troops. Two months later, Texan settlers occupied the town of San Antonio. Determined to stamp out the rebellion, Santa Anna marched north with a large army.

READING CHECK **Identify Cause and Effect** Why were U.S. settlers opposed to Mexican laws?

Analyze Images As a young officer in the Spanish army, Antonio López de Santa Anna fought against Mexican independence. Later, he became president of Mexico. **Summarize** What was Santa Anna's role in Texas history?

Independence for Texas

While Santa Anna was on the move, a group of Texans declared independence for the Republic of Texas on March 2, 1836. Sam Houston took command of its army. Volunteers from the United States and other nations, including African Americans and Tejanos, joined the fight for Texan independence.

Siege at the Alamo By the time Santa Anna reached San Antonio, the Texans had taken up positions in an old Spanish mission called the **Alamo**. A young lieutenant colonel, William B. Travis, was in command. Among the volunteers at the Alamo were the famous frontiersmen Jim Bowie and Davy Crockett. Poorly equipped and badly outnumbered, the rebels waited for the Mexican attack.

On February 23, 1836, Mexican troops began the **siege** of the Alamo. In a siege, enemy forces try to capture a city or fort by surrounding and often bombarding it. The Texan defenders barely held out as cannons pounded the walls for 12 days.

At dawn on March 6, Mexican cannons finally shattered the mission walls. Thousands of Mexican soldiers poured over the broken walls, shouting *"Viva Santa Anna!"* ("Long live Santa Anna!"). In the end, about 180 Texans and almost 1,500 Mexicans lay dead. Most of the few Texans who survived were executed.

INTERACTIVE

The Defenders of the Alamo

The Battle of San Jacinto The fall of the Alamo sparked Texan cries for revenge.

On April 21, 1836, the Texans caught their enemies by surprise camped near the San Jacinto (juh SIN toh) River. With cries of "Remember the Alamo!" Texans charged into battle.

Although the Texans were outnumbered, they were victorious. They captured Santa Anna and forced him to sign a treaty granting Texas independence.

READING CHECK **Identify Cause and Effect** What was the key to the Texans' victory at San Jacinto?

The Republic of Texas Is Born

After winning independence, Texas declared itself a republic. A constitution was written using the United States Constitution as a model.

Issues Facing the New Country Texas's new constitution treated Mexicans in Texas harshly. It denied Mexicans citizenship and property rights if they could not prove that they had supported the revolution. Many chose to give up their lands and flee.

Analyze Images In this painting, Texans defend the Alamo against the Mexican siege. Twelve feet high and two feet thick, the Alamo walls were good protection but unable to endure days of bombardment. **Hypothesize** How might the defenders' confidence have changed during the siege?

INTERACTIVE

Texas: From Settlement to Statehood

The new country faced other problems. First, the government of Mexico refused to accept the treaty that Santa Anna had signed. Mexicans insisted that Texas was still part of Mexico. Second, Texas was nearly bankrupt.

Third, Comanche and other Indian groups threatened to attack small Texan communities. Most Texans thought that the best way to solve these problems was to become part of the United States.

The United States Considers Annexation In the United States, people were divided over whether to annex, or add on, Texas to the Union. The arguments reflected sectional divisions in the country. White southerners **generally** favored the idea. Many northerners opposed it. The main issue was slavery. By the 1830s, antislavery feeling was growing in the North. Because many white Texans enslaved people, northerners feared that Texas would join the Union as an enslaving state, strengthening support for slavery in the U.S. government.

Academic Vocabulary

generally • *adv.*, in most cases

In addition, President Andrew Jackson worried that annexing Texas would lead to war with Mexico. As a result, Congress refused to annex the Republic of Texas.

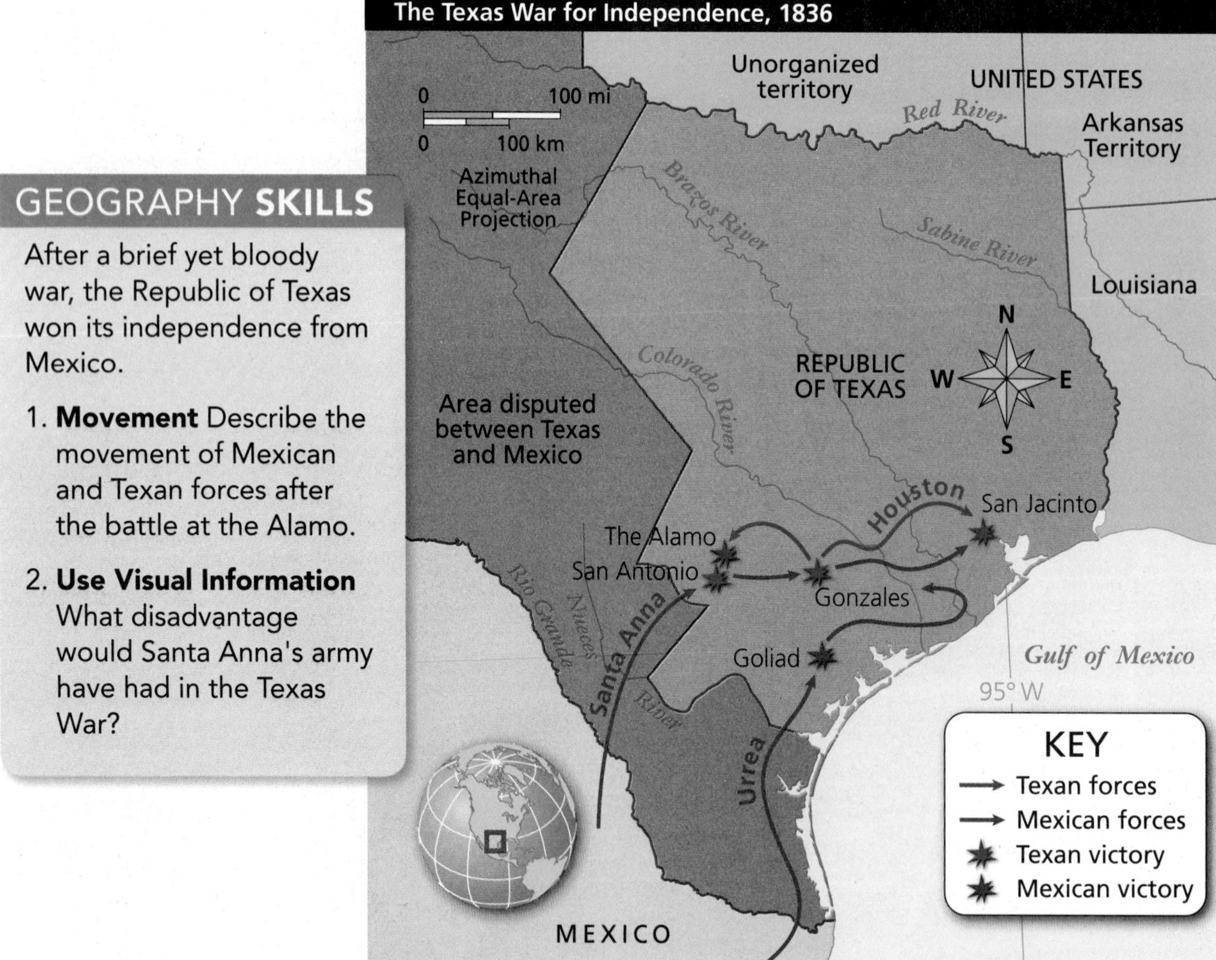

GEOGRAPHY SKILLS

After a brief yet bloody war, the Republic of Texas won its independence from Mexico.

1. **Movement** Describe the movement of Mexican and Texan forces after the battle at the Alamo.
2. **Use Visual Information** What disadvantage would Santa Anna's army have had in the Texas War?

Should the United States Annex Texas?

REASONS FOR	REASONS AGAINST
• Texans voted for annexation. • Statehood would guarantee defense against Mexican attacks and Native American raids. • The Republic would not survive for long as an independent nation. • The United States would benefit economically. • Britain might annex Texas if the United States did not.	• Tension between the North and South would increase if Texas were added as a slave state. • Mexico would see annexation as an act of war. • Annexation would heighten existing conflict between the Whig and Democratic parties. • Mexico might recognize Texas with the help of U.S. diplomacy, and the Republic of Texas could remain independent.

Analyze Images After gaining independence from Mexico, many Texans wanted to join the United States. **Evaluate Arguments** Do you think the argument for or against annexation was stronger? Why?

For the next nine years, leaders of the Republic of Texas worked to attract new settlers. The new Texas government encouraged immigration by offering settlers free land. During the Panic of 1837, thousands of Americans moved to Texas.

Settlers also arrived from Germany and Switzerland. They helped the new nation grow and prosper. By the 1840s, about 140,000 people lived in Texas, including many enslaved African Americans and some Mexicans. The Republic of Texas remained an independent country until the United States annexed it in 1845.

READING CHECK **Summarize** the three problems that faced the new Republic of Texas.

Lesson Check

Practice Vocabulary

1. Why did Santa Anna lay **siege** to the **Alamo**?
2. In what way were the California **missions** **self-sufficient**?

Critical Thinking and Writing

3. **Identify Cause and Effect** Why did the Republic of Texas remain an independent country for nine years?
4. **Summarize** How did the arrival of the missionaries affect American Indians living in California?
5. **Writing Workshop: Use Descriptive Details and Sensory Language** In your Active Journal, revise one of the passages you have written about an event that occurs on your journey west. Include descriptive details and sensory language to make your narrative more vivid and specific.

LESSON 7

Manifest Destiny in California and the Southwest

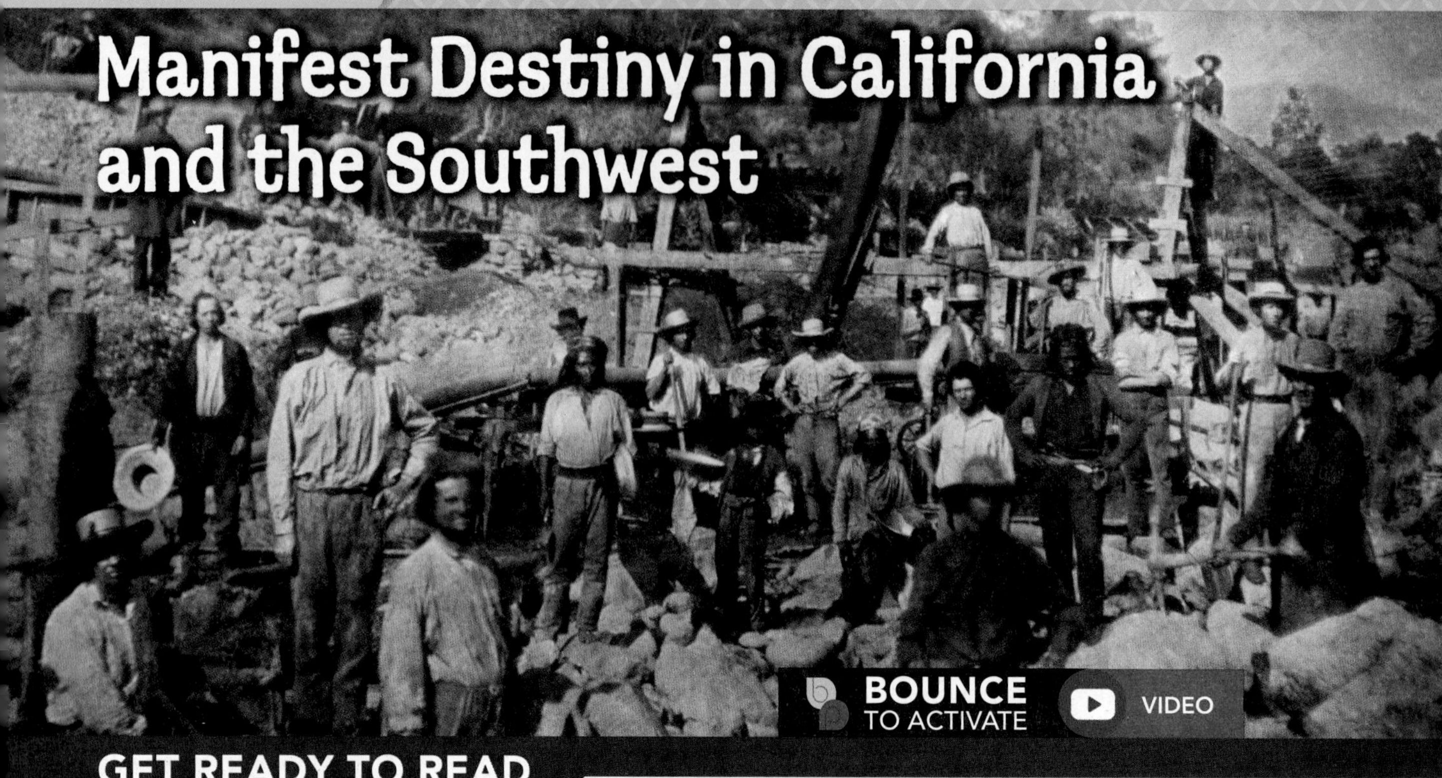

GET READY TO READ

START UP

Write three questions you might like to ask these miners at work during the California gold rush.

GUIDING QUESTIONS

- How did Manifest Destiny contribute to American expansion?
- What were the causes and consequences of the Mexican-American War?
- How did Utah and California grow?
- How did the gold rush and migration affect life in California?

TAKE NOTES

Literacy Skills: Identify Cause and Effect

Use the Graphic Organizer in your Active Journal to take notes as you read the lesson.

PRACTICE VOCABULARY

Use the Vocabulary Builder in your Active Journal to practice the vocabulary words.

Vocabulary		Academic Vocabulary
Manifest Destiny	Mexican Cession	allocation
Bear Flag Republic	forty-niner	consequently
Treaty of Guadalupe-Hidalgo		

In the mid-1840s, only about 700 people from the United States lived in California. Every year, however, more Americans were moving west.

Manifest Destiny

There were many economic, social, and political causes for this westward expansion. On several occasions, the United States government offered to buy California from Mexico. Some officials were eager to gain control of the ports at San Francisco and San Diego. Soon westward expansion became a major priority for the nation.

The Roots of Manifest Destiny In the 1840s, an editor named John L. O'Sullivan created the slogan ***Manifest Destiny***. The slogan suggested that the United States had the right to spread across the continent. *Manifest* means clear or obvious. *Destiny* means something that is fated to happen. The idea of Manifest Destiny was rooted in the belief that Americans had the right and the duty to spread their culture across the continent all the way to the Pacific Ocean.

Americans who believed in Manifest Destiny thought that westward expansion would also open new opportunities. To many Americans, the fertile farmland and natural resources in the West were prime opportunities for economic growth.

Manifest Destiny and westward expansion had some negative effects, however. Many white Americans believed that they were superior to American Indians and Mexicans. They used this belief to justify taking lands belonging to people whom they considered inferior.

Polk and Westward Expansion The political roots of Manifest Destiny and westward expansion took hold during the election of 1844. The Whigs nominated the well-known national leader Henry Clay for President. Clay had opposed the annexation of Texas. The Democrats chose James Polk, a little-known candidate from Tennessee who wanted to add Texas and Oregon Country to the Union.

On Election Day, Americans showed their support for westward expansion by electing Polk president. Acting on his campaign promise, Polk reached an agreement with the United Kingdom in 1846 over Oregon Country. The two countries divided the territory at latitude 49°N. Britain got the lands north of the line, and the United States got the lands south of the line.

Texas proved a more difficult problem. The United States at first had refused to annex Texas. Senators feared that annexing Texas would cause a war with Mexico.

Roots of Manifest Destiny

Social	• Belief in America as an exceptional nation • Desire to spread American democracy and ideals • Belief that it was God's will for America to expand • View that white Americans were superior to American Indians
Political	• Monroe Doctrine warning against European colonization in the Western Hemisphere • Desire to acquire Oregon from Britain • Desire to acquire Texas from Mexico • Success of Democrats, who supported expansion, over Whigs, who did not
Economic	• Farmland for settlers • Access to rich resources • Land for southern crops such as cotton

Analyze Images People had different reasons for supporting Manifest Destiny. **Analyze Charts** How might people's values lead them to support Manifest Destiny?

◀ This election banner shows James Polk and his running mate George Dallas.

Meanwhile, Mexico feared the United States would go ahead with annexation. Out of desperation, Mexico offered a deal: It would accept the independence of Texas if Texas rejected annexation. Texans, however, would not give up on joining the union. They spread rumors that Texas might ally itself with the United Kingdom. This scared Congress into passing a joint resolution, in 1845, admitting Texas to the Union. The annexation of Texas set the stage for conflict with Mexico.

READING CHECK **Identify Main Ideas** How did President Polk support the idea of Manifest Destiny?

Quest CONNECTIONS

What were the causes of the war? Note your ideas in your Active Journal.

The Mexican-American War

The annexation of Texas outraged Mexicans. They had not accepted Texan independence, much less annexation. They also worried that Americans might encourage rebellions in California and New Mexico as they had in Texas.

At the same time, Americans resented Mexico. They were annoyed when Mexico rejected President Polk's offer of $30 million to buy California and New Mexico. Many Americans felt that Mexico stood in the way of their country's Manifest Destiny.

The Clash Begins A border dispute finally caused war. Both the United States and Mexico claimed the land between the Rio Grande and the Nueces (noo AY says) River. In January 1846, Polk ordered General Zachary Taylor to set up posts in the disputed area. Polk knew the move might lead to war. In April 1846, Mexican troops crossed the Rio Grande and clashed with the Americans. At Polk's urging, Congress declared war on Mexico.

Americans were divided over the conflict. Many in the South and West were eager to fight, hoping to win new lands. Some northerners opposed the war. They saw it as a southern plot to add slave states to the Union. Still, the war was generally popular. When the army called for volunteers, thousands of recruits flocked to the cause.

Analyze Images The roots of the Mexican-American War lay in events that happened long before the war started. **Analyze Charts** How did land disputes lead to the war?

Causes of the Mexican-American War

Causes of the Mexican-American War
Texas wins independence from Mexico.
Supporters of Manifest Destiny seek more U.S. territory in the West.
The United States annexes Texas, outraging Mexicans.
Mexico and Texas both claim an area of land.
Supporters of Manifest Destiny push to gain control of Mexican lands.
President Polk sends U.S. troops into the area claimed by both Mexico and Texas.
Mexican troops enter that area and clash with U.S. troops.

The Mexican-American War, 1846–1848

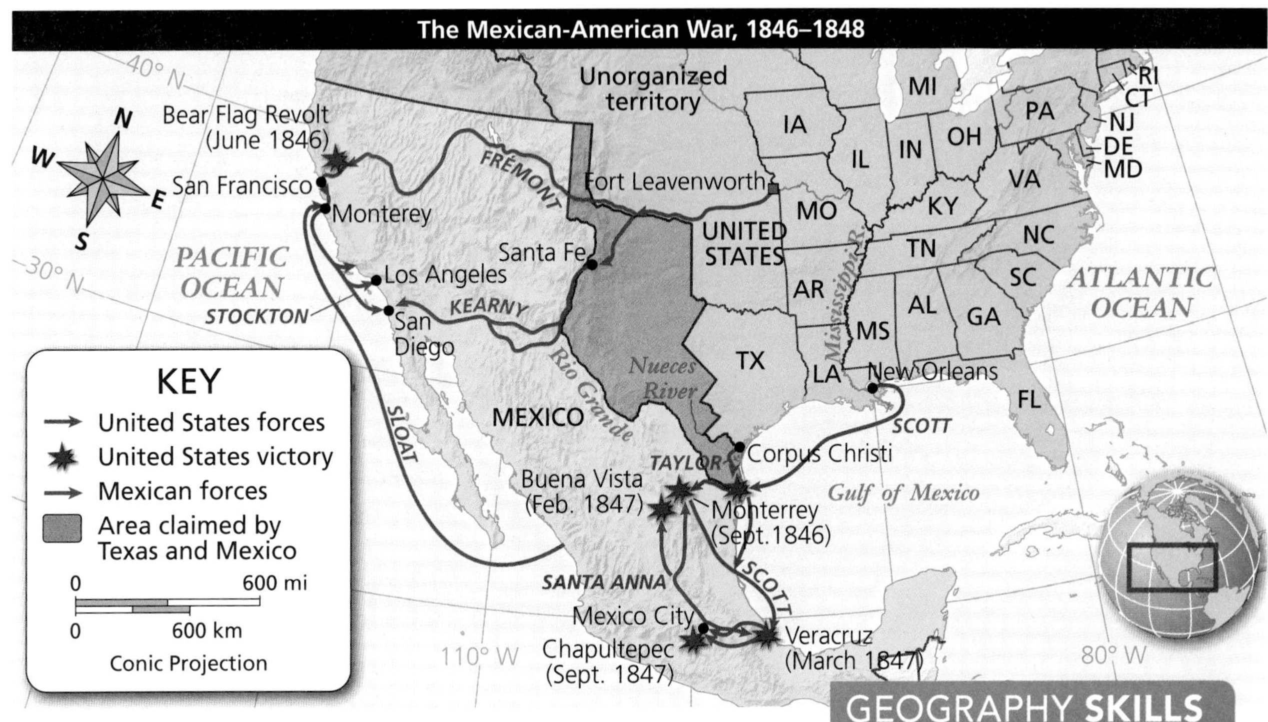

GEOGRAPHY SKILLS

The Mexican-American War was fought over a vast amount of territory.

1. **Movement** What were the similarities between American land and sea strategies?
2. **Infer** Why do you think the Americans attacked Mexico by sea instead of sending the armies overland through Texas?

Fighting on Multiple Fronts During the Mexican-American War, the United States attacked on several fronts at once.

General Taylor crossed the Rio Grande into northern Mexico. In February 1847, he met Mexican General Santa Anna at the Battle of Buena Vista. The Americans were outnumbered more than two to one, but they were better armed and better led. After fierce fighting and intense artillery fire, they forced Santa Anna to retreat.

A second army under General Winfield Scott landed at the Mexican port of Veracruz. After a long battle, Scott took the city. He then headed toward Mexico City, the capital.

A third army, led by General Stephen Kearny, captured Santa Fe without firing a shot. Kearny then hurried on to San Diego. After several battles, he won control of southern California early in 1847.

Even before hearing of the war, Americans in northern California had begun a revolt against Mexican rule. The rebels declared California an independent republic on June 14, 1846. They nicknamed their new nation the **Bear Flag Republic**. Within a month, U.S. forces claimed California for the United States. Led by John C. Frémont, rebel forces drove the Mexican troops out of northern California.

By 1847, the United States controlled all of New Mexico and California, and Scott was headed for Mexico City. Blocking his way was the Mexican army in a well-protected position. But in the ensuing Battle of Cerro Gordo, American troops outmaneuvered the Mexicans, who suffered heavy losses and were forced to retreat.

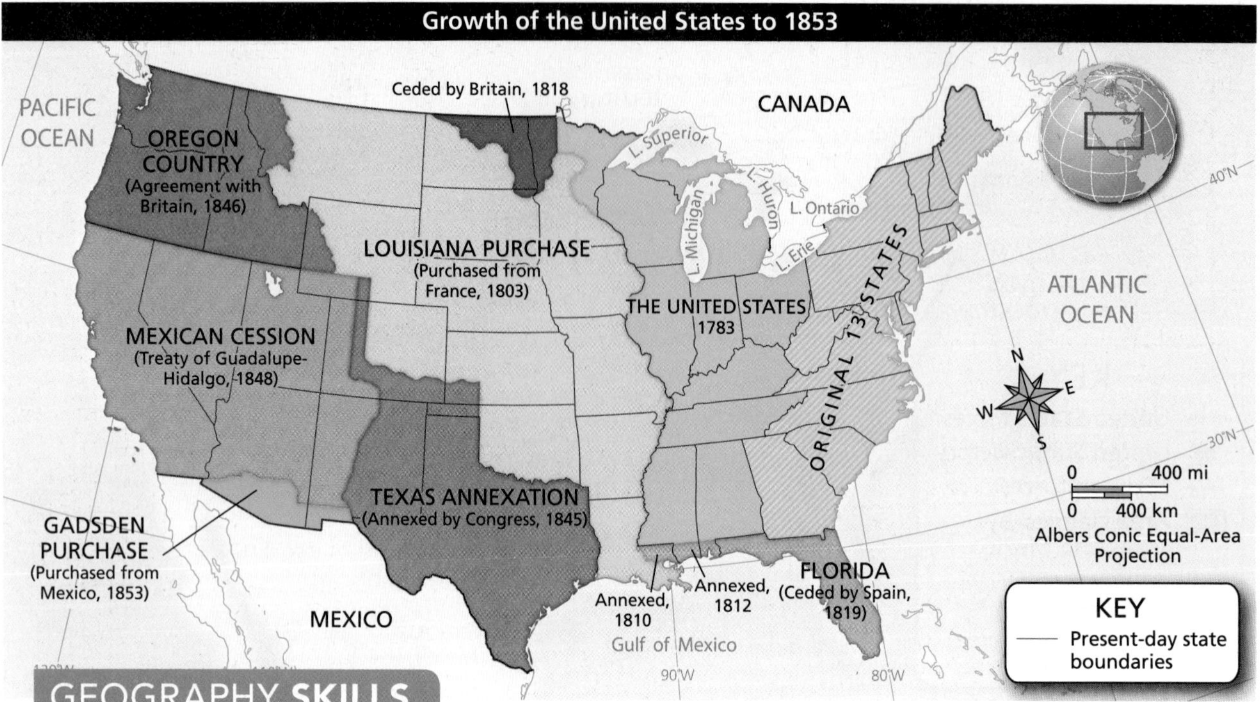

GEOGRAPHY **SKILLS**

By 1848, the United States extended from the Atlantic Ocean to the Pacific Ocean.

1. **Interaction** How would expansion of the United States across the continent change the character of the land?
2. **Identify Main Ideas** What was the impact of the Mexican-American War on the growth of the United States?

Then, at the edge of Mexico City, Scott's forces faced one last obstacle. Teenage Mexican cadets, or soldiers in training, made a heroic stand at Fort Chapultepec (chah POOL tuh pehk). Today, Mexicans honor those young cadets as heroes. At the battle's end, however, American forces captured Mexico City, and the war was essentially over. Scott's Mexico City campaign remains one of the most successful in U.S. military history.

The War Ends The Mexican-American War officially ended in 1848 when Mexico and the United States signed the **Treaty of Guadalupe-Hidalgo** (gwah duh LOOP ay hih DAHL goh). The treaty required Mexico to cede, or give up, all of California and New Mexico to the United States. These lands were called the **Mexican Cession**. In return, the United States paid Mexico $15 million.

In 1853, the United States paid Mexico an additional $10 million for a strip of land in present-day Arizona and New Mexico. Americans needed the land to complete a railroad. The land was called the Gadsden Purchase. With the Gadsden Purchase, many Americans felt that their dream of Manifest Destiny had been fulfilled.

READING CHECK **Identify Cause and Effect** Why were Mexicans worried about the annexation of Texas by the United States?

Mormons Settle the Mexican Cession

Winning the Mexican-American War ushered in a new era of growth. New Mexico Territory, now the southwestern part of the United States, came to be known as the Southwest. After 1848, English-speaking settlers flocked to the Southwest. The largest group was the Mormons.

CONNECTIONS

What was the effect of the war? Note your ideas in your Active Journal.

The Mormons Move West Mormons belonged to the Church of Jesus Christ of Latter-Day Saints. The church was founded in 1830 by Joseph Smith, a farmer in upstate New York.

Some of Smith's teachings differed from those of other Christian churches. These new teachings angered many non-Mormons, who forced the Mormons to leave New York.

The Mormons moved west and, in the 1840s, built a community they called Nauvoo on the banks of the Mississippi River in Illinois. Once again, the Mormons and their neighbors clashed. In 1844, an angry mob killed Joseph Smith, and Brigham Young was chosen as their new leader.

A New Home in Utah Young sought a place where Mormons would be safe from persecution. In 1847, he led an advance party into the valley of the Great Salt Lake. Soon, waves of Mormon families followed. For several years, Mormon wagon trains struggled across the plains and over the Rockies to Utah.

Young drew up plans for a large city, called Salt Lake City, to be built in the desert. The Mormon settlements in Utah grew, and eventually, in 1896, Utah became a state.

READING CHECK **Identify Cause and Effect** Why did the Mormons go to Utah?

The 31st State

While the Mormons were moving to what would become Utah, thousands of other Americans were racing even farther west. The great California gold rush had begun.

Did you know?

Five companies of Mormon settlers walked all the way to Salt Lake City pushing their belongings in handcarts like the one shown here.

The Rush to California In 1848, John Sutter was having a sawmill built on the American River, north of Sacramento, California. Sutter had hired James Marshall to supervise the job. Early on January 24, Marshall was out making inspections. He later recalled the events of that day:

Primary Source

"As I was taking my usual walk, . . . my eye was caught with the glimpse of something shining in the bottom of the ditch. . . . I reached my hand down and picked it up; it made my heart thump, for I was certain it was gold."

—James Marshall, quoted in *Hutchings' Illustrated California Magazine,* 1857–1858

Analyze Images Two Chinese American forty-niners. **Use Visual Information** What difficulties did forty-niners face?

Sutter tried to keep the news a secret, but word spread quickly. Soon, thousands of Americans caught "gold fever," along with people from Europe, China, Australia, and South America. More than 80,000 people made the journey to California in 1849. They became known as **forty-niners**, a nickname created in reference to the year they arrived.

Very few miners actually struck it rich, and many went broke. In some cases, wives made more money at home than their husbands did in the mines. "I have made about $18,000 worth of pies," one woman boasted.

INTERACTIVE

Growth of the West to 1860

Many miners left the gold fields, but they stayed in California. In time, they found jobs or took up farming.

Conflicts Over Water While California has a variety of climates and landscapes, many areas of California are naturally dry, especially in the south. Not surprisingly, as the population grew, people quarreled over water **allocation**.

Academic Vocabulary
allocation • *n.,* the dividing up of something for a special purpose

Two systems of water rights developed. One system, based in common law, gives water rights to the people who live in a place where water is. This system commonly gave first water rights to missions and pueblos, which were normally built near rivers or lakes.

The other system of water rights developed in the gold rush mining areas. To the miners, water was like gold: whoever found it owned it. If your neighbor upstream took water from a river, there might not be any left for you. Conflicts over water rights led to legal and political battles between missions, ranchers, miners, and farmers.

Many conflicts involved farmers who needed water for their crops or missions that needed water for their residents. Farmers complained that the mining process polluted the water, making it unfit for agriculture. The conflicts over water were never completely resolved and continue to the present time.

Statehood for California The gold rush brought big changes to California. Almost overnight, San Francisco grew into a bustling city. In the gold fields, towns sprang up just as quickly. Greed led some forty-niners into crime. Murders and robberies plagued many mining camps.

Californians realized that they needed a strong government to stop such lawlessness. **Consequently**, in November of 1849, they drafted a state constitution and then asked to be admitted to the Union. Their request caused an uproar because of the slavery issue. After a heated debate, California was admitted to the Union as a free state as part of the Compromise of 1850. But the question of whether new states could allow slavery would continue to cause bitter disagreements that further divided the nation.

Quick Activity

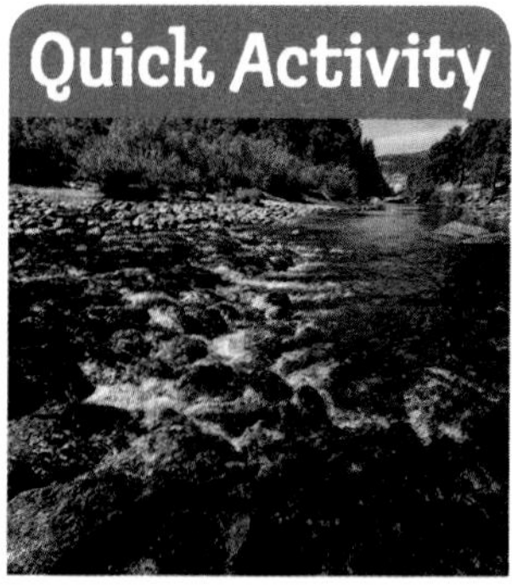

Investigate ways in which rivers and streams helped determine where people settled in California.

Academic Vocabulary
consequently • *adv.*, as a result

READING CHECK **Sequence** How did California grow to statehood?

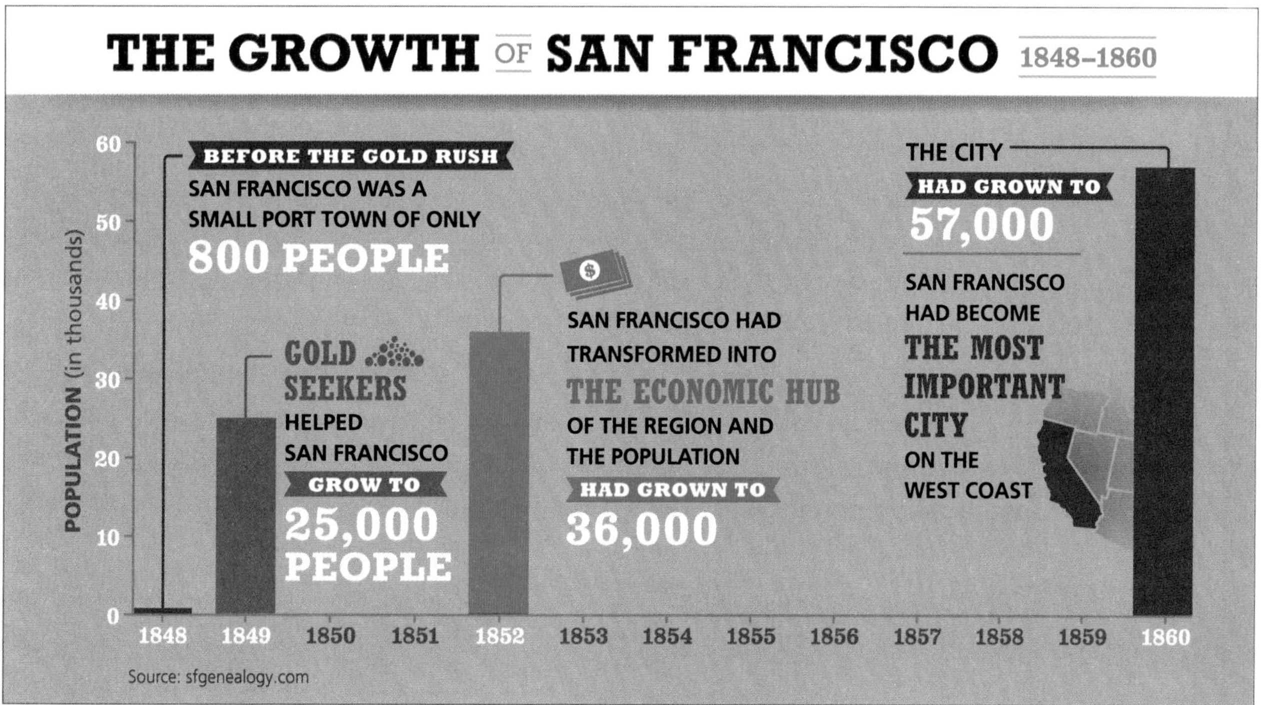

Analyze Images The gold rush transformed San Francisco from a small port town into a major city. **Analyze Charts** How did immigration and migration impact the settlement of San Francisco?

INTERACTIVE

The People of California

The Effects of Migration to California

Westward expansion had many effects on the cultures and peoples of California. The gold rush brought diverse groups of people into contact with each other in the West.

A Mix of Cultures Most newcomers were white Americans from the East. Far more white men than women had joined the quest for gold. As a result, white men far outnumbered white women, making single women very sought after. This increased women's bargaining position and their stature, enabling them to achieve some rights that women elsewhere were denied.

The shortage of women also helped break down barriers between groups. In some areas, intermarriage between white men and Mexican women became more common.

California's mining camps included African Americans who had escaped from slavery in the South, free African Americans, and American Indians. There were also people from Hawaii, China, Peru, Chile, France, Germany, Italy, Ireland, and Australia.

Before the gold rush, California's population had included large numbers of Mexicans. Mexican Americans faced serious hardships. In the years following California statehood, many Mexican Americans lost land that their families had owned for generations.

Analyze Images People of all races came to California from across the country and around the world. **Identify Supporting Details** How did the gold rush change California's population?

American Indians fared even worse. Many were driven off the lands where they lived. Without any means to earn a living, large numbers died of starvation or disease brought by the newcomers. Others were murdered. In 1850, about 100,000 American Indians lived in California. By the 1870s, their population had dwindled to 17,000.

Lured by tales of a "mountain of gold," thousands of Chinese immigrants crossed the Pacific Ocean to California. At first, they were welcomed because California needed workers. When Chinese people staked claims in the gold fields, however, white miners often drove them off. Despite such injustice, many Chinese Americans stayed in California. Their contributions helped the state to grow. They shaped the environment by draining swamplands and digging irrigation systems to turn dry land into fertile farmland.

Analyze Images This 1868 photo shows environmental damage near Dutch Flat, California, caused by hydraulic gold mining. **Sequence** Based on details in the photograph, describe how hydraulic mining damaged the environment.

Free Black people also joined the gold rush. Some became well-off by starting and running businesses. By the 1850s, California had the wealthiest African American population of any state. Yet, African Americans faced discrimination and were denied certain rights.

Changes to the Region In spite of its problems, California continued to grow and prosper. Settlers from other states and immigrants from all over the world kept arriving. With their diverse backgrounds, the newcomers helped create California's identity. The economy grew as commerce and mining expanded. Agricultural production and the growth of the oil industry accounted for much of California's early economic growth. Cities and roads grew to accommodate the increase in people and goods.

READING CHECK **Identify Cause and Effect** Why did so many American Indians die of disease as newcomers moved westward?

Lesson Check

Practice Vocabulary

1. What happened to the **Bear Flag Republic**?
2. What did Mexico cede in the **Treaty of Guadalupe-Hidalgo**?
3. Who were the **forty-niners**?

Critical Thinking and Writing

4. **Identify Main Ideas** How were Americans influenced by the idea of Manifest Destiny?
5. **Draw Conclusions** Why do you suppose Brigham Young chose the isolated valley of the Great Salt Lake as a new home for the Mormons?
6. **Writing Workshop: End Strongly** In your Active Journal, write a final paragraph for your narrative. Bring it to an end in a way that will make it memorable for readers.

TOPIC 6

Review and Assessment

VISUAL REVIEW

Events in the Age of Andrew Jackson

EVENTS IN THE AGE OF ANDREW JACKSON

Social
- Tocqueville observes rising equality
- Life in the West expands women's roles
- American Indian removal
- Slavery extended in the South

Political
- Suffrage extended
- Common people support Jacksonian democracy
- Whigs and Democrats disagree about the role of government
- Nullification Crisis
- Jackson defies Supreme Court

Military
- War for Texas Independence
- Mexican-American War
- Bear Flag Revolt

Economic
- Second Bank of the United States closes
- Development of steamboats, the National Road, and canals
- Panic of 1837
- California Gold Rush

Manifest Destiny

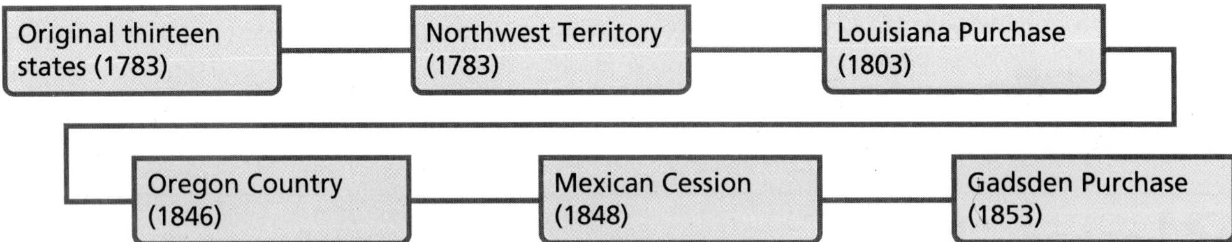

READING REVIEW

Use the Take Notes and Practice Vocabulary activities in your Active Journal to review the topic.

INTERACTIVE

Practice vocabulary using the Topic Mini-Games

Quest FINDINGS

Conduct Your Civic Discussion

Get help for conducting your discussion in your Active Journal.

ASSESSMENT

Vocabulary and Key Ideas

1. **Describe** How did **suffrage** change during the early years of the Age of Jackson?
2. **Check Understanding** Why did many people disapprove of the **spoils system**?
3. **Define** What was the **frontier**?
4. **Recall** What happens during a **depression**?
5. **Describe** How is a **caucus** different from a **nominating convention**?
6. **Use** What was the significance of the **National Road**?
7. **Check Understanding** What happened when Mexico signed the **Treaty of Guadalupe-Hidalgo**?

Critical Thinking and Writing

8. **Identify Point of View** Write a paragraph identifying the points of view the Whig Party and the Democratic Party held on major issues. What can you conclude about each party's point of view on the government's role in the economy?
9. **Explain an Argument** Explain how the issues of states' rights and nullification affected the nation during the Age of Jackson.
10. **Summarize** What is Manifest Destiny and how did this idea affect Americans and the people they encountered in the West?
11. **Revisit the Essential Question** Why did people move into the West? Think about the varied groups of people who settled in the West and their reasons for leaving their homes.
12. **Writing Workshop: Write a Narrative** Using the passages and notes you have written in your Active Journal, write a narrative from the perspective of a person moving westward during this time period. Tell about important or memorable events during your journey. Include description and sensory details to bring the narrative alive for readers. Create a strong opening and a memorable ending.

Analyze Primary Sources

13. The quotation presents one view of the conflict about
    A. the Second Bank of the United States.
    B. the Indian Removal Act.
    C. the "corrupt bargain."
    D. states' rights.

"When the laws undertake . . . to make the rich richer and the potent more powerful, the humble members of the society—the farmers, mechanics, and laborers—who have neither the time nor the means of [getting] favors for themselves . . . have a right to complain of the injustices of their government."

—President Andrew Jackson

Analyze Maps

Use the map to answer the following questions.

14. The Trail of Tears ended in which territory? Where did these American Indians live before they were relocated?
15. How did the Oregon Trail get its name? In which territory did the Oregon Trail begin?
16. Which territory did the United States acquire following the Mexican-American War? Which states were formed from this territory?

▼ U.S. Growth to 1853

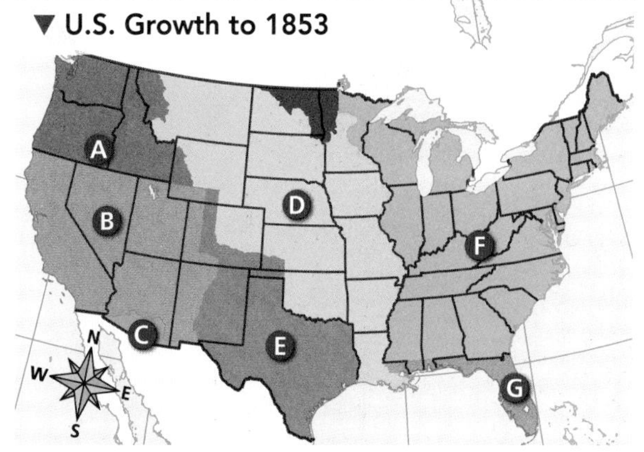

TOPIC 7

Society and Culture Before the Civil War (1820–1860)

GO ONLINE to access your digital course

VIDEO

AUDIO

ETEXT

INTERACTIVE

WRITING

GAMES

WORKSHEET

ASSESSMENT

Go back two centuries

to explore American SOCIETY AND CULTURE BEFORE THE CIVIL WAR. See how kids your age and younger worked in factories or picked cotton—10 to 14 hours a day. See how African Americans fought for their freedom and courageous women fought for their rights.

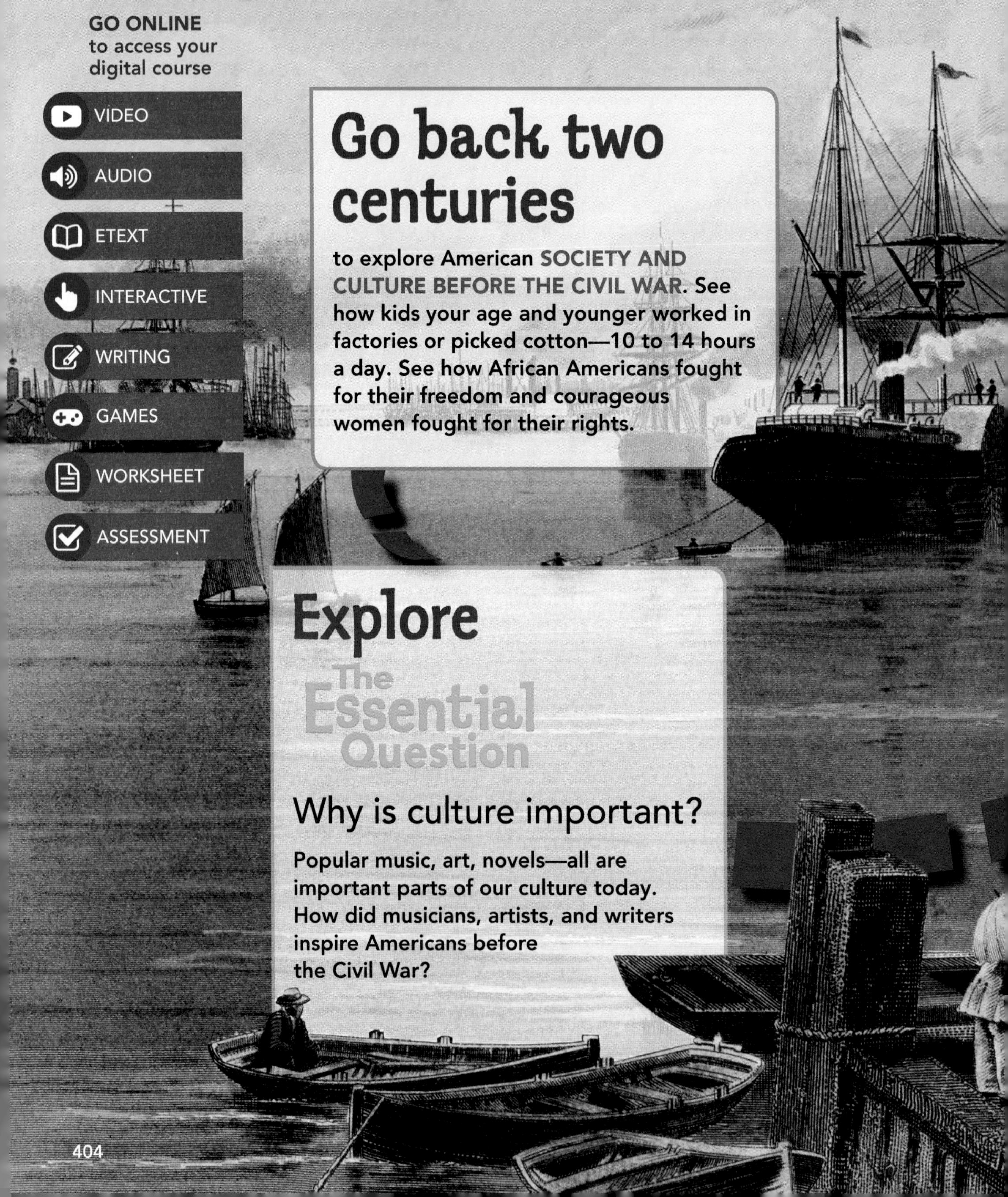

Explore The Essential Question

Why is culture important?

Popular music, art, novels—all are important parts of our culture today. How did musicians, artists, and writers inspire Americans before the Civil War?

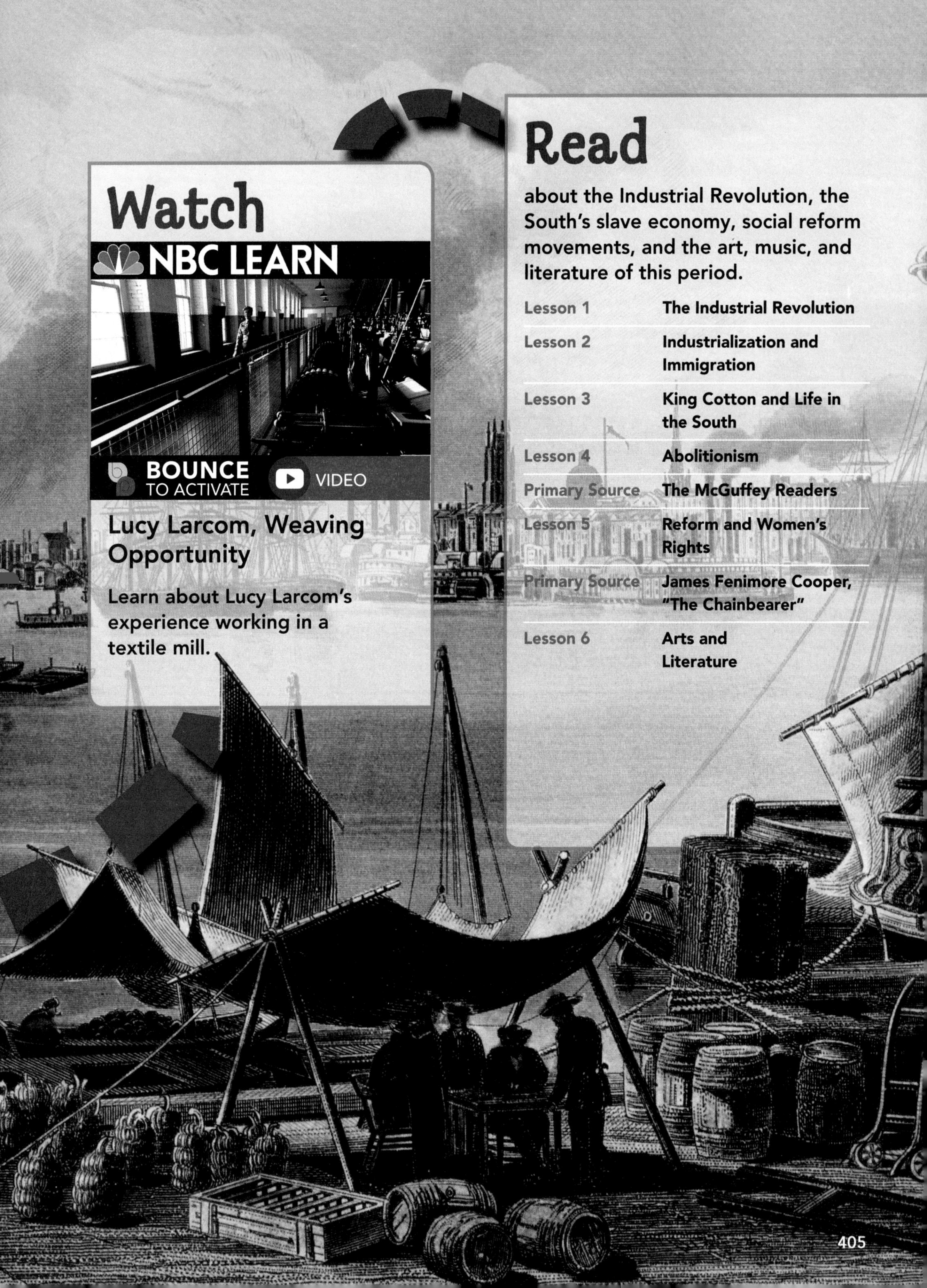

Watch

NBC LEARN

BOUNCE TO ACTIVATE ▶ VIDEO

Lucy Larcom, Weaving Opportunity

Learn about Lucy Larcom's experience working in a textile mill.

Read

about the Industrial Revolution, the South's slave economy, social reform movements, and the art, music, and literature of this period.

TOPIC 7

Society and Culture Before the Civil War (1820–1860)

Learn more about the pre–Civil War era by making your own map and timeline in your Active Journal.

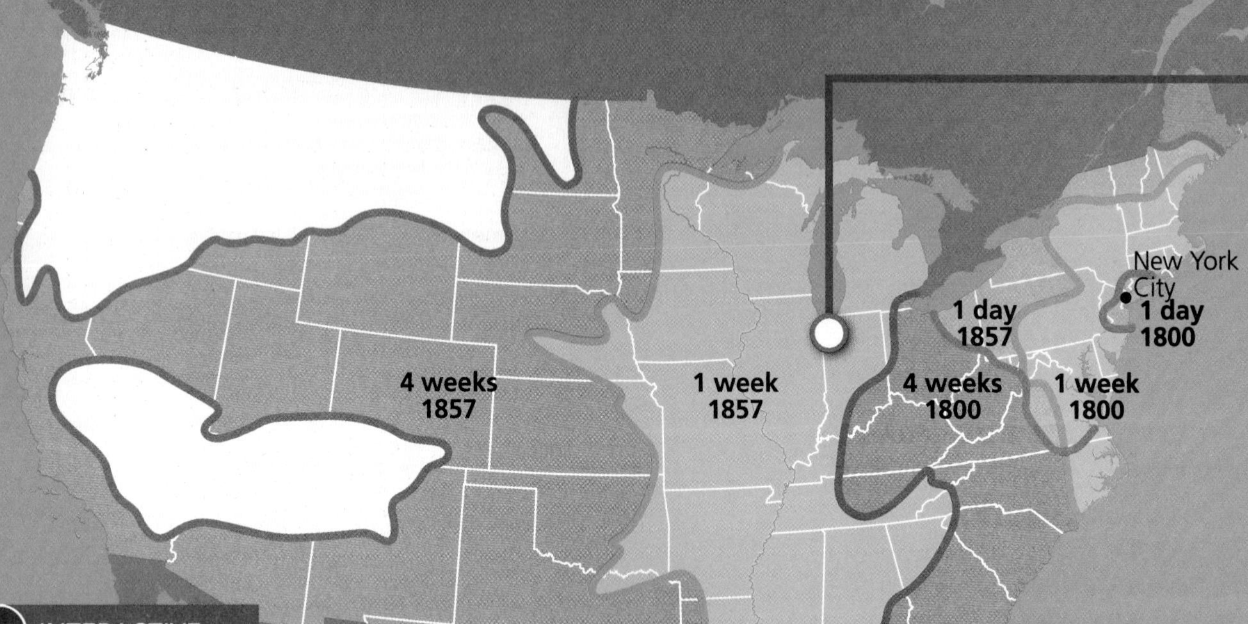

INTERACTIVE

Topic Timeline

What happened and when?

Noise and dust of the factory . . . women demanding equal rights . . . Explore the timeline to see some of what was happening in the United States and in the rest of the world.

1820
The Second Great Awakening begins.

TOPIC EVENTS

1810 **1820** **1830**

WORLD EVENTS

1833
British Factory Act limits child labor.

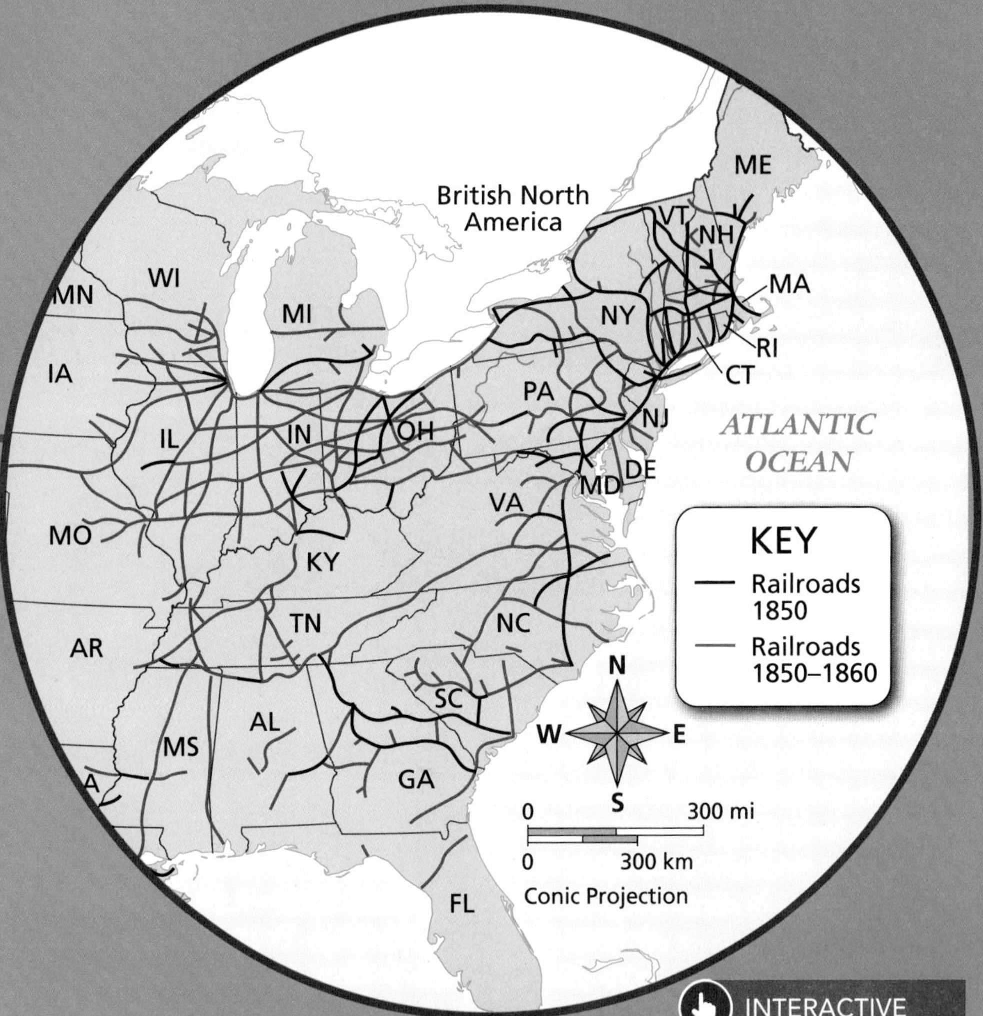

British North America

MN WI MI IA IL IN OH PA NY VT NH ME MA RI CT NJ DE MD VA MO KY TN NC AR MS AL GA SC FL LA

ATLANTIC OCEAN

KEY
Railroads 1850
Railroads 1850–1860

N S E W

0 300 mi
0 300 km
Conic Projection

INTERACTIVE
Topic Map

Who will you meet?

Eli Whitney, inventor of the cotton gin

Frederick Douglass, abolitionist

Susan B. Anthony, advocate for women's rights

How did the railroad change travel?

The growth of railroads greatly reduced travel time. Going from New York to Kentucky took a month in 1800. By 1857, travelers could go all the way to California in that time.

1844
Robert Morse patents the telegraph.

1848
Seneca Falls Convention

1854
Henry David Thoreau publishes *Walden.*

1840 | 1850 | 1860 | 1870

1848
Revolutions shake Germany, Italy, and France.

1853
Great Exhibition displays products of the Industrial Revolution.

1858
Great Britain takes control of India.

Document-Based Writing Inquiry

Slavery and Abolition

Quest KICK OFF

In the South, the increase in cotton production led to an increase in the number of enslaved people. In the 1830s, a movement called abolition began, with the goal of ending slavery. Americans expressed strong feelings for and against abolition.

What points of view did people have toward slavery and abolition?

How did people on both sides of this issue explain their position? Explore the Essential Question "Why is culture important?" in this Quest.

▶ Once enslaved, Frederick Douglass became a leading abolitionist.

1 Ask Questions

What questions would you ask people on both sides of the slavery issue? Write your questions in your Active Journal.

2 Investigate

As you read the lessons in this topic, look for Quest CONNECTIONS that will help you understand differing points of view toward slavery and abolition. Record notes in your Active Journal.

3 Examine Primary Sources

Study the primary sources from the 1800s. They provide several points of view on both sides of the slavery issue. Record notes in your Active Journal.

Quest FINDINGS

4 Write Your Essay

The opinions that Americans expressed before the Civil War about slavery and abolition reflected both cultural differences and personal attitudes. At the end of the topic, you will use the primary sources and your own knowledge of history to write an essay stating your own conclusions about these opinions. Get help for this task in your Active Journal.

LESSON 1

The Industrial Revolution

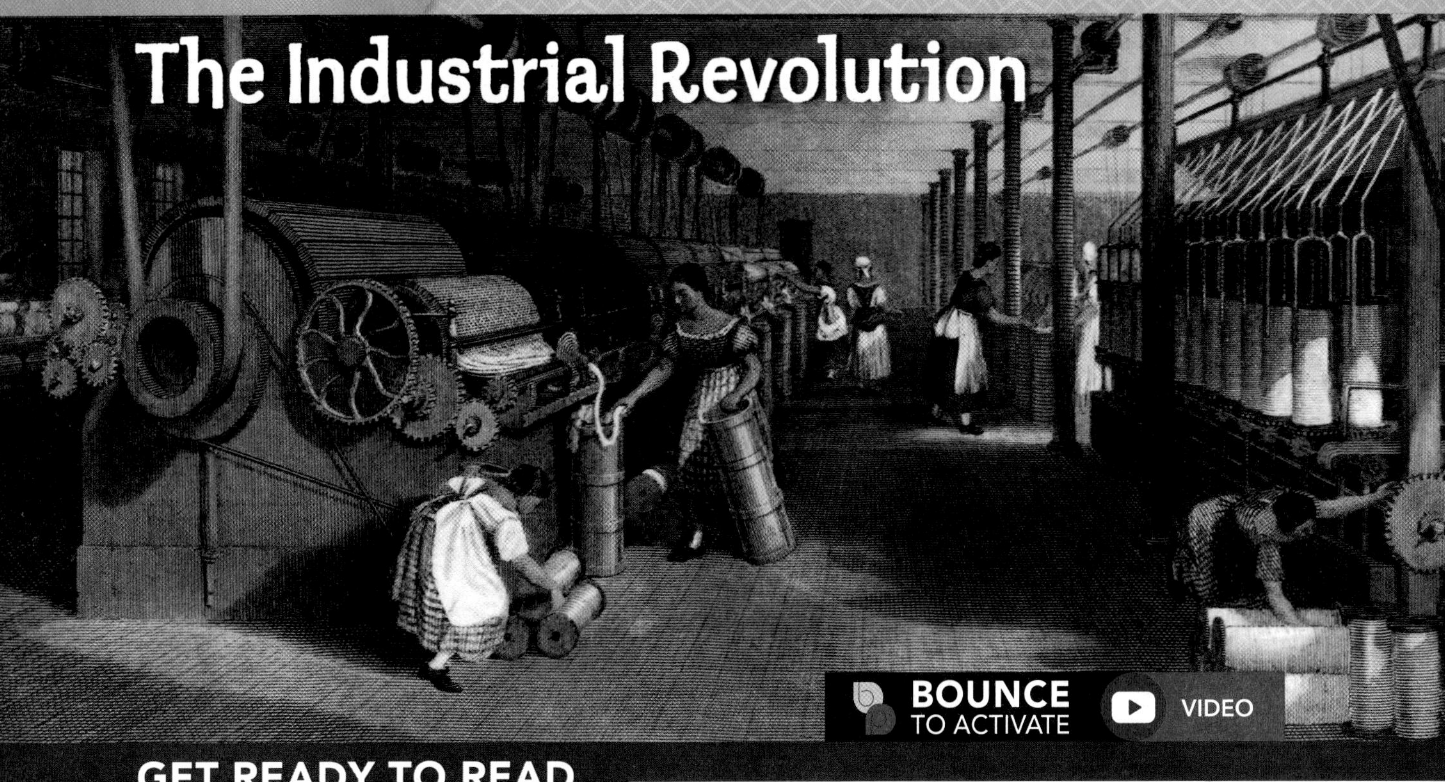

GET READY TO READ

START UP

Examine the illustration of workers in a textile mill. What would it be like to work here, in a large room filled with rapidly spinning machines?

GUIDING QUESTIONS

- How did work change between 1800 and 1850?
- What was family life like in different regions of the country during this period?

TAKE NOTES

Literacy Skills: Cite Evidence

Use the graphic organizer in your Active Journal to take notes as you read the lesson.

PRACTICE VOCABULARY

Use the vocabulary activity in your Active Journal to practice the vocabulary words.

Vocabulary

Industrial Revolution
capital
capitalist
scarcity
supply
interchangeable parts
Lowell girls
urbanization

Academic Vocabulary

profit
credit

In the early 1800s, busy factories and whirring machinery were part of a revolution that was spreading to the United States. Unlike the American Revolution, this one had no battles or fixed dates. The new revolution—the **Industrial Revolution**—was a long, slow process that completely changed the way goods were produced and where many people worked and lived.

The Industrial Revolution Begins

Before the 1800s, most Americans were farmers and most goods were produced by hand. As a result of the Industrial Revolution, this situation slowly changed. Machines replaced hand tools. New sources of power, such as steam, replaced human and animal power. While most Americans continued to farm for a living, the economy began a gradual shift toward manufacturing.

Technological Innovations The Industrial Revolution started in Britain in the mid-1700s. New machines transformed the textile industry.

Analyze Images The spinning jenny invented by James Hargreaves allowed workers to spin multiple spools of yarn at once. **Draw Conclusions** How did this invention affect the supply and cost of producing textiles?

Since the Middle Ages, workers had used spinning wheels to make thread. A spinning wheel, however, could spin only one thread at a time. In 1764, James Hargreaves developed the spinning jenny, a machine that could spin several threads at once. Other inventions sped up the process of weaving thread into cloth. In the 1780s, Edmund Cartwright built a loom powered by water. It allowed a worker to produce a great deal more cloth in a day than was possible before. These technological innovations would change how goods were made not only in Britain, but also in America and around the world.

New Ways to Produce Goods New inventions led to a new system of producing goods. Before the Industrial Revolution, most spinning and weaving took place in the home. Industrial production involved large machines, however, and these had to be housed in large mills near rivers. Water flowing downstream or over a waterfall turned a wheel that captured the power to run the machines.

To set up and operate a spinning mill required large amounts of **capital**, or invested money. Capitalists supplied this money. A **capitalist** is a person who invests in a business to make a **profit**. Capitalists built factories and hired workers to run the machines.

Academic Vocabulary
profit • *n.*, the difference between the cost of a good and its selling price

The new factory system brought workers and machinery together in one place to produce goods. Factory workers earned daily or weekly wages. They had to work a set number of hours each day.

In Britain, investors saw an opportunity. Because a single worker could produce much more with a machine than by hand, the cost of goods made by machine was much lower and more of those goods could be sold. If an investor built a factory that could produce cloth more cheaply, the investor could make a profit. Investors' desire to make a profit brought about rapid industrialization.

During the Industrial Revolution, the demand for factory-made products grew. In economics, demand is the readiness of people to purchase goods or services. The **supply**, or amount of goods available to sell, depended in part on the natural resources factories could get. To make products, factories needed raw materials, power, and laborers to run machinery. Some resources, such as cotton and iron, were in short supply. This **scarcity**, or limited supply, resulted in high prices. In response to high prices, farmers began to grow more cotton to supply spinning mills. Miners and others searched for new sources of iron and other materials used in machinery. The growing demand for products and for the supplies needed to make them led to a great change in standards of living.

INTERACTIVE

Early Textile Mill

READING CHECK **Summarize** How did the Industrial Revolution affect the forces of supply and demand?

America's First Factories

Britain wanted to keep its technological innovations, or new technologies, secret. It did not want rival nations to copy the new machines. Therefore, the British Parliament passed a law forbidding anyone to take plans of the new machinery out of the country.

Slater Emigrates to the United States Samuel Slater soon proved that this law could not be enforced. Slater was a skilled mechanic in a British textile mill. He knew that his knowledge and skills would be in demand in the United States. In 1789, Slater boarded a ship bound for New York City. British officials searched the baggage of passengers sailing to the United States to make sure they were not carrying plans for machinery with them. Slater, however, did not need to carry any plans. Having worked in the British mills from an early age, Slater knew not only how to build the mills and machinery but also how to operate them.

The First American Mill Slater soon visited Moses Brown, a Quaker capitalist who had a mill in Pawtucket, Rhode Island. The mill was not doing well because its machinery constantly broke down. Slater set to work on improving the machinery. By 1793, in Pawtucket, he built what became the first successful textile mill in the United States that was powered by water.

Slater's factory was a huge success. Before long, other American manufacturers began using his ideas.

Interchangeable Parts American manufacturers also benefited from the pioneering work of American inventor Eli Whitney. Earlier, skilled workers made goods by hand. For example, gunsmiths spent days making the barrel, stock, and trigger for a single musket. Because the parts were handmade, each musket differed a bit from every other musket. If a part broke, a gunsmith had to make a new part to fit that particular gun.

Analyze Images A restored water wheel stands outside a New England mill. **Infer** Water wheels had been used for many years at grain mills. Did they differ significantly from those that powered textile mills?

▲ Eli Whitney's development of interchangeable parts, while making muskets, revolutionized manufacturing.

Whitney wanted to speed up the making of guns by having machines manufacture each part. All machine-made parts would be alike—for example, one trigger would be identical to another. Identical parts would fit together with all other parts, and gunsmiths would not have build each gun from scratch. **Interchangeable parts** would save time and money.

Because the government bought many guns, Whitney went to Washington, D.C., to try to sell his idea. At first, officials laughed at his plan. Carefully, Whitney sorted parts for 10 muskets into separate piles. He then asked an official to choose one part from each pile. In minutes, the first musket was assembled. Whitney repeated the process until 10 muskets were complete.

In 1798, Whitney began producing muskets in the first factory to rely on interchangeable parts. The idea of interchangeable parts spread rapidly. Inventors designed machines to produce interchangeable parts for clocks, locks, and many other goods. With such machines, small workshops grew into factories.

Factories Spread The War of 1812 provided a boost to American industries. The British blockade cut Americans off from their supply of foreign goods. As a result, they had to produce more goods themselves. American merchants and bankers sought new ways to meet the increased demand. To profit from the efficiency provided by manufacturing, they built more factories. As American investors took advantage of new technologies and built more factories, the American economy grew.

Where Were Factories Built? The natural resources available to the people of a region shaped their economic activities. The first factories were built in the Northeast. Pennsylvania had abundant forests and iron ore. Lumbermen felled great swaths of forest for the timber used to make charcoal. Pennsylvania factories used the charcoal for power. These factories turned iron ore, which was mined and smelted locally, into machines, tools, and guns.

In New England, textile factories were built alongside the hilly region's numerous fast-moving streams. Falling water provided power for the mills. Humans also modified the landscape by building dams and canals to help power the mills. These modifications spurred economic growth. Wool and cotton produced in the South provided the raw materials for thread, yarn, and fabric. In Lynn, Massachusetts, businesses developed a step-by-step shoemaking process in the early 19th century. The large factories attracted new workers to the town, and the economy grew rapidly. New England became the first region in the United States to develop manufacturing on a wide scale.

The Market Economy and the Industrial Revolution In the United States, the Industrial Revolution took place in a period marked by the growth of a free enterprise, or market, economy. British restrictions on trade had been lifted. Hamilton's reforms had strengthened the banking system, and banks were able to lend more money. New access to **credit**, or borrowed money, allowed people to start mills and factories in cities and in rural places where swift streams provided power.

A market revolution was taking place. Mills and factories sprouted throughout the Northeast. New technologies, such as interchangeable parts and the steamboat, allowed for more efficient production and the transportation of goods. New roads and canals linked towns, expanding opportunities for commerce.

Businesses operated, for the most part, without much government control. Nor did the government own factories or intervene heavily in the market. The government, however, protected contracts and property. People could buy, sell, or use property as they saw fit.

Most Americans wanted the freedom to try new things. They believed in competition, which encouraged new inventions. In 1792, a group of 24 investors had started the New York Stock Exchange. This stock market raised private capital to pay for new ventures. Success meant profits and brought new wealth to investors. Profits led to new investment and further economic growth.

Low taxes allowed businesses to hold on to large amounts of capital and use it to expand and create even more wealth. The desire for profit and accumulated wealth sparked new ventures under new investors.

The Role of Market Forces Investors looked to the market to decide where to invest or what businesses to start. In a market economy, goods are bought and sold, and wages are determined, by the market. If a product is in high demand and the supply is limited,

Academic Vocabulary

credit • *n.*, an agreement or contract in which a borrower receives money or goods now, with an agreement to repay a greater amount later

Analyze Images The Pemberton Mill in Lawrence, MA, collapsed January 10, 1860, because the building's structure could not support the load placed on it. More than 145 workers, mostly women from Ireland, died in the collapse. **Draw Conclusions** What does this disaster tell you about the mill owners' attitude toward the mill's workers?

the price will be high. Entrepreneurs started businesses to supply high-priced or high-demand products. They abandoned businesses where the demand and price were low.

Workers faced the same market forces. People with skills that were in demand in factories could expect higher wages than those whose skills had less value in the market.

READING CHECK **Understand Effects** How did transportation boost the market revolution in the early 1800s?

Daily Life in Factory Towns

Slater and Whitney's innovations were just the first steps in America's Industrial Revolution. During the early 1800s, entire cities began to emerge around factories.

Mills in Lowell During the War of 1812, Francis Cabot Lowell, a Boston merchant, found a way to improve on British textile mills. In Britain, one factory spun thread and a second factory wove it into cloth. Why not, Lowell wondered, combine spinning and weaving under one roof? The new mill that he built in Waltham, Massachusetts, had all the machines needed to turn raw cotton into finished cloth.

After Lowell's death, his partners took on a more ambitious project. They built an entire factory town and named it after him. In 1821, Lowell, Massachusetts, was a village of five farm families.

By 1836, it boasted more than 10,000 people. Visitors to Lowell described it as a model community composed of "small wooden houses, painted white, with green blinds, very neat, very snug, very nicely carpeted."

Analyze Images The town of Lowell was set up to be a factory town. **Compare and Contrast** Map 1 shows Lowell in 1821, and map 2 shows the town in 1845. What changes can you see?

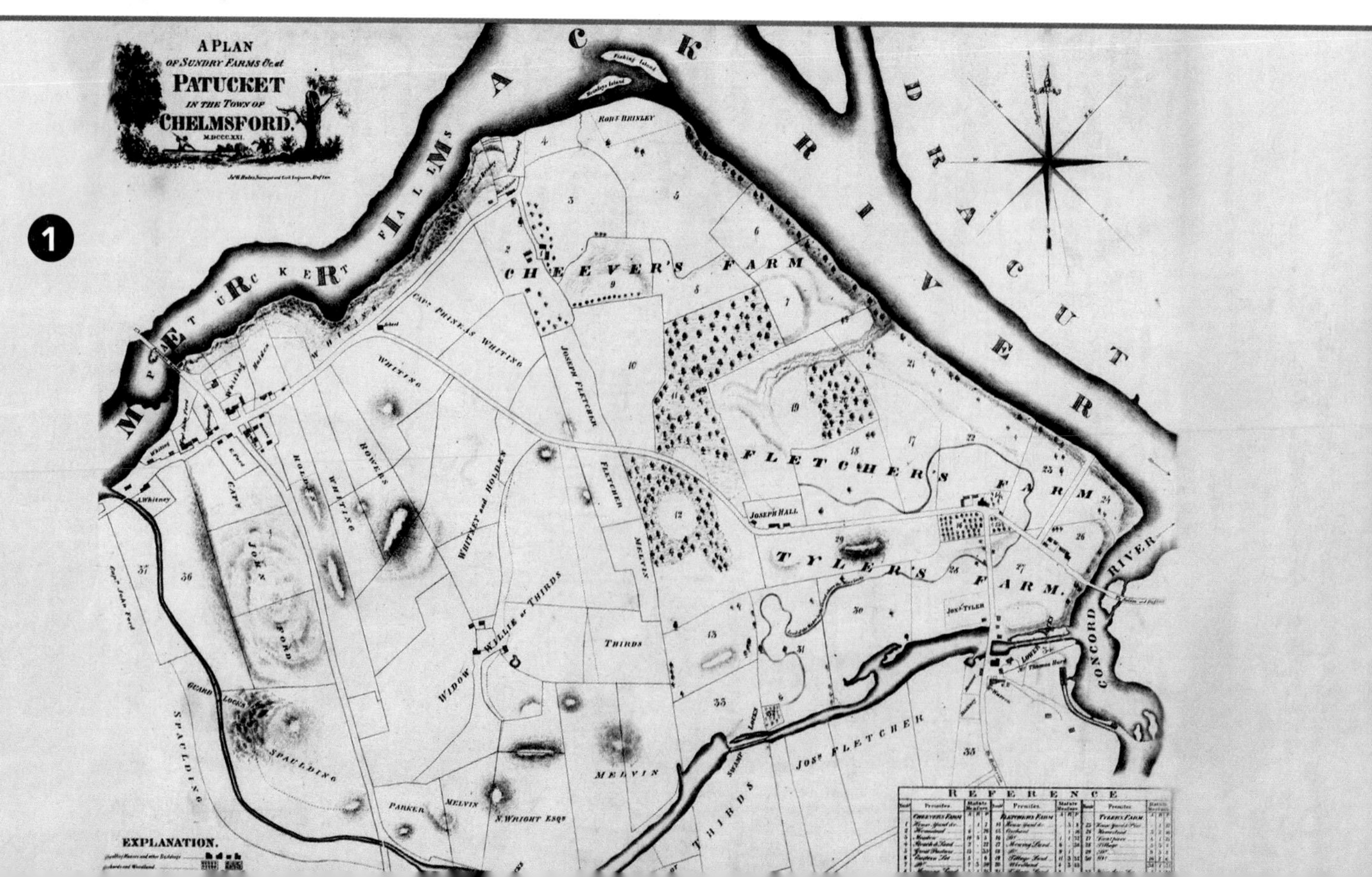

"Lowell Girls" To work in their new mills, the company hired young women from nearby farms. The **Lowell girls**, as they came to be called, usually worked for a few years in the mills before returning home to marry. These young women, and women like them in other mill towns, made an important economic contribution to American society by providing labor for the Industrial Revolution. Most sent their wages home to their families.

At first, parents hesitated to let their daughters work in the mills. To reassure parents, the company built boardinghouses, or buildings with many shared bedrooms and a kitchen that served meals. The company also made rules to protect the young women.

British author Charles Dickens toured Lowell in 1842. The Lowell girls impressed him. He later wrote:

Primary Source

"It is their station to work. And they do work. They labour in these mills, upon an average, twelve hours a day, which is unquestionably work, and pretty tight work too."

—Charles Dickens, *American Notes and Pictures from Italy*

Although factory work was often tedious, hard, and dangerous, many women valued the economic freedom they got from working in the mills. One worker wrote her sister Sarah back on a farm in New Hampshire:

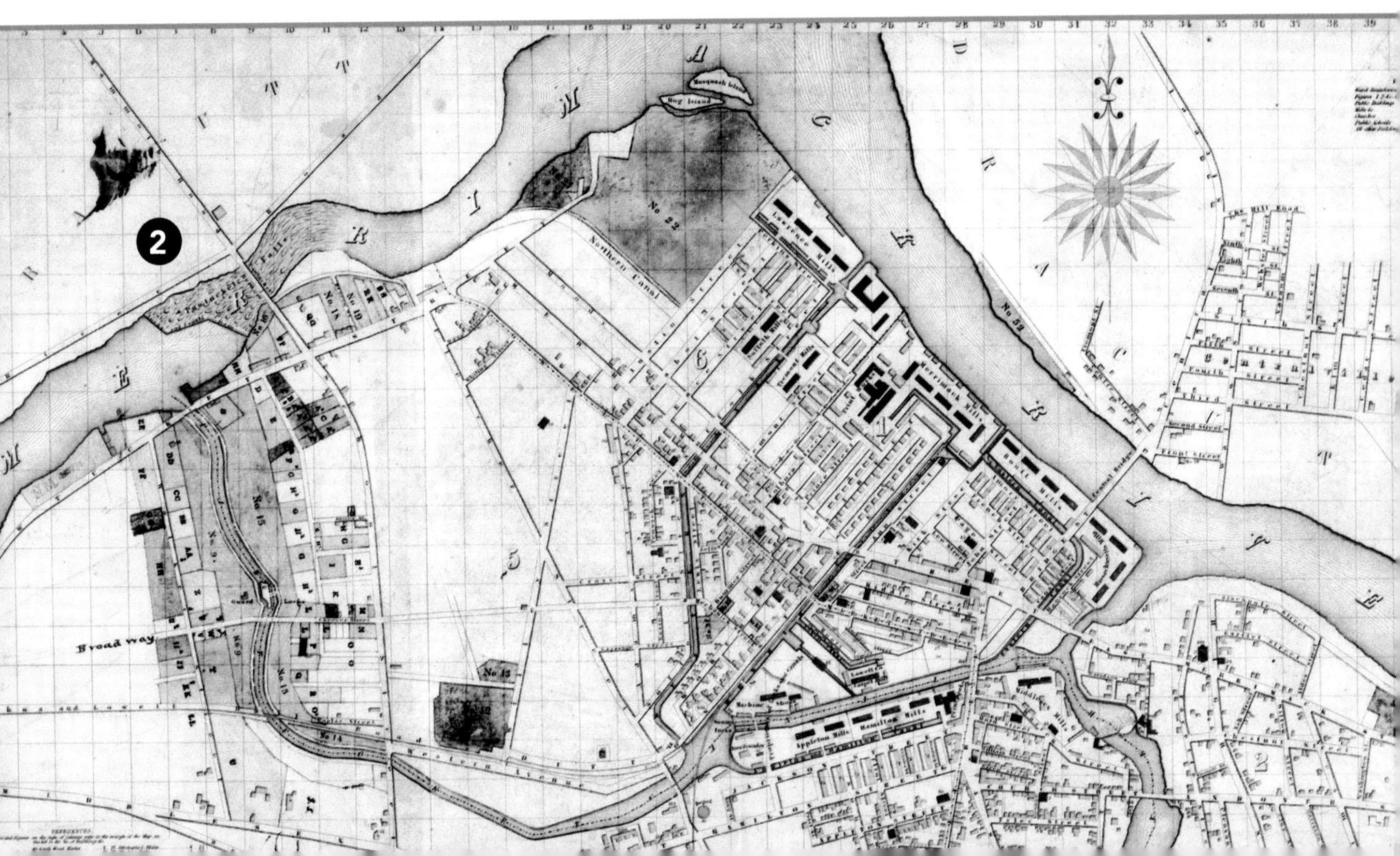

Primary Source

"Since I have wrote you, another pay day has come around. I earned 14 dollars and a half . . . I like it well as ever and Sarah don't I feel independent of everyone!"

— from *Lowell Offering: Writings by New England Mill Women*

In Lowell and elsewhere, mill owners hired mostly women and children. They did this because they could pay women and children half of what they would have had to pay men.

Child Labor Boys and girls as young as seven worked in factories. Small children were especially useful in textile mills because they could squeeze around the large machines to change spindles.

Today, most Americans look upon child labor as cruel. Yet in the 1800s, farm children also worked hard. Most people did not see much difference between children working in a factory or on a farm. Often, a child's wages were needed to help support the family.

Long Hours Working hours in the mills were long—12 hours a day, 6 days a week. True, farmers also put in long hours. However, farmers worked shorter hours in winter. Mill workers, in contrast, worked nearly the same hours all year round.

As industries grew and competition increased, employers took less interest in the welfare of their workers. Working conditions eventually declined.

Changes at Home The Industrial Revolution had a great impact on home life. Previously, most Americans worked in agriculture. The entire family lived at home and farmed the land together. In the Northeast, some families took part in cottage industries, making goods at home. Local merchants supplied them with materials, such as wool. Home workers, usually women and girls, would spin the wool into yarn and

Analyze Images Although farm work was hard, it varied. Factory workers did the same task for many hours at a time all year round. **Draw Conclusions** Do you think mill workers found their jobs satisfying?

weave it into cloth. Other cottage workers made shoes. As the factory system spread, the family economy gave way to industrial production. More family members left the home to earn a living.

These changes affected ideas about the role of women. In poorer families, women often had to go out to work. In wealthier families, husbands supported the family while wives stayed at home. For many husbands, having a wife who stayed at home became a sign of success. Men and women began to be viewed as fundamentally different, with distinct gender-based roles. Women were judged to be best suited to the domestic life, while men were expected to go out and earn a living in the world. As a result, women and men formed close bonds with one another inside their separate spheres, while at the same time were also expected to marry and raise a family.

Analyze Images In cottage industries, women were able to work at home and earn money for doing things such as weaving and spinning. **Infer** After factory work replaced cottage industry, how did family life change?

READING CHECK **Draw Conclusions** How did competition and the quest for profit change working conditions in American mills?

How Did Cities Expand?

In 1800, nearly five million Americans lived in rural areas, compared to 322,000 who lived in cities. During the Industrial Revolution, many people left farms for cities, attracted by the job opportunities to be found in factories. As investors found that factories produced a profit, they invested those profits in building more factories, which attracted still more workers from farms. Older cities expanded rapidly, while new cities sprang up around factories. This movement of the population from rural areas to cities is called **urbanization**. Urbanization increased as industry grew.

Urbanization was a steady but gradual process. In 1800, only 6 percent of the nation's population lived in urban areas. By 1850, the number had risen to 15 percent. Not until 1920 did more Americans live in cities than in rural areas.

By today's standards, these early cities were small. A person could walk from one end of any American city to the other in as little as 30 minutes. Buildings were, at most, only a few stories tall. As the factory system spread, the nation's cities grew.

Problems in Cities Growing cities had numerous problems. Many of these resulted from the human modification of the environment. Dirt and gravel streets turned into mud-holes when it rained. Cities had no sewers, and people threw garbage into the streets. A visitor to New York reported that "The streets are filthy, and the stranger is not a little surprised to meet the hogs walking about in them, for the purpose of devouring the vegetables and trash thrown into the gutter."

Untreated sewage and garbage often seeped into wells or flowed into streams and rivers, polluting the water. The contaminated water spread disease. Epidemics of cholera (KAHL ur uh) raged through cities, killing thousands of people.

At about the same time, coal became an important source of industrial and home heating power. The smoke and soot from burning coal seriously modified the environment, polluting the air and dirtying cities. It also caused health problems.

Attractions Besides work opportunities, cities also had attractions. Theaters, museums, and circuses created an air of excitement. In cities, people could shop in fine stores that sold the latest fashions from Europe. Some offered modern "ready-to-wear" clothing. While most women continued to sew their own clothes, many enjoyed visiting hat shops, china shops, shoe stores, and "fancy-goods" stores.

READING CHECK **Summarize** What were some drawbacks of urbanization?

New Inventions

Northern industry grew steadily in the mid-1800s. Most northerners still lived on farms. However, more and more of the northern economy began to depend on manufacturing and trade.

The 1800s brought a flood of new inventions in the North. "In Massachusetts and Connecticut," a European visitor exclaimed, "there is not a laborer who has not invented a machine or a tool." Americans of the period were a practical people. Americans, and especially northerners, looked to science for new and useful applications that could be put to work at once. They expected technology to bring economic development and to change the way people lived.

Technology refers to ways of doing things, sometimes involving advanced scientific knowledge, or tools that make use of advanced knowledge. Innovation is coming up with new ways of doing things.

New technologies during the colonial period, such as Franklin's lightning rod, had brought limited and modest changes to daily life in America. By comparison, the scientific and technological innovations of the 1800s transformed American life.

In 1834, Philo Stewart developed a cast-iron stove small enough for use in an average kitchen. His factory-built wood-burning stove was a great success. About 90,000 were sold. The cast-iron stove was only

Analyze Images New stoves and new farm equipment were among the inventions of this era. **Draw Conclusions** How did inventions like these affect the way food was grown and prepared?

one sign of the way northern factories were changing the lives of ordinary people.

Analyze Images Telegraph offices like this one were communication hubs. **Infer** When a telegram came in to such an office, how do you think it might have been handled?

Joseph Henry, a New Yorker, showed that electric current could be sent through a wire over long distances to ring a bell. His work paved the way for later inventions. Thomas Davenport, a blacksmith, invented an early type of electric motor in 1834.

Both inventions were adapted and marketed. Competition among inventors brought about more innovation.

In 1846, Elias Howe patented a sewing machine. A few years later, Isaac Singer improved on Howe's machine. Soon, clothing makers bought hundreds of the new sewing machines. Workers could now make dozens of shirts in the time it took a tailor to sew one by hand.

Farm Machines Some new inventions made work easier for farmers. In 1825, Jethro Wood began the manufacture of an iron plow with replaceable parts. John Deere improved on the idea when he invented a lightweight steel plow. Earlier plows made of iron or wood had to be pulled by oxen, which were strong but slow. A horse, less strong but faster than an ox, could pull a steel plow through a field more quickly.

In 1847, Cyrus McCormick opened a factory in Chicago that produced mechanical reapers. The reaper was a horse-drawn machine that cut and gathered wheat and other grains. McCormick's reaper could do the work of five people using hand tools.

Other farm machines followed. There was a mechanical drill to plant grain, a threshing machine to beat grain from its husk, and a horse-drawn hay rake. These machines helped farmers raise more grain with fewer hands. As a result, thousands of farmworkers left the countryside. Some went west to start farms of their own. Others found jobs in new factories in northern cities.

The Telegraph Connects the Nation Samuel F. B. Morse received a patent for a "talking wire," or telegraph, in 1844. The telegraph was a device that sent electrical signals along a wire. It was a new technology that was made possible by scientific discoveries about electricity. Morse also devised a code of dots, dashes, and spaces so messages could be sent. The dots stood for short tones, the dashes for long tones. This system of dots and dashes became known as the Morse code.

Congress gave Morse funds to run wire from Washington, D.C., to Baltimore. On May 24, 1844, Morse set up his telegraph in the Supreme Court chamber in Washington.

New Inventions Improve Life

Analyze Images When something new was invented, other inventors started trying to improve it. A British inventor created this version of the telegraph. **Infer** Why might piano-style keys have been easier to use?

As a crowd of onlookers watched, Morse tapped out a short message: "What hath God wrought!" A few seconds later, the operator in Baltimore tapped back the same message. The telegraph worked!

Morse's invention was an instant success. Telegraph companies sprang up everywhere. Thousands of miles of wire soon stretched across the country. News could now travel long distances in a few minutes.

The telegraph helped many businesses thrive. Merchants and farmers could have quick access to information about supply, demand, and prices of goods in different areas of the country. The availability of nearly instant information about markets changed the way goods were sold and contributed to the development of a nationwide market.

The telegraph connected the nation in a completely new way. Almost every American town eventually had a telegraph, providing rapid communication from coast to coast.

Ordinary people could communicate quickly with distant family and friends. The presence of telegraph offices in cities and towns was yet another of the many attractions that helped drive urbanization. The telegraph is an example of how scientific discoveries influenced daily life during the 1800s.

READING CHECK **Identify Implied Main Ideas** How did the invention of new farm machines contribute to urbanization in the North?

Lesson Check

Practice Vocabulary

1. What key role did **capitalists** play in the **Industrial Revolution**?
2. How would a **scarcity** of natural resources affect the **supply** of goods to a market?

Critical Thinking and Writing

3. **Identify Cause and Effect** How did the use of interchangeable parts contribute to the Industrial Revolution?
4. **Summarize** Explain how the willingness of factory owners to hire women and children changed family life.
5. **Writing Workshop: Introduce Characters** In your Active Journal, write a brief description of each character, including yourself, to appear in the narrative essay you will write at the end of the Topic. Include where each one lives, where they work, relationships, and any other interesting characteristics.

Detect Changing Patterns

Follow these steps to learn to identify causes of change in a society.

INTERACTIVE
Identify Trends

1 **Gather information about the society.** Look at different resources to learn about life in the society you are studying. What resources could help you find information about why and how United States society changed during the period 1820–1860?

2 **Identify possible sources of change in the society.** Sources of change can be economic, political, social, or cultural.

a. What was the most revolutionary change during this period?

b. Were there other sources of change linked to that major change—in other words, effects that themselves became agents of change?

3 **Determine how the sources of change led to new patterns of living.** What do the "before and after" images below tell you about a new pattern of living that resulted from the major change that you have identified?

4 **Summarize what you discover.** Use the information you have learned in order to make a general statement. What can you say about the effects on society of this major change?

Secondary Source

▲ The loom was an important tool used by the women and other family members who produced yarn and cloth at home for textile merchants.

Secondary Source

▲ Young women (often helped by children) operated complex machinery to produce yarn and cloth at a factory for the textile industry.

LESSON 2

Industrialization and Immigration

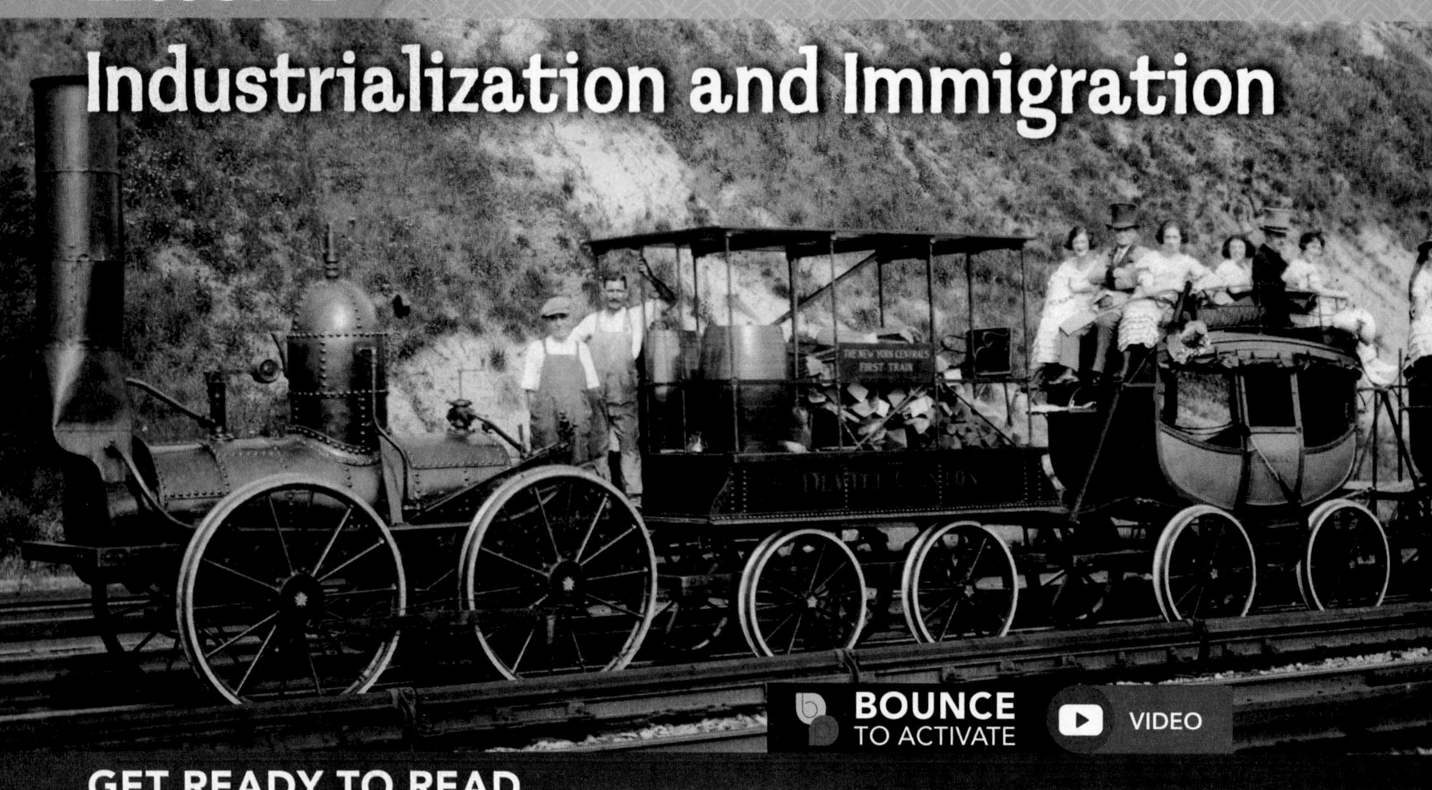

GET READY TO READ

START UP

Look at the photograph. What do you think Americans' reactions were to the first trains?

GUIDING QUESTIONS

- How did the use of steam power affect the Industrial Revolution?
- What was family life like in the growing cities?
- What was the impact of the Industrial Revolution on working conditions and social class?

TAKE NOTES

Literacy Skills: Identify Main Ideas

Use the graphic organizer in your Active Journal to take notes as you read the lesson.

PRACTICE VOCABULARY

Use the vocabulary activity in your Active Journal to practice the vocabulary words.

Vocabulary		Academic Vocabulary
artisan	nativist	organize
trade union	Know-Nothing Party	immigrant
strike	discrimination	
famine		

Where early industry had been powered by water, the Industrial Revolution went farther when it harnessed steam. Factory efficiency increased, and with improvements to locomotive technology, markets continued to expand.

What Changes Did the Age of Steam Power Bring?

At first, railroads were used to provide transportation to canals. Horses or mules pulled cars along wooden rails covered with strips of iron. Then, in 1829, an English family developed a steam-powered locomotive engine to pull rail cars. The engine, called the Rocket, barreled along at 30 miles per hour.

Early Difficulties Not all Americans welcomed the new railroads. Workers who moved freight on horse-drawn wagons feared that they would lose their jobs. People who had invested in canals worried that competition from the railroads might cause them to lose their investments.

There were problems with the early railroads. They were not always safe or reliable. Soft roadbeds and weak bridges often led to accidents. Locomotives often broke down. Even when they worked, their smokestacks belched thick black smoke and hot embers. The embers sometimes burned holes in passengers' clothing or set nearby buildings on fire.

Part of the problem was the way in which railroads were built. Often, instead of two tracks being laid—one for each direction—only one was set. Signals to control traffic on a single track did not yet exist. This increased the likelihood of a collision.

Another problem with early railroads was that there was no standard gauge, or distance between the rails. As a result, different railroads often used different gauges. To transfer from one railroad line to another, people and goods had to be moved off one train and then loaded onto another.

A Network of Railroads Gradually, railroad builders overcame problems and removed obstacles. Engineers learned to build sturdier bridges and solid roadbeds. They replaced wooden rails with iron rails. Railroads developed signaling systems and agreed on a standard gauge. Such improvements made railroad travel safer and faster.

By the 1850s, the American landscape had changed. A network of railroads crisscrossed the nation. The major lines were concentrated in the North and West. New York, Chicago, and Cincinnati became major rail centers. The South, less reliant on industry, had much less track than the North.

GEOGRAPHY SKILLS

This map shows the explosive growth of railroads between 1850 and 1860.

1. **Region** In which region were the most new rail lines?
2. **Infer** What does the increase in rail service tell you about the population of that region?

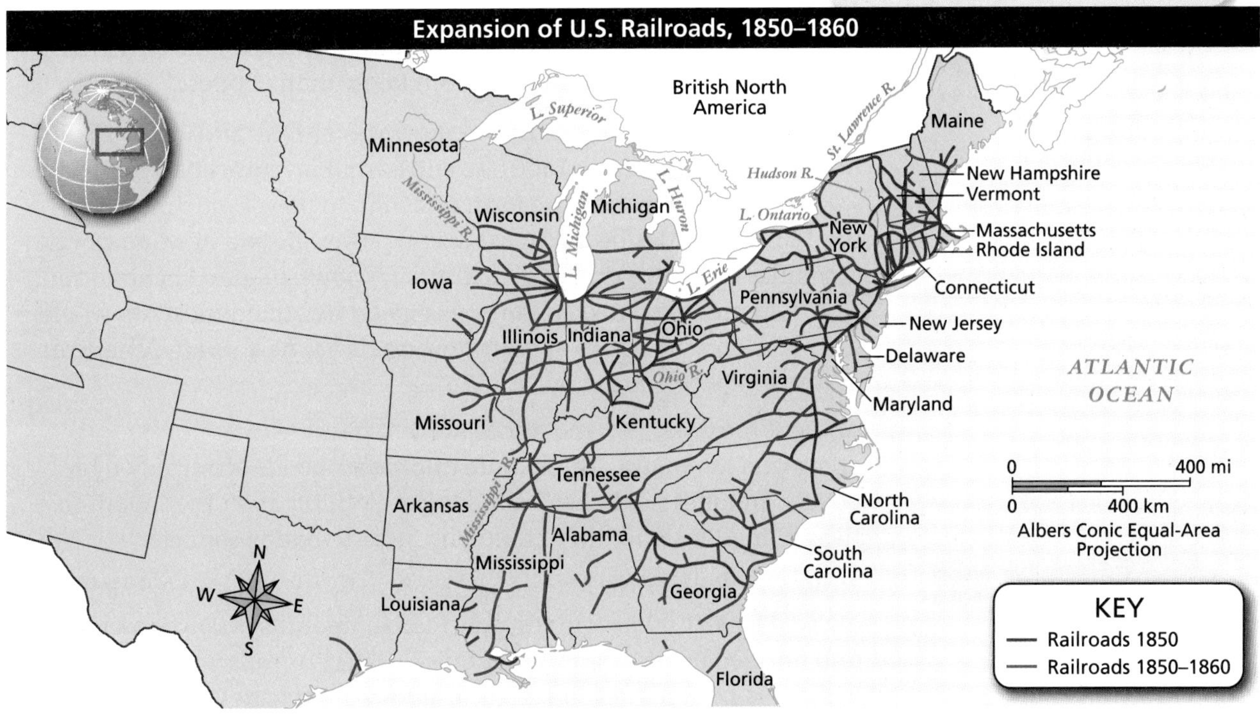

Railroads played an important role in urban growth. Cities with good rail connections attracted factories and other businesses. Railroads also made it possible for people to migrate more easily to new cities, increasing urban populations.

Analyze Images
Introduced in 1830, the "Best Friend of Charleston," lifted the city's economy by connecting the ports, canals, and inland markets. **Draw Conclusions** How could a train, even a small one, make a huge difference in a city?

What Were Yankee Clippers? Railroads increased commercial development in the United States. At the same time, trade with other nations also increased. At seaports in the Northeast, captains loaded their ships, the famed Yankee clippers, with cotton, fur, wheat, lumber, and tobacco. Then they set sail for other parts of the world.

Speed was the key to successful trade at sea. In 1845, an American named John Griffiths launched the *Rainbow*, the first of the clipper ships. These sleek vessels had tall masts and huge sails that caught every gust of wind. Their narrow hulls clipped swiftly through the water. These technological innovations traded cargo space for speed, which gave American merchants an advantage.

In the 1840s, American clipper ships broke every speed record. One clipper ship sped from New York to Hong Kong in 81 days, flying past older ships that took many months to reach China. The speed of the clippers helped the United States win a large share of the world's sea trade in the 1840s and 1850s.

The golden age of clipper ships was brief. In the 1850s, Britain launched the first oceangoing iron steamships. These sturdy vessels carried more cargo and traveled even faster than clippers.

What Were the Effects of Technological Developments? In the late 1700s and early 1800s, scientists and inventors had found ways to harness heat, in the form of steam, to power machines. By the 1830s, factories began to use steam power instead of water power. Machines that were driven by steam were powerful and cheap to run. Also, factories that used steam power could be built almost anywhere, not just along the banks of swift-flowing rivers. As a result, American industry expanded rapidly.

At the same time, new machines made it possible to produce more goods at a lower cost. These more affordable goods attracted eager buyers. Families no longer had to make clothing and other goods in their homes. Instead, they could buy factory-made products.

INTERACTIVE

The Steam Locomotive

How Did Railroads Advance the Market Revolution? Railroads allowed factory owners to transport large amounts of raw materials and finished goods cheaply and quickly. Also, as railroads stretched across the nation, they linked distant towns with cities and factories.

These towns became new markets for factory goods. Railroads greatly increased the size of the American marketplace and fueled even more factory production.

The growth of railroads also affected northern farming. Railroads brought cheap grain and other foods from the West to New England. New England farmers could not compete with this new source of cheap foods. Many left their farms to find new jobs in towns and cities as factory workers, store clerks, and sailors.

Rising Standards of Living The early rise of industrialization in the United States under a market economy brought striking economic and social benefits. Mass production lowered prices and raised Americans' purchasing power and standard of living. Wages increased for average workers. Food canned in factories improved peoples' year-round diets.

The use of stoves improved meals and home heating. Factory-made clothing was cheaper than homemade. Great numbers of newspapers and magazines reported regularly about the new inventions and advertised the new products. Along with these changes, though, there were also challenges.

READING CHECK **Draw Conclusions** What was the principal advantage of steam power over water power?

How Did Workers Respond to Challenges?

Factories of the 1840s and 1850s differed greatly from the mills of the early 1800s. As industrialization grew, life changed for workers. The factories were larger, and they used steam-powered machines. Laborers worked longer hours for lower wages. Usually, workers and their families lived in dark, dingy houses in the shadow of the factory. Cramped quarters, poverty, and pollution made the lives of many of these families miserable.

Changing Roles The emphasis on mass production changed the way workers felt about their jobs. Before the growth of factories, skilled workers, or **artisans**, were proud of the goods they made. The factory owner, however, was more interested in how much could be produced than in how well it was made. Workers could not be creative. Furthermore, unlike the artisan who could have his or her own business, the factory worker was not likely to rise to a management position.

Families in Factories As the need for workers increased, entire families labored in factories. In some cases, a family agreed to work for one year. If even one family member broke the contract, the entire family might be fired.

The factory day began when a whistle sounded at 4 A.M. The entire family—father, mother, and children—headed off to work.

Analyze Images Workers tend machines in a mill. **Infer** How did work like this affect the workers' physical health?

Many factories, at that time, employed young children. The workday did not end until 7:30 P.M., when a final whistle sent the workers home.

Hazards at Work Factory workers faced discomfort and danger. Few factories had windows or heating systems. In summer, the heat and humidity inside the factory were stifling. In winter, the extreme cold contributed to frequent sickness.

Factory machines had no safety devices, and accidents were common. There were no laws regulating factory conditions, and injured workers often lost their jobs.

Labor Organizations and Strikes Poor working conditions and low wages led workers to organize into groups to improve their conditions. The first workers to organize were artisans. In the 1820s and 1830s, artisans in each trade united to form **trade unions**. Trade unions were part of a labor reform movement.

The concentration of workers in cities helped the formation of unions by allowing people working in the same industry for different companies to organize together. Their trade unions called for a shorter workday, higher wages, and better working conditions. Sometimes, unions went on strike to gain their demands. In a **strike**, union workers refuse to do their jobs until managers agree to address their concerns.

Academic Vocabulary
organize • *v.,* to set up or establish a group, such as a labor union

In the early 1800s, strikes were illegal in many parts of the United States. Strikers faced fines or jail sentences. Employers often fired strike leaders. Employers were politically opposed to workers organizing.

Progress for Artisans Slowly, however, the labor reform movement made progress. In 1840, President Van Buren approved a ten-hour workday for government employees. Workers celebrated another victory in 1842 when a Massachusetts court declared that they had the right to strike.

Analyze Images Women, such as these working in a Massachusetts factory, received low pay although they worked long hours. **Identify Cause and Effect** Why would workers go out on strike?

Artisans won better pay because factory owners needed their skills. Unskilled workers, however, were unable to bargain for better wages since their jobs required little or no training. Because these workers were easy to replace, employers did not listen to their demands.

During the Industrial Revolution, a new awareness of class differences began to emerge. As a farming people, Americans had long viewed labor with deep respect. The changing conditions of factory labor and the gaps between the wages of unskilled workers, managers, and business owners led to a sense of people grouped in classes with shared interests. The interests of these classes were often different. By bringing together workers and managers in the same factories and cities, urbanization led to a rise in conflicts resulting from differences in social class.

Women Organize The success of trade unions encouraged other workers to **organize**. Workers in New England textile mills were especially eager to protest cuts in wages and unfair work rules. Many of these workers were women.

Women workers faced special problems. First, they had always earned less money than men did. Second, most union leaders did not want women in their ranks. Like many people at the time, they believed that women should not work outside the home. In fact, the goal of many unions was to raise men's wages so that their wives could leave their factory jobs.

Analyze Images Starving Irish people ransack a government potato store in 1845, during the potato famine. **Identify Cause and Effect** How did the failure of potato crops in Ireland affect immigration to the United States?

Despite these problems, women workers organized. They staged several strikes at Lowell, Massachusetts, in the 1830s. In the 1840s, Sarah Bagley organized the Lowell Female Labor Reform Association. The group petitioned the state legislature for a 10-hour workday.

READING CHECK **Draw Conclusions** Why could artisans command higher wages while other workers could not?

How Did Ethnic Minorities Fare in the North?

By the late 1840s, many factory workers in the North were **immigrants**. An immigrant is a person who enters a new country in order to settle there. In the 1840s and 1850s, about 4 million immigrants arrived in the United States. They were attracted, in large part, by the opportunities for farming the land or working in the cities. Economic opportunity, then, was a key "pull" factor—it pulled immigrants into the country. Among the new arrivals were immigrants from Britain who came to earn higher wages. There was a greater demand in the United States for skilled machinists, carpenters, and miners.

Academic Vocabulary
immigrant • *n.*, a person who enters another country in order to settle there

From Ireland and Germany In Ireland in the 1840s, a disease destroyed the harvest of potatoes, which were the main food of the poor people. Other crops, such as wheat and oats, were not affected. At the time, Ireland was under British rule and most Irish crops were exported to England. When a large part of the potato crop was lost to disease, British landowners continued to ship the wheat and oats to England. There was little left for the Irish to eat. This situation caused a **famine**, or severe food shortage. Thousands of people died of starvation.

Nearly as many died from disease. This disaster became known as the "Great Irish Famine." Between 1845 and 1860, over 1.5 million Irish fled to the United States seeking freedom from hunger and British rule. Famine, then, was a "push" factor—it pushed the Irish to leave their country.

Meanwhile, many Germans were also arriving in the United States. Harsh weather conditions from 1829 to 1830 resulted in severe food shortages in Germany. By 1832, more than 10,000 Germans were coming to the United States every year, seeking fertile land to farm and a better life. In 1848, revolutions had broken out in several parts of Germany. The rebels fought for democratic reforms. When the revolts failed, thousands had to flee. Attracted by its democratic political system, many came to the United States.

Analyze Images Many German immigrants settled in the Midwest, including this Wisconsin town, which features a German heritage historic site. **Infer** How would the arrival of immigrants change these communities?

Many other German immigrants came simply to make a better life for themselves. Between 1848 and 1860, nearly one million Germans arrived in the United States.

Immigrants Enrich the Nation Immigrants supplied much of the labor that helped the nation's economy grow. Although most of the Irish immigrants had been farmers, few had money to buy farmland. Many settled in the northern cities where low-paying factory jobs were available. Other Irish workers transformed the environment by helping to build many new canals and railroads. Irish women often worked as servants in private homes.

Immigrants from Germany often had enough money to move west and buy good farmland. These immigrants transformed the environment by turning prairie into farmland. Others were artisans and merchants. Cities of the Midwest such as St. Louis, Milwaukee, and Cincinnati had German grocers, butchers, and bakers.

A small minority of the immigrants from Germany were Jewish. German Jews began immigrating to the United States in the 1820s. By the early 1860s, there were about 150 communities in the United States with substantial Jewish populations.

READING CHECK **Compare and Contrast** In what ways were Irish and German immigrants alike? Different?

A Reaction Against Immigrants

Not everyone welcomed the flood of immigrants. One group of Americans, called **nativists**, wanted to preserve the country for native-born, white citizens. Using the slogan "Americans must rule America," they called for laws to limit immigration. They also wanted to keep immigrants from voting until they had lived in the United States for 21 years. At the time, newcomers could vote after only 5 years in the country.

Did you know?

German Americans are the largest single ethnic group in the United States.

Some nativists protested that newcomers "stole" jobs from native-born Americans because they worked for lower pay. Furthermore, when workers went out on strike, factory owners often hired immigrant workers to replace them. Many distrusted the different languages, customs, and dress of the immigrants. Others blamed immigrants for the rise in crime in the growing cities. Still others mistrusted Irish newcomers because many of them were Catholics. Until the 1840s, most immigrants from Europe had been Protestants. As American cities attracted Catholic immigrants, these cities became centers of conflicts over religion.

Did you know?

Anti-Irish sentiment ran so high during this time that ads for jobs and housing would state bluntly, "No Irish need apply."

By the 1850s, hostility to immigrants was so strong that nativists formed a new political party. Members of the party were anti-Catholic and anti-immigrant. Many meetings and rituals of the party were kept secret. It was called the **Know-Nothing Party** because members answered, "I know nothing," when asked about the party. The message of the party did gain supporters, but its support was limited to the North, where most immigrants settled. In 1856, Millard Fillmore, the Know-Nothing candidate for President, won 21 percent of the popular vote. Soon after, however, the party died out.

Quest CONNECTIONS

Find out how men like William Whipper and John Russwurm were involved in the abolitionist movement. Record your findings in your Active Journal.

READING CHECK **Infer** Why do you think the members of the Know-Nothing Party answered as they did?

African Americans Face Discrimination

During the nation's early years, slavery was legal in the North. By the early 1800s, however, all of the northern states had passed laws to bring an end to slavery. In some states, only the children of slaves gained freedom at first. Many did not completely abolish slavery until the mid-1800s. Still, thousands of free African Americans lived in the North, and their number grew steadily during the early 1800s.

Free African Americans in the North faced discrimination. **Discrimination** is a policy or an attitude that denies equal rights to certain groups of people. As one writer pointed out, African Americans were denied "the ballot-box, the jury box, the halls of the legislature, the army, the public lands, the school, and the church."

Even skilled African Americans had trouble finding good jobs. One African American woodworker was turned away by every furniture maker in Cincinnati. At last, a shop owner hired him. However, when he entered the shop, the other woodworkers dropped their tools. Either he must leave or they would, they declared. Similar experiences occurred throughout the North.

Some African Americans Find Success

Despite such obstacles, some northern African Americans achieved notable success in business.

Analyze Images Built in 1806, the African Meeting House in Boston is the oldest standing African American church in the United States. **Sequence** What other developments in the African American community followed the founding of this church?

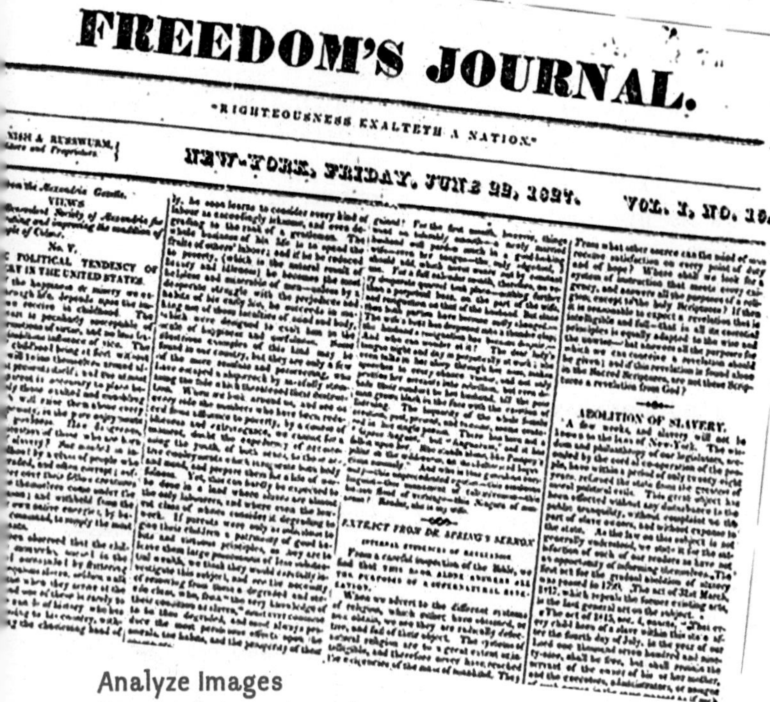

FREEDOM'S JOURNAL.

"RIGHTEOUSNESS EXALTETH A NATION."

NEW-YORK, FRIDAY, JUNE 22, 1827. VOL. I. NO. 16.

ABOLITION OF SLAVERY.

EXTRACT FROM DR. SPRING'S SERMON.

Analyze Images *Freedom's Journal* was the first newspaper owned by African Americans. **Infer** Do you think the editors of this paper were politically active? Why or why not?

William Whipper grew wealthy as the owner of a lumberyard in Pennsylvania. Henry Boyd operated a profitable furniture company in Cincinnati.

African Americans made strides in other areas as well. Henry Blair invented farm equipment. In 1845, Macon Allen became the first African American licensed to practice law in the United States. After graduating from Bowdoin College in Maine, John Russwurm edited *Freedom's Journal*, the first African American newspaper.

In the North, African Americans looked for ways to support one another. They set up schools to educate their youth. In 1852 in Philadelphia, an institute opened to train young African Americans for skilled jobs. Four years later, in Ohio, Wilberforce University was established. It was the first private university owned and run by African Americans.

The African Methodist Episcopal (AME) Church had purchased the land on which Wilberforce was built. Established in Philadelphia as an independent church in 1816 by Richard Allen, Absalom Jones, and others, the AME Church spread to major cities throughout the Northeast and Midwest. In these cities, the church worked to strengthen the African American community.

READING CHECK **Identify Supporting Details** Why did skilled African Americans have trouble finding jobs in the North?

Lesson Check

Practice Vocabulary

1. Why were **artisans** the first to organize **trade unions** and launch **strikes**?
2. Why were the **Know-Nothings** considered a **nativist** party?

Critical Thinking and Writing

3. **Understand Effects** How did the construction of a large railroad network contribute to urban growth?
4. **Compare and Contrast** What "push" factors caused Irish and Germans to leave their homelands for the United States?
5. **Identify Supporting Details** How did schools and churches help strengthen African American communities?
6. **Writing Workshop: Establish Setting** Write a sentence in your Active Journal that identifies a setting related to the workers described in this lesson. You will use this setting or another appropriate setting in the essay you will write at the end of the Topic.

LESSON 3

King Cotton and Life in the South

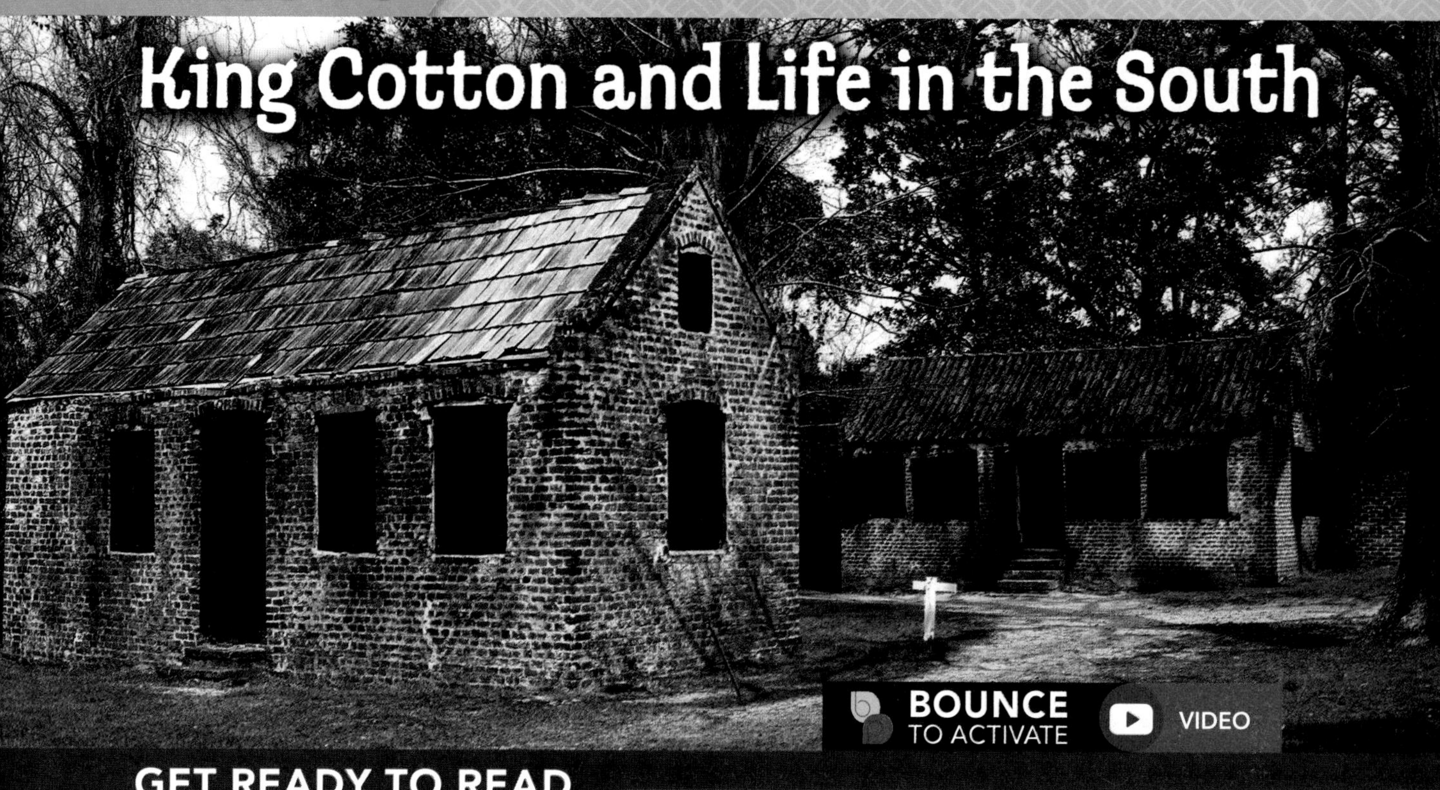

GET READY TO READ

START UP

Look at the cabins of enslaved people in the photograph. Describe what life might have been like for enslaved African Americans.

GUIDING QUESTIONS

- How did the invention of the cotton gin affect the Southern economy?
- What was the impact of slavery on the United States?
- What were the lives of enslaved people like?
- How did enslaved African Americans resist their enslavement?

TAKE NOTES

Literacy Skills: Compare and Contrast

Use the graphic organizer in your Active Journal to take notes as you read the lesson.

PRACTICE VOCABULARY

Use the vocabulary activity in your Active Journal to practice the vocabulary words.

Vocabulary		Academic Vocabulary
boom	slave code	cash crop
cultivate	extended family	discrimination
"cottonocracy"		

During the 1800s, cotton continued to grow in importance in the South. It was so profitable that southerners did not even feel a need to invest in factories. Even though southerners grew other crops, cotton remained the region's leading export. Cotton plantations—and the slave system on which they depended—shaped the way of life in the South.

The South's Cotton Kingdom

The Industrial Revolution greatly increased the demand for southern cotton. Textile mills in the North and in Britain needed more and more cotton to make cloth. At first, southern planters could not meet the demand. They could grow plenty of cotton, because the South's soil and climate were ideal. However, removing the seeds from the cotton by hand was a slow process. Planters needed a better way to clean cotton.

Eli Whitney Invents the Cotton Gin

Eli Whitney, a young teacher from Connecticut, traveled to Georgia in 1793. He planned to be a tutor on a plantation.

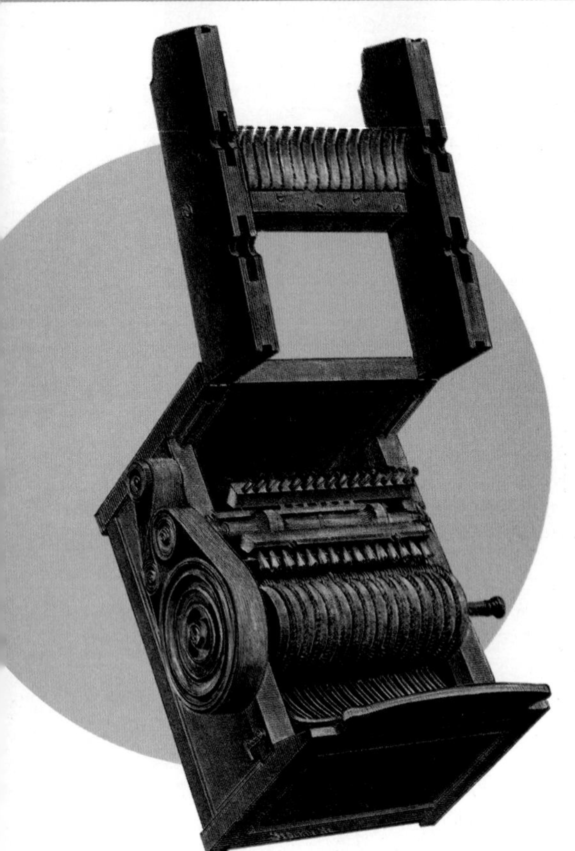

Analyze Images Workers fed cotton bolls through the gin's teeth and barbed roller to separate out the seeds and straighten the fibers. The gin let workers produce much more cotton in a day. **Predict Consequences** How would this invention affect the demand for enslaved workers?

INTERACTIVE

The Cotton Gin

At that time, there were few public schools in the South. Whitney was also a tinkerer. He loved to fix things. When he learned of the planters' problem, he decided to build a machine to clean cotton.

In only ten days, Whitney came up with a model. His cotton engine, or gin, had two rollers with thin wire teeth. When cotton was swept between the rollers, the teeth separated the seeds from the fibers.

This machine led to a dramatic expansion of plantation agriculture across the South. A single worker using a cotton gin could do the work of 50 people cleaning cotton by hand. Planters could now grow cotton at a huge profit. As a result, this new technology brought economic growth.

The Cotton Kingdom and Slavery The cotton gin led to a **boom**, or swift growth, in cotton production. In 1792, planters grew only 6,000 bales of cotton a year. By 1850, they were producing more than 2 million bales.

In the southern states along the Atlantic coast, there was not enough farmland to meet demand. Cotton farmers wanted new land to **cultivate**, or prepare for planting. After the War of 1812, cotton planters began to move west. They took enslaved African Americans with them. The huge demand for cotton, the efficiency offered by cotton gins, and southern planters' use of enslaved labor led to the growth of large plantations, each with many enslaved workers.

By the 1850s, cotton plantations extended in a belt from South Carolina to Texas. This area of the South became known as the Cotton Kingdom. Physical aspects of the environment in this part of the South, including rich soils, warm temperatures, and abundant rainfall, encouraged an economy focused on cotton farming.

Tragically, as the Cotton Kingdom spread, so did slavery. Even though cotton could now be cleaned by machine, it still had to be planted and picked by hand. The result was a cruel cycle in which enslaved labor brought profits to planters, who then used the profits to buy more land and more enslaved workers.

How Did the North and West Promote Slavery?

Slavery was a southern institution. However, northern and western factories, businesses, and banks indirectly promoted the enslavement of people through their commercial links with the South. Enslaved labor produced the cotton and other raw materials that fed the textile factories and other industries in the North and West. Slavery enabled those industries to thrive. When families in the North and West bought goods produced by enslaved workers, they too helped support enslavement in the South.

READING CHECK **Identify Cause and Effect** How did the invention of the cotton gin lead to an increase in slavery in the South?

Reliance on Plantation Agriculture

Cotton was the South's most profitable **cash crop**. However, the best soils and climate for growing cotton could be found mostly in a belt stretching across inland South Carolina, Georgia, Alabama, Mississippi, Louisiana, and Texas. In other areas of the South, rice, sugar cane, and tobacco were major crops. In addition, southerners raised much of the nation's livestock. Characteristics of the physical environment in different regions of the South influenced what farmers in those regions produced.

Academic Vocabulary
cash crop • *n.*, a crop sold for money at market

Rice was an important crop along the coasts of South Carolina and Georgia. Sugar cane was important in Louisiana and Texas. Growing rice and sugar cane required expensive irrigation and drainage systems and a warm, moist climate, all found mainly along the coasts.

Cane growers also needed costly machinery to grind their harvest. Small-scale farmers could not afford such expensive equipment, however. As a result, rice and sugar farmers relied on the plantation system, just as cotton farmers did.

Tobacco had been an export of the South since 1619, and it continued to be planted in Virginia, North Carolina, Tennessee, and Kentucky. However, in the early 1800s, the large tobacco plantations of colonial days had given way to small tobacco farms. On these farms, a few field hands tended five or six acres of tobacco.

In addition to the major cash crops of cotton, rice, sugar, and tobacco, the South also led the nation in livestock production. Southern livestock owners profited from hogs, oxen, horses, mules, and beef cattle, raised on land unsuitable for crops.

▼ African Americans enslaved on a plantation load rice onto a barge for transport on the Savannah River.

Livestock farming thrived in the woods of North Carolina and the hills of Georgia, western Virginia, Kentucky, Tennessee, and Arkansas. Kentucky developed a rural economy that included the breeding of horses.

Limited Southern Industry Because the South relied on agriculture, most of the industry in the South remained small and existed only to meet the needs of an agrarian society. This contrasted with the North, with its increasingly urban society and large and diverse industries. Southern factories made agricultural tools such as cotton gins, planters, and plows. They also made goods such as ironware, hoes, and jute or hemp cloth, which was used to make bags for holding bales of cotton. Cheap cotton cloth was made for use in enslaved workers' clothing. Some southerners wanted to encourage the growth of industry in the South. William Gregg, for example, modeled his cotton mill in South Carolina on the mills in Lowell, Massachusetts. Gregg built houses and gardens for his paid workers and schools for their children.

The South also developed a few other successful industries. In Richmond, Virginia, for example, the Tredegar Iron Works turned out railroad equipment, machinery, tools, and cannons. Flour milling was another important southern industry.

Even so, the South lagged behind the North in manufacturing. This difference had several causes. Rich planters invested their money in land and in purchasing enslaved African Americans rather than in factories.

Slavery also reduced the need for southern industry. In the North, most people had enough money to buy factory goods. In the South, however, millions of enslaved African Americans could not buy anything. As a result, the demand for manufactured goods in the South was not as great as it was in the North.

Analyze Data Although figures varied from state to state, all southern states had agricultural economies. **Use Visual Information** Why did the number of slaves in South Carolina increase even though its share of cotton production declined?

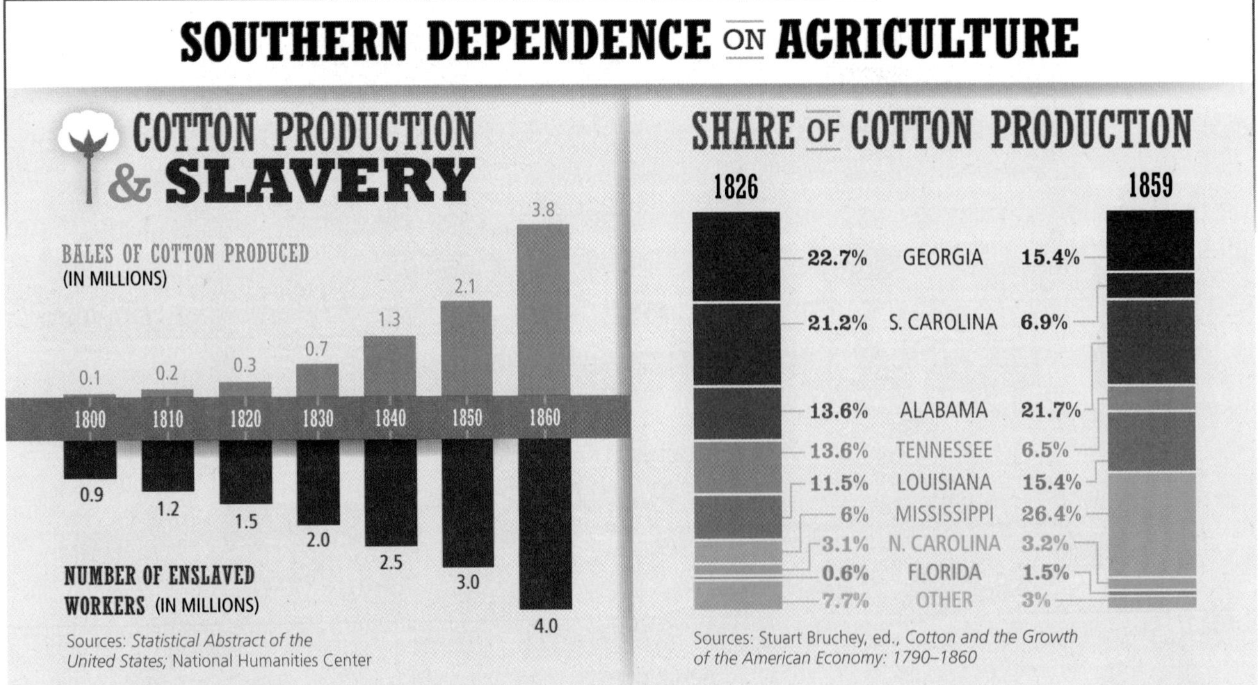

Southern Cities Although the South was mainly rural, there were some cities. The major ones were New Orleans, Louisiana; Charleston, South Carolina; and Richmond, Virginia. These cities had the same problems as northern cities, including poor housing and poor sanitation.

Fewer than 8 percent of white southerners lived in towns of more than 4,000 people. Many free African Americans lived in towns and cities.

Economically Dependent The South's lack of industry had a number of effects on the region. Because there were few industrial jobs, people in the South had few ways to escape the poverty of life on a small farm, whereas northern farmers could move to cities and take factory jobs. With little industry of its own, the South also came to depend more and more on the North and on Europe. Southern planters often borrowed money from northern banks. They also purchased much of their furniture, farm tools, and machines from northern or European factories.

Many southerners resented this situation. One described a burial to show how the South depended on the North for many goods:

Primary Source

"The grave was dug through solid marble, but the marble headstone came from Vermont. It was in a pine wilderness but the pine coffin came from Cincinnati. An iron mountain overshadowed it but the coffin nails and the screws and the shovel came from Pittsburgh. . . . A hickory grove grew nearby, but the pick and shovel handles came from New York. . . . That country, so rich in underdeveloped resources, furnished nothing for the funeral except the corpse and the hole in the ground."

—Henry Grady, Speech to the Bay Street Club, Boston, 1889

READING CHECK **Draw Conclusions** Why was the South dependent on the North and Europe for non-agricultural goods?

Agriculture in the South, 1860

KEY
Cotton
Rice
Sugar
Tobacco

Kansas Territory
Unorganized territory
TX
MO
AR
LA
MS
AL
GA
FL
IL
IN
OH
KY
TN
VA
NC
SC
MD
DE
Richmond
Charleston
New Orleans
ATLANTIC OCEAN
Gulf of Mexico
N
S
E
W
0 400 mi
0 400 km
Conic Projection

GEOGRAPHY SKILLS

This map shows the major crops grown in various regions of the South in 1860.

1. **Region** What advantages did the South have in terms of the physical environment over the North?
2. **Use Visual Information** Which crop was grown in the most limited geographic area?

What does this reliance on other places for manufactured goods tell you about the South's stance on slavery?

Different Ways of Life in the South

What Were the Characteristics of White Southern Society?

The Old South is often pictured as a land of vast plantations worked by hundreds of enslaved African Americans. Such grand estates did exist in the South. However, most white southerners were not rich planters. In fact, most whites owned no enslaved African Americans at all.

The "Cottonocracy" A planter was someone who enslaved at least 20 people. In 1860, only one white southerner in 30 belonged to a planter family. An even smaller number—less than 1 percent—enslaved 50 or more people. These wealthy families were called the **"cottonocracy"** because they made huge amounts of money from cotton. These rich planters lived mainly in the cotton belt of the lowland South and in coastal areas of South Carolina, Georgia, and Louisiana. Though few in number, their views and way of life dominated the South.

The richest planters built elegant homes and filled them with expensive furniture from Europe. They entertained lavishly. They tried to dress and behave like European nobility.

Because of their wealth and influence, many planters became political leaders. Planters hired white overseers to run day-to-day affairs on their plantations and to manage the work of enslaved people. Sometimes, enslaved African Americans, called drivers, were allowed to oversee their fellow workers.

Analyze Images Some wealthy white southerners lived in elegant homes on plantations, like this plantation home in Mississippi. **Use Visual Information** How does this dining room reflect its owners' wealth?

Small Farmers About 75 percent of southern whites lived on small family farms. These "plain folk" owned the land they farmed. They might also enslave one or two African Americans. Unlike planters, plain folk worked with their enslaved workers in the fields. Small farmers could be found in most parts of the South, but their numbers were fewer in the cotton belt and in coastal regions of the South, where plantation agriculture dominated.

Among these farm families, helping one another was an important duty. "People who lived miles apart counted themselves as neighbors," wrote a farmer in Mississippi. "And in case of sorrow or sickness, there was no limit to the service neighbors provided."

Poor White People Lower on the social ladder were poor white people. These people did not enslave any African Americans. Many did not own land. Instead, they rented it, often paying the owner with part of their crop. Many barely made a living.

Poor white people often lived in the hilly, wooded areas north and west of the cotton belt. They planted crops such as corn, potatoes, and other vegetables. They also herded cattle and pigs. Poor white people had hard lives, but they enjoyed rights that were denied to all Black people, enslaved or free.

Analyze Images The lives of the white and the African American children in this image were vastly different. **Identify Supporting Details** Identify details in the image that support this statement.

Comparing Northern and Southern White People Like white people in the North, most in the South were farmers. Most white farmers in both regions were small farmers. However, there were important differences in the white populations of the two regions. In the South, the wealthiest were planters who made their money from the work of enslaved African Americans. In the North, the wealthiest were capitalists who made their money from investing in industry. There were many white industrial workers and middle class people living in cities in the North. Relatively few southerners of any class lived in cities.

READING CHECK **Summarize** Tell how the lives of white southerners differed.

What Was Life Like for African Americans in the South?

Both free and enslaved African Americans lived in the South. Their legal and political conditions were different. Although free under the law and with certain legal rights, free African Americans faced harsh **discrimination**. Enslaved African Americans had no rights at all.

Academic Vocabulary
discrimination • *n.*, a policy or practice that denies equal rights to certain groups of people

Free African Americans Most free African Americans were descendants of enslaved people who were freed during and after the American Revolution. Others had bought their freedom. In 1860, more than 200,000 free African Americans lived in the South. Most lived in Maryland and Delaware, where slavery was in decline. Others lived in cities such as New Orleans, Richmond, and Charleston.

Many free African Americans reached an impressive level of success. Working as farmers, laborers, and artisans, such as blacksmiths, carpenters, and cobblers, they contributed to and influenced southern life. Some ran their own businesses, such as inns and barbershops.

A few became large plantation owners, growing cotton and owning enslaved workers.

White slave owners did not like free African Americans living in the South. They feared that free African Americans set a dangerous example, encouraging enslaved African Americans to rebel. Also, slave owners justified slavery by claiming that African Americans could not take care of themselves. Free African Americans proved this idea wrong.

To discourage free African Americans, southern states passed laws that limited their freedom and economic opportunities. Free African Americans were not allowed to vote or travel. In some southern states, they had to move out of the state or risk the chance of being kidnapped and enslaved.

Despite these limits, free African Americans were able to make a life for themselves and make valuable contributions to southern life. For example, Norbert Rillieux (RIHL yoo) invented a machine that revolutionized the way sugar was refined. Another inventor, Henry Blair, patented a seed planter.

Enslaved African Americans By 1860, enslaved African Americans made up one third of the South's population. Most worked as field hands on cotton plantations. Both men and women cleared new land and planted and harvested crops. Children helped by pulling weeds, collecting wood, and carrying water to the field hands. By the time they were teenagers, they worked between 12 and 14 hours a day. Daily labor in the fields bound enslaved workers into a community of people who tried to help and protect one another.

Analyze Images In 1849, Henry Brown thought of an ingenious way to escape slavery: He had himself mailed from Virginia to Philadelphia. **Infer** What do you think happened to the people in Virginia who helped Brown escape?

On large plantations, some enslaved African Americans had better positions. They might work as household servants or as skilled artisans, such as carpenters and blacksmiths. Such jobs might entitle workers to better food or clothing than field hands.

A few enslaved people worked in cities. Their earnings, however, belonged to their owners. Unlike free African Americans, enslaved African Americans could not easily start their own businesses.

Another major difference between the social circumstances of free and enslaved African Americans was that enslaved African American families could be broken up by their owners, with family members sold separately and to different owners. While they faced discrimination, free African American families were not forced to separate.

Analyze Images A child, a group of women and a man, probably enslaved African Americans, sit on the steps of the Florida Club in St. Augustine, Florida, in the mid-1800s. **Draw Conclusions** What role did the white woman standing behind them play in their lives?

READING CHECK **Compare and Contrast** How was life in the South similar and different for free and enslaved African Americans?

Slavery in the South

The life of enslaved African Americans was determined by strict laws and the practices of individual slave owners. Conditions varied from plantation to plantation. Some owners made sure their enslaved workers had clean cabins, decent food, and warm clothes. Other planters spent as little as possible on their enslaved workers.

Slave Codes Southern states passed laws known as **slave codes** to keep enslaved African Americans from either running away or rebelling. Under the codes, enslaved African Americans were forbidden to gather in groups of more than three.

They could not leave their owner's land without a written pass from their owner. They were not allowed to own guns.

Slave codes also made it a crime for enslaved African Americans to learn how to read and write. Owners hoped that this law would make it hard for African Americans to escape slavery. They reasoned that uneducated enslaved African Americans who escaped their owners would not be able to use maps or read train schedules. They would not be able to find their way north.

Some laws were meant to protect enslaved African Americans, but only from the worst forms of abuse. However, enslaved African Americans did not have the right to testify in court. As a result, they were not able to bring charges against owners who abused them.

INTERACTIVE

Lives of Free and Enslaved African Americans

Enslaved African Americans had only one real protection against mistreatment. Owners looked on their enslaved workers as valuable property. Most slave owners wanted to keep this human property healthy and productive. However, they would not hesitate to punish enslaved African Americans to keep them in line.

Frances Kemble, a British actress married to a southern slave owner, kept a journal about plantation life. She wrote about who had the right to whip an enslaved person:

Primary Source

"The common drivers are limited in their powers of chastisement, not being allowed to administer more than a certain number of lashes to their fellow slaves. Head man Frank, as he is called, has alone the privilege of exceeding this limit; and the overseer's latitude of infliction is only curtailed by the necessity of avoiding injury to life or limb. The master's irresponsible power has no such bound."

—Frances Anne Kemble, *Journal of a Residence on a Georgian Plantation in 1838–1839*

Hard Work Even the kindest owners insisted that their enslaved workers work long, hard days. Enslaved African Americans worked from "can see to can't see," or from dawn to dusk, up to 16 hours a day.

Analyze Images Music served as a source of solace and hope for enslaved African Americans. The spiritual is closely associated with the culture of slavery. **Infer** Why did people find hope in music?

Family Life It was hard for enslaved African Americans to keep their families together. Southern laws did not recognize enslaved people's marriages or families. As a result, enslavers could sell a husband and wife to different buyers. Children were often taken from their parents and sold.

On large plantations, many enslaved families did manage to stay together. For those African Americans, the family was a source of strength, pride, and love. Grandparents, parents, children, aunts, uncles, and cousins formed a close-knit group. This idea of an **extended family** had its roots in Africa.

Enslaved African Americans preserved other traditions as well. Parents taught their children traditional African stories and songs. They used folk tales to pass on African history and moral beliefs.

Religion Offers Hope By the 1800s, many enslaved African Americans were devout Christians. Planters often allowed white ministers to preach to people they enslaved. African Americans also had their own preachers and beliefs.

Religion helped African Americans cope with the harshness of life in slavery. Bible stories about how the ancient Israelites had escaped from slavery to freedom inspired a new type of religious song called a spiritual. Yet, enslaved African Americans had to be cautious even in their religious practice. While they sang of freedom in spirituals, the words of the spirituals suggested that this freedom would come after death, so as not to alarm enslavers.

READING CHECK **Identify Supporting Details** Why was it difficult for enslaved African Americans to keep their families together?

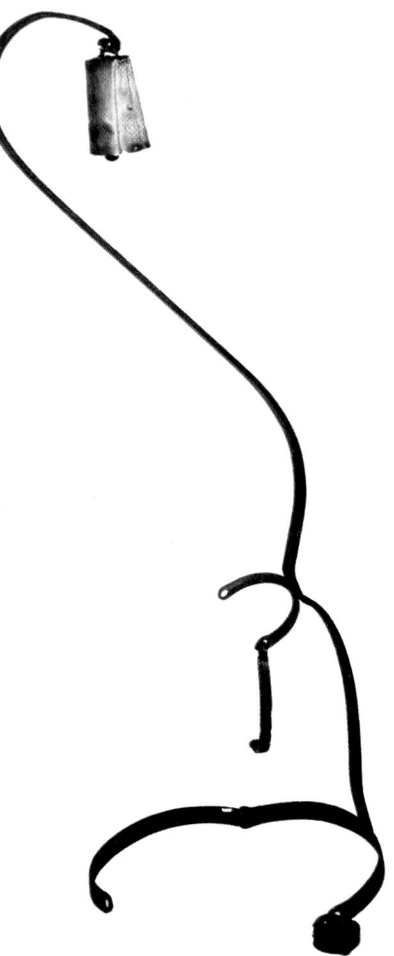

Analyze Images Enslaved people who tried to escape but were recaptured were forced to wear devices like this, which locked around their necks. **Use Visual Information** How would this device have affected a person wearing it?

How Did Enslaved African Americans Resist?

Enslaved African Americans struck back against the system that denied them both freedom and wages. Some slowed the pace of their work, broke tools, destroyed crops, or pretended they were ill. Some passively resisted by learning to read and write. Others took much bolder action.

Many enslaved African Americans tried to escape to the North. Because the journey was long and dangerous, very few made it to freedom. Every county had patrols and sheriffs looking for and ready to stop Black people.

Because southern laws offered no means to resist slavery, a few African Americans turned to violence. Gabriel Prosser, an enslaved African American, organized an uprising in Richmond, Virginia, but it failed. Denmark Vesey, a free African American, planned a revolt in 1822. Vesey was betrayed before the revolt began. Both Prosser and Vesey were executed, along with dozens of their followers.

Other armed uprisings against slavery took a toll on both Black and white people. The Stono Rebellion in South Carolina in 1739 resulted in the deaths of some 30 enslaved African American rebels and a similar number of white colonists.

In 1831, an African American named Nat Turner led a major uprising. An enslaved worker on a plantation in Southampton County, Virginia, Turner believed his mission was to take revenge on plantation owners.

Turner led his followers through Virginia, killing more than 57 white people. For nearly two months terrified white people hunted the countryside looking for Turner. They killed many innocent African Americans before catching and hanging him.

Analyze Images In 1831, Nat Turner led other enslaved African Americans in an uprising against enslavers. In this image, Turner is planning an attack. **Predict Consequences** How would Turner's rebellion affect the lives of enslaved African Americans who did not rebel?

Nat Turner's actions increased southern fears of an uprising of enslaved African Americans. Whites now became even more suspicious of the African Americans, free or enslaved. Southern states reacted to the revolt by further limiting African Americans' rights. At first, the Virginia legislature seriously debated ending slavery in the state, but decided against it. Virginia then, like other southern states, increased its restrictions on African Americans.

Overall, uprisings against slavery were rare. Because white southerners were well armed and kept careful track of African Americans, an uprising by African Americans had almost no chance of success.

READING CHECK **Draw Conclusions** What do the actions of leaders of uprisings against slavery reveal about the conditions under which enslaved Africans were forced to live?

Lesson Check

Practice Vocabulary

1. How did the **boom** in cotton production lead to the rise of the **"cottonocracy"**?
2. How did the physical characteristics of the environment affect a planter's decision about what crops to **cultivate**?

Critical Thinking and Writing

3. **Recognize Multiple Causes** What are three reasons that cotton became "king" in the South?
4. **Understand Effects** Why were there few factories in the South?
5. **Explain an Argument** Did their resistance to enslavement generally help or hurt enslaved African Americans? Explain.
6. **Writing Workshop: Organize Sequence of Events** Plan the events that you will describe in your narrative essay. In your Active Journal, write out those events in the order in which they will happen.

LESSON 4

Abolitionism

GET READY TO READ

START UP

Look at the image of the abolitionist being attacked. Why was abolition such a volatile issue? Write a few sentences to explain your answer.

GUIDING QUESTIONS

- How did people work to end slavery?
- What opposition did those people face?
- How did the Underground Railroad function?

TAKE NOTES

Literacy Skills Summarize

Use the graphic organizer in your Active Journal to take notes as you read the lesson.

PRACTICE VOCABULARY

Use the vocabulary activity in your Active Journal to practice the vocabulary words.

Vocabulary	Academic Vocabulary
American Colonization Society	public opinion
abolitionist	interest group
The Liberator	
Underground Railroad	
civil disobedience	

In the Declaration of Independence, Thomas Jefferson had written that "all men are created equal." Yet many Americans, including Jefferson himself, did not believe that this statement applied to enslaved African Americans. A growing number of reformers began to think differently.

What Form Did Early Opposition to Slavery Take?

Jefferson, owner of a slave plantation, may not have believed in the equality of whites and African Americans, but he did believe slavery should be ended. He wrote as much in his draft of the Declaration of Independence. The passage, which was later removed, criticized the existence of "a market where Men should be bought & sold."

In 1777, the constitution of the new state of Vermont banned slavery. Three years later, the Massachusetts constitution did the same, with the words "All men are born free and equal." In the years that followed, other northern states enacted policies aimed at eventually ending slavery.

Analyze Images This image of an enslaved African in chains was originally adopted as the seal of the Society for the Abolition of Slavery in England in the 1780s. **Draw Conclusions** Why do you think it took so long for slavery to become a major issue in the United States?

Religious beliefs led some Americans to oppose slavery. Since colonial times, Quakers had taught that it was a sin for one human being to own another. All people, they said, were equal in the sight of God. Benjamin Franklin, who owned two slaves, had a change of heart about slavery. He joined an early abolitionist society in Pennsylvania that was founded by Quakers. Later, during the Second Great Awakening, ministers such as Charles Grandison Finney called on Christians to join a massive effort to stamp out slavery.

In the North, with a population in 1800 of 50,000 enslaved African Americans, slavery was not very important to the economy. As growing numbers of northerners opposed it, slavery gradually came to an end in the North. By 1804, all the states from Pennsylvania through New England had ended slavery or promised to free their enslaved African Americans over time. The Northwest Ordinance of 1787 had banned slavery in the Northwest Territory, which became the Midwestern states north of the Ohio River and east of the Mississippi River. In 1807, Congress voted to end the slave trade. No more Africans could be enslaved and brought into the country.

These efforts to end slavery had little effect in the South, with its nearly one million slaves.

In fact, the South was growing ever more dependent on slavery. As you have learned, plantation agriculture expanded rapidly in the South in the early 1800s. As a result, there was little support in the South for ending slavery.

The Colonization Movement The **American Colonization Society** proposed to end slavery by setting up an independent colony in Africa for Africans and African Americans who had gained freedom from slavery. In 1822, President Monroe helped the society set up a colony in western Africa. This colony gained control over a territory that later became the nation of Liberia.

Some African Americans favored colonization, believing that they would never have equal rights in the United States. Most, however, opposed the movement. Nearly all, enslaved or free, had been born in the United States. They wanted to stay in their homeland. In the end, only a few thousand African Americans settled in Liberia.

READING CHECK **Summarize** What early efforts attempted to end slavery?

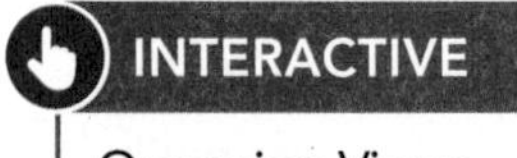
INTERACTIVE

Opposing Views on Slavery

How Did Abolitionism Gain Momentum?

A growing number of reformers, known as **abolitionists**, wanted to end slavery completely in the United States. Some abolitionists favored a gradual end to slavery. They expected slavery to die out if it was kept out of the western territories. Other abolitionists demanded that slavery end everywhere, at once. Almost all abolitionists were northerners. The abolitionist movement gradually gained strength from the 1820s through the 1840s. It grew more quickly during the 1850s.

A forceful voice for ending slavery was John Quincy Adams. A diplomat for many years, Adams served as President from 1824 to 1828. In the 1830s, he won election to the House of Representatives. There he proposed a constitutional amendment that would eventually end slavery by declaring all newborn children free. A few years earlier, however, southern members of Congress had agreed to abide by a "gag rule." They would not discuss anything having to do with slavery. As a result, Adams's proposal was ignored.

Quest CONNECTIONS

Who opposed slavery in the early years of the United States?

African American Abolitionists Free African Americans played a key role in the abolitionist movement by actively challenging the existence of slavery. Some tried to end slavery through lawsuits and petitions. In the 1820s, Samuel Cornish and John Russwurm set up an abolitionist newspaper, *Freedom's Journal.* They hoped to turn **public opinion** against slavery by printing stories about the brutal treatment of enslaved African Americans.

Academic Vocabulary

public opinion • *n.*, the views held by people, in general

Other African American abolitionists called for stronger measures. In *An Appeal to the Colored Citizens of the World*, David Walker encouraged enslaved African Americans to free themselves by any means necessary:

Primary Source

"Now, I ask you, had you not rather be killed than to be a slave to a tyrant, who takes the life of your mother, wife, and dear little children? Look upon your mother, wife, and children, and answer God Almighty; and believe this, that it is no more harm for you to kill a man, who is trying to kill you, than it is for you to take a drink of water when thirsty."

—David Walker, *Walker's Appeal*, 1829

Interpret Images William Lloyd Garrison's paper, *The Liberator*, was a leading abolitionist publication. **Use Visual Information** The illustration shows people being sold under a sign, "Horse-Market." What effect would that have had on someone who was seeing the paper for the first time?

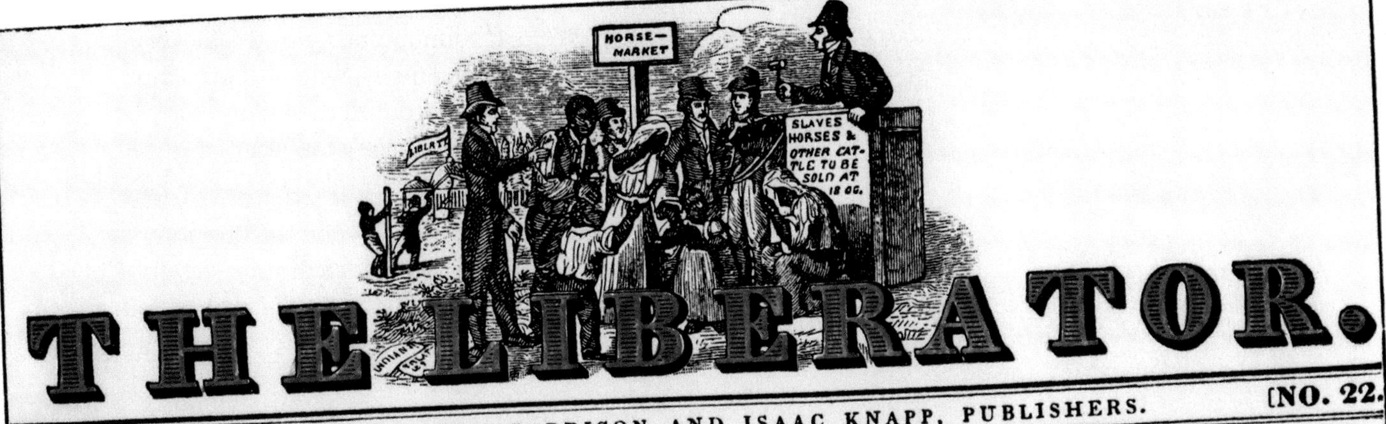
HORSE-MARKET

SLAVES HORSES & OTHER CATTLE TO BE SOLD AT 12 OC.

THE LIBERATOR.

VOL. I.] WILLIAM LLOYD GARRISON AND ISAAC KNAPP, PUBLISHERS. [NO. 22.

BOSTON, MASSACHUSETTS.] OUR COUNTRY IS THE WORLD—OUR COUNTRYMEN ARE MANKIND. [SATURDAY, MAY 28, 1831.

Analyze Images Frederick Douglass escaped slavery and became a leading voice in the abolitionist movement. **Infer** Why could Douglass appeal to listeners in a unique way?

Walker's friend Maria Stewart also spoke out against slavery. Stewart was the first American woman to make public political speeches.

Frederick Douglass The best-known African American abolitionist was Frederick Douglass. Douglass was born into slavery in Maryland. As a child, he defied the slave codes by learning to read.

Douglass escaped in 1838 and made his way to New England. One day at an antislavery meeting, he felt a powerful urge to speak. Rising to his feet, he talked about the sorrows of slavery and the meaning of freedom. The audience was moved to tears. Soon, Douglass was lecturing across the United States and Britain. In 1847, he began publishing an antislavery newspaper, which he called the *North Star.*

William Lloyd Garrison Speaks Out The most outspoken white abolitionist was a fiery young man named William Lloyd Garrison. To Garrison, slavery was an evil to be ended immediately. In 1831, Garrison launched ***The Liberator***, the most influential antislavery newspaper. On the first page of the first issue, Garrison revealed his commitment:

Primary Source

> "I will be as harsh as truth, and as uncompromising as justice. . . . I am in earnest. . . . I will not excuse—I will not retreat a single inch—and I WILL BE HEARD."
>
> —William Lloyd Garrison, *The Liberator*, January 1831

A year later, Garrison helped to found the New England Anti-Slavery Society. Members included Theodore Weld, a young minister and follower of Charles Grandison Finney, who had preached against slavery. Weld brought the energy of a religious revival to antislavery meetings.

The Grimké Sisters Contribute to Reform Angelina and Sarah Grimké were the daughters of a South Carolina slaveholder. Hating slavery, they moved to Philadelphia to work for abolition. Their lectures drew large crowds.

Some people, including other abolitionists, objected to women speaking out in public. "Whatsoever it is morally right for a man to do," replied Sarah Grimké, "it is morally right for a woman to do." As you will see, this belief helped spark a movement for women's rights.

INTERACTIVE

The Underground Railroad

Civil Disobedience and the Underground Railroad Some abolitionists formed the **Underground Railroad**. It was not a real railroad, but a network of abolitionists who secretly helped enslaved African Americans escape to freedom in the North or Canada.

"Conductors" guided runaways to "stations" where they could spend the night. Some stations were homes of abolitionists. Others were churches or even caves. Conductors sometimes hid runaways under loads of hay in wagons with false bottoms. It was illegal to help enslaved African Americans escape, but these conductors felt strongly about disobeying laws they considered unjust. Such acts of **civil disobedience** led thousands of enslaved people to freedom.

One daring conductor, Harriet Tubman, had escaped slavery herself. She felt deeply committed to freeing others from slavery. Risking her freedom and her life, Tubman returned to the South 19 times. She led more than 300 enslaved African Americans, including her parents, to freedom. Admirers called her the "Black Moses," after the biblical leader who led the Israelites out of slavery in Egypt. Slave owners offered a $40,000 reward for her capture.

Another escaped slave, Mary Pleasant, became a conductor on the Underground Railroad in the 1840s. In 1851, she feared being caught as a runaway and returned to slavery. She fled to California, a new state with a constitution that prohibited slavery. Pleasant became a successful businesswoman in San Francisco, where she worked to help other escaped slaves.

GEOGRAPHY **SKILLS**

The Underground Railroad provided routes African Americans fleeing slavery could take to reach the North or Canada.

1. **Movement** From which southern states did fugitives and their conductors travel by ship?
2. **Use Visual Information** After getting to Rochester, New York, what last physical obstacle did a fugitive face?

The Underground Railroad

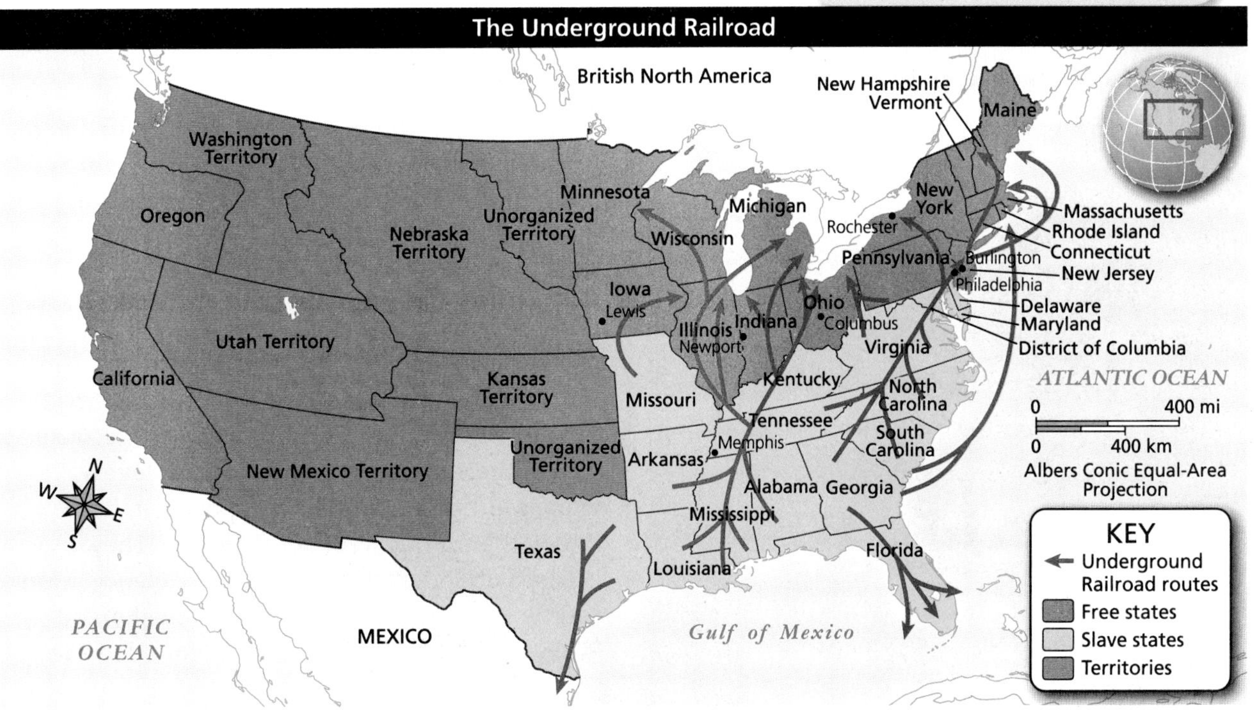

Quick Activity

Write an editorial about the work of abolitionists in your Active Journal.

A Novel Promotes Abolitionism In 1852, a writer named Harriet Beecher Stowe published *Uncle Tom's Cabin*, a novel describing the suffering of enslaved African Americans.

The novel's characters were often unrealistic and stereotyped, or based on inaccurate assumptions and beliefs about supposed characteristics of African Americans. However, the novel sold widely and convinced many northerners during the 1850s that slavery was evil and should be outlawed.

As abolitionism spread during the 1850s, it had a powerful impact on the United States. It increased tensions between the North and the South and helped set the stage for the Civil War.

READING CHECK **Use Evidence** Did the press play an important role in the abolition movement? Explain.

Who Opposed the Abolitionists?

By the mid-1800s, slavery existed only in the South. Still, abolitionists like Douglass and Garrison made enemies in the North as well.

Academic Vocabulary
interest group • *n.*, people who have a certain concern or belief in common

Northerners Against Abolition As you have learned, abolitionists were one **interest group** in the controversy over slavery. Their view was that slavery had to end.

However, northern mill owners, bankers, and merchants depended on cotton from the South. Some saw attacks on slavery as a threat to their livelihood. Some northern workers also opposed abolition. They feared that African Americans might come north and take their jobs by working for low pay.

These interest groups in the North took the view that slavery should be left up to individual states. Because few white southerners opposed slavery, their view was that slavery should be allowed to continue.

▼ This advertisement promotes the abolitionist novel *Uncle Tom's Cabin*.

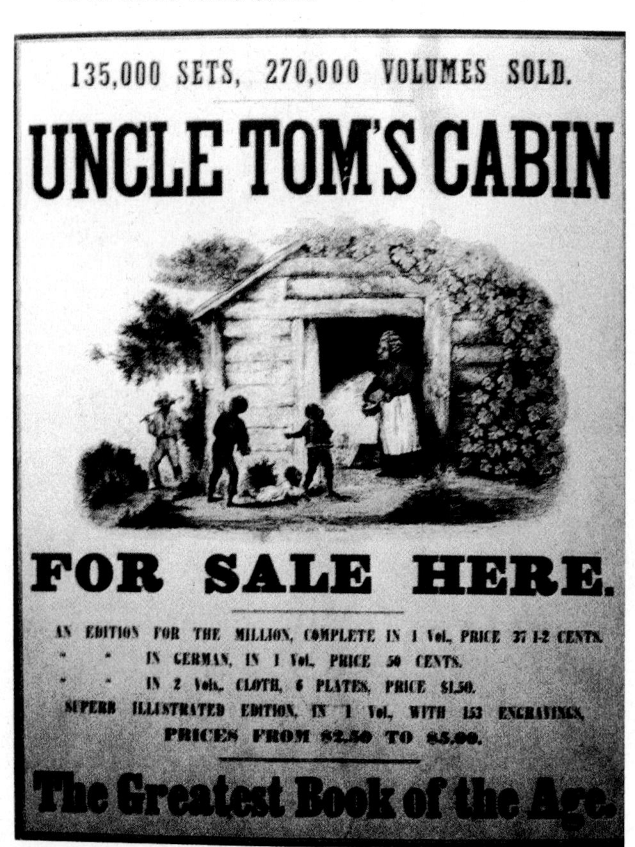

In northern cities, mobs sometimes broke up antislavery meetings or attacked homes of abolitionists. At times, the attacks backfired and won support for the abolitionists. One night, a Boston mob dragged William Lloyd Garrison through the streets at the end of a rope. A witness wrote, "I am an abolitionist from this very moment."

Southerners Defend Slavery Against the North Most white southerners were disturbed by the growing abolitionist movement. Because the southern economy depended on slavery, white southerners strongly supported it, even if they themselves were not enslavers. They accused abolitionists of preaching violence. Many southerners blamed Nat Turner's rebellion on William Lloyd Garrison, who had founded *The*

Analyze Images This engraving shows the burning of the print shop of Elijah P. Lovejoy, an abolitionist who published a newspaper opposed to slavery in Illinois. Anti-abolition rioters murdered Lovejoy during their attack on his shop. **Identify Implied Main Ideas** Why did some northerners resist abolition?

Liberator only a few months earlier. David Walker's call for a revolt against slavery seemed to confirm the worst fears of southerners.

Enslavers responded to the abolitionist effort by defending slavery even more. If enslaved African Americans were treated well, wrote one enslaver, they would "love their master and serve him . . . faithfully." Others argued that enslaved African Americans were better off than northern workers who labored long hours in dusty, airless factories.

Many white southerners believed northern support for the antislavery movement was stronger than it really was. They began to fear that northerners wanted to destroy their way of life.

READING CHECK **Summarize** Provide a summary of the reasons many northerners opposed abolition.

Lesson Check

Practice Vocabulary

1. Do you think most **abolitionists** supported the **American Colonization Society**? Why or why not?
2. In what way was taking part in the **Underground Railroad** an act of **civil disobedience**?

Critical Thinking and Writing

3. Use Evidence Why was the movement to abolish slavery successful in the North but strongly opposed in the South?
4. Infer Why did William Lloyd Garrison, a white man, devote his professional life to the abolitionist movement?
5. Draw Conclusions What can you tell about Harriet Tubman from her actions?
6. Writing Workshop: Use Narrative Techniques How can you best tell your story to the reader? One way is to use the first person point of view—"I lived . . ." or "I saw . . ." In your Active Journal, identify your point of view, what tense you will use (present or past), and whether you will include dialogue.

Update an Interpretation

INTERACTIVE

Draw Inferences

Follow these steps to learn ways to update interpretations of history, as new information is uncovered.

1 **Identify the interpretation that may need to change.** People in the South had long heard tales of runaway slaves living together in the Great Dismal Swamp, a wetland region in southeastern Virginia and northeastern North Carolina. But no evidence existed that the runaways had actually formed a community. Historians considered it a myth. According to the primary source, what was the existing interpretation of history regarding runaway slaves in the Great Dismal Swamp?

2 **Study new information about the subject.** Archaeologist Dan Sayers, a professor at American University, has found physical evidence of a community of runaways he thinks successfully lived in the swamp for 10 generations. Read the story below to learn what he discovered. What was Dan Sayers's key finding, and why was it important?

3 **Revise the interpretation, if needed, to reflect the new information.** As Dan Sayers once said, "Historical archaeology does require interpretation." Based on his discoveries in the Great Dismal Swamp, historians have revised their views. Most no longer question the ability of a community of escaped African Americans to adapt to an extreme environment in order to stay free. What part of the story about Dan Sayers confirms that the earlier interpretation of history has been updated?

Primary Source

[In the Great Dismal Swamp] Black men and women—escaped slaves—once scratched out lives, maybe even raised families, in what was once a 2,000-square-mile swamp, . . . The slaves established what historians call "Maroon Communities," . . .

Dan Sayers . . . has no doubts that escaped slaves lived in the swamp. . . . He wonders if researchers have shied away from searching for the Dismal's Maroons because they believe such a settlement couldn't exist in an era where the government and slave owners hunted down slaves who escaped. . . .

Sayers and a few volunteers surveyed likely settlement spots that took advantage of higher, drier ground. . . . Then, every 16 or so feet, he dug a careful hole no more than a foot wide and about 25 inches deep. . . . One of the very first pieces [he found], is the size of a quarter. . . . ceramic . . . Could it be that Maroons had [connected] with disenfranchised Native Americans and traded, or learned pottery-making skills? He hopes the context of this tiny piece will build and widen as he excavates more of the site.

—Kimberly Lenz, SunHerald.com, February 18, 2004

Primary Sources

McGuffey Readers

The *McGuffey Readers* were widely used in American schools from the mid-1800s to the mid-1900s. They were filled with stories and poems that promoted religious values, proper behavior, and patriotism in children. Their moral and cultural influence helped shape the national character.

◀ The textbooks known as *McGuffey Readers* first appeared in 1836.

TRY, TRY AGAIN. 1. 'T is ① a lesson you should heed, Try, try again; If at first you don't succeed, Try, try again; ② Then your courage should appear, For, if you will persevere, ③ You will conquer, never fear; Try, try again. 2. Once or twice though you should fail, Try, try again; If you would at last prevail, ④ Try, try again; If we strive, 'tis no disgrace Though we do not win the race; What should you do in the case? Try, try again. 3. If you find your task is hard, Try, try again; Time will bring you your reward, ⑤ Try, try again. All that other folks can do, Why, with patience, should not you? Only keep this rule in view: Try, try again.

—William Holmes McGuffey, editor, *McGuffey's Fourth Eclectic Reader*

WORK. 1. Work, work, my boy, be not afraid; Look labor boldly in the face; Take up the hammer or the spade, And blush not for your humble place. 2. There's glory in the shuttle's song; There's triumph in the anvil's stroke; There's merit in the brave and strong Who dig the mine or fell the oak. 3. The wind disturbs the sleeping lake, And bids it ripple pure and fresh; It moves the green boughs till they make Grand music in their leafy mesh. 4. And so the active breath of life Should stir our dull and sluggard wills; For are we not created rife With health, that stagnant torpor kills? 5. I doubt if he who lolls his head Where idleness and plenty meet, Enjoys his pillow or his bread As those who earn the meals they eat. 6. And man is never half so blest As when the busy day is spent So as to make his evening rest A holiday of glad content.

—William Holmes McGuffey, editor, *McGuffey's Fifth Eclectic Reader*

Reading and Vocabulary Support

① A question in the *Reader* asks students, "What does the mark before 'T is' mean?" What does that mark stand for?

② The saying "If at first you don't succeed, try, try again" is still popular today. What does that say about the continuity of American culture?

③ The *Reader* defines perseverance as "continuance in anything once begun."

④ The *Reader* defines prevail as "overcome."

⑤ According to the *Reader*, your reward is "anything given in return for good or bad conduct."

Analyzing Primary Sources

Cite evidence from the introduction and the primary source to support your answers.

1. **Support Ideas with Examples** What "national character" traits do you think the *McGuffey Readers* helped shape?
2. **Analyze Style and Rhetoric** What effect do you think the repetition in these poems had on young readers?

LESSON 5

Reform and Women's Rights

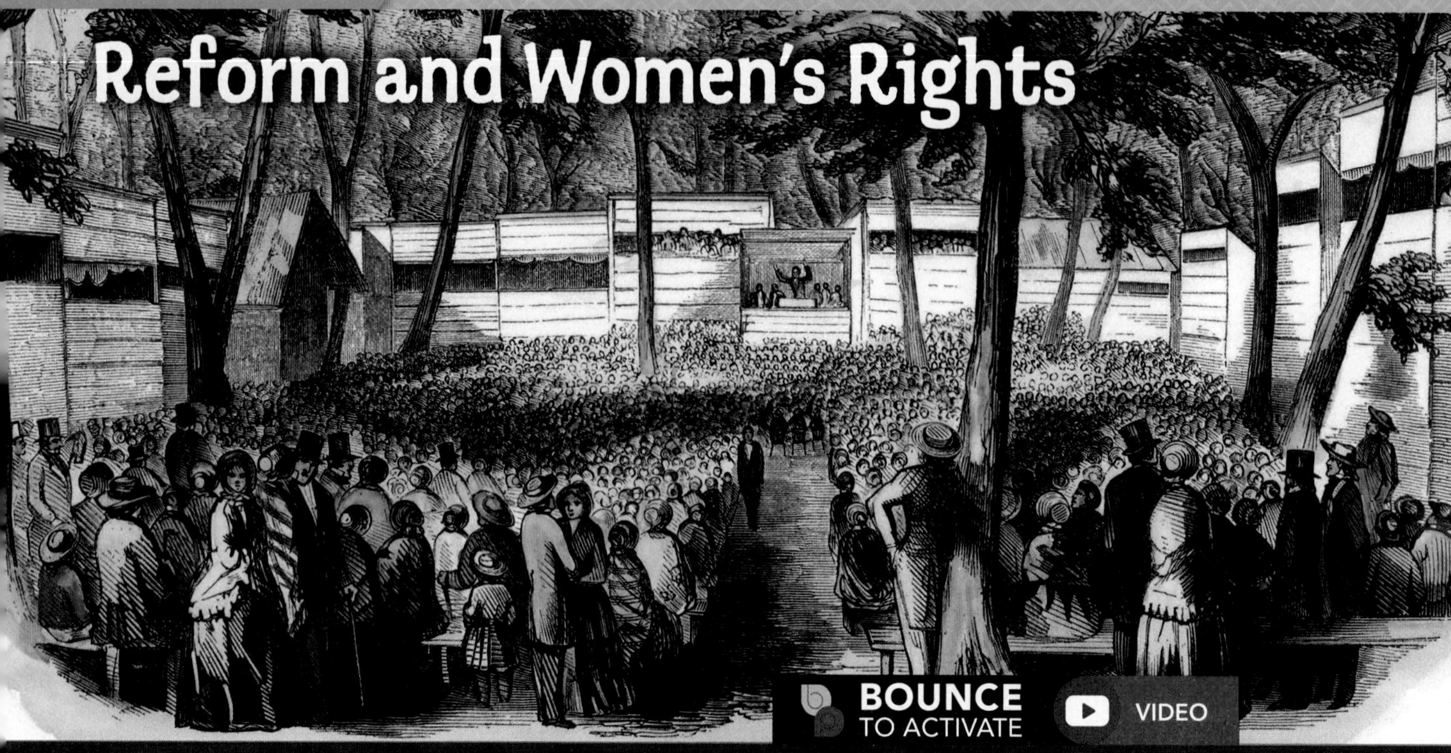

GET READY TO READ

START UP

Look at the image. What could all those people be listening to? Write a list of ideas.

GUIDING QUESTIONS

- How did political and religious trends spark reform movements?
- How did family life change during this time?
- What effect did the women's rights movement have on opportunities for women?

TAKE NOTES

Literacy Skills: Draw Conclusions

Use the graphic organizer in your Active Journal to take notes as you read the lesson.

PRACTICE VOCABULARY

Use the vocabulary activity in your Active Journal to practice the vocabulary words.

Vocabulary		Academic Vocabulary
social reform	Seneca Falls Convention	salvation
Second Great Awakening	women's rights movement	conservation
debtor		
temperance movement		

The period between 1815 and 1860 in the United States is sometimes called the Era of Reform because there were so many movements for social reform during this period. Reformers fought to end slavery, increase access to education, improve conditions in prisons, expand women's rights, and more.

The Era of Reform

Social reform is an organized attempt to improve what is unjust or imperfect in society. The impulse toward social reform had political, social, and religious causes.

Political Ideals Lead to Reform As you have read, during the Jacksonian era, politics was becoming more democratic. More people could vote and take part in government than ever before.

Still, some critics said American society was not living up to its ideals. They pointed to the promise of liberty and equality expressed in the Declaration of Independence. A society based on these ideals, they argued, would not allow slavery. Others asked why women had fewer rights than men. By changing such injustices, reformers hoped to move the nation closer to its political ideals.

Social Conditions Call for Reform As you have learned, the Industrial Revolution was changing the American economy and working conditions, especially in the North, and cities were growing rapidly. Crowded cities created new challenges for social well-being. At the same time, there was a growing need for an educated workforce. As American society changed, it required new institutions to meet its changing needs.

The Second Great Awakening and Its Causes During the colonial era, many American Protestant Christians believed in predestination. According to this idea, God decided in advance which people would attain **salvation** after death. This belief led many people to worry that they could do nothing to be saved.

Academic Vocabulary
salvation • *n.*, deliverance from sin

During the 1700s, Protestant thinkers in England and the colonies began to argue that salvation depended on a person's actions in this life. Its leaders stressed free will rather than predestination. They taught that individuals could choose to save their souls by their own actions. In the early 1800s, a dynamic religious movement known as the **Second Great Awakening** swept the nation. Arguments by religious thinkers were the main cause of this movement. Another cause was the democratic spirit of the Jacksonian era, which encouraged people to think independently and not blindly obey established religious authorities.

To stir religious feelings, preachers held revivals, huge outdoor meetings. Revivals might last for days and attract thousands of people. A witness recalled the excitement of a revival at Cane Ridge, Kentucky:

Analyze Charts The reform movement was an important part of the 1800s. **Use Visual Information** How did the reform movement reflect American culture at the time?

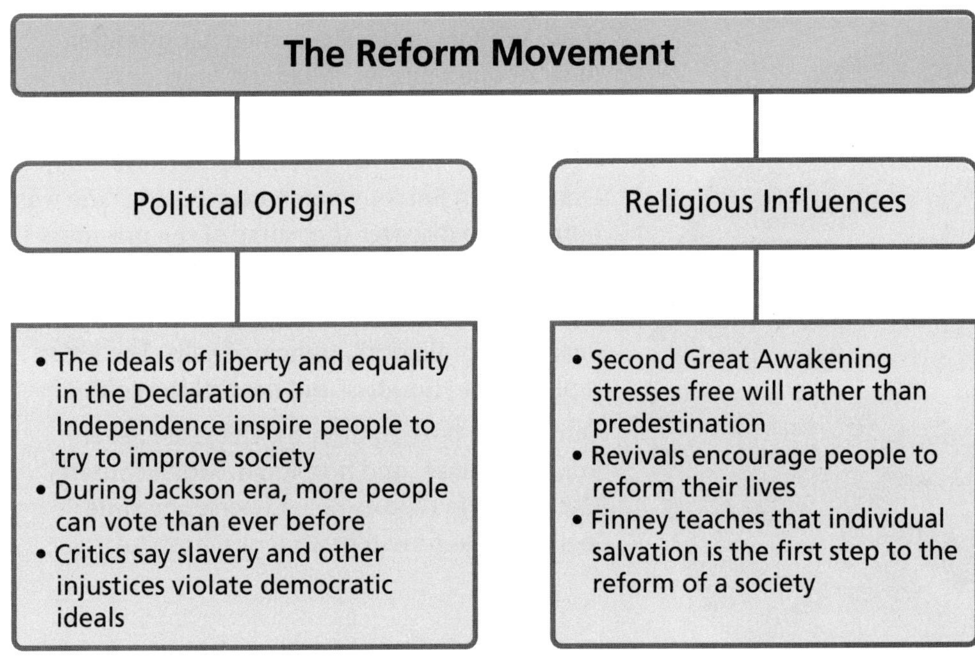

Did you know?

Dorothea Dix wrote a book, *Conversations on Common Things; or, Guide to Knowledge: With Questions*, that reflected her belief that men and women should receive equal educations.

Primary Source

"The vast sea of human beings seemed to be agitated as if by storm. I counted seven ministers all preaching at once. . . . Some of the people were singing, others praying, some crying for mercy."

—James B. Finley, *Autobiography*

One leader of the Second Great Awakening was a minister named Charles Grandison Finney. A powerful speaker, Finney taught that individual salvation was the first step toward "the complete reformation of the whole world."

Such teachings had effects that changed the country, inspiring a number of new social reform movements. These ranged from equal education for women and African Americans to the abolitionist movement. Inspired by religion, these social reformers began a lasting tradition in American culture of working to improve society.

READING CHECK **Identify Implied Main Ideas** What was the central premise on which the Second Great Awakening rested?

Social Reform Movements

The emphasis that the Second Great Awakening placed on improving society inspired many Americans. These Americans launched a number of reform movements, with far-reaching effects on prisons, care of the disabled, education, and attitudes toward slavery. Women often played a leading role in these reform movements.

▼ Dorothea Dix, a former schoolteacher, became an advocate for social reform.

One of the most vigorous social reformers was Dorothea Dix, a Boston schoolteacher whose strong religious beliefs spurred her to care for those less fortunate. She turned her attention to what one minister called the "outsiders" in society: criminals and the mentally ill.

Reforming Care of the Disabled In 1841, Dix visited a jail for women near Boston. She was outraged to discover that some of the prisoners were not criminals, but mentally ill.

Dix demanded to know why these women were locked in small, dark, unheated cells. The jailer replied that "lunatics" did not feel the cold.

During the next 18 months, Dix visited every jail, poorhouse, and hospital in Massachusetts. Her shocking reports helped persuade state legislators to fund a new mental hospital:

Primary Source

"I proceed, gentlemen, briefly to call your attention to the present state of Insane Persons confined . . . in cages, closets, cellars, stalls, pens! Chained, naked, beaten with rods, and lashed into obedience."

—Dorothea Dix, "Memorial to the State Legislators of Massachusetts"

Analyze Images Criminals, debtors, and the mentally ill were housed in terrible conditions. **Infer** Why do you think people were treated this way?

Dix went on to inspect jails as far away as Louisiana and Illinois. Her reports persuaded most legislatures to treat the mentally ill as patients, not criminals.

The Impact of Prison Reform Dix also joined a growing movement to improve conditions in prisons. Men, women, and children were often crammed together in cold, damp rooms. When food supplies were low, prisoners went hungry—unless they had money to buy meals from jailers.

Five out of six people in northern jails were **debtors**, or people who could not pay money they owed. While behind bars, debtors had no way to earn money to pay back their debts. As a result, many debtors remained in prison for years.

Dix and others called for changes in the prison system. As a result, some states built prisons with only one or two inmates to a cell. Cruel punishments were banned, and people convicted of minor crimes received shorter sentences. Slowly, states stopped treating debtors as criminals.

The Impact of the Temperance Movement Alcohol abuse was widespread in the early 1800s. At political rallies, weddings, and funerals, men, women, and sometimes even children drank heavily. Men could buy whiskey in candy stores or barbershops.

The **temperance movement**, a campaign against alcohol abuse, took shape in the late 1820s. Women often took a leading role in the battle. They knew that "demon rum" could lead to the physical abuse of wives and children and the breakup of families.

As a teenager in Washington, D.C., Annie Bidwell took up the temperance cause. She continued to work for laws banning alcohol after she married and moved to California. Bidwell also actively promoted the causes of women's suffrage and **conservation**.

Some temperance groups urged people to drink less. Others sought to end drinking altogether. They won a major victory in 1851, when Maine banned the sale of alcohol.

Academic Vocabulary

conservation • *n.*, the protection of natural resources

Analyze Images Students in a one-room schoolhouse recite for their teacher. **Compare and Contrast** How was a school of the mid-1800s different from today's schools? How was it similar?

Eight other states passed "Maine laws." Most were later repealed, but the temperance crusade would gain new strength in the late 1800s.

READING CHECK **Summarize** Provide a summary of Dorothea Dix's legacy as a social reformer.

What Impact Did Reformers Have on Education?

In colonial times, children's education started in the home. Some children also received an education through their church or were privately taught. In Puritan New England, education focused mainly on religion, with the aim of ensuring salvation. In other regions, church-based schools added reading and writing. Wealthier students often had private tutors or attended "dame schools," run by a local teacher, usually a woman, in her home.

Several colonies and, later, states partly funded public grammar schools. The books used in these schools helped students gain reading skills, but they also had social and civic purposes. The *Columbian Orator,* a book of orations, or public speeches, was used in many schools. Its readings ranged from "A Dialogue on Learning and Usefulness" and "The Dignity of Human Nature" to "President Washington's Address to the People of the United States" and "Description of the First American Congress." The popular *McGuffey Readers* also provided students with numerous moral lessons.

Still, until the mid-1800s, few American children attended any school. In 1827, Massachusetts became the first state to require free community-supported public schools for all children. Teachers, however, were poorly trained and ill paid. Students of all ages crowded together in a single room.

As more men won the right to vote, reformers acted to improve education. They argued that a republic required educated citizens. They also believed that children should not spend their whole day working in a factory. They belonged in school. In 1836, Massachusetts passed a law that required child laborers under age 15 to attend school at least three months of the year. Other states followed. Some of them limited children to a 10-hour day in the factory.

INTERACTIVE

Changes in American Schools

Education Reform Gives Rise to Public Schools Horace Mann became head of the Massachusetts Board of Education in 1837. A Unitarian inspired by the Second Great Awakening, Mann believed that education would help citizens become better Christians. He hounded legislators to provide more money for education. Under his leadership, Massachusetts built new schools, sorted children into grades by age, extended the school year, and raised teachers' pay. The state also opened three colleges to train teachers.

Other states followed the lead of Massachusetts. By the 1850s, most northern states had set up free tax-supported elementary schools. Schools in the South improved more slowly. In both the North and the South, schooling usually ended in the eighth grade. There were few public high schools.

Expanding Education for African Americans In most areas, African Americans had little chance to attend school. A few cities, like Boston and New York, set up separate schools for Black students. However, these schools received less money than schools for white students. In the North, African American men and women often opened their own schools to educate their children.

Some attempts to educate African Americans met with hostility. In the 1830s, Prudence Crandall, a Connecticut Quaker, began a school for African American girls. Crandall continued to teach even as rocks smashed through the window. Finally, a mob broke in one night and destroyed the school.

Despite such obstacles, some African Americans went on to attend private colleges such as Middlebury, Dartmouth, and Oberlin. The first African American known to have earned a college degree was Alexander Lucius Twilight, who graduated from Middlebury College in Vermont in 1823. The first institute of higher learning for African Americans, the Institute for Colored Youth, was founded in Pennsylvania in 1837. It was later followed by Lincoln University, also in Pennsylvania (1854), and Wilberforce University in Ohio (1856).

Reforms for People With Disabilities Some reformers improved education for people with disabilities. In 1817, a Christian evangelical Thomas Gallaudet (gal uh DEHT) set up a school for the deaf in Hartford, Connecticut. Now in Washington, D.C., Gallaudet University is the world's only college that is free of barriers for deaf and hard-of-hearing students.

Analyze Images Alexander Lucius Twilight, below, was the first African American to graduate from college in the United States. **Infer** What do you think Twilight did after graduating from college?

Physician Samuel Gridley Howe founded the first American school for the blind in 1832. Howe was active in many reform movements spurred by the Second Great Awakening, working for improvements in public schools, prisons, and treatment of the disabled. Howe used a system of raised letters to enable students to read with their fingers. One of Howe's pupils, Laura Bridgman, was the first deaf and blind student to receive a formal education.

READING CHECK **Identify Cause and Effect** Why did reformers insist that states set up publicly funded schools for their residents?

Early Calls for Women's Rights

Women had few political or legal rights in the mid-1800s. They could not vote or hold office. When a woman married, her husband became owner of all her property. If a woman worked outside the home, her wages belonged to her husband. A husband also had the right to hit his wife as long as he did not seriously injure her.

Many women, such as Angelina and Sarah Grimké, had joined the abolitionist movement. As these women worked to end slavery, they became aware that they lacked full social and political rights themselves. They and many other women felt limited by their gender when society was so dominated by men. Both white and African American abolitionists, men and women, joined the struggle for women's rights.

Analyze Images Born into slavery but later freed, Isabella Van Wagener took the name "Sojourner Truth" because she believed God wanted her to travel, or sojourn, across the nation preaching abolition. **Draw Conclusions** Would she have been as effective a speaker if she had not changed her name? Why or why not?

What Were the Contributions of Sojourner Truth? One of the most effective women's rights leaders was born into slavery in New York. After gaining freedom, she came to believe that God wanted her to fight slavery. Vowing to sojourn, or travel, across the land speaking the truth, she took the name Sojourner Truth.

Truth was a spellbinding speaker. Her exact words were rarely written down. However, her message spread by word of mouth. According to one witness, Truth ridiculed the idea that women were inferior to men by nature:

Primary Source

"I have as much muscle as any man, and can do as much work as any man. I have plowed and reaped and husked and chopped and mowed, and can any man do more than that?"

—Sojourner Truth, speech at Akron Women's Rights Convention, 1851

INTERACTIVE

The Early Women's Rights Movement

The Contributions of Lucretia Mott and Elizabeth Cady Stanton Other abolitionists also turned to the cause of women's rights. The two most influential were Lucretia Mott and Elizabeth Cady Stanton. Lucretia Mott was a Quaker and the mother of five children. A quiet speaker, she won the respect of many listeners with her persuasive logic. Mott also organized petition drives across the North.

Elizabeth Cady Stanton was the daughter of a New York judge. As a child, she was an excellent student and an athlete. However, her father gave her little encouragement. Stanton later remarked that her "father would have felt a proper pride had I been a man."

Both women attended a series of classes in Boston known as "conversations." These women-only discussions were hosted by Margaret Fuller, a young literary critic. Fuller linked the advance of women's rights with a better understanding of liberty:

Primary Source

"It should be remarked that, as the principle of liberty is better understood, and more nobly interpreted, a broader protest is made in behalf of Woman. As men become aware that few men have had a fair chance, they are inclined to say that no women have had a fair chance."

—Margaret Fuller, *Woman in the Nineteenth Century*, 1844

In 1840, Stanton and Mott joined a group of Americans at a World Antislavery Convention in London. However, convention officials refused to let women take an active part in the proceedings. Female delegates were even forced to sit behind a curtain, hidden from view. After returning home, Mott and Stanton took up the cause of women's rights with new energy.

READING CHECK **Draw Conclusions** How did their early experiences influence Sojourner Truth and Elizabeth Cady Stanton?

▼ Lucretia Mott used her persuasive logic and organizing skills to support the cause of women's rights.

Quick Activity

Explore the similarities between the Declaration of Sentiments and the Declaration of Independence in your Active Journal.

How Did the Women's Movement Start?

Even in London, Mott and Stanton had begun thinking about holding a convention to draw attention to the problems women faced. "The men . . . had [shown] a great need for some education on that question," Stanton later recalled. The meeting finally took place in 1848 in Seneca Falls, New York.

Different Views of Suffrage at the Seneca Falls Convention

About 200 women and 40 men attended the **Seneca Falls Convention**. Stanton's greatest contribution to the convention was the *Declaration of Sentiments*, which she had modeled on the Declaration of Independence. The delegates approved the declaration. It proclaimed, "We hold these truths to be self-evident: that all men and women are created equal."

The women and men at Seneca Falls voted for resolutions that demanded equality for women at work, at school, and at church. Only one resolution met with any opposition at the convention. It demanded that women be allowed to vote. Even the bold reformers at Seneca Falls hesitated to take this step. In the end, the resolution narrowly passed.

Analyze Images Elizabeth Cady Stanton addresses the Seneca Falls Convention. **Infer** Do you think public speaking was acceptable for women at this time?

Women Struggle for Justice The Seneca Falls Convention marked the start of an organized campaign for equal rights, or the **women's rights movement**. This movement was one of the most important reform movements of the Reform Era. In a speech the year after the convention, Lucretia Mott described what this movement would seek to gain:

Primary Source

"The question is often asked, 'What does woman want, more than she enjoys? What is she seeking to obtain? Of what rights is she deprived? What privileges are withheld from her?' I answer, she asks nothing as favor, but as right, she wants to be acknowledged a moral, responsible being."

—Lucretia Mott, "Discourse on Woman," 1849

New leaders took up the struggle. Susan B. Anthony built a close working partnership with Elizabeth Cady Stanton. While Stanton usually had to stay at home with her seven children, Anthony was free to travel across the country. Anthony was a tireless speaker. Even when audiences heckled her and threw eggs, she always finished her speech.

Around the country, Anthony campaigned for women's suffrage. She petitioned Congress repeatedly, and was even arrested in 1872 for trying to vote. After paying a $100 fine, she lashed out at the injustice:

▲ Susan B. Anthony was probably the most powerful and influential leader of the women's rights movement during the 1800s.

Primary Source

"It was we, the people; not we, the white male citizens; nor yet we, the male citizens; but we, the whole people, who formed the Union. And we formed it, not to give the blessings of liberty, but to secure them; not to the half of ourselves and the half of our posterity, but to the whole people—women as well as men."

—Susan B. Anthony, "Women's Rights to the Suffrage," 1873

In the years after 1848, women worked for change in many areas. They won additional legal rights in some states. For example, New York passed laws allowing married women to keep their own property and wages. Still, many men and women opposed the women's rights movement. The struggle for equal rights would last many years.

READING CHECK **Identify Supporting Details** For what act of civil disobedience was Susan B. Anthony arrested in 1872?

Women Gain New Opportunities

The women at Seneca Falls believed that education was a key to equality. Elizabeth Cady Stanton said:

Primary Source

"The girl must be allowed to romp and play, climb, skate, and swim. Her clothing must be more like those of the boy—strong, loose-fitting garments, thick boots. . . . She must be taught to look forward to life of self-dependence and, like the boy, prepare herself for some [profitable] trade profession."

—Elizabeth Cady Stanton, Letter, 1851

Such an idea was startling in the early 1800s. Women from poor families had little hope of learning even to read. Middle-class girls who went to school learned dancing and drawing rather than science or mathematics. After all, people argued, women were expected to care for their families. Why did they need an education?

Opportunities for Women's Education Possibly the greatest impact of the women's movement in the mid-1800s was the creation of greater opportunities for women in education. Emma Willard opened a high school for girls in Troy, New York. Here, young women studied "men's" subjects, such as mathematics and physics.

Mary Lyon opened Mount Holyoke Female Seminary in Massachusetts in 1837. She did not call the school a college because many people thought it was wrong for women to attend college. In fact, however, Mount Holyoke was one of the first women's colleges in the United States.

New Employment Opportunities for Women At about this time, a few men's colleges began to admit women. As their education improved, women found jobs teaching, especially in grade schools.

A few women entered fields such as medicine. Elizabeth Blackwell attended medical school at Geneva College in New York. To the surprise of school officials, she graduated first in her class. Women had provided medical care since colonial times, but Blackwell was the first woman in the United States to earn a medical degree. She later helped found the nation's first medical school for women.

Women made their mark in other fields as well. Maria Mitchell was a noted astronomer. Sarah Josepha Hale edited *Godey's Lady's Book*, an influential magazine for women.

Analyze Graphs The infographic below shows some of the changes in women's lives in the first half of the 1800s. **Use Visual Information** What details in the graphs support the conclusion that women's educational opportunities expanded during the mid-1800s?

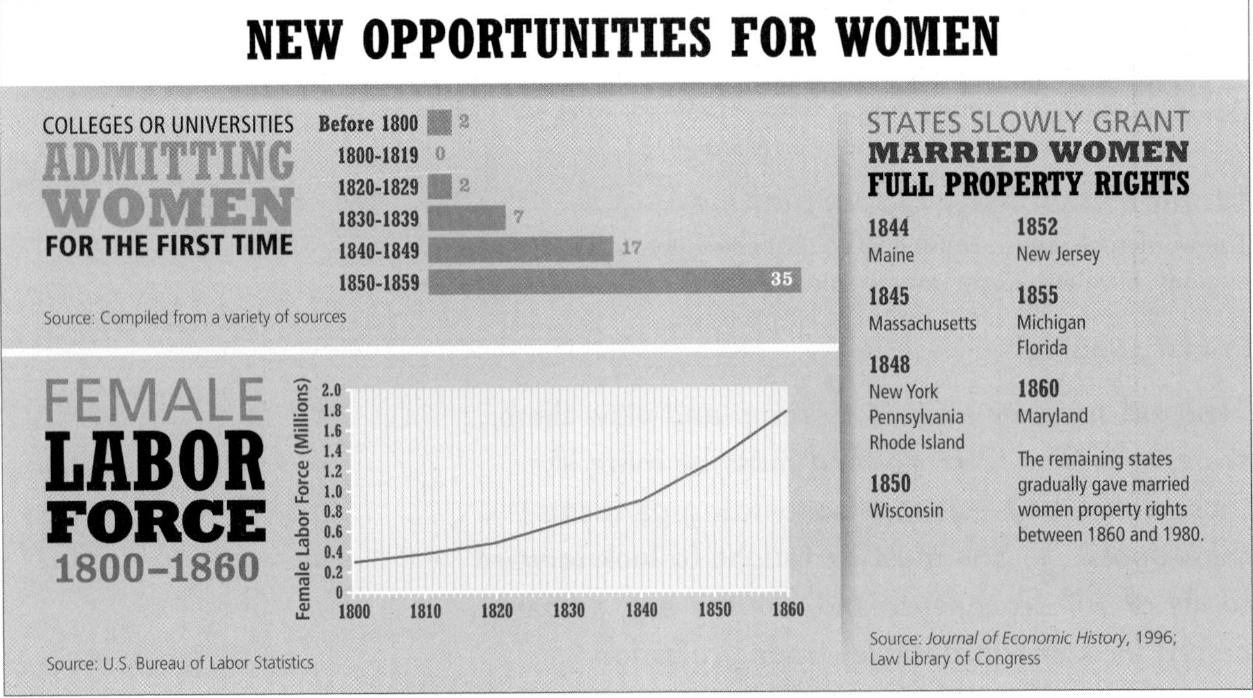

Antoinette Blackwell became the first American woman ordained as a minister. She also campaigned for abolitionism, temperance, and women's right to vote.

Analyze Images Women began attending medical school during the 1800s. **Infer** Why would women have been good candidates for medical training?

The Struggle Continues

The struggle for women's rights continues today. As in the 19th century, different groups have differing points of view.

One issue on which women's groups differ today is whether companies or the government should be required to pay women on maternity leave, or a period away from their jobs to give birth and take care of babies. Some women's groups today, such as the National Organization for Women, believe that employers, including the government, should be required to pay women during maternity leave. They argue that women need this support. Other groups, such as the Independent Women's Forum, argue that requiring employers to pay for maternity leave might make them less willing to hire women.

READING CHECK **Draw Conclusions** What effects did the women's movement have during the 1800s?

Lesson Check

Practice Vocabulary

1. How did the teachings of the **Second Great Awakening** inspire movements for **social reform**?
2. What role did the **Seneca Falls Convention** play in the **women's rights movement**?

Critical Thinking and Writing

3. Identify Main Ideas What did social reformers believe was unjust about American society?
4. Summarize Summarize the changes in how children were educated from colonial times through the mid-1800s.
5. Cite Evidence Do you consider the women's rights movement in the mid-1800s successful or not? Explain.
6. Writing Workshop: Use Descriptive Details and Sensory Language Look around yourself right now. What do you see, what do you hear, what do you feel or smell? Write a few sentences in your Active Journal to describe these sensations. You will find that descriptive words and sensory language will add life and excitement to your narrative essay.

James Fenimore Cooper, "The Chainbearer"

James Fenimore Cooper wrote about life on the early American frontier. In this passage, the narrator is sailing up the Hudson River on his way to a frontier settlement in northern New York.

◀ Axes were essential for clearing forests.

On the main-deck were six or eight sturdy, decent, quiet, respectable-looking labourers, who were evidently of the class of husbandmen. ① Their packs were lying in a pile, near the foot of the mast, and I did not fail to observe that there were as many axes as there were packs.

The American axe! It has made more real and lasting conquests than the sword of any warlike people that ever lived; but, they have been conquests that have left civilization in their train, ② instead of havoc and desolation. ③ More than a million of square miles of territory have been opened up from the shades of the virgin forest, to admit the warmth of the sun; and culture and abundance have been spread where the beast of the forest so lately roamed. . . . A brief quarter of a century has seen these wonderful changes wrought; and at the bottom of them all lies this beautiful, well-prized, ready, and efficient implement, the American axe!

It would not be easy to give the reader a clear notion of the manner in which the young men and men of all ages of the older portions of the new republic poured into the woods to commence the business of felling the forests, and laying bare the secrets of nature, as soon as the nation rose from beneath the pressure of war, ④ to enjoy the freedom of peace.

—James Fenimore Cooper, *The Chainbearer*

Reading and Vocabulary Support

① A farmer was called a husbandman.

② The phrase *in their train* literally means "behind them," but its implied meaning is "as a result of."

③ Explain, in your own words, how Cooper's "conquests" of the axe "left civilization in their train" instead of destruction.

④ What is the war that Cooper is referring to here?

Analyzing Primary Sources

Cite specific evidence from this source to support your answers.

1. **Determine Author's Purpose** Why does Cooper glorify the axe?
2. **Determine Author's Point of View** How does Americans' image of the forest today differ from that of Cooper's time?

LESSON 6

Arts and Literature

GET READY TO READ

START UP

Examine the painting by American artist Robert S. Duncanson. Write a sentence or two suggesting how this painting might reflect a theme common to writers and artists of this period.

GUIDING QUESTIONS

- What was life like in the early years of the republic?
- What themes did American painters pursue in the early to mid-1800s?
- What themes marked the works of writers during this period?
- How did transcendentalism affect American culture?

TAKE NOTES

Literacy Skills: Identify Cause and Effect

Use the graphic organizer in your Active Journal to take notes as you read the lesson.

PRACTICE VOCABULARY

Use the vocabulary activity in your Active Journal to practice the vocabulary words.

Vocabulary

Hudson River School
transcendentalist
individualism

Academic Vocabulary

idealize

Before 1800, most American painters studied in Europe. Benjamin West of Philadelphia was appointed historical painter to King George III. Many American painters journeyed to London to study with West. Two of them, Charles Wilson Peale and Gilbert Stuart, later painted famous portraits of George Washington.

A New American Art Style

By the mid-1800s, American artists began to develop their own style. The first group to do so became known as the **Hudson River School**. Artists such as Thomas Cole and Asher B. Durand painted vivid landscapes of New York's Hudson River region and other parts of the Northeast. African American painter Robert S. Duncanson depicted the beauty of nature.

Other artists painted scenes of hard-working country people in a natural setting. George Caleb Bingham of Missouri created a timeless picture of frontier life. George Catlin and Alfred Jacob Miller traveled to the Far West to record the daily life of American Indians.

Analyze Images John James Audubon's paintings of birds, like these Columbia jays, and other wildlife are still admired for their beauty and scientific accuracy. **Infer** Why did Audubon find endless subjects to paint in the United States?

John James Audubon, a wildlife artist, traveled across the country painting birds and mammals. His collection of 435 life-size prints, titled *The Birds of America,* portrayed every bird known in the United States at the time.

American artists in the early and mid-1800s proved that the American landscape and people were worthy subjects of art. Their paintings portrayed the continuity in the American way of life—in the timelessness of the country's geography and in the patterns of farm work. They also showed the great changes that were underway in this new era. Artists depicted the westward movement of white settlers, capturing the nation's expansion and growth. In their attention to these themes, the work of these painters reflected American society in their day.

READING CHECK **Identify Main Ideas** What were common themes in the works of American artists during the early to mid-1800s?

New Forms of Literature and Music

Like painters, early American writers also depended on Europe for their ideas and inspiration. In the 1820s, however, a new crop of poets and fiction writers began to write about American themes. At the same time, uniquely American forms of music began to emerge. These new forms of literature and music reflected American society in the early and mid-1800s.

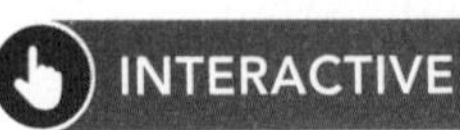

INTERACTIVE

Painting America

American Poetry Henry Wadsworth Longfellow was the favorite poet of Americans in the mid-1800s. Longfellow based many of his poems on historical events. "Paul Revere's Ride" honored the Revolutionary War hero. "The Song of Hiawatha" **idealized** Native American life. His poems gave Americans a sense of where they came from and, in the process, helped establish a national identity.

Academic Vocabulary

idealized • *v.,* to see in the best possible light

Other poets spoke out on social issues. John Greenleaf Whittier, a Quaker from Massachusetts, and Frances Watkins Harper, an African American woman from Maryland, reflected change in American society as abolitionism gained supporters. They used their pens to make readers aware of the evils of slavery.

After a career as a journalist, Walt Whitman became a groundbreaking poet. His greatest work was *Leaves of Grass*. Like Longfellow, Whittier, and Harper, he focused on uniquely American themes. His poetry celebrated democracy. He wrote proudly of being part of a "nation of many nations":

INTERACTIVE

Early American Music and Literature

Primary Source

"At home on the hills of Vermont or in the woods of Maine, or the Texan ranch, comrade of Californians, comrade of free North-Westerners, . . . of every hue and caste am I, of every rank and religion."

—Walt Whitman, *Song of Myself*

Whitman was also one of the first modern poets to write about love between men. His romantic view of friendship between men has been an inspiration to modern gay culture.

Only seven of Emily Dickinson's more than 1,700 poems were published in her lifetime. A shy woman who rarely left her home, Dickinson called her poetry "my letter to the world / That never wrote to me." Her close friendship with her brother's wife, Susan, has led some scholars to speculate that the two women had a romantic relationship, although there is no definite evidence of this. Today, Dickinson is recognized as one of the nation's greatest poets.

Writers Begin to Tell American Stories One of the most popular American writers was Washington Irving, a New Yorker. Irving first became known for *The Sketch Book,* a collection of tales published in 1820. Two of his best-loved tales are "Rip Van Winkle" and "The Legend of Sleepy Hollow."

The exciting novels of James Fenimore Cooper were also set in the American past. Several of his novels, including *The Deerslayer* and *The Last of the Mohicans,* feature Natty Bumppo, a heroic model of a strong, solitary frontiersman. Cooper's novels gave an idealized view of relations between whites and Native Americans on the frontier.

Like Longfellow's poems, the stories of Cooper and Irving gave Americans a sense of the richness of their past. Their appeal went beyond the United States, however. Washington Irving was the first American writer to enjoy fame in Europe.

Later Writers In 1851, Herman Melville published *Moby-Dick*. The novel tells the story of Ahab, the crazed captain of a whaling ship. Ahab vows revenge on the white whale that years earlier bit off his leg. *Moby-Dick* had only limited success when it was first published. Today, however, critics rank it among the finest American novels.

Analyze Images Emily Dickinson, shown here in an early photograph, wrote poems that reflected the loneliness of her life. **Draw Conclusions** Why do you think Dickinson is still considered one of the greatest American poets?

▲ Whalers face the angry whale Moby-Dick in a scene from Herman Melville's epic tale *Moby-Dick,* considered one of the greatest American novels.

Nathaniel Hawthorne often drew on the history of New England in his novels and short stories. In *The Scarlet Letter,* published in 1850, Hawthorne explored Puritan notions of sin and salvation. The novel shows how a young man is consumed by guilt when he tries to hide his wrongdoing from the world.

Edgar Allan Poe became famous for his many tales of horror. His short story "The Tell-Tale Heart" is about a murderer, driven mad by guilt, who imagines he can hear his victim's heartbeat. Poe is also known as the father of the detective story for his mystery stories, such as "The Murders in the Rue Morgue."

William Wells Brown was the first African American to earn his living as a writer. He published *Clotel,* a novel about slave life, in 1853. Brown also wrote a play inspired by his own experiences as a fugitive slave and a conductor on the Underground Railroad. His lectures and readings drew large audiences in Europe as well as throughout the North.

Women Writers Flourish Women wrote many of the best-selling novels of the period. Some novels told about young women who gained wealth and happiness through honesty and self-sacrifice. Others showed the hardships faced by widows and orphans.

Perhaps the best known of these women writers was Louisa May Alcott. Alcott wrote numerous short stories, poems, and books. Her most famous work was a novel written for girls, called *Little Women*. Centered on a strong-willed young woman who loves reading and writing, it remains a popular book today.

The novels of other writers, such as Catherine Sedgwick and Fanny Fern, have few readers today. Yet these writers earned far more than Hawthorne or Melville. Hawthorne complained about the success of a "mob of scribbling women."

American Music American classical music in the 1800s continued to follow European traditions. Yet, as American society changed and grew and different groups of people came into contact with one another, distinctly American musical forms began to emerge. Early songs were often patriotic or religious, such as "My Country Tis of Thee," written by Samuel Francis Smith in 1831, or "Amazing Grace," published in 1835.

Did you know?

The four sisters in *Little Women* were based on Alcott and her own sisters.

The 1800s saw the rise of a middle class interested in music that was entertaining and emotionally stirring. The songs of Stephen Foster, which drew on American themes, were especially popular. Although Foster was a northerner, many of his songs referred to southern traditions and were popular in the South. Another song popular in the South, "Dixie," was written by Ohio native Daniel Emmett. Western expansion, immigration, and migration mingled musical traditions together, creating new American sounds.

African American music in particular had a strong influence on the new forms that were developing. African American spirituals and work songs combined African and European musical traditions. During the 1800s, a new style of music now known as gospel music began to develop in African American religious congregations. These styles would later combine with European and American folk traditions to shape blues, jazz, country, and rock music.

READING CHECK **Draw Conclusions** What do many of the works of American literature of the early to mid-1800s have in common?

Transcendentalism Develops

In New England, a small but influential group of writers and thinkers emerged. They called themselves **transcendentalists**, because they believed that the most important truths in life transcended, or went beyond, human reason. They produced a unique body of literature reflecting transcendentalist thought. Transcendentalists valued the spark of deeply felt insights more than reason.

Analyze Images Although considered uniquely American, the banjo has roots in sub-Saharan Africa. **Cite Evidence** What other American musical traditions or instruments have African origins?

LOUISA MAY ALCOTT

Author of *Little Women* (1832–1888)

- Her father was an educator, philosopher, abolitionist, and women's rights supporter.
- As a child, she spent time with her father's Boston-area friends Ralph Waldo Emerson and Henry David Thoreau.
- At the start of the Civil War, she served as a nurse at a Union hospital, where she contracted typhoid fever.
- She published two *Little Women* books, in 1868 and 1869, and their success allowed her to pay off her family's extensive debts.
- She wrote in her book *Little Men* (1871): "Money is the root of all evil, and yet it is such a useful root that we cannot get on without it any more than we can without potatoes."

Critical Thinking Why do you think Alcott immediately began a second *Little Women* book after publishing the first?

Did you know?

The land where Thoreau built his cabin was owned by Emerson and was about 20 minutes by foot from Thoreau's family home.

They believed that each individual should live up to the divine possibilities within. This belief influenced many transcendentalists to support social reform.

Emerson on the Importance of the Individual The leading transcendentalist was Ralph Waldo Emerson. Emerson was the most popular essayist and lecturer of his day. Audiences flocked to hear him talk on subjects such as self-reliance and character. Emerson believed that the human spirit was reflected in nature. Civilization might provide material wealth, he said, but nature exhibited higher values that came from God.

In his essays and lectures, Emerson stressed **individualism**, or the importance of each individual. In its individual focus, transcendentalism is unique to American culture. Individualism and individual responsibility are central to America's democracy. Each person, Emerson said, has an "inner light." He urged people to use this inner light to guide their lives and improve society. "Trust thyself," he wrote. "Every heart vibrates to that iron string."

Thoreau and Civil Disobedience Henry David Thoreau (thuh ROH), Emerson's friend and neighbor, believed that the growth of industry and the rise of cities were ruining the nation. He urged people to live as simply and as close to nature as possible. In *Walden,* his best-known work, Thoreau describes spending a year alone in a cabin on Walden Pond in Massachusetts.

Analyze Images This replica of Henry David Thoreau's cabin sits near the site of his original cabin beside Walden Pond in Concord, Massachusetts. **Understand Effects** How might living in a small cabin like this have inspired Thoreau?

Like Emerson, Thoreau believed that each individual must decide what is right or wrong. "If a man does not keep pace with his companions," he wrote, in *Walden,* "perhaps it is because he hears a different drummer. Let him step to the music he hears."

Thoreau's "different drummer" told him that slavery was wrong. He argued in favor of civil disobedience and once went to jail for refusing to pay taxes to support the U.S.-Mexican War, which he felt promoted slavery. Thoreau wrote an essay titled "Civil Disobedience" that explained why an individual may feel the need to break laws that are unjust without resorting to violence.

He argued, though, that anyone who chooses this course has to be prepared to be imprisoned or otherwise punished. This essay had a great impact on future leaders. Thoreau's ideas on civil disobedience and nonviolence later influenced Mohandas Gandhi, who led a struggle in India for independence from Britain, and Martin Luther King, Jr., an American civil rights leader during the mid-1900s.

READING CHECK **Identify Main Ideas** What was the core belief of the transcendentalists?

▲ Ralph Waldo Emerson was one of the most influential of the transcendentalists.

Lesson Check

Practice Vocabulary

1. What role did **individualism** play in the beliefs of the **transcendentalists**?
2. What distinguished the artists of **Hudson River School** from other artists?

Critical Thinking and Writing

3. Summarize How did writers in the 1800s contribute to social reform movements?
4. Evaluate Arguments How would you respond to the argument that American artists and writers explored common themes during this period?
5. Generate Explanations How did transcendentalism affect American culture?
6. Writing Workshop: Prepare a Final Draft Review your writing as you prepare to create your final draft. You may want to share it with a partner. Check your structure, spelling, and grammar. Have you said what you wanted to say?

TOPIC 7

Review and Assessment

VISUAL REVIEW

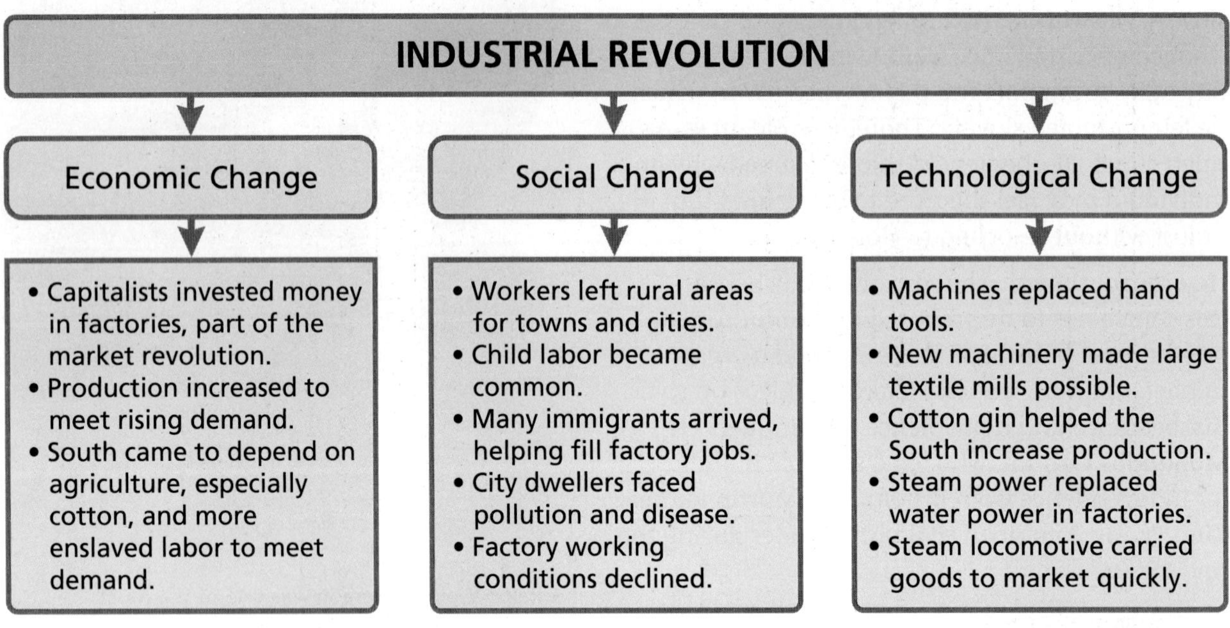

READING REVIEW

Use the Take Notes and Practice Vocabulary activities in your Active Journal to review the topic.

INTERACTIVE

Practice vocabulary using the Topic Mini-Games.

Quest FINDINGS

Write Your Essay

Get help for writing your essay in your Active Journal.

ASSESSMENT

Vocabulary and Key Ideas

1. **Check Understanding** Why did the spread of the factory system rely on **capitalists**?
2. **Identify Supporting Details** How did work in a factory differ from farm work?
3. **Identify** Who were the people in the South said to make up the **"cottonocracy"**?
4. **Define** What was the **Underground Railroad?**
5. **Recall** What political advantage did the **Know-Nothing Party** gain by opposing Irish immigrants?
6. **Locate** Which state took the lead in reforming its educational system and establishing public schools?
7. **Identify** What philosophy is associated with **individualism** and reliance on nature?

Critical Thinking and Writing

8. **Compare and Contrast** How did interchangeable parts differ from the parts that had been used before in manufacturing products, and why did that matter?
9. **Draw Conclusions** Do you think social reforms such as the abolition of slavery would have been pursued even if the Second Great Awakening had not occurred? Why or why not?
10. **Sequence** How could the building of a factory along a river in the early 1800s lead eventually to the existence of a growing city?
11. **Infer** What role did the Seneca Falls Convention play in sparking the women's rights movement?
12. **Revisit the Essential Question** American writers, artists, and musicians of the 1800s focused on themes that were unique to American culture. Do you agree or disagree? Explain your answer.
13. **Writing Workshop: Write Narratives** Using the outline you created in your Active Journal, write a three-paragraph narrative from the point of view of a young person working in northern industry during this time period.

Analyze Primary Sources

14. Who was the author of this dialogue?
    - **A.** Emily Dickinson
    - **B.** Ralph Waldo Emerson
    - **C.** Louisa May Alcott
    - **D.** Herman Melville

"Well, sir, I want to see what whaling is. I want to see the world."

"Want to see what whaling is, eh? Have ye clapped eye on Captain Ahab?"

Analyze Maps

Use the map at right to answer the following questions:

15. What does the dark green area in Tennessee indicate?
16. Which state had the largest area devoted to producing sugar?

▼ **Agriculture in the South**

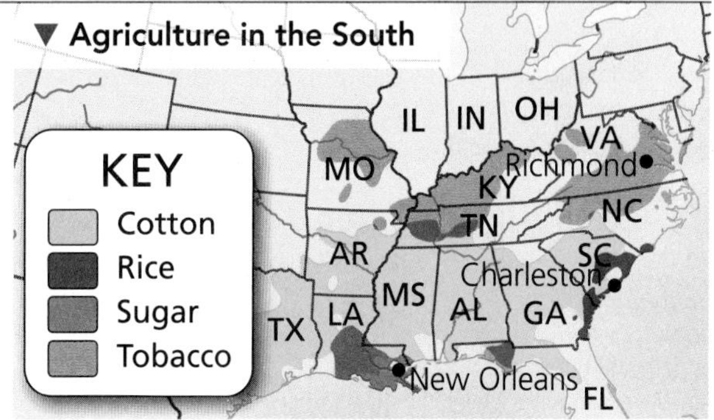

TOPIC 8

Sectionalism and Civil War

(1820–1865)

GO ONLINE to access your digital course

- VIDEO
- AUDIO
- ETEXT
- INTERACTIVE
- WRITING
- GAMES
- WORKSHEET
- ASSESSMENT

Go back to the 1820s

and the era of SECTIONALISM AND THE CIVIL WAR. Why? Because it was during this time that the seeds of the Civil War were sown. Learn what caused this terrible conflict.

Explore The Essential Question

When is war justified?

In 1861, southern states quit the Union. President Lincoln had to decide if that was a good enough reason to go to war. What did Lincoln have to consider in making the decision?

Unlock the Essential Question in your Active Journal.

Read

about events leading up to the Civil War, the decisions leaders made, and the conflict that raged for four years.

Watch

NBC LEARN

BOUNCE TO ACTIVATE VIDEO

Robert E. Lee, the Marble Man

Learn about Robert E. Lee's leadership at the Battle of Chancellorsville.

▲ The Battle of Gettysburg, 1863

TOPIC 8

Sectionalism and Civil War

Learn more about Sectionalism and the Civil War by making your own map and timeline in your Active Journal.

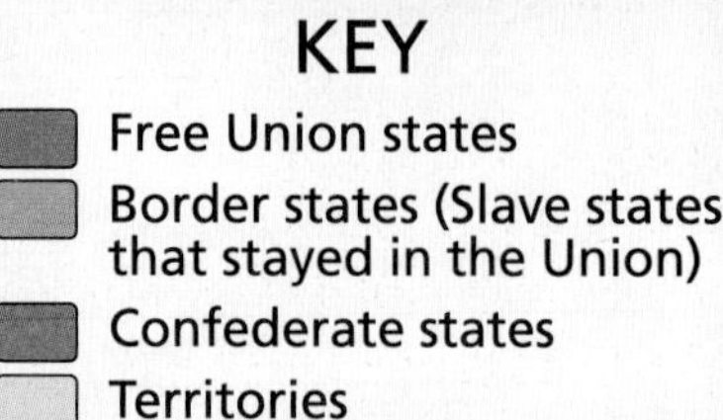

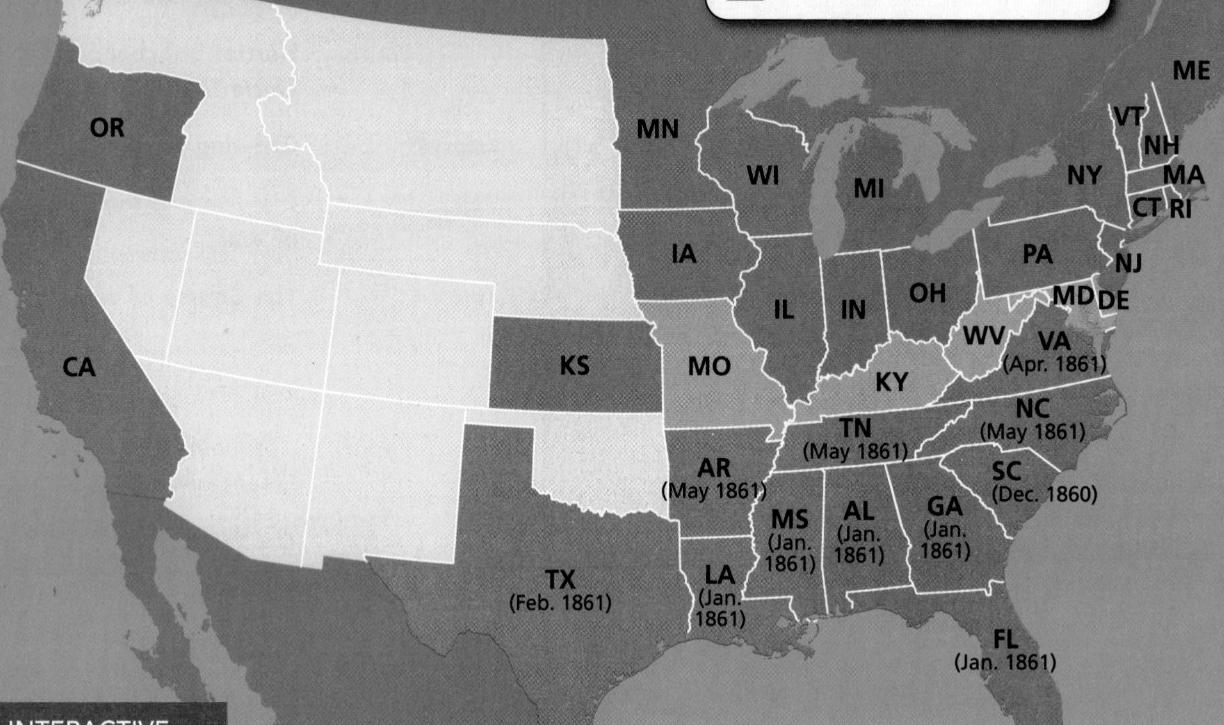

INTERACTIVE
Topic Timeline

What happened and when?

Tensions between states over slavery . . . compromises to keep the nation together . . . political divisions and courtroom drama. . . and then a long and bloody civil war. Explore the timeline to see some of what was going on in the United States and in the rest of the world.

1850
Compromise of 1850, Fugitive Slave Act

TOPIC EVENTS

1820	1830	1840

WORLD EVENTS

1820
African American colonists set sail for Liberia

1821
Mexico and most of Central America gain independence from Spain

Topic Map

Where was the Civil War fought?

The Civil War involved the whole United States, but most of the battles occurred in the Southern states that seceded from the Union and formed the Confederate States of America.

BY TELEGRAPH.

Sunday, April 14, 1861

Fort Sumpter Surrendered!

MAJ. ANDERSON

A PRISONER OF WAR

&c. &c. &c.

Who will you meet?

Abraham Lincoln, war President

Clara Barton, battlefield nurse

Jefferson Davis, leader of the Confederacy

1845 Great Famine begins in Ireland

1854 Kansas-Nebraska Act

1857 *Dred Scott* v. *Sandford* decision

1861 Shots fired at Ft. Sumter, Civil War begins

1865 Lee surrenders at Appomattox Court House

1866 Transatlantic cable completed

1850 | 1860 | 1870

Project-Based Learning Inquiry

A Lincoln Website

Quest KICK OFF

It is 1863, and you have come to hear President Lincoln dedicate a cemetery. As you listen to him speak, his words sound familiar.

How did Abraham Lincoln's writings and speeches relate to the Declaration of Independence?

With your team, explore the answer in this Quest, and then create a website to share your findings.

▲ President Lincoln, 1862

1 Ask Questions

In your Active Journal write questions about Lincoln and the Declaration of Independence to guide your Quest.

2 Investigate

As you read the lessons in this Topic, look for Quest CONNECTIONS to help you make connections between Lincoln's speeches and writings and the Declaration of Independence. Take notes about what you learn in your Active Journal.

3 Conduct Research

Now examine some of Lincoln's speeches and writings. In particular, read the Emancipation Proclamation (1863) Primary Source feature in Lesson 5, the "House Divided" speech (1858), the Gettysburg Address (1863), and the first and second inaugural addresses (1861, 1865). As you read, look for more connections.

Quest FINDINGS

4 Create a Web Site

Working with your team, create a two-page website so you can share your findings. Get help for this task in your Active Journal.

LESSON 1

Conflicts and Compromises

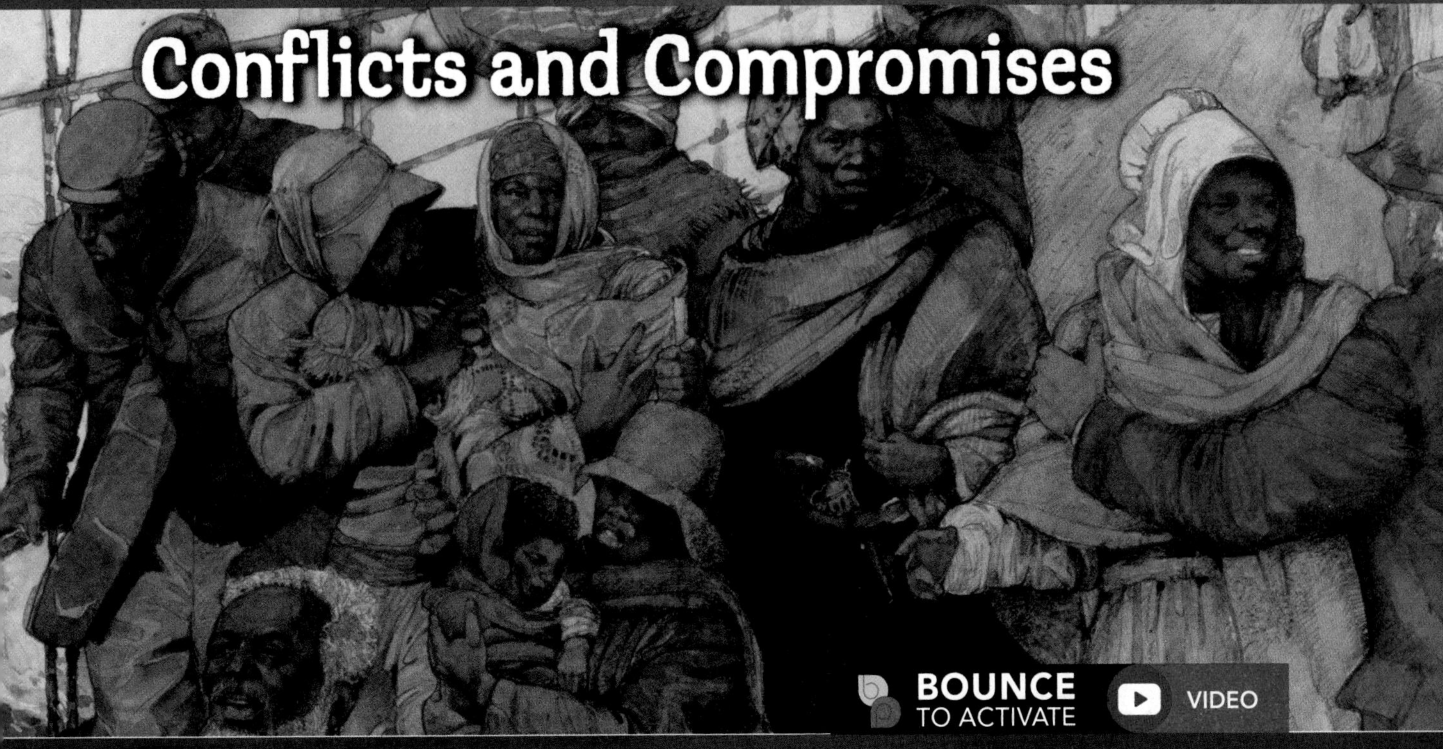

GET READY TO READ

START UP

This picture shows enslaved people escaping to freedom. What kinds of risks did they face?

GUIDING QUESTIONS

- Why did conflict arise over the issue of slavery in the western territories?
- How did Congress try to resolve the issue of slavery?
- How did *Uncle Tom's Cabin* affect attitudes toward slavery?

TAKE NOTES

Literacy Skills Compare and Contrast

Use the Graphic Organizer in your Active Journal to take notes as you read the lesson.

PRACTICE VOCABULARY

Use the Vocabulary Builder in your Active Journal to practice these words.

Vocabulary

- Missouri Compromise
- popular sovereignty
- Free-Soil Party
- secede
- fugitive
- civil war
- Compromise of 1850
- Fugitive Slave Act

Academic Vocabulary

- resolve
- propose

In 1819, there were 11 free states in the North and 11 slave states in the South. The North and South had different economies, political views, and ideas about slavery. These differences created a growing sectionalism. Sectionalism is a rivalry or tension that develops between people who are loyal to their section, or region, of the country. This era of sectionalism lasted from the 1810s to the 1860s. As a result of sectionalism, there were many political conflicts over issues important to each region.

The Missouri Compromise

Before 1819, the equal number of slave and free states balanced the sectional divide. In that year, however, Missouri applied to join the Union as a slave state. Immediately, a crisis erupted. Missouri's admission would give the South a majority in the Senate. Determined not to lose power, northerners opposed letting Missouri enter as a slave state.

Missouri Compromise, 1820

GEOGRAPHY SKILLS

The map shows how the Missouri Compromise divided the territories at latitude 36°30′ N. All states that would be formed from the territory north of this line would be free states.

1. **Location** Based on the map, how was Missouri an exception to the terms of the Missouri Compromise?
2. **Analyze Maps** Based on the information in the map, how did the Missouri Compromise preserve a balance of power in the Senate?

The argument lasted many months. During the long debate, Maine had also applied for statehood. Finally, Senator Henry Clay suggested admitting Missouri as a slave state and Maine as a free state. His plan, the **Missouri Compromise**, kept the number of slave and free states equal.

Under the provisions of the Missouri Compromise, Congress drew an imaginary line extending the southern border of Missouri at latitude 36°30′ N. Slavery was permitted in the part of the Louisiana Purchase south of that line. It was banned north of the line. The only exception was Missouri itself.

READING CHECK **Check Understanding** Why did Missouri's application to join the Union as a slave state spark a crisis?

How Did Western Expansion Increase Tensions?

The Missouri Compromise applied only to the Louisiana Purchase. By 1846, however, there were rumblings of a war with Mexico, and the United States expected to gain vast new lands. Once again, the question of slavery in the territories arose.

The Wilmot Proviso Divides Congress Many northerners feared that the South would extend slavery into the West. Congressman David Wilmot of Pennsylvania called for a law to ban slavery in any territories won from Mexico. Southern leaders angrily opposed this Wilmot Proviso. They said that Congress had no right to ban slavery in the West.

The House passed the Wilmot Proviso in 1846, but the Senate defeated it.

Opposing Views As the debate over slavery heated up, people took sides. Abolitionists believed slavery was morally wrong and wanted it banned throughout the country. Southern slaveholders thought that slavery should be allowed in any territory. They also demanded that enslaved African Americans who escaped to the North be returned to them. Even white southerners who did not enslave African Americans generally agreed with these ideas.

Between these two extremes, some moderates argued that the Missouri Compromise line should be extended west all the way to the Pacific. Any new state north of the line would be a free state. Any new state south of the line could allow slavery. Other moderates felt that slavery should be allowed where it existed, but it should not be expanded to new territories.

Still others supported the idea of **popular sovereignty**, or the right of people to create their government. Under popular sovereignty, voters in a territory would decide for themselves whether or not to allow slavery.

READING CHECK **Draw Conclusions** Why did the Missouri Compromise fail to solve the issue of slavery?

The Free-Soil Party Opposes Slavery in the West

By 1848, many northern Democrats and Whigs opposed the spread of slavery. However, with the presidential election ahead, leaders of both parties refused to take a stand for fear of losing southern votes. Some also feared that the slavery issue would split the nation.

In 1848, antislavery members of both parties met in Buffalo, New York. There, they founded the **Free-Soil Party**. The party's main goal was to keep slavery out of the western territories. Only a few Free-Soilers were abolitionists who wanted to end slavery in the South.

In the 1848 presidential campaign, Free-Soilers named former President Martin Van Buren as their candidate. Democrats chose Lewis Cass of Michigan. The Whigs selected Zachary Taylor, a hero of the 1848 Mexican-American War.

For the first time, slavery was an important election issue. Van Buren called for a ban on slavery in the Mexican Cession—the land ceded by Mexico after the 1848 war. Cass supported popular sovereignty. Taylor did not speak on the issue, but he was a slave owner from Louisiana, so many southern voters assumed that he supported slavery.

Analyze Images As Americans debated the issue of slavery, slave auctions, like this one in Virginia, continued in the South. **Infer** How did the slave system affect African American family life?

Presidential Election of 1848

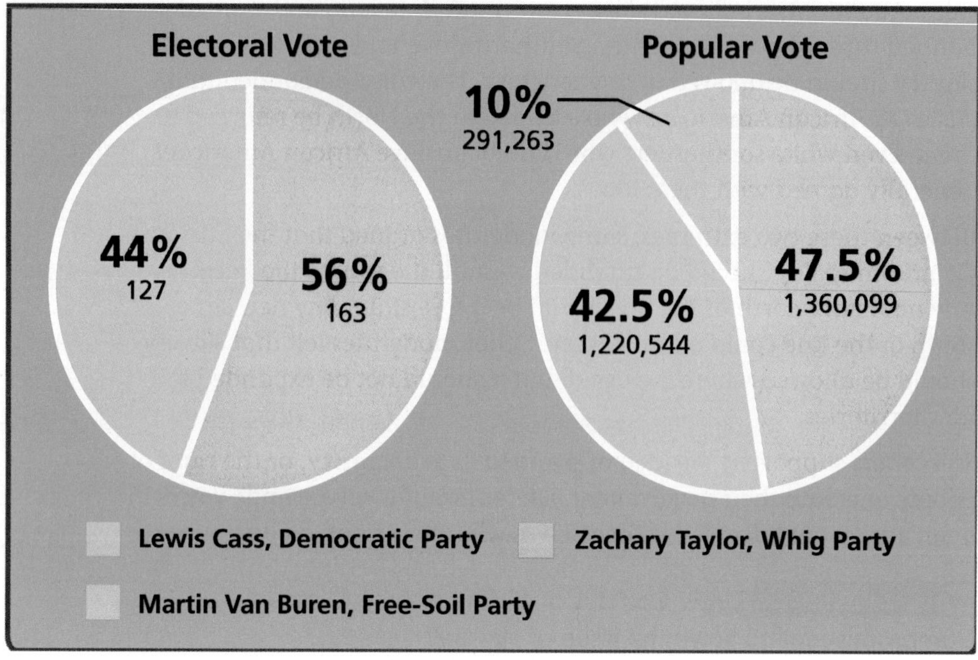

Analyze Graphs These graphs show the results of the 1848 presidential election. **Draw Conclusions** According to both pie graphs, what effect did Martin Van Buren's candidacy have on the other two candidates' electoral votes?

Zachary Taylor won the election. Still, Van Buren took 10 percent of the popular vote, and 13 other Free-Soil candidates won seats in Congress. The Free-Soil Party's success showed that slavery had become a national issue.

READING CHECK **Identify Central Issues** What was significant about the Free-Soil Party and the fact that slavery was a political issue for the first time?

California Reignites the Slavery Debate

For a time after the Missouri Compromise, both slave and free states entered the Union peacefully. However, when California requested admission to the Union as a free state in 1850, the balance of power in the Senate was once again threatened.

Conflict and Compromise In 1849, there were 15 slave states and 15 free states. Admitting California as a free state would upset the balance. Moreover, it seemed possible that Oregon, Utah, and New Mexico might also join the Union as free states.

Many white southerners feared that the South would be hopelessly outvoted in the Senate. Some even suggested that southern states might want to **secede**, or remove themselves, from the United States. Northern congressmen, meanwhile, argued that California should enter the Union as a free state because most of the territory lay north of the Missouri Compromise line.

It was clear that the nation faced a crisis.

Conflicts Between Henry Clay and John C. Calhoun Henry Clay had won the nickname "the Great Compromiser" for working out the Missouri Compromise and the compromise Tariff of 1833, which **resolved** the Nullification Crisis. Now, decades later, the 73-year-old Clay was frail and ill. Still, he pleaded for northern and southern politicians to reach an agreement. If they failed to do so, Clay warned, the nation could break apart.

Academic Vocabulary
resolve • *v.*, to find an answer or solution to something

Senator John C. Calhoun of South Carolina had worked with Clay to pass the compromise Tariff of 1833, but now he opposed compromise over the extension of slavery to the West. He drafted a speech expressing his opposition.

Calhoun was dying of tuberculosis and could not speak loudly enough to address the Senate. He stared defiantly at his northern foes while Senator James Mason of Virginia read his speech.

Calhoun insisted that slavery be allowed in the western territories. In addition, he demanded that **fugitives**, or African Americans who had fled slavery, be returned to their owners. He wanted northerners to admit that slaveholders had the right to reclaim their "property."

▼ The U.S. Senate debating California admission. ❶ Henry Clay sought compromise between northern and southern politicans. ❷ Daniel Webster feared the possibility of a civil war more than the spread of slavery. ❸ John C. Calhoun insisted on states' rights and preserving slavery.

Did you know?

In February 1850, President Taylor threatened to personally lead the U.S. Army to capture secessionist rebels and have them hanged for treason. He died two months later.

Calhoun's demands were based on his belief in states' rights. He believed the federal government's power over the states was limited. As Calhoun saw it, states had chosen to give authority to the federal government; therefore, he believed, states had the right to decide how much authority to give, and they could cancel the agreement if they wished.

If the northerners rejected white southerners' demands, Calhoun told the Senate, "let the states . . . agree to part in peace. If you are unwilling that we should part in peace, tell us so, and we shall know what to do." Everyone knew what Calhoun meant. If an agreement could not be reached, white southerners would use force to leave the Union.

Daniel Webster Offers Compromise Daniel Webster of Massachusetts spoke next. He had opposed Clay's compromise Tariff of 1833. Now, he supported Clay's plea to save the Union. Webster stated his position clearly:

Primary Source

"I speak today not as a Massachusetts man, nor as a northern man, but as an American. . . . I speak today for the preservation of the Union. . . . There can be no such thing as a peaceable secession."

—Daniel Webster, Speech in the U.S. Senate, July 17, 1850

Webster opposed the concept of states' rights. He believed that in a union the federal authority was supreme. He feared that the states could not separate without suffering a bloody civil war. A **civil war** is a war between people of the same country.

Like many northerners, Webster viewed slavery as evil. The breakup of the United States, however, he believed was worse. To save the Union, Webster was willing to compromise. He would support southern demands that northerners be forced to return fugitives from slavery.

READING CHECK **Check Understanding** Why did Daniel Webster, an avowed opponent of slavery, agree to support returning to their enslavers African Americans who had escaped slavery?

A Compromise Holds the Union Together

In 1850, as the debate raged, both Calhoun and President Taylor died. The new president was Millard Fillmore. Unlike Taylor, he encouraged Clay to seek a compromise.

The Compromise of 1850 Addresses Regional Concerns

Henry Clay gave more than 70 speeches in favor of a compromise. At last, Clay **proposed** the **Compromise of 1850**. By then, however, he had become too sick to continue. Stephen Douglas of Illinois took up the fight for him and guided Clay's plan through Congress.

Academic Vocabulary

propose • *v.*, to suggest something for people to consider

The Compromise of 1850 had five main provisions. First, it allowed California to enter the Union as a free state. There would be 16 free states and 15 slave states. Second, it divided the rest of the Mexican Cession into the territories of New Mexico and Utah. Voters in each state would decide the slavery question by popular sovereignty.

Third, it ended the slave trade in Washington, D.C., the nation's capital. Congress, however, declared that it had no power to ban the slave trade between slave states. Fourth, it included a strict fugitive slave law. Fifth, it settled a border dispute between Texas and New Mexico.

The Fugitive Slave Act Helps the South The **Fugitive Slave Act** of 1850 replaced the Fugitive Slave Act of 1793, which slave owners believed was too weak. Under the 1793 law, many northerners had refused to cooperate with slave owners who were trying to capture escapees and return them to slavery. The new law required all citizens to help catch African Americans trying to escape slavery. People who let fugitives escape could be fined $1,000 and jailed.

The Fugitive Slave Act also set up special courts to handle the cases of runaways. Suspects were not allowed a jury trial. Judges received $10 for sending an accused runaway to slavery but only $5 for setting someone free. Lured by the extra money, some judges sent African Americans to the South whether or not they were runaways.

Northern Anger Over the Fugitive Slave Act The Compromise of 1850 had the effect of holding the union together for a while longer. However, the conflict between northerners and white southerners over the issues of slavery and its expansion remained. Members of both groups were not satisfied with the compromise.

Analyze Graphs The graphic shows some effects of the Compromise of 1850. **Infer** Based on the information in the circle graph, what can you infer about the reason congressional representatives from slave states agreed to the Compromise of 1850?

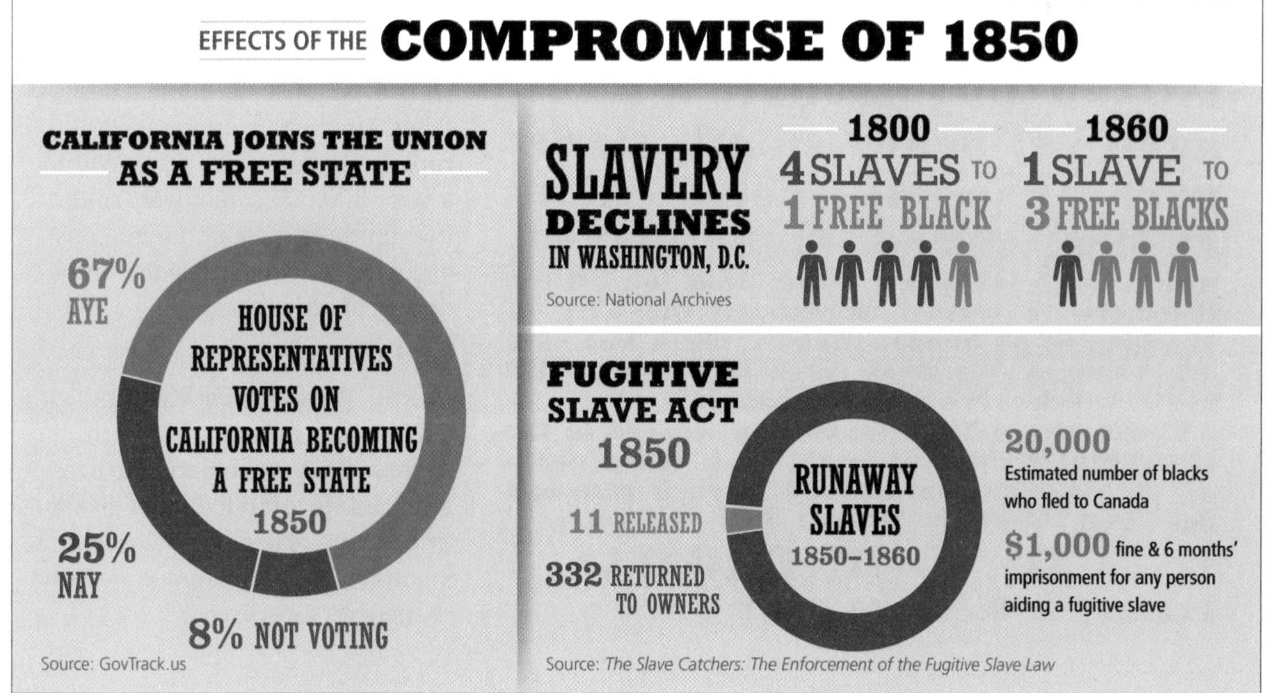

INTERACTIVE

The Fugitive Slave Act

Antislavery northerners were particularly angry about the Fugitive Slave Act. By forcing them to catch runaways, the law made northerners part of the slave system. Northerners found it harder to believe that slavery was a southern problem that they could ignore. In several northern cities, crowds protested by trying to rescue fugitives from their captors.

To counter the Fugitive Slave Act, many northern states passed personal liberty laws. These laws made it harder to recapture those accused of running away. The laws brought suspects before judges, provided jury trials, and prohibited kidnapping.

Some laws also gave legal assistance. One state, Vermont, declared free any enslaved person who entered the state. White southerners were outraged by these laws and called any interference with the Fugitive Slave Act unconstitutional.

READING CHECK **Generate Explanations** How did the Fugitive Slave Act of 1850 increase tensions between northerners and southerners?

A Book Sways the North Against Slavery

In 1852, Harriet Beecher Stowe of New England published a novel called *Uncle Tom's Cabin*. The novel shows the evils of slavery and the injustice of the Fugitive Slave Act.

Analyze Images This poster advertised a $100 reward for the capture and return of Robert Porter, who had escaped from enslavement. **Draw Conclusions** How did slavery affect people who lived in free states?

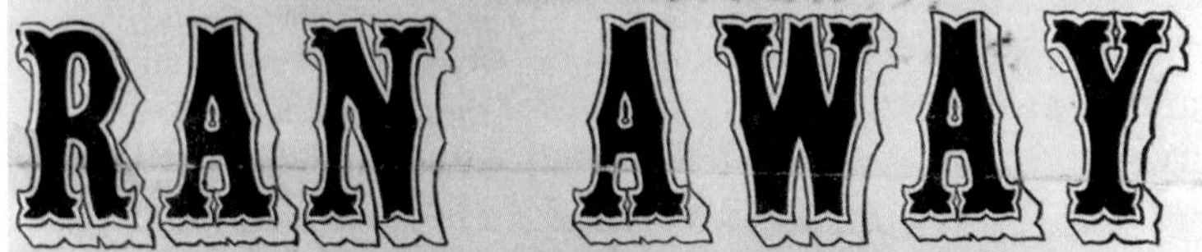

A Powerful Story Appeals to Northerners

Stowe told the story of Uncle Tom, an enslaved African American known for his kindness and piety. Tom's world is shattered when he is bought by the brutal Simon Legree. When Tom refuses to reveal the whereabouts of two runaways, Legree whips him to death.

The novel quickly became a best seller. The first printing of 5,000 copies sold out in two days. Within a year, 300,000 copies were sold. Eventually, the book sold millions of copies and was translated into dozens of languages.

Nationwide Reaction Is Mixed

Although *Uncle Tom's Cabin* was popular in the North, white southerners objected to it. They claimed that it did not give a true picture of life under slavery and ignored what they claimed were the "benefits" of slavery.

Despite such objections, *Uncle Tom's Cabin* helped change the way northerners felt about slavery. No longer could they ignore slavery as a political problem for Congress to settle. More and more northerners now saw slavery as a moral problem facing every American. For this reason, *Uncle Tom's Cabin* was one of the most important books in American history.

Analyze Images This painting shows a family attempting to escape from slavery. **Use Visual Information** What do you imagine each of these people is thinking?

READING CHECK **Check Understanding** What was the political significance of *Uncle Tom's Cabin*?

INTERACTIVE

Uncle Tom's Cabin

Lesson Check

Practice Vocabulary

1. What did it mean when the **Compromise of 1850** allowed **popular sovereignty** to decide the slavery question?
2. Why did both John C. Calhoun and Daniel Webster suggest that a **civil war** would result if a state tried to **secede**?
3. Who were African American **fugitives**?

Critical Thinking and Writing

4. **Understand Effects** What were the long-term effects of the Missouri Compromise?
5. **Compare and Contrast** the actions of Northern states to nullify the Fugitive Slave Act with the actions of Southern states to nullify the tariff of 1832.
6. **Writing Workshop: Consider Your Purpose** You will be writing an informative essay on the differences between the North and South before, during, and after the Civil War. In your Active Journal, describe what you will need to do to satisfy the requirements of the task.

Harriet Beecher Stowe, *Uncle Tom's Cabin*

Stowe's 1852 novel brought attention across the North to the evils of slavery. In this excerpt, Simon Legree explains to a stranger how he treats enslaved people.

◀ Harriet Beecher Stowe

Reading and Vocabulary Support

① Here, *constitution* refers to the health or physical condition of a person.

② Why does Simon say he doesn't try to "make 'em hold out"?

③ *Repressed* means to hold in feelings and not express them.

④ What do you think *humane* means?

⑤ *Sanction* means to approve or consent to. How is the planter sanctioning slavery?

"I don't go for savin' ['em]. Use up, and buy more, 's my way; . . . and I'm quite sure it comes cheaper in the end;" and Simon sipped his glass.

"And how long do they generally last?" said the stranger.

"Well, donno; 'cordin' as their constitution ① is. . . . I used to, when I fust begun, have considerable trouble fussin' with 'em and trying to make 'em hold out ②,—doctorin' on 'em up when they's sick, and givin' on 'em clothes and blankets, and what not, tryin' to keep 'em all sort o' decent and comfortable. . . . Now, you see, I just put 'em straight through, sick or well. When one [of 'em's] dead, I buy another. . . ."

The stranger turned away, and seated himself beside a gentleman, who had been listening to the conversation with repressed ③ uneasiness.

"You must not take that fellow to be any specimen of Southern planters," said he. . . . "[T]here are also many considerate and humane ④ men among planters."

"Granted," said the young man; "but, in my opinion, . . . if it were not for your sanction ⑤ and influence, the whole system could not keep foothold for an hour. If there were no planters except such as that one," said he, . . . "the whole thing would go down like a millstone. It is your respectability and humanity that licenses and protects his brutality."

Analyzing Primary Sources

Cite specific evidence from the document to support your answers.

1. **Identify Implied Main Ideas** How might Simon's dialogue about his enslaved workers make readers feel about slaveholders and slavery?
2. **Explain an Argument** According to the young man, how did "considerate and humane" planters keep slavery from dying out?
3. **Determine Author's Purpose** Based on this excerpt, why did Stowe write this novel?

LESSON 2
Growing Tensions

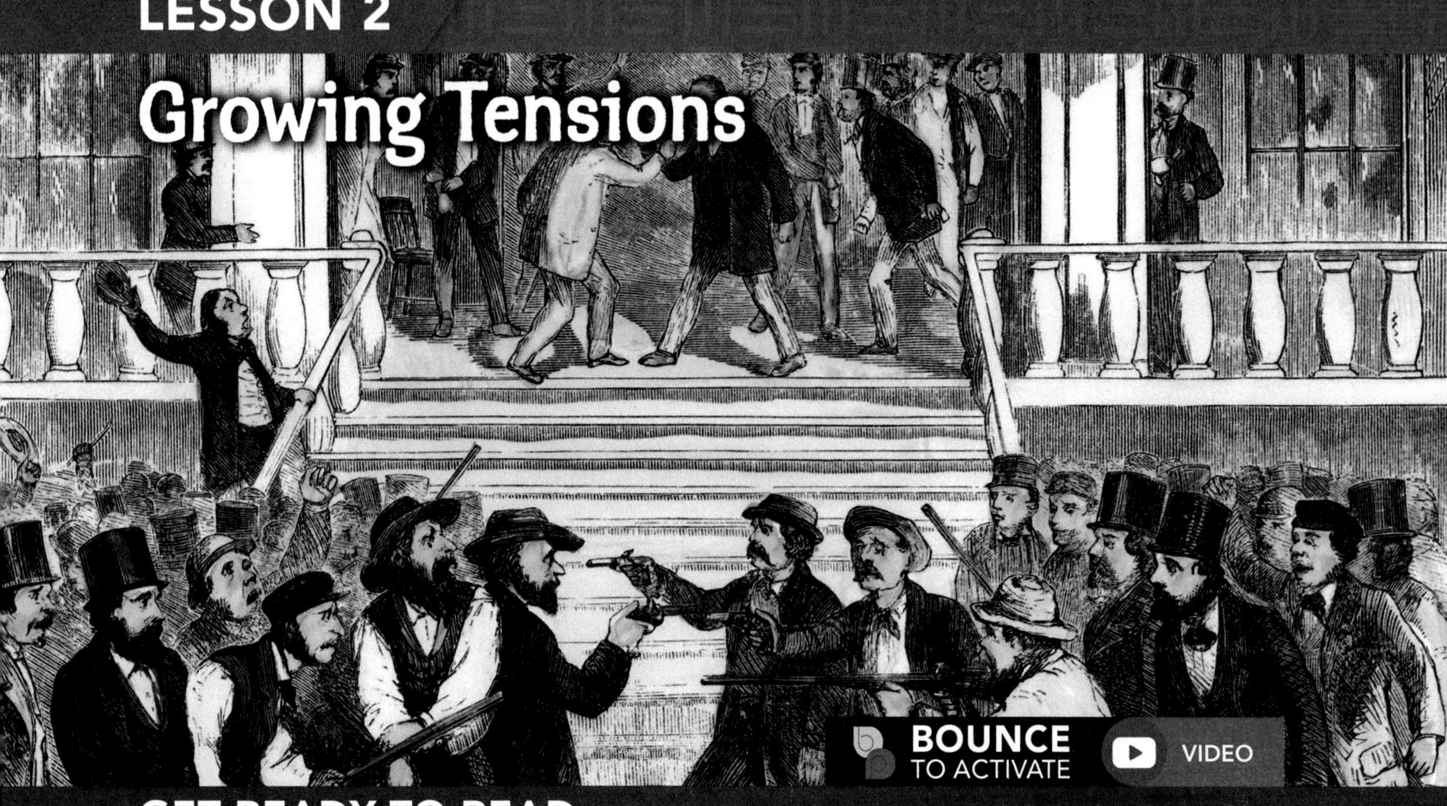

GET READY TO READ

START UP

Why do you think people, such as these Border Ruffians in Kansas, were so determined in their support of slavery?

GUIDING QUESTIONS

- What were the goals and outcomes of the Kansas-Nebraska Act?
- How did the Dred Scott case impact the nation?
- Why was the Republican Party founded, and how did Abraham Lincoln emerge as its leader?

TAKE NOTES

Literacy Skills Identify Cause and Effect

Use the graphic organizer in your Active Journal to practice the vocabulary words.

PRACTICE VOCABULARY

Use the vocabulary activity in your Active Journal to practice the vocabulary words.

Vocabulary		Academic Vocabulary
Kansas-Nebraska Act	Republican Party	denounce
Border Ruffian	arsenal	maintain
guerrilla warfare	treason	
Dred Scott v. *Sandford*	martyr	

The Compromise of 1850 dealt mainly with the Mexican Cession lands. It did not change the slavery policies for lands that had been part of the Louisiana Purchase—policies set by the Missouri Compromise. However, the Compromise of 1850 caused some people to question whether the Missouri Compromise needed to be changed.

Slavery in Kansas and Nebraska

In January 1854, Senator Stephen Douglas introduced a bill to set up a government for the lands in the northwestern part of the Louisiana Purchase. This territory stretched from present-day Oklahoma north to present-day Canada, and from Missouri west to the Rockies.

Congress Chooses Popular Sovereignty Douglas knew that white southerners did not want to add another free state to the Union. He proposed that this large region be divided into two territories, Kansas and Nebraska. The settlers in each territory would decide the issue of slavery by popular sovereignty.

Kansas-Nebraska Act, 1854

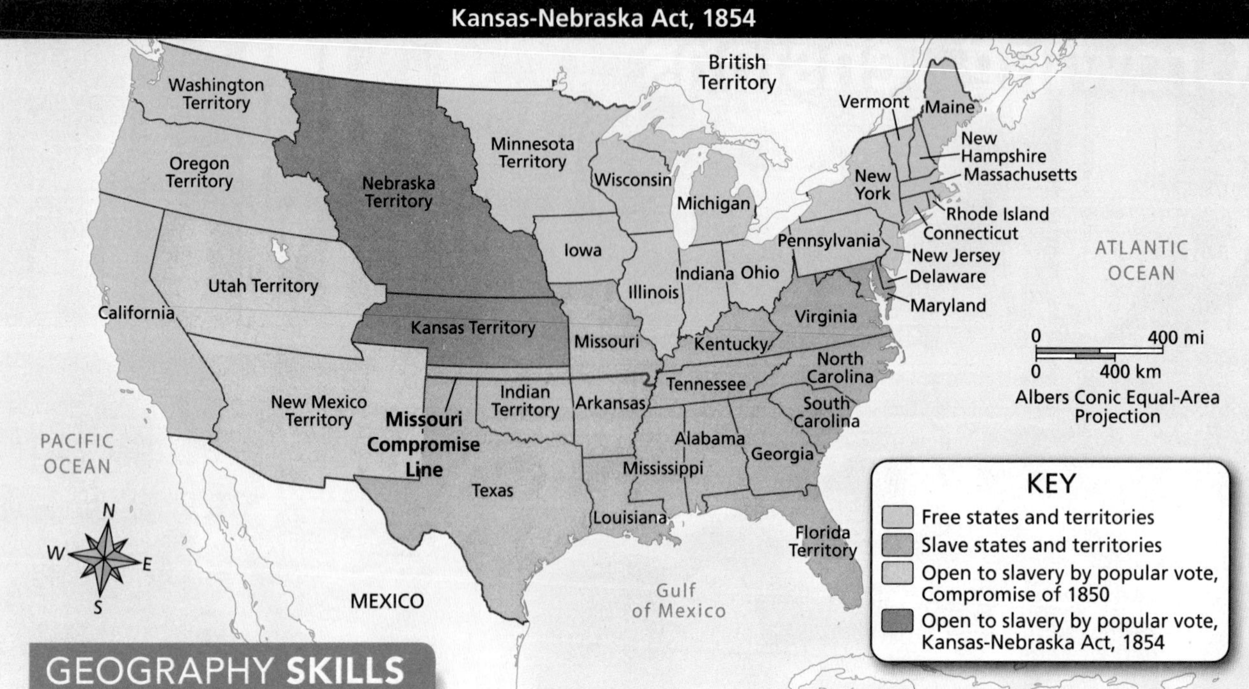

GEOGRAPHY SKILLS

The Missouri Compromise of 1820 prohibited slavery in territory north of the 36′ 30′ parallel.

1. **Locate** Which territories were opened to popular vote for slavery as a result of the Compromise of 1850?
2. **Analyze Information** How did the Kansas-Nebraska Act of 1854 conflict with the Missouri Compromise of 1820?

Douglas's bill was known as the **Kansas-Nebraska Act.** The Kansas-Nebraska Act seemed fair to many people. After all, the Compromise of 1850 had applied popular sovereignty in New Mexico and Utah. Southern leaders especially supported the Kansas-Nebraska Act. They expected slave owners from neighboring Missouri would move with their enslaved African Americans across the border into Kansas, and that in time, Kansas would become a slave state.

President Franklin Pierce, a Democrat elected in 1852, also supported the bill. With the president's help, Douglas pushed the Kansas-Nebraska Act through Congress.

The Kansas-Nebraska Act Ignites Sectionalist Disputes

Douglas did not realize it at the time, but he had lit a fire under a powder keg. Sectionalist arguments over slavery once again erupted, this time bringing the nation closer to civil war.

Many northerners were unhappy with the new law. The Missouri Compromise had already banned slavery in Kansas and Nebraska, they insisted. In effect, the Kansas-Nebraska Act would repeal the Missouri Compromise.

The northern reaction to the Kansas-Nebraska Act was swift and angry. Opponents of slavery called the act a "criminal betrayal of precious rights." Slavery could now spread to areas that had been free for more than 30 years.

INTERACTIVE

The Effects of the Kansas-Nebraska Act

READING CHECK **Check Understanding** Why did northerners consider the Kansas-Nebraska Act a betrayal?

Violent Clashes in Kansas

Kansas now became a testing ground for popular sovereignty. Stephen Douglas hoped that settlers would decide the slavery issue peacefully. Instead, proslavery and antislavery forces sent settlers to Kansas to fight for control.

Activists Populate Kansas Most of the new arrivals were farmers from neighboring states. Their main interest in moving to Kansas was to acquire cheap land. Few of these settlers owned enslaved African Americans. At the same time, abolitionists brought in more than 1,000 settlers from New England.

Proslavery settlers moved into Kansas as well. They wanted to make sure that antislavery forces did not overrun the territory. Proslavery bands from Missouri often rode across the border. These **Border Ruffians**, as they were called, battled the antislavery forces in Kansas.

Rival Governments in Kansas In 1855, Kansas held elections to choose lawmakers. Hundreds of Border Ruffians crossed into Kansas and voted illegally. They helped to elect a proslavery legislature.

The new legislature quickly passed laws to support slavery. One law said that people could be put to death for helping enslaved African Americans escape. Another made speaking out against slavery a crime punishable by two years of hard labor. Refusing to accept these laws, antislavery settlers elected their own governor and legislature. With two rival governments, Kansas was in chaos.

Analyze Images Angry citizens in Boston protested an 1854 court order to return Anthony Burns to slavery in Virginia. **Sequence** How did the Fugitive Slave Act lead to violence in the North?

Analyze Images Proslavery Representative Preston Brooks beat abolitionist Senator Charles Sumner on the Senate floor. **Analyze Political Cartoons** How does the cartoon portray northerners and southerners differently?

Open Fighting in Kansas In 1856, a band of proslavery men, including the town sheriff, raided the town of Lawrence. Lawrence was known as an antislavery stronghold. The attackers destroyed the Free State hotel as well as private homes and smashed the press of a Free-Soil newspaper.

John Brown, an abolitionist, decided to strike back. Brown and his five sons had moved to Kansas to help make it a free state. He claimed that God had sent him to punish supporters of slavery.

Three days after the Lawrence attacks, Brown rode with four of his sons and two or three other men to a settlement on Pottawatomie (paht uh WAHT uh mee) Creek. In the middle of the night, they dragged five proslavery settlers from their beds and murdered them.

The killings at Pottawatomie Creek led to even more violence. Both sides engaged in **guerrilla warfare**, or warfare in which small, informal military groups use surprise attacks and hit-and-run tactics. By late 1856, more than 200 people had been killed. Newspapers started calling the territory "Bleeding Kansas."

READING CHECK **Understand Effects** How did events in Kansas foreshadow the looming Civil War?

Violence Over Slavery Breaks Out in the Senate

Even before John Brown's attack, the battle over Kansas had spilled into the Senate. Charles Sumner of Massachusetts was the leading abolitionist senator. In one speech, the sharp-tongued Sumner **denounced** the proslavery legislature of Kansas. He then viciously criticized his southern foes, singling out Andrew Butler, an elderly senator from South Carolina.

Academic Vocabulary
denounce • *v.*, to publicly say that someone or something is wrong or bad

Butler was not in the Senate on the day Sumner spoke. A few days later, Butler's nephew, Congressman Preston Brooks, marched into the Senate chamber. Using a heavy cane, Brooks beat Sumner until he fell, bloody and unconscious, to the floor. Sumner did not fully recover from the beating for three years.

Many white southerners thought Sumner got what he deserved. Hundreds of people sent canes to Brooks to show their support.

To northerners, however, the brutal act was more evidence that slavery led to violence. The violence in the Senate was another warning that the nation was veering toward a civil war over slavery.

READING CHECK **Draw Conclusions** What does the violence in the Senate tell you about the mood of the country in the late 1850s?

The Dred Scott Case

How Did the Dred Scott Case Affect the Nation?

With Congress in an uproar, many Americans looked to the Supreme Court to settle the slavery issue and restore peace. In 1857, the Court ruled on a case involving an enslaved man named Dred Scott. Instead of bringing harmony, however, the Court's decision further divided the North and the South.

Dred Scott had been enslaved for many years in Missouri. Later, his enslaver took him to Illinois and then to the Wisconsin Territory, where slavery was not allowed. After they returned to Missouri, Scott's enslaver died. Antislavery lawyers helped Scott to file a lawsuit, a legal case brought to settle a dispute between people or groups. Scott's lawyers argued that, because Dred Scott had lived in a free territory, he had become a free man.

Analyze Images Dred Scott, who had once lived in a free territory, appealed for his freedom after his enslaver died. **Predict Consequences** How did the Supreme Court ruling against Dred Scott challenge the Missouri Compromise?

The Supreme Court Rules on *Dred Scott* v. *Sandford*

In time, the case reached the Supreme Court as ***Dred Scott* v. *Sandford***. The Court's decision shocked and dismayed Americans who opposed slavery. First, the Court ruled that Scott could not file a lawsuit because, as an enslaved person, he was not a citizen. Also, the Court's written decision clearly stated that enslaved persons were considered to be property.

The Court's ruling did not stop there. Instead, the Justices went on to make a sweeping decision about the larger issue of slavery in the territories. According to the Court, Congress did not have the power to outlaw slavery in any territory. This meant that the Missouri Compromise was unconstitutional.

Quick Activity

How might an enslaved person planning an escape to the North have felt about the Dred Scott decision? Write a few sentences In your Active Journal examining this issue.

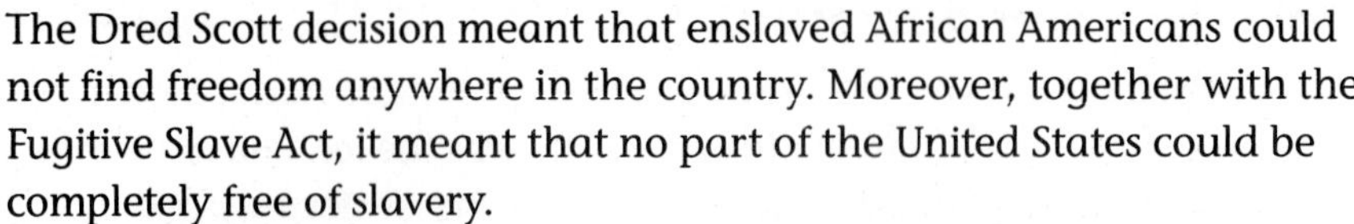

The Dred Scott decision meant that enslaved African Americans could not find freedom anywhere in the country. Moreover, together with the Fugitive Slave Act, it meant that no part of the United States could be completely free of slavery.

The Democratic Party began to divide over the issue of slavery. The decision also increased support for abolition in the North.

Reactions to *Dred Scott* v. *Sandford* White southerners rejoiced at *Dred Scott* v. *Sandford*. It meant slavery was legal in all the territories.

African Americans responded angrily to the decision. In the North, many held public meetings to condemn the ruling. At one meeting in Philadelphia, a speaker hoped that the ruling would lead more whites to "join with us in our efforts to recover the long lost boon of freedom."

White northerners were shocked by the ruling. Many had hoped that slavery would eventually die out. Now, slavery could spread throughout the West. A newspaper in Cincinnati declared, "We are now one great . . . slaveholding community."

Academic Vocabulary
maintain • *v.*, to keep in an existing state

Abolitionist Frederick Douglass also spoke out against *Dred Scott* v. *Sandford*: "This infamous decision," he declared, "**maintains** that slaves . . . are property in the same sense that horses, sheep, and swine are property . . . that [people] of African descent are not and cannot be citizens of the United States." He told his listeners:

Primary Source

"All I ask of the American people is that they live up to the Constitution, adopt its principles, [take in] its spirit, and enforce its provisions. When this is done . . . liberty . . . will become the inheritance of all the inhabitants of this highly favored country."

—Frederick Douglass, *Collected Speeches*, 1857

Analyze Images Frederick Douglass, who had once been enslaved, became a powerful spokesperson for abolition. **Infer** How do you think reactions to Frederick Douglass differed in the North and South?

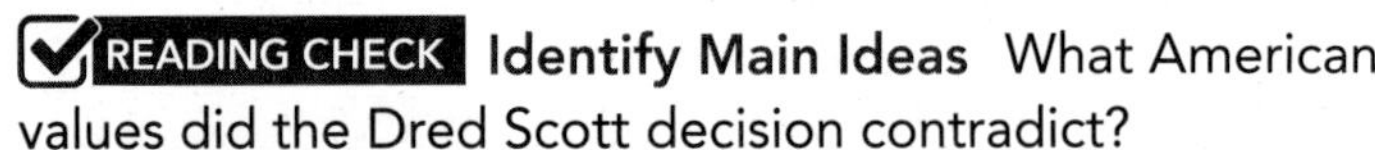

READING CHECK **Identify Main Ideas** What American values did the Dred Scott decision contradict?

The Republican Party Forms

By the mid-1850s, people who opposed slavery in the territories sought a new political voice. Neither Whigs nor Democrats, they maintained, would take a strong stand against slavery. "We have submitted to slavery long enough," an Ohio Democrat declared.

Analyze Images American Party candidate Millard Fillmore separates Republican John Frémont (left) and Democrat James Buchanan (right) before they can harm one another. **Analyze Political Cartoons** What can you infer about Fillmore's view on sectional tensions?

Birth of the Republican Party A group of Free-Soilers, northern Democrats, and antislavery Whigs gathered in Michigan in 1854. There they formed the **Republican Party**. While some Republicans hoped to completely abolish slavery throughout the country, the new party's main goal was to keep slavery from spreading to the western territories.

The Election of 1856 The new party grew quickly. In 1856, Republicans selected John C. Frémont to run for president. Frémont was a frontiersman who had fought for California independence. He had little political experience, but he opposed the spread of slavery.

Frémont's main opponent was Democrat James Buchanan of Pennsylvania. Many Democrats saw Buchanan as a "northern man with southern principles." Former President Millard Fillmore also ran as the candidate of the American, or "Know-Nothing," party. Fillmore, a strong supporter of the Union, feared that a Republican victory would split the nation apart.

Buchanan won the election with support from a large majority of white southerners and many northerners. Still, the Republicans made a strong showing. Without the support of a single southern state, Frémont won one third of the popular vote. White southerners worried that their influence in the national government was fading.

READING CHECK **Check Understanding** Why was the Republican Party established in 1854?

▲ Abraham Lincoln had to teach himself to read by firelight.

How Did Abraham Lincoln Come to Lead the Republican Party?

The next chance for the Republican Party came in 1858 in Illinois. Abraham Lincoln, a Republican, challenged Democrat Stephen Douglas for his seat in the Senate. Because most Americans expected Douglas to run for president in 1860, the race captured the attention of the whole nation.

Lincoln's Early Career Abraham Lincoln was born on the Kentucky frontier. Like many frontier people, his parents moved often to find better land. The family lived in Indiana and later in Illinois. As a child, Lincoln spent only a year in school, but he taught himself to read.

After Lincoln left home, he opened a store in Illinois. There, he studied law on his own and launched a career in politics. He served eight years in the state legislature and one term in Congress.

Bitterly opposed to the Kansas-Nebraska Act, Abraham Lincoln decided to run for the U.S. Senate in 1858. When the race began, Lincoln was not a national figure. Still, people in Illinois knew him well and liked him. To them, he was "just folks"—someone who enjoyed picnics, wrestling contests, and all their favorite pastimes. His honesty, wit, and plain-spoken manner made him a good speaker.

Lincoln strongly opposed the Dred Scott decision and used his political platform to speak against it. In his "House Divided" speech, which he delivered upon being nominated for senator in 1858, he attacked the ruling. He expressed concern that popular sovereignty would lead to slavery throughout the country.

Lincoln continued to voice his opposition in debates with Stephen Douglas and later during his presidential campaign. He rallied Republicans to oppose the Court's decision.

Lincoln and Douglas Debate During the Senate campaign, Lincoln challenged Douglas to a series of debates. Douglas was not eager to accept, but he did. During the campaign, the question of slavery in the territories was the most important issue.

Douglas wanted to settle the slavery question by popular sovereignty, or a popular vote in each territory. He personally disliked slavery, but stated that he did not care whether people in the territories voted it "down or up."

Lincoln was not an abolitionist, either. He did not want to end slavery in the states where it already existed. And, like nearly all white people of his day, he did not believe in "perfect equality" between Black and white people. He did, however, believe that slavery was wrong.

Quest CONNECTIONS

Read the passage in the Declaration of Independence that explains the rights of all men. How do Lincoln's comments support the meaning expressed in the Declaration of Independence? Record your findings in your Active Journal.

Primary Source

"There is no reason in the world why the negro is not entitled to all the natural rights [listed] in the Declaration of Independence, the right to life, liberty, and the pursuit of happiness. . . . In the right to eat the bread, without the leave of anybody else, which his own hand earns, he is my equal and the equal of Judge Douglas, and the equal of every living man."

—Abraham Lincoln, Speech at Ottawa, Illinois, August 21, 1858

Since slavery was a "moral, social, and political wrong," said Lincoln, Douglas and other Americans should not treat it as an unimportant question to be voted "down or up." No one's liberty, he thought, should be subject to a popular vote, nor should it be decided by the sort of violence that arose in Kansas.

Lincoln Becomes a Leader Week after week, both men spoke nearly every day to large crowds. Newspapers reprinted their campaign speeches. The more northerners read Lincoln's words, the more they thought about the injustice of slavery.

In the end, Douglas won the election by a slim margin. Still, Lincoln was now known throughout the country. Two years later, the two rivals would again meet face to face—both seeking the office of president.

READING CHECK **Describe** the contradiction in Lincoln's position on slavery.

Analyze Images In 1858, Abraham Lincoln and Stephen Douglas debated over the spread of slavery. **Draw Conclusions** What was the significance of the Lincoln-Douglas debates?

John Brown Fights Slavery

In the meantime, more bloodshed inflamed divisions between the North and the South. In 1859, the radical abolitionist John Brown led a group of followers, including five African Americans, to the town of Harpers Ferry, Virginia.

There, Brown raided a federal **arsenal**, or weapons and ammunition warehouse. He thought that enslaved African Americans would join him there. He then planned to arm them and lead them in a revolt. No slave uprising took place, however. Instead, troops under the command of Robert E. Lee killed ten raiders and captured Brown.

John Brown's Raid Most people, in both the North and the South, thought that Brown's plan to lead a slave revolt was insane. First of all, there were few enslaved African Americans in Harpers Ferry to join a revolt. Furthermore, after seizing the arsenal, Brown did nothing further to encourage a slave revolt.

At his trial, however, Brown seemed perfectly sane. He sat quietly as the court found him guilty of murder and **treason**, or actions against one's country. Before hearing his sentence, he gave a moving defense of his actions. He showed no emotion as he was sentenced to death.

A Symbol of the Nation's Divisions Because he conducted himself with such dignity during his trial, Brown became a hero to many northerners. Some considered him a **martyr** because he was willing to give up his life for his beliefs. On the morning he was hanged, church bells rang solemnly throughout the North. In years to come, New Englanders would sing a popular song with the chorus: "John Brown's body lies a mold'ring in the grave, but his soul is marching on." When poet Julia Ward Howe heard the song, she was inspired to write the

Analyze Graphs The chart shows results of three votes in which slavery was a central issue. **Draw Conclusions** Did the Kansas-Nebraska Act influence the outcome of the Kansas election for territorial legislature in 1855? Explain.

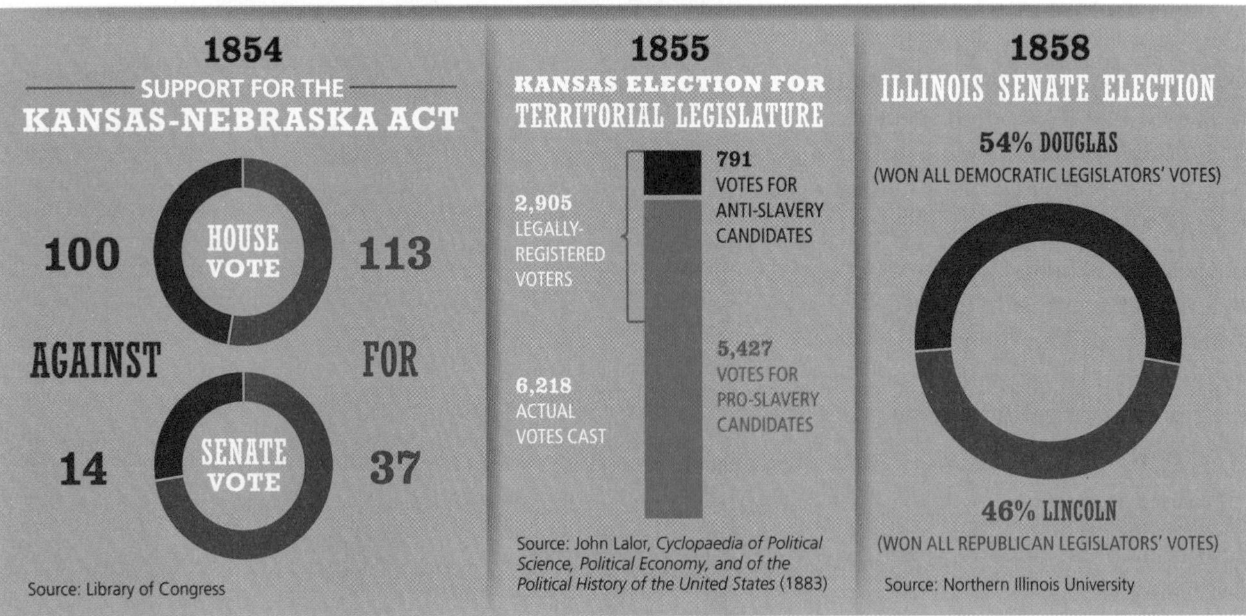

poem "The Battle Hymn of the Republic," which became a popular Civil War song set to the same tune.

To white southerners, the northern response to John Brown's death was outrageous. People were singing the praises of a man who had tried to lead a revolt against slavery. Many white southerners became convinced that the North wanted to destroy slavery—and the South along with it. The nation was poised for a violent clash.

Analyze Images This illustration shows John Brown's band attacking the federal arsenal at Harpers Ferry. **Explain an Argument** Why did people say John Brown's raid was insane?

READING CHECK **Check Understanding** Why did the northern response to John Brown's execution outrage white southerners?

Lesson Check

Practice Vocabulary

1. Why was the **Republican Party** formed?
2. Why did a court decide John Brown had committed **treason**?
3. In what way was John Brown a **martyr**?

Critical Thinking and Writing

4. **Draw Conclusions** Some northerners were outraged by the passage of the Kansas-Nebraska Act. What did that outrage have to do with the location of the Kansas Territory?
5. **Summarize** the issue that was brought to the Supreme Court in *Dred Scott* v. *Sandford.*
6. **Identify Main Ideas** Neither Stephen Douglas nor Abraham Lincoln approved of slavery, so what disagreement did they have?
7. **Writing Workshop: Pick an Organizing Strategy** Begin thinking about how you will organize your essay on the differences between the North and South before, during, and after the Civil War. Take notes in your Active Journal.

Distinguish Relevant from Irrelevant Information

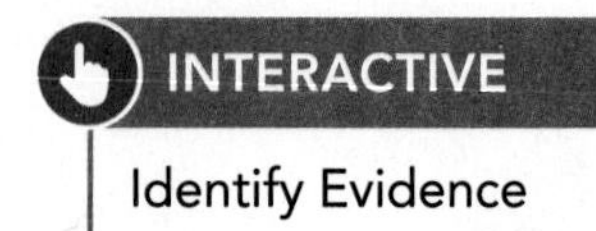

Follow these steps to learn to distinguish relevant from irrelevant information.

1 **Identify your focus or topic** By clearly defining your topic, you can better determine which pieces of information will be relevant or irrelevant.

2 **Locate sources and read about the topic** Based on the topic you identified, select a number of sources that will likely offer information on this topic. You may find sources online or in your school's media center.

3 **Identify the information that is relevant to your topic** Scan your sources to find passages that may relate to your topic. Then, read these passages closely to determine whether or not they provide relevant information.

4 **Identify the information that is irrelevant to your topic** Irrelevant information, such as anecdotes, may be interesting, but not central to the topic. In the source, what passages are not relevant to the topic of attitudes toward popular sovereignty?

The letter below is historical fiction. In the letter, William, a farmer who had moved to Kansas Territory, writes to his brother Joseph in Vermont.

November 20, 1854

Dear Joseph,

I was pleased to receive your last letter. The success of your store is a great achievement. Our new farm continues to prosper and little Sarah has recovered from the fever that had sickened her for a month. Of course, the issue of the Kansas-Nebraska Act continues to trouble me. I do not agree with your support of Senator Stephen Douglas of Illinois; however, I enjoy reading his speeches. Those who oppose slavery, as I do, do not want that cruel system in place in a territory where it had been banned. Under the terms of the Kansas-Nebraska Act, it is up to the people to decide the issue peacefully by voting their hearts. Yet, settlers who are for and against slavery in the territory seem intent on using force, instead of the ballot box. The elections next year will settle the issue once and for all.

Your loving brother,

William

LESSON 3

Division and the Outbreak of War

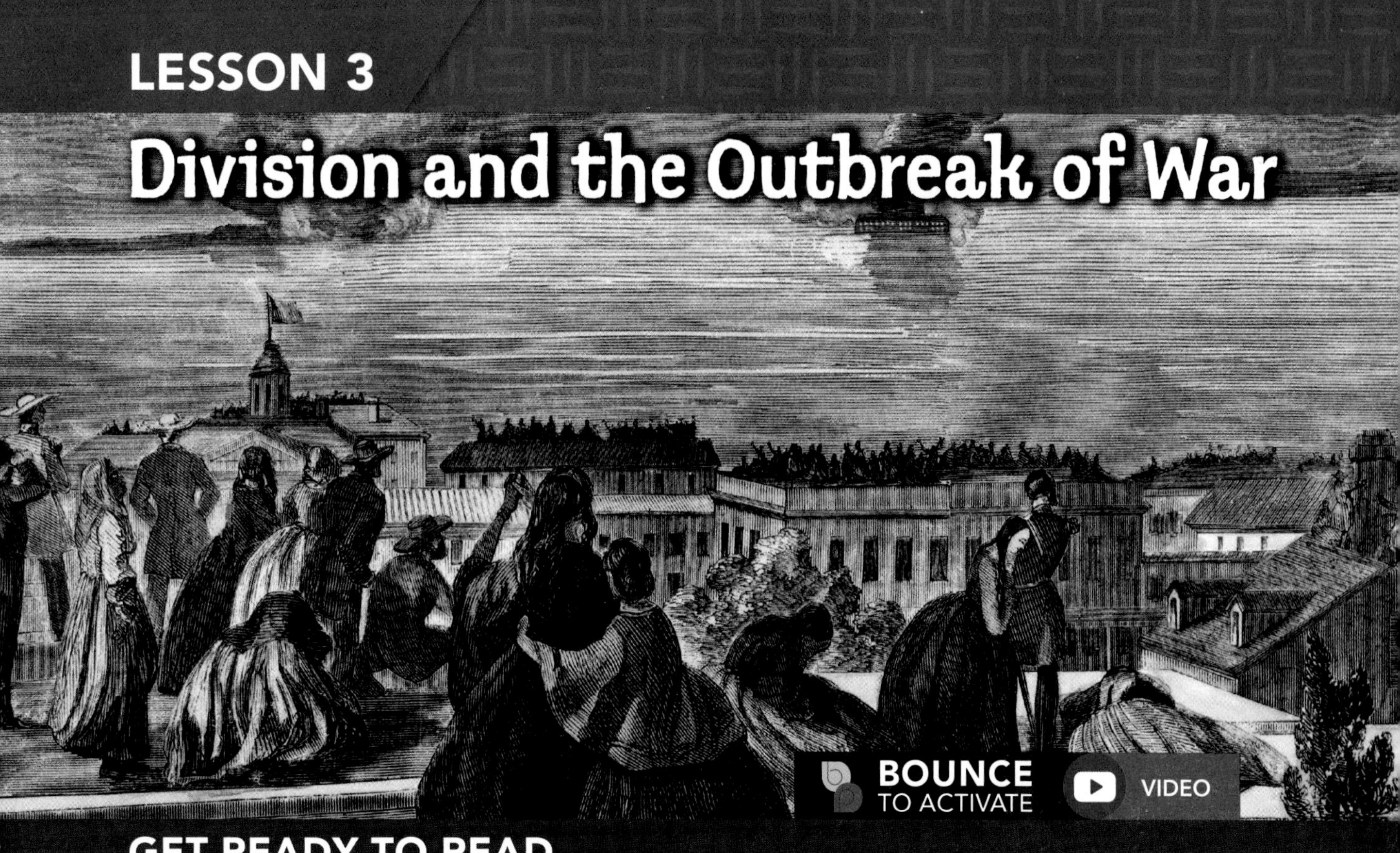

GET READY TO READ

START UP

Examine the civilians who have come to watch the bombardment of Fort Sumter. Why do you think these people have come, and what might they be thinking?

GUIDING QUESTIONS

- Why was there a Civil War?
- How did the 1860 election reflect sectional differences?
- Why did southern states secede from the Union following the election of 1860?
- What were the strengths and weaknesses of the North and South as the war began?

TAKE NOTES

Literacy Skills Compare and Contrast

Use the graphic organizer in your Active Journal to take notes as you read the lesson.

Practice Vocabulary

Use the vocabulary activity in your Active Journal to practice the vocabulary words.

Vocabulary		Academic Vocabulary
unamendable	border state	comprise
acquiescence		conducive

The Republican National Convention for the presidential election of 1860 took place in Chicago, Illinois. Abraham Lincoln faced William Seward for the nomination. Seward was a U.S. senator for New York. Lincoln, whose fame had increased during the Lincoln-Douglas debates in 1858, won the nomination.

Why Did Abraham Lincoln Win the Election of 1860?

The Democrats held their convention in Charleston, South Carolina, where a lack of party unity proved costly. Southern members wanted the party to call for slavery in all new territories, but northern Democrats refused. In the end, the party split in two. Northern Democrats chose Stephen Douglas to run for president. Southern Democrats picked John Breckinridge of Kentucky.

Some Americans tried to heal the split between the northern and southern states by forming a new party. The Constitutional Union party chose John Bell of Tennessee to run for president. Bell was a moderate who wanted to keep the Union together.

Douglas was sure that Lincoln would win, but he believed Democrats "must try to save the Union." He urged white southerners to stay with the Union, no matter who was elected.

When the votes were counted, Lincoln had won the election. He benefited from the division in the Democratic Party. Interestingly, southern votes did not affect the outcome, because Lincoln's name was not even on the ballot in ten southern states. Outnumbered and outvoted, many white southerners lost hope that the national government would ever again serve their interests.

READING CHECK **Understand Effects** How did the split in the Democratic Party in the 1860 election reflect the split in the country?

A Move Toward Civil War

White southerners reacted strongly to Lincoln's election. A South Carolina woman described white southerners' reactions:

Primary Source

"The excitement was very great. Everybody was talking at the same time. One . . . more moved than the others, stood up saying . . . 'No more vain regrets—sad forebodings are useless. The stake is life or death.'"

—Mary Boykin Chesnut, *A Diary From Dixie*, 1860

GEOGRAPHY SKILLS

The results of the 1860 election showed a nation deeply divided.

1. **Region** How did the electoral vote reflect sectional divisions?
2. **Synthesize Visual Information** Discuss with a partner: How might the election have turned out differently had Bell and Douglas not run for president?

Election of 1860

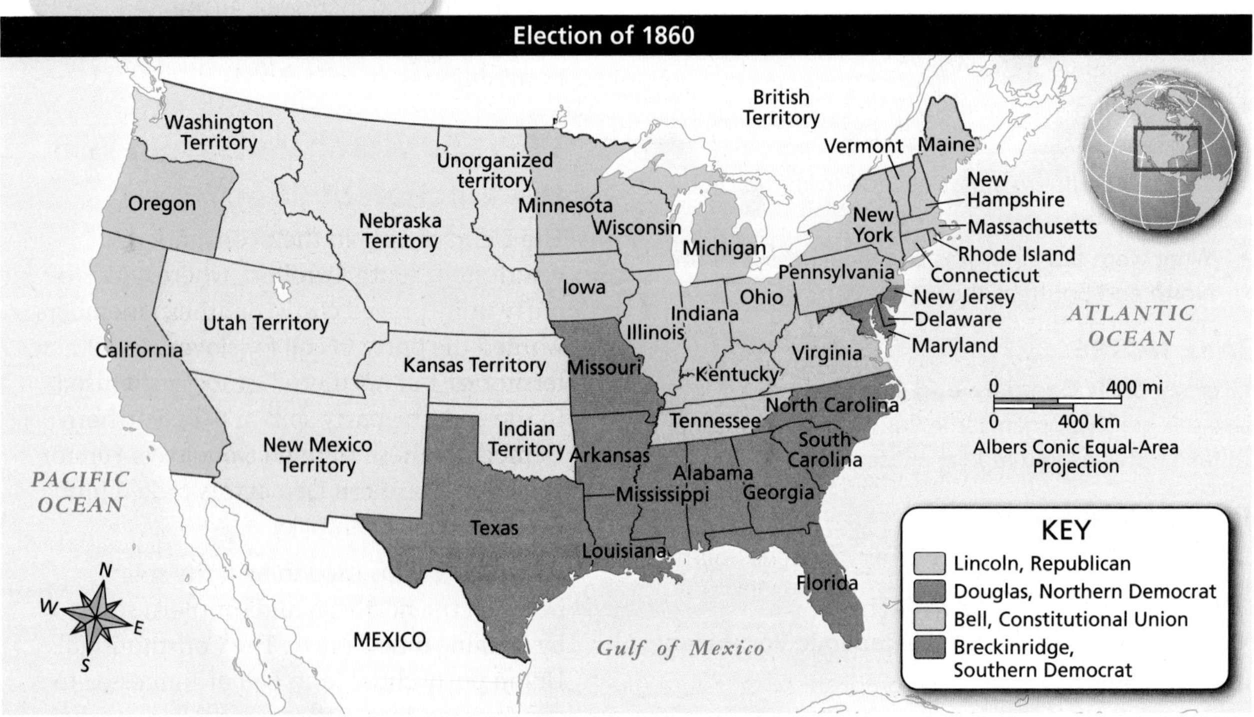

Secessionists leaving the Union.

Even before the election, South Carolina's governor had written to other southern governors. If Lincoln won, he wrote, it would be their duty to leave the Union. This sentiment revealed the strong currents of sectionalism running through the country. Many in the South felt stronger ties to their region than to the nation.

The Nation Splits Senator John Crittenden of Kentucky made a last effort to save the Union. In December 1860, he proposed a package of legislation that he said would forever guarantee slavery south of the Missouri Compromise line and prohibit it north of the line. His proposal included a Constitutional amendment that he said would be **unamendable**, one that could not be changed.

The Crittenden Compromise received little support. The issue was no longer just slavery in the West. Many white southerners believed the North had put an abolitionist in the White House and that secession was now their only chance to preserve slavery. Most Republicans also were unwilling to surrender what they had won in the national election.

On December 20, 1860, South Carolina became the first state to secede. By late February 1861, Alabama, Florida, Georgia, Louisiana, Mississippi, and Texas had also seceded.

At a convention in Montgomery, Alabama, the seven states formed a new nation, the Confederate States of America. Jefferson Davis of Mississippi became its first president.

Causes Leading to War Several of the states that seceded issued official statements explaining their reasons for leaving the Union. These statements emphasized the states' wish to defend the right to enslave African Americans as the main reason for secession. Lincoln, they believed, would deny them the right to force African Americans to live and work in slavery.

White southerners argued that they had the right to leave the Union in order to preserve their system of slavery. They rejected loyalty to a federal government that was opposed to extending slavery to new territories or arresting refugees from slavery. They claimed that protecting slavery gave them the right to leave the Union and to form a Confederacy **comprised** of states enforcing slavery.

Lincoln disagreed. He maintained that the Constitution shared powers between national and state governments but did not allow states to secede for any reason. The root causes of the Civil War were thus disagreements over slavery and over southern states' right to leave the Union in order to protect slavery.

READING CHECK **Check Understanding** Why did white southerners want to secede from the Union?

Analyze Images In this cartoon, two secessionists are sawing off the branch of the tree upon which they are sitting. **Analyze Political Cartoons** What effect do you think the artist believes secession would have on the South?

Quest CONNECTIONS

The Declaration of Independence says people have the right to "alter or to abolish" a government. What does Lincoln say about this in his speeches? Record your findings in your Active Journal.

Academic Vocabulary

comprise • *v.*, to be made up of

▲ Confederate troops, 1861

The Outbreak of War

When Lincoln took the oath of office on March 4, 1861, he faced a dangerous situation. Seven southern states had seceded from the United States and had joined together to form the Confederacy.

Lincoln's First Inaugural Address When he took office, Lincoln delivered an inaugural address. In the speech, Lincoln warned that "no state . . . can lawfully get out of the Union." Still, he pledged that there would be no war unless the South started it:

Primary Source

> "In YOUR hands, my dissatisfied fellow-countrymen, and not in MINE, is the momentous issue of civil war. . . . We are not enemies, but friends. We must not be enemies. Though passion may have strained, it must not break our bonds of affection."
>
> —Abraham Lincoln, First Inaugural Address, March 4, 1861

Lincoln's First Inaugural Address expressed ideas about union, liberty, equality, and government. Regarding union, Lincoln emphasized that the Constitution set limits on the actions of states, and that there was no provision in the Constitution for secession. That is, the Constitution required that the Union be preserved. On liberty, again, Lincoln emphasized that the states' liberty was constrained by their acceptance of the Constitution and did not include a right to secede.

Lincoln also stated his willingness to enforce the Fugitive Slave Act, but only if the liberty of free African Americans from kidnapping and enslavement could be ensured. Regarding equality, Lincoln assured Americans that he would provide government services and enforce federal law equally in all states, whether they were slave or free states.

Finally, Lincoln stated that government required **acquiescence**, or the willingness to accept laws whether or not a person agreed with those laws. The unwillingness of the South to accept his legal election under the Constitution, he implied, was a threat to government.

Jefferson Davis's Inaugural Address By the time Lincoln gave his address, the Confederate States of America had already sworn in Jefferson Davis as president. Davis's inaugural speech was very different from Lincoln's. Whereas Lincoln pledged to keep the Union together, Davis explained why the South had decided to secede from the Union. Davis said secession was based on "the desire to preserve our own rights and promote our own welfare."

Davis also said, "It is joyous, in the midst of perilous times, to look around upon a people united in heart, where one purpose of high resolve animates and actuates the whole—where the sacrifices to be made are not weighed in the balance against honor and right and liberty and equality."

For Davis, liberty and equality existed only between white men. Lincoln, in contrast, believed secession countered the principles of liberty and equality on which the nation was founded and its government was based. In a later speech, Lincoln would extend the idea of equality to all Americans.

Davis emphasized that government exists only with the consent of the governed. Since white southerners no longer consented to this government, they had to break away and form a government to which they could consent. This was in contrast to Lincoln's argument that government sometimes requires citizens to acquiesce to, or obey, laws with which they disagree. He described secession as "the essence of anarchy."

Davis also argued that each state had the right to reclaim powers that it had given to the federal government. Lincoln disagreed. He argued that the Constitution was an agreement among all the states, and that no state could leave the Union without the agreement of the others.

Lincoln Faces War Lincoln said in his inaugural address that he did not want war, but Jefferson Davis had already ordered Confederate forces to begin seizing federal forts in the South. Lincoln faced a difficult decision. Should he let the Confederates take over federal property? If he did, he would seem to be admitting that states had the right to secede. Yet if he sent troops to hold the forts, he might start a civil war and lose the support of the eight slave states that had not yet seceded.

Analyze Timelines The timeline shows some important events that led up to the outbreak of the Civil War. **Identify Cause and Effect** How did the election of Lincoln as president contribute to the attack on Fort Sumter?

Events Leading Up to the Civil War

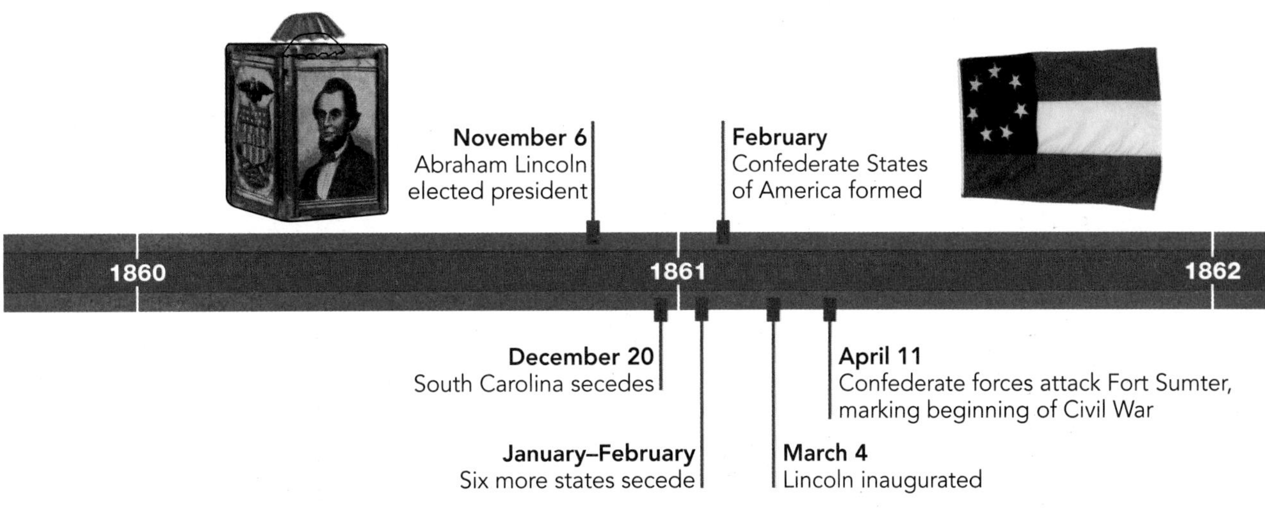

In April, the Confederacy forced Lincoln's hand. By then, Confederate troops controlled nearly all forts, post offices, and other federal buildings in the South. The Union held only three forts off the Florida coast and Fort Sumter in South Carolina. Fort Sumter was important to the Confederacy because it guarded Charleston Harbor.

Confederate Troops Attack Fort Sumter President Lincoln learned that food supplies at Fort Sumter were running low. He notified the governor of South Carolina that he was going to ship food to the fort. Lincoln promised not to send troops or weapons.

The Confederates refused to allow any shipments to the fort. On April 11, 1861, they demanded that Fort Sumter surrender. Major Robert Anderson, the Union commander, refused to give in, and Confederate guns opened fire. The Union troops quickly ran out of ammunition. On April 13, Anderson surrendered the fort.

The bombardment marked the start of the Civil War, which would last four terrible years, from 1861 to 1865.

READING CHECK **Summarize** Lincoln's dilemma over southern states taking control of federal property.

How Did Americans Take Sides?

When the war began, each side believed that its cause was just. Southern politicians believed states had the right to leave the Union. They called the conflict the War for Southern Independence. White southerners wanted independence so that they could preserve their control over enslaved African Americans.

Northerners believed that they were fighting to save the Union. Abolishing slavery was not an official goal. In fact, many northerners,

Analyze Images This photograph shows one of a set of Civil War trading cards issued in 1887. **Identify Main Ideas** Why did Confederate troops attack Fort Sumter?

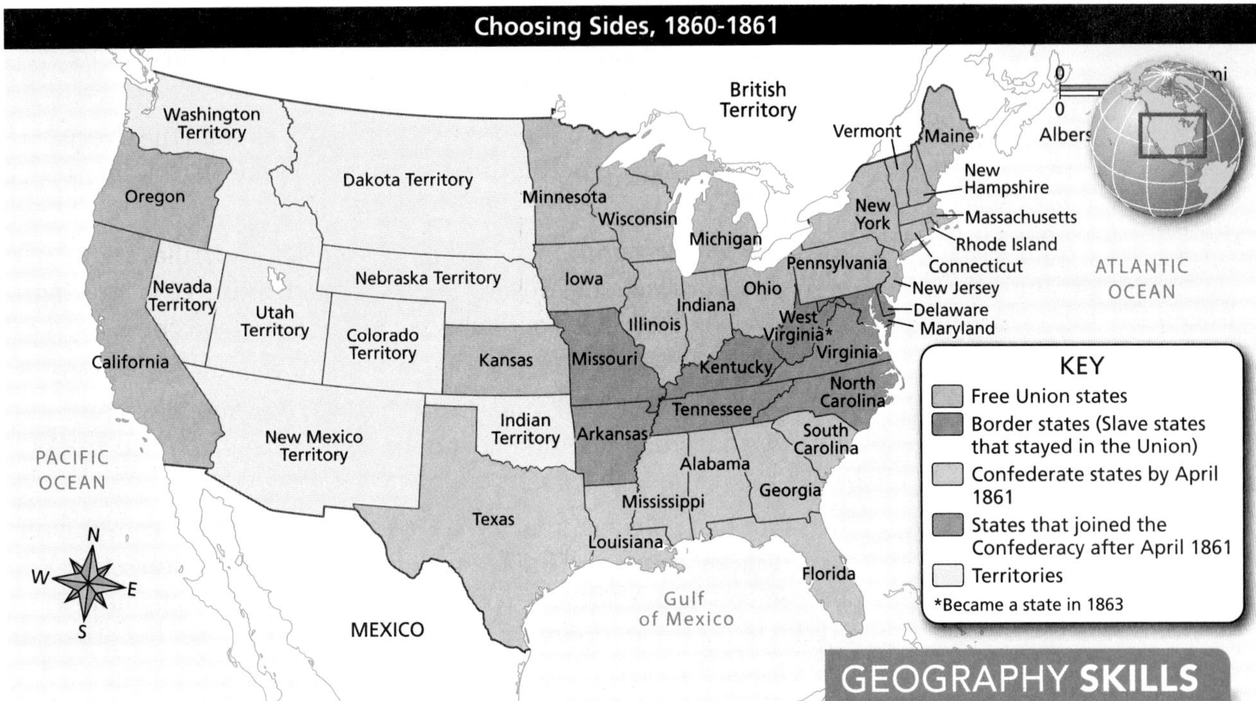

Choosing Sides, 1860-1861

GEOGRAPHY SKILLS

1. **Location** Based on the map, why were Missouri, Kentucky, West Virginia, Maryland, and Delaware called border states?
2. **Analyze Maps** Based on the information in the map, approximately what percentage of Union states were slave states during the Civil War?

guided by feelings of racism, approved of slavery. Racism is the false belief that people are divided into biological races with differences between them that justify one having privileges or power over the others.

In April 1861, eight slave states had not yet decided whether to remain in the Union. These states had more than half of the South's population and food crops and many of the South's factories. They would be important assets to whichever side they joined.

Four of these states—Virginia, North Carolina, Tennessee, and Arkansas—quickly joined the Confederacy. After some indecision, each of the four **border states**—Kentucky, Missouri, Maryland, and Delaware—decided to remain in the Union.

READING CHECK **Understand Effects** Why were both the North and South trying to attract border states?

Strengths and Weaknesses of the North and South

The South had the advantage of fighting a defensive war. "We seek no conquest," said Confederate President Jefferson Davis. "All we ask is to be let alone." If the North did not move its forces into the South, the Confederacy would remain a separate country.

The South White southerners believed that they were fighting a war for independence, similar to the American Revolution. Defending their homeland and their way of life gave them a strong reason to fight. "Our men must prevail in combat," one Confederate said, "or they will lose their property, country, freedom—in short, everything."

Confederate soldiers also knew the southern countryside better. Friendly civilians aided them, often guiding soldiers along obscure roads that did not appear on maps.

The South, however, had serious weaknesses. These were the effects of economic and geographic differences between the North and the South.

Academic Vocabulary
conducive • *adj.*, making it easy for something to happen

The South had an agrarian, or farming, economy. Its fertile land, ample rainfall, and long growing season were **conducive** to growing cash crops, such as cotton and tobacco, rather than food crops.

Likewise, the South had few factories to produce weapons and other vital supplies, and few railroads to move troops and supplies. The railroads that it did have often did not connect to one another. Tracks simply ran between two points and then stopped.

The South had political problems as well. The Confederate constitution favored states' rights and limited the authority of the central government. As a result, the Confederate government often found it difficult to get things done. On one occasion, for example, the governor of Georgia insisted that only Georgian officers should command Georgian troops.

Finally, the South had a small population of only 9 million people. Of these, about 40 percent were enslaved African Americans. Meanwhile, the Union had 22 million people, including 3.8 million men of military age. In the South, just 1.1 million were free men of military age, and it had to recruit 80 percent of them for the war. As a result, the South did not have enough people to both fight the war and run the economy.

Analyze Graphs The graphic provides economic data comparing the North and the South at the start of the Civil War. **Compare and Contrast** Based on the information in the graphs, what advantages did the North have over the South?

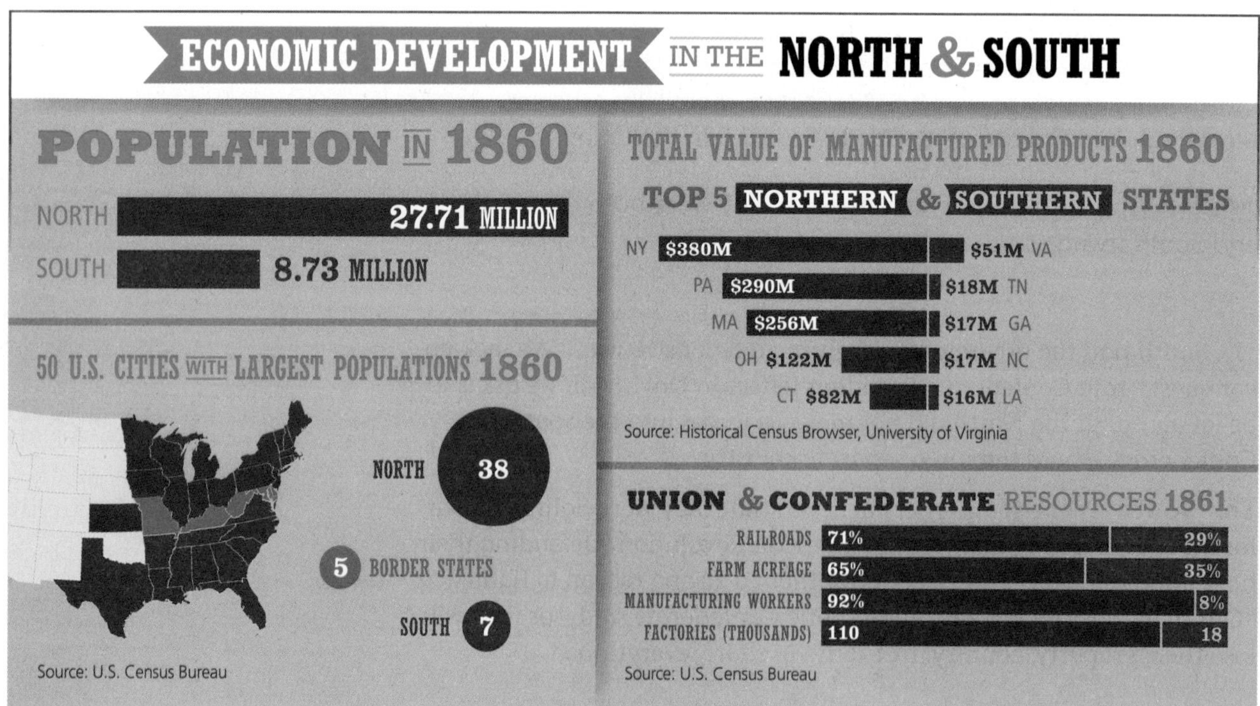

Analyze Images As these Union troops marched through Baltimore, Maryland, on their way to defend Washington, D.C., a pro-Confederate mob attacked them. **Identify Main Ideas** What was the significance of the border states?

The North The North had many people to grow food and to work in factories. But the war was unpopular among northerners, and extremely high war casualties continued to make it unpopular.

The North's biggest advantage was its strong industrial economy. Before the war, the North had ten times the industrial capacity of the South. Once the war began, these factories began making guns, bullets, cannons, boots, uniforms, and other supplies for the Union army. In addition, the North had more than double the miles of railroad line, which it used to transport both troops and supplies.

The geography of the North gave it another advantage. The prairie that rolled from Ohio in the east to Iowa and beyond in the west produced enormous food supplies. The South had nothing compared to it.

The North also benefited from a strong navy and a large fleet of trading ships. With few warships and only a small merchant fleet, the South was unable to compete with the North at sea.

The North had one other major advantage. West Point, the best military academy in the country, was located in New York. While the South had many West Point–trained officers, the Union could continue to train officers throughout the war.

Despite these advantages, the North faced a difficult military challenge. To force the South to rejoin the Union, northern soldiers had to conquer a huge area. Instead of defending their homes, they were invading unfamiliar land where their lines of supply would be long and open to attack.

READING CHECK **Summarize** how a weak economy and weak industry can be problematic during wartime.

 INTERACTIVE

Resources in the North and South, 1860

Comparing Lincoln and Davis

Lincoln's Experience	Davis's Experience
• Self-taught lawyer • Eight years in Illinois state legislature • One term in U.S. Congress • Generally regarded as winner of Lincoln-Douglas debates	• Attended West Point Military Academy • Officer in the Mexican War • Secretary of War under President Pierce

Analyze Charts This chart compares the experience of Lincoln and Davis as they took office as presidents of the Union and Confederacy. **Cite Evidence** Why might people think Davis was better prepared than Lincoln to be president?

INTERACTIVE

Abraham Lincoln and Jefferson Davis

How Did Lincoln and Davis Lead Their People?

Leadership was a crucial factor in the Civil War. President Davis, President Lincoln, and military leaders on both sides played key roles in determining the war's outcome.

Jefferson Davis Leads the South Many people had expected Davis to be a stronger leader than Lincoln. However, Davis did not want the presidency. As one observer stated:

Primary Source

> "Mr. Davis's military instincts still predominate, and his eager wish was to have joined the army instead of being elected president."
>
> —Arthur James Freemantle, from *The Freemantle Diary*

Davis's experience had prepared him for the position. He had attended the United States Military Academy at West Point and served as an officer in the Mexican-American War. Later, he was Secretary of War under President Franklin Pierce.

Davis was regarded as honest and courageous and was widely respected. However, he did not like to turn over to others the details of military planning. As a result, he spent much time worrying about small matters and arguing with advisers.

The Leadership Qualities of Abraham Lincoln At first, some northerners had doubts about Lincoln's ability to lead as President of the United States and commander-in-chief of the U.S. military. He had little experience in national politics or military matters. However, Lincoln proved to be a patient but strong leader and a fine war planner.

Day by day, Lincoln gained the respect of those around him. Many liked his sense of humor. They noted that Lincoln even accepted criticism with a smile. When Lincoln's Secretary of War, Edwin Stanton, called him a fool, Lincoln commented, "Did Stanton say I was a fool? Then I must be one, for Stanton is generally right, and he always says what he means."

The Role of Robert E. Lee, Military Leader As the war began, army officers in the South had to decide whether to stay in the Union army and fight against their home states, or join the Confederate forces.

Robert E. Lee of Virginia faced this dilemma when Lincoln asked him to command the Union army. He explained in a letter to a friend:

Primary Source

"If Virginia stands by the old Union, so will I. But if she secedes . . . , then I will still follow my native State with my sword and, if need be, with my life."

—Robert E. Lee, quoted in Carl Sandburg's *Abraham Lincoln*

Analyze Images This illustration shows how one artist imagined General Robert E. Lee of Virginia. **Infer** What impression of Lee do you think the artist was trying to convey?

Virginia did secede, and Lee refused Lincoln's offer. Later, Lee became commander of the Confederate army.

Many of the prewar United States Army's best officers served the Confederacy. As a result, President Lincoln had trouble finding generals to match those of the South.

READING CHECK **Check Understanding** What advantages in leadership did the South have over the North?

Lesson Check

Practice Vocabulary

1. Why did Senator Crittenden say his proposed amendment on extending the Missouri Compromise line to the Pacific should be **unamendable**?
2. How were the **border states** different from the other states that stayed in the Union?
3. Why did Lincoln think government required **acquiescence**?

Critical Thinking and Writing

4. **Identify Main Ideas** What motivated the South to fight in the Civil War?
5. **Summarize** the principal disadvantages the North faced in fighting the Civil War.
6. **Writing Workshop: Develop Your Thesis** Begin to draft a thesis on the differences between the North and South before, during, and after the Civil War. Write your thesis in your Active Journal. You can revise your thesis statement as your essay develops.

Assess Credibility of a Source

Follow these steps to assess the credibility of a source.

Analyze Primary and Secondary Sources

1 Identify who created the source and when it was created

a. Who wrote and delivered the speech excerpted below?

b. When was it delivered?

2 Identify the topic What is the main idea presented in this excerpt from the speech?

3 Identify the facts, opinions, and possible inaccuracies or biases

a. What facts does Lincoln present in this speech?

b. What opinions does he express?

c. What inaccuracies or biases can you detect?

4 Assess the credibility of the source When a source has credibility, it means it is believable and trustworthy. Are the ideas expressed by President Lincoln credible? Why do you think so?

Primary Source

On March 4, 1861, Abraham Lincoln delivered this speech at his first inauguration as President of the United States. Six weeks later, on April 12, the Civil War began.

> Apprehension seems to exist among the people of the Southern States that by the accession of a Republican Administration their property and their peace and personal security are to be endangered. There has never been any reasonable cause for such apprehension. Indeed, the most ample evidence to the contrary has all the while existed and been open to their inspection. It is found in nearly all the published speeches of him who now addresses you. I do but quote from one of those speeches when I declare that—
>
> I have no purpose, directly or indirectly, to interfere with the institution of slavery in the States where it exists. I believe I have no lawful right to do so, and I have no inclination to do so. . . .
>
> [T]o the extent of my ability, I shall take care, as the Constitution itself expressly enjoins upon me, that the laws of the Union be faithfully executed in all the States. . . . I trust this will not be regarded as a menace, but only as the declared purpose of the Union that it will constitutionally defend and maintain itself.
>
> — *President Abraham Lincoln, March 4, 1861*

LESSON 4

The Course of War

GET READY TO READ

START UP

How do you think fighting in battle would have changed a soldier's attitude toward the war? Write a few sentences expressing your ideas.

GUIDING QUESTIONS

- How was the Civil War conducted?
- How did the early battles of the war reflect broader patterns in the war?
- Which battles did the Confederacy and the Union win in the early years of the war?

TAKE NOTES

Literacy Skills Sequence

Use the graphic organizer in your Active Journal to take notes as you read the lesson.

PRACTICE VOCABULARY

Use the vocabulary activity in your Active Journal to practice the vocabulary words.

Vocabulary

Battle of Bull Run
Virginia
Monitor
Battle of Antietam
Battle of Fredericksburg
Battle of Chancellorsville
Battle of Shiloh

Academic Vocabulary

reluctant
demonstrate

As the war began, each side was confident that its strengths would lead it to victory.

How Did the Strategies of the North and South Differ?

The North and South had quite different strategies. The Union planned an aggressive, three-pronged campaign against the South.

The Union Strategy First, the Union planned to use its navy to blockade southern ports. This would cut off the South's supply of manufactured goods from Europe and its ability to earn money from cotton exports.

In the East, Union generals aimed to seize Richmond, Virginia, the Confederate capital. They thought they might end the war quickly by capturing the Confederate government.

In the West, the Union planned to seize control of the Mississippi River. This would prevent the South from using the river to supply its troops. It would also separate Arkansas, Texas, and Louisiana from the rest of the Confederacy.

Academic Vocabulary
reluctant • *adj.,* not eager

The Union's Strategies to Win the Civil War

The Confederate Strategy The South's strategy was simpler: The Confederate army would fight a defensive war until northerners tired of fighting. If the war became unpopular in the North, President Lincoln would have to stop the war and recognize the South's independence.

The Confederacy counted on European money and supplies. Southern cotton was important to the textile mills of England and other countries. Southerners thought that Europeans would recognize the Confederacy as an independent nation and that the South could continue to sell them cotton.

READING CHECK **Understand Effects** How was the Union plan for victory more aggressive than the Confederate plan?

Analyze Images Southern soldiers, like those shown here, prepared for a defensive war. **Identify Supporting Details** Why did the Confederates adopt a defensive strategy?

Early Battles

"Forward to Richmond! Forward to Richmond!" Every day for more than a month, the influential *New York Tribune* blazed this war cry across its front page. The Union army seemed **reluctant** to go on the offensive, however. At last, three months after the fall of Fort Sumter, Lincoln responded to public pressure and ordered an attack.

Stonewall Jackson Makes a Stand at Bull Run

The Confederate army was camped just 30 miles southwest of Washington, D.C. On July 21, 1861, Union troops set out from the nation's capital to attack the rebel forces. Hundreds of Washingtonians, in a festive mood, rode out along with the army to watch the battle. Many thought the Union army would crush the Confederates.

The Union troops had not gone far when they encountered Confederate troops near a small stream known as Bull Run, close by the town of Manassas, Virginia.

At first, Union forces succeeded in breaking up Confederate battle lines. "The war is over!" yelled some soldiers from Massachusetts. But General Thomas Jackson rallied the Virginia troops on a nearby hill. "Look!" cried a Confederate officer to his men, "There is Jackson standing like a stone wall! Rally behind the Virginians!"

From that day on, the general was known as "Stonewall" Jackson. Historians consider him one of the most gifted tactical commanders in the Civil War.

In the end, it was the Union troops who panicked and ran. "Off they went," reported one observer, "across fields, toward the woods, anywhere, everywhere, to escape."

The **Battle of Bull Run** (also referred to as the Battle of Manassas by the Confederates) showed how badly both Union and Confederate soldiers needed training. It also proved that the Confederate army could stand up to the Union, meaning the war would be long and bloody.

The Union Army Under George McClellan Northerners were shocked by the disaster at Bull Run. Almost immediately, President Lincoln appointed General George McClellan as commander of the Union army of the East, known as the Army of the Potomac. McClellan was a superb organizer who transformed inexperienced recruits into battle-ready soldiers.

McClellan, however, was very cautious. Newspapers reported "all quiet along the Potomac" so often that the phrase became a national joke. President Lincoln lost patience. "If General McClellan does not want to use the army," the president snapped, "I would like to borrow it."

At last, in March 1862, McClellan and most of his troops left Washington. They sailed down the Potomac River and Chesapeake Bay and landed south of Richmond on the Virginia Peninsula. McClellan slowly moved toward the Confederate capital.

General Lee launched a series of counterattacks. At the same time, Lee sent Jackson north to threaten Washington, D.C. Lincoln was forced to retain troops in Washington to defend the capital. This prevented him from sending reinforcements to help McClellan. Cautious as usual, McClellan abandoned the attack and retreated. The Peninsula Campaign, as it became known, had failed.

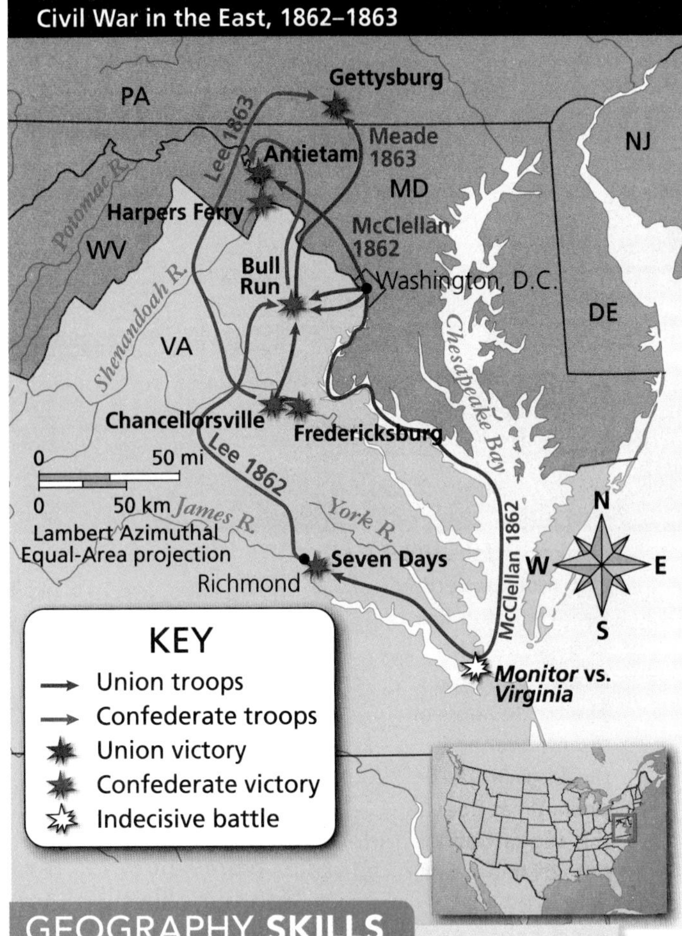

GEOGRAPHY **SKILLS**

This map shows the movement of troops and the major battles that took place from 1861 to 1862.

1. **Location** Using the scale of miles, measure the distance between the U.S. capital and the Confederate capital. How might the locations of the two capitals have influenced the battles and troop movements shown on the map?
2. **Synthesize Visual Information** Based on this map, which army seems to have had the advantage in the war during these years? Why?

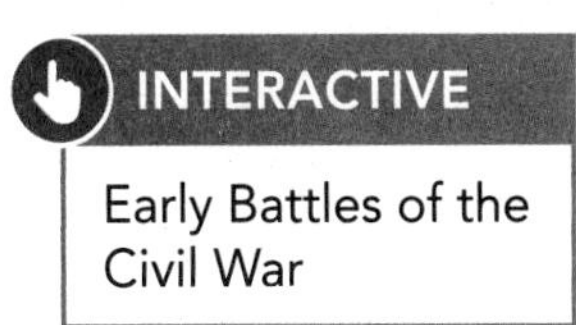

INTERACTIVE

Early Battles of the Civil War

Analyze Images The Confederate ship *Virginia* and the Union ship *Monitor* battled near Hampton Roads, Virginia, in 1862. **Draw Conclusions** The battle between the *Monitor* and the *Virginia* was a draw. What does this suggest about the advantages of ironclads?

Academic Vocabulary

demonstrate • *v.*, to prove something by being an example of it

The Blockade and the Ironclads Early in the war, Union ships blockaded southern ports. Because the South had few factories, it depended on imports for manufactured goods, such as weapons. A blockade could cripple the Confederate war effort.

At first, some small, fast ships slipped through the blockade. These "blockade runners" brought everything from matches to guns to the Confederacy.

In time, however, the blockade became more effective. Trade through southern ports dropped by more than 90 percent. The South desperately needed to break the Union blockade. One method it tried was the ironclad ship. *Clad* means *clothed*, or *covered*. Ironclad ships were covered with iron for protection.

Confederates modified an abandoned Union warship, the USS *Merrimack*. They covered it with iron plates and renamed it the ***Virginia***. On its first day out in March 1862, the *Virginia* **demonstrated** the advantages of ironclads. It destroyed two Union ships and drove three more aground. Union cannonballs bounced harmlessly off the *Virginia's* metal skin.

The Union countered with its own ironclad, the ***Monitor***. Soon, the two ships clashed near the mouth of Chesapeake Bay. This was the first time two ironclad warships battled one another.

Despite an exhausting battle, neither vessel seriously damaged the other, and both withdrew. Two months later, Confederates had to sink the *Virginia* when the Union captured Norfolk.

As ironclad ships became a standard part of naval forces, they changed naval warfare. The Union built 50 more ironclads during the Civil War and continued to build them for decades after. Other nations built them as well. They were later used in World War I.

Because of the North's ironclads, the South was never again able to mount a serious attack against the Union navy. The Union blockade held throughout the war.

Did you know?

In the 1970s, the USS *Monitor* was rediscovered 230 feet deep in the Atlantic Ocean. Some parts of the ship are now on display at the Mariner's Museum in Virginia.

The Battle of Antietam In September 1862, General Lee went on the offensive and marched his troops north into Maryland. He believed that a southern victory on northern soil would be a great blow to northern morale.

Luck was against Lee, however. At an abandoned Confederate campsite, a Union officer found a copy of Lee's battle plan. It was wrapped around three cigars, left behind by a careless general. General McClellan was overjoyed. "If I cannot whip 'Bobbie Lee,' I will be willing to go home," he boasted.

However, McClellan was slow to act. After a few days, he finally attacked Lee's main force near a creek called Antietam (an TEE tuhm) in the town of Sharpsburg, Maryland, on September 17. In the battle that followed, more than 23,000 Union and Confederate soldiers were killed or wounded—in one day. September 17, 1862, remains the bloodiest day in American military history.

On the night of September 18, Lee ordered his troops to slip back into Virginia. McClellan chose not to follow.

Neither side was a clear winner at the **Battle of Antietam** (also called the Battle of Sharpsburg by the Confederates). The battle was significant, however: Because Lee had withdrawn, the North was able to claim victory. As a result, northern morale improved. Still, President Lincoln was keenly disappointed. General McClellan had failed to follow up his victory by pursuing the Confederates. In November, Lincoln appointed General Ambrose Burnside to replace McClellan as commander of the Army of the Potomac.

READING CHECK **Draw Conclusions** What conclusions can you draw from the first battles of the Civil War?

Analyze Images General George B. McClellan's Union forces met the Confederates at the Battle of Antietam. **Summarize** What was the significance of the Battle of Antietam?

Victories in the East for Confederate Forces

Two stunning victories for the Confederacy came in late 1862 and 1863. In December 1862, Burnside led Union forces once again toward Richmond. They soon confronted the Confederates outside Fredericksburg, Virginia. Lee's forces dug into the crest of a hill. There, in a strong defensive position, the outnumbered Confederates mowed down wave after wave of charging Union troops. The **Battle of Fredericksburg** was one of the Union's worst defeats. Soon after, Burnside was relieved of his command.

Half a year later, in May 1863, Lee, aided by Stonewall Jackson, again outmaneuvered Union forces. The **Battle of Chancellorsville** took place on thickly wooded ground near Chancellorsville, Virginia. Lee and Jackson defeated the Union troops in three days.

Victory came at a high price for the South, however. During the battle, nervous Confederate sentries fired at what they thought was an approaching Union soldier. The "Union soldier" turned out to be General Stonewall Jackson. Several days later, Jackson died, and the Confederacy lost one of its best generals.

READING CHECK **Draw Conclusions** How might the Confederates have felt after the Battles of Fredericksburg and Chancellorsville?

Analyze Images These are some of the cannons used by Confederate forces. **Use Visual Information** Why were cannons dug into fortified positions?

Union Success in the West

In the West, Union forces had better results. As you have read, part of the Union strategy was to seize control of the Mississippi River. In February 1862, General Ulysses S. Grant attacked and captured Fort Henry and Fort Donelson in Tennessee. These forts guarded two important tributaries of the Mississippi.

Grant then pushed south to Shiloh, a village on the Tennessee River. There, on April 6, he was surprised by Confederate forces, who drove the Union troops back to the banks of the river.

Instead of retreating, Grant rushed reinforcements to the battle. That night, one of Grant's generals approached him. The officer thought Union forces should retreat. But, seeing Grant's stubborn face, the officer only said, "Well, Grant, we've had the devil's own day, haven't we?"

"Yes," Grant replied. "Lick 'em tomorrow, though."

And they did. On April 7, 1862, reinforcements arrived, and Grant's army beat back the Confederates and won the **Battle of Shiloh**. It was one of the bloodiest encounters of the Civil War. Because of the success at Shiloh, the Union was able to capture a crucial railroad crossing at Corinth.

Meanwhile, the Union navy moved to gain control of the Mississippi River. By June 1862, Union gunboats captured New Orleans, Louisiana, and Memphis, Tennessee. By capturing these ports, the Union controlled both ends of the southern Mississippi. The South could no longer use the river as a supply line.

Analyze Images General Ulysses S. Grant, pictured here, was Lincoln's most trusted general. **Draw Conclusions** How did individual personalities affect the conduct of the war?

READING CHECK **Understand Effects** Why was the capture of Fort Henry and Fort Donelson critical to the Union's overall war strategy?

Lesson Check

Practice Vocabulary

1. What was important about the ***Virginia*** and the ***Monitor***?
2. What disaster happened at the **Battle of Chancellorsville**?

Critical Thinking and Writing

3. Draw Conclusions What can you conclude from the fact that spectators accompanied Union troops to Bull Run to watch the battle and were in a festive mood?
4. Summarize the problems that a successful blockade of southern ports would cause.
5. Use Evidence What do the battles and events that you have read about so far lead you to predict about the war?
6. Writing Workshop: Support Thesis with Details In your Active Journal, begin listing details about the differences between the North and South. You will use these details as you write the essay at the end of the Topic.

LESSON 5

Emancipation and Life in Wartime

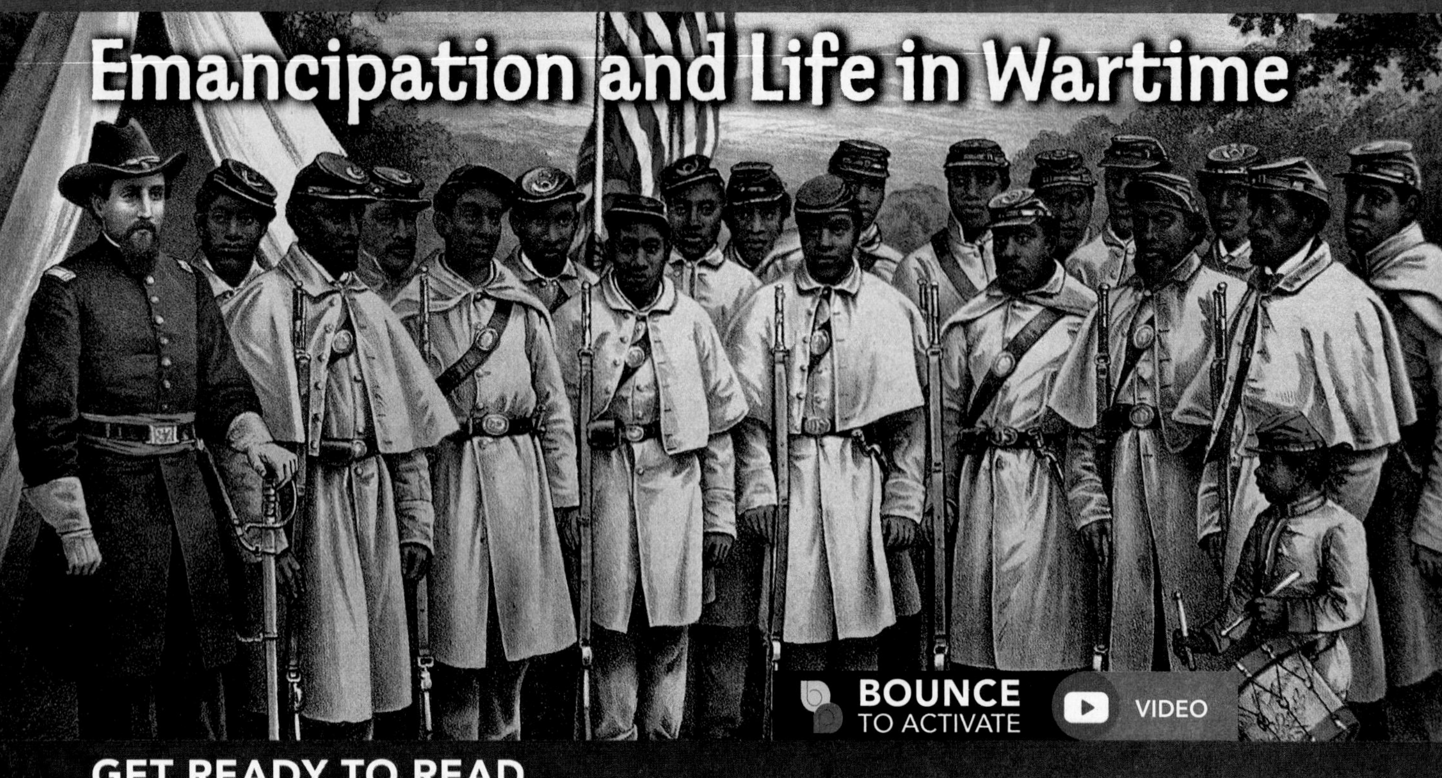

GET READY TO READ

START UP

These men have just enlisted in the Union Army. Write three questions you would like to ask them.

GUIDING QUESTIONS

- How and why did the Civil War become a war to end slavery?
- In what ways did African Americans contribute to the Union war effort?
- What roles did women play in the war?

TAKE NOTES

Literacy Skills Summarize

Use the graphic organizer in your Active Journal to take notes as you read the lesson.

PRACTICE VOCABULARY

Use the vocabulary activity in your Active Journal to practice the vocabulary words.

Vocabulary		Academic Vocabulary
Emancipation Proclamation	Copperhead	preliminary
54th Massachusetts Regiment	draft	essentially
Fort Wagner	habeas corpus	
	inflation	
	income tax	

The Civil War began as a war to restore the Union, not to end slavery. President Lincoln made this point clear in a letter that was widely distributed:

Primary Source

"If I could save the Union without freeing any slave, I would do it; and if I could save it by freeing all the slaves, I would do it; and if I could do it by freeing some and leaving others alone, I would also do that."

—Abraham Lincoln, August 22, 1862, quoted in Carl Sandburg, *Abraham Lincoln*

Lincoln's Emancipation Proclamation

Lincoln had a reason for handling the slavery issue cautiously. As you have read, four slave states remained in the Union, and the president did not want to do anything that might cause these states to join the Confederacy.

By mid-1862, however, Lincoln came to believe that he could save the Union only by broadening the goals of the war and emancipating, or freeing, the enslaved African Americans.

Academic Vocabulary
preliminary • *adj.,* something that comes before or is introductory

Lincoln Moves Slowly Lincoln knew that emancipation would weaken the Confederacy's ability to carry on the war. At the start of the war, Southerners held more than 3 million African Americans in slavery. They grew food that fed Confederate soldiers. They also worked in iron and lead mines that were vital to the South's war effort. Some served as nurses and cooks for the army.

However, Lincoln knew that many northerners opposed abolition. He hoped to introduce the idea of emancipation slowly, by limiting it to territory controlled by the Confederacy.

The President had another motive. Lincoln believed that slavery was wrong. When he felt that he could act to free enslaved African Americans without threatening the Union, he did so.

Lincoln needed a Union victory to announce his plan. He did not want Americans to think emancipation was a desperate effort to save a losing cause. On September 22, 1862, following the moderate success at Antietam, Lincoln announced a **preliminary** proclamation. He issued the formal **Emancipation Proclamation** on January 1, 1863.

The Emancipation Proclamation freed people enslaved in Confederate-held territory. It did not free enslaved African Americans in the four loyal slave states or those in Confederate lands that had already been captured by the Union, such as the city of New Orleans, Tennessee, and parts of Virginia.

GEOGRAPHY **SKILLS**

This map shows those parts of the United States that were under Union control and those parts that were controlled by the Confederacy in 1862.

1. **Interaction** Why might some southern regions have been exempted from the Emancipation Proclamation?
2. **Synthesize Visual Information** Where had the Union had its greatest successes?

Analyze Images In this painting, Lady Liberty rides a chariot labeled EMANCIPATION, and Lincoln holds a scroll labeled PROCLAMATION. **Use Visual Information** What does this painting say about the Emancipation Proclamation?

The Proclamation Changes the Purpose of the War Because the rebelling states were not under Union control, no African Americans actually gained their freedom on January 1, 1863. Still, the Emancipation Proclamation changed the war's purpose. Now, Union troops were fighting to end slavery as well as to save the Union.

The opponents of slavery greeted the proclamation with joy. Frederick Douglass witnessed a celebration in Boston:

Primary Source

"The effect of this announcement was startling . . . and the scene was wild and grand. . . . My old friend Rue, a Negro preacher, . . . expressed the heartfelt emotion of the hour, when he led all voices in the anthem, 'Sound the loud timbrel o'er Egypt's dark sea, Jehovah hath triumphed, his people are free!'"

—Frederick Douglass, *Life and Times of Frederick Douglass*

The proclamation also won the sympathy of Europeans, making it less likely that Britain or any other European country would come to the aid of the South. However, in the South, Lincoln's proclamation was seen as a "fiend's act" that destroyed valuable property.

READING CHECK **Understand Effects** How did the Emancipation Proclamation change the purpose of the Civil War?

Why Did African Americans Fight for the Union?

When the war began, thousands of free African Americans volunteered to fight for the Union, but federal law forbade them to serve as soldiers. When Congress repealed that law in 1862, both free African Americans and African Americans who had escaped from slavery enlisted in the Union army.

Military Service The army assigned African American volunteers to all-Black units, commanded by white officers. At first, the Black troops served only as laborers. They performed noncombat duties such as building roads and guarding supplies. Black troops received only half the pay of white soldiers.

African American soldiers protested against this discrimination. Gradually, conditions changed. By 1863, African American troops were fighting in major battles. In 1864, the War Department announced that all soldiers would receive equal pay. By the end of the war, about 200,000 African Americans had fought for the Union. Nearly 40,000 lost their lives.

For the families of African American soldiers, the war was just as horrible as it was for the families of white soldiers. They struggled on without fathers, brothers, and sons. They worried if loved ones would come home.

Analyze Images This monument in Boston honors the 54th Massachusetts Regiment. **Draw Conclusions** Why were Union regiments segregated by race?

The 54th Regiment One of the most famous African American units in the Union army was the **54th Massachusetts Regiment**. The 54th accepted African Americans from all across the North. Frederick Douglass helped recruit troops for the regiment, and two of his sons served in it.

On July 18, 1863, the 54th led an attack on **Fort Wagner** near Charleston, South Carolina. Under heavy fire, troops fought their way into the fort before being forced to withdraw. Almost half the regiment was killed.

The courage of the African American regiments helped to win respect for African American soldiers. Sergeant William Carney of the 54th Massachusetts was the first of 16 African American soldiers to win the Congressional Medal of Honor in the Civil War. Secretary of War Stanton said such Union heroes had "proved themselves among the bravest of the brave."

Analyze Graphs The graph shows the numbers of free and enslaved African Americans in the North and in the South. **Use Evidence** Based on the information in the graph, approximately what percentage of enslaved African Americans from the South escaped to the North during the Civil War?

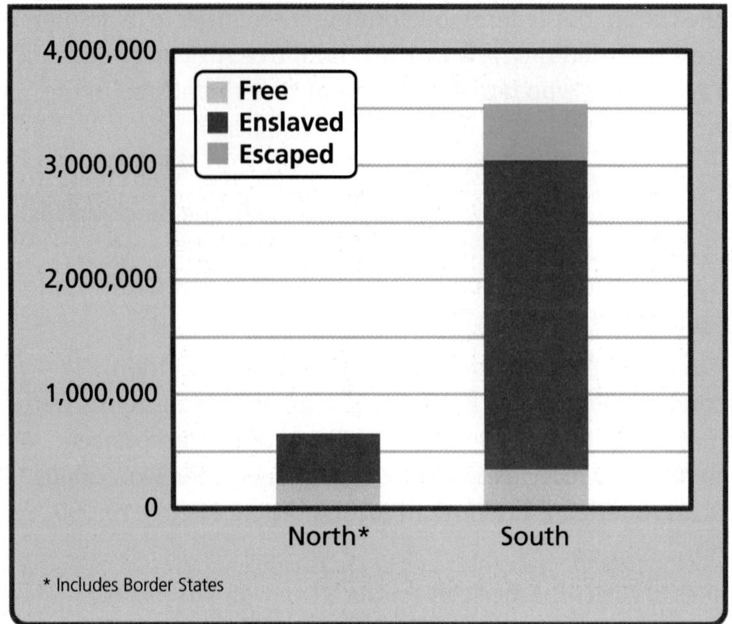

Quick Activity

In your Active Journal, explain how you can use a primary source to learn how the Civil War affected the lives of soldiers, African Americans, women, and others.

An Opportunity for Freedom Despite enslavement, many African Americans in the South contributed to the Union cause. To weaken the South's war effort, they worked more slowly or refused to work at all. They knew that when victorious Union troops arrived in their area, they would be free.

Thousands also took direct action to free themselves. Whenever a Union army moved into a region, enslaved African Americans fled across the Union lines to freedom. By the end of the war, about one-fourth of the South's enslaved population had escaped to freedom.

READING CHECK **Identify Supporting Details** Why were many African Americans on plantations able to escape during the war?

The Horrors of War

On both sides, most soldiers were under the age of 21. As the death toll rose, age restrictions for soldiers were relaxed. The South drafted boys as young as 17 and men as old as 50. Boys learned to stand firm as cannon blasts shook the earth and bullets whizzed past their ears.

Soldiers drilled and marched for long hours. They slept on the ground even in rain and snow. Often their clothing was inadequate and uncomfortable. Many soldiers had no shoes, particularly in the Confederacy.

Outdated military tactics contributed to heavy casualties. For example, soldiers attacked in straight lines or bunched together. This made them easy targets for artillery and rifle fire.

INTERACTIVE

The Hardships of Soldiers

Modern War Technology New technology added to the horror of war. Cone-shaped bullets and guns with rifling, or grooves cut on the inside of the barrel, made rifles twice as accurate. Improved cannons hurled exploding shells several miles and were much more deadly. Machine guns were introduced, and the first land mines brought unexpected horrors to war. Not surprisingly, soldiers began, for the first time, to dig trenches to escape gun and artillery fire. Even so, in most battles, one-fourth or more of the soldiers were killed or wounded.

Technology also brought the horror of modern warfare to civilians. Photographer Mathew Brady and his team of 20 battlefield photographers recorded the Civil War as had never before been done. Said one newspaper, "Mr. Brady has done something to bring home to us the terrible reality and earnestness of war."

Photography and the Civil War

The Civil War extended warfare into the skies and under water. Overhead, balloons gave commanders information about the enemy. It was the first war in which balloons were used extensively. At sea, submarines capable of sinking enemy ships were used for the first time.

Primitive Medical Technology Sick and wounded soldiers faced other horrors. Medical care was crude, especially on the battlefield. Surgeons routinely amputated injured arms and legs. Doctors did not know how germs cause infection and disease. As a result, minor wounds often became infected, and poor sanitary conditions in the army camps allowed disease to spread rapidly. Diseases such as pneumonia and malaria killed more men than guns or cannons did. Improper diet also caused sickness.

On both sides, prisoners of war faced horrifying conditions. At Andersonville, a prison camp in Georgia, many Union prisoners died of disease or starvation. The difficult life of soldiers led many to desert. One out of every seven Union soldiers and one out of every nine Confederate soldiers deserted.

READING CHECK **Identify Main Ideas** How did disease affect Civil War troops?

Analyze Images This hospital was set up after the Battle of Antietam. **Compare and Contrast** How does this battlefield hospital compare to a modern hospital?

Analyze Images Rioters who opposed the draft law in New York City destroyed multiple buildings. **Identify Supporting Details** Why didn't all northerners support the war?

Other Challenges in the North and South

Many northerners opposed using force to keep the South in the Union. Supporters of the war called these people **Copperheads**, after the poisonous snake. Other northerners supported the war but opposed how Lincoln was conducting it.

Congress Imposes a Draft As the war dragged on, public support dwindled, and there was a shortage of volunteers for the Union army. In response, Congress passed a **draft** law in 1863. It required all able-bodied males between the ages of 20 and 45 to serve in the military if they were called.

A man could avoid the draft by paying $300 (about as much as an unskilled worker could earn in a year) or by hiring someone to serve in his place. Many people began to see the Civil War as "a rich man's war and a poor man's fight."

The Draft Leads to Riots Opposition to the draft led to riots in several northern cities. Because the law went into effect soon after Lincoln issued the Emancipation Proclamation, some white northerners believed that they were being forced to fight to end slavery. Many people in northern cities, especially recent immigrants, saw little reason for wanting slavery abolished. Freed African Americans, they thought, would compete with them for jobs and drive down wages. **Essentially**, they feared the draft would force them to fight against their self-interest.

Academic Vocabulary
essentially • *adv.*, basically, fundamentally, in essence

The worst riot occurred in New York City in July 1863. For four days, white workers attacked free African Americans along with rich New Yorkers who had paid to avoid serving in the army. At least 74 people were killed.

President Lincoln moved to stop the riots and other "disloyal practices." Several times, he suspended **habeas corpus** (HAY bee uhs KOR puhs), the right to be charged or have a hearing before being jailed. Lincoln argued that the Constitution allowed him to deny this right "when in the cases of rebellion or invasion, the public safety may require it." Eventually, nearly 14,000 people were arrested. However, most were never brought to trial.

A Draft Comes to the South President Jefferson Davis struggled to create a strong federal government for the Confederacy. Many white southerners firmly believed in states' rights. They resisted paying taxes to a central government. At one point, Georgia even threatened to secede from the Confederacy.

Like the North, the South was forced to pass a draft law to fill its army. Men who enslaved or supervised more than 20 enslaved people were exempt. Southern farmers who enslaved few or no African Americans resented this law.

Near the end of the war, the South no longer had enough white men to fill the ranks. Desperate, the Confederate Congress enlisted enslaved African Americans in the military. The war ended, however, before more than a few thousand enslaved men fought for the Confederacy.

READING CHECK **Identify** How did draft problems differ in the South and North?

Analyze Graphs As the war wore on, the Union blockade of southern ports began to have a greater and greater impact. **Summarize** Based on the information in the graph, what were the effects of the North blockading southern ports?

★ BLOCKADE OF SOUTHERN PORTS ★

PRICES FOR BASIC GOODS IN THE SOUTH (IN CONFEDERATE DOLLARS)

Bacon	$8 a pound
Flour	$300 a barrel
Turkeys	$60 each
Milk	$4 a quart
Tea	$18 – $20 a pound
Sugar	$20 a pound

Source: *A Woman's Wartime Journal*

TRAVEL EXPENSES FOR ONE ARMY OFFICER: RICHMOND TO ATLANTA, 1865

March 11	Meal on the road	$20
March 20	Eyeglasses	$135
March 23	Coat, vest, pants	$2,700
March 30	Cavalry boots (1 pr)	$450
April 24	Matches	$25
April 24	Penknife	$125

Source: *The Nation: A Weekly Journal Devoted to Politics, Literature, Science, and Art*, Vol. 63

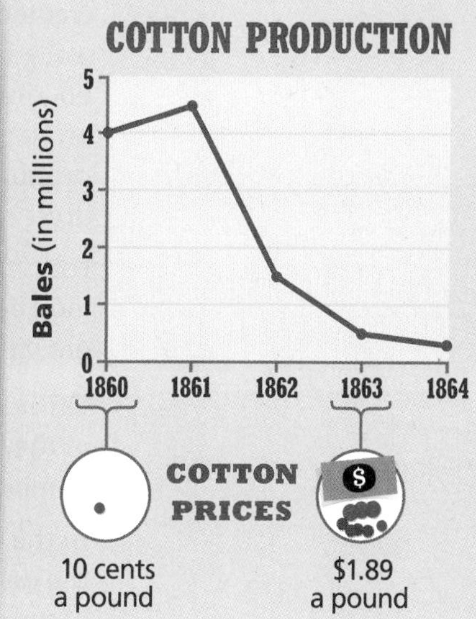

COTTON PRODUCTION

Analyze Images This photo shows Charleston, South Carolina, in 1865. **Understand Effects** What would be the effects of such destruction across the South?

War Devastates the Southern Economy

The Civil War cost far more than any previous war. For the South, war brought economic ruin. The South struggled with the cost of the war, the loss of the cotton trade, and severe shortages brought on by the Union blockade.

A Weak Wartime Economy To raise money, the Confederacy imposed an income tax and a tax-in-kind. The tax-in-kind required farmers, who had little cash, to turn over one tenth of their crops to the government.

The South also printed paper money, which led to wild **inflation**. Inflation is a general rise in prices and a decrease in the value of money. By 1865, one Confederate dollar was worth only two cents in gold. In Richmond, a barrel of flour was $275 in early 1864, potatoes were $25 a bushel, and butter was $15 a pound.

The war seriously damaged the cotton trade, the South's main source of income. Early in the war, President Davis halted cotton shipments to Britain. He offered to renew the shipments in exchange for Britain's support. But the tactic backfired when Britain bought its cotton from Egypt and India. Davis succeeded only in cutting the South's income.

The Union Blockade Creates Shortages The Union blockade created severe shortages in the South. Confederate armies sometimes waited weeks for supplies. With few factories of its own, the South bought many of its weapons in Europe. However, after the blockade cut off most deliveries, the Confederate government began building and running factories. Private manufacturers were offered contracts and draft exemptions for their workers if they produced war goods.

For civilians, the blockade brought food shortages. The production of food became critical to the economy. Many plantations switched from growing cotton to raising grain and livestock, or animals raised for food.

Widespread Destruction The impact of the war was everywhere in the South, where most of the fighting occurred. Many towns were bombarded. Homes and buildings were destroyed and burned.

In the countryside, trenches, defensive structures, cannon balls, and the debris of war spread across the land. Even where battles had not occurred, barns had been burned or stripped and fences torn down for firewood. Hungry armies destroyed fields of grain and seized livestock, mules, and other animals.

READING CHECK **Identify Cause and Effect** What were the causes of wartime economic difficulties for the Confederacy?

How Did the War Affect the Northern Economy?

The Union used several strategies to pay for the war. In some ways, war helped the North's economy.

Taxation and Inflation To pay for the war, Congress established the nation's first **income tax**, or tax on people's earnings, in 1861. A new agency, the Internal Revenue Bureau, oversaw the collection process. The Union also issued bonds worth millions of dollars, and, like the Confederacy, it printed more than $400 million in paper money, which led to inflation. During the war, prices for goods nearly doubled in the North.

Economic Benefits of the War The war also helped the North's economy in several ways. As farmers went off to fight, there was a greater need for machines to plant and harvest crops. The purchase of reapers rose to nearly 165,000 during the war. As a result, farm production actually went up during the war.

The wartime demand for clothing, shoes, guns, and other goods helped many northern industries. Some manufacturers made fortunes by profiteering. Profiteers charged excessive prices for goods that the government desperately needed for the war.

READING CHECK **Check Understanding** How did the Civil War strengthen the North's economy?

BIOGRAPHY 5 Things to Know About MARY EDWARDS WALKER

Doctor during the Civil War (1832–1919)

- Walker served as assistant surgeon in battlefield hospitals for the Union Army.
- She was captured by the Confederate army and later exchanged for a Confederate prisoner of war.
- Walker lectured on women's rights, suffrage, and on reforming standards for acceptable female clothing.
- Walker did not support the suffrage amendment, saying women's right to vote was already included in the Constitution.
- She was the first woman to be awarded the Congressional Medal of Honor.

Critical Thinking Do you think Dr. Mary Walker was ahead of her time? Explain.

Analyze Images Clara Barton was one of the many women who cared for wounded soldiers at Union field hospitals. **Recognize Multiple Causes** How were women essential to the war effort?

Women Contribute to the War Effort

Women in the North and South played vital roles during the war. As men left for the battlefields, women took over their jobs in industry and on farms. They also had to raise their families on their own.

In rare instances, some women disguised themselves as men and enlisted in the army. Others served as spies. Many served in army camps, choosing to accompany their husbands to war.

Women formed aid societies to help supply the troops with food, bedding, clothing, and medicine. Throughout the North, women held fairs and other fund-raising events to pay for supplies.

Helping the Wounded Women on both sides worked as nurses. At first, doctors were unwilling to permit even trained nurses to work in military hospitals. When wounded men began to swamp army hospitals, however, this attitude changed. Women performed so well that nursing became an accepted occupation for women.

Dorothea Dix, famous for her work reforming prisons and mental hospitals, and Clara Barton, who later founded the American Red Cross, both became nurses for the Union army. Of her reasons for serving as a nurse, Clara Barton said, "What could I do but go with them [Civil War soldiers], or work for them and my country?" Mary Edwards Walker, an important advocate of women's rights, served as both a nurse and an assistant surgeon during the war.

Sojourner Truth, the African American antislavery leader, worked in Union hospitals and in camps for African Americans freed from slavery. In the South, Sally Tompkins set up a hospital in Richmond, Virginia.

READING CHECK **Identify Main Ideas** What are some ways that women contributed to the war effort?

Lesson Check

Practice Vocabulary

1. How did the **Emancipation Proclamation** change the purpose of the Civil War?
2. What did the **54th Massachusetts Regiment** accomplish at **Fort Wagner**?
3. What happens during a period of **inflation**?

Critical Thinking and Writing

4. **Draw Conclusions** Why did the roles of women change during the Civil War?
5. **Summarize** how the treatment of African American soldiers in the Union army changed as the war progressed.
6. **Writing Workshop: Write an Introduction** In your Active Journal, write an introduction to your essay about the differences between the North and South. Include your thesis statement in your introduction.

Primary Sources

Abraham Lincoln, The Emancipation Proclamation

In 1863, in the midst of the Civil War, Abraham Lincoln believed it was necessary to give people more reasons to support the war. Until then, it had been about keeping the Union together. He chose to make it also about ending slavery.

▶ President Lincoln

That on the first day of January, in the year of our Lord one thousand eight hundred and sixty-three, all persons held as slaves within any State or designated ① part of a State, the people whereof shall then be in rebellion against the United States, shall be then, thenceforward ②, and forever free; and the Executive Government of the United States . . . will recognize and maintain the freedom of such persons, and will do no act or acts to repress ③ such persons, or any of them, in any efforts they may make for their actual freedom.

That the Executive will . . . designate the States and parts of States, if any, in which the people thereof, respectively, shall then be in rebellion against the United States; and the fact that any State, or the people thereof, shall on that day be, in good faith, represented in the Congress of the United States by members chosen thereto at elections wherein a majority of the qualified voters of such State shall have participated, shall, in the absence of strong countervailing testimony, be deemed . . . not then in rebellion against the United States.

Now, therefore I, Abraham Lincoln, President of the United States, . . . in time of actual armed rebellion against the authority and government of the United States, and as a fit and necessary war measure for suppressing ④ said rebellion, do. . . order and designate as the States and parts of States wherein the people thereof respectively, are this day in rebellion against the United States the following, to wit: Arkansas, Texas, Louisiana, . . . Mississippi, Alabama, Florida, Georgia, South Carolina, North Carolina, and Virginia.

Reading and Vocabulary Support

① *Designate* means "to name or point out for a particular purpose."

② What do you think the word *thenceforward* means?

③ *Repress* means "to control someone by force."

④ What does the word *suppressing* mean?

Quest CONNECTIONS

Read the passage in the Declaration of Independence that discusses the responsibility of governments to protect the safety and happiness of the people. How is that passage reflected in the Emancipation Proclamation? Record your findings in your Active Journal.

Analyzing Primary Sources

Cite specific evidence from the document to support your answers.

1. **Determine Author's Purpose** Why is Lincoln only freeing the slaves in certain states or parts of states?
2. **Summarize** According to Lincoln, what does a state have to do to prove it is not in rebellion?
3. **Cite Evidence** What reason does Lincoln give for freeing the enslaved people?

Recognize the Role of Chance, Oversight, and Error

INTERACTIVE

Interpret Sources

Follow these steps to recognize the role of chance, oversight, and error in shaping events.

1 **Identify the topic** When reading about an event, begin by focusing on what the passage is about. For example, is the passage about a military campaign or the rise of a new leader? Where did the event happen? Who were the key figures?

a. What event is the subject of Lee's letter?

b. What role did Lee play in the event?

2 **Identify the goal or expected outcome** Ask, "What was the leader trying to accomplish?" "What was expected to happen if everything had gone as planned?"

a. According to this letter, how did Lee expect the battle to progress?

b. What outcome did Lee expect?

3 **Identify any unexpected outcomes** As you consider the event or time period, ask, "Did events happen as the leader expected?" "Did something go wrong?" "Did key people achieve their stated goals?"

a. What happened that surprised Lee?

4 **Analyze the cause of the unexpected outcomes** Look for explanations for unexpected outcomes. Did something that nobody could have predicted go wrong—a storm or illness, for example? Did a person make a key mistake? Did someone forget some key step?

a. How did Lee explain what went wrong?

Primary Source

The following is a letter written by Confederate General Robert E. Lee to Jefferson Davis, president of the Confederacy.

Mr. President

Your note of the 27 [sic] enclosing a slip from the Charleston Mercury relative to the battle of Gettysburg is received. I much regret its general censure upon the operations of the army, as it is calculated to do us no good either at home or abroad. . . . No blame can be attached to the army for its failure to accomplish what was projected by me, nor should it be censured for the unreasonable expectations of the public. I am alone to blame, in perhaps expecting too much of its prowess & valor. . . . But with the knowledge I then had, & in the circumstances I was then placed, I do not know what better course I could have pursued. With my present knowledge, & could I have foreseen that the attack on the last day would have failed to drive the enemy from his position, I should certainly have tried some other course. What the ultimate result would have been is not so clear to me. Our loss has been heavy, that of the enemy's proportionally so. His crippled condition enabled us to retire from the country comparatively unmolested. The unexpected state of the Potomac was our only embarrassment.

— Robert E. Lee, Letter to Jefferson Davis, July 31, 1863

LESSON 6

The War's End

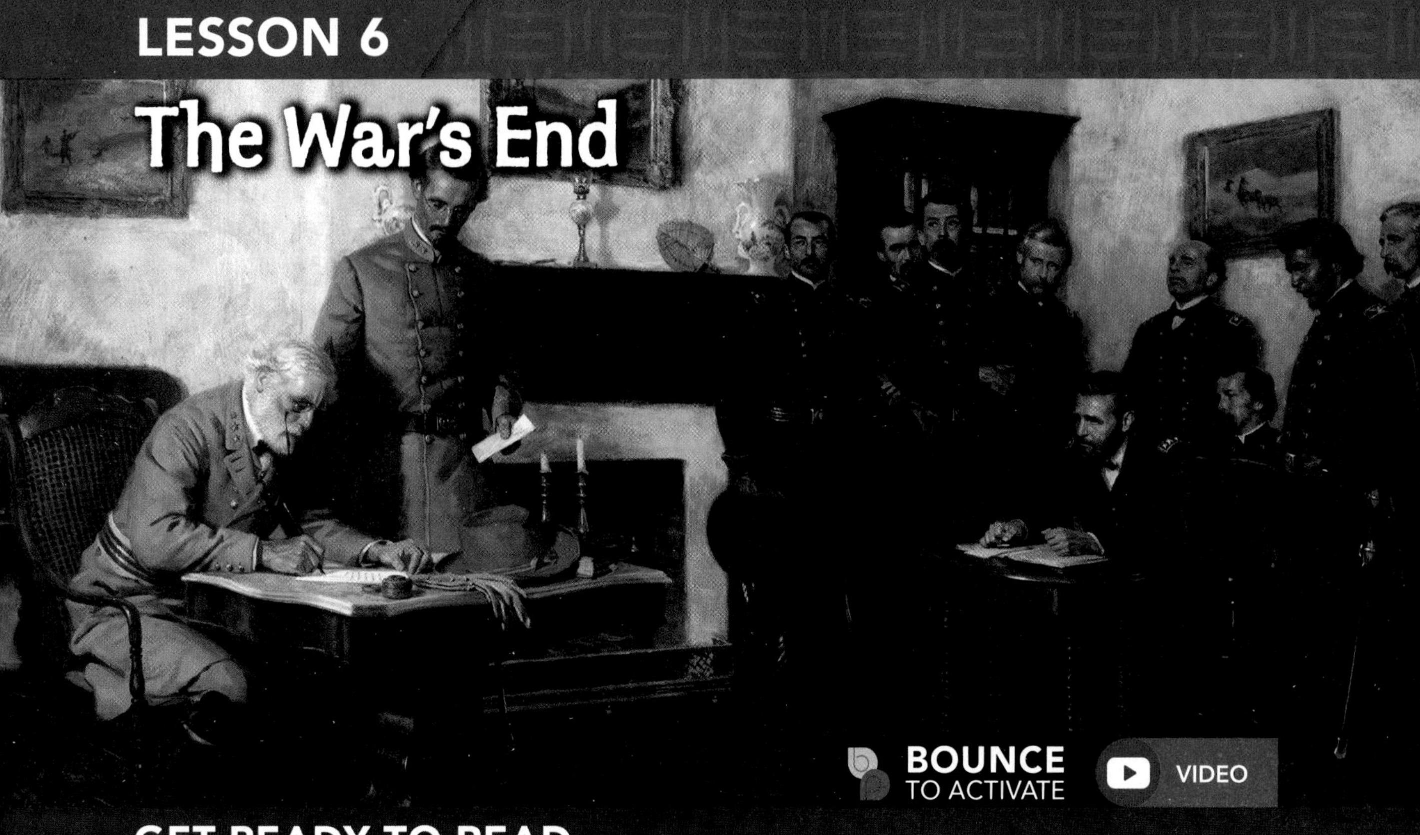

GET READY TO READ

START UP

Lee (left) surrendered April 9, 1865. After all the bloodshed and destruction, how would the country heal? Write a few sentences stating your ideas.

GUIDING QUESTIONS

- How did the Civil War change the United States?
- What was the significance of Union victories at Vicksburg and Gettysburg?
- What was Grant's plan for ending the war?

TAKE NOTES

Literacy Skills Sequence

Use the graphic organizer in your Active Journal to take notes as you read the lesson.

PRACTICE VOCABULARY

Use the vocabulary activity in your Active Journal to practice the vocabulary words.

Vocabulary	Academic Vocabulary
siege	significant
Battle of Gettysburg	imply
Pickett's Charge	
Gettysburg Address	
Appomattox Court House	

Confederate armies won major battles at Fredericksburg in December 1862 and at Chancellorsville in May 1863. These were gloomy days for the North. Then, in July 1863, the tide of war turned against the South as Union forces won major victories in both the East and the West.

The Union Captures Vicksburg

In the West, by the summer of 1863, the Union had captured New Orleans and Memphis, giving them control of both ends of the southern Mississippi River. Still, the Confederates held Vicksburg, Mississippi.

Grant Targets Vicksburg Vicksburg was a crucial Mississippi River crossing, linking the eastern and western Confederate states. Vicksburg sat on a cliff high above the eastern shore of the river, which made it difficult to attack from the west.

Grant was desperate to capture Vicksburg, and the Confederates were desperate to keep it. Early in 1863, Grant's forces tried again and again but failed to seize Vicksburg.

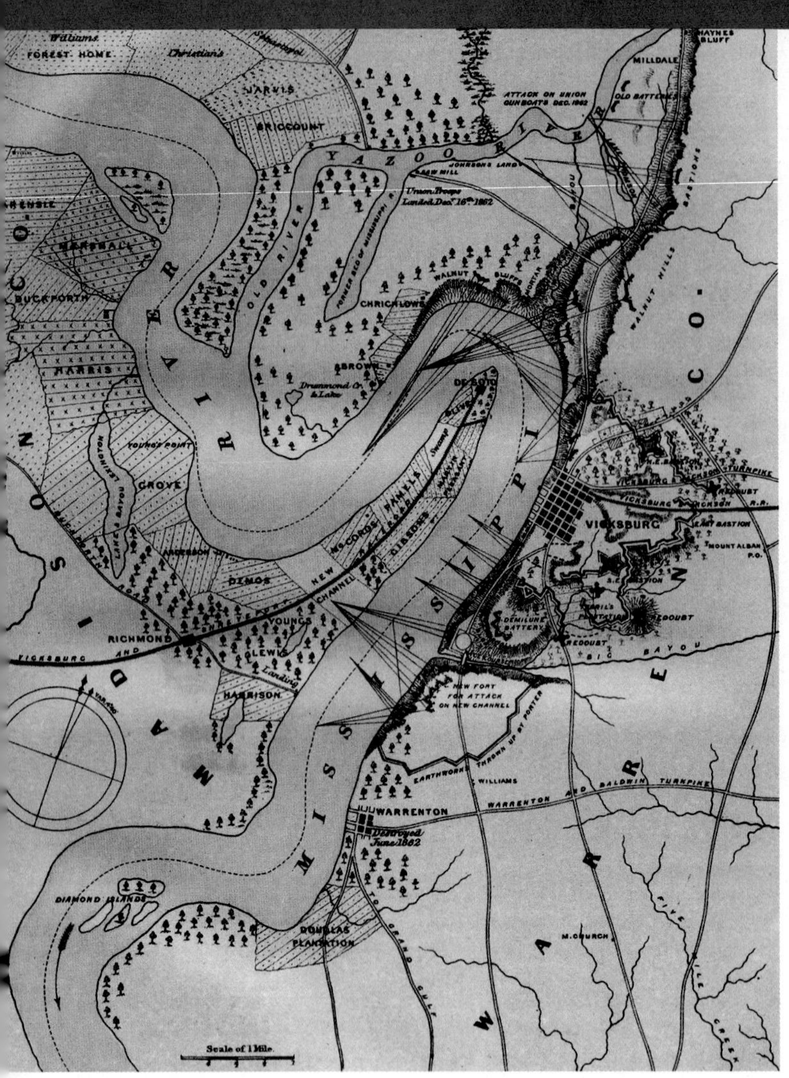

Analyze Images For more than six weeks, General Grant's forces encircled Vicksburg, cutting off its supplies. **Synthesize Visual Information** Why did Grant circle around and approach Vicksburg from the East?

At last, Grant devised a brilliant plan. Landing at an unguarded spot on the river, Grant marched inland eastward to launch a surprise attack on Jackson, Mississippi. Then, he turned back and attacked Vicksburg from the rear. On the side facing away from the river, no physical barriers protected Vicksburg.

The Siege of Vicksburg For more than six weeks, Grant's forces laid siege to Vicksburg. In a **siege**, a military force encircles an enemy position and blockades and bombards it in order to force it to surrender. Finally, on July 4, 1863, the Confederates surrendered Vicksburg.

On July 9, Union forces also captured Port Hudson, Louisiana, gaining control of the entire Mississippi River. The Confederacy was split in two. Cut off from the rest of the Confederacy, Texas, Arkansas, and Louisiana were no longer able to supply food, weapons, and other goods to the eastern Confederate states. This was a devastating blow.

READING CHECK Check Understanding Why was Union control of the Mississippi River a blow to the Confederacy?

A Union Victory at Gettysburg

Meanwhile, in the East, after his victory at Chancellorsville, General Lee moved his army north into Pennsylvania. He hoped to take Union forces by surprise. If he succeeded in Pennsylvania, Lee planned to swing south and capture Washington, D.C. The Union army followed the Confederates, making sure to remain between the Confederates and Washington.

The Battle Begins On June 30, 1863, the Union Army of the Potomac, now under command of General George C. Meade, met part of Lee's army at the town of Gettysburg, Pennsylvania. Both sides quickly sent in reinforcements. The three-day **Battle of Gettysburg** that followed was one of the most **significant** events of the Civil War.

Academic Vocabulary
significant • *adj.*, very important

INTERACTIVE
The Battle of Vicksburg

On the first day of battle, July 1, the Confederates drove the Union forces out of Gettysburg. The Union army, however, took up strong positions on Cemetery Ridge, overlooking the town. Union troops fortified these positions throughout the night.

The next day, Lee ordered an attack on both ends of the Union line, much of which was positioned on high ground, making the attacks difficult. Southern troops fought hard, but the Union army was well positioned. At the end of a day of savage fighting, Lee's forces had suffered heavy casualties but failed to dislodge the Union army.

INTERACTIVE

The Battle at Gettysburg

Some of the Union's success lay in its use of the Spencer repeating rifle. It permitted soldiers to fire shot after shot very quickly. The Spencer became widely used by Union soldiers. The South lacked this technology. Rifles with similar repeating action became standard weapons in later wars.

A Disastrous Decision for the Confederacy Despite his losses, Lee attacked again. He wanted to "create a panic and virtually destroy the [Union] army." On July 3, he ordered General George Pickett to lead 15,000 men in a daring charge against the center of the Union line. This attack is known as **Pickett's Charge**. To reach their target, Pickett's men would have to march about 1,000 yards across sloping, open ground—all within clear view of the enemy.

When Pickett gave the order to charge, the Confederates marched forward, and Union guns opened fire. Row after row of soldiers fell to the ground, dead or wounded. The battle noise, one soldier recalled, was "strange and terrible, a sound that came from thousands of human throats . . . like a vast mournful roar."

Pickett's Charge failed. The steady barrage of bullets and shells kept all but a handful of Confederate soldiers from penetrating Union lines. The next day, a Union officer inspecting the battlefield found that "the dead and wounded lay too thick to guide a horse through them."

Analyze Images This photograph shows the cyclorama in the Museum and Visitor Center at Gettysburg National Military Park. **Explain an Argument** Why is it important to remember what happened at Gettysburg?

As the survivors limped back, Lee rode among them. "It's all my fault," he admitted gravely. Lee had no choice but to retreat. The Confederates would never invade the North again.

General Meade was proud of the victory. He had protected Pennsylvania and Washington, D.C. Lincoln, however, was disappointed. He felt that the Union army had once again allowed the Confederate troops to get away.

The Union victories at Vicksburg and Gettysburg marked the turning point of the Civil War. It seemed just a matter of time before the Confederacy would fall. However, the South was still determined to fight. The war would last another two years.

READING CHECK Identify Main Ideas Why was the Union victory at Gettysburg significant?

Analyze Images This image shows President Lincoln with Union officers at a battlefield camp in 1862. **Draw Conclusions** What do Lincoln's visits to battlefields tell about him as a leader?

Lincoln Delivers the Gettysburg Address

The Battle of Gettysburg left more than 50,000 dead or wounded. On November 19, 1863, there was a ceremony to dedicate a cemetery to the memory of those soldiers. President Lincoln delivered a speech now known as the **Gettysburg Address**. The speech exemplified Lincoln's leadership at a time of grief and crisis.

Lincoln said that the Civil War was a test of whether or not a democratic government could survive. This claim **implied** that the nation's survival depended on the integrity of the Union. He also reminded Americans that their nation was founded on the belief that "all men are created equal." Lincoln told the audience:

Academic Vocabulary

imply • *v.*, to suggest without saying directly or plainly

Primary Source

"We here highly resolve that these dead shall not have died in vain—that this nation, under God, shall have a new birth of freedom—and that government of the people, by the people, for the people, shall not perish from the earth."

—Abraham Lincoln, Gettysburg Address, November 19, 1863

Lincoln connected the phrases "all men are created equal," taken from the Declaration of Independence, and "a new birth of freedom." Coming so soon after the Emancipation Proclamation, this **implied** that equality for African Americans was a core purpose of the nation. While the entire speech was only ten sentences long and took about three minutes to deliver, it is still honored as a profound statement of American ideals.

READING CHECK **Draw Conclusions** Lincoln said that the Civil War was a test. What was that test?

The Union Advances Into the South

Since the beginning of the war, Lincoln had searched for a general who could lead the Union to victory. More and more, he thought of Ulysses S. Grant.

General Grant Takes Charge General Ulysses S. Grant had led Union forces to victory at Shiloh. He developed an ingenious plan that led to the capture of Vicksburg. Then he continued to win battles in the West. In 1864, Lincoln appointed Grant commander of all Union forces. In this role, Grant would lead the final Union advance against the Confederacy.

Some questioned the choice of Grant, teasing that his initials stood for "Unconditional Surrender." But even back when Grant had been criticized for near disaster at the Battle of Shiloh, Lincoln had defended him: "I can't spare this man," Lincoln said. "He fights."

Grant's plan for ending the war was to destroy the South's ability to fight. To achieve this, Grant ordered his generals to wage total war. He wanted the Union army to destroy food, equipment, and anything else that might be useful to the enemy. At the start of the war, it was seen as an advantage of the Confederacy that the war would be fought on Southern soil, surrounded by Confederate supporters. Grant intended to turn this advantage into a liability. Confederate civilians would suffer hardship, and they would be unable to provide support to the military.

BIOGRAPHY 5 Things to Know About ULYSSES S. GRANT

Commanding general of the Union army during the Civil War (1822–1885)

- A graduate of West Point, Grant served in the Mexican-American War under General Zachary Taylor.
- Grant resigned from the army in 1854 but rejoined at the start of the Civil War.
- President Lincoln appointed him General-in-Chief of the Union Army in 1864.
- Grant was elected 18th president of the United States, serving from 1869 to 1877.
- Near the end of his life, Grant wrote a memoir to pay off debts and provide for his family. It earned $450,000.

Critical Thinking In what ways do you think a military career prepares someone to be President?

Analyze Images Sherman's troops destroyed railroad tracks, farms, and other civilian property. **Infer** Why would Sherman order his troops to destroy civilians' property?

Sheridan Spreads Destruction in the Shenandoah To set his plan in motion, Grant sent General Philip Sheridan and his cavalry into the rich farmland of Virginia's Shenandoah Valley. He instructed Sheridan:

Primary Source

"Leave nothing to invite the enemy to return. Destroy whatever cannot be consumed. Let the valley be left so that crows flying over it will have to carry their rations along with them."

—Ulysses S. Grant, quoted in Bruce Catton, *Grant Takes Command*

In the summer and fall of 1864, Sheridan marched through the valley, destroying farms and livestock. His troops burned 2,000 barns filled with grain. There was nothing left for Lee's troops or for southern civilians.

Sherman's March to the Sea Grant ordered General William Tecumseh Sherman to capture Atlanta, Georgia, and then march to Savannah, on the Atlantic coast. Like Sheridan, Sherman had orders to destroy everything useful to the South. In Sherman's words, he would "make them so sick of war that generations would pass away before they would again appeal to it."

Sherman's troops captured Atlanta in September 1864. They began their campaign by turning the people of Atlanta out of their homes and burning a large part of the city. Then, Sherman began his March to the Sea.

As they marched through Georgia, Sherman's troops ripped up railroad tracks, killed livestock, and tore up fields. They burned barns, homes, bridges, and factories. Civilian lives were spared.

READING CHECK **Summarize** Grant's concept of *total war.*

Contrasting Ideas of Liberty and Union

Lincoln ran for reelection in 1864. At first, his defeat seemed, in his own words, "exceedingly probable." Lincoln knew that many northerners were unhappy with his handling of the war.

The Democrats nominated General George McClellan to oppose Lincoln. They adopted a resolution demanding the immediate "cessation of hostilities" against the South. Although he had commanded the Union army, McClellan was willing to compromise with the Confederacy. If peace could be achieved, he would restore slavery.

Then, in September, Sherman took Atlanta, and the North rallied around Lincoln. Sheridan's victories in the Shenandoah Valley in October further increased Lincoln's popular support. In the election in November, the vote was close, but Lincoln remained President.

Lincoln's Second Inaugural In his Second Inaugural Address, Lincoln looked forward to the coming of peace:

Primary Source

"With malice toward none, with charity for all . . . let us strive . . . to bind up the nation's wounds . . . to do all which may achieve a just and a lasting peace among ourselves and with all nations."

—Abraham Lincoln, Second Inaugural Address

Lincoln's Second Inaugural Address, along with his First Inaugural and Gettysburg addresses, are landmark speeches in American history. Together, they present Lincoln's ideas about liberty, equality, union, and government.

In his First Inaugural, Lincoln emphasized the importance of the union of the states, which he viewed as "perpetual," or never-ending. In the Gettysburg Address, he emphasized the importance of maintaining the union of the country, especially since the country was based on freedom and equality. Lincoln's Second Inaugural highlighted slavery as a violation of equality and liberty, yet emphasized, again, the preservation of unity by urging people to "bind up the nation's wounds."

Analyze Images By the election of 1864, as this photograph clearly shows, the war had taken an emotional and physical toll on President Lincoln. **Draw Conclusions** What leadership qualities did Lincoln display?

Analyze Images Richmond, Virginia, shown here before (left) and after (right) the war, was the capital of the Confederacy. **Use Visual Information** What problems did the people of Richmond have to overcome after the war?

Two Contrasting Visions In Jefferson Davis's inaugural address, given four years earlier, the Confederate President had conveyed quite different views from Lincoln's. Davis explained the South's reasons for withdrawing from the Union as "a necessity, not a choice." Quoting the Declaration of Independence, Davis said:

Primary Source

"Our present condition . . . illustrates the American idea that governments rest upon the consent of the governed, and that it is the right of the people to alter or abolish governments whenever they become destructive of the ends for which they were established."

—President Jefferson Davis, First Inaugural Address, February 18, 1861

Lincoln had insisted in his First Inaugural Address that the Constitution required union. He had argued that "no state upon its own mere motion can lawfully get out of the Union." In the Emancipation Proclamation and the Gettysburg Address, Lincoln had extended the idea of liberty, enshrined in the nation's founding documents, to all Americans. While Lincoln's vision called for equality and liberty for enslaved African Americans, Davis called for the equality and liberty only of white southerners.

READING CHECK **Identify Main Ideas** What did the Union mean to Abraham Lincoln?

How Did the War Come to an End?

Grant began the drive to capture Richmond in May 1864. Throughout the spring and summer, he pursued Lee across eastern Virginia. Northerners read with horror that 60,000 men were killed or wounded in a single month at the Battles of the Wilderness, Spotsylvania, and Cold Harbor. Still, Grant pressed on with his Virginia Campaign. He knew that the Union could replace men and supplies. The South could not.

In June 1864, Lee dug in at Petersburg, near Richmond, and Grant began a siege. Nine months later, with a fresh supply of troops, Grant took Petersburg on April 2, 1865. The same day, Richmond fell.

The Confederacy Surrenders at Appomattox Lee withdrew his army to a small Virginia town called **Appomattox Court House**. There, a week later, they were trapped by Union troops. Lee knew that his men would be slaughtered if he kept fighting. On April 9, 1865, Lee surrendered.

At Appomattox Court House, Grant offered generous terms of surrender. Officers were allowed to keep their pistols, and soldiers who had horses could keep them. Grant knew the animals would be needed for spring plowing. Finally, ordered Grant, "each officer and man will be allowed to return to his home, not to be disturbed by the United States authorities."

As the Confederates surrendered, Union soldiers began to cheer. Grant ordered them to be silent. "The war is over," he said. "The rebels are our countrymen again."

Honoring Those Who Served The war was over, but the people who lived through it would remember it all of their lives. On both sides, home towns honored returning veterans with ceremonies—even up to 75 years later.

During the war, President Lincoln had signed into law what would later become the Medal of Honor, the highest honor in the American military. Over 1,500 soldiers were awarded the Medal of Honor for their heroic actions during the Civil War.

INTERACTIVE

Key Battles of the Civil War

Analyze Images The Union Army took over this family's home in the town of Appomattox Court House, Virginia. There, Lee signed his formal surrender. **Understand Effects** How did the war affect civilians?

One Medal of Honor recipient was O.S. (ordinary seaman) Philip Bazaar, an immigrant from Chile who enlisted in the Union Navy. Although his rank was low, his actions proved him a hero. Bazaar earned the Medal of Honor carrying vital messages between commanders while serving on the USS *Santiago de Cuba* during the assault on Fort Fisher, North Carolina, on January 15, 1865:

Primary Source

"As one of a boat crew detailed to one of the generals on shore, O.S. Bazaar bravely entered the fort in the assault and accompanied his party in carrying dispatches at the height of the battle. He was 1 of 6 men who entered the fort in the assault from the fleet."

—Medal of Honor Citation for Philip Bazaar, June 22, 1865

Analyze Graphs The graphic organizer points out some of the immense costs that Americans paid for fighting the Civil War. **Analyze Data** Based on the information about the human costs of the war, which side had more casualties during the war?

READING CHECK **Recall** What was significant about how General Grant treated Confederate soldiers after they surrendered?

A New Chapter for the United States

The cost of the Civil War was immense. More than 360,000 Union soldiers and 250,000 Confederate soldiers died. No war has ever resulted in more American deaths. The war cost about $20 billion, more than 11 times the entire amount spent by the federal government between 1789 and 1861.

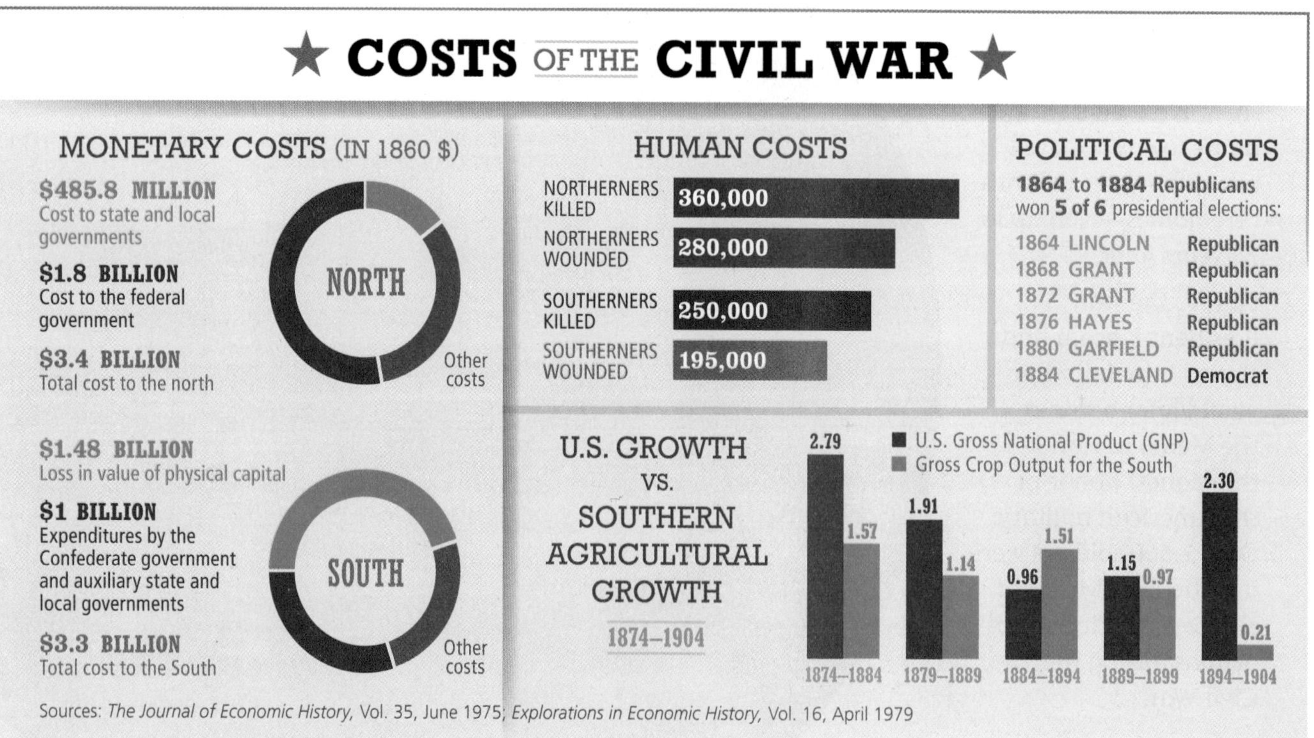

Sources: *The Journal of Economic History*, Vol. 35, June 1975; *Explorations in Economic History*, Vol. 16, April 1979

The Civil War was a major turning point in American history. No longer would Americans speak of the nation as a confederation of states. Before the war, Americans referred to "*these* United States." After, they began speaking of "*the* United States." The idea that each state might secede if it chose was dead. At the same time, the power of the federal government grew.

The war also ended slavery in the United States. For years, Americans had debated whether slavery could exist in a nation dedicated to liberty and equality. By the war's end, millions of African Americans had gained their freedom. Millions more Americans, both northern and southern, began to think about what it meant to be free and equal.

To be sure, a long and difficult struggle for equality lay ahead. Yet, Lincoln's words at Gettysburg were prophetic: "We here highly resolve . . . that this nation, under God, shall have a new birth of freedom." From out of a cruel, bitter, heart-rending war, the United States emerged a stronger, freer nation.

Analyze Images The carnage of the Civil War forced Americans to invent a variety of contraptions for transporting the dead and wounded. **Identify Supporting Details** List the human costs of the war.

Identify Main Ideas In what ways was the Civil War significant?

Lesson Check

Practice Vocabulary

1. Why was Grant's attack on Vicksburg called a **siege**?
2. What were some of the main points of Lincoln's **Gettysburg Address**?
3. What occurred at **Appomattox Court House**?

Critical Thinking and Writing

4. **Use Evidence** What elements of total war do you see in General Sherman's March to the Sea?
5. **Identify Cause and Effect** How might General Lee's goal of capturing Washington, D.C., have led him to order Pickett's Charge at the Battle of Gettysburg?
6. **Writing Workshop: Draft Your Essay** Begin writing the essay about the differences between the North and South before, during, and after the Civil War. Use the details you have been gathering to develop your ideas. Write your paragraphs in your Active Journal.

TOPIC 8

Review and Assessment

VISUAL REVIEW

Major Events Leading to War

Missouri Compromise divided Louisiana Purchase into slave and free states	**IMPACT:** Settled slavery issue in that territory
Fugitive Slave Act required citizens to capture runaways	**IMPACT:** Made northerners feel they were supporting slavery
Compromise of 1850 admitted California as a free state	**IMPACT:** Kept Union from going to war
Kansas-Nebraska Act allowed settlers to decide slavery by popular sovereignty	**IMPACT:** Opened territories to slavery; effectively repealed Missouri Compromise
Dred Scott* v. *Sandford ruled that African Americans could not be citizens	**IMPACT:** No part of United States could be completely free of slavery
John Brown's Raid attacked a federal arsenal in Harpers Ferry	**IMPACT:** In the North, made Brown a martyr, won sympathy for the anti-slavery cause
Lincoln's Election placed a northern Republican in the White House	**IMPACT:** Convinced southerners that they had no say in government

KEY EVENTS OF THE CIVIL WAR

Beginning	Middle	End
• Secession • Attack on Fort Sumter • Battle of Bull Run	• Battle of *Monitor* and *Virginia* • Battle of Antietam • Emancipation Proclamation	• Siege of Vicksburg • Battle of Gettysburg • Sherman's March • Virginia Campaign • Surrender at Appomattox Court House

READING REVIEW

Use the Take Notes and Practice Vocabulary activities in your Active Journal to review the topic.

INTERACTIVE

Practice vocabulary using the Topic Mini-Games

Create Your Website

Get help for creating your website in your Active Journal.

ASSESSMENT

Vocabulary and Key Ideas

1. **Identify Main Ideas** How did the **Missouri Compromise** affect slavery in the territories?
2. **Recall** Why were many people in the North angry over the **Fugitive Slave Act**?
3. **Check Understanding** How did the court justify convicting John Brown of **treason**?
4. **Recall** How did the South's defeat at the **Battle of Gettysburg** affect the war?
5. **Identify Main Ideas** How did the **Emancipation Proclamation** treat the **border states** differently from the Confederate states?
6. **Identify Main Ideas** How did the Supreme Court's ruling in ***Dred Scott* v. *Sandford*** increase sectional tensions?
7. **Recall** What did General Grant do at **Appomattox Court House**?

Critical Thinking and Writing

8. **Compare and Contrast** What different views did John C. Calhoun and Henry Clay express during the conflict over the extension of slavery in 1850?
9. **Identify Main Ideas** How did economic issues during the war impact the North and the South?
10. **Identify Cause and Effect** How did states' rights help cause the Civil War?
11. **Revisit the Central Question** Was the North's participation in the Civil War justified?
12. **Writing Workshop: Write an Informative Essay** Complete writing the essay you have begun on the differences between the North and South before, during, and after the Civil War. Finalize your thesis and introduction. Revise the body paragraphs, using transitions to connect ideas. Then write a conclusion.

Analyze Primary Sources

13. Read the quotation. What does Lincoln most want to achieve?
    - **A.** leave slavery just as it is
    - **B.** keep the Union together
    - **C.** free some enslaved persons
    - **D.** free all enslaved persons

"If I could save the Union without freeing any slave, I would do it; and if I could save it by freeing all the slaves, I would do it; and if I could do it by freeing some and leaving others alone, I would also do that."

—Abraham Lincoln, August 22, 1862, quoted in Carl Sandburg, *Abraham Lincoln*

Analyze Maps

The map shows Union states in blue and Confederate states in gray. Use the map to answer the following questions.

14. Which states were the last to join the Confederacy?
15. For which side did Missouri fight during the Civil War? Why was it called a border state?
16. How many states made up the Confederacy? Which was the farthest west?

▼ **North and South, 1861–1865**

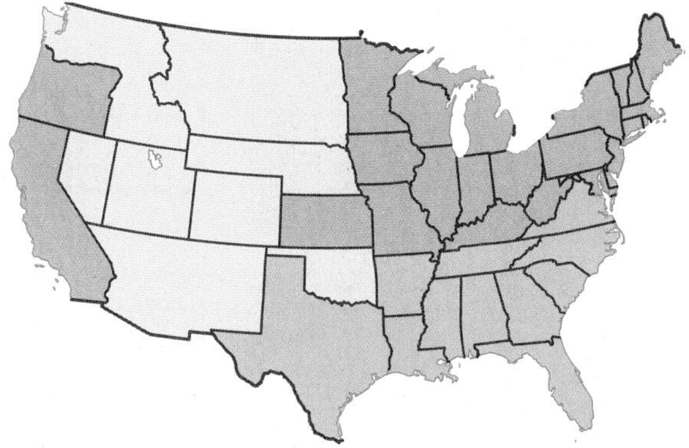

TOPIC 9

The Reconstruction Era (1865–1877)

GO ONLINE to access your digital course

- VIDEO
- AUDIO
- ETEXT
- INTERACTIVE
- WRITING
- GAMES
- WORKSHEET
- ASSESSMENT

Go back 150 years

to THE RECONSTRUCTION ERA following the Civil War. Why? The Union had survived, but big questions loomed: How would free African Americans fit into American society? How could the wounds of war be healed? How could the South be reconstructed?

Explore The Essential Question

How should we handle conflict?

The Reconstruction era was a time of uncertainty, distrust, and deep questioning. How did the United States find the answers?

Unlock the Essential Question in your Active Journal.

Read

how Americans met the challenges of the era and how the nation became one again.

Watch

NBC LEARN

BOUNCE TO ACTIVATE

VIDEO

Born Into Slavery

Learn about life in slavery and the changes that came with emancipation.

TOPIC 9

The Reconstruction Era (1865–1877)

Learn more about the Reconstruction Era by making your own map and timeline in your  Active Journal.

INTERACTIVE
Topic Timeline

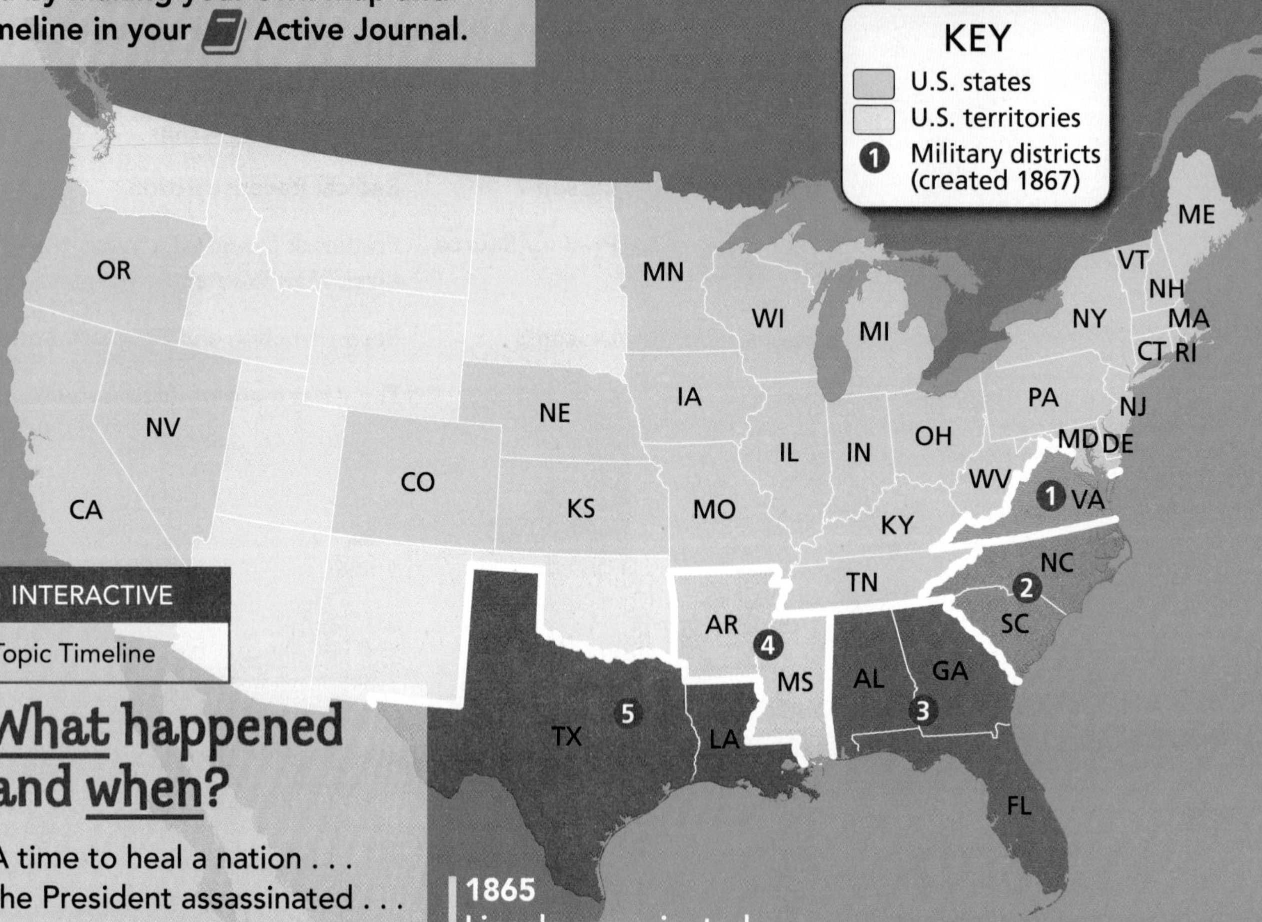

What happened and when?

A time to heal a nation . . . the President assassinated . . . four million African Americans learning to be free . . . many questions and no certain solutions. Explore the timeline to see some of what was going on in the United States and the rest of the world.

TOPIC EVENTS

1865 Lincoln assassinated; Thirteenth Amendment ratified

1866 Civil Rights Act

1867 First Reconstruction Act

1868 Johnson impeached; Fourteenth Amendment ratified; Grant elected president

1865 | **1870**

WORLD EVENTS

1866 Mendel publishes his laws of genetics

1869 Suez Canal opens

1871 End of feudal system in Japan

Topic Map

Where did the Reconstruction Era have its greatest effect?

Reconstruction affected the whole nation, but its greatest impact was on the South. There, state governments had to be rebuilt, the states brought back into the Union, and a ruined economy restarted. And there were four million African Americans who had to discover life as free people.

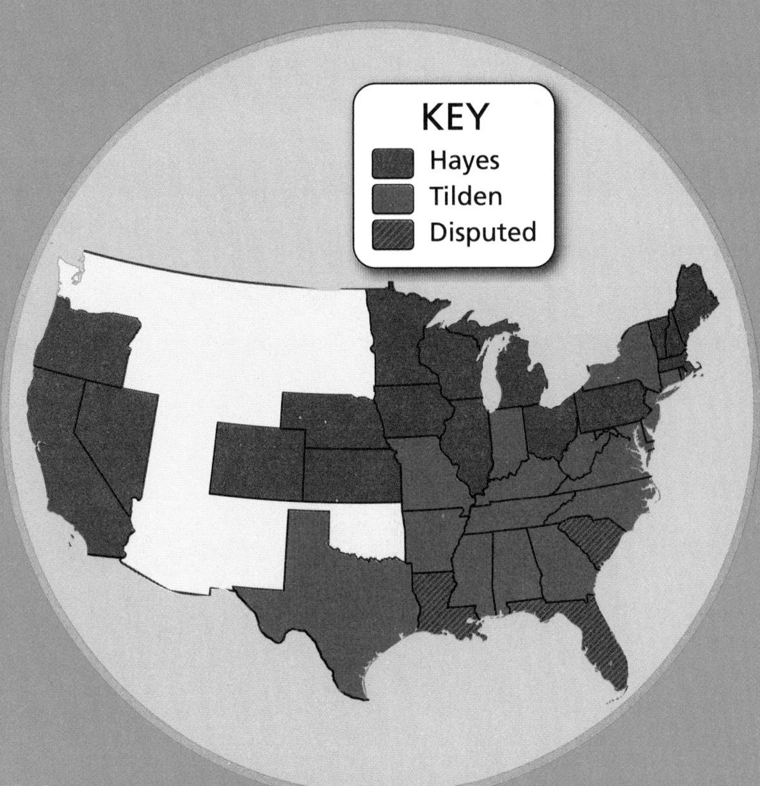

Who will you meet?

Andrew Johnson, president and opponent of strict Reconstruction

Thaddeus Stevens, representative and leader of the Radical Republicans

Blanche K. Bruce, U.S. senator born into slavery

1870 Fifteenth Amendment ratified

1876 Hayes-Tilden election

1875

1880

1872 Yellowstone—world's first national park

1876 Bell patents the telephone

Civic Discussion Inquiry

The End of Reconstruction

Quest KICK OFF

You are a leading scholar writing a multi-volume series on Reconstruction and its impact. Lately, you have been wrestling with a key question:

Should the United States have ended Reconstruction in 1877?

Be ready! Other historians will challenge your arguments. It's time to prepare!

1 Ask Questions

Get started by listing questions about the goals, the successes and failures, and the end of Reconstruction. Write the questions in your Active Journal.

2 Investigate

As you read this Topic, look for Quest Connections that provide information about Reconstruction. Collect your findings in your Active Journal.

3 Examine Sources

Next, explore primary sources that support differing viewpoints about Reconstruction. Capture notes in your Active Journal.

Quest FINDINGS

4 Discuss!

Next, prepare to discuss this question: Should the U.S. have ended Reconstruction in 1877? You will use your knowledge of Reconstruction as well as evidence from sources to make convincing arguments to support your answer.

▼ A Freedman's Bureau School classroom

LESSON 1

Early Reconstruction

GET READY TO READ

START UP

Examine this photograph showing the destruction suffered by the South. List three or four steps the South would have to take to begin rebuilding.

GUIDING QUESTIONS

- What economic, political, and social problems did the United States face after the Civil War?
- What steps were taken initially during Reconstruction?
- How did the assassination of Lincoln and the inauguration of a new President lead to conflict?

TAKE NOTES

Literacy Skills Identify Cause and Effect

Use the graphic organizer in your Active Journal to take notes as you read the lesson.

PRACTICE VOCABULARY

Use the vocabulary activity in your Active Journal to practice the vocabulary words.

Vocabulary		Academic Vocabulary
freedmen	Thirteenth Amendment	alternative
Reconstruction		intervene
amnesty		
Freedmen's Bureau		

At the end of the Civil War, the future looked bleak to many southerners. Across the South, cities and farms lay in ruins. All southerners, Black or white, faced an unfamiliar new world. At the same time, a shattered nation had to find a way to become whole again.

The Effects of the Civil War

After four years of war, both northerners and southerners had to adjust to a changed world. The adjustment was far more difficult in the South.

Problems in the North Despite their victory, northerners faced a number of economic problems. Some 800,000 returning Union soldiers needed jobs. The government was canceling its war orders, and factories were laying off workers. Still, the North's economic disruption was temporary. Boom times quickly returned.

The North lost more soldiers in the war than the South did. However, only a few battles had taken place on northern soil.

Quest CONNECTIONS

What problems did the country face after the Civil War? What problems should Reconstruction be expected to solve? Record your findings in your Active Journal.

Northern farms and cities were hardly touched. One returning Union soldier remarked, "It seemed . . . as if I had been away only a day or two, and had just taken up . . . where I had left off." However, thousands of soldiers suffered wounds from the war, many of which included missing limbs and other painful injuries.

The North faced political problems, too. There was disagreement about how to bring the South back into the Union and what to do with newly freed African Americans. Many wanted to punish southerners for what they had done, while others wanted a more moderate approach.

Problems in the South Economic conditions in the South were far worse than in the North. Confederate soldiers had little chance of taking up where they had left off. In some areas, every house, barn, and bridge had been destroyed.

INTERACTIVE

The Downfall of the Southern Economy

Two thirds of the South's railroad tracks had been turned into twisted heaps of scrap. The cities of Columbia, Richmond, and Atlanta had been leveled.

The war wrecked the South's financial system. After the war, Confederate money was worthless. People who had loaned money to the Confederate government were never repaid. Many southern banks closed, and depositors lost their savings.

The war changed southern society forever. Almost overnight, there was a new class of nearly four million people known as **freedmen**—men and women who had been freed from slavery. Under slavery, they could not own property or learn to read or write. What would become of them? How could the South cope with this drastic change?

These economic and social problems combined with political problems. It was unclear how the southern states would run their governments.

Analyze Images Like other major southern cities, Atlanta lay in ruins after the Civil War. **Use Visual Information** Examine the image and list the types of structures that were destroyed.

No legal systems were in place to protect African Americans, and many white southerners feared African Americans gaining political power. Also, many white politicians who had held office in the Confederacy were forbidden from politics.

Analyze Images For this family, as for many other freedmen, life after emancipation still involved working in the fields for white people. **Draw Conclusions** After their emancipation, why did many freedmen continue to work as farm laborers?

Overall, the economic differences between the agrarian South and industrial North increased after the war. The northern economy picked up, while the South struggled to rebuild. Many white southerners resented northerners coming in to "fix" southern problems. The ruined economy made recovery especially hard.

Environmental Damage from the War Because most of the fighting had been in the South, the region's physical environment suffered heavily from the war.

Many southern farms had become battlefields. Fields and buildings were destroyed, and battle debris littered the landscape. Other farms in the South were deliberately destroyed by Union troops.

Forests were destroyed as well. Soldiers cut down trees to build fortifications and campfires, and artillery and fires damaged other forests.

Animals also suffered. Mules and horses used in the war died by the thousands. Hungry soldiers captured livestock for food. Union soldiers killed the livestock they found as they swept through Georgia.

READING CHECK **Summarize** the political, economic, and social difficulties faced by the South after the war.

Causes and Effects of Reconstruction

The era following the Civil War became known as **Reconstruction**, or the physical, political, and social rebuilding of the South. Lincoln wanted to make it easy for southern states to rejoin the Union. The sooner that happened, he believed, the faster the South could rebuild.

Lincoln's Plan for Reconstruction As early as 1863, Lincoln outlined his Ten Percent Plan for Reconstruction. Under this plan, a southern state could form a new government after 10 percent of its voters swore an oath of loyalty to the United States. The new government had to abolish slavery. Voters could then elect members of Congress and take part in the national government once again.

INTERACTIVE

Lincoln and Reconstruction

Lincoln's plan also offered **amnesty**, or a government pardon, to Confederates who swore loyalty to the Union. Amnesty would not apply to the former leaders of the Confederacy, however.

Quick Activity

What would a Congressional Republican in 1864 have said if asked why the Wade-Davis Bill was the best plan for Reconstruction?

Lincoln Rejects a Rival Proposal Many Republicans in Congress thought the Ten Percent Plan was too generous to the rebels. In 1864, they passed an **alternative** plan, the Wade-Davis Bill. It required a majority of white men in each southern state to swear loyalty to the Union. It also denied the right to vote or hold office to anyone who had volunteered for the Confederacy. Lincoln refused to sign the Wade-Davis Bill because he felt it was too harsh.

Academic Vocabulary
alternative • *adj.*, offering a choice

The Freedmen's Bureau Addresses Economic and Social Needs One month before Lee surrendered, Congress passed a bill creating the **Freedmen's Bureau**, a government agency to help former slaves. Lincoln signed the bill.

The Freedmen's Bureau gave food and clothing to former slaves. It also tried to find jobs for freedmen. The bureau helped poor whites as well. It provided medical care for more than one million people.

One of the bureau's most important tasks was to set up schools for freedmen. Most of the teachers were volunteers, often women from the North. Grandparents and grandchildren sat side by side in the classroom. Charlotte Forten, an African American volunteer from Philadelphia, wrote:

Primary Source

"It is wonderful how a people who have been so long crushed to the earth . . . can have so great a desire for knowledge, and such a capacity for attaining it."

—Charlotte Forten, article in the *Atlantic Monthly*

Analyze Images
Freedmen's Bureau schools like this one aimed to provide skills needed for employment and civic life. **Infer** What do you think would be the most important skills and subjects to teach the former slaves?

The Freedmen's Bureau laid the foundation for the South's public school system. It also created colleges for African Americans, including today's Howard University, Morehouse College, and Fisk University. Many graduates of these schools became teachers themselves. By the 1870s, African Americans were teaching in grade schools throughout the South.

READING CHECK **Check Understanding** Why did President Lincoln want to make it easy for the South to rejoin the Union?

Analyze Images The first stage of Lincoln's funeral processed from the White House to the Capitol. **Compare and Contrast** How did Confederate and Union sympathizers feel about Lincoln's assassination?

Abraham Lincoln Is Assassinated

President Lincoln hoped to persuade Congress to accept his Reconstruction plan. However, he never got the chance.

On April 14, 1865, just five days after Lee's surrender, President Lincoln attended a play at Ford's Theatre in Washington, D.C. A popular actor who supported the Confederate cause, John Wilkes Booth, crept into the President's box and shot Lincoln in the head. Lincoln died the next morning. Booth was later caught and killed in a barn outside the city.

The nation was plunged into grief. The assassination was significant because Lincoln was the first American President to be assassinated. Also, millions who had been celebrating the war's end now mourned Lincoln's death. His body was transported by train for burial in Springfield, Illinois, his hometown. Millions of Americans came to pay their respects along the route. "Now he belongs to the ages," commented Secretary of War Edwin Stanton.

Booth was part of a group of ten conspirators who had long been plotting to kill Lincoln, Vice President Andrew Johnson, and Secretary of State William Seward. None of the other assassinations took place, although Seward was attacked by one of the conspirators. Four of Booth's co-conspirators were hanged for their crimes, including Mary Surratt, the first woman executed by the United States.

READING CHECK **Summarize** the meaning behind Secretary of War Edwin Stanton's statement about Lincoln.

Academic Vocabulary
intervene • *v.*, to interfere in order to stop or change something

President Johnson's Reconstruction Plan

Vice President Andrew Johnson was now President. Johnson had represented Tennessee in Congress. When his state seceded, Johnson had remained loyal to the Union.

The Thirteenth Amendment Changes Life in the United States Republicans in Congress believed Johnson would support a strict Reconstruction plan. But his plan was much milder than expected. It called for a majority of voters in each southern state to pledge loyalty to the United States. Each state also had to ratify the **Thirteenth Amendment**, which banned slavery throughout the nation. (As you read, the Emancipation Proclamation did not free slaves in areas already under Union control.) Congress proposed the Thirteenth Amendment in January 1865. It was ratified in December that year.

The Thirteenth Amendment had a significant impact on life in the United States. Without slavery, the South developed new social and economic systems. Many newly freed African Americans were hired on plantations. Others moved to towns or to the North to find work. Many thousands searched for and reunited with the family members who had been torn away by slavery. For many, Reconstruction meant a chance to rebuild the kinship ties that slavery had severed. And African Americans founded churches, freeing them from another form of white dominance.

Politically, the amendment overturned previous state laws and Supreme Court decisions upholding slavery. The Thirteenth Amendment gave Congress the power to **intervene**, and later to pass additional legislation protecting civil rights.

Fighting in Congress The southern states quickly met Johnson's conditions. While Congress was in recess, the President approved their new state governments in late 1865. Voters in the South then elected representatives to Congress. Many of those elected had held office in the Confederacy. For example, Alexander Stephens, the former vice president of the Confederacy, was elected senator from Georgia.

Analyze Images Although they had been freed, African Americans like this laborer had few opportunities and would struggle for many years to gain even the most basic civil rights. **Use Visual Information** What attitude does this man appear to express? Why do you think he posed for this picture?

Republicans in Congress were outraged. The men who had led the South out of the Union were being elected to the House and Senate. Plus, no southern state allowed African Americans to vote.

When the new Congress met, Republicans refused to let southern representatives serve. Instead, they set up a Joint Committee on Reconstruction to form a new plan for the South. The stage was set for a showdown between Congress and the President.

READING CHECK Compare and Contrast Which key difference between Lincoln's and Johnson's Reconstruction plans caused problems in 1865?

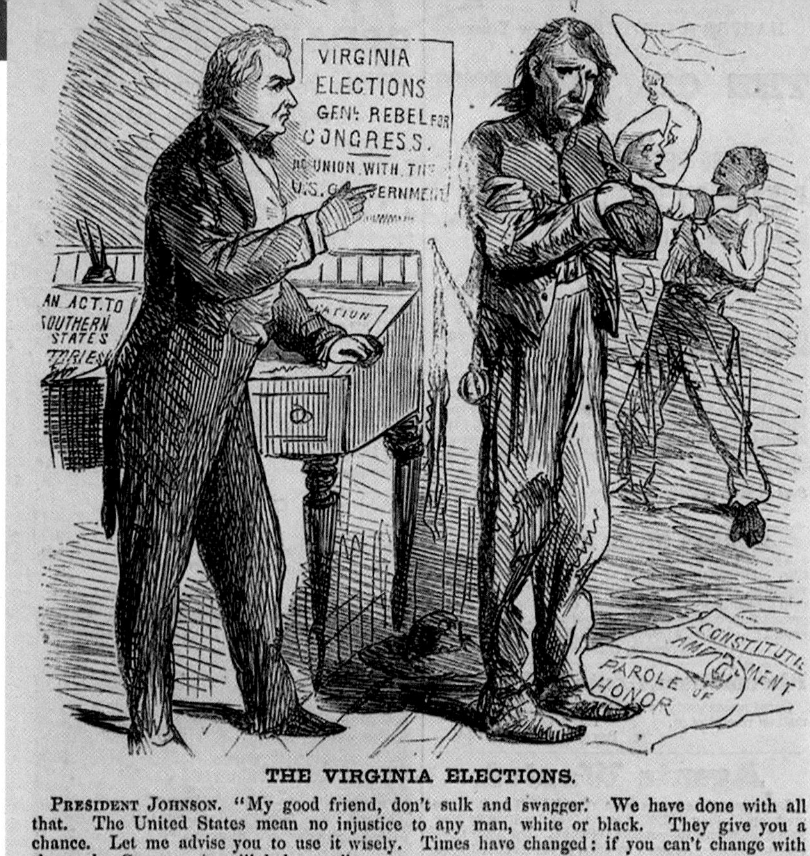

THE VIRGINIA ELECTIONS.

PRESIDENT JOHNSON. "My good friend, don't sulk and swagger. We have done with all that. The United States mean no injustice to any man, white or black. They give you a chance. Let me advise you to use it wisely. Times have changed: if you can't change with them, the Government will help you."

Analyze Political Cartoons In this cartoon, President Johnson sympathizes with a former rebel while ignoring cruelty to a former slave. **Draw Conclusions** Which side of the debate between Johnson and Congress does the cartoonist support? How do you know?

Lesson Check

Practice Vocabulary

1. In what ways was **amnesty** an important part of **Reconstruction**?
2. Who were the **freedmen**, and what was the purpose of the **Freedmen's Bureau**?
3. What was the purpose of the **Thirteenth Amendment**?

Critical Thinking and Writing

4. **Identify Main Ideas** What problems did the South face after the Civil War that the North did not?
5. **Understand Effects** Why did Republicans in Congress refuse to let newly elected southern representatives take their seats?
6. **Writing Workshop: Generate Questions to Focus Research** You will be writing a research paper on the Freedmen's Bureau and its effects, and the restrictions placed on the rights and opportunities of African Americans in the Reconstruction-era South. In your Active Journal, write questions that will help you narrow your research on the topic.

LESSON 2

Radical Reconstruction

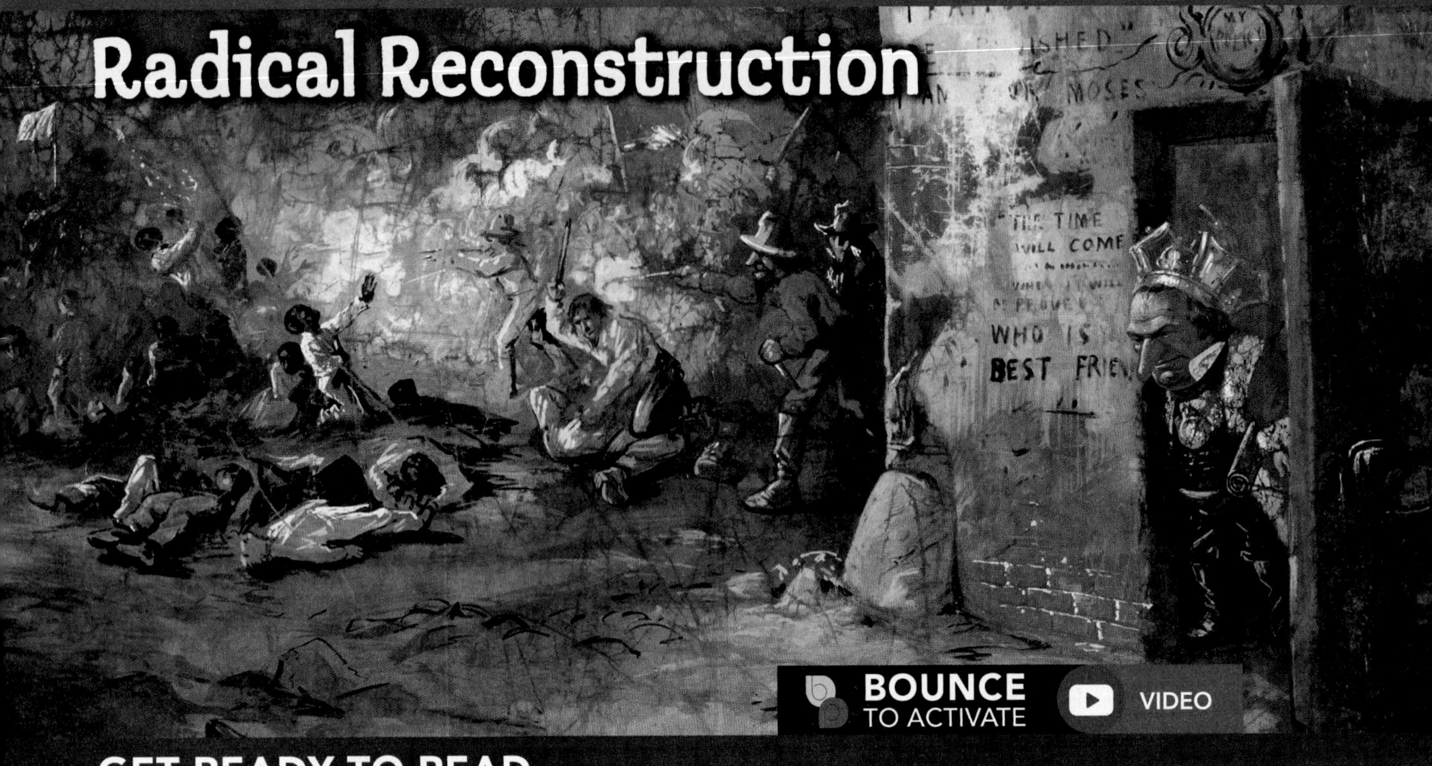

BOUNCE TO ACTIVATE VIDEO

GET READY TO READ

START UP

According to the cartoon, what role did President Johnson (shown with a big, red nose) have in the 1866 New Orleans race riots?

GUIDING QUESTIONS

- How did Congress react to the Black codes?
- Why was President Johnson impeached?
- How did Reconstruction redefine what it meant to be an American?

TAKE NOTES

Literacy Skills Identify Supporting Details

Use the graphic organizer in your Active Journal to take notes as you read the lesson.

PRACTICE VOCABULARY

Use the vocabulary activity in your Active Journal to practice the vocabulary words.

Vocabulary		Academic Vocabulary
Black codes	Reconstruction Act	capability
Radical Republicans	impeach	imposition
Fourteenth Amendment	Fifteenth Amendment	

Under Johnson's Reconstruction plan, most southern states promptly ratified the Thirteenth Amendment. However, southern legislatures also passed **Black codes**, laws that severely limited the rights of freed African Americans. Their purpose was to confine African Americans to an underclass to serve as a source of cheap labor.

Continuing Conflict Over Reconstruction

The Black codes did grant some rights. For example, African Americans could marry legally and own some kinds of property. Still, the codes were clearly meant to keep them from gaining political and economic power.

Restrictions in the South Black codes forbade African Americans to vote, own guns, and serve on juries. In some states, African Americans were permitted to work only as servants or farm laborers. In others, they had to sign contracts for a year's work. Those without contracts could be arrested and sentenced to work on a plantation.

Reconstruction Turns Radical Republicans charged that Johnson's Reconstruction plan was so lenient that it had encouraged southern legislatures to pass the Black codes. Republicans were also outraged by reports of violence against African Americans. In 1866, white police officers in Memphis, Tennessee, attacked African American Union soldiers, who fired back at the officers. A protest against the police ended in violence, and rioting broke out. Angry white people burned homes and schools in a Black neighborhood. Moves to vote by African Americans sparked similar riots in New Orleans.

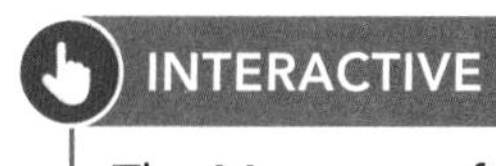

The Massacre of New Orleans

A report by the Joint Committee on Reconstruction accused the South of trying to "preserve slavery . . . as long as possible." When President Johnson ignored the report, members of Congress called **Radical Republicans** vowed to take control of Reconstruction.

READING CHECK **Understand Effects** Why were Radical Republicans outraged at President Johnson's approach to Reconstruction?

The Radical Reconstruction Congress

The Radicals were led by Thaddeus Stevens of Pennsylvania in the House and Charles Sumner of Massachusetts in the Senate. Radical Republicans had two main goals. First, they wanted to break the power of wealthy planters who had long ruled the South. Second, they wanted to ensure that people freed from slavery received the right to vote.

Legislative Reform Radicals needed the support of moderate Republicans, the largest group in Congress. Despite disagreements, Moderates and Radicals shared a common interest. Most white southerners were Democrats. With former Confederates barred from Congress, Republicans could control both houses.

To combat the Black codes, Congress passed the Civil Rights Act in April 1866. It gave citizenship to African Americans. When Johnson vetoed the bill, Congress overrode the veto.

▼ Senator Charles Sumner of Massachusetts

The Fourteenth Amendment Republicans feared that the Supreme Court might use its power of judicial review to declare the Civil Rights Act unconstitutional. To avoid such a ruling, Republicans supported the **Fourteenth Amendment**. It defines citizens as "all persons born or naturalized in the United States." Thus, the amendment voided the Dred Scott decision of 1857, in which Chief Justice Roger B. Taney wrote that African Americans were not and never could be citizens.

The Fourteenth Amendment guarantees citizens "equal protection of the laws" and forbids states to "deprive any person of life, liberty, or property without due process of law." Thus, states could not legally discriminate against a citizen on unreasonable grounds, such as race. The amendment did not apply to most American Indians.

Academic Vocabulary
capability • *n.*, ability, capacity

Under the Fourteenth Amendment, any state that denied any male citizen age 21 or older the right to vote would have its representation in Congress reduced. Republicans believed that African Americans would have the **capability** to defend their rights if they could vote.

The Fourteenth Amendment was proposed by Congress in 1866. It was not ratified for another two years. Republicans hoped the amendment would secure basic political rights for African Americans in the South. That goal would take a century to achieve. In the 1950s, the Fourteenth Amendment's Equal Protection Clause became a powerful tool in the struggle for civil rights.

READING CHECK **Identify Cause and Effect** Why did Republicans believe that the Fourteenth Amendment was necessary?

Analyze Images Thaddeus Stevens led the House in nullifying President Johnson's Reconstruction plan. **Draw Conclusions** What ideals motivated Stevens and the Radical Republicans?

New Rules for the South

President Johnson encouraged former Confederate states to reject the Fourteenth Amendment. He also decided to make the amendment an issue in the 1866 congressional elections.

Republicans Take Over Congress Across the North, Johnson urged voters to reject the Radicals. When a heckler yelled for Johnson to hang Jefferson Davis, Johnson shouted, "Why not hang Thad Stevens?"

In July, riots in New Orleans killed 34 African Americans who had gathered in support of a convention backing voting rights. White mobs attacked the crowd and fired into the convention. The violence convinced many northerners that stronger measures were needed. In the end, Republicans won majorities in both houses of Congress. African Americans were beginning to participate in elections. Almost all were Republicans and helped contribute to the Republicans' majority in Congress.

Rival Plans for Reconstruction

PLAN	TEN PERCENT PLAN	WADE-DAVIS BILL	JOHNSON PLAN	RECONSTRUCTION ACT
Proposed by	President Abraham Lincoln (1863)	Republicans in Congress (1864)	President Andrew Johnson (1865)	Radical Republicans (1867)
Conditions for Former Confederate States to Rejoin Union	• 10 percent of voters must swear loyalty to Union • Must abolish slavery	• Majority of white men must swear loyalty • Former Confederate volunteers cannot vote or hold office • Wartime debts by states will not be recognized	• Majority of white men must swear loyalty • Must ratify Thirteenth Amendment • Former Confederate officials may vote and hold office • Each state would be appointed a governor chosen by the president	• Must disband state governments • Must write new constitutions • Must ratify Fourteenth Amendment • African American men must be allowed to vote • Must disqualify former officials of the Confederacy from holding public office

Military Rule in the South In 1867, Republicans in Congress prepared to take charge of Reconstruction. With huge majorities in both houses, Congress could easily override vetoes. The period that followed is often called Radical Reconstruction.

Congress passed the first **Reconstruction Act** in March 1867. It threw out the state governments that had refused to ratify the Fourteenth Amendment—all the former Confederate states except Tennessee. The Military Reconstruction Acts of 1867 divided the southern states into five military districts, each governed by a military general.

Military rulers in these military districts had nearly unlimited power. They sometimes conducted trials without juries. Many white southerners bitterly resented the **imposition** of military rule. They argued that the military occupation violated their rights because it was done without their consent or representation.

Congress, however, imposed strict requirements. To rejoin the Union, former Confederate states had to write new constitutions and ratify the Fourteenth Amendment. The Reconstruction Act also required that southern states allow African Americans to vote.

With the new constitutions in place, reconstructed states held elections to set up new state governments. The Fourteenth Amendment barred former Confederate officials from voting. Many other white southerners avoided voting in protest. Protected by the army, African Americans proudly exercised their new right to vote. Most favored the Republican party, since it had supported their rights. As a result, Republicans gained control of all of the new southern state governments.

READING CHECK **Generate Explanations** On what basis did white southerners argue against the Military Reconstruction Acts?

Analyze Charts Four plans for reconstructing the states that had seceded were proposed. **Compare and Contrast** In what ways did the Reconstruction Act of 1867 place more restrictions on former Confederate states than had previous plans?

Academic Vocabulary
imposition • *n.*, something applied or created based on authority

Did you know?

As a U.S. senator in 1861, Andrew Johnson continued to serve in the Senate even though his home state of Tennessee had seceded.

Political Problems and a New President

Congress passed other Reconstruction acts over Johnson's veto. As President, Johnson had a duty to execute, or carry out, the new laws. However, Johnson did what he could to limit their effect. For instance, he fired military commanders who supported Radical Reconstruction. Republicans in Congress decided to try to remove Johnson from office.

President Johnson on Trial On February 24, 1868, the House of Representatives voted to **impeach**, or bring formal charges against, Johnson. According to the Constitution, the House may impeach a president for "treason, bribery, or other high crimes and misdemeanors." The president is removed from office if found guilty by two thirds of the Senate.

During Johnson's trial, it became clear that he was not guilty of high crimes and misdemeanors. Even Charles Sumner, Johnson's bitter foe, admitted that the charges were "political in character." Despite intense pressure, seven Republican senators refused to vote for conviction. The Constitution, they said, did not allow Congress to remove a president just because they disagreed with him. In the end, the vote was 35 to 19—one vote shy of the two thirds needed to convict.

Grant Wins the Election of 1868 Johnson served out the few remaining months of his term. In May 1868, Republicans nominated the Union's greatest war hero, Ulysses S. Grant, for president.

In July 1868, the Fourteenth Amendment was ratified, granting citizenship to African Americans and guaranteeing equal protection of the laws. Former Confederate states were still required to ratify the amendment before they could be readmitted to the Union.

Analyze Graphs Once the Radical Republicans got into office, Congress's stand on protecting African Americans' rights was surprisingly consistent. **Summarize** How would you describe congressional support for the Fourteenth and Fifteenth Amendments?

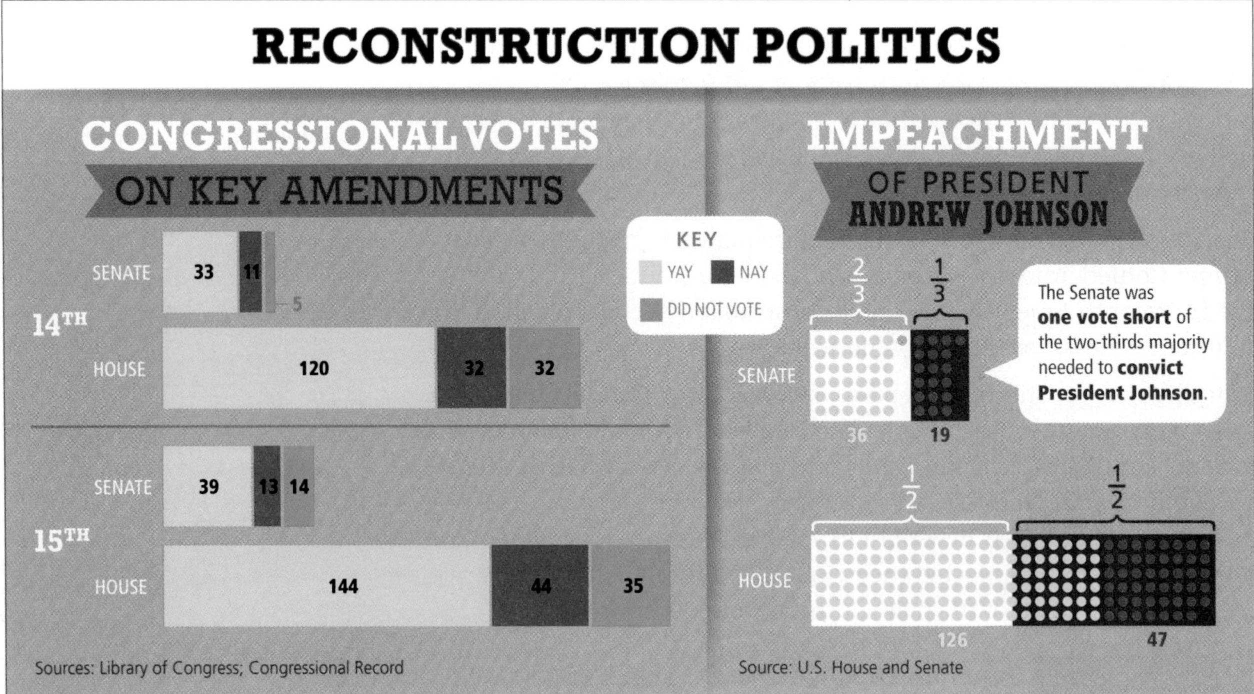

By election day, Texas, Mississippi, and Virginia had still not ratified the Fourteenth Amendment and were unable to vote. Most southern states had ratified the amendment and rejoined the Union, but some former Confederates in these states were still not allowed to vote. In addition, as required by the 1867 Reconstruction Act, the southern states allowed African American men to vote. About 500,000 Black men voted—nearly all of them for Grant. Grant won six states that had been part of the Confederacy. With support from most northerners as well, he easily won the election.

The Fifteenth Amendment In 1869, Congress proposed the **Fifteenth Amendment**. It forbids any state to deny any citizen the right to vote because of "race, color, or previous condition of servitude."

Republicans had moral and political reasons for supporting the Fifteenth Amendment. They remembered the great sacrifices made by African American soldiers in the Civil War. They also felt it was wrong to let African Americans vote in the South but not in the North. In addition, Republicans knew that if African Americans could vote in the North, they would help Republicans win elections there.

Analyze Images This illustration shows African Americans voting for the first time in 1868. **Draw Conclusions** Why did the artist show different types of African American citizens?

The Fifteenth Amendment was ratified in 1870. At last, all African American men over age 21 had the right to vote.

The Fifteenth Amendment was difficult to enforce, and white southern conservatives were determined to find ways around it. It was not until the mid-1900s that new legislation began to effectively protect voting rights and the full impact of the amendment was felt.

READING CHECK **Identify Cause and Effect** Why did some Republican senators refuse to vote to convict Johnson?

Lesson Check

Practice Vocabulary

1. What rights were secured for African Americans by the **Fourteenth Amendment** and the **Fifteenth Amendment**?
2. Why did Republicans **impeach** President Johnson?

Critical Thinking and Writing

3. **Generate Explanations** Why were the Black codes so restrictive?
4. **Draw Conclusions** Why was the Republican plan for Reconstruction called Radical Reconstruction?
5. **Writing Workshop: Find and Use Credible Sources** Begin doing research on your paper on the Freedmen's Bureau. Look for reliable sources. Take notes on information you may use in your paper. Record web addresses and other source information in your Active Journal so you can find them again.

Primary Sources

Frederick Douglass, "What the Black Man Wants"

In April 1865, millions of enslaved Americans were on the verge of being freed. White Americans wondered what to do. Douglass explained what he thought Black people wanted.

◀ Frederick Douglass

Reading and Vocabulary Support

① *Deprivation* means the fact of having something valuable taken away.

② To "exercise the elective franchise" means to make use of the right to vote.

③ Benevolence is kindness.

④ What is the meaning of this metaphor about the apples?

We may be asked, I say, why we want [the right to vote]. I will tell you why we want it. We want it because it is our right, first of all. No class of men can, without insulting their own nature, be content with any deprivation ① of their rights. We want it, again, as a means for educating our race. Men are so constituted that they derive their conviction of their own possibilities largely from the estimate formed of them by others. If nothing is expected of a people, that people will find it difficult to contradict that expectation. By depriving us of suffrage, you affirm our incapacity to form an intelligent judgment respecting public men and public measures; you declare before the world that we are unfit to exercise the elective franchise ②, and by this means lead us to undervalue ourselves, to put a low estimate upon ourselves, and to feel that we have no possibilities like other men. . . .

What I ask for the negro is not benevolence ③, not pity, not sympathy, but simply justice. The American people have always been anxious to know what they shall do with us. . . . I have had but one answer from the beginning. Do nothing with us! Your doing with us has already played the mischief with us. Do nothing with us! If the apples will not remain on the tree of their own strength, if they are worm-eaten at the core, if they are early ripe and disposed to fall, let them fall! ④ . . . And if the negro cannot stand on his own legs, let him fall also. All I ask is, give him a chance to stand on his own legs! Let him alone! If you see him on his way to school, let him alone,—don't disturb him! If you see him going to the dinner-table at a hotel, let him go! If you see him going to the ballot-box, let him alone,—don't disturb him!

Quest CONNECTIONS

What did Frederick Douglass want Reconstruction to achieve? How did his goals for Reconstruction compare with those of others? Record your findings in your Active Journal.

Analyzing Primary Sources

Cite specific evidence from the document to support your answers.

1. **Understand Effects** What effect does depriving Black men of suffrage have on them?
2. **Determine Author's Point of View** What is Douglass's main message in this excerpt?

Distinguish Essential from Incidental Information

INTERACTIVE

Identify Evidence

Follow these steps to help you distinguish essential from incidental information.

1 **Identify a focus or topic.** Set a purpose for your research. What exactly are you trying to find out? What key questions are you trying to answer? What idea or event are you trying to understand?

2 **Locate your sources.** The sources you choose will depend on your focus and topic.

3 **Identify information that is essential to your topic.** Based on your focus, what information will help you achieve your goal? What kinds of data will answer questions or increase your understanding?

4 **Identify Information that is incidental to your topic.** Remember the focus you have set for your research. Information that is not related to this focus is incidental. For example, suppose you want to use the information in the chart to learn about Andrew Johnson's plan for Reconstruction. Information about Johnson's impeachment might be accurate, but it is incidental to your topic. Which of the statements are incidental to your research? Which are essential?

President Andrew Johnson and Radical Reconstruction
Johnson supported a mild Reconstruction plan that called for a majority of voters in each southern state to pledge loyalty to the United States.
Johnson required states to ratify the Thirteenth Amendment as a condition of re-entering the union.
When southern states met his requirements for readmission to the Union, Johnson quickly approved their new state governments.
When President Lincoln was assassinated, Johnson became President. He took over the task of implementing Reconstruction.
Republicans were outraged when southern states that had been readmitted elected former Confederate officeholders to Congress.
The Radical Republicans were led in the House by Thaddeus Stevens of Pennsylvania and in the Senate by Charles Sumner of Massachusetts.
Republicans were angry when southern states enacted Black codes that restricted the rights of African Americans.

LESSON 3

Reconstruction and Southern Society

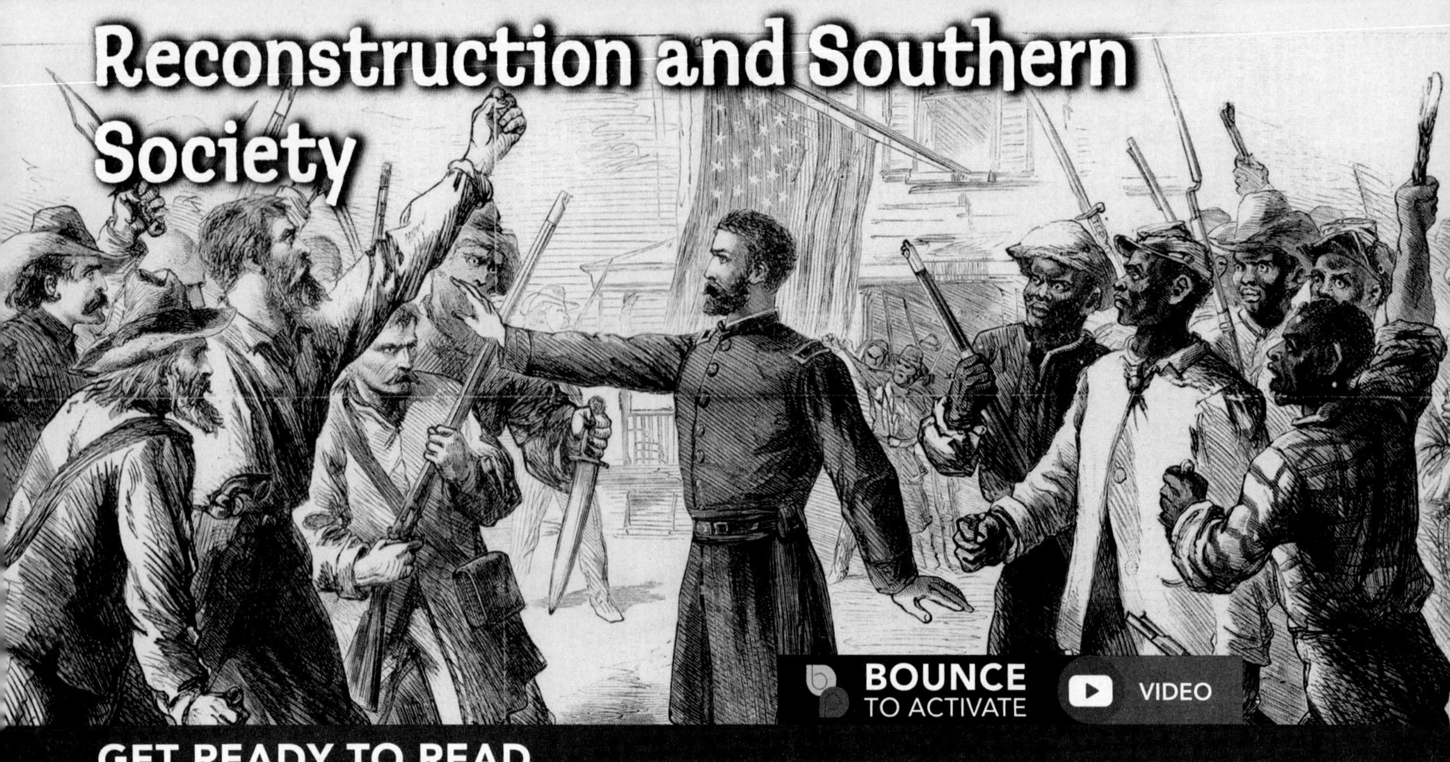

GET READY TO READ

START UP

In this image, a member of the Freedmen's Bureau holds off outraged white men. Look at other images and headings in this topic, then write two predictions of what you will read about.

GUIDING QUESTIONS

- How did white southerners resist Reconstruction?
- What economic, political, and social challenges faced Reconstruction governments?
- How did Reconstruction redefine what it meant to be an American?

TAKE NOTES

Literacy Skills Summarize

Use the graphic organizer in your Active Journal to take notes as you read the lesson.

PRACTICE VOCABULARY

Use the vocabulary activity in your Active Journal to practice the vocabulary words.

Vocabulary		Academic Vocabulary
scalawag	Ku Klux Klan	notorious
carpetbagger	sharecropper	anticipate

Before the Civil War, a small group of rich planters dominated politics in the South. During Reconstruction, however, new groups tried to reshape southern politics.

How Did New Political Groups Shape the South?

The state governments created during Radical Reconstruction were different from any governments the South had known before. The old leaders had lost much of their influence. Three groups stepped in to replace them.

White Southern Republicans One group to emerge consisted of white southerners who supported the new Republican governments. Many were businesspeople who had opposed secession in 1860. They wanted to forget the war and get on with rebuilding the South.

However, many white people in the South felt that any southerner who helped the Republicans was a traitor. They called the white southern Republicans **scalawags**, a word used for small, scruffy horses.

Northerners Many northerners came to the South after the war. White southerners accused the new arrivals of hoping to get rich from the South's misery. White southerners jested that these northerners were in such a hurry to move south that they had time only to fling a few clothes into carpetbags, a type of cheap suitcase. They became known as **carpetbaggers**.

In fact, northerners went south for various reasons. While a few did hope to profit as the South rebuilt, many more were Union soldiers who had grown to love the South's rich land. Others, both white and Black, were teachers, ministers, and reformers who wanted to help the people freed from slavery succeed in their new lives.

INTERACTIVE

Reconstruction-Era Political Groups

African Americans African Americans were the third major new group in southern politics. Before the war, they had no voice in government. During Reconstruction, they not only voted in large numbers, but they also ran for and were elected to public office. They became sheriffs, mayors, and legislators in the new state and local governments. As well, sixteen African Americans were elected to the United States Congress between 1869 and 1880.

Two African Americans, both representing Mississippi, served in the Senate. In 1870, Hiram Rhodes Revels, a clergyman and teacher, became the nation's first Black senator. He completed the unfinished term of former Confederate president Jefferson Davis. In 1874, Blanche Kelso Bruce became the first African American elected to a full term in the Senate. Bruce served from 1875 to 1881.

Analyze Images This illustration shows the first seven African Americans to serve in Congress, including Hiram Revels (far left). **Identify Cause and Effect** What changes made it possible to elect freedmen to national office?

BIOGRAPHY
5 Things to Know About

BLANCHE K. BRUCE

First African American elected to a full term in the U.S. Senate (1841–1898)

- Although born into slavery, Bruce received a good education as a child and attended Oberlin College for two years.
- At age 21 he won his freedom by escaping to Kansas.
- In 1864, he opened the first school for African American children in Missouri.
- The Mississippi legislature elected Bruce to the U.S. Senate in 1874, while the state was under military governance.
- As Senator, Bruce spoke out for fair treatment of African Americans and Native Americans.

Critical Thinking What was the significance of African Americans being elected to public office?

Revels's election was an important victory for African Americans. He served on the Committee on Education and Labor, where he opposed attempts to segregate, or separate, schools for African American and white children. He also tried to help African American workers.

African Americans did not dominate any southern state, however. Only in South Carolina did African Americans win a majority in one house of the state legislature. No state elected a Black governor.

Did you know?

After Blanche Bruce's election in 1874, no African American was elected to the Senate until Edward Brooke, of Massachusetts, in 1966.

READING CHECK **Describe** how politics in the South changed during Reconstruction.

Why Did White Southerners Resist Reform?

Most white southerners who had held power before the Civil War resisted Reconstruction. These people resented the changes required by Congress and enforced by the military. Some white southerners were willing to let some African Americans vote and hold a few offices, but they were determined to keep real power in the hands of white people. A few wealthy planters tried to force African Americans back onto plantations. Many white small farmers and laborers wanted the government to take action against African Americans, who now competed with them for land and power.

Most white southerners were Democrats. They declared war on anyone who cooperated with the Republicans. "This is a white man's country," declared one southern senator, "and white men must govern it."

Academic Vocabulary

notorious • *adj.,* well known for some bad quality or effect

The Ku Klux Klan Some white southerners formed secret societies to help them regain power. The most **notorious** was the **Ku Klux Klan**, or KKK. The Klan worked to keep African Americans and white Republicans out of office.

Dressed in white robes and hoods to hide their identities, Klansmen rode at night to the homes of African American voters, shouting threats and burning wooden crosses. When threats did not work, the Klan turned to violence. Klan members murdered hundreds of African Americans and their white allies.

The Klan's Reign of Terror Many moderate white southerners condemned the Klan's violence, but most did little to stop the reign of terror. Turning to the federal government, African Americans pled for help, as in this letter from a group in Kentucky:

Primary Source

"We believe you are not familiar with the Ku Klux Klan's riding nightly over the country spreading terror wherever they go by robbing, whipping, and killing our people without provocation."

—Records of the U.S. Senate, April 11, 1871

In 1870, Congress made it a crime to use force to keep people from voting. Klan activities decreased, but the threat of violence remained. Some African Americans continued to vote and hold office, but others were frightened away from the ballot box.

READING CHECK **Explain** the social and political impact of white southern opponents of Reconstruction.

How Did Political Problems Slow Progress?

Republican-dominated governments tried to rebuild the South. They made notable advances. They established the first publicly financed school systems in the South. These provided education for both Black and white children.

Many states gave women the right to own property and otherwise expanded women's rights. In some cases, the legislatures provided debt relief for the poor.

In addition, Reconstruction governments rebuilt railroads, telegraph lines, bridges, and roads. Between 1865 and 1879, the South laid 7,000 miles of railroad track. However, progress was hindered by economic difficulties, white resistance to reform, and government corruption.

Analyze Political Cartoons Both the KKK and White League used violence to try to prevent African Americans from voting. **Infer** What does the phrase "worse than slavery" suggest about the effect of this violence on African American families?

Taxation and Voting Rights Before the war, southerners paid low taxes, but rebuilding the South cost money, and taxes rose sharply. This created discontent among many southern whites. Many former Confederate officers and officials resented being denied voting rights while people they considered inferior were allowed to vote. The tax increases also caused some landowners to lose their land.

Widespread Corruption Southerners were further angered by reports of widespread corruption in the Reconstruction governments. One state legislature, for example, voted $1,000 to cover a member's bet on a horse race. Other items billed to the state included hams, perfume, and a coffin.

Mixed Results for Legislative Reform State legislative reform in the South met with mixed success. New state constitutions allowed all adult men to vote, removed restrictions for holding office, and made public officials elected rather than appointed. Executive branches were given increased power to provide government services.

However, legislation to enroll voters was hindered by new restrictions that kept many African Americans from registering or voting. Many of the laws preventing former Confederates from voting and holding office did not last. In Georgia, African Americans were forced from the state legislature.

READING CHECK **Summarize** the problems that faced Reconstruction governments trying to rebuild the South.

Analyze Images This 1872 newspaper cartoon was titled "Lincoln, the Emancipator." **Synthesize Visual Information** What are the people in the cartoon doing? Why?

Economic Problems in the South

In the first months after the war, many freedmen left the plantations on which they had lived and worked. Some searched for family members. Others went in search of work. They found few opportunities, however.

Freedmen Have Limited Opportunities Some Radical Republicans talked about giving each freedman "40 acres and a mule" as a fresh start. This idea stemmed from a field order given by General William Tecumseh Sherman in 1865. Thaddeus Stevens suggested breaking up big plantations and distributing the land. Most Americans opposed the plan, however. In the end, former slaves received—in the words of a freedman—"nothing but freedom."

Through hard work or good luck, some people freed from slavery did become landowners. Most, however, felt they had little choice but to return to where they had lived in slavery. Meanwhile, large planters had land and needed people to work it.

Rebuilding the South's Economy Before the Civil War, southern planters enjoyed prosperity because of strong demand for cotton, tobacco, and other farm products in the North and in Britain and Europe. During the war, a Union blockade cut off those markets. As a result, worldwide prices for those products rose, and suppliers in Latin America, India, and elsewhere began producing more tobacco, cotton, sugar cane, and rice. When the war ended and southern farmers returned to the market, they faced much greater competition from foreign producers. Predictably, according to the laws of supply and demand, this led to lower prices and less income. Some farmers went into debt and lost their land.

Analyze Images This photograph shows a group of people freed from slavery in Richmond, Virginia. **Identify Main Ideas** Why did many such people have trouble finding jobs?

Meanwhile, the war had destroyed many of the South's cities and factories. Moreover, Southern planters had lost their enslaved workers, who were often a planter's main investment. As a result, the South had little money to invest in industry. It remained dependent on farming at a time when farming brought less income.

Poverty in the South During Reconstruction, many poor white and formerly enslaved people became **sharecroppers** on plantations. As sharecroppers, they rented and farmed a plot of land in exchange for a share of the crop at harvest time. They also often bought seed, fertilizer, and tools on credit, to be paid for with an additional share of their crop. To people newly free, sharecropping offered a measure of independence. Many **anticipated** owning their own land one day.

Academic Vocabulary
anticipate • *v.*, expect or look ahead to

In fact, this arrangement locked sharecroppers into a cycle of poverty. Each spring, they received supplies on credit. In the fall, they used their harvest to repay what they had borrowed. Since prices for farm products were low, the harvest often did not cover what they owed. Each year they fell further behind. Instead of rising toward independence, they sank deeper into debt.

The Cycle of Poverty

Analyze Images This photograph shows freedmen planting sugar cane in Georgia in the late 1860s. **Identify Cause and Effect** What impact did sharecropping have on African Americans' economic status?

Sharecropping was not the only way formerly enslaved people could be trapped in peonage, or debt slavery. Under new laws against vagrancy, Black men were stopped, arrested, and fined for being unemployed. Victims who could not pay the fine would be imprisoned and forced to work without pay. Sometimes, a local business owner would offer to pay the fine in exchange for a term of servitude. If the paperwork became lost, a victim might never regain his freedom.

READING CHECK **Express Problems Clearly** What was the biggest problem with sharecropping?

Lesson Check

Practice Vocabulary

1. What were the differences between **scalawags** and **carpetbaggers**?
2. What was the **Ku Klux Klan**, and what did it try to accomplish?
3. Why did **sharecroppers** often end up in debt?

Critical Thinking and Writing

4. **Summarize** why white southern Democrats resisted Reconstruction.
5. **Identify Main Ideas** What were the central challenges to rebuilding the South?
6. **Writing Workshop: Support Ideas With Evidence** Outline your research paper by writing your main ideas. Under each main idea, write facts and other evidence from your research that support that idea.

Interpret Thematic Maps

Follow these steps to review the ways to analyze a thematic map.

INTERACTIVE
Read Special-Purpose Maps

1 Identify the type and general topic of the thematic map. Often, the map title indicates both the general type of map and its specific topic. If it does not, look at the key to see what kind of information the map shows. After studying the map briefly, make a general statement about the topic of this map.

2 Determine the place shown on the map. Map titles often indicate the region shown. If not, look at the map. Do the colors give you any clues? Often, surrounding regions, states, or countries are shown in a single neutral color. Areas that are the main focus of the map may have colors that make them stand out. What do the colors used on the map suggest is the main area covered by the map?

3 Determine the time period shown on the map. If no dates are indicated in the map title or key, the map probably represents the present time. What time period is shown on this map?

4 Explain what the map shows. Use the key to analyze the information shown on the map. The key explains special symbols and colors used on the map and indicates what kinds of information you can find on the map. In a few sentences, summarize the information shown on this map.

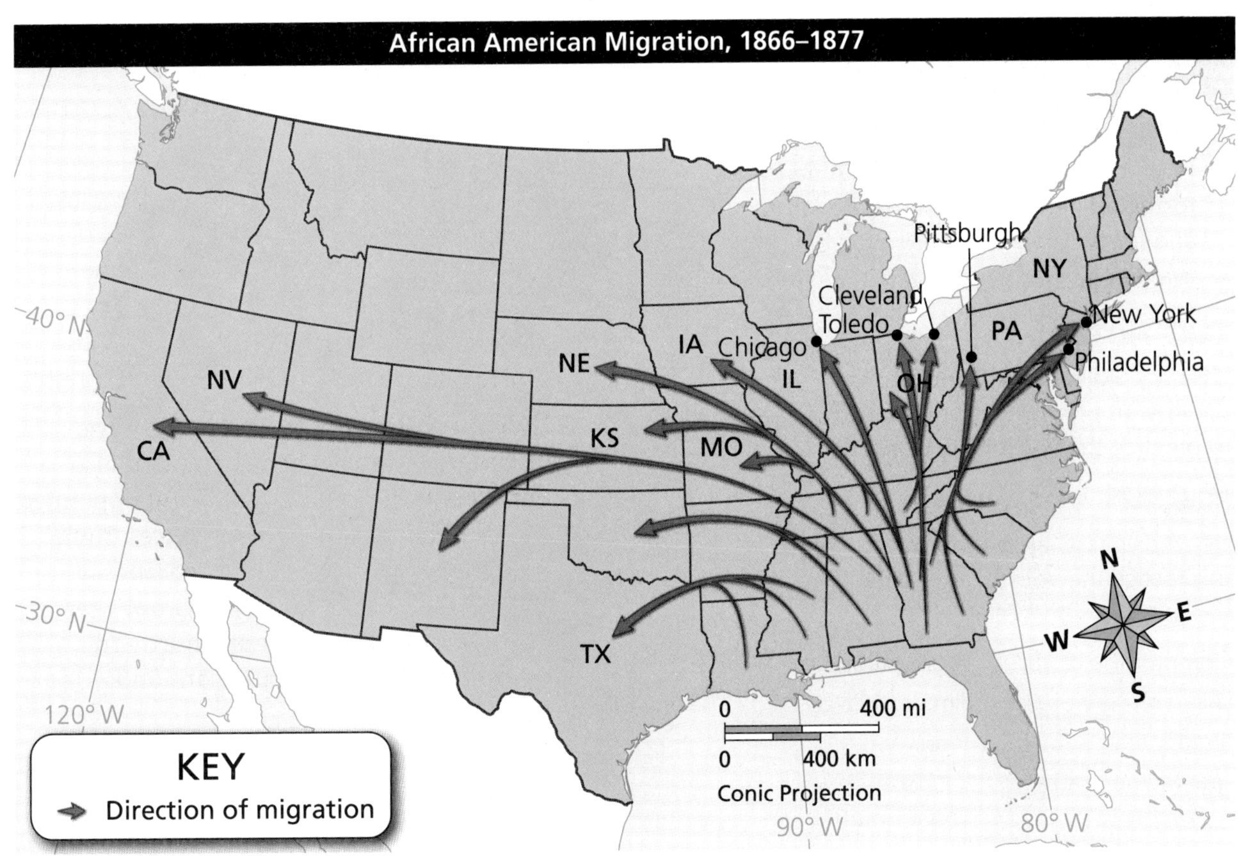

LESSON 4

The Aftermath of Reconstruction

GET READY TO READ

START UP

How might massive rebuilding in the South change these freedmen's lives and the future southern economy?

GUIDING QUESTIONS

- What events led to the end of Reconstruction?
- How were the rights of African Americans restricted in the South during Reconstruction and for decades afterward?
- What industries flourished in the "New South"?

TAKE NOTES

Literacy Skills Draw Conclusions

Use the graphic organizer in your Active Journal to practice the vocabulary words.

PRACTICE VOCABULARY

Use the vocabulary activity in your Active Journal to practice the vocabulary words.

Vocabulary

Compromise of 1877
poll tax
literacy test
grandfather clause
segregation
Jim Crow laws
Plessy v. *Ferguson*
"New South"

Academic Vocabulary

employ
specifically

Reconstruction had brought both positive change and turmoil to the South. The end of Reconstruction led to new hardships for African Americans in the South.

How Did Reconstruction Come to an End?

By the 1870s, Radical Republicans were losing power. Many northerners grew weary of trying to reform the South. It was time to let white southerners return to power, they believed—even if it meant that African Americans in the South might lose their rights.

Political Changes In the South The disclosure of widespread corruption also hurt Republicans. President Grant appointed many friends to government offices. Some used their position to steal large sums of money from the government. Grant won reelection in 1872, but many northerners had lost faith in Republicans and their policies.

Congress passed the Amnesty Act in 1872. It restored the right to vote to nearly all white southerners, including former Confederates.

These white southerners voted solidly Democratic. At the same time, they **employed** violence in order to prevent African Americans from voting. By 1876, only three southern states—South Carolina, Florida, and Tennessee—remained under Republican control.

Academic Vocabulary
employ • *v.*, make use of

A Disputed Election Leads to the End of Reconstruction The end of Reconstruction came with the election of 1876. The Democrats nominated Samuel Tilden, governor of New York, for president. The Republicans chose Ohio governor Rutherford B. Hayes. Both candidates vowed to fight corruption.

Tilden won the popular vote. However, he was one electoral vote short of victory. The outcome of the election hung on 20 disputed electoral votes. Of the 20, 19 were from the three states where federal troops still protected African Americans—South Carolina, Louisiana, and Florida. Democrats in these states accused Republican election officials of throwing out Democratic votes.

As inauguration day drew near, the nation still had no winner to swear in as president. The Republican-controlled Congress set up a special commission to settle the crisis. The commission, made up mostly of Republicans, gave all the disputed electoral votes to Hayes.

Southern Democrats could have fought the decision. Instead, they agreed to support the commission's decision in return for a promise by Hayes to end Reconstruction. This agreement is known as the **Compromise of 1877**. Once in office, Hayes removed all remaining federal troops from Louisiana, South Carolina, and Florida. Reconstruction was over.

GEOGRAPHY SKILLS

The 1876 presidential election was extremely close.

1. **Location** Why is the vote in New York, New Jersey, Connecticut, and Indiana surprising?
2. **Draw Conclusions** Based on the information shown here, why might Hayes's victory in the 1876 election have come as a surprise to some?

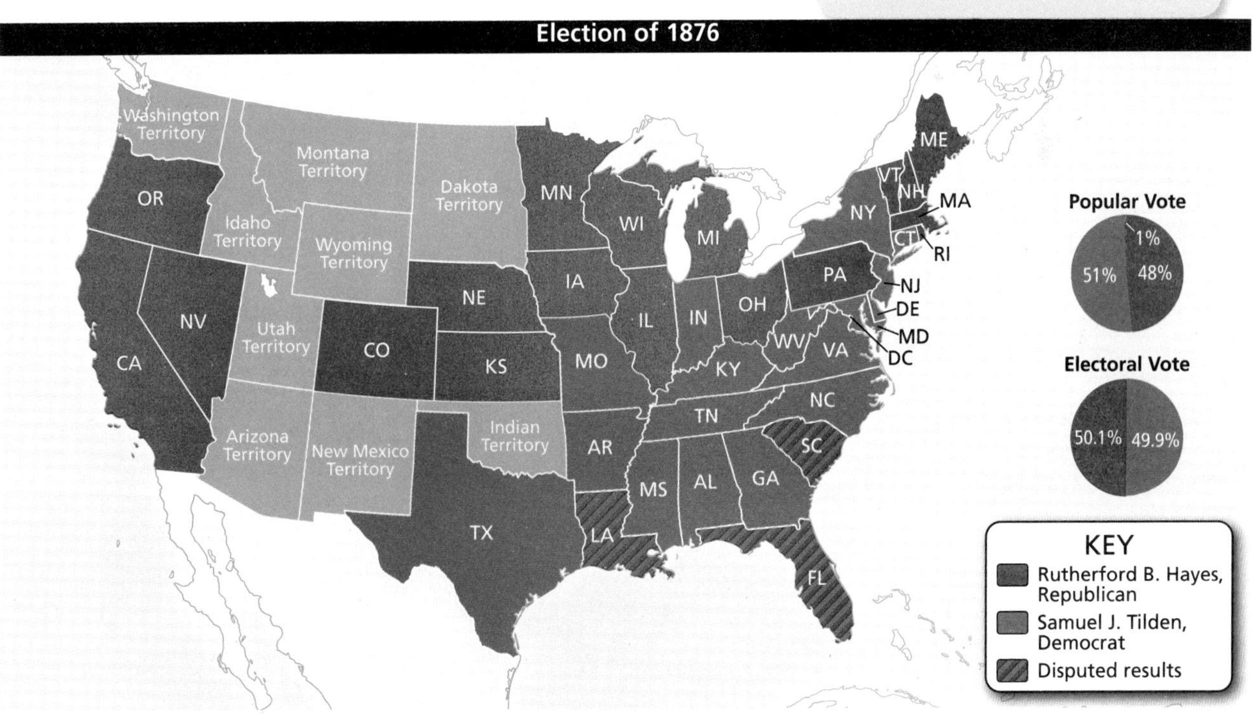

Quick Activity

Write a newspaper editorial taking a stand on the Compromise of 1877.

Reconstruction's Political Impact Reconstruction had a deep and lasting impact on southern politics. White southerners had bitter memories of Radical Republican policies and military rule. For the next hundred years, the South remained a stronghold of the Democratic party. At the same time, southern African Americans steadily lost most of their political rights.

READING CHECK **Sequence** Explain the sequence of events that resulted in the end of Reconstruction.

New Restrictions on African American Rights

As federal troops withdrew from the South, white southern Democrats found new ways to keep African Americans from exercising their rights. Many of these were laws **specifically** intended to prevent African Americans from voting.

Academic Vocabulary
specifically • *adv.*, for a particular purpose

Southern States Limit Political Participation Many southern states passed **poll taxes**, requiring voters to pay a fee each time they voted. As a result, African American men could rarely afford to vote.

States also imposed **literacy tests** that required voters to read and explain a section of the Constitution. Most African Americans had little education, so such tests kept them from voting. Election officials also applied different standards to Black voters, who often had to answer more difficult questions than white voters.

Analyze Political Cartoons This cartoon mocks the literacy tests that were intended to prevent African Americans from voting. **Synthesize Visual Information** How does this cartoon portray the new literacy tests?

Still, many poor white men could not have passed any literacy test. To increase the number of white voters, states passed **grandfather clauses**. These laws stated that if a voter's father or grandfather had been eligible to vote on January 1, 1867—a date after Johnson had restored rebels' right to vote—the voter did not have to take a literacy test. No African Americans in the South could vote before 1868, so the only effect of the grandfather clauses was to ensure that white men could vote.

Analyze Images Jim Crow laws made racial segregation legal in places such as this theater. **Draw Conclusions** What impact did these laws have on the equality of educational opportunities for white people and African Americans?

Jim Crow Laws Separate People by Race After 1877, **segregation**, or separation of races, became the law of the South. Blacks and white people were kept separate in schools, restaurants, theaters, trains, streetcars, playgrounds, hospitals, and even cemeteries by **Jim Crow laws**. In some cases, African Americans were restricted to completely separate facilities. In others, facilities were divided, with favorable areas reserved for white people. Louisiana novelist George Washington Cable described segregation as

Primary Source

"A system of oppression so rank that nothing could make it seem small except the fact that [African Americans] had already been ground under it for a century and a half."

—George Washington Cable, "The Freedman's Case in Equity"

INTERACTIVE

Oppression of African Americans

African Americans brought lawsuits to challenge segregation. In 1896, in the case of ***Plessy v. Ferguson***, the Supreme Court ruled that segregation was legal so long as facilities for blacks and whites were equal. In fact, facilities were rarely equal. For example, southern states spent much less on schools for Black children than for white children.

Despite such setbacks, the Constitution now recognized African Americans as citizens. Laws passed during Reconstruction—especially the Fourteenth Amendment—would become the basis of the civil rights movement almost 100 years later.

African Americans Leave the South Treatment as second-class citizens pushed many African Americans out of the South. They clung to the South because it was their home. Their families lived there. But they could also feel the pull of better opportunities elsewhere.

Quest CONNECTIONS

Did Reconstruction successfully rebuild society? Record your ideas in your Active Journal.

African Americans in northern cities published newspapers to help their brethren in the South cope with their new challenges. They often encouraged freedmen to come north. Factories needed more workers and sent recruiters to the South. They promised jobs, better housing, freedom to vote, and freedom from fear. Many African Americans began leaving the South for cities in the North and West.

Some freedmen were permitted to join the U.S. Army. Congress authorized four regiments of African Americans, to be commanded by white officers. Nicknamed "buffalo soldiers," African Americans served protecting settlers and enforcing federal laws in the western territories. Fourteen buffalo soldiers earned the medal of honor.

READING CHECK **Summarize** the ways in which southern governments restricted the rights of freedmen.

Change in Southern Industry

How Did the South Rebuild Its Economy?

During Reconstruction, the South made modest progress toward rebuilding its agricultural economy. By 1880, planters were growing as much cotton as they had in 1860.

After Reconstruction, a new generation of southern leaders worked to expand and diversify the economy. In stirring speeches, Atlanta journalist Henry Grady described a **"New South"** that used its vast natural resources to build up its own industry instead of depending on the North.

Old Industries Grow In 1880, the entire South still produced fewer finished textiles than Massachusetts. In the next decade, more communities built textile mills to turn cotton into cloth.

The tobacco industry also grew. In North Carolina, James Duke used new machinery to revolutionize the manufacture of tobacco products.

Analyze Graphs The war set back the South's development by many years, but by 1880, its economy began improving rapidly. **Use Evidence** Cite evidence from the charts that the southern economy diversified after Reconstruction ended.

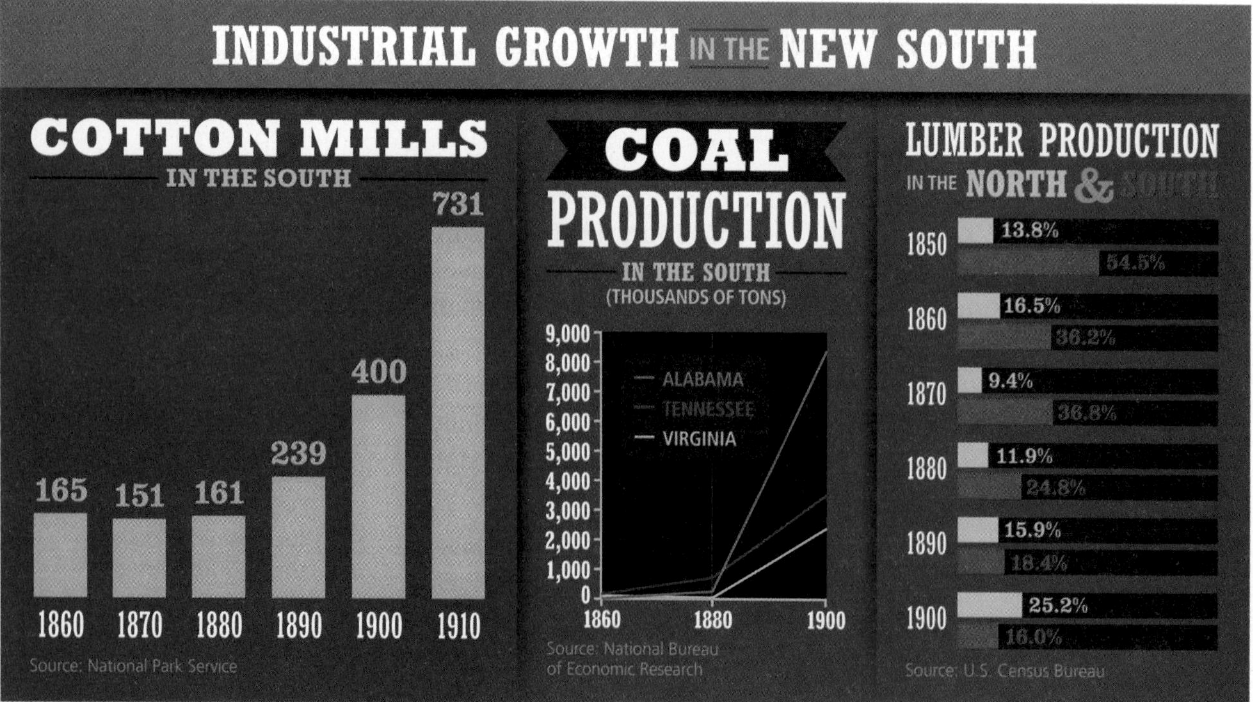

Duke's American Tobacco Company eventually controlled 90 percent of the nation's tobacco industry.

The Environment Shapes New Industries The New South also used its natural resources to develop new industries other than those based on farming. With its large deposits of iron ore and coal, Alabama became a center of the steel industry. Oil refineries sprang up in Louisiana and Texas. Other states produced copper, granite, and marble.

By the 1890s, many northern forests had been cut down. The southern yellow pine competed with the northwestern white pine as a lumber source. Southern factories produced cypress shingles and hardwood furniture.

Factories, farming, and mining modified the South's physical environment. Clearing land and using the natural resources provided jobs and opportunities. The South's wood, steel, and other products were used in industry around the country.

The South had developed a more balanced economy by 1900. "We find a South wide awake with business," wrote a visitor, "eagerly laying lines of communication, rapidly opening mines, building furnaces, foundries, and all sorts of shops." Still, the South did not keep up with even more rapid growth in the North and the West.

Analyze Images This poster advertised "OUR NATIONAL INDUSTRIES: METHODS OF IRON MINING AT CARTER'S FURNACE." **Summarize** How were companies like Carter's important to rebuilding the South?

READING CHECK **Compare and Contrast** the post-Reconstruction economy of the South with its pre-Civil War economy.

Lesson Check

Practice Vocabulary

1. How did **poll taxes** and **literacy tests** make it hard for African Americans to vote?
2. What were **Jim Crow** laws?
3. What was the effect of the **Compromise of 1877**?

Critical Thinking and Writing

4. **Analyze Information** How was the decision in *Plessy* v. *Ferguson* inconsistent with reality?
5. **Compare and Contrast** What was life like for African Americans in the South after Reconstruction ended? How did it differ from life under slavery?
6. **Writing Workshop: Cite Sources** In your Active Journal, create citations on all the sources you have used. Include the name of the article or text, the author, the publisher, the date of publication, and the web address.

TOPIC 9

Review and Assessment

VISUAL REVIEW

Causes and Effects of Reconstruction

Presidential Reconstruction: Southern states ratify Thirteenth Amendment; former Confederates swear loyalty to the Union.

President Johnson approves former Confederate states to rejoin Union.

Former Confederate leaders elected to government office. Southern states enact Black codes.

Radical Republicans win majority in Congress and reject Presidential Reconstruction.

Civil Rights Act grants citizenship to African Americans. Southern states required to ratify Fourteenth Amendment and allow African Americans to vote. Congress establishes military districts.

African Americans elected to local, state, and federal offices. Schools established for Black and white children.

White southerners dislike loss of power and work to end Reconstruction.

RADICAL RECONSTRUCTION AND ITS EFFECTS

Radical Reconstruction	After Reconstruction
• African American men gain right to vote. • African Americans become citizens. • African Americans gain right to own property.	• Poll taxes and literacy tests limit voting rights. • Jim Crow laws enforce segregation. • *Plessy* v. *Ferguson* endorses "separate but equal." • Rise of the "New South."

READING REVIEW

Use the Take Notes and Practice Vocabulary activities in your Active Journal to review the topic.

INTERACTIVE

Practice vocabulary using the Topic Mini-Games

Quest FINDINGS

Conduct your discussion

Get help for conducting your civic discussion in your Active Journal.

ASSESSMENT

Vocabulary and Key Ideas

1. **Identify Main Ideas** What was the significance of the **Thirteenth, Fourteenth**, and **Fifteenth Amendments**?
2. **Recall** Why were the **Radical Republicans** opposed to President Johnson's Reconstruction plan?
3. **Summarize** What was the **Ku Klux Klan**?
4. **Check Understanding** What was the **Compromise of 1877**, and what were the results?
5. **Identify Supporting Details** Why did the House of Representatives vote to impeach President Johnson, and why wasn't he convicted?
6. **Describe** How did the economy of the South change during Reconstruction?
7. **Identify Main Ideas** How did sharecropping affect African Americans?

Critical Thinking and Writing

8. **Identify Cause and Effect** How did the election of African Americans to public office affect people freed from slavery?
9. **Identify Cause and Effect** How were African Americans affected by the Black codes and the Radical Republican reaction to them?
10. **Summarize** What is the Fifteenth Amendment, and what was its impact?
11. **Draw Conclusions** What lasting effects did Reconstruction have on the South?
12. **Revisit the Essential Question** How should people handle the kind of conflict that divided the country during Reconstruction?
13. **Writing Workshop: Write a Research Paper** Complete your research paper on the Freedmen's Bureau and its effects. Include a discussion of the limits placed on the rights and opportunities of African Americans. Finalize your introduction. Revise the body paragraphs, using transitions to connect ideas. Then write a strong conclusion that summarizes your main ideas.

Analyze Primary Sources

14. What system is George Washington Cable most likely referring to in this quotation?
    A. Radical Reconstruction
    B. Lincoln's plan for amnesty
    C. Jim Crow laws
    D. the economy of the "New South"

"A system of oppression so rank that nothing could make it seem small except the fact that [African Americans] had already been ground under it for a century and a half."

—George Washington Cable, "The Freedman's Case in Equity"

Analyze Maps

Use the map to answer the following questions. [Map Key: red = Hayes; blue = Tilden; red/blue = disputed]

15. Which candidate won more states?
16. From which part of the country did Samuel Tilden get most of his support?
17. For whom did Florida vote? Explain.

▼ **Election of 1876**

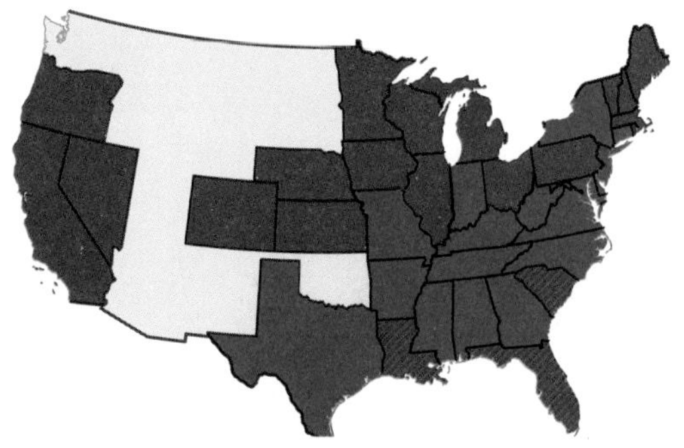

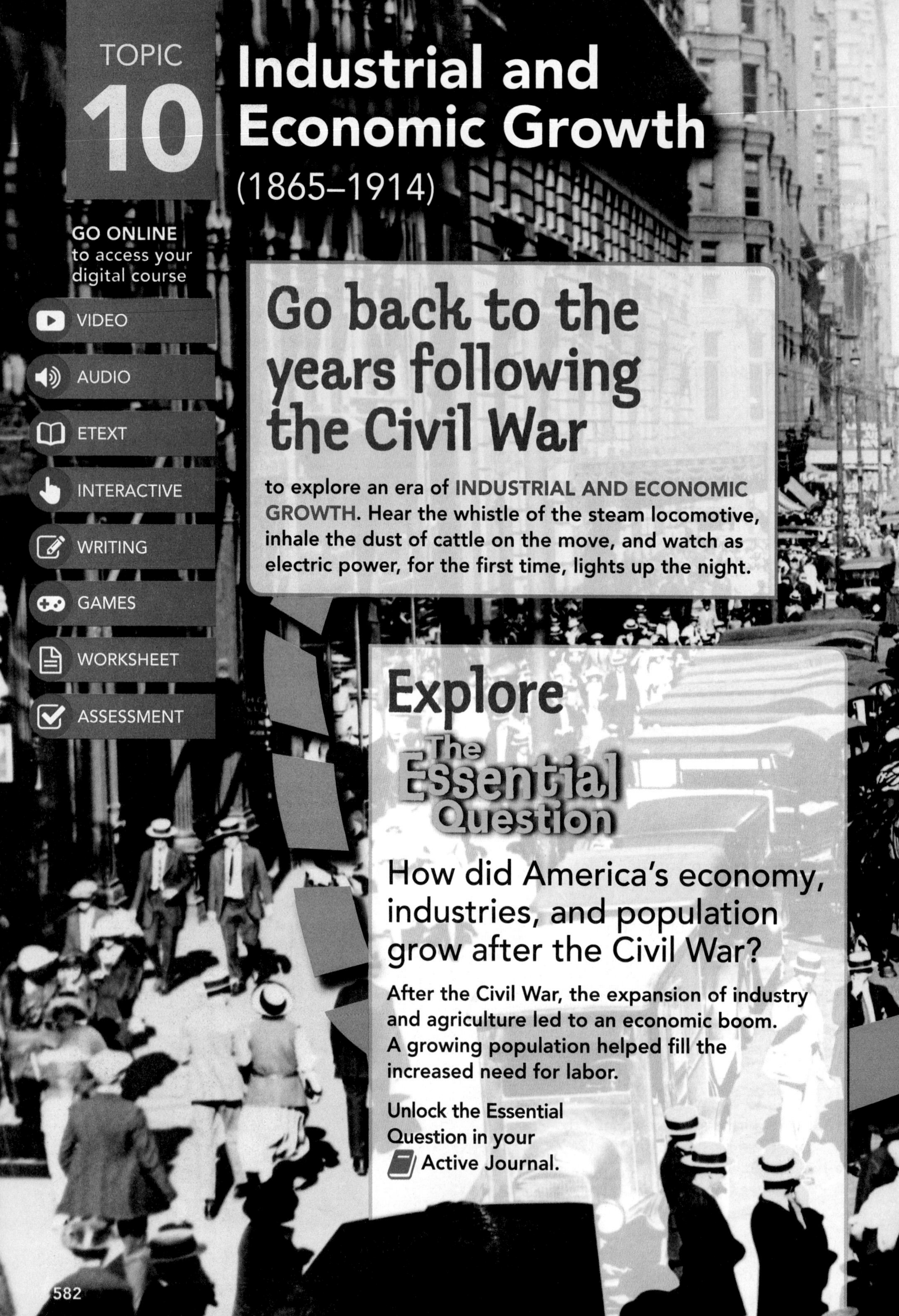

TOPIC 10

Industrial and Economic Growth (1865–1914)

GO ONLINE to access your digital course

- VIDEO
- AUDIO
- ETEXT
- INTERACTIVE
- WRITING
- GAMES
- WORKSHEET
- ASSESSMENT

Go back to the years following the Civil War

to explore an era of **INDUSTRIAL AND ECONOMIC GROWTH**. Hear the whistle of the steam locomotive, inhale the dust of cattle on the move, and watch as electric power, for the first time, lights up the night.

Explore The Essential Question

How did America's economy, industries, and population grow after the Civil War?

After the Civil War, the expansion of industry and agriculture led to an economic boom. A growing population helped fill the increased need for labor.

Unlock the Essential Question in your Active Journal.

Watch

NBC LEARN

BOUNCE TO ACTIVATE VIDEO

"The McCormicks, Strikes and Violence in Chicago"

Learn about the union strike that led to the Haymarket Riot of 1886.

Read

about changes in the American West, mining, railroads, and other industries, the corporations that ran them, the workers they employed, and the technologies that arose in the post–Civil War period.

TOPIC 10

Industrial and Economic Growth (1865–1914)

Learn more about Industrial and Economic Growth by making your own map and timeline in your Active Journal.

INTERACTIVE

Topic Timeline

What happened and when?

Explore the timeline to learn about events, inventions, and people that were changing life in the United States and the world.

TOPIC EVENTS

1865 Civil War ends

1869 Transcontinental railroad is completed

1876 Alexander Graham Bell invents the telephone

1886 Geronimo surrenders

1860 **1870** **1880**

WORLD EVENTS

1867 Japanese samurai overthrow shogun and restore emperor to leadership

1871 Germany is unified under William I

INTERACTIVE

Topic Map

How did industrialization affect the United States?

The years after the Civil War were marked by rapid change, including the addition of new states. Change is sometimes good, sometimes not.

1903
Wright Brothers invent the airplane

1890
Sherman Antitrust Act is passed

1911
Triangle Shirtwaist Company fire

1890 | 1900 | 1910 | 1920

1893
Columbian Exhibition is held in Chicago

1899
Boxer Uprising occurs in China

1914
World War I begins

Who will you meet?

John D. Rockefeller, business mogul

Chief Joseph, Nez Percé leader

Mother Jones, social reformer

Civic Discussion Inquiry

High-Speed Rail

▼ High-speed rail is common in Europe and Japan.

Quest KICK OFF

You are a member of the House of Representatives serving on the Subcommittee on Railroads. You are going to meet with other representatives in the subcommittee to decide whether the United States government should authorize high-speed rail programs. You will look at the U.S. government's original investment in rail transportation and its costs and impacts in the 1800s. You need to help answer a question about Americans' current and future needs:

Should America invest in high-speed rail?

Be ready! Other representatives will challenge your arguments. It's time to prepare!

1 Ask Questions

To find out the best course of action, start with a list of questions about railroads and other forms of transportation in the United States today. Write the questions in your Active Journal.

2 Investigate

As you read the lessons in this Topic, look for Quest CONNECTIONS that provide information about industrial and economic growth in the United States in the nineteenth century. Collect examples in your Active Journal.

3 Examine Sources

Next, explore a set of sources. They will support differing viewpoints about whether America should invest in high-speed rail. Capture notes in your Active Journal.

Quest FINDINGS

4 Discuss!

After you collect your clues and examine the sources, you will prepare to discuss this question: Should America invest in high speed rail? You will use your knowledge of this Topic as well as evidence from sources to make convincing arguments to answer YES or NO. You may also come up with answers of your own.

LESSON 1

Mining, Railroads, and the Economy

GET READY TO READ

START UP

Look at the image of the train speeding along the track. Write three sentences predicting effects that a boom in railroad building might have on the West after 1865.

GUIDING QUESTIONS

- What problems arose on the mining frontier?
- How did railroads spur development?
- How did railroads encourage economic growth?
- How did the government help railroads?

TAKE NOTES

Literacy Skills Identify Cause and Effect

Use the graphic organizer in your Active Journal to take notes as you read the lesson.

PRACTICE VOCABULARY

Use the vocabulary activity in your Active Journal to practice the vocabulary words.

Vocabulary

lode
vigilante
transcontinental railroad
subsidy
gauge
network
consolidate
rebate
pool

Academic Vocabulary

lure
consequently

The **lure** of silver and gold drew eager prospectors to the West starting well before the Civil War. After the war, the railroads carried hordes of eager settlers to the West, along with the goods they would need to make a life in this region. In the process, the railroads promoted economic expansion and the growth of cities.

How Did Mining Change the West?

The western mining boom had begun with the California gold rush of 1849. When the gold rush ended, miners looked for new opportunities. A mere rumor sent them racing east or north in search of new strikes.

The Comstock Lode Two prospectors struck gold in Nevada in 1859. Then another miner, Henry Comstock, appeared. "The land is mine," he cried, demanding to be made a partner. From then on, Comstock boasted about "his" mine. The strike became known as the Comstock Lode. A **lode** is a rich vein of gold or silver.

Analyze Images Virginia City, Nevada, became a boomtown due to mining activities from the Comstock Lode. **Identify Cause and Effect** How did silver and gold rushes affect settlement of the West?

Academic Vocabulary
lure • *n.,* a thing that tempts or entices a person to go somewhere or do something

Comstock and his partners often complained about the heavy blue sand that was mixed in with the gold. It clogged the devices used for separating out the gold and made the gold hard to reach. When Mexican miners took the "danged blue stuff" to an expert in California, tests showed that it was loaded with silver. Comstock had stumbled onto one of the richest silver mines in the world.

Miners moved into many other areas of the West. Some found valuable ore in Montana and Idaho. Others struck it rich in Colorado. In the 1870s, miners discovered gold in the Black Hills of South Dakota. In the late 1890s, thousands rushed north to Alaska after major gold strikes were made there.

Boomtowns and Ghost Towns Gold and silver strikes attracted thousands of prospectors. Towns sprang up almost overnight near all the major mining sites.

First, miners built a tent city near the diggings. Then, traders brought mule teams loaded with tools, food, and clothing. Merchants hauled in wagon-loads of supplies and set up stores.

Soon, wood-frame houses, hotels, restaurants, and stores replaced the tents. In less than a year, the Comstock Lode mining camp became the boomtown of Virginia City, Nevada.

Most settlers in the boomtowns of the mining frontier were men. However, enterprising women also found ways to profit. Some women ran boardinghouses and laundries. Others opened restaurants, where miners gladly paid high prices for home-cooked meals.

Many boomtowns lasted for only a few years. When the gold or silver ore was gone, the miners moved away. Without the miners for customers, businesses often had to close. In this way, a boomtown could quickly go bust and turn into a ghost town.

Some boomtowns survived and prospered after the mines shut down, as miners stayed and found new ways to make a living.

READING CHECK **Identify Main Ideas** Why did boomtowns spring up throughout the West?

Boomtowns and Ghost Towns

What Problems Came With the Mining Boom?

The surge of miners in the West created problems, as did the arrival of cattle ranchers and homesteaders. Mines and towns polluted clear mountain streams. Miners cut down forests to get wood for buildings. They also forced American Indians from the land.

Foreign miners were often treated unfairly. In many camps, mobs drove Mexicans from their claims. Chinese miners were heavily taxed or forced to work claims abandoned by others.

Few miners ever got rich. Much of the gold and silver lay deep underground. It could be reached only with costly machinery. Eventually, most mining in the West was taken over by large companies that could afford to buy this equipment. **Consequently**, independent prospectors like Henry Comstock largely disappeared. They were replaced by paid laborers who worked for the large companies.

Academic Vocabulary
consequently • *adv.*, as a result

Maintaining Order in Mining Towns Lawlessness and disorder often accompanied the rapid growth of a town. Stories have exaggerated the number of fights and killings that took place in these towns, but some towns actually were violent places. In response, miners sometimes resorted to organizing groups of **vigilantes**, or self-appointed law enforcers. Vigilantes tracked down outlaws and punished them, usually without trials. Lynching was a common punishment.

Occasionally, vigilante groups formed for other reasons. At least one San Francisco group organized to take political control of the city.

Informal methods of governing gradually gave way to more formal arrangements. In 1861, Colorado, Dakota, and Nevada were organized into territories. Idaho and Arizona followed in 1863 and Montana in 1864. The process of permanent settlement and government had begun.

READING CHECK **Identify Cause and Effect** How did informal methods of governance gradually become more formal?

Analyze Images The Chinese prospectors in this image are using a sluice box, which washed gold free of soil. **Infer** Do you think most miners became wealthy? Why or why not?

Railroads Encourage Economic Growth

To many American Indians, the railroad was a menace, an "iron horse" belching smoke and bringing settlers who would take their land. However, for the people of mining towns, railroads meant supplies, new townsfolk, and a rapid means of transporting their gold and silver.

Investors in the West needed a transportation system that could carry heavy loads over great distances at a cost low enough to guarantee a profit. It is no wonder, then, that railroad companies raced to lay track to the mines and boomtowns. In time, rail technology opened the West and fostered economic growth for the nation.

Government Support In 1863, two companies began a race to build the first transcontinental railroad. A **transcontinental railroad** is one that stretches across a continent from coast to coast. The Union Pacific Railroad started building a rail line westward from Omaha, Nebraska. The Central Pacific Railroad began in Sacramento, California, and was built eastward.

The market revolution that had begun in the first half of the 1830s relied on capitalists willing to invest in industry. Capitalists backed the Union Pacific and the Central Pacific railroads. However, those private companies also relied on government aid. The coming years would see increasing government support for industries involved in creating a national infrastructure.

The federal government helped the railroad companies because it believed that rail lines in the West would benefit the entire nation. The government's aid, aimed at encouraging expansion, came in the form of subsidies.

A **subsidy** is financial aid or a land grant from the government. Congress lent money to the railroad companies and gave them land.

Analyze Images This wooden trestle, the Dale Creek Bridge in Wyoming, was a great challenge for railroad engineers. **Use Visual Information** What were some of the challenges that this bridge presented?

For every mile of track completed, the railroad companies received 20 sections of land in the states along the route and 40 sections per mile in the territories. By the time the Central Pacific and Union Pacific railroads were completed, they had received about 45 million acres of land. Often, both business and government ignored the fact that American Indians lived on the land.

Building the Transcontinental Railroad Both companies had trouble getting workers. Labor was scarce during the Civil War. Also, the work was backbreaking and dangerous, and the pay was low.

The railroad companies hired immigrant workers, who accepted low wages. The Central Pacific brought in thousands of workers from China. The Union Pacific hired newcomers from Ireland. African Americans and Mexican Americans also worked for each line.

Analyze Images Even though the pay was low, workers like these on the Union Pacific took on the dangerous task of building the railroad. **Infer** What do you think these workers would have written in a letter to people back home?

The railroad workers faced a daunting task. The route would pass through environments as varied as forests, deserts, and mountains. Building the railroad forced workers to adapt to or modify the landscape. In some places, track was laid around mountains. In other places, however, workers relied on specialized tools, explosives, and other technological innovations to blast tunnels through mountains.

The Central Pacific had to carve a path across the rugged Sierra Nevada. The Union Pacific had to cut through the towering Rocky Mountains. Snowstorms and avalanches killed workers and slowed progress. At times, crews cutting tunnels through rock advanced only a few inches a day.

Railroads Encourage Urban and Rural Growth The Central Pacific and Union Pacific met at Promontory, Utah, on May 10, 1869. Leland Stanford, president of the Central Pacific, dropped a solid-gold spike into a pre-drilled hole in the rail. In doing so, he joined the two tracks and united the country. The nation's first transcontinental railroad was complete.

With the Civil War fresh in their minds, people cheered this new symbol of unity. The words that were engraved on the golden spike expressed their feelings:

Primary Source

> "May God continue the unity of our Country as the Railroad unites the two great Oceans of the world."
>
> —Engraved on the Golden Spike

Before long, other major rail lines linked the West and the East. The railroads brought economic growth and new settlement all across the West. They enabled people, supplies, and mail to move quickly and cheaply across the plains and mountains. Wherever rail lines went, settlements—"railroad towns"—sprang up along the tracks.

The Transcontinental Railroad

Larger towns and cities developed where major railroad lines met. Cities where sea and land transportation met, such as Seattle, San Francisco, and Los Angeles, experienced huge population growth with the coming of the railroads. Western cities, such as Denver, Cheyenne, and Wichita, grew when railroads were joined to the great cattle trails. Thus the railroad—the most advanced transportation system of its day—had a major impact on the urbanization of the United States.

Because of their rapid growth, western territories began to apply for statehood. Nevada became a state in 1864; Colorado, in 1876; North Dakota, South Dakota, Montana, and Washington, in 1889; Idaho and Wyoming, in 1890.

READING CHECK **Summarize** Why were immigrants brought in to help build the railroads?

Creating a National Railroad Network

The Civil War showed the importance of railroads. Railroads carried troops and supplies to the battlefields. They also moved raw materials to factories. After the war, railroad companies began to build new lines all over the country.

Racing to Construct New Lines Railroad builders raced to create thousands of miles of new tracks. In the years after completion of the first transcontinental rail line in 1869, Americans built three more. James Hill, a Canadian-born owner, finished the last major cross-country line in 1893. His Great Northern Railway wound from Duluth, Minnesota, to Everett, Washington.

Unlike other rail lines, the Great Northern was built without financial aid from Congress. To make his railroad succeed, Hill had to turn a profit from the start. He encouraged farmers and ranchers to move to

BIOGRAPHY 5 Things to Know About LELAND STANFORD

president of the Central Pacific Railroad (1824–1893)

- During the California gold rush, he sold supplies and groceries to miners.
- He helped finance and run the Central Pacific Railroad from 1861 to 1893.
- Among the people he contacted in Washington, D.C., while lobbying for the railroad, was Abraham Lincoln.
- He served as governor of California (1861–1863) and as a U.S. senator (1885–1893).
- He and his wife, Jane Stanford, founded Stanford University in Palo Alto, California, in 1891.

Critical Thinking How do you think being a railroad president helped Stanford get elected governor and senator?

Analyze Images This Golden Spike Ceremony marked the completion of the transcontinental railroad. **Summarize** Why was completing the railroad vital to the United States?

the Northwest and settle near his railroad. He gave seed to farmers and helped them buy equipment. He imported special bulls in order to breed hardier cattle. Not only was Hill's policy generous, it also made good business sense. In the end, Hill's railroad proved very successful even without government assistance, and it was a key to the development of the Northwest.

A National Transportation System Early railroads were short lines that served local communities. Many lines ran for no more than 50 miles. When passengers and freight reached the end of one line, they had to move to a train on a different line to continue their journey.

Even if the lines had been connected, the problem would not have been eliminated. Different lines used tracks of different **gauges**, or widths. As a result, the trains from one line could not run on the tracks of another line. In general, the tracks of northern lines used different gauges from those of southern lines.

In 1886, railroads in the South decided to adopt the northern gauge. On May 30, southern railroads stopped running so that work could begin. Using crowbars and sledgehammers, crews worked from dawn to dusk to move the rails a few inches farther apart. When they had finished, some 13,000 miles of track had been changed.

Once the track was standardized, American railroads formed a **network**, or system of connected lines. The creation of a rail network brought benefits to shippers. Often, rail companies arranged for freight cars on one line to use the tracks of another.

How did networks change railroads? Record your findings in your Active Journal.

Analyze Images Handcars like this one allowed workers, like these three Chinese men, to move materials during construction. **Summarize** What role did Chinese workers play in building the railroads?

For example, goods loaded in Chicago could stay on the same car all the way to New York, instead of being transferred from one car to another. As a result, the shipper had to pay only one fare for the whole distance.

New rails knit the sprawling nation together. By 1900, there were more miles of tracks in the United States than in Europe and Russia combined.

New Inventions Improve Rail Travel New inventions helped make railway travel safer and faster. On early trains, each railroad car had its own brakes and its own brake operator. If different cars stopped at different times, serious accidents could result. In 1869, George Westinghouse began selling his new air brake, which allowed a locomotive engineer to stop all the railroad cars at once. The air brake increased safety and allowed for longer, faster trains.

Train travel also became more comfortable. In 1864, George Pullman designed a railroad sleeping car that had bathrooms and sleeping berths. Rail lines also added dining cars. Porters (who carried baggage), conductors, and waiters attended to the needs of passengers.

The Railroads and Economic Growth The growth of the railroads in the 1800s showed how a market economy could lead to greater prosperity. As William Vanderbilt pointed out, the railroads "are built for men who invest their money." That is, the railroads were built to make money for the people who invested in them. Yet the railroads benefited many other people: the workers who laid the tracks, the employees who ran the trains, the passengers who rode the rails, and the businesses that filled cars with cargo. People who lived in the towns that sprouted up along the rail lines also benefited. Ultimately, the railroads benefited the country as a whole.

The expansion of the railroads brought significant changes to the way that goods were produced, distributed, and consumed. Businesses brought raw materials on railroads to factories. Finished goods from those factories could be shipped far and wide for a reasonable price. Consumers—especially those far from cities—could now have access to more goods than ever before. The same held true for farm goods: farmers had wider markets, and consumers had more food choices.

The Plight of Farmers and Small Businesses

Competition between railroad companies forces them to reduce rates.

↓

Railroad companies offer rebates and discounts to the biggest customers. Some railroad companies form pools and raise rates.

↓

Small farmers and shippers cannot afford to ship goods.

↓

Many small companies and farmers are forced out of business.

Analyze Charts This chart shows how railroad companies altered their pricing. **Infer** What can you infer about how rebates and discounts caused many small companies and farmers to go out of business in the 1800s?

Consolidation Brings Efficiency As railroads grew, they looked for ways to operate more efficiently. Small lines were often costly to run, so many companies began to **consolidate**, or combine. Larger companies bought up smaller ones or forced them out of business. The Pennsylvania Railroad, for example, consolidated 73 companies into its system.

Tough-minded business people led the drive for consolidation. Cornelius Vanderbilt was among the most powerful of these leaders. The son of a poor farmer, Vanderbilt earned one fortune in steamship lines. He then began to buy up railroad lines in New York State.

Vanderbilt sometimes used ruthless tactics to force smaller owners to sell to him. In the early 1860s, he decided to buy the New York Central Railroad. The owners refused to sell. Vanderbilt then announced that New York Central passengers would not be allowed to transfer to his trains. With their passengers stranded and business dropping sharply, the owners gave in and sold their line to Vanderbilt.

Analyze Political Cartoons This cartoon shows congressmen looking like train engines. **Synthesize Visual Information** What does this image suggest about the influence of the railroad industry in Congress?

Vanderbilt then bought up most of the lines between Chicago and Buffalo. By the time of his death in 1877, his companies controlled 4,500 miles of track and linked New York City to the Great Lakes region.

Other consolidations were soon under way. Before long, the major railroads of the United States were organized into a number of systems directed by a handful of wealthy and powerful men.

READING CHECK **Identify Supporting Details** What was significant about the way in which the Great Northern line was financed?

How Did Railroads Deal With Competition?

With builders rushing to share in the profits of the railroad boom, overbuilding occurred. Soon, there were too many rail lines in some parts of the country. Between Atlanta and St. Louis, for example, 20 different lines competed for business. There was not nearly enough rail traffic to keep all these lines busy.

Owners Look for New Ways to Make Profits Especially in the West, there were too few people—and therefore not enough paying customers—for the railroads to make a profit. Competition was fierce. Rate wars broke out as rival railroads slashed their fares to win customers. Usually, all the companies lost money as a result.

Often, railroads were forced to grant secret **rebates**, or discounts, to their biggest customers. The railroads preferred big customers for two reasons. First, big customers were more likely to pay their bills and keep being customers in the future. Second, it was less expensive to deal with a few big customers than many small customers.

Fewer customers meant less paperwork and simpler loading and unloading. Yet rebates hurt small shippers and drove some out of business.

Railroad owners soon realized that cutthroat competition was hurting even their large lines. They looked for ways to end the competition. One method was pooling. In a **pool**, railroad companies divided up the business in an area. They then fixed their prices at a high level.

Farmers React to High Railroad Prices Railroad rebates and pools angered small farmers in the South and the West. Both practices kept shipping prices high for them. Rates were so high that some farmers burned their crops for fuel rather than ship them to market.

Many farmers joined the Populist movement. Populists called for government regulation of rail rates. Some wanted the government to run the railroads. A debate began about whether government should interfere with business to protect the common good. Congress and several states passed laws regulating railroad companies. However, the laws did not end abuses. Railroad owners sometimes bribed officials to keep the laws from being enforced.

The Panic of 1893 In 1893, an economic panic hit the United States. About 15,000 businesses and 500 banks closed, leaving many workers unemployed.

Analyze Graphs Railroads had a profound effect on the U.S. economy. **Synthesize Visual Information** Why do you think certain professions grew so rapidly during this time? What effect did the growth of the railroad industry have on the U.S. economy in the late 1800s?

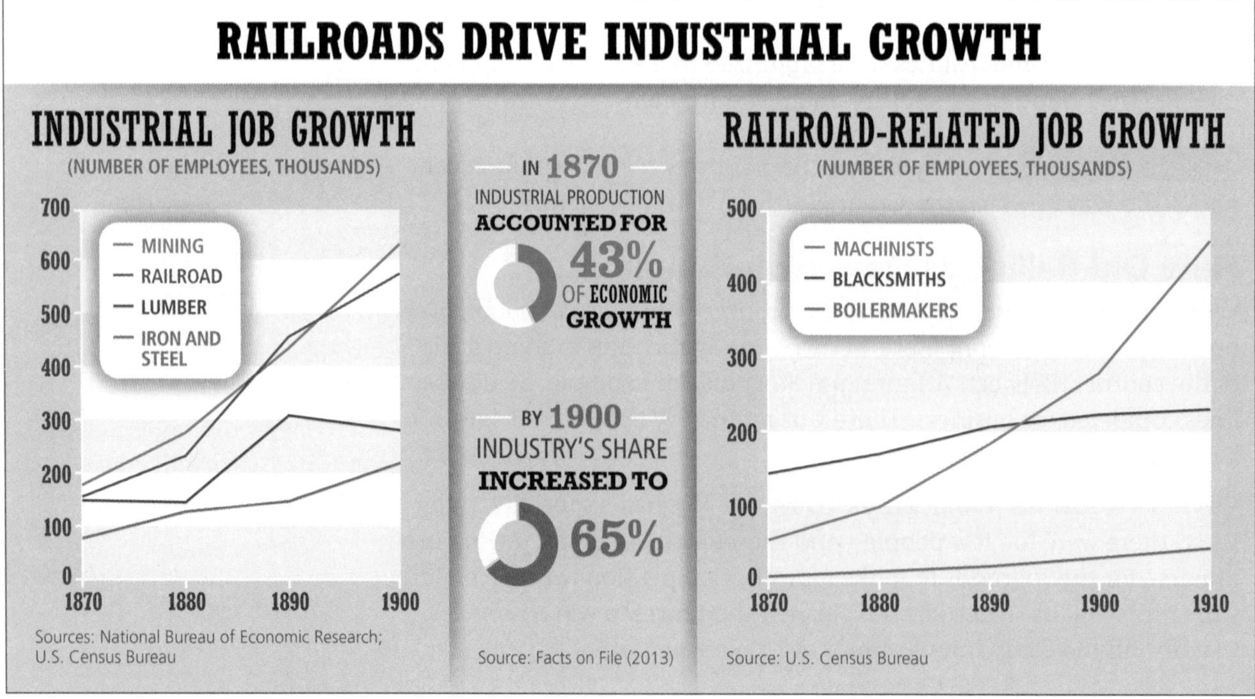

The railroads were both a cause and a victim of the economic downturn. Overbuilding in the 1860s meant that many railroad companies' finances were fragile—they were barely making money. In 1893, the Philadelphia and Reading Railroad went bankrupt, helping to start the panic. Many other leading railroads followed. Industries, like steel, and a wide variety of businesses that had come to depend on the railroad were hurt, as were businesses that depended on those businesses. Through a ripple effect, the whole economy suffered.

Analyze Political Cartoons Cornelius Vanderbilt, left, seldom failed when he tried to take over other railroads, but this image from 1870 depicts his loss to Daniel Drew for control of the Erie Railway Company. **Infer** Who do you think the cartoonist felt was the underdog in this battle?

READING CHECK **Summarize** How did railroad owners make profits?

How Did Railroads Help the Nation Expand?

Railroads caused some problems, but they also made possible the rapid growth of industry after 1865. Other industries, from mining to steel-making, grew because of railroad demand for their products. Railroads not only employed thousands of people but also developed new management techniques that spread to other businesses. Cities grew along rail lines. Now, with the railroad in place, the United States was poised to become the greatest industrial nation the world had ever seen.

READING CHECK **Identify Main Ideas** How did railroad companies change other large businesses?

Lesson Check

Practice Vocabulary

1. What role did **vigilantes** play on the western mining frontier?
2. Why was solving the **gauge** problem the key to creating an efficient rail **network**?

Critical Thinking and Writing

3. Generate Explanations Why might a sudden surge of people into an area cause problems other than environmental ones?
4. Express Problems Clearly What problems did an excess of competition cause for railroad companies and some customers?
5. Summarize Tell how railroads helped the United States grow and prosper.
6. Writing Workshop: Introduce Claims Recall how and why the federal government supported the construction of railroads. Write two sentences in your Active Journal to introduce your claim concerning what the government's role should be in the creation of a national infrastructure. This will get you started on the argument you will write at the end of the Topic.

LESSON 2

Western Agriculture

GET READY TO READ

START UP

Look at the image of the longhorn cattle. Write a paragraph to describe why it might be difficult to move this herd from trail to market.

GUIDING QUESTIONS

- How did the Cattle Kingdom form?
- What alliances did farmers make to try to improve their condition?
- What were some effects of the Homestead Act?

TAKE NOTES

Literacy Skills Classify and Categorize

Use the graphic organizer in your Active Journal to take notes as you read the lesson.

PRACTICE VOCABULARY

Use the vocabulary activity in your Active Journal to practice the vocabulary words.

Vocabulary		Academic Vocabulary
cattle drive	sodbuster	mechanization
vaquero	cooperative	pledge
cow town	wholesale	
Morrill Acts	inflation	

While Reconstruction shaped the South following the Civil War, other events were occurring throughout the American West. The vast landscape of the Great Plains offered both promise and problems.

How Did a Cattle Kingdom Start on the Plains?

In the 1860s, cattle ranching grew rapidly on the Great Plains. Before this time, the Spanish, and then the Mexicans, had set up cattle ranches in the Southwest. Over the years, strays from these ranches, along with American breeds, grew into large herds of wild cattle. These wild cattle were known as longhorns. They roamed freely across the grassy plains of Texas.

After the Civil War, the demand for beef increased. People in the growing cities in the East were eating more meat. Miners, railroad crews, farmers, and growing communities in the West added to the demand. The Texas longhorns were perfect for the commercial market. They could travel far on little water, and they required no winter feeding.

In response, Texas ranchers began rounding up herds of longhorns. They drove the animals hundreds of miles north to railroad lines in Kansas and Missouri on trips called **cattle drives**.

INTERACTIVE

Cattle Trails

Jesse Chisholm blazed one of the most famous cattle trails. Chisholm was half Scottish and half Cherokee. In the late 1860s, he began hauling goods by wagon between Texas and the Kansas Pacific Railroad. His route crossed rivers at the best places and passed by water holes. Ranchers began using the Chisholm Trail in 1867. Within five years, more than one million cattle had walked the road.

Tending Cattle in the West Ranchers employed cowhands to tend their cattle and drive herds to market. These hard workers rode alongside the huge herds in good and bad weather. They kept the cattle moving and rounded up strays. After the Civil War, veterans of the Confederate Army made up the majority of the cowhands who worked in Texas. However, it is estimated that nearly one in three cowhands was either Mexican American or African American. Some cowhands dreamed of setting aside enough money to start a herd of their own. Most, in the end, just worked to earn wages.

How does railroad access change people's lives? Record your findings in your Active Journal.

Spanish Influences American cowhands learned much about riding, roping, and branding from Spanish and Mexican vaqueros (vah KEHR ohs). **Vaqueros** were skilled riders who herded cattle on ranches in Mexico, California, and the Southwest.

The gear used by American cowhands was modeled on the tools of the vaquero. Cowhands used the leather lariat to catch cattle and horses. *Lariat* comes from the Spanish word for rope.

Their leather leggings, called chaps, were modeled on Spanish *chaparreras* (chah pah REH rahs). Chaps protected a rider's legs from the thorny plants that grow in the Southwest.

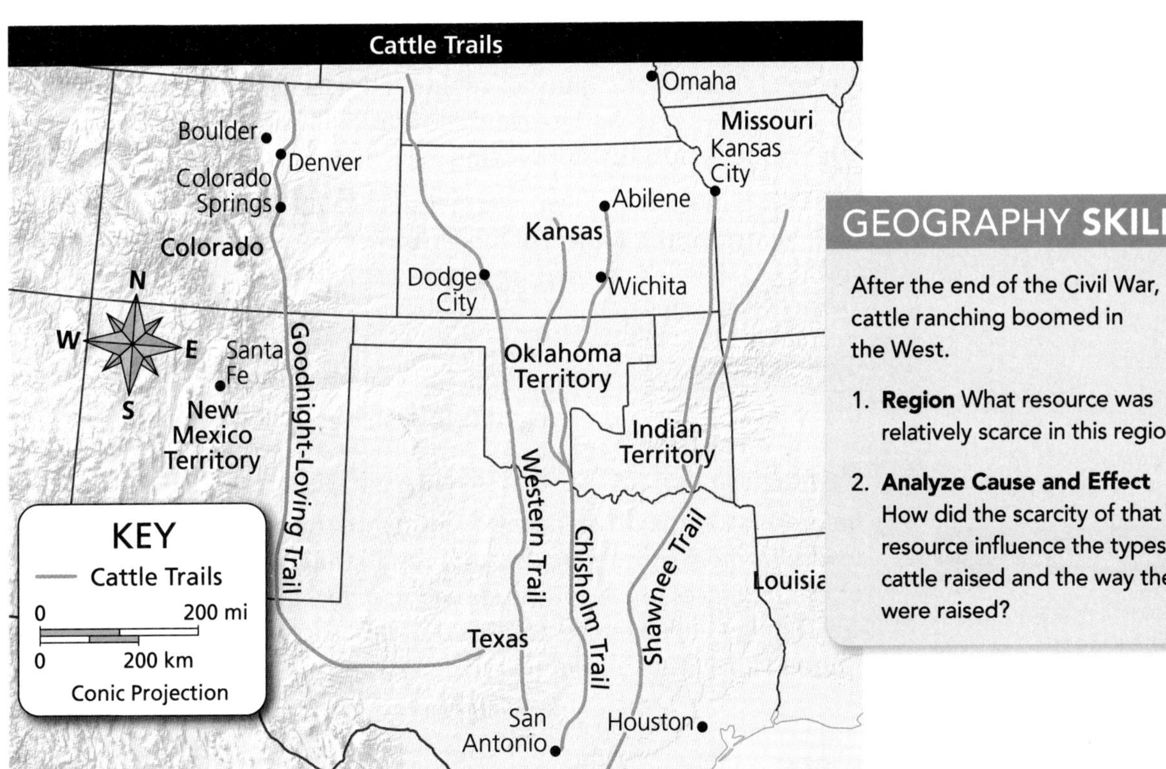

GEOGRAPHY **SKILLS**

After the end of the Civil War, cattle ranching boomed in the West.

1. **Region** What resource was relatively scarce in this region?
2. **Analyze Cause and Effect** How did the scarcity of that resource influence the types of cattle raised and the way they were raised?

Analyze Images A cowhand's life could be dangerous, as shown in this painting. **Infer** What role did the environment of the West play in the life of a cowhand?

The Life of a Cowhand A cattle drive was hot, dirty, tiring, and often boring. A cowboy's day could last for nearly 18 hours.

The work was so strenuous that cowhands usually brought a number of horses so that each day a fresh one would be available. Cowhands worked in all kinds of weather and faced many dangers, including prairie dog holes, rattlesnakes, and fierce thunderstorms. They had to prevent nervous cattle from drowning while crossing fast-flowing rivers. They had to fight raging grass fires. They also faced attacks from cattle thieves who roamed the countryside.

One of the cowhand's worst fears on a cattle drive was a stampede. A clap of thunder or a gunshot could set thousands of longhorns off at a run. Cowhands had to avoid the crush of hoofs and horns while attempting to turn the stampeding herd in a wide circle.

Most cowhands did not work for themselves. Instead, they were hired hands for the owners of large ranches. For all their hard work, cowhands were fed, housed, and lucky to earn $1 per day. Even in the 1870s, this was low pay.

READING CHECK **Identify Supporting Details** What influences did the vaqueros have on cowhand culture in the United States?

Ranching Affects Settlement Patterns

Cowhands and Their Gear

Before long, cattle drives began to influence the settlement of western towns. As more cattle were driven through these areas, businesses offering services to the cowhands began to form in towns. As a result, cattle drives ended in **cow towns** that had sprung up along the railroad lines. The Chisholm Trail, for example, ended in Abilene,

Kansas. Other cow towns in Kansas were Wichita, Caldwell, and Dodge City. In cow towns, cattle were held in large pens until they could be loaded into railroad cars and shipped to markets in the East.

In Abilene and other busy cow towns, dance halls, saloons, hotels, and restaurants catered to the cowhands. Sheriffs often had a hard time keeping the peace. Some cowhands spent wild nights drinking, dancing, and gambling.

The main street of a town was where people conducted business. Almost every town had a general store that sold groceries, tools, clothing, and all sorts of other goods. The general store also served as a social center where people could talk and exchange the latest news. As a town grew, drugstores, hardware stores, and even ice cream parlors lined its main street.

Religion also played an important role for the townspeople. Throughout the West, places of worship grew in number and membership. They served as spiritual and social centers and as symbols of progress and stability. "A church does as much to build up a town as a school, a railroad, or a fair," noted one New Mexico newspaper.

READING CHECK **Describe** How would you describe the settlement pattern of cow towns in the West?

Farming Spreads Across the Plains

In the 1870s, ranching spread north from Texas and across the grassy Plains. Soon, cattle grazed from Kansas to present-day Montana. Ranchers had built a Cattle Kingdom in the West. They came to expect high profits. Millions of dollars poured into the West from people in the East and in foreign countries who wanted to earn money from the cattle boom. However, the boom did not last.

Conflicts Over Land Ranchers let their cattle run wild on the open range. To identify cattle, each ranch had its own brand that was burned into a cow's hide.

Sometimes, there were conflicts on the range. When sheepherders moved onto the Plains, ranchers tried to drive them out. The ranchers complained the sheep nibbled the grass so low that the cattle could not eat it. To protect the range, which they saw as their own, ranchers sometimes attacked sheepherders and their flocks.

New Settlements Encroach on Cattle Land In the 1870s, farmers began moving onto the range. They fenced their fields with barbed wire, which kept cattle and sheep from pushing over fences and trampling plowed fields.

Analyze Images People who settled on the Great Plains had to be self-sufficient. **Cite Evidence** What do you think was the most precious item these settlers owned? Why?

Quick Activity

Explore how natural resources affected population growth in the West in your Active Journal.

As more farmers bought land, the open range began to disappear. Large grants of land to the railroads also limited it. As a result, a more organized system began to develop in which ranchers bought and maintained private property. This protection of property rights further boosted settlement in the West.

Nature, however, imposed limits on the cattle boom. After a time, there was not enough grass to feed all the cattle that lived on the Plains. The need to buy feed and land pushed up the costs. Diseases such as "Texas fever" sometimes destroyed entire herds. The bitterly cold winters of 1886 and 1887 killed entire herds of cattle. In the summer, severe heat and drought dried up water holes and scorched the grasslands.

Cattle owners began to buy land and fence it in. Soon, farmers and ranchers divided the open range into a patchwork of large fenced plots. The days of the Cattle Kingdom were over.

READING CHECK **Understand Effects** What effect did the arrival of growing numbers of farmers have on the open range system?

How Did the Homestead Act Affect the West?

Congress passed the Homestead Act in 1862. It was the centerpiece of the government's land policy. The law promised 160 acres of free land to anyone who was head of a household, who had not fought for the Confederacy, and who paid a small filing fee and improved the land over five years.

Free Land and Hidden Costs A stream of immigrants and easterners took up the offer of free land. Many planted their 160 acres with wheat and corn. By 1900, half a million Americans had set up farms under the Homestead Act.

Under the Homestead Act the land was free, but setting up a farm required money and hard work. Many people did not have the money to move west and start a farm.

Also, only about 20 percent of the homestead land went directly to small farmers. Land-owning companies took large areas of land illegally and resold it to farmers at a high price. As a result, many settlers struggled to make ends meet.

Analyze Images On the first day of the Oklahoma land rush, nearly 100,000 people set out to stake new claims, only to find other settlers already there. **Use Visual Information** Based on this image, how would you describe the first day of the land rush?

Analyze Images African Americans, including this family, were among the Americans who moved west. **Infer** What do you think this couple hoped to provide for their children by moving west?

African Americans Move West At the end of Reconstruction, many formerly enslaved African Americans left the South. They sought more freedom and greater economic opportunity. Many of them joined the rush for land in the West. Some were able to take advantage of the Homestead Act. By 1881, between 40,000 and 70,000 African Americans had moved to Kansas, including a group called the Exodusters. They took their name from a book of the Bible that tells the story of the Jews escaping slavery in Egypt. Unlike many homesteaders, the Exodusters paid for their land when they moved to Kansas in 1879.

Among the African Americans who moved West were the men of the 9th and 10th Cavalry. The men in these military units were all African Americans, although their officers were white. Given the nickname "Buffalo Soldiers" by the American Indians, they were known for their discipline and courage. Between 1870 and 1890, 14 Buffalo Soldiers were awarded the Medal of Honor, the U.S. armed force's highest decoration for bravery. Like African Americans everywhere at that time, however, those in the West continued to experience racism and discrimination.

Anglos and Mexicanos in the Southwest Easterners who moved to the Southwest found a large established Spanish-speaking population there. As you recall, the United States had gained much of the Southwest through the Mexican War. Many of its inhabitants were people of Spanish or Mexican origin who had lived in the region before it became part of the United States.

Spanish-speaking southwesterners called themselves Mexicanos. White Americans who lived in the region were known as Anglos. Most Mexicanos lived in small villages, where they farmed and raised sheep. A few wealthy Mexicanos were large landowners and merchants.

As more Anglos settled in the Southwest, they acquired the best jobs and land. Often, Mexicanos found themselves working as low-paid laborers on Anglo farms. In New Mexico, in the 1880s, angry farmers known as *Las Gorras Blancas*, or "White Caps," demanded fair treatment. Other Mexicanos in Arizona founded the Hispanic-American Alliance in 1894 to protect and fight for their rights.

Settlements on Oklahoma Farmland As settlers spread across the West, free land began to disappear. The last major land rush took place in Oklahoma. Several American Indian nations lived there, but the government forced them to sell their land. The government then announced that farmers could claim free homesteads in Oklahoma. They could not stake their claims, however, until noon on April 22, 1889.

Analyze Images Among the new Westerners were these California businessmen in 1890. **Use Visual Information** Describe the tools these men used to run their business.

On that day, as many as 100,000 land seekers lined up at the Oklahoma border. At noon, the "boomers" charged into Oklahoma, but they found that others were already there. "Sooners" sneaked into Oklahoma before the official opening and staked out much of the best land.

The physical characteristics of the Oklahoma environment meant that farmers needed good land in order to succeed. Those who settled on fertile farmland had better chances than those who ended up with less fertile land.

Academic Vocabulary

mechanization • *n.*, to change a process or action so it is performed with machines

Farming in California Only 10 percent of California's public land went to homesteaders. Farming in California was largely industrial agriculture rather than small family farms. Agriculture became the main driver of the early California economy.

From the 1850s on, after the Gold Rush, many former miners became migrant farm workers, helping plant and harvest wheat, corn, and barley. **Mechanization** came later, in the form of steam tractors and harvesters. This machinery helped the agricultural industry become more efficient and productive.

Immigrants from China, Korea, Japan, the Philippines, and India also worked the fields. Before coming to the United States, many of them had labored on plantations in Hawaii. In California, they helped build irrigation systems, and some established large farms of their own.

As knowledge of soil and climate improved, many farmers began growing vegetables and planting fruit and nut orchards. Canneries and packing plants shipped California produce by rail across the country and by ship around the world.

READING CHECK **Identify Supporting Details** Who worked to get around the rules of the Homestead Act in order to profit from the land, and how did they profit?

What Did the Morrill Acts Do?

At the same time industry was growing, agriculture was becoming more of a business as farmers increasingly grew food for the market. To train professionals for both agriculture and industry, publicly supported agricultural and mechanical colleges were needed. The Morrill Land-Grant Colleges Act of 1862 gave states 30,000 acres of public land per congressional representative to set up colleges. Colleges founded on this land had to teach science, classics, agriculture, mechanics, and military tactics.

In 1890, a second Morrill Act was passed to extend land-grant funding to African American students. It required states either to admit students of all races to their land-grant colleges or to set up separate land-grant colleges for African Americans. The South chose the latter.

Many of these agricultural colleges grew into historically Black colleges and universities serving African Americans in the South.

Both of the **Morrill Acts** had important effects on the country. Private colleges were expensive. The new public schools were more affordable. They made college more available to Americans and affirmed that the government would play a role in supporting higher education.

READING CHECK **Draw Conclusions** Why were the Morrill Acts important for the average American student?

Life on the Plains

Farmers on the western plains faced many hardships. The first problem was shelter. Because wood was scarce on the Great Plains, many farmers built houses of sod—soil held together by grass roots. Rain was a serious problem for sod houses. One woman complained that her sod roof "leaked two days before a rain and for three days after."

Sodbusting The fertile soil of the Great Plains was covered with a thick layer of sod that was tough enough to crack wood or iron plows. A new sodbusting plow made of steel reached the market by 1877. It enabled **sodbusters**, as Plains farmers were called, to cut through the sod to the soil below.

Technology helped farmers in other ways. On the Great Plains, water often lay hundreds of feet underground. Farmers built windmills to pump it to the surface. New reapers, threshing machines, and binders helped farmers harvest crops.

Environmental Challenges The dry climate was a constant threat. When too little rain fell, the crops shriveled and died. Dry weather also brought the threat of fire. A grass fire traveled "as fast as a horse could run." The summers often brought swarms of grasshoppers that ate everything in their path—crops, food, tree bark, even clothing. In winter, with few trees or hills to block the wind, icy gusts built huge snowdrifts. Deep snow buried farm animals and sometimes trapped families inside their homes.

Did you know?

As a joke, farmers referred to sod as "Nebraska marble," because it was as important in construction on the prairie as marble stone was back east.

Analyze Images The roofs of sod houses were extremely strong because of the intertwined roots that made up the sod. **Understand Effects** How would rain affect people living in sod houses?

Analyze Images Pioneer families spent most of their time tending to their farms, but they also came together for certain tasks, such as educating children, as shown here. **Infer** Do you think people looked forward to times when neighbors worked together? Why or why not?

Pioneer Women on the Plains Pioneer life on the Great Plains was challenging, and people had to be strong and self-sufficient. Because there were few stores, women made clothing, soap, candles, and other goods by hand. They also preserved food needed for the long winter. Women served their communities in many ways. Most schoolteachers were women. When there were no doctors nearby, women treated the sick and injured.

Growing up on the Plains, Laura Ingalls Wilder experienced the hardships of pioneer life as a child. She wrote about that life in a series of books. In one of them, *Little Town on the Prairie,* she summarized the attitude that helped pioneer families survive:

Primary Source

"This earthly life is a battle," said Ma. "If it isn't one thing to contend with, it's another. It always has been so, and it always will be. The sooner you make up your mind to that, the better off you are, and more thankful for your pleasures."

—Laura Ingalls Wilder, *Little Town on the Prairie*

Relying on the Physical Environment Homesteaders depended on the environment for their livelihood. They needed the right amounts of water, sunlight, rain, and soil for their crops. This made homesteading risky. Those who owned their farms worked hard to keep the land productive. They wanted to ensure that their property would continue to supply the resources they needed to survive. Homesteaders were extremely self-sufficient. They used resources from the environment to meet their needs.

Economic Challenges Farmers began to thrive in the West. Before long, they were selling huge amounts of wheat and corn in the nation's growing cities and even in Europe. Then, farmers faced an unexpected problem. The more they harvested, the less they earned.

In 1881, a bushel of wheat sold for $1.19. By 1894, the price had plunged to 49 cents. Western farmers were hurt most by low grain prices. They had borrowed money during good times to buy land and machinery. When wheat prices fell, they could not repay their debts.

INTERACTIVE

Nineteenth-Century Sod House

READING CHECK **Identify Supporting Details** What effects did the isolation of western farms have on the women of the Plains?

How Did Farmers Help Each Other?

Farmers began to work together. They learned that they could improve their condition through economic cooperation and political action.

The National Grange Supports Cooperation In 1867, farmers formed the National Grange. Grangers wanted to boost farm profits and reduce the rates that railroads charged for shipping grain.

Grangers helped farmers set up cooperatives. In a **cooperative** a group of farmers pooled their money to buy seeds and tools wholesale. **Wholesale** means buying or selling something in large quantities at lower prices. Grangers built cooperative warehouses so that farmers could store grain cheaply while waiting for better selling prices.

Leaders of the Grangerism movement urged farmers to use their vote. In 1873, western and southern Grangers **pledged** to vote only for candidates who supported their aims. They elected officials who understood the farmers' problems. As a result, several states passed laws limiting what could be charged for grain shipment and storage. Nevertheless, crop prices continued to drop. Farmers sank deeper into debt.

Academic Vocabulary
pledge • *v.*, to promise

The Farmers' Alliance Spreads Another group, the Farmers' Alliance, joined the struggle in the 1870s. Like the Grange, the Alliance set up cooperatives and warehouses. The Alliance spread from Texas through the South and into the Plains states. Alliance leaders tried to join with factory workers and miners angered by poor treatment.

READING CHECK **Identify Main Ideas** What was the principle upon which the National Grange and the Farmers' Alliance were formed?

Analyze Graphs Granges grew quickly between 1873 and 1874. A ton of wheat includes 36.7 bushels. **Cite Evidence** Based on the information in the charts, why did farmers form Granges?

FARMERS UNITE TO BATTLE FREIGHT PRICES

FREIGHT COSTS VARY WIDELY

NEW YORK → CHICAGO
1 TON
$5–$38

NEW YORK → ST. LOUIS
1 TON
$7–$46

Sources: *Wholesale Prices, Wages, and Transportation*, U.S. Senate Report, 1893

GRANGE MEMBERSHIP

Granges (per 100,000 agricultural population)
1,000
750
500
250
0
1873 1874 1875 1876
Iowa
Minnesota
Wisconsin
Illinois

Source: National Bureau of Economic Research

PRICE OF WHEAT & FREIGHT RATES FROM CHICAGO TO NEW YORK

PRICE PER BUSHEL		FREIGHT RATE
$1.44	1867	32.38¢
$1.10	1872	31.13¢
$1.03	1877	19.56¢
$0.88	1882	14.47¢
$0.68	1887	15.75¢
$0.62	1892	13.80¢
$0.73	1896	12.00¢

Source: Department of Agriculture Report, 1897

What Was Populism?

In 1892, farmers and labor unions joined to form the People's Party, also known as the Populists. Populists demanded that the government help to raise farm prices and to regulate railroad rates. They also called for an income tax, an eight-hour workday, and immigration limits.

The key Populist Party demand was "free silver." Populists wanted all silver mined in the West to be coined into money. They said that farm prices dropped because there was not enough money in circulation. Free silver would increase the money supply and make it easier for farmers to repay their debts.

Eastern bankers and factory owners opposed this. They argued that increasing the money supply would cause **inflation**, or increased prices, and wreck the economy. They favored the gold standard, a system in which the government backs every dollar with a certain amount of gold. Since the supply of gold is limited, there would be less money in circulation. Prices would drop.

Bryan Versus McKinley The Populists looked toward the election of 1896 with high hopes. Their program had been endorsed by one of the great orators of the age: Democrat William Jennings Bryan.

Like the Populists, Bryan believed that the nation needed to increase the supply of money. At the Democratic convention in 1896, Bryan made a powerful speech against the rich and for free silver.

Analyze Political Cartoons William Jennings Bryan was the Democratic and Populist parties' choice for president in 1896. **Use Visual Information** What does the cartoonist think about Bryan's turn toward Populism?

At the end of his speech, referring to the rich, Bryan proclaimed, "You shall not crucify mankind upon a cross of gold."

Both Democrats and Populists supported Bryan for President. However, business people feared that Bryan would ruin the economy. They supported William McKinley, the Republican candidate. McKinley and the Republican Party supported the gold standard.

Bryan narrowly lost the election of 1896. He carried the South and the West, but McKinley won the heavily populated North and East.

The People's Party broke up after 1896. One reason was that, with Bryan as a candidate, the Democrats adopted several Populist causes. Also, prosperity returned in the late 1890s. People worried less about railroad rates and the gold standard.

READING CHECK **Identify Cause and Effect** Why were eastern bankers opposed to the Populists' "free silver" demand?

Analyze Images William McKinley won the 1896 Presidential election. **Compare and Contrast** How are the images of McKinley and Bryan alike? Different?

Lesson Check

Practice Vocabulary

1. How did the **cattle drives** lead to the rise of **cow towns**?
2. How did technology help the **sodbuster**?

Critical Thinking and Writing

3. **Draw Conclusions** Why were immigrants and easterners the main groups who took advantage of the Homestead Act?
4. **Compare and Contrast** Why did Congress create each of the Morrill Acts?
5. **Summarize** How did farmers cooperate economically and politically?
6. **Explain an Argument** Do you think the Homestead Act was a wise way for the government to distribute public lands? Explain.
7. **Writing Workshop: Support Claims** Write a few sentences in your Active Journal to explain why your claim makes sense as a response to the question of how much the government should do to create a national infrastructure.

LESSON 3

Hardship for American Indians

GET READY TO READ

START UP

Look at the photo of American Indians on horseback. Make a list of ways the Plains Indians might have benefited from having horses.

GUIDING QUESTIONS

- What role did the bison play in the life of the Plains Indians?
- How did shifting federal policy toward American Indians cause ongoing problems?
- Why did reforms aimed at improving federal policy fail American Indians?

TAKE NOTES

Literacy Skills Summarize

Use the graphic organizer in your Active Journal to take notes as you read the lesson.

PRACTICE VOCABULARY

Use the vocabulary activity in your Active Journal to practice the vocabulary words.

Vocabulary		Academic Vocabulary
travois	reservation	resist
tepee	allotment	recount
jerky		
corral		

What Was the Early History of the Plains Indians?

American Indians had been living for centuries on the Great Plains. A number of them, such as the Arikaras, had lived on the Plains for hundreds of years. Others, such as the Lakotas, did not move to the Plains until the early 1700s.

Farming and Hunting Plains Indians had rich and varied cultures. They were skilled artists. They also had well-organized religions and warrior societies. Each nation had its own language. Sign language, or "hand-talk" also allowed people from different nations to communicate.

At one time, most Plains Indians were farmers who lived in semi-permanent villages. They sent out hunting parties on foot to pursue herds of buffalo and other animals. Agriculture, however, was their main source of food. They grew a variety of crops, including corn, beans, and sunflowers.

READING CHECK **Identify Supporting Details** During their early history, how did Plains Indians obtain most of their food?

Horses Transform Life on the Plains

Christopher Columbus had brought horses to the Americas in the late 1400s, and the Spanish brought them to the North American mainland in the 1500s. Under Spanish rule, American Indians were not allowed to own horses, but they did learn how to care for them and ride them. After the Pueblo revolted against the Spaniards in 1680, they were left with thousands of horses. They started trading these horses to neighboring American Indians. Eventually, the horses reached the people of the northern plains.

The horse transformed the lives of the Plains Indians. Horses allowed hunters to pursue and kill bison more easily than they could on foot. Stronger than dogs, horses could haul heavier loads on sleds called **travois** (truh-VOY), which allowed entire villages to follow the herds of bison as they migrated. During these times of following the herds, the Plains Indians lived in cone-shaped tents called **tepees**. Teepees consisted of long poles covered with bison hides. A flap at the top released the smoke of the hearth fire.

Hunting Bison Although the American Indians of the plains also hunted deer and elk, they mainly depended on the bison. Bison meat, rich in protein, was a staple in their diet. Women cut up and dried the meat on racks. The dried meat was called **jerky**. Bison hides were used for tepee covers, transformed into clothing, and even used to make boats. Bison horns were crafted into spoons and weapon points. Even the bison's tails were incorporated into hoop-shaped toys.

The movement of the Plains Indians mirrored the migration of the bison. In winter, small groups of bison moved to protected valleys and forests. In summer, huge herds gathered on the Plains where the grass was plentiful. In the same way, Plains Indians spent the winter in small bands and gathered in large groups during the summers. Some, such as the Arikara, planted their crops in the spring, followed the bison in the summer, and returned in time to harvest.

Did you know?

True buffalo live in Africa and Asia. The proper name for what we call the buffalo is "American bison."

Interpret Images Plains Indians had hunted bison before they obtained horses. **Infer** How would having horses change hunting methods?

Before horses came to the Plains, hunting bison was difficult. A group of hunters would shout and wave colored robes at the bison. The hunters would gradually drive a herd of buffalo into a **corral**, or enclosure.

There they killed the trapped bison. Then, everyone, including the children helped cut up the bison and take the meat and other materials back to camp.

Once they had horses, the bison hunters could ride right into the herd and kill their targets with bows and arrows, and, later, guns.

Councils and Ceremonies Many American Indian groups met on the Plains. They hunted together and attended special events. Summer gatherings were the time for councils. At the councils, the elders were consulted about the problems that affected an entire Plains Indian nation.

An important religious ceremony among the Plains peoples was the Sun Dance. Each nation performed it slightly differently, but the ritual was a means of renewing the relationship between the people, the land, and the spirit world. However, neither the Canadian nor United States government saw the ritual in that way; the Sun Dance was outlawed until the mid-1900s.

READING CHECK **Recall** How was the bison useful to the Plains Indians?

Division of Labor in Plains Indian Society

In Plains Indian nations, men and women had distinct jobs within society. While their roles were different, there was more flexibility than in white society. Some tribes had "two spirit" traditions, which were later lost when new Anglo-American gender roles were imposed. In some nations, women took part in hunting and governing. A Blackfoot woman, Running Eagle, led many hunting parties herself.

Women's Responsibilities Women's responsibilities included gathering food and making meals, yet they also tanned the hides of the bison and used them to make clothing, including shoes and mittens.

Analyze Images Men and women had different responsibilities within Plains Indian societies. **Infer** Do you think Plains Indian society enforced rigid gender roles?

Interpret Images Soldiers of the U.S. Cavalry attack a Cheyenne village at Sand Creek. More than 150 Cheyenne men, women, and children lost their lives in the massacre. **Draw Conclusions** What effect did the Sand Creek Massacre have on the relationship between the Plains Indians and the government?

Women not only made the tepees, but also raised and took them down. They cared for the children and, along with the men, passed along the traditions of their people.

Men's Responsibilities Men hunted to provide food and other materials they needed. They passed on their valuable skills and knowledge to the boys. They led religious ceremonies and waged war to protect their people, to defend or extend territory, and to gain horses.

READING CHECK **Classify and Categorize** What role did women play in the Plains Indian society?

Broken Promises

Before white settlers arrived on the Plains, the Plains Indians often fought with one another over territory or other resources, including horses. But as white settlers began to encroach on Plains Indians' lands, their attention turned toward this new threat.

Conflict on the Plains began as early as the 1840s, when settlers and miners began to cross Plains Indian hunting grounds on their way west. The settlers and miners asked for government protection from the American Indians.

A Treaty Quickly Forgotten The U.S. government built a string of forts to protect settlers and miners. In 1851, federal government officials met with Plains Indian nations near Fort Laramie in Wyoming. The officials asked each nation to keep to a limited area. In return, they promised money, domestic animals, farm tools, and other goods.

 INTERACTIVE

Native American Losses, 1850–1890

Officials told the American Indians that the lands that were reserved for them would be theirs forever. This promise would not be kept, however. Under federal policy toward American Indians established under President Andrew Jackson, American Indian peoples would be moved to make way for white expansion. Promises would be made and later broken.

Analyze Images These American Indian children wear the uniforms of the government school they were forced to attend. **Infer** How did forcing American Indian children to dress this way affect them culturally?

American Indian leaders agreed to the terms of the Fort Laramie Treaty. However, in 1858, gold was discovered at Pikes Peak in Colorado. A wave of white miners rushed to land that the government had promised to the Cheyenne and Arapaho peoples. Federal officials forced American Indian leaders to sign a new treaty giving up the land around Pikes Peak. Some American Indians refused to accept the agreement. They attacked white settlers.

The Sand Creek Massacre The settlers struck back. In 1864, Colonel John Chivington led his militia against a Cheyenne village whose leaders had come to a fort asking for protection. When Chivington attacked, the Cheyenne raised both a white flag of surrender and the flag of the United States. Chivington had thought the Cheyenne were hostile. He either ignored or did not see the flags. He ordered his men to destroy the village and take no prisoners. In what would become known as the Sand Creek Massacre, the militia slaughtered more than 150 men, women, and children.

After the massacre, soldiers said they found scalps of whites in the camp, indicating that there had been some hostile American Indians there. A congressional committee that investigated the massacre condemned Chivington's actions, but Chivington had already left the army. As a result of the massacre, Plains Indians went to war. They attacked white settlers and U.S. troops. U.S. troops responded by attacking American Indians.

Changing Traditional Ways of Life In 1867, federal officials established a peace commission to end the wars on the Plains. The government sent many American Indian children to government-run boarding schools, which forced them to dress in European-style clothes and learn English. They were discouraged from practicing their own culture or speaking their own language.

The Reservation System In 1867, the Kiowas, Comanches, and other southern Plains Indians signed a new treaty with the government. They promised to move to Indian Territory in present-day Oklahoma. The soil there was poor. Also, most Plains Indians were hunters, not farmers. They did not like the treaty but knew they had no choice.

The Lakotas and Arapahos of the northern Plains also signed a second Fort Laramie Treaty in 1868. They agreed to live on **reservations** in present-day South Dakota. A reservation is a limited area set aside for American Indians.

Bison Populations Fall Dramatically The Plains Indians suffered from lost battles and broken treaties. Even worse for them, however, was the destruction of the bison.

The decline of the bison began before the arrival of white settlers. Great herds lived in areas west of the Mississippi and east of the Rockies. However, with disease, drought, and destruction of the areas in which they lived, the herds were slowly growing smaller. As the market demand for bison robes increased during the 1830s and 1840s, professional hunters killed more of the animals. In addition, bison hunting became a pastime for railroad passengers, who could shoot at the animals from moving trains. Dead, dying, and wounded bison littered the plains.

American Indians learned to hunt more efficiently. Some, such as the Pawnee, continued to hunt bison even though they knew the number of bison was decreasing.

The bison hunt was a part of their culture that they did not want to give up. As the bison disappeared, so did the Plains Indians' way of life.

READING CHECK **Identify Cause and Effect** Why were the terms of the Fort Laramie treaty broken?

Analyze Images Bison run as passengers and crew aboard this train shoot at them for sport. This contributed to the rapid decline of the bison population in the mid to late 1800s. **Use Visual Information** How does this image sum up the attitude of Americans of this time toward the natural world?

Analyze Images General George A. Custer (front, on horse) and his soldiers attacked a Lakota and Cheyenne camp at Little Bighorn. Far outnumbered, the U.S. soldiers were all killed, including Custer. **Synthesize Visual Information** What impression of Custer does this painting give the viewer?

Conflict in the West Continues

White settlers and miners continued to move into the West. They wanted more and more land for themselves. Even on reservations, American Indians were not left in peace.

The Battle of Little Bighorn In 1874, prospectors found gold in the Black Hills region of the Lakota, or Sioux, reservation. Thousands of white miners rushed to the area.

To protect the miners, the federal government sent George A. Custer. The rash cavalry leader decided to attack a group of Lakota led by Sitting Bull. Custer divided his 600 men and led 225 of them into battle. Sitting Bull led nearly 2,000 warriors against them. Some of the other U.S. troops escaped, but the Lakota killed Custer and all his men at the Battle of Little Bighorn, the first battle of the Sioux War of 1876.

The American Indian victory at the Little Bighorn was short lived. The army soon defeated the Lakotas and Cheyennes. Then, Congress said no food could be distributed to the American Indians until they agreed to the government's demands. To avoid starvation, the Lakotas gave up most claims to the Black Hills and other territory. They surrendered about one third of the lands that the U.S. government had guaranteed them in the Fort Laramie Treaty of 1868.

Lakota leaders Sitting Bull and Crazy Horse had taken their few remaining followers to Canada. Eventually, both men returned.

Chief Joseph Resists Further Settlement The Nez Percé people lived in the Snake River valley, at the place where today Oregon, Washington, and Idaho meet. In 1855, some Nez Percé signed a treaty with the U.S. government in which they gave up part of their land.

In the 1860s, gold discoveries brought miners onto Nez Percé land. The government ordered the Nez Percé to move to a reservation in Idaho. Those who had not signed the treaty refused. Led by Chief Joseph, about 700 Nez Percé fled north toward Canada. Army troops followed close behind.

In the months that followed, the Nez Percé fought off or eluded pursuing army units. Finally, after a tragic journey of more than 1,000 miles, Chief Joseph decided that he had to surrender. Of the approximately 700 people who had set out with him, fewer than 450 remained. They were only 40 miles from the border.

Geronimo Surrenders in the Southwest In the arid lands of the Southwest, the Apaches fiercely **resisted** the loss of their lands. One leader, Geronimo, continued fighting the longest. In 1876, he assumed leadership of a band of Apache warriors when the government tried to force his people onto a reservation.

Academic Vocabulary
resist • *v.*, to fight against

Geronimo waged war off and on for the next ten years. From Mexico, he led frequent raids into Arizona and New Mexico. His surrender in 1886 marked the end of formal warfare between American Indians and whites.

READING CHECK **Identify Supporting Details** Why did the Sioux War of 1876 begin?

Longing for a Lost Way of Life

Many American Indians longed for their lost way of life. On the reservations, the Lakotas and other Plains Indians turned to a religious ceremony called the Ghost Dance. It celebrated the time when American Indians lived freely on the Plains.

What Was the Ghost Dance? In 1889, word spread that a prophet named Wovoka (woh VOH kuh) had appeared among the Paiute people of the region around Nevada. Wovoka said there would come a new world, free of white people and filled with plenty. To bring about this new world, he said, all the American Indians had to do was perform the Ghost Dance.

Analyze Charts Geronimo and Chief Joseph both led their tribes during difficult times. **Identify Supporting Details** How would you describe each man's leadership?

Two American Indian Leaders

Chief Joseph (1840–1904)	Geronimo (1829–1909)
• Of the Nez Percé in northeastern Oregon. • Given name was Hin-mah-too-yah-lat-kekt, or Thunder Rolling Down the Mountain. • Elected chief after his father died in 1871. • Met with President Rutherford B. Hayes in 1879 but could not persuade him to return the Nez Percé to their Oregon lands. • Quote: "If you tie a horse to a stake, do you expect him to grow fat? If you pen an Indian up on a small spot of earth, and compel him to stay there, he will not be contented, nor will he grow and prosper."	• Of the Chiricahua Apache in northern Mexico (present-day Arizona–New Mexico border) • Given name was Goyathlay, or The One Who Yawns. • Trained as a shaman, or holy man, but became a fearsome warrior after Mexican soldiers killed his mother, wife, and three of his children. • Attended the inauguration of President Theodore Roosevelt in 1905. • Quote, said just before he died: "I should never have surrendered. I should have fought until I was the last man alive."

In their ceremonies, Ghost Dancers joined hands in a large circle in which they danced, chanted, and prayed. As they danced, some felt a "growing happiness." Others saw a glowing vision of a new world.

Settlers Misinterpret the Ghost Dance Many settlers grew alarmed. The Ghost Dancers, they said, were preparing for war. The settlers persuaded the government to outlaw the Ghost Dance.

In December 1890, police officers entered a Lakota reservation to arrest Sitting Bull. They claimed that he was spreading the Ghost Dance among the Lakotas. In the struggle that followed, Sitting Bull was accidentally shot and killed.

Tragedy at Wounded Knee Upset by Sitting Bull's death, groups of Lakotas fled the reservations. Army troops pursued them to Wounded Knee Creek, in South Dakota. On December 29, the Lakota were preparing to surrender. As nervous troops watched, the Indians began to give up their guns.

Suddenly, a shot rang out. One account says a rifle went off by accident. The army opened fire. By the time the shooting stopped, nearly 300 Lakota men, women, and children lay dead. About 25 soldiers had also died. The massacre at Wounded Knee marked the end of warfare between the Plains Indians and the U.S. Army.

READING CHECK **Identify** What was the purpose of the Ghost Dance?

Interpret Images Wearing dresses covered with small metal bells, these jingle dancers are preparing for a competition. **Infer** What does the advent of the jingle dance in the 20th century say about American Indian society?

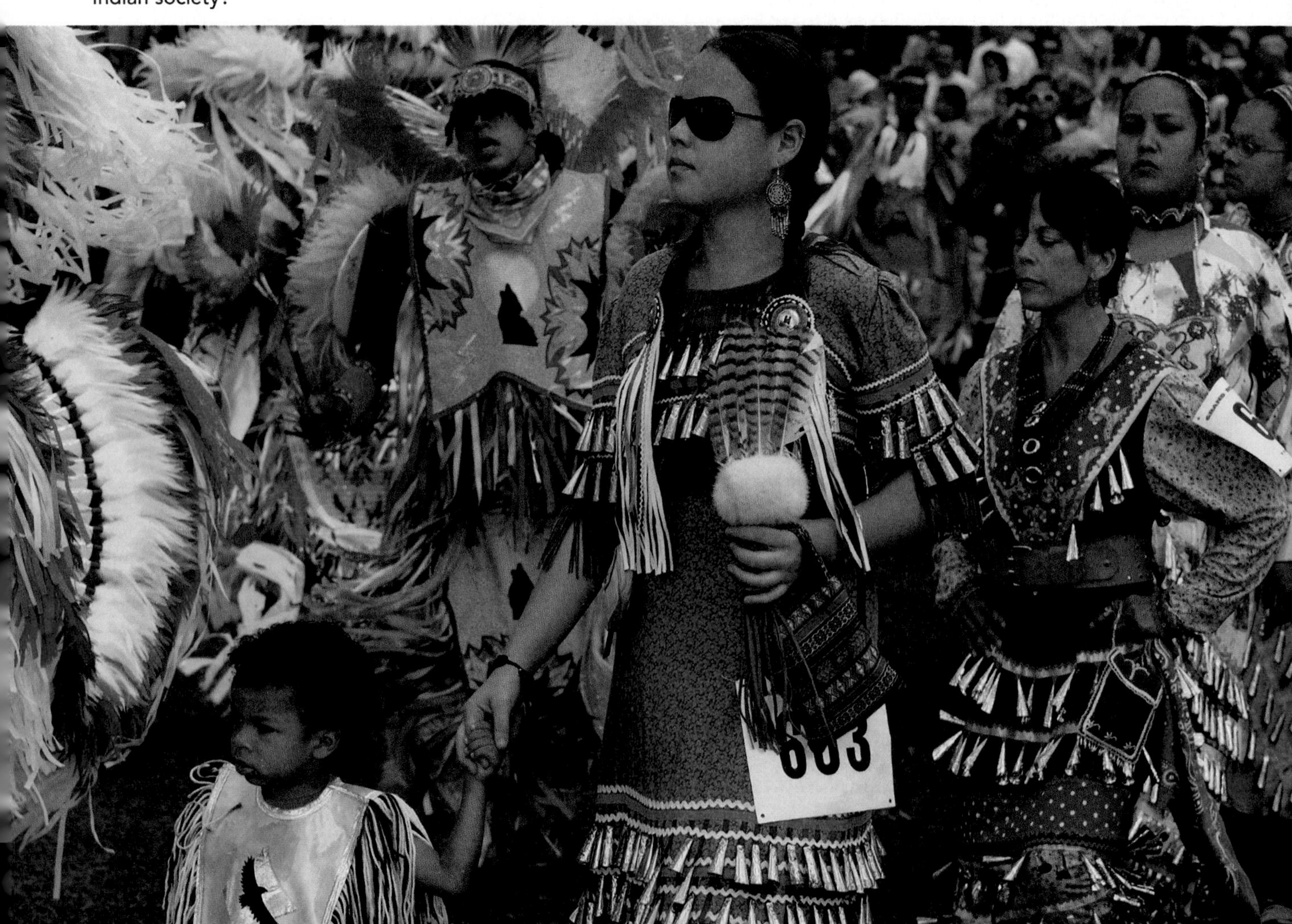

American Indian Policy Reform

The American Indians were no longer able to resist the U.S. government. During the late 1800s, more American Indians were forced onto reservations.

Publicizing Tragedies American Indians and white people spoke out against the tragedy that was occurring. Susette La Flesche, the daughter of an Omaha chief, wrote and lectured about the destruction of the Indian way of life. Another reformer, Helen Hunt Jackson, wrote *A Century of Dishonor* in 1881. The book **recounts** the history of broken treaties between the United States and the American Indians.

Dawes Act Calls for reform led Congress to pass the Dawes Act in 1887. The act encouraged American Indians to become farmers. It called for the **allotment**, or distribution, of reservation land to individual Indian families.

The Dawes Act was a major change in federal policy toward American Indians. Before the Act, Indians had been removed from their land and placed on reservations. With the Dawes Act, the government tried to lessen traditional influences on Indian society by making land ownership private rather than shared. The Act also ended some elements of female authority respected in many tribal societies.

The Dawes Act did not have the desired effect, however. Much of the land American Indians were assigned was not fertile. As a result, they often sold the land to white people for low prices. Reservation life changed American Indian culture. The federal government took away the power of Indian leaders. In their place, it appointed government agents to make most decisions.

▲ This monument memorializes those who died at Wounded Knee.

Academic Vocabulary
recount • *v.,* to tell about something that happened

READING CHECK **Identify Main Ideas** Describe the purpose and effects of the Dawes Act.

Lesson Check

Practice Vocabulary

1. How did the **tepee** and the **travois** make it easier for Plains Indians to follow the bison?
2. How did a **reservation** limit the activities of Plains Indians?

Critical Thinking and Writing

3. Why did conflict develop between white settlers and Plains Indians?
4. Given what you have learned about the treatment of American Indians at the hands of the U.S. government, what best explains the reaction of Chief Joseph and some Nez Percé Indians when they were ordered to move to a reservation in Idaho after gold was discovered on their land?
5. Why did the new federal policy outlined in the Dawes Act fail as a reform measure?
6. **Writing Workshop: Distinguish Claims from Opposing Claims** Write a few sentences in your Active Journal to explain how your claim, or argument, varies from the opposing claim.

Primary Sources

Chief Joseph, "I Will Fight No More Forever"

In 1877, Chief Joseph and other Nez Percé fled their home territory to avoid being forced to move to a reservation. After a journey of 1,000 miles, army troops finally caught up with them. An exhausted Chief Joseph sent his surrender to General Oliver Howard.

◀ Chief Joseph became chief after his father died.

Reading and Vocabulary Support

① Looking Glass was a Nez Percé warrior. Too-hul-hul-suit and the "old men" were elders.

② With the old Nez Percé men dead, who does Joseph say are making the decisions?

③ Chief Joseph here refers to his brother, Ollicut.

④ Who else, besides his own family, might the chief be referring to here?

⑤ What is the meaning of the phrase "From where the sun now stands"?

"I am tired of fighting. Our chiefs are killed; Looking Glass is dead. Too-hul-hul-suit is dead. The old men are all dead. ① It is the young men, now, who say yes or no. ② He who led on the young men is dead. ③ It is cold and we have no blankets. The little children are freezing to death. My people—some of them—have run away to the hills, and have no blankets, no food. No one knows where they are—perhaps freezing to death. I want to have time to look for my children ④ and see how many of them I can find; maybe I shall find them among the dead. Hear me, my chiefs; my heart is sick and sad. From where the sun now stands, ⑤ I will fight no more forever!"

—Chief Joseph, October 5, 1877

Analyzing Primary Sources

Cite specific evidence from the document to support your answers.

1. **Analyze Structure** Which sentence actually contains Chief Joseph's words of surrender?
2. **Analyze Style and Rhetoric** What is the overall emotion that Chief Joseph expressed in this surrender statement?

Frame Questions

Follow these steps to frame questions.

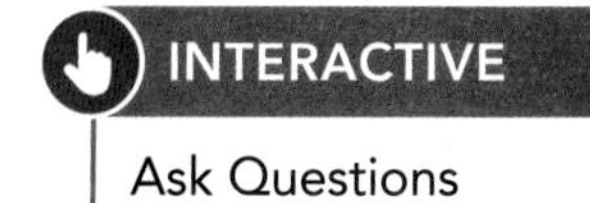

1 Identify your focus When studying an event, begin by focusing on what the passage is about and what you are trying to learn. As you read, ask yourself: *Who? What? Where? When? Why?* and *How?* Asking yourself "Who?" as you read will establish that the writer is Lone Wolf, a Blackfoot man recalling his childhood.

2 Identify the information provided As you review a source, note the questions it clearly answers. This source answers more than just the "Who?" question. The "Where?" question is partly answered—"Fort Shaw."

3 Frame remaining questions Now think about what you still need to learn after having studied your source. Which questions remain to be answered? As you read the source, form these and other missing pieces of information into questions. The intensely personal nature of this source might lead you to ask, "Why?"

4 Plan your research With your list of questions, plan how you will seek answers. Ask yourself, "What kinds of sources would help me answer this question?"

Primary Source

It was very cold that day when we were loaded into the wagons. None of us wanted to go and our parents didn't want to let us go. Oh, we cried for this was the first time we were to be separated from our parents. I remember looking back at Na-tah-ki and she was crying too. Nobody waved as the wagons, escorted by the soldiers, took us toward the school at Fort Shaw.

Once there our belongings were taken from us, even the little medicine bags our mothers had given us to protect us from harm. Everything was placed in a heap and set afire.

Next was the long hair, the pride of all the Indians. The boys, one by one, would break down and cry when they saw their braids thrown on the floor. All of the buckskin clothes had to go and we had to put on the clothes of the White Man.

If we thought that the days were bad, the nights were much worse. This was the time when real loneliness set in, for it was then we knew that we were all alone. Many boys ran away from the school because the treatment was so bad but most of them were caught and brought back by the police. We were told never to talk Indian and if we were caught, we got a strapping with a leather belt.

I remember one evening when we were all lined up in a room and one of the boys said something in Indian to another boy. The man in charge of us pounced on the boy, caught him by the shirt, and threw him across the room. Later we found out that his collar-bone was broken.

— Lone Wolf, Blackfoot

LESSON 4

Industry and Corporations

BOUNCE TO ACTIVATE VIDEO

GET READY TO READ

START UP

Study the photo of the Pittsburgh region. Write a few sentences about some of the positive and negative effects of industrial development.

GUIDING QUESTIONS

- What led to the expansion of the steel industry?
- What strategies and practices helped some entrepreneurs and bankers establish great fortunes for themselves?
- What are some arguments for and against trusts and monopolies?

TAKE NOTES

Literacy Skills Cite Evidence

Use the graphic organizer in your Active Journal to take notes as you read the lesson.

PRACTICE VOCABULARY

Use the vocabulary activity in your Active Journal to practice the vocabulary words.

Vocabulary		Academic Vocabulary
stock	monopoly	efficiency
corporation	capitalism	revenue
dividend	scarcity	
trust		

The railroads that arose after the Civil War were big businesses. Other big businesses followed as entrepreneurs, industrialists, and bankers found new ways to increase economic **efficiency** and the output of goods. In the process, they brought prosperity to the country and fabulous wealth to themselves.

The Steel Industry Expands

After the Civil War, the expansion of railroads spurred the growth of the steel industry. Early trains ran on iron rails that wore out quickly. Railroad owners knew that steel rails were much stronger and not as likely to rust as iron rails. Steel, however, was costly and difficult to make.

A New Way to Produce Steel In the 1850s, William Kelly in the United States and Henry Bessemer in England each discovered a new way to make steel. The Bessemer process, as it came to be called, used oxygen and other materials to purify molten iron ore into steel. It enabled steel makers to produce strong steel at a lower cost, and railroads began using steel rails.

Other industries also took advantage of the cheaper steel. Manufacturers made steel nails, screws, needles, and other items. Steel girders supported the great weight of "skyscrapers"—the new tall buildings going up in cities.

Academic Vocabulary
efficiency • *n.,* a way of working that is most productive and least wasteful at the same time

Midwestern Steel Mills Steel mills sprang up in cities throughout the Midwest. Pittsburgh became the steel-making capital of the nation. Nearby coal mines and good transportation helped Pittsburgh's steel mills thrive.

The boom in steel making brought jobs and prosperity to Pittsburgh and other steel towns. It also caused problems. Years of pouring industrial waste into nearby waterways had severely polluted them. Steel mills belched thick black smoke that turned the air gray. Soot blanketed houses, trees, and streets.

READING CHECK **Identify** What effects did the growth of the steel industry have on industrial cities?

How Did Andrew Carnegie Build an Empire?

Many Americans made fortunes in the steel industry. Richest of all was a Scottish immigrant, Andrew Carnegie. Carnegie's ideas about how to make money—and how to spend it—had a wide influence.

Controlling Steel Production During a visit to Britain, Carnegie had seen the Bessemer process in action. Returning to the United States, he borrowed money and began his own steel mill.

Analyze Images The Bessemer process changed iron into steel in a large, fireproof container. **Summarize** Explain how iron is changed during the Bessemer process.

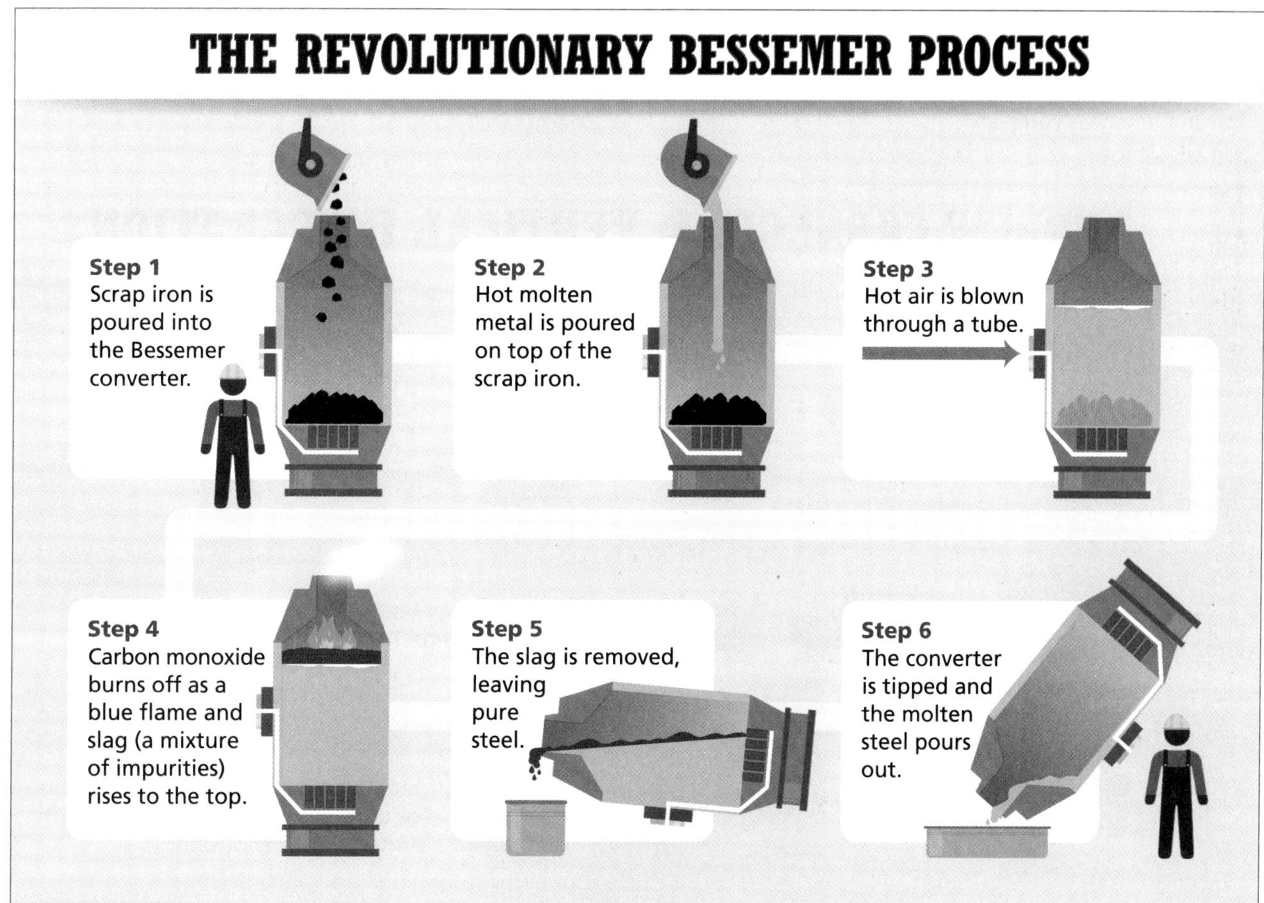

Shortly, Carnegie was earning huge profits. He used the money to buy out rivals. He also bought iron mines, railroad and steamship lines, and warehouses. Soon, Carnegie controlled all phases of the steel industry—from mining iron ore to shipping finished steel. Gaining control of all the steps used to change raw materials into finished products is called vertical integration.

Vertical integration gave Carnegie a great advantage over other steel producers. By 1900, his steel mills were turning out more steel than was produced in all of Great Britain.

The "Gospel of Wealth" Like other business owners, Carnegie drove his workers hard. Still, he believed that the rich had a duty to help the poor and to improve society. He called this idea the "gospel of wealth." Carnegie gave millions of dollars to charities. After selling his steel empire in 1901, he spent his time and money helping people.

Academic Vocabulary
revenue • *n.*, money, especially money collected by a government for public use

READING CHECK **Identify Cause and Effect** Why did Andrew Carnegie have an advantage over other steel producers?

What Led to the Rise of Corporations and Banks?

Before the railroad boom, nearly every American town had its own small factories. They produced goods for people in the area. By the late 1800s, however, big factories were producing goods more cheaply than small factories could. Railroads distributed these goods to markets all over the country. As demand for local goods fell, many small factories closed. Big factories then increased their output.

By increasing output, big factories were able to earn greater **revenue**, or income earned from a business after covering costs.

Analyze Diagrams Andrew Carnegie dominated the steel industry by using the process of vertical integration in building his business. **Identify Cause and Effect** How might vertical integration have given Carnegie's company an advantage?

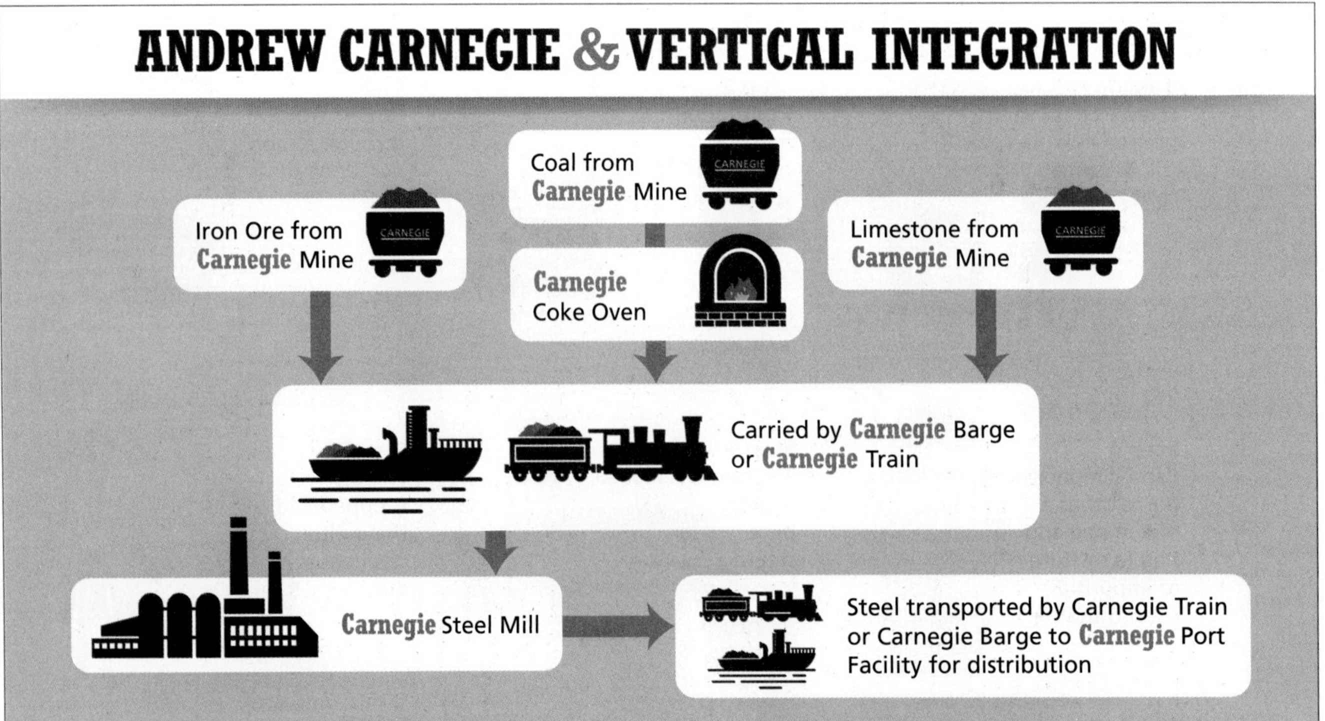

Factories often used revenue to expand operations or buy out rivals. Revenues allowed them to grow.

Companies using revenues to expand increased their capital. Capital is money used to invest in the long-term health and success of a company.

However, sometimes companies borrowed money for capital investment. Other companies gave investors **stock**, or partial ownership of the company, in return for capital. Companies might use this capital to build factories, buy new equipment, or buy out other companies. To raise capital and invest in future growth, Americans adopted new ways of organizing their businesses. They created corporations.

Interpret Images American banker J. P. Morgan merged several companies into one large corporation in the early 1900s. **Infer** How did Morgan's position as a banker help him as a businessman?

Businesses Become Corporations A **corporation** is a business that is owned by investors. Laws and court rulings allow corporations to enjoy many of the rights of individuals.

Investors in stock, or stockholders, hope to receive **dividends**, or shares of a corporation's profit. Stockholders elect a board of directors to run the corporation.

Owners of stock in a corporation face fewer risks than owners of private businesses do. If a private business goes bankrupt, the owner must pay all the debts of the business. By law, stockholders cannot be held responsible for a corporation's debts.

Corporations and Banks In the years after the Civil War, corporations attracted large amounts of capital from American investors. Corporations also borrowed millions of dollars from banks. Some of this money came from national banks backed by the federal government and some came from state banks. Loans helped American industry grow at a rapid pace. At the same time, bankers made huge profits.

The most powerful banker of the late 1800s was J. Pierpont Morgan. Morgan's influence was not limited to banking. He used his banking profits to gain control of major corporations.

During economic hard times in the 1890s, Morgan and other bankers bought up troubled corporations. They then adopted policies that reduced competition and ensured big profits. "I like a little competition, but I like combination more," Morgan used to say.

Morgan gained control of several major rail lines. He then began to buy up steel companies, including Carnegie Steel, and to merge them into a single large corporation. By 1901, Morgan had become head of the United States Steel Company. It was the first American business worth more than $1 billion.

Railroads and Industry

READING CHECK **Identify Cause and Effect** Why did many businesses become corporations?

How Did Rockefeller Take Control of the Oil Industry?

Industry could not have expanded so quickly in the United States without the nation's rich supply of natural resources. Iron ore was plentiful, especially in the Mesabi Range of Minnesota. Pennsylvania, West Virginia, and the Rocky Mountains had large deposits of coal. The Rockies also contained minerals, such as gold, silver, and copper. Vast forests provided lumber for building.

In 1859, Americans discovered a valuable new resource: oil. Drillers near Titusville, Pennsylvania, made the nation's first oil strike. An oil boom quickly followed. Hundreds of prospectors rushed to western Pennsylvania ready to drill wells in search of oil.

The Standard Oil Empire Among those who came to the Pennsylvania oil fields was young John D. Rockefeller. Rockefeller, however, did not rush to drill for oil. He knew that oil had little value until it was refined, or purified, to make kerosene. Kerosene was used as a fuel in stoves and lamps. So Rockefeller built an oil refinery.

Rockefeller believed that competition was wasteful. He used the profits from his refinery to buy up other refineries. He then combined the companies into the Standard Oil Company of Ohio.

Rockefeller was a shrewd businessman. He was always trying to improve the quality of his oil. He also did whatever he could to get rid of competition. Standard Oil slashed its prices to drive rivals out of business. It pressured its customers not to deal with other oil companies. It forced railroad companies eager for its business to grant rebates to Standard Oil. Lower shipping costs gave Rockefeller an important advantage over his competitors.

The success of Rockefeller's empire reflects the economic law of demand. By lowering the price of oil, Rockefeller was able to attract more buyers. By providing enough oil to meet that demand, he could increase total sales.

Rockefeller's success would not have been possible without the rise of national markets. Railroads could distribute products nationally, not just locally. National corporations marketed products widely, and railroads delivered them to consumers across the country.

Analyze Images In 1859, the first oil well was built in Titusville, Pennsylvania, and this photo depicts the National Historic Site that marks that accomplishment. **Infer** How might the discovery of oil have changed the lives of the people of the region?

The Oil Monopoly To tighten his hold over the oil industry, Rockefeller formed the Standard Oil trust in 1882. A **trust** is a group of corporations run by a single board of directors.

Stockholders in dozens of smaller oil companies turned over their stock to Standard Oil. In return, they got stock in the newly created trust. The trust paid the stockholders high dividends. However, the board of Standard Oil, headed by Rockefeller, managed all the companies, which had previously been rivals.

The Standard Oil trust created a monopoly of the oil industry. A **monopoly** controls all or nearly all the business of an industry. The Standard Oil trust controlled 95 percent of all oil refining in the United States.

Other businesses followed Rockefeller's lead. They set up trusts and tried to build monopolies. By the 1890s, monopolies and trusts controlled some of the nation's most important industries.

INTERACTIVE

Advantages and Disadvantages of Big Business

READING CHECK **Identify Supporting Details** What detail from the text shows that Standard Oil was a monopoly?

Americans Debate Over Trusts

Some Americans charged that the leaders of giant corporations were abusing capitalism. Under **capitalism**, businesses are owned by private citizens. Owners decide what products to make, how much to produce, where to sell products, and what prices to charge. Companies compete in a free market to win customers by making the best product at the lowest price.

Analyze Political Cartoons This cartoon shows the Senate dominated by trusts, shown as oversized men watching over senators. **Synthesize Visual Information** Many people argued against trusts and monopolies. What message does the artist convey in this 1889 cartoon?

All people in a free-market system have to make choices about what products to buy. This is because there is a limited supply of resources, a principle known as **scarcity**. Companies compete for scarce resources and for customers. Customers then make choices about what to buy to meet their needs, keeping in mind their scarce income or savings. People have fewer options when there are fewer companies competing.

Arguments Against Trusts Critics argued that trusts and monopolies reduced competition. Without competition, companies had no reason to keep prices low or to improve their products. It was also hard for new companies to compete with trusts.

Critics were also upset about the political influence of trusts. Some people worried that millionaires were using their wealth to buy favors from elected officials. These critics pointed to government policies that advanced the interests of big business.

Trusts, for example, used their money and influence to persuade Congress to enact protective tariffs, or taxes on imported goods. By making imports more expensive, the government encouraged the purchase of American-made goods. At the same time, they protected the trusts from foreign competition. John Reagan, a member of Congress from Texas, said:

Primary Source

"There were no beggars till Vanderbilts . . . shaped the actions of Congress and molded the purposes of government. Then the few became fabulously wealthy, the many wretchedly poor."

—John Reagan, *Austin Weekly Democratic Statesman*, 1877

Analyze Charts The rise of trusts brought economic growth, but their concentrated power sometimes led to tensions with workers or government. **Identify Cause and Effect** Using evidence from the chart, identify drawbacks to the rise of trusts.

Causes and Effects of Trusts

CAUSES	EVENTS	EFFECTS
Population growth and migration attract investment in railroads.	The Northern Securities Company controls three of the nation's railways by 1901.	The Supreme Court forces the Northern Securities Company to break apart in 1904.
Investors seek market control by forming trusts in the steel and oil industries.	Carnegie Steel Company produces 45.7% of U.S. steel output by 1900. The Standard Oil Company controls 90–95% of U.S. oil production by 1880	Conflicts with labor unions lead to violent strikes. The Supreme Court forces Standard Oil to break apart.
Investors seek market control over the coal and tobacco industries and face little or no government regulation to protect workers.	Pennsylvania coal companies control 96% of national output by 1900. American Tobacco controls 80% of the tobacco industry by 1904.	Strikes bring federal intervention. Factory workers face harsh conditions. Children are used as a source of cheap labor.

SOURCE: *Industrial Genius: The Working Life of Charles Michael Schwab; E.H. Harriman: Master Railroader; Big Steel: The First Century of the United States Steel Corporation 1901–2001; Encyclopædia Britannica*

Under pressure from the public, the government slowly moved toward controlling giant corporations. Congress approved the Sherman Antitrust Act in 1890, which banned the formation of trusts and monopolies. However, it was too weak to be effective. Some state governments passed laws to regulate business, but the corporations usually sidestepped them.

Arguments for Trusts Naturally, some business leaders defended trusts. Andrew Carnegie published articles arguing that too much competition ruined businesses and put people out of work. In an article titled "Wealth and Its Uses," he wrote:

Analyze Images Andrew Carnegie became a millionaire in the steel industry and later donated large sums of money to build educational institutions and to help the poor. **Identify Cause and Effect** How did Carnegie's being an immigrant affect this attitude toward wealth and its use?

Primary Source

"It will be a great mistake for the community to shoot the millionaires, for they are the bees that make the most honey, and contribute most to the hive even after they have gorged themselves full."

—Andrew Carnegie, "Wealth and Its Uses"

Defenders of big business argued that the growth of giant corporations brought lower production costs, lower prices, higher wages, and a better quality of life for millions of Americans. They pointed out that by 1900 Americans enjoyed the highest standard of living in the world.

READING CHECK **Check Understanding** Why was Andrew Carnegie in favor of trusts?

Lesson Check

Practice Vocabulary

1. Why would individuals buy **stock** in a **corporation**?
2. In what way is a **trust** a form of **monopoly**?

Critical Thinking and Writing

3. **Summarize** How did Andrew Carnegie process natural resources more efficiently and use vertical integration to make huge profits?
4. **Assess an Argument** According to critics, trusts and other monopolies were abusing capitalism. Do you agree? Why or why not?
5. **Generate Explanations** Why do you think the Sherman Antitrust Act and other attempts at regulating monopolies and trusts were not effective?
6. **Revisit the Essential Question** How did industrialists like Carnegie and Rockefeller help the economy grow and prosper?
7. **Writing Workshop: Use Credible Sources** What might Andrew Carnegie or John D. Rockefeller have thought of government involvement in the economy? Make a list in your Active Journal of sources that you can trust to contribute to the debate over government's role in creating a national infrastructure.

Draw Sound Conclusions from Sources

Follow these steps to learn how to draw sound conclusions from sources.

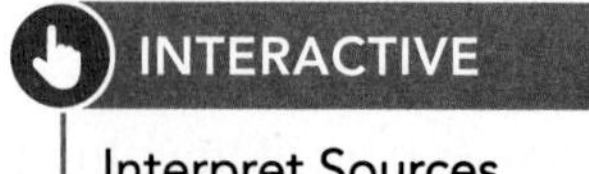

Interpret Sources

1 **Study the facts and main ideas in a source** Identify the main ideas of the source, and sort out the facts and opinions.

2 **Formulate questions about the source** Ask, "What points does this source try to make about those who have enormous wealth?"

3 **Draw conclusions from the source** Ask, "What conclusion do you draw from this source about what wealthy individuals should do with their wealth?"

4 **Test any conclusions for soundness** Ask, "Do the facts in the source support the conclusion?" For this source, ask, "Do the opinions in the source seem sound?"

Primary Source

There are but three modes in which surplus wealth can be disposed of. It can be left to the families of the decedents; or it can be bequeathed for public purposes; or, finally, it can be administered during their lives by its possessors. . . . Let us in turn consider each of these modes. The first is the most [unwise]. . . . Why should men leave great fortunes to their children? If this is done from affection, is it not misguided affection? Observation teaches that, generally speaking, it is not well for the children that they should be so burdened. Neither is it well for the state. . . .

As to the second mode, that of leaving wealth at death for public uses, it may be said that this is only a means for the disposal of wealth, provided a man is content to wait until he is dead before it becomes of much good in the world. . . .

There remains, then, only one mode of using great fortunes: but in this way we have the true antidote [remedy] for the temporary unequal distribution of wealth, the reconciliation of the rich and the poor—a reign of harmony. . . . Under its sway we shall have an ideal state, in which the surplus wealth of the few will become, in the best sense, the property of the many, because administered for the common good. . . .

This, then, is held to be the duty of the man of Wealth: First, to set an example of modest, unostentatious living, shunning [avoiding] display or extravagance; to provide moderately for the legitimate wants of those dependent upon him; and after doing so to consider all surplus revenues which come to him simply as trust funds, which he is called upon to administer . . . in the manner which, in his judgment, is best calculated to produce the most beneficial result for the community—the man of wealth thus becoming the sole agent and trustee for his poorer brethren, bringing to their service his superior wisdom, experience, and ability to administer—doing for them better than they would or could do for themselves.

— Andrew Carnegie, *"The Gospel of Wealth,"* 1889

LESSON 5

The Labor Movement

BOUNCE TO ACTIVATE VIDEO

GET READY TO READ

START UP

Examine the photo of the workers on strike. Write a paragraph about why they are facing soldiers.

GUIDING QUESTIONS

- Why did American workers form labor unions?
- What issues did women face in the workplace?
- What challenges did labor face?

TAKE NOTES

Literacy Skills Analyze Text Structure

Use the graphic organizer in your Active Journal to take notes as you read the lesson.

PRACTICE VOCABULARY

Use the vocabulary activity in your Active Journal to practice the vocabulary words.

Vocabulary	Academic Vocabulary
sweatshop	endorse
strikebreaker	prohibit
anarchist	
trade union	
collective bargaining	
Triangle Fire	

Before the Civil War, most factories were small and family-run. Bosses knew their workers by name and chatted with them about their families. Because most workers had skills that the factory needed, they could bargain with the boss for better wages. By the late 1800s, though, factories had changed, and workers needed to adapt.

How Did Working Conditions Change in the Late 1800s?

By the 1880s, the relationship between worker and boss had changed. People worked all day tending machines in a large, crowded, noisy room. Because their skills were easily replaced, many workers were forced to work for low wages. In the garment trade and other industries, sweatshops became common. A **sweatshop** is a workplace where people labor long hours in poor conditions for low pay. Most sweatshop workers were young women or children.

Child Labor The 1900 census reported nearly 2 million children under age 15 at work throughout the country.

Boys and girls labored in hazardous textile mills, tobacco factories, and garment sweatshops. In coal mines, they picked stones out of the coal for 12 hours a day, 6 days a week. Working children had little time for schooling. Lack of education reduced their chances of building better lives as adults.

A Dangerous, Unregulated Workplace Factories were filled with hazards. Lung-damaging dust filled the air of textile mills. Cave-ins and gas explosions plagued mines. In steel mills, vats of molten metal spilled without warning. Some workers developed long-term health problems. Others were severely injured or killed in industrial accidents. In just one year, 195 workers died in the steel mills of Pittsburgh.

The federal government continued its hands-off policy toward business. Congress did little to regulate conditions in the workplace or otherwise ensure the safety of workers—even child laborers.

READING CHECK **Identify Supporting Details** What were the working conditions like in sweatshops?

Why Did Workers Organize Unions?

Many workers found ways to fight back. Some workers slowed their work pace. Others went on strike. Strikes were usually informal, organized by workers in individual factories.

Sometimes workers banded together to win better conditions. However, most early efforts to form unions failed.

Analyze Images Large, fast-moving machines were a mainstay of factories. **Draw Conclusions** What kind of hazards would the women in this image face when the machine was running?

The Knights of Labor In 1869, workers formed the Knights of Labor. At first, the union was open to skilled workers only. The members held meetings in secret because employers fired workers who joined unions.

In 1879, the Knights of Labor elected Terence Powderly as their president. Powderly worked to strengthen the union by opening its membership to immigrants, African Americans, women, and unskilled workers.

Powderly did not believe in strikes. Rather, he relied on rallies and meetings to win public support. Goals of the Knights included a shorter workday, an end to child labor, and equal pay for men and women. Most important, Powderly wanted workers and employers to share ownership and profits.

In 1885, some members of the Knights of Labor launched a strike that forced the Missouri Pacific Railroad to restore wages that it had previously cut. The Knights did not officially support the strike. Still, workers everywhere saw the strike as a victory for the union. Membership soared to 700,000, including 60,000 African Americans.

Analyze Images In 1886, a bomb exploded during a workers' rights protest in Haymarket Square in Chicago. The Haymarket Riot damaged the labor movement's image. **Infer** Why would the labor movement's image have suffered, even though labor organizers were not responsible for the bombing?

How Did the Haymarket Riot Hurt Workers? The following year, the Knights of Labor ran into serious trouble. Workers at the McCormick Harvester Company in Chicago went on strike. Again, the Knights did not **endorse** the strike.

Like many companies at the time, the McCormick company hired **strikebreakers**, or replacements for striking workers. On May 3, 1886, workers clashed with strikebreakers outside the factory. Police opened fire, and four workers were killed.

The next day, thousands of workers gathered in Haymarket Square to protest the killings. The rally was led by **anarchists**, people who oppose all forms of organized government. Suddenly, a bomb exploded, killing seven police officers.

Eight anarchists were arrested for their part in the Haymarket Riot, as the incident was called. No real evidence linked these men to the bombing, but four were tried, convicted, and hanged. A wave of antilabor feeling swept the nation. Many Americans thought that the unions were controlled by anarchists. As a result, membership in the Knights of Labor dropped sharply.

A New Union Forms Despite the failure of the Knights of Labor, the labor movement continued to grow. In 1886, an immigrant cigar maker named Samuel Gompers organized a new union in Columbus, Ohio. The American Federation of Labor (AFL) was open to skilled workers only.

Academic Vocabulary
endorse • *v.,* to support publicly

Workers did not join the AFL directly. Rather, they joined a **trade union**, a union of persons working in the same trade. For example, a typesetter joined a typesetter's union. The union then joined the AFL. Thus, the AFL was a large organization made up of many unions.

Unlike the Knights of Labor, the AFL stressed practical goals. It focused on higher wages, shorter hours, and improved working conditions. It led the fight for **collective bargaining**, the right of unions to negotiate with management for workers as a group. The AFL also supported the use of strikes to achieve its goals.

Union Membership

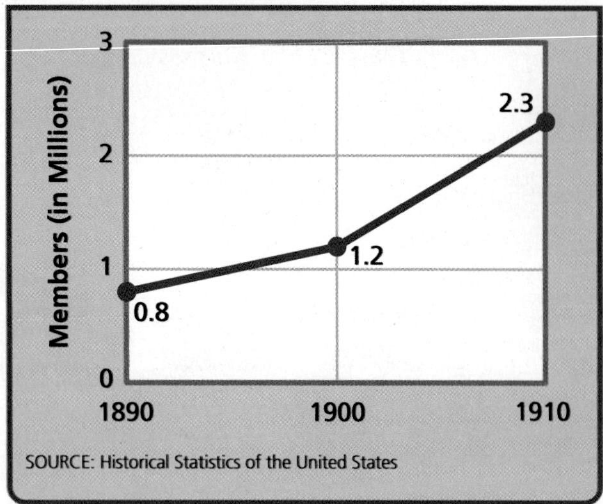

Analyze Graphs Union membership increased significantly between 1890 and 1910. **Understand Effects** What would joining a union have done for a typical worker?

Its practical approach helped the AFL become the most powerful labor organization in the nation. Between 1886 and 1910, membership in the AFL swelled from 150,000 to more than one and a half million. However, because African Americans, immigrants, and unskilled workers were barred from most trade unions, they could not join the AFL.

READING CHECK **Identify Supporting Details** What were the goals of the Knights of Labor?

Women in the Workplace

By 1890, one million women worked in American factories. In the textile mills of New England and the tobacco factories of the South, women made up the majority of workers. In New York City's garment industry, women outnumbered men.

During the 1800s, some women formed their own unions. A few, like the Washerwomen's Association of Atlanta, which had all African American members, went out on strike for higher wages. None of these unions succeeded, however.

Who Was Mother Jones? The best-known woman in the labor movement was Irish-born Mary Harris Jones, known as Mother Jones. Jones devoted much of her adult life to the cause of workers.

Jones spoke out about the hard lives of children in textile mills, "barefoot . . . reaching thin little hands into the machinery." By calling attention to such abuses, Mother Jones helped pave the way for reform.

Organizing Garment Workers In 1900, garment workers organized the International Ladies' Garment Workers Union (ILGWU). More than 20,000 women and men in the ILGWU walked off their jobs in 1909. After a few weeks, employers met union demands for better pay and shorter hours. The ILGWU became a key member of the AFL.

Despite the efforts of the ILGWU and other labor groups, most women with factory jobs did not join unions. They continued to work long hours for low pay. Many labored under unsafe conditions. Then a tragic event focused attention on the dangers faced by women workers.

The Triangle Fire On a cool day in March 1911, the workday was just ending when a fire broke out in the Triangle Shirtwaist Factory, a sweatshop in New York City. Within minutes, the factory's upper stories were ablaze. Hundreds of workers raced for the exits, only to find them locked. The company had locked the doors to keep workers at their jobs. In their panic, workers ran headlong into the doors, blocking them with their bodies.

Did you know?

Labor Day, the first Monday of September, has been a legal holiday since 1894.

Fire trucks arrived almost immediately, but their ladders could not reach the upper floors. One after another, workers trying desperately to escape the flames jumped to their deaths.

Primary Source

"As I looked up . . . there, at a window, a young man was helping girls to leap out. Suddenly one of them put her arms around him and kiss[ed] him. Then he held her into space and dropped her. He jumped next. Thud . . . dead. Thud . . . dead."

—The *New York Times*, March 26, 1911

Nearly 150 people, mostly young women, lost their lives in the **Triangle Fire**. The deaths shocked the public. As a result, New York and other states approved new safety laws to help protect workers.

READING CHECK **Understand Effects** How did the Triangle Fire affect labor reform in New York and other states?

Labor Faces Challenges

The new era of industry led to vast economic growth. At the same time, it created economic strains. In the rush for profits, many industries expanded too fast. As goods flooded the market, prices dropped. To cut their losses, factory owners often fired workers.

As the supply of goods fell, prices rose again. In turn, factories geared up again, and workers returned to their jobs.

The economy swung wildly between good times and bad. These boom and bust cycles challenged labor. Between 1870 and 1900, two major depressions and three smaller recessions rocked the country. In such hard times, workers lost their jobs or faced pay cuts.

Strikes Turn Violent After suffering several forced pay cuts, rail workers went on strike in 1877. Riots erupted as workers burned rail yards and destroyed track.

Analyze Images Despite the efforts of firefighters, many people lost their lives in the Triangle Fire. **Infer** How did the public react to the event?

Violent strikes also broke out in the West. In the 1870s, miners in Idaho tried to shut down two large mines. In 1893, after another bitter strike, miners formed the Western Federation of Miners. This union gained great strength in the Rocky Mountain states. Between 1894 and 1904, it organized strike after strike.

Authorities Act Against Unions The federal and state governments usually sided with factory owners. Several Presidents sent in troops to end strikes. Courts usually ruled against strikers, too.

In 1892, a Carnegie steel mill in Homestead, Pennsylvania, cut wages. When the mill manager refused to bargain, the workers went on strike. The manager shut down the mill and called in a private army to end the Homestead strike. A deadly clash followed. The governor sent in the state militia to stop the violence. Four months later, most of the men went back to work, but afterward the mill **prohibited** unions.

Academic Vocabulary
prohibit • *v.*, to refuse to allow; to forbid

In 1894, a Chicago court dealt a serious blow to unions. A year earlier, George Pullman had cut the pay of workers at his railroad car factory. Yet he did not reduce the rents he charged them for company-owned houses. Workers walked off the job in protest.

A federal judge ordered the Pullman workers to end their strike. The strike's leaders were jailed for violating the Sherman Antitrust Act. This act had been meant to keep trusts from limiting free trade. The courts, however, said that the strikers were limiting free trade.

Gains and Losses Union workers staged thousands of strikes during the late 1800s. However, many Americans opposed the strikes. Some were afraid that unions were run by foreign-born radicals. Because unions were unpopular, owners felt free to try to crush them.

Analyze Graphs
Industrialization led to profound changes in the American workforce around the year 1900. **Analyze Graphs** What effect might industrialization have had on farm productivity during this time?

Employment Trends, 1890 to 1910

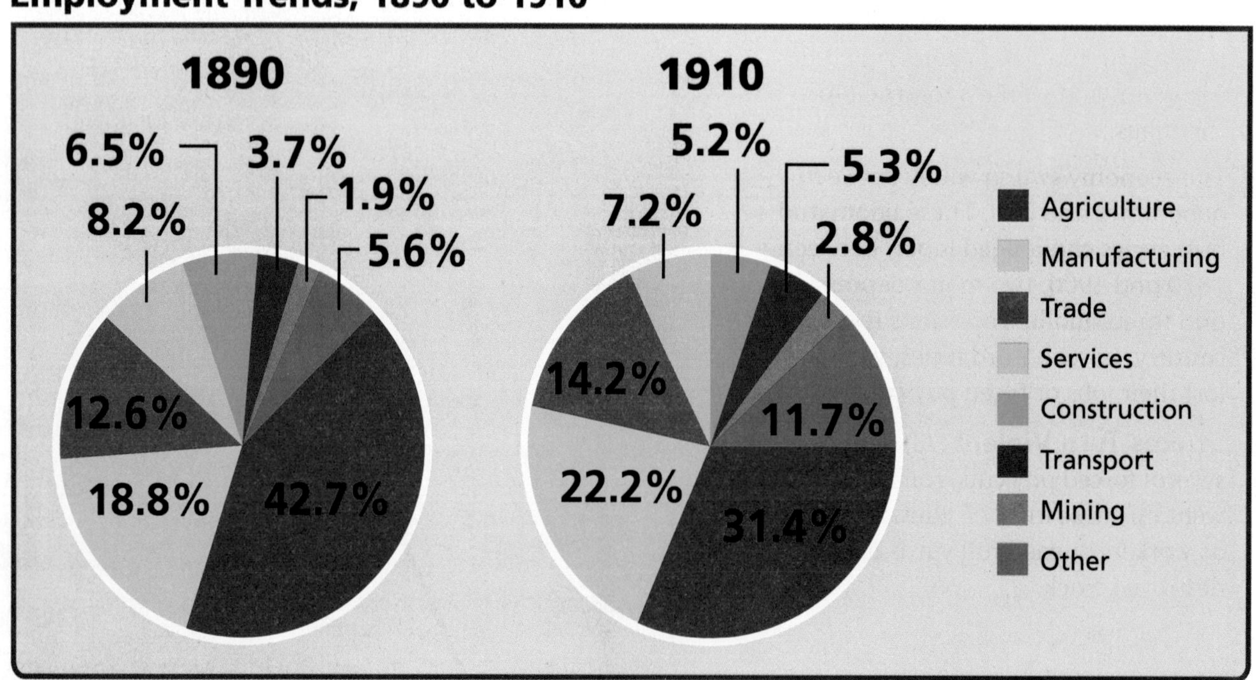

Workers did make some gains. Overall, wages rose slightly between 1870 and 1900. Still, union growth was slow. In 1910, only one worker in 20 belonged to a union. Some 30 years would pass before large numbers of unskilled workers were able to join unions.

Analyze Images Violence, including this train crash, marked the Pullman Strike. **Cite Evidence** Is violence an effective tool for striking workers? Why or why not?

READING CHECK **Identify Cause and Effect** Why were unions unpopular with many Americans?

Lesson Check

Practice Vocabulary

1. What role did **anarchists** play in the Haymarket Riot?
2. Why was it important for **trade unions** to engage in **collective bargaining**?

Critical Thinking and Writing

3. **Identify Main Ideas** How did the employer-worker relationship change over the course of the 1800s?
4. **Support Ideas with Examples** What do working conditions at the Triangle Shirtwaist Factory tell you in general about the attitude of sweatshop employers toward their workers' health and safety?
5. **Identify Cause and Effect** How did economic recessions and depressions affect workers during the late 1800s, and how did workers respond to these challenges?
6. **Writing Workshop: Shape Tone** How would you feel if your already low factory wages were cut? In a collective bargaining session with the factory owner, would your words reflect your emotions, or would your tone be calm? Write a few sentences in your Active Journal to help establish a tone for the argument essay you will write at the end of the topic.

LESSON 6

New Technologies

GET READY TO READ

START UP

Look at the image of the first flight of an airplane. Write a diary entry expressing how you might have felt standing on the beach that day.

GUIDING QUESTIONS

- How did new devices speed up communication during the late 1800s?
- How did automobiles and airplanes transform transportation?
- How did the inventions of this era improve businesses and Americans' quality of life?

TAKE NOTES

Literacy Skills Identify Supporting Details

Use the graphic organizer in your Active Journal to take notes as you read the lesson.

Practice Vocabulary

Use the vocabulary activity in your Active Journal to practice the vocabulary words.

Vocabulary	Academic Vocabulary
patent	determination
transatlantic	devise
moving assembly line	
mass production	

The U.S. Patent Office had never seen a year like 1897. An average of nearly 60 **patents**, or licenses for new inventions, were being granted every day. By year's end, Americans had registered some 21,000 patents, more than the total recorded in the entire 1850s.

How Did Communication Technology Change?

The market revolution of the early to mid-1800s had transformed the United States into an industrial powerhouse. Inventors continued to drive industrialization. By the late 1800s, the United States had become a land of invention.

Between 1870 and 1900, patent officers issued more than 500,000 new patents. Some newly patented inventions helped agriculture and industry grow and become more efficient. Others made daily life easier in many American homes.

Better communication was vital to American industries. The telegraph, in use since 1844, connected businesses around the nation.

How Was Transatlantic Communication Achieved? The telegraph sped up communication within the United States. Newspapers could share news from around the country. It still took weeks, however, for news from Europe to arrive by ship.

Cyrus Field had the idea of laying a cable under the ocean so that telegraph messages could go back and forth between North America and Europe. He began working in 1854, making five attempts to lay the cable. Each time, the cable snapped.

In 1858, two American ships managed to lay a cable between Ireland and Newfoundland, linking Europe and North America. Field then arranged for Britain's Queen Victoria in London to send the first **transatlantic**, or across-the-Atlantic, message to President James Buchanan in Washington, D.C.

For three weeks, Field was a hero. Then the cable broke. Nobody could say he lacked **determination**—Field would simply not give up. In 1866, the ship *Great Eastern* succeeded in laying a more durable cable. Field's transatlantic cable brought the United States and Europe closer together and made him famous.

Academic Vocabulary

determination • *n.*, the will to keep trying

Primary Source

"In five months . . . the cable had been manufactured, shipped . . . stretched across the Atlantic, and was sending messages . . . swift as lightning from continent to continent."

—Cyrus Field, speech, 1866

Analyze Images This historic map shows that path along which the transatlantic cable was laid. **Summarize** What challenges did Cyrus Field have to overcome to make the cable a reality?

What Did Alexander Graham Bell Do? The telegraph sent only dots and dashes over the wire. Several inventors were looking for a way to transmit voices. One of them was Alexander Graham Bell, a Scottish-born teacher of the deaf.

Bell had been working on his invention since 1865. In March 1876, he was ready to test his "talking machine." Bell sat in one room and spoke into his machine. His assistant, Thomas Watson, sat in another room with the receiver. "Mr. Watson, come here. I want to see you," Bell said. Watson heard the words faintly and rushed to Bell's side. "Mr. Bell," he cried, "I heard every word you said!" The telephone worked.

Bell's telephone aroused little interest at first. Scientists praised the invention. Most people, however, saw it as a toy. Bell offered to sell the telephone to the Western Union Telegraph Company for $100,000. The company refused—a costly mistake. In the end, the telephone earned Bell millions.

Analyze Images Alexander Graham Bell demonstrates the telephone. **Infer** Why would the telephone have increased the rate at which American businesses could operate?

Bell formed the Bell Telephone Company in 1877. By 1885, he had sold more than 300,000 phones, mostly to businesses. With the telephone, the pace of business sped up even more. People no longer had to go to a telegraph office to send messages. Business people could find out about prices or supplies by picking up the telephone.

READING CHECK **Summarize** How did new communication devices help American businesses?

Who Was Thomas Edison?

INTERACTIVE

American Inventors That Changed Society

In an age of invention, Thomas Edison was right at home. In 1876, he opened a research laboratory in Menlo Park, New Jersey. There, Edison boasted that he and his co-workers created a "minor" invention every 10 days and "a big thing every six months or so." Edison, who lost much of his hearing during childhood, sometimes credited his deafness with allowing him to focus on his work.

The "Wizard of Menlo Park" The key to Edison's success lay in his approach. He turned inventing into a system. Teams of experts refined Edison's ideas and translated them into practical inventions. The work was long and grueling. "Genius," Edison said, "is one percent inspiration and ninety-nine percent perspiration."

The results were amazing. Edison became known as the "Wizard of Menlo Park" for inventing the light bulb, the phonograph, and hundreds of other devices.

One invention from Edison's laboratory launched a new industry: the movies. In 1893, Edison introduced his first machine for showing moving pictures. Viewers watched short films by looking through a peephole in a cabinet. Later, Edison developed a motion picture projector, making it possible for many people to watch a film at the same time. By 1908, thousands of silent-movie houses had opened in cities across the United States.

The Age of Electricity One of Edison's most important creations was the electric power plant. He built the first power plant in New York City in 1882. He wired the business district first in hopes of attracting investors. With the flip of a switch, Edison set the entire district ablaze with light.

Within a year, Edison's power plant was supplying electricity to homes as well as businesses. Soon, more power plants were built. Factories replaced steam-powered engines with safer, quieter, electric engines. Electric energy powered streetcars in cities and lighted countless homes. The modern age of electricity had begun.

READING CHECK **Understand Effects** What impact did electricity have on American homes and businesses?

How Did Inventions Change Everyday Life?

Almost every day, it seemed, Americans were inventing new devices. As new technologies spread, businesses became more efficient, as did work around the home. Inventions improved the quality of life for all Americans.

Refrigeration In the 1880s, Gustavus Swift came up with an idea that transformed the American diet. Swift introduced refrigeration to the meatpacking industry. In the past, cattle, pigs, and chickens had been raised and sold locally. Meat spoiled quickly, so it could not be shipped over long distances.

Swift set up a meatpacking plant in Chicago, a railroad hub midway between the cattle ranches of the West and the cities of the East. Cattle were shipped by train to Chicago. At Swift's plant, the animals were slaughtered and carved up into sides of beef. The fresh beef was quickly loaded onto refrigerated railroad cars and carried to market. Huge blocks of ice kept the cars cold. Even in summer, Swift sent fresh meat to cities in the East.

Later, fruit and vegetable producers also began relying on refrigerated railroad cars. By 1920, thanks in part to refrigeration, California had become a leading supplier of lettuce, grapes, and other produce to markets across the country.

Improvements in Offices and Homes New inventions also affected life in the office and at home. Christopher Sholes perfected the typewriter in 1868. What Sholes did for words, William Seward Burroughs did for figures when he invented the adding machine in 1892. Both inventions made business more efficient.

Quick Activity

In your Active Journal, create an exhibit for a virtual Museum of Invention.

INTERACTIVE

Inventions Improve Daily Life

Analyze Images Thomas Edison's light bulb and electrical stations revolutionized American life. **Identify Main Ideas** How did electricity improve the quality of life in many homes?

Analyze Images The first vacuum cleaners were carriage-based devices that were brought to homes and businesses. **Infer** How would vacuums have improved people's lives?

A wide range of household appliances were created during the mid to late 19th century. The sewing machine, the clothes washer, the carpet sweeper (and later, the vacuum cleaner), shortened the time needed to perform necessary household chores.

Time-saving inventions gave people something new—time to play. In 1891, James Naismith invented the game of basketball. In 1888, George Eastman introduced the lightweight Kodak camera. No longer did photography require bulky equipment and chemicals. After taking 100 photographs, the owner returned the camera to Kodak. The company printed the pictures and sent them back, along with a reloaded camera. Taking photos became a popular pastime.

America's inventiveness was put on display at the 1893 Columbian Exposition. Held in Chicago, the fair showcased advances in engineering, agriculture, and other fields. Among the exhibitors was the electrical genius Nikola Tesla; among the fairgoers was Henry Ford, who would become one of America's leading industrialists.

African American Inventors African Americans contributed to the flood of inventions. In 1872, Elijah McCoy created a special device that oiled engines automatically. Granville T. Woods, found a way to send telegraph messages between moving railroad trains. Jan Matzeliger **devised** a machine that could perform almost all the steps in shoemaking that had previously been done by hand. Patented in 1883, the machine was eventually used in shoe factories across the country.

Academic Vocabulary
devise • *v.*, to think of or invent

Many African-American inventors had trouble getting patents for their inventions. Even so, in 1900, an assistant in the patent office compiled a list of patents issued to African-American inventors. The list, together with drawings and plans of all the inventions, filled four huge volumes.

READING CHECK **Identify Cause and Effect** How did new technology affect the American diet in the late 1800s?

When Did the Automobile Become Popular?

No single person invented the automobile. Europeans had produced motorized vehicles as early as the 1860s. In the 1890s, several Americans began building cars. Still, only the wealthy could afford them.

Henry Ford's Assembly Line It was Henry Ford who made the auto a part of everyday American life. In 1893, he attended the Chicago World's Fair. The fair's exhibits showcased the progress of the "modern" age. Inspired, Ford went on to design his own gas-powered vehicles.

In 1913, Ford introduced the **moving assembly line**. With this method of production, workers stay in one place as products move along on a track or belt. At Ford's auto plant, one group of workers would bolt seats onto a passing car frame, the next would add the roof, and so on. The assembly line greatly reduced the time needed to build a car. Other industries soon adopted the method.

Ford's assembly line allowed the mass production of cars. **Mass production** means making large quantities of a product quickly and cheaply. Because of mass production, Ford could sell his cars at a lower price than other automakers.

"Horseless Carriages" Catch On It took a number of years for the automobile to catch on. At first, most people laughed at it. Some thought the "horseless carriage" was a nuisance. Others thought it was dangerous. A backfiring auto engine could scare a horse right off the road. Towns and villages across the nation posted signs: "No horseless carriages allowed." In Tennessee, a person planning to drive a car had to advertise the fact a week ahead of time. This warning gave others time to prepare for the danger!

Over time, attitudes toward the automobile changed. No other means of travel offered such freedom. As prices dropped, more people could afford to buy cars. In 1900, only 8,000 Americans owned cars. By 1917, more than 4.5 million autos were traveling American roads.

Automobiles were at first regarded as machines for men only. Automakers soon realized, however, that women could drive—and buy—cars. Companies began to direct advertisements to women. Driving gave women greater independence.

READING CHECK **Identify Main Ideas** How did the introduction of the moving assembly line make automobiles more popular?

Interpret Images Jan Matzeliger's lasting machine automated shoe manufacturing. **Draw Conclusions** How did the machine change the status of the shoemaker?

Interpret Images On an assembly line, such as this one at the Ford Motor Company, cars were built piece by piece as they moved along a track. **Infer** Why would this have made cars cheaper to build?

Analyze Images People watch as the Wright Military Flyer soars overhead. **Draw Conclusions** Was the airplane an instant success? Why or why not?

The Wright Brothers Take to the Skies

Meanwhile, two Ohio bicycle mechanics, Orville and Wilbur Wright, were experimenting with another new method of transportation: flying. The Wright brothers owned a bicycle shop in Dayton, Ohio. During the 1890s, they read about Europeans who were experimenting with glider planes. The brothers were soon caught up in the dream of flying.

After trying out hundreds of designs, the Wright brothers tested their first "flying machine" on December 17, 1903, at Kitty Hawk, North Carolina. Orville's first flight lasted 12 seconds and went 120 feet. He flew three more times that day, the longest flight lasting 59 seconds.

Improvements came quickly after the first flight. By 1905, the Wrights had built a plane that could turn, make figure-eights, and remain in the air for up to half an hour.

Surprisingly, the first flights did not attract much interest. No one could see any practical use for the flying machine. It was the United States military that first saw a use for airplanes. In 1908, the Wrights demonstrated how planes could fly over battlefields to locate enemy positions. Then they produced an airplane for the military that could reach the amazing speed of 40 miles per hour!

In time, the airplane would achieve its vast potential. It would change the world by making travel quicker and trade easier.

READING CHECK **Identify Supporting Details** What details show the usefulness of the Wrights' "flying machine"?

Lesson Check

Practice Vocabulary

1. What was the importance of the **transatlantic cable**?
2. How did Henry Ford's **moving assembly line** enable the **mass production** of automobiles?

Critical Thinking and Writing

3. **Cite Evidence** How did Edison's light bulb and the electric power plant increase the amount of goods a factory was able to produce?
4. **Summarize** How did businesses benefit from American inventiveness?
5. **Infer** Why do you think Americans responded weakly to the newly invented telephone and automobile, and to the first airplane flight?
6. **Writing Workshop: Write a Conclusion** At the end of your essay, you must be ready to focus all of your key arguments into a persuasive and hard-hitting conclusion. In your Active Journal, write a list of those arguments.

Quotations from Thomas Edison

Besides being a great inventor, Thomas Edison was noted for his quick wit. One of his remarks, "Genius is one percent inspiration, ninety-nine percent perspiration," inspires creative people to this day.

▶ Thomas Edison at work

"A genius is often merely a talented person who has done all of his or her homework."①

"Opportunity is missed by most people because it is dressed in overalls and looks like work."

"I'd put my money on the sun and solar energy. What a source of power! I hope we don't have to wait until oil and coal run out before we tackle that.② I wish I had more years left."

"The world owes nothing to any man, but every man owes something to the world."

"I never did a day's work in my life. It was all fun."

"I have more respect for the fellow with a single idea who gets there ③ than for the fellow with a thousand ideas who does nothing."

"The man who doesn't make up his mind to cultivate the habit of thinking misses the greatest pleasure in life."

Reading and Vocabulary Support

① Based on this quote, what do you think Edison felt were the necessary ingredients for genius?

② By "that," Edison means developing technology that harnesses solar energy.

③ By "there," Edison means that the single idea is worked on and made a reality.

Analyzing Primary Sources

Cite specific evidence from the quotes to support your answers.

1. What does Edison mean when he describes opportunity as being "dressed in overalls"?
2. Based on these quotations, how do you think Thomas Edison felt about the work he did?

How could new technology improve railroads? Record your findings in your Active Journal.

TOPIC 10

Review and Assessment

VISUAL REVIEW

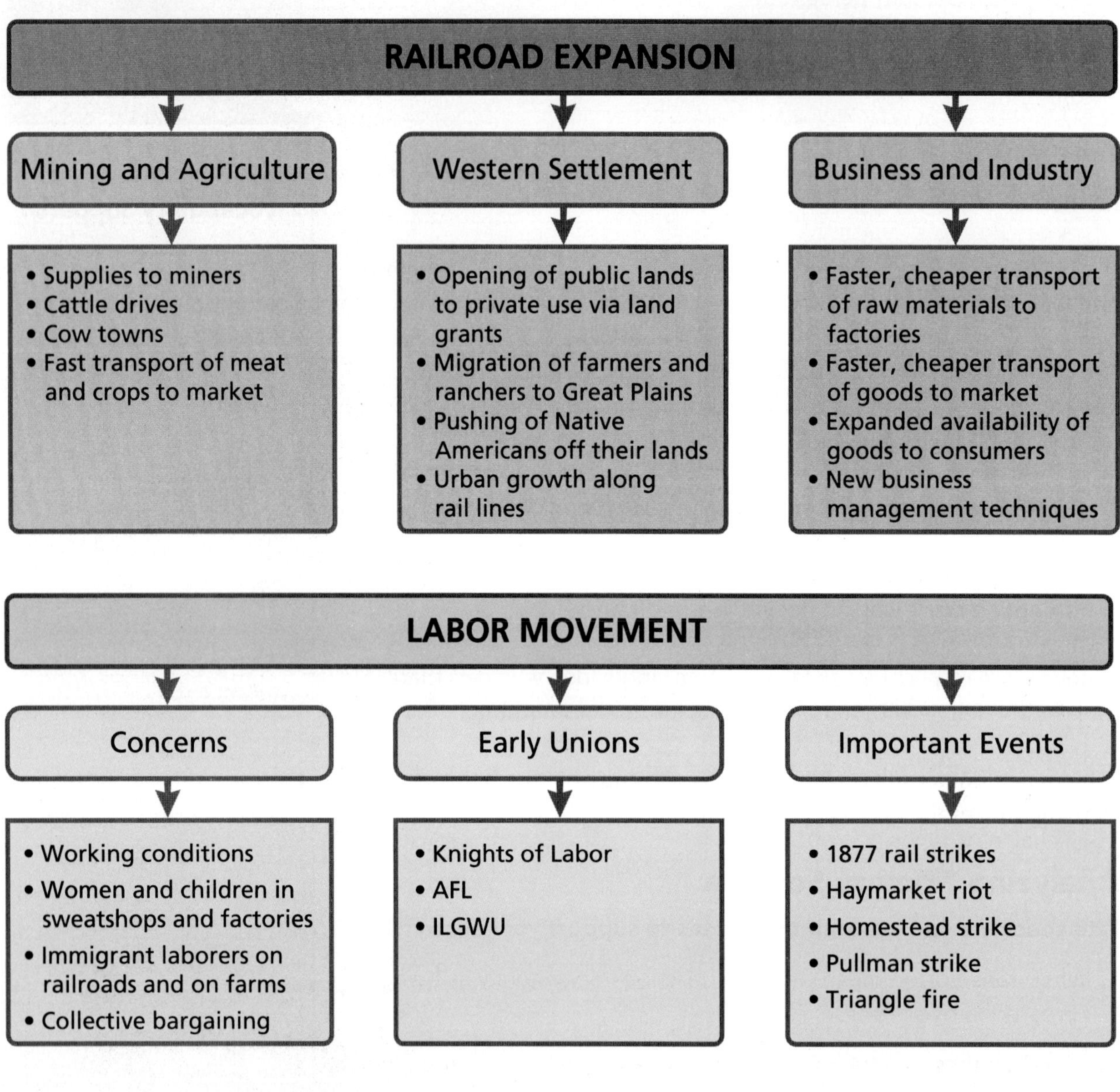

READING REVIEW

Use the Take Notes and Practice Vocabulary activities in your Active Journal to review the topic.

Quest FINDINGS

Share your thoughts about high-speed rail.

INTERACTIVE

Practice vocabulary using the Topic Mini-Games.

ASSESSMENT

Vocabulary and Key Ideas

1. **Check Understanding** What was the main purpose of building the **transcontinental railroad**?
2. **Define** Why were farmers on the Great Plains called **sodbusters**?
3. **Describe** What was the **travois**, and how did the Plains Indians use it?
4. **Explain** Why did investors in a **corporation** hope to receive **dividends**?
5. **Identify** Who was the most powerful banker of the late 1800s, who gained control of several major railroads and took over Carnegie Steel?
6. **Recall** What was the Triangle Fire?
7. **Identify Supporting Details** What did George Pullman do that led to a major labor strike in 1894?
8. **Identify** Why are Orville and Wilbur Wright famous?

Critical Thinking and Writing

9. **Identify Main Ideas** Why did the federal government offer the railroads subsidies in the form of land grants?
10. **Identify Cause and Effect** Why did many farmers decide to join the Grangers, the Populists, and other cooperative organizations?
11. **Recognize Multiple Causes** What reasons did American Indians on the Great Plains have for not wanting to move onto reservations?
12. **Explain an Argument** Some industrialists argued that competition should be reduced. What reasons did they give?
13. **Revisit the Essential Question** How did new technologies contribute to the growth of the economy after the Civil War?
14. **Writing Workshop: Write Arguments** Using the outline you created in your Active Journal, write a persuasive three-paragraph argument to answer this question: How much should the federal government do to support the creation of a national infrastructure?

Analyze Primary Sources

15. Who most likely made this statement?
    - **A.** John D. Rockefeller
    - **B.** Mother Jones
    - **C.** Alexander Graham Bell
    - **D.** Samuel Gompers

"I believe it is my duty to make money and still more money and to use the money I make for the good of my fellow man according to the dictates of my conscience."

Analyze Maps

16. Which cattle trail began farthest south?
17. Which cattle trail went to Denver?

▼ **Cattle Trails**

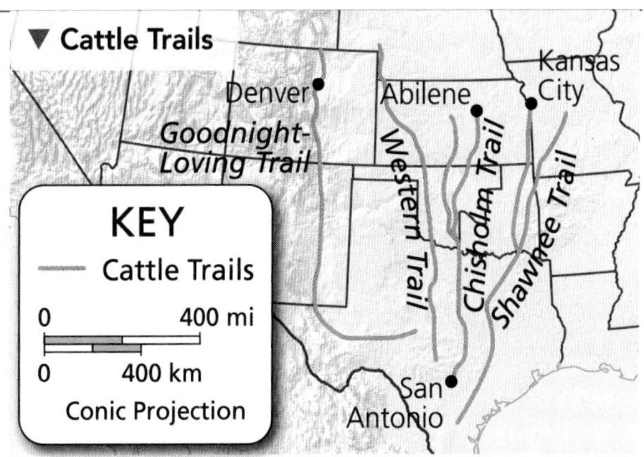

TOPIC 11

The Progressive Era

(1865–1920)

GO ONLINE to access your digital course

- VIDEO
- AUDIO
- ETEXT
- INTERACTIVE
- WRITING
- GAMES
- WORKSHEET
- ASSESSMENT

Go back to the year 1900,

when THE PROGRESSIVE ERA was building up steam. Why? To witness cities bursting at the seams with newly arrived immigrants and social reformers crying out for justice and equality.

Explore The Essential Question

What can individuals do to affect society?

In the late 1800s, a handful of very wealthy individuals dominated society. By 1900, Progressives had begun to create a fairer and more just society.

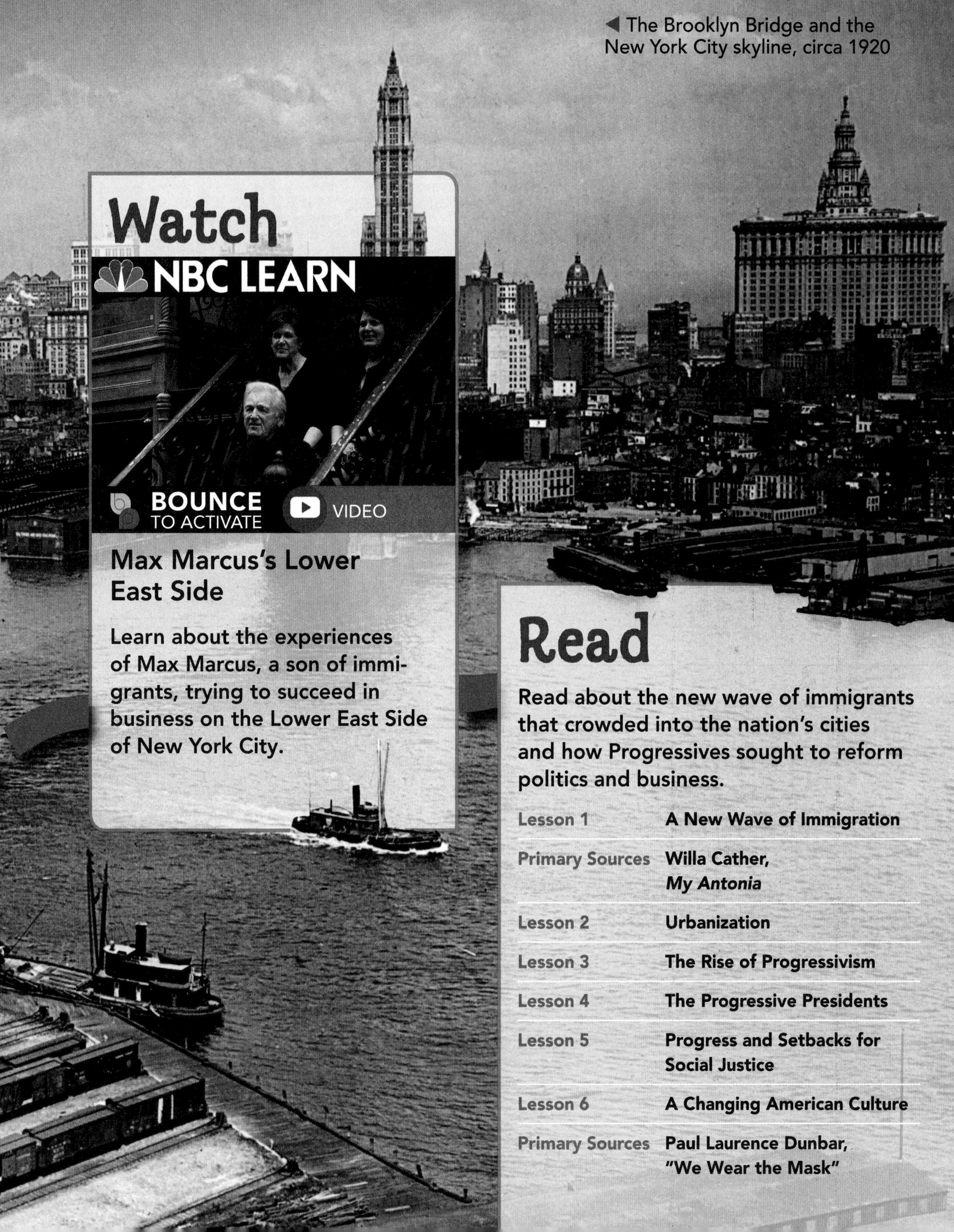

◀ The Brooklyn Bridge and the New York City skyline, circa 1920

Watch

Max Marcus's Lower East Side

Learn about the experiences of Max Marcus, a son of immigrants, trying to succeed in business on the Lower East Side of New York City.

Read

Read about the new wave of immigrants that crowded into the nation's cities and how Progressives sought to reform politics and business.

TOPIC 11
The Progressive Era (1865–1920)

Learn more about The Progressive Era by making a map and a timeline in your Active Journal.

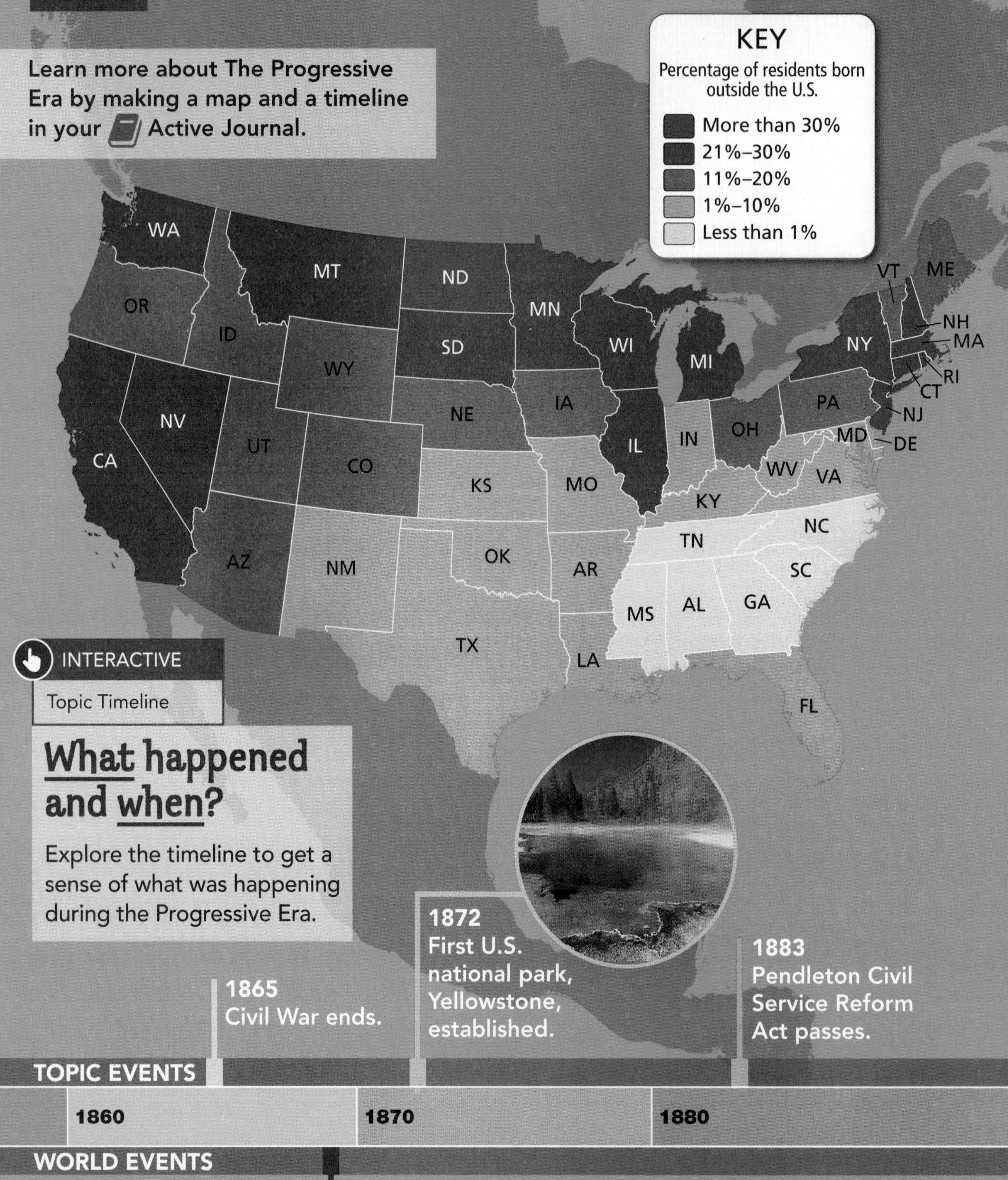

INTERACTIVE

Topic Timeline

What happened and when?

Explore the timeline to get a sense of what was happening during the Progressive Era.

TOPIC EVENTS

1865 Civil War ends.

1872 First U.S. national park, Yellowstone, established.

1883 Pendleton Civil Service Reform Act passes.

1860 | 1870 | 1880

WORLD EVENTS

1869 Suez Canal opens.

INTERACTIVE

Topic Map

Where did new arrivals settle?

The map shows the percentage of each state's residents who had been born in other countries, as of 1900. Why were immigrants more likely to settle in some states than in others?

Who will you meet?

W.E.B. Du Bois, civil rights activist

Jacob Riis, reporter and photographer

Carrie Chapman Catt, suffrage leader

1906 San Francisco earthquake

1920 Women gain the right to vote.

1901 Theodore Roosevelt becomes President.

1910 Angel Island Immigration Station opens.

1890 | 1900 | 1910 | 1920

1901 Britain's Queen Victoria dies.

1914 World War I begins.

1920 Russian Revolution ends.

Document-Based Writing Inquiry

Effects of Immigration

Quest KICK OFF

Starting after the Civil War, immigrants poured into the United States. This new wave of immigration changed the country.

How did immigration affect the United States around the year 1900?

Some Americans worked to improve conditions by promoting social reforms. Explore the Essential Question "What can individuals do to affect society?" in this Quest.

1 Ask Questions

Immigration changed the United States. Begin this Quest by writing several questions whose answers will provide information on the immigrant experience and on how some Americans viewed immigrants. Write the questions in your Active Journal.

2 Investigate

As you read the lessons in the topic, look for Quest CONNECTIONS that offer some insight into immigrant experiences. Record notes in your Active Journal.

3 Examine Primary Sources

Next explore a group of primary sources about immigrants and how people viewed them. Take notes in your Active Journal.

▼ Immigrants' experiences varied widely, depending on where they came from and where they settled.

Quest FINDINGS

4 Write Your Essay on the Immigrant Experience

At the end of the topic you will write an essay discussing the immigrant experience and the perceptions some Americans had of immigrants. Get essay-writing help in your Active Journal.

LESSON 1

A New Wave of Immigration

GET READY TO READ

START UP

Look at the image of new arrivals. Imagine yourself aboard that ship and write a few sentences about how you feel. Include one or more sensory details—sight, sound, smell, touch, or taste.

GUIDING QUESTIONS

- How did America's population grow after the Civil War?
- Why did immigrants make the difficult trip to the United States?
- What problems did immigrants face in the United States?

TAKE NOTES

Literacy Skills Summarize

Use the graphic organizer in your Active Journal to take notes as you read the lesson.

PRACTICE VOCABULARY

Use the vocabulary activity in your Active Journal to practice the vocabulary words.

Vocabulary		Academic Vocabulary
push factor	acculturation	persecution
pull factor	nativist	undergo
pogrom	Chinese Exclusion Act	
steerage		

Between 1865 and 1915, more than 25 million immigrants poured into the United States. They came full of hope and excitement but also with some anxiety.

Why Did People Immigrate?

O. E. Rölvaag, who came from Norway, captures a new immigrant's anxiety:

Primary Source

"New York is a terribly large city. Imagine the difficulties a poor immigrant woman meets with there—one who can neither speak nor understand the language! And this woman hadn't a single friend in all America. When she landed, and saw the great throngs of people, and looked at the whirlpool of traffic, she got terribly frightened, poor soul!"

—O. E. Rölvaag, *Giants in the Earth: A Saga of the Prairie*, 1927

Analyze Images The prospect of jobs lured immigrants to the United States in great numbers. This 1900 photo shows women working in a paper factory in Massachusetts. **Infer** What skills did these women need to do this work?

Immigrants such as Rölvaag came to the United States for many reasons. **Push factors** are conditions that drive people from their homes. **Pull factors** are conditions that attract immigrants to a new area. For example, an industrial boom in the United States had created a huge need for workers and that drew many immigrants.

Push Factors European immigrants were often small farmers or landless farmworkers. As European populations grew, land became scarce. Small farms could barely support the families that worked them. In some areas, new farm machines replaced farmworkers.

Academic Vocabulary

persecution • *n.*, the mistreatment or punishment of a group of people because of their beliefs

Political or religious **persecution** drove many people from their homes. In Russia, the government supported multiple waves of **pogroms** (poe-gruhmz), or organized anti-Jewish riots that left thousands dead or injured. In the Ottoman Empire (now Turkey), the genocide committed against them led many Armenian Christians to leave their homes.

Political unrest was another push factor. After 1910, a revolution erupted in Mexico. Many Mexicans came to the United States.

Pull Factors Industrial jobs were the chief pull factor for immigrants. American factories needed labor. Factory owners sent agents to Europe and Asia to hire workers at low wages. Steamship companies offered low fares for the ocean crossing. Railroads posted notices in Europe advertising cheap land in the American West.

Often, one family member—usually a young, single male—made the trip. Once settled, he would send for other family members. As immigrants wrote home describing the "land of opportunity," they pulled other neighbors from the "old country." For example, one out of every ten Greeks immigrated to the United States in the late 1800s.

The promise of freedom was another pull factor. Many immigrants were eager to live in a land where police could not arrest or imprison them without a reason and where freedom of religion was guaranteed.

Look at the photo of women in a factory. Why was it so important for a new immigrant to find a job? Record your findings in your Active Journal.

READING CHECK **Identify Supporting Details** Name two push factors and two pull factors.

What Was an Immigrant's Journey Like?

Leaving home required great courage. The voyage across the Atlantic or Pacific was often miserable. Most immigrants could afford only the cheapest berths. Shipowners jammed up to 2,000 people in **steerage**, the airless rooms below deck. On the return voyage, cattle or cargo filled the same spaces.

In such close quarters, disease spread rapidly. An outbreak of measles infected every child on one German immigrant ship. The dead were thrown into the sea "like cattle," reported a horrified passenger.

Academic Vocabulary
undergo • *v.*, to experience something, especially something painful or unpleasant

Ellis Island For most European immigrants, the voyage ended in New York City. Sailing into the harbor, they were greeted by the giant Statue of Liberty. Dedicated in 1886, it became a symbol of hope and freedom. A poem of welcome was carved on the base:

Primary Source

"Give me your tired, your poor,
Your huddled masses yearning to breathe free,
The wretched refuse of your teeming shore.

Send these, the homeless, tempest-tost to me:
I lift my lamp beside the golden door!"

—Emma Lazarus, "The New Colossus"

Analyze Images The Statue of Liberty greeted immigrants as their ships entered New York harbor. **Infer** What feelings do think this statue inspired in new arrivals?

In 1892, a new receiving station opened on Ellis Island. Here, immigrants had to **undergo** a dreaded medical inspection. Doctors watched newcomers climb a long flight of stairs. Anyone who limped or appeared out of breath might be stopped. Doctors also examined eyes, ears, and throats. The sick had to stay on Ellis Island until they got well. A small percentage who failed to regain full health were sent home.

Whether people's names were misspelled on the ships' passenger lists or purposely changed later in an effort to fit in to the new American culture, the names of many new immigrants changed on or shortly after their arrival in the United States. Krzeznewski became Kramer. Smargiaso ended up as Smarga.

Lucky immigrants went directly into the welcoming arms of friends and relatives. Many others stepped into a terrifying new land whose language and customs they did not know.

Angel Island Chinese immigrants had come to California in great numbers starting in the late 1840s. Other Asian groups followed later. Many Koreans, Japanese, and Filipinos sought jobs as agricultural laborers, as did Hindus and Sikhs. The California gold rush and the building of the transcontinental railroad also attracted immigrants. Some found work first in Hawaii before immigrating to the mainland.

Quick Activity

Work with a small group to create a song about an immigrant's new life in your Active Journal.

After 1910, many of these Asian immigrants were processed on Angel Island in San Francisco Bay. Because Americans wanted to discourage Asian immigration, new arrivals often faced long delays. Asian immigrants sometimes used the walls of the rooms in which they were housed to scratch poetry about their feelings:

Primary Source

"Lin, upon arriving in America,
Was arrested, put in a wooden building,
And made a prisoner.
I was here for one autumn.
The Americans did not allow me to land.
I was ordered to be deported."

—Daoist from the Town of Iron

Despite such obstacles, many Asians were able to make a home in the United States. However, they often faced a difficult adjustment.

READING CHECK **Summarize** What was the voyage to the United States like for most immigrants?

What Was the Immigrant Experience in America?

Many immigrants had heard stories that the streets in the United States were paved with gold. Once they arrived, they had to adjust to reality. "First," reported one immigrant, "the streets were not paved with gold. Second, they were not paved at all. Third, they expected me to pave them."

▼ Surrounded by their belongings, immigrants on Angel Island wait.

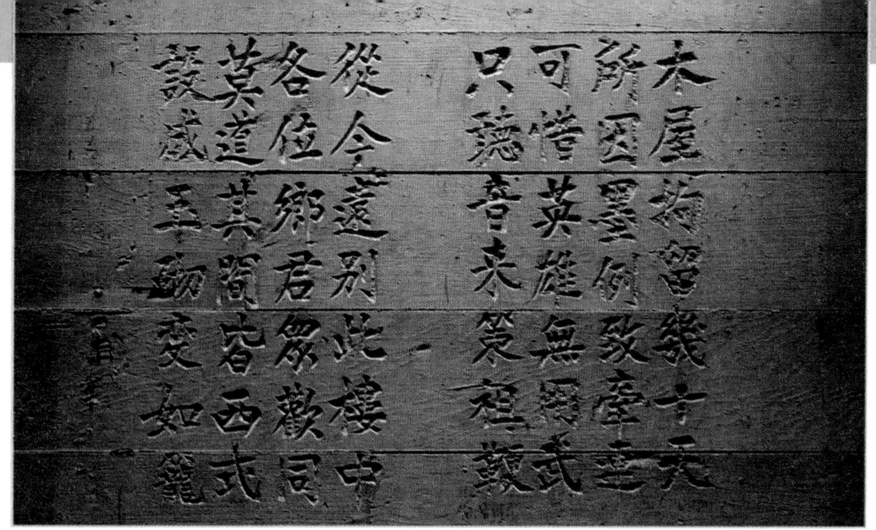

Analyze Images While waiting on Angel Island, some Asian immigrants carved poetry into the walls. **Cite Evidence** How different were the experiences of Angel Island immigrants from those who came through Ellis Island?

Newcomers immediately set out to find work. European peasants living off the land had had little need for money, but it took cash to survive in the United States. Through friends, relatives, labor contractors, and employment agencies, the new arrivals found jobs.

Immigrants often stayed in the cities where they landed. Cities were the seats of industrial work. City slums soon became packed with poor immigrants. By 1900, one neighborhood in New York's Lower East Side had become the most crowded place in the world.

A New Wave Brings New People Immigration patterns changed in the late 1800s. Most earlier immigrants had been Protestants from northern and western Europe. Those from England and some from Ireland already spoke English. The early wave of English, Irish, Germans, and Scandinavians became known as "old immigrants." At first, Irish Catholics and other groups faced discrimination. In time, they were drawn into American life.

After 1885, millions of "new immigrants" arrived from southern and eastern Europe. They included Italians, Poles, Greeks, Russians, and Hungarians. Their labor helped turn the United States into an industrial powerhouse.

On the West Coast, a smaller but growing number of Asian immigrants arrived, mostly from Japan. A few immigrants also arrived from Korea, India, and the Philippines. Many of them labored on California farms or ran farms themselves. They contributed greatly to the construction of the irrigation systems that helped agriculture flourish in the state.

Few of the new immigrants spoke English. Many of the Europeans were Catholic, Jewish, or Eastern Orthodox. Immigrants from Asia might be Buddhist or Daoist. Set apart by language and religion, they found it harder to adapt to a new life.

Home Away from Home Immigrants eased into their new lives by settling in their own neighborhoods. Large American cities became patchworks of Italian, Irish, Polish, Hungarian, Greek, German, Jewish, and Chinese neighborhoods. Within these neighborhoods, even while trying to "Americanize," newcomers spoke their own language, celebrated special holidays, and prepared foods as in the old country. Jews established many communal philanthropic organizations and enjoyed thriving Yiddish theatre.

Did you know?

The Angel Island immigration station was built to help enforce the Chinese Exclusion Act.

INTERACTIVE

Immigration 1870–1910

INTERACTIVE

Issues Facing Immigrants

Religion stood at the center of immigrant family life. Houses of worship both united and separated ethnic groups. Catholics from Italy, Ireland, and Poland, for example, worshipped in their own neighborhood parishes. Jewish communities largely belonged to three major religious movements, or branches: Orthodox, Reform, and Conservative.

Bridging Cultures As newcomers struggled to adjust, they were often torn between old traditions and American ways. The first generation to arrive went through a process of acculturation. **Acculturation** is the process of adapting to a new culture and making changes while holding on to older traditions. Immigrants learned how to use American institutions such as schools, factories, and the political system. At the same time, they tried to keep their traditional religions, family structures, and community life.

In their effort to adapt, immigrants blended old and new ways. For example, some newcomers mixed their native tongues with English. Italians called the Fourth of July "Il Forte Gelato," a phrase that actually means "the great freeze." In El Paso, Texas, Mexican immigrants developed *Chuco*, a blend of English and Spanish.

Children adapted to the new culture more quickly than their parents. They learned English in school and then helped their families speak it. Because children wanted to be seen as Americans, they often gave up customs that their parents honored. They played American games and dressed in American-style clothes.

READING CHECK **Compare and Contrast** What was one main difference between "old" and "new" immigrants?

Analyze Graphs Compare the graphs showing the proportion of immigrants by place of origin. **Summarize** trends reflected in these graphs.

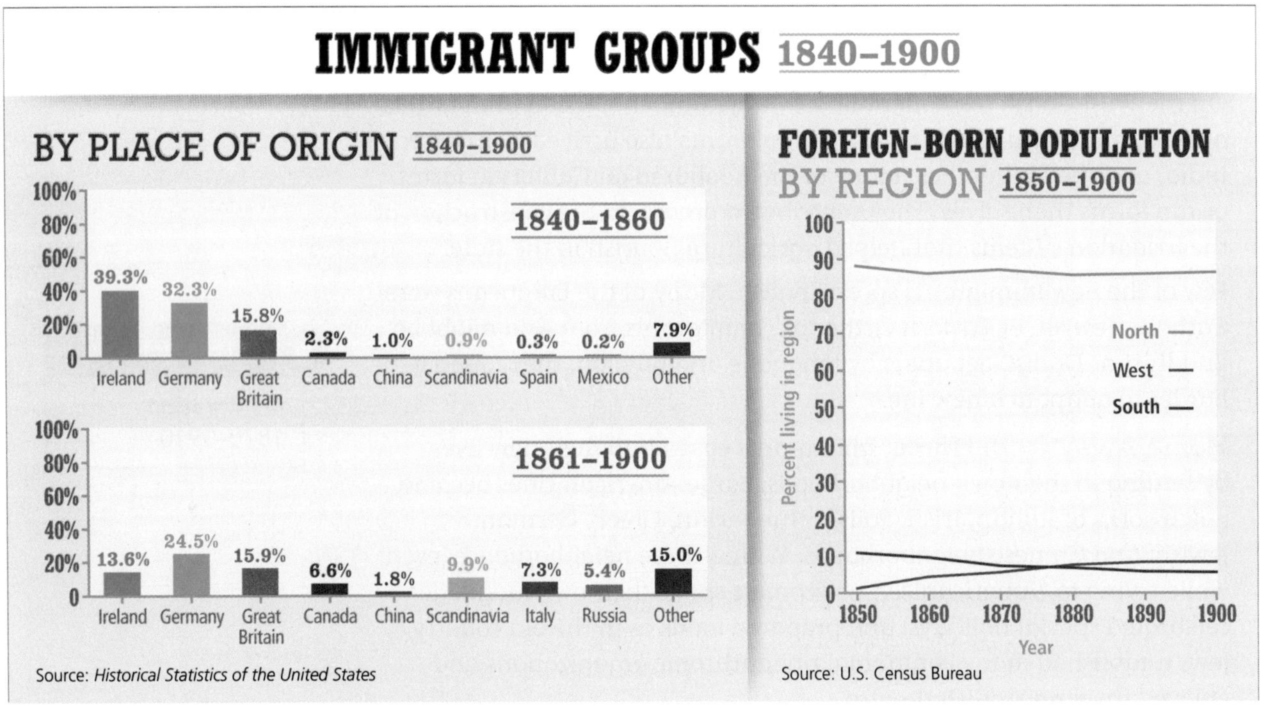

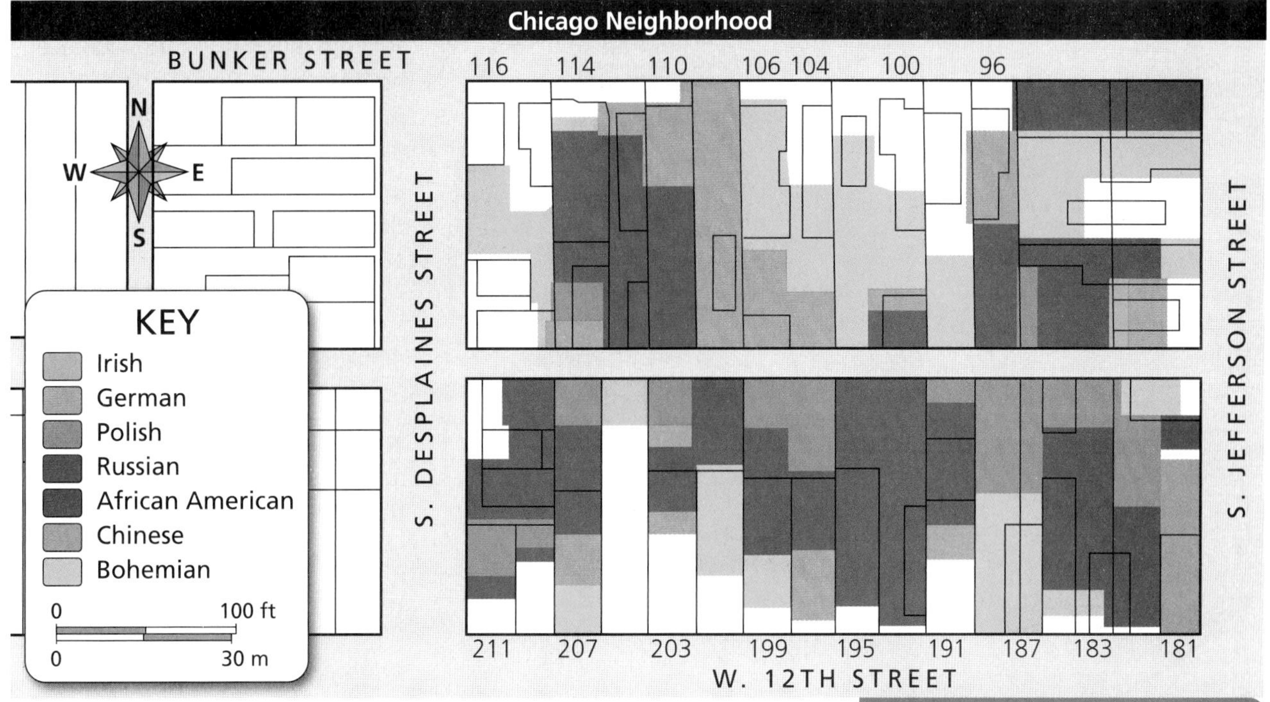

Why Did Nativists Oppose Immigration?

Even before the Civil War, Americans known as **nativists** sought to limit immigration and preserve the country for native-born, white Protestants. As immigration boomed in the late 1800s, nativist feelings reached a new peak.

Nativists argued that immigrants would not fit into American culture because their languages, religions, and customs were too different. Many workers resented the new immigrants because they took jobs for low pay. Others feared them because they were different.

Wherever new immigrants settled, nativist pressure grew. Nativists targeted Jews and Italians in the Northeast and Mexicans in the Southwest. On the West Coast, nativists worked to end immigration from China.

Chinese Exclusion Since the California Gold Rush, Chinese immigrants had helped build the West. Most lived in cities in tight-knit communities called "Chinatowns." Others farmed for a living. One Chinese immigrant, Ah Bing, spent decades working on a farm in Oregon, where he had a variety of cherry named after him. Today, the Bing cherry is the most widely produced cherry in the United States.

Most Americans did not understand Chinese customs. Also, some Chinese did not try to learn American ways. Like many other immigrants, they planned to stay only until they made a lot of money. They hoped to then return home to live out their lives as rich and respected members of Chinese society. When that dream failed, many Chinese settled in the United States permanently.

GEOGRAPHY **SKILLS**

This 1895 map shows a Chicago city block and uses a color key to identify the residents of each building.

1. **Interaction** What must it have been like to live on this block?
2. **Infer** Do you think the immigrant children played together? Why or why not?

Analyze Images Merchants tend their wares in a shop in San Francisco's Chinatown, around 1890. **Draw Conclusions** How did settling in ethnic neighborhoods make immigrants' lives easier?

As the numbers of Chinese grew, so did the prejudice and violence against them. Gangs attacked and sometimes killed Chinese people. Congress responded to this anti-Chinese feeling by passing the **Chinese Exclusion Act** in 1882. It barred Chinese laborers from entering the country. In addition, no Chinese person who left the United States could return , including cherry farmer Ah Bing, who went to China in the 1880s and was barred from returning to the United States.

The Chinese Exclusion Act was the first law to exclude a specific national group from immigrating to the United States. Congress renewed the original 10-year ban several times. It was finally repealed in 1943.

Congress Limits Immigration In 1887, nativists formed the American Protective Association. The group campaigned for laws to restrict immigration. Congress responded by passing a bill that denied entry to people who could not read their own language.

President Grover Cleveland vetoed the bill. It was wrong, he said, to keep out peasants just because they had never gone to school. Three later Presidents vetoed similar bills. However, in 1917, Congress overrode President Woodrow Wilson's veto, and the bill became law.

READING CHECK **Identify Main Ideas** What was the main goal of the nativists?

Lesson Check

Practice Vocabulary

1. Were the expanding industries of the United States a **pull factor** or a **push factor** for immigrants? Explain.
2. Would a **nativist** have believed that immigrants could achieve **acculturation**? Why or why not?

Critical Thinking and Writing

3. **Summarize** What challenges did immigrants face, starting with their journey to the United States?
4. **Analyze Information** What was the significance of the Chinese Exclusion Act?
5. **Writing Workshop: Generate Questions to Focus Research** At the end of the topic, you will write a research paper on a significant change in American culture or society. Once you have a general topic, write some "What," "Why," and "How" questions related to it in your Active Journal. Your goal is a single question that will focus your research.

Primary Sources

Willa Cather, *My Antonia*

In 1883, 9-year-old Willa Cather migrated with her family from Virginia to the Nebraska prairie. In her novel *My Antonia* she describes how immigrants carved out a new life on the Great Plains.

▶ Willa Cather was inspired by the immigrants she grew up among in Nebraska.

She greeted me ① gaily, and began at once to tell me how much ploughing she had done that day.

"No, we didn't. . . . I came to ask you something, Tony ②. Grandmother wants to know if you can't go to the term of school that begins next week over at the sod schoolhouse. She says there's a good teacher, and you'd learn a lot."

Antonia stood up, lifting and dropping her shoulders as if they were stiff. "I ain't got time to learn. I can work like mans now. My mother can't say no more how Ambrosch ③ do all and nobody to help him. I can work as much as him. School is all right for little boys. I help make this land one good farm."

She clucked to her team and started for the barn. . . . Before we reached the stable, I felt something tense in her silence, and glancing up I saw that she was crying. She turned her face from me and looked off at the red streak of dying light, over the dark prairie.④

I climbed up into the loft and threw down the hay for her, while she unharnessed her team. We walked slowly back toward the house. Ambrosch had come in from the north quarter, and was watering his oxen at the tank.

Antonia took my hand. "Sometime you will tell me all those nice things you learn at the school, won't you Jimmy?" she asked with a sudden rush of feeling in her voice.

—Willa Cather, *My Antonia*, 1918

Reading and Vocabulary Support

① The "me" refers to the narrator, whose name is Jim.

② Jim sometimes calls Antonia "Tony."

③ Ambrosch is Antonia's brother.

④ To what does the "red streak of dying light" refer?

Analyzing Primary Sources

Cite specific evidence from the source to support your answers.

1. **Vocabulary: Analyze Word Choices** How does the author show that English is not Antonia's first language?
2. **Express Problems Clearly** Why did Antonia start crying and then speak "with a sudden rush of feeling in her voice"?

Perform the dialogue between Jim and Antonia as a dramatic reading.

Analyze Sequence, Causation, and Correlation

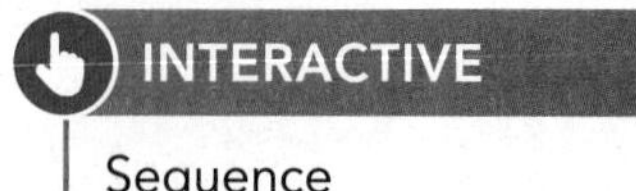

Follow these steps to help you identify sequence and distinguish between causation and correlation.

1. **Choose an event or a condition as a starting point.** You might want to choose an event at the beginning of the passage. Read the first paragraph of the passage below. What is the main event described there?

2. **Identify sequence.** Understand where that event occurred in time. Create a rough timeline of events or conditions that led up to that event and events or conditions that occurred after that event.

3. **Identify cause-and-effect relationships.** Look for text clues, like *because, led to, as a result,* and *therefore*. These terms signal cause-and-effect relationships.

4. **Look at other events or conditions for possible correlations.** Look for clue words and phrases like *meanwhile, at the same time,* and *also*. Terms like this suggest that although events and conditions may have something in common, such as a time period, one thing is not *caused* by the other.

5. **Summarize.** Make a table or chart showing the different relationships.

In the early 1800s, the United States underwent rapid geographical expansion and industrialization. The availability of jobs and land led people from a number of countries to immigrate to the United States. Many of the earliest immigrants came from China. The first wave of Chinese immigrants consisted largely of single men who sailed to California hoping to strike it rich in the gold rush. When the gold ran out, these Chinese needed other means of support. Therefore, many of them settled in cities on the West Coast, where they found jobs and opened businesses.

Meanwhile, a potato disease triggered a famine in Ireland. This prompted a massive wave of Irish immigration. In 1863, during the building of a transcontinental railroad, Chinese and Irish immigrants made up most of the workforce.

In addition to their work on the railroads, Chinese immigrants also labored in factories and on farms. Their eagerness to work, along with their acceptance of lower wages, led to bitter feelings. White laborers argued that Chinese workers were taking their jobs. Nativists, too, spoke out against the continuing stream of Chinese entering the country.

As a result, in 1882, Congress passed the Chinese Exclusion Act. Chinese laborers, skilled or unskilled, would no longer be allowed to enter the country. This new law caused employers on the West Coast to seek cheap labor elsewhere. They began hiring workers from Japan, the Philippines, Korea, and India. The steady immigration of workers from Asia would continue into the 1900s.

LESSON 2

Urbanization

GET READY TO READ

START UP

Look at the image of this growing city. Write about how people's lives changed as cities flourished.

GUIDING QUESTIONS

- Why did cities grow rapidly in the late 1800s?
- How did city dwellers' social and economic conditions determine where they lived?
- What was the settlement house movement?

TAKE NOTES

Literacy Skills Identify Cause and Effect

Use the graphic organizer in your Active Journal to take notes as you read the lesson.

PRACTICE VOCABULARY

Use the vocabulary activity in your Active Journal to practice the vocabulary words.

Vocabulary	Academic Vocabulary
urbanization	differentiate
tenement	
building code	
Social Gospel	
settlement house	
Hull House	

Economic opportunity meant jobs, and the nation's ever-expanding industries provided them. New immigrants, along with Americans fresh off the farm, poured into the cities in search of factory work. City populations swelled.

Why Did Cities Expand?

"We cannot all live in cities," declared newspaper publisher Horace Greeley, "yet nearly all seem determined to do so." **Urbanization**, the movement of population from farms to urban areas, or cities, began slowly in the early 1800s. As the nation industrialized, the pace quickened. In 1860, only one American in five lived in an urban area. By 1890, one in three did.

Jobs drew people to cities. As industries grew, so did the need for workers. New city dwellers took jobs in steel mills, meatpacking plants, and garment factories. Others worked as salesclerks, waiters, barbers, bank tellers, and secretaries.

Quick Activity

Use maps like the one below to trace the growth of a city.

Immigration and Domestic Migration The flood of immigrants swelled city populations. So, too, did migrations from farm to city within the country. In fact, many Americans left farms and migrated to cities to find a better life. One young woman summed up the feelings of many farmers toward their backbreaking work:

Primary Source

"If I were offered a deed to the best farm . . . on the condition of going back to the country to live, I would not take it. I would rather face starvation in town."

—quoted in *The Good Old Days—They Were Terrible!* (Bettmann)

African American Migration African Americans, too, sought a better life in the cities. By the 1890s, the south side of Chicago had a thriving African American community. Detroit, New York, Philadelphia, and other northern cities also had growing African American neighborhoods. The migration to the north began gradually, but increased rapidly after 1915.

African American migration usually began with one family member moving north. Later, relatives and friends followed. Many faced the challenge of adjusting to urban life.

READING CHECK **Identify Main Ideas** What caused the rapid urbanization of the late 1800s?

GEOGRAPHY SKILLS

Boston grew rapidly during the late 1800s. Unlike other cities, it was surrounded by water. The city had to fill in wetlands to create more building space.

1. **Place** What clues hint at the watery origin of parts of Boston?
2. **Draw Conclusions** Could a city use this solution to solve a space problem today? Why or why not?

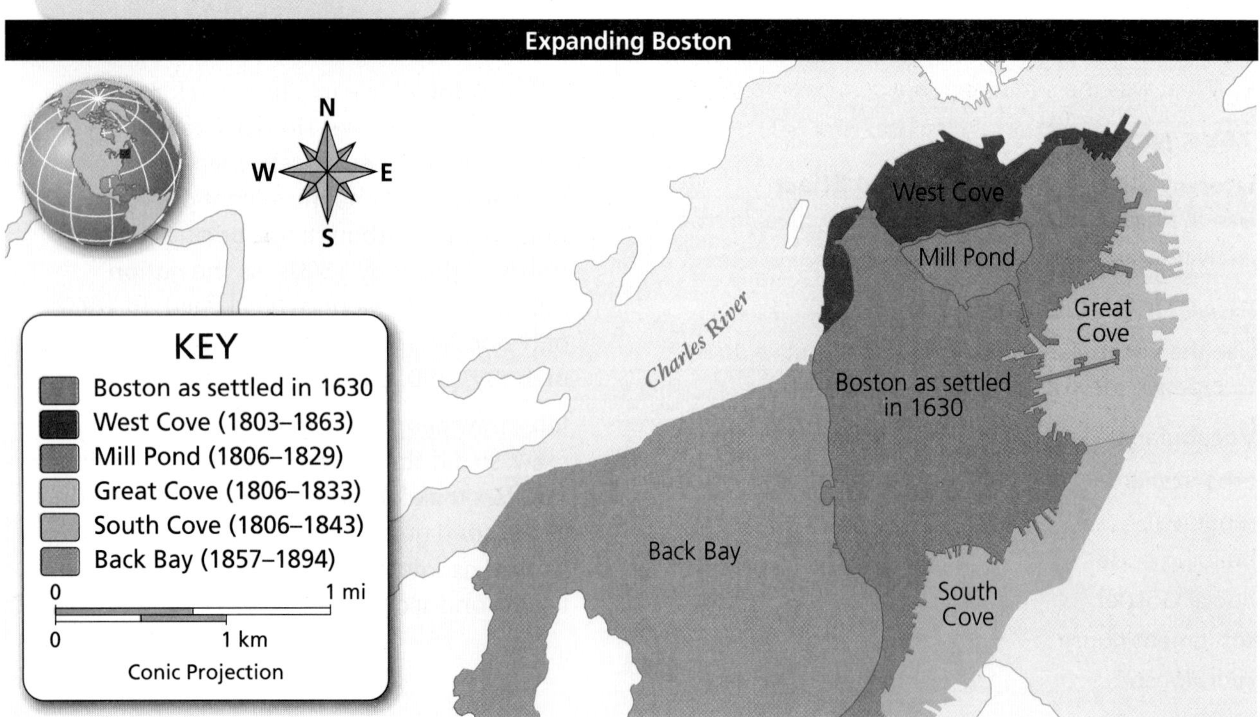

How Did Status Define City Neighborhoods?

Cities grew outward from their old downtown sections. Before long, many cities took on a similar shape. Neighborhoods were **differentiated** by the status, or condition, of the people living there.

The Poor Poor families often clustered near the city's center, the oldest section. They struggled to survive in crowded slums. The streets were jammed with people, horses, pushcarts, and garbage.

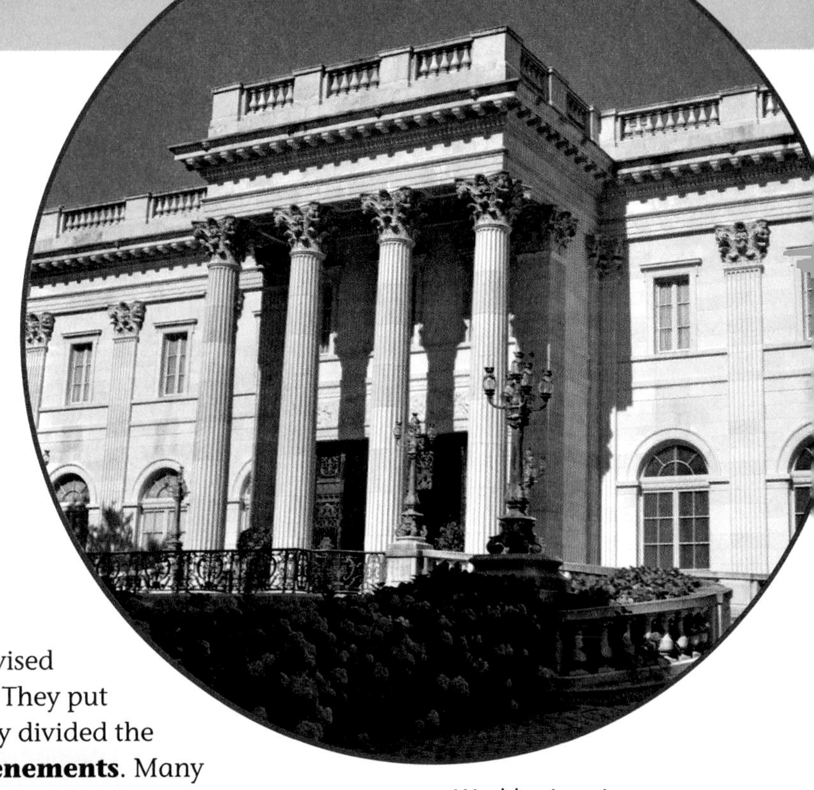

▲ Wealthy Americans used their wealth to build magnificent mansions that stood in stark contrast to the nearby slums.

Because space was so limited, builders devised a new kind of house to hold more people. They put up buildings six or seven stories high. They divided the buildings into small apartments, called **tenements**. Many tenements had no windows, heat, or indoor bathrooms. Often, 10 people shared a single room.

Crowding increased as businesses built factories near the city centers to take advantage of good rail connections and cheap labor. They forced more and more people into fewer and fewer apartments.

Typhoid and cholera raged through the tenements. Tuberculosis, a lung disease, was the biggest killer, accounting for thousands of deaths each year. Babies, especially, fell victim to disease. Around 1900, more than half of all babies in one Chicago slum died before they were one year old. Despite the poor conditions, the populations of slums grew rapidly.

The Middle Class Beyond the slums stood the homes of the new middle class, including doctors, lawyers, business managers, and office workers. Rows of neat, spacious houses lined tree-shaded streets. Here, disease broke out less frequently than in the slums.

Academic Vocabulary
differentiate • *v.*, to tell what makes one thing or person different from another

Leisure activities gave middle-class people a sense of community and purpose. They joined clubs, singing societies, bowling leagues, and charitable organizations. As one writer said, the clubs "bring together many people who are striving upward, trying to uplift themselves."

The Wealthy Beyond the slums stood the mansions of the very rich, protected by iron gates or brick walls. In New York, huge homes dotted upper Fifth Avenue, then on the outskirts of the city. In Chicago, 200 millionaires lived along the exclusive lakefront by the 1880s. In San Francisco, the wealthy lived the exclusive Nob Hill area.

Rich Americans modeled their lives on those of European royalty. They filled their mansions with priceless artwork and gave lavish parties. At one banquet, the host handed out cigarettes rolled in hundred-dollar bills.

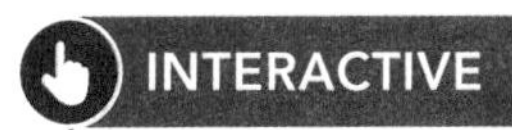

INTERACTIVE
New York City Changes, 1840 to 1900

READING CHECK **Identify Supporting Details** What was life like for the urban poor?

INTERACTIVE
Urban Problems

Effects of Rapid Urbanization

As more and more people crowded into cities, problems grew. Garbage rotted in the streets. Factories polluted the air. Crime flourished. Thieves and pickpockets haunted lonely alleys, especially at night.

Tenement buildings were deathtraps if a fire broke out. News reporter Jacob Riis brought readers into the tenements in his startling exposé, *How the Other Half Lives*:

Primary Source

"Step carefully over this baby—it is a baby, spite of its rags and dirt—under these iron bridges called fire-escapes, but loaded down . . . with broken household goods, with washtubs and barrels, over which no man could climb from a fire."

—Jacob Riis, *How the Other Half Lives*

What Did the Government Do to Help? By the 1880s, reformers pressured city governments for change. **Building codes** set standards for construction and safety. New buildings were required to have fire escapes and decent plumbing. Cities also hired workers to collect garbage and sweep the streets.

Analyze Images This family worked together to make cigars in their tenement home. **Use Visual Information** Who do you think did the bulk of the work?

To reduce pollution, zoning laws kept factories out of neighborhoods where people lived. Safety improved when cities set up professional fire companies and police forces. Gas—and later electric—lights made streets less dangerous at night. As you will read, many cities built new systems of public transportation as well, and developed new water systems that provided clean water to city dwellers every day.

How Did Religious Groups Help? Religious groups worked to ease the problems of the poor. The Catholic Church ministered to the needs of Irish, Polish, and Italian immigrants. An Italian-born nun, Mother Cabrini, helped found dozens of hospitals for the poor. In cities, Protestant ministers preaching a new

Analyze Images Cities purchased newly developed equipment, such as this firefighting pump, to improve the safety of crowded neighborhoods. **Infer** Why do you think the increase in tenement housing could be a safety hazard?

Social Gospel called on their well-to-do members to help the poor. Founded in 1865 in England, the Salvation Army offered food and shelter to those in need.

READING CHECK **Identify Supporting Details** What did the government do to improve the lives of city dwellers?

What Was the Settlement House Movement?

Some people looked for ways to help the poor. By the late 1800s, individuals began to organize **settlement houses**, community centers that offered services to the poor. The leading figure of the settlement house movement was a Chicago woman named Jane Addams.

Who Was Jane Addams? Jane Addams came from a well-to-do family but had strong convictions about helping the poor. After college, she moved into one of the poorest slums in Chicago. There, in an old mansion, she and her romantic partner, Ellen Starr, opened a settlement house named **Hull House** in 1889.

Other idealistic young women soon joined Addams. They took up residence in Hull House so that they could experience firsthand some of the hardships of the slum community in which they worked. Hull House volunteers offered a wide variety of services. They taught classes in American government and the English language. Other volunteers gave instruction in health care or operated day nurseries for children whose mothers worked outside the home.

Quest CONNECTIONS

How were urbanization and immigration connected? Record your findings in your Active Journal.

Analyze Images Hull House in Chicago offered many activities to help immigrants feel more at home in their new surroundings. **Use Visual Information** Do you think these children are enjoying themselves? Why or why not?

Hull House provided recreational activities for young people, such as sports, a choral group, and a theater.

The settlement house movement spread quickly. By 1900, about 100 such centers had opened in American cities.

INTERACTIVE

Living in a Tenement

How Did Addams and Hull House Promote Reform? Addams and her staff helped bring about reform legislation. They studied the slum neighborhoods where they worked. They realized that the problems were too big for any one person or group, and they urged the government to act.

Alice Hamilton, a Hull House doctor, campaigned for better health laws. Florence Kelley worked to ban child labor. Jane Addams herself believed that reform legislation would pass more quickly if women were allowed to vote. She joined the continuing campaign for women's suffrage.

READING CHECK **Use Evidence** How did the settlement house movement help immigrants?

Lesson Check

Practice Vocabulary

1. How did **building codes** improve the quality of life for **tenement** dwellers?

Critical Thinking and Writing

2. **Identify Cause and Effect** What was the main cause of urbanization?
3. **Identify Cause and Effect** What was the key factor that determined in which area of the city a person would live? Who lived in which areas?
4. **Revisit the Essential Question** How did Jane Addams and other members of Hull House have a positive effect on American society?
5. **Writing Workshop: Find and Use Credible Sources** Start a list in your Active Journal of a variety of reliable, established research sources. Use these sources to find answers to the question that is the focus of your research.

Conduct a Cost-Benefit Analysis

INTERACTIVE

Make Decisions

Follow these steps to analyze the decision-making process.

1 **Identify the decision that has to be made.** A decision often starts with a problem. For example: How can I make my government stronger? How can I improve the economy? What problem does Jacob Riis refer to in the source below?

2 **Identify a possible solution.** What is a step you could take that might solve your problem? What solution did Mayor Low offer to the problem Riis identified?

3 **Identify the costs and benefits of your solution.** Ask, "What might this solution cost to put into place?" Then ask, "What are the benefits that might occur?" Be thorough in listing costs and benefits.

a. What was the cost to build the six new schools? What other possible costs can you think of?

b. What were the benefits that Riis identified? What other benefits might there have been?

4 **Compare the benefits to the costs.** A good solution offers benefits that are far greater than the costs. Compare the ratio of costs to benefits for several options. Make a chart to list the costs and benefits of building the six new schools, and then compare the ratio of costs to benefits.

Primary Source

"The East Side, that had been orderly, became a hotbed of child crime. . . . Yesterday, Mayor Low's reform government voted six millions of dollars for new schools. . . . In that most crowded neighborhood in all the world, where the superintendent lately pleaded in vain for three new schools, half a dozen have been built, the finest in this or any other land—great, light, and airy structures, with playgrounds on the roof; and all over the city the like are going up. The briefest of our laws . . . says that never one shall be built without its playground.

And not for the child's use only. The band shall play there yet and neighbor meet neighbor in such social contact as the slum has never known to its undoing. . . . Clergymen applaud the opening of the school buildings on Sunday for concerts, lectures, and neighborhood meetings. Common sense is having its day. The streets are cleaned."

—Jacob Riis, *The Battle With the Slum*, 1902

LESSON 3

The Rise of Progressivism

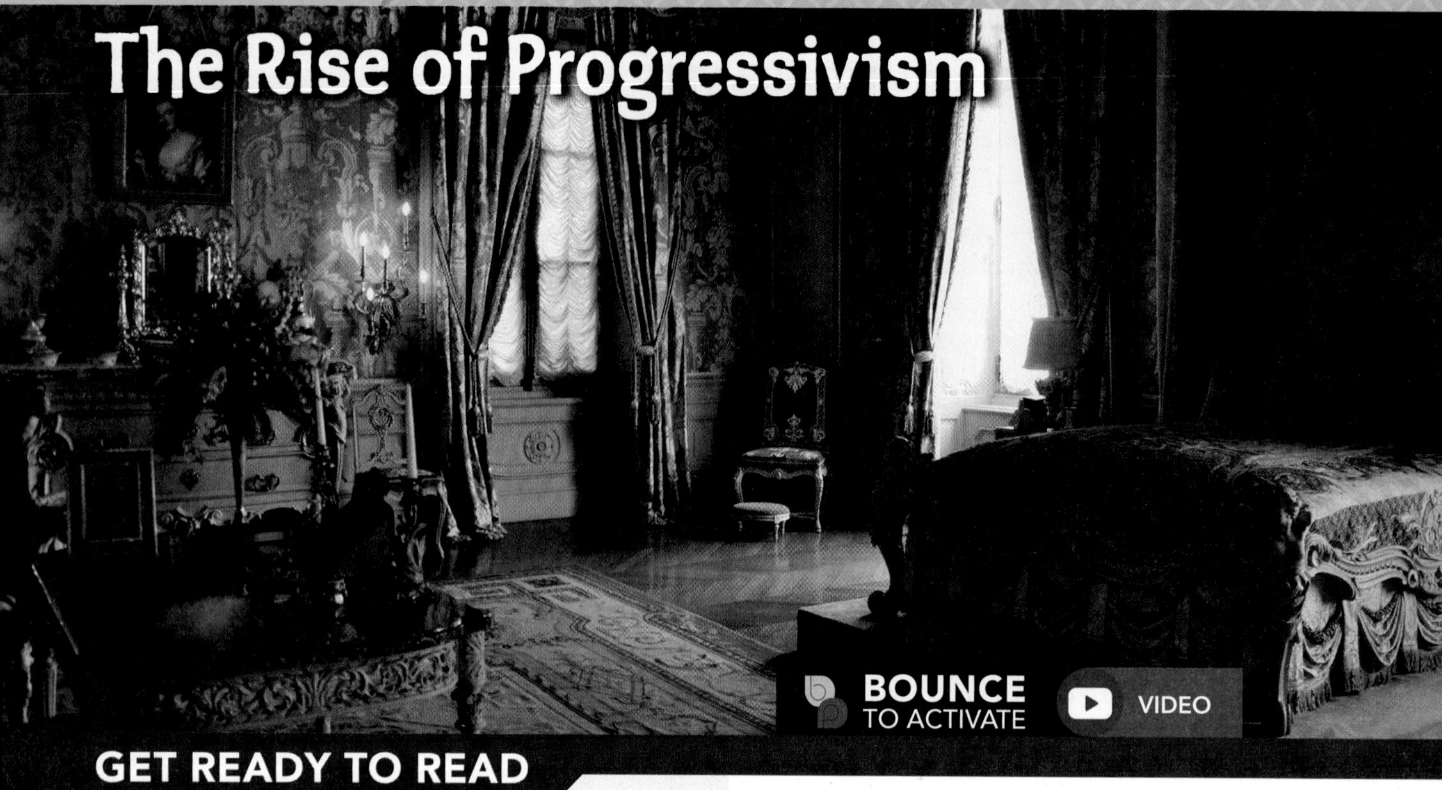

GET READY TO READ

START UP

Look at the photo of a mansion from the late 1800s. Why do you think the wealthiest Americans were often able to influence government policy?

GUIDING QUESTIONS

- What bothered reformers about politics during the Gilded Age?
- What reforms marked the Progressive Era?
- How did the federal government affect the country's growth after the Civil War?

TAKE NOTES

Literacy Skills Identify Supporting Details

Use the graphic organizer in your Active Journal to take notes as you read the lesson.

PRACTICE VOCABULARY

Use the vocabulary activity in your Active Journal to practice the vocabulary words.

Vocabulary		Academic Vocabulary
patronage	primary	merit
civil service	initiative	forum
muckraker	referendum	
Progressive	recall	

The late 1800s has been called the Gilded Age. The name came from an 1873 novel by Mark Twain and Charles Dudley Warner titled *The Gilded Age*, which poked fun at the era's greed and political corruption. *Gilded* means coated with a thin layer of gold. It implies that a surface glitter hides a darker reality. For many Americans, the novel captured the spirit of the time. In the words of one observer, it was government "of, by, and for the rich."

Gilded Age Politics

The Gilded Age lasted from the 1870s through the 1890s. During this time, reformers struggled to clean up political corruption.

Political power in the Gilded Age was split between the two major parties. Usually, the North and West voted Republican, and the South voted Democratic. Neither party controlled Congress for more than a term or two, although Republicans held the White House for nearly 25 years. However, Presidents generally had less power than Congress during the period.

For Americans of the Gilded Age, elections provided great entertainment. Campaigns featured brass bands, torchlight parades, picnics, and long speeches. Americans marched, ate, drank, and listened. Voter turnout has never again been as high—almost 80 percent of eligible voters went to the polls.

Two concerns shaped politics. Many Americans worried about the power of the rich. They feared that bankers, industrialists, and other wealthy men were controlling politics at the expense of the public good. The other worry was corruption, especially bribery and voter fraud. Reformers blamed much of the problem on the spoils system, the practice of rewarding political supporters with government jobs.

How did city governments become so corrupt? As cities grew, they needed to expand services such as sewers, garbage collection, and roads. Often, politicians accepted money to give away these jobs. As a result, bribes and corruption became a way of life.

Corruption at the Top Powerful politicians called political bosses gained power in many cities. Political bosses also ruled county and state governments. Bosses controlled work done locally and demanded payoffs from businesses. City bosses were popular with the poor, especially with immigrants. They provided jobs and made loans to the needy. They handed out extra coal for heating in winter and turkeys at Thanksgiving. In exchange, the poor voted for the boss or his chosen candidate.

Boss Tweed In New York City, Boss William Tweed carried corruption to new extremes. During the 1860s and 1870s, he cheated the city out of more than $100 million. Journalists exposed Boss Tweed's wrongdoing. For example, cartoonist Thomas Nast pictured Tweed as a vulture who had fed on the city. Nast's cartoons especially angered Tweed. His supporters might not be able to read, he said, but they could understand Nast's cartoons.

Primary Source

"The way to have power is to take it."

—William M. "Boss" Tweed

Faced with prison, Tweed fled to Spain. There, local police arrested him when they recognized him from Nast's cartoons. When Tweed died in jail in 1878, thousands of poor New Yorkers mourned for him.

READING CHECK Identify Cause and Effect Why were political bosses popular with the poor?

Analyze Political Cartoons The Tammany Tiger represented the strength of "Boss" Tweed and his cronies. **Infer** Why do you think the tiger is so large?

Federal and Local Reform Efforts

The spoils system had grown since the days of Andrew Jackson. When a new President took office, job seekers swarmed into Washington. They demanded government jobs as rewards for their political support. Giving jobs to followers is called **patronage**.

Patronage often led to corruption. Some jobholders simply stole public money. Others had no skills for the jobs they were given. In New York, for example, one man was made court reporter even though he could neither read nor write.

Initial Reforms Calls for reform slowly brought change. In 1877, President Rutherford B. Hayes took steps toward ending the spoils system. He ordered an investigation of the New York customhouse. There, investigators found hundreds of appointed officials receiving high salaries but doing no work. Despite the protests of local Republican leaders, Hayes dismissed two customhouse officials.

Academic Vocabulary
merit • *n.*, ability, achievement, or worthiness

In 1881, James Garfield entered the White House and was soon swamped with office seekers. He thought that government jobs should be awarded on the basis of **merit**, or ability, not politics.

That July, however, a disappointed office seeker, Charles Guiteau (gee TOH), shot the President. Garfield died two months later. The assassination sparked new efforts to end the spoils system.

How Did Civil Service Reform Federal Jobs? Vice President Chester A. Arthur succeeded Garfield. Arthur was a product of the spoils system. In fact, he was one of the New York customhouse officials dismissed by Hayes a few years earlier! Yet, as President, Arthur worked

Analyze Images His rejection of the spoils system led to President James Garfield's assassination in 1881 at the age of 49. **Synthesize Visual Information** Based on the image, which person depicted is probably the assassin?

with Congress to reform the spoils system.

In 1883, Congress passed the Pendleton Act. It created the Civil Service Commission to conduct exams for federal jobs. The **civil service** includes all federal jobs except elected offices and the military. The aim of the Civil Service Commission was to fill jobs on the basis of merit. People who scored highest on the civil service exams earned the posts.

At first, the Civil Service Commission controlled only a few federal jobs. However, under pressure from reformers, later Presidents placed more jobs under the Civil Service Commission. By 1900, the commission controlled about 40 percent of all federal jobs.

Analyze Images Theodore Roosevelt's campaign against trusts was often the subject of cartoons. **Interpret Political Cartoons** Why do you think the cartoonist represented the trusts as a pig?

How Did Cities Encourage Honest Government? In many cities, reformers set up good-government leagues. Their goal was to replace corrupt officials with honest leaders. The leagues had some successes. Cleveland reformers helped elect Tom Johnson mayor. Johnson gave out contracts honestly, improved garbage and sewer systems, and set up services for the poor.

READING CHECK **Summarize** What was the role of the Civil Service Commission in political reform?

The Power of Big Business

Part of the Gilded Age's excess and corruption stemmed from the philosophical work of Herbert Spencer. Spencer took the scientific idea of another Englishman, Charles Darwin, and applied it to human society. Using Spencer's interpretation of Darwin's work about "survival of the fittest" as justification, Gilded Age barons believed that they deserved more wealth and power because they were naturally more "fit" than other people. This philosophy became known as Social Darwinism. It was used to justify poor treatment of workers, racism, and unrestricted, unregulated capitalism.

Social Darwinism supported actions like those taken by Collis Huntington. In 1877, Huntington, builder of the Central Pacific Railroad, tried to bribe members of Congress to kill a railroad bill that would be unfavorable to his interests. "It costs money to fix things," Huntington explained.

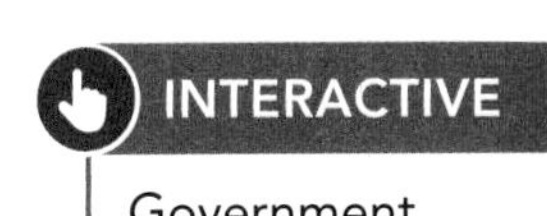

Government Reforms in the Progressive Era

Analyze Images Chinese laborers and their skills were essential to building rail lines. **Evaluate Arguments** Some people say that when a business spends so much money on infrastructure, such as building railroad lines, it should not have to share what it built with its competition. What do you think?

Government Regulation of Business The behavior of men like Huntington convinced many Americans that big businesses controlled the government. They demanded that something be done to limit the power of big business.

In response, the government began to regulate railroads and other large businesses. Under the Constitution, the federal government had the power to regulate interstate commerce, or business that crossed state lines. In 1887, President Grover Cleveland signed the Interstate Commerce Act. It forbade practices such as pools and rebates. It also set up the Interstate Commerce Commission (ICC) to oversee the railroads.

At first, the ICC was weak. In court challenges, most judges ruled in favor of the railroads. Still, Congress had shown that it was ready to regulate big business. Later laws made the ICC more effective.

Promoting Competition In 1888, Grover Cleveland lost his bid for another term as President to Benjamin Harrison. In 1890, Harrison signed the Sherman Antitrust Act. The act prohibited businesses from trying to limit or destroy competition.

The Sherman Antitrust Act sounded strong, but enforcing it proved difficult. Opponents claimed that the law was an illegal attempt by the government to control private property.

Courts even used the law against labor unions. They said strikes blocked free trade and thus threatened competition. Later on, as the reform spirit spread, the courts began to use the Sherman Antitrust Act to regulate monopolies.

READING CHECK **Identify Supporting Details** How did the courts use the Sherman Antitrust Act to help big business?

How Did Muckrakers Push for Reforms?

Reformers used the press to turn public opinion against corruption. Newspaper reporters described how corruption led to inadequate fire and police protection and poor sanitation services. Jacob Riis (reess), a photographer and writer, provided shocking images of slum life.

Crusading journalists like Riis became known as **muckrakers**. People said they raked the dirt, or muck, and exposed it to public view. One muckraker, Ida Tarbell, targeted the unfair practices of big business. Her articles about the Standard Oil Company led to demands for more controls on trusts.

In 1906, Upton Sinclair's novel *The Jungle* shocked the nation. Although the book was fiction, it was based on facts. It revealed grisly details about the meatpacking industry, including descriptions of the horrid working conditions and the unsanitary practices in the plants. Sinclair told how the packers used meat from sick animals. He described how rats often got ground up in the meat, which was then dyed to make it look healthy. He explained just how little thought was given to the health of the consumer.

Sinclair claimed that his purpose in writing *The Jungle* was to alert the public to the unfit working conditions of meatpackers. However, the public outrage focused on the contaminated food they were unknowingly eating. Soon after the novel's publication, the federal government passed the Pure Food and Drug and Meat Inspection Acts. Sinclair's writing did impact reform.

BIOGRAPHY 5 Things to Know About

IDA TARBELL

Muckraking journalist who exposed the unfair business practices of Standard Oil (1857–1944)

- Tarbell was born and raised in Pennsylvania, the center of the oil industry at the time.
- A rebate scheme between railroads and John D. Rockefeller's Standard Oil Company left many businesses in ruins—including her father's.
- Hired in 1894 as an editor by *McClure's Magazine*, she wrote a series of articles about Abraham Lincoln that brought her great praise and brought the magazine many more readers.
- In 1902, she started a 19-part series titled "The History of Standard Oil," which exposed Rockefeller's anti-competitive practices and earned her a reputation as a muckraker.
- In spite of her Progressive attitude toward big business, she opposed the struggle for women's suffrage.

Critical Thinking How did muckraking journalists like Tarbell contribute to society?

Analyze Images Workers, including young boys, make sausages at a Chicago factory in 1893. **Cite Evidence** Do you think this food was manufactured in a sanitary way? Support your answer.

As magazines became affordable, muckrakers began publishing in them to reach a wider middle-class audience. *McClure's Magazine* was a popular **forum** for crusading journalists. Lincoln Steffens, who published with *McClure's Magazine*, eventually gathered his articles in a book about the political corruption that plagued cities across the nation.

Muckrakers helped change public opinion. For years, middle-class Americans had ignored the need for reform. When they saw how dishonest politicians and businesses corrupted the nation—and even the food they ate—they, too, demanded change.

Academic Vocabulary
forum • *n.*, a setting where people exchange views, ideas, and opinions

READING CHECK **Classify and Categorize** Why were some reformers called muckrakers?

Progressive Reforms

By 1900, reformers were calling themselves **Progressives**. By that, they meant that they were forward-thinking people who wanted to improve American life. Progressives won many changes during the period from 1898 to 1917. As a result, this period is called the Progressive Era.

Progressives were never a single group with a single goal. Instead, they came from many backgrounds and backed different causes. They were united by a belief that the ills of society could be solved. Progressives wanted the government to act in the public interest, for the good of the people.

Both religion and science inspired Progressives. The Social Gospel movement of the late 1800s stressed the duty of Christians to improve society. At the same time, Progressives used scientific studies and statistics to find ways to solve society's problems.

Progressives valued education. John Dewey, a Progressive educator, wanted schools to promote reform. Schools must teach democratic values by example, he argued. He therefore urged students to ask questions and to work together to solve problems. He believed that students should be able to apply what they learned in school to their lives outside of school

The Wisconsin Idea Robert La Follette of Wisconsin was another influential Progressive. "The will of the people shall be the law of the land," was his motto. His fighting spirit won him the nickname "Battling Bob."

As governor of Wisconsin, La Follette introduced various Progressive reforms that became known as the Wisconsin Idea. For example, he lowered railroad rates. The result was increased rail traffic, which helped both railroad owners and customers.

Empowering Voters Progressives like La Follette wanted voters to participate more directly in government. Since Andrew Jackson's time, party leaders had picked candidates for local and state offices. Progressives called, instead, for primaries. In a **primary**, voters choose their party's candidate for the general election. In 1903, Wisconsin was the first state to adopt a primary run by state government officials. By 1917, all but four states had done so.

Other reforms gave voters more power. They included the **initiative**, which gave voters the right to put a bill before a state legislature. A certain number of qualified voters must sign initiative petitions to propose a law. The **referendum** allowed voters to put a bill on the ballot and vote it into law. The **recall** allowed voters to remove an elected official from office. That reform let voters get rid of corrupt officials.

Progressives from other states visited Wisconsin to study La Follette's reforms. A number of states elected Progressive governors eager for reforms.

Amending the Constitution Progressives fought for other changes, too. They favored lowering tariffs on imported goods. If American industry had to compete against foreign imports, they argued, consumers would benefit from lower prices.

Some reforms led to changes in the U.S. Constitution. Many reformers backed a graduated income tax, which taxes people at different rates. The wealthy pay taxes at a higher rate than the poor or the middle class. However, the Supreme Court had held that a federal income tax was unconstitutional.

Analyze Images In the early 1900s, Governor Robert La Follette of Wisconsin promoted a number of Progressive reforms known as the Wisconsin Idea. **Summarize** In what ways did La Follette inspire others?

INTERACTIVE

Progressive Political Reforms

So, Progressives sought an amendment to give Congress the power to pass an income tax. By 1913, the states had ratified the amendment.

The states approved another amendment in 1913. Since 1789, state legislatures had elected senators. Powerful interest groups had sometimes bribed lawmakers to vote for certain candidates. Progressives wanted to end such abuses by having voters elect senators directly. In 1912, Congress approved the Seventeenth Amendment, which allowed for the direct election of senators. It was ratified a year later.

READING CHECK **Identify Main Ideas** What belief united the Progressive movement?

Analyze Images In many states, Progressive reforms shifted political power to voters. **Draw Conclusions** What responsibilities does a citizen have when voting on a referendum?

Progressive Political Reforms

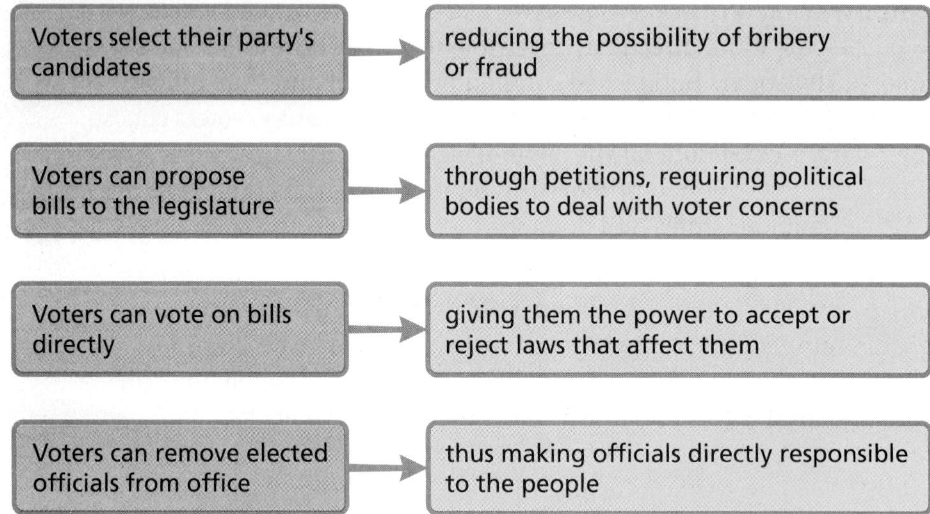

Lesson Check

Practice Vocabulary

1. How was **patronage** linked to the spoils system?
2. Of the **initiative**, **referendum**, and **recall**, which one allows voters to put a bill directly onto the ballot?

Critical Thinking and Writing

3. **Draw Conclusions** Why did cartoonist Thomas Nast depict Boss Tweed as a vulture?
4. **Identify Supporting Details** What were Congress's first attempts to regulate big business, and why were they ineffective at first?
5. **Summarize** What successes did Progressive reformers achieve?
6. **Writing Workshop: Find and Use Credible Sources** Read through your sources and start taking notes in your Active Journal. Write specific facts and ideas from the sources in your own words or summarize broader, more general ideas. Any directly quoted material must be enclosed in quotation marks in your paper.

Identify Central Issues and Problems

Follow these steps to learn ways to identify central issues and problems.

INTERACTIVE

Identify Main Ideas and Details

1. **Identify the subject of the passage.** Read the passage to find out what it is about. The passage below lacks a true topic sentence that identifies the main idea or subject. Based on the first paragraph, what is the subject of the passage?

2. **Identify the people, time, and place discussed in the passage.** Look for clues in the passage.
   - **a.** What can you guess about the profession of the writer?
   - **b.** Who is the intended audience for this article?
   - **c.** During what era did this article appear?

3. **Determine the central issue or problem.** Read the details of the passage to find its main focus. What is the central problem or issue that the passage focuses on?

4. **Explain why this issue was important.**
   - **a.** Why was this particular issue important at the time?
   - **b.** Have people at other times and places faced similar issues?

Primary Source

IV—The Subtle Poisons

Ignorance and credulous hope make the market for most proprietary remedies. . . . Of these concealed drugs the headache powders are the most widely used, and of the headache powders, Orangeine is the most conspicuous. . . . Orangeine, like practically all the headache powders, is simply a mixture of acetanilid with less potent drugs. . . . The wickedness of the fraud lies in this: That whereas the nostrum, by virtue of its acetanilid content, thins the blood, depresses the heart, and finally undermines the whole system, it claims *to strengthen the heart and to produce better blood*. . . .

Recent years have added to the mortality records of our cities a surprising and alarming number of sudden deaths from heart failure . . . and there is every reason to believe that the increased mortality, which is still in evidence, is due largely to the secret weakening of the heart from acetanilid. . . .

Obscurity as to the real nature of the drug . . . is the safeguard of the acetanilid vendor. . . . And were the even more important fact that the use of these powders becomes a habit . . . understood by the public, the repeated sales which are the basis of Orangeine's prosperity would undoubtedly be greatly cut down.

—Samuel Hopkins Adams, *The Great American Fraud*, 1905

LESSON 4

The Progressive Presidents

GET READY TO READ

START UP

Examine the photograph of Theodore Roosevelt, a Progressive President. Based on this image, do you think he wanted to protect natural resources?

GUIDING QUESTIONS

- What were Theodore Roosevelt's reform goals?
- How did William Howard Taft's policies compare and contrast with those of Theodore Roosevelt?
- What economic reform policies did Woodrow Wilson pursue?

TAKE NOTES

Literacy Skills Classify and Categorize

Use the graphic organizer in your Active Journal to take notes as you read the lesson.

PRACTICE VOCABULARY

Use the vocabulary activity in your Active Journal to practice the vocabulary words.

Vocabulary

- trustbuster
- Square Deal
- conservation
- Bull Moose Party
- New Freedom
- Federal Reserve Act
- Federal Trade Commission

Academic Vocabulary

- committed
- expose

The Progressive reform movement received a huge boost when Theodore Roosevelt became President in 1901. He was the first of three Presidents who used their power as the nation's chief executive to fight for Progressive causes.

Theodore Roosevelt's Path to the White House

Theodore Roosevelt—also known as Teddy Roosevelt or "TR"—came from a wealthy New York family. As a child, he suffered from asthma and was often sick. To build his strength, he lifted weights, ran, and boxed. He improved his physical condition and remained active his entire life.

A Life of Public Service Roosevelt could have enjoyed a life of ease. Instead, he decided to enter politics. He was determined to end corruption and devote himself to working for the public interest.

Roosevelt's friends mocked his decision to devote his life to public service. He later recalled that they said, "that the men I met would be rough and brutal and unpleasant to deal with." He replied that he would not quit until he "found out whether I was really too weak to hold my own in the rough and tumble."

By age 26, Roosevelt was serving in the New York state legislature. Then tragedy struck. In 1884, his mother and his wife died on the same day. Overcome by grief, Roosevelt quit the legislature. He went west to work on a cattle ranch. There, he noticed the damage being done to the environment and wildlife and became concerned.

After two years, Roosevelt returned to the East and to politics. He served on the Civil Service Commission. He then headed New York City's police department and later became assistant secretary of the navy.

In 1898, the United States went to war against Spain. Roosevelt led a unit of troops in some daring exploits. He returned home to a hero's welcome and was elected governor of New York.

A Progressive Leader Since his days in the legislature, Roosevelt had pushed for reform. As governor, he continued to work for Progressive reforms. Other lawmakers called him a "goo goo," a mocking name for someone who wanted good government.

New York Republican bosses were relieved when Roosevelt resigned from the office of governor to become Vice President. Then, after President McKinley was shot in September 1901, Roosevelt became President. He was **committed**, he later wrote, to "making an old party Progressive."

Academic Vocabulary
committed • *v.,* devoted

READING CHECK **Sequence** What were the major events in Theodore Roosevelt's life leading up to his presidency?

Encouraging Fair Business Practices

Roosevelt promised to continue McKinley's pro-business policies. He was not against big business. In fact, he believed business was a positive force and that giant corporations were here to stay.

Roosevelt saw a difference, however, between good trusts and bad trusts. Good trusts, he said, were efficient and fair and should be let alone. Bad ones took advantage of workers and cheated the public. He believed that the government needed to either control bad trusts or break them up.

Regulating Trusts Roosevelt wanted to test the power of the government to break up bad trusts. In 1902, he asked the Attorney General, the government's chief lawyer, to bring a lawsuit against the Northern Securities Company. Northern Securities was a trust that had been formed to control competition among railroads. Roosevelt argued that the company used unfair business practices in violation of the Sherman Antitrust Act.

At news of the lawsuit, stock prices fell. "Wall Street is paralyzed at the thought that a President of the United States would sink so low as to try to enforce the law," one newspaper joked.

Analyze Images President Roosevelt spoke forcefully in favor of Progressive reforms during his presidency (1901–1909). **Draw Conclusions** In what area did Roosevelt make the greatest impact?

While business leaders worried, many ordinary Americans cheered Roosevelt's bold action against big business.

In 1904, the Supreme Court ruled that Northern Securities had violated the Sherman Antitrust Act. It ordered the trust to be broken up. The decision was a victory for Progressives. For the first time, the Sherman Antitrust Act had been used to break up trusts, not unions.

Next, Roosevelt had the Attorney General file suit against other trusts, including Standard Oil and the American Tobacco Company. In time, the courts ordered the breakup of both trusts because they blocked free trade.

Some business leaders called Roosevelt a **trustbuster**, a person who wanted to destroy all trusts. "Certainly not," replied Roosevelt, only those that "have done something we regard as wrong." He preferred to control or regulate trusts, not "bust" them.

A Pro-Labor President Roosevelt also clashed with mine owners. In 1902, Pennsylvania coal miners went on strike for better pay and a shorter workday. Mine owners refused to negotiate with the miners' union.

As winter approached, schools and hospitals ran out of coal. Furious at the mine owners, Roosevelt threatened to send in troops to run the mines. Finally, owners sat down with the union and reached an agreement. Roosevelt was the first President to side with labor.

READING CHECK **Identify Main Ideas** How did Roosevelt feel about big business?

What Was the Square Deal?

Roosevelt ran for President in his own right in 1904. During the campaign, he promised Americans a **Square Deal**. By this he meant that everyone from farmers and consumers to workers and owners

Analyze Political Cartoons In this cartoon from a British magazine, John Mitchell, president of the United Mine Workers, wrestles a bull labeled "Coal Operators' Combine" during the Anthracite Coal Strike of 1902. **Infer** Do you think the cartoonist thought the union would succeed?

The Square Deal

REGULATING CORPORATIONS	CONSUMER PROTECTION	CONSERVATION OF NATURAL RESOURCES
• Bureau of Corporations was created to gather information from companies. • Elkins Act outlawed railroad rebates. • Northern Securities Company (a monopoly-holding group of railroad companies) was dismantled.	• The Pure Food and Drug Act required ingredients to be listed on packages. • The Meat Inspection Act required regular inspection of meatpacking houses. • The use of the press to expose consumer abuse and scandals increased.	• National parks and wildlife refuges were established. • The federal government took over natural resources management from state and local governments. • The Newlands Reclamation Act used federal land sales to fund irrigation and reservoir projects in the western United States.

Analyze Charts This chart summarizes the Square Deal. **Draw Conclusions** What does the Square Deal suggest about Roosevelt's view of the proper role of government? Explain your answer.

should have the same opportunity to succeed. That promise helped Roosevelt win a huge victory.

Railroads were a main target of the Square Deal. The Interstate Commerce Act of 1887 had done little to end rebates and other abuses. Roosevelt therefore urged Congress to outlaw rebates. In 1906, Congress gave the Interstate Commerce Commission (ICC) the power to set railroad rates.

Primary Source

"I do not believe that any president ever had as thoroughly good a time as I have had, or has ever enjoyed himself as much."

—Theodore Roosevelt, in a letter to Sir George Otto Trevelyan, British historian

Pushing for Regulations Roosevelt wanted reforms to protect consumers. He had been shocked by Upton Sinclair's novel *The Jungle*. In response, he sent more government inspectors to meatpacking houses. The owners refused to let them in.

Roosevelt then gave the newspapers copies of a government report that **exposed** conditions in meatpacking plants. The public was outraged. This forced Congress to pass a law in 1906 allowing more inspectors to enter meatpacking houses.

Academic Vocabulary
expose • *v.*, to reveal or bring to light

Muckrakers had exposed drug companies for making false claims about medicines. They also showed how food companies added harmful chemicals to canned foods. In 1906, Congress passed the Pure Food and Drug Act, which required food and drug makers to list ingredients on packages. It also tried to end false advertising and the use of impure ingredients.

Analyze Images Theodore Roosevelt, left, found a kindred spirit in Scotsman John Muir, who urged him to protect the wilderness. **Identify Cause and Effect** Was Muir the main influence on Roosevelt's actions to protect the environment? Why or why not?

Protecting Natural Resources Roosevelt also took action to protect the nation's wilderness areas. To fuel industrial growth, lumber companies were cutting down whole forests. Miners were taking iron and coal from the earth at a frantic pace and leaving gaping holes.

Roosevelt loved the outdoors and worried about the destruction of the wilderness. He pressed for **conservation**, the protection of natural resources. "The rights of the public to natural resources outweigh private rights," he said.

Roosevelt wanted some forest areas left as wilderness. Others could supply needed resources. He wanted lumber companies to plant new trees in the forests they were clearing. Mining, too, should be controlled. In 1905, with the support of Congress, Roosevelt created the National Forest Service.

Under Roosevelt, the government also set aside about 194,000 acres for national parks. A national park is an area set aside to preserve the natural or historic treasures of the country.

READING CHECK **Summarize** What was Roosevelt's stance on the environment?

Did President Taft Continue Roosevelt's Progressive Work?

Roosevelt did not want to run for re-election in 1908. Instead, he backed William Howard Taft, his Secretary of War. Taft won easily. Roosevelt then left for a 10-month safari in Africa and a tour of Europe.

Taft's approach to the presidency was far different from Roosevelt's. Unlike the hard-driving, energetic Roosevelt, Taft was quiet and careful. Roosevelt loved power. Taft feared it.

Nevertheless, Taft supported many Progressive causes. He broke up even more trusts than Roosevelt had. He favored the graduated income tax, approved new safety rules for mines, and signed laws giving government workers an eight-hour day.

Despite such successes, Taft lost Progressive support. In 1909, he signed a bill that raised most tariffs. Progressives opposed the new law, arguing that tariffs raised prices for consumers. Also, Taft fired a high-level Forest Service official during a dispute over the sale of wilderness lands in Alaska. Progressives accused him of blocking conservation efforts.

INTERACTIVE

National Land Conservation

READING CHECK **Identify Supporting Details** What Progressive reforms did Taft support?

Wilson Wins the Presidency

When Roosevelt returned from overseas, he found Taft under attack by reformers. In 1912, Roosevelt decided to run against Taft for the Republican nomination. Although Roosevelt had a great deal of public support, Taft controlled the Republican party leadership. At its convention, the party nominated Taft.

A Republican Split Progressive Republicans stormed out of the convention. They set up a new Progressive Party and chose Roosevelt as their candidate. He accepted saying, "I feel as strong as a bull moose." Roosevelt's supporters became known as the **Bull Moose Party**.

The Democratic Nominee Democrats chose Woodrow Wilson, a Progressive, as their candidate. As a boy, Wilson made up his mind always to fight for what he thought was right. Wilson served as president of Princeton University and as governor of New Jersey. He was known as a brilliant scholar and a cautious reformer.

Together, Taft and Roosevelt won more votes than Wilson. However, they split the Republican vote. Their quarrel helped Wilson win the election of 1912 by beating Taft and Roosevelt in many states.

Increasing the Government's Role in the Economy At first, Wilson tried to break up trusts into smaller companies. By doing so, he hoped to increase competition in the American economy. "If America is not to have free enterprise, then she can have freedom of no sort whatever," he said. Wilson called his program the **New Freedom**.

To spur competition, Wilson asked Congress to lower tariffs on goods. A lower tariff would force U.S. producers to face foreign competition. After a struggle, Congress did lower tariffs. To make up for lost revenues, it then passed a graduated income tax.

Analyze Graphs These circle graphs show the results for the 1912 Presidential election. **Use Visual Information** Was the 1912 election a close race or an easy victory? Explain your answer.

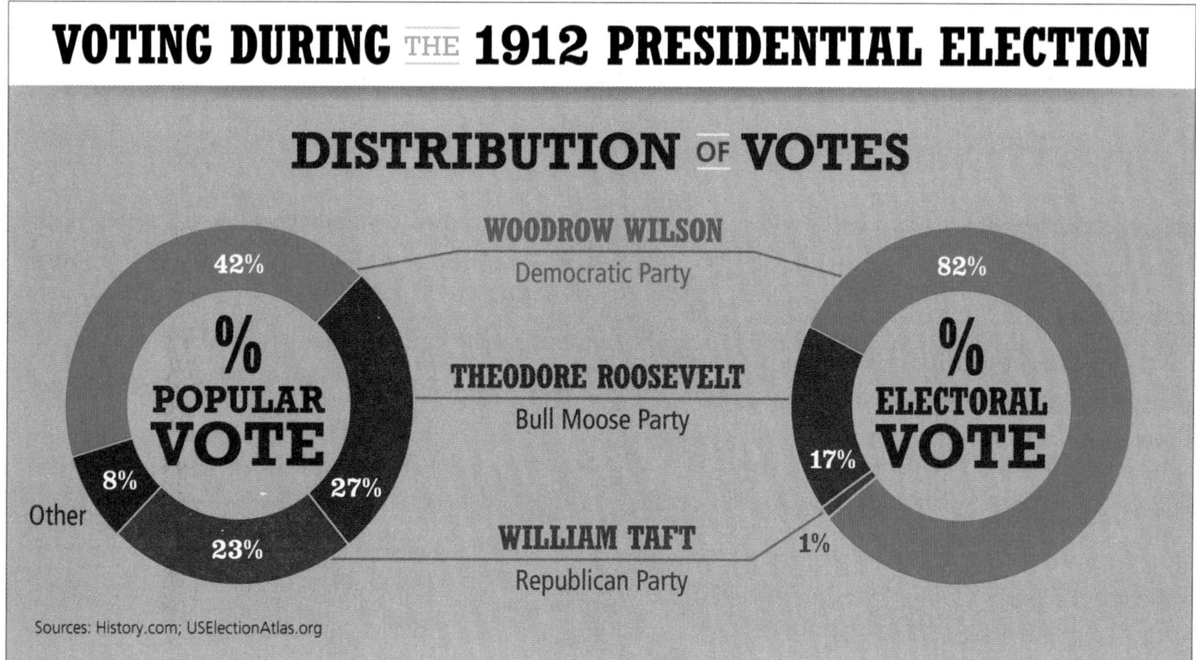

To regulate banking, Congress passed the **Federal Reserve Act** in 1913. It set up the Federal Reserve System, an organization that would control the supply of money to the U.S. financial system. The Federal Reserve would also have the power to raise or lower interest rates.

Protecting Competition To ensure fair competition, President Wilson set up the **Federal Trade Commission** (FTC) in 1914. The FTC could investigate companies and order them to stop using unfair practices to destroy competitors.

Wilson signed the Clayton Antitrust Act in 1914. He had wanted a much stronger law, but the new law did ban some business practices that limited free enterprise. In addition, it stopped antitrust laws from being used against unions, a major victory for labor.

Despite Wilson's successes, the Progressive movement slowed after 1914. By then, Progressives had achieved many of their goals. Also, the outbreak of war in Europe in 1914 drew Americans' attention. They worried that the war might soon affect them.

Analyze Images "I will not fail them," Wilson said of the American people at his presidential inauguration. **Cite Evidence** Do you think Wilson was as progressive as Roosevelt? Why or why not?

INTERACTIVE

Three Presidents' Accomplishments

READING CHECK **Identify Main Ideas** What was Wilson's New Freedom?

Lesson Check

Practice Vocabulary

1. Why was Theodore Roosevelt known as a **trustbuster**?
2. Did Congress regulate banking by passing the **Federal Reserve Act** or creating the **Federal Trade Commission**?

Critical Thinking and Writing

3. **Draw Conclusions** Why did Roosevelt's vice presidency please New York party bosses?
4. **Compare and Contrast** How closely did the policies of William Howard Taft match those of Theodore Roosevelt?
5. **Identify Cause and Effect** What were the causes and effects of the split in the Republican Party?
6. **Writing Workshop: Support Ideas with Evidence** You have gathered ideas for your research paper. Now add supporting details to each in your Active Journal.

LESSON 5

Progress and Setbacks for Social Justice

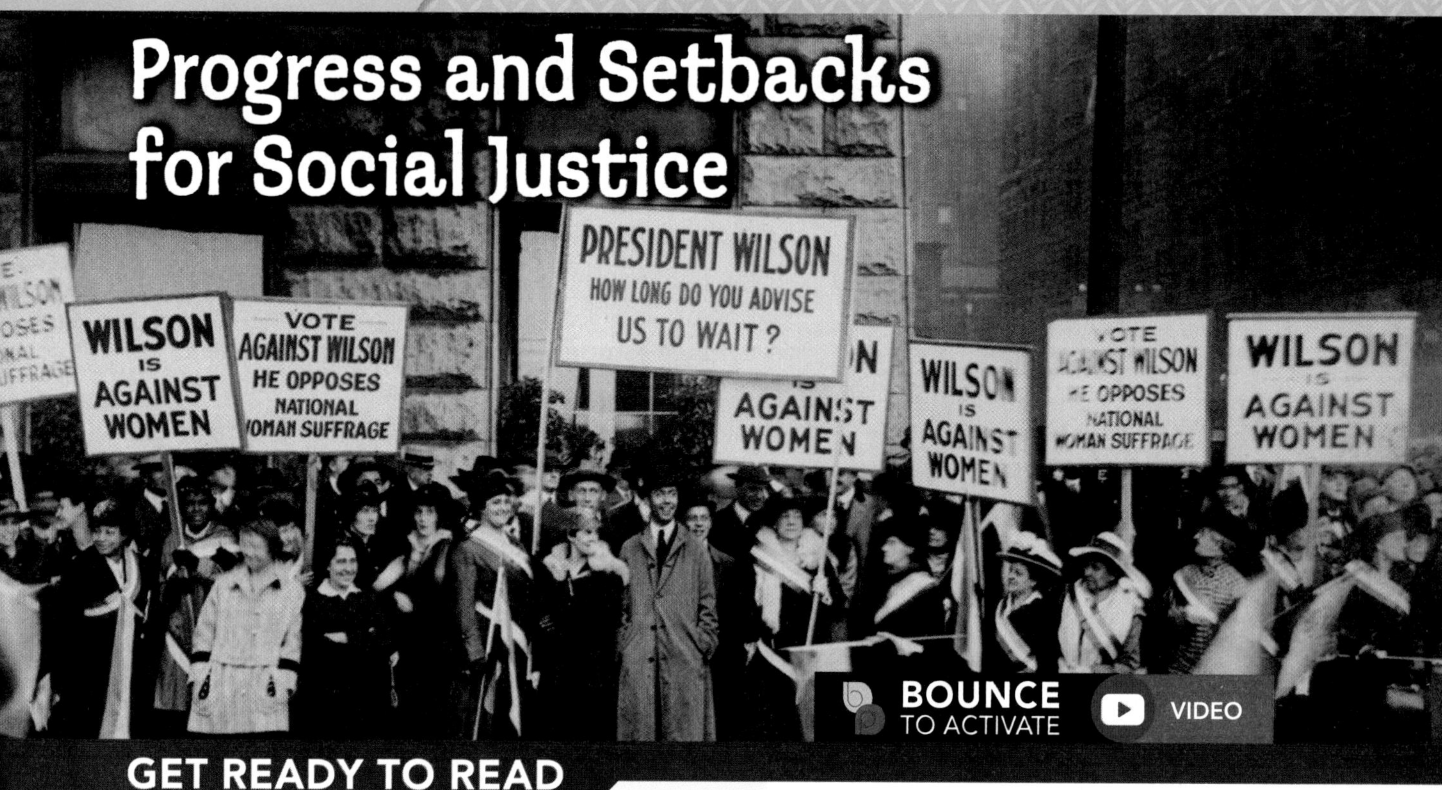

GET READY TO READ

START UP

Look at the image of people protesting for women's suffrage. Write a sentence or two about the effect this protest might have had on onlookers.

GUIDING QUESTIONS

- How did women work to win rights?
- Why was the campaign against alcohol especially important to women?
- What hardships did other groups face in the Progressive Era?

TAKE NOTES

Literacy Skills Determine Central Ideas

Use the graphic organizer in your Active Journal to take notes as you read the lesson.

PRACTICE VOCABULARY

Use the vocabulary activity in your Active Journal to practice the vocabulary words.

Vocabulary		Academic Vocabulary
suffrage	NAACP	radical
prohibition	barrio	Ph.D.
lynch	*mutualista*	

The struggle of women for **suffrage**, or the right to vote, went back many years. The Seneca Falls Convention in 1848 called for many reforms, including women's suffrage.

What Was the Path to Women's Suffrage?

After the Civil War, Elizabeth Cady Stanton and Susan B. Anthony renewed calls for suffrage. They had opposed the Fifteenth Amendment because it gave the vote to African American men but not to women. In 1869, Stanton and Anthony set up the National Woman Suffrage Association, a group that worked for a constitutional amendment to give women the right to vote.

Beginnings in the West In most states, leading politicians opposed women's suffrage. Nevertheless, in the late 1800s, women won the right to vote in four western states: Wyoming, Utah, Colorado, and Idaho. Pioneer women had worked alongside men to build farms and cities. By giving women the vote, these states recognized the women's contributions.

When Wyoming applied for statehood in 1890, many members of Congress wanted the state to change its law that gave women the vote. Wyoming lawmakers replied, "We may stay out of the Union for 100 years, but we will come in with our women." Wyoming barely won admission.

Pioneer woman Annie Bidwell worked to secure the right to vote for women in her home state of California. She helped form the California Equal Suffrage Association in 1904. She was also a member of the National Woman Suffrage Association. Like many reform-minded women of the time, she had gained important experience in the movement to establish laws banning the sale of alcohol.

▲ A dedicated suffragist and highly effective organizer, Carrie Chapman Catt followed Susan B. Anthony as president of the National Woman Suffrage Association in 1900.

Women Gain Support In the early 1900s, the women's suffrage movement gained strength. More than 5 million women were earning wages outside the home. Although women were paid less than men, wages gave them some power. Many demanded a say in making the laws that affected them.

After Stanton and Anthony died, a new generation of leaders took up the cause. Among the most outspoken was Carrie Chapman Catt. She had worked as a school principal and a reporter before she became a leader of the National Woman Suffrage Association.

Catt was a brilliant organizer. She created a detailed plan to fight for suffrage, state by state. Across the nation, suffragists, or people who worked for women's right to vote, followed her strategy.

Gradually, their efforts succeeded. One by one, states in the West and Midwest gave women the vote. Generally, women in these states could vote only in state elections. At the same time, more and more women were demanding a constitutional amendment to give them the right to vote in all elections.

READING CHECK **Identify Supporting Details** What was Carrie Chapman Catt's main contribution to women's suffrage?

What Did the Nineteenth Amendment Guarantee?

Academic Vocabulary
radical • *adj.*, extreme

As the struggle dragged on, some suffragists, such as Alice Paul, took more **radical** steps to win the vote. Paul had marched with British suffragists in London. She had been jailed and gone on hunger strikes to help British women win the vote. When Paul returned home, she fought for suffrage for American women.

Taking the Fight to the Capital Soon after Woodrow Wilson became President, he met with Paul and other suffragists. Wilson did not oppose women's suffrage, but he also did not back a constitutional amendment.

Paul told the President that suffragists wanted such an amendment. "And then," she recalled, "we sent him another delegation and another and another and another and another and another and another."

Early in 1917, Rose Winslow, Paul, and other women began to picket the White House. Within a few months, police started to arrest the silent protesters. Winslow and Paul were jailed for obstructing the sidewalk. A public outcry soon won their release. The women then resumed their picketing.

New Opportunities for Women

Women Win Suffrage By early 1918, the tide had finally turned in favor of suffrage. President Wilson agreed to support the suffrage amendment. In 1919, Congress passed the Nineteenth Amendment. It guaranteed women the right to vote. By August 1920, three fourths of the states had ratified the amendment, and it became part of the Constitution. The amendment doubled the number of eligible voters.

READING CHECK **Identify Main Ideas** What was the purpose of the Nineteenth Amendment?

What New Opportunities Opened Up for Women?

Besides working for the vote, women struggled to gain access to jobs and education. Most states refused to grant women licenses to practice law or medicine. Myra Bradwell taught herself law, just as Abraham Lincoln had done. Still, Illinois denied her a license in 1869 because she was a woman. In 1890, Illinois finally allowed her to practice law.

GEOGRAPHY SKILLS

Some states took longer than others to ratify the Nineteenth Amendment.

1. **Region** Which two regions gave women the right to vote earlier than other regions? (Choose from West, Southwest, Midwest, Northeast, and Southeast.)
2. **Understand Effects** How did Wilson's support affect the ratification of the suffrage amendment?

The Vote for Women

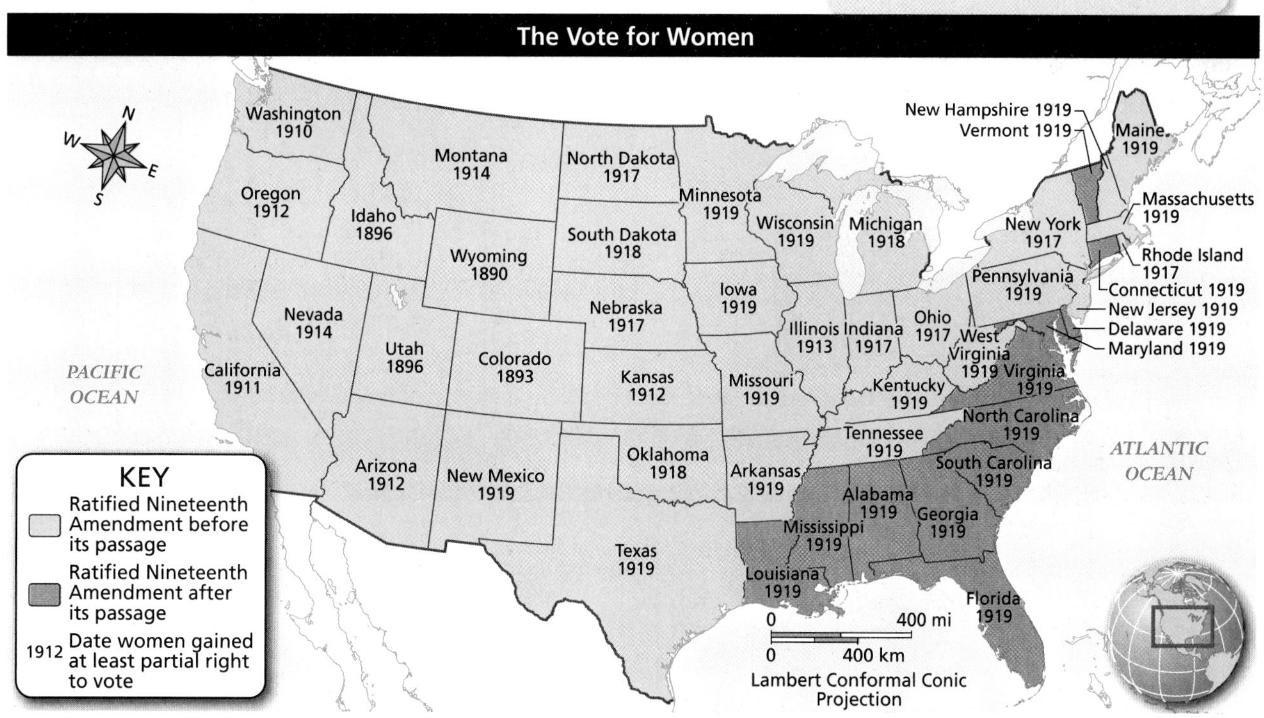

Academic Vocabulary

Ph.D. • *n.*, in the United States, the highest academic degree awarded in a field other than law or medicine

Access to Higher Education Despite obstacles, a few women managed to get the higher education needed to enter the professions. In 1877, Boston University granted the first **Ph.D.** to a woman. Slowly, more women entered graduate schools and earned advanced degrees. By 1900, the nation had about 1,000 women lawyers and 7,000 women doctors.

Forming Groups to Take Action During the late 1800s, middle-class women joined women's clubs. At first, most club women read books and sought other ways to improve their minds. In time, many became eager reformers. They raised money for libraries, schools, and parks. They pressed for laws to protect women and children, to ensure pure food and drugs, and to win the vote.

Faced with racial barriers, African American women formed their own clubs, such as the National Association of Colored Women. They battled to end racial injustice and worked for suffrage and other reforms.

Seeking Reform During the Progressive Era, many women became committed to reforming society. Some women entered the new profession of social work. Others campaigned to end social evils, such as child labor. Florence Kelley investigated conditions in sweatshops. In time, she was made the chief factory inspector for the state of Illinois. Kelley's main concern, though, was child labor. She organized a boycott of goods produced by child labor. She helped publish a list of manufacturers whose factories met basic standards.

READING CHECK **Identify Main Ideas** Why did Illinois at first deny Myra Bradwell the right to practice law?

The Temperance Movement

The temperance movement to end the sale of alcoholic beverages began in the early 1800s. Many in the movement wanted the government to

Analyze Timeline
Prohibition had been building for many years. **Infer** What do you think will happen to the U.S. crime rate after 1933?

Timeline of Prohibition

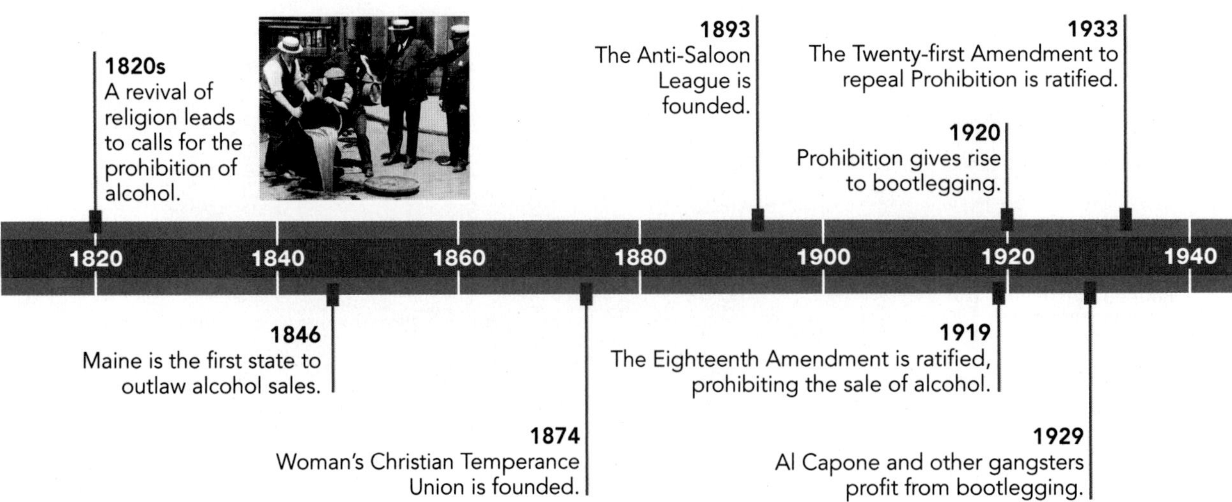

enact **prohibition**, or a ban on the manufacture and sale of alcoholic beverages. By 1900, the movement was gaining strength.

Women often led the temperance drive. Many wives and mothers recognized alcohol as a threat to their families. Drinking often caused violence and economic hardship at home.

For political reasons, women also opposed saloons, where alcohol was served. In saloons, male political bosses made political decisions out of the reach of women. Most saloons refused entry to women.

The Woman's Christian Temperance Union Forms In 1874, a group of women organized the Woman's Christian Temperance Union (WCTU). Frances Willard became its president in 1880. Willard recalled an incident at a Pittsburgh saloon:

Analyze Images Members of the Woman's Christian Temperance Union (WCTU) march on Washington, D.C., in 1909. **Cite Evidence** Were marches like this successful? Explain your answer.

Primary Source

"The tall, stately lady who led us placed her Bible on the bar and read a psalm. . . . Then we sang 'Rock of Ages' as I thought I had never sung it before. . . . This was my Crusade baptism."

—Frances E. Willard, *Glimpses of Fifty Years, the Autobiography of an American Woman, 1889*

Willard spoke tirelessly about the evils of alcohol. She called for state laws to ban the sale of liquor. She also worked to close saloons. In time, Willard joined the suffrage movement, bringing many WCTU members along with her.

Carrie Nation was a more radical temperance crusader. She dedicated her life to fighting "demon rum." After her husband died from heavy drinking, Nation often stormed into saloons. Swinging a hatchet, she smashed beer kegs and liquor bottles. Nation won publicity, but her actions embarrassed the WCTU.

Prohibition Becomes Law Temperance crusaders wanted a constitutional amendment banning the production and sale of liquor. Support for such an amendment grew after 1917, when the United States entered World War I. Temperance supporters argued that grain used to make liquor should be used instead to feed American soldiers.

Temperance leaders finally persuaded Congress to pass the Eighteenth Amendment in 1917. By 1919, three fourths of the states had ratified it. The amendment made it illegal to sell alcoholic drinks anywhere in the United States.

READING CHECK **Identify Main Ideas** What was the main purpose of the WCTU?

Discrimination Against African Americans

After Reconstruction, African Americans in the South lost many hard-won rights. Jim Crow laws led to segregation in schools, trains, and other public places. In the North, too, African Americans faced prejudice and discrimination. Landlords refused to rent homes in white areas to African Americans. Across the nation, African Americans were hired only for low-paying jobs.

The depression of 1893 made life even harder. In the South and elsewhere, jobless whites took out their anger on African Americans. In the 1890s, more than 1,000 African Americans were **lynched**—murdered by mobs.

The murders outraged Ida B. Wells, an African American journalist. In her newspaper, *Free Speech,* Wells urged African Americans to protest the lynchings. She called for a boycott of streetcars and white-owned stores. Wells spoke out despite threats to her life.

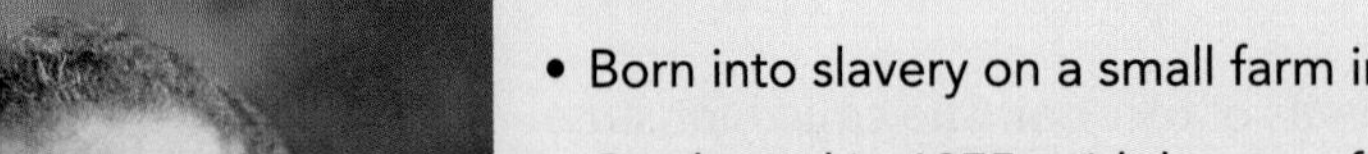

BIOGRAPHY 5 Things to Know About BOOKER T. WASHINGTON

Educator, reformer, and the voice for many African Americans (1856–1915)

- Born into slavery on a small farm in Virginia
- Graduated in 1875, with honors, from Hampton Institute in Virginia
- In 1881, helped establish the Tuskegee Institute in Alabama
- As an advisor to Theodore Roosevelt and William Howard Taft, recommended African Americans for low-level jobs in government
- Pursued a practical education and economic advancement for African Americans, but avoided actively taking up the fight against segregation and the denial of voting rights

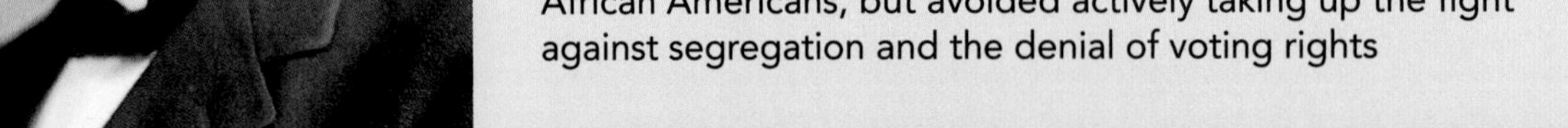

Critical Thinking Why do you think Washington chose to avoid the bigger fights against segregation and the denial of voting rights?

A Moderate Approach to Gain Equality During this period, Booker T. Washington spoke for many African Americans. He called on blacks and whites to live in harmony. In *Up From Slavery,* his autobiography, Washington told his own success story. Although born into slavery, he had taught himself to read. As a youth, he worked in coal mines, attending schools whenever he could. In 1875, he graduated from the newly founded Hampton Institute. Six years later, he helped found the Tuskegee Institute in Alabama to offer higher education to blacks.

African Americans, said Washington, must work patiently to move up in society. First, he urged them to learn trades and earn money. Then they would have the power to demand equality.

Business tycoons like Andrew Carnegie and John D. Rockefeller backed Washington. They helped him build trade schools for African Americans. Presidents also sought his advice on racial issues.

Analyze Images Madame C.J. Walker became the first female American millionaire. **Identify Cause and Effect** How did providing hair care products lead Walker to success?

A More Radical Approach to Gain Equality Other African Americans, like W.E.B. Du Bois (doo BOYSS), took a different approach. Du Bois agreed with Booker T. Washington's view on the need for "thrift, patience, and industrial training." However, he added, "So far as Mr. Washington apologizes for injustice, . . . we must firmly oppose him." Instead of patiently accepting discrimination, Du Bois urged African Americans to fight it actively.

In 1909, Du Bois, along with Jane Addams, Lincoln Steffens, and other reformers, organized the National Association for the Advancement of Colored People, or **NAACP**. Members of the NAACP worked for equal rights for African Americans.

Successes Despite Discrimination Most Progressives, though, failed to support African Americans. When African American soldiers were falsely accused of shootings in Brownsville, Texas, President Roosevelt had their whole regiment dishonorably discharged. Later, President Wilson ordered the segregation of African American and white government workers. When African Americans protested, Wilson replied that "segregation is not humiliating, but a benefit."

Despite many obstacles, some African Americans succeeded. George Washington Carver discovered hundreds of new uses for peanuts and other crops grown in the South. His writings about crop rotation changed southern farming practices. Sarah Walker, better known as Madame C. J. Walker, created a line of hair care products for African American women. She became the first American woman to earn more than $1 million.

INTERACTIVE

African American Reform Movement, 1895–1915

African Americans established their own companies, including insurance firms and banks, to serve the needs of African Americans. Other businesses provided personal services that whites refused to offer African Americans. Among these were restaurants, beauty parlors and barber shops, and funeral parlors. Colleges such as Wilberforce and Tuskegee trained young African Americans for their professions. Churches like the African Methodist Episcopal Church were training grounds for African American leaders.

READING CHECK **Identify Supporting Details** Which African American leader called for fighting discrimination aggressively?

The Mexican American Experience

Thousands of Americans of Mexican or Spanish descent lived in the United States, especially in the Southwest and West. They lived in areas acquired by the United States from Mexico under the Treaty of Guadalupe-Hidalgo and the Gadsden Purchase. In the early 1900s, however, large numbers of immigrants began arriving from Mexico.

In 1910, revolution and famine swept Mexico. Thousands of *Mexicanos,* or native-born Mexicans, fled their homeland into the United States. To them, it was *el norte* "the north." The immigrants came from all levels of Mexican society. Many were poor farmers, but some came from middle-class and upper-class families. Although many *Mexicanos* later returned home, some remained.

Life in the United States Some Mexican immigrants worked as field hands, built roads and rail lines, and dug irrigation ditches. In California, Mexican families helped cultivate and harvest the grains, vegetables, fruits, and nuts of that fast-growing agricultural state. Other immigrants from Mexico worked in city factories, where they faced harsh conditions. They were paid less than white workers and were denied skilled jobs.

Analyze Images Many people of Mexican descent, including these Californians, lived in the United States even before large numbers immigrated in 1910 to escape war and famine. **Compare and Contrast** How did the experience of *Mexicanos* differ from that of other immigrants? How was it similar?

Mexicans in California, 1880–1930

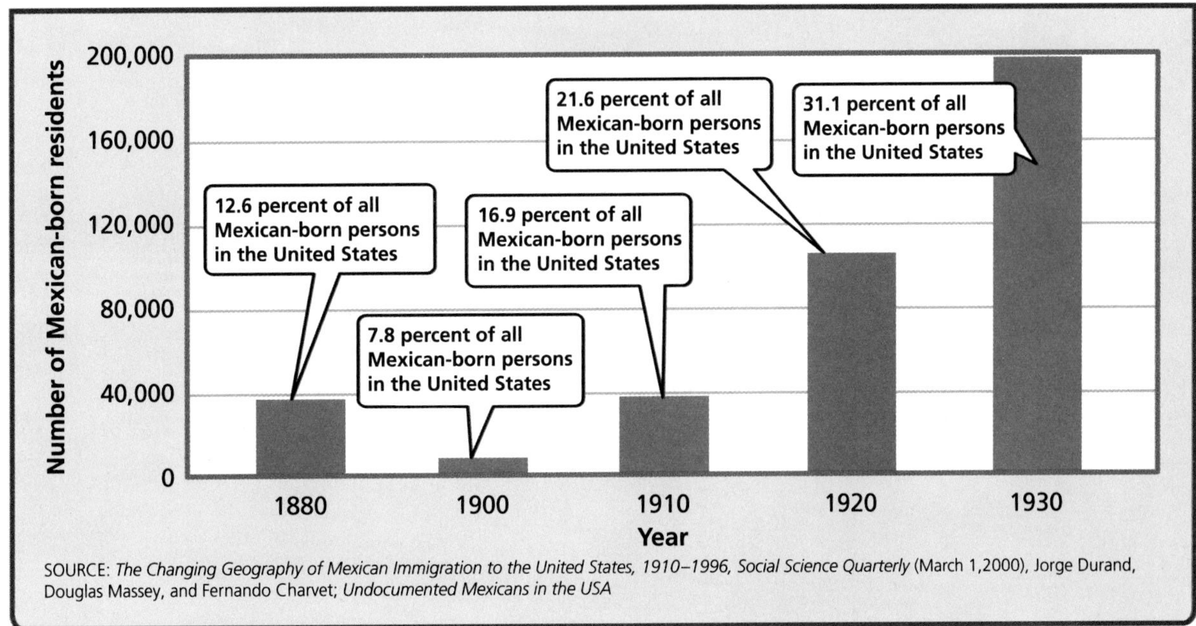

SOURCE: *The Changing Geography of Mexican Immigration to the United States, 1910–1996, Social Science Quarterly* (March 1,2000), Jorge Durand, Douglas Massey, and Fernando Charvet; *Undocumented Mexicans in the USA*

Analyze Graphs The number of Mexican immigrants to California rose significantly in 30 years. **Use Visual Information** About how many times more people in California had been born in Mexico in 1930 than in 1910?

Like other immigrants who settled in cities, Mexicans created their own neighborhoods, or **barrios**. There, they preserved their language and culture, celebrated traditional festivals, and shared memories of Mexico. Los Angeles became home to the nation's largest barrio. Its population almost tripled between 1910 and 1920. Seeking jobs, many moved to the Midwest and the Rocky Mountain region.

Mutual Aid Within the barrio, Mexican immigrants and Mexican Americans took many steps to help each other. Some formed ***mutualistas***, or mutual aid groups. These groups worked like other immigrant aid societies. Members of *mutualistas* pooled money to buy insurance and pay for legal advice. They also collected money for the sick and needy.

Most *mutualistas* were for men, although larger groups often had versions for women. One of the few women to lead a *mutualista* with both male and female members was Luisa González. She was a midwife who served as president of the San Antonio, Texas, chapter of Alianza Hispano-Americana in the 1920s.

READING CHECK **Draw Conclusions** How did *mutualistas* benefit the barrio?

The Government Restricts Asian Immigration

White racism toward Chinese immigrants on the West Coast led to calls for a Chinese Exclusion Act. This 1882 law kept Chinese from settling in the United States. As a result, the Chinese population declined.

Japanese Immigrants Still, the demand for cheap labor remained high. White employers on the West Coast and in Hawaii therefore got around the Chinese Exclusion Act by hiring workers from other Asian countries.

How did immigration policies change during this time? Record your findings in your Active Journal.

Analyze Images Asian and Latino men harvest grapes on a southern California vineyard in 1905. **Cite Evidence** What might a vineyard owner have felt about restrictions on immigration?

Sugar planters in Hawaii brought in workers from Japan, Korea, and the Philippines. They deliberately hired workers from diverse groups. They hoped these differences would keep workers from uniting and demanding fair treatment and pay on par with whites.

When the United States annexed Hawaii in 1898, a number of Japanese saw the opportunity for a better life on the mainland. More than 100,000 Japanese entered the United States in the early 1900s.

Many newcomers from Japan were farmers. They settled on dry, barren land that Americans thought was useless. Through hard work and careful management of resources, the Japanese made their farms profitable. Soon, they were producing a large percentage of southern California's fruits and vegetables. Mantsuchi Nakamura, for example, moved to California from Hawaii in 1902. He eventually bought a grape farm, which he used to produce raisins.

A "Gentlemen's Agreement" Prejudice against immigrants from Asia remained high. Many white farmers and factory workers resented the success of the Japanese. In California, the Japanese were barred from owning land and from many economic pursuits. In 1906, San Francisco forced all Asian students, including Japanese children, to attend separate schools. Japan protested the insult, and the issue threatened to cause an international crisis.

Unions and other groups also put pressure on President Roosevelt to limit immigration from Japan. Because Japan was a growing naval power in the Pacific, Roosevelt tried to soothe Japanese feelings. He condemned the segregated schools and offered his own solution. If San Francisco ended its segregation order, he would restrict further Japanese immigration.

In 1907, Roosevelt reached a "Gentlemen's Agreement" with Japan. Japan would stop any more workers from going to the United States. The United States, in exchange, would allow Japanese women to join their husbands who were already in this country.

Anti-Japanese feeling did not decrease with the "Gentlemen's Agreement." In 1913, California passed a law that banned Asians who were not American citizens from owning land. Before long, the United States would take more drastic steps to stop immigration from Asia.

READING CHECK **Identify Supporting Details** What were the terms of Roosevelt's "Gentleman's Agreement" with Japan?

How Were American Indians Treated During the Progressive Era?

Through the Dawes Act of 1887, the government hoped American Indians would adopt white ways and become farmers. Although it was unmistakably a failure, white people kept trying to force American Indians to adopt white culture.

American Indians had been robbed of their lands, forced to abandon their traditional ways, and pushed to adopt white American customs. American Indian children were taken away to boarding schools. There they were given new names, haircuts, and clothing, according to white American practices, and punished if they spoke their own language.

Analyze Graphs Theodore Roosevelt bowed to pressure to restrict Asian immigration. **Summarize** Look at the graph and summarize the trends it depicts.

Asian Immigration to the United States

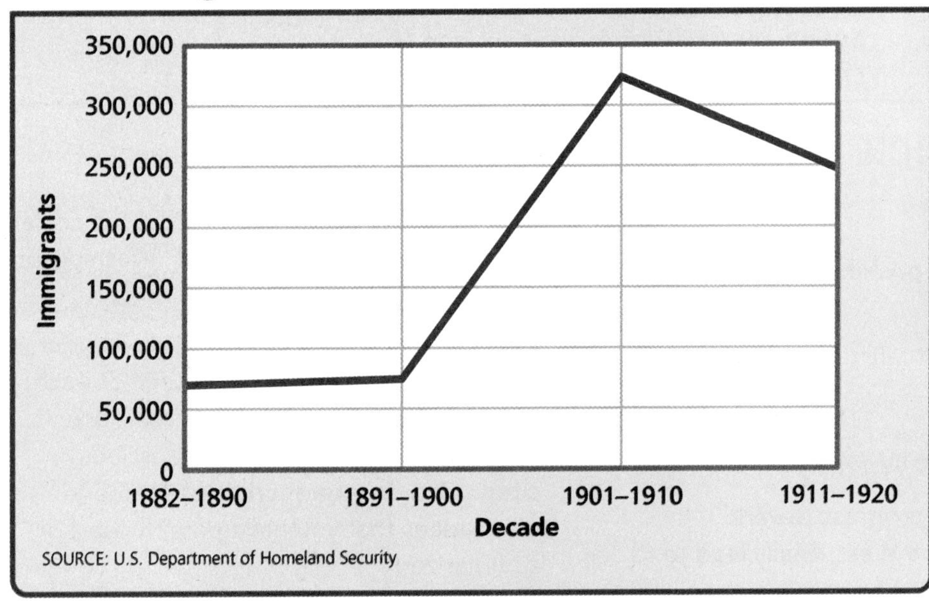

Analyze Images Relatively little changed for American Indians during the Progressive Era. **Use Visual Information** What was one significant change in the lives of these family members?

For American Indians, little really changed during the Progressive Era. Those who lived on reservations continued to rely on the federal government for assistance. On the reservation many struggled with poverty, alcohol, and a lack of employment. Outside the reservation, many faced prejudice and discrimination.

In the early 1900s, a new generation of American Indian leaders emerged. One group set up the Society of American Indians. It included artists, writers, Christian ministers, lawyers, and doctors from many different peoples.

The Society worked for social justice and tried to educate white Americans about American Indian life. However, it supported policies to force American Indians into the mainstream by abolishing reservations. This created so much opposition among American Indian groups that the Society went out of existence in 1925.

READING CHECK **Identify Supporting Details** What actions did the Society for American Indians support?

Lesson Check

Practice Vocabulary

1. Why was the fight for **prohibition** especially important to women?
2. What services did ***mutualistas*** provide in the **barrio**?

Critical Thinking and Writing

3. Summarize How did progress toward suffrage, starting in the West, finally lead to women gaining the right to vote?
4. Compare and Contrast How did the social and political ideas of Booker T. Washington and W.E.B. Du Bois differ?
5. Writing Workshop: Cite Sources In your Active Journal write the source of each note you have taken. In your essay, any words quoted from a source must be cited. Also cite the sources of someone else's ideas that you have paraphrased or summarized.

LESSON 6

A Changing American Culture

GET READY TO READ

START UP

In this photo, one of the first great baseball players, Honus Wagner, prepares to swing at a pitch. What does the rise of sports tell you about America at this time?

GUIDING QUESTIONS

- How did cities change in the Progressive Era?
- What new forms of theater, music, art, and literature appeared during this time?
- What advances occurred in public education in the Progressive Era?

TAKE NOTES

Literacy Skills Analyze Text Structure

Use the graphic organizer in your Active Journal to take notes as you read the lesson.

PRACTICE VOCABULARY

Use the vocabulary activity in your Active Journal to practice the vocabulary words.

Vocabulary		Academic Vocabulary
skyscraper	yellow journalism	convey
suburb	realist	compulsory
vaudeville	local color	
ragtime		

Progressives fought for reforms in government and society. The Progressive Era also was a time of enormous change in American culture. Cities, sports, education, and the arts all broke new cultural ground.

Changes and Challenges in City Life

A building boom changed the face of American cities. Cities such as Chicago and New York gradually began to run out of space in their downtown areas. Resourceful developers decided to build up instead of out.

Touching the Sky After fire leveled downtown Chicago in 1871, planners tried out many new ideas as they rebuilt the city. Using new technology, they designed **skyscrapers**, tall buildings with many floors supported by a lightweight steel frame. The first skyscraper, only nine stories tall, was built in Chicago in 1885. As technology improved, builders competed to raise taller and taller skyscrapers.

Skyscrapers and larger apartment buildings featured newly invented electric elevators.

As they carried residents and workers to upper floors, elevators moved so quickly, according to one rider, that "the passenger seems to feel his stomach pass into his shoes."

Transportation Innovations As skyscrapers crowded more people into smaller spaces, they added to a growing problem: traffic. Downtown streets were jammed with horse-drawn buses, carriages, and carts.

Electricity offered one solution. Frank Sprague, an engineer from Richmond, Virginia, designed the first electric streetcar system in 1887. Streetcars, or trolleys, were fast, clean, and quiet. Many trolley lines ran from the center of a city to the outlying countryside, creating the first suburbs. A **suburb** is a residential area on or near the outskirts of a city.

Academic Vocabulary
convey • *v.*, to carry

Other cities built steam-driven passenger trains on overhead tracks. In 1897, Boston built the first American subway, or underground electric railway. Subways and elevated railroads **conveyed** workers rapidly to and from their jobs.

Some cities needed ways to move masses of people and goods across rivers. In 1874, James B. Eads designed and built a three-arched bridge across the Mississippi River at St. Louis. The Eads Bridge was more than a quarter of a mile long. Nine years later, the Brooklyn Bridge, linking Manhattan Island and Brooklyn, was completed. More than a mile long, this suspension bridge carried a footpath, roadways, and two railroad lines. Four huge cables suspended the bridge, which was soon carrying 33 million people a year.

Places to Relax While cities grew up and out, some planners wanted to preserve open spaces. They believed that open land would calm busy city dwellers.

Analyze Images Along with a subway, this elevated railway was built to relieve Boston's traffic problems. **Infer** Why would an elevated rail line improve street congestion?

Analyze Images Large department stores such as Marshall Field & Company, located in a Chicago skyscraper, offered customers a variety of items available for purchase all in a single location. **Use Visual Information** What advances of the era can you identify in this photograph?

In the 1850s, landscape architect Frederick Law Olmsted planned spacious Central Park in New York City. Other cities followed this model. They set aside land for public parks that contained zoos and gardens so that city people could enjoy green grass and trees during their leisure time.

A New Pastime Shopping areas also got a new look. In the past, people had bought shoes in one store, socks in another, and dishes in a third. The new department stores sold all kinds of goods in different sections or departments. As the American economy was able to produce more goods at cheaper prices, American consumers were better able to afford them. Americans were therefore both producers and consumers of goods and services, encouraging new department stores to open across the country.

In New York, R. H. Macy opened a nine-story department store in 1902. Its motto stated, "We sell goods cheaper than any house in the world." Soon, other cities had department stores. Shopping became a popular pastime. People browsed through each floor, looking at clothes, furniture, and jewelry. On the street, "window-shoppers" paused to view elaborate displays behind enormous new plate-glass windows.

READING CHECK **Identify Cause and Effect** How did developers respond when cities began running out of space in their downtown areas?

Why Did Sports Become Popular?

The rise of the factory split the worlds of work and play more sharply than ever. With less chance to socialize on the job, there was more interest in leisure. Sports provided a great escape from the pressures of work.

Analyze Images This Smith College women's basketball team played in front of all-female audiences because their uniforms were considered too "immodest" for men to see. **Infer** How have sports changed over the last hundred years?

"Play Ball!" Baseball was the most popular sport in the nation. Organized baseball was first played in New York. During the Civil War, New York soldiers showed other Union troops how to play. By the 1870s, several cities had professional baseball teams and the first professional league was organized.

Early baseball was somewhat different from today's game. Pitchers threw underhanded. Catchers caught the ball after one bounce. Fielders did not wear gloves. As a result, high scores were common. One championship baseball game ended with a score of 103 to 8!

At first, African Americans played professional baseball. In time, though, the major leagues barred Black players. In 1885, Frank Thompson organized a group of waiters into one of the first African American professional teams, the Cuban Giants of Long Island. They took the name "Cuban," not because they were from Cuba, but in hopes that all-white teams might be willing to play them.

An Early Version of Football Football grew out of informal English games that also gave rise to rugby. Americans had played forms of football since colonial times. Early football called for lots of muscle and little skill. On every play, the opposing teams crashed into each other like fighting rams. The quarterback ran or jumped over the tangle of bodies.

Players did not wear helmets and were often hurt. In 1908 alone, 33 college football players died from injuries. Some colleges banned the sport or drew up stricter rules of play for the game.

Basketball Begins In 1891, James Naismith invented basketball. Naismith taught physical education at a Young Men's Christian Association (YMCA) in Springfield, Massachusetts. He wanted a sport that could be played indoors in winter. He nailed two bushel baskets to the gym walls. Players tried to throw a soccer ball into the baskets.

Basketball caught on quickly. It spread to other YMCAs and then to schools and colleges around the country.

READING CHECK **Draw Conclusions** Why might all-white baseball teams be willing to play African Americans who called themselves "Cubans"?

New Forms of Entertainment

By the late 1800s, American cities supported a wide variety of cultural activities. Talented immigrants contributed to new forms of music and theater. People from different cultures sang the same songs and enjoyed the same shows.

In urban centers, public socializing increased. Before this time, young men and women got together in the home, under the watchful eye of parents. Now many single women had jobs in the cities, often as teachers, clerks, or secretaries. With more places to go, such as theaters, dance halls, and amusement parks, dating became more common. Men, who generally earned a higher wage than women, usually paid for the entertainment.

As railroads grew, circuses, acting companies, and "Wild West" shows toured the country. These traveling groups helped spread American culture beyond the cities to the small towns.

An Evening Out Many large cities organized symphony orchestras and opera companies. Generally, only the wealthy attended the symphony or the opera. For other city dwellers, an evening out often meant a trip to a vaudeville house. **Vaudeville** (VAWD vil) was a variety show that included comedians, song-and-dance routines, and acrobats.

Vaudeville provided opportunities for people from many ethnic backgrounds, such as Irish American dancer-singer George M. Cohan and Jewish comedians like the Marx Brothers. Will Rogers, a performer of Cherokee descent, was one of the best-loved entertainers in the nation. He began his career doing lariat tricks on stage. Later, Rogers, wearing a cowboy hat and twirling a rope, used gentle wit to comment on American life. "Everybody is ignorant," he said, "only on different subjects."

Popular Music Songwriters produced many popular tunes, such as "Shine On, Harvest Moon." Later, Thomas Edison's phonograph sparked a new industry. By 1900, millions of phonograph records had been sold.

Ragtime was a new kind of music with a lively, rhythmic sound. Scott Joplin, an African American composer, helped make ragtime popular. His "Maple Leaf Rag" was a nationwide hit.

In towns and cities, marching bands played the military music of John Philip Sousa. Sousa wrote more than 100 marches, including "The Stars and Stripes Forever." His marches are still favorites at Fourth of July celebrations.

READING CHECK **Draw Conclusions** How did Edison's phonograph affect the music industry?

Analyze Images Will Rogers began his career in vaudeville doing rope tricks, but became renowned for his gentle wit. **Infer** Why was show business so attractive to diverse performers?

Analyze Images Reading, writing, and arithmetic were the focus of schools in the late 1800s. **Compare and Contrast** How is a modern classroom different from this one? How is it similar?

Why Did More Americans Attend School?

Before 1870, fewer than half of American children went to school. Many who did attended one-room schoolhouses, with only one teacher. Often, several students shared a single book.

Government-Funded Schools As industry grew, the nation needed an educated work force. As a result, states improved public schools at all levels. By 1900, there were 4,000 kindergartens across the nation.

Academic Vocabulary
compulsory • *adj.*, required, as by law

In the North, most states passed **compulsory** education laws that required children to attend school, usually through sixth grade. In the South, which had no tradition of public schools, the Freedmen's Bureau had built grade schools for both African American and white students. By 1900, most southern schools were segregated.

In cities such as Boston and New York, public schools taught English to young immigrants. Children also learned about the duties and rights of citizens. In the 1880s, Catholics became worried that public schools stressed Protestant teachings. They opened their own parochial, or church-sponsored, schools.

A Typical School Day The typical school day lasted from 8:00 A.M. to 4:00 P.M. Pupils learned the "three Rs": reading, 'riting, and 'rithmetic. Students memorized and recited passages from the most widely used textbook, *McGuffey's Eclectic Reader.* With titles like "Waste Not, Want Not," the poems and stories taught not only reading but also religion, ethics, and values.

Schools emphasized discipline and obedience. Students had to sit upright in their seats, often with their hands folded in front of them. Punishment was swift and severe—a rap on the head for whispering or a paddling for arriving late.

Higher Learning After the Civil War, many cities and towns built public high schools. By 1900, there were 6,000 high schools in the country. Higher education also expanded. New private colleges for both women and men opened. Many states built universities that offered free or low-cost education.

To help meet the need for trained workers, the Chicago Manual Training School opened in 1884. It offered courses in "shop work," such as electricity and carpentry, as well as in a few academic subjects. Soon, most public schools in the nation had programs to prepare students for jobs in business and in industry.

READING CHECK **Compare and Contrast** How did public and parochial schools differ?

A Newspaper Boom

"Read all about it!" cried newsboys on city street corners. As education spread, people read more, especially newspapers. The number of newspapers grew dramatically. By 1900, half the newspapers in the world were printed in the United States.

The newspaper boom was linked to the growth of cities. In towns and villages, neighbors shared news face to face. In the crowded and busy cities, people needed newspapers to stay informed.

Newspapers reported on major events of the day. Most of them featured stories about local government, business, fashion, and sports. Many immigrants learned to read English by spelling their way through a daily paper. They also learned about American life.

Competition Creates Yellow Journalism Joseph Pulitzer, a Hungarian immigrant, created the first modern, mass-circulation newspaper. In 1883, Pulitzer bought the New York *World*. He set out to make it lively and "truly democratic."

To win readers, Pulitzer slashed prices and added comic strips. Pictures and bold "scare" headlines attracted reader attention. The *World* splashed crimes and political scandals across its front page.

Analyze Graphs
Education was a priority for the Progressives. **Draw Conclusions** What conclusions can you draw about trends in the level of education, based on this graph?

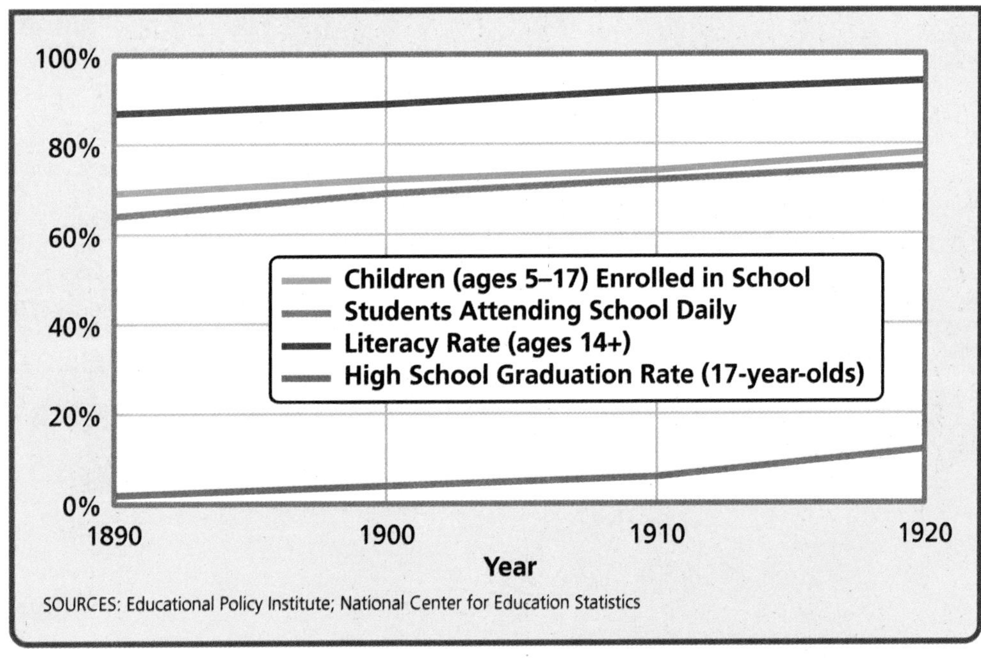

Did you know?

Nellie Bly exposed much corruption as a reporter for the New York *World.*

William Randolph Hearst challenged Pulitzer. Hearst's New York *Journal* began to outdo the *World* in presenting scandals, crime stories, and gossip. Critics complained that the papers offered less news and more scandal every day. They coined the term **yellow journalism** for the sensational reporting style of the *World* and the *Journal.*

The Female Readership Newspapers competed for women readers. They added special sections on fashion, social events, health, homemaking, and family matters. Newspapers rarely pushed for women's rights, however. Most were afraid to take bold positions that might anger some readers.

Magazines and Novels Americans also read more books and magazines. New printing methods lowered the cost of magazines. Magazines also added eye-catching pictures to attract readers.

Each magazine had its special audience. *The Ladies' Home Journal* appealed mostly to middle-class women. By 1900, it had one million readers. Other magazines, such as *Harper's Monthly* and *The Nation,* specialized in politics or current events.

Low-priced paperbacks, known as dime novels, offered thrilling adventure stories. Many told about the "Wild West." Young people loved dime novels, but parents often disapproved. One critic complained, "Stories for children used to begin, 'Once upon a time . . . .' Now they begin, 'Vengeance, blood, death,' shouted Rattlesnake Jim.'"

Analyze Images
News carriers wait for newspapers "hot off the press" in Cincinnati. **Use Visual Information** What role did these men and boys play in the newspaper business?

Horatio Alger wrote more than 100 dime novels for children. Most told of poor boys who became rich and respected through hard work, luck, and honesty. "Rags-to-riches" stories offered the hope that even the poorest person could succeed in the United States.

READING CHECK **Draw Conclusions** Why did serious newspaper readers criticize yellow journalism?

Analyze Images American author Samuel Clemens, otherwise known as Mark Twain, gained national renown through his depiction of southern life in novels like *The Adventures of Huckleberry Finn* and *The Adventures of Tom Sawyer.* **Compare and Contrast** How was the work of a realist like Twain different from that of authors who had preceded him?

New American Writers and Artists

In the 1880s, a new crop of American writers appeared. For the first time, Americans were reading more books by American authors than by British authors.

Depicting Reality One group of writers, called **realists**, tried to show the harsh side of life as it was. Many realists had worked as newspaper reporters. They had seen poverty and wanted to make people aware of the costs of urbanization and industrial growth.

Stephen Crane was best known for his Civil War novel, *The Red Badge of Courage*. Crane also wrote about the shattered lives of young city slum dwellers in novels such as *Maggie: A Girl of the Streets.* Jack London, born in California, wrote about miners and sailors on the West Coast who put their lives at risk in backbreaking jobs.

Kate Chopin found an audience in women's magazines for her short stories about New Orleans life. Chopin's stories showed women breaking out of traditional roles.

Paul Laurence Dunbar was the first African American to make a living as a writer. He wrote poems, such as "We Wear the Mask," in a serious, elegant style. In other poems, he used everyday language to express the feelings of African Americans of the time.

Mark Twain The most famous and popular author of this period was Mark Twain, the pen name of Samuel Clemens. Twain had his first success in 1865 with his comical short story "The Celebrated Jumping Frog of Calaveras County."

Like many other writers, Twain used local color to make his stories more realistic. **Local color** refers to the speech and habits of a particular region. Twain captured the speech patterns of southerners who lived and worked along the Mississippi River.

In his novels Twain used homespun characters to poke fun at serious issues. Huckleberry Finn, a country boy, and Jim, an escaped slave, raft down the Mississippi River together in the days before the Civil War. Huck comes to respect Jim and to view slavery as wrong.

Here, Huck talks about Jim's love for his family:

Primary Source

"He was saying how the first thing he would do when he got to a free state he would go to saving up money, . . . and when he got enough he would buy his wife, and then they would both work to buy the two children, and if their master wouldn't sell them, they'd get an Ab'litionist to go and steal them."

—Mark Twain, *The Adventures of Huckleberry Finn*

Analyze Images American artist Mary Cassatt used bold colors to paint scenes of everyday life, such as *The Boating Party* (1893). **Infer** Why do you think Cassatt moved to France?

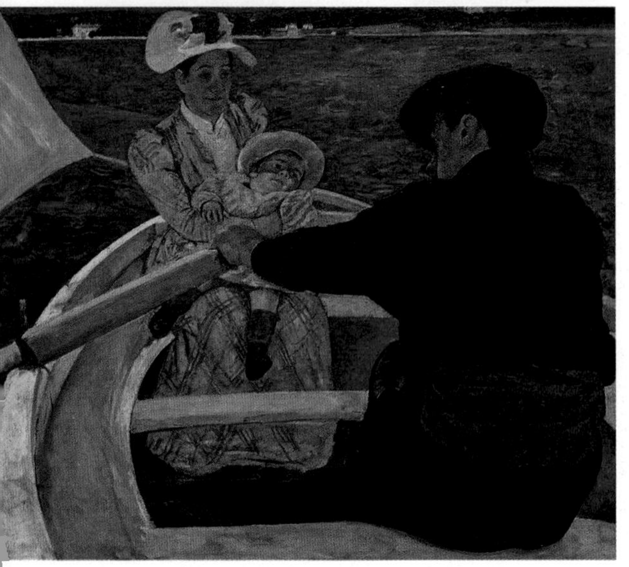

Lifelike Art Like writers of the period, many artists sought to capture local color and the gritty side of modern life. In the late 1800s, leading artists painted realistic everyday scenes.

During the Civil War, Winslow Homer drew scenes of brutal battles for magazines. Later, he gained fame for realistic paintings of the New England coast. Henry Tanner, an African American, won fame for paintings of Black sharecroppers. Later, Tanner moved to Paris to enjoy greater freedom.

Other American artists preferred to work in Europe, too. James Whistler left Massachusetts for Paris and London. His use of color and light influenced young European artists. Mary Cassatt painted bright, colorful scenes of people in everyday situations, especially mothers and children.

READING CHECK **Identify Main Ideas** What was the main goal of writers referred to as realists?

Lesson Check

Practice Vocabulary

1. Where would you have found a **skyscraper** in 1900—in the city center or in a **suburb**? Explain.
2. What did the writing of **realists** have in common with **yellow journalism**?

Critical Thinking and Writing

3. **Summarize** How did city life change during the Progressive Era?
4. **Infer** Why did education become available to more people during the Progressive Era?
5. **Writing Workshop: Use Technology to Produce and Publish** You are nearly ready to write the research paper, based on the notes in your Active Journal. Technology will help you efficiently produce and publish a well-organized paper that clearly answers the question that you posed earlier.

Paul Laurence Dunbar, "We Wear the Mask"

Paul Laurence Dunbar is best known for his poems expressing his views of the African American experience.

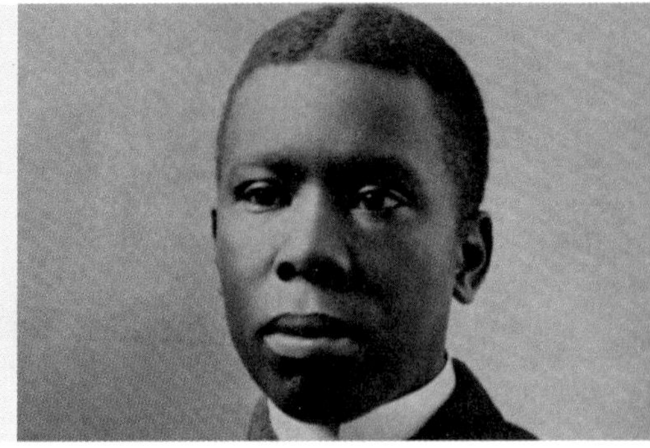

▶ Paul Laurence Dunbar was the son of freed slaves, and was born in Ohio.

We Wear the Mask

We wear the mask that grins and lies,
It hides our cheeks and shades our eyes,—
This debt we pay to human guile; ①

With torn and bleeding hearts we smile,
And mouth with myriad subtleties. ②

Why should the world be over-wise,
In counting all our tears and sighs?
Nay, let them only see us, while
We wear the mask. ③

We smile, but, O great Christ, our cries
To thee from tortured souls arise.
We sing, but oh the clay is vile ④
Beneath our feet, and long the mile;
But let the world dream otherwise,
We wear the mask! ⑤

Reading and Vocabulary Support

① The term *guile* means "slyness" or "deceit."

② The phrase *myriad subtleties* means "a great number of subtle, or indirect, actions."

③ Summarize this stanza (group of four lines) in your own words. What is the poet saying here?

④ The word *vile* means "disgusting" or "extremely unpleasant."

⑤ Why does the poet end this line with an exclamation point, when the same line earlier in the poem ended in a period?

Analyzing Primary Sources

Cite specific evidence from the document to support your answers.

1. Why do you think African Americans often felt the need to "wear the mask"?
2. Does the poet believe that African Americans should "wear the mask"? What words or sentences does he use to support his opinion?

TOPIC 11

Review and Assessment

VISUAL REVIEW

A NEW WAVE OF IMMIGRATION

From southern and eastern Europe

- Entered via East Coast, Ellis Island
- Non-English speakers
- Catholic, Jewish, Eastern Orthodox
- Settled mainly in cities
- Worked in factories, steel mills, meatpacking plants

From Mexico

- Entered via southern border
- Non-English speakers
- Catholic
- Settled in Southwest; later in Midwest, Rocky Mountain region, California
- Worked on farms and building roads, railroads, and irrigation projects

From Asia: China, Japan, the Philippines, Korea, and India

- Entered via West Coast, Angel Island
- Non-English speaking
- Buddhist, Daoist, Hindu, Sikh
- Settled mainly on West Coast
- Worked in mines, on railroads, in canneries and lumber mills, and owned shops

READING REVIEW

Use these resources in your Active Journal to help you to review your notes and topic vocabulary.

Practice vocabulary using the Topic Mini-Games.

Write Your Immigration Essay

Find writing help in your Active Journal.

ASSESSMENT

Vocabulary and Key Ideas

1. **Check Understanding** Why is warfare a **push factor** and not a pull factor?
2. **Identify Supporting Details** How does the **initiative** and **referendum** give the people of a state more political power?
3. **Identify Supporting Details** What industry did the **Federal Reserve Act** regulate?
4. **Define** What did the people who supported **prohibition** want to do?
5. **Check Understanding** How did the difficulties of pioneer life affect the decision by western states to grant women the right to vote?
6. **Identify Main Ideas** Why are Theodore Roosevelt, William Howard Taft, and Woodrow Wilson considered **Progressive** Presidents?
7. **Summarize** How did government try to make sure that the educational system met the needs of a steadily industrializing nation?

Critical Thinking and Writing

8. **Understand Effects** Why was the immigrant population especially high in cities?
9. **Infer** How did the establishment of the Civil Service Commission help get rid of the spoils system?
10. **Recognize Multiple Causes** Why did nativists push so hard to keep Chinese people out of the country?
11. **Draw Conclusions** Why do you think Mark Twain was such a popular writer during this period?
12. **Revisit the Essential Question** How did Progressive reformers improve American society?
13. **Writing Workshop: Write a Research Paper** Using the notes you created in your Active Journal, write a research paper on the subject that you chose.

Analyze Primary Sources

14. Who most likely made the statement quoted here?
    A. Mark Twain
    B. Ida Tarbell
    C. Jacob Riis
    D. Mary Cassatt

"Rockefeller and his associates did not build the Standard Oil Co. in the board rooms of Wall Street banks. They fought their way to control by rebate and drawback, bribe and blackmail, espionage and price cutting, by ruthless . . . efficiency of organization."

Analyze Maps

15. Which letter on the map shows the location of Ellis Island?
16. Which letter on the map indicates where women first gained the right to vote?
17. Which letter on the map shows the point of entry for most Asian immigrants?

▼ **Immigration and Suffrage**

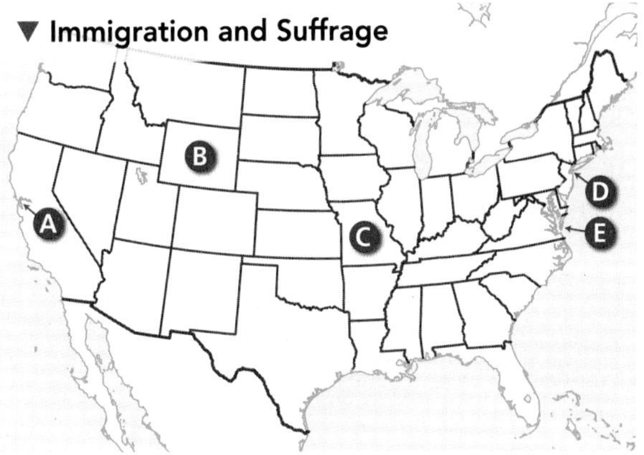

TOPIC 12

Imperialism and World War I (1853–1919)

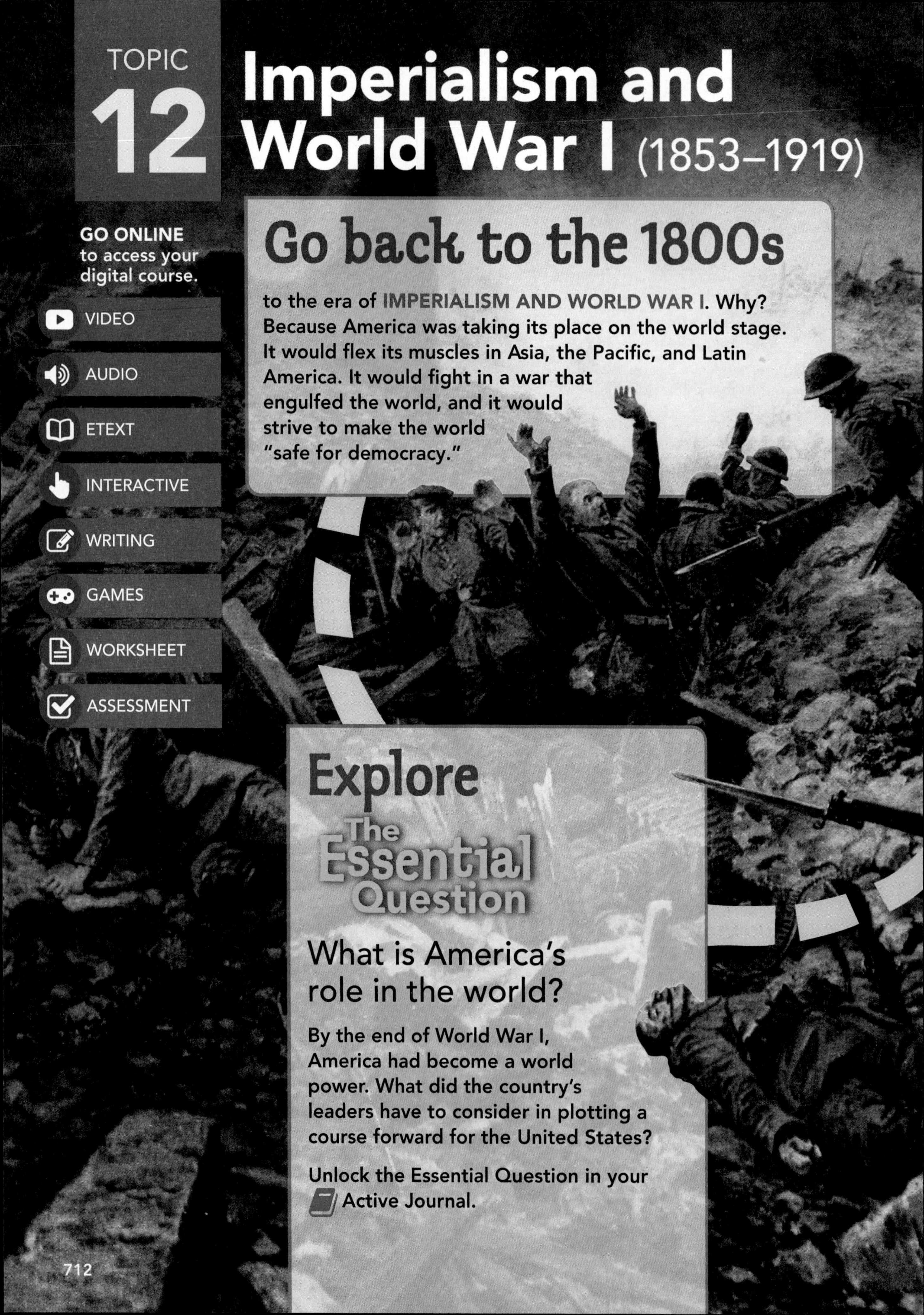

GO ONLINE to access your digital course.

- VIDEO
- AUDIO
- ETEXT
- INTERACTIVE
- WRITING
- GAMES
- WORKSHEET
- ASSESSMENT

Go back to the 1800s

to the era of IMPERIALISM AND WORLD WAR I. Why? Because America was taking its place on the world stage. It would flex its muscles in Asia, the Pacific, and Latin America. It would fight in a war that engulfed the world, and it would strive to make the world "safe for democracy."

Explore The Essential Question

What is America's role in the world?

By the end of World War I, America had become a world power. What did the country's leaders have to consider in plotting a course forward for the United States?

Unlock the Essential Question in your Active Journal.

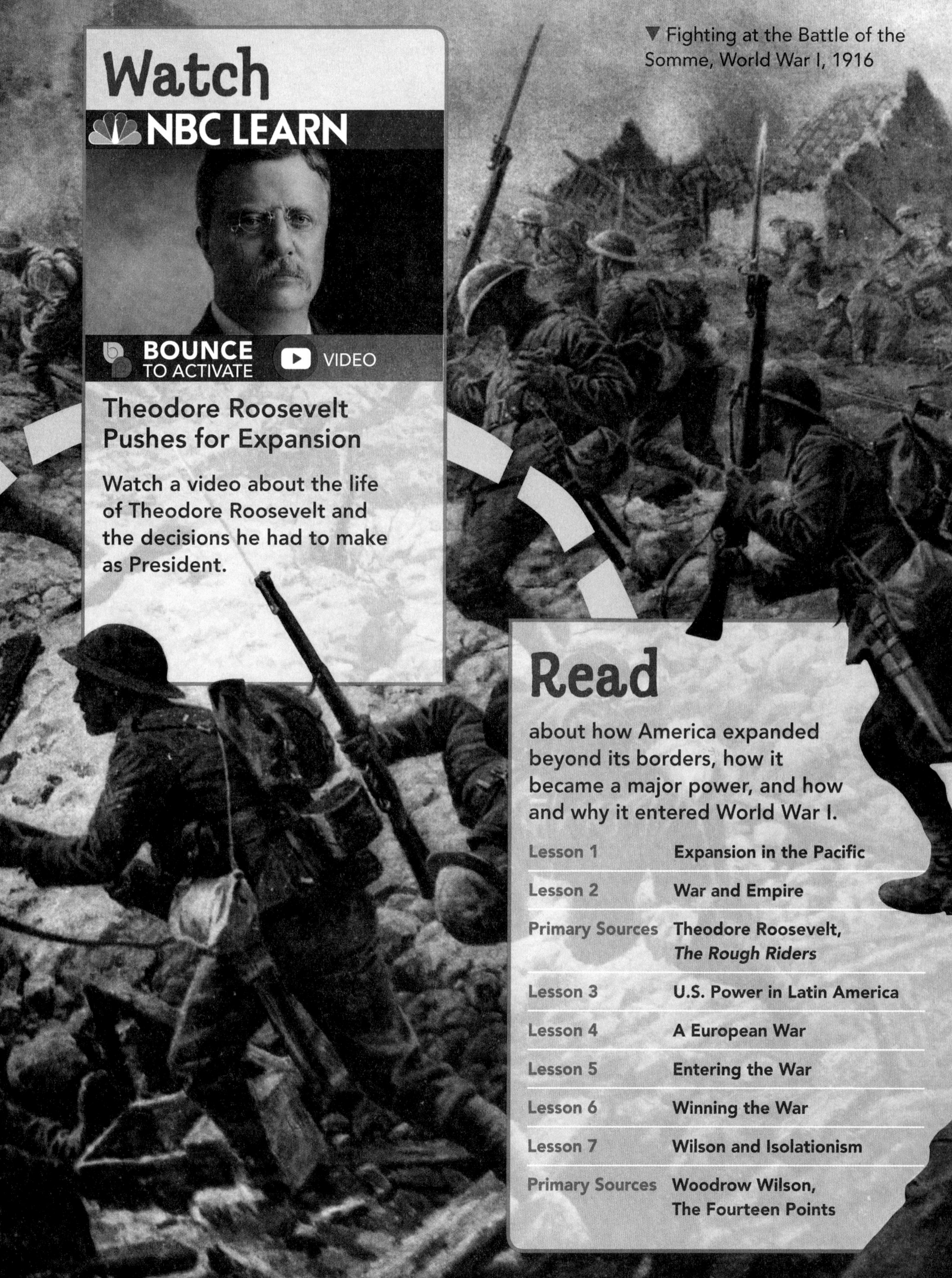

▼ Fighting at the Battle of the Somme, World War I, 1916

Watch

Theodore Roosevelt Pushes for Expansion

Watch a video about the life of Theodore Roosevelt and the decisions he had to make as President.

Read

about how America expanded beyond its borders, how it became a major power, and how and why it entered World War I.

TOPIC 12

Imperialism and World War I (1853–1919)

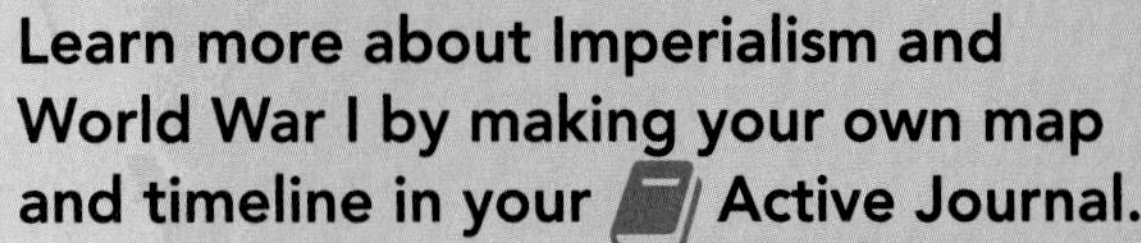

Learn more about Imperialism and World War I by making your own map and timeline in your Active Journal.

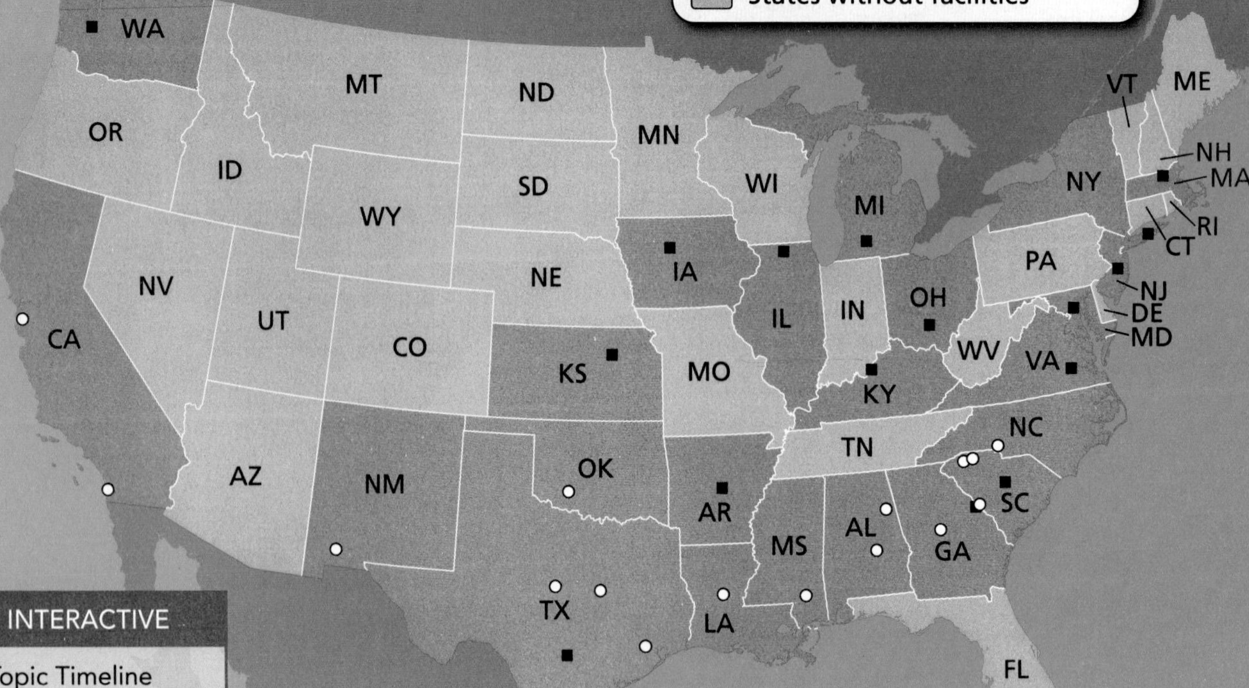

INTERACTIVE

Topic Timeline

What happened and when?

America finds opportunity in far parts of the world . . . and becomes involved in the bloodiest war the world had known. Explore the timeline to see some of what was happening in the United States and in the rest of the world.

TOPIC EVENTS

1854
Commodore Perry opens Japan to trade

1867
Secretary of State Seward purchases Alaska

1850 **1875**

WORLD EVENTS

1853
France, Britain, and Turkey fight Russia in Crimean War

1870
Franco-Prussian War begins

Topic Map

Where was America's influence felt?

The United States became a world power as it won influence throughout the Pacific and in Latin America. During World War I, training bases across the country helped America prepare for an important role in the future of Europe.

1898
Spanish-American War

1904
Work begins on Panama Canal

1917
U.S. enters World War I

1898
U.S. annexes Hawaii

1918
Armistice ends fighting in World War I

1900 — 1925

1889
Eiffel Tower built in Paris for International Exposition

1903
Marie Curie wins Nobel Prize for Physics for discovery of radioactivity

1914
World War I begins in Europe

Who will you meet?

Liliuokalani, last queen of Hawaii

Theodore Roosevelt, soldier and President

Woodrow Wilson, wartime President

Imperialism and Annexation

Quest KICK OFF

Recently, a U.S. citizen discovered a tiny island that was previously unknown in the Pacific Ocean. You are a U.S. State Department official and you're deciding whether the United States should annex the island. To help you decide, you will look to history. You will need to answer this question:

Should the U.S. have annexed Hawaii?

Be ready! Other U.S. State Department officials will challenge your arguments. It's time to prepare!

▼ The islands of Hawaii

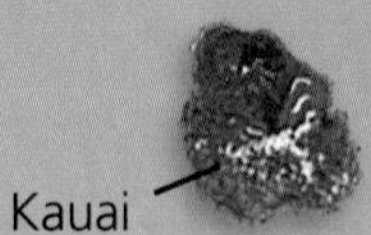

Kauai

Oahu

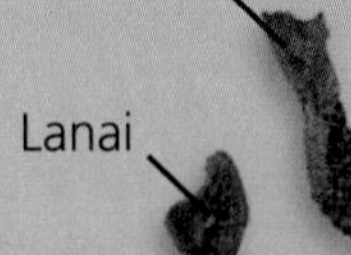

Molokai

Lanai

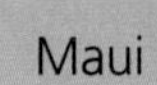

Maui

Hawaii

1 Ask Questions

You are determined to know the best answer to the Guiding Question. Get started by making a list of questions about the annexation of Hawaii. Write the questions in your Active Journal.

2 Investigate

As you read the lessons in this topic, look for Quest CONNECTIONS that provide information about the annexation of Hawaii. Collect examples in your Active Journal.

3 Examine Sources

Next, explore primary sources related to the annexation of Hawaii. They will support differing viewpoints about whether the U.S. should have annexed Hawaii. Capture notes in your Active Journal.

Quest FINDINGS

4 Discuss!

After you collect your clues and examine the sources, you will prepare to discuss this question: Should the U.S. have annexed Hawaii? You will use your knowledge of the annexation of Hawaii as well as evidence from sources to make convincing arguments to answer YES or NO to the question. You may also come up with answers of your own.

LESSON 1

Expansion in the Pacific

GET READY TO READ

START UP

Examine the painting of the American fleet on its way to Japan. Then preview other images in the lesson. Write two predictions of how you think America's role in the world will change.

GUIDING QUESTIONS

- How did the United States gain control of territories in the Pacific?
- What is the meaning of imperialism, and why did nations pursue it?
- How did the United States protect its trade with China?

TAKE NOTES

Literacy Skills Summarize

Use the graphic organizer in your Active Journal to take notes as you read the lesson.

PRACTICE VOCABULARY

Use the vocabulary activity in your Active Journal to practice the vocabulary words.

Vocabulary		Academic Vocabulary
isolationism	Great White Fleet	divest
Treaty of Kanagawa	Open Door Policy	sustain
imperialism		

In his Farewell Address in 1796, George Washington had advised the nation to have little to do with the political affairs of other nations. He was concerned about forming dangerous alliances with other nations. He preferred that the United States stay out of international affairs except to protect its economic interests.

How Did Expansion Lead to Trade With Japan?

Washington's beliefs influenced the policy of later Presidents. For over a hundred years, U.S. Presidents professed a policy of **isolationism**, or staying out of world affairs. Americans had no wish to be dragged into Europe's frequent wars.

Expansion and Trade Yet Americans had goals beyond isolationism. From the beginning, the United States had also followed a policy of expansionism, or extending its national boundaries. Americans were constantly pressing westward across the continent until the country stretched from sea to shining sea.

Commodore Perry's Arrival in Japan

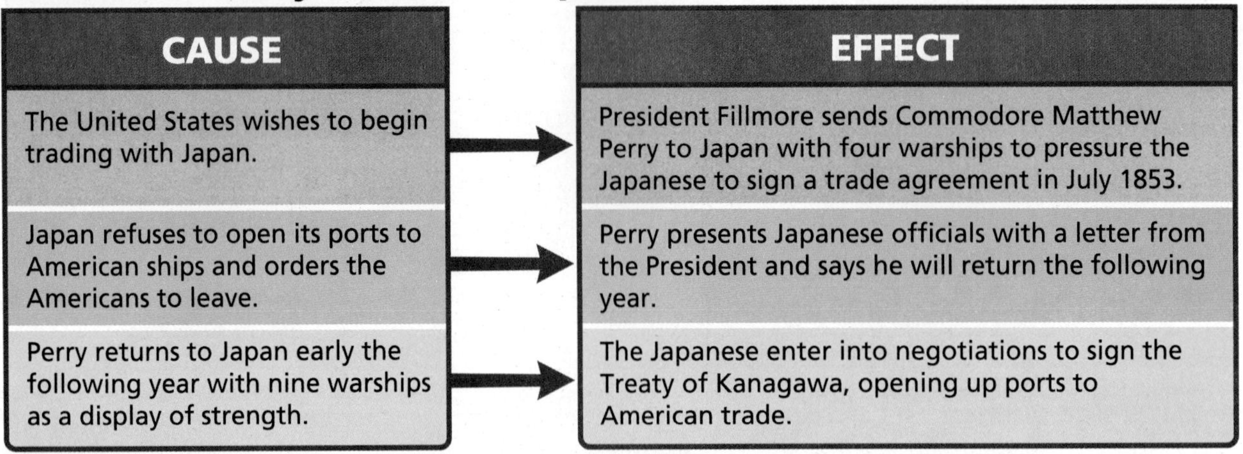

CAUSE	EFFECT
The United States wishes to begin trading with Japan.	President Fillmore sends Commodore Matthew Perry to Japan with four warships to pressure the Japanese to sign a trade agreement in July 1853.
Japan refuses to open its ports to American ships and orders the Americans to leave.	Perry presents Japanese officials with a letter from the President and says he will return the following year.
Perry returns to Japan early the following year with nine warships as a display of strength.	The Japanese enter into negotiations to sign the Treaty of Kanagawa, opening up ports to American trade.

SOURCES: PBS; Asia for Educators

Analyze Charts
Commodore Perry's visits to Japan proved to be a turning point in American relations with Asia. **Infer** Why did the Japanese refuse to see Perry on his first visit?

At the same time, Americans were also engaged in a lively foreign trade. Merchant ships carried American goods to Europe, as well as to Asian nations such as China. The success of many U.S. industries depended on exports. The island nation of Japan, however, refused to open its doors to American trade.

Foreign Trade With Japan Fearing outsiders, Japanese rulers had cut themselves off from the world in the 1600s and expelled all westerners. Only a few Dutch merchants were permitted to trade once a year at the port of Nagasaki. Any foreign sailors who were shipwrecked on the shores of Japan were not allowed to leave.

Americans wanted Japan to open its ports to trade and to help shipwrecked sailors. To achieve these goals, President Millard Fillmore sent Commodore Matthew Perry to Japan. Perry entered Tokyo Bay with four warships in July 1853.

The Japanese had never before seen steam-powered ships. Japanese rulers ordered the Americans to leave. Perry complied, but before departing, he presented Japanese officials with a letter from President Fillmore. It asked the Japanese to open trading relations with the United States. Perry said he would return the following year for an answer.

Perry returned in February 1854, this time with nine warships. Impressed by this show of strength, the Japanese emperor signed the **Treaty of Kanagawa**. In the treaty, Japan accepted demands to help shipwrecked sailors, and it opened two ports to American trade.

Perry's visit launched trade between Japan and the West. It also made the Japanese aware of the power of the western industrial nations. Japan soon set out to become a modern industrial nation itself, with the United States as one of its models.

READING CHECK **Understand Effects** How did U.S. expansion and economic growth impact Japan?

U.S. Interest in the Pacific

American interest in Asia and the Pacific continued. In the 1860s, Secretary of State William Seward wanted the United States to dominate trade in the Pacific. In 1867, he persuaded Congress to annex, or take over, Midway Island, in the middle of the Pacific Ocean. The island became part of the United States. Seward also made a bold deal to buy the vast territory of Alaska from Russia.

A Late-Night Land Deal Seward saw Alaska as an important stepping stone for increasing U.S. trade in Asia and the Pacific. For their part, the Russians were eager to **divest** themselves of the territory, which was too far away to be governed effectively.

Academic Vocabulary
divest • *v.*, to rid or free

One night in 1867, Seward was playing cards when he was interrupted by a message from the Russian ambassador. The czar, or emperor, of Russia was willing to sell Alaska to the United States for $7.2 million. Seward agreed to buy the land then and there.

"But your Department is closed," said the ambassador.

"Never mind that," Seward replied. "Before midnight you will find me at the Department, which will be open and ready for business."

Next morning, Seward completed the deal. The cost came to 2 cents an acre. The purchase of Alaska increased the area of the United States by almost one fifth.

Analyze Political Cartoons In this cartoon making fun of Seward's purchase of Alaska, the man on the right, representing the Russian ruler, carries a chunk of ice labeled "Russian America." **Draw Conclusions** What opinion of Alaska does the cartoon express?

"Seward's Folly" At the time, the purchase seemed foolish to many Americans. They thought Alaska was a barren land of icy mountains and frozen fish. They mockingly called the new territory "Seward's Ice Box" and referred to the purchase as "Seward's Folly."

Minds changed in the 1890s, after prospectors found gold in Alaska. Miners rushed to the new territory as they had once rushed to California. Since then, Seward's vision of Alaska as a valuable territory has proved correct. Northern Alaska contains vast reserves of oil. The land is also rich in timber, copper, petroleum, and natural gas. In 1959, Alaska became the forty-ninth state.

READING CHECK **Identify Main Ideas** Why did Seward buy Alaska?

How Did the Age of Imperialism Begin?

The period between 1870 and 1914 has often been called the Age of Imperialism. **Imperialism** is the policy of powerful countries seeking to control the economic and political affairs of weaker countries or regions. Between 1870 and 1914, European nations, such as the United Kingdom (Britain), Germany, and France, seized control of almost the entire continent of Africa and much of southern Asia. During this period, the United States and Japan also became imperial powers.

Reasons for Imperialism There were several reasons for the growth of imperialism. First, the industrial nations of Europe needed raw materials and new markets. European factories used raw materials from Africa and Asia to manufacture goods. Some of these goods were then sold in Africa and Asia.

GEOGRAPHY **SKILLS**

The map shows how the world's imperialist nations divided up the world.

1. **Location** Based on the map, which nations held the greatest worldwide influence through their colonies?
2. **Synthesize Visual Information** Which nation's colonies were most widely spread around the world?

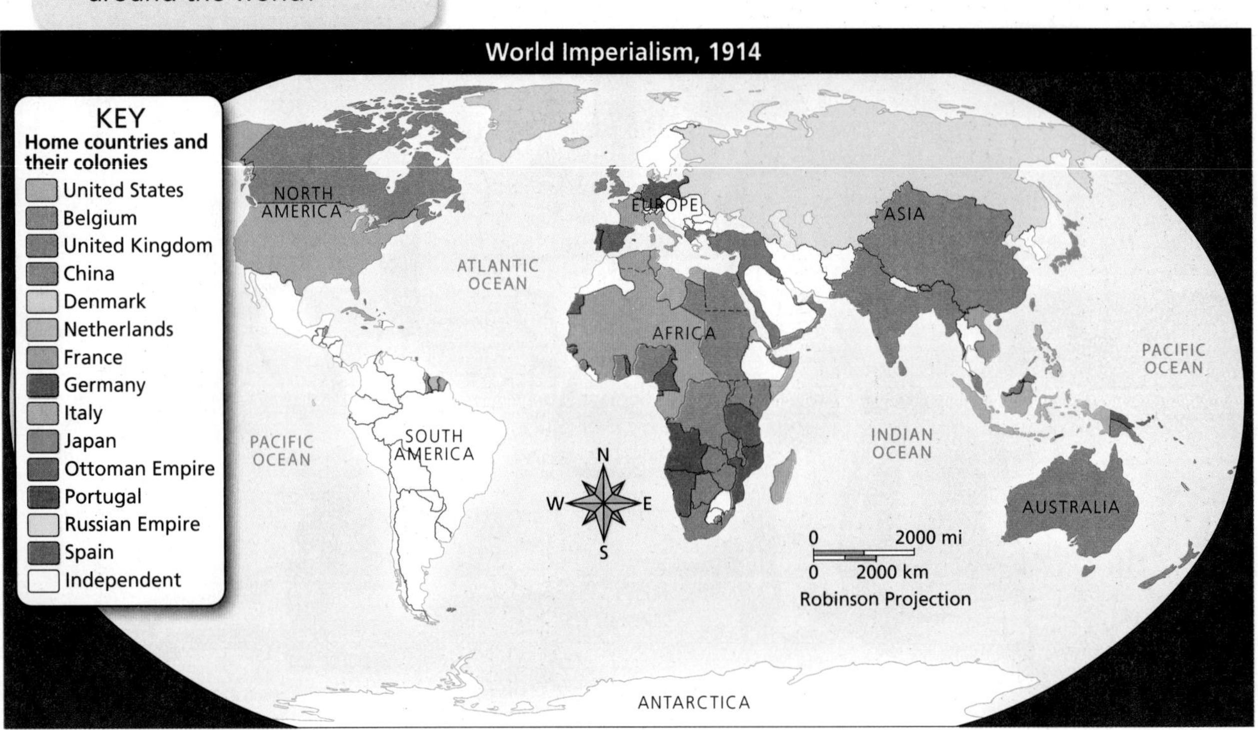

American Foreign Trade, 1865–1915

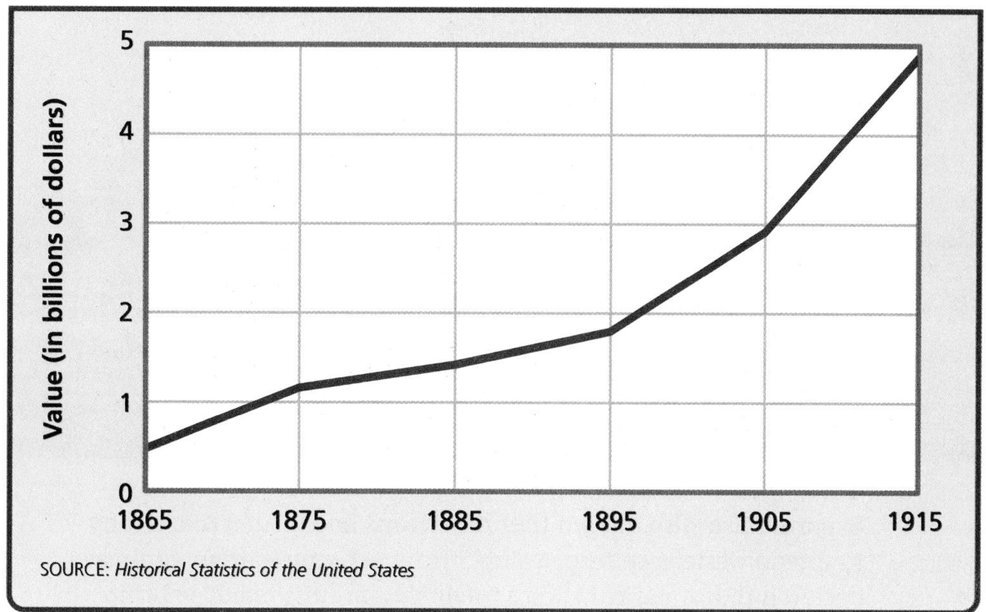

Analyze Graphs This graph shows how American foreign trade increased between the years 1865 and 1915. **Identify Cause and Effect.** Based on what you have read, list at least two causes for the increase in foreign trade.

Imperialism was also based on racism, or the false belief that people are divided into races and that one race deserves power over another. Many Europeans felt that they had a duty to spread their culture to people they considered less civilized. British writer Rudyard Kipling called this responsibility "the white man's burden." Such thinking ignored the existing rich cultures of Africans and Asians.

A third cause was competition. When a European country colonized an area, it often closed those markets to other countries. A European nation might take over an area just to keep rival nations out.

American Expansionists Make Their Case Americans could not ignore Europe's race for colonies. By the 1890s, the United States was a world leader in industry and agriculture. American factories turned out huge amounts of steel, and American farms grew surpluses of corn, wheat, and cotton. The nation was growing rapidly, and arguments in favor of expansion were popular.

Many people believed that the American economy would collapse unless the United States gained new foreign markets.

Primary Source

"Today we are raising more than we can consume. Today we are making more than we can use. Today our industrial society is congested; there are more workers than there is work. . . . Therefore we must find new markets for our produce, new occupations for our capital, new work for our labor."

—Albert Beveridge, quoted in Bowers, *Beveridge and the Progressive Era*

Analyze Images The Great White Fleet, shown here departing Virginia in 1907, was sent around the globe to impress the world with U.S. naval power. **Infer** Why do you think President Roosevelt wanted to demonstrate U.S. naval power around the world?

Expansionists also argued that Americans had a right and a duty to spread western culture. Josiah Strong, a Congregational minister, declared that Americans were "divinely commissioned" to bring democracy and Christianity "down upon Mexico, down upon Central and South America, out upon the islands of the sea."

Other expansionists stressed the need to replace the vanishing frontier. For 100 years, the economy had boomed as Americans settled the West. The 1890 census declared, however, that the frontier was gone. People in crowded eastern cities had no new land to settle. The solution, said some, was to take new land overseas.

Naval Power One leading advocate of American imperialism was naval captain Alfred Mahan. In an influential 1890 book, *The Influence of Sea Power Upon History*, Mahan argued that the prosperity of the United States depended on foreign trade. Furthermore, he said, a bigger navy was needed to protect American merchant ships. "When a question arises of control over distant regions," Mahan wrote, "it must ultimately be decided by naval power."

Academic Vocabulary
sustain • *v.*, to preserve and support

In Mahan's view, the United States could not **sustain** a world-class navy unless it controlled naval bases throughout the world. Mahan was especially interested in acquiring harbors in the Caribbean and the Pacific as links to Latin America and Asia.

Even before Mahan's appeal, Congress had begun to enlarge and modernize the navy. By 1900, a powerful American navy was ready for action. Its steam-powered ships were called the **Great White Fleet** because their steel hulls were all painted white.

READING CHECK **Summarize** What reasons account for the increase in American expansionism?

The United States Expands in the Pacific

As its naval power grew, the United States showed increasing interest in Samoa, a chain of islands in the South Pacific. Samoa had a fine harbor that could serve as a naval base and commercial port.

Competition for Samoa Germany and the United Kingdom also realized the value of the harbor. As the three nations competed for control, a military clash seemed likely. In 1889, German ships fired upon Samoan villages that were friendly to the Americans. For months, German and American sailors eyed each other nervously from their warships. Then, with tensions at their highest, a powerful storm sank ships of both countries. The disaster helped ease the crisis.

U.S. Expansion in the Pacific, 1867–1899

Later, the three nations reached a peaceful settlement. The United States and Germany divided Samoa, while the United Kingdom received territories elsewhere in the Pacific. The United States had demonstrated that it would assert its power in the Pacific Ocean.

Interest in Hawaii Another Pacific territory that had long interested the United States was Hawaii. Hawaii is a chain of eight large islands and more than 100 smaller islands. Hawaii's rich soil, warm climate, and plentiful rainfall allow farmers to grow crops all year round.

Westerners first learned about Hawaii in 1778. In that year, James Cook, a British sea captain, dropped anchor in the islands on his way to China. In the early 1800s, American ships bound for China began stopping in Hawaii, and a few American sailors and traders settled there.

Missions and Plantations In 1820, American missionaries began going to Hawaii to convert the Hawaiians to Christianity. The missionaries and other Americans became valued advisers to the rulers of Hawaii. Americans helped write Hawaii's first constitution in 1840.

GEOGRAPHY **SKILLS**

During the second half of the 1800s, the United States expanded its territories across the Pacific, all the way to the Philippines.

1. **Location** Which of the islands are closest to the U.S. mainland? About how far away are they?
2. **Understand Effects** Why would possession of the islands shown on the map be important to American trade with China and Japan?

U.S. Expansion in the Pacific, 1857–1898

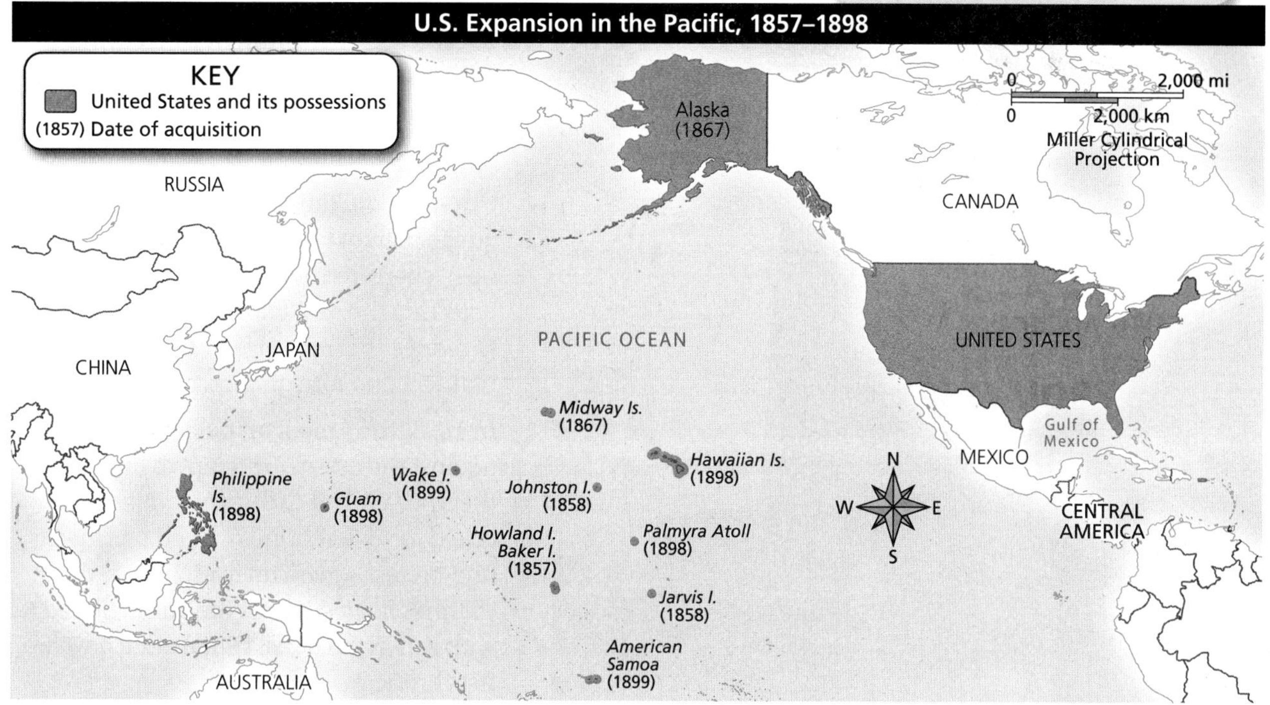

By the mid-1800s, Americans had set up large sugar plantations in Hawaii. Needing cheap labor, the planters imported thousands of workers from China, Korea, the Philippines, and Japan. By 1900, one fourth of Hawaii's population had been born in Japan.

As the sugar industry grew, so did the wealth and political power of American planters. In 1887, they forced the Hawaiian king, Kalakaua, to accept a new constitution. It reduced royal power and increased the planters' influence.

Analyze Images This statue of Queen Liliuokalani stands in front of her former palace in Honolulu. **Infer** Why do you think Liliuokalani was opposed to foreign influence in Hawaii?

American Involvement Changes Hawaii American influence in Hawaii significantly changed the social structure and cultural traditions of the native Hawaiians. New rules outlawed Hawaiian traditions. They prohibited teaching the Hawaiian language in schools and banned dances such as the Hula.

Imperialism also changed the relationship between the environment and Hawaii's people. Traditionally, the lands of Hawaii had been divided among the Hawaiian crown, the government, and the ruling elite. As American influence increased, control of much of Hawaii's land was given to American plantation owners instead.

American businesses cleared native forests and diverted water for agricultural use. Foreigners further altered the environment by clearing native species and bringing in new animals and plants.

American Plantation Owners Seek Power Kalakaua died in 1891. The new queen, Liliuokalani (lih lee oo oh kah LAH nee), cherished Hawaiian independence. Rejecting the new constitution, she sought to reduce the influence and privileges of planters and foreign merchants.

In 1893, the American planters rebelled against the queen's attempt to limit their power. The American ambassador called for U.S. marines to land on Hawaii and protect American lives. In fact, the marines helped topple the queen. Faced with American guns, Liliuokalani gave up her throne:

Primary Source

"I yield to the superior force of the United States of America. . . . To avoid any collision of armed forces and perhaps the loss of life, I do this under protest, and impelled by said force, yield my authority."

—Liliuokalani, letter to the United States government, 1893

Analyze Images These men were probably brought to Hawaii by a wealthy planter to work on this pineapple plantation. **Draw Conclusions** How did American planters change the culture of Hawaii?

The United States Annexes Hawaii With Liliuokalani no longer in power, the planters quickly set up a republic and asked the United States to annex Hawaii. A debate raged in Congress for months. President Grover Cleveland blocked moves to take over the islands. "Our interference in the Hawaiian Revolution of 1893 was disgraceful," he later said.

Congress finally annexed Hawaii in 1898, after Cleveland left office. Two years later, Hawaii was made a United States territory. In 1959, Hawaii became the fiftieth state.

READING CHECK **Identify Cause and Effect** What were one social, one economic, and one political impact of America's interest in Hawaii?

A Worldwide Rivalry for Chinese Trade

Despite its new footholds in the Pacific, the United States was a latecomer to the race for Pacific and Asian territory. The United Kingdom, Germany, Japan, and other industrial nations were already competing for colonies in Asia. The rivalry was especially fierce in China.

Once the most advanced empire in the world, China had been weakened by years of civil war. In addition, China had refused to industrialize in the 1800s. It was unable to fight off industrialized nations seeking profits from its vast resources and markets.

The Open Door Policy In the late 1800s, the United Kingdom, France, Germany, Russia, and Japan carved spheres of influence in China. A sphere of influence was an area, usually around a seaport, where a nation had special trading privileges. Each nation made laws for its own citizens in its own sphere.

The United States was eager to gain a share of the China trade. However, Secretary of State John Hay feared that the imperial powers would cut off China to American merchants. To prevent this, Hay sent a letter in 1899 to all the nations that had spheres of influence in China. He urged them to keep an "open door" in China permitting any nation to trade in the spheres of others. Reluctantly, the imperialist powers accepted the **Open Door Policy**.

Quest CONNECTIONS

What reasons favored annexing Hawaii, and why did President Cleveland oppose it? Record your findings in your Active Journal.

U.S. Influence in Foreign Nations

Analyze Political Cartoons The United States faced resistance in its effort to gain an "open door" to China. **Identify Implied Main Ideas** How does this cartoon represent the resistance faced by the United States?

The Boxer Rebellion Many Chinese resented foreign influence. Some formed a secret society called the Righteous Fists of Harmony, or Boxers. Encouraged by the Chinese government, in 1900, the Boxers attacked westerners, whom they called "foreign devils." During the Boxer Rebellion more than 200 foreigners were killed. Hundreds of others were trapped in Beijing, the Chinese capital.

Foreign governments quickly sent an international army to China that included 2,500 Americans. Armed with modern weapons, they fought their way into Beijing. They freed the trapped foreigners and crushed the uprising.

Several nations saw the Boxer Rebellion as an excuse to seize more land in China. Secretary of State Hay sent another Open Door letter, urging all nations to respect China's independence. Britain, France, and Germany officially accepted Hay's letter. Fearing war, Japan and Russia quietly observed Hay's policy, too.

Hay's Open Door letters were effective because they were backed by U.S. military power. In the next lesson you will read how the United States proved its military strength on the world stage.

READING CHECK **Identify Main Ideas** Why did the United States want an "open door" policy with China?

Lesson Check

Practice Vocabulary

1. How was the **Treaty of Kanagawa** an example of American expansionism?
2. Why and how did the United States advance the **Open Door Policy**?
3. How did the **Great White Fleet** support American **imperialism**?

Critical Thinking and Writing

4. **Evaluate Explanations** How did racism shape imperialism, and how was the racist logic of imperialism flawed?
5. **Identify Cause and Effect** What economic factors influenced territorial expansion during the Age of Imperialism?
6. **Writing Workshop: Consider Your Purpose** You will be writing an essay describing U.S. expansion and intervention during the late 1800s and early 1900s. In your Active Journal, write a thoughtful statement of what you must do to meet the requirements of this writing task.

LESSON 2

War and Empire

GET READY TO READ

START UP

Many people believed the USS *Maine* had been sunk in a Cuban harbor by Spain. How might the United States react to this news? Why?

GUIDING QUESTIONS

- How did tensions in Cuba lead Americans to call for war with Spain?
- How did the United States win such a quick victory in the Spanish-American War?
- How did the United States acquire and rule its empire?

TAKE NOTES

Literacy Skills Identify Main Ideas

Use the graphic organizer in your Active Journal to take notes as you read the lesson.

PRACTICE VOCABULARY

Use the vocabulary activity in your Active Journal to practice the vocabulary words.

Vocabulary

atrocity
yellow journalism
Spanish-American War
Platt Amendment
protectorate
Foraker Act

Academic Vocabulary

subsequently
ultimately

For many years, Americans had looked longingly at Cuba, a Spanish-ruled island just 90 miles off the coast of Florida. As early as 1823, Secretary of State John Quincy Adams had compared Cuba to a ripe apple. A storm, he said, might tear that apple "from its native tree"—the Spanish empire—and drop it into the hands of the United States.

By the 1890s, Spain's once-vast empire in the Western Hemisphere had shrunk to two islands in the Caribbean: Cuba and Puerto Rico. Then, Cuban rebels created the storm that Adams had hoped for.

A Revolution in Cuba

In 1868, the Cuban people had rebelled against Spanish rule. The revolution was finally crushed after 10 years of fighting. Some of the revolutionaries fled to New York, where they kept up the battle for freedom. There, some gathered in the home of exiled Puerto Rican revolutionary Lola Rodríguez de Tió. A renowned poet, Rodríguez de Tió wrote patriotic poems in support of Puerto Rican and Cuban independence.

Another Cuban exile, José Martí, worked day and night raising funds and giving speeches in support of Cuban independence. In his newspaper *Patria,* he told sympathetic Americans of the Cuban struggle for freedom.

"Free Cuba!" In 1895, Martí returned to Cuba. With cries of *Cuba Libre!*—"Free Cuba!"—rebels launched a new fight against Spain. Martí was killed early in the fighting, but the rebels continued the fight and won control of much of Cuba.

The rebels burned sugar cane fields and sugar mills all over Cuba. They hoped that this would make the island unprofitable for Spain and persuade the Spanish to leave. The rebels killed workers who opposed them. They even blew up some passenger trains.

In response, Spain sent a new governor to Cuba, General Valeriano Weyler (WAY ee lair). Weyler used brutal tactics to crush the revolt. In a policy known as reconcentration, his men forced about half a million Cubans into detention camps so that they could not aid the rebels. At least 100,000 Cubans in reconcentration camps died from starvation and disease.

Americans Are Divided In the United States, people watched the revolt in nearby Cuba with concern. The United States had vital economic links to the island. Americans had invested about $50 million in Cuban sugar and rice plantations, railroads, tobacco, and iron mines. Trade with Cuba was worth about $100 million a year.

Opinion split over whether the United States should intervene in Cuba. Many business leaders opposed American involvement, arguing that it might hurt foreign trade.

Analyze Images This photo shows a Cuban sugar plantation around 1910. **Generate Explanations** Why might some Cubans have opposed the rebels?

Analyze Images This illustration shows Cuban rebels leading a charge against Spanish troops in the late 1890s. **Infer** Why did José Martí return to Cuba in 1895?

Other Americans, however, sympathized with Cuban desires for freedom. They called on the government to take action. Senator Henry Cabot Lodge of Massachusetts compared the Cuban rebels to the Patriots in the American Revolution:

Primary Source

"They have risen against oppression, compared to which the oppression which led us to rebel against England is as dust in the balance; and they feel that for this reason, if no other, they should have the sympathy of the people of the United States."

—Henry Cabot Lodge, Record of the 54th Congress, 1896

READING CHECK **Identify Cause and Effect** Why were Americans interested in Cuba?

How Did Americans Push for War?

The press whipped up American sympathies for the people of Cuba. Two New York newspapers—Joseph Pulitzer's *World* and William Randolph Hearst's *Journal*—competed to print the most grisly stories about Spanish **atrocities**, or wartime acts of cruelty and brutality. The publishers knew that war with Spain would boost sales of their newspapers.

Sensational News To attract readers, Hearst and Pulitzer used **yellow journalism**, or reporting that relied on sensational stories and headlines. Often, these reports were biased or untrue. According to one story, a photographer bound for Cuba told Hearst that there was no war. "You supply the pictures," Hearst supposedly replied. "I'll supply the war." News stories described events in Cuba in graphic and horrifying detail.

In response to the news reports, many Americans demanded that the President take action to help the Cubans. Yet despite growing pressure, President Cleveland wanted to avoid war with Spain. He called the war fever in the United States an "epidemic of insanity." Stories in the press, he grumbled, were nonsense.

When William McKinley became President in 1897, he also tried to keep the country neutral. However, remaining neutral would soon become difficult.

The Battleship *Maine* Early in 1898, fighting broke out in Havana, the Cuban capital. Acting promptly, President McKinley sent the battleship *Maine* to Havana to protect American citizens and property.

On the night of February 15, the *Maine* lay at anchor in Havana harbor. Just after the bugler played taps, a huge explosion ripped through the ship. The explosion killed at least 260 of the 350 American sailors and officers on board.

The yellow press pounced on the tragedy. "DESTRUCTION OF THE WARSHIP *MAINE* WAS THE WORK OF AN ENEMY," screamed one New York newspaper. "THE WARSHIP *MAINE* SPLIT IN TWO BY AN ENEMY'S SECRET INFERNAL MACHINE?" blared the front page of another.

Analyze Images The New York *World* trumpeted the shocking news of the *Maine*'s destruction. **Distinguish Between Fact and Opinion** In what way is the newspaper headline misleading?

863,956 WORLDS CIRCULATED YESTERDAY — The World. — 863,956 WORLDS CIRCULATED YESTERDAY

"Circulation Books Open to All."

Department of State

NEW YORK, THURSDAY, FEBRUARY 17, 1898.

MAINE EXPLOSION CAUSED BY BOMB OR TORPEDO?

Capt. Sigsbee and Consul-General Lee Are in Doubt---The World Has Sent a Special Tug, With Submarine Divers, to Havana to Find Out---Lee Asks for an Immediate Court of Inquiry---Capt. Sigsbee's Suspicions.

CA I. SIGSBEE, IN A SUPPRESSED DESPATCH TO THE STATE DEPARTMENT, SAYS THE ACCIDENT WAS MADE POSSIBLE BY AN ENEMY.

Dr. E. C. Pendleton, Just Arrived from Havana, Says He Overheard Talk There of a Plot to Blow Up the Ship---Capt Zalinski, the Dynamite Expert, and Other Experts Report to The World that the Wreck Was Not Accidental---Washington Officials Ready for Vigorous Action if Spanish Responsibility Can Be Shown---Divers to Be Sent Down to Make Careful Examinations.

The New York World a day after

The real cause of the explosion remains a mystery. Most historians believe that a boiler blew up or that there was an accident in the ship's ammunition hold. But Americans, urged on by Pulitzer and Hearst, clamored for war. "Remember the *Maine!*" they cried.

Still hoping to avoid war, McKinley tried to get Spain to talk with the Cuban rebels. In the end, however, he gave in to war fever. At 4 A.M. on April 25, 1898, McKinley signed a declaration of war against Spain.

READING CHECK **Identify Main Ideas** How did newspapers generate support for the war, and why?

The Spanish-American War

The **Spanish-American War** lasted only four months. The battlefront stretched from the nearby Caribbean to the distant Philippine Islands off the coast of Southeast Asia.

Capturing the Philippines Two months before the war started, Assistant Secretary of the Navy Theodore Roosevelt had begun making preparations for a possible war with Spain. Roosevelt realized that a conflict with Spain would be fought not only in the Caribbean but wherever Spanish sea power lay. The Philippine Islands, a Spanish colony and Spain's main naval base in the Pacific, would be a major military objective.

Analyze Images This illustration shows the American navy defeating the Spanish fleet in the Battle of Manila. **Synthesize Visual Information** How did naval war change between the U.S. Civil War and the Spanish-American War?

Roosevelt believed it necessary to attack the Spanish in the Philippines as soon as war began. **Subsequently**, he wired secret orders to Commodore George Dewey, commander of the Pacific fleet:

Primary Source

"Secret and confidential. Order the squadron . . . to Hong Kong. Keep full of coal. In the event of declaration of war Spain, your duty will be to see that the Spanish squadron does not leave the Asiatic coast, and then offensive operations in Philippine Islands."

—Theodore Roosevelt, Telegram, February 25, 1898

Academic Vocabulary
subsequently • *adv.,* happening after something else

When war was declared, Dewey sailed to Manila, the main city of the Philippines. On April 30, 1898, his ships slipped into Manila harbor under cover of darkness. There, the Spanish fleet lay at anchor.

At dawn, Dewey told his flagship commander, Charles Gridley, "You may fire when you are ready, Gridley." The Americans bombarded the surprised Spanish ships. By noon, the Spanish fleet had been destroyed.

By July, American ground troops had landed in the Philippines. As in Cuba, local people there had been fighting for independence from Spain for years. With the help of these Filipino rebels, led by Emilio Aguinaldo (ah gwee NAHL doh), the American forces quickly captured Manila.

Victory in Cuba Meanwhile, American troops had also landed in Cuba. The expedition was badly organized. Soldiers wore heavy woolen uniforms in the tropical heat, and they often had to eat spoiled food. Yet, most were eager for battle.

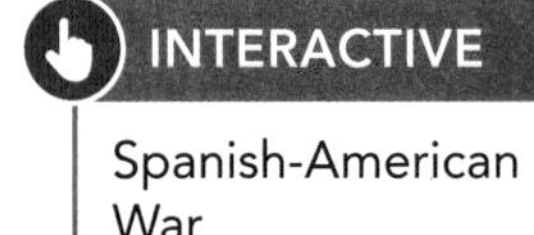

None was more eager than Theodore Roosevelt. When the war broke out, Roosevelt resigned his position as Assistant Secretary of the Navy. He then organized the First Volunteer Cavalry Regiment, later called the Rough Riders. The Rough Riders were a mixed crew, ranging from cowboys to college students and adventurers.

The Rough Riders joined regular troops in the most notable land battle of the war. During the fight for the key Cuban city of Santiago, Americans had to gain control of the San Juan Heights overlooking the city. Under withering fire, charging American forces took two strategic hills.

African American members of the 9th and 10th Cavalries, nicknamed Buffalo Soldiers, played a major role in the bloody victory. John J. Pershing, commander of the 10th Cavalry, later described how the troops united in what came to be called the Battle of San Juan Hill:

Primary Source

> "White regiments, black regiments, regulars and Rough Riders, representing the young manhood of the North and South, fought shoulder to shoulder, unmindful of race or color, . . . mindful of their common duty as Americans."
>
> —John J. Pershing, quoted in MacAdam, *The Life of General Pershing*

Two days later, on July 3, the Americans destroyed the Spanish fleet in Santiago Bay. The Spanish army in Cuba surrendered.

GEOGRAPHY **SKILLS**

Although many Americans had hoped to avoid war, the United States attacked the Spanish in Cuba and soon afterwards in Puerto Rico.

1. **Location** Why did the United States have an interest in Cuba based on its location?
2. **Synthesize Visual Information** How did the United States Navy approach Santiago Bay for its battle with the Spanish fleet?

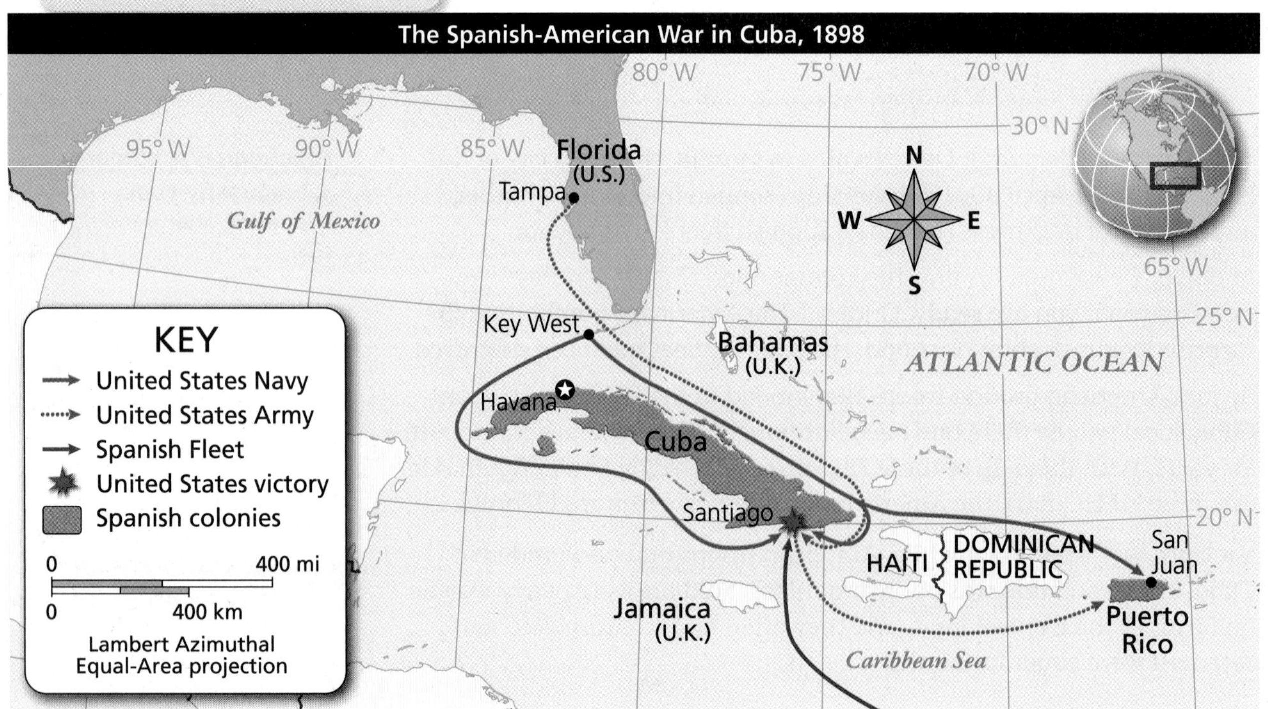

American troops then landed on Puerto Rico and claimed the island.

Spanish Defeat Spain was defeated. On August 12, Spain and the United States agreed to end the fighting. American battle losses were fairly light—379 killed. However, more than 5,000 Americans died of other causes, such as yellow fever, typhoid, and malaria.

John Hay, who was soon to become Secretary of State, summed up the outlook of many Americans: "It's been a splendid little war." A malaria-ridden veteran of the war had a different view: "I was lucky—I survived."

READING CHECK **Identify Cause and Effect** In what areas of the world was the Spanish-American War fought? Why did the war extend to so many regions?

Analyze Images This photo shows Theodore Roosevelt surrounded by his Rough Riders atop San Juan Hill. **Summarize** How did the Americans win the Spanish-American War in Cuba?

The United States Becomes a Colonial Power

The United States and Spain signed a peace treaty in Paris in December 1898. The treaty ended Spain's colonial rule in the Western Hemisphere. It granted Cuba its freedom and gave the United States two islands: Puerto Rico in the Caribbean and Guam in the Pacific. Finally, in return for $20 million, Spain handed over the Philippines to the United States.

Americans Debate Colonialism Before the Senate approved the treaty, a great debate occurred. Many Americans objected to the treaty. They argued it violated American principles of democracy by turning the United States into a colonial power.

Expansionists favored the treaty. They claimed that the navy needed bases in the Caribbean and the Pacific. Besides, the Philippines and Puerto Rico opened new territory for American businesses. Also, many Americans agreed with President McKinley, who said that the United States would "uplift and civilize and Christianize [the Filipinos]." In fact, most Filipinos already were Christians.

Urged on by McKinley, in February 1899, the Senate narrowly ratified the treaty. At last, the United States possessed a true overseas empire.

An American Protectorate in Cuba When the war with Spain began, the United States pledged to "leave the government and control of [Cuba] to its people." That promise, however, was not kept. After the war, American soldiers remained in Cuba. Many in Congress believed that Cuba was not ready for independence. American business leaders feared that an independent Cuba might threaten their investments.

INTERACTIVE

Causes and Effects of the Spanish-American War

Quest CONNECTIONS

How did U.S. treatment of Cuba and the Philippines compare to U.S. treatment of Hawaii? Record your findings in your Active Journal.

Academic Vocabulary
ultimately • *v.*, at the end of a period of time

In the end, the United States let the Cuban people write their own constitution. However, Cuba had to accept the **Platt Amendment**. The Platt Amendment allowed the United States to intervene in Cuba and gave the United States control of the naval base at Guantanamo Bay. In effect, it made Cuba an American **protectorate**, a nation whose independence is limited by the control of a more powerful country.

The United States pulled its army out of Cuba in 1902. However, American soldiers would return to Cuba in 1906 and again in 1917.

New Government in Puerto Rico In Puerto Rico, the United States set up a new government under the **Foraker Act** of 1900. The Foraker Act gave Puerto Ricans only a limited say in their own affairs. In 1917, Puerto Ricans were made citizens of the United States. Americans set up schools, improved healthcare, and built roads on the island. Even so, many Puerto Ricans wanted to be free of foreign rule.

Filipinos Revolt Filipino nationalists had begun fighting for independence long before the Spanish-American War. When the United States took over their land after the war, Filipinos felt betrayed. Led by Emilio Aguinaldo, they now fought for freedom against a new imperial power: the United States.

Analyze Cartoons This 1902 political cartoon illustrates independent Cuba's attitude toward its new relationship with the United States. **Draw Conclusions** According to the cartoon, what is Cuba's response to the choices given it by the United States?

Aguinaldo, who had fought beside the Americans against Spain, accused the United States of forgetting its beginnings. The United States, he said, was using military force to keep the Filipinos from attaining "the same rights that the American people proclaimed more than a century ago."

The Philippine-American War was the first all-out Asian war in which the United States fought. It dragged on for years. At one point, about 60,000 American troops were fighting there. **Ultimately**, Aguinaldo was captured in 1901, and the war came to an end officially in 1902.

The Philippine-American War was longer and more costly than the Spanish-American War. More than 4,000 Americans died in the Philippines. Nearly 20,000 Filipino soldiers were killed. Another 200,000 civilians died from shelling, famine, and disease.

Analyze Images Emilio Aguinaldo led Filipino nationalists in a war first against Spain and later against the United States. **Infer** How do you think Aguinaldo is regarded by Filipinos today?

In 1902, the United States set up a government in the Philippines similar to the one in Puerto Rico. Filipinos, however, were not made American citizens because the United States planned to give them independence in the future. It was not until 1946, however, that the United States allowed Filipinos to govern themselves.

READING CHECK **Summarize** How did the United States become a colonial power?

Lesson Check

Practice Vocabulary

1. What were the purpose and consequences of the **Platt Amendment**?
2. Why did newspapers engage in **yellow journalism**?
3. What was the effect of making Cuba an American **protectorate**?

Critical Thinking and Writing

4. Generate Explanations Explain how the rebellion in Cuba affected U.S. economic interests.
5. Identify Cause and Effect Explain how the United States got involved in the Spanish-American War.
6. Writing Workshop: Develop a Clear Thesis A thesis is a concise statement of the main idea of an essay. In your Active Journal, write a thesis for your essay describing the expansion and intervention of the United States during the late 1800s and early 1900s.

Theodore Roosevelt, *The Rough Riders*

In 1898, Theodore Roosevelt resigned as Assistant Secretary of the Navy to join in the fight against Spain. He was appointed to form his own regiment. It became known as the Rough Riders.

◀ Theodore Roosevelt

Reading and Vocabulary Support

① Why does Roosevelt describe his regiment as having a "peculiar character"?

② Sinews are muscles and tendons. *Sinewy* means "strong and tough."

③ Someone who is resolute is very determined.

④ When people live under adverse circumstances, they deal with difficult, challenging conditions. Why would Roosevelt want men who had lived under these conditions in his regiment?

We drew recruits from Harvard, Yale, Princeton, and many another college. . . . after they had shown that they knew how to ride and shoot. I may add that in no case was I disappointed in the men thus taken. . . .

These men formed but a small fraction of the whole. . . . I went down to San Antonio myself, where I found the men from New Mexico, Arizona, and Oklahoma. . . .

These were the men who made up the bulk of the regiment, and gave it its peculiar character ①. . . . They were a splendid set of men, these Southwesterners—tall and sinewy ②, with resolute ③, weather-beaten faces, and eyes that looked a man straight in the face without flinching. They included in their ranks men of every occupation; but the three types were those of the cowboy, the hunter, and the mining prospector. . . .

In all the world there could be no better material for soldiers than that afforded by these grim hunters of the mountains, these wild rough riders of the plains. They were accustomed to handling wild and savage horses; they were accustomed to following the chase with the rifle, both for sport and as a means of livelihood. . . . They were hardened to life in the open, and to shifting for themselves under adverse circumstances ④. They were used, for all their lawless freedom, to the rough discipline of the round-up and the mining company. Some of them came from the small frontier towns; but most were from the wilderness, having left their lonely hunters' cabins and shifting cow-camps to seek new and more stirring adventures beyond the sea.

Analyzing Primary Sources

Cite specific evidence from the document to support your answers.

1. **Draw Conclusions** Why do you think the regiment was called the Rough Riders?
2. **Determine Author's Point of View (a)** What are Roosevelt's feelings toward his regiment? **(b)** What can you infer about his attitude toward the war itself?

LESSON 3

U.S. Power in Latin America

GET READY TO READ

START UP

Examine this scene of the construction of the Panama Canal. What challenges do you think the builders of the canal would have had to overcome? Write three or four ideas.

GUIDING QUESTIONS

- Why and how did the United States build the Panama Canal?
- What was Theodore Roosevelt's "big stick" policy in Latin America?
- How did the crisis between the United States and Mexico develop and how did it end?

TAKE NOTES

Literacy Skills Use Evidence

Use the graphic organizer in your Active Journal to take notes as you read the lesson.

PRACTICE VOCABULARY

Use the vocabulary activity in your Active Journal to practice the vocabulary words.

Vocabulary		Academic Vocabulary
isthmus	dollar diplomacy	suppress
Roosevelt Corollary	moral diplomacy	previous

When Theodore Roosevelt became President in 1901, he was determined to build a canal through Panama in Central America. Roosevelt knew that a canal would greatly benefit American commerce and military capability. By avoiding the long trip around South America, ships could shorten the journey from New York City to San Francisco by nearly 8,000 miles.

Taking Land for the Panama Canal

Roosevelt wanted a canal to reduce the cost of shipping goods between the Atlantic and Pacific coasts. In addition, in the event of a war, a canal would enable the navy to quickly move ships back and forth between the Pacific Ocean and the Atlantic Ocean. As President, Roosevelt took on the job of seeing that the canal was built.

Roosevelt Makes an Offer A unique geographical feature, the Isthmus of Panama, provided an ideal location to build a canal.

Academic Vocabulary
suppress • *v.*, to end or stop

An **isthmus** is a narrow strip of land, with water on each side, that connects two larger bodies of land. At the canal site, only 50 miles of land separated the Caribbean Sea and the Pacific Ocean.

To build the canal, Roosevelt had to deal with Colombia, which owned the isthmus. Roosevelt asked Secretary of State John Hay to approach Colombia. Hay offered $10 million cash plus $250,000 a year to rent a strip of land across Panama.

Taking the Canal Zone When Colombia rejected Roosevelt's offer, he was furious. He did not think that the United States should allow Colombians "permanently to bar one of the future highways of civilization."

At times like this, Roosevelt was fond of quoting an African proverb: "Speak softly and carry a big stick, and you will go far." He meant that words should be supported by strong action. Roosevelt knew that some Panamanians wanted to break away from Colombia. He made it known that he would not help Colombia **suppress** the rebels. In fact, he might even support the rebellion.

On November 2, 1903, the American warship *Nashville* dropped anchor in the port of Colón, Panama. The next day, Panamanians rebelled against Colombia.

American forces stopped Colombian troops from crushing the revolt. Panama then declared itself an independent republic. The United States recognized the new nation at once. Panama in turn agreed to let the United States build a canal on terms similar to those Hay had offered to Colombia.

Geography Skills

The Panama Canal was cut through the Isthmus of Panama, a narrow strip of land separating the Atlantic Ocean from the Pacific Ocean.

1. **Movement** In which direction did ships travel to get from the Caribbean Sea to the Pacific Ocean?
2. **Use Visual Information** What natural feature did the engineers take advantage of as they built the canal?

The Panama Canal, 1903–1914

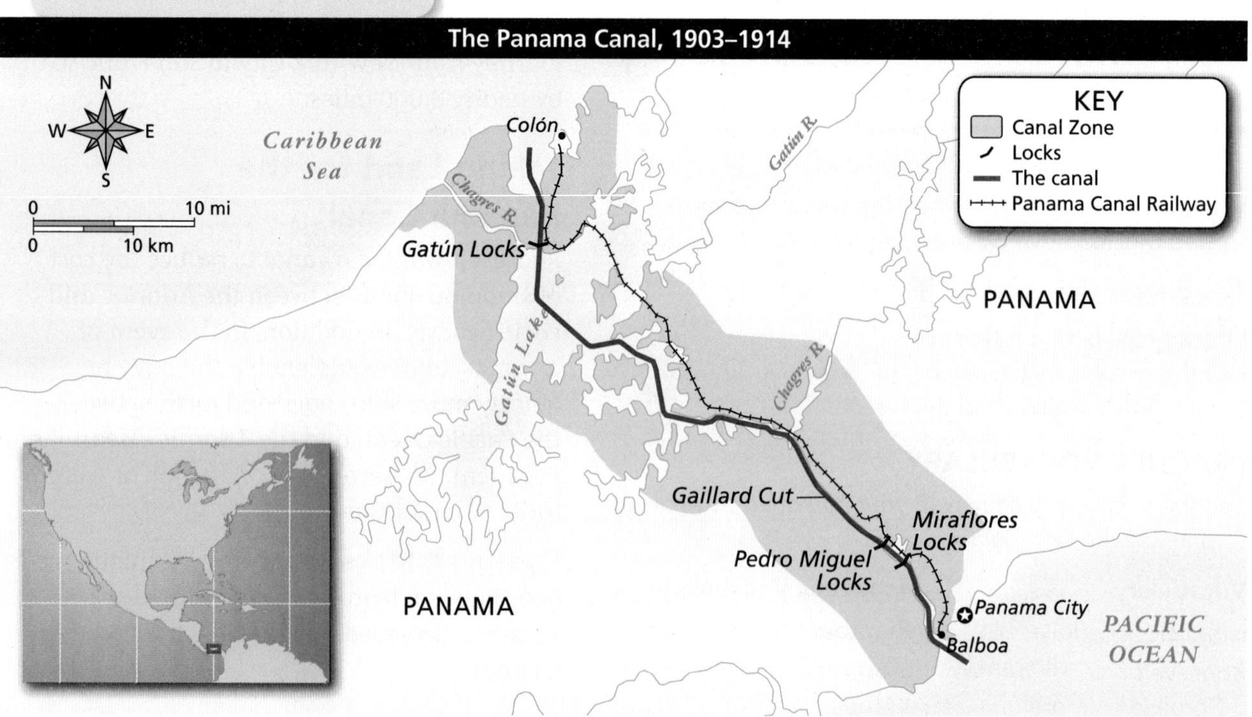

BIOGRAPHY
5 Things to Know About
THEODORE ROOSEVELT

Lieutenant colonel of the Rough Riders and President of the United States (1858–1919)

- As President, Roosevelt moved the United States toward a greater role in world politics.
- Roosevelt won the Nobel Peace Prize for negotiating a peace treaty that ended the Russo-Japanese War.
- As President, Roosevelt aggressively acquired the land and had the Panama Canal constructed.
- An avid outdoorsman, as President, Roosevelt promoted conservation, greatly expanding the national forests and public lands.
- To combat poor health as a child, Roosevelt adopted a strenuous lifestyle of vigorous exercise.

Critical Thinking Why was Roosevelt's presidency significant?

Roosevelt's action in Panama angered many Latin Americans. It also upset some members of Congress. The President, however, proudly stated, "I took the Canal Zone and let Congress debate."

INTERACTIVE
The Panama Canal

READING CHECK **Identify Cause and Effect** Why did Roosevelt get involved in the Panamanian rebellion against Colombia?

Challenges With Construction

Roosevelt now had the right to build his canal. However, before work could begin, Americans had to conquer a deadly enemy: disease.

Preventing Tropical Disease With its tropical heat, heavy rainfall, and plentiful swamps, Panama was a "mosquito's paradise." This presented serious difficulties for the canal builders. Mosquitoes carry two of the deadliest tropical diseases: malaria and yellow fever.

Dr. William Gorgas, an army physician, arrived in Panama in 1905 to help control the mosquitoes and the spread of disease. He ordered workers to locate all pools of water where mosquitoes laid their eggs. Day after day, the workers drained swamps, sprayed tons of insecticide, and spread oil on stagnant water to kill mosquito eggs.

By 1906, Gorgas had won his battle. Yellow fever disappeared from Panama, and malaria cases dropped dramatically. Work on the Panama Canal could proceed.

Difficult Work Under the supervision of army engineer Colonel George Goethals, more than 40,000 workers struggled for over six years to dig the canal route. Most were Caribbean islanders. They blasted a path through mountains and dammed what became the largest artificial lake in the world at that time. In all, they removed more than 200 million cubic yards of earth.

Quick Activity

What do you think was the most difficult part of building the Panama Canal? Write your ideas in your Active Journal.

Then, they built gigantic locks to raise and lower ships as they passed through the canal. Finally, in 1914, the first ocean-going steamship traveled through the Panama Canal.

The new waterway helped the trade of many nations. American merchants and manufacturers benefited most. They could now ship goods cheaply to South America and Asia. However, many Latin American nations remained bitter about the way in which the United States had gained control of Panama.

READING CHECK **Identify Supporting Details** What challenges did the canal builders have to overcome?

INTERACTIVE

Roosevelt's Big Stick Diplomacy

U.S. Intervention in Latin America

The Panama Canal involved the United States more than ever in Latin America. Gradually, President Roosevelt and succeeding Presidents established a policy of intervening in Latin America—especially when disturbances threatened American lives, property, and interests.

Extending the Monroe Doctrine In 1902, several European countries sent warships to force Venezuela to repay its debts. The United States did not want Europeans to interfere in Latin America. President Roosevelt decided that the United States must step in to keep Europeans out. He declared:

Primary Source

"If we intend to say 'Hands off' to the powers of Europe, then sooner or later we must keep order ourselves."

—Theodore Roosevelt, quoted in Brands, *T. R.: The Last Romantic*

Analyze Political Cartoons This 1904 cartoon shows President Roosevelt aggressively swinging his "Big Stick." **Analyze Information** How might the "Big Stick" in the cartoon relate to the Roosevelt Corollary?

In 1904, Roosevelt announced an extension of the Monroe Doctrine. This extension came to be called the **Roosevelt Corollary**. A corollary is an immediate, natural result. The Roosevelt Corollary claimed that the United States had a right to intervene in Latin America to preserve law and order.

By using what he called "international police power," the United States would force Latin Americans to pay their debts to European nations. It would also keep those nations from meddling in Latin American affairs. For the next 20 years, Presidents used the Roosevelt Corollary to justify U.S. intervention in Latin America.

GEOGRAPHY **SKILLS**

The map shows areas of Latin America where the United States chose to exercise its power to influence events.

1. **Interaction** Which of the areas shown on the map were governed directly by the United States?
2. **Analyze Information** Based on the map, when did American involvement in the affairs of these nations begin?

Dollar Diplomacy Roosevelt's successor, William Howard Taft, also favored a strong role in Latin America. However, he wanted to "substitute dollars for bullets." He urged American bankers to invest in Latin America. Taft's policy of building strong economic ties to Latin America became known as **dollar diplomacy**.

American investors responded eagerly. They helped build roads, railroads, and harbors in Latin America. These improvements increased trade, benefiting both the United States and local governments. The new railroads, for example, brought minerals and other resources to Latin American ports. From there, they were shipped all over the world.

Dollar diplomacy created problems, too. American businesses, such as the United Fruit Company, often meddled in the political affairs of host countries. Sometimes, the United States used military force to keep order and protect American-owned plantations, mines, and other business interests. In 1912, when a revolution erupted in Nicaragua, the United States sent in marines to protect American investments.

Moral Diplomacy The next President, Woodrow Wilson, condemned the heavy-handed foreign policy of earlier Presidents. "The force of America," he said, "is the force of moral principle." The stated goals of Wilson's **moral diplomacy** were to condemn imperialism, spread democracy, and promote peace. Nevertheless, Wilson ordered military intervention in Latin America more than any **previous** President. He sent marines to Haiti in 1915 and the Dominican Republic in 1916. American troops remained in Haiti until 1934.

Academic Vocabulary
previous • *v.*, earlier

Wilson declared that U.S. intervention had a moral purpose. Still, many Latin Americans denounced the United States for invading their countries and interfering in their internal affairs.

READING CHECK **Identify Main Ideas** How did Taft's dollar diplomacy differ from Wilson's moral diplomacy?

U.S. Involvement in Mexico

Moral diplomacy faced its greatest test in Mexico. Porfirio Díaz, Mexico's president from 1884 to 1911, welcomed American investment. By 1912, Americans had invested about $1 billion to develop mines, oil wells, railroads, and ranches. Yet, most Mexicans remained poor. They worked the land of a few wealthy families, receiving very little for their labor.

Mexican Revolution Mexicans rebelled against Díaz in 1910. The new leader, Francisco Madero, promised democratic reform. Then, in 1913, Madero was himself overthrown and killed by General Victoriano Huerta (WEHR tuh). As civil war raged, Wilson refused to recognize what he called Huerta's "government of butchers."

Analyze Images In this 1911 photo, *soldaderas*, or women soldiers, train for their role in the Mexican Revolution. **Use Visual Information** What does this image suggest about the importance to Mexicans of the Revolution?

Wilson tried to stay neutral. He hoped that Mexico would develop a democratic government without American interference. As Huerta's dictatorship grew more brutal, however, Wilson authorized the sale of arms to Huerta's rival, Venustiano Carranza.

The United States Intervenes A minor incident led to American intervention. In 1914, Huerta's troops arrested several American sailors. The sailors were quickly released and an apology issued. Still, Wilson ordered the United States Navy to occupy the Mexican port of Veracruz. Rallied by the American show of strength, Carranza's forces drove Huerta from power. The United States troops withdrew.

Still, civil war continued in Mexico. Now, General Francisco "Pancho" Villa led a force in an attempt to overthrow President Carranza. The United States supported Carranza.

In January 1916, Villa's soldiers removed 17 American citizens from a train in Mexico and shot them. In March, Villa raided Columbus, New Mexico, killing 18 Americans.

Villa hoped that his actions would weaken relations between the United States and the Carranza government in Mexico City. But the plan backfired.

The United States Invades Wilson sent General John J. Pershing with several thousand troops into Mexico to capture Pancho Villa. When Mexico demanded that the troops be withdrawn, Wilson refused. Still, both Wilson and Carranza resisted calls for war. After 11 months, Wilson ordered Pershing to withdraw without capturing Villa. The United States had again shown its willingness to use force to protect its interests. The incident strained relations with Mexico.

Analyze Images This photograph shows Mexican leader Pancho Villa (fifth from left) with his staff, in 1911. **Identify Cause and Effect** Why did the U.S. Army pursue Villa?

As United States troops headed home from Mexico, many Americans realized that their nation's role in world affairs had dramatically changed over the years. Now, the United States stationed troops and ships in both Asia and Latin America. American business interests spanned the globe. At the same time, an enormous war had begun in Europe in 1914. With its increased role in international affairs, the United States would find it impossible to stay out of the conflict.

READING CHECK **Summarize** How did U.S. foreign policy toward Mexico change over the course of Wilson's presidency?

Lesson Check

Practice Vocabulary

1. Why did the United States choose an **isthmus** for building the Panama Canal?
2. How was **Roosevelt's Corollary** a result of the Monroe Doctrine?
3. Who established the policy of **moral diplomacy** and what were its goals?

Critical Thinking and Writing

4. Generate Explanations Do you approve of how the United States gained the right to build the Panama Canal? Explain.
5. Draw Conclusions Describe the advantages and disadvantages of dollar diplomacy.
6. Writing Workshop: Pick an Organizing Strategy How will you organize your essay on U.S. expansion and intervention? You might organize it in time order, from most important to least important events, or in some other manner. Write your strategy in your Active Journal.

LESSON 4

A European War

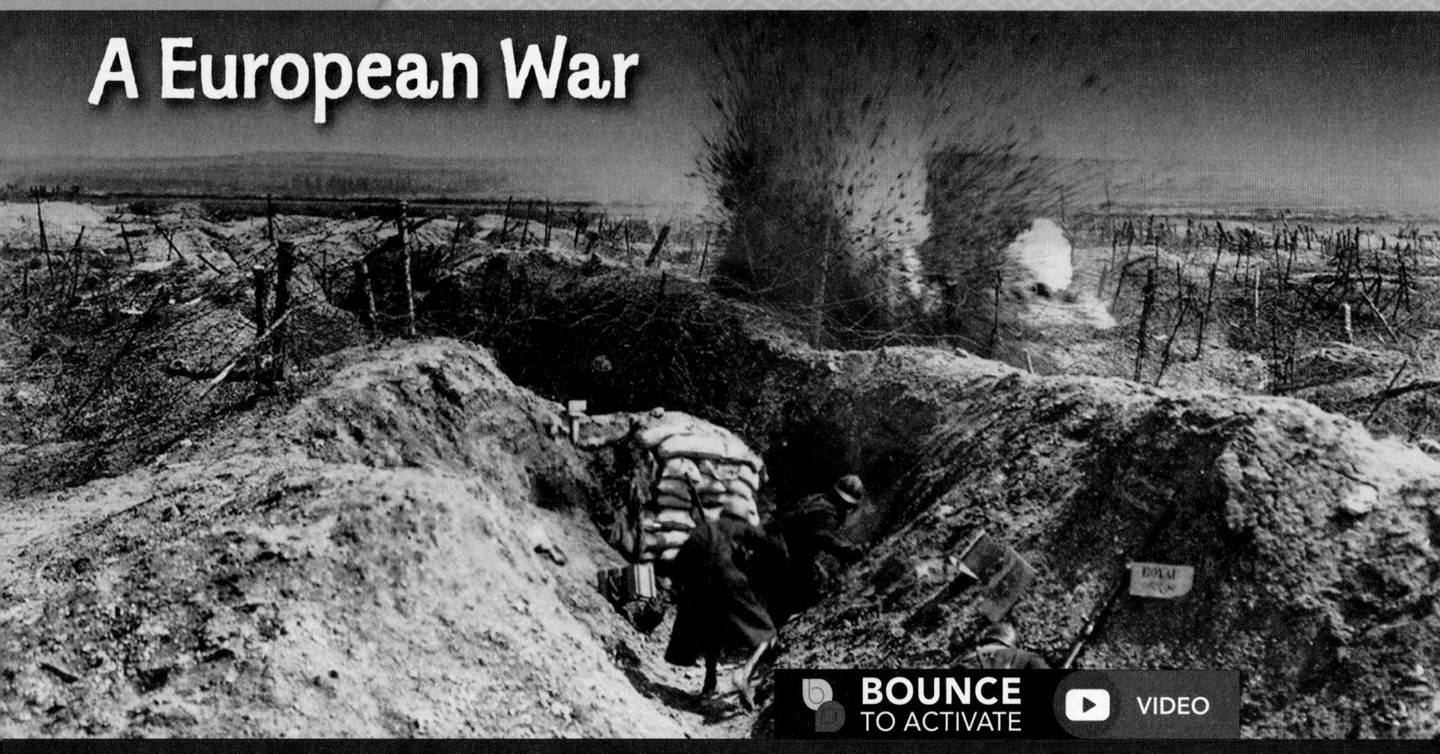

GET READY TO READ

START UP

Examine this photograph of the trenches used in World War I and then preview the lesson. Write three facts you already know about the war.

GUIDING QUESTIONS

- What were the causes of World War I?
- How was war fought in the trenches?
- How did Germany's use of submarine warfare affect American neutrality?

TAKE NOTES

Literacy Skills Sequence

Use the graphic organizer in your Active Journal to take notes as you read the lesson.

PRACTICE VOCABULARY

Use the vocabulary activity in your Active Journal to practice the vocabulary words.

Vocabulary		Academic Vocabulary
nationalism	trench warfare	embroil
militarism	neutral	incline
terrorist	propaganda	
Central Powers	U-boat	
Allied Powers	*Lusitania*	

The First World War ravaged Europe and the Middle East from 1914 to 1918. It was the first war with chemical weapons, aerial warfare, and tank battles. It was called The Great War, but its main feature was carnage. Well over half of soldiers involved became casualties. Why did the United States choose to join in Europe's war?

How Did Tensions in Europe Lead to a Crisis?

The war in Europe was caused by tensions that had been building for years. When they erupted and war began in 1914, few Europeans were surprised.

Nationalism Creates Rivalries One cause of this tension came from the extreme feelings of **nationalism**, or pride in one's nation. In the 1870s, European nationalists demanded freedom and self-government. They believed that people with a common language and culture should throw off foreign rule and form their own countries.

While nationalism encouraged unity, it also created mistrust and bitter rivalry between nations. For example, France and Germany had gone to war in 1870. When France lost the war, it had to give Germany the iron-rich territory of Alsace-Lorraine. The French never forgot this blow to their national pride. They hoped for an opportunity to regain their lost territory.

Chain of Events, 1914

In Eastern Europe, nationalism deepened hostility between Austria-Hungary and Russia. Russia encouraged Serbs and other minorities in Austria-Hungary to rise up against their rulers.

Imperialism and Militarism Another cause of problems in Europe came from imperialism. Between 1870 and 1914, rivalries expanded among powerful nations such as Britain, France, Germany, Italy, and Russia as they scrambled for colonies in Africa, Asia, and the Pacific. Often, several nations competed for power in the same region. This competition sometimes led to wars in places far from Europe.

Militarism was a third source of tension. **Militarism** is the policy of building up strong armed forces to prepare for war. European nations expanded their armies and navies, creating new stresses. For example, when Germany built up its navy, the British responded by adding more ships to their fleet. This race for naval dominance strained relations between the two nations.

The Alliance System To protect themselves, European powers formed rival alliances. Germany organized the Triple Alliance with Austria-Hungary and Italy. France responded by linking itself to Russia and Britain in the Triple Entente (ahn TAHNT).

Analyze Graphs Because of both imperialism and militarism, many European nations had large standing armies. **Draw Conclusions** Were the Allies or the Central Powers better prepared for war?

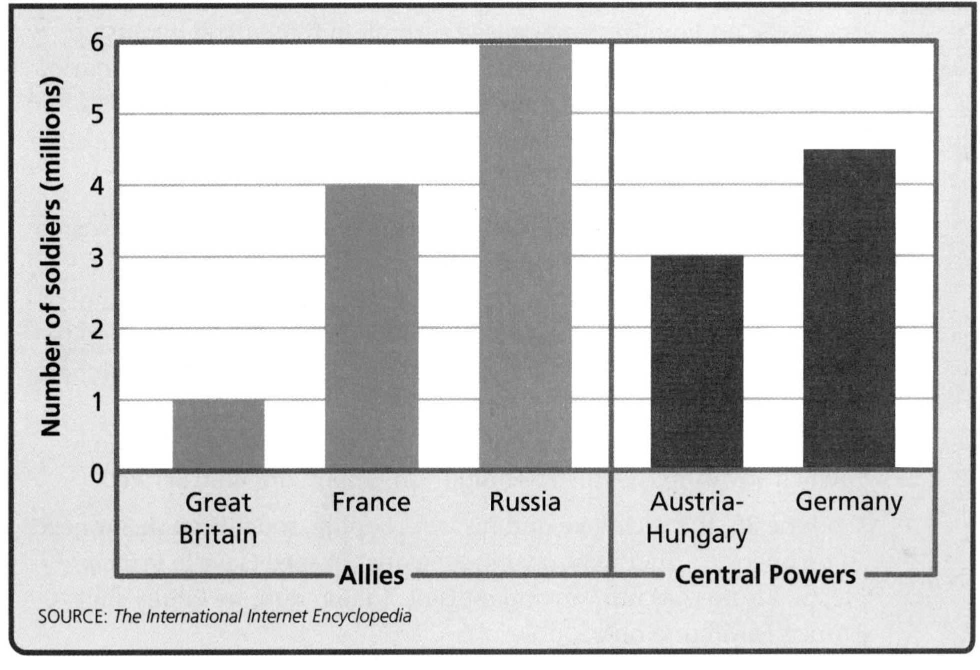

Events Leading to World War I

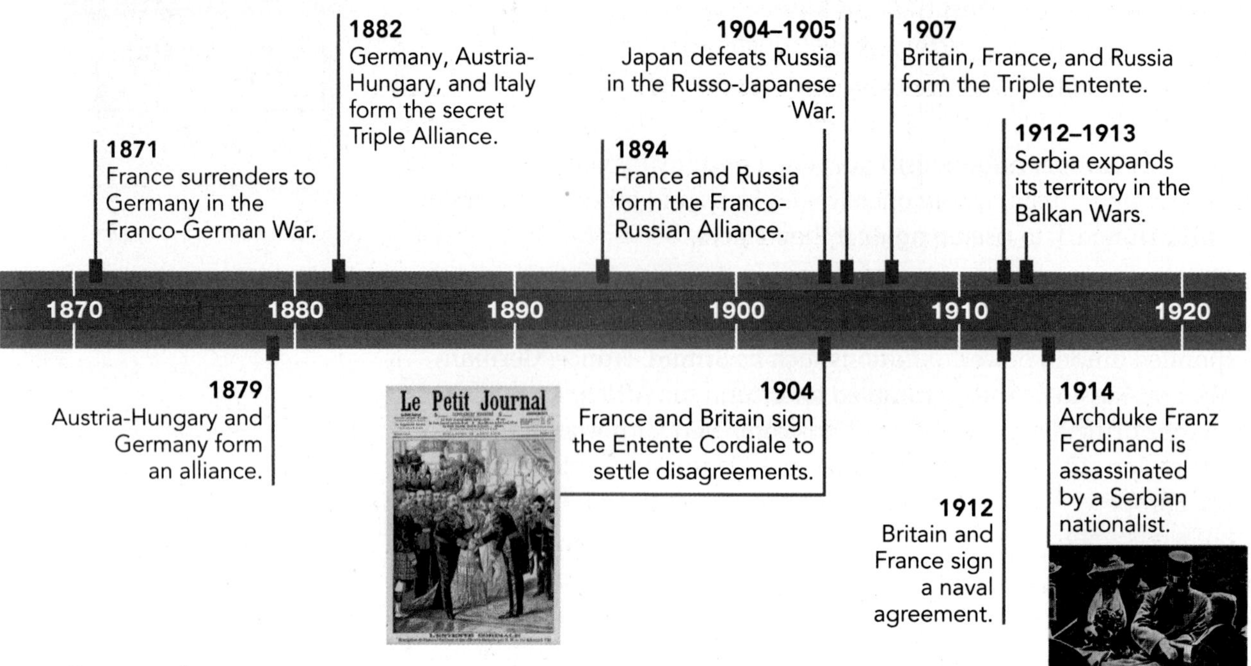

Analyze Timelines
Many events, not just one, contributed to the outbreak of World War I. **Use Evidence** How do the events in the timeline demonstrate the ease with which many European countries could fall into war?

The alliance system posed a new danger. Allies agreed to support one another in case of an attack. Thus, a crisis involving one member of an alliance also affected that nation's allies. This meant that a minor incident could spark a major war. On June 28, 1914, such an incident took place.

READING CHECK **Summarize** What is militarism, and how did it contribute to World War I?

War Breaks Out

For years, nationalism had caused turmoil in the Balkan peninsula in southeastern Europe. There, the rival nations of Albania, Bulgaria, Greece, Montenegro, Romania, and Serbia battled for territory. At the same time, Balkan nationalists called on related ethnic groups in Austria-Hungary to throw off Austrian rule.

Academic Vocabulary
embroil • *v.*, to involve in conflict or difficulties

An Assassination In June 1914, a crisis that would have a devastating effect **embroiled** the region. Archduke Francis Ferdinand, heir to the throne of Austria-Hungary, was visiting Sarajevo, the capital of Bosnia. At the time, Bosnia was part of the Eastern European empire ruled by Austria-Hungary. Francis Ferdinand's visit angered members of the Black Hand, a Serbian terrorist group. A **terrorist** uses threats and violence to promote a cause. The Black Hand wanted Bosnia to break away from the Austro-Hungarian Empire and join Serbia.

On June 28, the archduke and his wife, Sophie, rode through Sarajevo in an open car. Suddenly, a young terrorist named Gavrilo Princip stepped from the curb, waving a pistol. Taking aim, he fatally shot Francis Ferdinand and Sophie.

Allies Declare War In the days that followed, Austria-Hungary accused the Serbian government of organizing the archduke's assassination. When Austria-Hungary threatened war, Russia moved to protect Serbia. Diplomats rushed to ease tensions, but they could not stop the system of alliances from running its fateful course.

On July 28, Austria-Hungary declared war on Serbia. The very next day, Russia ordered its forces to mobilize, or prepare for war. Austria-Hungary's ally, Germany, called on Russia to cancel the mobilization order. When it received no reply, Germany declared war on Russia on August 1.

On August 3, Germany declared war on Russia's ally France. The next day, when German armies sliced through neutral Belgium on their march to France, Britain declared war on Germany. Long before, Britain had promised to defend Belgium if it were attacked. Austria-Hungary declared war on Russia on August 6. In this way, what began as a local crisis in Bosnia exploded into a major war.

READING CHECK **Identify Supporting Details** What details support the idea that the alliance system turned a local crisis into a world war?

A Lengthy Stalemate

The war pitted the **Central Powers**—Germany and Austria-Hungary—against the **Allied Powers**, which were France, Britain (United Kingdom), and Russia, as well as Serbia. In time, other nations joined each side.

GEOGRAPHY SKILLS

The map shows how Europe was divided between the Allies and the Central Powers during World War I.

1. **Location** Name the countries that comprised the Allies and the Central Powers at the start of the war in 1914.
2. **Use Visual Information** Which of the Allies were in a particularly dangerous location? Why?

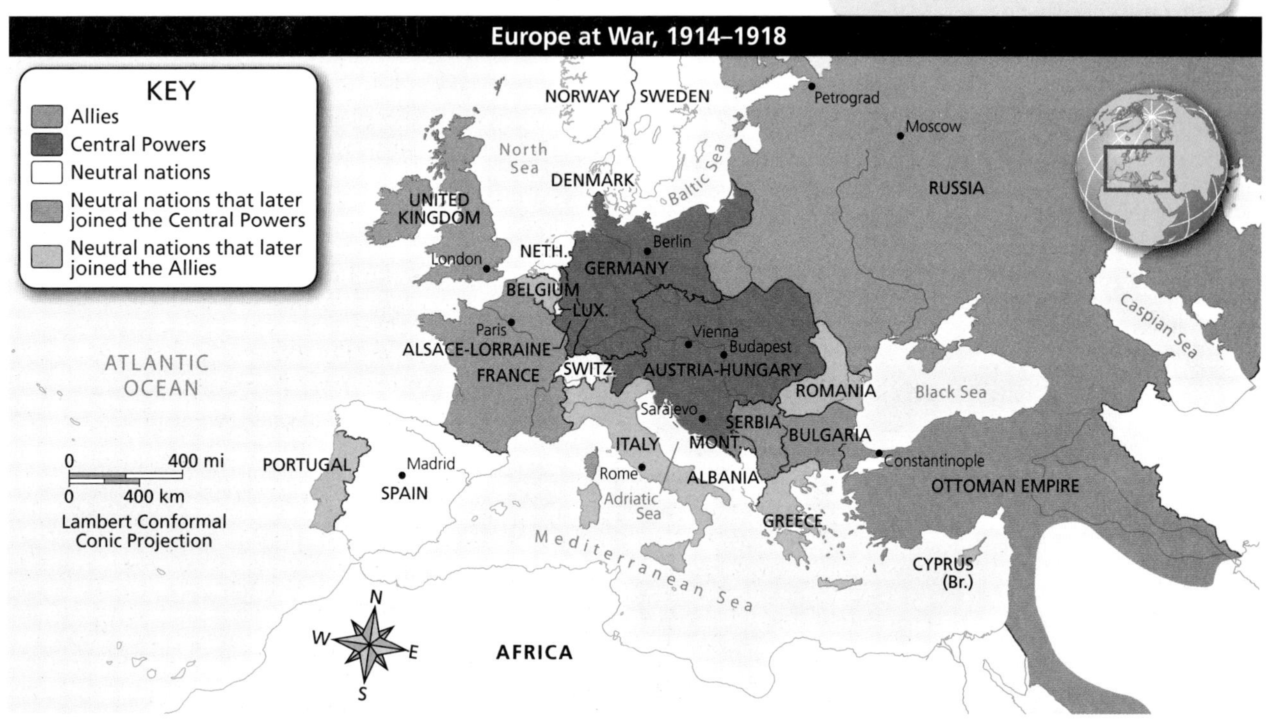

INTERACTIVE

Trench Warfare

The Fighting Begins "You will be home before the leaves have fallen from the trees," the kaiser, or German emperor, promised his troops as they marched off to war. Europeans on both sides of the conflict thought the war would end soon. They were mistaken. The war dragged on for four blood-soaked years, from 1914 to 1918. At the time, the conflict was called the Great War. Later, it became known as the First World War or World War I.

By November 1914, a German advance and an Allied counterattack had produced nothing but a deadly stalemate. A stalemate is a deadlock in which neither side is strong enough to defeat the other. For three years, the two armies fought huge battles with little to show for them.

Quick Activity

What would it be like to live in a trench? Write down your thoughts in your Active Journal.

Both sides dug in, creating a maze of trenches protected by barbed wire. Some trenches were shallow ditches. Others were elaborate tunnels that served as headquarters and first-aid stations. Between the frontline trenches of each side lay a "no man's land" of barbed wire.

Death in the Trenches In **trench warfare**, soldiers spent day after day shelling the enemy trenches. An attack would begin with hours of heavy artillery fire. Then, on orders from an officer, the troops charged "over the top" of the trenches. Armed with their rifles, soldiers raced across no man's land to attack the enemy. With luck, they might overrun a few trenches. Before long, the enemy would launch a counterattack, with similar results. In this way, the struggle went on, back and forth, over a few hundred yards of territory.

A new weapon used on both sides was poison gas—chlorine and mustard were two types. The clouds of gas floated into the trenches, burning, choking, blinding, and often killing the soldiers.

▼ World War I was characterized by trench warfare, a brutal form of fighting that claimed many lives. ❶ Trenches were muddy and infested with rats, frogs, and lice. ❷ Trenches eventually stretched almost 500 miles. ❸ Diseases infected men living in trenches ❹ Between Allied and enemy trenches lay no man's land, a deadly zone for anyone caught there.

Analyze Images This August 1914 anti-war meeting in New York City drew a large crowd. **Identify Main Ideas** Why did some Americans in 1914 favor joining the war?

Because of the nature of trench warfare, most offensives were long and deadly. The Battle of Verdun lasted for 10 months in 1916. The Germans lost some 400,000 men trying to overrun French lines. The French lost even more lives defending their positions.

Meanwhile, in the East, the vast armies of Germany and Austria-Hungary faced off against those of Russia and Serbia. Stalemate and trench warfare brought deadly results there as well. By mid-1916, the Russians had lost more than one million soldiers. Yet, neither side could win a decisive victory.

READING CHECK **Identify Cause and Effect** What were the effects of trench warfare?

The United States Tries to Avoid the Conflict

When war broke out in Europe, the United States was determined to avoid being dragged into the conflict. The government adopted an official position of neutrality. **Neutral** means not taking sides in a conflict.

Public opinion, however, was divided, often along ethnic lines. Most Americans were **inclined** to support the Allies because of long-standing ties of language, history, and culture through Britain. Also, the United States and France had been allies in the American Revolution.

Academic Vocabulary
incline • *v.,* to tend or to become drawn toward an opinion or action

On the other hand, many of the 8 million Americans of German or Austrian descent favored the Central Powers. Millions of Irish Americans also sympathized with the Central Powers. They hated the British, who had ruled Ireland for centuries.

Because some of them had fled persecution in Russia only a few years earlier, many American Jews initially favored Germany over Russia. When the United States entered the war, many Jews enlisted and fought in the American armed forces.

World War I Technology

Effects on the United States The war had several immediate effects on the United States. First, the economy boomed as American farmers and manufacturers rushed to fill orders for war goods. By 1917, trade with the Allies had greatly increased. Trade with the Central Powers also increased but by a much smaller amount. This trade imbalance meant that the United States was not strictly neutral.

Both sides waged a propaganda war in the United States. **Propaganda** is the deliberate spreading of ideas that help a cause or hurt an opposing cause. Each side pictured the other as savage beasts who killed innocent civilians.

U-boats Attack Early in the war, Britain blockaded German ports, hoping to starve Germany into surrender. In response, Germany set up a blockade around Britain. To enforce the blockade, Germany used a powerful new weapon—a fleet of submarines known as **U-boats**. German U-boats attacked any ship that entered or left British ports. This meant that neutral ships were also attacked.

U-boat attacks on neutral shipping raised a storm of protest. Under international law, a country at war could stop and search a ship suspected of carrying war goods. However, German submarines were not equipped to conduct a search. They simply torpedoed enemy and neutral ships, often killing scores of civilians.

As a neutral nation, the United States claimed the right to trade with either side in the conflict. However, Germany warned the United States and other neutral nations to keep their ships out of the blockade zone.

Analyze Images This photo shows the engine room of a WWI German U-boat. **Use Visual Information** Describe what you see in the photo. What does this suggest about the dangers of serving on a U-boat?

President Wilson responded by vowing to hold Germany responsible if its U-boats caused any loss of American life or property.

Germany Sinks the Lusitania Germany ignored Wilson's warning. On May 7, 1915, a German submarine torpedoed the **Lusitania**, a British passenger ship, off the coast of Ireland. Nearly 1,200 people died, including 128 Americans. An outraged Wilson threatened to break off diplomatic relations, or official ties, if Germany did not stop sinking passenger ships.

Germany was not ready to strengthen the Allies by drawing the United States into the war. It agreed to restrict its submarine campaign. Before attacking any ship, U-boats would surface and give warning. This agreement, called the Sussex Pledge, kept the United States out of the war a little longer.

Analyze Images Nearly 1,200 people, including 128 American citizens, died when a German U-boat sank the *Lusitania* in 1915. **Infer** How do you think images like this made Americans feel about Germany?

READING CHECK **Summarize** What difficulties did the United States face in attempting to stay neutral during World War I?

Lesson Check

Practice Vocabulary

1. How did a **terrorist** start World War I?
2. Which nations made up the **Central Powers** and the **Allied Powers**?
3. Why were **U-boats** such a danger to ships like the *Lusitania*?

Critical Thinking and Writing

4. **Draw Conclusions** How did nationalism increase tensions between European countries?
5. **Compare Points of View** Describe American public opinion regarding World War I, and explain how this related to the official position of the United States.
6. **Writing Workshop: Write an Introduction** Write an introduction to your essay about U.S. expansion and intervention during the late 1800s and early 1900s. Be sure to include your thesis statement in your introduction.

LESSON 5

Entering the War

GET READY TO READ

START UP

When war came, American women like these went to work in munitions factories and other jobs. How did the war change their lives?

GUIDING QUESTIONS

- Why did the United States declare war?
- How did the government prepare for and manage the war effort?
- How did the war affect Americans at home?

TAKE NOTES

Literacy Skills Summarize

Use the graphic organizer in your Active Journal to take notes as you read the lesson.

PRACTICE VOCABULARY

Use the vocabulary activity in your Active Journal to practice the vocabulary words.

Vocabulary

- warmonger
- Zimmermann telegram
- Selective Service Act
- illiterate
- bureaucracy
- Liberty Bond
- pacifist
- socialism

Academic Vocabulary

- exposure
- embark

Early in the war, President Wilson tried to bring both sides to peace talks. He believed that the United States, as a neutral nation, could lead warring nations to a fair peace, a "peace without victory." But Wilson's peace efforts failed.

How Did the U.S. Move Toward War?

Even as he was trying to make peace, Wilson knew that the United States might be drawn into the war. Thus, the President began to lobby for a stronger army and navy.

In 1916, Wilson ran for reelection against Republican Charles Evans Hughes. Although Hughes also favored neutrality, Democrats were able to portray him as a **warmonger**, or person who tries to stir up war. At the same time, they boosted Wilson's image with the slogan "He kept us out of war!"

The race was close. On election night, Hughes went to bed believing he had won. Just after midnight, his telephone rang. "The President cannot be disturbed," a friend told the caller.

"Well, when he wakes up," the caller replied, "just tell him he isn't President." Late returns from California had given Wilson the election.

Diplomacy Ends In January 1917, Wilson issued what proved to be his final plea for peace. It was too late.

In a desperate effort to break the Allied blockade, Germany had already decided to renew submarine warfare. Germany warned neutral nations that after February 1, 1917, its U-boats would have orders to sink any ship nearing Britain. German leaders knew that renewed U-boat attacks would probably bring the United States into the war. They gambled that they would defeat the Allies before American troops could reach Europe.

To protest Germany's action, Wilson broke off diplomatic relations with Germany.

The Zimmermann Note A few weeks later, in February, a startling discovery moved the United States closer to war. President Wilson learned that Arthur Zimmermann, Germany's foreign secretary, had sent a secret note to the German minister in Mexico. The **Zimmermann telegram** instructed the minister to urge Mexico to attack the United States if the United States declared war on Germany. In return, Germany would help Mexico win back its "lost provinces" in the American Southwest, which would include all of Texas, Arizona, and New Mexico. When Americans heard about the Zimmermann telegram, anti-German feeling soared.

The Russian Revolution Two other events in early 1917 pushed the United States still closer to war. First, German submarines sank several American merchant ships. Second, a revolution in Russia drove Czar Nicholas II from power.

Analyze Graphs The race for president in 1916 was between Woodrow Wilson and Charles Hughes. **Draw Conclusions** Based on the graphs, what conclusions can you draw about the American public's opinion of Woodrow Wilson?

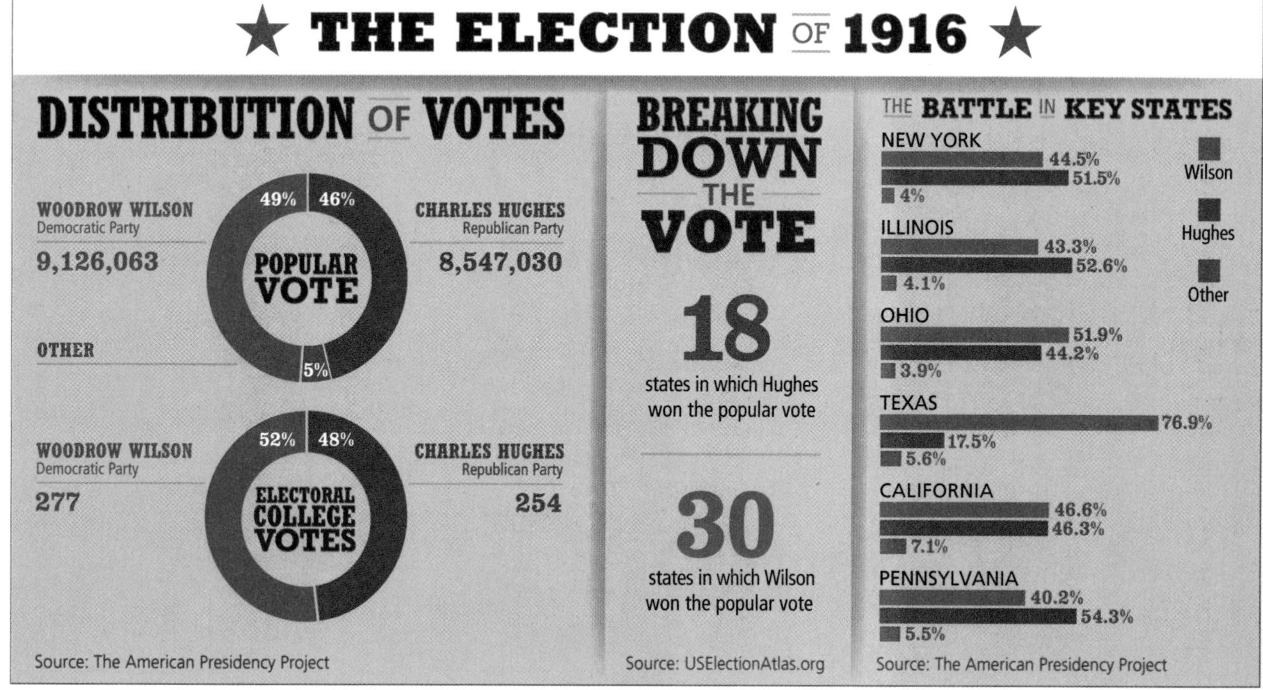

For hundreds of years, czars, or Russian emperors, had ruled with absolute power. Several times in the 1800s and early 1900s, Russians revolted against czarist rule. Their efforts ended in failure.

When the war in Europe began in 1914, Russians united behind the czar. However, as the war brought heavy losses at the front and economic hardship at home, discontent resurfaced. In March 1917, riots protesting the shortage of food turned into a revolution. The czar was forced to step down. Revolutionaries then set up a provisional government and called for democratic reforms.

President Wilson welcomed the Russian Revolution. He was a firm believer in democracy, and it was against his principles to be an ally of an absolute ruler. Without the czar, it would be easier for Wilson to support the Allied cause.

Declaration of War Finally, President Wilson went before Congress on April 2, 1917, to ask for a declaration of war. "The world must be made safe for democracy," he declared. His war message assured the American people that entering the war was not only just; it was noble.

Congress voted for war 455 to 56. Among those who voted against the declaration was Jeannette Rankin of Montana, the first woman elected to Congress. She hated war as much as she loved her country. "I want to stand by my country, but I cannot vote for war. I vote no!" she said.

On April 6, the President signed the declaration of war. It thrust Americans into the deadliest war the world had yet seen.

READING CHECK **Sequence** Outline the events that led the United States into World War I.

Americans Prepare for War

The day after Congress declared war, George M. Cohan wrote a new song. The patriotic tune swept the nation. Its opening lines expressed the confidence that Americans felt:

Analyze Images Less than five months after his re-election in November 1916, President Wilson read his war message to Congress. **Identify Cause and Effect** What made President Wilson change his mind about entering the war?

★ BUILDING THE ARMED FORCES ★

THE U.S. MILITARY 1917–1918

4,700,000 U.S. DRAFTEES

- 4,281,800 WHITE
- 400,000 AFRICAN AMERICAN
- 5,700 MEXICAN AMERICAN
- 12,500 AMERICAN INDIAN

Source: National Center for Biotechnology Information

WOMEN'S JOBS IN THE MILITARY

- Clerk
- Nurse
- Driver
- Translator
- Cryptologist
- Telephone operator

30,000 WOMEN joined the United States military between 1917 and 1918

Source: National Women's History Museum

TRAINING THE RECRUITS

1,600%	increase in size of U.S. Navy training facilities between 1917 to 1918
29,650	cadets trained as pilots from 1917–1918
500	colleges and universities establish Student Army Training Corps programs

Source: National Center for Biotechnology Information

MILITARY EXPENDITURES 1916–1918

Billions of current dollars

0, 2, 4, 6, 8, 10

1916, 1917, 1918

Source: EH.net

3.5 MILLION rifles produced during the war

Analyze Graphs As soon as the United States entered the war, it had to build up its armed forces and prepare them to go overseas. **Draw Conclusions** Based on the data, what can you conclude about the popularity of the war among Americans?

Primary Source

"Over there, over there,
Send the word, send the word, over there,
That the Yanks are coming . . ."

—George M. Cohan, "Over There," 1917

Its closing message promised, "We'll be over, we're coming over, And we won't come back till it's over over there."

Americans had to do more than sing patriotic tunes, however. They had to prepare to fight—and quickly. The Allies needed everything from food to arms. Britain and France were on the verge of collapse. In Russia, soldiers were deserting to join the Russian Revolution.

The Military Expands Before it could fight, the United States needed to enlarge its armed forces. On May 18, 1917, Congress passed the **Selective Service Act**. It required all men from ages 21 to 30 to register for the military draft. A draft is a law requiring people of a certain age to serve in the military.

In the next 18 months, 4 million men and women joined the armed forces. People from every ethnic group enlisted. About 20,000 Puerto Ricans served in the armed forces, as did many Filipinos. Scores of soldiers were immigrants who had recently arrived in the United States.

Many American Indians were not citizens, so they could not be drafted. Large numbers of American Indians enlisted anyway. One family of Winnebago Indians provided 35 volunteers. They served together in the same unit.

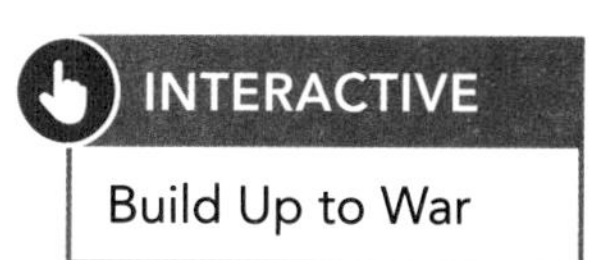

More than 2 million African Americans registered for the draft, although at first the armed forces did not allow them in combat. When the government abandoned this policy, nearly 400,000 were accepted for duty. They were formed into segregated "Black only" units that were commanded mostly by white officers. Still, African Americans rallied to the war effort.

Academic Vocabulary
exposure • *n.,* the condition of experiencing something or being affected by something

Educating Recruits For many recruits, the army offered several firsts. It was their first **exposure** to military authority and discipline. It was the first time most had ventured outside their farms and villages, let alone outside their country. Some had never taken regular baths or eaten regular meals before. Others had never used indoor plumbing. About 25 percent were **illiterate**, that is, unable to read or write. The army became a great educator. It taught millions of young Americans not only how to fight but also how to read, how to plan and eat nutritious meals, and how to care for their daily health needs.

Shocking rates of illiteracy and other low test scores among recruits fueled a drive to reform public education. State and local school boards lengthened the school day and required students to spend more years in school. They raised teacher-training standards. More truancy officers patrolled the streets. By 1920, nearly 75 percent of all school-age children were enrolled in school.

READING CHECK **Summarize** How did the United States expand its military?

Organizing a Massive War Effort

The United States reorganized its economy to produce food, arms, and the many other goods needed to fight the war. President Wilson set up government agencies to oversee the effort. A huge bureaucracy (byoo ROK ruh see) emerged to manage the war effort. A **bureaucracy** is a system of managing government through departments run by appointed officials.

Analyze Images This image shows new recruits training to use machine guns. **Use Visual Information** What does the picture tell you about how recruits were prepared?

Food Production Wilson chose Herbert Hoover to be head of the Food Administration. Hoover's job was to boost food production to feed American troops and send food to the Allies. Hoover relied on cooperation rather than force. He tried to win support for his programs with publicity campaigns that encouraged Americans to act voluntarily. "Food Will Win the War," proclaimed one Food Administration poster.

In response, citizens planted "victory gardens" to raise their own vegetables. People went without wheat on "wheatless Mondays" and without meat on "meatless Tuesdays." The food they saved helped feed the men in the trenches.

U.S. farm production also increased. The war in Europe decreased worldwide food supplies. That caused food prices to rise, which encouraged American farmers to grow more crops.

Industry War caught the nation short of military supplies. The U.S. Army had on hand only around 600,000 rifles, 2,000 machine guns, and fewer than 1,000 pieces of artillery. Disorder threatened as the military competed with private industry to buy scarce materials.

To meet this crisis, President Wilson set up a new government agency, the War Industries Board. It told factories what they had to produce. It also provided for the sharing of limited resources and decided what prices should be set.

Without the support of workers, industry could not mobilize. In 1918, Wilson created the War Labor Board. It settled disputes over working hours and wages and tried to prevent strikes. With workers in short supply, unions were able to win better pay and working conditions. Railroad workers, for example, gained a large wage increase and an eight-hour workday. With the President supporting workers, union membership rose sharply and labor unrest declined.

Analyze Images This poster encouraged Americans to plant "victory gardens." **Infer** *Munition* means "military weapon or equipment." What does the caption "Every Garden a Munition Plant" mean?

Financing the War Conducting a war also required paying for it. The War Revenue Act sharply raised taxes on personal and corporate income. Additionally, movie stars, such as Charlie Chaplin and Mary Pickford, helped sell **Liberty Bonds**. By buying bonds, American citizens were lending money to the government to pay for the war. The sale of Liberty Bonds raised $21 billion, just over half of what the United States spent on the war.

To rally public support for the war, the government sent out 75,000 men known as "Four-Minute Men" to speak to the American people. The name reminded people of the heroic minutemen of 1776. It also referred to the four-minute speeches the men gave at public events, movies, and theatrical productions. The speakers urged Americans to make sacrifices for the goals of freedom and democracy.

READING CHECK **Summarize** How did United States domestic policy boost production during the war?

Analyze Images Celebrities such as movie star Charlie Chaplin, shown here, encouraged Americans to buy Liberty Bonds. **Identify Supporting Details** Why did Americans buy Liberty Bonds?

Changes at Home

The changes brought about by the war affected Americans' lives in a variety of ways.

Women Join the Work Force As men joined the armed forces, women stepped into men's jobs. Women received better pay in war industries than they had in peacetime. Still, they earned less than the men they replaced.

In factories, women assembled military goods such as weapons and airplane parts. Some women drove trolley cars and delivered the mail. Others served as police officers, railroad engineers, or electric-lift truck drivers. By performing well in jobs once reserved for men, women helped change the view that they were fit only for "women's work." Most of the gains made by women later disappeared when the men returned to the workforce at the end of the war. Thousands of women lost jobs as army defense workers.

Anti-German Prejudice German Americans endured suspicion and intolerance during the war. Newspapers questioned their loyalty. Mobs attacked them on the streets. In 1918, a mob lynched Robert Prager, whose only crime was that he had been born in Germany. A jury later refused to convict the mob leaders.

Anti-German prejudice led some families to change their names. Schools stopped teaching the German language. Americans began referring to German measles as "liberty measles" and sauerkraut as "liberty cabbage."

INTERACTIVE

World War I Homefront

Urban Migration The war spurred migration within the nation. Immigration from abroad had stopped. The draft drained cities and factories of needed workers. But cities soon swelled with newcomers.

During the war, almost a half million African Americans and thousands of Mexican Americans **embarked** on a great migration from the South and Southwest to cities in the North.

Academic Vocabulary
embark • *v.*, to make a start

In northern cities, many African Americans found better-paying jobs in war industries. As a result, African American migration continued after the war ended. At the same time, however, they ran into prejudice and even violence. Competition for housing and jobs sometimes led to race riots. Thirty-nine African Americans were killed during a 1917 riot in East St. Louis, Illinois. A New York parade protested the deaths. Marchers carried signs demanding, "Mr. President, Why Not Make AMERICA Safe for Democracy?"

International Migration In the Southwest, ranchers pressed the government to let more Mexicans cross the border. Almost 100,000 Mexicans entered the United States to work on farms. By 1920, Mexicans were the leading foreign-born group in California. Some Mexicans moved on to northern cities to work in factories.

Throughout the war, Mexicans worked in cotton and beet fields, in copper mines, and in steel mills. All these jobs were important to the war effort. Yet after the war, when veterans returned and unemployment grew, the United States tried to force Mexican workers to return to Mexico.

READING CHECK **Classify and Categorize** Which groups saw permanent changes in their situations because of the war? Which groups experienced only temporary changes?

Analyze Images This photo shows African American women preparing leg wraps known as spiral puttees for shipping in a New York factory in 1917. **Recognize Multiple Causes** Why did African Americans move north in the early years of the 1900s?

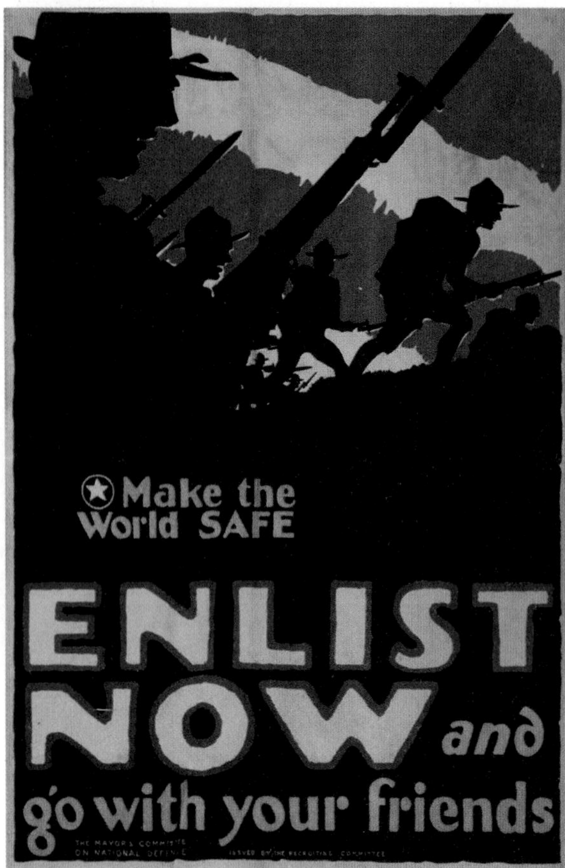

Analyze Images Once America entered the war, recruiting posters like this one from 1917 began to appear. **Summarize** Why did the United States need to persuade Americans to enlist?

Silencing Opposition

Some Americans opposed the war. Among them were Progressives such as Jane Addams. Many of these critics were **pacifists**, people who refuse to fight in any war because they believe that all war is wrong.

Antiwar feeling also ran high among Socialists and radical labor groups. **Socialism** is an economic system in which individuals own personal property but the public owns the means of production, such as factories and natural resources. Socialists argued that the war benefited factory owners but not workers.

To encourage unity, Congress passed laws making it a crime to criticize the government or to interfere with the war effort. Nearly 1,600 men and women were arrested for breaking these laws. Eugene V. Debs, Socialist Party candidate for President five times, was jailed for protesting the draft.

The government also jailed "Big Bill" Haywood, head of the Industrial Workers of the World (IWW), a radical union. Using special powers granted under the wartime laws, government authorities ransacked the IWW's offices.

A few people questioned these laws. They argued that silencing critics violated the Constitution's guarantee of freedom of speech. Most Americans, however, felt that the laws were necessary in wartime.

READING CHECK **Understand Effects** How were freedom of speech, of the press, and of association restricted during the war?

Lesson Check

Practice Vocabulary

1. How did the **Zimmermann telegram** help draw the United States into World War I?
2. What was the **Selective Service Act**, and why did the United States adopt it during World War I?
3. Why would a **pacifist** oppose the U.S. entry into World War I?

Critical Thinking and Writing

4. **Summarize** What changes occurred in United States migration patterns because of the war?
5. **Identify Main Ideas** How did women's roles change in the United States during World War I?
6. **Writing Workshop: Support Thesis with Details** Write details you have learned from reading this topic that support your thesis statement. You will use these details as you draft your essay. Based on your reading, you may also wish to revise your thesis statement.

LESSON 6

Winning the War

GET READY TO READ

START UP

These soldiers are celebrating the end of the war. Write three specific questions you would like to ask these soldiers about their experiences in the war.

GUIDING QUESTIONS

- What setbacks did the Allies suffer in 1917 and 1918?
- How did the American Expeditionary Forces help the Allies win the war?
- What was the toll on human life during World War I?

TAKE NOTES

Literacy Skills Analyze Text Structure

Use the graphic organizer in your Active Journal to take notes as you read the lesson.

PRACTICE VOCABULARY

Use the vocabulary activity in your Active Journal to practice the vocabulary words.

Vocabulary

- American Expeditionary Forces (AEF)
- Battle of Belleau Wood
- Battle of the Argonne Forest
- armistice
- epidemic

Academic Vocabulary

- intense
- prerequisite

For two years, the war in Europe was largely stalemated. As an example: From July to November 1916, over a million soldiers were killed in the Battle of the Somme. In those five months of fighting, the Allies advanced only five miles.

Both sides had trouble keeping troops in the field. An Italian soldier despaired:

Primary Source

"Do not think that this is war. This is not war. It is the ending of the world."

—A wounded soldier, quoted in *World War One: The Global Conflict that Defined a Century*

Allied Setbacks

In 1917 and early 1918, as the United States was preparing for battle and starting to send troops to Europe, the Allies suffered major setbacks. One of those was the loss of a key partner.

Analyze Images The German army overwhelmed Belgium. This image shows German troops occupying Brussels' central square. **Summarize** How did the Germans plan to win the war?

Russia Withdraws From the War

In November 1917, a group known as the Bolsheviks seized power in Russia. Led by Vladimir I. Lenin, the Bolsheviks staged a Communist revolution. Lenin embraced the ideas of Karl Marx, a German thinker of the 1800s. Marx had predicted that workers around the world would unite to overthrow the ruling class. After the workers revolted, they would do away with private property and set up a classless society.

Lenin opposed the war, arguing that it benefited only the ruling class. Once in power, he opened peace talks with Germany. In March 1918, Russia and Germany signed the Treaty of Brest-Litovsk, ending Russia's participation in the war. The treaty was harsh, requiring Russia to give up large amounts of land to Germany. Still, Lenin welcomed peace. With Russia out of the war, he could focus on the Communist revolution.

The Allies saw the treaty as a betrayal. Besides land, it gave Germany coal mines and other valuable resources. More important, with Russia out of the struggle, Germany now moved its armies away from the Russian, or eastern, front to support its armies in France.

The German Offensive In early 1918, the Germans mobilized their troops for what they called a "peace offensive"—an all-out attack on the Allies. They hoped that a final push would end the war before the Americans could rescue the Allies.

By March 21, dozens of German divisions had massed near the French town of Amiens. Late at night, 6,000 German cannons began pounding a small British force. Despite the heavy fire, the British held on for two weeks. At last, on April 4, the Germans gave up their attack.

The Germans continued their offensive elsewhere. By late May, they had smashed through Allied lines along the Aisne (EHN) River.

On May 30, they reached the Marne River near Château-Thierry (SHA toh tee ER ee). Paris lay only 50 miles away. As France prepared to evacuate the capital, American troops entered the war in force.

READING CHECK **Identify Supporting Details** How did Russia's withdrawal from the war affect the Allies?

American Soldiers Arrive in Europe

By June 1918, American troops were reaching France in large numbers. More than one million American troops would arrive. Commanding the **American Expeditionary Forces (AEF)** was General John J. Pershing. Pershing was already well known at home. He had led American troops into Mexico in 1916 to hunt for Mexican rebel leader Francisco "Pancho" Villa.

Allied generals wanted the fresh troops to reinforce their own war-weary soldiers. Pershing refused. He insisted that American troops operate as separate units. The United States wanted to have an independent role in shaping the peace. Only by playing "a definite and distinct part" in the war would it win power at the peace table.

In the end, Pershing agreed to let some Americans fight with the British and French. At the same time, he set up an American operation to fight on its own.

African American Soldiers Among the first American units attached to the French Army was the 369th United States Infantry. This African American unit became known as the Harlem Hellfighters. Although the United States allowed few African Americans to train for combat, the French respected the bravery of African American soldiers and were glad to fight side by side with them.

The Harlem Hellfighters spent more time under fire than any other American unit. For their bravery, the French awarded them the *Croix de Guerre*, their highest military honor, and numerous other decorations.

Key Battles Fought by Americans in World War I

GEOGRAPHY **SKILLS**

This map shows major battles that American forces participated in and how the front lines shifted between July and November 1918.

1. **Location** Based on the position of the Allied front lines, summarize Germany's position in the war as of July 1918.
2. **Draw Conclusions** How did the entry of American forces into the war, change the momentum of the fighting? How do you know?

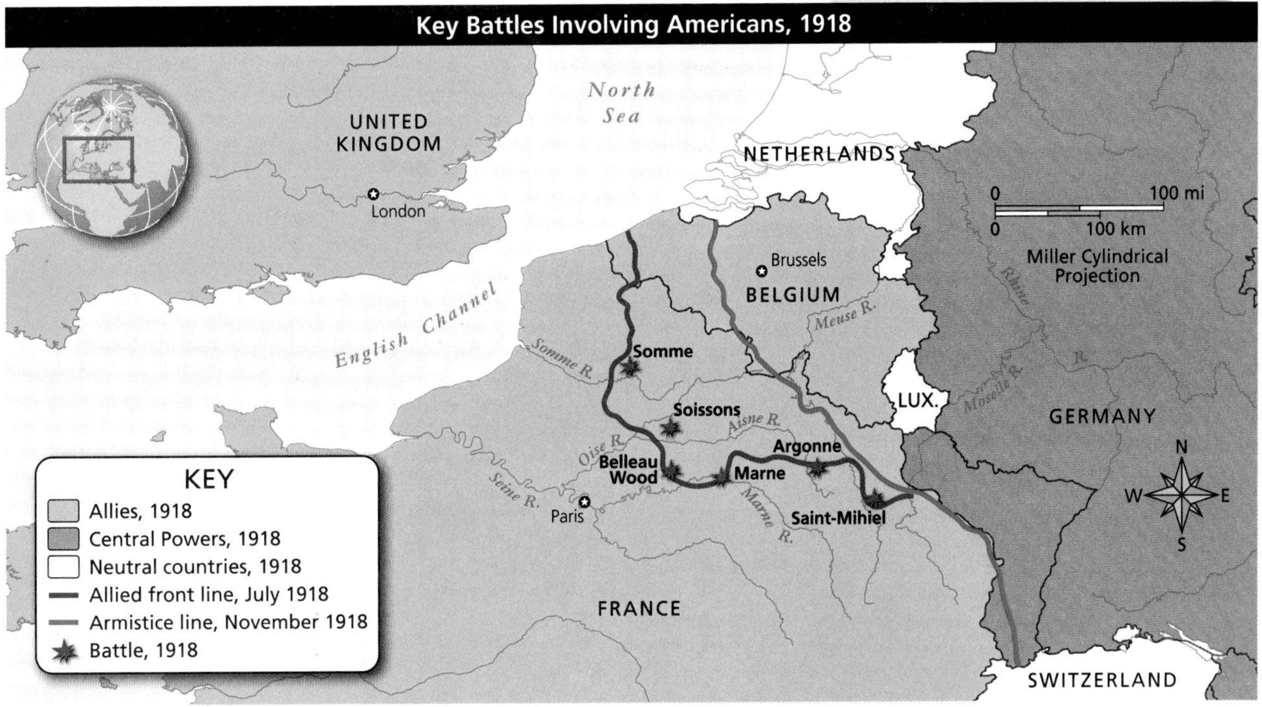

Analyze Images The African American soldiers known as Harlem Hellfighters served with distinction in the French army. **Infer** How do you think African American soldiers felt upon their return to the United States?

After the war, New Yorkers greeted the returning Hellfighters with a huge parade. "God bless you, boys!" they cheered. The unit commander felt a rush of joy. "They did not welcome us [as] a regiment of colored soldiers," he said, but as "a regiment of men who had done the work of men."

Did you know?

Around 2 million New Yorkers turned out for a parade to celebrate the Hellfighters upon their return from the war.

Battle of Belleau Wood In June 1918, American troops plunged into their first major battle in Belleau (BEH loh) Wood, outside Paris. A French general sent U.S. General James Harbord instructions: "Have your men prepare entrenchments some hundreds of yards to the rear in case of need." Harbord sent back a firm reply: "We dig no trenches to fall back on. The marines will hold where they stand."

During the three-week-long **Battle of Belleau Wood**, the inexperienced but combat-ready Americans performed bravely. Expert marksmen hit their targets from hundreds of yards away. Individual soldiers charged German machine gun nests. When one man fell, another stepped in promptly to take his place. The Americans suffered great casualties. But at last, on June 25, they emerged victorious from the woods. General Harbord passed along the good news: "Wood now exclusively U.S. Marine Corps."

READING CHECK **Summarize** Why did the American Expeditionary Forces remain separate from other Allied forces?

Victory for the Allies

In mid-July, the Germans launched another drive to take Paris. They pushed the Allies back until they came up against American troops. Within three days, the Allies, with American help, had forced the Germans to retreat.

INTERACTIVE

Life of American Soldiers in World War I

The Final Offensive The Allies now struck back. French Marshal Ferdinand Foch (FOHSH), commander of the Allied forces, ordered "Everyone to battle!" On September 26, 1918, more than one million

American soldiers began the assault that would become the **Battle of the Argonne Forest**. Years of fierce fighting had left the land scarred with trenches and shell holes, and the air still smelled of poison gas.

At first, the Americans advanced despite **intense** German fire. Then, rains and the thick woods slowed their progress. Small units drove forward to capture deadly German positions. Armed with a single rifle, Sergeant Alvin York of Tennessee wiped out a nest of German machine gunners. His brave act helped clear the way for advancing American troops. York became the most decorated American soldier of the war.

Academic Vocabulary
intense • *adj.*, existing in an extreme degree

Finally, after 47 days, the Americans broke through the German defense. However, the cost was high. Americans had suffered more than 100,000 casualties in the battle.

British, French, and Belgian forces also smashed through the German lines in their areas. By November, German forces were in retreat. After more than four years of fighting, the Great War was finally nearing its end.

Armistice In September, German generals told the kaiser that the war could not be won. On October 4, Prince Max of Baden, head of the German cabinet, secretly cabled President Wilson.

Primary Source

"To avoid further bloodshed, the German government requests the President to arrange the immediate conclusion of an armistice on land, by sea, and in the air."

—Max, Prince of Baden, Cable, October 4, 1918

5 BIOGRAPHY Things to Know About

SERGEANT ALVIN YORK

Recipient of the Congressional Medal of Honor for heroism during World War I (1887–1964)

- York identified himself as a conscientious objector, but was still drafted into the U.S. Army.
- He destroyed a machine gun emplacement by himself and captured 132 prisoners in all.
- In addition to the Medal of Honor, York was also awarded other medals by France and Italy.
- York achieved great fame when the movie *Sergeant York* was made about his life in 1941.
- After the war, York founded a high school and a Bible school in his home state of Tennessee.

Critical Thinking What made Sgt. York such a popular hero?

Academic Vocabulary
prerequisite • *n.,* something that is necessary for carrying out an act

An **armistice** is an agreement to stop fighting. President Wilson set two **prerequisites** for an armistice. First, Germany must accept his plan for peace. Second, the German emperor must abdicate, or give up power.

While German leaders debated a response, rebellion simmered in the ranks. Daily, the German army lost ground. Morale plunged among the troops. German sailors mutinied. People in several German cities threatened to revolt.

On November 9, the kaiser fled to Holland, and Germany became a republic. The new German leaders agreed to the armistice terms. At 11 A.M. on November 11, 1918—the eleventh hour of the eleventh day of the eleventh month—World War I ended at last.

READING CHECK **Identify Cause and Effect** How did the Battle of the Argonne Forest contribute to the end of the war?

What Were the Costs of the War?

The costs of the war were staggering. A generation of young Europeans lost their lives. Between 8 million and 9 million people died in battle—more than had died in all the wars fought during the previous 100 years. Germany alone lost close to 2 million men. The United States lost over 100,000 men. Many more died of diseases. More than 20 million soldiers on both sides were wounded.

No one knows exactly how many civilians died of disease, starvation, and other war-related causes. Some historians believe as many civilians died as soldiers.

Analyze Images A combination of two photographs shows the size of this Philadelphia celebration of the armistice, November 8, 1918. **Infer** What sort of peace terms do you predict the Allies will demand?

Casualties of World War I

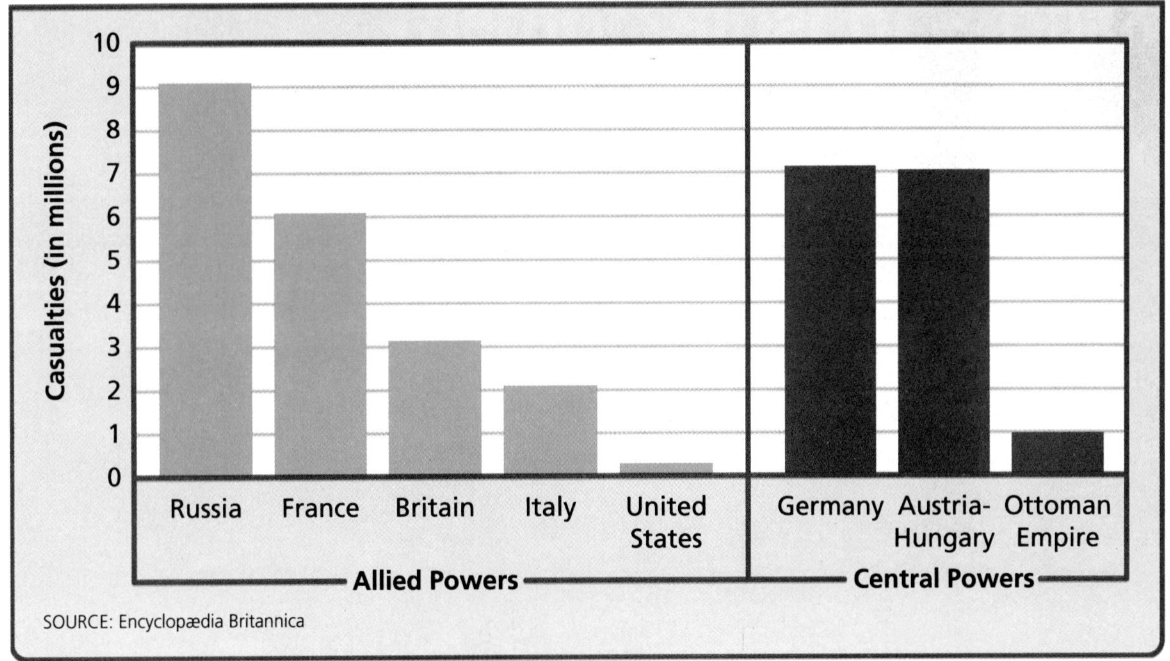

Much of northern France lay in ruins. Millions of Germans were near starvation. Children in many nations were left orphaned and homeless.

In 1918, as the world was reeling from the war, a new disaster struck. A terrible influenza **epidemic** spread around the globe. An epidemic is the rapid spread of a contagious disease among large numbers of people.

Between 1918 and 1919, more than half a million Americans died in the flu epidemic. The death toll in other countries was even higher. All told, the epidemic killed more than 30 million people worldwide.

Analyze Graphs As the graph shows, the human costs in injuries and deaths from World War I were enormous. **Compare and Contrast** Compare the U.S. casualty total to those of other Allied nations and explain why U.S. casualties might have been different.

READING CHECK **Identify Main Ideas** What were the costs of the war beyond the number of soldiers killed in battle?

Lesson Check

Practice Vocabulary

1. What did the **armistice** achieve?
2. What were the results of the battles of **Belleau Wood** and **Argonne Forest**?
3. What was the influenza **epidemic**, and what was the result?

Critical Thinking and Writing

4. Generate Explanations Why did many civilians die during World War I?
5. Identify Cause and Effect Why did Lenin choose to withdraw Russian troops from World War I?
6. Writing Workshop: Draft Your Essay Draft the body of your essay on U.S. expansion and intervention during the late 1800s and early 1900s. Begin each paragraph with a main idea. Add details in the rest of the paragraph that support and explain that main idea.

LESSON 7

Wilson and Isolationism

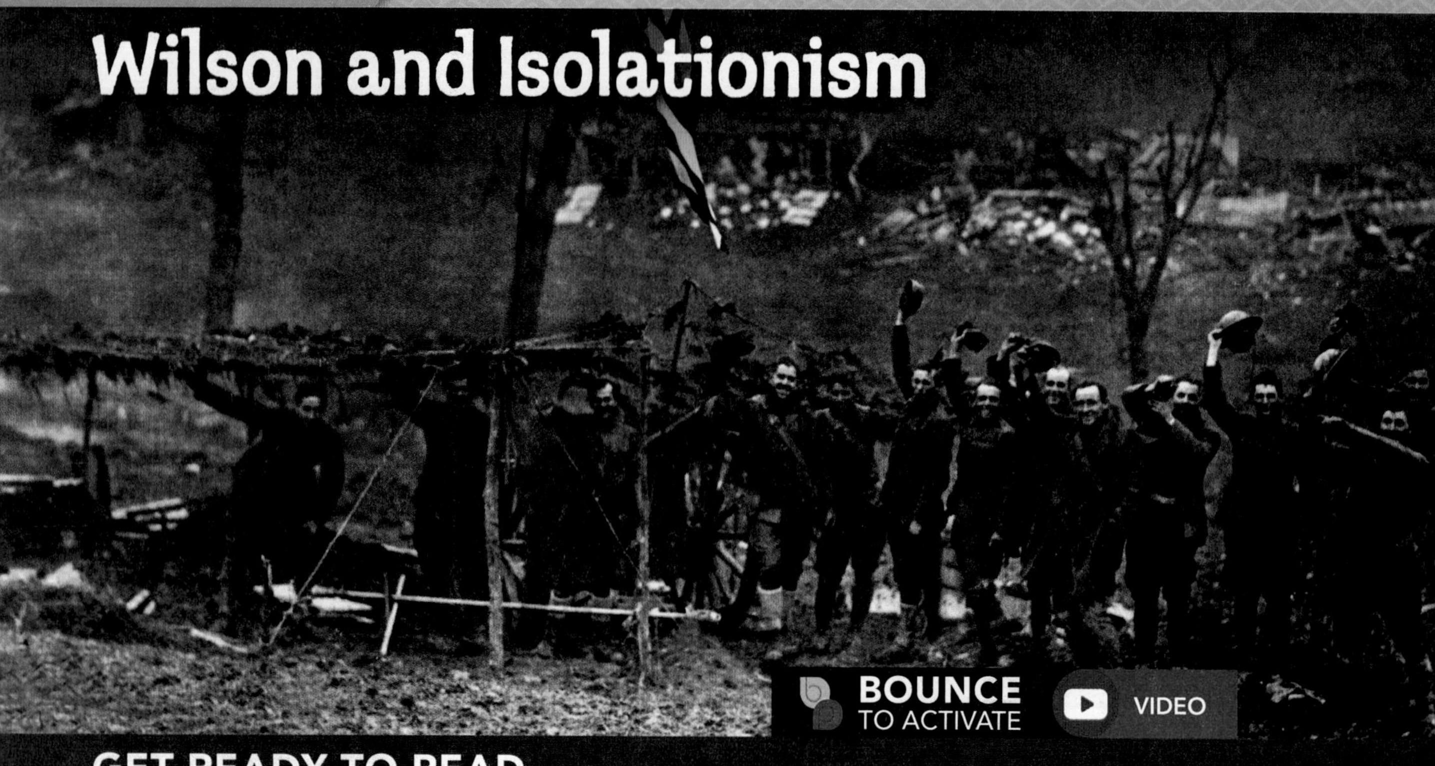

GET READY TO READ

START UP

The war won, American troops like these were eager to come home. Preview the rest of the lesson. Write some sentences about how the war might have affected these soldiers and the nation.

GUIDING QUESTIONS

- What were the components and the purpose of Wilson's fourteen-point peace plan?
- What did Wilson achieve at the Paris Peace Conference?
- Why did the Versailles Treaty and the League of Nations fail to win support in the United States?

TAKE NOTES

Literacy Skills Use Evidence

Use the graphic organizer in your Active Journal to take notes as you read the lesson.

PRACTICE VOCABULARY

Use the vocabulary activity in your Active Journal to practice the vocabulary words.

Vocabulary		Academic Vocabulary
Fourteen Points	reparations	negotiate
self-determination	Treaty of Versailles	incur
League of Nations	mandate	

On board the American naval ship *George Washington* were President Woodrow Wilson and his advisers. They were sailing to France in late 1918 to help the Allies set the terms of peace following World War I. As the ship passed the Statue of Liberty, a hopeful Wilson waved his hat to the crowd. At last, he would have a chance to keep his promise of making the world "safe for democracy."

The Fourteen Points

President Wilson was determined to do whatever was needed to achieve his vision of a just and lasting peace. In the end, however, Wilson failed. The other Allied leaders, it turned out, did not share his vision or his hopes. Even the American people disagreed over how to approach the postwar world.

In Europe, Wilson visited Paris, London, Milan, and Rome. Everywhere, cheering crowds welcomed him. He thought that the crowds shared his goal of peace without victory. In fact, he was wrong. The Europeans who greeted Wilson so warmly scoffed at his high-minded proposals for peace. They and their leaders were determined to punish the Germans for the war.

In January 1918, even before the war ended, Wilson outlined his peace plan. Known as the **Fourteen Points**, it was meant to prevent international crises from causing another war.

The first point in Wilson's plan called for an end to secret agreements. Secrecy, Wilson felt, had encouraged the web of rival alliances that had helped lead to war. Next, he called for freedom of the seas, free trade, and a limit on arms. He urged peaceful settlement of disputes over colonies. He also supported the principle of national **self-determination**, that is, the right of national groups to have their own territory and forms of government.

For Wilson, however, the fourteenth point was the most important. It called for a "general association of nations," or **League of Nations**. Its job would be to protect the independence of all countries, large or small. His goals were clear:

Primary Source

"An evident principle runs through the whole program that I have outlined. It is the principle of justice to all peoples and nationalities, and their right to live on equal terms of liberty and safety with one another, whether weak or strong."

—Woodrow Wilson, Speech, January 8, 1918

Wilson persuaded the Allies to accept the Fourteen Points as the basis for making peace. However, the plan soon ran into trouble. Some goals were too vague. Others conflicted with reality. In the peace conference, Wilson faced a constant battle to save his Fourteen Points. He discovered that the Allies were more concerned with protecting their own interests than with forging a lasting peace.

READING CHECK **Summarize** What was the purpose of creating a League of Nations?

INTERACTIVE

Woodrow Wilson

▲ President Woodrow Wilson

Analyze Charts This chart summarizes several of the major ideas in Wilson's Fourteen Points. **Cite Evidence** Which do you think is the most important point in terms of maintaining peace? Why?

Selected Details From Wilson's Fourteen Points

Selected Details From Wilson's Fourteen Points
All treaties between nations should be made public in order to avoid secret treaties such as the Triple Alliance.
All countries should be able to freely navigate the oceans and seas in times of peace.
Strengthening trade between countries will help create a lasting peace.
Nations should only keep enough weapons to be able to defend themselves against the possibility of attack.
An international organization of nations will help prevent the possibility of another world war.
Colonial claims must be settled with the involvement of local populations.

SOURCE: *Encyclopædia Britannica*

Analyze Images The "Big Four" Allied leaders (from left, George, Orlando, Clemenceau, and Wilson) met in Paris in 1919 to negotiate a peace treaty after World War I.
Infer Why did the Allies grant four countries special peace-making powers?

Peace Treaties Shape the Postwar World

Diplomats from more than 30 nations met in Paris and Versailles (vuhr SI) to **negotiate** five separate peace treaties known as the Peace of Paris. Key issues were decided by the leaders of the Allied nations known as the Big Four: Woodrow Wilson of the United States, David Lloyd George of United Kingdom, Georges Clemenceau (kleh mahn SOH) of France, and Vittorio Orlando of Italy.

Allied Nations Disagree Each leader had his own aims. Wilson had called for "peace without victory." He opposed punishing the defeated powers.

The other Allies, however, ached for revenge. Germany must pay, they said. They insisted on large **reparations**, or cash payments, for the losses they had **incurred** during the war. Further, they wanted to include a "war guilt clause" that would force Germany to accept responsibility for the war.

Academic Vocabulary

negotiate • *v.*, to confer with others in order to reach agreement

incur • *v.*, to become liable for

The Allies were also determined to prevent Germany from rebuilding its military strength. In particular, Clemenceau wanted to weaken Germany so that it could never again threaten France. "Mr. Wilson bores me with his Fourteen Points," he complained. "Why, God Almighty has only ten!"

The haggling continued for months. In the end, Wilson had to compromise on his Fourteen Points in order to save his key goals, especially the League of Nations. However, he would not budge on the League. With the League in place, he believed, any mistakes made in Paris could later be corrected.

Humiliation for Germany By June 1919, the **Treaty of Versailles**, the most important treaty of the Paris Peace Conference, was ready. None of the Allies was satisfied with it. Germany, which had not even been allowed to send delegates to the peace talks, was shocked by the terms of the treaty. Still, its representatives had no choice but to sign.

Under the treaty, Germany had to take full blame for the war.

Primary Source

"The Allied and Associated Governments affirm, and Germany accepts, the responsibility of Germany and her allies for causing all the loss and damage to which the Allied and Associated Governments and their nationals have been subjected as a consequence of the war imposed on them by the aggression of Germany and her allies."

—Article 231, Treaty of Versailles, June 28, 1919

Germany also had to pay the Allies huge reparations, including the cost of pensions for Allied soldiers or their widows and children. The total cost of German reparations would come to over $300 billion.

Other provisions of the Treaty of Versailles were aimed at weakening Germany. The treaty severely limited the size of the German military. It returned Alsace-Lorraine to France. In addition, the treaty stripped Germany of its overseas colonies, which were put under the control of Britain or France. The Germans, wrote one reporter, "suffered a horrible humiliation."

Britain and France were also given **mandates**, or authorization, by the League of Nations to govern territory in what had been parts of the Ottoman Empire. The purpose of the mandates was to govern these territories until they could function as independent nations. The British would control the former Turkish provinces of Iraq and Palestine, while the French would control Syria and Lebanon.

Wilson Preserves the League of Nations Despite opposition to many of his Fourteen Points, Wilson succeeded in keeping some of them. In Eastern Europe, the Allies provided for several new nations to be formed on the principle of **self-determination**, including Czechoslovakia and Yugoslavia. They were created out of lands once ruled by Germany, Russia, and Austria-Hungary. In addition, Poland regained its independence as a nation.

Analyze Images Twenty-seven countries sent delegates to the Versailles Peace Conference, but Russia and the Central Powers were not invited. **Cite Evidence** What resulted from excluding the defeated countries from the peace conference?

Some people were dissatisfied with the new boundaries. Many Germans, for example, had settled in Poland and Czechoslovakia. Before long, Germany would seek to regain control of German-speaking peoples in Eastern Europe.

To Wilson, however, his greatest achievement was persuading the Allies to include the League of Nations in the treaty. Wilson was certain that the League would prevent future wars by allowing nations to talk over their problems. If talk failed, members would join together to fight aggressors. "A living thing is born," he declared. The League "is definitely a guarantee of peace."

INTERACTIVE

Europe Before and After World War I

READING CHECK **Identify Central Ideas** How was the Treaty of Versailles a humiliation for Germany?

How Did Wilson Fight for the Peace Treaty?

When President Wilson returned home, he faced a new battle. He had to persuade the Senate to approve the Treaty of Versailles and American participation in the League of Nations.

American Opposition Most Americans favored the treaty, but a vocal minority opposed it. Some believed that it was too soft on the defeated powers. Many German Americans felt that it was too harsh. Some Republicans hoped to embarrass President Wilson, a Democrat, by rewriting or defeating the treaty. Isolationists, people who wanted the United States to stay out of world affairs, opposed the League of Nations. They considered the League a dangerous "entangling alliance." Other people who were against the League felt that it did not have enough authority to solve any pressing economic

GEOGRAPHY SKILLS

The map shows how Europe changed as a result of World War I.

1. **Region** Which new countries bordered Russia?
2. **Understand Effects** What effect might these new nations have on the relationships between European countries?

Europe after WWI, 1919

problems. They thought that it could lead to another war.

Senator Lodge Opposes the Treaty Critics of the treaty found a leader in Senator Henry Cabot Lodge of Massachusetts. Lodge, a Republican, chaired the Senate Foreign Relations Committee, which would have to approve the treaty before it could be presented to the entire Senate for a vote.

Lodge accepted the idea of the League of Nations, but he wanted changes in some provisions relating to the League. He believed that Americans were being asked to "subject our own will to the will of others."

Specifically, Lodge objected to Article 10 of the treaty. It called for the League to protect any member whose independence or territory was threatened. Lodge argued that Article 10 interfered with United States sovereignty because it could compel the United States to join in future European wars. He wanted changes in the treaty that would ensure that the United States remained independent of the League. He also wanted Congress to have the power to decide on a case-by-case basis whether the United States would follow League policy.

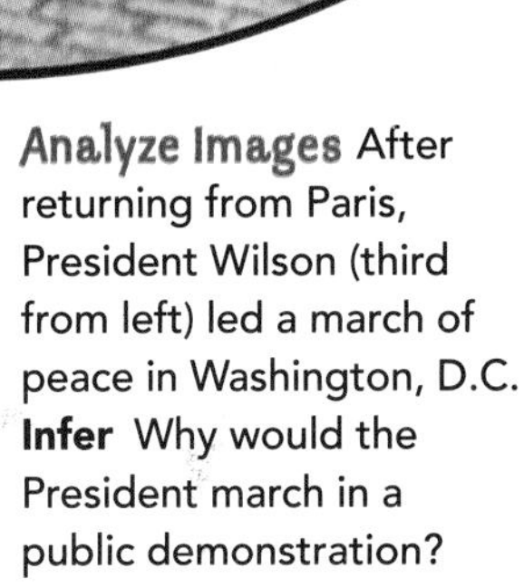

Analyze Images After returning from Paris, President Wilson (third from left) led a march of peace in Washington, D.C. **Infer** Why would the President march in a public demonstration?

Wilson believed that Lodge's changes would hobble the League. Advisers urged the President to compromise, to give up some of his demands in order to save the League. Wilson replied, "Let Lodge compromise." He refused to make any changes.

The Senate Rejects the Treaty As the battle grew hotter, the President took his case to the people. In early September 1919, Wilson set out across the country. He traveled nearly 8,000 miles and made 37 speeches in 29 cities. He urged Americans to let their senators know that they supported the treaty.

Wilson kept up a relentless pace. On September 25, the exhausted Wilson complained of a headache. His doctors canceled the rest of the trip, and President and Mrs. Wilson returned to Washington. A week later, his wife Edith found the President unconscious. He had suffered a stroke that left him bedridden for weeks.

For the remainder of his term, Edith Wilson would manage the executive branch, protecting the President from the pressures of his office.

Analyze Political Cartoons This 1919 cartoon shows President Wilson giving an olive branch marked "League of Nations" to a dove. **Infer** What does the size of the branch suggest about the League of Nations?

Wilson had done all he could. In November 1919, the Senate rejected the Treaty of Versailles. "It is dead," Wilson mourned, "[and] every morning I put flowers on its grave." Gone, too, was Wilson's cherished goal—American membership in the League of Nations.

The United States did not sign a peace treaty with Germany until 1921. Many nations had already joined the League of Nations. Without the United States, though, the League failed to live up to its goal of protecting members against aggression. Wilson's dream of a world "safe for democracy" would have to wait.

READING CHECK **Check Understanding** Why did some Americans oppose the Treaty of Versailles?

Lesson Check

Practice Vocabulary

1. What was Wilson's view on the principle of **self-determination** as it applied to national groups?
2. Why did the Allies, apart from the United States, seek large **reparations** from Germany, and how did Germany feel about it?
3. Why did some Americans oppose the **Treaty of Versailles**?

Critical Thinking and Writing

4. **Summarize** What were the main components of President Wilson's Fourteen Points?
5. **Compare and Contrast** What did Wilson and the other members of the Big Four at the Paris Peace Conference disagree about?
6. **Writing Workshop: Write a Conclusion** Write a concluding paragraph for your essay on U.S. expansion and intervention. Summarize the main idea of your essay and tell why it is important.

Primary Sources

Woodrow Wilson, The Fourteen Points

In his Fourteen Points, Woodrow Wilson outlined his goals for the Paris Peace Conference. It was an idealistic statement that did not fully correspond to the views of many Europeans.

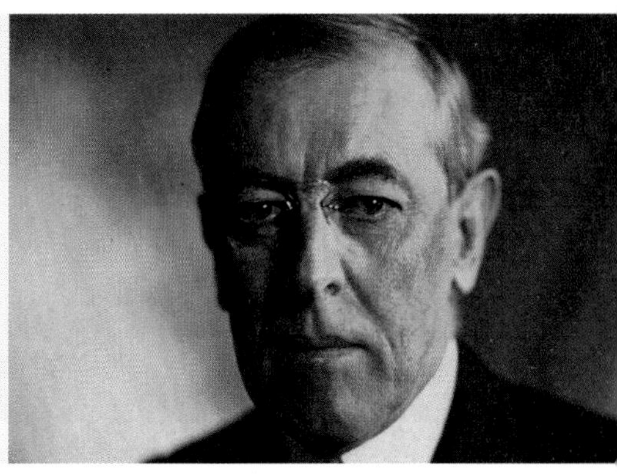

▶ Woodrow Wilson

It will be our wish and purpose that the processes of peace, when they are begun, shall be absolutely open and that they shall involve and permit henceforth no secret understandings of any kind. The day of conquest and aggrandizement ① is gone by; so is also the day of secret covenants ② entered into in the interest of particular governments and likely at some unlooked-for moment to upset the peace of the world. It is this happy fact, now clear to the view of every public man whose thoughts do not still linger in an age that is dead and gone, which makes it possible for every nation whose purposes are consistent with justice and the peace of the world to avow ③ nor or at any other time the objects it has in view.

We entered this war because violations of right had occurred which touched us to the quick ④ and made the life of our own people impossible unless they were corrected and the world secure once for all against their recurrence ⑤. What we demand in this war, therefore, is nothing peculiar to ourselves. It is that the world be made fit and safe to live in; and particularly that it be made safe for every peace-loving nation which, like our own, wishes to live its own life, determine its own institutions, be assured of justice and fair dealing by the other peoples of the world as against force and selfish aggression. All the peoples of the world are in effect partners in this interest, and for our own part we see very clearly that unless justice be done to others it will not be done to us.

Reading and Vocabulary Support

① To aggrandize is to increase power, wealth, or status.

② What is a covenant?

③ *Avow* means "to acknowledge or admit."

④ What does "touched us to the quick" mean?

⑤ *Recurrence* means "happening again."

Analyzing Primary Sources

Cite specific evidence from the document to support your answers.

1. **Determine Author's Point of View** Why does Wilson think it is possible that the Paris Peace Conference will adopt his approach for making the world permanently safe?
2. **Determine Author's Purpose (a)** What is Wilson demanding from the leaders attending the Paris Peace Conference? **(b)** Why does he think other nations will join in bringing this about?

Quest CONNECTIONS

Based on the principles Wilson expresses, how might he have judged U.S. actions in annexing Hawaii? Make notes in your Active Journal.

TOPIC 12

Review and Assessment

VISUAL REVIEW

United States Imperialism, 1854–1903

Year	Event
1854	Admiral Perry opens Japan for trade.
1867	U.S. annexes Midway Island.
1867	U.S. purchases Alaska from Russia.
1898	U.S. wins Cuba, Puerto Rico, and Philippines from Spain.
1898	U.S. Marines help topple Hawaiian government. U.S. annexes Hawaii.
1899	U.S. promotes Open Door Policy in China.
1903	U.S. supports Panamanian revolt and acquires canal zone.

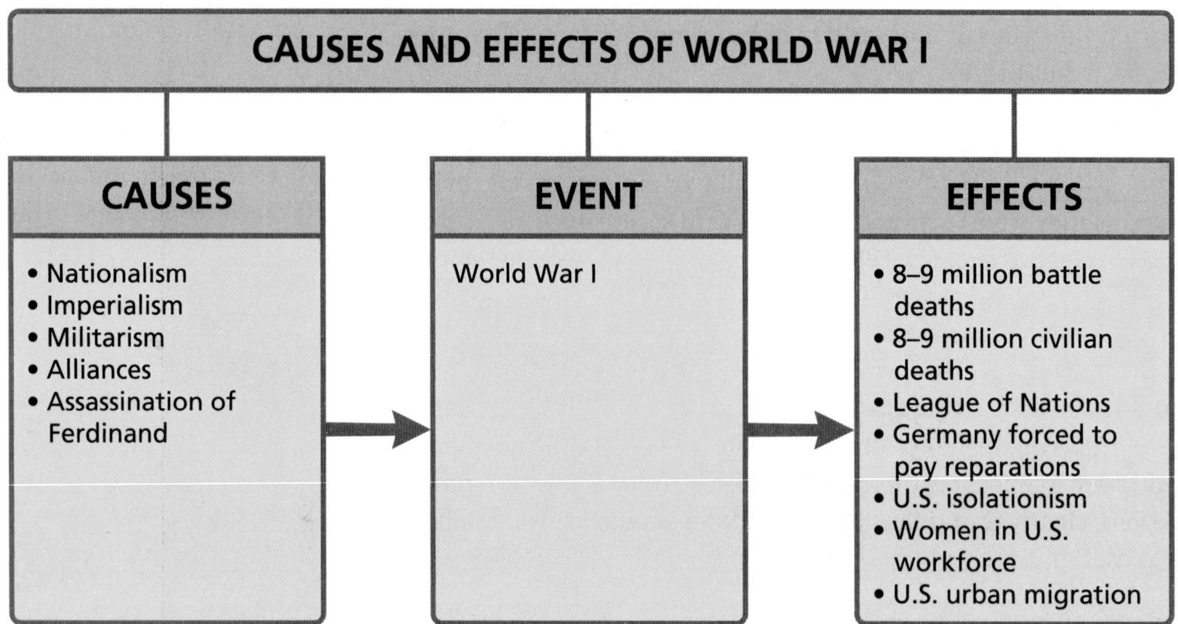

READING REVIEW

Use the Take Notes and Practice Vocabulary activities in your Active Journal to review the topic.

Practice vocabulary using the Topic Mini-Games

Quest FINDINGS

Conduct Your Civic Discussion

Get help for conducting your discussion in your Active Journal.

ASSESSMENT

Vocabulary and Key Ideas

1. **Recall** How did **yellow journalism** contribute to America's involvement in the **Spanish-American War**?
2. **Check Understanding** Why was an **isthmus** a desirable place to build the Panama Canal?
3. **Identify** Which nations made up the **Allied Powers** and the **Central Powers**?
4. **Identify Main Ideas** Why were most European nations drawn into World War I?
5. **Trace** How did the Russian Revolution influence President Wilson's decision to enter the war?
6. **Trace** How did America's entry into World War I impact the labor force?
7. **Identify Main Ideas** How did President Wilson's goals for peace differ from the aims of the other Allies?

Critical Thinking and Writing

8. **Identify Cause and Effect** What economic factors drew the United States into the Spanish-American War?
9. **Recognize Multiple Causes** What were the causes of World War I?
10. **Understand Effects** How was America's entry into World War I a turning point in the war?
11. **Compare and Contrast** What are the pros and cons of American participation in international organizations?
12. **Revisit the Essential Question** Based on your readings in this topic, what is America's role in the world?
13. **Writing Workshop: Write an Informative Essay** Finalize your informative essay describing U.S. expansion and intervention during the late 1800s and early 1900s. Revise your thesis, introduction, body paragraphs, and conclusion as needed. Add transitions to connect ideas. Make sure that you have strong details to support each main idea.

Analyze Primary Sources

14. Based on Lodge's statement, what is his position on America participating in an international organization?
    - **A.** International alliances prevent wars.
    - **B.** International treaties promote trade.
    - **C.** International service helps the nation.
    - **D.** International commitments are dangerous.

"I will go as far as anyone in world service, but the first step to world service is the maintenance of the United States. . . . and when I think of the United States first in an arrangement like this I am thinking of what is best for the world, for if the United States fails, the best hopes of mankind fail with it."

—Henry Cabot Lodge, speech, 1919

Analyze Maps

Use the map to answer the following questions.

15. Which letter identifies the Caribbean Sea? Which identifies the Atlantic Ocean?
16. Which letter identifies Puerto Rico?
17. Approximately how far is Cuba from the United States?

▼ **War in the Caribbean**

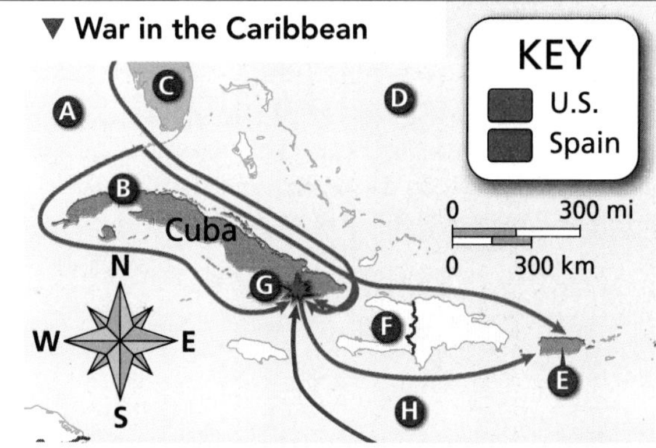

TOPIC 13 Prosperity and Depression (1919–1939)

GO ONLINE to access your digital course

- VIDEO
- AUDIO
- ETEXT
- INTERACTIVE
- WRITING
- GAMES
- WORKSHEET
- ASSESSMENT

Go back to the years after World War I,

to an era of PROSPERITY AND DEPRESSION. Enjoy the music! the dancing! the freedom! But beware: The good times will not last. The future will bring hardship and suffering.

Explore The Essential Question

What should governments do?

The economy rocketed higher and then came the crash. Should the government take steps to rebuild the economy, or let free market forces do the restoration?

Unlock the essential question in your Active Journal.

Watch

NBC LEARN

BOUNCE TO ACTIVATE VIDEO

Billie Holiday, Lady Day

Learn more about the famed jazz singer Billie Holiday.

▲ Despite a nationwide ban on alcohol, parties and music were hallmarks of the Jazz Age—until the economy collapsed.

Read

about 1920s politics and society and the severe economic downturn that followed.

TOPIC 13

Prosperity and Depression (1919–1939)

Learn more about the period following World War I by making your own map and timeline in your Active Journal.

INTERACTIVE

Topic Timeline

What happened and when?

A booming economy, new fads and fashions, a high-flying stock market. . . . What could go wrong? Explore the timeline to see what happened during the up-and-down decades following World War I.

1920 Ratification of the Nineteenth Amendment gives women the right to vote.

1920 Prohibition begins.

1925 John Scopes tried for teaching evolution.

TOPIC EVENTS

1915 **1919** **1924**

WORLD EVENTS

1922 Benito Mussolini comes to power in Italy.

1923 Turkey gains its independence.

INTERACTIVE

Topic Map

When did the United States hit the road?

As the automobile became more affordable, it became more popular. The map shows the increase in vehicle registrations in just eight years. How did that change Americans' lives?

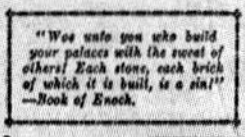

The Milwaukee Leader

"Unawed by Influence and Unbribed by Gain"

HOME EDITION

Vol. 18—No. 275. MONDAY EVENING, OCTOBER 28, 1929. PRICE THREE CENTS

BILLIONS LOST IN NEW STOCK CRASH

PRINCIPALS IN COAST CASE

TRUNK PLANT FIRE DAMAGE IS $75,000

Thirtieth St. Industrial Area Menaced by Blaze.

May Punish Senator for Aiding Tariff Lobbyists

FIRE MENACES INDUSTRIAL AREA

BINGHAM SAYS IT'S FRAME-UP, IS CRITICISED

Norris Planning to Offer Resolution in Senate.

BANKERS' AID FAILS TO END SELLING WAVE

United States Steel Leads List in Plunge.

PANTAGES IS FOUND GUILTY; PRISON LOOMS

Newsies Call Srike, Won't Handle Paper

Flashes Badge at Hotel, Pays $5 Fine

STATE TO AID FEDERALS IN HURLEY CASES

Snook Files Appeal As Execution Nears

WARNS OF NEW 30-MILE GALE

Six Inches Water Drowns Baby Girl

RADIUM PAINT TRAGEDY NEAR

HEART OUT OF PLACE, BULLET IS NOT FATAL

VON BUELOW, EX-CHANCELLOR

Who will you meet?

Franklin Roosevelt promised a new deal for Americans suffering through the Great Depression

Frances Perkins, secretary of labor, first woman to serve in the Cabinet

Langston Hughes, acclaimed poet of the Harlem Renaissance

1929 The New York Stock Exchange crashes.

1933 Franklin D. Roosevelt becomes President.

1929 | 1934 | 1939

1933 Adolf Hitler takes power in Germany.

1937 Japanese army seizes China's capital.

1939 Germany invades Poland.

Document-Based Writing Inquiry

The Role of Government in the Economy

Quest KICK OFF

The Great Depression caused economic hardship for Americans, many of whom lost their jobs and could no longer support themselves and their families.

In times of economic distress, what should governments do to help or support their citizens?

How did the federal government respond to the needs of its citizens during this severe economic downturn? Explore the Essential Question "What should governments do?" in this Quest.

▼ People who lost their jobs during the Great Depression, like this man, had to think of new ways to earn money.

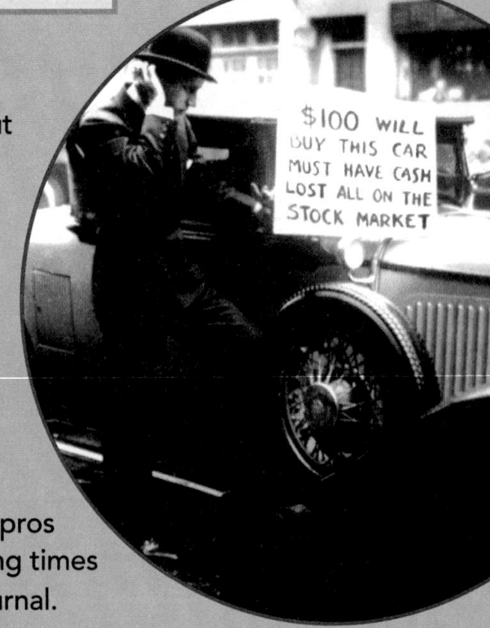

1 Ask Questions

First, list questions that will help you draw conclusions about the government's role during times of economic trouble. Write the questions in your Active Journal.

2 Investigate

As you read the lessons in the topic, look for Quest CONNECTIONS that provide insights into differing opinions on government intervention in the economy. Capture notes in your Active Journal.

3 Examine Primary Sources

Next, explore a group of primary sources dealing with the pros and cons of government involvement in the economy during times of need. Take notes on these sources in your Active Journal.

Quest FINDINGS

4 Write About the Government's Role in the Economy

Finally, write an essay evaluating what, in your opinion, government should do to help citizens during tough economic times. Get essay-writing help in your Active Journal.

LESSON 1

Harding and Coolidge

GET READY TO READ

START UP

As seen in this window display, home appliances became available during the 1920s. Write a few sentences from the viewpoint of a first-time buyer.

GUIDING QUESTIONS

- How did corruption hurt Warren G. Harding's presidency?
- Why did the economy grow under President Calvin Coolidge?
- Why did the United States limit its role in world affairs?

TAKE NOTES

Literacy Skills: Summarize

Use the graphic organizer in your Active Journal to take notes as you read the lesson.

PRACTICE VOCABULARY

Use the vocabulary activity in your Active Journal to practice the vocabulary words.

Vocabulary		Academic Vocabulary
recession	bull market	consumer goods
installment buying	margin	pact
interest	communism	
stock	disarmament	

World War I had greatly boosted the economy. Europeans, and later the U.S. military, ordered vast amounts of supplies and equipment from American factories. The end of the war, however, brought cutbacks.

Republicans Regain the White House

When the war ended, more than 2 million soldiers came home and began to look for jobs. At the same time, factories stopped turning out war materials. The result was a sharp **recession**, or economic slump.

A Landslide Victory The recession fed voter discontent with the Democrats, who had held power for eight years. In the 1920 election, Warren Harding swamped his Democratic opponent.

For the top cabinet posts, Harding chose able men who strongly followed pro-business policies. Andrew Mellon, a wealthy banker, became secretary of the treasury. Mellon balanced the budget and lowered taxes.

Did you know?

In 1922, Americans bought 11,000 electric refrigerators. Sales in 1929 reached 630,000.

Herbert Hoover became the new secretary of commerce. During World War I, Hoover had earned the world's admiration by organizing efforts to supply food to millions of starving Belgians. As secretary of commerce, he worked to help American businesses expand overseas.

The Ohio Gang To fill most other cabinet posts, however, Harding brought in his old friends. They became known as the "Ohio Gang." Harding himself was honest and hardworking, but the Ohio Gang saw government service as a way to enrich themselves. A series of scandals resulted. For example, Harding made Charles Forbes head of the Veterans Bureau. Forbes was later convicted of stealing millions of dollars from the Bureau.

Harding looked upon Forbes's crime as a betrayal. When rumors of new scandals surfaced, he grew even more distressed. In August 1923, Harding died of a heart attack. Many believed that the scandals contributed to his sudden death.

After Harding died, new scandals came to light. The most serious involved Secretary of the Interior Albert Fall. Two oil executives had bribed Fall. In return, he secretly leased them government land in California and at Teapot Dome, Wyoming. As a result of the Teapot Dome Scandal, Fall became the first cabinet official ever sent to prison.

Coolidge Becomes President On the day Harding died, Vice President Calvin Coolidge was visiting his father's farm in Vermont. Coolidge recalled, "I was awakened by my father. . . . I noticed that his voice trembled." Coolidge's father, a justice of the peace, used the family Bible to swear his son in as President.

Analyze Images This 1924 cartoon comments on the Teapot Dome Scandal during Warren Harding's administration. **Interpret Cartoons** Why is the teapot drawn to look like a steamroller?

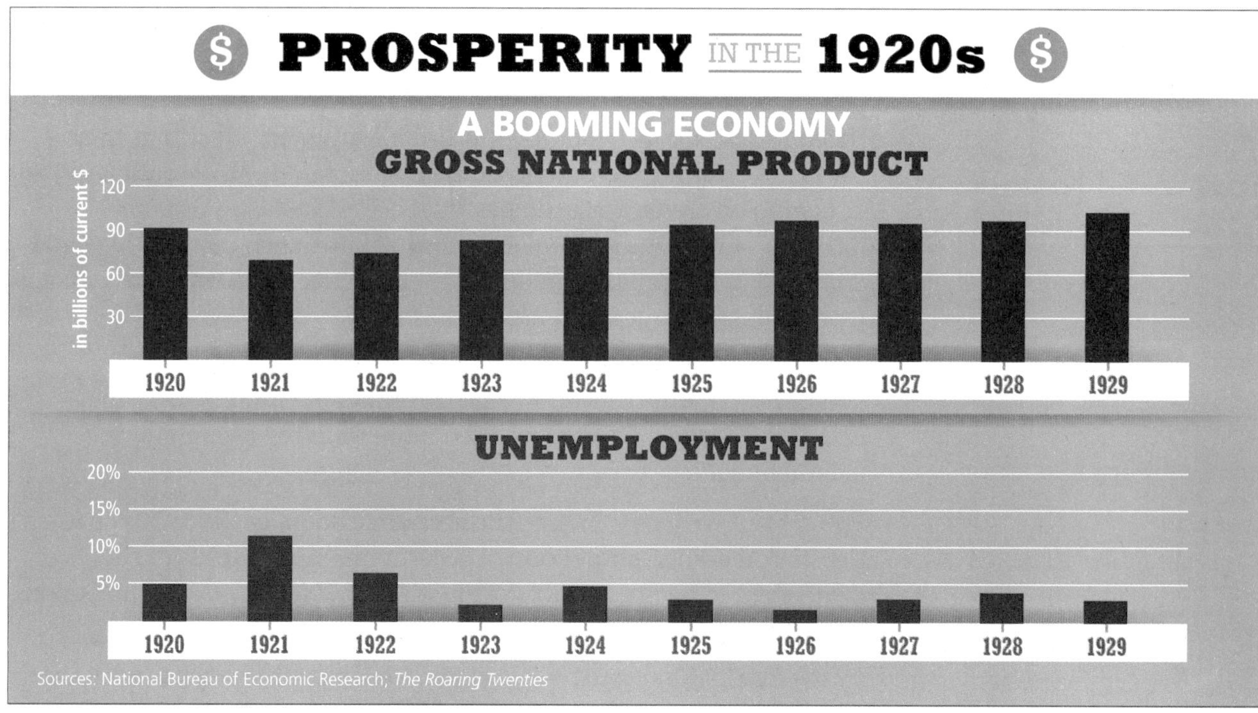

Analyze Graphs The Gross National Product (GNP) is the value of all the products and services that the nation produces. **Draw Conclusions** What do you notice about the relationship between changes in the GNP and the unemployment rate?

"Silent Cal" Coolidge was very different from Harding. Harding loved throwing parties and making long speeches. Coolidge was tight with both money and words. A woman reportedly told Coolidge she had bet that she could get him to say more than two words. "You lose," Coolidge replied.

Coolidge set out to repair the damage caused by the scandals. He forced the officials involved in scandals to resign. In 1924, Coolidge ran against Democrat John Davis and Progressive Robert La Follette. Voters chose to "Keep Cool with Coolidge" and returned the cautious New Englander to office.

READING CHECK **Identify Cause and Effect** What fueled American discontent with Democrats?

How Did the Economy Perform Under President Coolidge?

Like Harding, Coolidge believed that prosperity for all Americans depended on business prosperity. Coolidge cut regulations on business. He also named business leaders to head government agencies.

Academic Vocabulary
consumer goods • products bought for personal or home use

Production Increases Coolidge's pro-business policies contributed to a period of rapid economic growth. People referred to this boom as "Coolidge prosperity." As factories switched to **consumer goods**, the postwar recession ended. From 1923 to 1929, the quantity of goods made by industry almost doubled.

For most Americans, incomes rose. As a result, they were able to buy a flood of new consumer products. Electric refrigerators, radios, phonographs, vacuum cleaners, and many other appliances took their places in American homes.

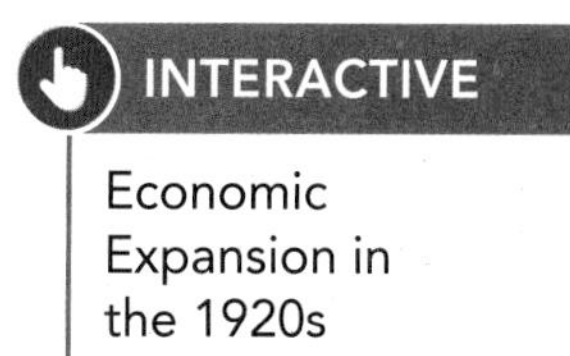

Businesses used advertising to boost sales of consumer goods. Advertisements encouraged people to think that their happiness depended on owning a wealth of shiny new products.

Faced with so many goods, people often wanted to buy things they could not afford. In response, businesses allowed **installment buying**, or buying on credit. For example, buyers could take home a new refrigerator by putting down just a few dollars. Each month, they paid an installment until they had paid the full price, plus **interest**, which is a percentage charged as a fee for the loan.

The new policy of "buy now, pay later" increased the demand for goods. At the same time, however, consumer debt jumped. By the end of the decade, consumers owed more than the amount of the federal budget.

The Stock Market Soars The economic boom of the 1920s gave the stock market a giant boost. Corporations sold **stocks**, or shares of ownership, to investors. Investors made or lost money depending upon whether the price of the shares went up or down.

By the late 1920s, more people were investing in the stock market than ever before. Stock prices rose so fast that some people made fortunes almost overnight. Stories of ordinary people becoming rich drew others into the stock market. Such a period of increased stock trading and rising stock prices is known as a **bull market**.

Many people bought stocks on **margin**. Under this system, an investor bought a stock for as little as a 10 percent down payment, or margin. The buyer held the stock until the price rose and then sold it at a profit. Margin buying worked as long as stock prices kept going up.

Analyze Graphs The graph below shows the economic growth of major nations after World War I. **Compare and Contrast** Compare the state of the U.S. economy in the 1920s and 1930s.

World Economies After World War I

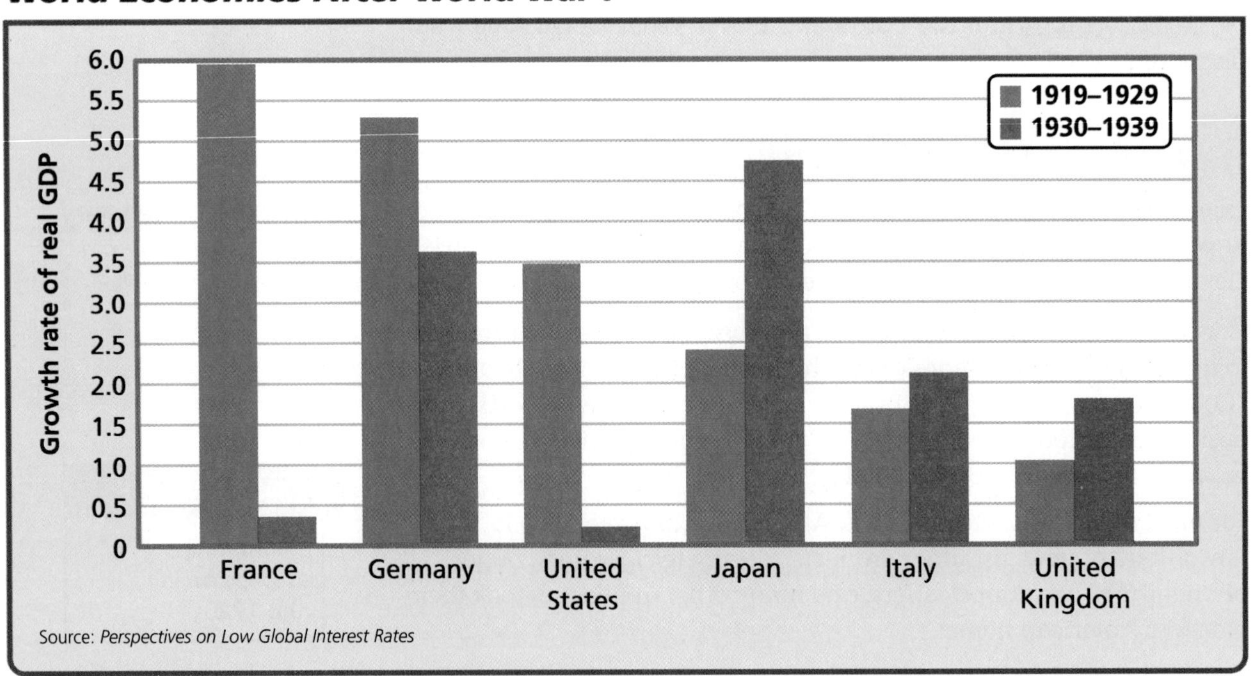

Source: *Perspectives on Low Global Interest Rates*

In 1928 and 1929, however, the prices of many stocks rose faster than the value of the companies themselves. A few experts warned that the bull market could not last forever. Still, most investors ignored the warnings.

READING CHECK Use Evidence What evidence supports the idea that Coolidge's policies were pro-business?

Analyze Images From 1909 until the early 1930s, the United States sent marines like these to Nicaragua to help keep revolutionary groups from taking power there. **Infer** How did this vehicle give U.S. troops an advantage?

Why Did the United States Return to Isolationism?

After World War I, the United States was the world's leading economic power. Europeans expected the United States to take a major role in world affairs. Presidents Harding and Coolidge wanted to keep the hard-won peace in Europe. However, they did not want to commit the United States to the job of keeping world peace. The United States sent observers to the League of Nations, but refused to join. Most Americans supported this return to prewar isolationism.

Latin American Investments During the war, Latin American nations had been cut off from Europe because of wartime threats to shipping. As a result, United States trade and investment in Latin America increased. This trend continued after the war. However, the United States limited its role abroad for fear that more involvement might push the country into another war.

At times, the United States intervened in Latin America. In 1926, for example, a revolution broke out in Nicaragua, where Americans owned plantations and railroads. Coolidge sent marines to oversee new elections.

In 1927, Mexico announced plans to take over foreign-owned oil and mining companies. American investors called on President Coolidge to send in troops. Instead, Coolidge sent a diplomat, Dwight Morrow, to Mexico. After much hard bargaining, Morrow was able to work out a compromise with the Mexican government.

The First Communist State Meanwhile, the Soviet Union became the world's first Communist state. **Communism**, as practiced in the Soviet Union, was an economic system in which all wealth and property were owned by the government.

The United States refused to recognize Vladimir Lenin's government. Most Americans disliked communism. It shocked them when the Soviet government did away with private property and attacked religion. Still, Congress voted to provide $20 million in aid when famine threatened the Soviet Union in 1921. American aid may have saved as many as 10 million Soviet lives.

INTERACTIVE

Points of View on Foreign Affairs in the 1920s

Analyze Images During a famine in the Soviet Union in 1921, the American Relief Service, funded by Congress, used camels to haul food to remote villages. **Use Visual Information** What can you assume about the area this aid caravan is traveling through?

Pursuing Peace An arms race in Europe had helped cause World War I. For this reason, many people in the 1920s favored the reduction of armed forces and weapons of war, or **disarmament**. Pacifist groups such as the Women's International League for Peace and Freedom, founded by Jane Addams, led the call for disarmament in the United States and Europe.

Presidents Harding and Coolidge also backed peace efforts. At the Washington Conference of 1921, the United States, Britain, and Japan agreed to limit the size of their navies. Seven years later, the United States and 61 other nations signed the Kellogg-Briand **Pact**. This treaty outlawed war.

The treaty, however, had a fatal flaw. It did not set up any means for keeping the peace. One nation could still use force against another without fear of punishment. Still, many hailed the Kellogg-Briand Pact as the beginning of a new age of peace.

Academic Vocabulary
pact • a formal agreement or treaty

READING CHECK **Identify Cause and Effect** Why did the United States intervene in Latin America?

Lesson Check

Practice Vocabulary

1. What did **installment buying** help people do?
2. What happens to the price of **stocks** during a **bull market**?

Critical Thinking and Writing

3. **Use Evidence** How did members of President Harding's cabinet prove unfit for office?
4. **Draw Conclusions** How did advertising contribute to the bull market of the 1920s?
5. **Identify Main Ideas** Why did most Americans support a return to isolationism after World War I?
6. **Writing Workshop: Generate Questions to Focus Research** At the end of this topic, you will write a research paper on the New Deal. Write a few questions in your Active Journal that will help you focus your research on a specific aspect of the New Deal and its impact on Americans. Start with this one: What was the New Deal?

LESSON 2
Social Change

GET READY TO READ

START UP

Look at the photograph of the driver above. Consider social limits placed on women in earlier times. Write about what it meant that more women were learning to drive and buying cars in the 1920s.

GUIDING QUESTIONS

- Why was Prohibition called the "noble experiment"?
- How did women's lives change in the 1920s?
- What changes did the automobile bring to American society?

TAKE NOTES

Literacy Skills: Draw Conclusions

Use the graphic organizer in your Active Journal to take notes as you read the lesson.

PRACTICE VOCABULARY

Use the vocabulary activity in your Active Journal to practice the vocabulary words.

Vocabulary		Academic Vocabulary
Prohibition	repeal	undermine
bootlegger	Equal Rights Amendment	
organized crime	mass culture	

By 1920, the Progressive social reformers had seen their efforts bear fruit in the form of constitutional amendments. Prohibition and suffrage became the law of the land. The effects of those new laws, however, were not all positive.

Prohibition

For nearly a century, reform groups such as the Woman's Christian Temperance Union had worked to ban alcoholic beverages. They finally achieved this when the states ratified the Eighteenth Amendment in January 1919. One year later, **Prohibition**, often referred to as the "noble experiment," went into effect. Prohibition was the legal ban on the manufacture, sale, or transportation of alcohol.

In 1920, as today, alcohol abuse was a serious problem. Many Americans hoped the ban on liquor would improve American life. In fact, the ban did have some positive effects. Alcoholism declined during Prohibition. However, in the end, the ban did not work.

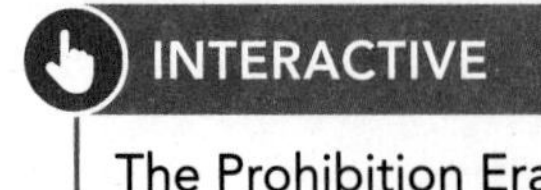

Going Underground Many Americans found ways to get around the law. Some made their own alcohol, while others smuggled liquor into the country. These smugglers became known as rum-runners or **bootleggers**. Meanwhile, illegal bars, called speakeasies, opened in nearly every city and town. In some ways, speakeasies made drinking liquor more popular than ever. To enforce the ban, the government sent out federal Prohibition agents. These "g-men" traveled around the country, shutting down speakeasies and stopping smugglers.

Organized Crime Prohibition gave a huge boost to **organized crime**, or criminal activity organized as a business. Every speakeasy needed a steady supply of liquor. Professional criminals, or gangsters, took over the job of meeting this need. Gangsters divided up cities and forced speakeasy owners in their "territories" to buy liquor from them. Sometimes, gangsters bribed police officers, public officials, and judges.

Academic Vocabulary
undermine • *v.,* to make someone or something weaker or less effective

The Experiment Ends Gradually, more Americans began to think that Prohibition was a mistake. The ban reduced drinking but never stopped it. Worse, argued critics, Prohibition was **undermining** respect for the law. Every day, millions of Americans were buying liquor in speakeasies. By the mid-1920s, almost half of all federal arrests were for Prohibition-related crimes.

By the end of the decade, many Americans were calling for the **repeal**, or ending, of Prohibition. In 1933, the states ratified the Twenty-first Amendment, which repealed the Eighteenth Amendment. The noble experiment was over.

READING CHECK **Identify Cause and Effect** Why did Americans begin to think that Prohibition was a mistake?

Analyze Graphs The number of Americans in prison rose sharply after 1920. **Identify Cause and Effect** Explain why prison populations rose so sharply during Prohibition.

Prohibition and the Prison Population

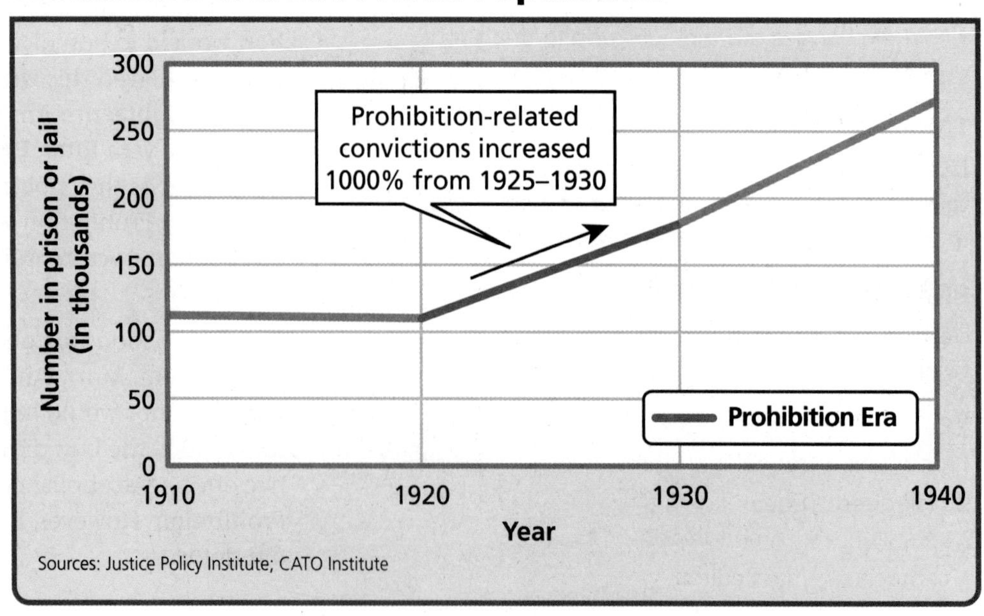

How Did Women's Lives Change During the 1920s?

Another constitutional amendment, the Nineteenth Amendment, also changed American life, but in a very different way. Ratified in 1920, it gave women the right to vote.

▲ The Nineteenth Amendment gave women the right to vote in 1920. This photo shows women voting in New York City in 1922.

Women Cast a Vote Women went to the polls nationwide for the first time in November 1920. Their votes helped elect Warren Harding President. Women did not vote as a group, however, as some people had predicted. Like men, some women voted for Republicans and some for Democrats, and many did not vote at all.

In 1920, Carrie Chapman Catt, head of the National Woman Suffrage Association, set up the League of Women Voters. The organization worked to educate voters, as it does today, and to protect other rights, such as women's right to serve on juries.

Women served as delegates in the 1924 Republican and Democratic conventions. That year, the first two women governors were elected—Nellie Tayloe Ross of Wyoming and Miriam A. Ferguson of Texas.

Women in Puerto Rico asked if they now had the right to vote. They were told that they did not. Led by Ana Roqué de Duprey, an educator and writer, Puerto Rican women crusaded for the vote. In 1929, their crusade finally succeeded.

An Equal Rights Amendment Leaders in the suffrage movement began to work for new goals. Alice Paul, who had been a leading suffragist, pointed out that women still lacked many legal rights. For example, many professional schools still barred women, and many states gave husbands legal control over their wives' earnings. Paul called for a new constitutional amendment in 1923. Paul's proposed **Equal Rights Amendment** (ERA) stated that "equality of rights under the law shall not be denied or abridged by the United States or by any State on account of sex."

Many people feared that the ERA went too far. Some argued that women would lose legal safeguards, such as laws that protected them in factories. Paul worked hard for the ERA until her death in 1977. The amendment passed in Congress but was never ratified by the states.

Women in the Workforce Women's lives changed in other ways in the 1920s. During World War I, thousands of women had worked outside the home for the first time. They filled the jobs of men who had gone off to war. When the troops came home, many women were forced to give up their jobs. Still, some remained in the workforce.

INTERACTIVE

Changes in American Life in the 1920s

Analyze Images As cars became popular, entrepreneurs built many new filling stations, such as this one in Maryland in 1921. **Compare and Contrast** How does this gas station compare to a modern one?

For some women, working outside the home was nothing new. Working-class women had been cooks, servants, and seamstresses for many years. In the 1920s, they were joined by middle-class women who worked as teachers, typists, secretaries, and store clerks. Some became doctors and lawyers despite discrimination.

Life at home also changed for women. More of them bought ready-made clothes for the whole family rather than sewing them at home as they had done in the past. Electric appliances such as refrigerators, washers, irons, and vacuum cleaners made housework easier. However, women who worked outside the home found that they had to work a second shift when they came home. Most husbands expected their wives to cook, clean, and care for children even if they held full-time jobs.

READING CHECK **Summarize** Why did the proposed Equal Rights Amendment fail to gain ratification?

How Did the Automobile Change America?

"Why on earth do you need to study what's changing this country?" one man asked the experts. "I can tell you what's happening in just four letters: A-U-T-O." In the 1920s, Americans traveled to more places and moved more quickly than ever before—all because of the automobile.

The auto industry played a central role in the business boom of the 1920s. Car sales grew rapidly during the decade. The auto boom spurred growth in related industries such as steel and rubber.

Cars Become Affordable Lower prices sparked the auto boom. By 1924, the cost of a Model T had dropped from $850 to $290. As a result, an American did not have to be rich to buy a car. Car prices fell because factories became more efficient.

As you have read, Henry Ford introduced the assembly line in his automobile factory in 1913. Before the assembly line, it took 14 hours to put together a Model T. In Ford's new factory, workers could assemble a Model T in 93 minutes. Other companies copied Ford's methods. In 1927, General Motors passed Ford as the top automaker. Unlike Ford, General Motors sold cars in a variety of models and colors.

Henry Ford had once boasted that people could have his cars in "any color so long as it's black." When General Motors introduced a low-priced car available in different colors, Ford lost many customers. Faced with the success of General Motors, he changed his mind. His next car, the Model A, came in different colors. Soon, car companies were offering new makes and models every year.

Americans hit the road. Between 1920 and 1928, vehicle registrations boomed. In some areas of the country, they increased more than 200 percent.

A Boost for the Economy Car sales spurred growth in other parts of the economy. By 1929, some four million Americans owed their jobs to the automobile, directly or indirectly. Tens of thousands of people worked in steel mills, producing metal used in cars. Others made tires, paint, and glass for cars. Some drilled for oil in the Southwest or worked in the oil refineries where crude petroleum was converted into usable gasoline.

Analyze Graphs Throughout the decade, more than a million cars were sold each year. **Make Predictions** Predict one reason for the rise in auto sales in 1927–1929.

Rise in Auto Sales, 1920–1929

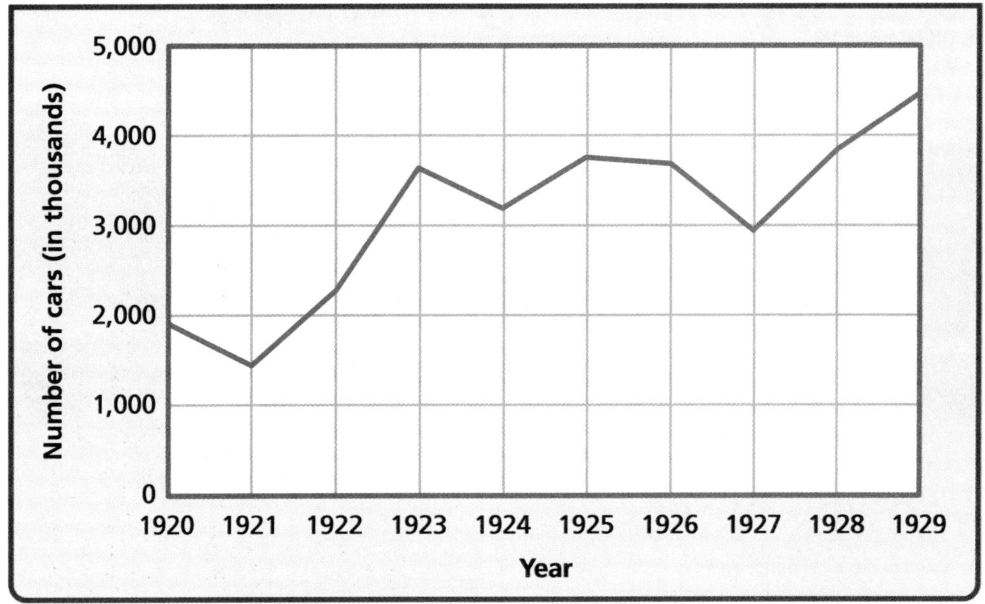

The car boom had other effects. States and cities paved more roads and built new highways. In 1925, the Bronx River Parkway in New York was the first of many highways in parklike settings. Gas stations, car dealers, motels, and roadside restaurants sprang up across the country to serve the millions who traveled by car. In 1920, there were only about 1,500 filling stations in the entire United States. By 1929, there were more than 120,000. Auto-repair shops also became a necessity.

Social Effects of Car Ownership Cars shaped life in the city and in the country. Many city dwellers wanted to escape crowded conditions. They moved to nearby towns in the country, which soon grew into suburbs. A suburb is a community located outside a city. With cars, suburban families could drive to the city even though it was many miles away. They could also drive to stores, schools, or work. No longer did people have to live where they could walk or take a trolley to work.

Another major shift came when suburban housewives refused to be confined to the passenger seat. Instead, they took their place behind the wheels of their own automobiles. As they did, they broke down still another barrier that separated the worlds of men and women.

In rural areas, cars brought people closer to towns, shops, and the movies. One farm woman bought a car before she got indoor plumbing. "You can't go to town in a bathtub," she explained.

READING CHECK **Identify Main Ideas** How did the automobile boost the American economy?

Analyze Images The new field of advertising helped popularize the automobile. **Use Visual Information** Who was the target of this advertisement?

Analyze Images As more people went to the movies, massive new theaters were built in a style that lived up to the name "movie palace." Today, the Chicago Theatre (built in 1921) has been restored to its past beauty. **Infer** Why do you think movie palaces were made so spectacular?

The Rise of a National Culture

By making travel easier, cars helped Americans from different parts of the country learn more about one another. They played a role in creating a new national culture that crossed state lines.

New forms of entertainment also contributed to the rise of a **mass culture**. Mass culture is the set of values and practices that arise from watching the same movies, listening to the same music, and hearing the same news reports as others around the nation. In the 1920s, rising wages and labor-saving appliances gave families more money to spend and more leisure time in which to spend it.

Entertainment at Home Radio became very popular in the 1920s. The country's first commercial radio station, KDKA, started broadcasting in Pittsburgh in 1920. By 1929, more than 10 million American families owned radios.

A new lifestyle emerged. Each night after dinner, families gathered around the radio to tune in to shows such as "Roxy and His Gang" or "Jack Frost's Melody Moments." Radio listeners enjoyed comedies and westerns, classical music and jazz, news reports and play-by-play sports broadcasts.

Going to the Movies In the 1920s, the movie industry came of age. Southern California's warm, sunny climate allowed filming all year round. Soon, Hollywood became the movie capital of the world.

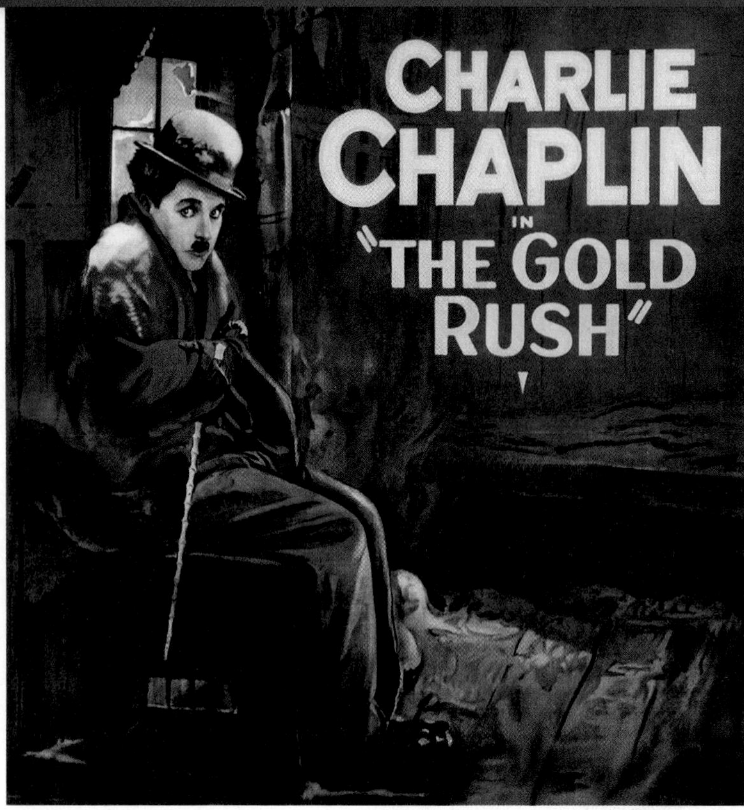

▲ Charlie Chaplin's fame as a silent film star began in the 1910s and continued through the 1920s and beyond. Chaplin continued to make popular silent films years after the shift to "talking pictures" in 1927.

Movies contributed to the new mass culture. Millions of Americans went to the movies at least once a week. They were thrilled to watch westerns, romances, adventures, and comedies. In small towns, theaters were bare rooms with hard chairs. In cities, they were huge palaces with red velvet seats.

The first movies had no sound. Audiences followed the plot by reading "title cards" that appeared on the screen. A pianist played music that went with the action.

Fans adored Hollywood movie stars. Cowboy stars like Tom Mix thrilled audiences with their heroic adventures. Clara Bow won fame playing restless, fun-seeking young women. The most popular star of all was comedian Charlie Chaplin, nicknamed "The Little Tramp." In his tiny derby hat and baggy pants, Chaplin presented a comical figure. His attempts to triumph over the problems of everyday life moved audiences to both laughter and tears.

In 1927, Hollywood caused a sensation when it produced *The Jazz Singer*. The film was a "talkie"—a movie with a soundtrack. Soon, all new movies were talkies.

READING CHECK **Identify Main Ideas** How did radio contribute to a new national culture in America?

Lesson Check

Practice Vocabulary

1. How did **Prohibition** support the growth of **organized crime**?
2. Why did many women demand an **Equal Rights Amendment**?

Critical Thinking and Writing

3. **Assess an Argument** Warren Harding won the presidency in 1920 because of his overwhelming support by women, who finally had the right to vote. Do you agree with the preceding statement? Why or why not?
4. **Support Ideas with Evidence** How did the automobile change America?
5. **Identify Main Ideas** How did a mass culture develop in the 1920s?
6. **Writing Workshop: Find and Use Credible Sources** What types of sources will offer you credible information about the subject of your New Deal research paper? Start finding possible sources now, and list them in your Active Journal.

LESSON 3

Roaring Twenties Culture

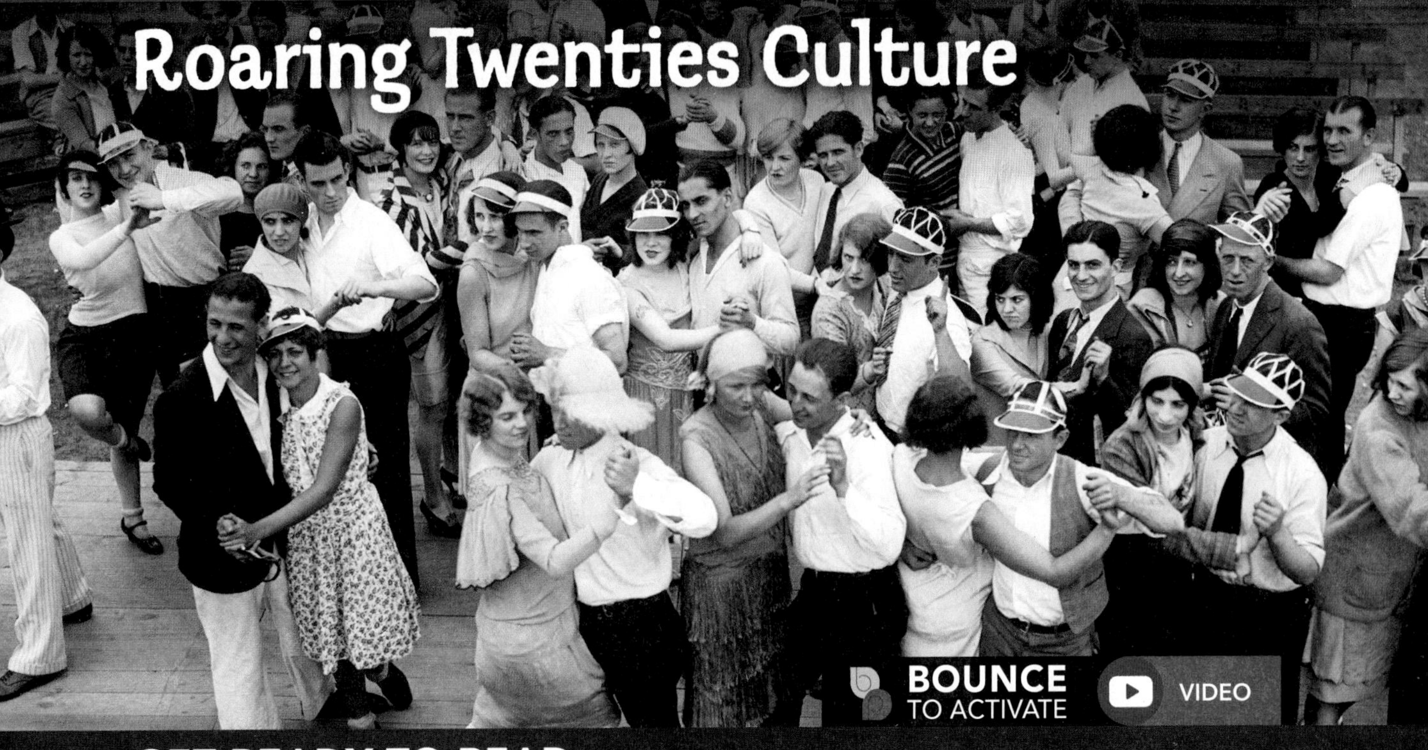

GET READY TO READ

START UP

Look at the photograph. Based on this photo, write one word that describes the 1920s and explain why you chose that word.

GUIDING QUESTIONS

- What were some of the fads and fashions popular during the 1920s?
- What new kinds of music and writing appeared during the 1920s, and how did they reflect the mood of the era?
- Who were the best-loved heroes of the 1920s?

TAKE NOTES

Literacy Skills: Summarize

Use the graphic organizer in your Active Journal to take notes as you read the lesson.

PRACTICE VOCABULARY

Use the vocabulary activity in your Active Journal to practice the vocabulary words.

Vocabulary	Academic Vocabulary
fad	exploit
flapper	prominent
jazz	
expatriate	

The 1920s brought economic prosperity and social change to the United States. At the same time, the culture underwent a radical shift. The era was called the Roaring Twenties with good reason. Like a roaring lion, it was loud and wild and exciting.

What Were the Main Trends of the 1920s?

"Ev'ry morning, ev'ry evening, ain't we got fun?" went a hit song of 1921. During the "Era of Wonderful Nonsense"—yet another nickname for the 1920s—fun came in many forms.

Fun Fads Fads caught on, then quickly disappeared. A **fad** is an activity or a fashion that is taken up with great passion for a short time. Flagpole sitting was one fad of the 1920s. Young people would perch on top of flagpoles for hours, or even days. Another fad was the dance marathon, where couples danced for hundreds of hours at a time to see who could last the longest. Crossword puzzles and mah-jongg, a Chinese game, were other popular fads of the 1920s.

Analyze Images Young women known as flappers defied expectations. **Synthesize Visual Information** In what ways did flappers depart from tradition?

Dance crazes came and went rapidly. The most popular new dance was probably the Charleston. First performed by African Americans in southern cities such as Charleston, South Carolina, the dance became a national craze after 1923. Moving to a quick beat, dancers pivoted their feet while kicking out first one leg, and then the other, backward and forward.

Flapper Fashion Perhaps no one pursued the latest fads more intensely than the **flappers**. These young women rebelled against traditional ways of thinking and acting. Flappers wore their hair bobbed, or cut short. They wore their dresses short, too—shorter than Americans had ever seen. Flappers shocked their parents by wearing bright red lipstick.

To many older Americans, the way flappers behaved was even more shocking than the way they looked. Flappers smoked cigarettes in public, drank bootleg alcohol in speakeasies, and drove fast cars. "Is 'the old-fashioned girl,' with all that she stands for in sweetness, modesty, and innocence, in danger of becoming extinct?" wondered one magazine in 1921.

Only a few young women were flappers. Still, they set a style for others. Slowly, older women began to cut their hair and wear makeup and shorter skirts. For many Americans, the bold fashions pioneered by the flappers symbolized a new sense of freedom.

The Rise of Jazz Music Another innovation of the 1920s was **jazz**. Born in New Orleans, jazz combined West African rhythms, African American work songs and spirituals, and European harmonies and band music. Jazz also had roots in the ragtime rhythms of composers such as Scott Joplin.

American Culture in the 1920s

Louis Armstrong was one of the brilliant young African American musicians who helped create jazz. Armstrong learned to play the trumpet in the New Orleans orphanage where he grew up. Armstrong had the ability to take a simple melody and experiment with the notes and the rhythm. This allowed his listeners to hear many different versions of the basic tune. Other great early jazz musicians included "Jelly Roll" Morton and singer Bessie Smith.

Jazz quickly spread from New Orleans to Chicago, Kansas City, and the mainly African American section of New York City known as Harlem. White musicians, such as trumpeter Bix Beiderbecke, also began to adopt the new style. Before long, the popularity of jazz spread to Europe as well.

Many older Americans worried that jazz and the new dances were a bad influence on the nation's young people. Despite their complaints, jazz continued to grow more popular. Today, jazz is recognized as an original art form developed by African Americans. It is considered one of the most important cultural contributions of the United States.

Analyze Images Jazz musicians such as Louis Armstrong, right, brought crowds of listeners into the Cotton Club in Harlem. **Infer** Why did jazz appeal to so many people?

Athletic Heroes Radio, movies, and newspapers created celebrities known across the country. Americans followed the **exploits** of individuals whose achievements made them stand out from the crowd. Some of the best-loved heroes of the decade were athletes. Each sport had its stars. Bobby Jones won almost every golf championship. Bill Tilden and Helen Wills ruled the tennis courts. Jack Dempsey reigned as world heavyweight boxing champion for seven years. At the age of 19, Gertrude Ederle became the first woman to swim across the English Channel.

College football also drew huge crowds. Many Americans who had never attended college rooted for college teams. They were thrilled to watch the exploits of football stars like Red Grange, the "Galloping Ghost" of the University of Illinois.

Americans loved football, but baseball was their real passion. The most popular player of the 1920s was Babe Ruth. He became the star of the New York Yankees. Fans flocked to games to see "the Sultan of Swat" hit home runs. The 60 home runs he hit in one season set a record that lasted more than 30 years. His lifetime record of 714 home runs was not broken until 1974.

"Lucky Lindy" The greatest hero was Charles A. Lindbergh. On a gray morning in May 1927, he took off from an airport in New York to fly nonstop across the Atlantic Ocean—alone. His was the first solo, nonstop transatlantic flight.

For more than 33 hours, Lindbergh piloted his tiny single-engine plane, the *Spirit of St. Louis,* over the stormy Atlantic. He carried no map, no parachute, and no radio. At last, he landed in Paris, France. The cheering crowd carried him across the airfield. "Lucky Lindy" returned to the United States as the hero of the decade.

READING CHECK **Classify and Categorize** What traits defined a flapper?

New American Writers Emerge

A new generation of American writers earned worldwide fame in the 1920s. Many of them were horrified by their experiences in World War I. They criticized Americans for caring too much about money and fun. Some became so unhappy with life in the United States that they moved to Paris, France. There, they lived as **expatriates**, people who leave their own country to live in a foreign land.

Hemingway and Fitzgerald Ernest Hemingway was one of the writers who lived for a time in Paris. Still a teenager at the outbreak of World War I, he traveled to Europe to drive an ambulance on the Italian front. Hemingway drew on his war experiences in *A Farewell to Arms,* a novel about a young man's growing disgust with war. In *The Sun Also Rises,* he examines the lives of American expatriates in Europe.

Analyze Images Babe Ruth hit 714 home runs in his career, a record that stood for nearly 40 years. **Understand Effects** How would an exciting player like Ruth cause baseball to surge in popularity?

Academic Vocabulary
exploits • *n.,* heroic or daring acts

Hemingway became one of the most **prominent** writers of the 1920s. His simple but powerful style influenced many other writers.

The young writer who best captured the mood of the Roaring Twenties was Hemingway's friend, F. Scott Fitzgerald. In *The Great Gatsby* and other novels, Fitzgerald examined the lives of wealthy young people who attended endless parties but could not find happiness. His characters included flappers, bootleggers, and moviemakers. Fitzgerald became a hero to college students and flappers, among others.

Other Important Contributions Sinclair Lewis grew up in a small town in Minnesota and later moved to New York City. In novels such as *Babbitt* and *Main Street,* he presented small-town Americans as dull and narrow-minded. Lewis's attitude reflected that of many city dwellers toward rural Americans. In fact, the word *babbitt* became a popular nickname for a smug businessman uninterested in literature or the arts. In 1930, Lewis was the first American to win the Nobel Prize in Literature.

Poet Edna St. Vincent Millay, who grew up in Maine, was enormously popular. She expressed the frantic pace of the 1920s in her verse, such as her short poem "First Fig."

Primary Source

My candle burns at both ends;
It will not last the night;
But ah, my foes, and oh, my friends—
It gives a lovely light.

—Edna St. Vincent Millay, "First Fig," 1920

Another writer, Eugene O'Neill, revolutionized the American theater. Most earlier playwrights had presented romantic, unrealistic stories. O'Neill shocked audiences with powerful, realistic dramas based on his years at sea. In other plays, he used experimental methods to expose the inner thoughts of tormented young people.

READING CHECK **Compare and Contrast** Which author best captured the Roaring Twenties?

A Renaissance in Harlem

In the 1920s, large numbers of African American musicians, artists, and writers settled in Harlem, in New York City. "Harlem was like a great magnet for the Negro Intellectual," said one African American writer.

Quick Activity

Explore changes in American culture during the 1920s in your Active Journal.

Academic Vocabulary
prominent • *adj.,* well-known

Analyze Images Edna St. Vincent Millay won the Pulitzer Prize in 1924 for her fourth book of poetry. **Infer** How did her work reflect the pace of the 1920s?

INTERACTIVE

Key Figures of the Harlem Renaissance

This gathering of African American artists and musicians led to the Harlem Renaissance, a rebirth of African American culture.

During the Harlem Renaissance, young Black writers celebrated their African and American heritages. They also protested prejudice and racism. For the first time, too, a large number of white Americans took notice of the achievements of African American artists and writers.

Langston Hughes Probably the best-known poet of the Harlem Renaissance was Langston Hughes. He published his first poem, "The Negro Speaks of Rivers," soon after graduating from high school. The poem connected the experiences of African Americans living along the Mississippi River with those of ancient Africans living along the Nile and Niger rivers. Like other writers of the Harlem Renaissance, Hughes encouraged African Americans to be proud of their heritage.

In other poems, Hughes protested racism and acts of violence against African Americans. In addition to his poems, Hughes wrote plays, short stories, and essays about the African American experience.

Other Poets and Novelists Other poets such as Countee Cullen and Claude McKay also wrote of the experiences of African Americans. Orphaned when his grandmother died, Cullen was raised by a Harlem minister and his wife. He went on to graduate from New York University and Harvard. He published award-winning books of poetry in the 1920s, and later wrote novels and plays.

McKay came to the United States from Jamaica. In his poem "If We Must Die," he condemned the lynchings and other mob violence that African Americans suffered after World War I. The poem concludes with the lines "Like men we'll face the murderous, cowardly pack, / Pressed to the wall, dying but fighting back!"

Analyze Graphs The Harlem Renaissance was a time of immense change. **Infer** What changes in the south might have encouraged African Americans to move north?

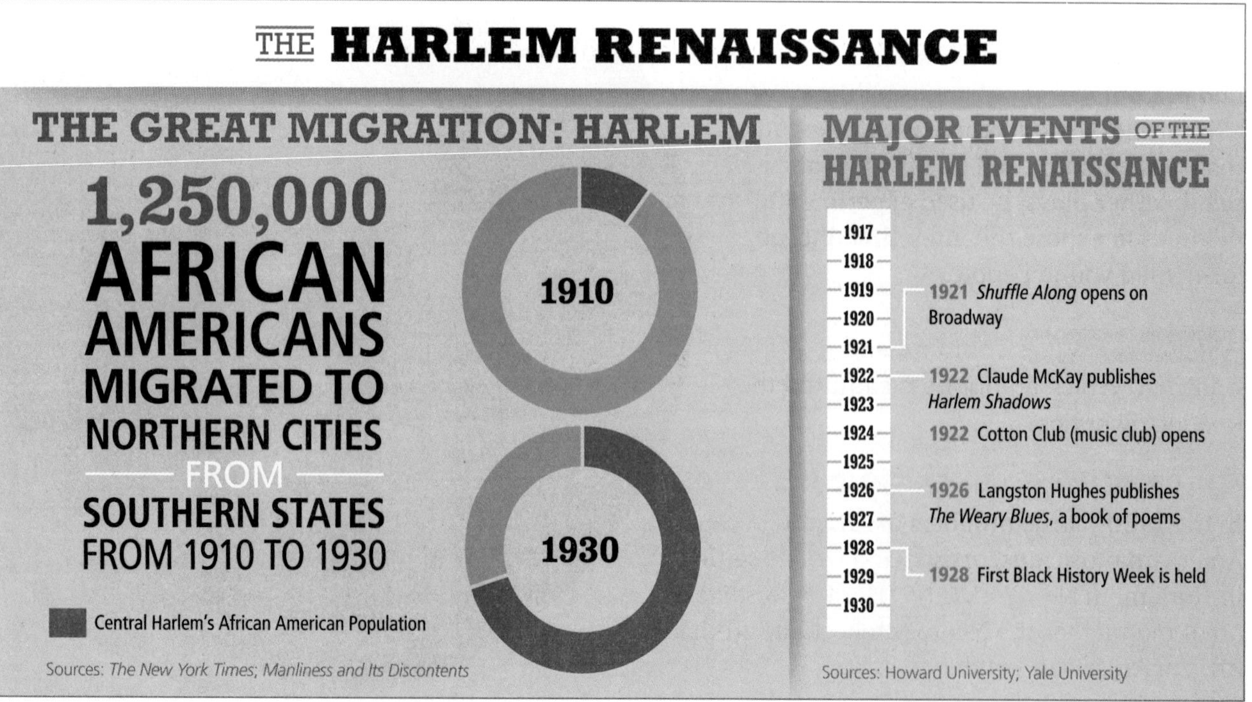

BIOGRAPHY 5 Things to Know About

ZORA NEALE HURSTON

Harlem Renaissance novelist, essayist, and folklorist (1891–1960)

- Her father, who was once enslaved, was mayor of the first all-black town in the country, Eatonville, Florida.
- After her mother died, she moved in with her sister.
- An anthropologist (one who studies humans and their ancestors), she traveled the South, Haiti, and Jamaica to gather folklore.
- Although it garnered little notice when published in 1937, her novel *Their Eyes Were Watching God* is today widely read.
- She died penniless and was buried in an unmarked grave.

Critical Thinking How did Hurston's travels to gather folklore help her preserve her heritage?

Zora Neale Hurston, who grew up in Florida, wrote novels, essays, and short stories. Hurston grew concerned that African American folklore "was disappearing without the world realizing it had ever been."

In 1928, she set out alone to travel through the South in a battered car. For two years, she collected the folk tales, songs, and prayers of African American southerners. She later published these in her book *Mules and Men*.

READING CHECK **Identify Main Ideas** What did many Harlem Renaissance writers hope to achieve with their writing?

Lesson Check

Practice Vocabulary

1. Would you expect a **flapper** to follow various **fads**? Why or why not?
2. Why do you think **jazz** has been popular for so long?

Critical Thinking and Writing

3. Draw Conclusions Why did some older people think jazz and the new dance styles were a bad influence on the nation's young people?
4. Support Ideas with Examples Do you think Charles Lindbergh deserved to be called a hero? Explain.
5. Generate Explanations Why was it important for writers of the Harlem Renaissance to express their feelings about racism and prejudice?
6. Writing Workshop: Find and Use Credible Sources Gather relevant information from the reliable sources you have found by taking careful notes from each one. Write the notes in your Active Journal, making sure you either paraphrase ideas, using your own words, or put quotation marks around information that comes directly from a source. Indicate, in your research paper, the source of any idea that is not your own.

Langston Hughes, "The Negro Speaks of Rivers" and "My People"

Langston Hughes wrote about how it felt to be African American, from the pain of racial prejudice to his deep pride in his culture and heritage. These two poems are among his most famous.

◀ Langston Hughes (1902–1967)

Reading and Vocabulary Support

① The Euphrates is a river in Mesopotamia, the Middle Eastern site of one of the earliest civilizations.

② The Congo is a river in Central Africa.

③ The Nile River Valley in Egypt was the location of another very early civilization.

④ Why did the poet make reference to Abraham Lincoln?

⑤ What connection is the poet making here between "The night" with "the faces of my people"?

The Negro Speaks of Rivers

I've known rivers:
I've known rivers ancient as the world and older than the flow of human blood in human veins.
My soul has grown deep like the rivers.
I bathed in the Euphrates ① when dawns were young.
I built my hut near the Congo ② and it lulled me to sleep.
I looked upon the Nile ③ and raised the pyramids above it.
I heard the singing of the Mississippi when Abe Lincoln ④ went down to New Orleans, and I've seen its muddy bosom turn all golden in the sunset.
I've known rivers:
Ancient, dusky rivers.
My soul has grown deep like the rivers.

My People

The night is beautiful,
So the faces of my people. ⑤
The stars are beautiful,
So the eyes of my people.
Beautiful, also, is the sun.
Beautiful, also, are the souls of my people.

Analyzing Primary Sources

Analyze the poems to answer the following questions.

1. **Determine Author's Point of View** What is the author's attitude toward being of African descent?

2. **Analyze Style and Rhetoric** How do the last lines of each poem create a link between the ideas expressed in each poem?

LESSON 4

Division and Inequality

GET READY TO READ

START UP

The trial for robbery and murder of Italian immigrants Nicola Sacco and Bartolomeo Vanzetti, shown here, divided the nation. Why do you think many Americans feared foreigners in the 1920s?

GUIDING QUESTIONS

- Why did some Americans face economic hardship during the 1920s?
- What did the Scopes Trial and the Red Scare reveal about American society?
- How did nativism and racism affect American society in the 1920s?

TAKE NOTES

Literacy Skills: Identify Cause and Effect

Use the graphic organizer in your Active Journal to take notes as you read the lesson.

PRACTICE VOCABULARY

Use the vocabulary activity in your Active Journal to practice the vocabulary words.

Vocabulary		Academic Vocabulary
company union	deport	setback
sabotage	quota system	hostility
anarchist	Great Migration	

Although it is often called "The Roaring Twenties" and remembered for dancing and jazz music, the decade of the 1920s was not all fun and games for everyone. Farmers, laborers, immigrants, and African Americans struggled to make progress in an era of widespread prosperity.

The Downside of the 1920s

Many Americans did not share in the boom of the 1920s. Workers in the clothing industry, for example, were hurt by changes in women's fashions. Shorter skirts meant that less cloth was needed to make dresses. Coal miners also faced hard times as oil replaced coal as a source of energy. Railroads slashed jobs because trains were losing business to cars and trucks.

Farmers Suffer Farmers were hit the hardest. During World War I, Europeans had bought American farm products, sending prices up. Farmers borrowed money to buy more land and tractors. They planned to pay off these loans with profits from increased production.

Quest CONNECTIONS

In the 1920s, many farmers could not pay their debts. Should the government have helped them? Record your responses in your Active Journal.

When the war ended, however, European farmers were again able to produce enough for their own needs. As a result, prices for American farm products dropped sharply throughout the 1920s. Farmers were unable to pay their debts. By the end of the decade, the farmers' share of national income had shrunk by almost half.

Labor Faces Losses For labor unions, too, the 1920s were a disaster. During the war, unions had worked with the government to keep production high. Labor's cooperation contributed to victory. In return, union leaders expected the government to support labor.

During the war, wages had not kept up with prices. Now, with the war over, workers demanded higher pay. When employers refused, unions launched a wave of strikes. Management moved quickly to crush the strikes. Because the government did not step in to help them, workers felt betrayed and management gained power.

Academic Vocabulary

setback • *n.*, a defeat or a reversal of progress

The strikes turned much of the public against labor. One strike in particular angered many Americans. In 1919, the city of Boston fired 19 police officers who had tried to join the American Federation of Labor (AFL). In protest, Boston police went out on strike. The sight of police officers leaving their posts shocked the country.

The later 1920s saw even more **setbacks** for labor. In one court case after another, judges limited the rights of unions. At the same time, employers created **company unions**, labor organizations that were actually controlled by management. As a result, membership in independent unions dropped from 5 million in 1920 to 3.4 million by 1929. Without strong unions, labor had little power to win higher wages.

READING CHECK **Identify Main Ideas** What workers in different areas of the economy suffered economic losses during the 1920s?

Analyze Images A Boston police officer appeals to a mounted state trooper during the Boston Police Strike of 1919. **Summarize** Why did the police go on strike?

What Cultural Clashes Gained National Attention?

In the 1920s, cities drew thousands of people from farms and small towns. Those who stayed in rural areas often feared that new ways of life in the city were a threat to traditional values. Changes abroad also spurred nationwide worries about people with differing political views.

The Scopes Trial One clash between old and new values erupted in the small town of Dayton, Tennessee. At the center of the controversy was Charles Darwin's theory of evolution. Darwin, a British scientist, had claimed that all life had evolved, or developed, from simpler forms over a long period of time.

Analyze Images High-school teacher John T. Scopes (center) was convicted and fined for teaching evolution to his students in the state of Tennessee. **Cite Evidence** Do you think Scopes should have been convicted?

While biologists accepted Darwin's theory, some churches condemned it, saying it contradicted the teachings of the Bible. Tennessee, Mississippi, and Arkansas passed laws that banned the teaching of Darwin's theory. In 1925, John Scopes, a biology teacher in Dayton, taught evolution to his class. Scopes was arrested and tried.

Two of the nation's best-known figures opposed each other in the Scopes trial. William Jennings Bryan, who had run for president three times, argued the state's case against Scopes. Clarence Darrow, a Chicago lawyer who had helped unions, defended Scopes.

As the trial began, the nation's attention was riveted on Dayton. Reporters recorded every word of the battle between Darrow and Bryan. "Scopes isn't on trial," Darrow thundered at one point, "civilization is on trial." In the end, Scopes was convicted and fined. Later, the laws against teaching evolution were overturned, or defeated.

Worries Cause a Red Scare During World War I, Americans had been on the alert for enemy spies and **sabotage**, or the secret destruction of property or interference with work in factories. These wartime worries led to a growing fear of foreigners.

The rise of communism in the Soviet Union fanned that fear. Lenin, the Communist leader, called on workers everywhere to overthrow their governments. Many Americans saw the strikes that swept the nation as the start of a Communist revolution.

INTERACTIVE

Contrasts in American Society

The First Red Scare

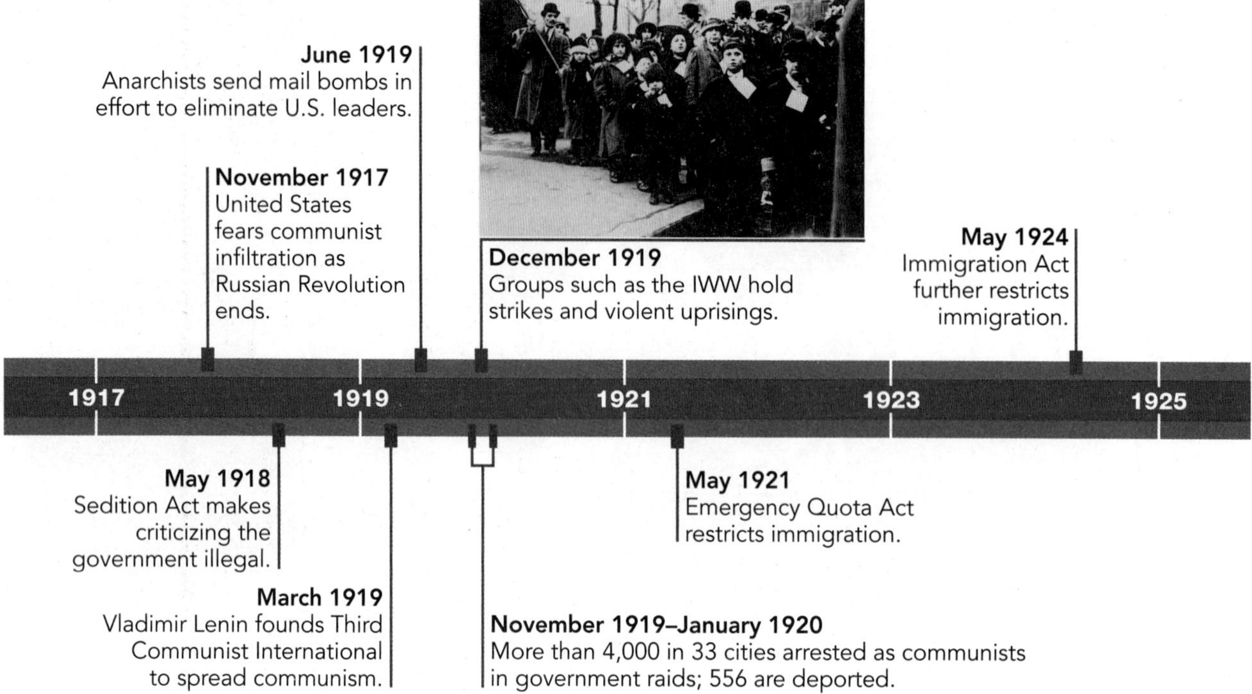

Analyze Images Increasing alarm about communism led to many reactions. **Identify Supporting Details** Explain the relationship between immigration laws and Americans' fear of Communists.

Eliminating Extremists The actions of **anarchists**, or people who oppose organized government, added to the sense of danger. One group of anarchists plotted to kill well-known Americans, including John D. Rockefeller, the head of Standard Oil. Because many anarchists were foreign-born, their attacks led to an outcry against all foreigners.

The government took harsh actions against both anarchists and Communists, or "reds." During the Red Scare, thousands of radicals were arrested and jailed. Many foreigners were **deported**.

Sacco and Vanzetti The trial of two Italian immigrants in Massachusetts came to symbolize the anti-foreign feeling of the 1920s. Nicola Sacco and Bartolomeo Vanzetti were arrested for robbery and murder in 1920. The two men admitted being anarchists, but insisted they had committed no crime. A jury convicted them, however. Sacco and Vanzetti were then sentenced to death.

The Sacco and Vanzetti trial created a furor across the nation. The evidence against the two men was limited. The judge was openly prejudiced against the two immigrants. Many Americans thought that Sacco and Vanzetti were convicted because they were immigrants and radicals, instead of being guilty. The two men waited in jail during a six-year fight to overturn their convictions. In 1927, they were executed.

The issue of whether Sacco and Vanzetti received a fair trial has been debated ever since. In the meantime, some Americans thought the case proved that the United States had to keep out dangerous radicals.

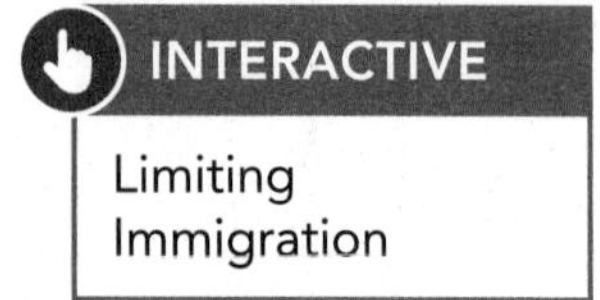

READING CHECK **Identify Main Ideas** What was the key issue in the Scopes trial?

How Was Immigration Restricted?

In the end, the Red Scare died down. Yet **hostility** toward foreigners led to a new move to limit immigration. As you recall, this kind of anti-foreign feeling is known as nativism.

Academic Vocabulary
hostility • *n.*, an unfriendly feeling or action

Immigration Quotas After the war, millions of Europeans hoped to find a better life in the United States. American workers feared that too many newcomers would force wages down. Others worried that Communists and anarchists would flood in.

Congress responded by passing the Emergency Quota Act in 1921. The act set up a **quota system** that allowed only a certain number of people from each country to enter the United States. Only 3 percent of the people in any national group already living in the United States in 1910 could be admitted.

The quota system favored immigrants from northern Europe, especially Great Britain. In 1924, Congress passed new laws that further cut immigration, especially from eastern Europe, which was seen as a center of anarchism and communism. In addition, Japanese were added to the list of Asians denied entry to the country.

Hispanics Immigrate Latin Americans and Canadians were not included in the quota system. As a result, Mexican immigrants continued to move to the United States. Farms and factories in the Southwest depended on Mexican workers. The pay was low, and the housing was poor. Still, immigrants were drawn by the chance to earn more money than they could at home. By 1930, a million or more Mexicans had crossed the border.

The Jones Act of 1917 granted American citizenship to Puerto Ricans. Poverty on the island led to a great migration to the north. In 1910, about 1,500 Puerto Ricans lived on the mainland. By 1930, there were about 53,000.

READING CHECK **Identify Supporting Details** Why did Congress cut immigration from Eastern European countries more than from other countries?

Analyze Images The Ku Klux Klan marches in Washington, D.C., in 1926. **Infer** How did the rise of the Klan signal a growing fear among Americans?

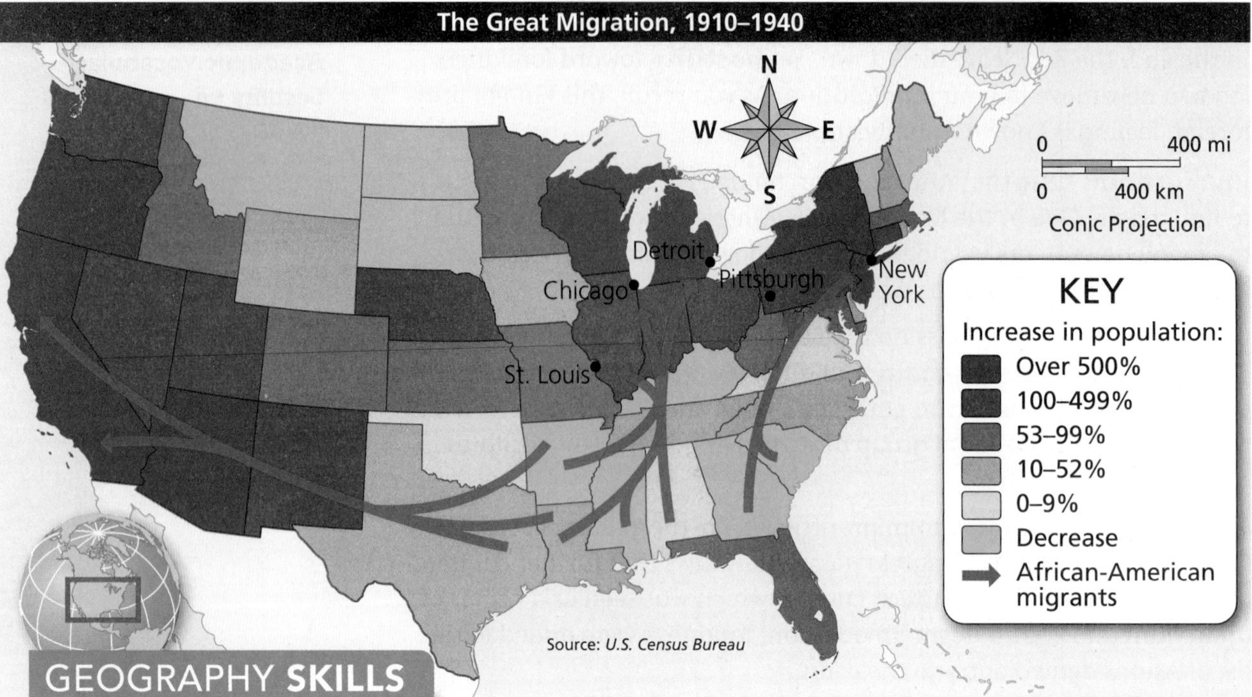

GEOGRAPHY **SKILLS**

Between 1910 and 1940, most states saw increases in their African American populations as African American migrants moved from the South.

1. **Region** Which region saw the greatest number of new arrivals?
2. **Infer** Why were certain northern cities the primary destinations for African Americans during the Great Migration?

Racial Tensions Rise

As African American soldiers returned from serving their country in the war, they began demanding equal rights. This, along with the large African American migration to northern cities, led to heightened racial tension and race riots. White racists formed a new Ku Klux Klan. Groups called the Universal Negro Improvement Association and the National Association for the Advancement of Colored People, or NAACP, organized to defend the rights of African Americans.

The New Klan Fear of change gave new life to an old organization. In 1915, a group of white men in Georgia declared the rebirth of the Ku Klux Klan. The original Klan had used terror to keep African Americans from voting after the Civil War. The new Klan had a broader aim: to preserve the United States for white, native-born Protestants.

The new Klan waged a campaign not only against African Americans but also against immigrants, especially Catholics and Jews. Klan members burned crosses outside people's homes. They used whippings and lynchings to terrorize immigrants and African Americans. The Klan strongly supported efforts to limit immigration.

Because of its large membership, the Klan gained political influence. In the mid-1920s, however, many Americans became alarmed at the Klan's growing power. At the same time, scandals surfaced that showed Klan leaders had stolen money from members. Klan membership dropped sharply.

The Great Migration African Americans had hoped that their service during World War I would weaken racism at home. However, returning African American soldiers found that the South was still a segregated society. In the North, too, racial prejudice was widespread.

Many African Americans moved north during and after the war. The large-scale movement north of African Americans during the early to mid-1900s is known as the **Great Migration**. African Americans took factory jobs in Chicago, Detroit, New York, Philadelphia, and other large cities. They often found that the only jobs open to them were low-paying ones. Also, due to discrimination, there were only a few neighborhoods where landlords would rent apartments to African Americans.

At the same time, many newly arrived African Americans wanted to live near friends and family members. This reinforced residential segregation due to racism in northern cities.

Many northern white workers resented the arrival of so many African Americans competing for jobs. In 1919, white attacks sparked race riots in several cities. The worst took place in Chicago, leaving 38 dead.

A Black Nationalist Leader Shocked by the racism they found, African Americans looked for new ways to cope. Marcus Garvey became one of the most popular African American leaders. He started the first widespread Black nationalist movement in the United States. Garvey organized the Universal Negro Improvement Association. He hoped to promote unity and pride among African Americans. He believed that African Americans needed to rely on themselves rather than white people to get ahead. "I am the equal of any white man," Garvey said.

Garvey urged African Americans to seek their roots in Africa. Although few actually went to Africa, the movement built racial pride.

READING CHECK **Identify Cause and Effect** What caused racial tensions to increase during the 1920s?

The Election of 1928

By 1928, Republicans had led the nation for eight years. They pointed to prosperity as their outstanding achievement. President Coolidge chose not to run for re-election. Instead, Secretary of Commerce Herbert Hoover easily won the Republican nomination. The Democrats chose as their candidate Alfred E. Smith, the governor of New York.

The contrast between the candidates revealed the tensions lurking below the surface of American life. Smith, the grandson of Irish, Italian, and German immigrants, was the first Catholic to run for President. City dwellers, including many immigrants and Catholics, rallied around Smith. Hoover was a self-made millionaire from the Midwest who was respected for his management skill in working to supply troops during World War I.

Analyze Images Marcus Garvey helped spark movements from African nationalist independence to American civil rights. **Infer** How was Garvey an inspiration?

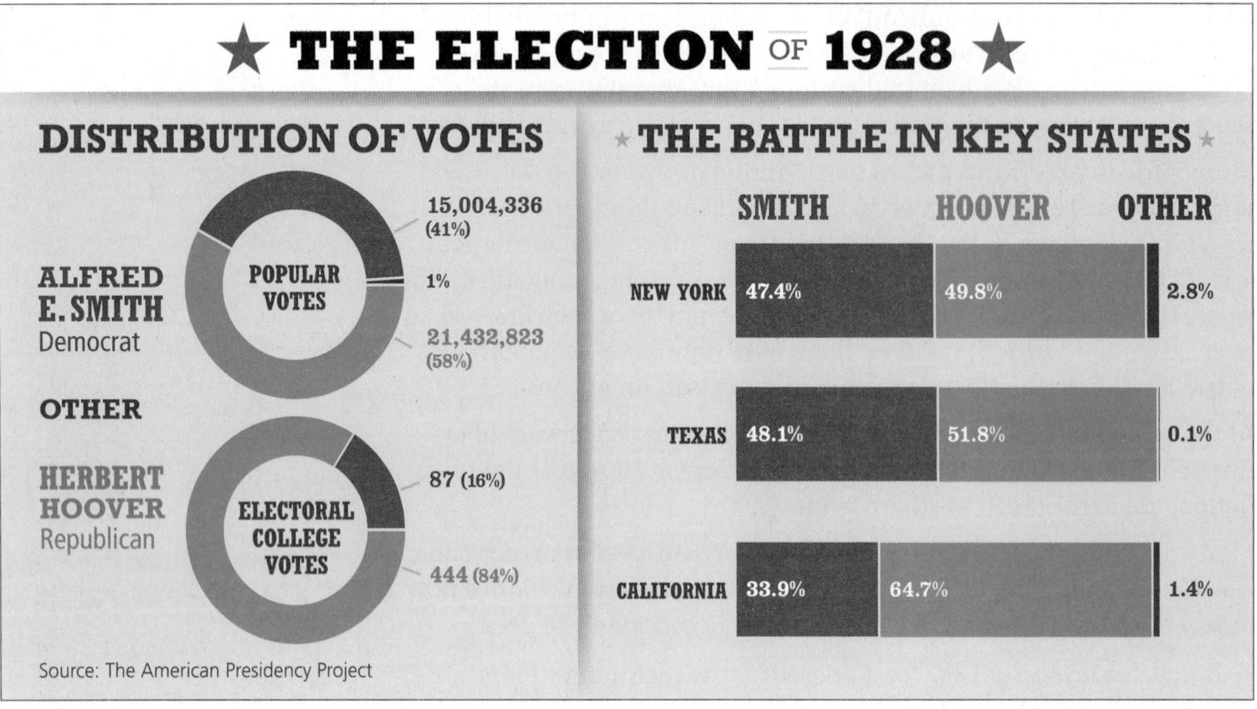

Analyze Graphs Voters chose Herbert Hoover over Alfred E. Smith in the 1928 presidential election. **Use Visual Information** What do the graphs tell you about the American population at the time?

He won votes from rural Americans and big business. Supporters of Prohibition also supported Hoover because Smith favored repeal.

In the election, Smith won the country's 12 largest cities. Rural and small-town voters supported Hoover. He won by a landslide. Americans hoped Hoover would keep the country prosperous. Less than a year after he took office, however, the economy would come crashing down.

READING CHECK **Compare and Contrast** How did Al Smith's background differ from that of Herbert Hoover?

Lesson Check

Practice Vocabulary

1. Why might an **anarchist** attempt **sabotage**?
2. Where in the country did the **Great Migration** generally start and end?

Critical Thinking and Writing

3. **Compare Points of View** Why do you think presidents refused to intervene in labor strikes in the 1920s—unlike Theodore Roosevelt, who had intervened in a major 1902 coal strike?
4. **Analyze Information** According to the quota system, the number of people allowed to immigrate from a nation would be a set percentage of the people from that nation already living in the United States. Why did that quota system favor northern Europeans?
5. **Identify Cause and Effect** Why did calls for political and social equality for minority groups increase after World War I?
6. **Writing Workshop: Support Ideas With Evidence** Your note-taking has given you a number of ideas that you will incorporate into your research paper. Write the key ideas in your Active Journal, and include evidence that supports each idea.

LESSON 5

Entering the Great Depression

GET READY TO READ

START UP

Look at the photo of the man who lost everything during the Great Depression. Write three questions you would ask him.

GUIDING QUESTIONS

- What led to the stock market crash of 1929?
- How did the early years of the Great Depression affect Americans?
- How did President Hoover respond to the economic downturn?

TAKE NOTES

Literacy Skills: Sequence

Use the graphic organizer in your Active Journal to take notes as you read the lesson.

PRACTICE VOCABULARY

Use the vocabulary activity in your Active Journal to practice the vocabulary words.

Vocabulary		Academic Vocabulary
on margin	soup kitchen	relief
Great Depression	public works	bonus
bankrupt	Hooverville	
	Bonus Army	

During his successful 1928 campaign for president, Herbert Hoover assured voters, "We in America are nearer the final triumph over poverty than ever before in the history of any land." The voters had no reason to doubt that the good times would continue.

What Led to the Crash?

Most Americans had great confidence in President Hoover when he was inaugurated in March 1929. For most of the 1920s, Hoover had served in the cabinet as secretary of commerce. In that role, he had helped create the greatest prosperity the country had ever seen.

Then, only seven months after Hoover's inauguration, the stock market crashed. The United States began a plunge into the worst economic depression in its history. Everywhere, stunned people asked: How could this have happened?

An Economic Slowdown When Hoover took office in 1929, he saw a growing economy. Along with most of the nation's leaders, he did not recognize the signs of trouble.

FRIDAY, OCTOBER 25, 1929.

Daily Mail

CONTINENTAL EDITION

PRICE (France): ONE FRANC.

GREATEST CRASH IN WALL STREET'S HISTORY

DELUGE OF PANIC SELLING OVERWHELMS MARKET

19,000,000 SHARES CHANGE HANDS

PRICES TUMBLE LIKE AN AVALANCHE

WILD SCENES TILL GREAT FINANCIERS COME TO RESCUE

The New York Stock Exchange.

The worst crash in the history of Wall Street took place yesterday, when 19,226,400 shares changed hands, the values of securities were reduced by billions of dollars and the big stocks dropped to record low figures.

SCARE SELLING BY SMALL INVESTORS.

MEETING OF MILLIONS

BIG BANKERS' EFFORT TO STOP PANIC

BANKERS' REASSURING STATEMENT

MR. CHARLES E. MITCHELL'S OPTIMISM

TRADERS' PANIC

SABOTAGE SCARE

'PLANE MISSING IN CHANNEL GALE

NO NEWS FROM 3 MEN ABOARD

SHIPS KEEP WATCH

WHIRLWIND'S HAVOC

GREAT FILM FIRE AT HOLLYWOOD

NEGATIVES DESTROYED.

ATTEMPT TO KILL PRINCE HUMBERT

BETROTHAL DAY DRAMA

SHOT AT BY SOCIALIST

PRINCE'S COURAGE

EXCHANGE RATES

SEARCH FOR NEW FRENCH PREMIER

(Continued in Page 5, Col. 1.)

CANADA

THE ROYAL BANK OF CANADA

Lucile PARIS

SALE OF MODELS TO-DAY AND TO-MORROW

london trades

SHOWING DEMI-SAISON COLLECTION TO-DAY, FRIDAY, at 3 p.m.

Au Coin de Venise

GREAT HANDKERCHIEF WEEK.

MONTE CARLO

NOW OPEN THE HOTEL METROPOLE

Analyze Images
Newspapers around the country spread the word about the stock market crash. **Infer** Why do you think the crash was international news?

Hoover did realize that some Americans had not shared in the prosperity of the 1920s. As you have read, farmers already faced hardship in the 1920s. So did workers in the textile and coal industries. For workers in those industries, a booming economy was something they only read about in the newspapers. The words on a Pennsylvania mining town tombstone reflected their feelings of frustration.

Primary Source

> For forty years beneath the sod
> With pick and spade I did my task
> The coal king's slave, but now,
> thank God I'm free at last.
>
> —Tombstone inscription, Pennsylvania

In the mid-1920s, the overall economy began to slow down. No one noticed the slowdown because at that time the government did not keep detailed statistics.

The Crash By August 1929, some investors worried that the boom might soon end. They began selling their stocks. In September, more people decided to sell. The rash of selling caused stock prices to fall. Hoover reassured investors that the "business of the country . . . is on a sound and prosperous basis." Despite the President's calming words, the selling continued and stock prices tumbled.

Many investors had bought stocks on margin. Buyers of stocks **on margin** pay only part of the cost of the stock when they make the purchase. They borrow the rest from their stockbrokers. With prices falling, brokers asked investors to pay back what they owed. Investors sold their stock to repay their loans.

A panic quickly set in. Between October 24 and October 29, desperate people tried to unload millions of shares. As a result, stock prices dropped even further.

When the stock market opened on Tuesday, October 29, a wild stampede of selling hit the New York Stock Exchange. Prices plunged because there were no buyers. People who thought they owned valuable stocks were left with worthless paper.

After Black Tuesday, as it came to be called, business leaders tried to restore confidence in the economy. John D. Rockefeller told reporters, "My son and I have for some days been purchasing some common stocks." Replied comedian Eddie Cantor, "Sure, who else has any money left?"

READING CHECK **Identify Supporting Details** What happened on Black Tuesday?

The Great Depression Begins

The period of economic hard times that followed the crash is known as the **Great Depression**. It lasted from 1929 to 1941.

The stock market crash did not cause the Great Depression, but it did shake people's confidence in the economy. As the Depression worsened, people tried to understand how the prosperity of the 1920s had vanished.

Causes of the Great Depression Among the chief causes of the Great Depression was overproduction. American factories and farms produced vast amounts of goods in the 1920s. Vast corporate profits made from increased production were not passed on to workers. As a result, the gap between rich and poor widened with the middle class slipping into poverty. In fact, over one third of American assets were owned by one percent of Americans—those with the most money.

Having such a small number of people in control of so much wealth contributed to an economic slump. First, the wealthy were more likely to save the money than spend it like those who were less wealthy. Second, those who were less wealthy saw their buying power fall.

Because wages did not keep up with prices, workers could not afford to buy the goods that corporations continued to produce. Factories and farms were producing more goods than people were buying. As orders slowed, factories laid off workers.

Another cause of the Depression was weakness in the banking system. During the 1920s, banks made unwise loans. For example, banks lent money to people who invested in the stock market. When the stock market crashed, borrowers could not repay their loans.

Analyze Graphs American factories and farms increased production in the 1920s. **Use Visual Information** What effect did the overproduction of goods have on prices?

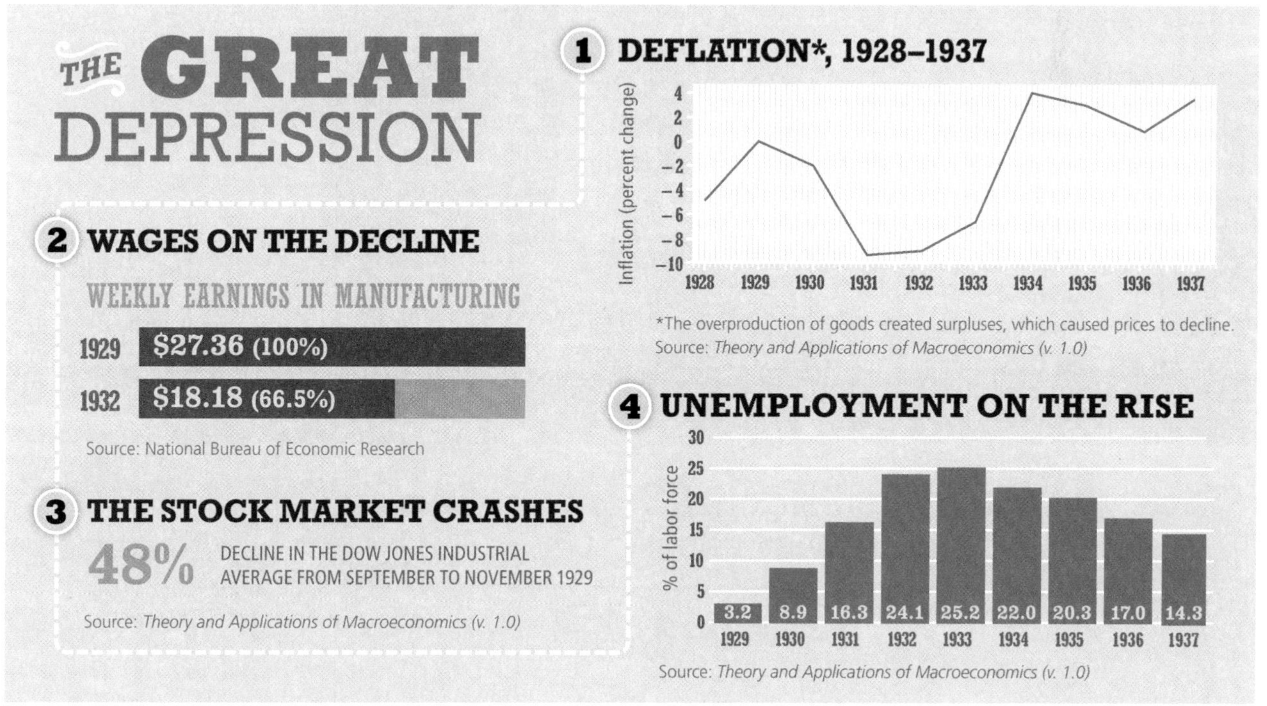

Because banks could not give depositors their money when they asked for it, many banks were forced to close.

More than 5,000 banks closed between 1929 and 1932. When a bank closed, depositors lost their money. Often, a family's lifetime savings disappeared overnight.

A Series of Economic Problems After the stock market crash, the economy slid downhill at a fast pace. One disaster triggered another. The stock market crash, for example, ruined many investors. Without capital, or money, from investors, businesses could no longer grow and expand. Businesses could not turn to banks for capital because the banks were also in trouble.

As factories cut back on production, they cut wages and laid off workers. Unemployed workers, in turn, had little money to spend, so demand for goods fell further. In the end, many businesses went **bankrupt**—they were unable to pay their debts. As bankrupt businesses closed, even more people were thrown out of work.

The Great Depression led to a worldwide economic crisis. In the 1920s, the United States had loaned large sums to European nations. When American banks stopped making loans or demanded repayment of existing loans, European banks began to fail. The depression spread from nation to nation. By 1930, a worldwide economic crisis occurred.

READING CHECK **Identify Main Ideas** What were two main causes of the Great Depression?

Analyze Charts A series of events led to the Great Depression. **Summarize** How does the timeline show a relationship between the U.S. economy and the economies of other nations?

Events Leading to Global Economic Collapse, 1919–1930

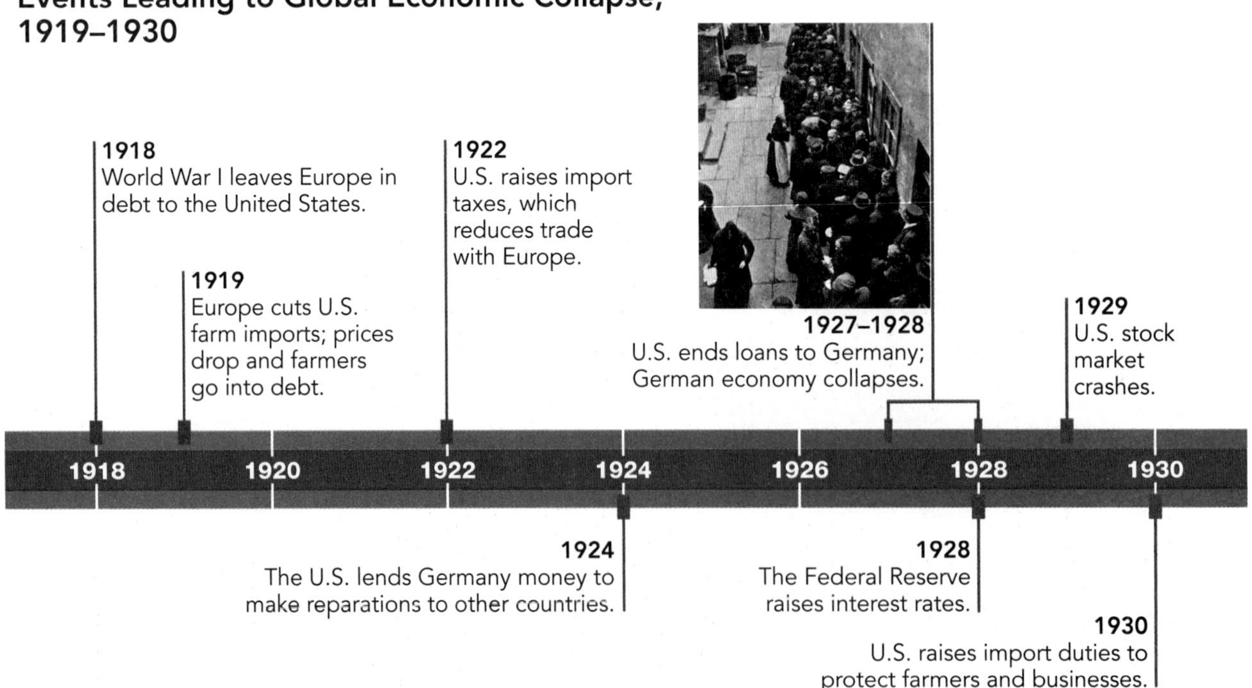

Daily Life for Americans

The United States had suffered earlier economic depressions. None, however, was as severe as the Great Depression. In earlier times, most Americans lived on farms and grew their own food. In the 1930s, millions of Americans lived in cities and worked in factories. When factories closed, the jobless had no money for food and no land on which to grow it.

The Jobless As the Depression spread, the unemployment rate soared. By the early 1930s, one in every four workers was jobless. Millions more worked shortened hours or took pay cuts. Many of the jobless lost their homes. On city streets, people sold pencils and begged for money.

The chance of finding work was small. On an average day, one New York job agency had 5,000 people looking for work. Only about 300 found jobs. In another city, police had to keep order as 15,000 women pushed and shoved to apply for six jobs cleaning offices. Some of the jobless shined shoes on street corners. Others set up sidewalk stands and sold apples.

Analyze Images Like many others, this family faced huge challenges during the Depression. **Compare and Contrast** Describe how rural and urban families dealt with the struggles of daily life.

Challenges for Families During the Depression, families suffered. Marriage and birth rates dropped. Hungry parents and children searched through city dumps and restaurant garbage cans for food. In one school, a teacher ordered a thin girl to go home to eat. "I can't," replied the girl. "This is my sister's day to eat."

The pressure of hard times led some families to split up. The scarcity of food and work caused fathers and even children as young as 13 or 14 years old to leave home to hunt for work. Their leaving meant the family had fewer people to feed, but it also came at a cost: there were fewer people to care for any young children or elderly at home.

Jobless men and women drifted from town to town looking for work. Some "rode the rails," living in railroad cars and hitching rides on freight trains. Louis Banks, a young African American, later described what it was like to ride the rails.

Primary Source

"Twenty-five or thirty would be out on the side of the rail, white and colored. They didn't have no mothers or sisters, they didn't have no home, they were dirty, they had overalls on, they didn't have no food, they didn't have anything."

— Louis Banks, Interview, 1970

The Impact of the Great Depression

▲ As joblessness multiplied during the Great Depression, an increasing number of people relied on charity for food.

Americans did their best to cope. They attempted to meet their basic needs by utilizing the scarce resources they possessed. Neighbors shared what little they had. Some families doubled up, taking in aunts, uncles, and cousins. Some families began to grow vegetables and can foods instead of shopping in stores.

The Great Depression shook Americans' belief in themselves. Many Americans defined their self-worth partly on their ability to produce and consume goods and services. Without the opportunity to be productive members of the economy, many found their self-worth diminished. "No matter that others suffered the same fate, the inner voice whispered, 'I'm a failure,'" one unemployed man wrote.

READING CHECK **Identify Supporting Details** How did urbanization worsen the effects of the Depression?

How Did the President Respond?

President Hoover was deeply concerned about the suffering. However, Hoover thought that government should not become directly involved in helping end the business crisis. He feared that government might become too powerful. It was up to businesses, he believed, to work together to end the economic downturn.

Academic Vocabulary
relief • *n.,* help for the needy, often in the form of money or food

Aid for the Needy At first, Hoover also opposed government **relief** programs—projects aimed at helping the needy. Instead, the President urged business leaders to keep workers employed and to maintain wages.

Hoover also called on private charities to help the needy. Churches set up **soup kitchens**, places where the hungry could get a free meal. Ethnic communities organized their own relief efforts. In San Francisco's Chinatown, fraternal societies gave out food and clothing. Father Divine, an African American religious leader in New York's Harlem, fed 3,000 hungry people a day. Mexican Americans and Puerto Ricans turned to aid societies. Still, the numbers of the needy soon overwhelmed private charities.

President Hoover's strong belief in limited government affected his initial response to the economic crisis. Soon after taking office in 1930, he declared, "Prosperity cannot be restored by raids upon the public Treasury." However, as the Depression continued, he adopted some policies that he hoped would help people help themselves and stimulate the economy.

The Great Depression—Causes and Effects

He set up public works programs. **Public works** are projects built by the government for public use. The government hired workers to build schools, construct dams, and pave highways. By providing jobs, these programs enabled people to earn money.

Hoover also asked Congress to approve the Reconstruction Finance Corporation, or RFC, in 1932. The RFC loaned money to banks, railroads, and insurance companies to help them stay in business. Saving these businesses, Hoover hoped, would save thousands of jobs.

Quest CONNECTIONS

What does the Hoover Dam's construction tell you about President Hoover's opinion about government helping citizens in times of need? Record your responses in your Active Journal.

A Deepening Depression Hoover did more to reverse hard times than any previous President. However, his efforts were too little and came too late. In 1931, as the third winter of the Depression approached, more and more people joined the ranks of the hungry and homeless. "Men are sitting in the parks all day long and all night long," wrote one man in Detroit.

Many people blamed the President for doing too little. He refused to establish a welfare system for those out of work, believing it would further devastate American morale. However, people were desperate for any help they could get. They gave the name **Hoovervilles** to the clusters of shacks where the homeless lived. People spoke of "Hoover blankets," the newspapers used by the homeless to keep warm when they slept outside. A cardboard patch that covered a hole in a shoe was called "Hoover leather." Men, women, and children lined up for "Hoover stew," the name they gave to the thin soup they received in soup kitchens.

Academic Vocabulary

bonus • *n.*, an additional sum of money

The Bonus Army While people waited for the government to help, one group of Americans took action. After World War I, Congress had voted to give veterans a **bonus**, to be paid in 1945. In 1932, more than 20,000 jobless veterans marched to Washington to demand the bonus right away. For two months, the **Bonus Army**, as the group of veterans were called, camped in a tent city along the Potomac River.

The House of Representatives voted to give the veterans the bonus at once, but the Senate rejected the bill. Senators thought that the cost would prevent government action to aid the country's recovery. While many discouraged veterans went home, thousands stayed.

Local police tried to force the veterans to leave. Battles with police left four people dead. Hoover then ordered General Douglas MacArthur to clear out the veterans.

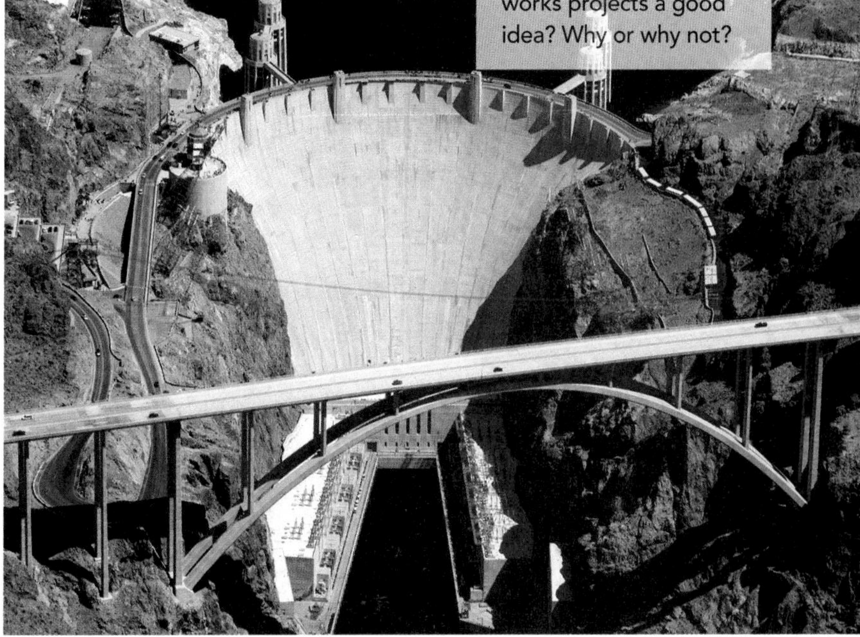

Analyze Images Public works projects, like the Hoover Dam, gave Americans jobs. **Cite Evidence** Were public works projects a good idea? Why or why not?

Using cavalry, tanks, machine guns, and tear gas, MacArthur moved into the camp and burned it to the ground.

An editorial in the *Washington News* years later expressed the shock many Americans felt at the time.

Primary Source

What a pitiful spectacle is that of the great American Government, mightiest in the world, chasing unarmed men, women, and children with Army tanks. . . . If the Army must be called out to make war on unarmed citizens, this is no longer America.

—*Washington News,* "The Summer of the BEF," November 23, 1946

▲ In 1932, Bonus Army members occupied a portion of Washington, D.C., in this camp.

After the attack on the Bonus Army, Hoover lost what little support he still had. Convinced that the country needed a change, many Americans looked for a new leader.

READING CHECK **Compare and Contrast** How do public works differ from private projects?

Lesson Check

Practice Vocabulary

1. When a business went **bankrupt** during the Great Depression, how did that affect the community?
2. What did **Hoovervilles** and the **Bonus Army** camp have in common?

Critical Thinking and Writing

3. **Express Problems Clearly** Why did buying on margin seem, to some investors, like an acceptable way to purchase stock, but turn out to be unwise?
4. **Generate Explanations** Why do you think President Hoover ordered the military to clear the Bonus Army out of Washington, D.C.?
5. **Revisit the Essential Question** Do you think President Hoover did enough to try to boost the economy and help Americans hurt by the Great Depression?
6. **Writing Workshop: Support Ideas with Evidence** Look at the list of ideas and evidence that you wrote earlier in your Active Journal. Make sure your evidence fully supports your ideas and includes information such as statistics and direct quotations.

LESSON 6

Roosevelt's New Deal

BOUNCE TO ACTIVATE

VIDEO

GET READY TO READ

START UP

Look at the poster. Why would the government pay artists to create beautiful images during the Great Depression?

GUIDING QUESTIONS

- Why did Franklin D. Roosevelt win the election of 1932?
- How did Roosevelt's New Deal change government's relationship to the economy?
- What did critics have to say about New Deal policies?
- What was the impact of the New Deal?

TAKE NOTES

Literacy Skills: Analyze Text Structure

Use the graphic organizer in your Active Journal to take notes as you read the lesson.

PRACTICE VOCABULARY

Use the vocabulary activity in your Active Journal to practice the vocabulary words.

Vocabulary

- bank holiday
- fireside chat
- Hundred Days
- New Deal
- collective bargaining
- pension
- deficit spending
- national debt

Academic Vocabulary

- stabilize
- tactic

By the time of the presidential election of 1932, any optimism about a quick end to the economic downturn had melted away. The unemployment rate continued to climb, banks were failing, and Americans demanded action. Franklin Roosevelt promised bold new policies to beat back the Great Depression.

Roosevelt Becomes President

Franklin Delano Roosevelt, known as FDR, came from a wealthy, influential family. He attended Harvard University and Columbia Law School. In 1905, he married a distant cousin, Anna Eleanor Roosevelt.

During World War I, Roosevelt served as assistant secretary of the navy. In 1920, he was the Democratic candidate for Vice President but lost in the Harding landslide.

Physical Challenges Then, in the summer of 1921, Roosevelt was stricken with a severe case of polio, which left his legs paralyzed. He spent years building up his strength.

In time, Roosevelt returned to public life. In 1928, he won election as governor of New York. Then, in 1932, the Democrats made him their presidential candidate.

The Republicans again nominated Herbert Hoover, even though many believed he had little chance of winning after his struggles to cope with the Great Depression and his treatment of the Bonus Army.

Winning the Election Roosevelt set a new tone right from the start. He broke with tradition by flying to the Democratic convention to accept the nomination in person. Standing before the delegates, he declared: "I pledge myself to a new deal for the American people."

Roosevelt did not spell out what he meant by "a new deal." Still, he sounded a hopeful note. In campaign speeches, he promised to help the jobless, poor farmers, and the elderly.

Voters responded to Roosevelt's confident manner and personal charm. On election day, he won a landslide victory. Democrats also gained many seats in Congress. On inauguration day, the new President addressed the American people with optimism:

Primary Source

> This great nation will endure as it has endured, will revive and will prosper. So, first of all, let me assert my firm belief that the only thing we have to fear is fear itself—nameless, unreasoning, unjustified terror which paralyzes needed efforts to convert retreat into advance.

—Franklin D. Roosevelt, Inaugural Address, March 4, 1933

Analyze Images Franklin Roosevelt takes the oath of office March 4, 1933. **Sequence** Trace the political path that Roosevelt followed to the White House.

President Roosevelt then issued a call to action. "This nation asks for action and action now," he said. Many Americans welcomed this energetic new President, especially since Hoover's more cautious approach had failed to end the nation's economic crisis.

Analyze Images A key member of President Roosevelt's Brain Trust, Secretary of Labor Frances Perkins—the woman in black directly behind the President—looks on as he signs a bill into law in 1935. **Infer** How do you think people reacted to Perkins being named to the cabinet?

READING CHECK **Summarize** the major steps in Roosevelt's path to the presidency.

How Did FDR Fight the Depression?

During his campaign for the presidency, Roosevelt had sought advice on how to fight the Depression. He turned to a number of college professors who were experts on economic issues. These experts, nicknamed the Brain Trust, helped Roosevelt to plan bold new programs.

Once in office, President Roosevelt chose able advisers. Harold Ickes (ik eez), a Republican reformer from Chicago, became secretary of the interior. The President named social worker Frances Perkins the secretary of labor. Perkins was the first woman to hold a cabinet post.

The new President moved forward on many fronts. He urged his staff to "take a method and try it. If it fails, admit it and try another. But above all try something."

Strengthening Banks Roosevelt's first challenge was the nation's crumbling banking system. Many banks had closed. Fearful depositors had withdrawn their savings from other banks. People hid their money under mattresses or buried it in their yards.

The President knew he had to **stabilize** the banking system; without sound banks, the economy could not recover. On his second day in office, he declared a **bank holiday**. He closed every bank in the country for four days. He then asked Congress to pass the Emergency Banking Relief Act. Under this act, only those banks with enough funds to meet depositors' demands could reopen. Others had to stay closed.

Academic Vocabulary

stabilize • *v.,* to make steady or keep at a given level

A week after taking office, President Roosevelt spoke to Americans by radio. Under the new law, the President told the people, "it is safer to keep your money in a reopened bank than under your mattress."

The radio broadcast worked. Roosevelt explained things so clearly, said humorist Will Rogers, that even the bankers understood the situation. Reassured by the President, depositors returned their money to banks, and the banking system grew stronger.

Roosevelt gave 30 radio talks while in office. They became known as **fireside chats**. The President liked to imagine that his listeners were sitting around a fireplace with him. In fact, all across the nation, families gathered around their radios to listen to Roosevelt. Many believed the President understood their problems.

Selected Laws Passed During FDR's First 100 Days

LAW	OBJECTIVE
Federal Unemployment Relief Act	Provide jobs that help to protect parks, forests, and public lands
National Industrial Recovery Act	Establish codes of fair practice for industries
Securities Act	Provide government oversight of stock trading to prevent fraud
Emergency Banking Act	Give the President power over banks
Tennessee Valley Authority Act	Provide electricity to poor areas in Tennessee and surrounding states

Sources: *Encyclopædia Britannica;* Archives.gov; Library of Congress; PBS

Analyze Charts This table lists examples of the laws put into place during Roosevelt's first hundred days in office. **Cite Evidence** Which do you think was the most important to aid the struggling nation? Explain your answer.

Laws for Recovery The bank bill was the first of many bills that Roosevelt sent to Congress during his first three months in office. Between March 9 and June 16, 1933, Congress passed a record 15 major new laws. Even the President admitted he was "a bit shellshocked" by the **Hundred Days**, as this period was called.

The bills covered programs from job relief to planning for economic recovery. Together, they made up Roosevelt's New Deal. The **New Deal** laid out three main goals: relief for the jobless, plans for economic recovery, and reforms to prevent another Depression.

Early Relief Programs In 1933, when Roosevelt took office, 13 million Americans were out of work. The President asked Congress for a variety of programs to help the jobless.

Among the earliest New Deal programs was the Civilian Conservation Corps (CCC). The CCC hired unemployed single men between the ages of 18 and 25. For $1 a day, they planted trees, built bridges, worked on flood-control projects, and developed new parks. The Federal Emergency Relief Administration (FERA) gave federal money to state and local agencies, which distributed it to the unemployed.

The WPA The Works Progress Administration (WPA) came into existence in 1935. The WPA put the jobless to work making clothes and building hospitals, schools, parks, playgrounds, and airports.

The WPA also hired artists, photographers, actors, writers, and composers. Artists painted murals on public buildings.

WPA writers collected information about American life, folklore, and traditions. Some WPA writers interviewed African Americans who had lived under slavery. Today, scholars still use these interviews to learn firsthand about slave life.

Critics accused the WPA of creating make-work projects that did little to benefit the nation in the long run. "People don't eat in the long run," replied a New Dealer. "They eat every day."

READING CHECK **Define** What happened during the Hundred Days?

Making Economic Reforms

New Deal Programs

To bring about recovery, the President had to boost both industry and farming. He developed programs that greatly expanded the government's role in the economy. With these and other programs, he hoped to prevent another Depression.

Regulating Industry Overproduction and declining prices had been a major cause of the Depression. Low prices during the Depression had caused businesses to fail and created widespread unemployment. Aiming to boost the economy, New Dealers drew up plans to control production, stabilize prices, and keep workers on the job.

A key new law was the National Industrial Recovery Act (NIRA). Under this law, each industry wrote a code, or set of rules and standards, for production, wages, prices, and working conditions. The NIRA tried to end price cutting and worker layoffs.

To enforce the new codes, Congress set up the National Recovery Administration (NRA). Companies that followed the NRA codes stamped a blue eagle on their products.

The government encouraged people to do business only with companies displaying the NRA eagle. The NRA soon ran into trouble, however. Many companies ignored the codes. Also, small businesses believed that the codes favored the biggest firms.

The NIRA also set up the Public Works Administration (PWA). It promoted recovery by hiring workers for thousands of public works projects. PWA workers built projects such as the Grand Coulee Dam in Washington, public schools in Los Angeles, two aircraft carriers for the navy, and a deep-water port in Brownsville, Texas. Despite these efforts, the PWA did little to bring about recovery.

Subsidizing Farms On farms, overproduction remained the main problem. Surpluses kept prices and farmers' incomes low. A surplus occurs when farmers produce more than they can sell.

To help farmers, the President asked Congress to pass the Agricultural Adjustment Act (AAA). Under the AAA, the government paid farmers not to grow certain crops. Roosevelt hoped this action would increase prices.

Analyze Images This poster promoting the National Park Service was one of many created by the Works Progress Administration (WPA) during the Depression. **Infer** Why did the government invest in the arts during this time?

Analyze Images This 1936 photograph, "Migrant Mother" by Dorothea Lange, came to symbolize the struggles of migrant farm worker families during the Depression. **Use Visual Information** How does this photograph express the struggles of families during the Great Depression?

The government also paid farmers to plow surplus crops under the soil and to destroy surplus cows and pigs. Many Americans were outraged that crops and livestock were being destroyed when people in the cities were going hungry. Yet, the plan seemed necessary to help farmers recover and keep them growing food.

The Rural Electrification Administration (REA) was created to help people in rural areas get the same electrical service as people in urban areas. The REA provided money to extend electric lines to rural areas. As a result, the number of farms with electricity rose from 10 percent to 25 percent.

Electricity helped save many farms from ruin. For example, with refrigeration, dairy farmers did not have to worry about milk going sour before it could be sent to market.

Tennessee Valley Authority Perhaps the boldest program of the Hundred Days was the Tennessee Valley Authority (TVA). It set out to remake the Tennessee River Valley. This vast region often suffered from terrible floods. Because the farmland was so poor, more than half the region's families were on relief.

The TVA was a daring experiment in regional planning. To control flooding, TVA engineers built 49 dams in seven states. The dams also produced cheap electric power. In addition to building dams, the TVA deepened river channels for shipping. It planted new forests to conserve soil and developed new fertilizers to improve farmland. The agency also set up schools and health centers.

The TVA sparked a furious debate. Critics argued that the government had no right to take business away from private companies in the region. Power companies in the Tennessee River Valley were especially outraged. They pointed out that the government, which did not have to make a profit for shareholders, could supply electrical power more cheaply than a private company could. Having to compete with the government, they said, might force them out of business.

Supporters replied that the TVA showed how the government could use its resources to help private enterprise. In the end, the program helped transform a region of desperate poverty into a prosperous and productive area.

Reforming the Economic System The third New Deal goal was to prevent another depression by reforming the economic system. During the Hundred Days, Congress passed laws regulating the stock market and the banking system. The Truth-in-Securities Act was designed to end the risky buying and selling of stocks in the hope of making a quick profit. Experts agreed that uncontrolled buying and selling was a leading cause of the 1929 crash.

Another law set up the Federal Deposit Insurance Corporation (FDIC). It insured depositors' accounts in banks approved by the government. If a bank insured by the FDIC failed, the government would make sure depositors received their money.

Later New Deal laws brought about other kinds of reforms. Laws regulated gas and electric companies. In 1938, a new law extended the Pure Food and Drug Act of 1906. It protected consumers by requiring manufacturers to list the ingredients in certain products. It also made sure that new medicines passed strict tests before they were put on the market.

READING CHECK **Understand Effects** How did the Rural Electrification Act benefit farmers?

GEOGRAPHY **SKILLS**

The Tennessee Valley Authority was an ambitious project.

1. **Location** What land features made this location ideal for the TVA?
2. **Use Visual Information** How many dams were constructed in Tennessee by the TVA?

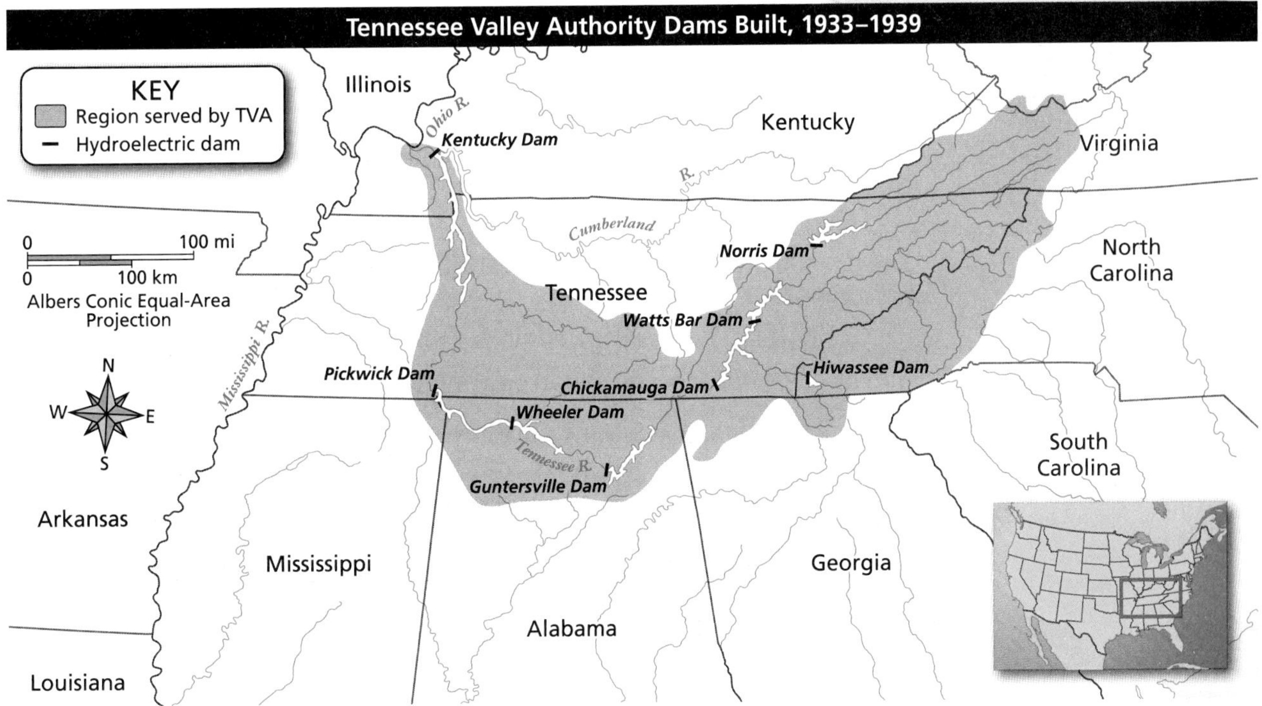

Analyze Images Workers at a General Motors plant staged a sit-down strike when company owners refused to recognize the United Auto Workers (UAW) union in 1936. **Infer** Why do you think this sit-down strike worked?

New Programs to Help Workers and the Elderly

During the years of the New Deal, Roosevelt supported programs to help workers and the elderly. Both groups faced particular hardship during the Great Depression.

Strengthening Unions In 1935, Congress passed the National Labor Relations Act, or Wagner Act. Senator Robert Wagner of New York, the act's sponsor, was a strong supporter of labor. The Wagner Act protected American workers from hostile management practices, such as firing a worker for joining a union. It also guaranteed workers the right to collective bargaining. **Collective bargaining** is the process by which a union representing a group of workers negotiates with management for a contract. Workers had fought for this right since the late 1800s.

The Wagner Act helped union membership grow from 3 million to 9 million during the 1930s. Union membership got a further boost when John L. Lewis set up the Congress of Industrial Organizations (CIO). The CIO represented workers in whole industries, such as steel, automobiles, and textiles.

With more members, unions increased their bargaining power. They also became a powerful force in politics.

A New Labor Strategy Despite the Wagner Act, employers tried to stop workers from joining unions. Violent confrontations often resulted. Workers then tried a new strategy. At the Goodyear Tire Factory in Akron, Ohio, workers staged a sit-down strike. They stopped all machines and refused to leave the factory until Goodyear recognized their union.

The **tactic** worked. Workers at other factories made use of sit-down strikes until the Supreme Court outlawed them in 1939.

Academic Vocabulary

tactic • *n.*, a method of achieving a goal

Social Security Meanwhile, the President sought to help the elderly. In the 1930s, the United States was the only major industrial nation that did not have a formal pension program. A **pension** is a sum of money paid to people on a regular basis after they retire. Roosevelt and Secretary of Labor Perkins pushed to enact an old-age pension program.

Second, the new act set up the nation's first system of unemployment insurance. People who lost their jobs received small payments until they found work again.

Third, the act gave states money to support dependent children and people with disabilities.

Criticism of Social Security Critics condemned the Social Security law. Some liberals pointed out that it did not include farm workers, domestic servants, or the self-employed—many of whom were women or members of minority groups. Some conservatives, on the other hand, saw Social Security as another way for the government to take money away from people who had jobs. Others saw it as an unacceptable expansion of the role of government.

Despite these attacks, the Social Security system survived and expanded over the years. Today, it provides medical benefits and pensions to older Americans, as well as unemployment insurance to workers.

READING CHECK **Identify Supporting Details** What were the three parts of Social Security?

Why Did Critics Attack the New Deal?

Some of Roosevelt's most severe critics were people who had supported him in 1932. Among the most outspoken of these was Senator Huey Long of Louisiana. Long believed that the New Deal had not gone far enough to help the poor. Adopting the motto "Share Our Wealth," Long called for heavy taxes on the rich.

Reformer Francis Townsend, a California doctor, claimed the government had turned its back on older citizens. Townsend wanted everyone over age 60 to get a pension of $200 a month. People receiving the pension would have to retire, thus freeing up a job for someone else. They would also agree to spend the pension money at once to boost the economy.

On the other hand, many conservatives opposed the programs that were part of the New Deal.

Analyze Images The Trojan Horse refers to an ancient incident in which Greek soldiers hid inside a huge wooden horse given to Troy as a gift. Once inside Troy, the Greeks let the rest of their army into the kingdom. **Analyze Political Cartoons** Why do you think the New Deal is portrayed as a Trojan Horse?

The New Deal Political Cartoon

They did not like the government intervention in business or in the lives of individuals. Big names in industry and finance, including the DuPont family and Alfred P. Sloan of General Motors, formed the Liberty League in an effort to combat the New Deal.

The League accused Roosevelt of abusing power and suggested that the New Deal was based on a socialist agenda. The government, they warned, was taking away basic American freedoms. In the end, the Liberty League lacked political savvy and ended up angering many Americans while alienating many of Roosevelt's other critics.

The Supreme Court Strikes Down Key Programs In 1935, members of the Supreme Court began to attack the New Deal. In that year, the Supreme Court ruled that the National Industrial Recovery Act was unconstitutional. A year later, the Court struck down the Agricultural Adjustment Act. Then it overturned eight other New Deal laws on constitutional grounds. To Roosevelt, the Supreme Court rulings threatened not only the New Deal but also his ability to lead the nation.

Roosevelt waited until after the 1936 election to take action. In that election, he easily beat his Republican opponent, Alf Landon of Kansas. Soon after his inauguration in January 1937, Roosevelt put forward a plan to enlarge the federal courts. He called for raising the number of Justices on the Supreme Court from 9 to 15. The change would make it possible for him to appoint six new Justices who supported his programs.

Analyze Images In 1937, Roosevelt sought the ability to appoint more justices to the Supreme Court to assure support of his programs. **Analyze Political Cartoons** Explain how this cartoonist represents Roosevelt's attitude toward the Supreme Court.

"Court Packing" The President's move raised a loud outcry. Both supporters and critics of the New Deal accused him of trying to "pack" the Court with Justices who supported his views. They saw his move as a threat to the principle of separation of powers. For six months, the President fought for his plan. Even his allies in Congress deserted him. Finally, he withdrew his proposal.

Still, in the end, Roosevelt got the Supreme Court majority he wanted without a battle. One Justice who had voted against many New Deal laws changed his views. Another retired. Roosevelt filled his place with a new Justice who was favorable to his programs.

READING CHECK **Draw Conclusions** Why was the "Court Packing" plan a threat to the principle of separation of powers?

THE NEW DEAL IN THE 1930s

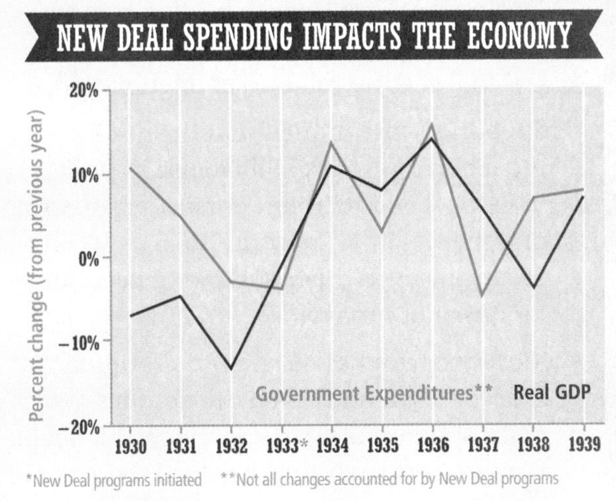

*New Deal programs initiated **Not all changes accounted for by New Deal programs

Sources: *Theory and Applications of Macroeconomics* (v. 1.0); John Wallis "The Political Economy of New Deal Spending Revisited, Again," *Explorations in Economic History* Vol. 35 (1998)

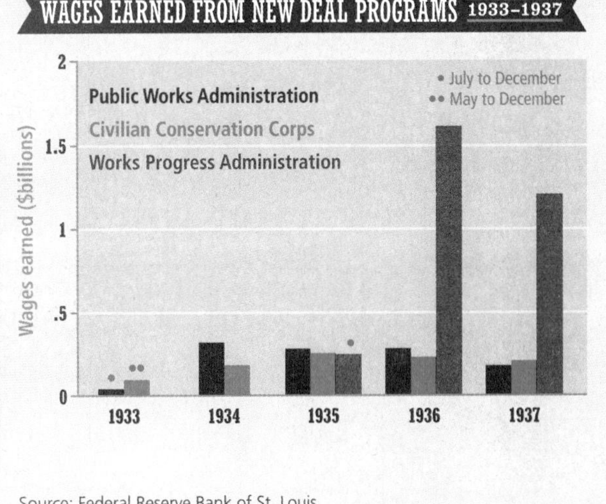

Source: Federal Reserve Bank of St. Louis

Analyze Graphs The New Deal affected the economy in various ways. **Use Visual Information** Based on the information provided about gross domestic product (GDP), which is a measure of an economy's size, describe the New Deal's impact on the economy.

Debating the New Deal

The New Deal changed American government forever. Ever since, Americans have debated whether the change was good or bad for the country. Many of the programs that Franklin Roosevelt instituted during this difficult time in the nation's history still impact the lives of Americans today. One example is Social Security, which provides support to the elderly and the disabled.

Criticism of the New Deal Before the 1930s, most Americans had little contact with the federal government. New Deal programs, however, touched almost every citizen. The federal government grew in size and power.

Many people worried about the increased power of government. They complained that the government was intruding in people's lives, threatening both individual freedoms and private property. These critics called for a return to the traditional policy of laissez faire—the idea that government should play as small a role as possible in the functioning of the nation's economy.

Critics also expressed alarm because the government was spending more than it took in. This practice of **deficit spending** was creating a huge increase in the **national debt**, or the total sum of money the government owes.

Finally, despite its vast spending, the New Deal had not achieved its major goal—ending the Depression. In fact, full economic recovery did not come until 1941. This recovery was partly the result of increased U.S. production for nations fighting in World War II.

Did you know?

The Twentieth Amendment, ratified in 1933, shifted the date of the President's inauguration from March 4 to January 20.

▲ This 1935 poster promoted the newly established Social Security system, which gave financial assistance to the elderly, the unemployed, and the disabled.

Support for the New Deal Supporters of the New Deal noted that FDR had steered the nation through the worst days of the Depression. New Deal legislation had ended the banking crisis, protected farmers, and created work for millions of unemployed.

Supporters also argued that the government had a responsibility to use its power to help all of its citizens, not just businesses and the wealthy. Programs such as Social Security, New Dealers said, were necessary for national survival.

Most important of all, supporters argued, the New Deal had saved the nation's democratic system. Elsewhere in the world, people were turning to dictators to lead them out of hard times. President Roosevelt, on the other hand, restored the nation to economic health while preserving its democracy.

Over the years, Americans have continued to debate the expanded role of government that began during the New Deal. The question whether government intervention in the economy helps or harms Americans' well-being remains a lively one today.

READING CHECK **Identify Supporting Details** What is one argument for and one against the New Deal?

Lesson Check

Practice Vocabulary

1. Why had workers long sought the right of **collective bargaining**?
2. Why does **deficit spending** increase the **national debt**?

Critical Thinking and Writing

3. **Understand Effects** Why did President Roosevelt's fireside chats have a positive effect on Americans?
4. **Infer** How was life for families different after the Social Security Act was passed?
5. **Revisit the Essential Question** Why did some Americans criticize the New Deal?
6. **Writing Workshop: Cite Sources** In your Active Journal, write the source of each note you have taken. In your research paper, any direct quotes from a source must be cited. Also cite the sources of someone else's ideas that you have paraphrased or summarized.

Franklin Roosevelt, Fireside Chat on Banking

President Franklin Roosevelt delivered his first fireside chat on March 12, 1933, six days after he had declared a bank holiday on March 6, 1933.

▶ Franklin D. Roosevelt

By the afternoon of March 3d scarcely a bank in the country was open to do business. . . . It was then that I issued the proclamation providing for the nationwide bank holiday, and this was the first step in the Government's reconstruction of our financial and economic fabric. . . .

There will be, of course, some banks unable to reopen without being reorganized. The new law ① allows the Government to assist in making these reorganizations quickly and effectively and even allows the Government to subscribe to at least a part of new capital which may be required. . . . ②

It has been wonderful to me to catch the note of confidence from all over the country. I can never be sufficiently grateful to the people for the loyal support they have given me in their acceptance of the judgment that has dictated our course, even though all our processes may not have seemed clear to them. ③

After all, there is an element in the readjustment of our financial system more important than currency, more important than gold, and that is the confidence of the people. Confidence and courage are the essentials of success in carrying out our plan. You people must have faith; you must not be stampeded by rumors or guesses. Let us unite in banishing fear. We have provided the machinery to restore our financial system; it is up to you to support and make it work.

It is your problem no less than it is mine. Together we cannot fail.

Reading and Vocabulary Support

① The new law was the Emergency Banking Relief Act, passed quickly by Congress and signed by the President on March 9, 1933.

② The new law allowed the government to provide money so banks could reopen by buying stock (subscribing) or making loans.

③ Do you think it was an effective approach for the President to take? Why or why not?

Analyzing Primary Sources

Cite evidence from the primary source to support your answers.

1. **Assess an Argument** Some of Roosevelt's critics claimed that his New Deal programs represented socialism or communism. How did the President, in this speech, argue against that accusation?
2. **Analyze Style and Rhetoric** Why is the last line of this speech an effective way to end the fireside chat?

Quest CONNECTIONS

Based on the document, what was Roosevelt's point of view on how involved the government should be in the country's financial affairs? Record your responses in your Active Journal.

LESSON 7

Life During the Depression

GET READY TO READ

START UP

Look at the photograph of a family struggling with the effects of the severe drought that turned a large area of the Great Plains into the Dust Bowl. Write a brief diary entry that a farmer in this region might have written concerning his or her future.

GUIDING QUESTIONS

- What caused the Dust Bowl, and what effects did it have?
- What impact did the Depression have on women, African Americans, and other groups?
- How did the arts reflect life during the Depression?

TAKE NOTES

Literacy Skills: Summarize

Use the graphic organizer in your Active Journal to take notes as you read the lesson.

PRACTICE VOCABULARY

Use the vocabulary activity in your Active Journal to practice the vocabulary words.

Vocabulary		Academic Vocabulary
Dust Bowl	civil rights	nurturing
migrant worker	Indian New Deal	advocate
Black Cabinet		

The Great Depression ruined the lives of numerous Americans who lost their jobs, their homes, and their savings. Hundreds of thousands of farmers and others on the Great Plains suffered the additional burden of having to flee the land that had sustained them. Many would never return.

The Dust Bowl

During much of the 1930s, states from Texas to the Dakotas suffered a severe drought. One region in the central Great Plains was especially hard hit. The topsoil dried out. High winds carried the soil away in blinding dust storms. As a result, this area became known as the **Dust Bowl**.

Causes of the Dust Bowl Dust storms buried farmhouses, fences, and even trees over large areas of the plains. People put shutters over doors and windows, but the dust blew in anyway. Even food crunched when it was chewed. One storm blew dust from Oklahoma to Albany, New York. A Kansas farmer sadly reported that he sat by his window counting the farms going by.

What caused the disaster? Years of overgrazing by cattle and plowing by farmers destroyed the grasses that once held the soil in place. The drought of the 1930s and high winds did the rest.

Effects of the Dust Bowl Hardest hit by the drought and dust storms were poor farmers in Oklahoma and other Great Plains states. Thousands of these "Okies" packed their belongings into cars and trucks and headed west. They became **migrant workers**—people who move from one region to another in search of work. They hoped to find jobs in the orchards and farms of California, Oregon, or Washington.

Once they reached the West Coast, the migrants faced a new hardship—they were not wanted. Local citizens feared that the newcomers would take away their jobs. Sometimes, angry crowds blocked the highways and forced the migrants to go elsewhere. Those migrants who did find work were paid little.

Academic Vocabulary
nurturing • *n.*, caring and attention

READING CHECK **Identify Cause and Effect** What caused the Dust Bowl?

How Did the Depression Affect Women?

Traditional roles took on added importance during the Depression. Homemakers had to stretch family budgets to make ends meet. Some women took in laundry to earn extra money. Others took in boarders to help pay the rent. Wives also found that unemployed husbands sometimes needed more **nurturing** to feel worthwhile.

Working women faced special problems during the Depression. If jobs were available, employers hired men before they would hire women. In order to spread jobs around, the federal government refused to hire a woman if her husband had a job.

GEOGRAPHY SKILLS

The center of the nation was most affected during the Dust Bowl.

1. **Place** Identify the states most severely affected.
2. **Infer** What challenges would Dust Bowl migrants face when they moved west?

The Dust Bowl

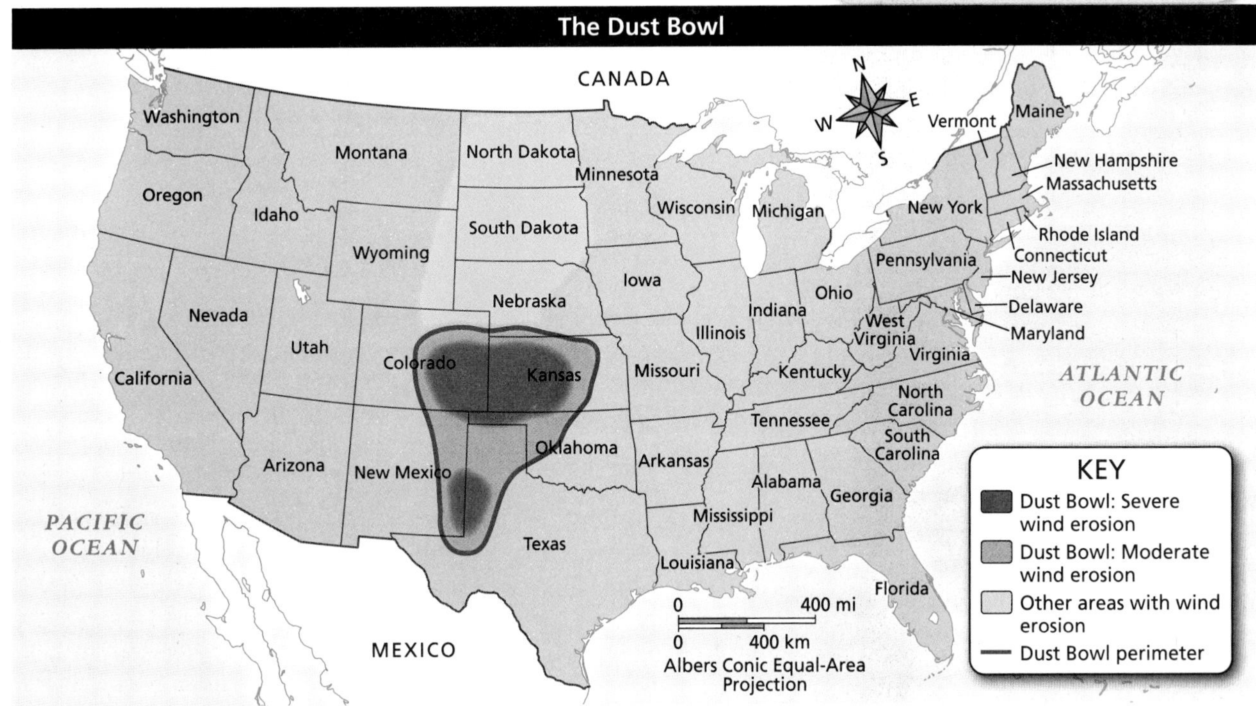

Analyze Images First Lady Eleanor Roosevelt became an advocate for Americans all over the country. **Cite Evidence** How was the First Lady an important part of the administration?

Working Women Despite such obstacles, millions of women earned wages in order to support themselves and their families. During the 1930s, the number of married women in the workforce increased by 52 percent. Educated women took jobs as secretaries, schoolteachers, and social workers. Other women earned livings as maids, factory workers, and seamstresses.

Some women workers struck for better pay. In San Antonio, Texas, at least 80 percent of the pecan shellers were Mexican American women. When employers lowered their pay, a young worker, Emma Tenayuca, organized the shellers and led them off the job. Tenayuca said later, "I had a basic faith in the American idea of freedom and fairness. I felt something had to be done."

The First Lady Takes a Stand Eleanor Roosevelt created a new role for the First Lady. Acting as the President's "eyes and ears," she toured the nation. She visited farms and American Indian reservations and traveled deep into a coal mine. She talked to homemakers, studying the condition of their clothing on the wash line to measure how well they were doing. In this way she became a spokesperson for Americans all over the country.

The First Lady did more than just aid the President. She used her position to speak out for women's rights, as well as other issues. In her newspaper column, "My Day," she called on Americans to live up to the goal of equal justice for all. By speaking out on social issues, Eleanor Roosevelt angered some people. However, many other Americans admired her strong stands.

READING CHECK **Identify Main Ideas** How did the Depression affect women's lives?

BIOGRAPHY 5 Things to Know About

ELEANOR ROOSEVELT

First Lady, journalist, and social activist 1884–1962

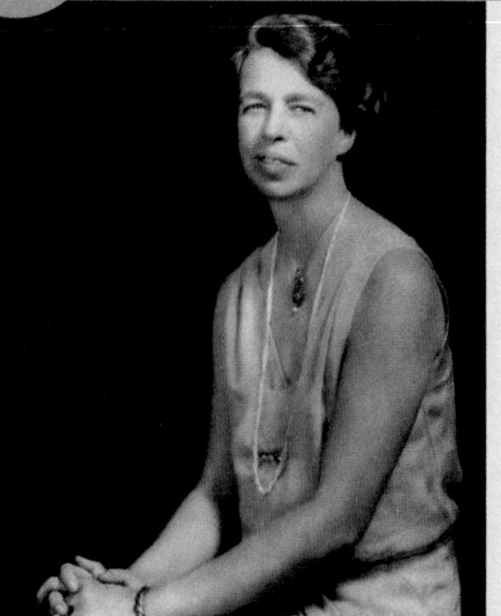

- She was born Anna Eleanor Roosevelt, niece of Theodore Roosevelt and fifth cousin, once removed, of Franklin.
- One of her and Franklin's six children died as an infant.
- While Franklin was first ill, she kept the Roosevelt name in the news by advocating for social reforms and leading a women's delegation at the 1924 Democratic Convention.
- Ever gracious and charming, she felt equally at ease among immigrants, labor leaders, veterans, and the unemployed.
- In 1946, a year after Franklin's death, she continued to serve the United States as a diplomat at the newly formed United Nations in New York City.

Critical Thinking How did Eleanor Roosevelt help her husband politically?

Analyze Images The Civilian Conservation Corps gave an opportunity to work to African Americans. **Use Visual Information** How did their CCC jobs make a difference to these women?

African Americans Face Hard Times

INTERACTIVE

The Great Depression's Impact

When the Great Depression hit, African American workers were often the first to lose their jobs. By 1934, Black workers were suffering a 50 percent unemployment rate, more than twice the national average. Often, they were denied public works jobs. Some charities even refused to serve African Americans at centers giving out food to the needy.

Eleanor Roosevelt and **advocates** urged the President to improve the situation of African Americans. The President responded to their needs. For example, thousands of young African American men learned a trade through the Civilian Conservation Corps (CCC).

Academic Vocabulary

advocate • *n.*, a person who argues for or supports a cause or policy

In aiding African Americans, Roosevelt won their support for the Democratic Party. The President invited African American leaders to the White House to advise him. These unofficial advisers became known as the **Black Cabinet**. They included Robert C. Weaver, a Harvard-educated economist, and Mary McLeod Bethune, a well-known Florida educator. Roosevelt appointed Bethune to head the National Youth Administration's Division of Negro Affairs. She was the first African American to head a government agency.

Often, Roosevelt followed the advice of the Black Cabinet. However, when African American leaders pressed him to support an anti-lynching law, he refused. He feared that by doing so he would lose the support of white southerners in Congress for his New Deal programs.

Many Black leaders called on African Americans to unite to obtain their **civil rights**—the rights due to all citizens. African Americans used their votes, won higher-level government jobs, and kept up pressure for equal treatment. Slowly, they made a few gains. However, the struggle for civil rights would take many more years.

READING CHECK **Draw Conclusions** What was the purpose of Roosevelt's "Black Cabinet"?

Quick Activity

Explore important events that took place during the Great Depression in your Active Journal.

How Did Other Americans Weather the Depression?

The hard times of the Great Depression created fear and insecurity among many Americans. These feelings sometimes erupted in discrimination and hostility toward Americans with different ethnic backgrounds.

Mexican Americans By the 1930s, Mexican Americans worked in many cities around the country. A large number, however, were farmworkers in the West and Southwest. There, they faced discrimination in education and jobs and at the polls.

In good times, employers had encouraged Mexicans to move north and take jobs in factories or on farms. When hard times struck, however, many Americans wanted Mexicans to be sent back to Mexico. More than 400,000 people were rounded up and sent to Mexico. Some of them were in fact American citizens, not Mexicans.

Asian Americans Some Americans resented Chinese, Japanese, and Filipino workers who competed with them for scarce jobs. Sometimes, violence against Asians erupted. Responding to pressure, the government sought to reduce the number of Asians in the United States. In 1935, FDR signed a law that provided free transportation for Filipinos who agreed to return to the Philippines and not come back.

American Indians In 1924, Congress had granted all American Indians citizenship. Still, most Indians continued to live in deep poverty. President Roosevelt encouraged new policies toward American Indians.

In the 1930s, Congress passed a series of laws that have been called the **Indian New Deal**. The laws gave Indian nations greater control over their own affairs.

Analyze Images African American educator Mary McLeod Bethune, standing at the center of this photo, promoted the interests of African Americans across the country and served as advisor to President Roosevelt in the 1930s and 1940s. **Infer** How did having advisers like Bethune make Roosevelt a better President?

Analyze Images Dorothea Lange took this 1935 photo of Filipino immigrants harvesting lettuce in California. **Draw Conclusions** How might jobless Americans have viewed immigrants at this time?

The President chose John Collier, a longtime defender of American Indian rights, to head the Bureau of Indian Affairs. Collier ended the government policy of breaking up American Indian landholdings. In 1934, Congress passed the Indian Reorganization Act (IRA). It protected and even expanded landholdings of Indian reservations. The Roosevelt administration also strengthened American Indian governments by letting reservations organize corporations and develop their own business projects.

To provide jobs during the Depression, the government set up the Indian Emergency Conservation Work Group. It employed American Indians in programs of the control of topsoil erosion, irrigation, and land development.

READING CHECK **Identify Supporting Details** What was the purpose of the Indian New Deal?

The Arts During the Depression

Creative artists powerfully portrayed the hardships of Depression life. Many writers depicted the hard times Americans faced across the country. In his 1939 novel *The Grapes of Wrath*, John Steinbeck told the heartbreaking story of the Okies streaming over the mountains trying to build new lives in California.

Many painters turned to familiar themes. The huge murals of Thomas Hart Benton brought the history of the frontier to life. In *American Gothic*, Grant Wood painted an Iowa farmer and his daughter who look determined enough to survive any hardship.

The government sent out photographers to create a lasting record of American life during the Great Depression. The vivid photographs of Dorothea Lange showed the suffering of Dust Bowl farm families. Margaret Bourke-White photographed poor tenant farmers in the South.

Entertainment on the Radio Americans found ways to escape the hard times of the 1930s. Listening to the radio and going to the movies were among their favorite pastimes.

Every night, millions of Americans tuned in to their favorite radio programs. Comedians, such as the husband-and-wife team of George Burns and Gracie Allen, made people forget their troubles for a time. With so many people out of work, daytime radio shows became popular. People listened to dramas like "Ma Perkins" that told the story of families weathering the Depression. Because soap companies sponsored many of these serials, the programs became known as soap operas.

Analyze Images Movies now had both sound and color, and moviegoers enjoyed both as they watched two of 1939's most popular films, *The Wizard of Oz* and *Gone with the Wind*. **Infer** Why do you think people enjoyed movies so much during this time?

Perhaps the most famous broadcast took place in 1938. On Halloween night, actor Orson Welles presented a "newscast" based on a science fiction novel, *The War of the Worlds*. Welles grimly reported the landing of invaders from the planet Mars. People who tuned in late mistook the program for a real newscast. Thousands of terrified people ran into the streets, seeking ways to escape the Martian invasion.

Going to the Movies In the 1930s, movie makers tried to restore Americans' faith in the future. Movies told optimistic stories about happy families or people finding love and success. Shirley Temple became a hugely popular star at the age of five. When Temple sang "On the Good Ship Lollipop," her upbeat spirit cheered up audiences.

One of the most popular movies was Walt Disney's *Snow White and the Seven Dwarfs*. It was the first full-length animated film. In 1939, Judy Garland won American hearts in *The Wizard of Oz*. The movie told of a young girl's escape from a bleak life in Depression-era Kansas to the magical land of Oz.

The most expensively made and most popular movie of the 1930s was *Gone With the Wind*. It showed the Civil War in a romantic light. For more than three hours, many Americans forgot their worries as they watched the story of love and loss in the Old South. The movie also encouraged many Americans. They had survived hard times before. They would do so again.

READING CHECK **Identify Main Ideas** What purposes did the arts serve during the Depression?

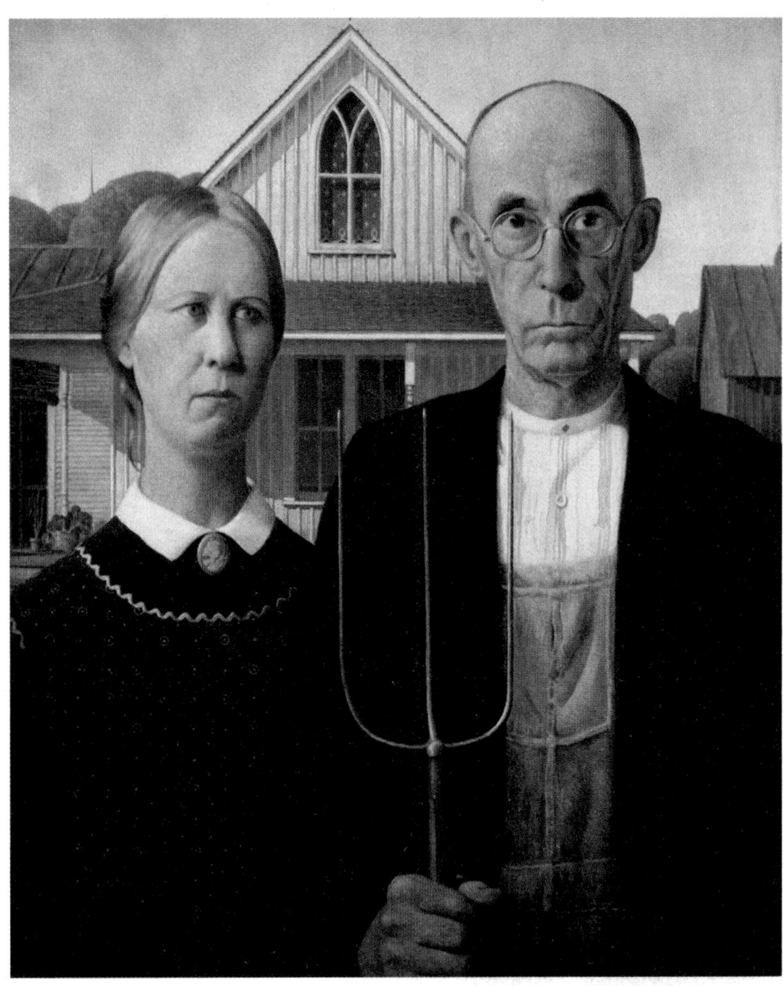

Analyze Images Grant Wood completed his painting *American Gothic* in 1930. **Use Visual Information** In what ways might the painting have reflected the attitudes of people living through the Depression?

Lesson Check

Practice Vocabulary

1. How did the **Dust Bowl** expand the number of **migrant workers**?
2. How did the **Indian New Deal** restore some pride to American Indians?

Critical Thinking and Writing

3. **Identify Cause and Effect** How did the Great Depression affect how Dust Bowl migrants were treated after they reached the West Coast?
4. **Compare and Contrast** How did President Roosevelt both help and hurt the struggle of African Americans for their civil rights?
5. **Writing Workshop: Use Technology to Produce and Publish** Soon you will write your New Deal research paper, using the notes you have written in your Active Journal. To produce and publish a thoroughly researched and clearly presented paper, take advantage of available technology.

TOPIC 13

Review and Assessment

VISUAL REVIEW

Comparing the 1920s and 1930s

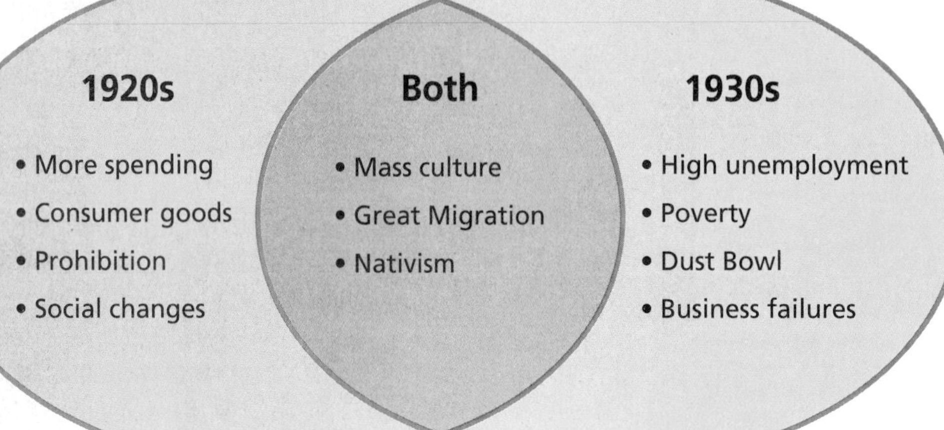

THREE PRESIDENCIES

Calvin Coolidge (1923–1929)	Herbert Hoover (1929–1933)	Franklin Roosevelt (1933–1945)
• Cut business regulations • Rapid economic growth ended postwar recession • Intervention in Latin America	• Stock market crash started Great Depression • Wage cuts and layoffs • Economies collapse around the world	• New laws to regulate banks and industry • New Deal programs (WPA, Social Security Act)

READING REVIEW

Use the Take Notes and Practice Vocabulary activities in your Active Journal to review the topic.

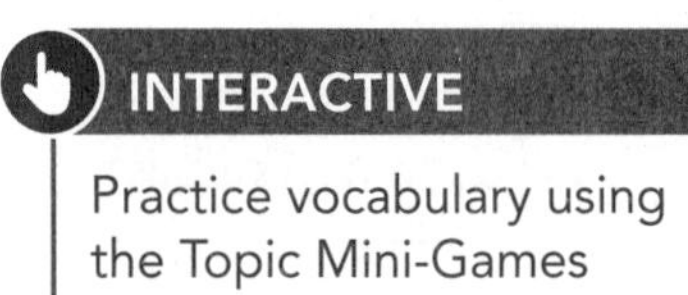

ASSESSMENT

Vocabulary and Key Ideas

1. **Identify** Under which President did the **bull market** end?
2. **Check Understanding** How did movies help give rise to a **mass culture**?
3. **Define** Was **jazz** one of the **fads** of the 1920s? Why or why not?
4. **Describe** How did the **quota system** put in place in 1921 change who could immigrate to the United States?
5. **Recall** What was the main fear that led to the Red Scare?
6. **Identify Main Ideas** Why did Hoover arrange for the government to oversee the building of schools, construction of dams, and paving of highways?
7. **Identify** What method did Franklin Roosevelt use to communicate his ideas to the American people?

Critical Thinking and Writing

8. **Draw Conclusions** How do you think Calvin Coolidge would have responded to the Great Depression if he had been President in the early 1930s?
9. **Explain an Argument** Why did many Americans in the early 1930s conclude that Prohibition was a mistake and that the law should be repealed?
10. **Understand Effects** What impact did the Harlem Renaissance have on the way African Americans viewed themselves?
11. **Revisit the Essential Question** How could President Roosevelt justify his use of deficit spending to fund the New Deal?
12. **Writing Workshop: Write a Research Paper** Using the notes and other materials that you have gathered in your Active Journal, write a research paper on how one aspect of the New Deal affected Americans, both positively and negatively.

Analyze Primary Sources

13. Who most likely made the statement quoted here?
    - **A.** Calvin Coolidge
    - **B.** Franklin Roosevelt
    - **C.** Frances Perkins
    - **D.** Langston Hughes

"After all, the chief business of the American people is business. They are profoundly concerned with producing, buying, selling, investing, and prospering in the world. I am strongly of the opinion that the great majority of people will always find these are moving impulses of our life."

Analyze Maps

Use the map at the right to answer the following questions.

14. What are the two easternmost states served by the Tennessee Valley Authority (TVA)?
15. Which of the dams are located in Alabama?
16. What were the main functions of the TVA dams?

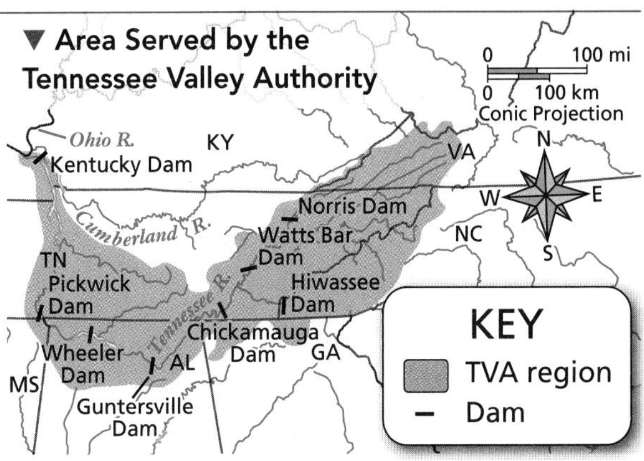

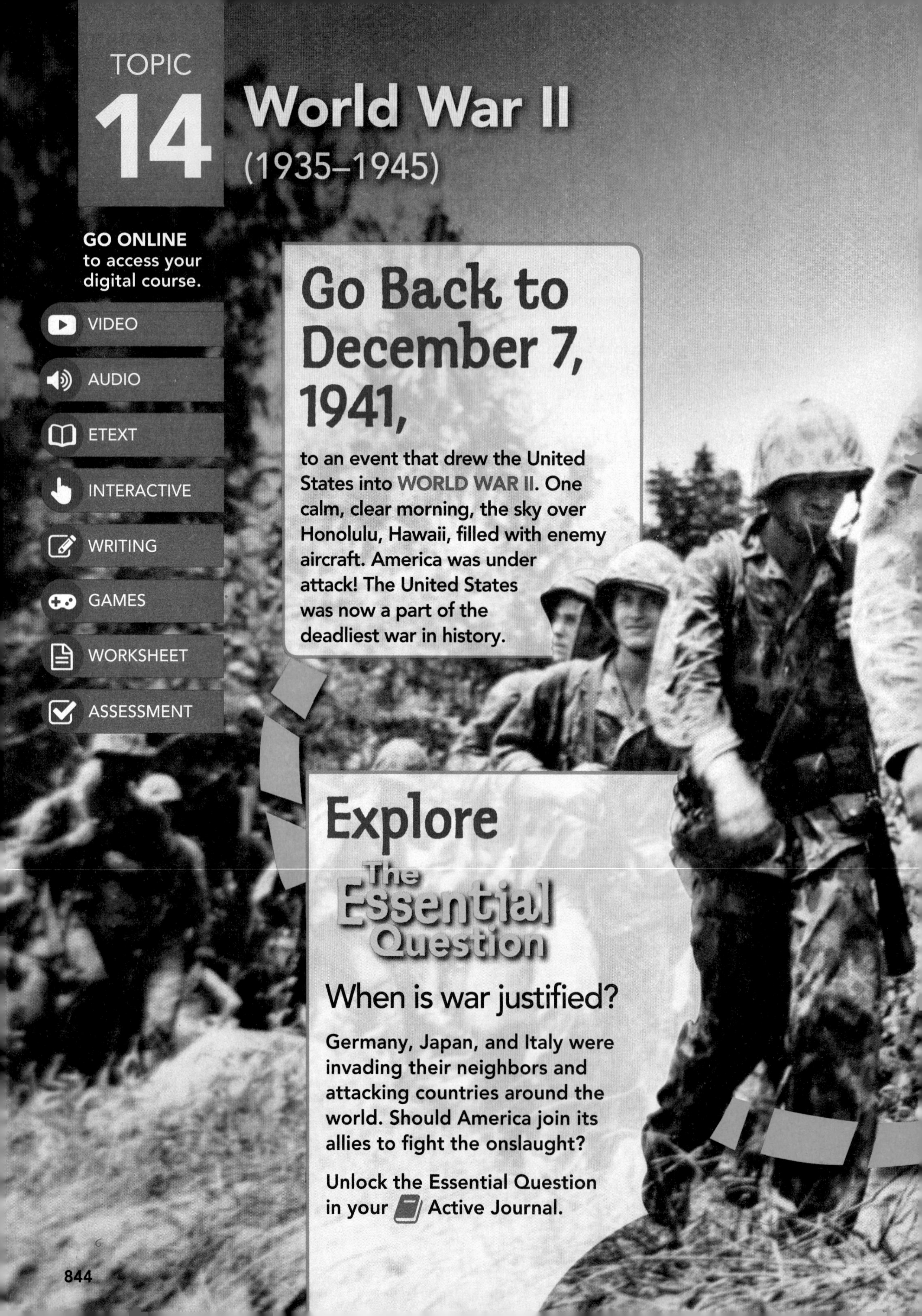

TOPIC 14

World War II
(1935–1945)

GO ONLINE to access your digital course.

VIDEO

AUDIO

ETEXT

INTERACTIVE

WRITING

GAMES

WORKSHEET

ASSESSMENT

Go Back to December 7, 1941,

to an event that drew the United States into WORLD WAR II. One calm, clear morning, the sky over Honolulu, Hawaii, filled with enemy aircraft. America was under attack! The United States was now a part of the deadliest war in history.

Explore The Essential Question

When is war justified?

Germany, Japan, and Italy were invading their neighbors and attacking countries around the world. Should America join its allies to fight the onslaught?

Unlock the Essential Question in your Active Journal.

Read

about events leading up to the outbreak of World War II, the battles, the strategy it took to win the war, and the massive costs of the war.

Watch

NBC LEARN

BOUNCE TO ACTIVATE VIDEO

A Liberation Story

Learn about the liberation of the Dachau concentration camp near the end of World War II.

◀ U.S. Marines in Papua New Guinea, 1943

TOPIC 14

World War II (1935–1945)

Learn more about World War II by making your own map and timeline in your Active Journal.

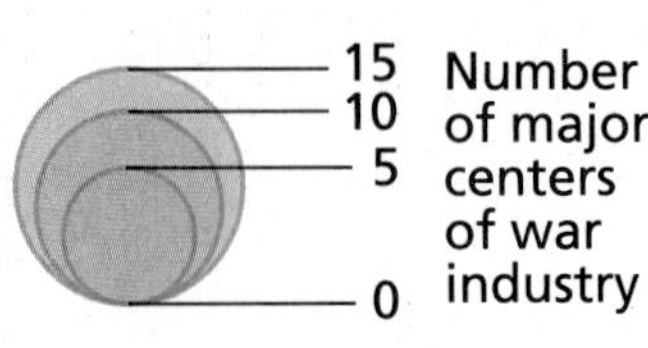

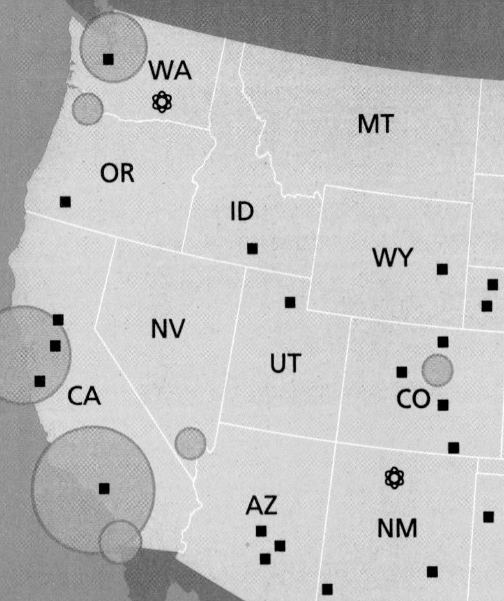

INTERACTIVE

Topic Timeline

What happened and when?

A shocking attack on America . . . a brutal war engulfs the globe . . . atomic bombs change everything . . . Explore the timeline to see some of what was happening during the World War II years.

TOPIC EVENTS

1933 Hitler becomes chancellor of Germany, ending democratic rule.

1937 Japan invades China.

1938 Britain and France give in to Hitler's demands.

1938 Jews persecuted in Germany and Austria in night of terror called *Kristallnacht*.

1939 Germany invades Poland, starting World War II.

1930 | **1935**

WORLD EVENTS

1936 The Spanish Civil War begins.

1937 As she attempts to fly around the world, Amelia Earhart disappears over the Pacific Ocean.

INTERACTIVE

Topic Map

Where did World War II take place?

World War II was fought across most of the world. The entire United States was involved in supporting the war effort.

▲ The Battle of Midway, 1942

Who will you meet?

Adolf Hitler, Chancellor of Germany

Winston S. Churchill, British Prime Minister

Dorie Miller, American war hero

1939
The Great Depression ends as nations mobilize for war.

1940

1941
Japan makes a surprise attack on the United States.

1944
D-Day—The Allies land in Normandy.

1945

1945
Germany surrenders.

1945
The United States drops atomic bombs on Hiroshima and Nagasaki; Japan surrenders.

1945
ENIAC, the first programmable computer, is built.

1950

Document-Based Writing Inquiry

Dropping the Atomic Bomb

Quest KICK OFF

President Truman had an important decision to make. He was told the atomic bomb—what he called "this awful weapon"—was the key to ending the war. Should he use it?

Was President Truman justified in dropping the atomic bomb?

What you learn in this Quest from investigating the President's decision will help you think about the Essential Question, "When is war justified?"

1 Ask Questions

People have debated Truman's decision since the first bomb was dropped on Hiroshima. What do you need to know to form your opinion? In your Active Journal, list questions that will help you form your answer.

2 Investigate

As you read the lessons in the topic, look for Quest CONNECTIONS that provide information that would influence the decision on using the bomb. Capture notes in your Active Journal.

3 Examine Primary Sources

Next, explore primary sources about World War II and the atomic bombs. They will help you form a sound basis for making your judgment. Capture notes in your Active Journal.

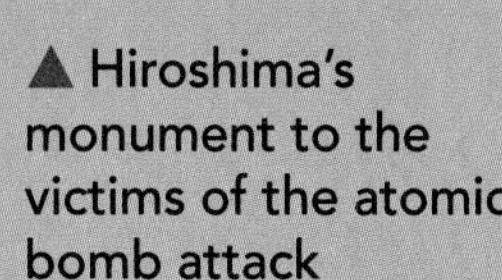

▲ Hiroshima's monument to the victims of the atomic bomb attack

Quest FINDINGS

4 Write an Essay Expressing Your Opinion

In deciding whether to use the bomb, President Truman looked at the question from many angles. However, nobody could predict with certainty the effects of this new weapon.

Did Truman make the right choice? Do your own investigation. At the end of the topic, you'll write an essay spelling out your opinion and how you arrived at it. Get help for writing your essay in your Active Journal.

LESSON 1

Aggression Overseas and Isolationism at Home

GET READY TO READ

START UP

The Hitler Youth salute German dictator Adolf Hitler in this 1938 photograph. Write three ideas about how Germany reacted to its treatment following World War I.

GUIDING QUESTIONS

- How did fascist governments come to power in Italy and Germany?
- How did Stalin rule the Soviet Union?
- Why did the United States adopt a policy of isolationism?

TAKE NOTES

Literacy Skills: Summarize

Use the graphic organizer in your Active Journal to take notes as you read the lesson.

PRACTICE VOCABULARY

Use the vocabulary activity in your Active Journal to practice the vocabulary words.

Vocabulary		Academic Vocabulary
fascism	concentration camp	initiate
aggression	totalitarian state	dynamic
Nazi	Neutrality Acts	
scapegoat	Good Neighbor Policy	

In the 1930s, a storm was gathering around the globe. New rulers had come to power in Europe and Asia. These leaders drew on resentment about their countries' fates after World War I. They also aimed to spread their influence. Their hunger for power would change the lives of millions of people and cause mass destruction around the world.

Dictators Take Power in Italy and Germany

In Italy and Germany, totalitarian leaders exerted complete control over the government and society. These dictators were fascists (FASHists). **Fascism** is rooted in militarism, extreme nationalism, and blind loyalty to the state. Fascist dictators vowed to create new empires. Unlike communists, who drew much of their support from the working classes, fascists found allies among business leaders and landowners.

Fascist Italy In 1922, Benito Mussolini and his Fascist Party seized power in Italy. He played on anger about the Treaty of Versailles ending World War I.

Many Italians felt cheated because the treaty did not grant Italy the territory it wanted. Mussolini promised to make Italy a mighty empire.

Mussolini also used fear to gain and hold power. Economic unrest and fears of a communist revolution plagued Italy, and many looked to Mussolini to stabilize the nation.

Once in power, Mussolini outlawed all political parties except his own. He controlled the press and banned criticism of the government. Critics were jailed or simply murdered. In schools, children recited the motto "Mussolini Is Always Right!"

Mussolini Conquers Ethiopia In the 1930s, Mussolini used foreign conquest to distract Italians from economic problems. Promising to restore the greatness of ancient Rome, he **initiated** a program of military aggression. **Aggression** is a hostile or warlike act by one country against another without provocation.

Academic Vocabulary
initiate • *v.*, to begin

Mussolini invaded the African nation of Ethiopia in 1935. The Ethiopians fought bravely, but their cavalry and outdated rifles were no match for Italy's modern tanks and airplanes. Ethiopian emperor Haile Selassie (HIlee suhLASee) asked the League of Nations for aid. The League responded weakly. Britain and France were caught up in their own economic problems and unwilling to risk another war. Without help, Ethiopia fell.

Nazi Germany In Germany, Adolf Hitler brought the National Socialist German Workers' Party, or **Nazis**, to power. Like Mussolini, Hitler played on anger about the Treaty of Versailles. Germans bitterly resented the treaty because it blamed their country for World War I and made them pay heavy war costs.

Analyze Charts The chart shows the severe economic situation that existed in Germany in the years following World War I. **Identify Cause and Effect** What evidence from the graph partly explains why many Germans would support a change in government?

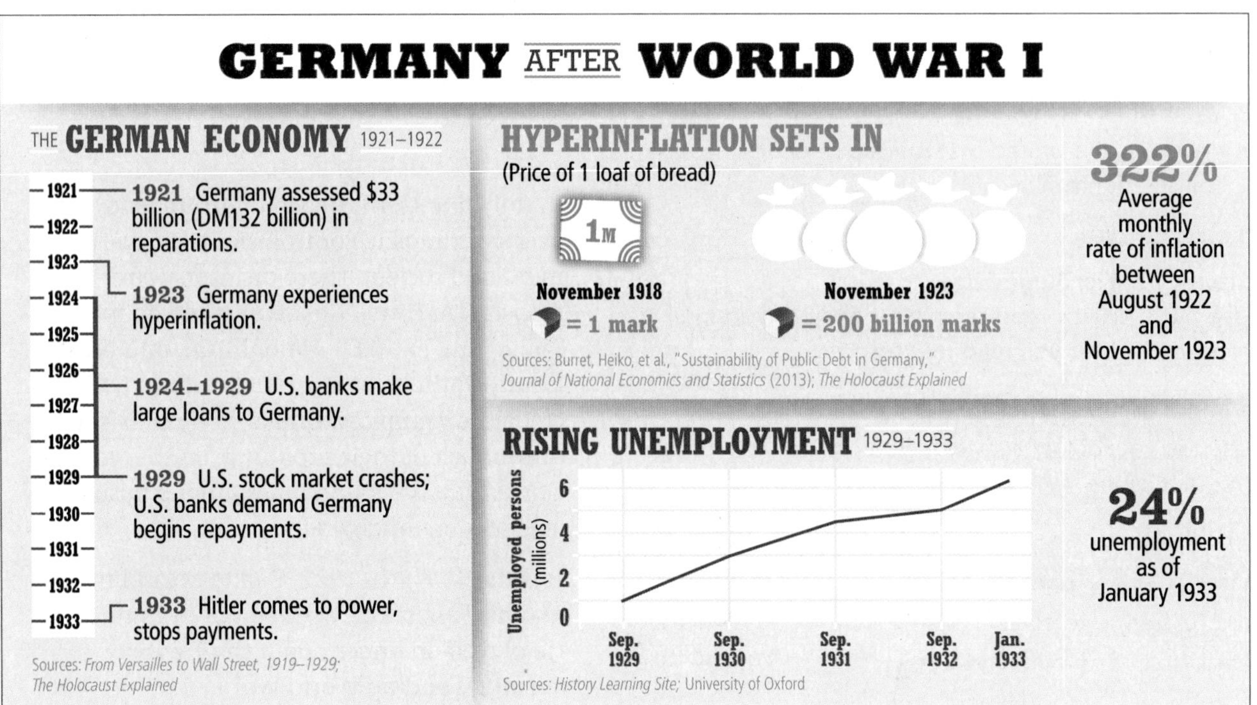

Analyze Images Germans observe the aftermath of *Kristallnacht* (Night of Broken Glass). On November 9–10, 1938, Nazi troops ransacked Jewish homes, businesses, and synagogues, and killed at least 91 Jewish people. **Infer** What can you infer from the people's expressions about their response to *Kristallnacht*?

Hitler's Rise to Power Hitler assured Germans that they had not lost the war. Rather, he said, Jews and other traitors had "stabbed Germany in the back." The argument was false, but in troubled times people were eager to find a **scapegoat**—a person or group on whom to blame their problems.

Hitler was a **dynamic** speaker and skillful politician. By the time the Great Depression struck, many Germans looked to him as a strong leader with answers to their problems.

Academic Vocabulary
dynamic • *adj.*, forceful and energetic

In 1933, Hitler was named chancellor, or head of the German government. Within two years, he ended democratic rule and created a militaristic totalitarian state. In Nazi Germany, the government controlled the press, the schools, and religion.

The following year, Hitler organized a week-long rally in Nuremberg. Crowds chanted slogans praising Hitler. Uniformed soldiers marched in seemingly endless parades and engaged in mock battles. American reporter William Shirer described the Nuremberg rally:

Primary Source

"It is difficult to exaggerate the frenzy of the three hundred thousand German spectators when they saw their soldiers go into action, heard the thunder of the guns, and smelt the powder."

— William L. Shirer, *Berlin Diary*

Nazis Persecute Jews Hitler preached that Germans belonged to a race that was biologically superior to Jews; Roma, or Gypsies; and other peoples. The Nazi government singled out the Jews for special persecution. Jews were deprived of their citizenship, forbidden to use public facilities, and driven out of almost every type of work.

Analyze Images This 1940 Soviet poster reads "Long Live the Victorious Nation! Long Live Our Dear Stalin." **Synthesize Visual Information** What emotions did this poster try to stir in the Soviet people?

Later, Jews were rounded up and sent to **concentration camps**, originally prison camps for civilians whom the Nazis declared "enemies of the state." Many camps became death camps. In time, Hitler would unleash a plan to kill all the Jews in Europe.

Germany Moves Toward War Hitler claimed that Germany had a right to expand to the east. In defiance of the Treaty of Versailles, he began to build up Germany's armed forces. Although the League of Nations condemned his actions, Hitler predicted that the rest of Europe would "never act. They'll just protest. And they will always be too late."

In 1936, German troops moved into the Rhineland, near the border with France and Belgium. The Treaty of Versailles had banned German troops from this region. France and Britain protested Germany's illegal action but took no other action.

READING CHECK **Identify Supporting Details** How did political change in Germany result in military aggression in Europe?

Strong Leaders in the Soviet Union and Japan

Totalitarian leaders also came to power in the Soviet Union and Japan. Unlike those in Italy and Germany, however, these leaders were not fascist—but they did seek complete control. They were unhappy with the terms of the Treaty of Versailles and hoped to bring new glory to their nations. As in Western Europe, the political changes underway in these regions drew the world closer to war.

Totalitarianism in the Soviet Union Vladimir Lenin set up a communist government in the Soviet Union. After Lenin's death in 1924, Joseph Stalin gained power. Stalin ruled as a totalitarian dictator. In a **totalitarian state**, a single party controls the government and every aspect of people's lives. Citizens must obey the government without question. Criticism of the government is severely punished.

Stalin took brutal measures to modernize and communize Soviet industry and agriculture. He ordered peasants to hand over land and animals to government-run farms. Millions resisted and were executed or exiled to forced labor camps. More than 5 million people starved to death.

Stalin also purged, or got rid of, his political enemies. Many confessed to false charges under torture. These people were also killed or sent to labor camps. In all, it is estimated that 20 million or more people perished by the hand of Stalin's ruthless dictatorship.

Did you know?

Stalin sent perhaps 18 million people to hard labor camps, often for the most insignificant acts.

Military Rule in Japan Japan's economy suffered severely during the Great Depression. As many Japanese grew impatient with their democratic government, military leaders took power. Like Hitler, these leaders preached racial superiority. They believed that the Japanese were purer than, and superior to, other Asians as well as non-Asians.

The military rulers set out to expand into Asia. In 1931, Japanese forces seized a region in northeastern China known as Manchuria. The region was rich in coal and iron, two resources scarce in Japan. The Japanese set up a state in Manchuria called Manchukuo.

China called on the League of Nations for help. The League condemned Japanese aggression but did little else. The United States refused to recognize Manchukuo but took no action.

INTERACTIVE

Characteristics of Totalitarianism

READING CHECK **Identify Supporting Details** Why was the Soviet Union considered a totalitarian state?

The United States Remains Isolated

In the United States, the strong isolationist mood of the 1920s continued. As war clouds gathered overseas, Americans were determined to keep from becoming involved. In 1935, Congress passed the first of a series of **Neutrality Acts**, which banned arms sales or loans to countries at war. Congress also warned Americans not to travel on ships of countries at war. By limiting economic ties with warring nations, isolationists hoped to stay out of any foreign conflict.

Relations With Latin America Closer to home, the United States tried to improve relations with Latin American nations. In 1930, President Hoover rejected the Roosevelt Corollary. The United States, he declared, no longer claimed the right to intervene in Latin American affairs.

When President Franklin Roosevelt took office in 1933, he also worked to build friendlier relations with Latin America. His **Good Neighbor Policy** emphasized trade and cooperation. Under this policy, FDR withdrew American troops from Nicaragua and Haiti.

Analyze Charts This chart describes the main impacts of each of the three Neutrality Acts. **Use Evidence** What evidence shows that the United States hoped to minimize involvement in any overseas war?

The Neutrality Acts, 1935–1939

YEAR	IMPACT
1935	Prohibited the sale and export of weapons to nations at war and required American weapons manufacturers to apply for an export license
1937	Prohibited U.S. citizens from traveling on ships of nations at war and banned American merchant ships from transporting weapons produced outside the United States to warring nations
1939	Lifted the ban on weapons but prohibited American ships from transporting goods to ports of nations at war

Source: United States Department of State

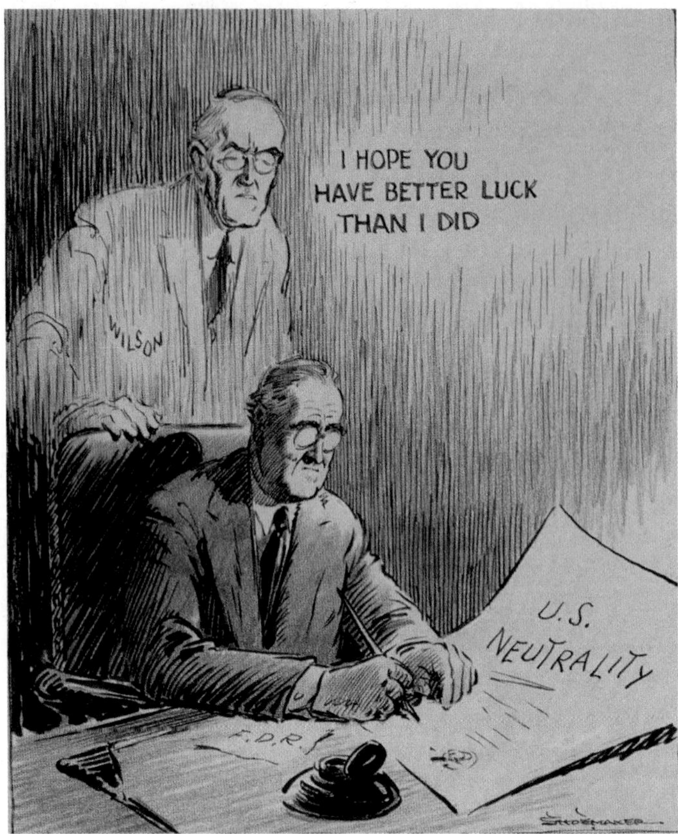

Analyze Images In this 1935 cartoon, "Only a Generation Apart," Woodrow Wilson tells President Roosevelt, "I hope you have better luck than I did." **Use Visual Information** What comparison does the cartoonist draw between Wilson and Roosevelt?

Roosevelt also canceled the Platt Amendment, which had limited the independence of Cuba.

Roosevelt believed that as world tensions increased, the need to strengthen ties in the Americas became more pressing. On a visit to Argentina, he warned that any foreign aggressor "will find a hemisphere wholly prepared to consult together for our mutual safety."

Relations With the Soviet Union President Roosevelt also improved relations with the Soviet Union. He restored diplomatic relations with the Soviet government in 1933, although he remained wary about allying America too closely with the communist nation. In addition to benefiting the American economy, Roosevelt hoped that improved relations with the Soviet Union would discourage Japanese expansion in Asia.

READING CHECK **Understand Effects** How did political changes in Europe and Asia lead to the Good Neighbor Policy?

Lesson Check

Practice Vocabulary

1. How did Germany, Japan, and Italy act with **aggression**?
2. What was the purpose of Hitler's **concentration camps**?
3. Why did Congress enact the **Neutrality Acts?**

Critical Thinking and Writing

4. **Summarize** How did Mussolini seize power in Italy in 1922, and what actions did he take that led to a fascist government?
5. **Draw Conclusions** How did the Nazi government justify its persecution of Jews during the early days of Hitler's rule?
6. **Writing Workshop: Introduce Characters** You will write a narrative from the perspective of either an American soldier during World War II or of an American on the home front. Decide which perspective you will use, and then think about who will be characters in your story. Write three sentences in your Active Journal describing your characters.

LESSON 2

Entering World War II

GET READY TO READ

START UP

U.S. battleships *West Virginia* and *Tennessee* were hit hard by Japan's surprise attack in 1941. How would you expect Americans to respond to such an attack?

GUIDING QUESTIONS

- How did aggression lead to war in Asia and Europe?
- How did the United States respond to the outbreak of World War II?
- Why did the United States enter World War II?

TAKE NOTES

Literacy Skills: Identify Cause and Effect

Use the graphic organizer in your Active Journal to take notes as you read the lesson.

PRACTICE VOCABULARY

Use the vocabulary activity in your Active Journal to practice the vocabulary words.

Vocabulary

Munich Conference
appeasement
Nazi-Soviet Pact
blitzkrieg
Axis
Allies
Battle of Britain
Lend-Lease Act
Atlantic Charter

Academic Vocabulary

denounce
convey

The totalitarian governments that arose in Japan and Germany had large imperial ambitions. They began advancing into surrounding territories. European leaders hoped to avoid war, and the United States was wary of getting involved. Yet the military aggression from these two nations would soon become impossible to ignore.

How Did War Begin?

Japan is an island nation that has few natural resources to fuel its economy and supply its military. Nearby places in Asia, however, had plentiful resources, and Japan intended to acquire them.

Japan Invades China In 1937, Japan began an all-out war against China. Japanese planes bombed China's major cities. Thousands of people were killed. In the city of Nanjing alone, some 300,000 civilians and prisoners of war were murdered in a six-week massacre. Japanese troops defeated Chinese armies and occupied northern and central China.

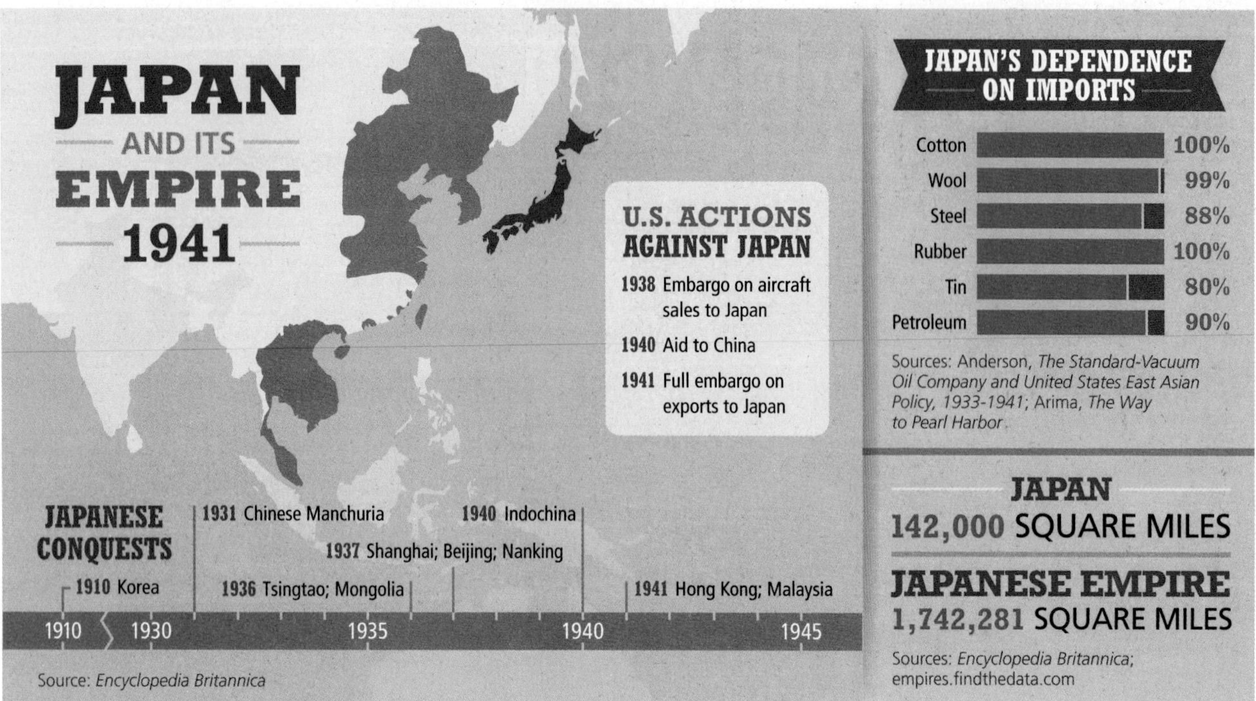

Analyze Charts The chart gives an overview of the growth of the Japanese Empire. **Draw Conclusions** What does the information about imports and U.S. actions suggest about the reasons Japan used its military?

The Japanese advance into China alarmed American leaders. They felt it undermined, or worked against, the Open Door Policy, which promised equal access to trade in China. It also threatened the Philippines, which the United States controlled. Nevertheless, isolationist feelings remained strong among the American people and kept the United States from taking a firm stand against the Japanese.

Americans React Americans were angered by Japan's invasion of China. The United States did not want Japan to become an imperial power in Asia. However, the public did not support going to war against Japan. The conflict in Asia was far away. Many Americans felt that it did not have a direct impact on their lives.

Academic Vocabulary
denounce • *v.*, to publicly state that some action or person is wrong or bad

President Roosevelt reacted to the invasion with a speech **denouncing** Japan's "reign of terror and international lawlessness," but he maintained his neutral stance. As you will read, Roosevelt would eventually try to apply economic pressure to Japan to halt its military aggression. Ignoring Roosevelt's harsh words, Japan sped up its attacks. It had its eye on British and Dutch colonies in Southeast Asia that were rich in oil, rubber, and other raw materials that its military could use.

Americans grew more concerned as the conflict in Asia spread. However, the United States would not go to war with Japan unless Japan attacked the United States directly.

Germany Expands In Europe, Hitler continued his plans for German expansion. In 1938, just two years after occupying the Rhineland, Hitler annexed Austria. This action violated the Treaty of Versailles once more. But again, Britain and France took no action against Germany.

Later that year, Hitler claimed the Sudetenland, the western part of Czechoslovakia. He justified his demand by claiming that the Sudetenland contained many people of German heritage.

Appeasement The United Kingdom (Britain) and France had signed treaties to protect Czechoslovakia but were reluctant to go to war. The two nations sought a peaceful solution.

In September 1938, the leaders of the United Kingdom, France, Italy, and Germany met in Munich, Germany, to discuss a solution. At the **Munich Conference**, Hitler promised that Germany would seek no further territory once it had acquired the Sudetenland. To preserve peace, the British and French agreed that Germany should have the Sudetenland. This practice of giving in to threats or aggression in order to avoid war is known as **appeasement**.

The policy of appeasement failed. Nazi Germany seized the rest of Czechoslovakia the very next year. At last, the United Kingdom and France realized that they had to take a firm stand against Nazi aggression.

Germany Invades Poland In August 1939, Hitler and Stalin signed the **Nazi-Soviet Pact**. The two rival dictators agreed not to attack each other. Secretly, they also agreed to divide Poland and other parts of Eastern Europe.

Confident that Russia would not retaliate, Hitler went after Poland. In September 1939, Hitler launched a **blitzkrieg**, or lightning war. This new tactic involved rushing concentrated forces with superior firepower into a specific area to scatter the enemy and penetrate deeply into enemy territory.

GEOGRAPHY SKILLS

The map shows Germany's steady expansion to the east and to the west.

1. **Interaction** Point out to a partner evidence from the map that shows that the German military aggressively expanded in the late 1930s.
2. **Use Visual Information** How far did the German empire extend from east to west by September 1939?

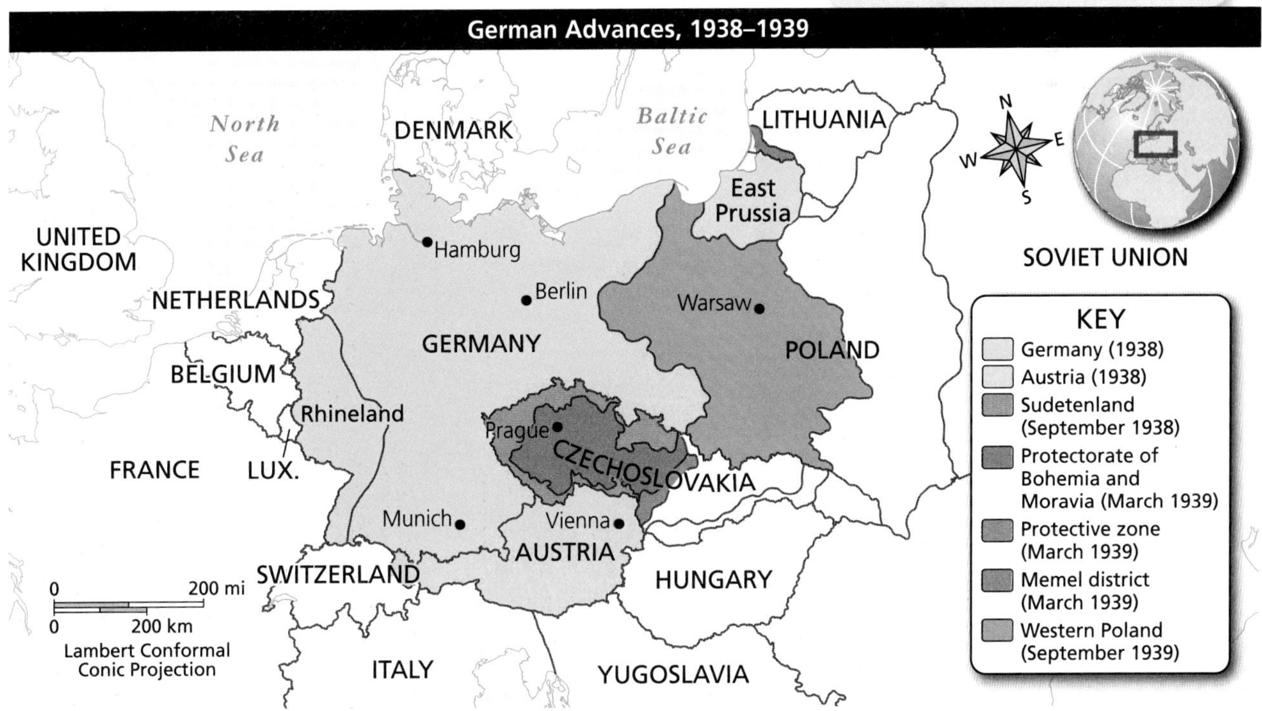

Unable to withstand modern German planes and tanks, the Poles soon surrendered.

Meanwhile, the Soviet Union seized eastern Poland. Stalin's forces also invaded Finland and later annexed Estonia, Lithuania, and Latvia. Stalin claimed that these steps were needed to build Soviet defenses.

READING CHECK **Summarize** What is appeasement and why was this policy not successful?

The War Expands

Two days after Hitler's invasion of Poland, Britain and France declared war on Germany. A new world war had begun.

World War II was truly a global conflict. Military forces fought all over the world. Italy, Japan, and six other nations joined Germany to form the **Axis** Powers. Opposing the Axis Powers were the **Allies**. Before the war was over, the Allies would include the United Kingdom, France, the Soviet Union, the United States, China, and 45 other countries.

Germany Conquers France In the spring of 1940, Hitler's armies marched north and west. In April, they smashed through Denmark and Norway. In May, they overran the Netherlands and Belgium and pushed into France. Germany's ally, Italy, also attacked France.

The British sent troops to help France resist the assault. The British and French, however, were quickly overpowered. By May, the Germans had forced them to retreat to Dunkirk, a French port on the English Channel. In a bold action, the British sent every available ship across the channel to rescue the trapped soldiers.

Unhindered, German armies entered France and marched on to Paris, the French capital. On June 22, 1940, barely six weeks later, France surrendered. The fall of France shocked the world.

Analyze Images In this 1940 photo, German troops parade on the Champs-Élysées, a grand avenue in the heart of Paris. **Understand Effects** What effect would this parade have had on the citizens of Paris?

Axis versus Allies World Map, July 1940

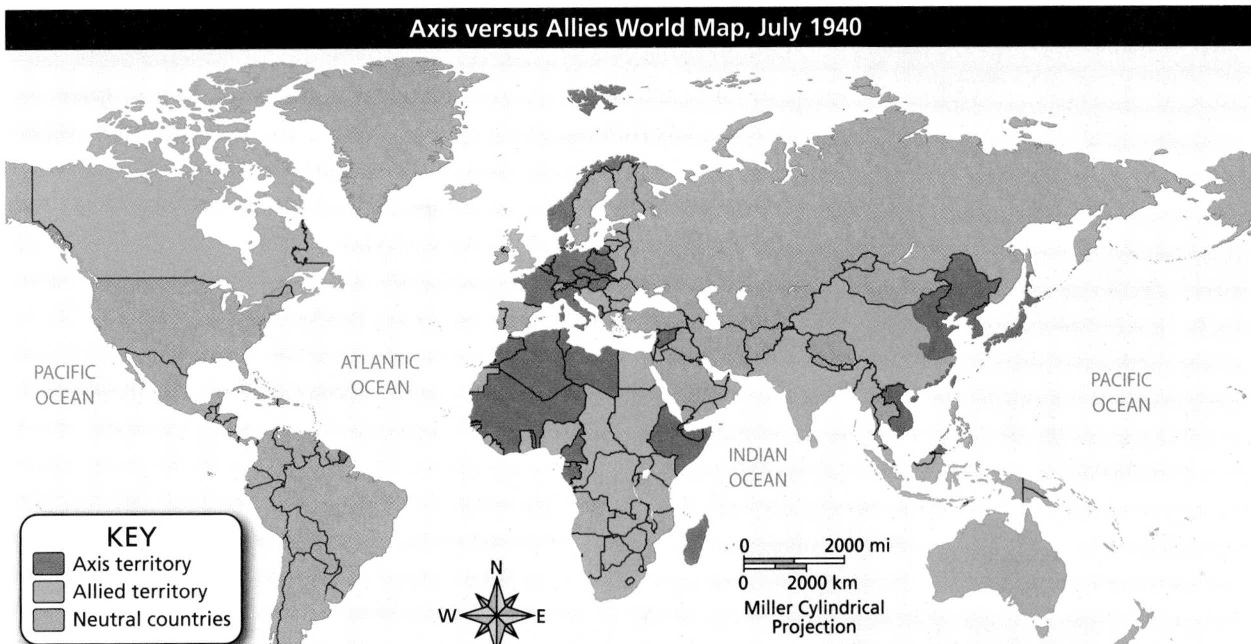

GEOGRAPHY SKILLS

The map shows areas of the world controlled by the Axis and Allied powers, and countries that were maintaining their neutrality.

1. **Region** How would the balance of power between the Axis and Allied powers change after the United States and Soviet Union joined the Allies?
2. **Use Visual Information** On which continents do the Axis Powers control territory?

Battle of Britain Britain now stood alone. Even so, the new prime minister, Winston Churchill, was confident:

Primary Source

"We shall fight on the beaches, we shall fight on the landing grounds, we shall fight in the fields and in the streets . . . we shall never surrender."

— Winston Churchill, Speech to House of Commons, June 4, 1940

Hitler's plan to invade Britain, codenamed Operation Sea Lion, became a massive air battle. German planes rained bombs down on London and other British cities during the **Battle of Britain**. British fighter pilots fought back, gunning down nearly 2,000 German planes. By late 1940, after months of bombing, Hitler gave up his planned invasion of Britain.

In the United States, Americans listened to radio reports from London. Hearing of Britain's brave stand against Hitler, Americans wondered how much longer they could stay out of the war.

READING CHECK **Identify Cause and Effect** Why did Britain and France declare war on Germany?

How Did the United States Aid the Allies?

After the invasion of Poland, President Roosevelt announced that the United States would remain neutral. He knew that most Americans favored the Allies but did not want to go to war.

INTERACTIVE

Axis and Allied Nations in Europe, 1939–1942

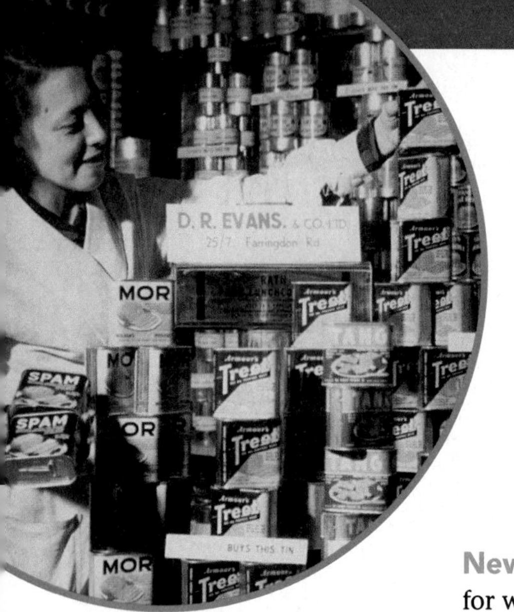

▲ The Lend-Lease program brought American-made goods to British shops.

Arms for the Allies At the same time, Roosevelt sought ways to help the Allies. He asked Congress to repeal the neutrality law that banned the sale of arms to warring nations. Isolationists blocked the move, but FDR won a compromise. The United States could sell arms to the Allies under a "cash-and-carry" plan. The Allies had to pay cash for the goods and carry them away in their own ships.

By 1940, German submarines had sunk many British ships. Roosevelt agreed to give the United Kingdom 50 old American destroyers. In exchange, the British gave the United States 99-year leases on military bases in Newfoundland and the Caribbean.

New Policies The United States also took several steps to prepare for war. Congress approved greater spending for the army and navy. Congress also passed the Selective Service Act of 1940, requiring all men between the ages of 21 and 36 to register for the draft. It was the first peacetime draft in the nation's history.

Isolationists opposed these moves, especially aid for the United Kingdom. "I have been forced to the conclusion that we cannot win this war for England, regardless of how much assistance we extend," warned Charles Lindbergh, the hero pilot of the 1920s. Many other Americans, however, felt that the United States had no choice. If Britain fell, Hitler might control the Atlantic Ocean.

Roosevelt Wins a Third Term The threat of war persuaded Roosevelt to run for a third term in 1940. He thought it was a dangerous time for a change in the country's leadership. His decision broke the precedent, set by George Washington, of seeking only two terms as President. Republicans nominated Wendell Willkie, an Ohio businessman.

BIOGRAPHY 5 Things to Know About WINSTON S. CHURCHILL

British Prime Minister (1874–1965)

- Churchill served as a high-ranking minister in the British government during World War I and later was a soldier in the war.
- He served as British prime minister from 1940 to 1945 and again from 1951 to 1955.
- After World War II, he made his famous "Iron Curtain" speech in Fulton, Missouri, in which he predicted the long Cold War between the West and the Soviet Union.
- Churchill's father was English, but his mother was an American. President John F. Kennedy awarded Churchill honorary American citizenship in 1963.
- Churchill was a gifted speaker, an exceptional historian and biographer, and a skilled painter.

Critical Thinking What do you think made Churchill popular with Americans?

Timeline of U.S. Entry Into World War II

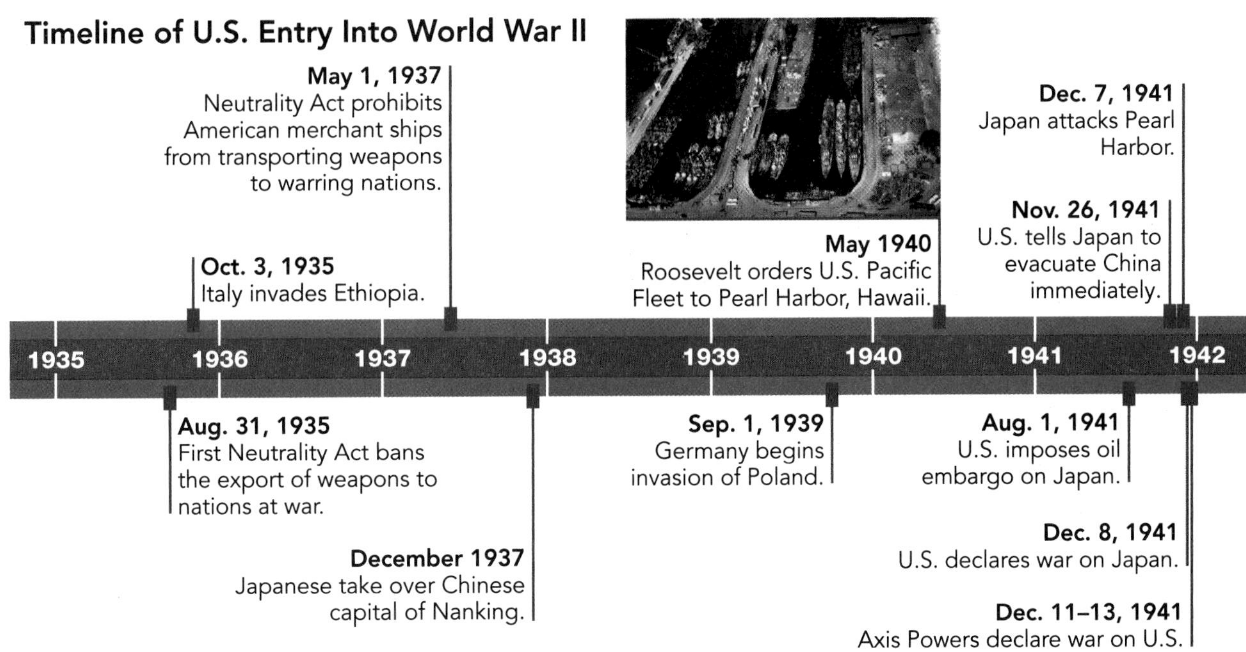

Sources: *Encyclopædia Britannica;* United States Department of State

Analyze Timelines The timeline shows the series of events that eventually led to America's entry into World War II. **Classify and Categorize** Which events in the timeline would isolationists in Congress have supported?

Willkie was a strong critic of Roosevelt's New Deal. Still, he agreed with Roosevelt on many issues, such as sending aid to the British. Both candidates also pledged not to send Americans into any foreign wars.

Republicans—and some Democrats—criticized Roosevelt for breaking the two-term tradition. Still, the voters gave Roosevelt a clear victory. After his defeat, Willkie worked to win Republican support for Roosevelt's war aims.

The Lend-Lease Act By late 1940, Britain was running out of cash. Roosevelt boldly suggested lending supplies to Britain. He proclaimed that Britain was defending democracy against totalitarian forces.

Despite continued opposition from isolationists, Congress passed the **Lend-Lease Act** in March 1941. It allowed sales or loans of war materials to "any country whose defense the President deems vital to the defense of the United States." Under Lend-Lease, the United States **conveyed** airplanes, tanks, guns, and ammunition to Britain and other Allied nations. British merchant ships transported the goods, with escorts of American warships providing protection as far as Iceland.

Academic Vocabulary
convey • *v.*, to carry

Lend-Lease Extends to the Soviet Union In June 1941, Hitler launched a surprise invasion of the Soviet Union. The invasion force was the largest in history. The invasion proved to be a vital turning point in the war, as it brought the Soviets over to the Allied side. Now the Germans would have to fight on two fronts instead of one.

American support for the Soviets was weak. Much of the American public remained anticommunist. President Roosevelt had condemned Stalin's totalitarian rule, but he decided to extend Lend-Lease aid to the Soviet Union. After much debate, Congress approved extending the aid to the Soviets.

Analyze Images This photograph shows Roosevelt (left) and Churchill at the Atlantic Charter Conference. **Summarize** What was the significance of the Atlantic Charter conference?

Creating Postwar Goals In August 1941, Roosevelt and Churchill issued the **Atlantic Charter**, which set goals for the postwar world. The two leaders agreed to seek no territory from the war. They pledged to support "the right of all peoples to choose the form of government under which they will live." The charter also called for a "permanent system of general security" similar to the League of Nations.

READING CHECK **Identify Supporting Details** Although the United States didn't formally join the war, what details indicate its support for the Allies?

The United States Enters the War

To Roosevelt, Japanese aggressions in Asia were as alarming as Germany's advance through Europe. By the late 1930s, the Japanese had seized much of China. After Germany defeated France in 1940, Japan took control of French colonies in Southeast Asia. In September 1940, the Japanese signed an alliance with Germany and Italy.

Limiting Trade With Japan The United States tried to stop Japanese aggression by refusing to sell oil and scrap metal to Japan. This embargo angered the Japanese because they badly needed these resources. "Sparks will fly before long," predicted an American diplomat.

Japanese and American officials met in November 1941. Japan asked the United States to lift its trade embargo. The United States called on Japan to withdraw its armies from China and Southeast Asia. Neither side would compromise. As the talks limped along, Japan completed plans for a secret attack on the United States.

"A Date Which Will Live in Infamy" On Sunday morning, December 7, 1941, much of the American Pacific Fleet was peacefully anchored at Pearl Harbor, Hawaii. Suddenly, Japanese planes swept through the sky. In less than two hours, they sank or seriously damaged 19 American ships, destroyed almost 200 planes, and killed about 2,400 people.

The attack was a desperate gamble by Japanese leaders. They knew they lacked the resources to defeat the United States in a long war. However, they believed Americans were weak and had no stomach for fighting. They thought the strike would force the United States to beg for peace immediately. Instead, Pearl Harbor united Americans in their resolve.

The Japanese made two other mistakes. First, they failed to sink any aircraft carriers, which were at sea at the time of the attack. Second, they did not destroy any fuel oil tanks. Oil and aircraft carriers would become two keys to American victory in the war that followed.

Declaring War The next day, a grave President Roosevelt addressed Congress. "Yesterday, December 7, 1941—a date which will live in infamy—the United States of America was suddenly and deliberately attacked by naval and air forces of the Empire of Japan," he began.

Quest CONNECTIONS

What reasons did Japan have for going to war? What role did the United States play in Japan's aggression? Record your findings in your Active Journal.

INTERACTIVE

Surprise Attack on Pearl Harbor

Primary Source

"No matter how long it may take us to overcome this premeditated invasion, the American people, in their righteous might, will win through to absolute victory."

— Franklin D. Roosevelt, War Message to Congress, December 8, 1941

Analyze Images "Battleship Row" (right of the island) and aircraft were the prime targets of the 183 planes in the first wave of the Japanese attack on Pearl Harbor. **Synthesize Visual Information** What made the United States' ships so vulnerable?

Analyze Images The attack on Pearl Harbor sunk the USS *Arizona*, killing 1,177 of its crew. This photo shows surviving crew members honored at Remembrance Day ceremonies on the 50th anniversary of the attack. **Explain an Argument** Why do you think it is important to honor war veterans?

Congress declared war on Japan. In response, Germany and Italy declared war on the United States. Americans were now united in the cause of freedom. Even isolationists backed the war effort.

The attack on Pearl Harbor had an immediate effect on Americans' lives. Young men left schools and jobs to enter the war. The economy sped up to provide the necessary supplies. A new wartime society developed with a surge in patriotic feeling. For Americans of Japanese, Italian, and German heritage, the war also brought difficulties. Many in the country viewed them with suspicion.

READING CHECK **Identify Cause and Effect** Why did Japan attack the United States?

Lesson Check

Practice Vocabulary

1. Why wasn't **appeasement** effective at the **Munich Conference**?
2. How did Hitler use the **blitzkrieg**?
3. Which were the chief nations that made up the **Allied** and **Axis** powers?

Critical Thinking and Writing

4. **Identify Main Ideas** How did the attack on Pearl Harbor immediately affect the lives of Americans?
5. **Summarize** How did President Roosevelt work with isolationists in Congress to support the British while still keeping the United States officially neutral?
6. **Writing Workshop: Establish Setting** Think about the setting for your narrative from the perspective of the American soldier or the American on the home front. Write a few sentences in your Active Journal describing your setting.

Primary Sources

Franklin D. Roosevelt, "Day of infamy" Speech

On December 8, 1941, the day after Japan's surprise attack on Pearl Harbor, President Franklin D. Roosevelt responded in an address before Congress.

▶ Roosevelt speaking to Congress

Yesterday, December 7, 1941—a date which will live in infamy ①—the United States of America was suddenly and deliberately attacked by naval and air forces of the Empire of Japan.

The United States was at peace with that Nation and, at the solicitation ② of Japan, was still in conversation with its Government and its Emperor looking toward the maintenance of peace in the Pacific. Indeed, one hour after Japanese air squadrons had commenced bombing in the American Island of Oahu, the Japanese Ambassador to the United States and his colleague delivered to our Secretary of State a formal reply to a recent American message. And while this reply stated that it seemed useless to continue the existing diplomatic negotiations, it contained no threat or hint of war or of armed attack....

The attack yesterday on the Hawaiian Islands has caused severe damage to American naval and military forces. I regret to tell you that very many American lives have been lost. In addition American ships have been reported torpedoed on the high seas between San Francisco and Honolulu....

No matter how long it may take us to overcome this premeditated ③ invasion, the American people in their righteous might will win through to absolute victory. I believe that I interpret the will of the Congress and of the people when I assert that we will not only defend ourselves to the uttermost but will make it very certain that this form of treachery shall never again endanger us....

I ask that the Congress declare that since the unprovoked ④ and dastardly ⑤ attack by Japan on Sunday, December 7, 1941, a state of war has existed between the United States and the Japanese Empire.

Reading and Vocabulary Support

① *Infamy* means being famous for a shocking, terribly bad action.

② What does *solicitation* mean?

③ When an act is premeditated, it has been thought through and planned.

④ What does it mean when an action is unprovoked?

⑤ A dastardly attack is one that is cruel and deceitful.

Quest CONNECTIONS

Consider Roosevelt's tone and the feelings he expresses about Japan's treachery. To what extent do you think he would have gone at that moment to punish Japan and end the war? Record your findings in your Active Journal.

Analyzing Primary Sources

Cite specific evidence from the document to support your answers.

1. **Use Evidence** What did the Japanese do to deceive the United States?
2. **Identify Main Ideas** What did President Roosevelt promise the American people?

LESSON 3

The Home Front

BOUNCE TO ACTIVATE VIDEO

GET READY TO READ

START UP

Airwoman Lillian Yonally of the Women Airforce Service Pilots (WASPs) flew warplanes to Europe. How might living through a war change women's lives after the war?

GUIDING QUESTIONS

- How did the United States mobilize its economy to produce materials and funds for World War II?
- How did working women help the war effort?
- How did the United States treat minority groups during the war?

TAKE NOTES

Literacy Skills: Classify and Categorize

Use the graphic organizer in your Active Journal to take notes as you read the lesson.

PRACTICE VOCABULARY

Use the vocabulary activity in your Active Journal to practice the vocabulary words.

Vocabulary		Academic Vocabulary
War Production Board	"Double V" campaign	allocate
rationing	Tuskegee Airmen	redeem
victory garden	internment	
Rosie the Riveter	Bracero Program	

During World War II, more than 15 million Americans served in the military. Many millions more spent the war years at home, far from the battlefields. To win the war, it was crucial to mobilize the home front to support and supply the armed forces.

Americans Mobilize for War

President Roosevelt had taken a number of steps even before war was declared to make sure America was ready if the time came. He was already building the armed forces through the draft, and manufacturers were turning out aircraft, artillery, and ammunition for Britain and other countries. Still, actually joining in the war meant even greater efforts were needed to prepare and supply America's forces.

Training Recruits In 1939, the United States military had just 334,500 servicemen. That was not nearly enough to combat the large and experienced armies of Germany and Japan. So, as war approached, America had to quickly recruit and train a huge number of civilians.

Army, navy, and air bases were built all over the country. Recruits were trained to fight in the jungles of the Pacific, the deserts of North Africa, and the towns and farmlands of Europe.

Throughout the war, recruitment and training continued to receive the highest priority. By the end of 1941, there were 1,800,000 men and women in the armed forces. By 1945, the number had risen to over 12 million.

A Wartime Economy Even more than in World War I, the government controlled the economy during World War II. Government agencies set the prices of goods, negotiated with labor unions, and decided what should be produced.

The **War Production Board** required factories to shift from making consumer goods to making guns, ships, and other war materials. Automobile makers, for example, produced tanks, aircraft, and artillery shells. From 1942 to 1945, no new cars were built in the United States. The War Production Board also **allocated** resources to ensure factories had the materials they needed.

Academic Vocabulary
allocate • *v.*, to apportion, distribute

A Nazi leader once scoffed that "Americans can't build planes, only electric iceboxes and razor blades." He was wrong. In 1942 alone, American workers produced more than 48,000 planes and shipped more than 8 million tons of goods.

Civilians Pitch In To control shortages and ensure that enough raw materials would be available for war production, the government imposed **rationing**, or limits on certain goods that people could buy. Americans were given ration coupons to purchase coffee, sugar, meat, gasoline, and other goods. When people ran out of coupons, they could not buy the items until new coupons were issued.

Analyze Charts The chart provides a glimpse of how the U.S. economy was performing during World War II. **Cite Evidence** What evidence shows that the United States supported the Allied war effort in the early 1940s?

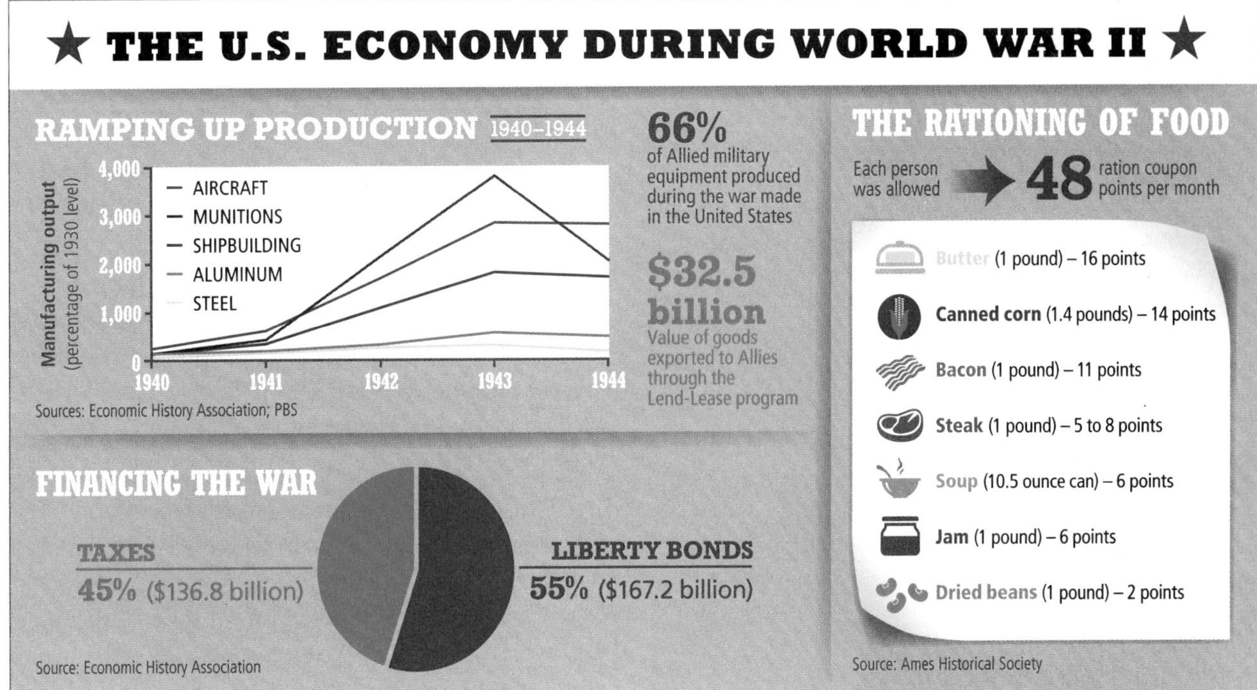

Academic Vocabulary
redeem • *v.*, to buy back

Consumer goods became scarce. To combat food shortages, many Americans planted **victory gardens**. At the height of the war, more than 20 million victory gardens produced 40 percent of all vegetables grown in the country.

To pay for the war, the government raised taxes. Also, as in World War I, the U.S. government borrowed money from millions of American citizens by selling war bonds. Americans could buy a bond with the promise that the government would **redeem** the bond after ten years, with interest. In the meantime, the government would use the money from bond sales to pay for the war. Movie stars took part in drives to sell bonds and boost patriotic spirit.

Quick Activity

In your Active Journal, write a couple of sentences exploring how a poster might encourage people to support the war.

The war quickly ended the Great Depression. Unemployment fell as millions of jobs opened up in factories. Minority workers found jobs where they had been rejected in the past.

READING CHECK **Draw Conclusions** How did America's entry into World War II affect the U.S. economy?

New Opportunities for Women and African Americans

"If you can drive a car, you can run a machine." Newspapers and magazines echoed this call to American women to work for victory. "Why do we need women workers?" asked a radio announcer. "You can't build ships, planes, and guns without them."

Analyze Images This poster aimed to recruit women ordinance workers, or WOWs. **Generate Explanations** Why was it so important to get women working?

Women Go to Work Women responded to the urgent demand for their labor. Almost five million women entered the work force. They replaced the men who joined the armed services. Many women worked in offices. Millions more kept the nation's factories operating around the clock. Some welded, ran huge cranes, or tended blast furnaces. Others became bus drivers, police officers, and gas station attendants. The image of **Rosie the Riveter**, a fictional factory worker, became a symbol of American women's contribution to the war effort.

Because women were badly needed in industry, they were able to win better pay and working conditions. The government agreed that women and men should get the same pay for the same job. Many employers, however, found ways to avoid equal pay.

The war also changed fashions for women. Instead of wearing skirts on the job, many women dressed in trousers. They wore overalls and tied scarves around their hair. More importantly, war work gave many women a new sense of confidence:

BIOGRAPHY 5 Things to Know About MARGARET "MAGGIE" GEE

World War II Pilot (1923–2013)

- Gee was one of the first two Chinese American women in the United States military.
- She joined the Women Airforce Service Pilots (WASPs) and spent most of her time training male recruits to fly.
- She earned degrees in physics and mathematics from the University of California, Berkeley.
- After World War II, Gee worked as a physicist for Livermore National Laboratories.
- In 2009, all surviving WASP veterans, including Gee, were awarded the Congressional Gold Medal for "distinguished achievements and contributions."

Critical Thinking What are some challenges Maggie Gee faced in her career?

Primary Source

"I will never regret my two years or more in the shipyards. It gave me a good start in life. . . . I decided that if I could learn to weld like a man, I could do anything it took to make a living."

—Nova Lee McGhee Holbrook, quoted in *A Mouthful of Rivets*

Women Join the Armed Forces Women joined all the armed services in great numbers. Almost 400,000 signed up for the army, navy, marines, and army air forces. Through their service, they replaced men who could be reassigned to combat units.

Women pilots logged 60 million air miles ferrying bombers from base to base, towing targets, and teaching men to fly. Many served overseas, and although they were not sent into combat, they faced some of the same dangers. Some were captured and made prisoners of war. Some died, and some earned Purple Hearts, Bronze Stars, and Legions of Merit, all medals given for courage and service.

Fighting a War Abroad and Discrimination at Home When the war began, African Americans rallied to their nation's cause, as they had during World War I. This time, however, African Americans decided to pursue a **"Double V" campaign**—victory over the enemy abroad and victory over discrimination at home.

Life on the Home Front During World War II

As industry geared up for war, factories replaced "No Help Wanted" signs with "Help Wanted, White" signs. African Americans, as well as Chinese Americans, Mexican Americans, and others, were excluded.

In 1941, A. Philip Randolph, head of the Brotherhood of Sleeping Car Porters, called for a protest march on Washington. The government, he said, "will never give the Negro justice until they see masses—ten, twenty, fifty thousand Negroes on the White House lawn."

Government officials worried that such a march would feed Hitler's propaganda machine. After meeting with Randolph, FDR ordered employers that did business with the government to end discrimination in hiring. As a result, the employment of skilled Black workers doubled during the war.

However, Black people faced increased hostility. Thousands of Americans—Black and white—moved to cities to work in industry. Scarce housing and persistent racism sparked violence. In 1943, race riots broke out in Detroit, New York, and other cities.

Heroism in the Military While FDR acted against discrimination in hiring, he refused to end segregation of the races in the military. Nearly a million African Americans enlisted or were drafted. They had to serve in all-Black units commanded by white officers.

African Americans served heroically in all branches of the armed forces. In the army, African American soldiers formed artillery and tank units. African Americans in the navy served as gunners' mates and helped build bases in the Pacific. African American marines helped defend American posts against Japanese attacks.

The **Tuskegee Airmen** were African American fighter pilots who trained at Tuskegee, Alabama. By the end of the war, the Tuskegee airmen had destroyed or damaged about 400 enemy aircraft.

Analyze Images Members of the Tuskegee airmen are briefed prior to the spring 1945 offensive in northern Italy. **Infer** Why were African Americans eager to serve in the military despite the discrimination?

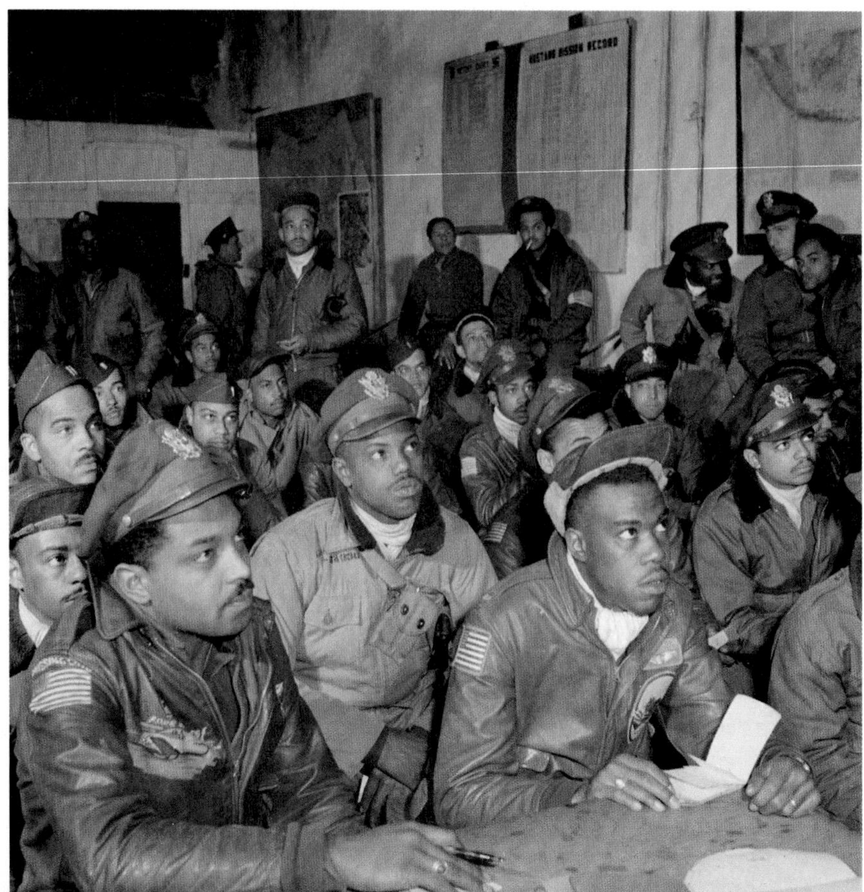

One of the earliest heroes of the war was Dorie Miller, an African American sailor serving on the battleship *West Virginia*. During the attack on Pearl Harbor, Miller dragged his wounded captain to safety. Then, though he had no training as a gunner, Miller manned a machine gun to defend his ship against enemy planes. For heroism in action, Miller was awarded the Navy Cross.

The contributions of African Americans to the war effort increased their determination to win justice at home. After the war, Black veterans would be at the forefront of a renewed campaign for civil rights.

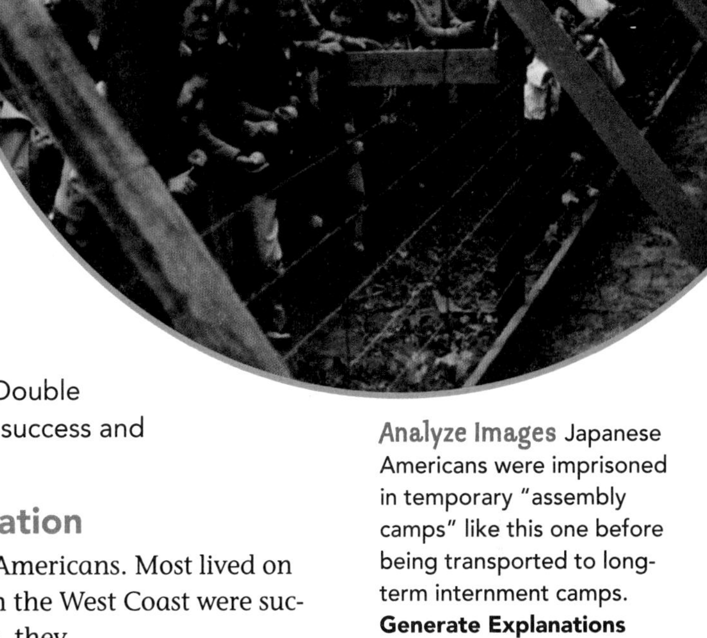

Analyze Images Japanese Americans were imprisoned in temporary "assembly camps" like this one before being transported to long-term internment camps. **Generate Explanations** Why did many people argue that these camps were not needed and unconstitutional?

READING CHECK **Summarize** Explain the "Double V" campaign and provide details showing its success and limitations.

Other Americans Face Discrimination

The war brought suffering to many Japanese Americans. Most lived on the West Coast or in Hawaii. Many of those on the West Coast were successful farmers and business people. For years, they had faced prejudice, in part because of their success.

Japanese American Relocation Camps After the attack on Pearl Harbor, many Americans questioned the loyalty of Japanese Americans. Some thought they might act as spies and help Japan invade the United States. No evidence of disloyalty existed. Yet, President Roosevelt signed an order allowing the army to move Japanese Americans from their homes to "relocation camps." Many were American citizens by birth. Later, a court case challenged the order, but the Supreme Court decided in *Korematsu* v. *United States* that such an order was constitutional in times of war.

About 110,000 Japanese Americans were forced to sell their homes, farms, or businesses at great loss. "We didn't know where we were going," recalled Peter Ota, who was 15 at the time. "We didn't know what to take. A toothbrush, toilet supplies, some clothes. Only what you could carry."

In the camps, Japanese Americans lived behind barbed wire in crowded barracks with little privacy.

Japanese American Service and Compensation Despite unfair treatment, thousands of Japanese American men served in the armed forces. Most were put in segregated units and sent to fight in Europe. There, they won many honors for bravery. The 442nd Nisei Regimental Combat Team became the most highly decorated military unit in United States history.

Did you know?

When detainees were released from the camps, they were given $25 and a train ticket.

The Experience of Japanese Internment

Years later, in 1988, Congress apologized to Japanese Americans who had suffered from **internment**, or temporary imprisonment, during World War II. Congress also approved compensation, or repayment for losses, in the amount of $20,000 to every survivor of the camps.

German Americans and Italian Americans Japanese Americans were not the only group to face wartime restrictions. About 11,000 German Americans and several hundred Italian Americans were also held in government camps as "enemy aliens." Other German Americans and Italian Americans faced curfews or travel restrictions.

Mexican Americans Because of the need for workers, the United States signed a treaty with Mexico in 1942. It allowed the recruitment of Mexican laborers to work in the United States. Under this **Bracero Program**, many Mexicans moved north to work on farms and railroads.

Analyze Images These Bracero Program participants have just arrived in Stockton, California, on their way to temporary jobs harvesting beets. **Identify Cause and Effect** Why were these workers needed in the United States?

At the same time, Mexican American citizens faced prejudice and discrimination. In June 1943, a group of sailors on leave attacked some young Mexican Americans, beating them on the streets. The incident led to several days of rioting in Los Angeles. Newspapers blamed the violence on the Mexican Americans. But in her newspaper column, Eleanor Roosevelt argued that the riots were the result of "longstanding discrimination against the Mexicans in the Southwest."

Still, like other groups, Mexican Americans served bravely in the military during World War II. Despite problems at home, Americans were united in their resolve to win in Europe and the Pacific.

READING CHECK **Understand Effects** Why did Japanese, German, and Italian Americans face unfair treatment during World War II?

Lesson Check

Practice Vocabulary

1. How did the **War Production Board** support the war effort?
2. What was the purpose of **rationing** and **victory gardens**?
3. What was the **"Double V" campaign**?

Critical Thinking and Writing

4. **Summarize** How did Rosie the Riveter show the significant changes in American society during World War II?
5. **Identify Cause and Effect** How did America's entry into World War II affect the nation's economy?
6. **Writing Workshop: Organize Sequence of Events** Consider the events you will describe in your narrative about life during World War II. What will happen first, second, and so on? Write your ideas in your Active Journal.

Primary Sources

Jean Faulk, Memories of Growing Up During World War II

Jean Faulk was a young girl in St. Petersburg, Florida, when the Japanese attacked Pearl Harbor. She would carry the memories of that day and of the war years throughout her life.

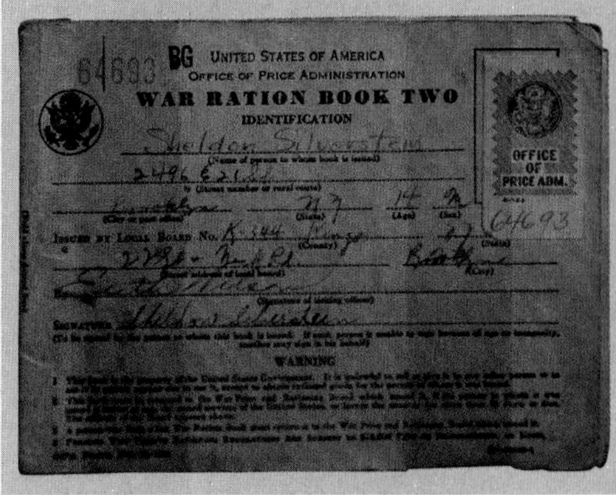

▶ A ration book, 1943

Sunday, December 7, 1941 . . . [We were out in the yard] when an uncle and aunt arrived. With a very solemn face he asked my dad what he thought of the news. . . .

That was the way we learned of the bombing of Pearl Harbor. Immediately the "grown-ups" . . . went into the house and turned the radio on. The women started crying. The men started talking in hushed tones.

A favorite uncle had recently been released after four years in the U. S. Marine Corps and knew he had to "re-up," or be drafted. All other draft age relatives immediately started flooding the Draft Boards and on Monday morning our family was well represented with volunteers. The young ex-Marine (age 22) reenlisted, and was later killed in the South Pacific. . . .

Ration books and coins ① were issued to all residents and were necessary for the purchase of butter, meat, sugar, and gasoline. Since my dad worked at night and there was no public transportation, he would mix his gas with kerosene ② to have enough to go back and forth to work six nights a week.

A garden was a necessity. We also had goats for milk, chickens for eggs, and rabbits for additional meat.

Everything that could be used in the "war effort" was collected by the school children. We took great pride in collecting newspapers, rubber bands, and the wrapping from chewing gum ③.

Reading and Vocabulary Support

① The federal Office of Price Administration issued ration books to limit how much of key goods any individual or family could obtain. No one could purchase rationed items, such as butter or beef, without having a ration stamp or coin.

② Kerosene is a fuel made from petroleum that was once commonly used for heating and lamps.

③ Recycled newspaper and other scrap paper was used for packing armaments. Rubber bands were recycled as tires. Recycled metal foil wrapping from gum, candy, and other products was used in making weapons.

Analyzing Primary Sources

Cite specific evidence from the document to support your answers.

1. **Identify Cause and Effect** Why were the women crying and the men talking in hushed voices after hearing of the attack?
2. **Analyze Information** How did children contribute to the war effort?

LESSON 4

Winning a Deadly War

GET READY TO READ

START UP

The Allies launched a massive invasion of Europe in June 1944. Why would this event have caused both dread and celebration among Americans at home?

GUIDING QUESTIONS

- What early defeats did the Allies suffer, and how did they turn the tide?
- Why did Japan finally surrender?
- What made World War II the deadliest war in history?

TAKE NOTES

Literacy Skills: Sequence

Use the graphic organizer in your Active Journal to take notes as you read the lesson.

PRACTICE VOCABULARY

Use the vocabulary activity in your Active Journal to practice the vocabulary words.

Vocabulary		Academic Vocabulary
Battle of Midway	death camp	encounter
Operation Overlord	Holocaust	vary
Battle of the Bulge	Nuremberg Trials	
island-hopping		
concentration camp		

When Adolf Hitler learned of the Japanese attack on Pearl Harbor, he was delighted. "Now it is impossible for us to lose the war," he predicted. "We now have an ally who has never been vanquished in 3,000 years." Although Germany's alliance with Japan did not require it, Hitler promptly declared war on the United States.

Early Defeats for the Allies

At first, Hitler's prediction looked as if it might come true. In early 1942, the situation looked bleak for the Allies. German armies occupied most of Europe and much of North Africa. German submarines were sinking ships faster than the Allies could replace them. The German war machine seemed unbeatable.

Meanwhile, Japan was sweeping across Asia and the Pacific. American forces were divided between two fronts, and everywhere the Allies were on the defensive. It was not until 1943 that the tide of battle turned. It took time for the Allies to develop new strategies, weapons, and forces to fight back and win the war against Hitler and Japan.

Germany Invades the Soviet Union In the Soviet Union, German armies were closing in on Moscow, Leningrad (St. Petersburg), and Stalingrad (Volgograd) during the summer of 1941. The Soviets resisted heroically. They burned crops and destroyed farm equipment so that the Germans could not use them. The harsh Russian winter that followed also greatly hindered the German advance.

The German attack caused massive suffering. During the 900-day siege of Leningrad that began in the fall of 1941, more than one million Russian men, women, and children died, mostly of starvation.

Japan Advances Across the Pacific Meanwhile, Japanese forces were on the move in the Pacific. After the bombing of Pearl Harbor, they seized Guam, Wake Island, Hong Kong, and Singapore.

General Douglas MacArthur commanded United States forces in the Southwest Pacific. In the Philippines, he also directed Filipino troops. This combined force was still too small to match the powerful Japanese attacks. But they fought bravely as they made their final stand on the Bataan Peninsula, on Manila Bay:

Primary Source

"Besieged on land and blockaded by sea, cut off from all sources of help in the Philippines and in America, these intrepid fighters have done all that human endurance could bear. . . . Bataan has fallen, but the spirit that made it stand—a beacon to all liberty-loving peoples of the world—cannot fall!"

— Norman Reyes, "Voice of Freedom" broadcast, 1942

Analyze Images Residents of Leningrad dig antitank ditches in expectation of the German invasion. **Use Visual Information** What can you tell from the photograph about the hardships the Soviet people faced during the war?

Pacific Theater, 1942

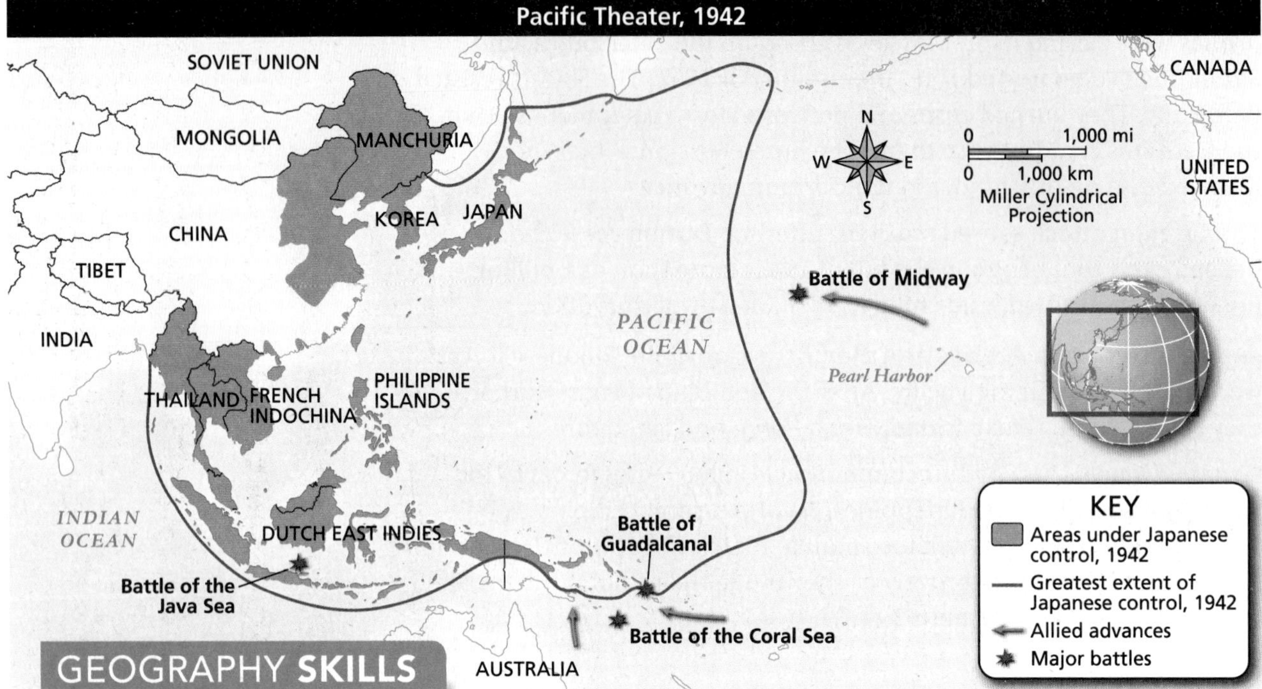

GEOGRAPHY SKILLS

This map shows the vast territory controlled by Japan in 1942. Beginning that year, the Allies pushed back and gradually freed those lands from Japan.

1. **Location** Based on the map, what challenges did the U.S. military face in the Pacific Theater?
2. **Infer** Why would the Japanese want to control tiny islands thousands of miles from Japan?

MacArthur was able to withdraw. However, about 75,000 troops he left behind to defend Bataan were captured. From the safety of Australia, MacArthur declared, "I shall return."

The Japanese pressed on. They captured Malaya (today's Malaysia) and Singapore, Burma, and the Dutch East Indies (today's Indonesia). They threatened India to the west and Australia and New Zealand to the south.

READING CHECK **Identify Supporting Details** What difficulties did the United States face in fighting a war in the Pacific?

The Allies Change the Course of the War

To succeed against the Axis powers, the Allies had to agree on a strategy. Even before Pearl Harbor, American and British leaders had decided that the Allies must defeat Germany and Italy first. Then, they would send their combined forces to fight Japan.

Quick Activity

Consider how each battle in the Pacific changed the course of the war with Japan.

Victories Over Japan Adopting a "beat Hitler first" strategy did not mean abandoning the war in the Pacific. Chester Nimitz, commander of Allied forces in the Pacific, sent a naval task force into the Coral Sea near Java in May 1942. The task force, strengthened by aircraft carriers that had survived the attack on Pearl Harbor, met a Japanese fleet there. After a three-day battle, the Japanese fleet turned back. It was the first naval battle in history in which the ships never engaged one another directly. All the damage was done by airplanes launched from the carriers.

One month later, the United States Navy won a stunning victory at the **Battle of Midway**. American planes sank four Japanese aircraft carriers. The battle severely hampered the Japanese offensive. It also kept Japan from attacking Hawaii again.

Pushing Across North Africa Allied forces began to push back the Germans in North Africa. In October 1942, the British won an important victory at El Alamein in Egypt. German forces under General Erwin Rommel were driven west into Tunisia.

Meanwhile, American troops under the command of Generals Dwight D. Eisenhower, Omar Bradley, and George S. Patton landed in Morocco and Algeria. They then pushed east and trapped Rommel's forces in Tunisia. In May 1943, his army had to surrender.

The Allies Invade Italy From bases in North Africa, the Allies organized the invasion of Italy. Paratroopers and soldiers brought by sea captured the island of Sicily. In early September 1943, the Allies crossed from Sicily to the mainland of Italy.

By then, Mussolini had been overthrown as leader of Italy. The Germans, however, still occupied much of Italy. In a series of bloody battles, the Allies slowly fought their way up the peninsula. On June 4, 1944, Allied troops marched into Rome. It was the first European capital to be freed from Nazi occupation.

The Eastern Front The Soviet army repelled the Germans from Leningrad in 1943. At Stalingrad, after months of fierce house-to-house fighting, Soviet soldiers forced the invading German army to surrender.

3-D Model: The B-24 Liberator

Analyze Images This photograph shows U.S. General George S. Patton in the North African desert. A light tank is in the background. **Use Visual Information** Based on the photograph, what particular difficulties do you think the armies fighting in North Africa would have faced?

Slowly, the Soviet army pushed the remaining German forces westward through Eastern Europe. Fighting in Russia and Eastern Europe was fierce. The Soviet Union would eventually lose some 9 million soldiers during the war, more than any other country.

For years, Stalin had urged Britain and the United States to send armies across the English Channel into France. Such an attack would create a second front in Western Europe and ease pressure in the East. However, not until 1944 were Churchill and Roosevelt prepared to attempt an invasion of Western Europe.

GEOGRAPHY SKILLS

This map shows the advance of Allied forces and the location of major battles.

1. **Interaction** What evidence from the map indicates that the Soviet Union gained territory previously taken by the Axis powers?
2. **Summarize** Based on the map, how would you describe Germany's situation during 1944 and 1945? Why was this the case?

Operation Overlord Years of planning went into **Operation Overlord**, the code name for the invasion of Europe. General Eisenhower, who was appointed commander of Allied forces in Europe, faced an enormous task. He had to organize a huge army, ferry it across the English Channel, and provide it with weapons, ammunition, food, and other supplies. By June 1944, almost 3 million troops were ready for the invasion.

The Germans knew that an attack was coming, but not when or where. To guard against the Allied invasion, they had mined beaches and strung barbed wire along the entire French coastline. Machine guns and concrete antitank walls stood ready to repel an advance.

D-Day in France In the early morning of June 6, 1944—D-Day as it was known—a fleet of 4,000 Allied ships carried the invasion force to France. Allied airplanes dropped thousands of paratroopers into occupied France behind German lines. Gliders landed in the French fields to deliver yet more troops and supplies. Allied warships shelled German defenses in preparation for the

World War II in Europe, 1942–1945

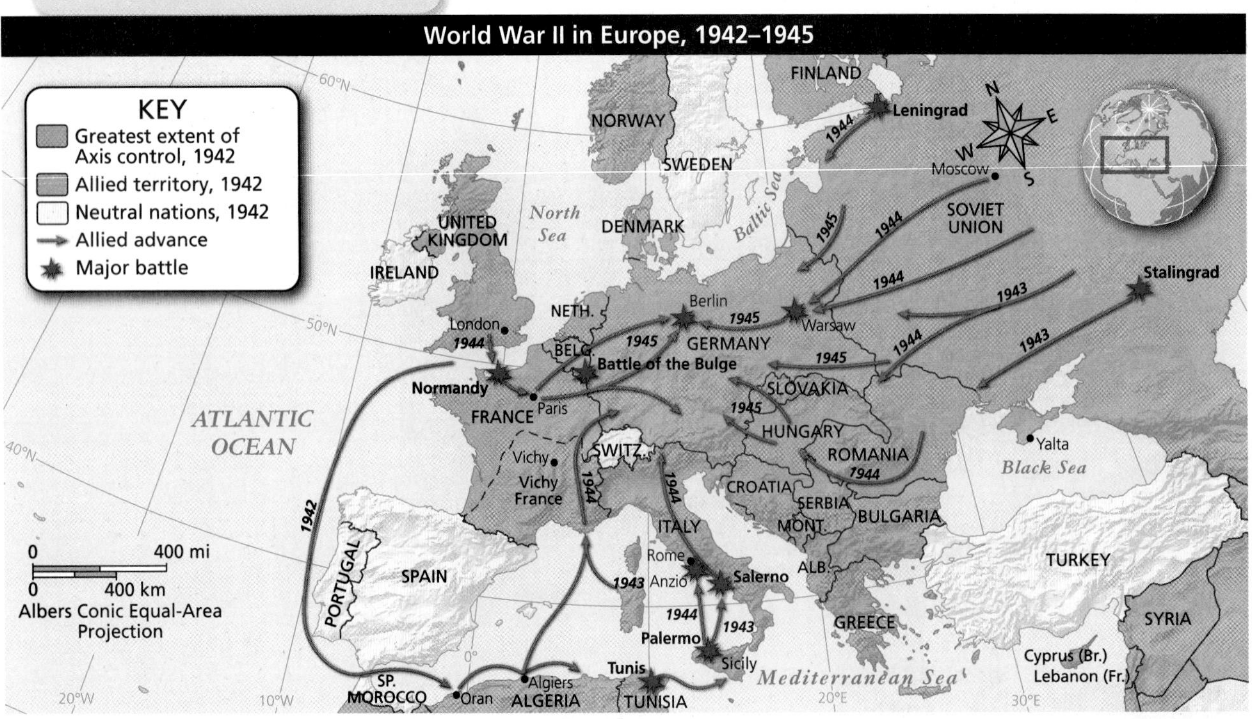

Analyze Images After the Allies captured the beaches at Normandy, the fighting moved inland, and the beach served as a supply center as more men and equipment were brought in. **Use Visual Information** What challenges were faced by General Eisenhower and others who planned Operation Overlord?

attack, but the main thrust of the invasion came from troop landings on five different beaches along Normandy. Allied troops scrambled ashore, with particularly tough resistance at a location code-named Omaha Beach. Americans suffered 2,400 casualties at "Bloody Omaha":

Primary Source

"It all seemed unreal, a sort of dreaming while awake, men were screaming and dying all around me. . . . I honestly could have walked the full length of the beach without touching the ground, [the bodies] were that thickly strewn about."

— Melvin B. Farrell, *War Memories*

Eventually, Allied forces captured all five beaches. Then, despite intense German gunfire and heavy losses, Allied forces surged on to capture more territory along the coast of France. Every day, more soldiers landed at Normandy to reinforce the advance. Progress after D-Day was extremely slow and dangerous due to French farm fields that provided thick cover for the enemy. But the Allied ground troops fought stubbornly and pushed German forces back.

The Allied liberation of France continued with the capture of Cherbourg, an important French port, by the end of June. Then the Allies swept east. On August 25, 1944, they entered Paris. After four years under Nazi rule, the Parisians greeted their liberators with joy. Within a month, all of France was free.

READING CHECK **Identify Main Ideas** What was the "beat Hitler first" strategy and what are some examples of its success?

Defeat for Germany

By September, the Allies were moving east toward Germany. However, a shortage of fuel for trucks, tanks, and other vehicles slowed the advance.

The German Counterattack On December 16, 1944, German forces began a fierce counterattack. They pushed the Allies back, creating a bulge in the front lines. During the **Battle of the Bulge**, as it was later called, the outnumbered American forces held the Germans back. Because of their own fuel shortage, the Germans were unable to power their tanks through the American defense. The Allies maintained their ground.

Analyze Images This scene occurred about 70 miles from Berlin, as American troops moving east met up with Soviet troops moving west. **Infer** Why were these Americans and Russians celebrating?

The Battle of the Bulge slowed the Allies but did not stop them. While Allied armies advanced on the ground, their planes bombed Germany. At night, British airmen dropped tons of bombs on German cities. By day, the Americans bombed factories and oil refineries. The bombing caused severe fuel shortages in Germany and reduced the nation's ability to produce war goods.

Roosevelt's Death Stuns the Nation Breaking all tradition, in 1944, President Roosevelt announced he would run for a fourth term. His Republican opponent was Governor Thomas E. Dewey of New York. Roosevelt was tired and ill. "All that is within me cries to go back to my home on the Hudson," he wrote. Still, he and his running mate, Senator Harry S. Truman of Missouri, campaigned strongly and won.

Five months later, on vacation in Georgia, the President complained of a headache. Within hours, he was dead.

All over the world, people mourned Roosevelt. His death especially shocked Americans. Many could hardly remember any other President. As for Truman, he was faced with taking over a country in the midst of war. "I felt like the moon, the stars, and all the planets had fallen on me," he later recalled.

Victory in Europe By April 1945, Germany was collapsing. American troops were closing in on Berlin from the west while Soviet troops were advancing from the east. On April 25, American troops **encountered** the Soviet army at Torgau, 60 miles south of Berlin.

Academic Vocabulary
encounter • *v.*, to meet or come upon

As Allied air raids pounded Berlin, Hitler hid in his underground bunker. Unwilling to accept defeat, he committed suicide. One week later, on May 7, 1945, Germany surrendered to the Allies. On May 8, the Allies celebrated the long-awaited V-E Day—Victory in Europe.

READING CHECK **Identify Cause and Effect** Why did the United States bomb German factories and oil refineries?

Japan Surrenders

While war raged in Europe, the Allies kept up pressure on Japan. The United States had two main goals in the Pacific war: to regain the Philippines and to invade Japan. Both tasks would prove difficult. American forces encountered stubborn resistance as they advanced into Japanese territories. Japanese soldiers were trained not to surrender, even if it was clear they were not going to win.

Capturing Japanese Islands To gain control of the Pacific Ocean, American forces used a strategy of capturing a few vital Japanese-held islands and going around others. In this **island-hopping** campaign, each island that was won became another stepping-stone to Japan.

A deadly routine developed. First, American ships and planes shelled and bombed an island. Next, troops waded ashore under heavy gunfire. Then, they slowly advanced across the island, often engaging in hand-to-hand fighting against determined Japanese resistance.

American Indian soldiers known as code-talkers made a key contribution. They helped create a code based on the Navajo language and used it to radio vital messages from island to island. The Japanese intercepted many messages but were totally unable to decode them.

In October 1944, American forces under General MacArthur finally recaptured the Philippines. In hard-fought battles, other forces captured the islands of Iwo Jima (EE woh JEE muh) and Okinawa (oh kuh NAH wuh) from the Japanese. Capturing Iwo Jima was important because of the air base located there. Okinawa, just 340 miles from the mainland of Japan, was intended to be used as a launching point for the invasion of Japan.

Analyze Charts This chart summarizes important ideas about the war against Japan. **Identify Supporting Details** Approximately how many casualties did the U.S. Army suffer in the Pacific theater during World War II?

THE PACIFIC THEATER

THE ALLIED EFFORT

UNITED STATES, BRITAIN, NEW ZEALAND, AUSTRALIA, CANADA, FIJI

Source: In Their Words: AETN's World War II Oral History Project

U.S. CASUALTIES IN THE PACIFIC 1941–1945

Branch	Casualties
Navy	27,876
Marines	18,446
Army	211,528

Total Pacific Theater Casualties: 252,850

Sources: Naval History & Heritage Command; Association of the United States Army

MAJOR EVENTS IN THE PACIFIC THEATER

December 1941 Japan attacks Pearl Harbor

June 1942 Battle of Midway

June 1944 Battle of the Philippine Sea

February–March 1945 Battle of Iwo Jima

April–June 1945 Battle of Okinawa

August 1945 U.S. drops atomic bombs on Hiroshima and Nagasaki, Japan

August 14, 1945 Japan surrenders; World War II ends

Sources: The National WWII Museum; University of Virginia; PBS

U.S. NAVY VESSELS IN THE PACIFIC

- Aircraft Carriers 575 ft.
- Battleships 550 ft.
- Heavy Cruisers 550 ft.
- Destroyers 300 ft.
- Gun Boats 300 ft.
- Submarines 280 ft.
- Torpedo Boats 70 ft.

Sources: PBS; Naval History & Heritage Command

Quest CONNECTIONS

Truman agonized over the decision to drop the first bomb on Hiroshima. How might he have felt three days later when he chose to drop the second bomb? Record your findings in your Active Journal.

For the Japanese, defending their homeland became a desperate struggle. Japanese leaders stressed an ancient code known as *Bushido*, or the Way of the Warrior. It emphasized loyalty, honor, and sacrifice. To surrender was to "lose face" or be dishonored. In suicide missions, kamikaze (kah muh KAH zee) pilots loaded old planes with bombs and then deliberately crashed them into Allied ships.

Plans to Invade By April 1945, American forces were close enough to launch attacks against the Japanese home islands. American bombers pounded factories and cities. American warships bombarded the coast and sank ships. The Japanese people suffered terribly. Yet, their leaders promised a glorious victory.

United States military leaders made plans to invade Japan in the autumn. They warned that the invasion might cost between 150,000 and 250,000 American casualties.

INTERACTIVE

Hiroshima

A Secret Weapon Truman, Churchill, and Stalin met at Potsdam, Germany, in July 1945. While there, Truman received word that American scientists had successfully tested a secret new weapon, the atomic bomb. A single bomb was powerful enough to destroy an entire city. Some scientists believed that it was too dangerous to use.

From Potsdam, the Allied leaders sent a message warning Japan to surrender or face "prompt and utter destruction." Japanese leaders did not know about the destructive power of the atomic bomb, and, consequently, they ignored the Potsdam Declaration.

Atomic Bombs End the War With Japan On August 6, 1945, the American bomber *Enola Gay* dropped an atomic bomb on Hiroshima, Japan. The blast destroyed most of the city, killing at least 70,000 people and injuring an equal number.

Analyze Images These photographs show the city of Hiroshima before and after it was struck by the atomic bomb. **Explain an Argument** Do you think it was right to drop the atomic bombs? Why or why not?

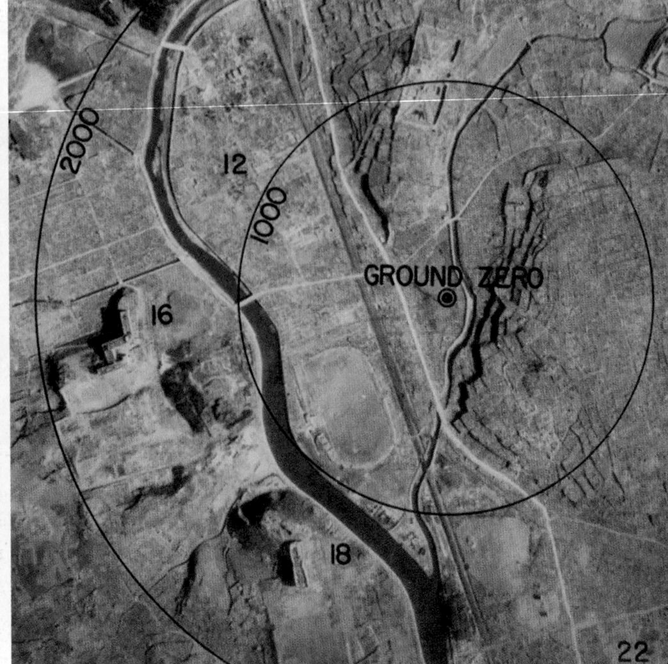

Analyze Images Americans in New York celebrated after living through the world's worst war. **Infer** Why would many Americans have mixed feelings at the end of the war?

On August 9, a second atomic bomb was dropped, on Nagasaki. About 40,000 residents died instantly. In both Nagasaki and Hiroshima, many more people later died from the effects of atomic radiation.

On August 14, 1945, the emperor of Japan announced that his nation would surrender. The formal surrender took place on September 2 aboard the USS *Missouri* in Tokyo Bay. The warship flew the same American flag that had waved over Washington, D.C., on the day that Japan bombed Pearl Harbor.

V-J (Victory in Japan) Day sparked wild celebrations across the United States. People honked their car horns. Soldiers and sailors danced in victory parades. World War II was over at last.

READING CHECK **Identify Main Ideas** Why did Japan surrender in 1945?

Widespread Devastation

World War II was the deadliest war in history. The exact number of casualties will probably never be known. Estimates of the number of people killed **vary** from 30 million to 60 million.

Academic Vocabulary
vary • *v.*, to range or differ

The fighting occurred on the land, sea, and air throughout many parts of the world. The war affected civilians more than any other war. Bombers destroyed houses, factories, and farms. By 1945, millions were homeless and had no way to earn a living. Well over half of the deaths from the war were civilians.

After the war, Americans heard horrifying stories of the brutal mistreatment of prisoners of war. When the Japanese captured the Philippines in 1942, they forced about 75,000 American and Filipino prisoners to march 65 miles with little food or water. About 10,000 prisoners died or were killed during the Bataan Death March.

The Holocaust In the last months of the European war, Allied forces uncovered other horrors. The Allies had heard about Nazi **concentration camps**—prison camps where members of targeted groups were confined. Some concentration camps were **death camps**, where people were systematically murdered. As the Allies advanced into Germany and Eastern Europe, they discovered the full extent of the **Holocaust**, the slaughter of Europe's Jews by the Nazis. During the war, the Nazis imprisoned Jews from Germany and the nations Germany conquered. More than 6 million Jews—two thirds of Europe's Jews—were tortured and murdered.

INTERACTIVE

Holocaust Aftermath and Remembrance

When Allied troops reached the death camps, they saw the gas chambers the Nazis had used to murder hundreds of thousands of people. The battle-hardened veterans wept at the sight of the dead and dying. After touring one death camp, General Omar Bradley wrote:

Primary Source

"The smell of death overwhelmed us even before we passed through. . . . More than 3,200 naked, emaciated bodies had been flung into shallow graves."

— Omar N. Bradley, *A General's Life*

Nearly 6 million Poles, Slavs, and Roma, or Gypsies, were also victims of the death camps. Nazis killed many prisoners of war, as well as physically or mentally disabled people. The Nazis also killed many they thought were "undesirable," including gay men, lesbians, beggars, alcoholics, and political enemies.

Analyze Graphs This graph compares the numbers of deaths suffered by the principal nations involved in World War II. **Use Visual Information** Approximately how many civilian casualties did the Allied Powers suffer in all?

World War II Deaths

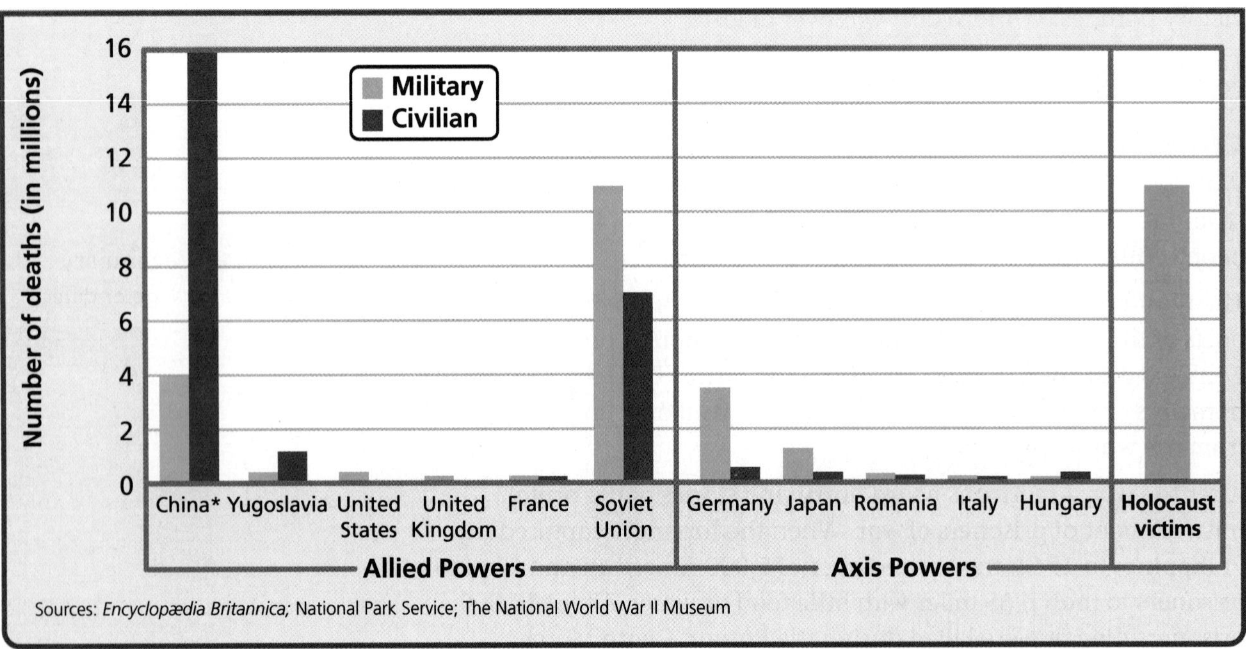

Sources: *Encyclopædia Britannica;* National Park Service; The National World War II Museum

War Crimes As the full truth of the Holocaust was revealed, the Allies decided to prosecute Nazis for war crimes and "crimes against humanity." The accused included government officials, military officers and enlisted men, businesspeople, and others. As a result of the **Nuremberg Trials**, 12 top Nazi leaders were sentenced to death. Thousands of others were convicted and imprisoned or executed.

The Allies also held war crimes trials in Tokyo. Over 4,000 Japanese officers and soldiers were convicted and over 900 were executed.

These postwar trials established the legal principle that individuals are responsible for their criminal actions even when they are following orders.

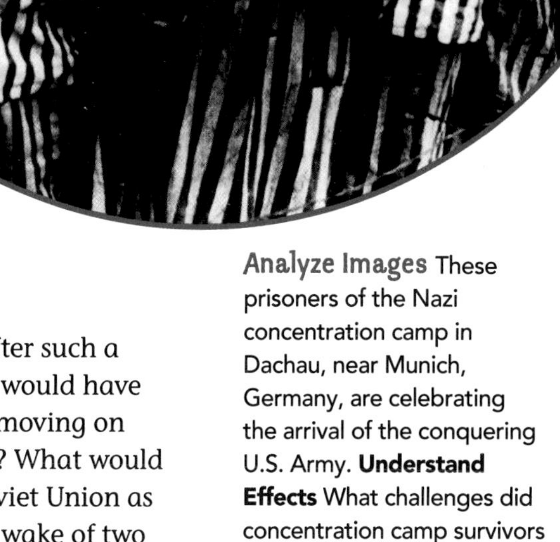

Analyze Images These prisoners of the Nazi concentration camp in Dachau, near Munich, Germany, are celebrating the arrival of the conquering U.S. Army. **Understand Effects** What challenges did concentration camp survivors face after the war?

Postwar Challenges Americans looked ahead to life after such a devastating war. More than ever before, the United States would have a critical influence on world affairs. The daunting task of moving on presented many challenges. How would Europe be rebuilt? What would happen to Germany? How would the emergence of the Soviet Union as a world power affect democracy around the world? In the wake of two terrible world wars, how could peace be maintained? World leaders struggled with these problems as they entered a new modern era.

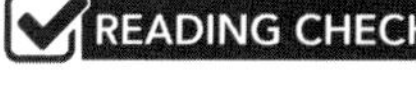

READING CHECK **Understand Effects** Why was World War II so deadly?

Lesson Check

Practice Vocabulary

1. What was the **Battle of Midway** and why was it important?
2. What was **Operation Overlord** and what were its results?
3. What happened during the **Holocaust**?

Critical Thinking and Writing

4. **Compare and Contrast** the Allies' strategy in the Pacific with their strategy in Europe.
5. **Use Evidence** What were the Nuremberg Trials, and why were they important?
6. **Writing Workshop: Use Narrative Techniques** In your Active Journal, draft the first part of your narrative. Use narrative techniques, such as dialogue, description, and similes. You will use this draft as a start for the narrative you will write at the end of the topic.

TOPIC 14

Review and Assessment

VISUAL REVIEW

Building Toward World War II

Building Toward WWII

- Mussolini's Italy invades Ethiopia (1935).
- Hitler's Germany annexes Austria, claims Sudetenland (1938).
- Munich Conference results in appeasement (1938).
- Nazi-Soviet Pact (1939): Germany and Soviet Union divide up Poland; Germany invades Poland.
- Japan seizes Manchuria (1931) and invades China (1937).

Major Events of World War II

WWII in Europe	WWII in the Pacific
• Hitler's armies invade France; France surrenders. • British and French soldiers escape at Dunkirk. • Battle of Britain • United States passes Lend-Lease Act to aid Allies. • After Pearl Harbor attack, U.S. enters the war. • Germany invades Soviet Union. • Allies win in North Africa. • Soviet Union defeats Germany at Stalingrad. • D-Day: Allies land on Normandy Beach. • Allies free Paris. • Allies win Battle of the Bulge. • Germany surrenders.	• Japan attacks Pearl Harbor. • U.S. enters the war. • Japanese advances continue. • Japan defeats General MacArthur in the Philippines. • U.S. wins stunning victory in Battle of Midway. • U.S. recaptures the Philippines. • Allies capture Iwo Jima and Okinawa. • U.S. drops atomic bombs on Hiroshima and Nagasaki. • Japan surrenders.

READING REVIEW

Use the Take Notes and Practice Vocabulary activities in your  Active Journal to review the topic.

INTERACTIVE

Practice vocabulary using the Topic Mini-Games

Quest FINDINGS

Answer the Document-Based Questions

Get help for writing your answers in your  Active Journal.

ASSESSMENT

Vocabulary and Key Ideas

1. **Describe** What were the purposes of the **concentration camps**?
2. **Check Understanding** How did Hitler use the **blitzkrieg** to invade and conquer neighboring countries?
3. **Recall** What was the **Bracero Program** and how did it help support the war effort?
4. **Describe** How did women's lives change during the war?
5. **Identify Main Ideas** How was the Battle of Stalingrad a turning point in World War II?
6. **Identify Main Ideas** Why did the United States change its plans to invade Japan?
7. **Recall** What were some of the big questions hanging over the world when World War II finally ended?
8. **Check Understanding** What was the significance of **Operation Overlord**?

Critical Thinking and Writing

9. **Understand Effects** What was appeasement and why was the policy a mistake?
10. **Draw Conclusions** Was President Roosevelt an effective international leader? Explain.
11. **Analyze an Argument** Why was the internment of Japanese Americans a mistake?
12. **Cite Evidence** How did World War II increase opportunities for African Americans?
13. **Revisit the Essential Question** Was America justified in going to war in 1941? Explain.
14. **Writing Workshop: Write Narratives** Complete a draft of your narrative from the perspective of an American soldier or of an American on the home front during World War II. Write a final paragraph that gives your narrative a strong ending, one that will make it memorable for readers.

Analyze Primary Sources

15. Read the quotation by J. Robert Oppenheimer, director of the program that developed the atomic bomb. According to him, how did the physicists feel about their role in developing the atomic bomb?
    - **A.** They wished they had never created the bomb.
    - **B.** They were proud of their achievement.
    - **C.** They did not expect the bomb to be used.
    - **D.** They recognized their role in killing so many people.

"The physicists felt a peculiarly intimate responsibility for... achieving the realization of atomic weapons. Nor can we forget that these weapons... dramatized so mercilessly the inhumanity and evil of modern war. In some sort of crude sense... the physicists have known sin; and this is a knowledge which they cannot lose."

—J. Robert Oppenheimer, Director of the Manhattan Project

Analyze Maps

Use the map to answer the questions.

16. Which letter represents Germany? Which letter represents the Rhineland?
17. Which letter represents where Germany invaded in September, 1939, starting World War II?

▼ **German Control, 1939**

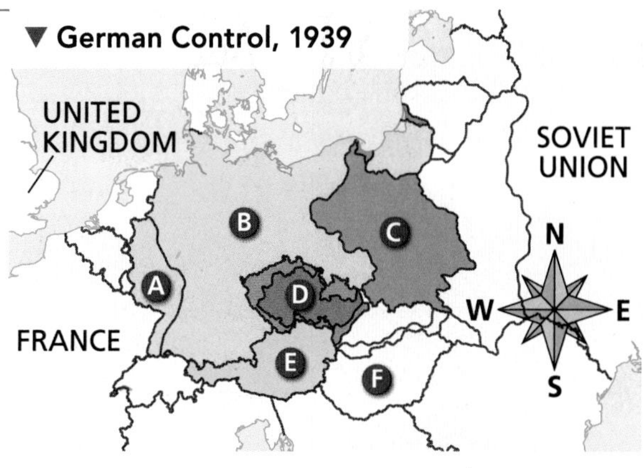

TOPIC 15

Postwar America (1945–1975)

GO ONLINE to access your digital course

VIDEO
AUDIO
ETEXT
INTERACTIVE
WRITING
GAMES
WORKSHEET
ASSESSMENT

Go back to the middle of the last century

to POSTWAR AMERICA. Why? It was a critical time in our country's history. It was a time when nuclear war could have erupted at any time, and nearly did. It was a time of worry, of deep questioning, and of hope for the future.

Explore The Essential Question

What is America's role in the world?

By the end of World War II, the United States had become the world's most powerful country. How would America use this new strength and influence?

Unlock the Essential Question in your Active Journal.

◁ Rev. Martin Luther King, Jr., speaks at the March on Washington for Jobs and Freedom, August 28, 1963.

Read

about postwar America, wars in Korea and Vietnam, the fight against communism, and the struggle for civil rights.

Watch

Minnijean Brown-Trickey, A Sojourn to the Past

Go on a journey with a key figure in the civil rights movement.

TOPIC 15 Postwar America (1945–1975)

Learn more about postwar America by making your own map and timeline in your Active Journal.

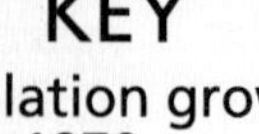

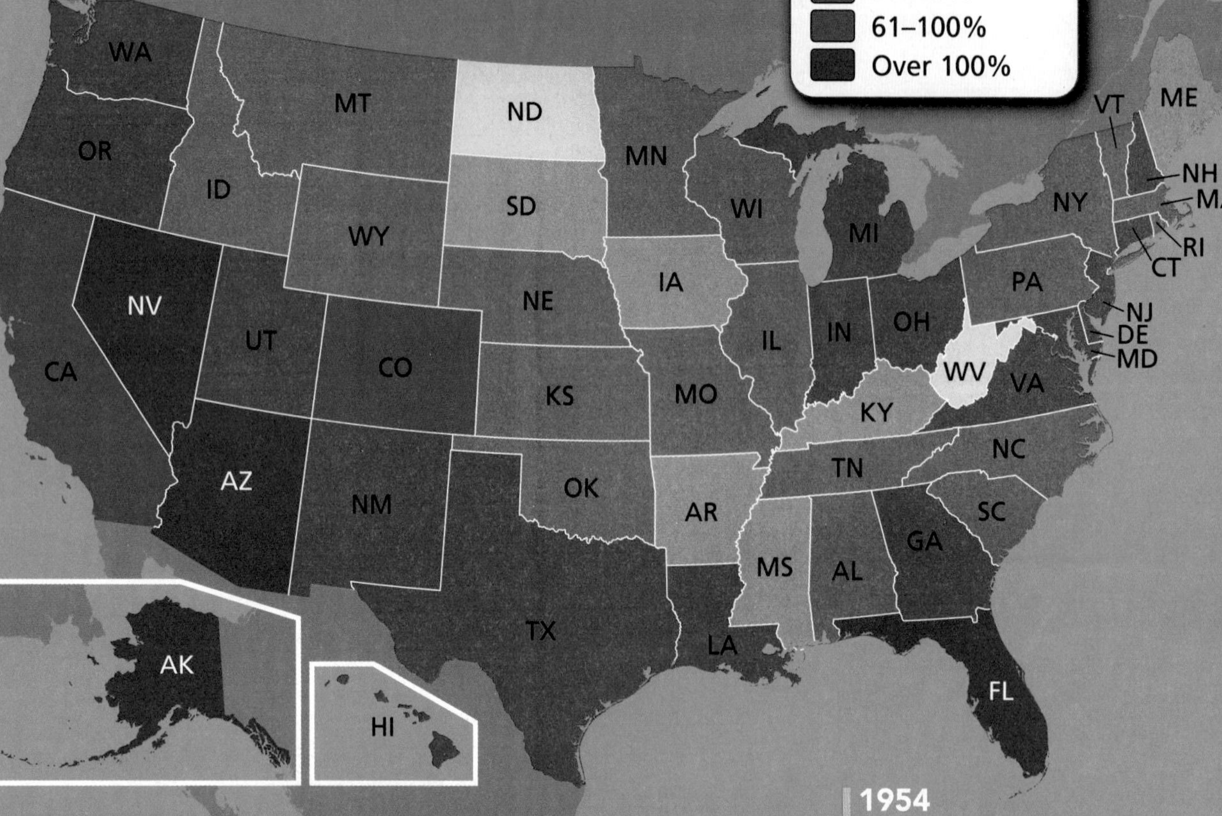

TOPIC EVENTS

1948 The Marshall Plan helps Europe rebuild.

1950 The Korean War begins.

1954 *Brown* v. *Board of Education* outlaws racially segregated schools.

1955 Rosa Parks is arrested, and the Montgomery bus boycott begins.

1940 | **1950**

WORLD EVENTS

1947 India and Pakistan gain their independence.

1949 Mao Zedong establishes the People's Republic of China.

INTERACTIVE

Topic Map

Where was the population growing?

America's population grew rapidly after World War II. Find the states on the map where the population really boomed.

INTERACTIVE

Topic Timeline

What happened and when?

Two superpowers face off, nuclear weapons at the ready . . . protests over segregation and an overseas war . . . Explore the timeline to see some of what was happening in postwar America and in other parts of the world.

1961
East Germany builds the Berlin Wall.

1961
Kennedy begins buildup of U.S. troops in Vietnam.

1962
Cuban Missile Crisis

1969
United States lands astronauts on the moon.

1960 | 1970 | 1980

1957
Six Western European nations form the European Economic Community.

1957
Soviet Union launches *Sputnik 1*, the world's first artificial satellite.

Who will you meet?

Cesar Chavez, organizer of migrant farm workers

Rosa Parks, civil rights activist

John F. Kennedy, U.S. President who confronted the Soviet Union

Project-Based Learning Inquiry

Reporting the Facts

Quest KICK OFF

People marched and demonstrated to draw attention to the civil rights movement, and reporters told America about these events.

How do the different ways a story is told and reported influence public opinion about social movements?

As you think about the Essential Question, "What is America's role in the world?," think about news stories you have heard and read. How do they influence your answer? You can explore these questions in this Quest.

▲ A reporter interviews James Meredith after a federal court ordered him admitted to the University of Mississippi.

1 Ask Questions

A reporter makes many choices when telling a story. How do these choices influence people's opinions of the event? Write questions that will help you form an answer to this question in your Active Journal.

2 Investigate

As you read about the civil rights movement, look for Quest CONNECTIONS that give clues about effects of news reporting. Capture notes in your Active Journal.

3 Conduct Research

Choose an event during the civil rights movement. Do your own research and read different stories reporting on the event. Consider how the way the story is reported influences your opinion. Capture notes in your Active Journal.

Quest FINDINGS

4 Create Your Newsletter

At the end of this project, your team will produce a newsletter analyzing how various reports influenced public opinion. Get help for writing your newsletter in your Active Journal.

The Beginning of the Cold War

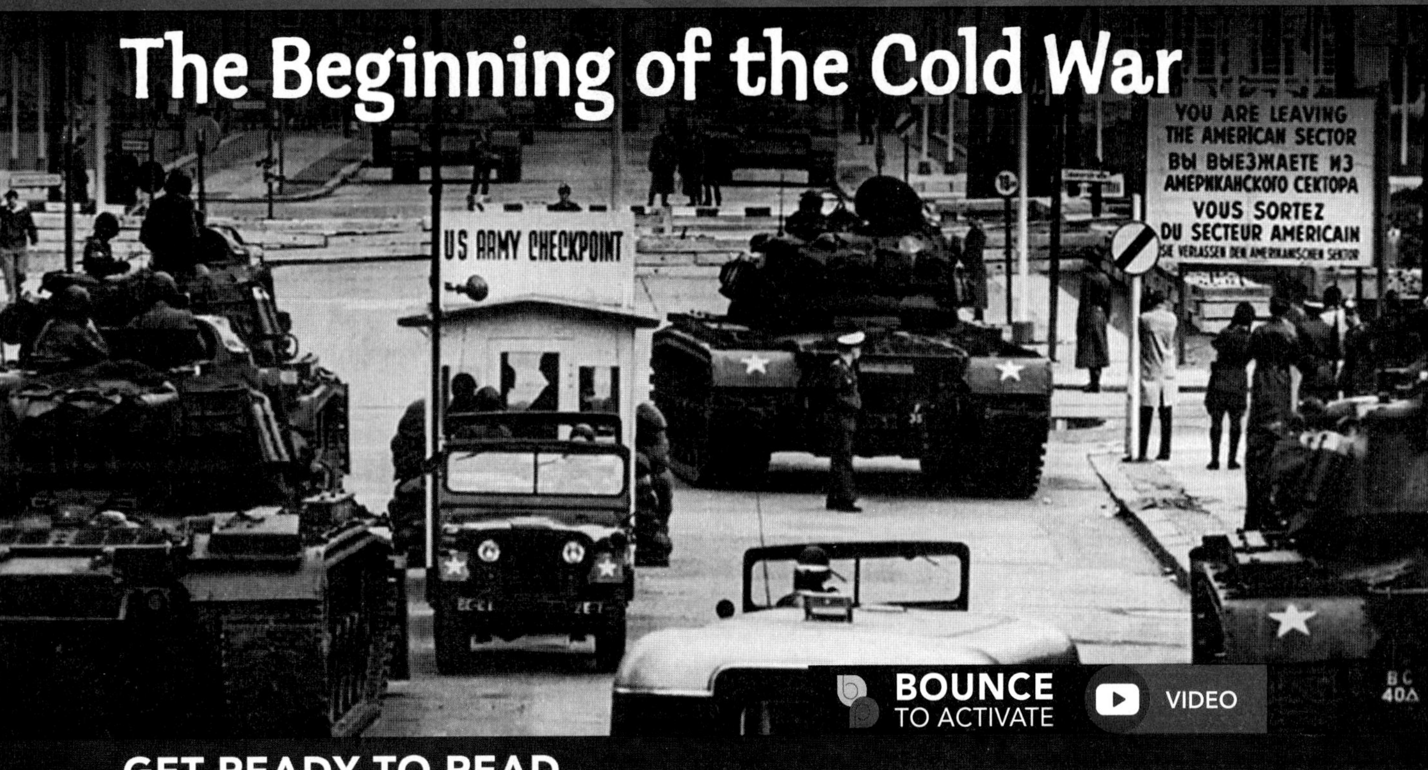

GET READY TO READ

START UP

Examine this photograph of a guard station at a crossing from West Berlin to Communist East Berlin. What would it be like to live in a divided city occupied by heavily armed soldiers?

GUIDING QUESTIONS

- Why did the United States take a leadership role in the world after World War II?
- How did the Cold War begin?
- How did the United States respond to Soviet expansion?

TAKE NOTES

Literacy Skills: Summarize

Use the graphic organizer in your Active Journal to take notes as you read the lesson.

PRACTICE VOCABULARY

Use the vocabulary activity in your Active Journal to practice the vocabulary words.

Vocabulary		Academic Vocabulary
Cold War	Berlin Wall	paralyze
iron curtain	North Atlantic Treaty Organization	reunification
containment	Warsaw Pact	
Marshall Plan	United Nations	
Berlin Airlift		

After the devastation of World War II, the United States and the Soviet Union were the only nations strong enough to exert global influence. However, the differences between the two countries led to a new kind of war.

What Caused the Cold War?

The United States and the Soviet Union did not clash directly in battle, but they competed for power and influence. Their intense rivalry became known as the **Cold War**. The Cold War lasted for nearly 50 years and led to numerous conflicts around the globe.

Distrust on Both Sides During World War II, the United States and the Soviet Union had worked together. Yet, even before the war ended, tensions surfaced.

The United States distrusted the Soviet Union and its communist rejection of religion and private property. Furthermore, the Soviets worked to overthrow noncommunist governments and boasted that communism would soon destroy free enterprise systems around the world.

INTERACTIVE

Cold War—Cause and Effect

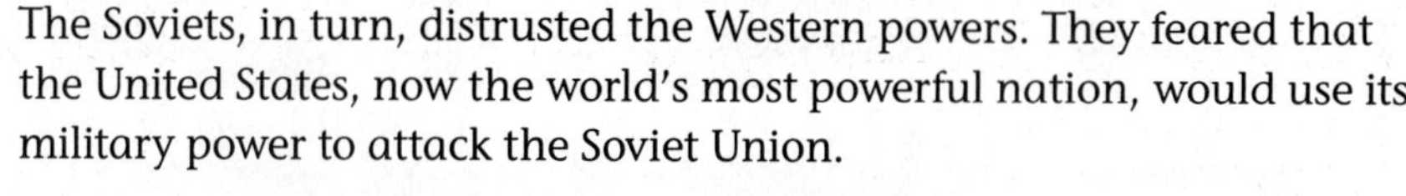

The Soviets, in turn, distrusted the Western powers. They feared that the United States, now the world's most powerful nation, would use its military power to attack the Soviet Union.

The Question of Eastern Europe Before World War II ended, Soviet armies had driven German forces out of Eastern Europe and back into Germany. As a result, Soviet troops occupied much of Eastern Europe. Josef Stalin, the dictator of the Soviet Union, promised to hold free elections in these Eastern European nations "as soon as possible." Stalin soon broke that promise. "A freely elected government in any of the Eastern European countries would be anti-Soviet," he said, "and that we cannot allow."

Academic Vocabulary
paralyze • *v.*, to make something unable to function

By 1948, Communists controlled the government of every Eastern European country. Except for Yugoslavia, these countries became satellite nations of the Soviet Union. A satellite nation is one that is dominated politically and economically by a more powerful nation. In each satellite nation, the Soviets backed harsh dictators. Citizens who protested were imprisoned and sometimes killed.

Communism Gains Ground As early as 1946, the British statesman Winston Churchill had warned against Soviet expansion into Eastern Europe. Naming two cities that were located in the north and south of Europe, he said: "From Stettin in the Baltic to Trieste in the Adriatic, an iron curtain has descended across the Continent." The **iron curtain** cut off Soviet-run Eastern Europe from the democratic governments of the West.

Analyze Political Cartoons This 1952 French cartoon shows a caricature of Josef Stalin holding a sign for "PEACE," a dove, and a mace—a medieval weapon of war. **Recognize Point of View** What does this cartoon suggest about how people in the West regarded the Soviet Union?

Western fears of communism deepened as Communist parties, backed by Stalin, achieved success in other parts of Europe. Italian Communists won many seats in the Italian parliament. In Greece, Communist rebels waged a civil war to topple the Greek government. Communist-led unions conducted strikes that **paralyzed** their nations' weak economies.

READING CHECK **Identify Main Ideas** What was the basic conflict that fueled the Cold War?

The Aftermath of War

President Harry S. Truman was determined to keep Soviet influence contained within existing boundaries. Thus, his Cold War policy was known as **containment**.

The Truman Doctrine In March 1947, President Truman asked Congress for $400 million in military and economic aid for Greece and Turkey. Eventually, with American aid, both countries held off Communist threats. Truman's program to encourage nations to resist Communist expansion became known as the Truman Doctrine:

The Iron Curtain, 1949

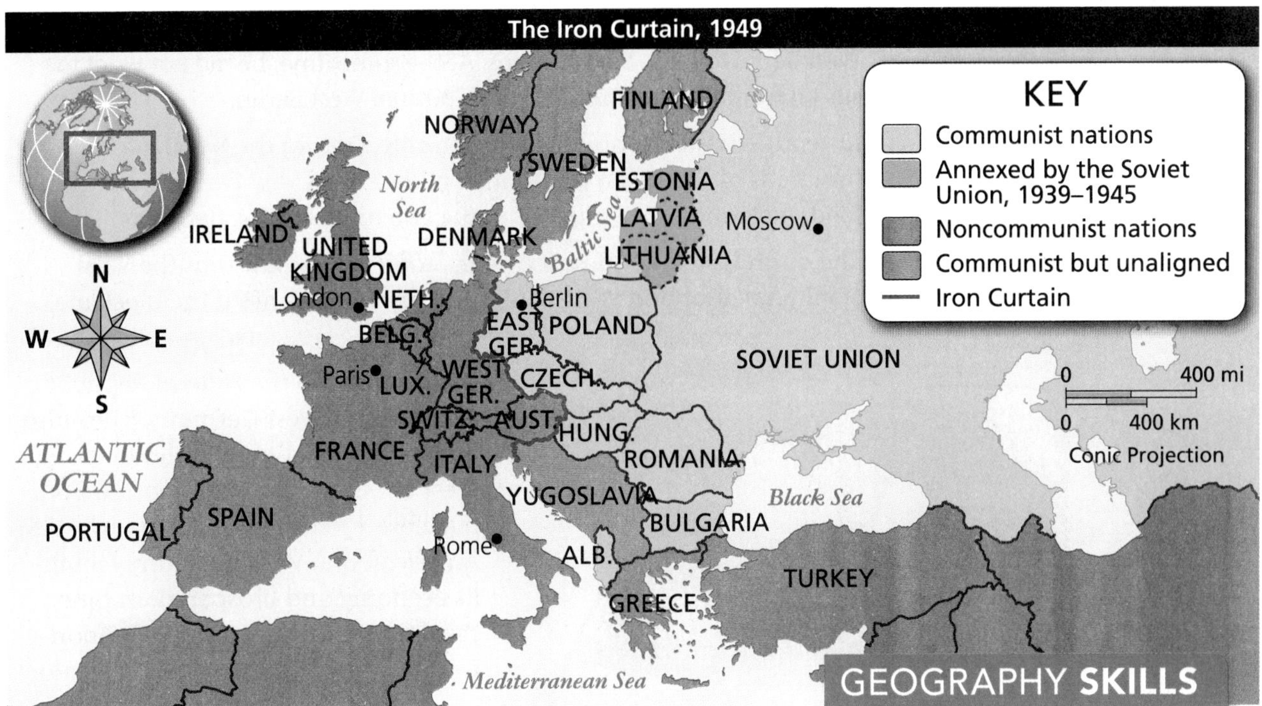

GEOGRAPHY SKILLS

After World War II ended, Europe became divided between communist and noncommunist countries.

1. **Interaction** Discuss with a partner how the division of Europe between communist and noncommunist countries might affect the interaction of people in these two regions.
2. **Infer** What was the iron curtain?

Primary Source

"The free peoples of the world look to us for support in maintaining their freedoms. If we falter in our leadership, we may endanger the peace of the world—and we shall surely endanger the welfare of our own nation."

—Harry Truman, Speech, March 12, 1947

The Marshall Plan Other European nations needed aid, too. The war had left Europe's homes, roads, and factories in ruins. When Secretary of State George Marshall toured Europe, he saw millions of homeless, hungry refugees.

In June 1947, Marshall proposed an ambitious aid plan to help Europe rebuild. The ultimate purpose of the **Marshall Plan** was to reduce the threat of communist revolutions. The President and Congress accepted the Marshall Plan. Between 1948 and 1952, it provided more than $12 billion in aid to Western European countries.

A Divided City In 1948, a crisis developed in Berlin, Germany's former capital and largest city. After the war, the Allies had divided Germany into four zones. American, British, French, and Soviet troops each occupied a zone. Berlin, too, was divided among the four Allies, even though it lay entirely inside the Soviet zone.

By 1948, the United States, Britain, and France wanted to reunite their zones in Berlin and the rest of Germany. Stalin opposed that plan. To prevent **reunification**, he closed all roads, railway lines, and river routes connecting West Berlin with the outside world.

Academic Vocabulary
reunification • *n.*, joining again to make a single thing

Did you know?

During the Berlin airlift, American pilots dropped candy to thousands of Berlin's children as part of "Operation Little Vittles." The candy was dropped by tiny parachutes made of handkerchiefs.

Sending Supplies to West Berlin President Truman would not let West Berlin fall into Soviet hands. At the same time, he did not want to start a war by using force to open a path to West Berlin.

Instead, Truman approved a huge airlift. During the **Berlin Airlift**, hundreds of American and British planes every day carried tons of food, fuel, and other supplies to the two million West Berliners.

The airlift lasted for almost a year. Stalin finally saw that the West would not abandon West Berlin. In May 1949 he lifted the blockade.

Four months later, the Allies merged their zones into the Federal Republic of Germany, or West Germany. They also merged their zones in Berlin to form West Berlin, which was separate from but closely tied to West Germany. With American aid, West Germany rebuilt its economy and prospered. In time, the Soviet zone became the German Democratic Republic, or East Germany.

The Berlin Wall Communist East Germany was much poorer than West Germany. For years, East Germans fled communism by crossing into West Berlin. The flight embarrassed the Communists and drained the country of many people.

In 1961, the East German government built the **Berlin Wall**, a huge concrete wall topped with barbed wire, to seal off East Germany from West Berlin. Border guards shot East Germans who tried to scale the wall. The Berlin Wall broke apart families and friends and became a bitter symbol of the Cold War that divided Europe and the world.

READING CHECK **Compare and Contrast** What did the Truman Doctrine and the Marshall Plan have in common?

What Postwar Alliances Were Formed?

New military alliances emerged during the Cold War. A world peace-keeping organization was also established.

NATO and the Warsaw Pact To contain Soviet influences, the United States set up alliances with friendly nations. In 1949, the United States joined with many Western European countries to form a security alliance, the **North Atlantic Treaty Organization** (NATO). NATO countries agreed to defend each other against any attack.

Early Cold War Alliances

In 1955, the Soviet Union formed its own military alliance, the **Warsaw Pact**. The Soviet Union dominated its Warsaw Pact neighbors, forcing them to follow its policies.

The United Nations Many international disputes were brought before a new world organization, the **United Nations** (UN). Fifty-one nations ratified the UN charter in October 1945. Over time, membership in the United Nations expanded as new nations were admitted.

Under the UN charter, member nations agree to bring disputes before the body for peaceful settlement. Every member has a seat in the General Assembly, where problems can be discussed. A smaller Security Council also discusses conflicts that threaten peace.

Over the years, the UN has succeeded best in fighting hunger and disease and in improving education. UN relief programs have provided food, medicine, and supplies to victims of famine, war, and other disasters. Preserving peace has proved more difficult. Some nations have rejected UN resolutions, which are formal recommendations for courses of action. Still, UN negotiators and peacekeeping forces have sometimes eased dangerous crises.

Communist Advancements Until 1949, most Americans felt that their country had the upper hand in the Cold War. Then, in September 1949, the United States learned that the Soviet Union had tested an atomic bomb.

GEOGRAPHY SKILLS

The map shows the postwar partition of Germany and of the city of Berlin.

1. **Interactivity** What problems could result from dividing the control of Germany and Berlin among four countries?
2. **Location** How would Berlin's location have made it particularly difficult for the United States, Britain, and France to govern their portions of the city?

Germany Divided, 1945–1949

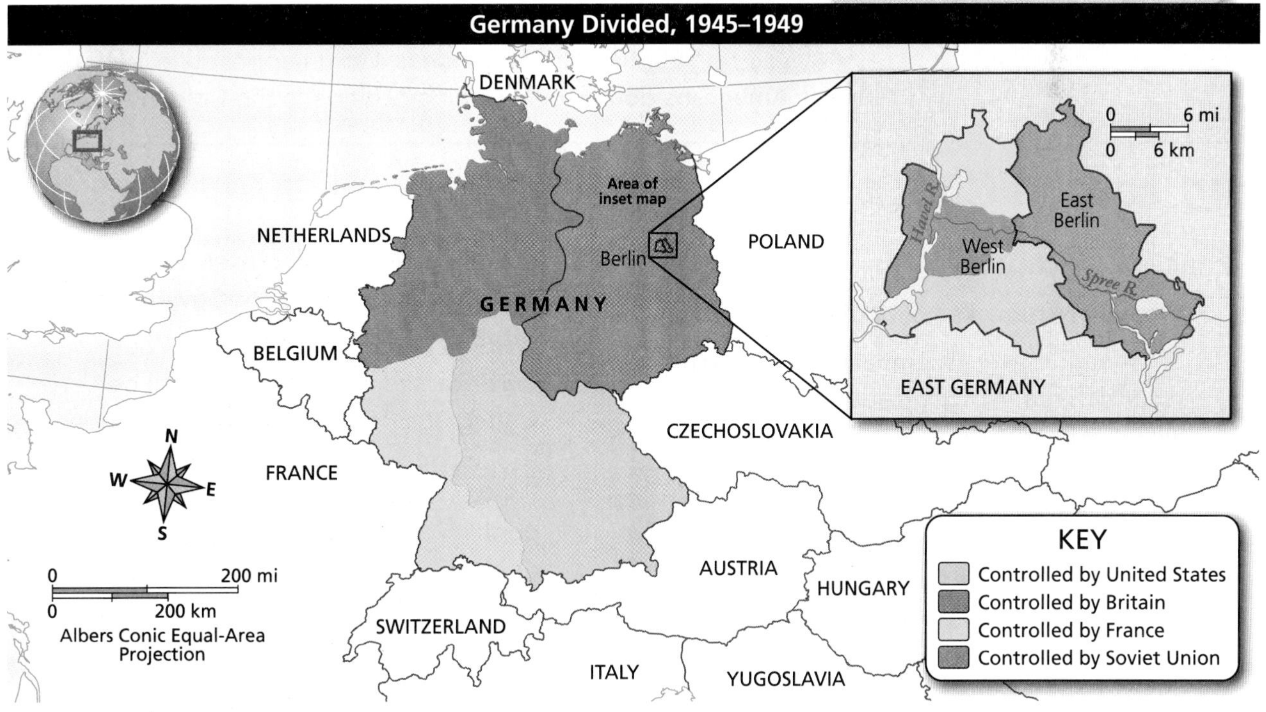

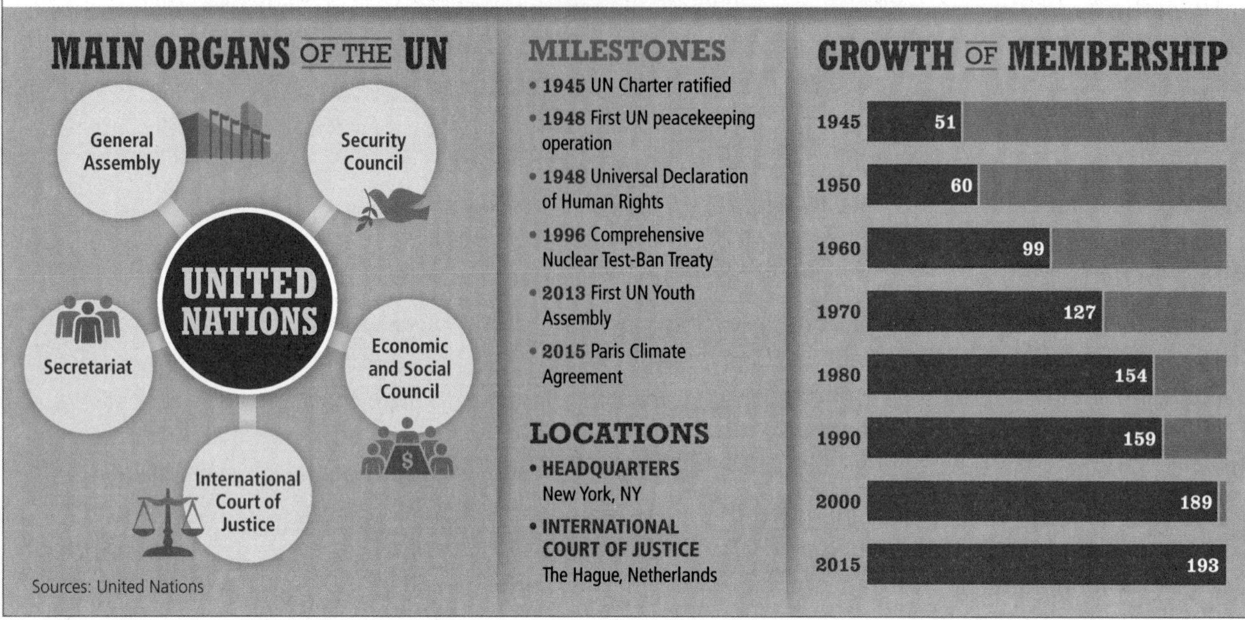

Analyze Charts The chart outlines the organization and growth of the United Nations. **Summarize** How would you describe the main purpose of the United Nations, based on some of the milestones listed?

A second shock followed. Communist forces, led by Mao Zedong (mow dzuh doong), gained power in China. The United States had long backed the Nationalists, led by Jiang Jieshi (jahng jeh shih), also known as Chiang Kai-shek. In 1949, after a long civil war, Mao's Red Army forced Jiang and his forces to retreat to Taiwan, an island off the coast of China. On the mainland, Mao set up the People's Republic of China.

Communist leaders in China and the Soviet Union often disagreed with each other. Yet together, the two nations controlled almost a quarter of the globe. Many Americans feared that communism would spread still farther.

READING CHECK **Identify Main Ideas** What happened in 1949 that made Americans doubt their winning position in the Cold War?

Lesson Check

Practice Vocabulary

1. What was Truman's policy of **containment**?
2. What nations were members of the **North Atlantic Treaty Organization** and the **Warsaw Pact**?
3. What was the purpose of the **United Nations**?

Critical Thinking and Writing

4. Compare and Contrast How did the Cold War differ from prior wars?
5. Recognize Multiple Causes Why did the United States oppose the Soviet Union?
6. Writing Workshop: Consider Your Purpose and Audience You will be writing an informative essay on changes to the United States after World War II. For example, you might write about the population change, developments in music, or equal rights. In your Active Journal, describe who your audience will be and what you will need to do to satisfy the requirements of the task.

LESSON 2

Korea and Other Postwar Conflicts

GET READY TO READ

START UP

This photograph shows a parade of Mao's Red Army. What do you think the purpose of such parades might have been?

GUIDING QUESTIONS

- Why did the United States become involved in the conflict in Korea?
- How did the fighting in Korea end?
- Why did the Cold War spread to Africa and other parts of Asia?
- Why were there hunts for Communists at home in the United States, and what were the results?

TAKE NOTES

Literacy Skills: Use Evidence

Use the graphic organizer in your Active Journal to take notes as you read the lesson.

PRACTICE VOCABULARY

Use the vocabulary activity in your Active Journal to practice the vocabulary words.

Vocabulary		Academic Vocabulary
38th parallel	McCarthyism	perceive
demilitarized zone	censure	inevitably
perjury		

Korea is a peninsula in East Asia. Russia and China border it to the north and the west. Japan lies to the east across the Sea of Japan (known in Korea as the East Sea). In the past, these powerful neighbors often competed to control Korea.

The Korean War

From 1910 to 1945, Japan ruled Korea as a colony. As World War II wound to an end, the Soviet Union moved into the northern portion of Korea. In September, following Japan's surrender, the United States entered southern Korea, setting the stage for the division of the Korean peninsula.

A Divided Nation The United States and the Soviet Union agreed to a temporary division of Korea at the **38th parallel** of latitude. The United States backed a non-Communist government in South Korea. The Soviet Union supported the Communist government of North Korea. Both nations also agreed that Korea would soon be reunited. As the Cold War deepened, however, Korea remained divided.

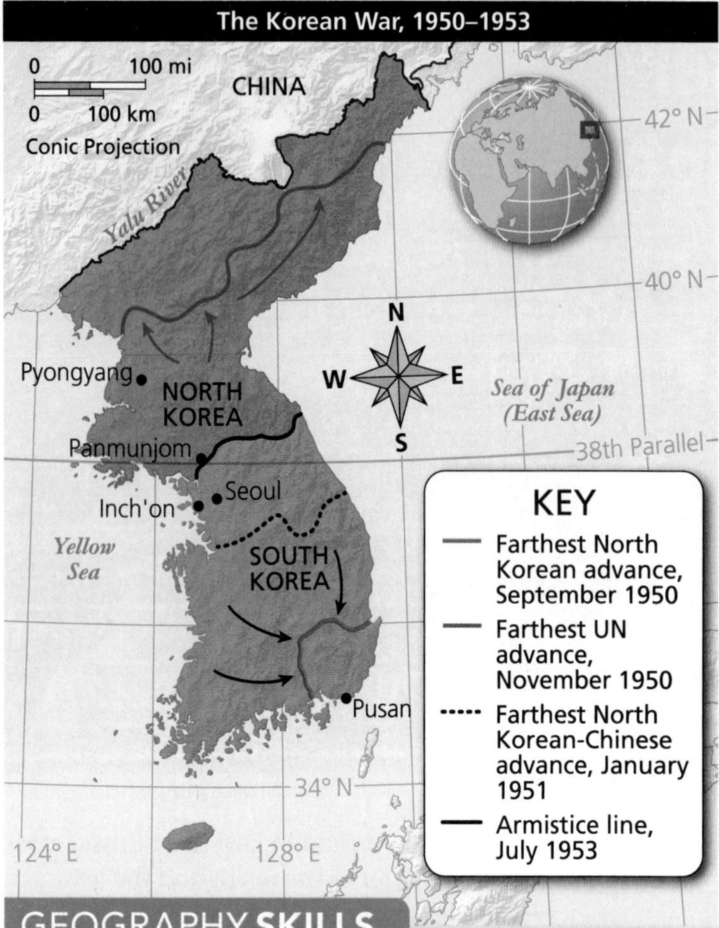

GEOGRAPHY **SKILLS**

The Korean War comprised a series of advances and reversals up and down the Korean peninsula.

1. **Location** Based on the map, how does the success of the UN forces in November 1950 help explain why China entered the war?
2. **Infer** How might the deep penetrations of the UN and of the North Korean forces have influenced the opposing sides in the war?

Communist Aggression In June 1950, North Korean troops swept across the 38th parallel, overwhelming the South Korean army. This marked the beginning of the Korean War. Within days, North Korean forces occupied Seoul (SOL), the capital of South Korea.

President Truman immediately asked the United Nations to authorize a military response to the invasion. The UN Security Council agreed. Although 16 nations joined the UN action in Korea, about 80 percent of the troops were American.

The military force would be commanded by a general chosen by Truman. The President chose General Douglas MacArthur, who had commanded Allied forces in the Pacific during World War II.

Strategic Advances At first, UN forces were outnumbered and poorly supplied. Armed with new Soviet tanks, the North Koreans continued their push southward and soon occupied almost all of South Korea. MacArthur then launched a daring counterattack by sea. He landed his forces at Inch'on, behind North Korean lines. Caught by surprise, the North Koreans were forced back across the 38th parallel.

MacArthur's original orders called for him only to drive the invaders out of South Korea. Truman and his advisers, however, wanted to punish North Korea for its aggression. They also wanted to unite Korea. With these goals in mind, they won UN approval for MacArthur to cross into North Korea.

China Joins the Fight While MacArthur advanced northward, the Chinese government warned that it would not "sit back with folded hands" if the United States invaded North Korea. As UN forces neared the Chinese border, Communist China **perceived** them as a threat to its own security. The Chinese were determined to fight off that threat. Masses of Chinese troops crossed the Yalu River into North Korea.

Academic Vocabulary
perceive • *v.*, to notice or become aware of

Once again, the fighting seesawed. The Chinese overwhelmed the UN forces, pushing them back deep into South Korea. Then, the UN forces regrouped and pushed the Chinese back into North Korea. By March 1951, UN troops had regained control of the south. The war then turned into a bloody deadlock.

INTERACTIVE

Phases of the Korean War

READING CHECK **Summarize** What is the best way to summarize American involvement in the Korean War?

When Did the Fighting End?

During the deadlock, a serious disagreement arose between General MacArthur and President Truman. MacArthur thought that to win the war, UN forces must attack China. Truman feared that an attack on China might lead to a world war. He ordered MacArthur to limit the war and restore the border at the 38th parallel.

Disagreement at the Top A frustrated MacArthur complained publicly that politicians in Washington were holding him back. "We must win," he insisted. "There is no substitute for victory." Angry that MacArthur was defying orders, Truman fired the popular general.

Truman's action outraged many Americans. They gave MacArthur a hero's welcome when he returned home. Truman, however, had the Constitution behind him. He pointed out that the President is commander in chief, responsible for key decisions about war and peace. MacArthur's statements, said Truman, undermined attempts to reach a peace settlement.

Analyze Images American soldiers in a North Korean prisoner-of-war camp celebrate the end of the Korean War. **Infer** How do you think these soldiers would have felt about what America accomplished in this war?

Armistice Peace talks began in mid-1951. At first there was little progress. Meanwhile, the deadly fighting continued.

Republicans nominated Dwight Eisenhower, the popular World War II general, as their presidential candidate in 1952. Eisenhower pledged that if he were elected, he would personally go to Korea. At the same time, he would work to get the stalled peace talks going again.

Eisenhower won the election and visited Korea within a few weeks of his victory. By then, both sides were eager for a cease-fire. The only remaining problem was the return of prisoners of war. After long negotiations, the two sides agreed to turn this issue over to an international commission.

Finally, in July 1953, the two sides signed an armistice to end the fighting. It redrew the border between North Korea and South Korea near the 38th parallel, where it had been before the war.

The armistice also set up along the border a **demilitarized zone** (DMZ), an area where no military forces were allowed. On either side of the DMZ, however, heavily armed troops dug in. They remain there today.

What Were the Effects of the Korean War? The human costs of the Korean War were staggering. Well over 30,000 Americans lost their lives in the war zone. Nearly 2 million Koreans and Chinese were also killed.

Politically, the Korean War changed nothing. Korea remained divided. To this day, relations between North Korea and South Korea remain poor. On the other hand, UN forces did push back North Korean forces during the war and kept communism out of South Korea. Through this action, the United States and its allies showed that they were ready to fight to prevent Communist expansion.

READING CHECK **Summarize** the terms of the Korean War armistice.

Analyze Graphs These graphs show the costs of the Korean War. **Draw Conclusions** Why do you think the graph shows civilian casualties for North Korea and South Korea but not for China and the United States?

COSTS OF THE KOREAN WAR

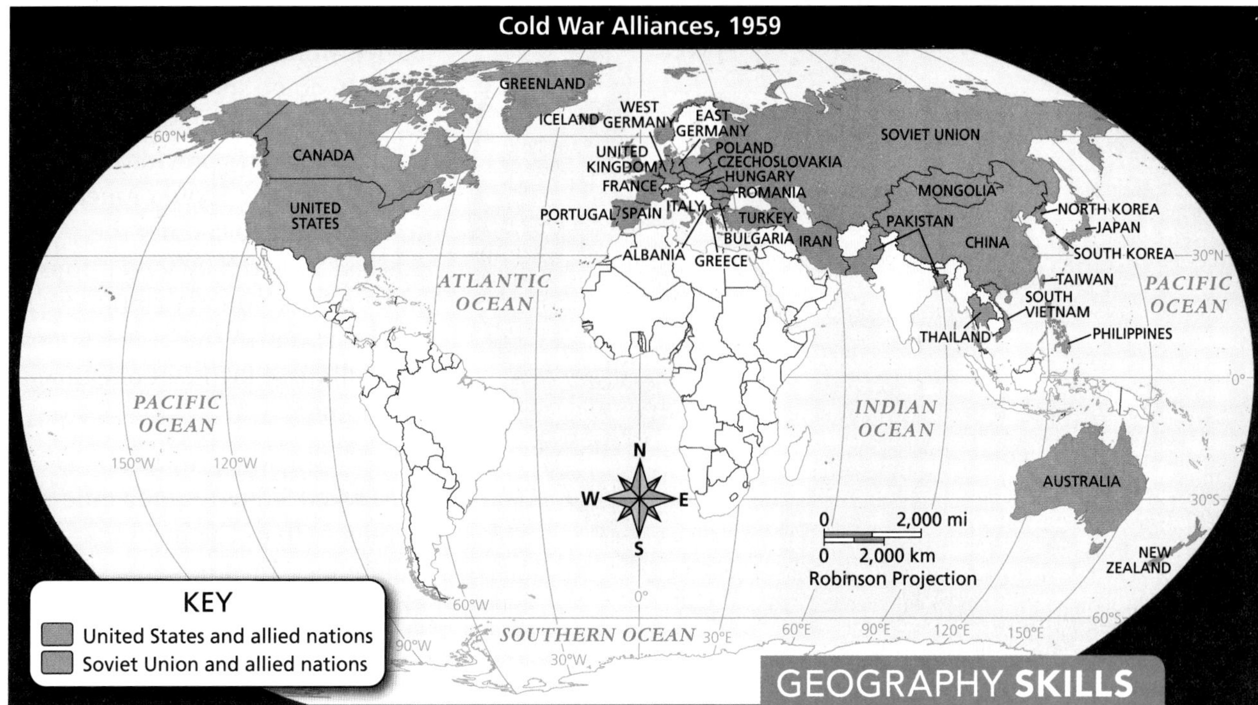

GEOGRAPHY **SKILLS**

During the Cold War, the United States and Soviet Union competed to gather allies and to gain influence in countries around the world.

1. **Interaction** What patterns can you find on the map regarding allies in Europe and Asia?
2. **Summarize** How would you describe the differences in where the allies of the United States and the Soviet Union were located?

A Global Cold War

The Korean War was not the only conflict resulting from the Cold War. Around the globe, rivalries sprang up between groups backed by the Soviet Union and the United States, respectively.

The Cold War Spreads In September 1959, the Soviet leader, Nikita Khrushchev (KROOSH chawf), arrived in New York to address the United Nations. Khrushchev, who had gained power a few years after Stalin died in 1953, spoke calmly at first. He expressed hopes that the Cold War between the United States and the Soviet Union would end. Then, gradually his manner changed. Twice, he became so angry that he took off his shoe and pounded it on the table.

Khrushchev's trip to the UN symbolized the fact that the Cold War had become global. Although the Cold War had started in Europe, the United States and the Soviet Union now competed for allies and influence among the members of the United Nations.

Struggle for Power Over Colonies For years, many of the nations of Africa and Asia had been governed as colonies of European and other foreign powers. After World War II, many colonial people demanded and won independence. Some achieved independence peacefully. Others had to fight for it.

In these colonies, Communists often joined other groups to fight foreign control. Khrushchev called these struggles "wars of national liberation." Both openly and secretly, the Soviets gave economic and military aid to rebel forces.

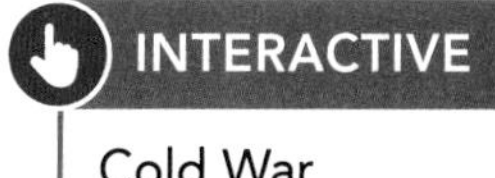

Cold War Actions—The United States and the Soviet Union

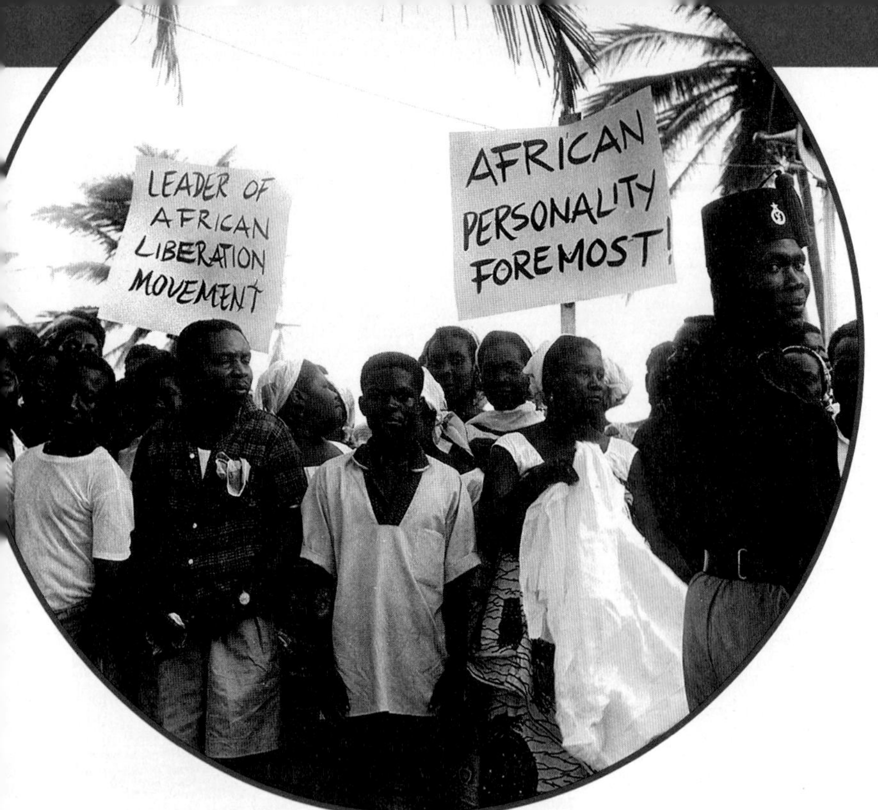

The West tried to prevent the Soviets from expanding their influence. In doing so, American leaders faced difficult choices. Should the United States provide aid to a colonial power? Should Americans use secret aid to counter the Soviets? Should they send troops into another nation to influence its internal affairs? The United States used all these tactics at one time or another.

The Philippines In 1946, the United States granted independence to its colony in the Philippines. Crowds in Manila cheered as the American flag was lowered and the Filipino flag was hoisted high.

▲ Throughout Africa, people demanded independence from colonial rule. This 1959 photograph shows Ghanaians rallying in support of African liberation. **Infer** Ghana gained independence in 1957. Why were Ghanaians still protesting colonialism two years after their nation's independence?

Since gaining independence, the Philippines has suffered from poverty, local uprisings, and dictatorships. Under the rule of Ferdinand Marcos, who was in power from 1965 to 1986, opposition parties were repressed. In the years that followed, the Philippines struggled to find a stable and honest government.

African Independence During the 1950s and 1960s, more than 30 African nations won freedom from European rule. Some of these new nations faced civil wars among rival ethnic or tribal groups. Some fought border wars with their neighbors. **Inevitably**, the United States and the Soviet Union backed opposing sides in these struggles. As a result, the Cold War turned local conflicts into international crises.

In East Africa, the United States and the Soviet Union took sides in a long war between Somalia and Ethiopia. The United States backed Somalia, while the Soviet Union supported Ethiopia. In southern Africa, the Cold War intensified a civil war in Angola.

South Asian Independence In 1947, India won independence from Britain. Soon, the Indian subcontinent was divided into two nations: India and Pakistan. Pakistan, feeling threatened by the Soviet Union to its north, became an ally of the United States. India accepted both American and Soviet aid but remained neutral in the Cold War.

French-ruled Indochina included present-day Laos, Cambodia, and Vietnam. In each country, separate nationalist groups fought for independence. The wars lasted for almost 30 years and eventually drew in the United States, as you will read in a later lesson.

Academic Vocabulary
inevitably • *adv.*, universally, in a way that cannot be avoided

READING CHECK **Understand Effects** How did the freedom of former colonies in Africa and Asia impact the Cold War?

Fears About Communism at Home

For many Americans, the Korean War increased worries about Communists at home. They feared that Communist sympathizers and spies might be secretly working to overthrow the U.S. government. These concerns helped spark a hunt for Communists within American society.

During the Great Depression, some Americans had turned against democracy and free enterprise. They had rejected the efforts of the New Deal as inadequate. To them, communism offered the only solution to the nation's deep economic troubles. In time, however, many American Communists recognized that Soviet leader Joseph Stalin was a brutal dictator, and they left the party.

Hunting Spies Still, some remained avid Communists. Between 1946 and 1950, several people in the United States, Canada, and Britain were arrested as Soviet spies. In the United States, Ethel and Julius Rosenberg were sentenced to death for passing atomic secrets to the Soviets. Despite protests, both were executed in 1953. The Rosenberg case made many Americans wonder if other Soviet spies were living among them as ordinary citizens.

Americans also worried that there were Communists in high government positions. In 1950, Alger Hiss, a State Department official, was imprisoned for **perjury**, or lying under oath. Hiss had denied that he was part of a Soviet spy ring. Later evidence would show that Hiss and several other government officials were passing secrets to the Soviet Union.

In 1947, President Truman ordered investigations of government workers to determine if they were loyal to the United States. Thousands of government employees were questioned. Some people were forced to resign. Many of those had done nothing disloyal to the United States.

Analyze Timelines
The Red Scare lasted for almost 20 years and included a number of major developments, as shown on the timeline. **Hypothesize** After McCarthy was reprimanded, do you think the fear of communism in the United States faded permanently?

The Second Red Scare

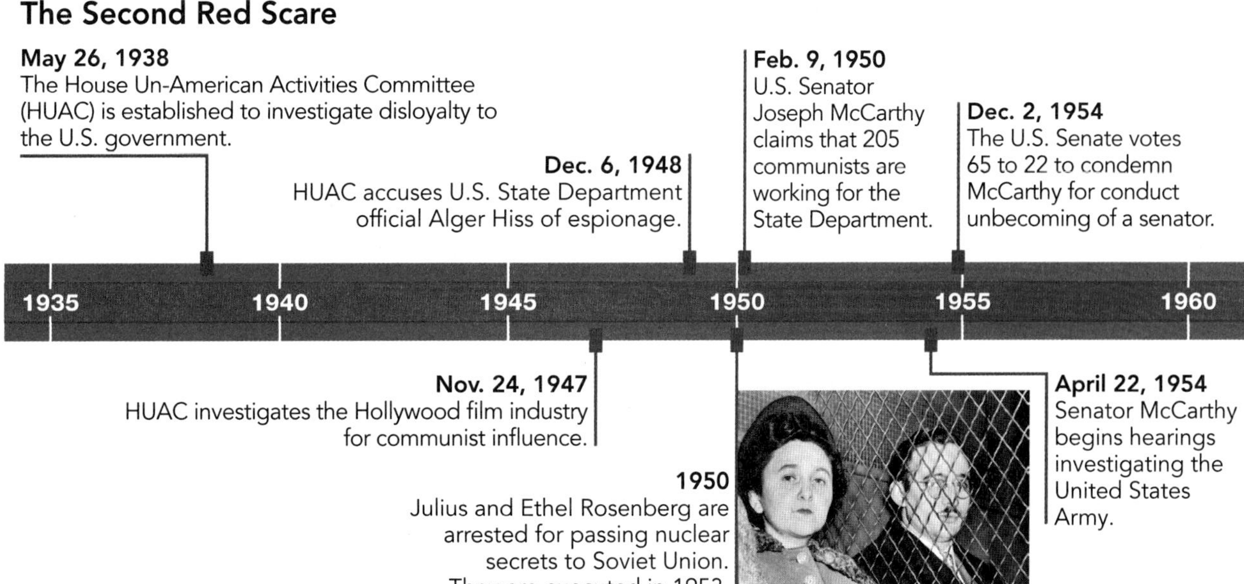

Analyze Images Senator Joseph McCarthy claimed to have proof that his opponents and enemies, such as Democratic presidential candidate Adlai Stevenson, associated with alleged subversive groups. **Infer** Why do you think McCarthy showed off documents but did not let news reporters read them?

The McCarthy Era In 1950, Senator Joseph McCarthy of Wisconsin made a shocking announcement. He claimed to have a list of 205 State Department employees who were Communist Party members.

McCarthy never offered evidence for his claims. Yet, McCarthy's dramatic charges won him national attention.

During the next four years, McCarthy's campaign spread suspicion across the nation. Businesses and colleges questioned employees. Many people were fired and forced out of their professions. The term **McCarthyism** came to refer to threatening people and repressing dissent through the use of reckless charges of disloyalty.

In 1954, the Senate held televised hearings to investigate a new McCarthy charge. He insisted that there were Communists in the United States Army. This time, McCarthy had gone too far. On national television, he came across as a bully, not a hero. His popularity plunged.

In December 1954, the Senate passed a resolution to **censure**, or officially condemn, McCarthy for "conduct unbecoming a member." As a result, McCarthy lost much of his support. By the time he died three years later, the Communist scare was mostly over.

READING CHECK **Draw Conclusions** How does the Rosenberg case demonstrate American attitudes toward communism during the Cold War?

Lesson Check

Practice Vocabulary

1. What was the significance of the **38th parallel** in Korea?
2. What was the effect of the **demilitarized zone**?

Critical Thinking and Writing

3. **Summarize** the hunt for Communists that occurred within the United States.
4. **Identify Main Ideas** How did the Cold War turn regional conflicts into international crises?
5. **Writing Workshop: Develop a Clear Thesis** Draft a thesis for your essay on changes to the United States after World War II. Write your thesis in your Active Journal. You can revise this statement as your essay develops.

LESSON 3

Eisenhower and Postwar America

GET READY TO READ

START UP

This 1950s photograph shows traffic on the Grand Central Parkway in Queens, New York. How did parkways and highways change the American landscape?

GUIDING QUESTIONS

- What postwar problems did Americans face?
- What factors contributed to the economic and baby booms of the 1950s?
- How did American lifestyles change in the 1950s?

TAKE NOTES

Literacy Skills: Classify and Categorize

Use the graphic organizer in your Active Journal to take notes as you read the lesson.

PRACTICE VOCABULARY

Use the vocabulary activity in your Active Journal to practice the vocabulary words.

Vocabulary

GI Bill of Rights
inflation
Fair Deal
baby boom
productivity
standard of living
suburb
Sunbelt
beatnik

Academic Vocabulary

pioneer
presume

In the decades after World War II, the United States experienced a boom like no other in its history. The population mushroomed, the economy prospered, and the American nation enjoyed the highest standard of living it had ever known.

Postwar Prosperity

When the war ended in 1945, two thirds of all American men between the ages of 18 and 34 were in uniform. Experts feared that with wartime production ceased, many returning soldiers might not find jobs. Unemployment would rise, and the economy would tumble.

Addressing Economic Issues Even before the war ended, Congress passed the **GI Bill of Rights** to help returning veterans. (The abbreviation *GI* refers to "government issued" materials and came to refer to soldiers, too.) The GI Bill of Rights authorized billions of dollars to help veterans set up farms and businesses. Many GIs received loans to pay for college or a new home. The law also provided a full year of unemployment benefits for veterans who could not find work.

Inflation, or a general decline in the value of money, was a major postwar problem. During the war, the government had controlled prices and wages. When the controls ended, Americans who had sacrificed during the war were eager to buy. The rising demand for goods led to price increases, which led workers to demand higher wages. When employers refused, labor unions called strikes.

President Harry Truman was sympathetic to workers but feared that higher wages would only add to inflation. He urged strikers to return to work.

The Election of 1948 In 1946, labor strikes and soaring prices had helped Republicans win majorities in both the House and the Senate for the first time since the 1920s. Now, as the election of 1948 approached, Truman and the Democrats seemed doomed. Unhappy liberals and conservatives deserted Truman to form parties of their own. The Republicans confidently nominated Governor Thomas Dewey of New York for President.

Truman fought back. During his campaign, Truman traveled thousands of miles across the country by train. At every stop, he attacked the Republicans as "do-nothings" and "gluttons of privilege." When all the votes were counted, Truman won a surprise victory over Dewey.

Analyze Political Cartoons This cartoon shows President Truman announcing his Fair Deal program of liberal reform. **Analyze Information** Is the Fair Deal program portrayed in a positive light or a negative one in this cartoon? Explain.

The Fair Deal During his presidency, Truman proposed a new round of reform he called the **Fair Deal**. He wanted to extend the liberal policies of his predecessor, Franklin D. Roosevelt.

In Congress, the Fair Deal faced heavy opposition from conservative Democrats and Republicans. Only a few of the proposals passed: a higher minimum wage, expanded Social Security benefits, and loans for buying low-cost houses. Congress rejected most of Truman's reforms, including a bold plan to provide government-financed health insurance.

A Moderate Takes Office In 1952, Truman chose not to run for reelection. Democrats nominated Adlai Stevenson of Illinois. Republicans chose General Dwight D. Eisenhower, a hero of World War II. Eisenhower, known as "Ike," promised to end the conflict in Korea and lead Americans through the Cold War.

For the first time, television played a major role in a presidential campaign. Instead of long speeches, Republicans used 20-second TV "spots" of Ike responding to questions from hand-picked citizens. Complained one critic: "It was selling the President like toothpaste." But it worked: Eisenhower won a landslide victory. In 1956, voters re-elected Ike to a second term of office.

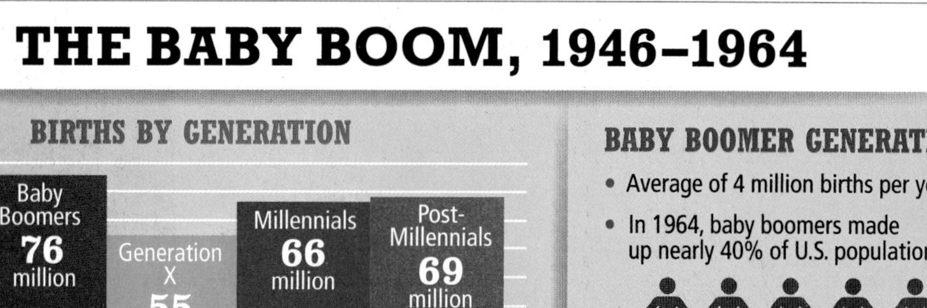

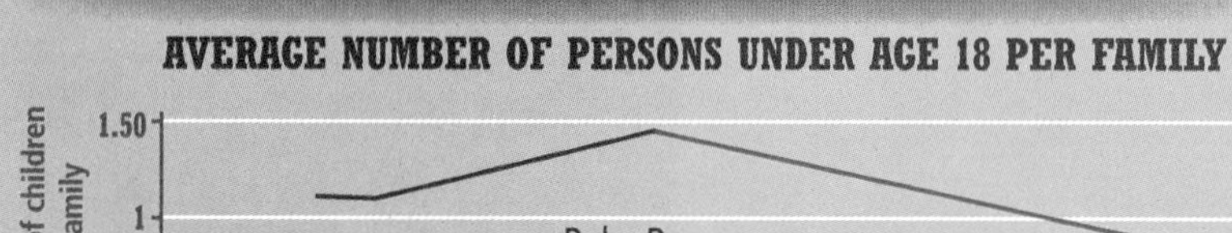

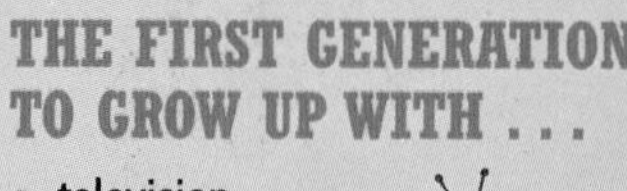

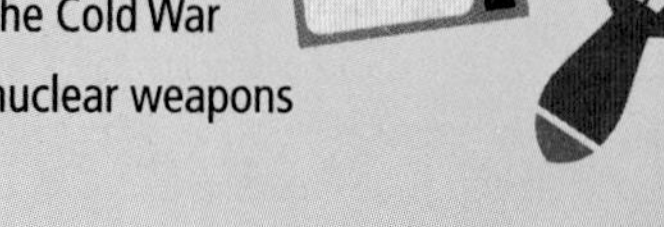

Source: U.S. Bureau of the Census

Like most Republicans, President Eisenhower believed in limiting federal spending and reducing federal regulation of the economy. He called his political course the "straight road down the middle." He favored cutting the federal budget overall, but expanding Social Security benefits and some other New Deal programs.

Analyze Charts These graphs show why the baby boom generation had such a large impact on the nation. **Synthesize Visual Information** The text says that married couples had an average of three children, yet the graph shows the average number of persons under age 18 per family was less than 1.5. Explain how this is possible.

Baby Boom During the Great Depression and World War II, many Americans had put off having families. When the war ended and prosperity returned, the number of births soared. Population experts called the phenomenon a **baby boom**.

In the 1930s, the population of the United States had grown by only 9 million. In the 1940s, it grew by 19 million, and in the 1950s by an astounding 29 million. Many couples married younger than was common during the Depression years, had an average of three children, and completed their families by their late twenties.

Improvements in healthcare and nutrition for both children and pregnant women contributed to the baby boom. Infants were born healthier, and fewer children died from childhood diseases.

Prosperity Abounds In addition to the baby boom, there was an economic expansion in the postwar years. When an economy expands, more goods are produced and sold, and more jobs are created.

Federal projects increased factory production. The government spent more money to build new roads, houses, and schools. In the middle of the Cold War, government spending on military goods spurred the economy, too.

New technology added to the boom by promoting steady rises in **productivity**, or the average output per worker. Corporations began using computers to perform calculations and keep records.

The Baby Boom Changes the Nation

Homeownership, 1940–1960

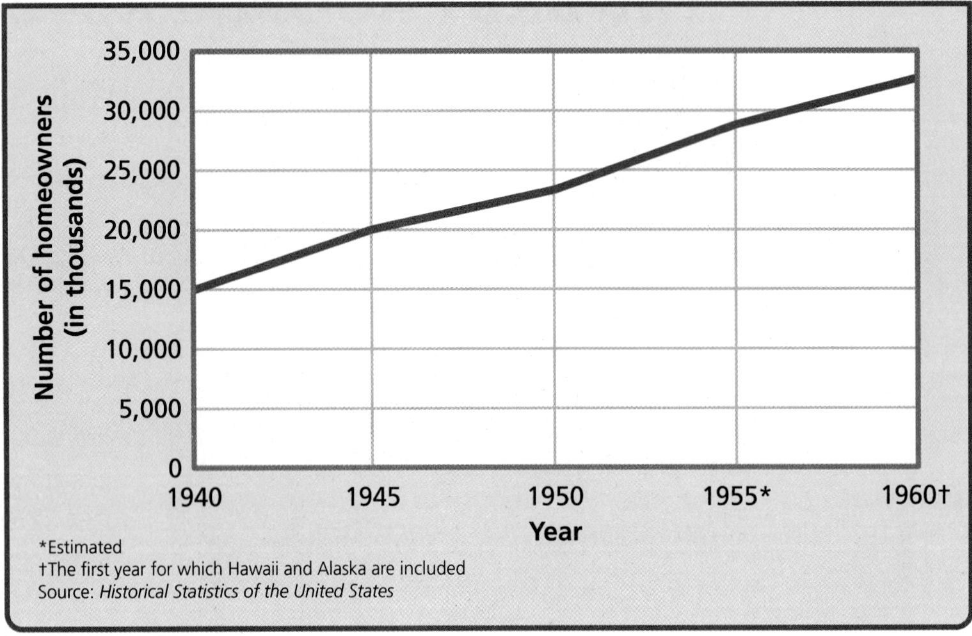

Analyze Graphs The graph shows how the number of people owning homes increased between 1940 and 1960. **Generate Explanations** Explain how the data on home ownership relates to standard of living.

High productivity allowed the United States to manufacture and consume, or use, more goods than any other country. The victory in World War II and the booming economy created a sense of public confidence in the United States. American citizens enjoyed a postwar prosperity that saw significant job growth throughout much of the nation.

READING CHECK **Identify Cause and Effect** What factors contributed to the postwar prosperity?

What Was Life Like in the 1950s?

The economic boom raised Americans' **standard of living**, a measurement of how well people live based on the amount of goods, services, and leisure time people have. Rising wages enabled Americans to buy washing machines, vacuum cleaners, televisions, automobiles, and many other consumer goods.

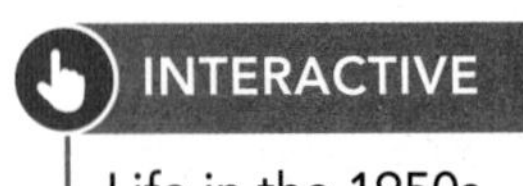

Life in the 1950s

Public confidence in the United States replaced many of the financial worries associated with the Great Depression and World War II. Few Americans worried that they were saving little. Instead, most Americans enjoyed a life in which they had more money to spend. This consumer spending reshaped the country.

The New Suburbs With their newfound wealth, many people bought homes in the **suburbs**, or communities outside the cities. The GI Bill encouraged home building in the suburbs by offering low-interest loans to veterans. During the 1950s, suburbs grew 40 times faster than cities.

Academic Vocabulary

pioneer • *v.*, to create new ideas for doing something

Builder William Levitt **pioneered** a new way of building suburban houses. He bought large tracts of land and then divided them into small, equal-sized lots. On each lot, he built a house identical to every other house in the tract. Using pre-assembled materials, teams of carpenters, plumbers, and electricians could put up a Levitt house in 16 minutes. These mass-produced houses cost much less to build than custom-made houses.

Levitt began his first big project in 1947 on Long Island, where he put up 17,000 new homes. It was the largest housing development ever built by an American. Levitt called the project Levittown. As in a great many areas of the country, African Americans were barred from owning or renting in Levittown. Levitt **presumed** that if he sold to African Americans, white people would not buy.

Academic Vocabulary
presume • *v.*, to expect or suppose without proof

Shopping centers with modern department stores sprang up near the suburban housing developments. Nationwide there were eight shopping centers in 1946. By the end of the 1950s, there were 4,000. No longer did consumers have to travel to the city to buy what they wanted.

As millions flocked to the suburbs, central cities began a slow decline. Suburbs and their shopping centers drained cities of businesses and taxes. Since most of those who moved were white, some critics complained that the United States was turning into a nation where African Americans lived in cities and white people lived in the suburbs.

Moving South Americans also flocked to the **Sunbelt**, a region stretching across the southern rim of the country. States from Florida to Texas to California began to experience dramatic growth.

For Americans on the move, the Sunbelt, both then and now, had many lures: a warm climate; good jobs; a prosperous economy based on agriculture, oil, and electronics; and national defense industries. The workforce included recent immigrants from Latin America and Asia. Like many ambitious newcomers, they were willing to work hard to establish new lives in the United States.

Analyze Images Construction of new homes in the suburbs like that shown here surged in the years after World War II. **Synthesize Visual Information** Why do you think more people chose to live in the suburbs?

Did you know?

President Eisenhower argued for better roads because, "In case of an atomic attack on our key cities, the road net must permit quick evacuation of target areas."

Taking to the Road During the 1950s, cars became more important to daily life. People living in the suburbs or the Sunbelt usually needed a car to drive to work. By 1960, nine out of ten families living in the suburbs owned a car. Since few people bought foreign cars, the American automobile companies, such as General Motors, profited greatly.

To accommodate the increase in automobiles, the federal government built thousands of miles of highways. In 1956, Congress passed the Federal Aid Highway Act. This act called for a network of high-speed roads linking the nation. It set aside $41 billion to build 40,000 miles of highway.

The new highway system boosted the economy, especially the automobile and trucking industries. Americans could travel more easily for business or pleasure. As a result, a new roadside culture of motels and fast-food restaurants emerged.

GEOGRAPHY SKILLS

During the 1950s, many Americans moved south to find good jobs and warm weather.

1. **Movement** Which states experienced the greatest population increases due to migration?
2. **Infer** Why do you think these states were called the "Sunbelt"?

Home Entertainment Television caught on slowly. At first, television screens displayed only in black and white, and they were very expensive. However, as TV sets shrank in price and grew in size, almost everybody wanted one. By 1960, 9 out of 10 households had at least 1 television. Television brought news and entertainment into people's homes. Commercials encouraged spending and buying.

Television also helped to make the 1950s a time when people wanted to look and act the same as everyone else. Many programs presented the same single view of the ideal white middle-class family: fathers knew best, mothers were loving and supportive, and children were always obedient.

Rock-and-Roll In the mid-1950s, a new type of music appeared. Rock-and-roll combined the sounds of rhythm, blues,

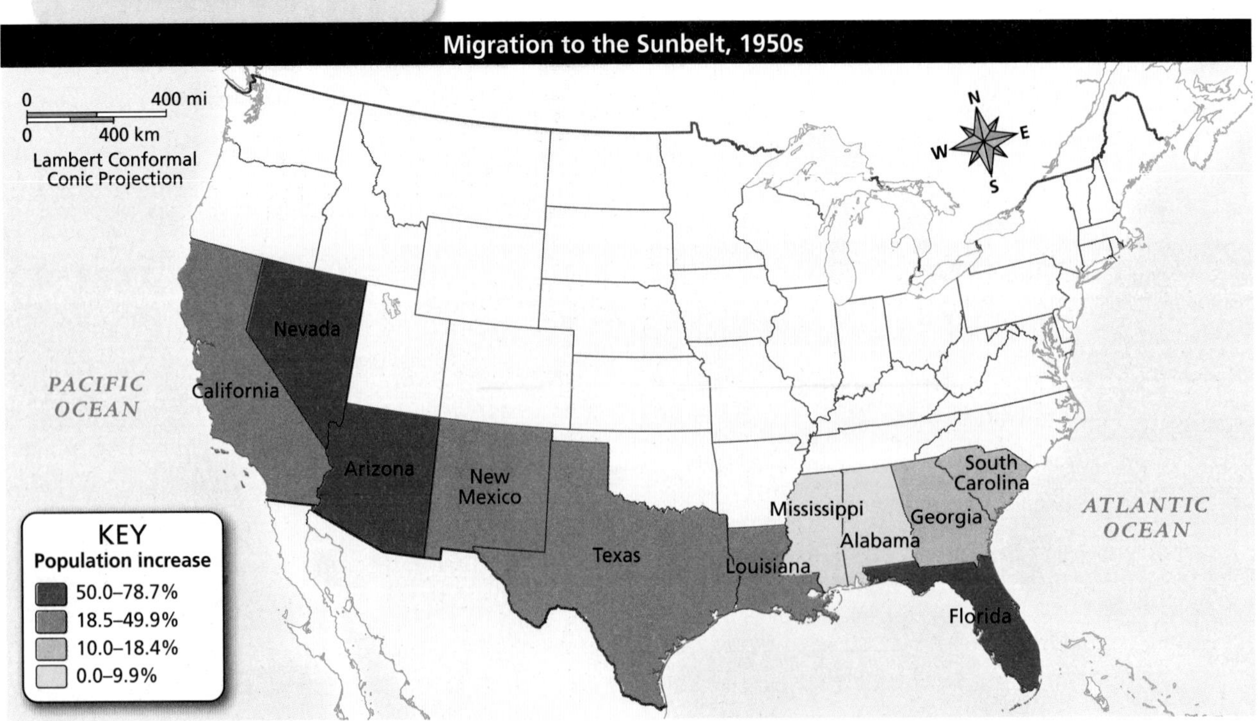

country, and gospel with a hard-driving beat. Adults worried that the music was too wild. However, many teenagers liked rock-and-roll because it provided an opportunity for them to show their independence. *Teenager* was a word first used in the 1950s to describe someone between 13 and 19 years old.

African American singers Chuck Berry and Little Richard gained national fame. From Texas came Buddy Holly, and from California, Latino singer Richie Valens. No one attracted more attention than Memphis's Elvis Presley. His slick hair, sideburns, and steamy dancing alarmed parents but made Elvis a hit with teenagers. They dressed like him, bought his records, and nicknamed him "the King."

▲ Chuck Berry does his famous "duck walk," 1964.

An Underlying Discontent Not all Americans in the 1950s were happy about the emphasis on getting and spending. A small group of writers and artists criticized what they saw as the growing materialism of American society and its lack of individuality. Novelist Jack Kerouac coined the term *beat,* meaning "weariness with all forms of the modern industrial state." Middle-class observers called Kerouac and others like him **beatniks**. Kerouac's best-selling novel, *On the Road,* influenced many young Americans.

Most Americans paid little attention to these signs of discontent. Soon, however, a growing outcry could not be ignored.

READING CHECK **Understand Effects** How did the increase in the popularity of cars affect the United States?

Lesson Check

Practice Vocabulary

1. Why did **inflation** become a problem after World War II ended?
2. How did the **GI Bill of Rights** help veterans returning from war?
3. What were the **beatniks** rebelling against?

Critical Thinking and Writing

4. **Recognize Multiple Causes** What factors contributed to the baby boom?
5. **Identify Cause and Effect** How did television change politics and society?
6. **Writing Workshop: Support Thesis with Details** In your Active Journal, begin listing details that support your thesis about changes to the United States after World War II. You will use these details as you write the essay at the end of the Topic.

Primary Sources

Levittown, New York

In 1947, Abraham Levitt's construction company built the first Levittown on 1200 acres of land on Long Island, New York. This neighborhood of mass-produced homes became the country's first suburb. The houses were affordable, with only a few basic models to choose from. Levitt & Sons also built communities in Pennsylvania and New Jersey. The article below describes the Levitts' assembly-line approach for turning out thousands of new homes.

◀ A family views models of homes in the new Levittown suburb.

Millions of newly liberated GIs, many with wives and children, were eager to buy homes. Unfortunately, wartime shortages had crippled the housing industry, and there simply weren't enough homes to meet the demand. Sensing a tremendous opportunity, the Levitts purchased 1,000 acres of land on Long Island, 25 miles east of Manhattan, and embarked on a bold venture to build 17,000 homes. . . .

They broke down the construction process into 27 separate tasks and assigned each task to a group of workers who would go from house to house repeating their specific task at each building site. Trucks would deliver parts and materials to homesites placed at 60-foot intervals. Then the carpenters, tilers, painters and roofers arrived each in turn. There was even one employee who did nothing but bolt washing machines to the floors. When the process was in high gear, houses were completed at the rate of as many as 36 per day. (Even at that pace, [the Levitts were] hard-pressed to keep up with demand. During the first weekend of building, [the Levitts] sold more than 300 houses.)

To keep down lumber costs, the Levitts bought their own forests and built a sawmill in Oregon. They purchased appliances directly from the manufacturer, cutting out the distributor's markup. They even made their own nails.

Analyzing Primary Sources

Cite specific evidence from the source to support your answers.

1. **Cite Evidence** Which group of people were the Levitts trying to reach with their affordable suburban homes?
2. **Express Ideas Clearly** What methods helped the Levitts build so many houses so quickly?
3. **Support Ideas with Examples** List two ways that the Levitts were able to cut costs.

Make a Difference

INTERACTIVE
Make a Difference

Follow these steps to make a difference.

1 Identify an issue in your community and learn all you can about it. Making a difference does not mean that you have to find a solution to a major global problem. Often, you may observe a need or a problem right within your community. You may hear about an issue from family members or read about an issue in the newspaper. Once you find an issue, do some research to learn about it. Look for more information online or in the newspaper. Also, there may be organizations already working on the issue. People at these organizations can tell you how you can get involved.

2 Organize a group to come up with a plan to solve the issue. Once you have learned all you can on your own about the issue, talk to friends and family about taking action. If you are concerned about the issue, other people in your community may want to help. If you organize a group of people to work together, you can do more than if you work on your own. Also, other people in the group may have good suggestions on how to make a difference. Work with your group to make a plan of action. Think carefully about the steps that you will take to address the issue.

3 Turn your plan into action to make a difference. Once you have a plan of action, you can get started. Even the most challenging tasks can be completed if you break them into simple steps. Make sure that there is good communication within the group. One person may run into difficulties, and you may find that a certain step is not as simple as you thought. Work together to find solutions to any problems that come up. Finally, when you have completed all or part of your plan, you may want to discuss whether or not the plan had the effect that you wanted. Many issues are very complex, and you will learn many new things as you put your plan into action.

Create a graphic organizer like the one below to help you get started.

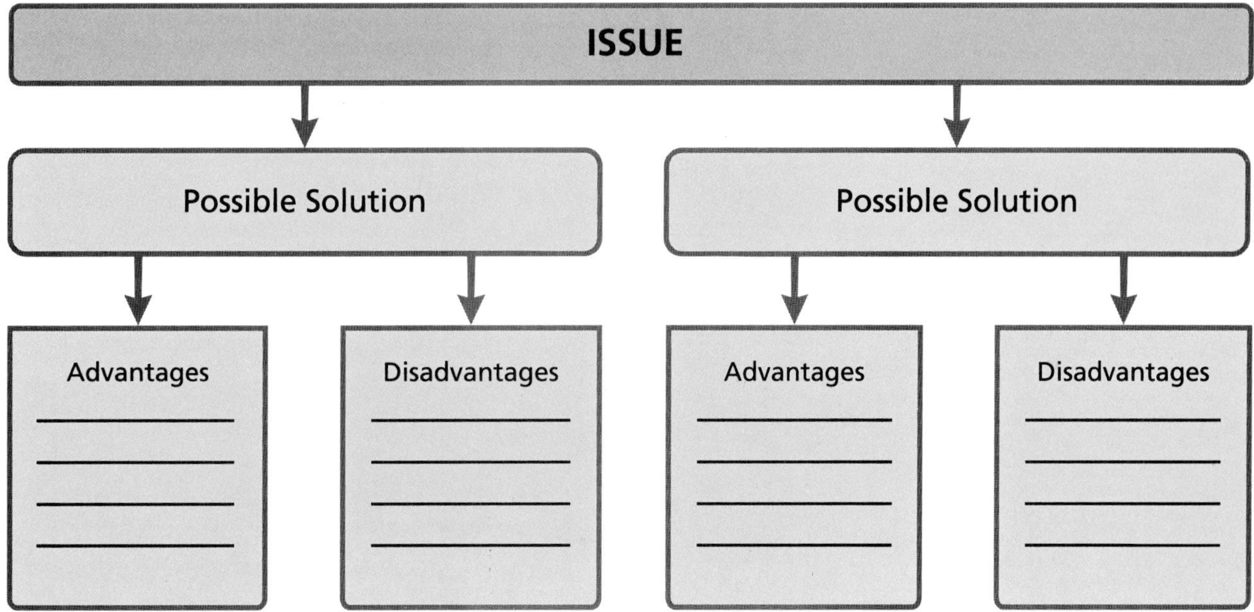

LESSON 4

The Civil Rights Movement

GET READY TO READ

START UP

These people marched from Selma to Montgomery, Alabama, demanding passage of the Voting Rights Act. What words would you use to describe the actions and attitudes of these people?

GUIDING QUESTIONS

- How did discrimination affect the lives of minorities in the United States?
- How did the courts, protests, and boycotts help minority groups achieve greater rights?
- What was the role of Martin Luther King, Jr., in the Civil Rights Movement?

TAKE NOTES

Literacy Skills: Sequence

Use the graphic organizer in your Active Journal to take notes as you read the lesson.

PRACTICE VOCABULARY

Use the vocabulary activity in your Active Journal to practice the vocabulary words.

Vocabulary		Academic Vocabulary
segregation	boycott	compose
integration	civil disobedience	prominent
Civil Rights Movement	sit-in	
	affirmative action	

From the late 1940s to the 1970s, mass protests and coordinated demonstrations made it clear that minorities would no longer tolerate discrimination. But full equality would take time, and the struggle to get there would often be brutal.

Why Did Discrimination Continue?

The Fourteenth Amendment, ratified in 1868, and the Fifteenth Amendment, ratified in 1870, were intended to provide African Americans with equal rights. In reality, these amendments were not adequate to ensure equality for all Americans.

African Americans Fight Segregation Throughout the nation, discrimination limited the lives of millions of Americans. Qualified African Americans found themselves barred from good jobs and decent housing in the North. In the South, laws enforced strict **segregation**, or separation, of the races in schools, theaters, restaurants, and other public places. Facilities for African Americans were inferior to those for whites.

For African Americans, the NAACP (National Association for the Advancement of Colored People) led the drive against discrimination. During World War II, NAACP membership rocketed from 50,000 to 500,000. Under Thurgood Marshall, the NAACP's Legal Defense Fund mounted several court battles against segregation. The NAACP also helped African Americans register to vote and fought for equal opportunity in housing and employment.

Legal Integration Two significant events occurred in the late 1940s that advanced the fight against segregation. First, Jackie Robinson broke the color barrier in Major League Baseball. In 1947 he joined the Brooklyn Dodgers. He was even named rookie of the year. Not since Moses Fleetwood Walker had a Black player played in the major leagues. Walker, the first African American player to join a major league team, played in 1884.

The second significant event occurred in 1948. Under pressure from civil rights groups, President Truman ordered **integration**, or the mixing of different racial groups, in the armed forces. During the Korean War, Black and white soldiers fought side by side.

After risking their lives abroad, returning veterans were unwilling to accept discrimination at home. Often they became leaders in the struggle for equal rights. "Veterans," explained an observer, "have acquired a new courage, and have become more vocal in protesting inequalities."

READING CHECK **Draw Conclusions** What did segregation suggest about American society at this time?

Analyze Images Racial discrimination took many forms. African Americans were forced to use segregated bathrooms and water coolers, as seen in this 1939 photo. **Identify Main Ideas** Why would white people subject African Americans to this treatment?

The Legal Struggle for Equality

During the 1950s, African Americans stepped up the struggle for legal and social equality. They took their cases to court and protested in the streets. Their efforts became known as the **Civil Rights Movement**.

Equal Educational Opportunities The U.S. Supreme Court had decided in 1896 in *Plessy* v. *Ferguson* that the U.S. Constitution did not prohibit "separate but equal" facilities for Black and white Americans. During the 1940s, the NAACP did not attack this idea head on. Instead, its lawyers argued that separate facilities for African American students were in fact not equal to white facilities.

This strategy required patience. Each type of facility and each type of inequality had to be attacked case by case. By the early 1950s, laws in 21 states and the District of Columbia still enforced separate Black and white public schools. Virtually all of the Black schools were inferior to the white ones.

Oliver Brown of Topeka, Kansas, decided to challenge the Kansas school segregation law. He asked the local school board to let his daughter, Linda, attend a nearby white school rather than the distant Black school to which she had been assigned. When board members refused, Brown filed a suit against the school board with the help of the NAACP. Eventually, the case of *Brown* v. *Board of Education of Topeka* reached the U.S. Supreme Court.

In court, the Browns were represented by Thurgood Marshall, who had served as legal director of the NAACP for more than ten years. Marshall and his team decided they had made enough progress to finally challenge the whole idea of "separate but equal." Segregated schools, he argued, could never provide equal education. By their very nature, said Marshall, segregated schools violated the Fourteenth Amendment, which promised "equal protection of the laws" to all citizens.

The Supreme Court ruled in Brown's favor in 1954. Chief Justice Earl Warren noted that segregation affected the "hearts and minds" of African American students "in a way unlikely ever to be undone":

Analyze Images Thurgood Marshall (center) and his legal team were a powerful weapon in the fight against discrimination. Marshall would later become the first African American Supreme Court justice. **Infer** Why would a legal approach to fighting discrimination be effective?

Primary Source

"We conclude that in the field of public education, the doctrine of 'separate but equal' has no place. Separate educational facilities are always unequal."

—Chief Justice Earl Warren, *Brown* v. *Board of Education of Topeka*

Analyze Images President Eisenhower sent federal troops to protect students integrating Little Rock's Central High School. **Draw Conclusions** What does this photo reveal about Americans' attitudes toward desegregation in the 1950s?

Desegregating Schools A year later, the Court ordered the schools to be desegregated "with all deliberate speed." In a few places, schools were desegregated without much trouble. In many others, officials resisted. White politicians in these places decided that the phrase "with all deliberate speed" could mean they could take years to integrate their schools. Or, perhaps they would never obey the decision.

The case that caught everyone's attention took place in 1957. Arkansas Governor Orval Faubus called out the National Guard in order to keep African American students from attending the all-white Central High School in Little Rock. President Eisenhower decided he had to act because the Arkansas governor was defying a federal court order. Eisenhower sent in federal troops to protect Black students as they entered Central High.

Eisenhower was the first President since Reconstruction to use armed troops in support of African American rights. The action showed that the federal government could play a key role in protecting civil rights.

Quest CONNECTIONS

The integration of Central High School was headline news in 1957. How did the national press cover it? How did the Little Rock newspaper cover it? Record your findings in your Active Journal.

READING CHECK **Identify Main Ideas** Why would a state governor refuse to follow a court order such as Orval Faubus did after the ruling of *Brown* v. *Board of Education*?

What Caused the Montgomery Bus Boycott?

Court cases were not enough to end discrimination, as Rosa Parks discovered. On Friday, December 2, 1955, she was riding home from work on a crowded bus in Montgomery, Alabama. The driver ordered her to move to the back of the bus so that a white man could have her seat, as Alabama's segregation laws required. Parks, a well-known activist and a former secretary of the local chapter of the NAACP, refused to leave her seat. She was arrested and put in jail.

Quick Activity

Identify the most important events during the Civil Rights Movement in your Active Journal.

Angered by Parks's arrest, a group of NAACP activists met that night to discuss a response. Martin Luther King, Jr., a Baptist minister, addressed them:

Primary Source

"You know, my friends, there comes a time when people get tired of being trampled over by the iron feet of oppression. . . . We are determined here in Montgomery . . . to work and fight until justice runs down like water, and righteousness like a mighty stream!"

—Martin Luther King, Jr., Speech, December 2, 1955

Academic Vocabulary
compose • *v.*, to create or write

Several of the women **composed** a letter asking all African Americans to **boycott**, or refuse to use, the city buses on the following Monday. The boycott, they hoped, would hurt the city financially and force an end to segregation on the buses. Thousands of copies of the letter were distributed. On Monday, only 10 percent of African Americans in Montgomery rode a bus.

Civil Disobedience The boycott was so well supported that Montgomery's Black leaders formed a new organization, the Montgomery Improvement Association (MIA), to keep the movement going. They chose Martin Luther King, Jr., as its head. King spoke at a meeting in the Holt Street Baptist Church. Hundreds packed the church. Thousands more stood outside. "We are here this evening . . . for serious business," King began. "Yes, yes!" the crowd shouted.

Analyze Charts This chart lists selected Supreme Court rulings that advanced civil rights in the United States. **Summarize** the purpose of bringing civil rights cases to the Supreme Court.

Civil Rights and the Supreme Court

CASE	YEAR	RULING
Brown v. Board of Education	1954	Racial segregation in public schools violates the Fourteenth Amendment; *Plessy* v. *Ferguson* ruling of 1896 reversed
Hernández v. Texas	1954	Discrimination based on class violates the Fourteenth Amendment, which guarantees equal protection
Boynton v. Virginia	1960	Segregation of passengers on buses traveling across interstate lines is unconstitutional
Heart of Atlanta Motel, Inc. v. United States	1964	Refusing to rent rooms to African Americans violates the Civil Rights Act of 1964, which prohibits racial discrimination in public places
Loving v. Virginia	1967	State laws prohibiting interracial marriage are unconstitutional; 16 states revise their laws

Sources: *Encyclopædia Britannica;* United States Department of Education; City of Norman; National Criminal Justice Reference Service

The boycott lasted more than a year. MIA carpools carried some 20,000 African Americans to and from work each day. Many people simply walked. One elderly woman coined a phrase that became a motto of the boycott: "My feets is tired, but my soul is rested."

Angry white people fought back. Employers threatened to fire African Americans if they did not abandon the boycott. Police handed out traffic tickets to harass boycotters, and they frequently stopped African American drivers and demanded to see their licenses. They arrested King for speeding and kept him in jail for several days. King's house was bombed. Still, the boycott continued.

King insisted that his followers limit their actions to **civil disobedience**, or nonviolent protests against unjust laws. He said, "We must use the weapon of love. We must have compassion and understanding for those who hate us."

Analyze Images
Montgomery police took this photograph of Rosa Parks when they arrested her for refusing to move to the back of a city bus. **Generate Explanations** What made Parks's action courageous?

Churches and Courthouses Throughout the bus boycott, African American churches were critical to its success. Churches played a central role in the lives of African Americans across the country. In Montgomery, mass meetings were held in Black churches. There, boycotters sang together, prayed together, and listened to stories of sacrifice. The churches kept morale high, provided leadership, and provided a place where boycotters could inspire and encourage one another.

Finally, the MIA filed a federal lawsuit to end bus segregation in Montgomery. In 1956, almost a year after Rosa Parks had refused to move to the back of the bus, the Supreme Court ruled that segregation on city buses was unconstitutional. The Montgomery bus company agreed to integrate the buses and to hire African American bus drivers.

Gaining National Attention The effects of the bus boycott reached far beyond Montgomery. The boycott brought national attention to the Civil Rights Movement and established nonviolent protest as a key tactic in the struggle for equality. What is more, the boycott introduced the nation to a new generation of African American leaders. Many were ministers from African American churches.

A Strong Leader One of the most important of these new national figures was Martin Luther King, Jr. He was the son of a **prominent** Baptist minister. King had graduated from Morehouse College, a leading African American college. Later, he had earned a Ph.D. in religion and served as pastor of an African American church in Montgomery.

Academic Vocabulary
prominent • *adj.,* well-known

Analyze Images
Martin Luther King, Jr., entertained activists as they planned a lunch counter sit-in. **Use Visual Information** Based on the photograph, how did King affect his followers?

King had studied a wide range of philosophers and political thinkers. He had come to admire especially Mohandas Gandhi, a political leader who had pioneered the use of nonviolence to end British rule in India.

Following the Montgomery victory, King and other African American leaders founded the Southern Christian Leadership Conference (SCLC) to carry on the crusade for civil rights. The group, consisting of nearly 100 Black ministers, elected King president and the Reverend Ralph Abernathy treasurer. The SCLC urged African Americans to fight injustice by using civil disobedience.

Primary Source

"Understand that nonviolence is not a symbol of weakness or cowardice, but as . . . demonstrated, nonviolent resistance transforms weakness into strength and breeds courage in the face of danger."

—SCLC statement, January 10–11, 1957

Still, discrimination and segregation remained widespread. The Civil Rights Movement of the 1950s would grow into a howling wind of protest that would sweep across the country.

READING CHECK **Sequence** What events led to the end of segregation on buses?

A Continuing Crusade for Equality

INTERACTIVE

Nonviolent Strategies in the Civil Rights Movement

In 1963, Anne Moody was a senior in college when she and two friends sat down at a "whites-only" lunch counter in Jackson, Mississippi. The server told them to move to the Black section, but Anne and her friends, all African Americans, stayed put. "We would like to be served," Anne said politely.

A crowd of white people pulled Anne and her friends from their seats. They beat one of Anne's friends, who was promptly arrested. When Anne and her other friend returned to their seats, they were joined by a white woman from her school. "Now there were three of us," Anne recalled, "and we were integrated." The crowd smeared them with ketchup and mustard and dragged them from the lunch counter.

Anne and her friends were using a form of protest called a **sit-in**, in which people sit and refuse to leave. The first sit-in took place at a lunch counter in Greensboro, North Carolina, in 1960. During the 1960s, thousands of Black and white Americans were conducting sit-ins at public places across the South.

Segregation laws in the South limited the rights of African Americans not only at lunch counters but also in bus stations, restrooms, and other public facilities. In the 1960s, sit-ins and other forms of protest fortified the crusade for equality. The protests signaled a new determination to end segregation and discrimination.

Nonviolent Direct Action Civil rights groups planned the protests, but it was often young people like Anne Moody who carried them out.

Analyze Images These African American students refused to leave when white waitstaff at this lunch counter refused to serve them **Infer** Why was this form of protest effective?

Analyze Images This was a recruiting and publicity poster for the Student Nonviolent Coordinating Committee, an interracial civil rights group that supported sit-ins, Freedom Rides, and the 1963 March on Washington. **Synthesize Visual Information** How does this poster relate to the goals and nonviolent methods of SNCC?

The Congress of Racial Equality (CORE), for example, organized "Freedom Rides." Busloads of young Freedom Riders—Black and white—rode from town to town to integrate bus terminals in the South.

These early civil rights groups held firmly to the tactics of what Martin Luther King, Jr., called "nonviolent direct action." Sit-ins, boycotts, marches, and other peaceful methods were used to achieve their goals.

Police sometimes responded by using attack dogs or water hoses against protesters. Houses and churches of Black leaders were bombed. Civil rights workers—Black and white—were sometimes injured or killed. By remaining nonviolent, protesters gained a moral advantage and the sympathy of many Americans.

In 1963, more than 200,000 Americans marched on Washington, D.C. They wanted Congress to pass laws to end discrimination and to help the poor. Among the speakers that day was Martin Luther King, Jr.

Primary Source

"When we let freedom ring . . . we will be able to speed up that day when all of God's children, black men and white men, Jews and Gentiles, Protestants and Catholics, will be able to join hands and sing in the words of the old Negro spiritual, 'Free at last! Free at last! Thank God Almighty, we are free at last!'"

—Martin Luther King, Jr., Speech, August 28, 1963

The Federal Government Protects Civil Rights The demonstrations spurred Presidents Kennedy and Johnson to press for federal civil rights laws. Kennedy failed, but Johnson succeeded in pushing through the Civil Rights Act of 1964, which protected the right of all citizens to vote. It also outlawed discrimination in hiring and ended segregation in public places.

At the Democratic National Convention in 1964, Fannie Lou Hamer, an African American, told of her experiences while trying to register to vote in Mississippi. Her efforts, along with the help of others, were successful in gaining voting rights for all citizens.

In 1965, the Voting Rights Act allowed federal officials to register voters in states practicing discrimination. It also ended literacy tests that were used to block African Americans from voting. As a result, tens of thousands of African Americans voted for the first time.

The new civil rights laws did not end all discrimination. In the North, no formal system of segregation existed. Informally, though, housing in certain neighborhoods and employment in many companies remained closed to African Americans.

Some Call for Separation Because progress was slow, some African Americans believed that nonviolent protest had failed. The Black Panthers and other radical groups told African Americans to arm themselves. Black Americans, they said, had to be ready to protect themselves and to fight for their rights.

Black Muslims, such as Malcolm X, argued that African Americans could succeed only if they separated themselves from white society. Before he was assassinated in 1965, Malcolm X began to change his views. He called for "a society in which there could exist honest white-Black brotherhood."

▼ After a lifetime of struggles with discrimination, Fannie Lou Hamer became a leader of the Mississippi Freedom Democratic Party in 1964. She went on to national prominence in the Civil Rights Movement.

Both moderates and radicals found common ground in talk of "Black Power." They urged African Americans to achieve economic independence by starting their own businesses and shopping in African American-owned stores. Leaders also called for "Black Pride," encouraging African Americans to learn more about their heritage and culture.

Race Riots In crowded city neighborhoods, many African Americans were angry about discrimination, lack of jobs, and poverty. Beginning in 1965, their anger boiled over into violence.

A confrontation between a white police officer and an African American man in Watts, an African American neighborhood in Los Angeles, triggered a riot there in August. During the next six days, rioters set fire to buildings and looted stores. Some 4,000 people were arrested, 34 were killed, and 1,000 were injured. Over the next two years, Chicago, Detroit, and dozens of other cities exploded with violence, destruction, and death.

King Is Assassinated Martin Luther King, Jr., continued to preach nonviolence. His high visibility made him a target of hate from those who opposed integration. In April 1968, he went to Memphis, Tennessee, to support a strike of Black sanitation workers. When he stepped outside his motel room, a white gunman killed him.

King's life has continued to inspire Americans to work for peaceful change. To honor his memory, his birthday was declared a national holiday in 1986.

Getting Results The Civil Rights Movement began to show some results in the 1970s when African Americans won public offices in small towns and large cities. Atlanta, Cleveland, Detroit, New Orleans, and Los Angeles had all elected Black mayors by 1979.

African Americans also made gains in the federal government. In 1967, Edward Brooke of Massachusetts became the first Black senator since Reconstruction. A year later, President Johnson appointed Thurgood Marshall to the Supreme Court.

Analyze Graphs This graph shows the unemployment rates for Black and white Americans. **Use Evidence** Through the 1950s and 1960s, did the difference between the Black and white unemployment rates increase, decrease, or stay about the same?

Unemployment, by Race, 1950–1970

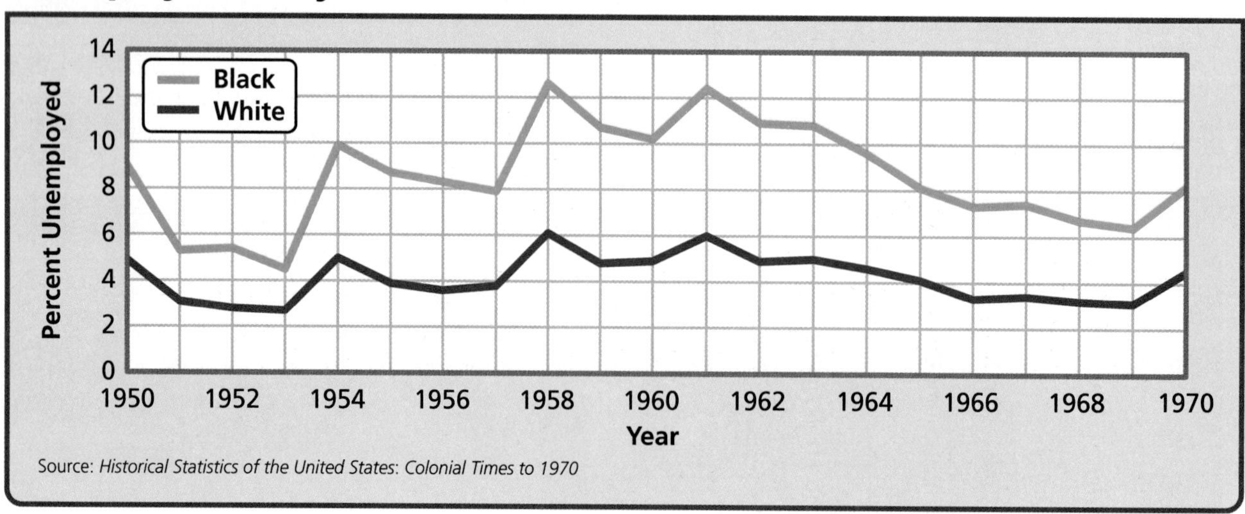

Source: *Historical Statistics of the United States: Colonial Times to 1970*

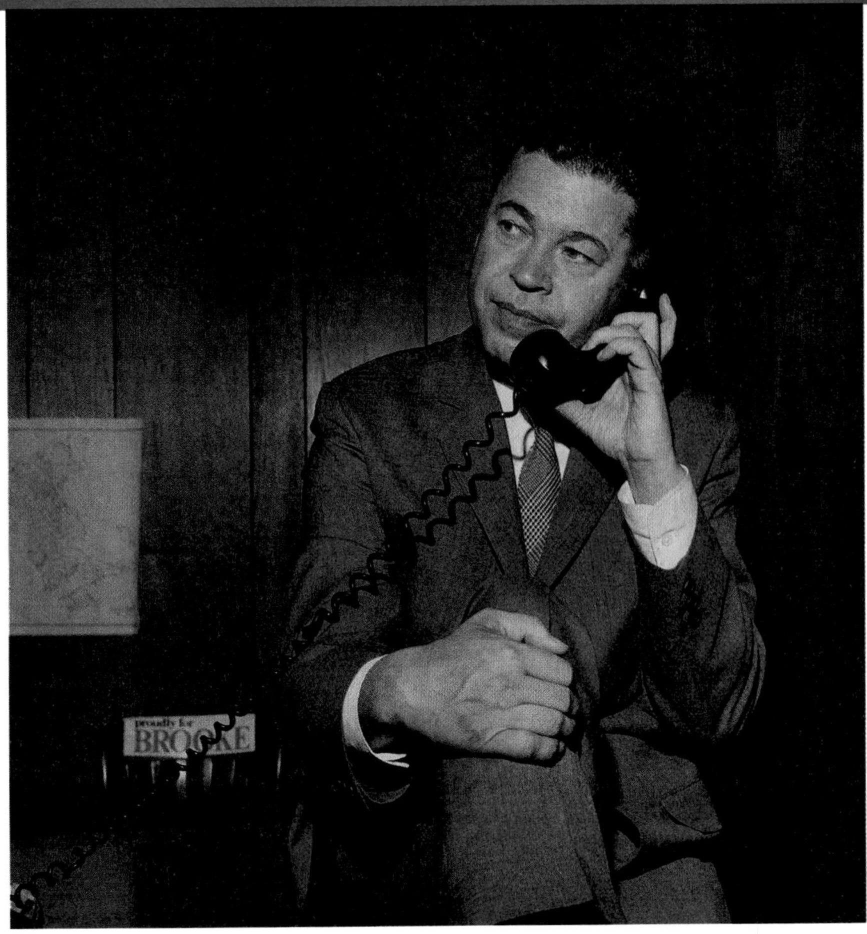

Analyze Images Before his election as senator, Edward Brooke was a decorated veteran of World War II and attorney general of Massachusetts. **Infer** How did the Civil Rights Movement change the federal and state governments?

Many businesses and universities adopted **affirmative action** programs. These programs sought to hire and promote minorities, women, and others who had faced discrimination. By the 1970s, more African Americans were entering such professions as medicine and law. Yet, for all their efforts, African Americans still had to contend with bias in hiring, promotions, and pay.

READING CHECK **Summarize** How did the Civil Rights Movement change over time?

Lesson Check

Practice Vocabulary

1. What was the **Civil Rights Movement**?
2. What were **boycotts** and **sit-ins** and how did they promote civil rights?
3. Why did Martin Luther King, Jr., encourage **civil disobedience**?

Critical Thinking and Writing

4. Identify Cause and Effect What effect did the Korean War have on integration?
5. Identify Main Ideas How did the Civil Rights Act of 1964 and affirmative action initiatives affect minorities?
6. Writing Workshop: Pick an Organizing Strategy Begin thinking about how you will organize your essay on changes to the United States after World War II. Take notes in your Active Journal.

Primary Sources

Martin Luther King, Jr., "I Have a Dream"

On August 28, 1963, 200,000 people joined in the March on Washington for Jobs and Freedom. They marched in protest against racial discrimination. Martin Luther King, Jr., spoke to them.

◀ King speaking at the March on Washington

Reading and Vocabulary Support

① What is "the American dream"? How is it related to King's "dream"?

② A creed is a set of basic beliefs.

③ Something that is transformed is changed.

④ How might you paraphrase "hew out of the mountain of despair a stone of hope"?

⑤ *Discord* has two meanings. One refers to an unpleasant combination of musical notes. The other refers to a disagreement among people or ideas.

Quest CONNECTIONS

King's speech was only a part of a big event, the March on Washington. How did reporters cover it? Did they focus on the crowd's reaction, the success of the march, or the speech itself? Record your findings in your Active Journal.

I say to you today, my friends, even though we face the difficulties of today and tomorrow, I still have a dream. It is a dream deeply rooted in the American dream ①.

I have a dream that one day this nation will rise up and live out the true meaning of its creed: ② "We hold these truths to be self-evident, that all men are created equal."

I have a dream that one day on the red hills of Georgia sons of former slaves and the sons of former slave owners will be able to sit down together at the table of brotherhood.

I have a dream that one day even the state of Mississippi, a state sweltering with the heat of injustice, sweltering with the heat of oppression, will be transformed ③ into an oasis of freedom and justice.

I have a dream that my four little children will one day live in a nation where they will not be judged by the color of their skin but by the content of their character. I have a dream. . . .

This is our hope. This is the faith that I go back to the South with. With this faith we will be able to hew out of the mountain of despair a stone of hope ④. With this faith we will be able to transform the jangling discords ⑤ of our nation into a beautiful symphony of brotherhood.

Analyzing Primary Sources

Cite specific evidence from the document to support your answers.

1. **Determine Author's Purpose** What is King's purpose in this portion of his speech?
2. **Analyze Style and Rhetoric** In the second paragraph, King uses the quote "We hold these truths to be self-evident, that all men are created equal." Where is this quote from and why does King use it?

LESSON 5

The Struggle for Equal Rights Continues

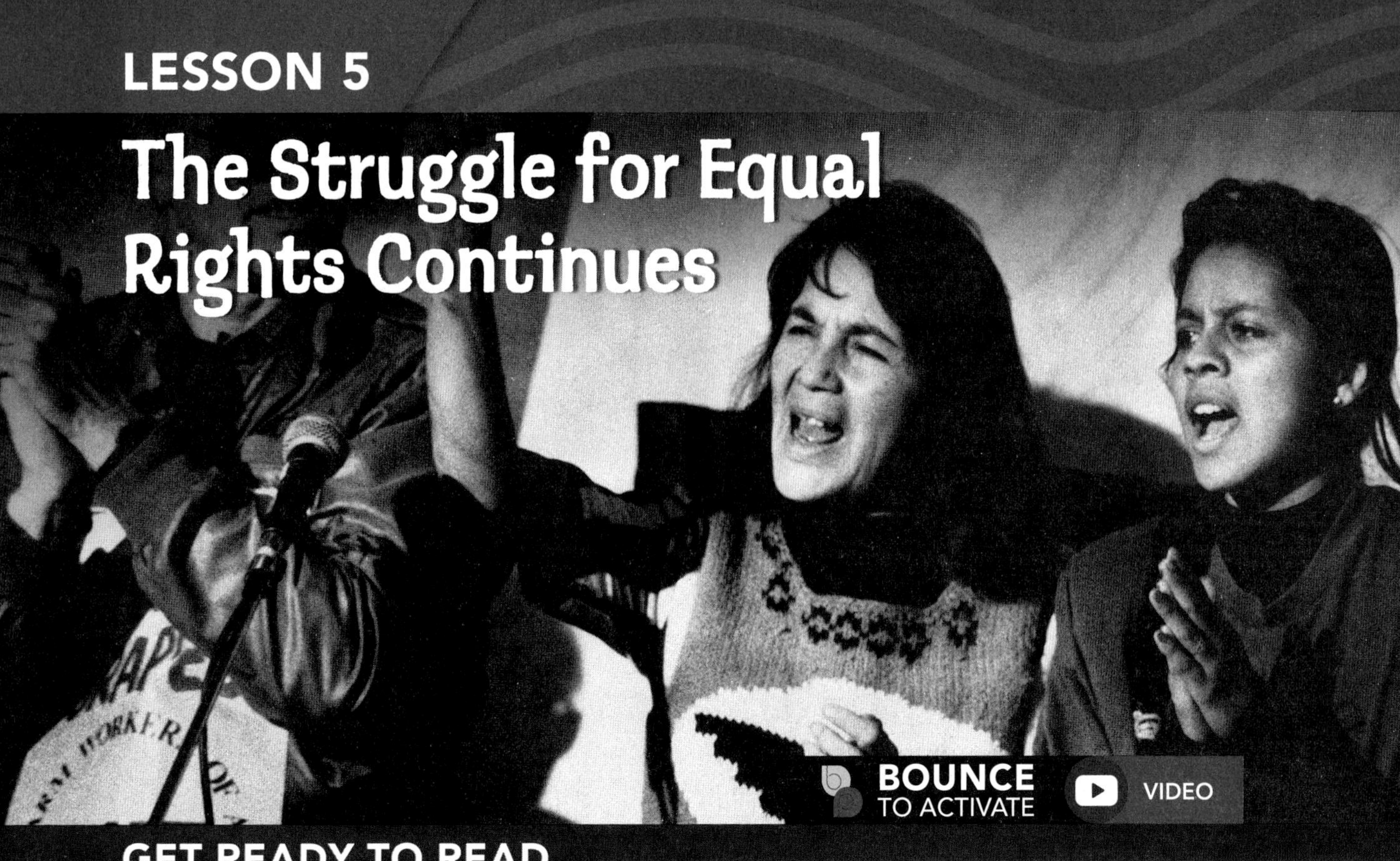

GET READY TO READ

START UP

In the 1960s, Dolores Huerta organized migrant farm workers to fight for better pay and working conditions. At this 1988 rally, Huerta led farm workers demanding less use of pesticides. How do environmental issues impact workers' rights?

GUIDING QUESTIONS

- How did different groups try to achieve equal rights?
- What obstacles did women face in achieving equal opportunities?
- Why were gay men and lesbians at a particular disadvantage in their fight for equality?

TAKE NOTES

Literacy Skills: Classify and Categorize

Use the graphic organizer in your Active Journal to take notes as you read the lesson.

PRACTICE VOCABULARY

Use the vocabulary activity in your Active Journal to practice the vocabulary words.

Vocabulary		Academic Vocabulary
migrant worker	Equal Pay Act	elusive
bilingual	Civil Rights Act	eliminate

By the end of the 1970s, more than 10 million Latinos lived in the United States, and they worked hard to gain equal rights. They were joined by Asian Americans and American Indians in the fight for equality.

Why Did Other Minorities Fight for Equality?

Discrimination limited Mexican Americans and other Latinos. They were not subject to strict segregation laws, but other laws—as well as traditions—worked against them. In the Southwest, all-white schools closed their doors to Mexican American children. Instead, they were segregated in poorly equipped "Mexican schools." Discrimination kept Mexican Americans from living in certain neighborhoods or using certain hotels or restaurants. Often, better-paying jobs were not open to them.

Mexican Americans Mexican Americans are the largest group of Latinos living in the United States today. From 1960 to 1980, the greatest number of immigrants to the United States came from Mexico.

Analyze Images In contrast to the 1960s, strawberry pickers today are provided breaks, toilets, clean drinking water, hand washing facilities, protection against pesticides, and safety and sanitary conditions in farm labor camps. **Use Visual Information** Why is fruit picking back-breaking work?

Many Mexican Americans lived and worked in cities. Many more labored as **migrant workers** who traveled from farm to farm looking for seasonal work. Low wages and harsh working conditions made life difficult for them. Discrimination made things worse. Mexican Americans were often barred from better-paying jobs and from better neighborhoods. Few schools offered programs for those whose first language was Spanish. Migrants moved so often that it was hard for their children to make steady progress in school or even to attend regularly.

Mexican Americans organized their own fight for civil rights. Mexican American veterans founded the American GI Forum of the United States (AGIF) in 1948 to campaign for equal rights. Similar to the NAACP, the AGIF supported legal challenges to discrimination.

A Legal Victory In 1954, the same year as *Brown* v. *Board of Education*, Mexican Americans won an important legal battle when the Supreme Court ruled on the case of *Hernández* v. *Texas*.

Pete Hernández, a Mexican American, had been convicted of murder by an all-white jury in Texas. Among the lawyers who appealed his conviction was Gus Garcia, one of the leaders of the AGIF. Attorney James DeAnda, another Mexican American, also helped. He had previously worked to desegregate areas of Corpus Christi, Texas, where Mexican Americans were not allowed to buy houses.

Hernández's lawyers argued that Mexican Americans in Texas were denied equality under the law because they were excluded from juries. The Supreme Court agreed. It overturned the conviction and ended the exclusion of Mexican Americans from juries. In the future, other minority groups would use this decision to help win their civil rights.

Puerto Rican Americans Latinos in the eastern United States often came from Puerto Rico. In the 1950s, thousands left Puerto Rico in search of work in the United States. Many took jobs in the factories of New York City, New Jersey, Connecticut, and Pennsylvania. Some went to Boston, Chicago, and San Francisco. Puerto Ricans also faced discrimination in housing and jobs wherever they settled.

Cuban Americans A third group of Latinos came in two waves from Cuba. Between 1959 and 1962, some 200,000 people fled to southern Florida when Fidel Castro set up a Communist government in Cuba. These immigrants were often middle class and well educated. They adapted quickly to their new home. A second wave of immigrants came in 1980 after Castro allowed thousands of people to leave the island. Many of these new refugees were unskilled. They had a hard time making a living.

As their numbers grew, Cuban Americans became a force in southern Florida. Miami took on a new look. Shop windows displayed signs in Spanish. Cuban restaurants and shops opened. Cubans published Spanish-language newspapers and operated radio and television stations. Cuban American politicians were soon elected.

Cooperation Yields Results In the 1960s, new Latino organizations sought change. Cesar Chavez formed a union of migrant workers, the United Farm Workers. When farm owners refused to talk to the union, Chavez called for a nationwide boycott of grapes and some other farm products. In the end, the owners recognized the union, and workers won higher wages.

By the mid-1960s, Latinos began to publicly take pride in their history and culture. Mexican Americans called themselves *Chicanos,* a name that comes from the Spanish word *Mexicano.*

Leaders for Change

BIOGRAPHY 5 Things to Know About CESAR CHAVEZ

Labor leader (1927–1993)

- Chavez was a farm laborer who later organized migrant workers to improve pay and working conditions for farm workers.
- He founded the National Farm Workers Association in 1962.
- To win better pay for workers, Chavez led a five-year strike beginning in 1965 by California grape pickers.
- He used nonviolent protests to earn publicity for his cause, including marches, boycotts, and hunger strikes.
- In 1994, Chavez's wife accepted the Presidential Medal of Freedom in his name for his nonviolent efforts to improve the lives of working people.

Critical Thinking What do you think motivated Chavez to become a labor organizer?

Latino groups also registered voters and made sure that voting laws were enforced. These new voters helped to elect more Latino officials to represent their interests.

One result of these efforts was the Voting Rights Act of 1975. It required areas with many non-English-speaking citizens to hold bilingual elections. **Bilingual** means in two languages. Many Latinos' native language is Spanish. A bilingual ballot makes it easier for people whose native language is not English to vote.

The Bilingual Education Acts of 1968 and 1973 promoted bilingual programs in public schools for Spanish-speaking and Asian students.

Asian Americans Asian Americans began their own fight against discrimination in 1968 when students at the University of California at Berkeley founded the Asian American Political Alliance (AAPA). Students of Chinese, Japanese, Filipino, and other Asian descent joined to promote the rights and culture of Asian Americans. As a result, many universities across the nation created programs in Asian American studies.

Analyze Images In 1973, members of the American Indian Movement (AIM) blocked roads and occupied the town of Wounded Knee, South Dakota, to call attention to their cause. **Infer** Why do you think these protesters chose to arm themselves?

American Indians American Indians also worked for their full rights. They claimed rights not only as individuals, but also as members of tribal groups.

Over the years, the federal government had recognized tribal governments by signing treaties with them. During the late 1940s and the 1950s, the federal government tried to break up tribal governments. They also encouraged American Indians to leave the reservations. By the late 1960s, more than half of all American Indians lived off the reservations, mainly in cities. Gradually, city life weakened traditional customs, and people became separated from their heritage. Yet, they were often unable to become fully integrated into the larger society.

American Indians organized against these government policies. The National Congress of American Indians regularly sent delegations to Washington to defend Indian rights.

The American Indian Movement (AIM) protested unfair treatment. In 1973, AIM members occupied Wounded Knee, South Dakota, for several weeks. As you have read, the United States Army had killed nearly 300 American Indians at Wounded Knee in 1890. AIM highlighted the government's unfair treatment of American Indians. Since Wounded Knee, protests and court cases have won public support and greater legal protection for American Indians.

READING CHECK **Draw Conclusions** Why did the rights of Latinos become a more prominent issue during the civil rights era?

The Women's and Gay Rights Movements

Women had long fought inequality. Following the success of the Civil Rights Movement, the Women's Rights Movement gained energy in the 1960s. Meanwhile, a movement for equal rights for gay men and lesbians began to gain attention.

Betty Friedan's 1963 book *The Feminine Mystique* challenged traditional male and female roles. While many men and women argued that women's natural role is to care for a traditional family, Friedan and others urged that women and men should have the same economic, social, and political opportunities.

New laws in the 1960s helped women make some gains toward equality. The **Equal Pay Act** of 1963 required equal pay for equal work. The **Civil Rights Act** of 1964 outlawed discrimination in hiring based on gender and on race. Still, to this day equal pay and full equality on other issues remain **elusive** for women.

Academic Vocabulary
elusive • *adj*, hard to find or achieve

Inequality at Work In the workplace, qualified women found that male employers were unwilling to hire them for certain jobs. Women were usually paid less than men, even for the same work. They were laid off before men and passed over for promotions in favor of men.

In 1966, 28 women including Friedan and Pauli Murray helped to set up the National Organization for Women (NOW), which worked for equal rights for women in jobs, pay, and education. It also helped women bring discrimination cases to court and campaigned for maternity leave and child-care centers. Urging women to be more politically active, NOW organized the Strike for Equality Parade in 1970. Some 50,000 women marched.

Quest CONNECTIONS

Was the Strike for Equality Parade widely covered in newspapers and on TV? What did these sources say? Did the coverage influence what people thought? Record your findings in your Active Journal.

The Equal Rights Amendment In the 1970s, the women's movement suffered a major defeat. In 1972, Congress passed the Equal Rights Amendment (ERA) to the Constitution. The amendment would ban discrimination based on gender.

Analyze Images Women march in favor of the Equal Rights Amendment (ERA), 1973. **Explain an Argument** Why did some people reject women's claims for equal rights?

After passage by Congress, the ERA went to the states for ratification. Phyllis Schlafly and other conservative women led a successful campaign against ratification of the amendment. They said the ERA would lead to women being drafted into the military and would harm the traditional family. Despite this defeat, the women's movement brought women more power and equality.

Since the defeat of the ERA, it has been reintroduced in every Congress.

Gay and Lesbian Rights Movement Gay rights was one of the most strongly debated social issues of the 1900s. In 1924, the first gay rights organization, the Society for Human Rights, was founded.

Gay men and lesbian women continued to face discrimination, even by their own government. In 1953, President Eisenhower banned the hiring of gay men and lesbians for government jobs. Around the nation, gay men and lesbians also suffered harassment by the police. At this time, gay male and lesbian sexuality was against the law in the United States.

Gay rights activists began to protest what they saw as unfair treatment. In 1950, Chuck Rowland and Harry Hay formed the Mattachine Society in Los Angeles. This was a gay rights group of mostly male members. In 1955, the Daughters of Bilitis, a lesbian group, was formed in San Francisco by Del Martin and Phyllis Lyon.

In 1967, Los Angeles police raided the Black Cat, a gay bar, and arrested more than a dozen people. Gay rights activists demonstrated in front of the bar during the following days. The voices of gay and lesbian people were beginning to be heard.

Two years later, police raided the Stonewall Inn in New York City—a bar serving gay men and lesbians—aiming to arrest people just for being there. Police had been making such arrests for years.

BIOGRAPHY 5 Things to Know About BETTY FRIEDAN

Women's rights activist and author (1921–2006)

- Friedan wrote *The Feminine Mystique*, (1963) a best-selling book that challenged traditional expectations for women.
- In 1966, Friedan co-founded the National Organization for Women, which sought to win equal opportunities for women.
- To promote increased participation of women in the political process, Friedan helped create the National Women's Political Caucus in 1971.
- Friedan led the fight for women's rights, including equal pay, fair hiring practices, and maternity leave.
- After her first child, Friedan returned to work as an editor only to be fired when she became pregnant with a second child.

Critical Thinking What methods did Friedan use to combat inequality?

That night and for several days afterward, gay men and lesbians from around New York City rioted against the police. The events of Stonewall inspired gay men and lesbians elsewhere to fight for equal rights.

The next year, 5,000 gay men and lesbians marked the first anniversary of the riots with a march in New York City. The event became a yearly celebration.

Many Americans opposed the growing demands for equal rights by gay men and lesbians. Many condemned gay and lesbian relationships because they considered them immoral for religious reasons. Due to this opposition, efforts to **eliminate** discrimination in jobs and housing had little success during the 1960s and 1970s.

Analyze Images On June 28, 1970, the first Gay Liberation Day, these marchers commemorated the first anniversary of the Stonewall riots. **Generate Explanations** Who was the audience for this form of protest?

READING CHECK **Summarize** the actions and results of the women's and gay rights movements.

Academic Vocabulary
eliminate • *v*, to get rid of or do away with

Lesson Check

Practice Vocabulary

1. Why was it difficult for the children of **migrant workers** to get an education?
2. How did **bilingual** ballots make it easier for Latinos to vote?
3. How did the **Civil Rights Act** help women and minorities?

Critical Thinking and Writing

4. Identify Main Ideas How did the United States government try to control American Indian groups during the 1950s?
5. Summarize the emergence of the gay and lesbian rights movement in the United States.
6. Writing Workshop: Write an Introduction In your Active Journal, write an introduction to your informative essay on changes to the United States after World War II. Include your thesis statement in your introduction.

LESSON 6

Kennedy, Johnson, and Vietnam

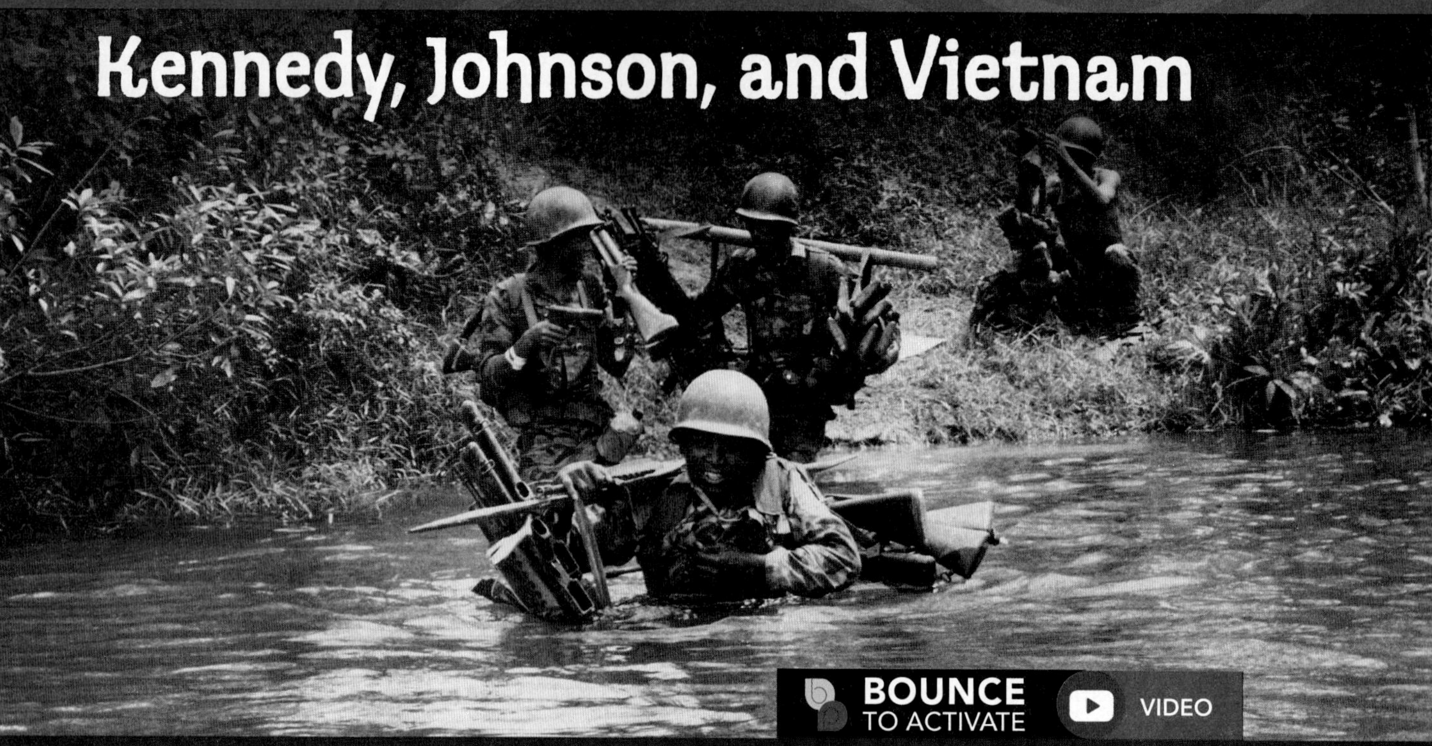

GET READY TO READ

START UP

How does this photo of U.S. troops in Vietnam show the challenges of combat in the Vietnam War?

GUIDING QUESTIONS

- What were President Kennedy's accomplishments?
- What were President Johnson's accomplishments?
- Why and how did the United States become so deeply involved in the Vietnam War?

TAKE NOTES

Literacy Skills: Analyze Text Structure

Use the graphic organizer in your Active Journal to take notes as you read the lesson.

PRACTICE VOCABULARY

Use the vocabulary activity in your Active Journal to practice the vocabulary words.

Vocabulary

superpower
Bay of Pigs invasion
Cuban missile crisis
Peace Corps
Organization of American States
Great Society
domino theory
Gulf of Tonkin Resolution
Tet Offensive
counterculture movement

Academic Vocabulary

resume
legacy

The presidential election of 1960 pitted Republican Vice President Richard Nixon against John F. Kennedy, a Democrat and senator from Massachusetts. It was a close contest that went to Kennedy by a narrow margin.

A New President

Many Americans voted against John F. Kennedy because they felt he did not have enough experience to be President. Others worried about Kennedy's religion, Catholicism. No Roman Catholic had ever been President. Many Americans feared that Kennedy might be more loyal to the Pope and the Roman Catholic Church than to the country. Kennedy reassured voters that he believed in the separation of church and state.

Television Helps Kennedy Win The Kennedy–Nixon race included the first televised presidential debates in history. They turned the tide for Kennedy.

It was a close race, with Nixon holding the advantage through much of the summer.

But on the day of the first debate, Nixon was recovering from the flu, plus, he spent the day campaigning, while Kennedy holed up in a hotel and practiced for the debate. When the two men appeared on stage, Kennedy appeared youthful and confident, in contrast with Nixon, who looked tired and nervous.

As debaters, the two were evenly matched. Those who listened to the debate on the radio considered it a draw, or even gave the edge to Nixon. In contrast, the TV audience rated Kennedy as the clear winner. In November, in one of the closest elections since Reconstruction, Kennedy won the popular vote with a margin of less than 120,000.

Kennedy Inspires the Nation John F. Kennedy took the presidential oath of office on January 20, 1961. At 43, he was the youngest man ever elected President and the first to be born in the twentieth century. "Let the word go forth," he said, "that the torch has been passed to a new generation of Americans."

Kennedy's youth and idealism had inspired Americans during the campaign. Now he called them to service.

Primary Source

"The trumpet summons us again . . . to bear the burden of a long twilight struggle . . . against the common enemies of man: tyranny, poverty, disease, and war itself. . . . And so, my fellow Americans: ask not what your country can do for you—ask what you can do for your country."

— John F. Kennedy, Inaugural Address, January 20, 1961

▼ John F. Kennedy was a youthful President who inspired people with his ideas and speaking.

For all his youth and high hopes, Kennedy and the presidents who followed him faced tough challenges. The 1960s and 1970s were years of idealism. They also turned out to be a time of uncertainty, tragedy, and turmoil for Americans of all ages.

READING CHECK **Identify Main Ideas** What were the strengths and weaknesses of Kennedy and Nixon as presidential candidates?

Why Was Communist Cuba a Threat?

By the time Kennedy entered the White House, the United States and the Soviet Union had emerged as **superpowers**—nations with enough military, political, and economic strength to influence events worldwide. As leader of a superpower, President Kennedy was given the task of negotiating the country's way through Cold War crises. In fact, the rivalry between the superpowers led to clashes in many places, including Cuba, an island in the Caribbean very close to the United States.

In 1959, Fidel Castro led a revolution that set up a Communist state in Cuba. Castro's government took over private companies, including many owned by American businesses. Thousands of Cubans, especially those from the upper and middle classes, fled to the United States.

A Failed Invasion The Soviet Union began supplying Cuba with large amounts of aid. The growing ties between the Soviet Union and Castro's Cuba worried American officials. Cuba lies just 90 miles off the coast of Florida.

In 1961, President John F. Kennedy approved a plan to support Cuban exiles in an invasion of Cuba to overthrow Castro. Exiles are people who have been forced to leave their own country.

A force of about 1,400 Cuban exiles landed at the Bay of Pigs on Cuba's south coast. The invasion was badly planned. Castro's forces outnumbered the invaders and quickly rounded them up and jailed them, killing about 100 of the invaders. The **Bay of Pigs invasion** strengthened Castro in Cuba and embarrassed the United States.

Impending Crisis After the Bay of Pigs invasion, the Soviet Union gave Cuba more weapons. In October 1962, President Kennedy learned that the Soviets were secretly building missile bases on the island. If the bases were completed, nuclear missiles launched from them could reach American cities within minutes.

Analyze Images Fidel Castro was a revolutionary leader who turned Cuba into the first communist state in the western hemisphere. **Use Visual Information** Based on this photograph, how would you describe Castro?

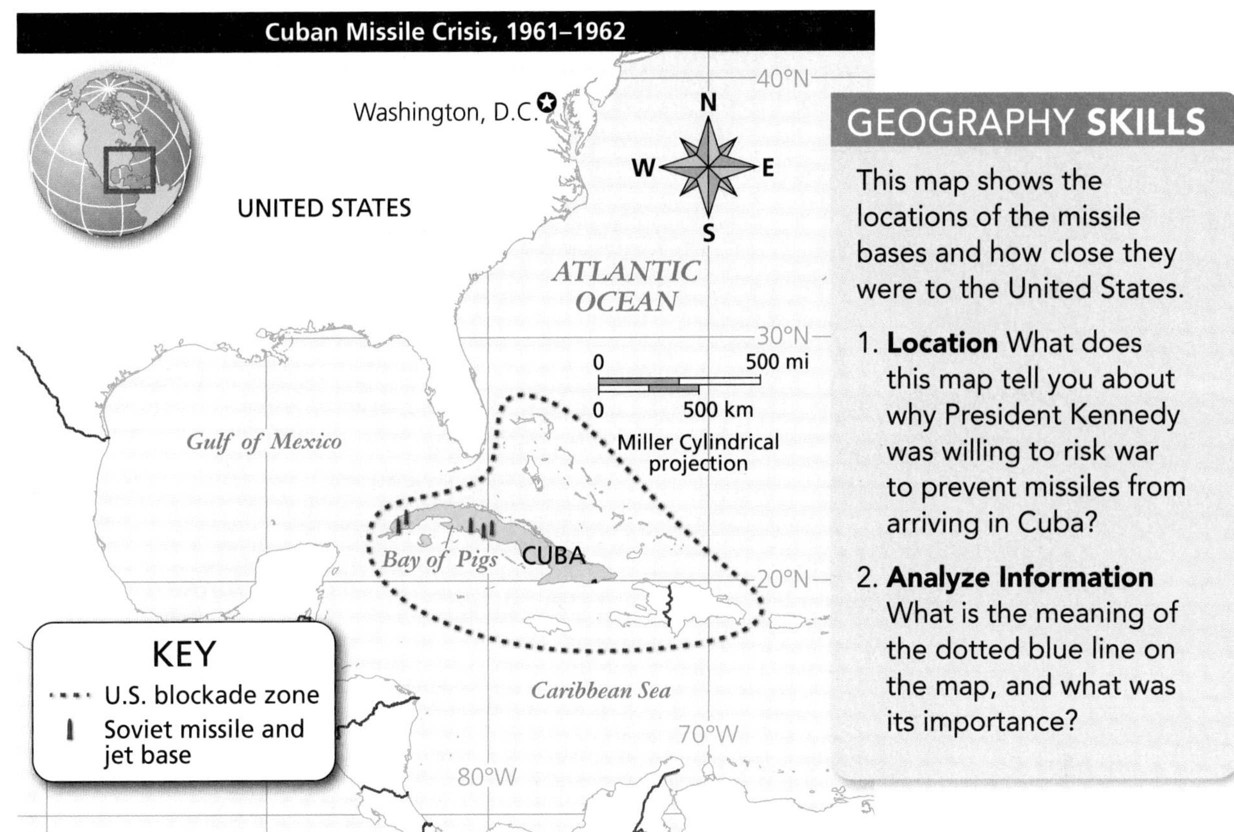

GEOGRAPHY SKILLS

This map shows the locations of the missile bases and how close they were to the United States.

1. **Location** What does this map tell you about why President Kennedy was willing to risk war to prevent missiles from arriving in Cuba?
2. **Analyze Information** What is the meaning of the dotted blue line on the map, and what was its importance?

Kennedy responded cautiously to the **Cuban missile crisis**. He announced that American warships would be positioned around Cuba with orders to stop any Soviet ships carrying missiles. For the next six days the world waited tensely as Soviet ships traveling toward Cuba approached the American blockade. At the last minute, the Soviet ships turned back. "We're eyeball to eyeball," said Secretary of State Dean Rusk, "and I think the other fellow just blinked."

Kennedy's strong stand led the Soviets to compromise. Soviet leader Nikita Khrushchev agreed to remove Soviet missiles from Cuba. In turn, the United States promised not to invade the island. Still, the crisis had shaken both American and Soviet officials. In all the years of the Cold War, the world had never come closer to a full-scale nuclear war.

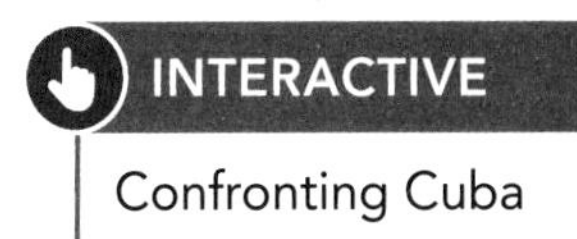

READING CHECK **Identify Main Ideas** What was the American government trying to accomplish with the Bay of Pigs invasion?

Reform and Progress

In the early 1900s, the United States had frequently intervened in the internal affairs of Latin American nations. Now, Cold War tensions led the United States under President Kennedy to **resume** its active role. Successive Presidents also tried to contain communism in Latin America.

Communism in Latin America Because of its colonial past, Latin America had long faced severe social and economic problems. A huge gap existed between the wealthy few and the majority of people.

Academic Vocabulary
resume • *v.*, to begin again after stopping

Analyze Images The Peace Corps sent volunteers to teach at this school in the Philippines. **Understand Effects** How did the Peace Corps promote America's influence in the world?

In most of Latin America, rural people lived in desperate poverty. When the poor migrated to cities seeking work, they were often forced to live in shacks without heat, light, or water.

Many poor Latin Americans saw communism as a solution to their problems. Communists called for land to be distributed to the poor and for governments to take over foreign corporations. Some non-Communists also supported these policies.

Kennedy Attempts Reform Many American leaders agreed with the need for reform in Latin America. They hoped that U.S. aid would help make Latin American nations more democratic, ease the lives of the people, and lessen Communist influence.

In 1961, President Kennedy created an ambitious aid program called the Alliance for Progress. He urged Latin American countries to make reforms to improve the lives of their people. In return, the United States contributed aid to build schools and hospitals and to improve farming and sanitation services. The Alliance brought a few improvements, but it did not end the causes of poverty.

Kennedy also set up the **Peace Corps**. Under this program, American volunteers worked in developing countries in Latin America, Asia, and Africa as teachers, engineers, and technical advisers. Volunteers lived with local people for two years, teaching or giving technical advice.

The United States was also a leading member of the **Organization of American States**, or OAS. Through the OAS, the United States promoted economic progress in the Americas by investing in transportation and industry.

To battle communism, the United States gave military aid to train and arm Latin American military forces. The United States spoke up for democracy and pressed governments to make reforms. Often, though, the United States ended up supporting military dictators because they opposed communism.

Academic Vocabulary
legacy • *n.*, something received by a predecessor or from the past

Kennedy Faces Challenges When Kennedy took office, he was handed the task of leading a country through the Cold War. In doing so, Kennedy took a hard line on many issues, responding directly to Soviet aggression in Cuba and Berlin. These actions were risky, but in both instances, the Soviet Union backed off. Still, the American people remained worried about the possibility of nuclear war.

Both the Soviet Union and the United States had developed large stocks of nuclear bombs and missiles. In fact, they had enough bombs to destroy civilization. When, in 1957, the Soviet Union launched *Sputnik I*, the world's first artificial satellite, Americans questioned whether Soviet rockets armed with atomic weapons could reach the United States.

As both superpowers raced to send larger satellites farther into space, the United States under President Kennedy's leadership set up NASA, the National Aeronautics and Space Administration. Its mission was to direct an American space program to compete with that of the Soviets.

Many programs that began with the Kennedy administration are part of his **legacy** today. For example, NASA continues research today, sending more and more satellites into space and bettering Americans' lives with its technology. The Peace Corps works around the world, continuing to provide support to people in developing nations.

READING CHECK **Identify Supporting Details** What are some aid programs established under President Kennedy's administration?

Analyze Charts The U.S. space program inspired millions of people in the United States and around the world during the 1960s and 1970s. **Draw Conclusions** What do the charts and graphs tell you about the United States' strategy for developing the space program? Explain.

★ THE U.S. SPACE PROGRAM ★

KEY U.S. SPACE ACHIEVEMENTS

1960 · 1965 · 1970 · 1975 · 1980 · 1985 · 1990 · 1995 · 2000 · 2005 · 2010 · 2015

- **1961** Alan Shepherd, first American in space
- **1962** John Glenn, first American to orbit Earth
- **1965** Edward White, first spacewalk
- **1967** Apollo 1 fails on launchpad, crew of three killed
- **1968** Apollo 8 mission, first to orbit moon
- **1969** Neil Armstrong, first person to step on moon
- **1981** Columbia Space Shuttle, first reusable spacecraft
- **2012** Voyager I space probe enters interstellar space

Source: NASA

FIRST U.S. CREWED SPACE PROJECTS

PROGRAM	CREW	CREWED FLIGHTS	GOAL
Mercury 1958–1963	1	6	Orbit Earth
Gemini 1965–1966	2	10	Prepare for Apollo
Apollo 1963–1972	3	12	Land a person on the moon

ROCKET HEIGHTS

What Was Johnson's Great Society?

Nearly two years into his term, President Kennedy had achieved much, but he still had work to do. However, he never got a chance to continue it. Kennedy's life was cut short by an assassin.

The Kennedy Assassination On November 22, 1963, Kennedy traveled to Dallas, Texas. As his convertible passed cheering crowds, shots rang out, and the President slumped in his seat. Later, John F. Kennedy died, and Vice President Lyndon Johnson was sworn in as President.

Stunned Americans reacted with grief and confusion, but more drama followed. Police caught Lee Harvey Oswald, the suspected gunman. However, after his arrest, Oswald himself was killed by another gunman.

Later a special government commission headed by Chief Justice Earl Warren concluded that a lone gunman, Oswald, had murdered the President. Today, most historians agree with the conclusions of the Warren Commission.

Analyze Political Cartoons In this cartoon, President Johnson holds a firearm labeled "domestic policy" and a water pistol labeled "foreign policy." **Identify Main Ideas** What does the cartoon suggest about how Johnson exercised his powers?

President Johnson Carries On "Let us continue," said Johnson. He steered many of Kennedy's proposals through Congress. In November 1964, voters returned Johnson to the White House in a landslide victory. Johnson had his own program. He called it the **Great Society**. It boldly aimed to create a decent living standard for every American. In a first step, Johnson declared a "war on poverty."

Congress had not supported Kennedy's poverty program. However, Johnson was more persuasive. Using his years of political experience, he pressured members of Congress individually and personally. In just two years, Johnson pushed 50 new laws through Congress.

Johnson's Plan The Great Society had many programs. Under Medicare, the government helped pay hospital costs for senior citizens. Medicaid gave states money to help poor citizens with medical bills. A new Office of Economic Opportunity created job-training programs for the unemployed. It gave loans to needy farmers and to businesses in poor sections of cities.

Programs to build housing for low-income and middle-income families were also part of the Great Society. To carry out these programs, Congress established the Department of Housing and Urban Development, or HUD. Robert Weaver headed the department. He was the first African American ever appointed to the Cabinet.

The Great Society had mixed success. It aided the poor but at great cost to taxpayers. Government grew in size, and corruption sometimes plagued antipoverty programs. Still, Medicare, Medicaid, and other reforms helped millions and continue to do so today.

READING CHECK **Summarize** President Johnson's Great Society.

War in Vietnam

Vietnam is a narrow country in Southeast Asia that stretches about 1,000 miles along the South China Sea. Starting in the 1950s, the United States gradually became deeply involved in a conflict there.

Since the late 1800s, France had ruled Vietnam as a colony. During the 1940s, Ho Chi Minh (hoh chee min), a Vietnamese nationalist and a Communist, had led the fight for independence. Ho's army finally defeated the French in 1954.

An international peace conference divided Vietnam into two countries. Ho Chi Minh led Communist North Vietnam. Ngo Dinh Diem (noh din dyem) was the leader of non-Communist South Vietnam. In the Cold War world, the Soviet Union supported North Vietnam, and the United States backed Diem in the south.

The Vietcong Diem quickly lost popular support. Many South Vietnamese thought that he favored wealthy landlords and was corrupt. He failed to help the nation's peasant majority and ruled with a heavy hand.

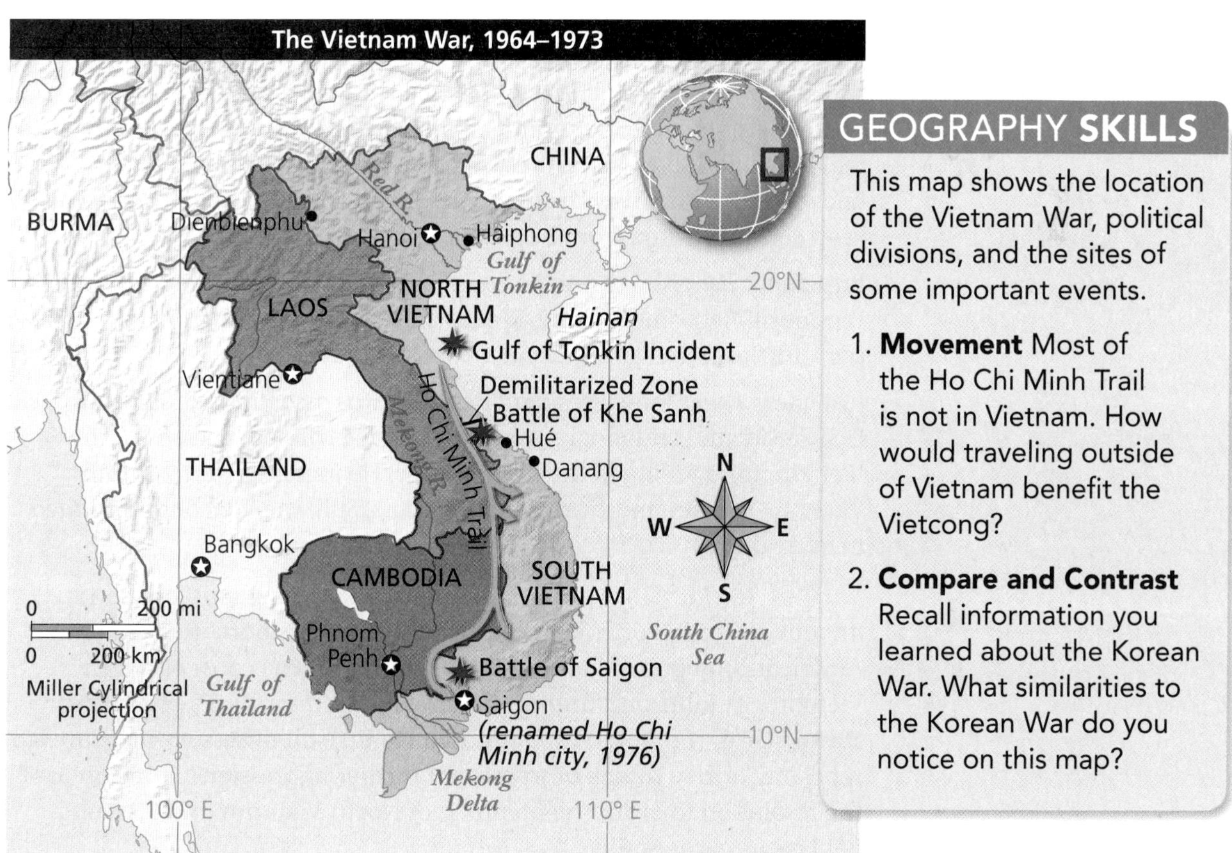

GEOGRAPHY **SKILLS**

This map shows the location of the Vietnam War, political divisions, and the sites of some important events.

1. **Movement** Most of the Ho Chi Minh Trail is not in Vietnam. How would traveling outside of Vietnam benefit the Vietcong?
2. **Compare and Contrast** Recall information you learned about the Korean War. What similarities to the Korean War do you notice on this map?

THE VIETNAM WAR

WAR DEATHS

U.S. military: **58,000**

North Vietnam and Viet Cong: **1.1 MILLION**

South Vietnam Army: **250,000**

Civilians: **2 MILLION**

Source: NARA

BY THE NUMBERS

Number of U.S. helicopters used: **12,000**

Tons of bombs dropped by U.S. planes: **nearly 8 MILLION**

Average age of U.S. infantry soldier: **22**

Average number of days of combat a U.S. soldier saw in one year: **240**

U.S. military personnel deployed: **3,403,000**

Cost to the United States: **$138-$168 BILLION**

Sources: 81st Training Wing; *Encyclopedia of the Vietnam War*; Vietnam Helicopter Flight Crew Network; *Congressional Quarterly Almanac*

U.S. TROOP LEVELS

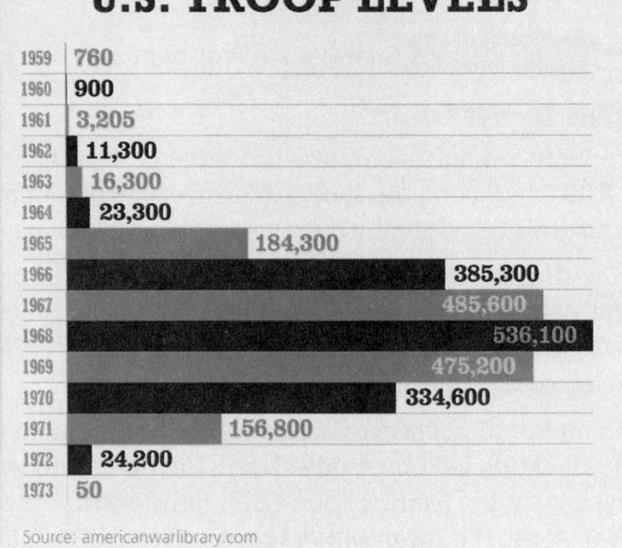

Source: americanwarlibrary.com

Analyzing Charts These data support the idea that the Vietnam War was one of the longest and hardest-fought wars in U.S. history. **Draw Conclusions** During what years do you think the fighting was the most intense? Why?

As discontent grew, many peasants joined the Vietcong—guerrillas who opposed Diem. Guerrillas (guh RIL uz) are fighters who make hit-and-run attacks on the enemy. They do not wear uniforms or fight in large battles. In time, the Vietcong became Communist and were supported by North Vietnam. Vietcong influence quickly spread, especially in the villages.

The Domino Theory Vietcong successes worried American leaders. If South Vietnam fell to communism, they believed, other countries in the region would follow—like a row of falling dominoes. This idea became known as the **domino theory**. The United States decided that it must keep South Vietnam from becoming the first domino.

Presidents Eisenhower and Kennedy sent military advisers to help train the South Vietnamese army. Meanwhile, Diem continued to lose support. In November 1963, Diem was assassinated.

Just a few weeks later, President Kennedy was assassinated. The new U.S. President, Lyndon Johnson, was also determined to keep South Vietnam from falling to the Communists. He increased aid to South Vietnam, sending more arms and advisers. Still, the Vietcong continued to make gains.

Gulf of Tonkin Resolution In August 1964, President Johnson announced that North Vietnamese torpedo boats had attacked an American ship patrolling the Gulf of Tonkin off the coast of North Vietnam. At Johnson's urging, Congress passed the **Gulf of Tonkin Resolution**. It allowed the President "to take all necessary measures to repel any armed attack or to prevent further aggression." Johnson used the resolution to order the bombing of North Vietnam and Vietcong-held areas in the south.

With the Gulf of Tonkin Resolution, the role of Americans in Vietnam changed from military advisers to active fighters. The war in Vietnam escalated, or expanded. By 1968, President Johnson had sent more than 500,000 troops to fight in Vietnam.

Guerilla Warfare The Vietnam War differed from other wars that Americans had fought. Rather than trying to gain ground, Americans attempted to destroy enemy positions. However, the Vietcong were hard to pin down. When Americans found an enemy stronghold, the guerrillas disappeared into the jungle. When the Americans left, the Vietcong returned. As a result, Americans found themselves going back again and again to fight in the same areas.

Worse still, American soldiers often could not tell which villagers were Vietcong. "The farmer you waved to from your jeep in the day," explained an American soldier, "would be the guy with the gun out looking for you at night."

The Tet Offensive In January 1968, the Vietcong launched numerous surprise attacks on cities throughout South Vietnam. Guerrillas even stormed the American embassy in Saigon, the capital of South Vietnam. The attack became known as the **Tet Offensive** because it took place during Tet, the Vietnamese New Year's holiday.

In the end, American and South Vietnamese forces pushed back the enemy. Still, the Vietcong had won a major political victory. The Tet Offensive showed that even with half a million U.S. troops, after years of fighting and thousands of American deaths, South Vietnam was no closer to victory. Many Americans began to protest the war.

Hoping to restore calm to a nation rocked by protests, a weary President Johnson announced that he would not seek re-election in 1968. He said that he needed to focus on his official duties rather than on campaigning. He was also concerned about his health.

READING CHECK **Summarize** What was the domino theory, and how was it applied in Vietnam?

Analyze Images Nurses assist wounded soldiers before they are airlifted from Tan Son Nhat airbase near Saigon, 1967. **Synthesize Visual Information** Do you think this photograph gives a fair, accurate picture of military nurses in the Vietnam War? Explain.

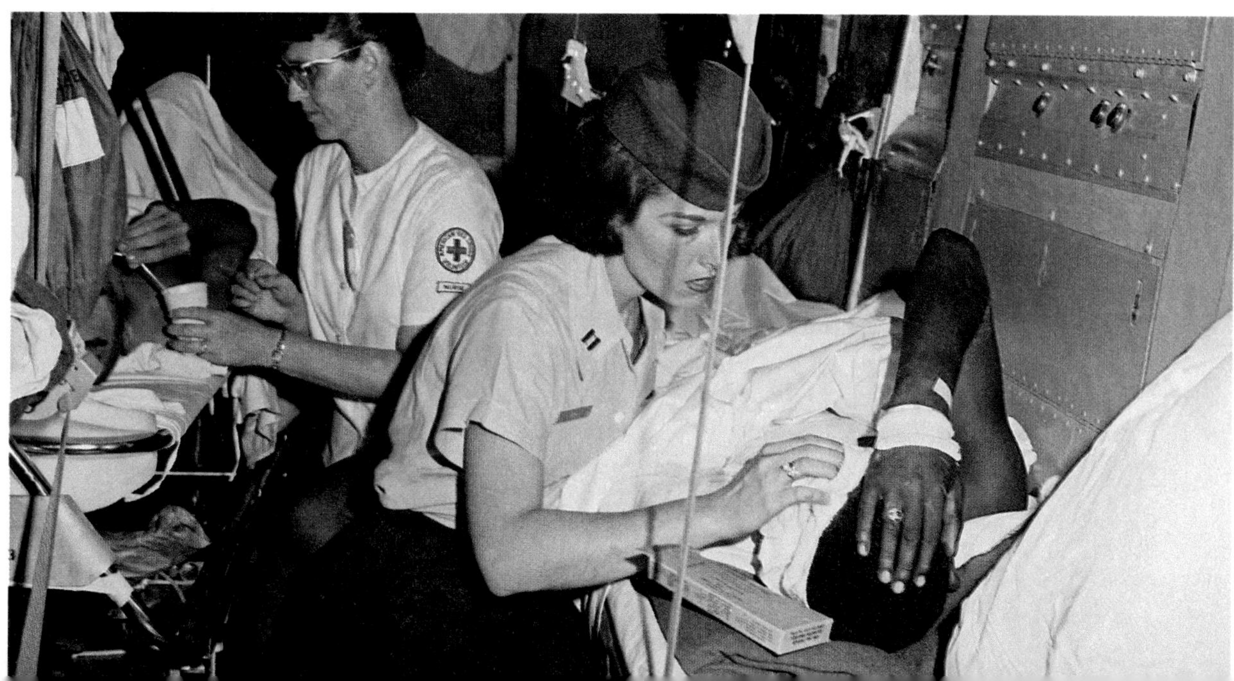

Quick Activity

What do you think are the most striking or interesting details about the progress of the war and the protests that resulted?

 INTERACTIVE

Hawks and Doves

What Caused Protests at Home?

Protest movements grew in the 1960s. The civil rights movement expanded. Some young people began to openly reject the values and lifestyles of their parents. Opposition to the war in Vietnam grew.

Protesting War As American casualties mounted, public support for the war faded. For the first time, Americans watched a war on television. They saw villages burned, children and the elderly caught in battle, and soldiers wounded and killed.

To build up troops, the United States expanded the draft, the system of mandatory enlistment into the armed forces. The draft affected American youth unequally. Many young upper-class and middle-class men found ways to avoid the draft, such as by attending college. As a result, many of the draftees sent to Vietnam were poor. A large number were African American and Latino.

As more and more young men were sent to fight in the Vietnam War, an antiwar movement gained strength. Protesters staged rallies, burned draft cards (notices that a person has been drafted), and refused to serve in the military. Many of the largest demonstrations took place on college campuses.

By the mid-1960s, the country split between "hawks" and "doves." Hawks supported the Vietnam War as a battle against communism. Doves opposed it. They saw it as a civil war that concerned the Vietnamese only.

Protesters also charged that American lives and money were being wasted on an unjust war. The South Vietnamese government, they said, was corrupt and brutal, and the United States should not support it. They wanted the huge sums being spent on the war to be spent on social programs at home.

Analyze Images Americans assembled in large numbers to protest their country's involvement in Vietnam. **Compare and Contrast** What similarities to the Civil Rights Movement that was going on at the same time do you see in this protest?

A Counterculture Emerges The antiwar protests fed a spirit of rebellion among young people. During the 1960s and early 1970s, many young people rejected traditional American values. Many young Americans joined the **counterculture movement**. They criticized competition and the drive for status and material gain. Instead of going to college, they "dropped out." Instead of traditional families, they lived together in groups or communes. Many listened to new forms of rock music. Some "turned on," or experimented with illegal drugs.

Inspired by the civil rights movement, counterculture protesters called for peace, justice, and social equality. They wore torn, faded jeans and work shirts to blur the differences between rich and poor. Men grew long hair and beards. Women refused to put on makeup. All wanted to look and to be more natural and less like their parents.

Like the beatniks of the 1950s, members of the counterculture said American life was empty and materialistic. Some turned to eastern religions such as Buddhism in search of spiritual meaning.

▲ This poster announced the counterculture event known today as Woodstock.

READING CHECK Compare and Contrast How did the hawks and the doves differ?

Lesson Check

Practice Vocabulary

1. What caused the **Cuban missile crisis** and how did it end?
2. How did the **Gulf of Tonkin Resolution** escalate the Vietnam War?
3. What was the **counterculture movement**?

Critical Thinking and Writing

4. **Identify Main Ideas** How did the Vietnam War differ from prior wars?
5. **Compare and Contrast** How were the policies of President Kennedy and President Johnson similar and different?
6. **Writing Workshop: Draft Your Essay** Begin writing your essay on changes to the United States after World War II. Use the details you have been gathering to develop your ideas. Write your paragraphs in your Active Journal.

LESSON 7

The Nixon Years

GET READY TO READ

START UP

Millions of people around the world watched on TV as Neil Armstrong became the first person to walk on the moon. What adventure do you foresee in the future that will equal the interest that landing on the moon held for so many people? Write your ideas.

GUIDING QUESTIONS

- What were President Nixon's accomplishments?
- How did the Vietnam War end, and what were the results of the war?
- What was the Watergate scandal, and how did it lead to Nixon's resignation?

TAKE NOTES

Literacy Skills: Determine Central Ideas

Use the graphic organizer in your Active Journal to take notes as you read the lesson.

PRACTICE VOCABULARY

Use the vocabulary activity in your Active Journal to practice the vocabulary words.

Vocabulary		Academic Vocabulary
silent majority	détente	stimulate
stagflation	SALT Agreement	legitimate
Khmer Rouge	Watergate	
boat people		

By 1968, the counterculture and antiwar movements were peaking. Protests took place at universities across the nation. Angry demonstrators protested at the Democratic National Convention in Chicago. As the elections of 1968 rolled around, enormous pressure was building for a change in course in Vietnam.

The Nixon Years

Johnson had already served as President for six years. Constitutionally, he could have run for another term, but his popularity had plummeted. To avoid angry protesters, Johnson stayed in the White House more and more. Early in 1968 he announced his decision not to run for another term.

The Election of 1968 Johnson's decision not to run for re-election opened the way for other Democrats to seek their party's nomination in 1968. New York senator Robert Kennedy, brother of the late President, made a strong run. However, tragedy again struck the Kennedy family. While campaigning in Los Angeles, Kennedy was shot and killed by a Palestinian who opposed the senator's support for Israel. The Democrats selected Vice President Hubert Humphrey as their candidate.

The Republicans again nominated former Vice President Richard Nixon. Nixon promised "peace with honor" in Vietnam and "law and order" at home. Alabama governor George Wallace entered the race as a third-party candidate. Helped by this and by divisions among Democrats over the Vietnam War, Nixon won a narrow victory.

The Silent Majority As President, Richard M. Nixon cut funds for many Great Society programs, including job training, education, and low-income housing. He also sought to return power to the states. He called this transfer of power the "New Federalism."

During his presidential campaign, Nixon said that he wanted to help those whom he called the **silent majority**. By this he meant Americans who were disturbed by the unrest of the 1960s but did not protest publicly. They were, Nixon maintained, the "great majority of Americans, the nonshouters, the nondemonstrators."

True to his campaign promise, Nixon began his law-and-order program. Federal funds were used to help local police departments. Nixon also named four conservative justices to the Supreme Court. They tended to favor dealing harshly with people accused of crimes.

The Moon Landing Nixon inherited the space program from Kennedy and Johnson. Its greatest triumph came in 1969 just as Nixon took office. That summer, two astronauts landed a small craft on the moon's surface. With millions of television viewers around the world watching, Neil A. Armstrong became the first person to step onto the moon. "That's one small step for a man—one giant leap for mankind," he radioed back to Earth. American astronauts visited the moon five more times.

Analyze Charts This chart shows data concerning Richard Nixon's narrow victory in the 1968 election. **Cite Evidence** In what key states did Nixon lose the popular vote to Humphrey? Why did he still win the election?

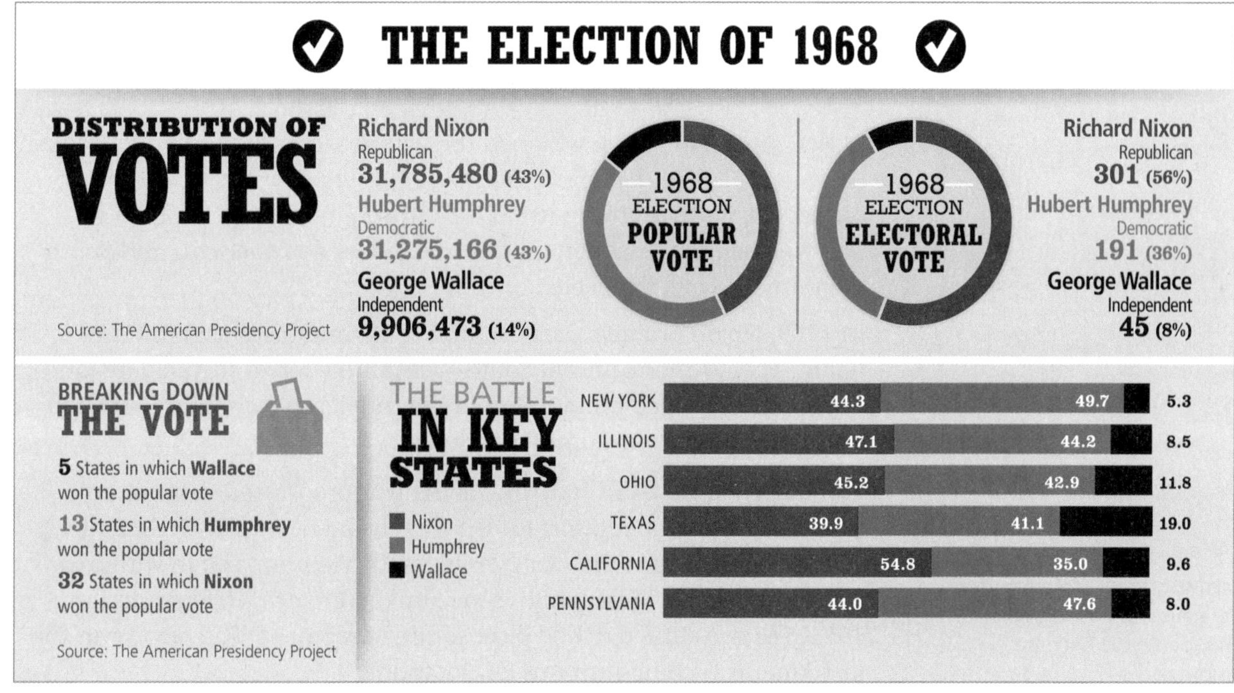

Inflation, 1945–1975

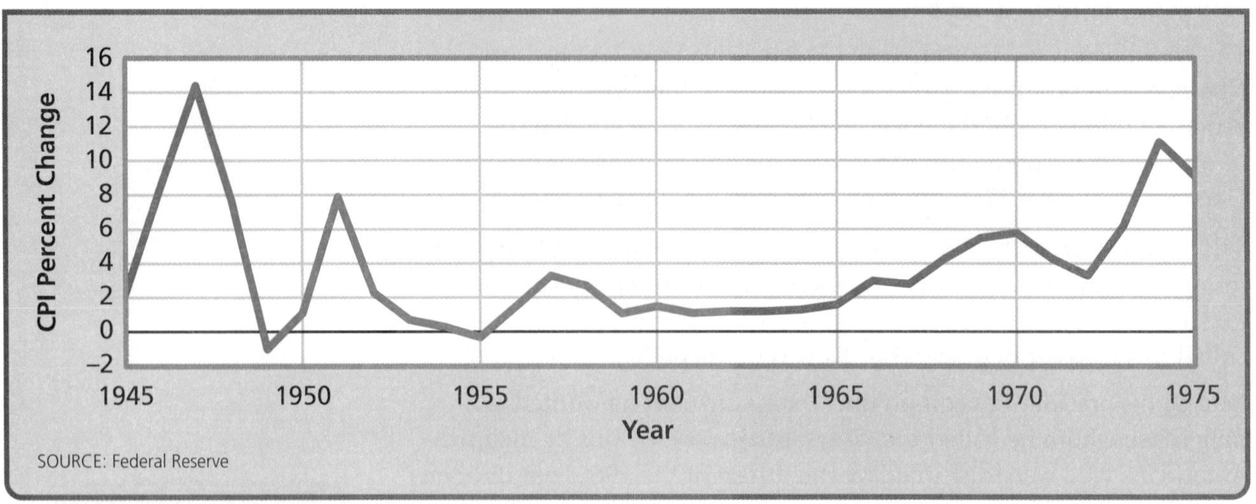

Analyze Graphs This graph shows the annual percent increase or decrease in the Consumer Price Index (CPI), a standard measure of inflation. **Compare and Contrast** How did the value of a dollar in the 1970s compare to the value of a dollar in the 1950s and 1960s?

The Economy Suffers During the Nixon years, the economy suffered from **stagflation**, a combination of rising prices, high unemployment, and slow economic growth. To halt inflation, Nixon froze wages and prices. To **stimulate** economic growth, he increased federal spending.

Still, economic problems would not go away. Increased federal spending caused federal budget deficits; that is, the government spent more than it received in revenues. Early in Nixon's second term, Arab nations imposed an oil embargo on the United States. Gas and other petroleum products were in short supply and prices increased. The shortage put added pressure on the economy as higher energy prices caused the price of goods to rise even more.

READING CHECK **Draw Conclusions** Why do you think the moon landing was important?

The Vietnam War Comes to an End

At first President Nixon widened the war in Vietnam, hoping to weaken the enemy. For years, North Vietnam had sent supplies to Vietcong soldiers in South Vietnam using trails through nearby Cambodia. The Vietcong also escaped into Cambodia when American and South Vietnamese units attacked.

In 1969, Nixon ordered the bombing of Communist bases in Cambodia. Then, American and South Vietnamese forces invaded by land. These moves helped plunge Cambodia into its own civil war between Communist and non-Communist forces.

Withdrawal of U.S. Troops As the war progressed without an end in sight, public support for U.S. involvement waned. President Nixon began to turn the war over to South Vietnam and to withdraw American troops. Meanwhile, peace talks were held in Paris. In January 1973, the two sides reached a cease-fire agreement. The next year, the last American combat troops left Vietnam.

Academic Vocabulary

stimulate • *v.*, to encourage or cause something to happen or to become more active

The United States continued to send large amounts of aid to South Vietnam. Even so, the South Vietnamese were unable to stop a North Vietnamese advance.

In April 1975, Communist forces captured Saigon. They renamed it Ho Chi Minh City. Soon after, Vietnam was united under a Communist government.

Communism in Cambodia Also in 1975, the Communist **Khmer Rouge** (kuh MER ROOZH) won the civil war in Cambodia. The Khmer Rouge imposed a brutal reign of terror on their own people. More than one million Cambodians starved to death or were killed.

In 1979, Vietnam invaded Cambodia and set up a new Communist government. It was less harsh than the Khmer Rouge, but it could not end the fighting. Not until the 1990s would a shaky peace be restored in Cambodia.

The Aftermath The Vietnam War was a costly conflict. More than 58,000 American soldiers lost their lives. Over 150,000 American soldiers were wounded, and hundreds of thousands of soldiers suffered lingering effects from the psychological stress of the war. More than one million Vietnamese soldiers and perhaps half a million civilians died. The war shattered the Vietnamese economy.

After 1975, hundreds of thousands of people fled Vietnam and Cambodia. Refugees from Vietnam escaped in small boats. Many of these **boat people** drowned or died of hunger and thirst. Others made it to safety. Eventually, many were allowed to settle in the United States.

Analyze Images In 1975, as the Vietcong were entering Saigon, American planes and helicopters flew almost nonstop into Saigon to rescue people desperately fleeing the Communist forces. **Infer** Why were South Vietnamese desperate to leave their country?

Academic Vocabulary
legitimate • *adj.*, real or official

The Vietnam War was a painful episode in American history. The war produced no victory and divided the nation. Instead of celebrations and parades, many returning soldiers were met with protests and with resentment by family and former friends. Vietnam left Americans wondering about how far the nation should go to fight communism.

READING CHECK **Identify Main Ideas** Why did Nixon order attacks on Cambodia?

Nixon Seeks to Ease Cold War Tensions

In 1971, while Americans were still fighting in Vietnam, the Cold War showed signs of a thaw. President Nixon wanted to ease world tensions, and his first move was to seek improved relations with the People's Republic of China.

Recognizing Mao's China Since 1949, the United States had refused to recognize Mao Zedong's Communist government in China. Instead, it recognized the Chinese Nationalists, now confined to the island of Taiwan. The United States gave arms and aid to the Nationalists and supported their claim to being the **legitimate** government of all China.

Richard Nixon had long been an outspoken opponent of giving official recognition to the Chinese government. As president, though, Nixon ordered secret talks with Chinese officials. As a show of goodwill, China invited the American table tennis team to a competition in Beijing.

To the surprise of many Americans, Nixon then visited the People's Republic of China in 1972. Television cameras captured the President walking along the Great Wall of China and attending state dinners with Chinese leaders.

Analyze Images President Nixon (center) visited the People's Republic of China in 1972 and met with Chinese Premier Chou En Lai (left). **Identify Main Ideas** What was significant about Nixon's trip to China?

The visit was a triumph for Nixon and the start of a new era in relations with China. As tensions eased, the United States and China established formal diplomatic relations in 1979.

Détente President Nixon followed his visit to China with another historic trip. In May 1972, he became the first U.S. President since the start of the Cold War to visit the Soviet Union. The trip was part of Nixon's effort to reduce tensions between the superpowers. This policy was known as **détente** (dayTAHNT).

Cold War Arms Buildup and SALT I and II

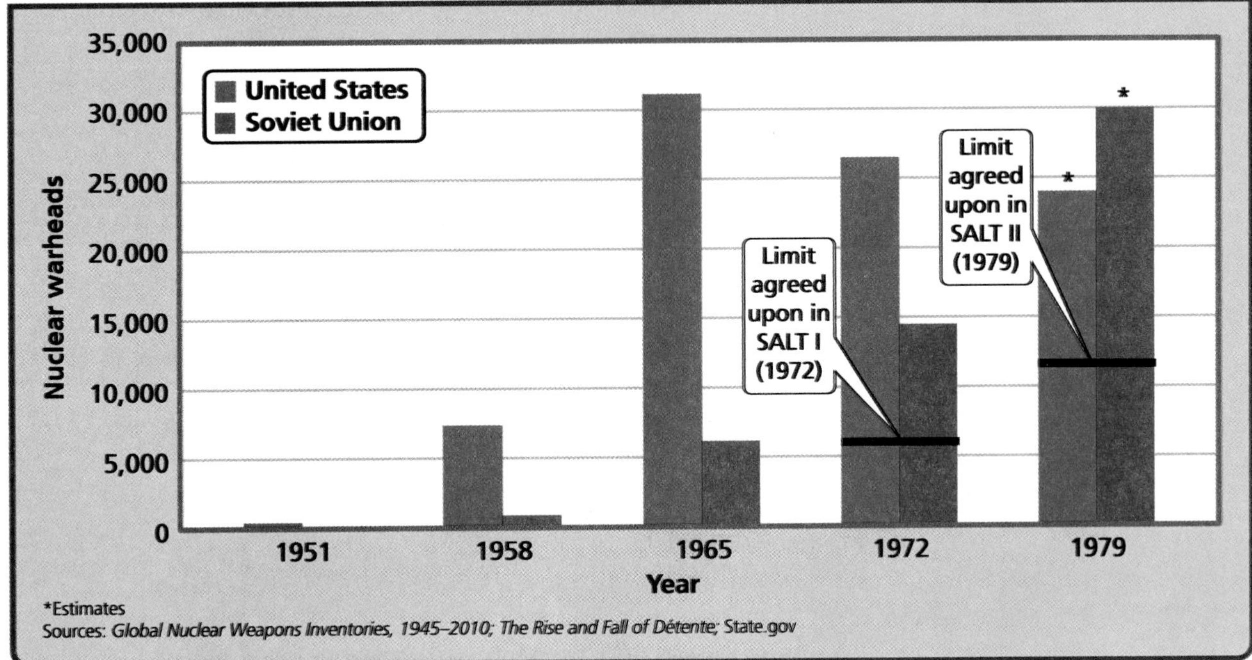

Analyze Graphs The graph shows how rivalry between the United States and the Soviet Union resulted in a massive buildup of nuclear warheads by both nations. **Identify Implied Main Ideas** What was the purpose of the SALT II agreement?

A French word meaning "loosening," *détente* represents an end to strained relations between countries.

Détente eased the tensions of the Cold War by establishing more trade and other contacts between the superpowers. It also led them to sign a treaty to limit the number of nuclear warheads and missiles. The treaty was known as the **SALT Agreement**. (*SALT* stands for Strategic Arms Limitation Talks.)

The next two Presidents, Gerald Ford and Jimmy Carter, continued the policy of détente. Trade between the United States and the Soviet Union increased. Under President Ford, Soviet and American astronauts conducted a joint space mission. In 1979, President Carter met with Soviet leader Leonid Brezhnev (BREZH nef). They worked out the details of a SALT II Treaty.

READING CHECK **Identify Cause and Effect** What were the results of Nixon's foreign policy in China and the Soviet Union?

The Watergate Scandal

During President Nixon's second term in office, an event that began while he was campaigning for reelection turned into a major scandal known as **Watergate**. On June 17, 1972, police caught five men breaking into Democratic party headquarters in the Watergate building in Washington, D.C. The burglars were there to steal information about the Democrats by taking secret documents and wiretapping phones. Though it was suspected that the spies were linked to Nixon, no solid evidence was found at first. The President assured the public that no one in the White House was involved in the break-in. He won the election by a landslide.

INTERACTIVE

Watergate

The Scandal Deepens Watergate did not go away with Nixon's re-election. The American people would learn that Nixon was indeed involved. After the break-in, he paid the spies to keep quiet about his involvement, and he enlisted the CIA to obstruct the investigation. However, seven men were charged in the scandal. Of those seven, two were convicted and five pleaded guilty.

Despite Nixon's denials of involvement, a Senate committee began public hearings in May 1973. The hearings revealed that Nixon had made secret tape recordings of conversations in his office. Nixon refused to give the committee the tapes, knowing that the tapes would prove his guilt.

In the fall of that same year, another unrelated scandal erupted. Vice President Spiro Agnew was accused of taking bribes and evading taxes. He was forced to resign. The President appointed Representative Gerald R. Ford of Michigan to replace him.

Nixon Resigns In July 1974, Nixon was ordered by the Supreme Court to surrender the tapes. The Watergate crisis came to a head when Nixon continued to hold onto the tapes. A House of Representatives committee passed articles of impeachment against the President. One of several charges was obstructing, or blocking, justice.

A month later, on August 5, Nixon handed over the tapes that proved he and several close advisers had tried to cover up the truth about the Watergate break-in. Three days later, before an impeachment trial could begin, Richard Nixon became the first President to resign from office.

Analyze Political Cartoons In this cartoon, the White House is crushed by the tapes that Nixon secretly made of his office conversations. **Recognize Point of View** What was the cartoonist trying to show about the importance of Nixon's tapes and the Watergate affair?

Analyze Images On August 8, 1974, Richard Nixon resigned from the presidency. **Understand Effects** Do you think it was better for the country that Nixon resigned rather than being found guilty in an impeachment trial?

Ford Takes Office Gerald Ford, the new President, had a difficult job. He faced a troubled economy and the challenge of helping the nation emerge from a major political scandal. In response to the nation's troubled mood, President Ford granted Nixon a "full, free, and absolute pardon." He did so a month after Nixon resigned. Some felt that Nixon should have been brought to trial. Ford, however, said that he wanted to save the country from more bitter debate over Watergate. Ford lost a great deal of public support because of his decision.

READING CHECK **Sequence** List the series of events that led to Nixon's resignation.

Lesson Check

Practice Vocabulary

1. Who were the **silent majority**?
2. How did **détente** ease Cold War tensions?
3. What was the **Watergate** scandal?

Critical Thinking and Writing

4. **Summarize** What economic pressures existed during Nixon's presidency?
5. **Identify Main Ideas** How did relations between the United States and China change during Nixon's presidency?
6. **Writing Workshop: Include Formatting and Graphics** Review your essay and think about how you can use formatting and graphics to better develop and explain your ideas. Consider using diagrams, charts, or graphs. Sketch some ideas you might use as you finalize your essay.

Review and Assessment

VISUAL REVIEW

CRUSADE FOR EQUALITY

Economic and Social Rights	Equality in Education	Political Rights	Social Action
• Jackie Robinson desegregates major league baseball. • Truman desegregates armed forces. • Civil Rights Act of 1964 outlaws discrimination in hiring. • Equal Pay Act of 1965	• *Brown* v. *Board of Education* desegregates schools. • Bilingual Education Acts of 1968 and 1973 • Minority studies programs created.	• Voting Rights Act of 1965 • *Hernandez* v. *Texas* integrates juries.	• Martin Luther King, Jr., preaches nonviolence and civil disobedience. • Boycotts, sit-ins, and protests draw national attention. • Riots break out in cities across nation. • Minority pride movements develop.

The United States Fights Communism

READING REVIEW

Use the Take Notes and Practice Vocabulary activities in your Active Journal to review the topic.

Practice vocabulary using the Topic Mini-Games

Write Your Newsletter

Get help for writing your newsletter in your Active Journal.

ASSESSMENT

Vocabulary and Key Ideas

1. **List** What were the effects of the **baby boom**?
2. **Recall** What did the Supreme Court rule in the case of *Brown* v. *Board of Education*, and what was the result?
3. **Describe** How did **McCarthyism** and the fear of communism affect the lives of people in the United States?
4. **Recall** How did **détente** make the world safer?
5. **Identify Main Ideas** What did Churchill mean when he spoke of the **iron curtain** that had descended upon Europe?
6. **Recall** What happened as a result of the **Watergate** scandal?
7. **Recall** Why did protestors of the 1960s and early 1970s oppose the Vietnam War?

Critical Thinking and Writing

8. **Draw Conclusions** How did the Marshall Plan help prevent communism from spreading into Western Europe?
9. **Understand Effects** Was the United States successful in the Korean War? Explain.
10. **Summarize** How did migration to the suburbs change the United States?
11. **Understand Effects** What were the effects of the Civil Rights Movement's use of nonviolent protest?
12. **Revisit the Essential Question** What was America's role in the world during the postwar years?
13. **Writing Workshop: Write an Informative Text** Review all the work you've done for your informative essay on changes to the United States after World War II. Revise and develop your ideas to clarify relationships between ideas. Create your graphic organizers and write a final draft.

Analyze Primary Sources

14. Read the quotation. Who most likely said these words?
    - **A.** Martin Luther King, Jr.
    - **B.** Betty Friedan
    - **C.** Rosa Parks
    - **D.** César Chávez

"The [police] asked if the driver had asked me to stand up, and I said yes, and they wanted to know why I didn't. I told them I didn't think I should have to stand up. After I had paid my fare and occupied a seat, I didn't think I should have to give it up."

Analyze Maps

Use the map to answer the following questions.

15. Which letter represents North Vietnam? Is this a democratic or a Communist country?
16. Which letter represents Cambodia? Which country lies to the east of Cambodia?
17. The city of Saigon is identified by which letter?

▼ Indochina, 1956

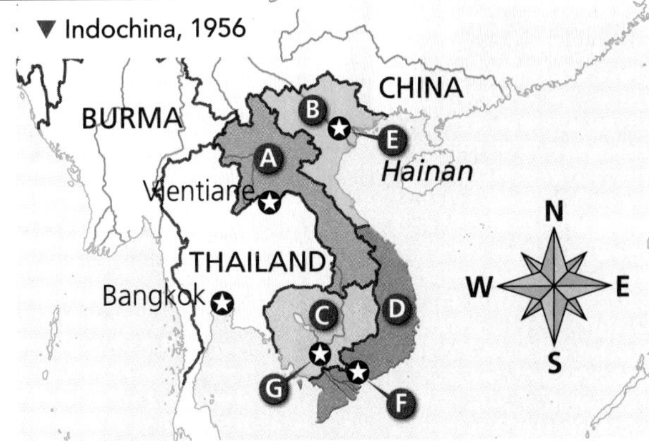

TOPIC 16

A Global Superpower Facing Change

(1975–2000)

GO ONLINE to access your digital course

- VIDEO
- AUDIO
- ETEXT
- INTERACTIVE
- WRITING
- GAMES
- WORKSHEET
- ASSESSMENT

Go back to the late 1900s,

to a time when the United States was **A GLOBAL SUPERPOWER FACING CHANGE**. See how a weak American economy grew stronger, how the collapse of the Soviet Union ended the Cold War, and how the United States responded to conflicts around the globe.

Explore The Essential Question

How should we handle conflict?

The United States, as a superpower, was drawn into dangerous and violent confrontations around the globe. How did it deal with conflict?

Unlock the Essential Question in your Active Journal.

Read

about a major shift in American political philosophy, a victory for democracy, and a series of conflicts across the globe.

Watch

NBC LEARN

BOUNCE TO ACTIVATE VIDEO

Irene Zoppi, Gulf War Veteran

Irene Zoppi describes her role as a military officer during the Persian Gulf War.

TOPIC 16

A Global Superpower Facing Change (1975–2000)

Learn more about national and global events during the last years of the 1900s by making your own map and timeline in your Active Journal.

INTERACTIVE

Topic Timeline

What happened and when?

The end of the 1900s saw major changes all over the world as the Cold War ended and democracy took root in new places. Explore the timeline to see some of what was happening.

TOPIC EVENTS

1977 Jimmy Carter becomes President.

1981 Ronald Reagan becomes President.

1970 **1980**

WORLD EVENTS

1973 Arab members of OPEC halt oil shipments to the U.S.

1985 Mikhail Gorbachev rises to power in the Soviet Union.

Topic Map

Where did change occur?

Where did new countries form when the Soviet Union crumbled? Where did new conflicts put Americans in danger?

Who will you meet?

Ronald Reagan, 40th President of the United States

Sandra Day O'Connor, first woman on the U.S. Supreme Court

Nelson Mandela, who fought to end the practice of apartheid in South Africa

1989 George H. W. Bush becomes President.

1990 East and West Germany reunite.

1991 Persian Gulf War begins.

1991 The Soviet Union breaks up.

1993 Bill Clinton becomes President.

1994 Nelson Mandela is elected president of South Africa.

1998 India and Pakistan test nuclear weapons.

1990 — 2000

Document-Based Writing Inquiry

Analyzing the Reagan Conservative Movement

Quest KICK OFF

In the **1970s** and early **1980s**, the U.S. economy suffered from high inflation. Americans struggled to pay the rising costs of essentials.

How did Reaganomics differ from liberals' and moderates' beliefs about how to achieve a healthy economy?

In this Quest, explore a range of opinions put forward in the 1980s on how to revive the economy.

▼ Ronald Reagan

1 Ask Questions

What questions would you ask politicians to get a clear picture of what they would do to improve the economy? Write your questions in your Active Journal.

2 Investigate

As you read, look for Quest CONNECTIONS that will help you understand the problems of the economy and differing points of view on how to address them. Record notes in your Active Journal.

3 Examine Primary Sources

Next, study a set of primary sources from the 1980s. They offer differing opinions about the best ways to improve the ailing economy. Record notes in your Active Journal.

Quest FINDINGS

4 Write Your Essay

Your notes and the information in the lessons will help you write an essay explaining how Reaganomics sought to improve the economy and describing the differing opinions of more moderate and liberal politicians. Get help for this task in your Active Journal.

LESSON 1

The Conservative Revolution

GET READY TO READ

START UP

Look at the photo of Ronald Reagan on the campaign trail. What promises do candidates make?

GUIDING QUESTIONS

- What challenges did the administration of President Jimmy Carter face?
- What was Ronald Reagan's agenda as President?
- How did President George H. W. Bush deal with domestic issues?
- What social and economic goals did President Bill Clinton pursue?

TAKE NOTES

Literacy Skills: Classify and Categorize

Use the graphic organizer in your Active Journal to take notes as you read the lesson.

PRACTICE VOCABULARY

Use the vocabulary activity in your Active Journal to practice the vocabulary words.

Vocabulary

- Moral Majority
- Reaganomics
- deregulation
- balanced budget
- downsizing
- NAFTA
- "Contract With America"

Academic Vocabulary

- monetary policy
- surplus

After the Nixon years, completed by Gerald Ford, Americans demanded change. Each of the next four presidents—Jimmy Carter, Ronald Reagan, George H. W. Bush, and Bill Clinton—had his own approach to meeting that demand. It was Reagan, however, who launched the most radical change—the conservative revolution.

President Carter's Administration

In 1976, Republicans nominated Ford for President. Democrats chose Jimmy Carter, the former governor of Georgia.

Carter had no experience in Washington, but used to his advantage the fact that he was a Washington outsider. He pointed out that "the vast majority of Americans . . . are also outsiders." After years of scandal in Washington, Carter's fresh face and promises of a new approach carried him to a narrow victory.

Carter's term began with a whirlwind of activity. In his first year, the new President sent Congress almost a dozen major bills.

They included reforms in the Social Security system and in the tax code. But Carter's lack of experience in Washington hurt him. Congress refused to support his legislation.

The President did not fare much better with the problem of inflation, a general increase in the level of prices. When the government tried to slow inflation, prices only kept rising. Many families had trouble paying for food, clothing, and housing.

Although Carter was a Democrat, he adopted conservative solutions to the problem of high inflation. He cut government spending and appointed Paul Volcker as chairman of the Federal Reserve. Volcker used **monetary policy** to attack inflation by reducing credit and raising interest rates.

Academic Vocabulary
monetary policy • *n.*, actions taken by a country's central bank to regulate the money supply

Carter also adopted a conservative position when he took steps toward **deregulation**, or decreased regulation, of the transportation industry. Reducing regulation increased free-market competition. In addition, new policies, such as the Airline Deregulation Act of 1978, brought lower prices for consumers.

In foreign affairs, Carter was a strong defender of human rights. The United States had signed the Helsinki Agreement just before he took office. Thirty-five nations pledged to respect basic rights such as religious freedom and freedom of speech. The United States, Carter said, should keep this pledge and not aid countries that violated human rights.

The Iranian Revolution and Hostage Crisis Even before Carter's presidency, the United States was deeply involved in conflicts in the Middle East. Iran was ruled by a shah who had U.S. support. Then, in 1979, the Iranian Revolution forced the unpopular shah to flee. A religious leader, Ayatollah Khomeini (i yuh TOH luh koh MAYN ee), took control of Iran.

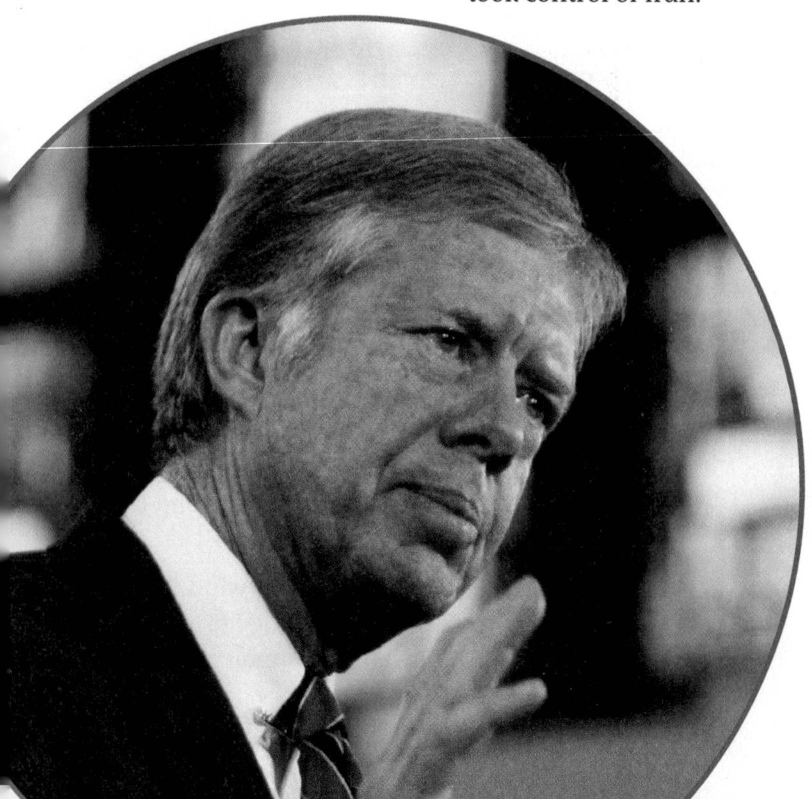

Analyze Images President Jimmy Carter, formerly governor of Georgia, attempted to use his position as a Washington "outsider" to bring change to the federal government. **Infer** Why might an "outsider" appeal to voters?

The shah had been a firm ally of the United States. The ayatollah was strongly anti-American. Where the shah had favored westernizing Iran, the new ruler wanted to enforce a strict, old-fashioned version of Islam. Neither leader, however, favored democracy.

In November 1979, President Carter let the shah enter the United States for medical treatment. In response, Iranian revolutionaries seized the American embassy and took 53 Americans hostage. The hostages were not freed until January 1981. The hostage crisis poisoned American relations with Iran for decades.

Analyze Images During the energy crisis of 1979, gas was in short supply in the United States. American drivers found themselves waiting in long lines at gas stations. **Cause and Effect** Do you think the crisis changed Americans' driving habits? Why or why not?

It also affected domestic politics. During the 1980 presidential election campaign, conservatives and Republicans criticized Carter for not successfully defending the overseas interests of the United States.

An Energy Crisis The Iranian Revolution seriously disrupted oil production in Iran, which had been a major source of oil on the world market. Oil prices shot up, and Americans began to line up in cars at gas stations to buy gasoline, fearing that shortages would develop. Panic buying did lead to shortages in some places. Many Americans blamed President Carter's foreign policy for the gas lines and shortages.

After Iranians took Americans hostage in late 1979, Carter blocked any further oil imports from Iran. Then, in September 1980, war broke out between Iran and its neighbor, Iraq. Both countries had been major oil producers. The war further reduced world oil supplies and kept gas prices high. The energy crisis undermined Americans' confidence and led many Americans to oppose Carter's re-election in 1980.

INTERACTIVE

Reacting to Crises Under Carter

READING CHECK **Identify Supporting Details** What conservative policies did Jimmy Carter adopt during his presidency to address economic problems?

Quest CONNECTIONS

During Jimmy Carter's presidency, what was the key problem with the economy? How did Carter try to fix that problem?

What Did the Conservative Movement Demand?

By the election of 1980, many Americans had come to believe that high taxes and "big government" were causing national problems. "Government," Ronald Reagan said, "is not the solution to our problems, government is the problem." These ideas contrasted sharply with the dominant ideas of the 1960s and 1970s.

Analyze Images A campaign button depicts the 1980 Republican candidates for President and Vice President, Ronald Reagan and George H. W. Bush. **Infer** How important are campaign slogans?

Smaller Federal Government Since the 1930s, the federal government had grown steadily. President Franklin D. Roosevelt had begun this trend to help people through the Great Depression. Harry Truman, John Kennedy, and Lyndon Johnson continued the expansion. These liberal presidents believed that government should play a large role in managing the economy and providing social programs.

Beginning in the 1960s, a conservative movement warned against growing federal power. Arizona Senator Barry Goldwater led the way. He argued for a smaller government nearer the people.

Primary Source

"Our towns and our cities, then our counties and our states, then our regional compacts—and only then the national government. That, let me remind you, is the ladder of liberty built by decentralized power."

—Barry Goldwater, Speech at Republican National Convention, July 16, 1964

By the 1980s, conservatives dominated the Republican Party. Led by Ronald Reagan, they believed that federal social programs had become too costly and that federal regulations kept businesses from growing. State and local governments, they argued, were closest to the people and should decide what regulations were needed.

Social and Political Causes After decades of social change, many conservatives called for a return to traditional values. These included religion, family, and patriotism.

Reflecting the renewed emphasis on traditional values, evangelical Christian churches grew rapidly during the 1970s and 1980s. Evangelicals stressed personal conversion and sought to convert others. Evangelical ministers used television to widen their audience.

Many evangelicals took an active role in conservative political causes. In 1979, the Reverend Jerry Falwell founded the **Moral Majority**. The group aided political candidates who favored conservative religious goals, such as a constitutional amendment to allow organized prayer in public schools. In 1980, strong support from the Moral Majority and the other conservative religious organizations helped put Reagan in the White House.

READING CHECK **Summarize** Why did conservatives support a more limited federal government?

The Reagan and Bush Presidencies

Reagan was a handsome man with a relaxed, friendly air. He had been a movie star before winning election as governor of California. His skill at presenting ideas in terms that ordinary people could understand earned him the nickname the Great Communicator.

In 1980, Reagan defeated Jimmy Carter for President. He was swept into office on a conservative tide. After an era of protests, high prices, and the humiliation of the Iran hostage crisis, voters embraced Reagan's promise to "make America great again." He was re-elected in 1984 by an even wider margin.

Reagan's Economic Program The new President's first priority was his economic program, often called **Reaganomics**. He persuaded Congress to cut taxes. Reagan hoped that taxpayers would use the extra money to buy more and save more. Buying more would spur business growth. Saving more would allow banks to invest in new business ventures. Reagan also promised to cut federal spending to reduce the size of government.

The President persuaded Congress to slow down spending increases on social programs, such as welfare and aid to education. Critics charged that those cuts hurt the poor and children. Supporters responded that Reagan was just trimming programs that did not work.

A third goal of Reaganomics was deregulation. Reagan sped up an earlier trend toward the reduction of restrictions on businesses. He opposed all laws, for example, that required industries to install expensive antipollution devices.

After a slow start, the economy was booming by 1984. When Reagan left office, there were 16 million more jobs, while inflation had been held in check.

Quest CONNECTIONS

Look at the graphic organizer. Which of the goals relate to improving the economy?

Analyze Charts One of the conservative goals listed was to reduce the size of the federal government. **Use Visual Information** Choose one of the other goals in this chart that might also have reduced the size of government, and explain how it might have done so.

The Conservative Movement

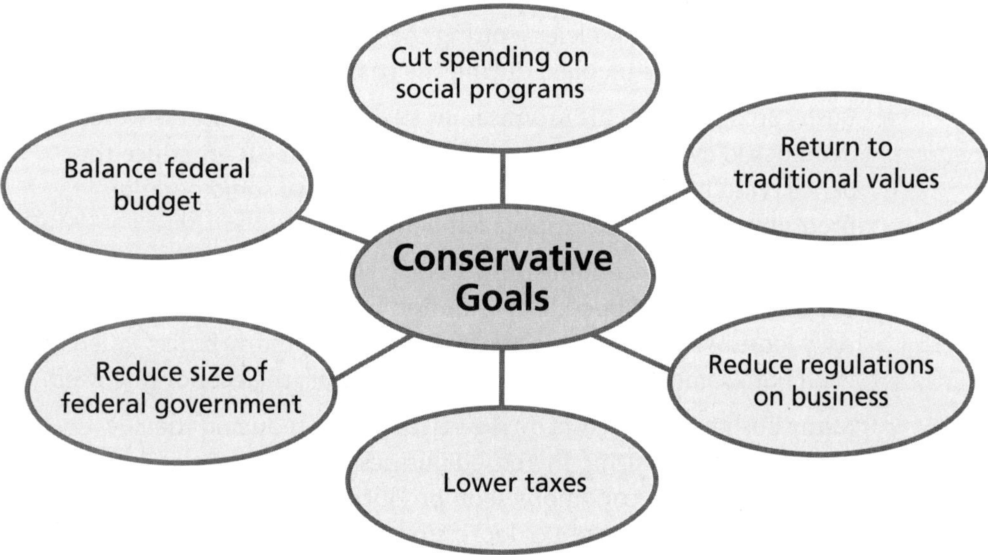

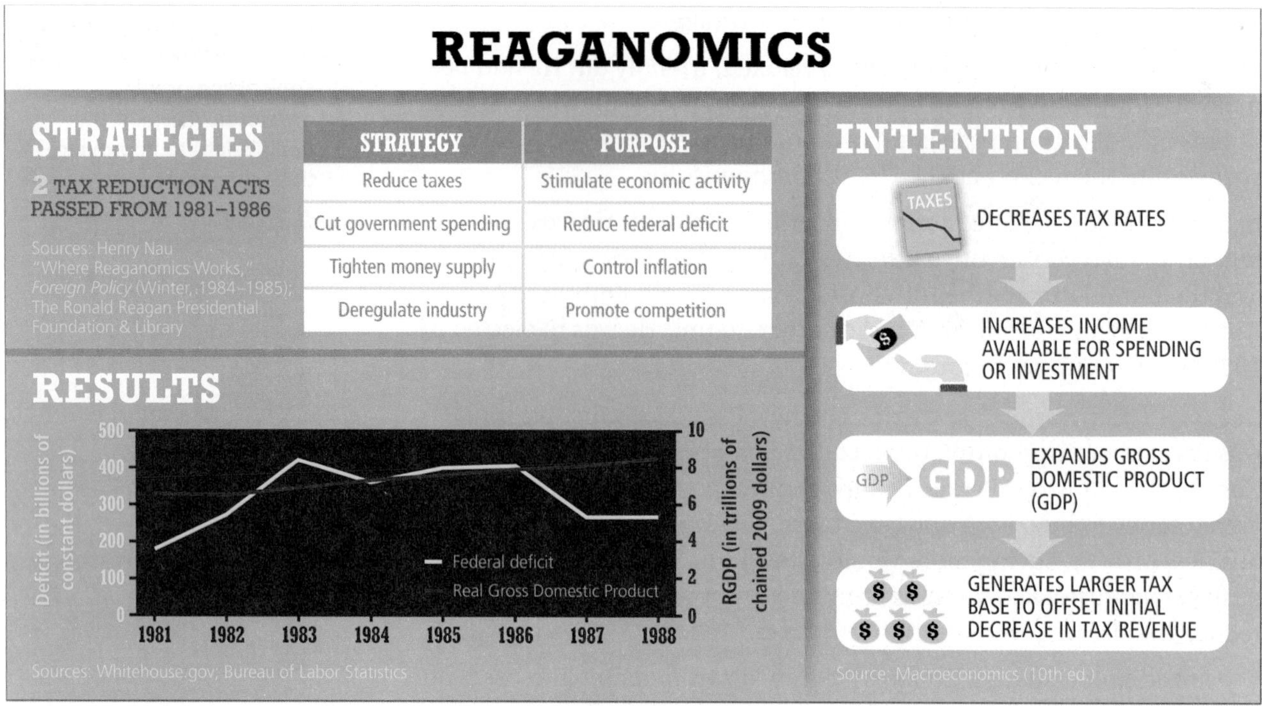

STRATEGY	PURPOSE
Reduce taxes	Stimulate economic activity
Cut government spending	Reduce federal deficit
Tighten money supply	Control inflation
Deregulate industry	Promote competition

Analyze Images These graphs summarize how Reaganomics was intended to affect the federal deficit. **Infer** Was this result achieved?

The Budget Deficit Another of Reagan's goals—a balanced budget—proved harder to achieve. A **balanced budget** requires the government to spend only as much as it takes in. While Reagan cut social spending, he sharply increased military spending. As military spending rose and taxes fell, the budget deficit soared. For 1986, the deficit jumped to $240 billion, more than twice as high as under any previous President.

Still, the economy continued to expand, and Reagan remained popular. For many Americans, he had succeeded in restoring faith in the presidency, which had been so badly tarnished in previous years.

Bush's Economic Troubles Reagan's Vice President, George H. W. Bush, won a big victory in 1988. Bush vowed to continue Reagan's economic policies, cutting the deficit without raising taxes. "Read my lips," he pledged during the campaign. "No new taxes."

Bush could not keep his promise. By 1990, he and Congress were deadlocked over which government programs to cut to reduce the deficit. Finally, Bush agreed to raise taxes to save some popular programs. Many conservatives felt betrayed.

As taxes rose, the economy grew weaker. To make matters worse, a banking crisis developed. Deregulation had led some banks to make risky loans. When those loans were not repaid, many banks failed. With banks unable or unwilling to make loans, the economy slowed.

Many businesses cut costs by **downsizing**, or reducing their workforces. Downsizing increased business profits, but also increased joblessness. These conditions soon produced a recession, an economic slump that is milder than a depression. The recession continued for more than a year.

Conservative Supreme Court Justices Reagan and Bush appointed a total of five justices to the Supreme Court. (One of Reagan's choices, Sandra Day O'Connor, was the first woman to serve on the Court.) The new justices were more conservative than the justices that they replaced.

The more conservative Court placed new limits on the rights of suspected criminals, as well as on the right of prisoners to appeal convictions. The Court made it harder for workers to win job discrimination cases. It also reduced busing, which some school districts had used since the 1960s to achieve racial integration in public schools.

How did economic policies pursued by President Bush contribute to a worsening of the economy?

READING CHECK **Identify Supporting Details** What were the three major ideas upon which Reaganomics was based?

President Clinton Turns Toward the Center

Bush faced a stiff re-election challenge in 1992. Recession and unemployment continued. Bickering between Congress and the President left voters unhappy with Washington politics. The Democratic nominee, Arkansas governor Bill Clinton, promised more government involvement in areas ignored by Reagan and Bush.

On Election Day, voters signaled their dissatisfaction. Only 38 percent voted for Bush. Although he received less than half the popular vote—43 percent—Clinton won the highest number of votes. The remaining 19 percent went to Ross Perot, a Texas billionaire who ran as an independent candidate.

BIOGRAPHY

5 Things to Know About

SANDRA DAY O'CONNOR

First woman to serve as a Supreme Court Justice (1930–)

- She spent much of her childhood on her family's cattle ranch in southeastern Arizona, where her chores included branding cattle.
- As an Arizona legislator, she became the first woman in the nation to serve as the majority leader of a state senate.
- Her appointment to the Supreme Court by Ronald Reagan in 1981 was confirmed by the U.S. Senate, 99–0.
- After retiring from the Court in 2006, she traveled around the country speaking and promoting civic education for young Americans.
- In 2009, she received the Presidential Medal of Freedom, the nation's highest civilian honor, from President Barack Obama.

Critical Thinking What impact do you think O'Connor's "firsts" had on young women at the time?

INTERACTIVE

Compare Four Presidents

Improvements and Setbacks President Clinton followed a middle-of-the-road course. On the one hand, he moved cautiously when he persuaded Congress to increase some taxes and reduce spending. Yet this caution brought success. Under Clinton, for the first time in over 40 years, the federal deficit began a steady decline.

On the other hand, Clinton pushed for bold reform of the healthcare system. In 1994, some 37 million Americans had no health insurance. Clinton called for a national system of health insurance for almost all Americans. After heated debate, however, Congress defeated the plan. Many Americans worried that it would be too costly and involve the government too deeply in their lives.

To many Americans, the struggle over healthcare showed that Washington was paralyzed. Democrats controlled both Congress and the White House, yet the President could not get his own plan enacted.

Expanding Trade During the term of President Bush, the United States had negotiated with Mexico and Canada to conclude the North American Free Trade Agreement (**NAFTA**). Bush signed the agreement in October 1992, but he was unable to persuade Congress to ratify the agreement before he left the White House in January 1993.

In the United States opponents argued that, by allowing free trade with Mexico, where pay was much lower and there were fewer laws protecting the environment, the agreement would result in American jobs leaving the country. Among those opposing NAFTA were much of the labor movement. Many U.S. business leaders, however, supported NAFTA, arguing that it would open up markets for U.S. products.

When Bush signed NAFTA in October 1992, he was in the midst of a presidential campaign against Bill Clinton. Clinton agreed to support

BIOGRAPHY

5 Things to Know About BILL CLINTON

42nd president of the United States (1946–)

- He was born William Jefferson Clinton in Hope, Arkansas. His father died before he was born, and he was raised largely by his mother and grandmother.
- Young Clinton played the saxophone in his high school band.
- At age 16, while visiting Washington, D.C., he shook hands with President John F. Kennedy. This meeting solidified Clinton's dream to be President.
- His wife, Hillary Clinton, helped run his election campaigns and later ran for President herself.
- He was the first Democratic president since Franklin Roosevelt to win election to two terms in office.

Critical Thinking Why do you think shaking hands with President Kennedy made such a big impression on Bill Clinton?

NAFTA if provisions were added to the agreement protecting the environment and labor rights.

Even after Canada and Mexico agreed to those changes, however, opponents of the agreement put up a fight. They believed the changes did not go far enough. In the end, though, Clinton convinced Congress to support the agreement.

NAFTA took effect on January 1, 1994. It opened the markets of all three North American countries to the free movement of trade and investment across borders. After the agreement took effect, trade among the three countries increased dramatically.

Analyze Images President Clinton signs a bill into law during a ceremony in the White House Rose Garden. **Summarize** What is the procedure for a bill to become a law?

An Economic Boom After Clinton took office in 1993, the U.S. economy recovered strongly from recession. Continuing for eight years, this was the longest uninterrupted period of economic growth in U.S. history.

The economy's strong performance helped Clinton win re-election by a large margin in 1996.

Historians disagree on the reasons for the boom. Some believe that Clinton's effort to trim the federal budget deficit strengthened the economy. Others point to sharply lower energy prices. Still others believe that economic growth was largely the result of using computers to make American workers more productive.

Clinton and the Conservatives Despite the improving economy, voter frustration with Clinton's healthcare plans helped Republicans win a resounding victory in the 1994 congressional elections. For the first time since the 1950s, Republicans held a majority in both the Senate and the House of Representatives.

Newt Gingrich of Georgia became Speaker of the House. Under his leadership, House Republicans drew up a "**Contract With America**." This set of proposed laws included reducing social spending and environmental regulations and slashing taxes.

The President attacked many of the proposals as unfair to poor and middle-class Americans. After a bitter fight, he compromised with Congress on a plan to balance the federal budget by the year 2002. In fact, the economy grew so strongly that in 1998 the government reported a budget **surplus**, in which income exceeded spending. Over the next two years, the surplus grew even larger.

Academic Vocabulary
surplus • *n.*, an excess, or an extra amount

Congress and Clinton also compromised on welfare reform. The government limited the length of time a person could receive welfare benefits. In this way, it hoped to encourage unemployed Americans to find jobs.

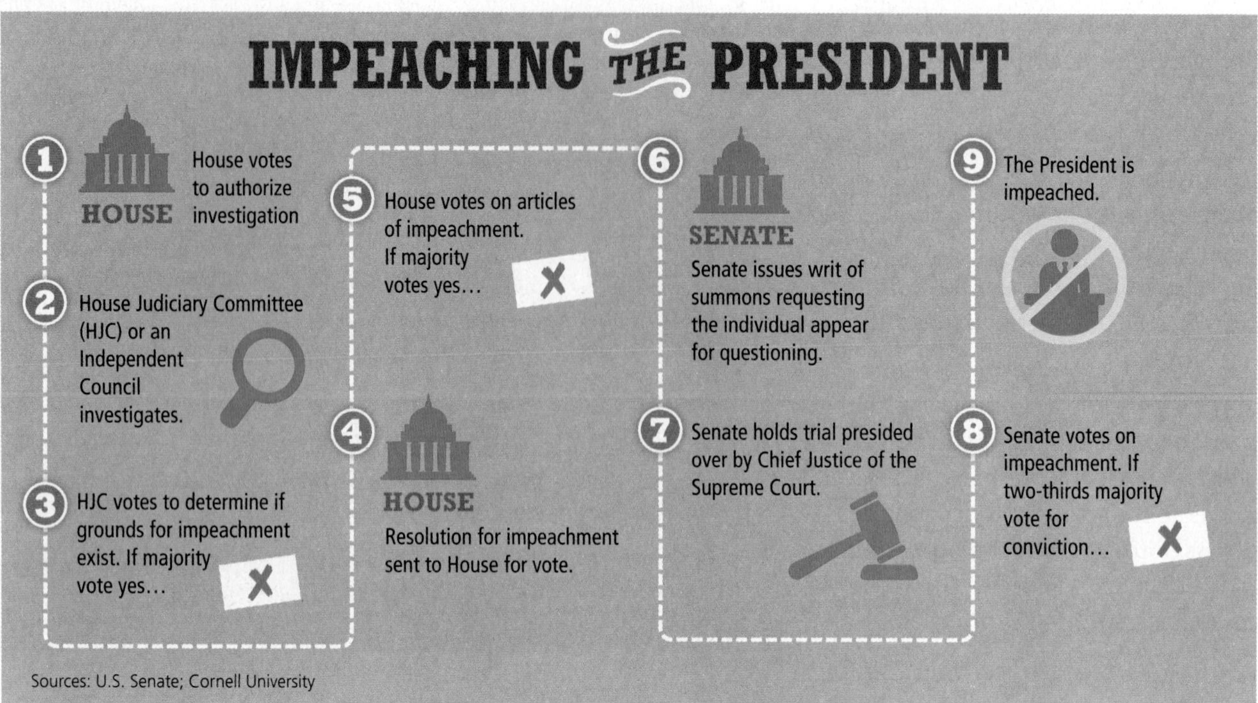

Analyze Images
Impeachment is a multi-step process. **Cite Evidence** How are checks and balances involved in the impeachment process?

Impeachment and Acquittal Controversy engulfed Clinton's second term. Federal prosecutors investigated Clinton for real estate dealings while he was governor of Arkansas. Prosecutors found no evidence of lawbreaking. However, they did accuse the President of lying under oath about an improper relationship with a White House intern.

Amid heated debate, the House voted to impeach President Clinton. For only the second time in history, the Senate tried a President. In February 1999, the Senate voted to acquit the President, and he continued in office until the end of his second term, in 2001.

READING CHECK **Identify Supporting Details** What factors encouraged economic growth during the Clinton administration?

Lesson Check

Practice Vocabulary

1. Did **Reaganomics** lead to a **balanced budget**? Explain.
2. What roles did Presidents Bush and Clinton play in the passage of **NAFTA**?

Critical Thinking and Writing

3. **Understand Effects** What was the Iran hostage crisis, and how did it affect President Carter's political image?
4. **Draw Conclusions** What impact did religion have on American politics in the 1980s?
5. **Identify Implied Main Ideas** What was the "Contract With America," and how did President Clinton respond to it?
6. **Writing Workshop: Develop a Clear Thesis** At the end of this topic, you will write an essay explaining what you've learned about the Cold War and the collapse of the Soviet Union. Do a little background research now—enough to decide on an interesting thesis, or central message. In your Active Journal, write this thesis in one or two sentences that clearly communicate your main idea.

LESSON 2

The End of the Cold War

GET READY TO READ

START UP

Look at the photograph of the Berlin Wall, long a symbol of the Cold War. Write down several things you already know about the Berlin Wall. How did it become a symbol of the *end* of the Cold War?

GUIDING QUESTIONS

- What event caused Cold War tensions to increase, starting in 1979?
- Why did communism fall in Eastern Europe and the Soviet Union?
- How did the end of the Cold War affect life in the United States?

TAKE NOTES

Literacy Skills: Sequence

Use the graphic organizer in your Active Journal to take notes as you read the lesson.

PRACTICE VOCABULARY

Use the vocabulary activity in your Active Journal to practice the vocabulary words.

Vocabulary		Academic Vocabulary
Star Wars	*glasnost*	condemn
Solidarity	summit meeting	verify
martial law		

The policy of détente pursued by Presidents Nixon, Ford, and Carter opened the door to trade and friendlier relations with the Soviet Union. The hostility that marked the Cold War seemed to be easing. Then, near the end of Carter's presidency, the Soviet Union took an action that the United States could not accept.

What Led to the End of Détente?

Efforts to reduce tensions during the Cold War had improved relations between the United States and the Soviet Union. However, this policy of détente ended suddenly in 1979. In December, troops from the Soviet Union invaded Afghanistan, a mountainous nation on the Soviet Union's southern border. Soviet troops were sent there to help a pro-Soviet government.

Opposing Soviet Action in Afghanistan

The United States **condemned** the Soviet invasion of Afghanistan. President Carter withdrew the SALT II Treaty from Senate approval hearings. The United States also refused to take part in the 1980 Olympic Games in Moscow.

Analyze Images The United States supported Afghan rebels such as these, seen here standing atop a Russian helicopter they had captured. **Use Visual Information** How, do you think, did the rebels succeed in resisting the Soviet military?

Despite worldwide criticism, Soviet troops remained in Afghanistan for ten years. They suffered heavy losses as Afghan rebels, supplied by the United States, battled the Communist government. The war in Afghanistan became so costly for the Soviets that it weakened the Soviet economy, and Soviet forces could not remain. In 1989, the Soviets were forced to pull all troops out of Afghanistan.

Reagan Reacts Ronald Reagan declared that the Soviet Union was "the focus of evil in the modern world." He called on Americans to "oppose it with all our might."

Reagan wanted to deal with the Soviets from a position of strength. To achieve this, he persuaded Congress to increase military spending by more than $100 billion during his first five years in office. His Strategic Defense Initiative (SDI) also called for the development of a new weapons system that Reagan hoped could destroy Soviet missiles from ground and from space. SDI was nicknamed **Star Wars** after a popular movie. Only the early stages of research were completed.

During Reagan's first term in office, the two superpowers continued to view each other with deep mistrust. In December 1981, with Soviet backing, Poland's Communist government cracked down on **Solidarity**, an independent labor union. Solidarity members had gone on strike at Polish shipyards to demand labor reforms.

Under Soviet pressure, the Polish government imposed **martial law**, or emergency military rule, on the country. President Reagan condemned the move. He urged the Soviets to allow Poland to restore basic human rights. The United States also put economic pressure on Poland to end martial law.

Academic Vocabulary
condemn • *v.*, to state in a strong way that something is bad or wrong

READING CHECK **Identify Supporting Details** Identify three details that support the claim that Reagan took a strong stand against the Soviet Union.

The Soviet Empire Crumbles

Cracks began to appear in the Soviet empire in the mid-1980s. Economic problems grew in part because of the huge sums the Soviets were spending on their military to try to keep up with the United States, which had a much stronger free-market economy. The Soviets had little money left for producing consumer goods. Soviet citizens stood in line for hours waiting for poorly made products. The Communist system was not working. The time was ripe for reform.

INTERACTIVE

Before and After: The Berlin Wall

Gorbachev Breaks With the Past In 1985 a new Soviet leader, Mikhail Gorbachev (mee kah EEL GOR buh chawf), rose to power. Gorbachev believed that only major reforms would allow the Soviet system to survive.

Gorbachev backed ***glasnost***, the Russian term for speaking out openly. *Glasnost,* Gorbachev hoped, would lead citizens to find solutions to pressing economic and social problems. This new openness was a break with the past, when any criticism of government policies had been quickly silenced.

Academic Vocabulary
verify • *v.,* to confirm that something is true; to fact-check

Improving Relations Gorbachev realized that he could not solve the Soviet Union's economic problems without cutting military spending sharply. To do so, he had to have better relations with the United States.

President Reagan and Gorbachev met at several summit meetings. A **summit meeting** is a conference between the highest-ranking officials of different nations. Reagan agreed to these meetings because he approved of Gorbachev's new policy of openness.

In 1987, the two leaders signed an arms control pact called the Intermediate Nuclear Force (INF) Treaty. In it, both nations agreed to get rid of their stockpiles of short- and medium-range missiles. To prevent cheating, each side would have the right to inspect the other's missile sites. Reagan summarized this aspect of the pact by reciting his favorite Russian proverb, "Trust, but **verify**."

Two years later, Gorbachev withdrew Soviet troops from Afghanistan. This action removed another barrier to cooperation between the superpowers.

Change Comes to Eastern Europe For more than 50 years, the Communist governments of Eastern Europe had banned any open discussion of political issues.

Analyze Images Mikhail Gorbachev (left) and Ronald Reagan made history when they signed agreements on human rights, nuclear arms reduction, and security. **Infer** Why would these agreements be beneficial to the entire world?

Quick Activity

Guess the mystery person. Take the "Who Am I?" quiz in your Active Journal.

As in the Soviet Union, only one political party, the Communist Party, was allowed to win elections. People were denied many basic rights, such as freedom of speech.

Now, in the late 1980s, Eastern European governments could no longer control the rising demands of their people for democratic and economic reforms. With opposition so widespread, most of those governments did not dare to use military force to oppose change. Furthermore, the Soviet Union did not have the power to suppress these protests. It was too busy trying to solve its own problems.

In 1989, Poland held its first free elections in 50 years. Polish voters rejected Communist candidates in favor of those put up by the trade union, Solidarity. Solidarity leader Lech Walesa (LEK vah WEN sah) had once been jailed by the Communists for almost a year. After the elections, he became head of a new Polish government.

One by one, Communist governments fell in Czechoslovakia, Hungary, Bulgaria, and Albania. In Romania, a violent revolt toppled Nicolae Ceausescu, the country's longtime Communist dictator.

In East Germany, protests in 1989 drove the Communists from power. The government was forced to open gates in the Berlin Wall when citizens demanded to be let through. By 1990, Germany was reunited under a democratic government.

Analyze Images In November 1989, the Berlin Wall fell. Here, jubilant East Germans rush past Checkpoint Charlie, the U.S. army's control point at the entrance to West Berlin. **Infer** Why do you think the East German military did not act against the people who took down the Wall?

The Soviet Union Dissolves

SOURCE: *The CIA World Factbook*

Analyze Charts After the first nations declared independence from the Soviet Union, the rest followed quickly. **Draw Conclusions** Why did the dissolution of the Soviet Union speed up in late 1991?

The Soviet Union Breaks Apart The Soviet Union was made up of 15 different republics held together by a strong central government in Moscow. Under Soviet rule, the republics had few powers. All important policy decisions were made in Moscow. Moscow was also the capital of the republic of Russia, containing most of the land and people of the Soviet Union.

By 1990, resentment of Moscow was high in the non-Russian republics. Some of their people demanded self-rule. Meanwhile, Gorbachev allowed political parties to form. For nearly 70 years, the Soviet Union had been a one-party Communist state.

Hard-line Communist officials were outraged. A group of them sent troops to oust Gorbachev. Their power grab did not last long. A Moscow politician who had rejected the Communist Party, Boris Yeltsin, led thousands of Russians in protest. They surrounded the Parliament building and forced troops to pull back.

As a Communist rejected by his own defeated party, Gorbachev was weakened. In the months that followed, republic after republic declared its independence from the Soviet Union. In late 1991, Gorbachev resigned. By then, the Soviet Union had collapsed.

Fifteen new nations emerged from the old Soviet Union. Of these, Russia was the largest and most powerful. It began the difficult task of building a new economy based on a free-market system. In a free market, individuals decide what and how much to produce and sell. Under communism, the government had made such economic decisions.

Promoting Democracy in Eastern Europe The United States and Western European nations provided economic aid to Russia, the other former Soviet republics, and Eastern European nations. American experts offered advice to political and business leaders in Russia and Eastern Europe on the free-market system.

The United States was eager to see stable, democratic governments emerge in the old Communist world. It also hoped that the new nations would become trading partners.

Meanwhile, nations formerly under Soviet domination in Eastern Europe sought to protect their new freedom. Former East Germany left the Warsaw Pact and became part of the North Atlantic Treaty Organization, or NATO, when Germany reunified in 1990. As a member of NATO, the United States promised to defend other members. In 1999, President Clinton welcomed Poland, the Czech Republic, and Hungary into NATO.

READING CHECK **Summarize** How did the United States respond to the collapse of the Soviet Union?

The Aftermath of the Cold War

For almost 50 years, the Cold War deeply affected American life. Students in the 1950s and 1960s practiced crouching under their desks in case of atomic attack. Hundreds of thousands of Americans went off to fight in the Korean and Vietnam wars. About 112,000 of them did not return.

The Costs of the Cold War Americans cheered the end of the Cold War and the emergence of democratic governments in Eastern Europe. Victory was costly, though. From 1946 to 1990, the United States spent more than $6 trillion on national defense. The development of nuclear weapons and the arms race had created new dangers for the world. During and after the Cold War, other nations besides the superpowers worked to develop their own nuclear weapons.

The Cold War had divided Americans at times. The search for Communists in the 1950s had created an atmosphere of fear and suspicion. The Vietnam War had split the American public in an often bitter debate. Many Americans greeted the end of the Cold War with relief.

Analyze Charts The Cold War had many effects around the world. **Use Visual Information** How did the Cold War affect U.S. military power?

Causes		Effects
• Soviet Union takes control of Eastern European nations. • Communism gains influence in developing nations. • Western powers fear Soviet expansion.	→ THE COLD WAR →	• Arms race between United States and Soviet Union results in heavy military spending. • Western powers and Soviet Union create separate military alliances. • Armed conflicts erupt in Korea and Vietnam. • United States and Soviet Union compete for influence in developing nations.

The Peace Dividend The collapse of the Soviet Union allowed President Clinton to cut military spending. Tens of thousands of U.S. troops stationed in Germany and other European countries to defend against a possible Soviet attack were brought home. U.S. military bases were closed.

The money saved by reducing military spending, sometimes called a "peace dividend," helped Clinton wipe out the federal budget deficit. Some economists believe that it contributed to the economic boom during the Clinton years.

There was another peace dividend that could not be measured in dollar terms. This was the feeling, after decades of living in fear of another world war, that the United States was free at last from serious external threats. This feeling of ease was short-lived, however. During the 1990s, the United States faced a number of new challenges around the world.

Analyze Images Members of the U.S. Army's 1st Armored Division fall out for the final time in Germany. The Division had been stationed in Germany from 1945 to 1994, when they were reassigned to the United States. **Infer** Why were military units such as this no longer needed in Germany after the Cold War?

READING CHECK **Identify Main Ideas** What were the costs of fighting the Cold War?

Lesson Check

Practice Vocabulary

1. In 1981, the Soviet-backed Polish government declared **martial law** as a means of dealing with a strike by **Solidarity**. How did the United States react?
2. Why can you be sure both Reagan and Gorbachev would have attended a **summit meeting** between the United States and the Soviet Union?

Critical Thinking and Writing

3. **Draw Conclusions** Why might Gorbachev's policy of ***glasnost*** have suggested to Americans that the Soviet Union might be open to a closer relationship?
4. **Sequence** How did Gorbachev's policy of openness trigger changes in Eastern Europe that eventually led to the collapse of the Soviet Union?
5. **Generate Explanations** Why were Americans optimistic about the country's future at the end of the Cold War?
6. **Writing Workshop: Support Thesis with Details** To support your thesis on the Cold War, you must find detailed information in reliable books, journal articles, and online sites. Write the details in your Active Journal and organize them in a way that best develops your thesis.

Primary Sources

Ronald Reagan, "Tear Down This Wall"

Near the end of the Cold War, on June 12, 1987, President Ronald Reagan visited West Berlin. Standing just outside the Berlin Wall, he gave an impassioned speech. He directed part of it at the Soviet leader, Mikhail Gorbachev.

◀ President Ronald Reagan raises his hand to thank the crowd after his speech.

Yet it is here in Berlin where the wall emerges most clearly; here, cutting across your city, where the news photo and the television screen have imprinted this brutal division of a continent upon the mind of the world. Standing before the Brandenburg Gate,① every man is a German, separated from his fellow men. Every man is a Berliner, forced to look upon a scar. . . .

We hear much from Moscow about a new policy of reform and openness.② Some political prisoners have been released. Certain foreign news broadcasts are no longer being jammed.③ Some economic enterprises have been permitted to operate with greater freedom from state control.

Are these the beginnings of profound changes in the Soviet state? Or are they token gestures, intended to raise false hopes in the West, or to strengthen the Soviet system without changing it? We welcome change and openness; for we believe that freedom and security go together, that the advance of human liberty can only strengthen the cause of world peace. There is one sign the Soviets can make that would be unmistakable, that would advance dramatically the cause of freedom and peace.

General Secretary Gorbachev, if you seek peace, if you seek prosperity for the Soviet Union and Eastern Europe, if you seek liberalization: Come here to this gate! Mr. Gorbachev, open this gate! Mr. Gorbachev, tear down this wall!

Reading and Vocabulary Support

① When it was built more than 200 years ago, the Brandenburg Gate was one of 18 entryways into the walled city of Berlin.

② What policy is Reagan referring to?

③ To keep people in Communist countries from hearing news broadcasts coming in from the West, the government would broadcast its own signals on the same wavelength as those coming in—a tactic known as jamming.

Analyzing Primary Sources

Use the primary source and your own knowledge of the Cold War to answer the following questions.

1. **Express Ideas Clearly** What did Reagan mean when he said, "Standing before the Brandenburg Gate, every man is a German, separated from his fellow men"?
2. **Generate Explanations** The Berlin Wall was built by the East German government. Why did Reagan direct his demands at Gorbachev?

Regional Conflicts

GET READY TO READ

START UP

South Africa experienced great change during this time. What other nations experienced upheaval?

GUIDING QUESTIONS

- How did the end of the Cold War change America's role in the world?
- How did the United States help promote democracy around the world?
- Why did the United States intervene in conflicts around the world?

TAKE NOTES

Literacy Skills: Summarize

Use the graphic organizer in your Active Journal to take notes as you read the lesson.

PRACTICE VOCABULARY

Use the vocabulary activity in your Active Journal to practice the vocabulary words.

Vocabulary		Academic Vocabulary
Strategic Arms Reduction Treaty	OPEC	foster
mediator	Camp David Accords	fraud
apartheid	PLO	
sanction		

The Soviet Union split apart in 1991. The breakup brought an end to the Cold War. It also left the United States as the world's lone superpower.

A Post–Cold War World

Americans debated their function in the post–Cold War world. Some people wanted to reduce the role of the United States in world affairs. "In the post–Cold War world, we will no longer require our people to carry an unfair burden for the rest of humanity," said Representative Dana Rohrabacher.

Others argued that the nation must not retreat from the world. They thought that the United States had a responsibility to use its power wisely. "The United States must lead, period," declared Speaker of the House Newt Gingrich.

Neither President George H. W. Bush nor President Bill Clinton reduced U.S. engagement around the world. Both believed that **fostering** freedom and democracy abroad would only strengthen the United States at home.

Academic Vocabulary
foster • *v.*, to encourage something to develop

INTERACTIVE
Nuclear Arms Reductions

Disarmament As the former Soviet Union collapsed, the world faced a menacing challenge, the spread of nuclear weapons. The United States and Russia still had thousands of nuclear missiles in their possession. Other nations were developing nuclear weapons, too.

The United States and the old Soviet Union had already agreed to several treaties reducing nuclear arms. In 1991, they signed the most important agreement yet, the **Strategic Arms Reduction Treaty**, or START. Even more reductions followed in 1993.

How Did Nuclear Weapons Spread? Despite such progress, a new arms race loomed. In 1970, the Nuclear Nonproliferation Treaty came into force. (*Nonproliferation* means "stopping the spread of something.") Under the treaty, nuclear powers such as the United States promised to reduce their stock of nuclear weapons and not to spread nuclear weapon technology to other nations. Nations without nuclear weapons promised not to develop them.

A few countries, including Israel, India, and Pakistan, never agreed to this treaty. According to U.S. government sources, Israel developed nuclear weapons in the late 1960s; however, Israel has never confirmed this.

In 1998, India confirmed the fears of other nations when it announced that it had conducted five nuclear tests. Two weeks later, Pakistan, its neighbor and deadly rival, exploded five nuclear devices of its own. World leaders saw the tests as the beginning of a dangerous new arms race.

President Clinton called for economic sanctions against both India and Pakistan. **Sanctions** are measures aimed at making a country change its policy. The sanctions had little effect. Pakistan was later found to have shared nuclear weapons technology with other countries, including North Korea.

READING CHECK **Identify Main Ideas** Why did the United States promote nuclear disarmament and nonproliferation?

Analyze Images After the United States, several other nations developed and tested nuclear weapons. **Use Visual Information** Of those shown, which nations were associated with the West?

Nuclear Proliferation, 1940–Present

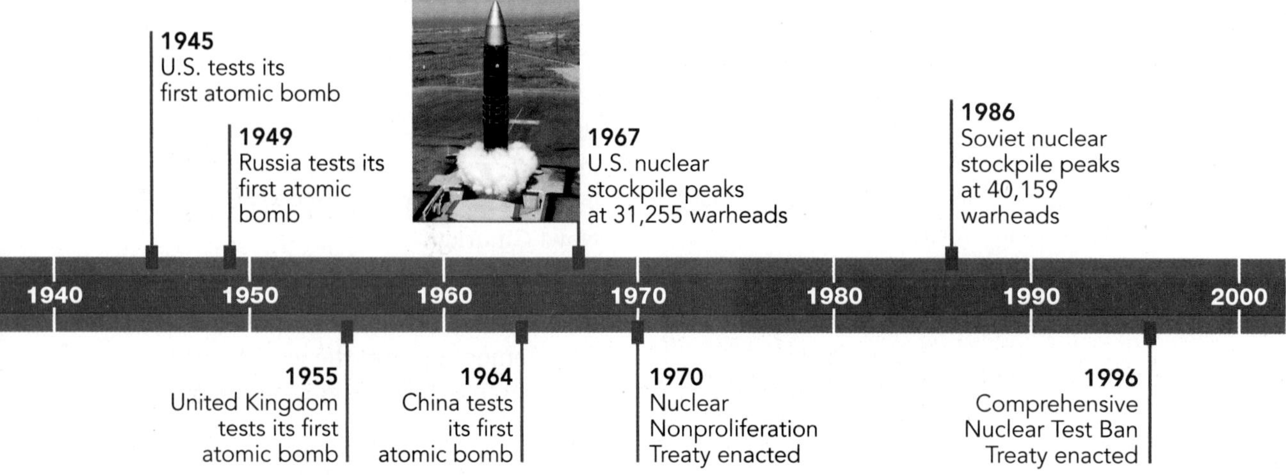

SOURCE: Washington *Post*, Brookings Institute, Arms Control Association

Analyze Images Pro-democracy protests in China were stopped by the government, but not before images like this reached the rest of the world. **Infer** What does this image tell about the confrontation between the protestors and government forces?

What Gains Did Democracy Make Around the Globe?

The efforts of Presidents Bush and Clinton to promote global democracy supported a process that was already under way. Political freedom was spreading across the globe. With it came economic freedom, including the development of free markets with less interference from the state. In the last years of the 20th century, the United States encouraged both of these trends. American leadership met with both failures and successes.

American leadership took many forms. Sometimes the United States worked to influence foreign governments through quiet diplomacy or economic pressure. Sometimes it acted as a mediator. A **mediator** is an agent that helps conflicting parties come to an agreement. Occasionally the United States used military force, often in cooperation with other nations.

Where Did Democracy Take Root in Asia? In 1986, thousands of Filipinos protested the rule of dictator Ferdinand Marcos. They accused Marcos of **fraud** in a recent presidential election.

Proclaiming "people power," they refused to recognize Marcos as president. After weeks of demonstrations, the Philippine army joined the demonstrators. Marcos fled. The United States backed Corazon Aquino, the woman who had run against him. During the 1990s, the United States continued to provide economic aid to support the young Filipino democracy.

Academic Vocabulary

fraud • *n.*, deception that is meant to lead to personal or financial gain

Analyze Images As the Cuban economy faltered, thousands of Cubans fled to the United States. **Cite Evidence** What effect did the fall of the Soviet Union have on Cuba?

What Reforms Were Made in China? After President Nixon's historic visit to China, many hoped that the Communist nation would begin to reform. During the 1980s, China did begin to build a free-market economy. However, Chinese leaders refused to accept political reforms.

In 1989, students and workers launched a bold campaign to bring democracy to China. Hundreds of thousands gathered at Tiananmen Square in the nation's capital, Beijing. However, the army crushed the demonstrations. Many people were killed or arrested.

President George H. W. Bush disapproved of the crackdown, but took no strong action against the Chinese government. He hoped to influence China by keeping communication open. President Clinton followed a similar policy. On a 1998 visit to China, he pledged to strengthen ties between the two nations. At the same time, he publicly debated human rights issues with China's president.

Communism in Cuba and North Korea Other Communist nations refused to reform even when their people faced hard times. The fall of the Soviet Union deprived Cuba of its main source of trade and economic aid. As the Cuban economy spiraled downward, some 30,000 Cubans fled by boat to the United States. Still, after four decades, Cuba's Communist dictatorship remained in power.

In 1994, the United States signed an agreement with Cuba to allow Cubans to emigrate more freely. At the same time, the United States continued to enforce a 40-year-old embargo that was aimed at toppling Fidel Castro.

On the Korean peninsula, the Cold War remained alive. There, the armies of Communist North Korea and democratic South Korea faced each other along a tense border. In the 1990s, famine struck North Korea. The famine was worsened by the economic policies of the North Korean dictator, Kim Jong Il.

Why Did South Africa End Apartheid? The cause of global democracy had its most dramatic success in South Africa. Since 1948, the government of South Africa had enforced a policy of **apartheid** (uh PAHRT hayt), or strict separation of races. The nation's nonwhite majority was segregated. By law, nonwhites and whites were required to use separate facilities. Nonwhites were allowed no voice in the South African government.

In 1986, Congress approved economic sanctions against South Africa to force an end to apartheid. American companies were forbidden to invest in South Africa or import South African products.

In the 1990s, in response to sanctions, South Africa moved to end white minority rule. Under a new constitution, all races were permitted to vote for the first time in 1994.

Nelson Mandela (mahn DEL uh), a Black man who had spent 27 years in prison for opposing apartheid, was elected president. Mandela called for peace and reconciliation, or an agreement to come together, among South Africa's peoples. He helped establish democracy, racial equality, and freedom in South Africa.

READING CHECK **Identify Supporting Details** How did the United States use economic pressure to promote the spread of democracy?

Analyze Images This graphic summarizes the sanctions the United States put in place against South Africa. **Cite Evidence** How did the sanctions affect American businesses?

IMPACT OF U.S. SANCTIONS ON SOUTH AFRICA

COMPREHENSIVE ANTIAPARTHEID ACT, 1986

TO PRESSURE SOUTH AFRICA TO END APARTHEID

- Banned U.S. businesses from making new investments in South Africa
- Banned imports from South Africa (steel, coal, iron, etc.)
- Canceled landing rights for South African airlines
- Stopped export of oil to South Africa

Source: Peterson Institute for International Economics

IMPACT ON INVESTMENT

U.S. companies with direct investments in South Africa

Year	Companies
1985	306
1986	266
1987	227
1988	136

Source: Peterson Institute for International Economics

IMPACT ON TRADE

South African Exports to U.S. (millions of current dollars)

Analyze Images Sarajevo residents duck a sniper's bullets during Bosnia's civil war in 1993. **Compare and Contrast** In what ways did life change in nations like Yugoslavia after the fall of communism?

What Challenges Did Russia and Eastern Europe Face?

After the Cold War, the nations that rejected communism struggled to adapt to their new freedoms. As the governments sold off state-run businesses to private enterprises, their economies were not able to adjust. The result was high unemployment and high inflation.

Russian president Boris Yeltsin sought to build a stable democracy. His efforts faltered when he failed to put down an independence movement in the Russian province of Chechnya. The United States supported Yeltsin's democratic efforts and offered the Russian government advice on transitioning to a free-market economy.

Bosnian Civil War In Eastern Europe, Yugoslavia faced a civil war. Yugoslavia was made up of several republics, including Croatia, Serbia, and Bosnia-Herzegovina. In 1991, Croatia and Bosnia declared their independence. However, Serbs in Croatia and Bosnia wanted to remain part of Yugoslavia. With help from Serbia, they fought to prevent the new governments from splitting away. Fighting ended quickly in Croatia, but continued in Bosnia. During four years of civil war, more than 250,000 people died, including many children and teenagers.

To end the violence, the United States sponsored a meeting in Dayton, Ohio. There an agreement was hammered out. To help guarantee the peace agreement, President Clinton sent about 20,000 American troops to Bosnia. There, they joined NATO and Russian forces in a peacekeeping mission. The troops helped restore order.

Kosovo Seeks Independence Kosovo, a province within Serbia, also sought greater independence. The Albanians living there were in the majority and resented Serbian rule.

In 1998, Serbs launched a series of attacks against Albanian rebels in Kosovo. Hundreds of thousands of Albanians fled the province. Many thousands of others were killed or wounded. President Clinton condemned the attacks, saying that they were "feeding the flames of ethnic and religious division."

In March 1999, American air forces joined the air forces of other NATO nations in bombing Serbia. This drove Serbian troops out of Kosovo. NATO peacekeeping forces then entered the province. The violence in Kosovo ended, and a slow process of rebuilding began.

READING CHECK **Summarize** How did President Clinton aid peacekeeping efforts in Bosnia and Kosovo?

Intervention in Latin America, Africa, and Europe

In the early 1900s, the United States had frequently intervened in the internal affairs of Latin American nations. In the late 1900s, Cold War tensions led the United States to resume its active role.

Civil Wars in Latin America During the Cold War, the United States returned to a policy of intervention in Latin American affairs. During the 1970s and 1980s, civil wars raged in several Central American countries. Rebels in El Salvador and Guatemala fought to overthrow harsh governments. The United States backed the governments because they were strongly anti-Communist. The wars cost tens of thousands of lives. To escape the fighting, thousands of refugees fled to the United States.

In Nicaragua, a rebel group known as the Sandinistas overthrew a longtime dictator in 1979 and set up a socialist government. President Reagan, afraid that Nicaragua would become another Cuba, aided a group opposed to the Sandinistas. They were known as "Contras," from the Spanish word for "against."

Many members of Congress disagreed with President Reagan's policy in Nicaragua, especially after the Sandinistas won a democratic election in Nicaragua in 1984. They passed laws banning military aid to the Contras. Even so, some people on the president's staff secretly arranged for military aid to the Contras. They arranged to sell weapons to Iran in violation of an arms embargo against the country. The administration sent over half of the millions that Iran paid for the weapons straight to the Contras to aid in their fight.

Analyze Images Marine Lt. Colonel Oliver North testified before Congress for six days during the Iran-Contra hearings, an investigation into a secret government arrangement to sell weapons to Iran and send the money to Nicaraguan rebels. **Identify Cause and Effect** What concern was the root of the arrangement?

INTERACTIVE

U.S. Engagement Around the World

When details of the "arms-for-hostages" deal became public, many Americans were outraged. The scandal became known as the Iran-Contra affair. Two Reagan officials were tried and convicted of lying to Congress, though the convictions were later successfully appealed. Finally, in 1990, Nicaragua held new elections. Nicaraguans rejected the Sandinistas and voted in new leaders.

Tragedy in Somalia Sometimes the American effort to bring stability to war-torn regions ended in tragedy. In 1992, American forces led a UN mission attempting to end civil war and famine in the African nation of Somalia. However, neither the American troops nor the UN were able to end the civil war. Gradually, the Americans found themselves the target of hostility. In 1993, 18 U.S. Army Rangers died in fighting while trying to restore order in the capital, Mogadishu. Shortly afterward, the United States withdrew its troops from Somalia.

Peace in Northern Ireland By contrast, the United States successfully used diplomacy to ease conflict in Northern Ireland. Most members of the Catholic minority there wanted the region to be reunited with Ireland. Most of the Protestant majority wanted to remain under British rule. Between 1969 and 1998, more than 3,000 people died in the fighting.

The United States sent former Senator George Mitchell of Maine to aid the Northern Ireland peace talks. He helped to produce an agreement in April 1998. Although the peace process was slow and often troubled, a lasting peace settlement seemed within reach.

READING CHECK **Summarize** Explain the Iran-Contra affair in your own words.

Analyze Images President Clinton greets an onlooker during his visit to Northern Ireland. **Cite Evidence** Was U.S. involvement in the Northern Ireland conflict a success? Why or why not?

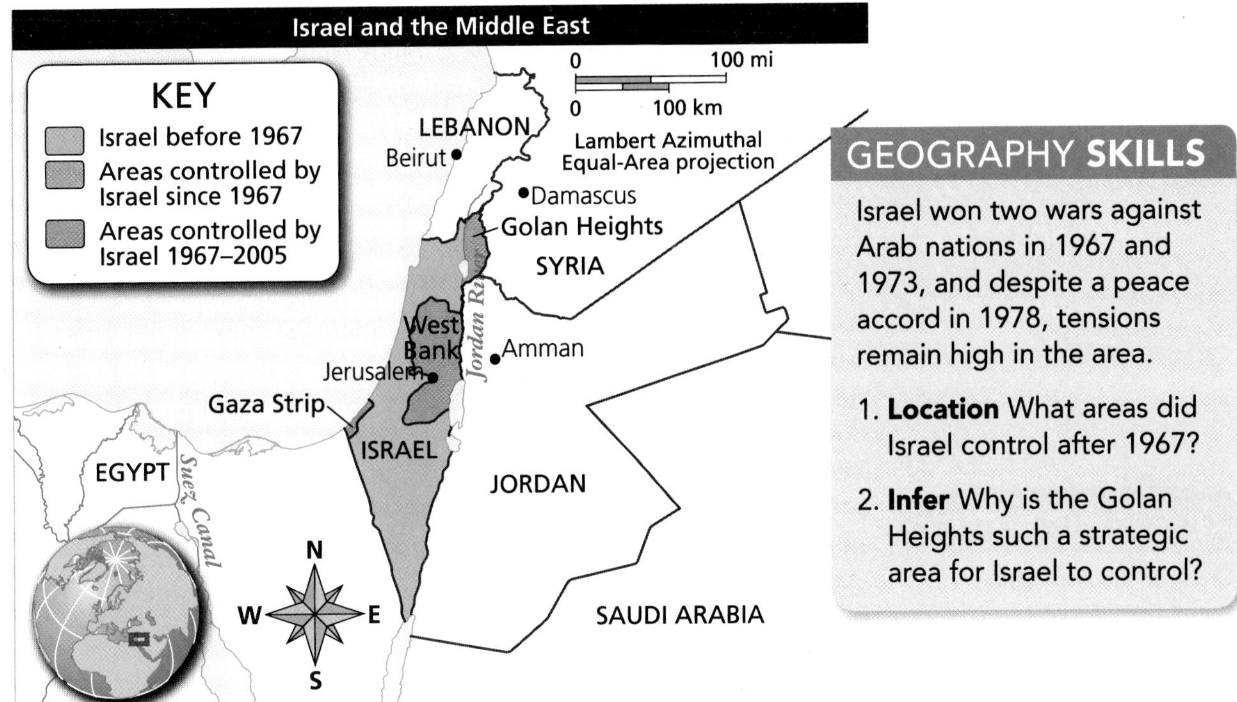

GEOGRAPHY SKILLS

Israel won two wars against Arab nations in 1967 and 1973, and despite a peace accord in 1978, tensions remain high in the area.

1. **Location** What areas did Israel control after 1967?
2. **Infer** Why is the Golan Heights such a strategic area for Israel to control?

What Caused Conflict in the Middle East?

Conflict had long troubled the Middle East, a region extending from southwestern Asia across North Africa. Over the centuries, friction among religious groups has led to violence. European attempts to colonize the Middle East and competition for large oil reserves in the region added to tensions.

The United States had conflicting interests in the Middle East. It strongly supported the Jewish state of Israel. Yet, it also had ties to the Muslim Arab states that dominated the region and opposed Israel. Arab nations such as Saudi Arabia supplied much of the oil used by Americans.

A Jewish State In the late 1800s, European Jews arrived in a region sometimes known as Palestine along the Mediterranean coast. They hoped to create a Jewish state in their ancient homeland. Jewish settlement grew in the 1930s as European Jews fled Nazi persecution.

In 1948, Arabs rejected a plan to divide the land into one Jewish and one Palestinian Arab state. Jews in the region announced the creation of the state of Israel. The United States and other nations quickly recognized the new nation.

Arab-Israeli Wars Neighboring Arab nations refused to recognize the Jewish state. Instead, they attacked, but Israel won the 1948 war. More than 500,000 Palestinian Arabs fled to refugee camps in the region surrounding Israel. Most were not permitted to return after the war and were not paid for their lands and homes. Meanwhile, hundreds of thousands of Jewish refugees from Arab nations fled to Israel, leaving their lands and homes behind.

Did you know?

In 1973, OPEC supplied almost 50 percent of the oil imported into the United States.

Arab nations fought Israel again in 1967 and 1973. Israel defeated its opponents in both wars. In 1967, it took control of territories neighboring Israel, including areas that were home to many Palestinian Arab refugees.

The United States sent aid to Israel in the 1973 war. Arab members of **OPEC**, the Organization of Petroleum Exporting Countries, retaliated. They cut off oil shipments to the United States and slowed down oil production. OPEC lifted the oil embargo in 1974.

A Move Toward Peace Egyptian president Anwar el-Sadat took a bold step toward peace in 1977. He became the first Arab head of state to visit Israel. When peace talks between the two nations broke down, President Jimmy Carter invited Sadat and Israeli Prime Minister Menachem Begin (muh NAHK um BAY gin) to Camp David, the president's retreat in Maryland.

Quick Activity

Organize the information about regional conflicts in your Active Journal.

In the **Camp David Accords** of 1978, Israel agreed to return the Sinai Peninsula to Egypt, and Egypt agreed to recognize Israel. The two nations signed a peace treaty in 1979.

The Palestinian Conflict Some Palestinian Arabs waged guerrilla war against Israel. Under Israeli rule, Palestinians in territories controlled by Israel had limited rights. Those living outside Israeli control wanted to return to their homeland under a Palestinian government. Many supported the Palestine Liberation Organization, or **PLO**. Its leader, Yasser Arafat, stated that the goal of the PLO was to destroy Israel.

In 1987, Palestinians in the Israeli-controlled West Bank and Gaza Strip took to the streets to protest Israeli rule. The unrest, called the *Intifada,* focused attention on the need to end the Israeli-Palestinian conflict.

After years of effort, the United States persuaded Israel and the PLO to come to the bargaining table. In 1993, the longtime enemies signed a pact in Washington, D.C. The PLO agreed to recognize Israel's right to exist and promised to give up violence. Israel agreed to limited self-rule for Palestinian parts of the Gaza Strip and West Bank. Despite this agreement, tensions persisted in the region.

▼ Egyptian President Anwar Sadat (left), U.S. President Jimmy Carter (center), and Israeli Prime Minister Menachem Begin (right) at the Camp David Summit of 1979.

The Iranian Revolution The United States was deeply involved in other Middle East conflicts. In 1953, the United States helped overthrow the elected government of Iran and return the dethroned Shah Muhammad Reza Pahlavi to power. Then, in 1979, a revolution forced the unpopular shah to flee. A religious leader, the Ayatollah Khomeini (i yuh TOH luh koh MAYN ee), took control of Iran.

▼ Kuwaiti troops were trained by the United States and used U.S.-supplied equipment, such as this tank, during the 1991 Persian Gulf War with Iraq.

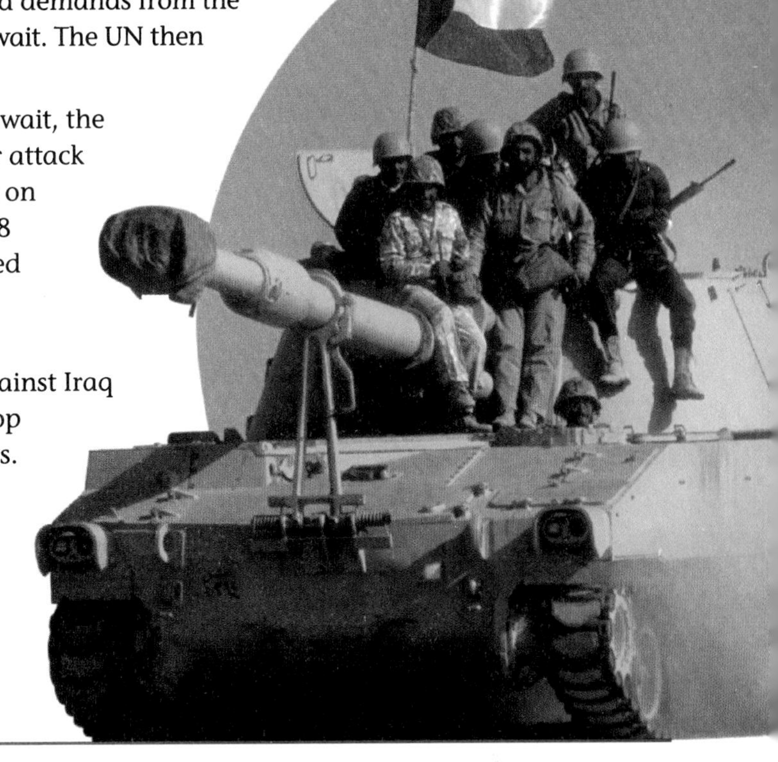

The Persian Gulf War In August 1990, Saddam Hussein, the dictator of Iraq, sent 100,000 troops to invade oil-rich Kuwait. President George H. W. Bush feared that the invasion was the start of a larger plan to gain control of Middle East oil. Hussein ignored demands from the United States and the UN to withdraw from Kuwait. The UN then imposed a trade boycott on Iraq.

In 1991, when Hussein still refused to leave Kuwait, the United States and its UN allies launched an air attack on Iraq. This was followed by a massive attack on Iraqi troops in Kuwait and Iraq. Troops from 28 nations—including some Arab countries—joined the effort. It took only six weeks to defeat the Iraqis and free Kuwait.

Although the war was over, the UN boycott against Iraq continued. The goal was to force Hussein to stop his chemical and biological weapons programs. However, Hussein refused to cooperate with UN arms inspectors.

READING CHECK **Summarize** What role did the United States play in the Camp David Accords?

Lesson Check

Practice Vocabulary

1. Did the **Strategic Arms Reduction Treaty** of 1991 end the spread of nuclear weapons?
2. How did the **Camp David Accords** reflect the role of the United States as a **mediator**?

Critical Thinking and Writing

3. **Draw Conclusions** What did events in Tiananmen Square in 1989 suggest about the chances for democracy to take hold in China?
4. **Compare and Contrast** How did the American intervention in the Kosovo and Iraq-Kuwait conflicts differ from that in the Northern Ireland and Palestinian conflicts?
5. **Recognize Point of View** Why do you think the United States was so eager to end apartheid that it applied sanctions against South Africa?
6. **Writing Workshop: Write an Introduction and Conclusion** You will need a paragraph to introduce the subject of your explanatory essay and your thesis. This introduction should provide the key ideas of your essay in a general way. The conclusion, or final paragraph, will restate your thesis and explain how the details in the essay support it. Draft an introduction and conclusion in your Active Journal.

Nelson Mandela, "Glory and Hope"

Nelson Mandela delivered this speech after having been elected president in South Africa's first multiracial election in 1994. Knowing that the injustices of apartheid would be hard to overcome, Mandela asked the people to work together for peace and justice.

◀ In 1990, Nelson Mandela was released from a South African prison.

Reading and Vocabulary Support

① What do you think the word *covenant* means?

② What do you think Mandela means by a "rainbow nation"?

③ *Reconciliation* means a settling of differences that results in harmony.

We have, at last, achieved our political emancipation. We pledge ourselves to liberate all our people from the continuing bondage of poverty, deprivation, suffering, gender and other discrimination. . . .

We have triumphed in the effort to implant hope in the breasts of the millions of our people. We enter into a covenant ① that we shall build the society in which all South Africans, both black and white, will be able to walk tall, without any fear in their hearts, assured of their inalienable right to human dignity—a rainbow nation ② at peace with itself and the world. . . . We understand it still that there is no easy road to freedom.

We know it well that none of us acting alone can achieve success.

We must therefore act together as a united people, for national reconciliation, ③ for nation building, for the birth of a new world.

Let there be justice for all. Let there be peace for all. Let there be work, bread, water, and salt for all. . . . The sun shall never set on so glorious a human achievement!

Analyzing Primary Sources

Cite specific evidence from the source to support your answers.

1. **Evaluate Arguments** White South Africans who had supported apartheid feared a backlash by Black South Africans. How does Mandela's speech respond to that danger?
2. **Determine Author's Point of View** How would you describe the tone of Mandela's speech? How does this tone reflect Mandela's view of his country and its future?
3. **Determine Author's Purpose** Why do you think Mandela talks about building a new world, not just a new South Africa?

Political Participation

INTERACTIVE
21st Century Skills

Follow these steps to become an informed citizen.

1 Volunteer for a political campaign. Political campaigns offer a wide variety of opportunities to help you become involved in the political process and become a responsible citizen by serving the public good. As a political campaign volunteer you may have the opportunity to attend events, make calls to voters, and explore your community while getting to know how other voters think about the responsibilities, duties, and obligations of citizenship. A good way to become involved in your school and community is to run for office. Student council and community positions offer a great opportunity for you to become familiar with the campaign and election process.

2 Reach out to others. Start or join an interest group. Interest groups enable people to work together on common goals related to the political process. Write a letter or email to a public official. By contacting an elected official from your area, you can either support or oppose laws or policies. You can also ask for help or support regarding certain issues.

Social networking sites and blogs offer a great way for people of all ages to interact and write about political issues. As you connect with others, you'll become more confident in your role as a citizen working for the public good.

3 Get Involved. Working for a candidate or supporting an issue can include writing on blogs, doing research, and attending rallies. As you learn more about issues, you will become more confident in your role as a citizen working for the public good.

Answer the following questions to help you decide what types of political participation you might be interested in:

1. In the last presidential election, which candidate would you have supported?
2. What party did that candidate represent?
3. If you could volunteer to help in a political campaign for that party, what could you do as a volunteer?
4. What local issues are important to you?
5. Are there interest groups that have been formed to work on these issues? What are the names of these groups?

TOPIC 16

Review and Assessment

VISUAL REVIEW

Four Presidents

Jimmy Carter (1977–1981)	Ronald Reagan (1981–1989)	George H. W. Bush (1989–1993)	Bill Clinton (1993–2001)
• Inflation and an energy crisis • Iran hostage crisis • Peace between Egypt and Israel	• Job growth; inflation kept in check • Military spending increased budget • Opposition to Soviet Union • Iran-Contra affair	• Raised taxes to save popular programs • Banking crisis • Persian Gulf War • Soviet Union breakup	• Economic boom • Balanced budget • Impeached by House, acquitted by Senate • Military intervention in Bosnia, Kosovo, and Palestine

The End of the Cold War

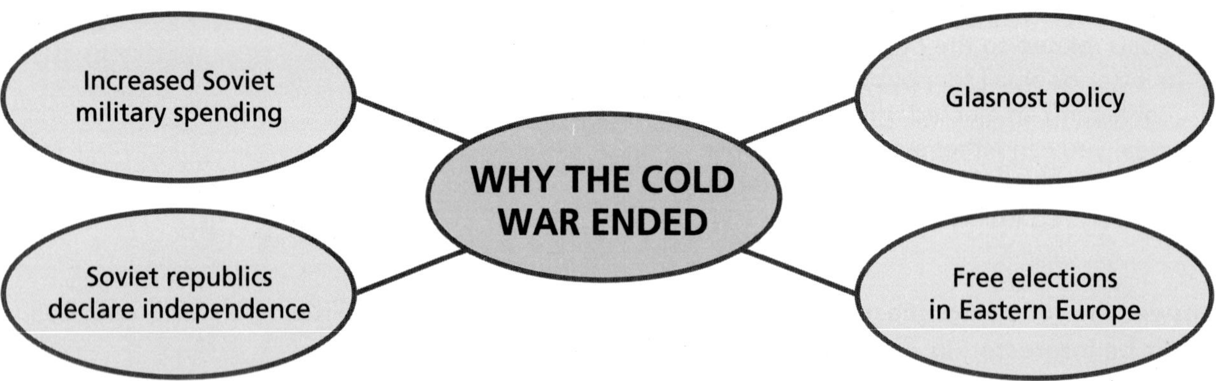

READING REVIEW

Use the Take Notes and Practice Vocabulary activities in your Active Journal to review the topic.

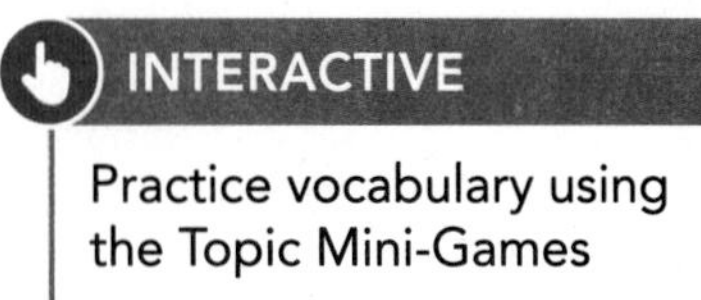

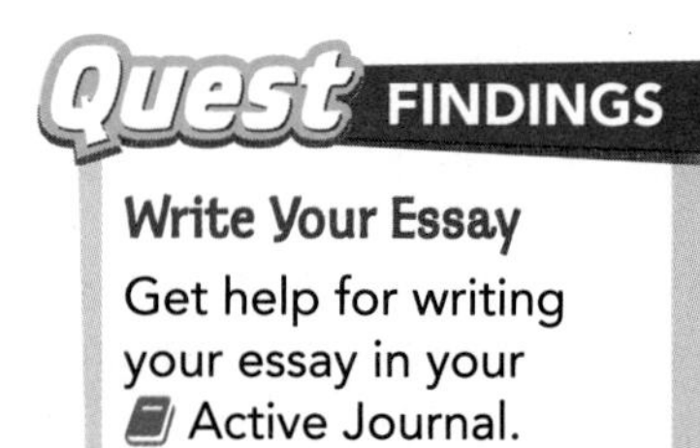

ASSESSMENT

Vocabulary and Key Ideas

1. **Check Understanding** Why did President Clinton oppose the "**Contract With America**"?
2. **Identify** What was the goal of **deregulation**?
3. **Recall** What was the **Star Wars** program?
4. **Check Understanding** What role did **sanctions** play in ending **apartheid** in South Africa?

Critical Thinking and Writing

5. **List** What events led to the Persian Gulf War?
6. **Recall** Who won the Arab-Israeli wars fought in 1948, 1967, and 1973?
7. **Describe** How did the United States attempt to bring peace to Northern Ireland?
8. **Compare and Contrast** How did the viewpoints of liberals and conservatives differ on the issues of taxation and the size of government?
9. **Draw Conclusions** Why did Jimmy Carter lose the 1980 election to Ronald Reagan?
10. **Cite Evidence** What evidence supports the idea that the policy of *glasnost* had unintended consequences?
11. **Revisit the Essential Question** Do you agree with the idea that the post–Cold War status of the United States as the world's only superpower meant that it had to get involved in regional conflicts? Why or why not?
12. **Writing Workshop: Write an Explanatory Essay** Now it is time to develop your thesis on the end of the Cold War and the collapse of the Soviet Union in an explanatory, or informative, essay. Use the introduction you wrote earlier, the details you have gathered to support your thesis, and the conclusion you drafted to write your essay in your Active Journal.

Analyze Primary Sources

13. Who most likely made the statement quoted below?
    A. Corazon Aquino
    B. Jerry Falwell
    C. Jimmy Carter
    D. Sandra Day O'Connor

"I care very much about women and their progress. I didn't go march in the streets, but when I was in the Arizona Legislature, one of the things that I did was to examine every single statute in the state of Arizona to pick out the ones that discriminated against women and get them changed."

Analyze Maps

Use the map at the right to answer the following questions.

14. Which letter marks the country that recognized the existence of Israel as part of the Camp David Accords?
15. Which letter marks the country that occupies the east bank of the Jordan River?
16. Syria and Egypt led the Arab attack on Israel in 1973. Why would Israel want to occupy the Golan Heights?

▼ **Israel in the Middle East**

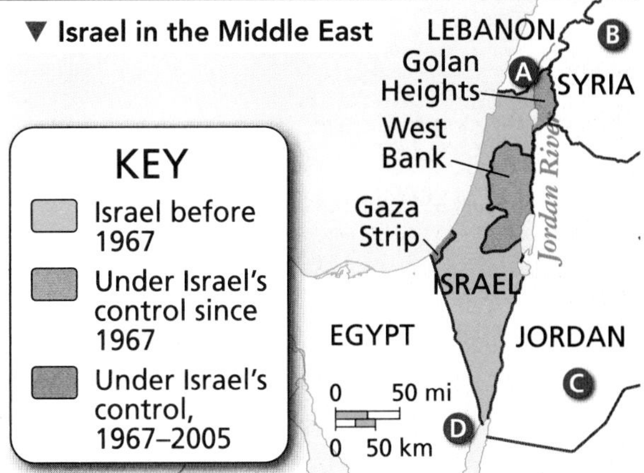

TOPIC 17

Meeting New Challenges (1975–Present)

GO ONLINE to access your digital course

- VIDEO
- AUDIO
- ETEXT
- INTERACTIVE
- WRITING
- GAMES
- WORKSHEET
- ASSESSMENT

Go back to the 1970s,

when many of the current issues facing our country began to emerge. In this topic, you will also learn about the events of September 11, 2001, the impact of terrorism, and how technology is affecting our lives.

Explore The Essential Question

What can individuals do to affect society?

In the twenty-first century, many people have shaped society. How have their decisions affected all of us?

Unlock the Essential Question in your Active Journal.

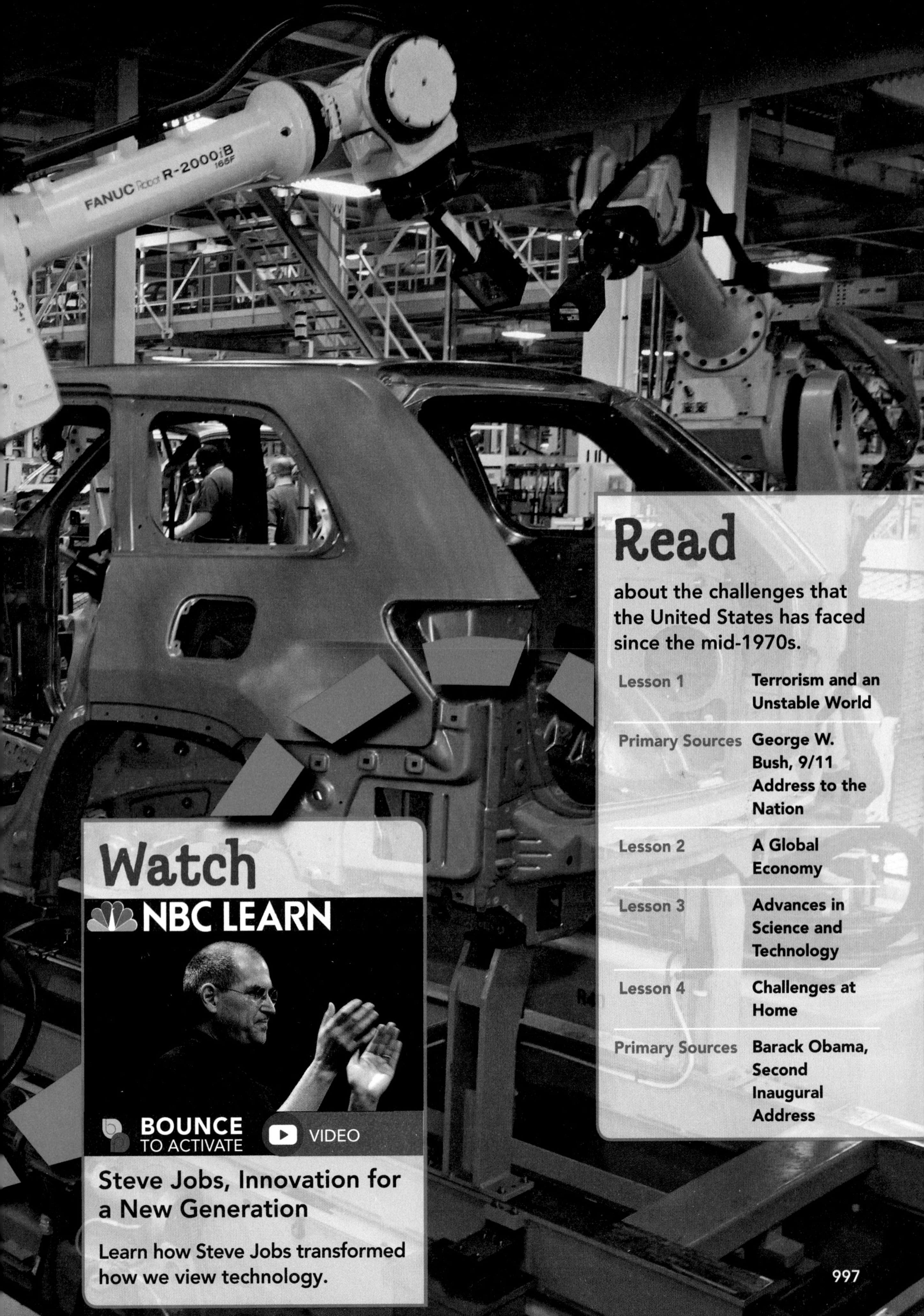

Read

about the challenges that the United States has faced since the mid-1970s.

Lesson 1	Terrorism and an Unstable World
Primary Sources	George W. Bush, 9/11 Address to the Nation
Lesson 2	A Global Economy
Lesson 3	Advances in Science and Technology
Lesson 4	Challenges at Home
Primary Sources	Barack Obama, Second Inaugural Address

Watch

NBC LEARN

BOUNCE TO ACTIVATE

VIDEO

Steve Jobs, Innovation for a New Generation

Learn how Steve Jobs transformed how we view technology.

TOPIC 17

Meeting New Challenges

Learn more about global trade by making your own map and timeline in your Active Journal.

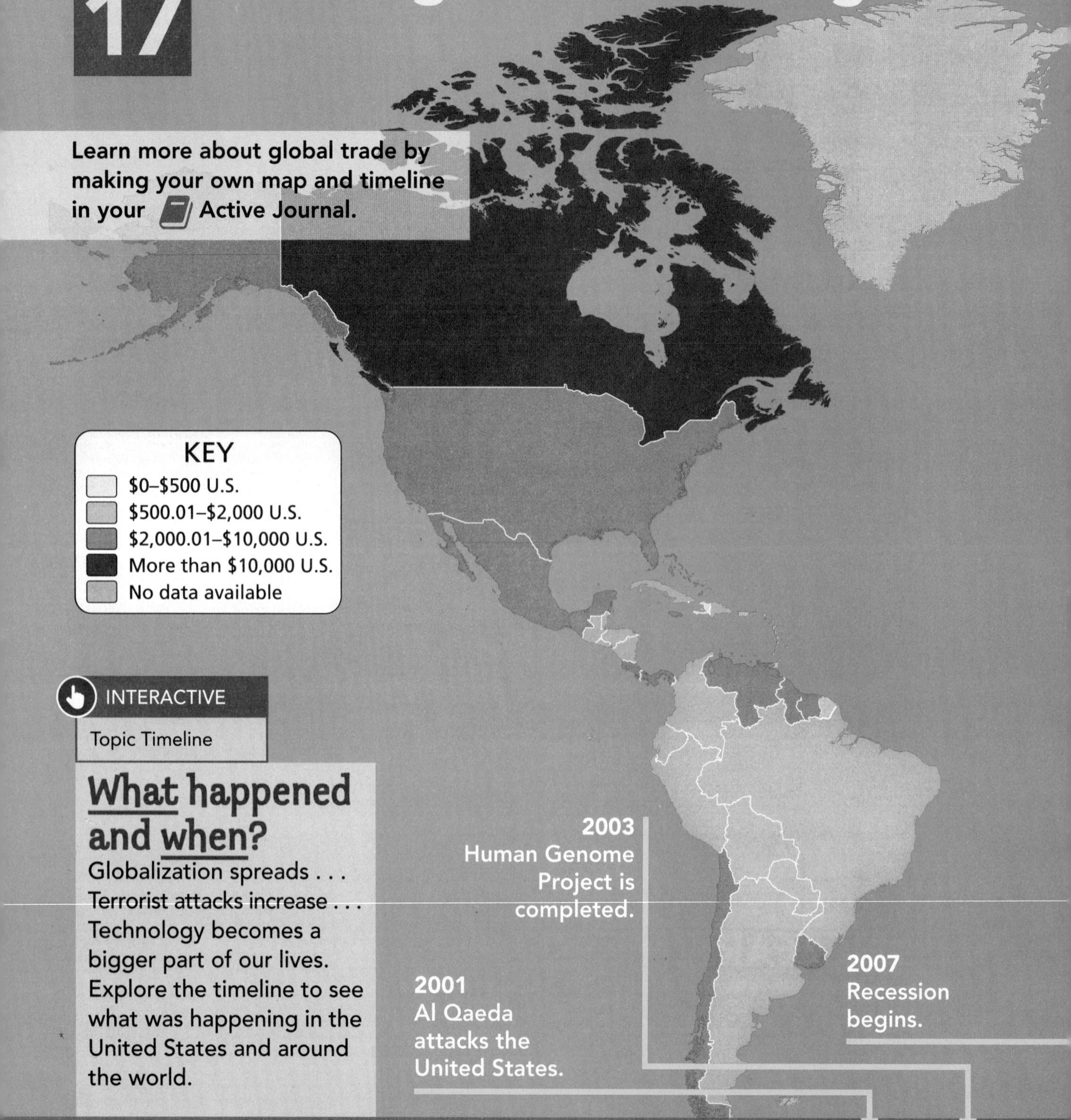

KEY
- $0–$500 U.S.
- $500.01–$2,000 U.S.
- $2,000.01–$10,000 U.S.
- More than $10,000 U.S.
- No data available

INTERACTIVE

Topic Timeline

What happened and when?

Globalization spreads . . . Terrorist attacks increase . . . Technology becomes a bigger part of our lives. Explore the timeline to see what was happening in the United States and around the world.

TOPIC EVENTS

2001 Al Qaeda attacks the United States.

2003 Human Genome Project is completed.

2007 Recession begins.

1990

2000

WORLD EVENTS

1989 Berlin Wall falls.

1993 Vaclav Havel becomes president of the Czech Republic.

2000 Vicente Fox is elected president of Mexico.

How does U.S. trade compare to that of other countries?

The map shows the value of international trade, per capita, for 2016. As you can see from the map, some nations dominate global trade.

Who will you meet?

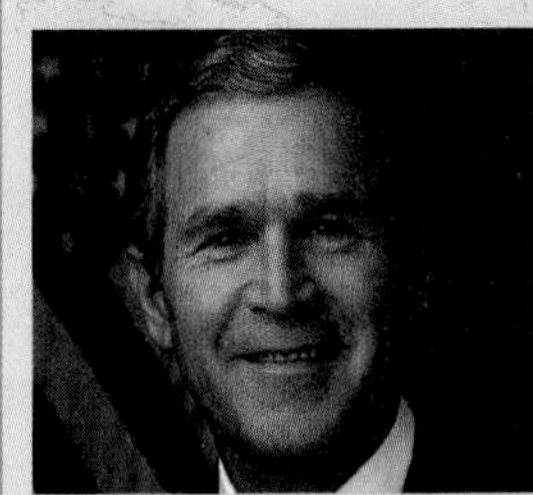
George W. Bush, President from 2001–2009

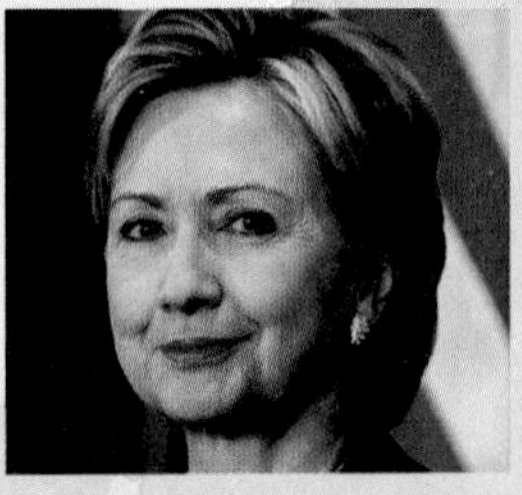
Hillary Clinton, first female candidate of a major party for U.S. President

Donald Trump, President from 2017–2021

2009 Barack Obama becomes President of the United States.

2010 Arab Spring begins.

2013 U.S. Supreme Court rules that federal government must recognize same-sex marriages.

2010

2020

2010 A volcanic explosion in Iceland sends ash across Europe.

2013 Pope Francis becomes the first Latin American to head the Roman Catholic Church.

Document-Based Writing Inquiry

Look Into the Future

Quest KICK OFF

The **twenty-first century** has featured many changes. Some of these changes have created challenges, but they have also created opportunities.

What do young Americans envision for themselves and their future?

How will the changes affect your life and the lives of your friends? Explore the Essential Question, "What can individuals do to affect society?"

▲ One way individuals can affect society is by working to help others, like this Peace Corps volunteer (left) teaching literacy in Niger.

1 Ask Questions

First, you'll need to review the events, changes, and developments that are discussed in this topic. Then make a list of questions you would like to ask about the things that have happened this century. Write down these questions in your Active Journal.

2 Investigate

As you study the topic, look for Quest CONNECTIONS that provide information on the state of the world and how it has changed. Record your notes in your Active Journal.

3 Examine Primary Sources

Next, explore sources of information about the future of our country. Capture your thoughts in your Active Journal.

Quest FINDINGS

4 Write Your Explanatory Essay

Develop an answer to the Guiding Question, and shape it into an essay explaining what you think young people envision for the future. Get help for this task in your Active Journal.

LESSON 1

Terrorism and an Unstable World

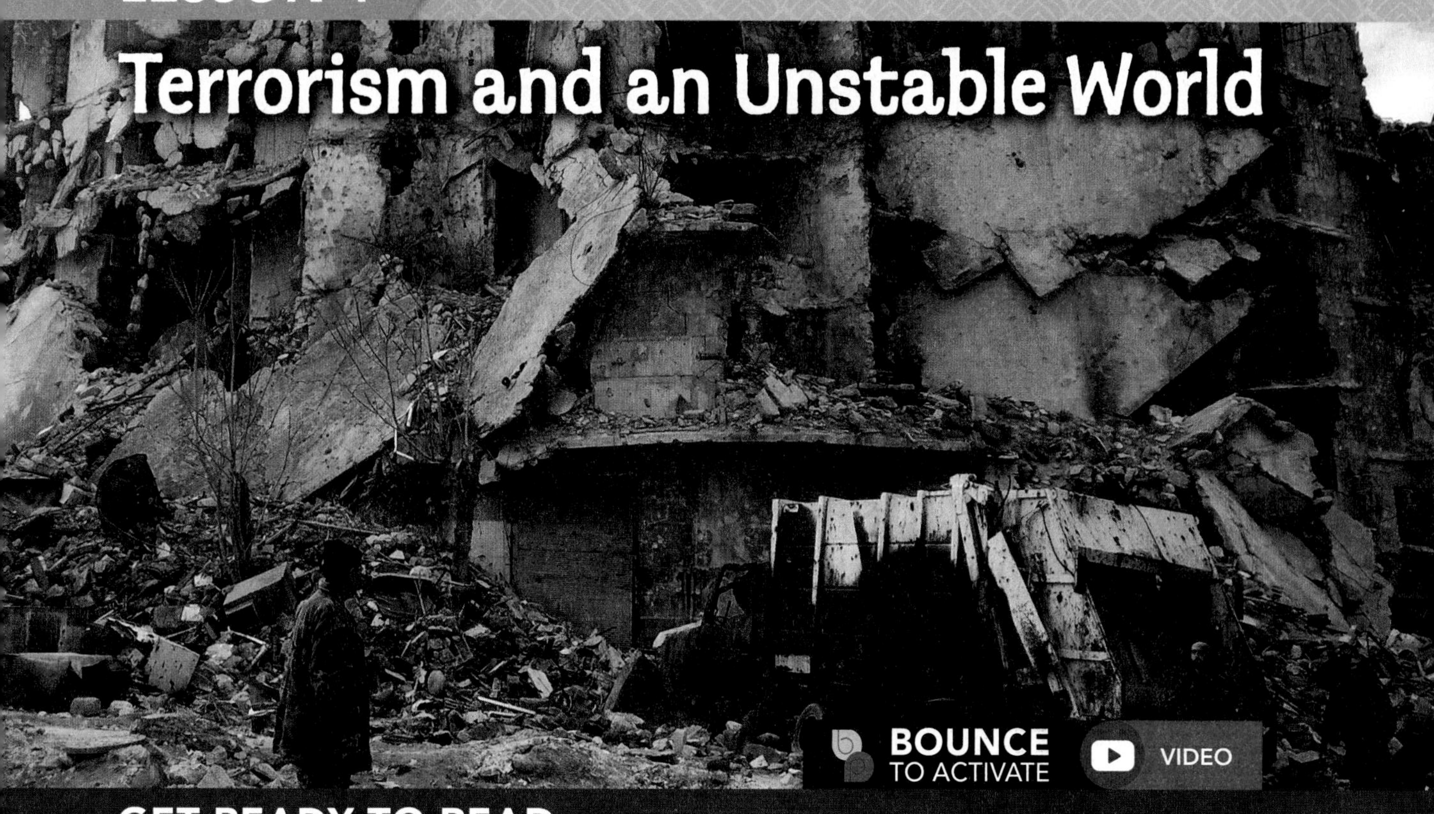

GET READY TO READ

START UP

Study the photo of war-torn Aleppo, Syria. How does it show challenges faced by the region?

GUIDING QUESTIONS

- What are the challenges posed by jihadism?
- Why are U.S. alliances important?

TAKE NOTES

Literacy Skills: Use Evidence

Use the graphic organizer in your Active Journal to take notes as you read the lesson.

PRACTICE VOCABULARY

Use the vocabulary activity in your Active Journal to practice the vocabulary words.

Vocabulary

jihadism
Islamic fundamentalist
terrorism
weapons of mass destruction
insurgency
Nuclear Non-Proliferation Treaty
Arab Spring
North Atlantic Treaty Organization

Academic Vocabulary

obtain
reaffirm

In this century, jihadism has played a significant role in global affairs. **Jihadism** is an Islamic fundamentalist movement that supports violence in the struggle against those seen as enemies of Islam.

Islamic fundamentalists believe that Islamic religious texts should be taken literally. Muslims, or people who follow Islam, define *jihad* as a struggle to achieve the goals of Islam. The struggle can take place inside a person who is trying to accept and devote himself or herself to the requirements of Islam. The struggle can also take place externally, as a person battles individuals who are opposed to Islam. Jihadists emphasize this second definition, which they use to justify violent actions that most Muslims oppose.

Believing that Islam is under attack, the goal of jihadists is to fight those they see as opponents of Islam throughout the world, often using terrorist methods. They want to remove unfriendly governments in Muslim countries and wage war against countries that they see as enemies.

▲ The September 11, 2001, terrorist attacks shocked Americans. When the World Trade Center towers in New York City were struck by hijacked aircraft, they burned and collapsed.

How Did the United States Respond to the Attacks of September 11, 2001?

On September 11, 2001, members of Al Qaeda, an international Islamist terrorist network, launched an attack against the United States. Osama bin Laden (oh SAH muh bin LAH dun) had founded Al Qaeda in 1988. Al Qaeda was based on the idea of jihadism. Most Islamic fundamentalists are not jihadists. Jihadists, however, are generally Islamic fundamentalists. They are also Islamists, or Muslims who believe that society should be governed by religious, Islamic law.

Al Qaeda pursued a strategy of **terrorism**, or the use of violence and cruelty to achieve political goals. Note that the vast majority of Muslims are not fundamentalists and oppose jihadism and terrorism.

INTERACTIVE

September 11, 2001

Al Qaeda opposed American influence in the Muslim world and launched a number of attacks against American targets beginning in the 1990s, including on U.S. embassies in Kenya and Tanzania. Hundreds of people died in these attacks, which led President Bill Clinton to order the bombing of bin Laden's headquarters in Afghanistan. In 2000, Al Qaeda attacked the USS *Cole,* a U.S. Navy destroyer, while it was anchored at a port in Yemen on the coast of the Arabian Peninsula.

Al Qaeda Attacks the United States The East Coast's clear blue sky on the morning of September 11, 2001, gave no indication that the day would end far differently than it began. As Americans began their day, 19 Al Qaeda terrorists prepared to seize four commercial airliners in an attack against the United States.

At 8:46 A.M., the hijackers crashed the first plane into one of the World Trade Center's twin towers, New York City's tallest buildings, a location later known as "ground zero." Another plane hit the second tower about 15 minutes later. Within the hour, a third plane crashed into the Pentagon, the U.S. military headquarters in Arlington, Virginia. Brave passengers on a fourth plane bound for Washington, D.C., stormed the cockpit, leading the hijackers to crash the plane into a field in Shanksville, Pennsylvania.

Within two hours of the attack, the twin towers of the World Trade Center had collapsed. The September 11 attacks killed nearly 3,000 people and stunned Americans. President George W. Bush quickly blamed Osama bin Laden and Al Qaeda.

In response, the Bush administration launched what it called a global war on terrorism, far different from other wars America had fought. The enemy, less clearly defined, included terrorist groups that threatened the United States and its allies.

This effort to wipe out terrorism led the United States into wars in Iraq and Afghanistan. It also led to the creation of the Department of Homeland Security, which was given the job of safeguarding security within the United States. Meanwhile, Congress passed the USA PATRIOT Act, which allows officials to conduct surveillance on suspected terrorists at home and abroad.

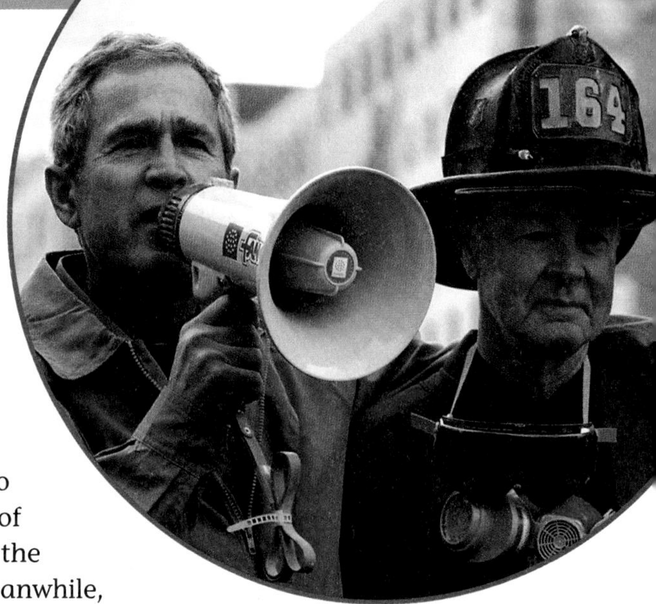
▲ When the 9/11 attacks occurred, George W. Bush was fewer than eight months into his first term as President. His response to the attacks would become a defining feature of his presidency.

The War in Afghanistan Shortly after the September 11 attacks, President Bush asked Afghanistan to surrender Osama bin Laden. The Taliban, the Islamic fundamentalist group that controlled Afghanistan, refused.

In October 2001, with authorization from Congress, American forces invaded Afghanistan. The war began with American-led bombing missions. By the end of 2001, the Northern Alliance, made up of Afghans who opposed the Taliban, had captured the capital city of Kabul. It established a new government that was friendly to the United States.

BIOGRAPHY 5 Things to Know About GEORGE W. BUSH

President of the United States (born 1946)

- George W. Bush served as Governor of Texas from 1995 until 2000 and President of the United States from 2001 until 2009.
- After the September 11 attacks, Bush sought to unite the country and spoke about the importance of respecting the beliefs of others.
- His administration formed the Department of Homeland Security to protect the country from terrorist attacks.
- He signed a law that expanded Medicare, a government health insurance program for elderly Americans. The law made it easier to obtain prescription drugs.
- Although he lost the popular vote in the 2000 election, Bush won re-election in 2004 with a majority of the electoral vote.

Critical Thinking Why do you think George W. Bush talked about respecting the beliefs of others after the September 11 attacks?

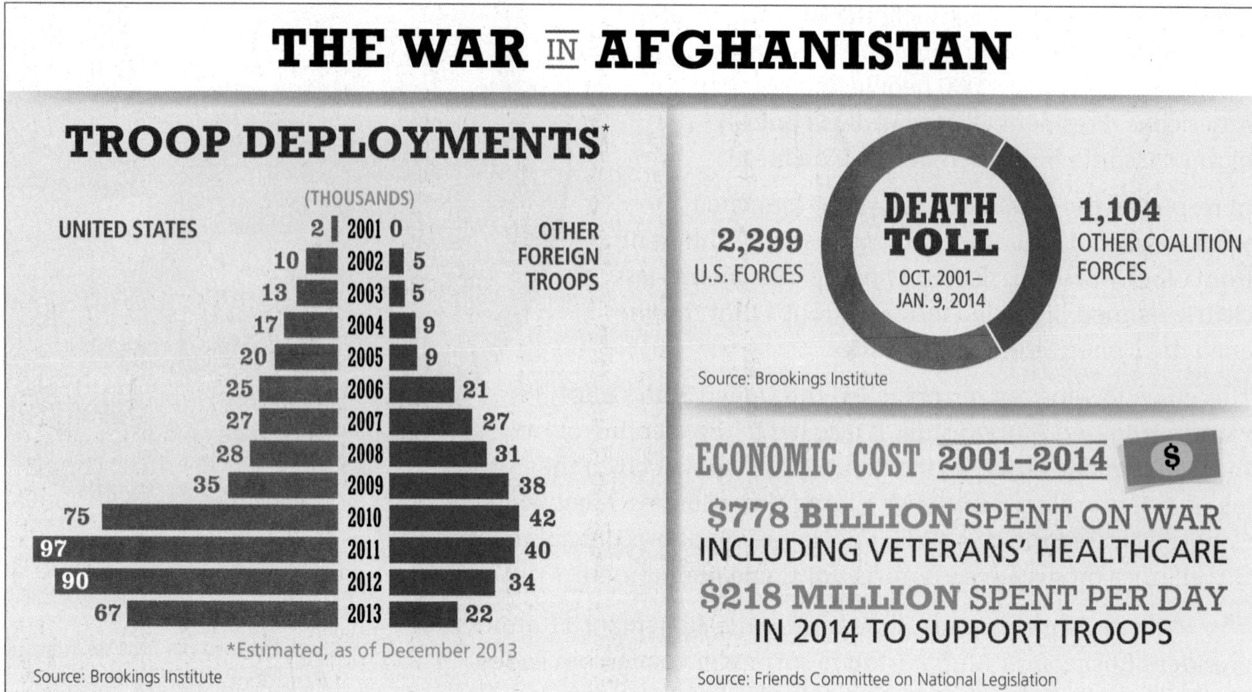

Analyze Graphs In October 2001, the United States and its allies invaded Afghanistan to try to drive out the Taliban. **Synthesize Visual Information** Based on the data in the bar graph on the left, summarize the role of the United States in the international coalition that fought in the war.

The United States provided money to support the new Afghan government, and American forces stayed in the country. In spite of this, the new government never gained full control of Afghanistan. During the war, bin Laden escaped to Pakistan. By 2007, the Taliban had regained some of its power in Afghanistan.

When Barack Obama became President in 2009, the war in Afghanistan was still underway. Obama sent additional troops to Afghanistan to provide protection and to train Afghan forces.

As the war dragged on, American support declined. In 2014, the United States ended its combat mission, but some soldiers remained to provide support to the Afghan army.

READING CHECK **Identify Cause and Effect** Why did the United States invade Afghanistan?

What Happened in the Iraq War?

In 2002 to 2003, tensions mounted between the United States and Iraq. Ever since the Gulf War of 1991, the United States and its allies had maintained a no-flight zone over parts of Iraq. They had also pushed for continued inspections of Iraqi military facilities. They aimed to prevent the development of chemical, biological, or nuclear weapons, also known as **weapons of mass destruction**, or WMDs—weapons that are capable of causing widespread and significant harm.

In his 2002 State of the Union Address, President Bush declared that Iraq formed an "axis of evil" with Iran and North Korea. Although none of the countries had a direct connection to the September 11 attacks, Bush accused them of protecting terrorists and hiding WMDs that threatened the United States.

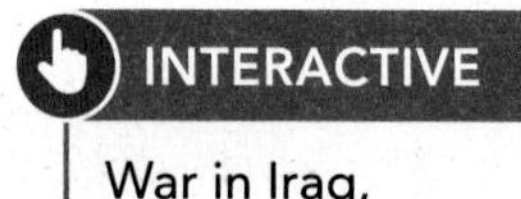

War in Iraq, 2003–2011

Iraq had blocked inspections and refused to destroy weapons that violated rules set by the United Nations. In early 2003, the United States and Britain claimed to have evidence that Iraq in fact possessed WMDs.

War Breaks Out Based on this evidence, the Bush administration wanted UN approval to go to war but said it would act with or without that approval. Congress approved a resolution that gave the President the power to use force, if necessary.

In March 2003, although Iraq had allowed UN officials to conduct inspections and had begun destroying weapons, U.S. officials said that Iraq had not done enough to address concerns. U.S. and British forces began bombing targets inside Iraq and then sent troops into the country. After a month, U.S. forces occupied the capital city of Baghdad. In May, Bush declared the war concluded. No working WMDs were ever found. In December, American forces captured Saddam Hussein and turned him over to an Iraqi court for trial. The court found him guilty and sentenced him to death in 2006.

In the meantime, the United States had transferred control to a temporary Iraqi government in 2004. The next year, Iraqis elected a national assembly that had the difficult job of organizing a government despite ongoing violent conflicts among the country's Sunni Muslim Arabs, Shia Muslim Arabs, and ethnic Kurds. Despite Bush's earlier claim, the Iraq War was not yet finished. U.S. forces faced the tasks of supporting the government and trying to end the violence. In fact, U.S. involvement in the war would continue until 2011.

Mixed Results and Withdrawal The United States paid a heavy price for the Iraq War. Almost 5,000 Americans and hundreds of thousands of Iraqis died. After eight years, the war cost more than a trillion dollars. Saddam Hussein was removed from power, but that did not bring peace to Iraq. Iraqis looted businesses and homes. Shiite and Sunni Arabs fought each other, and Arabs fought ethnic Kurds in the north. An **insurgency**, or armed rebellion, arose against American soldiers and the Iraqi government. The new Iraqi government was too weak to manage the country.

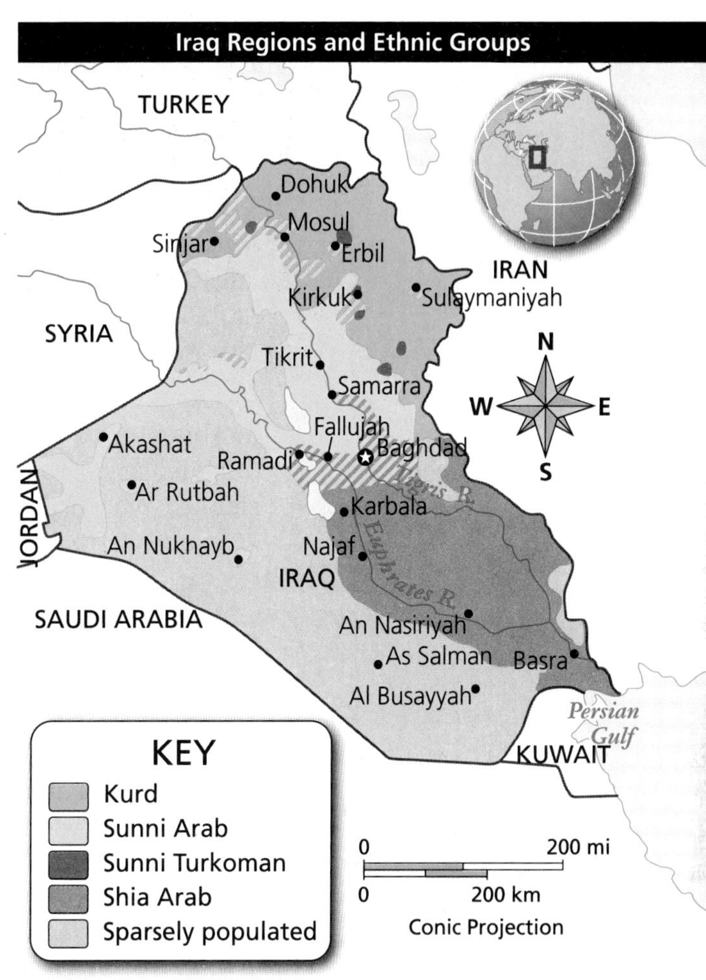

GEOGRAPHY SKILLS

The Iraqi population is composed of many different ethnic groups.

1. **Place** On which river is Baghdad located?
2. **Infer** Identify the areas in Iraq where ethnic conflicts might have been most likely to occur.

As the war continued, support for it decreased. In spite of this, the Bush administration increased the number of American forces with a troop surge. The surge reduced ethnic and religious violence in the country for a time but did not end it.

In 2008, Iraqis demanded a plan for the withdrawal of American troops. In 2011, President Obama ordered the removal of American troops from Iraq. In December of that year, the last 500 soldiers left Iraq, with the exception of a few guarding the American embassy.

The Islamic State During the war in 2014, a jihadist group based in Syria and calling itself the Islamic State in Iraq and the Levant (ISIL) gained control of much of western Iraq. The group, which follows an extreme form of Islam that most Muslims reject, ruled in a brutal, violent way. Its members often recorded their acts and shared them over social media to terrorize people all over the world. In summer and fall 2014, the United States and international partners, such as Saudi Arabia and Jordan, launched airstrikes to prevent ISIL, also known as ISIS, from taking more territory.

Groups affiliated with ISIL also had a presence in places such as northern Africa and carried out terrorist attacks. In Europe, ISIL-affiliated groups attacked an airport and a nightclub. People who claimed to be inspired by ISIL carried out attacks in the United States in 2015 and 2016.

READING CHECK **Identify Supporting Details** How did the United States and Britain justify attacking Iraq?

What Are the Continuing Challenges of Jihadism?

In 2011, nearly 10 years after the September 11 attacks, American forces captured and killed Osama bin Laden at his compound in Pakistan. Bin Laden's death, however, did not signal the end of jihadism, Al Qaeda, or the threat of terrorism.

▼ President Barack Obama and his advisers followed the raid of Osama Bin Laden's compound on closed-circuit television.

Indeed, organizations linked to Al Qaeda seemed to be expanding after 2010. Meanwhile, the United States faced questions about how it had conducted the war on terrorism.

Policy Questions Following the September 11 attacks, Bush administration officials argued that many areas of international law did not apply to the war on terrorism. They said this was especially true of laws on the treatment of prisoners, because members of Al Qaeda were not part of a regular national army. The Department of Defense approved methods of forcing prisoners to reveal information that some critics labeled as torture.

Analyze Images In Amman, Jordan, in 2012, jihadists protest the United States. **Understand Effects** How does jihadism in other countries affect the United States?

Relations with Afghanistan and neighboring Pakistan have also posed challenges. While the United States supported a new Afghan government led by Hamid Karzai during the early 2000s, his government faced widespread accusations of corruption. Karzai also grew increasingly hostile toward the United States.

Meanwhile, Pakistan, which received U.S. aid and provided an important supply route to Afghanistan, was accused of supporting the Taliban, which was fighting the Afghan government. Members of Pakistan's military were also accused of sheltering Osama bin Laden, who lived for years near a major Pakistani military base.

A Resilient Force By 2012, jihadist movements had taken root in Yemen, Pakistan, and Somalia, and the United States began attacking jihadists in these countries. Many of these jihadists were linked to Al Qaeda. Despite U.S. attacks, mainly by pilotless drone aircraft, jihadists seemed to remain strong in parts of these countries.

Meanwhile, jihadist groups had a growing presence in other parts of the Muslim world. They fought the government of Iraq after the U.S. withdrawal. Jihadist groups also launched violent attacks in Algeria, Mali, and Nigeria. U.S. policymakers were concerned about the spread of jihadists hostile to the United States and its allies. They struggled to find an effective way to counter them.

In Syria, a civil war broke out in 2011 between the government of Bashar al-Assad and forces who opposed it. Different groups later joined the fighting, including ISIL. As of 2017 the war had killed more than 250,000 civilians and caused widespread destruction. As a result of the conflict, millions of refugees fled Syria for Europe and other places.

READING CHECK **Draw Conclusions** What do you think the impact of the flood of refugees might be?

Quest CONNECTIONS
How have deals to limit the spread of nuclear weapons made the world a safer place? How does a safer world make our futures brighter? Record your findings in your Active Journal.

What Has Been Done to Stop the Spread of Nuclear Weapons?

The spread of nuclear weapons is known as nuclear proliferation. By the early 2000s, most countries in the world, including the United States, had signed the **Nuclear Non-Proliferation Treaty** (NPT). The NPT required countries that already had nuclear weapons to reduce their number of weapons.

The NPT also prohibited countries that did not have nuclear weapons from acquiring them. All countries, however, could use nuclear power for peaceful purposes. The goal of non-proliferation is to reduce the chance of nuclear war.

Nuclear Tensions With North Korea As the United States and the global community monitored nuclear proliferation, North Korea was one country that attracted attention. In 1985, North Korea joined the Nuclear Non-Proliferation Treaty. Since North Korea did not have nuclear weapons at that time, it was prohibited from **obtaining** them.

Academic Vocabulary
obtain • *v.*, to get

International concern about its nuclear program led North Korea to use the program as a negotiating tool. In the 1990s, North Korea offered to end its nuclear program if the United States and other nations assisted North Korea with the construction of nuclear power plants.

Both sides reached an agreement in 1994. However, both sides accused each other of failing to live up to the agreement. In 2001, President George W. Bush announced that he would not negotiate with North Korea until it met a list of conditions. In response, North Korea resumed its nuclear program and withdrew from the NPT. Since 2006, North Korea has conducted underground tests of nuclear weapons. The country has also developed missiles that might be able to reach the United States.

Analyze Diagrams Nuclear fuels (such as uranium) must be enriched to produce energy. Nuclear weapons require greater enrichment. **Identify Supporting Details** What step follows energy production in order to develop nuclear weapons?

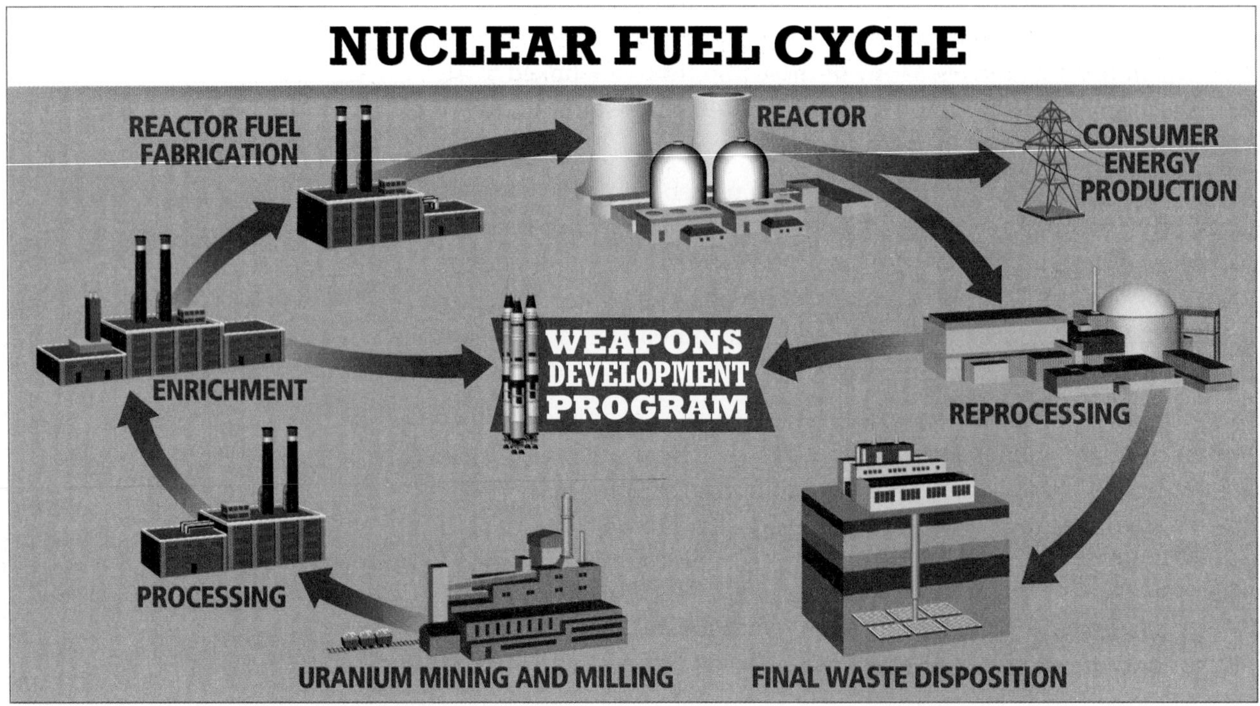

Analyze Visuals The North Korean government spends around a quarter of the country's gross domestic product on the military. **Use Visual Information** What elements in the visual verify the information in the image caption?

The United States and international organizations such as the United Nations (UN) launched efforts to respond to North Korea's nuclear program. North Korea's nuclear program caused international concern because of the possibility of nuclear attacks or a nuclear disaster.

The UN Security Council, including the United States, condemned North Korea's nuclear testing and imposed sanctions on trade with North Korea. Even China, North Korea's closest ally, supported UN Security Council resolutions requiring North Korea to end its nuclear program. In spite of this, North Korea continued constructing and testing nuclear weapons.

Iran's Nuclear Program Iran's nuclear program also alarmed the United States and other countries. Because the Iranian government had expressed strong hostility to Israel, a U.S. ally, Israel voiced special concern. In the 1980s, the U.S. government asked other countries not to sell nuclear technology to Iran. It imposed sanctions that harmed Iran's economy. The United States also partnered with other countries, as it had done before in attempts to end North Korea's nuclear program. Major Western powers moved to restrict Iran's access to the international financial system.

These efforts limited Iran's ability to sell oil, its most important export, which caused economic problems in Iran. In 2013, Iranians elected a new president, Hassan Rouhani, who was willing to negotiate with the United States and other powers over nuclear weapons. Negotiations to prevent Iran from developing nuclear weapons began in 2013. Three years later, six countries, including the United States, reached an agreement with Iran on its nuclear program. In exchange for the lifting of sanctions, Iran said it would stop enriching uranium for nuclear weapons. Critics were doubtful the deal would be effective.

READING CHECK **Identify Main Ideas** What is the main purpose of the NPT?

Did you know?

When Korea was divided following World War II, Kim Il-sung became the leader of North Korea. His son, Kim Jong-il, became the leader after his father's death in 1994. Today, Kim Jong-il's son, Kim Jong-un, leads North Korea.

GEOGRAPHY SKILLS

Israelis and Palestinians have disagreed over control of the West Bank for some 50 years.

1. **Interaction** Describe the way the Palestinian territories in the West Bank are organized.
2. **Draw Conclusions** Based on information from the map, why might the Israeli capital of Jerusalem be a site of conflict between Israelis and Palestinians?

Unrest in Southwest Asia and North Africa

The United States has strong ties to North Africa and Southwest Asia, the area sometimes called the Middle East. This region lies where the continents of Africa, Asia, and Europe meet. It is a region inhabited by Jews, Christians, and Muslims. As in past years, old conflicts in this region continued after 2000, and new conflicts emerged. The United States was a close ally of Israel, a mainly Jewish nation. At the same time, the U.S. economy relied on the oil production of Muslim nations, such as Saudi Arabia. The United States tried to resolve conflicts in this region. It remained committed to supporting democracy, its allies, and its own national interests.

Ongoing Arab–Israeli Tensions In 2003, President George W. Bush presented a "road map to peace" in the Israeli–Palestinian conflict. The goal was an independent Palestinian state and peaceful relations between Palestinians and Israelis.

Bush called for an end to the violence and for Israel to withdraw its troops permanently from Gaza and the West Bank, which Israel had occupied in 1967. However, resistance on both sides made the "road map" unworkable. Israeli Prime Minister Ariel Sharon, nonetheless, announced that he would withdraw Israeli forces from Gaza, home to more than 1.5 million Palestinians. Israel continued to control Gaza's boundaries, waters, and airspace. Israel also continued a policy of building Jewish settlements in the West Bank.

In 2007, tensions between Israel and Gaza increased when Hamas, an organization labeled as terrorist by Israel and the United States, came to power in Gaza. When rockets launched from Gaza killed Israeli civilians, Israel attacked Gaza in late 2008 and early 2009. These attacks resulted in Palestinian civilian deaths. Israel continued to restrict the flow of supplies and people across Gaza's borders. The U.S. government again supported Israel's actions as justified in terms of self-defense and continued to try to ease tensions between Israel and the Palestinians.

In 2014, another round of violence flared up between Hamas in Gaza and Israel. Hamas fired missiles into Israel, killing some civilians. Again, Israel bombarded Gaza and sent troops into the territory, resulting in many civilian deaths. An end to the cycle of violence seemed far away.

INTERACTIVE

The U.S. Role in the Middle East

What Has Caused Unrest in the Middle East? Unrest within the Arab world extended beyond the Arab–Israeli conflict. In early 2010, protests against undemocratic governments began in Tunisia and spread to other Arab countries. Together, these pro-democracy protests became known as the **Arab Spring**. In Egypt, protestors called for President Hosni Mubarak to step down after almost three decades of leading an undemocratic government. The United States agreed with the protestors, but the Obama administration moved cautiously in its support for the Arab Spring.

Pro-democracy movements spread to other Arab countries. In Syria, where the Arab Spring also triggered a civil war, the loss of life totaled 100,000 people or more. Meanwhile, in Egypt, the military overthrew the democratically elected government. The Obama administration expressed sympathy and gave limited support to democratic forces in both countries but worked to keep U.S. forces out of these conflicts.

READING CHECK **Identify Cause and Effect** Why did Israel attack Gaza in late 2008 and early 2009?

Analyze Visuals
Protesters gather in Cairo, Egypt, in 2011 to demand that Egyptian President Hosni Mubarak step down. **Draw Conclusions** Why might the sign in the photo be in English?

▲ The U.S. military often participates in relief operations, such as this one after a hurricane in Haiti in 2016.

How Did the United States Assist Other Nations?

In 2005, President George W. Bush declared that the United States must "extend democracy throughout the world." This commitment has led America to assist its allies and other nations.

As a member nation of the **North Atlantic Treaty Organization** (NATO), the United States has supported the addition of Eastern European countries to the military alliance. Russia opposed the addition of countries that were under Soviet rule during the Cold War. The growth of NATO reinforced the U.S. goal of a free and peaceful Europe.

After Russia invaded Ukraine in 2014, NATO **reaffirmed** its commitment to protecting its easternmost members. The United States and the European Union imposed sanctions on Russia.

Academic Vocabulary
reaffirm • *v.*, to express again a strong belief in

The United States also supported its allies through President Barack Obama's "pivot to Asia." This policy called for the United States to strengthen its relationships with nations in the Pacific Rim.

It also helped the United States monitor the actions of the Chinese government. China threatened the peace of the region by asserting claims to islands also claimed by Japan, the Philippines, Vietnam, and Malaysia. Besides protecting American interests in the Pacific, the "pivot to Asia" supported allies such as Japan.

READING CHECK **Draw Conclusions** Why do you think Russia opposed the addition of former Soviet countries to NATO?

Lesson Check

Practice Vocabulary

1. What role did **jihadism** play in the September 11 attacks?
2. What was the **Arab Spring**?

Critical Thinking and Writing

3. **Summarize** How has the United States supported its allies in Europe, Africa, and Asia since 2005?
4. **Understand Effects** What were the successes and failures of the U.S. war effort in Iraq?
5. **Identify Supporting Details** How did jihadists continue their mission after Osama bin Laden's death? How did the United States respond?
6. **Writing Workshop: Generate Questions to Focus Research** Write three to four questions in your Active Journal about societal changes in the United States following the attacks of September 11, 2001. These questions will help you focus your research on the topic of technological innovations and social changes for a research paper you will write at the end of the topic.

Primary Sources

George W. Bush, 9/11 Address to the Nation

On the evening of September 11, 2001, President George W. Bush delivered a speech to the American people from the Oval Office. The nation had just witnessed a devastating terrorist attack killing nearly 3,000 people and injuring more than 6,000 others.

▶ President George W. Bush

Good evening. Today, our fellow citizens, our way of life, ① our very freedom came under attack in a series of deliberate and deadly terrorist acts. The victims were in airplanes, or in their offices; secretaries, businessmen and women, military and federal workers; moms and dads, friends and neighbors. Thousands of lives were suddenly ended by evil, despicable ② acts of terror.

The pictures of airplanes flying into buildings, fires burning, huge structures collapsing, have filled us with disbelief, terrible sadness, and a quiet, unyielding ③ anger. These acts of mass murder were intended to frighten our nation into chaos and retreat. But they have failed; our country is strong. A great people has been moved to defend a great nation. Terrorist attacks can shake the foundations of our biggest buildings, but they cannot touch the foundation of America. These acts shattered steel, but they cannot dent the steel of American resolve.

America was targeted for attack because we're the brightest beacon for freedom and opportunity in the world. And no one will keep that light from shining. . . .

This is a day when all Americans from every walk of life unite in our resolve for justice and peace. America has stood down enemies before, and we will do so this time. None of us will ever forget this day. Yet, we go forward to defend freedom and all that is good and just in our world.

Reading and Vocabulary Support

① What does Bush mean when he says our "way of life" came under attack?

② *Despicable* means hateful or worthy of scorn.

③ What do you think the word *unyielding* means?

Analyzing Primary Sources

Cite specific evidence from the source to support your answers.

1. **Generate Explanations** Why do you think Bush compares America to "our biggest buildings"?
2. **Infer** What is meant by "no one will keep that light from shining"?
3. **Determine Author's Purpose** Why do you think Bush decided to give this speech to the American people?

Distinguish Real News from "Fake News"

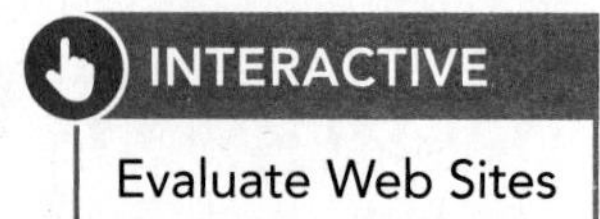

Follow these steps to help you to distinguish real news from "fake news."

1 **What is "fake news"?** Fake news is news that is reported but in reality is not accurate or reliable. It often appears on the Internet, and can appear in the form of written articles or as photographs or videos. It is often used to influence people, to shock people, or to gain attention.

2 **Identify false information.** Who is the author or creator of the site and what is their background? Is this someone who is just expressing his or her opinion, or is the author an expert on this particular topic? When you are looking for reliable information online, it is best to avoid sources that are anonymous. If you cannot find out who is responsible for putting the material on a site, then it's likely not accurate. A college professor or someone who works in a job related to the topic would obviously have more knowledge than someone who is just using the Internet to express their opinion. Read the headlines below. What sources would you use to identify whether these claims are real or fake?

3 **Rely on multiple sources.** Double-check the information on several different Web pages. Use established news sources and sources that are more likely to be reliable, such as

- government sites (end in .gov)
- educational sites (end in .edu)
- nonprofit organization sites (end in .org)

Many sites have been developed to monitor the factual accuracy of news stories, ads, and speeches. You can use these sources to determine what is real and what is fake on the Internet:

- FactCheck.org
- Snopes.com
- Politifact.com

4 **Trust your instincts.** Does the article or video seem real or probable based on what you already know? Do you have an emotional reaction to what you are reading or seeing? If something doesn't "seem" right, then it's important to verify the information with other sources.

5 **Be responsible before you click "send."** One reason that people create "fake news" sites is to get attention and to cause panic. If you have doubts about the reliability of what you find on a Web site, don't pass it on to your friends or family.

Headlines:

Congress Votes to Abolish the Electoral College

Sources: ______________________________

New Satellite Images Reveal That Antarctic Ice Is Melting

Sources: ______________________________

U.S. Billionaire Says He Earned His Fortune as a Russian Spy

Sources: ______________________________

A Global Economy

BOUNCE TO ACTIVATE VIDEO

GET READY TO READ

START UP

Look at the photo of workers in a Chinese factory. Predict how world trade might affect your everyday life.

GUIDING QUESTIONS

- How are the U.S. economy and the global economy connected?
- What were the reasons for the 2007 recession?
- Why did the U.S. economy recover slowly after the 2007 recession?

TAKE NOTES

Literacy Skills: Sequence

Use the graphic organizer in your Active Journal to take notes as you read the lesson.

PRACTICE VOCABULARY

Use the vocabulary activity in your Active Journal to practice the vocabulary words.

Vocabulary		Academic Vocabulary
globalization	American Recovery and Reinvestment Act	fraud
bubble	debt ceiling	stimulate
mortgage	default	
subprime mortgage		

Through its financial and trade relationships, America became part of a global economy. In the 1990s and early 2000s, America's trade with other countries grew dramatically.

Trade agreements with countries in the Americas and Asia strengthened U.S. relations and opened trade in new areas. American businesses benefited from lower production costs and the opening of new markets for trade. American consumers benefited from lower prices for goods and services.

How Did a Worldwide Economy Develop?

Globalization, or the spread of a global economy, also posed potential problems, though. Some American workers suffered when companies moved work overseas. Also, when one country suffered an economic crisis, the entire global community was at risk.

A Crash and Recovery In the 1990s, the American economy grew strongly. This growth was partly due to the creation of new businesses and jobs in the technology industry.

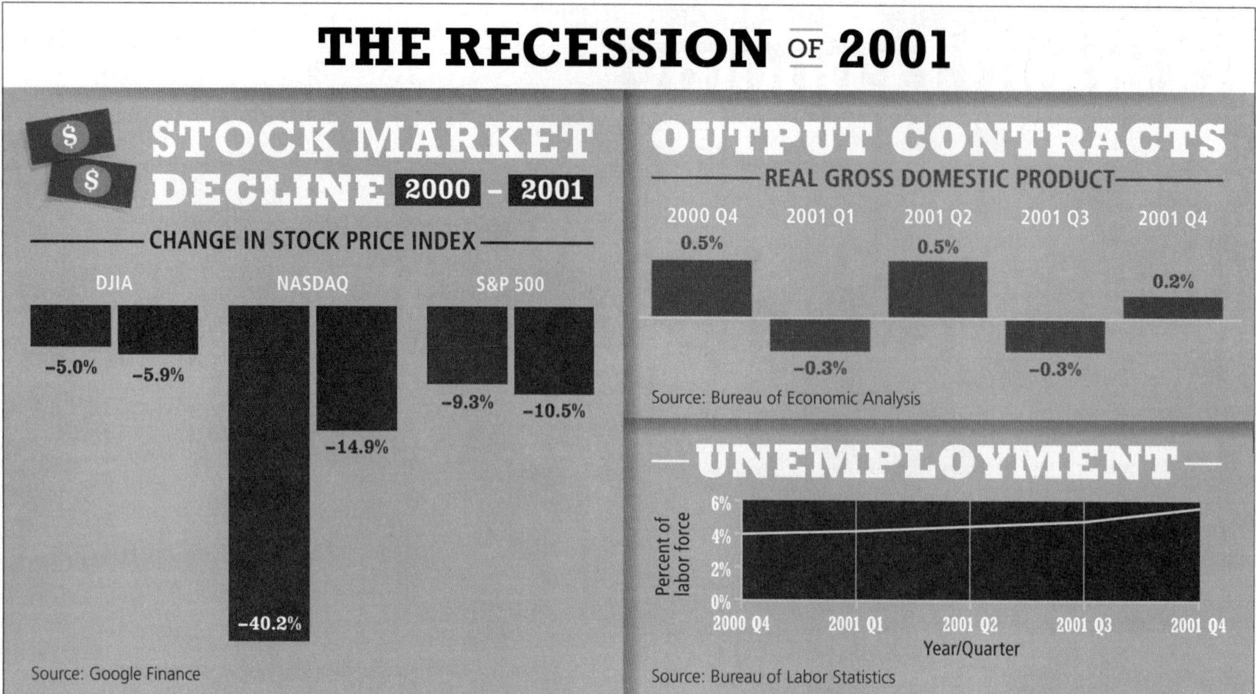

Analyze Charts The stock market and employment suffered as a result of the recession in 2001. **Use Visual Information** In which year did the NASDAQ experience its greatest drop?

Many Internet start-up companies, known as dot-coms, were founded during the decade. In some of these, owners and managers used risky business practices. They thought that if the number of customers increased, then profits would increase, too. This worked for some companies but not for all of them.

Investors saw the potential to make profits from dot-coms, so they bought stock in the companies. High demand for these stocks created a stock-market **bubble**. A bubble is an unstable condition of prices driven above the real value of an asset by buyers hoping that prices will rise further.

Effects of the Recession

When many dot-coms failed to yield a profit, the bubble burst and stock prices plunged. Investment in these companies dried up. Between 1999 and 2001, many dot-com businesses had to close. Other companies, such as Google and Amazon, suffered losses but survived and eventually grew.

In 2001, the American economy entered a recession, partly as a result of the dot-com bubble bursting. A recession occurs when the economy shrinks instead of growing. The September 11 attacks also hurt the stock market, and the transfer of American manufacturing jobs to other countries deepened the recession.

The federal government responded to the economic crisis by lowering taxes, while the Federal Reserve System lowered interest rates to encourage people and businesses to borrow. The economy gradually recovered in 2003 and 2004.

Academic Vocabulary

fraud • *n.*, using dishonest methods to take something valuable from another person

Questions of Fraud When the stock market crashed in 2000, Americans realized that **fraud** had helped trigger the 1990s boom. Accounting firms and banks had hidden companies' financial situations.

This increased their stock prices. Enron, a Houston energy company, exemplified this trend. Enron bought and sold electricity instead of producing it on its own. The company falsely reported billions of dollars in profits. A Texas jury convicted Enron executives of fraud, but it was too late to help investors. Fraud at Enron damaged Americans' trust of corporations in general.

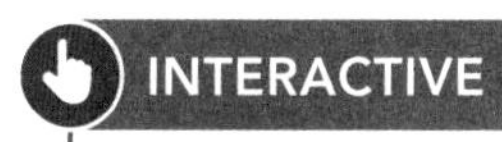

Pivot to Asia

Increasing Global Trade The North American Free Trade Agreement (NAFTA), established in 1993, linked the United States, Canada, and Mexico in a free-trade zone. In 1995, the United States became a member of the World Trade Organization (WTO). The WTO works to remove barriers to trade and encourage trade and investment among countries.

NAFTA and the WTO encouraged the United States to negotiate similar agreements in other areas of the world. In 2005, the Central America Free Trade Agreement (CAFTA-DR) created a free-trade zone between the United States and several Latin American countries. The United States also negotiated a free-trade agreement with South Korea in 2007.

Each of these agreements allowed U.S. businesses to sell more goods and services overseas. Meanwhile, foreign businesses were able to increase sales in the United States.

These free-trade agreements increased global trade, but they were controversial. They led some American businesses to move operations to other countries, where worker pay was lower and environmental regulations were weaker.

One of the world's main trading and investment alliances is the European Union (EU). The EU includes most European countries. In 2004, the EU expanded to include countries from Central and Eastern Europe and the Mediterranean.

Membership in the EU created new opportunities for these countries. It also attracted American investment. Many American banks and other firms opened branches within the EU to have access to its large market. As a result, what happened in the EU could affect the U.S. economy.

Analyze Visuals NAFTA links the United States, Canada, and Mexico in a free-trade zone and increases the trade of goods among the three nations. **Synthesize Visual Information** According to the images, what are three trade goods exchanged through NAFTA?

Growing Financial Ties Globalization brought benefits, such as the expansion of trade opportunities. It also created the potential for new problems for the United States. The banking system throughout the world became closely connected. If the European banking system or the American banking system were to face trouble, both sides would suffer the consequences.

In 1999, most countries in the European Union adopted a shared currency, known as the euro. The countries using the euro were known as the euro zone. By the 2010s, the euro was the second most widely used currency in the world, behind the American dollar. Euro-zone companies held large investments in the United States, and U.S. firms had large investments in the euro zone.

The EU was one of America's most important trade partners in the early 2000s. As a result, economic problems in Europe could hurt the United States. American entrepreneurs and businesses depend on investments from euro-zone countries to grow new or existing businesses. American businesses also depend on euro-zone customers to buy their products and services.

READING CHECK **Identify Cause and Effect** Why was the World Trade Organization formed?

What Caused a World Economic Crisis?

As you have read, to help the United States economy recover from the 2001 recession, the Federal Reserve System lowered interest rates. This enabled people to pay less to borrow money. Low interest rates encouraged Americans and American businesses to increase the amounts of money that they borrowed, spent, and invested.

▼ After the real estate bubble burst in 2007, many Americans lost their homes to foreclosure. Foreclosure is the process by which a bank takes ownership of a home from an owner that fails to pay a mortgage.

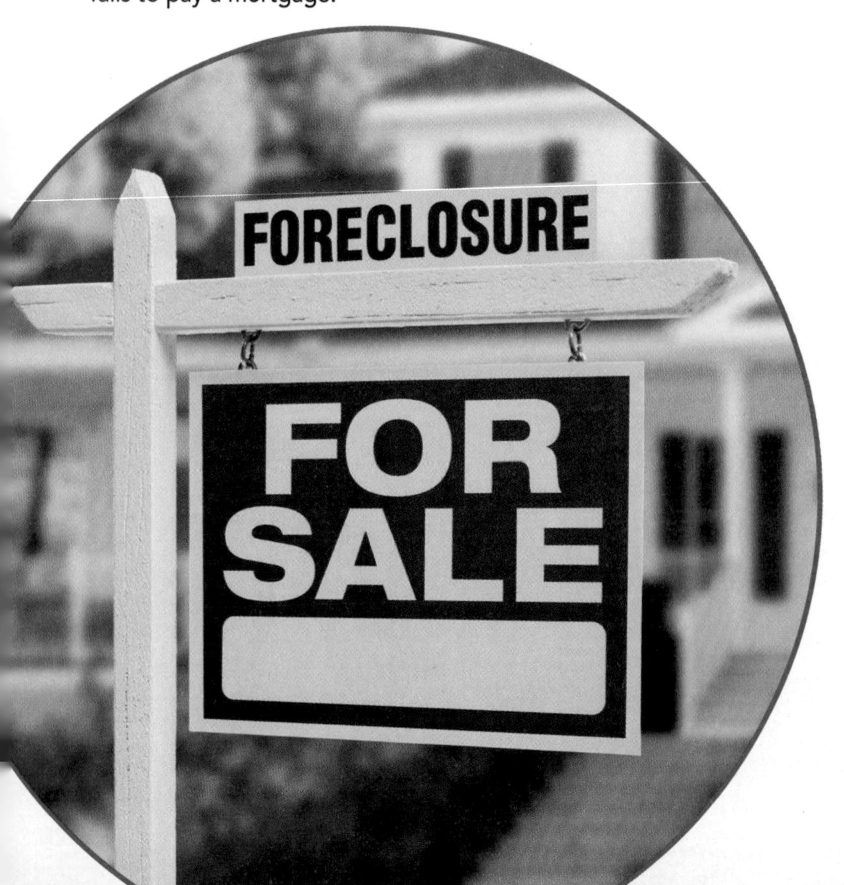

It also allowed more Americans to buy homes, and low interest rates made larger **mortgages** affordable. A mortgage is a loan to buy a piece of property, commonly with monthly payments. It allows the lender to claim the property if the mortgage is not paid.

As the demand for homes and mortgages increased, home prices also increased. This created a housing bubble much like the dot-com bubble.

Banks and mortgage companies thought that home prices would keep increasing. As a result, they offered mortgages to people who could not truly afford the payments. These risky loans were known as **subprime mortgages**.

Stock Fluctuations, 2000–2017

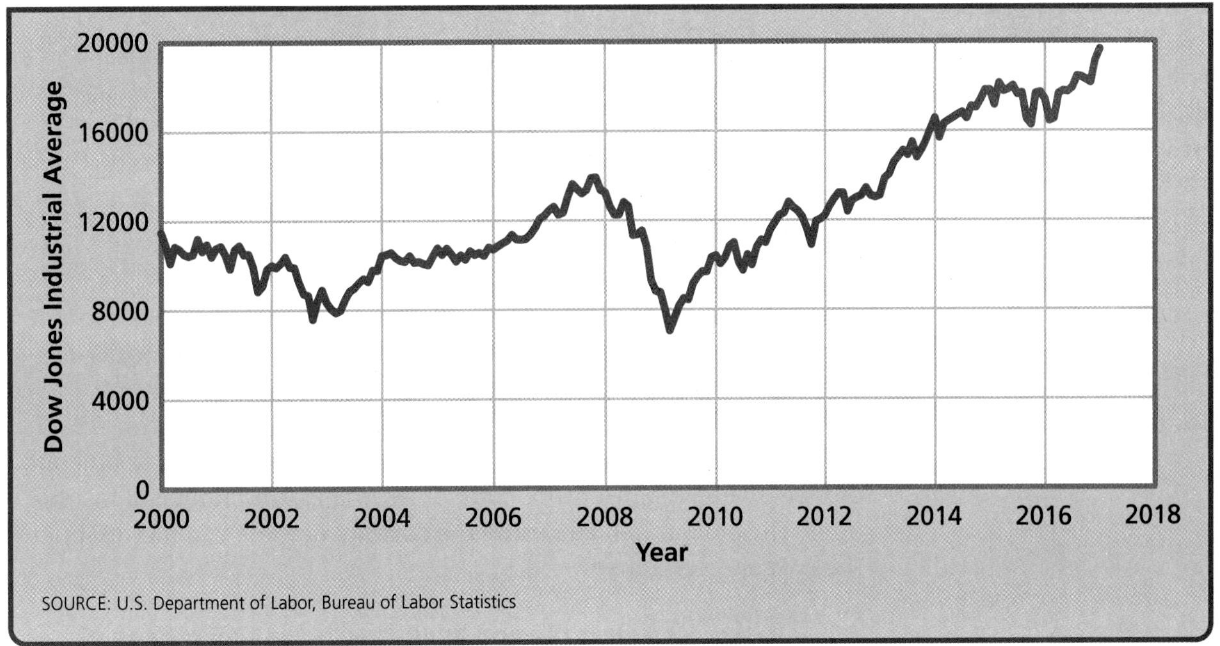

Analyze Graphs The financial crisis caused stock prices to plummet in 2008 and 2009, but they later recovered. **Use Visual Information** In which year did the stock market experience its greatest drop?

In 2006 and 2007, overbuilding and a flood of sellers seeking to cash in on high prices for their homes caused American home prices to drop, which burst the housing bubble. When prices dropped, many homeowners owed more on their mortgages than their homes were worth. When interest rates increased, some could not pay their mortgages. If they sold, they would lose their investment and still have a large debt.

Many of these borrowers defaulted on their mortgages, and banks repossessed, or foreclosed on, the homes. Foreclosures left Americans without homes and left banks with massive financial losses. This triggered an economic crisis in which banks stopped making loans, businesses stopped expanding, and the stock market crashed. The United States entered another recession in 2007.

What Were the Global Repercussions? The stock market crash and the mortgage crisis in 2007 led Americans to cut back on their spending. Reduced spending caused American businesses to downsize or even to fail, which increased unemployment. Consumers lost their jobs, their homes, their retirement savings, and their confidence in America.

Globalization, however, meant that the economic problems extended to the world. Decreases in American spending also caused job losses for U.S. trade partners, such as China and Mexico.

Because Europe's banks had bought subprime mortgages from American banks, the bursting of the housing bubble hurt European banks, too. It also made investors more aware of risk. They began to demand higher interest rates for loans to governments with poor finances. Governments across Europe were forced to cut back.

Economic Challenges in the 2000s

Quick Activity

In your Active Journal, create an illustrated timeline about economic developments and trends since the 1990s.

European banks stopped lending. Europe went into recession, too, which hurt American businesses because they lost sales in Europe.

For decades, the United States government had cut regulations, believing that government interference would damage banks. When the financial crisis resulted from what many saw as weak regulation, the government reversed its policy. The Bush administration allowed a bank called Lehman Brothers to fail, but it worried about the national and global implications of additional banking failures.

However, the Bush administration thought that many large banks and financial firms were "too big to fail." Administration officials believed that the connectedness of these companies to other businesses put the United States at risk of financial collapse and an economic depression. Thus, in 2008, Congress provided money to bail out, or save, struggling insurance companies, banks, and financial institutions. The bailout helped ensure the survival of these companies, but the economy remained weak.

READING CHECK **Draw Conclusions** How do you think people reacted when the government decided to bail out the insurance companies, banks, and financial institutions?

A Weak Recovery

When President Barack Obama took office in 2009, Americans were still experiencing the effects of the economic recession. The unemployment rate for the year averaged close to ten percent. Fourteen percent of Americans lived below the poverty line. Home prices continued to fall.

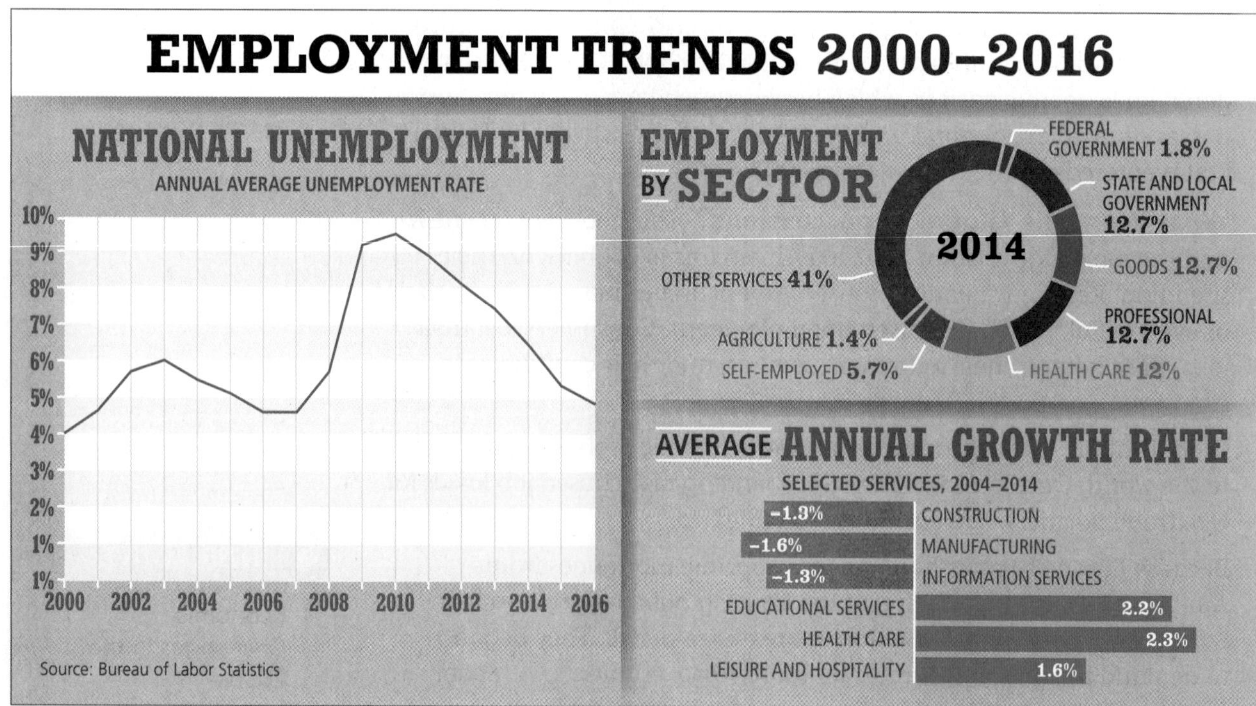

Analyze Graphs The financial crisis caused many people to lose their jobs, and the unemployment rate increased substantially. **Use Visual Information** How high was unemployment in October 2008?

Analyze Visuals
Construction projects like this one in Arizona were funded by the American Recovery and Reinvestment Act. **Draw Conclusions** Why do you think the orange sign was included with this road sign?

Why Was the Stimulus Controversial? In 2009, President Obama signed into law the **American Recovery and Reinvestment Act**. The act aimed to **stimulate** the economy and reduce unemployment. Through it, Congress supplied funds to create jobs and to increase unemployment, disability, and food stamp benefits. The bill also funded improvement projects at schools and airports and on highways to create jobs and help communities. It also reduced taxes.

A number of economists have argued that the recession would have been longer and more severe without this stimulus. Critics, however, found problems with the act. Some felt that it had been ineffective, was too expensive, and had increased the federal deficit for no purpose. Other critics argued that the stimulus was too small.

The act also reflected sharp political divides between the Democratic and Republican parties. All Republicans in the House of Representatives voted against the act. Only three Republican senators voted in favor of it.

A Paper Recovery American recovery from the 2007 economic recession occurred slowly. The stock market rallied, and it appeared as if the recession had ended by 2010, in the sense that the economy returned to growth.

Americans still struggled, though. State and local governments reduced their workforces. The national unemployment and poverty rates remained high. In some years, the number of new jobs was lower than the number of young people reaching working age. The number of manufacturing jobs rose, but job creation did not reach pre-recession levels.

Meanwhile, jobs and pay were unequally distributed. Most jobs were at the high and low ends of the pay scale. The financial industry had laid off workers, but employees who kept their jobs received high pay. This frustrated Americans whose taxes were used to bail out the companies that were "too big to fail."

The largest number of job increases occurred in low-paying jobs. Workers with these jobs had difficulty supporting themselves and their families. From 2009 until 2014, wages fell for most Americans. Incomes then started to rebound. By 2016, median earnings had finally risen to exceed the level they were at before the economic crisis. The unemployment rate, which peaked in 2009 at 10 percent, fell below 5 percent in 2016.

Academic Vocabulary
stimulate • *v.*, to cause something to grow or to happen

Analyze Images Workers in Greece demonstrate against cuts to their pay as a result of the debt crisis. **Identify Main Ideas** What caused Greece's economic troubles?

Economic Dangers Persist In the 2010s, debt crises in the United States and Europe threatened economic stability. Tax cuts, wars in Iraq and Afghanistan, and slow economic growth had pushed America's debt to near its limit.

The **debt ceiling** limits the amount of debt that the United States can owe. When the country nears the debt ceiling, Congress must vote to raise the limit, or the country risks **default**, or failure to repay a debt, and a possible financial crisis. Since 1960, Congress has acted 78 times to raise, extend, or revise the definition of the debt limit.

When President Obama asked Congress to raise the debt ceiling in 2011 and 2013, Republicans refused unless the President agreed to a compromise. Congress had to raise the debt ceiling to keep the country operating, but Republican members were only willing to do that if the President agreed to reduce spending.

Meanwhile, a debt crisis occurred in Europe. Between 2009 and 2012, six euro-zone countries acknowledged that they were struggling to pay their debts and were facing default. Greece was the first country to show signs of problems.

This situation presented an economic problem for the world by putting into question government bonds. If banks are worried about money they have lent to governments, they are less likely to lend money to businesses and individuals. Recognizing this, European and international agencies all provided bailout money.

This bailout brought a temporary solution to the European debt crisis, but a number of countries continued to face heavy debts and a lack of economic growth. It was not clear that the debt problem had been corrected. A danger remained that one or more countries might default on their debts and cripple the global financial system.

READING CHECK **Understand Effects** What did the American Recovery and Reinvestment Act do?

Lesson Check

Practice Vocabulary

1. Which asset **bubbles** popped in the first decade of the 2000s?
2. Why might a **default** on the national debt lead to a financial crisis?

Critical Thinking and Writing

3. **Summarize** Discuss the dot-com boom and how it affected the American economy.
4. **Use Evidence** What were some of the criticisms of NAFTA?
5. **Sequence** What events led to the U.S. economic recession in 2007?
6. **Writing Workshop: Support Ideas with Evidence** Gather credible sources to support your ideas about technological innovation and social change. Record them in your Active Journal.

LESSON 3

Advances in Science and Technology

GET READY TO READ

START UP

Examine the photo of the wind turbines. How do you think they generate electricity?

GUIDING QUESTIONS

- What are the world's environmental challenges?
- How have advances in biotechnology, medicine, digital technology, and communication affected the world?

TAKE NOTES

Literacy Skills: Analyze Text Structure

Use the graphic organizer in your Active Journal to take notes as you read the lesson.

PRACTICE VOCABULARY

Use the vocabulary activity in your Active Journal to practice the vocabulary words.

Vocabulary

fossil fuel
pollution
Environmental Protection Agency
climate change
drought
emission
biotechnology
AIDS
Internet
smart phone

Academic Vocabulary

organic
enhance

New Discoveries

During the early 2000s, the National Aeronautics and Space Administration (NASA) explored the solar system. Orbiters circled planets to gather information about each planet's chemical structure, magnetic field, and formation.

These studies required planning and patience. It could take years from the time an orbiter is launched until it reached its destination. It took the *Messenger* orbiter seven years after its launch from Earth in 2004 to reach orbit around the planet Mercury. The *New Horizons* space probe needed a nine-year voyage after its launch in 2006 to reach Pluto, and the *Juno* orbiter needed five years after its launch in 2011 to reach Jupiter.

NASA gave special attention to Mars. Presidents George W. Bush and Barack Obama expressed support for the idea of sending astronauts to Mars in the future. To explore the planet, NASA sent orbiters to Mars during the 2000s. The *Mars Odyssey*, *Mars Express*, and *Mars Reconnaissance* orbiters circled Mars and took photographs.

Analyze Images The *Curiosity* rover landed on the surface of Mars and was still exploring the planet in early 2017. **Explain an Argument** What can be learned from exploring other planets?

They also recorded the weather, mapped the terrain, and sent the information back to Earth.

Beginning in 2004, NASA also sent scientific rovers to explore Mars. The *Opportunity* and *Spirit* rovers traveled across the planet's surface and sent images back to Earth. The *Curiosity* science laboratory collected and analyzed Martian soil and rocks. NASA's goal was to look for evidence of water and for fossils or **organic** materials to find out whether ancient life existed on Mars.

NASA also explored space beyond our solar system. Through the Kepler mission, NASA studied our Milky Way Galaxy in a search for new planets. Instead of using rovers and orbiters for this mission, NASA used a space-based telescope. The Kepler orbiting telescope collected images from the galaxy and sent them back to Earth. Scientists analyzing those images identified more than 1,700 planets outside Earth's solar system.

READING CHECK **Identify Main Ideas** Why does NASA send orbiters and rovers to explore planets in the solar system?

Responding to Environmental Challenges

As the global economy grew, it consumed larger amounts of energy. Most of that energy came from **fossil fuels**, such as oil, coal, and natural gas.

Fossil fuels are fuels formed in the distant past that have limited supplies. Once they are burned, they are gone and cannot be replaced. They also cause environmental damage by polluting the air when they are burned. **Pollution**, or harmful impurities added to the environment, is a worldwide problem. Air or water pollution from other countries may affect the United States.

What Is the Environmental Movement? The modern environmental movement began in the 1960s with the publication of *Silent Spring*. In this book, Rachel Carson, a marine biologist, warned readers of the dangers of DDT. DDT is a chemical that farmers used to kill insects. Carson explained that DDT sprayed on crops did not just kill insects. It killed birds and fish and even threatened human food supplies.

Congress responded by passing a law to restrict the use of DDT. Soon environmental groups like the Sierra Club, the National Wildlife Foundation, and the Audubon Society lobbied Congress for additional protective laws. In 1970, President Richard Nixon created the **Environmental Protection Agency** (EPA). In the same year, environmentalists held the first Earth Day.

In the 2000s, environmentalists throughout the world continued to address global problems. They were concerned about many issues.

Academic Vocabulary
organic • *adj.* of, relating to, or obtained from living things

These included groundwater contamination, chemical spills, depletion of the ozone layer in Earth's atmosphere, nuclear waste disposal, reliance on fossil fuels, the extinction of plants and animals, and the destruction of the rainforest.

INTERACTIVE

The World Today

The Issue of Climate Change **Climate change** is any measurable long-term change in climate. Climate change may affect precipitation, wind patterns, or temperature. Global warming, defined as an increase in average temperatures near Earth's surface, is one form of climate change.

According to the Environmental Protection Agency, during the 1900s, the temperature near Earth's surface rose 1.4 degrees Fahrenheit. The EPA estimated that the temperature would increase another 2 to 11.5 degrees by 2100.

In the early 2000s, scientists expressed concern that climate change could affect farming, the water supply, personal health, and the weather. Scientific studies suggested that climate change had caused some areas, such as the eastern United States, to experience heavier rain and increased flooding.

Other areas, such as the western United States, had less precipitation and more frequent droughts. A **drought** is a shortage of water that affects plants and animals and energy production and increases the risk of wildfires.

Climate scientists concluded in the early 2000s that humans were the greatest contributors to climate change. Burning fossil fuels released carbon dioxide and other greenhouse gases into the atmosphere. Greenhouse gases, which blanket Earth, are gases that trap energy and cause the temperature to increase.

Analyze Images The water level of Lake Mead, shown here, has dropped significantly due to drought. **Draw Conclusions** How might climate change affect your environment?

Did you know?

China and the United States are the world's largest emitters of greenhouse gases.

Some amount of greenhouse gases is needed for a stable climate, but too much will permanently change Earth's climate. The main greenhouse gas, carbon dioxide, remains in the atmosphere for almost 100 years, so past and present human action will affect future generations.

In the 2000s, the EPA collected information on pollution and greenhouse gas **emissions**, or gases released into the air. It also encouraged energy conservation and the development of cleaner energy. The EPA worked to reduce greenhouse gas emissions. Since both pollution and climate change were global issues, the EPA also worked with international partners.

Progress on Cleaner Energy To reduce greenhouse gas emissions, the U.S. government encouraged the use of renewable energy sources. Unlike fossil fuels, renewable energy sources have potentially unlimited supplies. Energy from the sun, wind, moving water, Earth's heat (geothermal energy), and organic plant and waste material (biomass) can restore itself.

Environmentalists preferred these energy sources to fossil fuels. They had the potential to decrease America's dependence on foreign oil, diminish greenhouse gas emissions, and reduce pollution. Critics argued, however, that these sources are often more expensive than fossil fuels and that relying on them could harm the economy.

Nuclear power and biofuels provided additional alternatives to fossil fuels. The dangers of nuclear power made it controversial, though. In 1979, the Three Mile Island nuclear power plant near Harrisburg, Pennsylvania, experienced a meltdown in its reactor. This accident caused radioactive material to leak and forced people to evacuate.

Analyze Charts The use of fossil fuels has had a significant impact on the climate. **Synthesize Visual Information** How much is the global temperature predicted to rise between 1900 and 2100 with continued heavy use of fossil fuels?

GLOBAL CLIMATE CHANGE

INCREASE IN CARBON DIOXIDE LEVELS SINCE INDUSTRIAL REVOLUTION
43%

GLOBAL SURFACE TEMPERATURE CHANGE
°F (RELATIVE TO 1960–1999 AVERAGE)

DIFFERENT SCENARIOS:

20th century actual		Year 2000 carbon dioxide levels hold steady		Some shift toward non-fossil fuels		Continued heavy use of fossil fuels	
−1.1	+0.4	+0.4	+1.1	+0.4	+5.0	+0.4	+7.2
1900	2000	2000	2100	2000	2100	2000	2100

ARCTIC SEA ICE COVER

1980

2015

Sources: National Climate Data Center; National Oceanic and Atmospheric Administration

Radioactive material is harmful and can be deadly to people and other living things.

Nuclear power plants convert radioactive nuclear fuels into energy by capturing the force of splitting atoms. This process leaves behind nuclear waste, or radioactive material. Nuclear waste remains hazardous to people and other living things for hundreds of thousands of years. During the early 2000s, experts could not agree on a safe way to dispose of nuclear waste, so there was the risk that it could harm people for many generations to come.

Biofuels are alternative energy sources produced from converting biomass, plant, and waste material into liquid fuels. The most common forms of biofuels are ethanol and biodiesel. During the early 2000s, most ethanol in the United States was produced from corn. Beginning in 2005, federal law required a percentage of the gasoline sold in the United States to be mixed with at least small quantities of ethanol. Biodiesel is produced from crops such as soybeans. Both fuels can power automobiles.

Biofuels, however, were also controversial. Growing, processing, and transporting crops to create biofuels uses fossil fuels that contribute to pollution and consume energy. There were questions about whether the energy that biofuels produce was greater than the energy used to create the biofuels themselves. Critics also noted that using crops for fuel could increase food costs.

READING CHECK **Identify Supporting Details** Name two reasons why environmentalists prefer renewable energy sources to fossil fuels.

Analyze Images Solar farms trap energy from the sun. That energy is later converted into electricity that people can use. **Compare and Contrast** how using solar energy and burning fossil fuels change the environment.

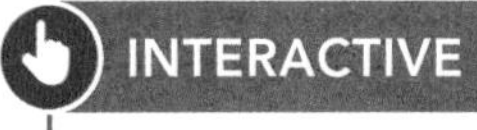

Advances in Energy Technology

GENETICALLY MODIFIED FOODS

GENETIC MODIFICATION

Sweet Potatoes	Golden Rice	Papaya	Corn	Cow Feed
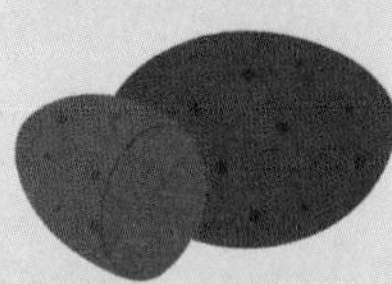		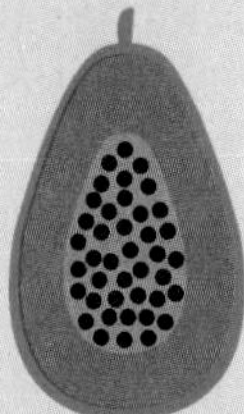	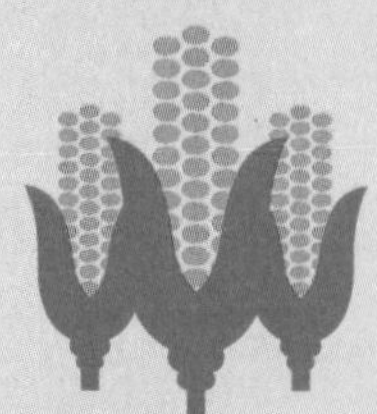	
Modified to resist Sweet Potato Feather Mottle Virus	Modified to increase amount of beta-carotene by 20 times	Modified to resist Papaya Ringspot Virus	Modified to resist certain insects	Modified to boost milk production

Sources: Encyclopedia Britannica, U.S. Department of Agriculture, U.S. Environmental Protection Agency, U.S. Food and Drug Administration

Analyze Charts Biotechnology companies employ scientists to create new ways of addressing human needs, from medicine to food to creating new materials, and more. **Identify Main Ideas** What needs are being addressed by the modifications to these particular crops?

What Are Some Advances in Biology and Medicine?

In the years after 2000, scientists made progress in identifying the building blocks of life, particularly genes. Genes are the hereditary material in organisms, including humans. Scientists, doctors, and other healthcare providers also made progress fighting disease.

The Biotech Revolution **Biotechnology** is technology based on biology. Advances in biotechnology helped feed, fuel, and heal the world. Biotechnology made rapid advances in the years after 2000. Not only did biotechnology improve medicine and agriculture, it also supported a growing industry based on creating products and services with biotechnology.

The medical field uses biotechnology to detect and fight disease. In 1990, the Human Genome Project brought the international scientific community together to map all the genes in the human body. The project was completed in 2003.

Scientists concluded that there are about 20,500 human genes. The complete set of genes in the human body is known as the human genome. Studying the human genome helped researchers understand human diseases. With this knowledge, they could develop new plans for the detection, treatment, and prevention of diseases.

Researchers also used biotechnology to make drugs to treat diseases. They learned to adjust the genes of microorganisms, such as bacteria, to make them produce useful drugs and other treatments. During the early 2000s, these efforts produced better and safer vaccines and brought down the cost of some medicines.

Quest CONNECTIONS

What do the advances in biotechnology mean for people's health? What advantages does a well-nourished, healthy person have? Record your findings in your Active Journal.

Farmers use biotechnology to increase crop production, develop crops that are resistant to insects and diseases, and **enhance** food nutrition. By adjusting the genes of crop plants, researchers were able to create varieties of crops that produced more food or that resisted drought, insects, and other agents that harmed crops. Ancient techniques of breeding also adjust the genes of plants and livestock, but biotechnology does so in a targeted way using scientific methods. These advances helped many farmers and consumers.

Academic Vocabulary
enhance • *v.,* to increase or improve the quality of

Fighting Disease Globalization increased the impact and reach of illnesses and infectious diseases. The frequency of travel intensified the rate at which diseases could be transmitted throughout the world. This increased rate of transmission led to increased concern about health security.

The U.S. Centers for Disease Control and Prevention (CDC) worked with governments around the world to address this concern. The CDC helped other countries learn how to detect and prevent the spread of potential disease epidemics.

The CDC also supported HIV/AIDS programs in more than 70 countries. *HIV* stands for human immunodeficiency virus. HIV can cause **AIDS**, acquired immunodeficiency syndrome, an often fatal disease that attacks the human immune system. Although the human body cannot get rid of HIV, medication can prolong the lives of people infected with the virus.

During the 1990s, medications for AIDS improved. By the 2000s, nearly all Americans had access to effective AIDS treatments.

The United States has been a leader in medicine since the 1900s. During the years after 2000, the United States continued to develop better drugs and better ways of treating and preventing disease.

For example, beginning in the early 2000s, the National Cancer Institute began developing drugs and other treatments that targeted cancer cells. These treatments were safer and more effective than earlier treatments for cancer. Researchers have also developed improved surgical methods and new vaccines.

READING CHECK **Identify Supporting Details** What was a primary goal of the Human Genome Project?

A Networked World

Computers allow information to be saved, analyzed, and exchanged. The first computers in the world were mainframes, which were so large they could fill a room. In the 1950s and 1960s, only private businesses, the government, and universities could afford to own them.

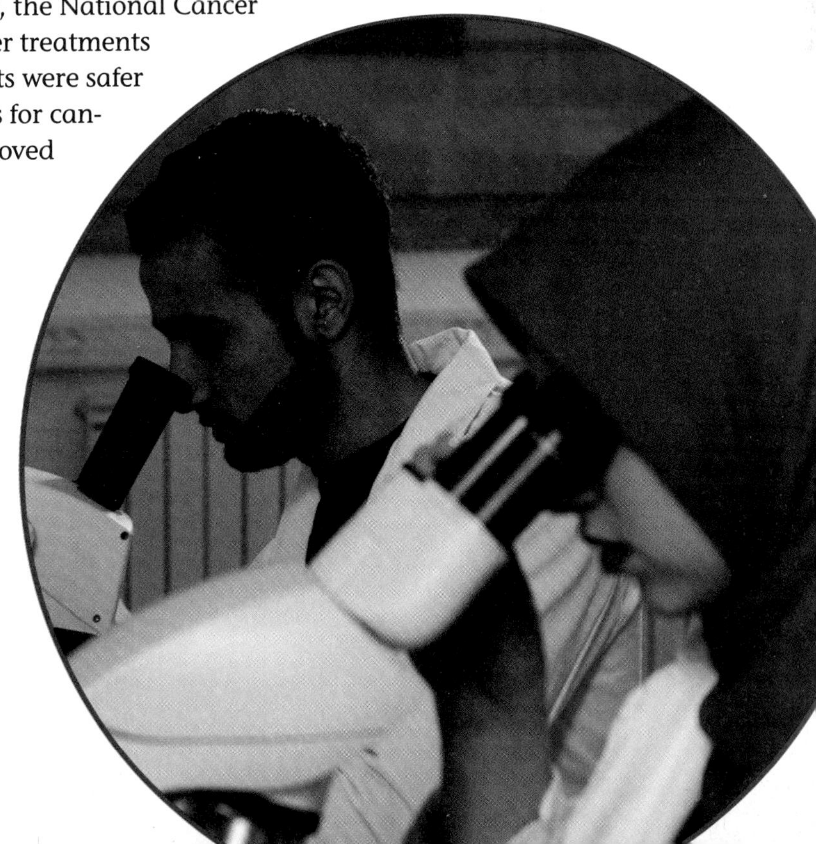

▼ Scientists work in a biochemistry lab. Biochemists play a major role in developing medicines that fight disease.

Quick Activity

Think of three events—real or imagined—that show important aspects of life in twenty-first-century America. Write newspaper headlines about these events in your Active Journal.

By the 1980s, affordability and smaller sizes made personal computers common in homes, small businesses, and schools. By the early 2000s, new technology had made computers faster, less expensive, and more portable. Some computers could fit in a pocket.

The Internet In the 1960s, a scientist at the Massachusetts Institute of Technology worked to develop a system to connect computers worldwide. His ideas provided the basis for the **Internet**, a system of linking computers that gives users access to information. In 1969, the United States Department of Defense began linking its computers to computers at American universities. In the 1990s, private companies made the Internet available to homes and businesses.

The Internet makes email communication, instant messaging, Voice over Internet Protocol (VoIP) calls, video calls, and use of the World Wide Web, often simply known as the Web, possible. The Web was created in the 1980s using technology developed by the United States, Britain, and France.

Although sometimes lumped together, the Web and the Internet are not the same. The Web is one of many services that run on the Internet. It links documents through hypertext. Web browsers let people view those documents as images, texts, and multimedia on the Internet.

Personal computers and the Internet changed the world. They increased business productivity and efficiency. E-commerce expanded the marketplace to make it digital and global. People regularly bought products, paid bills, and managed their bank accounts online. Digital lessons, textbooks, and library resources transformed teaching and learning.

The Internet and the Web introduced users to social networking. Social networks allow people with shared interests and backgrounds to connect digitally. Social network sites can be used for personal and business connections. They allow people to set up profiles and manage who has access to the information that they share.

Like the rest of the Internet, social networking sites presented risks when they did not adequately protect individual privacy. They also could be vulnerable to data theft and viruses.

Analyze Visuals Early computers, such as this IBM "702" model from 1954, were so large they had to be housed in an entire room. **Draw Conclusions** What might be the purpose of the object the man on the right of the photo is holding in his hand?

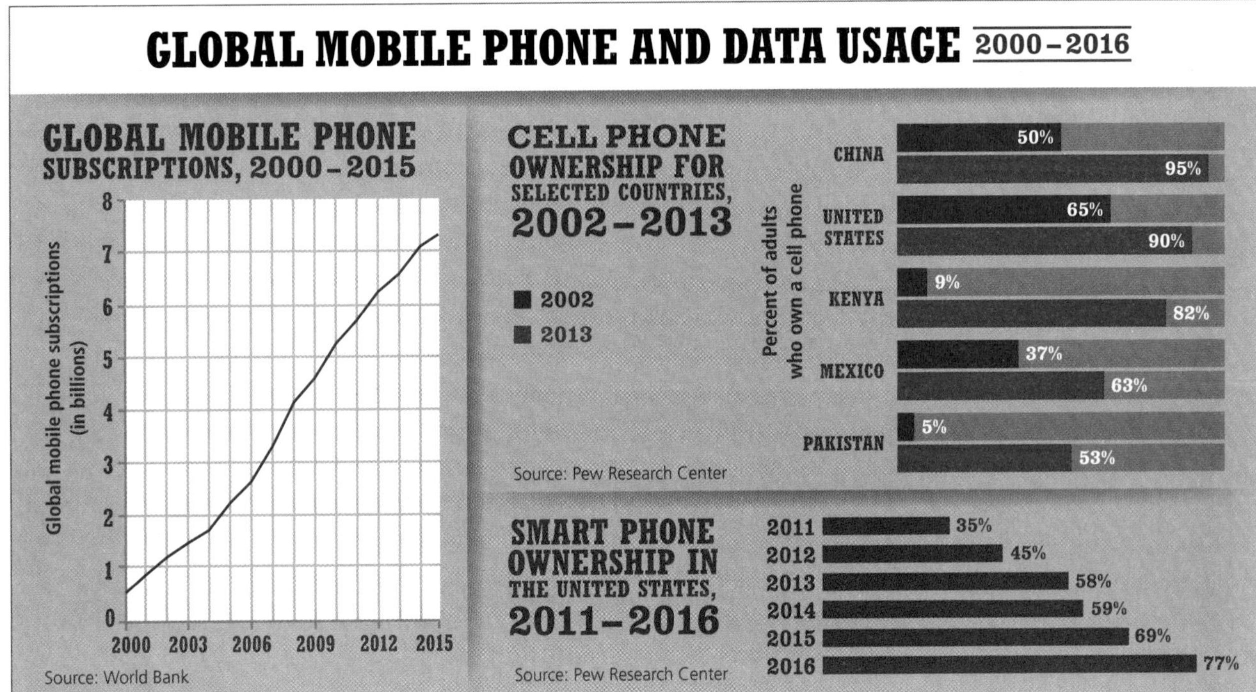

Analyze Graphs Since the turn of the century, cell phone use has increased significantly. **Use Visual Information** Which country has made the greatest jump in cell phone ownership since 2002?

The Mobile Revolution The first mobile phones were developed in the 1970s, but they were awkward and expensive. Mobile phones came into wider use in the 1990s.

By the early 2000s, many Americans owned **smart phones**, or small, handheld phones with sophisticated computing capability and an ability to connect to the Internet via radio signals. Many individuals and families also owned tablet computers. Tablets are small mobile computers with touch screens that also connect to the Internet.

Mobile devices such as smart phones and tablets use application software, or apps, to operate. Originally, apps were used for simple tasks like sending and receiving email, managing a calendar, or collecting contact information.

Public demand led software engineers to develop apps for games, magazines and books, banking, and shopping. Today, Americans use apps for social networking, viewing videos, searching for information, and reading books.

In spite of their popularity, mobile devices raised some concerns. Phone use in cars led to accidents. Many states required people to use hands-free devices while driving. People often found cell phone use disruptive in places such as restaurants, stores, and on public transportation. Smartphones contain chemicals that are toxic to humans and animals. The production and improper disposal of mobile devices damaged the environment.

Digital Security As use of the Internet and the Web increased, concern over cybercrime increased with it. Cybercrime includes identity theft, or collecting information about a person in order to engage in illegal activity.

Analyze Political Cartoons Internet attacks threaten both personal privacy and international security. **Identify Implied Main Ideas** What is the cartoonist's message about the potential effects of technology on the United States?

Many cybercriminals make fraudulent purchases with the information. Cybercrime also includes espionage and illegal intelligence gathering.

"Hackers," who tap into computers and threaten privacy, contribute to the spread of cybercrime. Today, most Internet attacks take place through computers based in the United States, China, and Russia.

Cyberwarfare is a digital form of warfare. It uses computers and other digital devices to attack an enemy's information system. It can be used in combination with military-based attacks, or it can be carried out on its own. Cyberwarfare can be directed toward businesses, agencies, organizations, and governments.

Politics or terrorism often motivate cyberattackers. If a cyberattack hit a country's power grid, it could cause traffic accidents, interrupt surgeries, and stop factory production.

During the 2000s, the Department of Defense's cyberwarfare unit and the National Security Agency (NSA) worked to protect the United States from cyberattacks. The NSA collected and processed data to protect the security of the nation.

Some of the NSA's data collection methods were controversial. In 2013, NSA contractor Edward Snowden leaked NSA documents to the press. Snowden's actions were also controversial. The U.S. government charged that he had damaged the nation's security. The case raised questions about government surveillance of U.S. citizens and American allies and the balance between individual privacy and national security.

READING CHECK **Understand Effects** What concern do many people share about social networking sites?

Lesson Check

Practice Vocabulary

1. What are examples of **fossil fuels**?
2. How have **greenhouse gases** caused **climate change**?

Critical Thinking and Writing

3. **Understand Effects** How was *Silent Spring* responsible for the creation of the modern environmental movement?
4. **Use Evidence** What examples can you give to support the idea that advances in biotechnology helped to feed, fuel, and heal the world?
5. **Summarize** How did the increased use of the Internet and the Web present new threats to its users?
6. **Writing Workshop: Cite Sources** Cite sources for your research paper in your Active Journal. You will write your research paper at the end of the Topic.

LESSON 4

Challenges at Home

GET READY TO READ

START UP

Examine the photo of Donald Trump on election night in 2016. How would you describe his mood?

GUIDING QUESTIONS

- What are significant events in George Bush's and Barack Obama's presidencies?
- What are some of the effects of immigration and expanded civil rights on American society?
- What happened during the presidential election of 2016?

TAKE NOTES

Literacy Skills: Summarize

Use the graphic organizer in your Active Journal to take notes as you read the lesson.

PRACTICE VOCABULARY

Use the vocabulary activity in your Active Journal to practice the vocabulary words.

Vocabulary		Academic Vocabulary
deficit	affirmative action	concede
Affordable Care Act	populist	enact
	temperament	

The election of 2000 was one of the most disputed in U.S. history. The Republican candidate, Governor George W. Bush of Texas, was the son of former President George H. W. Bush. Bush faced Vice President Al Gore, the Democratic candidate. When the election ended, Gore had won the popular vote by a margin of about 540,000 votes. According to the U.S. Constitution, however, the electoral vote, or the vote of the electoral college, determines who becomes President.

The Bush Era

With such a close election, the result rested on the electoral votes of one state: Florida. The initial results gave Bush a small lead, but winning Florida would have given Gore the votes he needed to win the election. Democrats expressed concern over confusion among Florida voters and problems with counting the ballots. They asked the Florida Supreme Court to force a recount of the Florida votes. The recount began, but in December 2000, the United States Supreme Court ordered the recount to stop.

Academic Vocabulary
concede • *v.*, to admit that you have been defeated

Bush, therefore, won the electoral votes of Florida and the presidential election of 2000. Al Gore **conceded** the election but voiced his disapproval of the Court's decision.

Standing Tall The election of 2000 showed sharp divisions within the country. Most Americans in the South and Mountain West voted for Bush. Most Americans in the Northeast, Upper Midwest, and on the West Coast voted for Gore. In the Senate, the Republican and Democratic parties were divided evenly with 50 seats each.

President Bush entered office in 2001 with plans for tax and education reform. The terrorist attacks on September 11, 2001, however, changed his presidency and the lives of Americans.

Bush led the nation as it fought back against the attacks. Americans showed an outpouring of patriotism in the months that followed. Bush benefited from that and from his strong response to the attacks, including the launch of a global war on terrorism. In September 2001, 90 percent of Americans approved of the job that Bush was doing.

In the same year, the United States slipped into an economic recession. Bush advocated for tax cuts to stimulate the economy. Congress responded by passing the largest tax cuts in American history. These cuts, when paired with the war on terrorism, increased the federal **deficit**, the amount of spending that is greater than income.

Recovery from the 2001 recession occurred slowly. Still, when Bush ran for reelection in 2004, his popularity was high. Many Americans were reluctant to change leaders when the wars in Iraq and Afghanistan were still underway. Bush easily won reelection over his Democratic opponent, Senator John Kerry of Massachusetts.

Analyze Graphs Deficits increased in 2009 but recovered as the economy improved. **Use Visual Information** In what year did the federal budget not show a deficit?

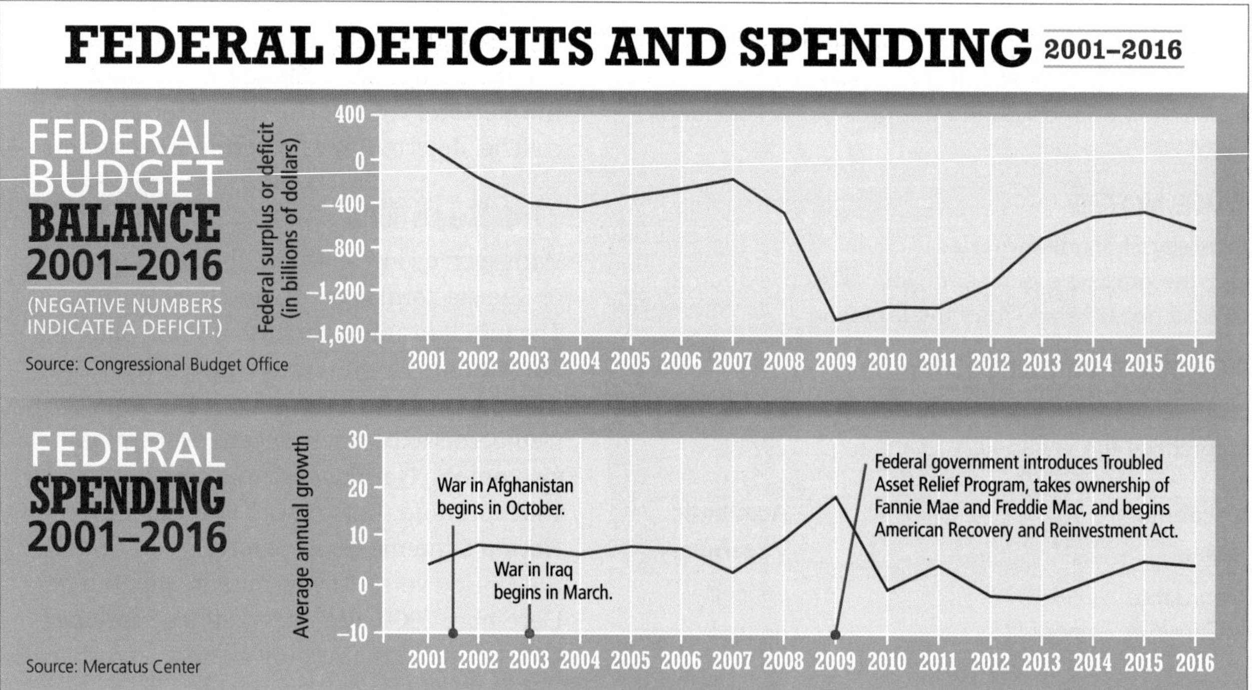

▲ In addition to economic and foreign-policy challenges, President Bush's response to Hurricane Katrina harmed his popularity in 2005. Here, he looks at the damage from Air Force One, the President's airplane.

Why Did President Bush's Popularity Decline? When Bush began his second term in 2005, more than half of Americans approved of the job he was doing. Over the next four years, however, Bush's popularity steadily declined. His average approval rating during his first term was 62 percent, but during his second term it averaged 37 percent.

Several factors caused President Bush's popularity to drop. The economy recovered from the 2001 recession by 2004, but not all Americans felt the recovery. Unemployment remained high, and the percentage of people living in poverty increased.

Then, beginning in 2007, the country experienced another recession as the housing bubble burst and home values tumbled. The huge federal deficit that resulted from Bush's prior tax cuts and the wars in Iraq and Afghanistan added to the problems. By 2008, the deficit totaled $455 million, the highest in history. Americans worried about their own economic future and the federal debt's effect on the next generation.

As Americans weathered the economic storm, residents of Louisiana and Mississippi faced an actual storm. In August 2005, Hurricane Katrina made landfall in New Orleans, Louisiana. When the storm hit, the city flooded with water. About 1,500 people died. Two thirds of the city's residents were displaced from their homes. The Federal Emergency Management Agency (FEMA) was not prepared to deal with the results of Katrina.

President Bush, vacationing in Texas, seemed unaware of the disaster's extent, even though television broadcasts showed the horrifying scenes. The Bush administration received heavy criticism for its handling of Katrina. Bush's popularity rating dropped. During the 2006 midterm elections, Democrats took control of Congress.

READING CHECK **Recognize Multiple Causes** What are two factors that caused Bush's popularity to decline?

▲ Barack Obama called for change during his successful 2008 run for the presidency.

Obama's Presidency

In 2008, Americans struggled with a deepening economic recession, and the wars in Iraq and Afghanistan grew increasingly unpopular. A Democratic presidential victory seemed likely. Senator John McCain of Arizona was the Republican candidate. McCain was a U.S. Navy veteran who emphasized his foreign policy experience and support for the war in Iraq.

The Democratic candidate was Senator Barack Obama of Illinois. Obama expressed his opposition to the war in Iraq and promised voters that he would bring "hope" and "change" to Washington. Voters responded to his promises and handed him a clear victory. The son of a Kenyan father and an American mother, Barack Obama became the nation's first African American President.

What Were the Challenges of Obama's First Term? President Obama entered office facing the economic recession and ongoing wars in Iraq and Afghanistan. In response to America's economic problems, he allowed some of the Bush-era tax cuts to expire and signed an economic stimulus bill.

The recession ended in 2010 as the economy resumed slow growth. Many Americans saw little economic improvement, though. Some faced foreclosure on their homes. Unemployment peaked at close to 10 percent. The poverty rate remained high.

Obama had campaigned on a promise to end the war in Iraq. In keeping with that promise, the last combat troops left Iraq in 2011. During his first term, however, Obama broadened the fight against terrorists. In 2012, Americans were involved in combat missions in Afghanistan, Yemen, Pakistan, and Somalia. President Obama also extended the USA PATRIOT Act and gave up on his promise to close the Guantanamo Bay prison. He found that making promises as a candidate was different from **enacting** those changes as a president.

Academic Vocabulary

enact • *v.*, to make something a law

Beyond foreign policy and the economy, Obama devoted his first term to reorganizing the country's healthcare system. In March 2010, Congress passed the **Affordable Care Act**, nicknamed "Obamacare." The act required all Americans to purchase private health insurance and provided funding to help lower-income Americans pay for insurance. It also expanded Medicaid, a government-run insurance program for people with low incomes.

Support for the act was divided along party lines. All Republicans voted against it. Critics argued that the act increased health insurance prices for some Americans who were already insured.

Government by Crisis In the 2010 elections, Republicans gained control of the House of Representatives. In the middle of his first term in office, Obama suddenly faced the challenge of working with a Republican-dominated House. Republicans also won seats in the Senate and several state governorships. Political gridlock resulted from the politically divided Congress. Republicans blocked passage of bills the President supported. Republicans were limited in what they could accomplish since Democrats controlled the Senate.

The congressional deadlock was apparent during debates about the federal budget and the debt ceiling from 2010 to 2012. Republicans wanted to cut spending and reduce taxes. Democrats wanted to protect federal programs and raise taxes on wealthy Americans to pay for them. They argued that economic hardship in America made support for existing federal programs essential.

In 2012, as President Obama ran for reelection, his approval rating hovered around 50 percent. Unemployment remained high, and economic recovery was still slow. Voters were frustrated by the political gridlock in Washington. American support for the war in Afghanistan had dwindled. In spite of these challenges, Obama won the election against his Republican opponent, Mitt Romney.

Economic Issues Unemployment was persistent after the recession of 2007 and 2008. Long-term unemployment reached record levels, and some Americans gave up on looking for work.

The movement of American jobs overseas contributed to these problems. Outsourcing of jobs lowered prices for consumers, but it resulted in job losses and global competition for American workers. Businesses using computers and robots also eliminated the need for many jobs.

READING CHECK **Identify Supporting Details** What were the main challenges of President Obama's first term?

Analyze Political Cartoons President Obama and Congress were often at odds over policy issues. **Use Visual Information** How does the cartoonist illustrate the concept of political gridlock?

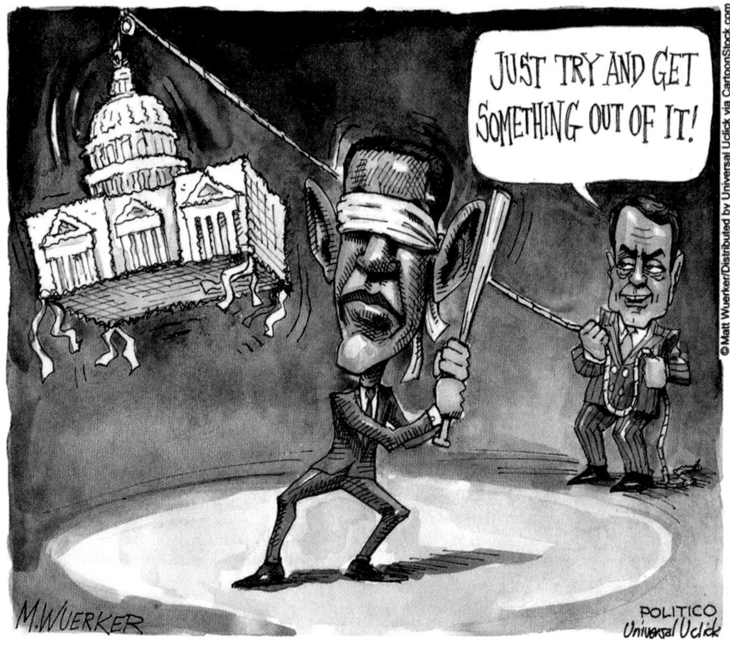

How Has Society Changed?

As the American population in the 2000s changed and grew, the country faced new challenges and revisited old ones. The United States saw increases in immigration, a changing ethnic makeup, and growing numbers of older Americans. Tensions over immigration echoed those the nation had faced during earlier waves of immigration.

Immigration Brings Changes and Challenges During the early 2000s, about one million immigrants entered the United States each year. Most of these immigrants came from Latin America and Asia. In 2010, just over half of the immigrants in the United States were Latino. *Latino* refers to people who were born in Latin America or are of Latin American descent. Latino immigrants came to the United States to escape political unrest and economic hardship and to seek opportunity. Asian immigrants came to the United States for many of the same reasons. In 2010, just over a quarter of the immigrants in the United States were Asian.

Americans' responses to immigrants varied. Some Americans valued immigrants' strong work ethic and the cultural diversity that they brought to the country. Other Americans worried about job competition and decreases in wages as the number of workers increased. They also worried about the cost of providing education, healthcare, and other services to immigrants. In response to these concerns, conservative politicians worked to restrict immigration and strengthen patrols of America's borders.

A Changing Mosaic Immigration has made America more diverse. In 2010, a little more than one in eight Americans were born in foreign countries. Latinos were the largest minority group in the United States, outnumbering African Americans.

Analyze Charts People from all over the world have immigrated to the United States. **Use Visual Information** From which single country does the largest percentage of immigrants come?

Origin of U.S. Immigrants, 1965–2015

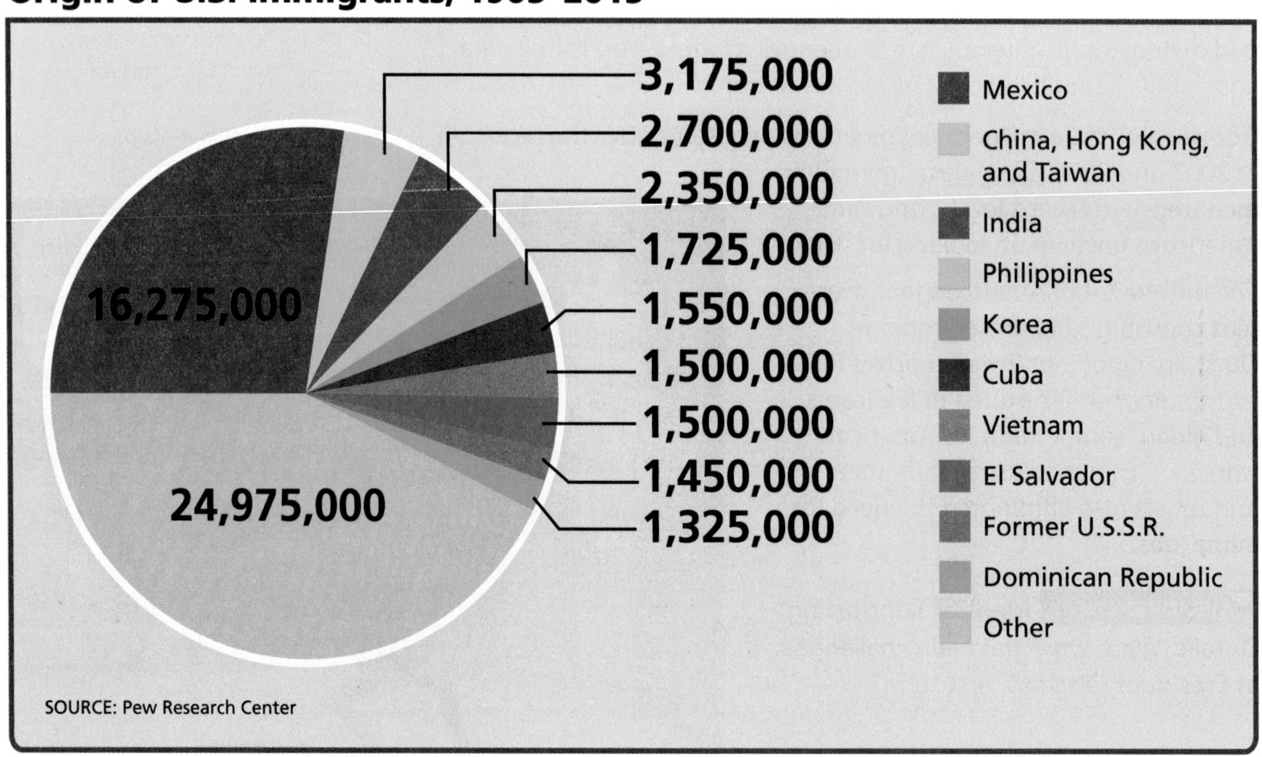

The United States population increased in number. Immigration contributed to this increase, but so did longer lifespans. Older Americans made up 13 percent of the U.S. population in 2014. That figure was expected to increase to 20 percent by the year 2040. This meant that Americans were enjoying longer lives than they did in the past. These changes raised concerns about healthcare costs and federal Social Security payments in the future.

As the American population increased in size, states also experienced demographic changes. In states such as California and New Mexico, and in the city of Washington, D.C., non-Latino whites were a minority of the population by the early 2000s. States in the South and Southwest were growing faster than the rest of the country. These Sunbelt states benefited from increases in population and more representation in Congress.

Analyze Images These new U.S. citizens attended a swearing in ceremony in Florida. **Revisit the Essential Question** How do immigrants affect American society?

Questions over Rights In the 2000s, questions over affirmative action and same-sex marriage brought changes to the legal landscape. The U.S. Supreme Court played a significant role in these changes. In the 1960s, policymakers began to promote **affirmative action**, or a preference for hiring African Americans, women, or members of other groups that had faced discrimination. Eventually, local governments and universities adopted affirmative action policies to make sure that employees and students came from diverse ethnic backgrounds.

In 2003, the U.S. Supreme Court decided on two affirmative action cases from the University of Michigan. After hearing the arguments, the Court decided that colleges and universities had the right to consider race when deciding whether to admit a student.

In 2013, the Supreme Court again considered the question of minority rights. This time, the court ruled on the question of same-sex marriages. In its decision, the Court declared parts of the 1996 Defense of Marriage Act (DOMA) unconstitutional. DOMA required the federal government to deny recognition to same-sex marriages performed in states where those marriages were legal.

Through its decision, the Court ruled that married same-sex couples must receive federal benefits, such as health insurance, retirement funds, and tax refunds, just like other married couples. The Court's decision reflected society's growing acceptance of lesbian, gay, bisexual, and transgender people.

READING CHECK **Identify Supporting Details** What changes have minorities experienced since 2000?

Quest CONNECTIONS

How have new opportunities for women and minority groups benefited everybody? Record your findings in your Active Journal.

What Happened During the 2016 Election?

Since the 1980s, Donald Trump has been part of American popular culture. As a real estate developer, he built apartment towers, hotels, and casinos and received attention from the media. He also starred on reality television programs. For years, he considered running for President.

The Democratic and Republican Primaries On June 16, 2015, Donald Trump announced he would run for President. Promising in his campaign slogan to "make America great again," Trump said his business success would help him create jobs. He caused controversy by saying that Mexican immigrants are, in general, criminals, despite this claim being false.

Trump was one of 17 candidates to compete for the nomination of the Republican party. Few experts expected him to win, but many voters liked his **populist** message. A populist is a person who claims to represent the common people. After a bruising campaign, he won the nomination, defeating senators Ted Cruz and Marco Rubio, Ohio Governor John Kasich, and the rest of the Republican challengers.

The Democratic primary featured fewer candidates than the Republican primary. The field eventually shrunk to two candidates, Hillary Clinton and Bernie Sanders. Clinton had been First Lady during President Bill Clinton's administration; she then served as a United States senator and as Secretary of State. Although he ran for the Democratic nomination, Sanders was an Independent senator from Vermont.

Clinton was the favorite to win the Democratic nomination, but Bernie Sanders's populist message, which placed more emphasis on economics than Trump's populism, excited voters.

Analyze Images Hillary Clinton inspired many voters, including young people and women. **Revisit the Essential Question** How do people affect society by voting and running for President?

However, Clinton's strength with minority voters helped her win the nomination. In doing so, she became the first woman to win the nomination for President from one of the two major political parties.

The General Election The campaign for the presidency was often harsh and negative. Clinton said Trump did not have the temperament to be the President. **Temperament** is the usual attitude, mood, or behavior of a person. She accused him of spreading "a steady stream of bigotry." Trump criticized her for taking inadequate security measures when she was Secretary of State. He also accused her of dishonest behavior.

During the campaign, Trump caused controversy by criticizing the Muslim parents of a soldier who had died in the Iraq War. Another controversy occurred following the release of a recording of comments he made about women.

BIOGRAPHY
5 Things to Know About

DONALD TRUMP
Real Estate Developer, Reality Television Star, and President of the United States (born 1946)

- Donald Trump was born in the Queens borough of New York City and eventually took over his father's real estate business.
- In the 1980s, Trump built and purchased many buildings in New York City and casinos in Atlantic City, New Jersey.
- In 2004, his reality television program, *The Apprentice*, debuted and soon became popular.
- Trump has coauthored many books, including *The Art of the Deal* and *Trump: The Art of the Comeback*.
- He was elected the 45th President of the United States on November 8, 2016.

Critical Thinking How do you think *The Apprentice* might have helped Donald Trump become President?

Shortly afterward, women came forward to announce that Donald Trump had behaved inappropriately with them.

Trade was one of the major issues discussed during the campaign. Trump argued that NAFTA (North American Free Trade Agreement) was a terrible agreement that cost the United States many manufacturing jobs. Both Trump and Clinton came out against the Trans-Pacific Partnership (TPP), a trade deal with Pacific Rim countries that the United States was considering signing. The two candidates also discussed globalization and large financial institutions.

Most experts expected Clinton to win, but Trump surprised many people by defeating her. Although he lost the popular vote by nearly 3 million votes, he won in the electoral college.

READING CHECK **Draw Conclusions** Based on Trump's positions on trade and immigration, who may have voted for him?

America's Promise

During the 1900s, the United States experienced dramatic changes that transformed Americans' lives. Technological advances led to the development of the Internet, electric cars, cell phones, and personal computers. Astronauts walked on the moon, scientists explored the depths of the ocean, and researchers developed cures for diseases. Literacy rates in the United States increased from 25 percent to 86 percent. Life expectancy rose.

America's Changing Demographics

By the 2000s, the diversity of Americans had increased. Civil rights and political opportunities for minorities had expanded. The African American civil rights movement of the mid-1900s helped Thurgood Marshall become the first African American Supreme Court justice.

Analyze Images In 2009, Sonia Sotomayor became the first Latina and the third woman justice of the U.S. Supreme Court. **Explain an Argument** What is the value of a diverse judiciary?

It helped Colin Powell to become the first African American Secretary of State under George W. Bush and enabled Barack Obama to become the first African American President.

Rights for women also expanded. In the early 2000s, more than half of medical school and law school students were women. Women served throughout government. In the Clinton administration, Madeleine Albright served as the first female Secretary of State. In 2007, Nancy Pelosi became the first female speaker of the House of Representatives. The number of women serving in Congress continued to rise.

Americans still had questions to consider and solutions to find at home and abroad. The United States remained a world leader. Its role in world affairs continued to change. Globalization increased America's importance in the world politically, economically, and militarily. It also increased Americans' responsibility to address worldwide problems, such as climate change, reliance on fossil fuels, economic crises, cyber-warfare, and the spread of infectious diseases.

At home, Americans adjusted to changing demographics. The number of immigrants, people in nontraditional relationships, and people of different racial, ethnic, and religious backgrounds was likely to increase.

Traditionally, America has welcomed people of diverse backgrounds and beliefs. National pride, a commitment to economic opportunity, and a devotion to freedom have guided the United States since its founding. These three principles will continue to guide Americans in years to come.

INTERACTIVE

Turning Points in U.S. History

READING CHECK **Summarize** According to the text, what is America's Promise?

Lesson Check

Practice Vocabulary

1. What caused the **deficit** to increase in the 2000s?
2. What is a **populist**?

Critical Thinking and Writing

3. Identify Supporting Details How did the recessions of 2001 and 2007 affect the American economy?
4. Use Evidence What evidence supports the idea that Congress was divided along party lines during Obama's presidency?
5. Summarize What demographic changes affected the American population in the 2000s?
6. Writing Workshop: Develop a Clear Thesis Think about the information you have collected on social changes and technological innovations for your research paper. What conclusions can you draw about how technology has been used and the impact that social changes have had? Organize your thinking to develop a clear thesis about the subject.

Barack Obama, Second Inaugural Address

On January 20, 2013, Barack Obama began his second term as President of the United States. He spoke about the responsibility of the American people to ensure that the nation carries out the vision of the country's founders.

▶ President Obama delivered his second inaugural address from the steps of the Capitol in Washington, D.C.

Each time we gather to inaugurate a President we bear witness to the enduring ① strength of our Constitution. We affirm the promise of our democracy. We recall that what binds this nation together is not the colors of our skin or the tenets [beliefs] of our faith or the origins of our names. What makes us exceptional—what makes us American—is our allegiance to an idea articulated [expressed] in a declaration ② made more than two centuries ago:

"We hold these truths to be self-evident, that all men are created equal; that they are endowed by their Creator with certain unalienable rights; that among these are life, liberty, and the pursuit of happiness." ③

Today we continue a never-ending journey to bridge the meaning of those words with the realities of our time. For history tells us that while these truths may be self-evident, they've never been self-executing; that while freedom is a gift from God, it must be secured by His people here on Earth. ④ The patriots of 1776 did not fight to replace the tyranny of a king with the privileges of a few or the rule of a mob. They gave to us a republic, a government of, and by, and for the people, entrusting each generation to keep safe our founding creed [set of beliefs]. ⑤

Reading and Vocabulary Support

① Something that is enduring is long-lasting.

② President Obama is referring to the Declaration of Independence.

③ How has the interpretation of these words changed over time?

④ Who is responsible for ensuring that the rights of the people are protected?

⑤ What is a government that is by and for the people?

Analyzing Primary Sources

Cite specific evidence from the document to support your answers.

1. **Identify Main Ideas** What idea does President Obama say binds our nation together?
2. **Draw Conclusions** How might the "privileges of a few or the rule of a mob" make it difficult to carry out the founders' vision that all people are created equal?

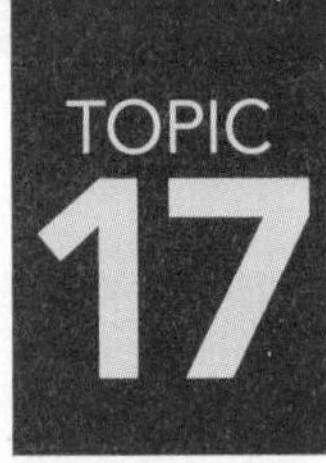

Review and Assessment

VISUAL REVIEW

U.S. Response to September 11

Al Qaeda attacks the United States. → The United States launches a global war on terrorism. → The United States invades Afghanistan. → The United States invades Iraq.

Advances in Science and Technology

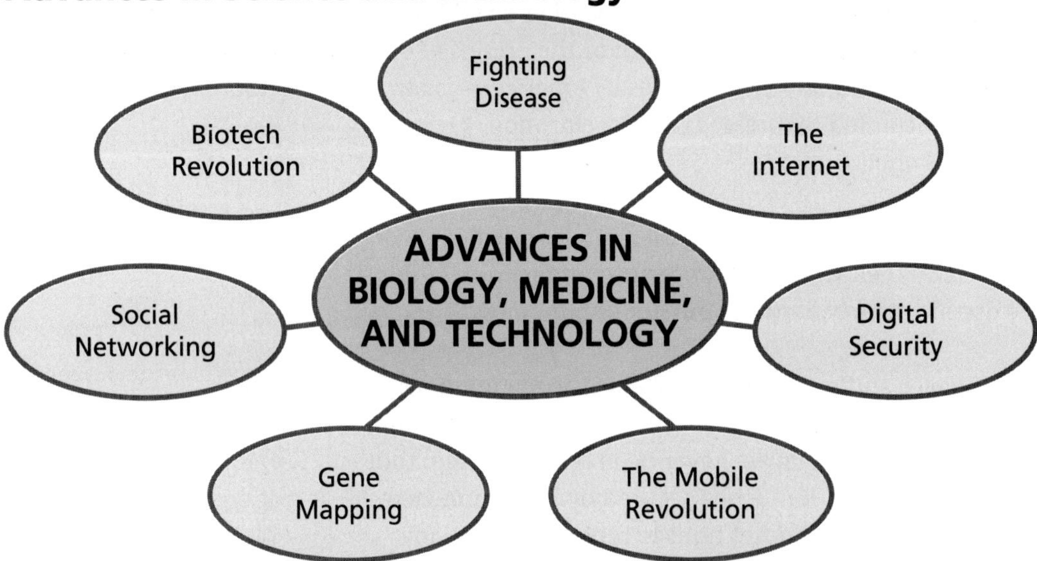

READING REVIEW

Use the Take Notes and Practice Vocabulary activities in your Active Journal to review the topic.

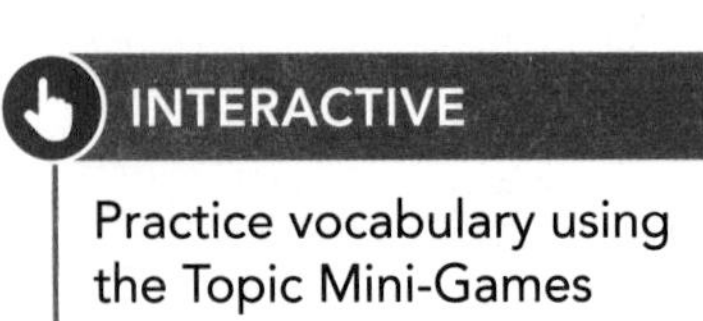

Look Into the Future

Complete your essay explaining what you think young people envision for the future in your Active Journal.

ASSESSMENT

Vocabulary and Key Ideas

1. **Recall** Why do **Islamic fundamentalists** pursue a strategy of **terrorism**?
2. **Describe** What was the effect of the **Arab Spring** in Egypt?
3. **Recall** What **bubbles** burst in the first decade of the 2000s?
4. **Identify Main Ideas** How have **greenhouse gases** contributed to **climate change**?
5. **Recall** Which event led directly to the creation of the Department of Homeland Security?
6. **Check Understanding** Why was the Internet initially designed?
7. **Identify Supporting Details** In what way was the election of George W. Bush in 2004 different from his election in 2000?

Critical Thinking and Writing

8. **Identify Cause and Effect** What caused public support for the war in Iraq to decline after the initial invasion?
9. **Draw Conclusions** What would be the likely consequence for the United States of an economic crisis in a euro-zone country?
10. **Summarize** Which events in the real estate market between 2001 and 2007 contributed to the recession that damaged the U.S. economy in later years?
11. **Recognize Multiple Causes** Explain why the United States and other countries have been concerned about the development of Iran's nuclear program.
12. **Revisit the Essential Question** What can individuals do to affect society? Use examples from the topic.
13. **Writing Workshop: Use Technology to Produce and Publish** Using the notes you have made and the sources you have found, write a research paper on a significant invention or change in society that you learned about in this topic.

Analyze Primary Sources

14. What event was Barack Obama referring to in the quote to the right?
    - **A.** Donald Trump's election victory
    - **B.** Obama's first election victory
    - **C.** Obama's second election victory
    - **D.** George W. Bush's second election victory

"If there is anyone out there who still doubts that America is a place where all things are possible, who still wonders if the dream of our founders is alive in our time, who still questions the power of our democracy, tonight is your answer."
—Barack Obama, November 2008

Analyze Maps

15. Which letter represents the Kurdish area of Iraq? Why do you think some people in the Kurdish area wanted to create their own country?
16. Which letter represents the Sunni region of Iraq? Why did the Sunni and Shia clash in the area around Baghdad?
17. Which letter represents the Shia region of Iraq? Which body of water do the Shia live near?

▼ **Iraq Regions**

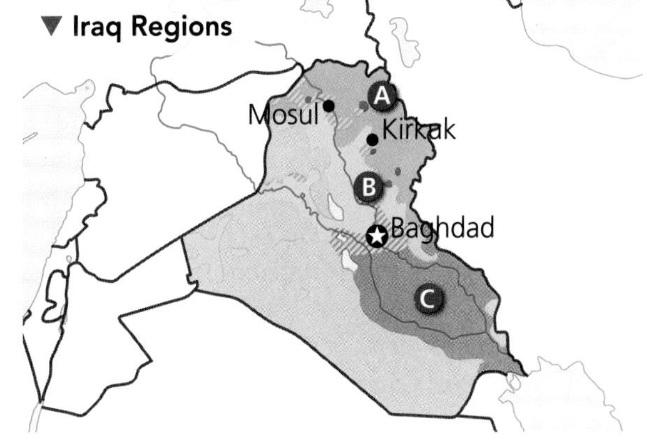

Declaration of Independence

Introduction

By signing the Declaration of Independence, members of the Continental Congress sent a clear message to Britain that the American colonies were free and independent states. Starting with its preamble, the document spells out all the reasons the people of the United States have the right to break away from Britain.

Primary Source

The Unanimous Declaration of the Thirteen United States of America

When in the Course of human events, it becomes necessary for one people to dissolve the political bands which have connected them with another, and to assume among the powers of the earth, the separate and equal station to which the Laws of Nature and of Nature's God entitle them, a decent respect to the opinions of mankind requires that they should declare the causes which impel [force] them to the separation.

We hold these truths to be self-evident, that all men are created equal, that they are endowed [gifted] by their Creator with certain unalienable [cannot be taken away] Rights, that among these are Life, Liberty and the pursuit of Happiness. That to secure these rights, Governments are instituted among Men, deriving their just powers from the consent of the governed. That whenever any Form of Government becomes destructive of these ends, it is the Right of the People to alter or to abolish it, and to institute new Government, laying its foundation on such principles and organizing its powers in such form, as to them shall seem most likely to effect their Safety and Happiness. Prudence [cautiousness], indeed, will dictate that Governments long established should not be changed for light and transient causes; and accordingly all experience hath shown that mankind are more disposed to suffer, while evils are sufferable, than to right themselves by abolishing the forms to which they are accustomed. But when a long train of abuses and usurpations [unjust uses of power], pursuing invariably the same Object evinces a design to reduce them under absolute Despotism [rule of absolute power], it is their right, it is their duty, to throw off such Government, and to provide new Guards for their future security.

Such has been the patient sufferance of these Colonies; and such is now the necessity which constrains them to alter their former Systems of Government. The history of the present King of Great Britain is a history of repeated injuries and usurpations, all having in direct object the establishment of an absolute Tyranny over these States. To prove this, let Facts be submitted to a candid world.

He has refused his Assent to Laws, the most wholesome and necessary for the public good.

He has forbidden his Governors to pass Laws of immediate and pressing importance, unless suspended in their operation till his Assent should be obtained; and when so suspended, he has utterly neglected to attend to them.

He has refused to pass other Laws for the accommodation of large districts of people, unless those people would relinquish [give up] the right of Representation in the Legislature, a right inestimable [priceless] to them and formidable to tyrants only.

He has called together legislative bodies at places unusual, uncomfortable, and distant from the depository of their public Records, for the sole purpose of fatiguing them into compliance with his measures.

He has dissolved Representative Houses repeatedly, for opposing with manly firmness his invasions on the rights of the people.

He has refused for a long time, after such dissolutions [closing down], to cause others to be elected; whereby the Legislative powers, incapable of Annihilation, have returned to the People at large for their exercise; the State remaining in the mean time exposed to all the dangers of invasion from without, and convulsions [riots] within.

He has endeavoured to prevent the population of these States; for that purpose obstructing the Laws for Naturalization of Foreigners; refusing to pass others to encourage their migrations hither, and raising the conditions of new Appropriations of Lands.

He has obstructed the Administration of Justice by refusing his Assent to Laws for establishing Judiciary powers.

He has made Judges dependent on his Will alone, for the tenure [term] of their offices, and the amount and payment of their salaries.

He has erected a multitude of New Offices, and sent hither swarms of Officers to harass our people, and eat out their substance.

He has kept among us, in times of peace, Standing Armies without the Consent of our legislatures.

He has affected to render the Military independent of and superior to the Civil power.

He has combined with others to subject us to a jurisdiction foreign to our constitution, and unacknowledged by our laws; giving his Assent to their Acts of pretended Legislation:

For quartering [lodging] large bodies of armed troops among us:

For protecting them, by a mock Trial, from punishment for any Murders which they should commit on the Inhabitants of these States:

For cutting off our Trade with all parts of the world:

For imposing Taxes on us without our Consent:

For depriving us in many cases, of the benefits of Trial by Jury:

For transporting us beyond Seas to be tried for pretended offences:

For abolishing the free System of English Laws in a neighbouring Province, establishing therein an Arbitrary government, and enlarging its Boundaries so as to render it at once an example and fit instrument for introducing the same absolute rule into these Colonies:

For taking away our Charters, abolishing our most valuable Laws, and altering fundamentally the Forms of our Governments:

For suspending our own Legislatures, and declaring themselves invested with power to legislate for us in all cases whatsoever.

He has abdicated Government here, by declaring us out of his Protection and waging War against us.

He has plundered our seas, ravaged our Coasts, burnt our towns, and destroyed the lives of our people.

He is at this time transporting large Armies of foreign Mercenaries [soldiers] to complete the works of death, desolation, and tyranny, already begun with circumstances of Cruelty and perfidy [dishonesty] scarcely paralleled in the most barbarous ages, and totally unworthy the Head of a civilized nation.

He has constrained our fellow Citizens taken Captive on the high Seas to bear Arms against their Country, to become the executioners of their friends and Brethren, or to fall themselves by their Hands.

He has excited domestic insurrections amongst us, and has endeavoured to bring on the inhabitants of our frontiers, the merciless Indian Savages whose known rule of warfare, is an undistinguished destruction of all ages, sexes and conditions.

In every stage of these Oppressions We have Petitioned for Redress [correction of wrongs] in the most humble terms: Our repeated Petitions have been answered only by repeated injury. A Prince, whose character is thus marked by every act which may define a Tyrant, is unfit to be the ruler of a free people.

Nor have We been wanting in attentions to our British brethren. We have warned them from time to time of attempts by their legislature to extend an unwarrantable jurisdiction over us. We have reminded them of the circumstances of our emigration and settlement here. We have appealed to their native justice and magnanimity [generosity], and we have conjured [begged] them by the ties of our common kindred, to disavow these usurpations, which would inevitably interrupt our connections and correspondence. They too have been deaf to the voice of justice and of consanguinity [relation by blood]. We must, therefore, acquiesce in the necessity, which denounces our Separation, and hold them, as we hold the rest of mankind, Enemies in War, in Peace Friends.

We, therefore, the Representatives of the United States of America, in General Congress, Assembled, appealing to the Supreme Judge of the world for the rectitude [justness] of our intentions, do, in the Name, and by Authority of the good People of these Colonies, solemnly publish and declare, That these United Colonies are, and of Right ought to be Free and Independent States; that they are Absolved from all Allegiance to the British Crown, and that all political connection between them and the State of Great Britain, is and ought to be totally dissolved; and that as Free and Independent States, they have full Power to levy War, conclude Peace, contract Alliances, establish Commerce, and to do all other Acts and Things which Independent States may of right do. And for the support of this Declaration, with a firm reliance on the protection of Divine Providence, we mutually pledge to each other our Lives, our Fortunes and our sacred Honor.

☑ Assessment

1. **Identify Cause and Effect** How might the ideas about equality expressed in the Declaration of Independence have influenced later historical movements, such as the abolitionist movement and the women's suffrage movement?
2. **Identify Key Steps in a Process** Why was the Declaration of Independence a necessary document for the founding of the new nation?
3. **Draw Inferences** English philosopher John Locke wrote that government should protect "life, liberty, and estate." How do you think Locke's writing influenced ideas about government put forth in the Declaration of Independence?
4. **Analyze Structure** How does the Declaration organize its key points from beginning to end?

Constitution Quick Study Guide

Amendments

1st Amendment:	**Freedom of Religion, Speech, Press, Assembly, and Petition**
2nd Amendment:	**Right to Keep, Bear Arms**
3rd Amendment:	**Lodging Troops in Private Homes**
4th Amendment:	**Search, Seizures, Proper Warrants**
5th Amendment:	**Criminal Proceedings, Due Process, Eminent Domain**
6th Amendment:	**Criminal Proceedings**
7th Amendment:	**Jury Trials in Civil Cases**
8th Amendment:	**Bail; Cruel, Unusual Punishment**
9th Amendment:	**Unenumerated Rights**
10th Amendment:	**Powers Reserved to the States**
11th Amendment:	**Suits Against the States**
12th Amendment:	**Election of President and Vice President**
13th Amendment:	**Slavery and Involuntary Servitude**
Section 1.	Slavery and Involuntary Servitude Prohibited
Section 2.	Power of Congress
14th Amendment:	**Rights of Citizens**
Section 1.	Citizenship; Privileges and Immunities; Due Process; Equal Protection
Section 2.	Apportionment of Representation
Section 3.	Disqualification of Officers
Section 4.	Public Debt
Section 5.	Powers of Congress
15th Amendment:	**Right to Vote—Race, Color, Servitude**
Section 1.	Suffrage Not to Be Abridged
Section 2.	Power of Congress
16th Amendment:	**Income Tax**
17th Amendment:	**Popular Election of Senators**
Section 1.	Popular Election of Senators
Section 2.	Senate Vacancies
Section 3.	Inapplicable to Senators Previously Chosen
18th Amendment:	**Prohibition of Intoxicating Liquors**
Section 1.	Intoxicating Liquors Prohibited
Section 2.	Concurrent Power to Enforce
Section 3.	Time Limit on Ratification
19th Amendment:	**Equal Suffrage—Sex**
Section 1.	Suffrage Not to Be Abridged
Section 2.	Power of Congress
20th Amendment:	**Commencement of Terms; Sessions of Congress; Death or Disqualification of President-Elect**
Section 1.	Terms of President, Vice President, members of Congress
Section 2.	Sessions of Congress
Section 3.	Death or Disqualification of President-Elect
Section 4.	Congress to Provide for Certain Successors
Section 5.	Effective Date
Section 6.	Time Limit on Ratification
21st Amendment:	**Repeal of 18th Amendment**
Section 1.	Repeal of Prohibition
Section 2.	Transportation, Importation of Intoxicating Liquors
Section 3.	Time Limit on Ratification
22nd Amendment:	**Presidential Tenure**
Section 1.	Restriction on Number of Terms
Section 2.	Time Limit on Ratification
23rd Amendment:	**Inclusion of District of Columbia in Presidential Election Systems**
Section 1.	Presidential Electors for District
Section 2.	Power of Congress
24th Amendment:	**Right to Vote in Federal Elections—Tax Payment**
Section 1.	Suffrage Not to Be Abridged
Section 2.	Power of Congress
25th Amendment:	**Presidential Succession; Vice Presidential Vacancy; Presidential Inability**
Section 1.	Presidential Succession
Section 2.	Vice Presidential Vacancy
Section 3.	Presidential Inability
26th Amendment:	**Right to Vote—Age**
Section 1.	Suffrage Not to Be Abridged
Section 2.	Power of Congress
27th Amendment:	**Congressional Pay**

United States Constitution

The Preamble states the broad purposes the Constitution is intended to serve—to establish a government that provides for greater cooperation among the States, ensures justice and peace, provides for defense against foreign enemies, promotes the general well-being of the people, and secures liberty now and in the future. The phrase We the People emphasizes the twin concepts of popular sovereignty and of representative government.

PREAMBLE

We the People of the United States, in Order to form a more perfect Union, establish Justice, insure domestic Tranquility, provide for the common defence, promote the general Welfare, and secure the Blessings of Liberty to ourselves and our Posterity, do ordain and establish this Constitution for the United States of America.

Legislative Department

Section 1. Legislative power; Congress

Congress, the nation's lawmaking body, is bicameral in form; that is, it is composed of two houses: the Senate and the House of Representatives. The Framers of the Constitution purposely separated the lawmaking power from the power to enforce the laws (Article II, the Executive Branch) and the power to interpret them (Article III, the Judicial Branch). This system of separation of powers is supplemented by a system of checks and balances; that is, in several provisions the Constitution gives to each of the three branches various powers with which it may restrain the actions of the other two branches.

Article I.

Section 1.

All legislative Powers herein granted shall be vested in a Congress of the United States, which shall consist of a Senate and House of Representatives.

Section 2. House of Representatives

▶ Clause 1. **Election** Electors means voters. Members of the House of Representatives are elected every two years. Each State must permit the same persons to vote for United States representatives as it permits to vote for the members of the larger house of its own legislature. The 17th Amendment (1913) extends this requirement to the qualification of voters for United States senators.

▶ Clause 2. **Qualifications** A member of the House of Representatives must be at least 25 years old, an American citizen for seven years, and a resident of the State he or she represents. In addition, political custom requires that a representative also reside in the district from which he or she is elected.

▶ Clause 3. **Apportionment** The number of representatives each State is entitled to is based on its population, which is counted every 10 years in the census. Congress reapportions the seats among the States after each census. In the Reapportionment Act of 1929, Congress fixed the permanent size of the House at 435 members with each State having at least one representative. Today there is one House seat for approximately every 700,000 persons in the population.

The words "three-fifths of all other persons" referred to slaves and reflected the Three-Fifths Compromise reached by the Framers at Philadelphia in 1787; the phrase was made obsolete, was in effect repealed, by the 13th Amendment in 1865.

* The blue words indicate portions of the Constitution altered by subsequent amendments to the document.

▶ Clause 4. **Vacancies** The executive authority refers to the governor of a State. If a member leaves office or dies before the expiration of his or her term, the governor is to call a special election to fill the vacancy.

Section 2.

▶1. The House of Representatives shall be composed of Members chosen every second Year by the People of the several States, and the Electors in each State shall have the Qualifications requisite for Electors of the most numerous Branch of the State Legislature.

▶2. No Person shall be a Representative who shall not have attained to the age of twenty-five Years, and been seven Years a Citizen of the United States, and who shall not, when elected, be an Inhabitant of that State in which he shall be chosen.

▶3. Representatives and direct Taxes* shall be apportioned among the several States which may be included within this Union, according to their respective Numbers, which shall be determined by adding to the whole Number of free Persons, including those bound to Service for a Term of Years and excluding Indians not taxed, three fifths of all other Persons. The actual Enumeration shall be made within three Years after the first Meeting of the Congress of the United States, and within every subsequent term of ten Years, in such Manner as they shall by Law direct. The Number of Representatives shall not exceed one for every thirty Thousand, but each State shall have at Least one Representative; and, until such enumeration shall be made, the State of New Hampshire shall be entitled to choose three, Massachusetts eight, Rhode Island and Providence Plantations one, Connecticut five, New York six, New Jersey four, Pennsylvania eight, Delaware one, Maryland six, Virginia ten, North Carolina five, South Carolina five, and Georgia three.

▶4. When vacancies happen in the Representation from any State, the Executive Authority thereof shall issue Writs of Election to fill such Vacancies.

▶5. The House of Representatives shall choose their Speaker and other Officers; and shall have the sole Power of Impeachment.

▶Clause 5. **Officers; impeachment** The House elects a Speaker, customarily chosen from the majority party in the House. Impeachment means accusation. The House has the exclusive power to impeach, or accuse, civil officers; the Senate (Article I, Section 3, Clause 6) has the exclusive power to try those impeached by the House.

Section 3.

▶1. The Senate of the United States shall be composed of two Senators from each State chosen by the Legislature thereof for six Years; and each Senator shall have one Vote.

▶2. Immediately after they shall be assembled in Consequences of the first Election, they shall be divided, as equally as may be, into three Classes. The Seats of the Senators of the first Class shall be vacated at the Expiration of the second Year; of the second Class, at the Expiration of the fourth Year; and of the third Class, at the Expiration of the sixth Year; so that one-third may be chosen every second Year; and if Vacancies happen by Resignation, or otherwise, during the Recess of the Legislature of any State, the Executive thereof may make temporary Appointments until the next Meeting of the Legislature, which shall then fill such Vacancies.

▶3. No Person shall be a Senator who shall not have attained to the Age of thirty Years, and been nine Years a Citizen of the United States, and who shall not, when elected, be an Inhabitant of that State for which he shall be chosen.

▶4. The Vice President of the United States shall be President of the Senate but shall have no Vote, unless they be equally divided.

▶5. The Senate shall choose their other Officers, and also a President pro tempore, in the Absence of the Vice President, or when he shall exercise the Office of President of the United States.

▶6. The Senate shall have the sole Power to try all Impeachments. When sitting for that Purpose, they shall be on Oath or Affirmation. When the President of the United States is tried, the Chief Justice shall preside: And no Person shall be convicted without the Concurrence of two thirds of the Members present.

▶7. Judgment in Cases of Impeachment shall not extend further than to removal from Office, and disqualification to hold and enjoy any Office of honor, Trust, or Profit under the United States: but the Party convicted shall nevertheless be liable and subject to Indictment, Trial, Judgment and Punishment, according to Law.

Section 3. Senate

▶ Clause 1. **Composition, election, term** Each State has two senators. Each serves for six years and has one vote. Originally, senators were not elected directly by the people, but by each State's legislature. The 17th Amendment, added in 1913, provides for the popular election of senators.

▶ Clause 2. **Classification** The senators elected in 1788 were divided into three groups so that the Senate could become a "continuing body." One-third of the Senate's seats are up for election every two years.

The 17th Amendment provides that a Senate vacancy is to be filled at a special election called by the governor; State law may also permit the governor to appoint a successor to serve until that election is held.

▶ Clause 3. **Qualifications** A senator must be at least 30 years old, a citizen for at least nine years, and must live in the State from which elected.

▶ Clause 4. **Presiding officer** The Vice President presides over the Senate, but may vote only to break a tie.

▶ Clause 5. **Other officers** The Senate chooses its own officers, including a president pro tempore to preside when the Vice President is not there.

▶ Clause 6. **Impeachment trials** The Senate conducts the trials of those officials impeached by the House. The Vice President presides unless the President is on trial, in which case the Chief Justice of the United States does so. A conviction requires the votes of two-thirds of the senators present.

No President has ever been convicted. In 1868 the House voted eleven articles of impeachment against President Andrew Johnson, but the Senate fell one vote short of convicting him. In 1974 President Richard M. Nixon resigned the presidency in the face of almost certain impeachment by the House. The House brought two articles of impeachment against President Bill Clinton in late 1998. Neither charge was supported by even a simple majority vote in the Senate, on February 12, 1999.

▶ Clause 7. **Penalty on conviction** The punishment of an official convicted in an impeachment case has always been removal from office. The Senate can also bar a convicted person from ever holding any federal office, but it is not required to do so. A convicted person can also be tried and punished in a regular court for any crime involved in the impeachment case.

Section 4. Elections and Meetings

▶ Clause 1. **Election** In 1842 Congress required that representatives be elected from districts within each State with more than one seat in the House. The districts in each State are drawn by that State's legislature. Seven States now have only one seat in the House: Alaska, Delaware, Montana, North Dakota, South Dakota, Vermont, and Wyoming. The 1842 law also directed that representatives be elected in each State on the same day: the Tuesday after the first Monday in November of every even-numbered year. In 1914 Congress also set that same date for the election of senators.

▶ Clause 2. **Sessions** Congress must meet at least once a year. The 20th Amendment (1933) changed the opening date to January 3.

Section 5. Legislative Proceedings

▶ Clause 1. **Admission of members; quorum** In 1969 the Supreme Court held that the House cannot exclude any member-elect who satisfies the qualifications set out in Article I, Section 2, Clause 2.

A majority in the House (218 members) or Senate (51) constitutes a quorum. In practice, both houses often proceed with less than a quorum present. However, any member may raise a point of order (demand a "quorum call"). If a roll call then reveals less than a majority of the members present, that chamber must either adjourn or the sergeant at arms must be ordered to round up absent members.

▶ Clause 2. **Rules** Each house has adopted detailed rules to guide its proceedings. Each house may discipline members for unacceptable conduct; expulsion requires a two-thirds vote.

▶ Clause 3. **Record** Each house must keep and publish a record of its meetings. The Congressional Record is published for every day that either house of Congress is in session, and provides a written record of all that is said and done on the floor of each house each session.

▶ Clause 4. **Adjournment** Once in session, neither house may suspend (recess) its work for more than three days without the approval of the other house. Both houses must always meet in the same location.

Section 4.

▶1. The Times, Places and Manner of holding Elections for Senators and Representatives, shall be prescribed in each State by the Legislature thereof; but the Congress may at any time by law make or alter such Regulations, except as to the Places of choosing Senators.

▶2. The Congress shall assemble at least once in every Year, and such Meeting shall be on the first Monday in December, unless they shall by Law appoint a different Day.

Section 5.

▶1. Each House shall be the Judge of the Elections, Returns and Qualifications of its own Members, and a Majority of each shall constitute a Quorum to do Business; but a smaller Number may adjourn from day to day, and may be authorized to compel the Attendance of absent Members, in such Manner, and under such Penalties, as each House may provide.

▶2. Each House may determine the Rules of its Proceedings, punish its Members for disorderly Behavior, and, with the Concurrence of two thirds, expel a Member.

▶3. Each House shall keep a Journal of its Proceedings, and from time to time publish the same, excepting such Parts as may in their Judgment require Secrecy; and the Yeas and Nays of the Members of either House on any question shall, at the Desire of one fifth of those Present, be entered on the Journal.

▶4. Neither House, during the Session of Congress, shall, without the Consent of the other, adjourn for more than three days, nor to any other Place than that in which the two Houses shall be sitting.

Section 6.

▶1. The Senators and Representatives shall receive a Compensation for their Services, to be ascertained by Law, and paid out of the Treasury of the United States. They shall in all Cases, except Treason, Felony, and Breach of the Peace, be privileged from Arrest during their Attendance at the Session of their respective Houses, and in going to and returning from the same; and for any Speech or Debate in either House, they shall not be questioned in any other Place.

▶2. No Senator or Representative shall, during the Time for which he was elected, be appointed to any civil Office under the Authority of the United States, which shall have been created, or the Emoluments whereof shall have been increased during such time; and no Person holding any Office under the United States, shall be a Member of either House during his Continuance in Office.

Section 7.

▶1. All Bills for raising Revenue shall originate in the House of Representatives; but the Senate may propose or concur with amendments as on other Bills.

▶2. Every Bill which shall have passed the House of Representatives and the Senate, shall, before it become a law, be presented to the President of the United States: If he approve, he shall sign it, but if not he shall return it, with his Objections to that House in which it shall have originated, who shall enter the Objections at large on their Journal, and proceed to reconsider it. If after such Reconsideration two thirds of the House shall agree to pass the Bill, it shall be sent, together with the Objections, to the other House, by which it shall likewise be reconsidered, and if approved by two thirds of that House, it shall become a Law. But in all such Cases the Votes of both Houses shall be determined by Yeas and Nays, and the Names of the Persons voting for and against the Bill shall be entered on the Journal of each House respectively. If any Bill shall not be returned by the President within ten Days (Sunday excepted) after it shall have been presented to him, the Same shall be a law, in like Manner as if he had signed it, unless the Congress by their Adjournment, prevent its Return, in which Case it shall not be a Law.

▶3. Every Order, Resolution, or Vote to which the Concurrence of the Senate and House of Representatives may be necessary (except on a question of adjournment) shall be presented to the President of the United States; and before the Same shall take Effect, shall be approved by him, or, being disapproved by him, shall be repassed by two thirds of the Senate and House of Representatives, according to the Rules and Limitations prescribed in the Case of a Bill.

Section 6. Compensation, Immunities, and Disabilities of Members

▶ Clause 1. **Salaries; immunities** Each house sets its members' salaries, paid by the United States; the 27th Amendment (1992) modified this pay-setting power. This provision establishes "legislative immunity." The purpose of this immunity is to allow members to speak and debate freely in Congress itself. Treason is strictly defined in Article III, Section 3. A felony is any serious crime. A breach of the peace is any indictable offense less than treason or a felony; this exemption from arrest is of little real importance today.

▶ Clause 2. **Restrictions on office holding** No sitting member of either house may be appointed to an office in the executive or in the judicial branch if that position was created or its salary was increased during that member's current elected term. The second part of this clause—forbidding any person serving in either the executive or the judicial branch from also serving in Congress—reinforces the principle of separation of powers.

Section 7. Revenue Bills, President's Veto

▶ Clause 1. **Revenue bills** All bills that raise money must originate in the House. However, the Senate has the power to amend any revenue bill sent to it from the lower house.

▶ Clause 2. **Enactment of laws; veto** Once both houses have passed a bill, it must be sent to the President. The President may (1) sign the bill, thus making it law; (2) veto the bill, whereupon it must be returned to the house in which it originated; or (3) allow the bill to become law without signature, by not acting upon it within 10 days of its receipt from Congress, not counting Sundays. The President has a fourth option at the end of a congressional session: If he does not act on a measure within 10 days, and Congress adjourns during that period, the bill dies; the "pocket veto" has been applied to it. A presidential veto may be overridden by a two-thirds vote in each house.

▶ Clause 3. **Other measures** This clause refers to joint resolutions, measures Congress often passes to deal with unusual, temporary, or ceremonial matters. A joint resolution passed by Congress and signed by the President has the force of law, just as a bill does. As a matter of custom, a joint resolution proposing an amendment to the Constitution is not submitted to the President for signature or veto. Concurrent and simple resolutions do not have the force of law and, therefore, are not submitted to the President.

Section 8. Powers of Congress

▶ Clause 1. The 18 separate clauses in this section set out 27 of the many expressed powers the Constitution grants to Congress. In this clause Congress is given the power to levy and provide for the collection of various kinds of taxes, in order to finance the operations of the government. All federal taxes must be levied at the same rates throughout the country.

▶ Clause 2. Congress has power to borrow money to help finance the government. Federal borrowing is most often done through the sale of bonds on which interest is paid. The Constitution does not limit the amount the government may borrow.

▶ Clause 3. This clause, the Commerce Clause, gives Congress the power to regulate both foreign and interstate trade. Much of what Congress does, it does on the basis of its commerce power.

▶ Clause 4. Congress has the exclusive power to determine how aliens may become citizens of the United States. Congress may also pass laws relating to bankruptcy.

▶ Clause 5. has the power to establish and require the use of uniform gauges of time, distance, weight, volume, area, and the like.

▶ Clause 6. Congress has the power to make it a federal crime to falsify the coins, paper money, bonds, stamps, and the like of the United States.

▶ Clause 7. Congress has the power to provide for and regulate the transportation and delivery of mail; "post offices" are those buildings and other places where mail is deposited for dispatch; "post roads" include all routes over or upon which mail is carried.

▶ Clause 8. Congress has the power to provide for copyrights and patents. A copyright gives an author or composer the exclusive right to control the reproduction, publication, and sale of literary, musical, or other creative work. A patent gives a person the exclusive right to control the manufacture or sale of his or her invention.

▶ Clause 9. Congress has the power to create the lower federal courts, all of the several federal courts that function beneath the Supreme Court.

▶ Clause 10. Congress has the power to prohibit, as a federal crime: (1) certain acts committed outside the territorial jurisdiction of the United States, and (2) the commission within the United States of any wrong against any nation with which we are at peace.

Section 8.

The Congress shall have Power

▶1. To lay and collect Taxes, Duties, Imposts and Excises to pay the Debts and provide for the common Defence and general Welfare of the United States; but all Duties, Imposts and Excises, shall be uniform throughout the United States;

▶2. To borrow Money on the credit of the United States;

▶3. To regulate Commerce with foreign Nations, and among the several States, and with the Indian Tribes;

▶4. To establish an uniform Rule of Naturalization, and uniform Laws on the subject of Bankruptcies throughout the United States;

▶5. To coin Money, regulate the Value thereof, and of foreign Coin, and fix the Standard of Weights and Measures;

▶6. To provide for the Punishment of counterfeiting the Securities and current Coin of the United States;

▶7. To establish Post Offices and post Roads;

▶8. To promote the Progress of Science and useful Arts, by securing, for limited Times to Authors and Inventors the exclusive Right to their respective Writings and Discoveries;

▶9. To constitute Tribunals inferior to the supreme Court;

▶10. To define and punish Piracies and Felonies committed on the high Seas, and Offences against the Law of nations;

▶11. To declare War, grant Letters of Marque and Reprisal, and make Rules concerning Captures on Land and Water;

▶ Clause 11. Only Congress can declare war. However, the President, as commander in chief of the armed forces (Article II, Section 2, Clause 1), can make war without such a formal declaration. Letters of marque and reprisal are commissions authorizing private persons to outfit vessels (privateers) to capture and destroy enemy ships in time of war; they were forbidden in international law by the Declaration of Paris of 1856, and the United States has honored the ban since the Civil War.

▶12. To raise and support Armies; but no Appropriation of Money to that Use shall be for a longer Term than two Years;

▶13. To provide and maintain a Navy;

▶ Clause 12 and 13. Congress has the power to provide for and maintain the nation's armed forces. It established the air force as an independent element of the armed forces in 1947, an exercise of its inherent powers in foreign relations and national defense. The two-year limit on spending for the army insures civilian control of the military.

▶14. To make Rules for the Government and Regulation of the land and naval Forces;

▶ Clause 14. Today these rules are set out in three principle statutes: the Uniform Code of Military Justice, passed by Congress in 1950, and the Military Justice Acts of 1958 and 1983.

▶15. To provide for calling forth the Militia to execute the Laws of the Union, suppress Insurrections and repel Invasions;

▶16. To provide for organizing, arming, and disciplining the Militia, and for governing such Part of them as may be employed in the Service of the United States, reserving to the States respectively the Appointment of the Officers, and the Authority of training the Militia according to the discipline prescribed by Congress;

▶ Clause 15 and 16. In the National Defense Act of 1916, Congress made each State's militia (volunteer army) a part of the National Guard. Today, Congress and the States cooperate in its maintenance. Ordinarily, each State's National Guard is under the command of that State's governor; but Congress has given the President the power to call any or all of those units into federal service when necessary.

▶17. To exercise exclusive Legislation in all Cases whatsoever, over such District (not exceeding ten Miles square) as may, by Cession of Particular States, and the Acceptance of Congress, become the Seat of the Government of the United States, and to exercise like Authority over all Places purchased by the Consent of the Legislature of the State in which the Same shall be, for the Erection of Forts, Magazines, Arsenals, Dockyards and other needful Buildings;—And

▶ Clause 17. In 1791 Congress accepted land grants from Maryland and Virginia and established the District of Columbia for the nation's capital. Assuming Virginia's grant would never be needed, Congress returned it in 1846. Today, the elected government of the District's 69 square miles operates under the authority of Congress. Congress also has the power to acquire other lands from the States for various federal purposes.

▶18. To make all Laws which shall be necessary and proper for carrying into Execution the foregoing Powers and all other Powers vested by this Constitution in the Government of the United States, or in any Department or Officer thereof.

▶ Clause 18. This is the Necessary and Proper Clause, also often called the Elastic Clause. It is the constitutional basis for the many and far-reaching implied powers of the Federal Government.

Section 9.

▶1. The Migration or Importation of such Persons as any of the States now existing shall think proper to admit, shall not be prohibited by the Congress prior to the Year one thousand eight hundred and eight, but a Tax or duty may be imposed on such Importation, not exceeding ten dollars for each Person.

Section 9. Powers Denied to Congress

▶ Clause 1. The phrase "such persons" referred to slaves. This provision was part of the Commerce Compromise, one of the bargains struck in the writing of the Constitution. Congress outlawed the slave trade in 1808.

▶ Clause 2. A writ of habeas corpus, the "great writ of liberty," is a court order directing a sheriff, warden, or other public officer, or a private person, who is detaining another to "produce the body" of the one being held in order that the legality of the detention may be determined by the court.

▶ 2. The Privilege of the Writ of Habeas Corpus shall not be suspended, unless when in Cases of Rebellion or Invasion the public safety may require it.

▶ Clause 3. A bill of attainder is a legislative act that inflicts punishment without a judicial trial. See Article I, Section 10, and Article III, Section 3, Clause 2. An ex post facto law is any criminal law that operates retroactively to the disadvantage of the accused. See Article I, Section 10.

▶ 3. No Bill of Attainder or ex post facto Law shall be passed.

▶ Clause 4. A capitation tax is literally a "head tax," a tax levied on each person in the population. A direct tax is one paid directly to the government by the taxpayer—for example, an income or a property tax; an indirect tax is one paid to another private party who then pays it to the government—for example, a sales tax. This provision was modified by the 16th Amendment (1913), giving Congress the power to levy "taxes on incomes, from whatever source derived."

▶ 4. No Capitation, or other direct, Tax shall be laid, unless in Proportion to the Census of Enumeration hereinbefore directed to be taken.

▶ Clause 5. This provision was a part of the Commerce Compromise made by the Framers in 1787. Congress has the power to tax imported goods, however.

▶ 5. No Tax or Duty shall be laid on Articles exported from any State.

▶ Clause 6. All ports within the United States must be treated alike by Congress as it exercises its taxing and commerce powers. Congress cannot tax goods sent by water from one State to another, nor may it give the ports of one State any legal advantage over those of another.

▶ 6. No Preference shall be given by any Regulation of Commerce or Revenue to the Ports of one State over those of another: nor shall Vessels bound to, or from, one State, be obliged to enter, clear or pay Duties in another.

▶ Clause 7. This clause gives Congress its vastly important "power of the purse," a major check on presidential power. Federal money can be spent only in those amounts and for those purposes expressly authorized by an act of Congress. All federal income and spending must be accounted for, regularly and publicly.

▶ 7. No Money shall be drawn from the Treasury, but in Consequence of Appropriations made by Law; and a regular Statement and Account of the Receipts and Expenditures of all public Money shall be published from time to time.

▶ Clause 8. This provision, preventing the establishment of a nobility, reflects the principle that "all men are created equal." It was also intended to discourage foreign attempts to bribe or otherwise corrupt officers of the government.

▶ 8. No Title of Nobility shall be granted by the United States: And no Person holding any Office of Profit or Trust under them, shall, without the Consent of the Congress, accept of any present, Emolument, Office, or Title, of any kind whatever, from any King, Prince, or foreign State.

Section 10. Powers Denied to the States

Section 10.

▶ Clause 1. The States are not sovereign governments and so cannot make agreements or otherwise negotiate with foreign states; the power to conduct foreign relations is an exclusive power of the National Government. The power to coin money is also an exclusive power of the National Government. Several powers forbidden to the National Government are here also forbidden to the States.

▶ 1. No State shall enter into any Treaty, Alliance, or Confederation; grant Letters of Marque and Reprisal; coin Money; emit Bills of Credit; make any Thing but gold and silver Coin a Tender in Payment of Debts; pass any Bill of Attainder, ex post facto Law, or Law impairing the Obligation of Contracts, or grant any Title of Nobility.

▶ Clause 2. This provision relates to foreign, not interstate, commerce. Only Congress, not the States, can tax imports; and the States are, like Congress, forbidden the power to tax exports.

▶ 2. No State shall, without the Consent of the Congress, lay any Imposts or Duties on Imports or Exports, except what may be absolutely necessary for executing its inspection Laws; and the net Produce of all Duties and Imposts, laid by any State on Imports or Exports, shall be for the Use of the Treasury of the United States; and all such Laws shall be subject to the Revision and Control of the Congress.

▶ 3. No State shall, without the Consent of Congress, lay any Duty of Tonnage, keep Troops, or Ships of War in time of Peace, enter into any Agreement or Compact with another State, or with a foreign Power, or engage in War, unless actually invaded, or in such imminent Danger as will not admit of delay.

▶ Clause 3. A duty of tonnage is a tax laid on ships according to their cargo capacity. Each State has a constitutional right to provide for and maintain a militia; but no State may keep a standing army or navy. The several restrictions here prevent the States from assuming powers that the Constitution elsewhere grants to the National Government.

Article II

Executive Department

Section 1.

Section 1. President and Vice President

▶ 1. The executive Power shall be vested in a President of the United States of America. He shall hold his Office during the Term of four Years, and, together with the Vice President, chosen for the same Term, be elected as follows:

▶ Clause 1. **Executive power, term** This clause gives to the President the very broad "executive power," the power to enforce the laws and otherwise administer the public policies of the United States. It also sets the length of the presidential (and vice-presidential) term of office; see the 22nd Amendment (1951), which places a limit on presidential (but not vice-presidential) tenure.

▶ 2. Each State shall appoint, in such Manner as the Legislature thereof may direct, a Number of Electors, equal to the whole Number of Senators and Representatives to which the State may be entitled in the Congress: but no Senator or Representative, or Person holding an Office of Trust or Profit, under the United States, shall be appointed an Elector.

▶ Clause 2. **Electoral college** This clause establishes the "electoral college," although the Constitution does not use that term. It is a body of presidential electors chosen in each State, and it selects the President and Vice President every four years. The number of electors chosen in each State equals the number of senators and representatives that State has in Congress.

▶ 3. The Electors shall meet in their respective States, and vote by Ballot for two Persons, of whom one at least shall not be an Inhabitant of the same State with themselves. And they shall make a List of all the Persons voted for, and of the Number of Votes for each; which List they shall sign and certify, and transmit sealed to the Seat of the Government of the United States, directed to the President of the Senate. The President of the Senate shall, in the Presence of the Senate and House of Representatives, open all the Certificates, and the Votes shall then be counted. The Person having the greatest Number of Votes shall be the President, if such Number be a majority of the whole Number of Electors appointed; and if there be more than one who have such Majority, and have an equal Number of Votes, then, the House of Representatives shall immediately choose by Ballot one of them for President; and if no Person have a Majority, then from the five highest on the List the said House shall in like Manner choose the President. But in choosing the President, the Votes shall be taken by States, the Representatives from each State having one Vote; a quorum for this Purpose shall consist of a Member or Members from two thirds of the States, and a Majority of all the States shall be necessary to a Choice. In every Case, after the Choice of the President, the Person having the greatest Number of Votes of the Electors shall be the Vice President. But if there should remain two or more who have equal Votes, the Senate shall choose from them by Ballot the Vice President.

▶ Clause 3. **Election of President and Vice President** **This** clause was replaced by the 12th Amendment in 1804.

▶ Clause 4. **Date** Congress has set the date for the choosing of electors as the Tuesday after the first Monday in November every fourth year, and for the casting of electoral votes as the Monday after the second Wednesday in December of that year.

▶4. The Congress may determine the Time of choosing the Electors, and the Day on which they shall give their Votes; which Day shall be the same throughout the United States.

▶ Clause 5. **Qualifications** The President must have been born a citizen of the United States, be at least 35 years old, and have been a resident of the United States for at least 14 years.

▶5. No Person except a natural born Citizen, or a Citizen of the United States, at the time of the Adoption of this Constitution, shall be eligible to the Office of President; neither shall any person be eligible to that Office who shall not have attained to the Age of thirty-five Years, and been fourteen Years a Resident within the United States.

▶ Clause 6. **Vacancy** This clause was modified by the 25th Amendment (1967), which provides expressly for the succession of the Vice President, for the filling of a vacancy in the Vice Presidency, and for the determination of presidential inability.

▶6. In Case of the Removal of the President from Office, or of his Death, Resignation, or Inability to discharge the Powers and Duties of the said Office, the Same shall devolve on the Vice President, and the Congress may by Law provide for the Case of Removal, Death, Resignation or Inability, both of the President and Vice President, declaring what Officer shall then act as President, and such Officer shall act accordingly, until the Disability be removed, or a President shall be elected.

▶ Clause 7. **Compensation** The President now receives a salary of $400,000 and a taxable expense account of $50,000 a year. Those amounts cannot be changed during a presidential term; thus, Congress cannot use the President's compensation as a bargaining tool to influence executive decisions. The phrase "any other emolument" means, in effect, any valuable gift; it does not mean that the President cannot be provided with such benefits of office as the White House, extensive staff assistance, and much else.

▶7. The President shall, at stated Times, receive for his Services, a Compensation, which shall neither be increased nor diminished during the Period for which he shall have been elected, and he shall not receive within that Period any other Emolument from the United States, or any of them.

▶ Clause 8. **Oath of office** The Chief Justice of the United States regularly administers this oath or affirmation, but any judicial officer may do so. Thus, Calvin Coolidge was sworn into office in 1923 by his father, a justice of the peace in Vermont.

▶8. Before he enter on the Execution of his Office, he shall take the following Oath or Affirmation:
"I do solemnly swear (or affirm) that I will faithfully execute the Office of President of the United States, and will to the best of my Ability, preserve, protect and defend the Constitution of the United States."

Section 2. President's Powers and Duties

Section 2.

▶ Clause 1. **Military, civil powers** The President, a civilian, heads the nation's armed forces, a key element in the Constitution's insistence on civilian control of the military. The President's power to "require the opinion, in writing" provides the constitutional basis for the Cabinet. The President's power to grant reprieves and pardons, the power of clemency, extends only to federal cases.

▶1. The President shall be Commander in Chief of the Army and Navy of the United States, and of the Militia of the several States, when called into the actual Service of the United States; he may require the Opinion, in writing, of the principal Officer in each of the executive Departments, upon any Subject relating to the Duties of their respective Offices, and he shall have Power to Grant Reprieves and Pardons for Offences against the United States, except in Cases of Impeachment.

▶2. He shall have Power, by and with the Advice and Consent of the Senate, to make Treaties, provided two thirds of the Senators present concur; and he shall nominate, and by and with the Advice and Consent of the Senate, shall appoint Ambassadors, other public Ministers and Consuls, Judges of the supreme Court, and all other Officers of the United States, whose Appointments are not herein otherwise provided for, and which shall be established by Law: but the Congress may by Law vest the Appointment of such inferior Officers, as they think proper, in the President alone, in the Courts of Law, or in the Heads of Departments.

▶ Clause 2. **Treaties, appointments** The President has the sole power to make treaties; to become effective, a treaty must be approved by a two-thirds vote in the Senate. In practice, the President can also make executive agreements with foreign governments; these pacts, which are frequently made and usually deal with routine matters, do not require Senate consent. The President appoints the principal officers of the executive branch and all federal judges; the "inferior officers" are those who hold lesser posts.

▶3. The President shall have Power to fill up all Vacancies that may happen during the Recess of the Senate, by granting Commissions which shall expire at the End of their next Session.

▶ Clause 3. **Recess appointments** When the Senate is not in session, appointments that require Senate consent can be made by the President on a temporary basis, as "recess appointments." Recess appointments are valid only to the end of the congressional term in which they are made.

Section 3.

He shall from time to time give to the Congress Information of the State of the Union, and recommend to their Consideration such Measures as he shall judge necessary and expedient; he may, on extraordinary Occasions, convene both Houses, or either of them, and in Case of Disagreement between them, with Respect to the Time of Adjournment, he may adjourn them to such Time as he shall think proper; he shall receive Ambassadors and other public Ministers; he shall take Care that the Laws be faithfully executed, and shall Commission all the Officers of the United States.

Section 3. President's Powers and Duties

The President delivers a State of the Union Message to Congress soon after that body convenes each year. That message is delivered to the nation's lawmakers and, importantly, to the American people, as well. It is shortly followed by the proposed federal budget and an economic report; and the President may send special messages to Congress at any time. In all of these communications, Congress is urged to take those actions the Chief Executive finds to be in the national interest. The President also has the power: to call special sessions of Congress; to adjourn Congress if its two houses cannot agree for that purpose; to receive the diplomatic representatives of other governments; to insure the proper execution of all federal laws; and to empower federal officers to hold their posts and perform their duties.

Section 4.

The President, Vice President and all Civil Officers of the United States, shall be removed from Office on Impeachment for and Conviction of, Treason, Bribery, or other high Crimes and Misdemeanors.

Section 4. Impeachment

The Constitution outlines the impeachment process in Article I, Section 2, Clause 5 and in Section 3, Clauses 6 and 7.

Article III

Section 1.

The judicial Power of the United States, shall be vested in one supreme Court, and in such inferior Courts as the Congress may from time to time ordain and establish. The Judges, both of the supreme and inferior Courts, shall hold their Offices during good Behaviour, and shall, at stated Times, receive for their Services, a Compensation, which shall not be diminished during their Continuance in Office.

Judicial Department

Section 1. Judicial Power, Courts, Terms of Office

The judicial power conferred here is the power of federal courts to hear and decide cases, disputes between the government and individuals and between private persons (parties). The Constitution creates only the Supreme Court of the United States; it gives to Congress the power to establish other, lower federal courts (Article I, Section 8, Clause 9) and to fix the size of the Supreme Court. The words "during good behaviour" mean, in effect, for life.

Section 2. Jurisdiction

▶ Clause 1. **Cases to be heard** This clause sets out the jurisdiction of the federal courts; that is, it identifies those cases that may be tried in those courts. The federal courts can hear and decide—have jurisdiction over—a case depending on either the subject matter or the parties involved in that case. The jurisdiction of the federal courts in cases involving States was substantially restricted by the 11th Amendment in 1795.

▶ Clause 2. **Supreme Court jurisdiction** Original jurisdiction refers to the power of a court to hear a case in the first instance, not on appeal from a lower court. Appellate jurisdiction refers to a court's power to hear a case on appeal from a lower court, from the court in which the case was originally tried. This clause gives the Supreme Court both original and appellate jurisdiction. However, nearly all of the cases the High Court hears are brought to it on appeal from the lower federal courts and the highest State courts.

▶ Clause 3. **Jury trial in criminal cases** A person accused of a federal crime is guaranteed the right to trial by jury in a federal court in the State where the crime was committed; see the 5th and 6th amendments. The right to trial by jury in serious criminal cases in the State courts is guaranteed by the 6th and 14th amendments.

Section 3. Treason

▶ Clause 1. **Definition** Treason is the only crime defined in the Constitution. The Framers intended the very specific definition here to prevent the loose use of the charge of treason—for example, against persons who criticize the government. Treason can be committed only in time of war and only by a citizen or a resident alien.

▶ Clause 2. **Punishment** Congress has provided that the punishment that a federal court may impose on a convicted traitor may range from a minimum of five years in prison and/or a $10,000 fine to a maximum of death; no person convicted of treason has ever been executed by the United States. No legal punishment can be imposed on the family or descendants of a convicted traitor. Congress has also made it a crime for any person (in either peace or wartime) to commit espionage or sabotage, to attempt to overthrow the government by force, or to conspire to do any of these things.

Section 2.

▶1. The judicial Power shall extend to all Cases, in Law and Equity, arising under this Constitution, the Laws of the United States, and Treaties made, or which shall be made, under their Authority;— to all Cases affecting Ambassadors, other public ministers, and Consuls;— to all Cases of Admiralty and maritime Jurisdiction;— to Controversies to which the United States shall be a Party;— to Controversies between two or more States;— between a State and Citizens of another State;— between Citizens of different States;— between Citizens of the same State claiming Lands under Grants of different States, and between a State, or the Citizens thereof, and foreign States, Citizens, or Subjects.

▶2. In all Cases affecting Ambassadors, other public Ministers and Consuls, and those in which a State shall be a Party, the supreme Court shall have original Jurisdiction. In all the other Cases before mentioned, the supreme Court shall have appellate Jurisdiction, both as to Law and Fact, with such Exceptions, and under such Regulations as the Congress shall make.

▶3. The trial of all Crimes, except in Cases of Impeachment, shall be by Jury; and such Trial shall be held in the State where the said Crimes shall have been committed; but when not committed within any State, the Trial shall be at such Place or Places as the Congress may by Law have directed.

Section 3.

▶1. Treason against the United States shall consist only in levying War against them, or in adhering to their Enemies, giving them Aid and Comfort. No Person shall be convicted of Treason unless on the Testimony of two Witnesses to the same overt Act, or on Confession in open Court.

▶2. The Congress shall have Power to declare the Punishment of Treason, but no Attainder of Treason shall work Corruption of Blood, or Forfeiture except during the Life of the Person attainted.

Article IV

Section 1.

Full Faith and Credit shall be given in each State to the public Acts, Records, and judicial Proceedings of every other State. And the Congress may by general Laws prescribe the Manner in which such Acts, Records and Proceedings shall be proved, and the Effect thereof.

Section 2.

▶1. The Citizens of each State shall be entitled to all Privileges and Immunities of Citizens in the several States.

▶2. A Person charged in any State with Treason, Felony, or other Crime, who shall flee from justice, and be found in another State, shall on Demand of the executive Authority of the State from which he fled, be delivered up, to be removed to the State having Jurisdiction of the Crime.

▶3. No Person held to Service or Labor in one State, under the Laws thereof, escaping into another, shall, in Consequence of any Law or Regulation therein, be discharged from Service or Labor, but shall be delivered up on Claim of the Party to whom such Service or Labor may be due.

Section 3.

▶1. New States may be admitted by the Congress into this Union; but no new State shall be formed or erected within the Jurisdiction of any other State; nor any State be formed by the Junction of two or more States, or Parts of States, without the Consent of the Legislatures of the States concerned as well as of the Congress.

▶2. The Congress shall have Power to dispose of and make all needful Rules and Regulations respecting the Territory or other Property belonging to the United States; and nothing in this Constitution shall be so construed as to Prejudice any Claims of the United States, or of any particular State.

Section 4.

The United States shall guarantee to every State in this Union a Republican Form of Government, and shall protect each of them against Invasion; and on Application of the Legislature, or of the Executive (when the Legislature cannot be convened) against domestic Violence.

Relations Among States

Section 1. Full Faith and Credit

Each State must recognize the validity of the laws, public records, and court decisions of every other State.

Section 2. Privileges and Immunities of Citizens

▶ Clause 1. **Residents of other States** In effect, this clause means that no State may discriminate against the residents of other States; that is, a State's laws cannot draw unreasonable distinctions between its own residents and those of any of the other States. See Section 1 of the 14th Amendment.

▶ Clause 2. **Extradition** The process of returning a fugitive to another State is known as "interstate rendition" or, more commonly, "extradition." Usually, that process works routinely; some extradition requests are contested however—especially in cases with racial or political overtones. A governor may refuse to extradite a fugitive; but the federal courts can compel an unwilling governor to obey this constitutional command.

▶ Clause 3. **Fugitive slaves** This clause was nullified by the 13th Amendment, which abolished slavery in 1865.

Section 3. New States; Territories

▶ Clause 1. **New States** Only Congress can admit new States to the Union. A new State may not be created by taking territory from an existing State without the consent of that State's legislature. Congress has admitted 37 States since the original 13 formed the Union. Five States—Vermont, Kentucky, Tennessee, Maine, and West Virginia—were created from parts of existing States. Texas was an independent republic before admission. California was admitted after being ceded to the United States by Mexico. Each of the other 30 States entered the Union only after a period of time as an organized territory of the United States.

▶ Clause 2. **Territory, property** Congress has the power to make laws concerning the territories, other public lands, and all other property of the United States.

Section 4. Protection Afforded to States by the Nation

The Constitution does not define "a republican form of government," but the phrase is generally understood to mean a representative government. The Federal Government must also defend each State against attacks from outside its border and, at the request of a State's legislature or its governor, aid its efforts to put down internal disorders.

Provisions for Amendment

This section provides for the methods by which formal changes can be made in the Constitution. An amendment may be proposed in one of two ways: by a two-thirds vote in each house of Congress, or by a national convention called by Congress at the request of two-thirds of the State legislatures. A proposed amendment may be ratified in one of two ways: by three-fourths of the State legislatures, or by three-fourths of the States in conventions called for that purpose. Congress has the power to determine the method by which a proposed amendment may be ratified. The amendment process cannot be used to deny any State its equal representation in the United States Senate. To this point, 27 amendments have been adopted. To date, all of the amendments except the 21st Amendment were proposed by Congress and ratified by the State legislatures. Only the 21st Amendment was ratified by the convention method.

Article V

The Congress, whenever two thirds of both Houses shall deem it necessary, shall propose Amendments to this Constitution, or, on the Application of the Legislatures of two thirds of the several States, shall call a Convention for proposing Amendments, which, in either Case, shall be valid to all Intents and Purposes, as Part of this Constitution, when ratified by the Legislatures of three fourths of the several States, or by Conventions in three fourths thereof, as the one or the other Mode of Ratification may be proposed by the Congress; Provided that no Amendment which may be made prior to the Year One thousand eight hundred and eight shall in any Manner affect the first and fourth Clauses in the Ninth section of the first Article; and that no State, without its Consent, shall be deprived of its equal Suffrage in the Senate.

National Debts, Supremacy of National Law, Oath

Section 1. Validity of Debts

Congress had borrowed large sums of money during the Revolution and later during the Critical Period of the 1780s. This provision, a pledge that the new government would honor those debts, did much to create confidence in that government.

Section 2. Supremacy of National Law

This section sets out the Supremacy Clause, a specific declaration of the supremacy of federal law over any and all forms of State law. No State, including its local governments, may make or enforce any law that conflicts with any provision in the Constitution, an act of Congress, a treaty, or an order, rule, or regulation properly issued by the President or his subordinates in the executive branch.

Section 3. Oaths of Office

This provision reinforces the Supremacy Clause; all public officers, at every level in the United States, owe their first allegiance to the Constitution of the United States. No religious qualification can be imposed as a condition for holding any public office.

Article VI

Section 1.

All Debts contracted and Engagements entered into, before the Adoption of this Constitution, shall be as valid against the United States under this Constitution, as under the Confederation.

Section 2.

This Constitution, and the Laws of the United States which shall be made in Pursuance thereof; and all Treaties made, or which shall be made, under the Authority of the United States, shall be the supreme Law of the Land; and the Judges in every State shall be bound thereby, anything in the constitution or Laws of any State to the Contrary notwithstanding.

Section 3.

The Senators and Representatives before mentioned, and the Members of the several State legislatures, and all executive and judicial Officers, both of the United States and of the several States, shall be bound by Oath or Affirmation, to support this Constitution; but no religious Test shall ever be required as a Qualification to any Office or public Trust under the United States.

Ratification of Constitution

The proposed Constitution was signed by George Washington and 37 of his fellow Framers on September 17, 1787. (George Read of Delaware signed for himself and also for his absent colleague, John Dickinson.)

Article VII

The ratification of the Conventions of nine States, shall be sufficient for the Establishment of this Constitution between the States so ratifying the same.

Done in Convention by the Unanimous Consent of the States present the Seventeenth Day of September in the Year of our Lord one thousand seven hundred and Eighty-seven and of the Independence of the United States of America the twelfth. In witness whereof We have hereunto subscribed our Names.

Attest:

William Jackson,
Secretary

George Washington,
President and Deputy from Virginia

New Hampshire

John Langdon
Nicholas Gilman

Massachusetts

Nathaniel Gorham
Rufus King

Connecticut

William Samuel Johnson
Roger Sherman

New York

Alexander Hamilton

New Jersey

William Livingston
David Brearley
William Paterson
Jonathan Dayton

Pennsylvania

Benjamin Franklin
Thomas Mifflin
Robert Morris
George Clymer
Thomas Fitzsimons
Jared Ingersoll
James Wilson
Gouverneur Morris

Delaware

George Read
Gunning Bedford, Jr.
John Dickinson
Richard Bassett
Jacob Broom

Maryland

James McHenry
Dan of St. Thomas Jenifer
Daniel Carroll

Virginia

John Blair
James Madison, Jr.

North Carolina

William Blount
Richard Dobbs Spaight
Hugh Williamson

South Carolina

John Rutledge
Charles Cotesworth Pinckney
Charles Pinckney
Pierce Butler

Georgia

William Few
Abraham Baldwin

The United States Constitution

Amendments

The first 10 amendments, the Bill of Rights, were each proposed by Congress on September 25, 1789, and ratified by the necessary three-fourths of the States on December 15, 1791. These amendments were originally intended to restrict the National Government—not the States. However, the Supreme Court has several times held that most of their provisions also apply to the States, through the 14th Amendment's Due Process Clause.

1st Amendment. **Freedom of Religion, Speech, Press, Assembly, and Petition**

The 1st Amendment sets out five basic liberties: The guarantee of freedom of religion is both a protection of religious thought and practice and a command of separation of church and state. The guarantees of freedom of speech and press assure to all persons a right to speak, publish, and otherwise express their views. The guarantees of the rights of assembly and petition protect the right to join with others in public meetings, political parties, interest groups, and other associations to discuss public affairs and influence public policy. None of these rights is guaranteed in absolute terms, however; like all other civil rights guarantees, each of them may be exercised only with regard to the rights of all other persons.

1st Amendment

Congress shall make no law respecting an establishment of religion, or prohibiting the free exercise thereof, or abridging the freedom of speech, or of the press; or the right of the people peaceably to assemble, and to petition the Government for a redress of grievances.

2nd Amendment. **Bearing Arms**

The right of the people to keep and bear arms was insured by the 2nd Amendment.

2nd Amendment

A well-regulated Militia being necessary to the security of a free State, the right of the people to keep and bear Arms, shall not be infringed.

3rd Amendment. **Quartering of Troops**

This amendment was intended to prevent what had been common British practice in the colonial period; see the Declaration of Independence. This provision is of virtually no importance today.

3rd Amendment

No Soldier shall, in time of peace be quartered in any house, without the consent of the Owner, nor, in time of war, but in a manner to be prescribed by law.

4th Amendment. **Searches and Seizures**

The basic rule laid down by the 4th Amendment is this: Police officers have no general right to search for or seize evidence or seize (arrest) persons. Except in particular circumstances, they must have a proper warrant (a court order) obtained with probable cause (on reasonable grounds). This guarantee is reinforced by the exclusionary rule, developed by the Supreme Court: Evidence gained as the result of an unlawful search or seizure cannot be used at the court trial of the person from whom it was seized.

4th Amendment

The right of the people to be secure in their persons, houses, papers, and effects, against unreasonable searches and seizures, shall not be violated, and no Warrants shall issue, but upon probable cause, supported by Oath or affirmation, and particularly describing the place to be searched, and the persons or things to be seized.

5th Amendment. **Criminal Proceedings; Due Process; Eminent Domain**

A person can be tried for a serious federal crime only if he or she has been indicted (charged, accused of that crime) by a grand jury. No one may be subjected to double jeopardy—that is, tried twice for the same crime. All persons are protected against self-incrimination; no person can be legally compelled to answer any question in any governmental proceeding if that answer could lead to that person's prosecution. The 5th Amendment's Due Process Clause prohibits unfair, arbitrary actions by the Federal Government; a like prohibition is set out against the States in the 14th Amendment. Government may take private property for a legitimate public purpose; but when it exercises that power of eminent domain, it must pay a fair price for the property seized.

5th Amendment

No person shall be held to answer for a capital, or otherwise infamous crime, unless on a presentment or indictment of a Grand Jury, except in cases arising in the land or naval forces, or in the Militia, when in actual service in time of War, or public danger; nor shall any person be subject for the same offence to be twice put in jeopardy of life or limb; nor shall be compelled in any criminal case to be a witness against himself, nor be deprived of life, liberty, or property, without due process of law; nor shall private property be taken for public use, without just compensation.

6th Amendment

In all criminal prosecutions, the accused shall enjoy the right to a speedy and public trial, by an impartial jury of the State and district wherein the crime shall have been committed, which district shall have been previously ascertained by law, and to be informed of the nature and cause of the accusation; to be confronted with the witnesses against him; to have compulsory process for obtaining witnesses in his favor, and to have the Assistance of Counsel for his defence.

6th Amendment. **Criminal Proceedings**

A person accused of crime has the right to be tried in court without undue delay and by an impartial jury; see Article III, Section 2, Clause 3. The defendant must be informed of the charge upon which he or she is to be tried, has the right to cross-examine hostile witnesses, and has the right to require the testimony of favorable witnesses. The defendant also has the right to be represented by an attorney at every stage in the criminal process.

7th Amendment

In Suits at common law, where the value in controversy shall exceed twenty dollars, the right of trial by jury shall be preserved, and no fact tried by a jury, shall be otherwise re-examined in any Court of the United States, than according to the rules of the common law.

7th Amendment. **Civil Trials**

This amendment applies only to civil cases heard in federal courts. A civil case does not involve criminal matters; it is a dispute between private parties or between the government and a private party. The right to trial by jury is guaranteed in any civil case in a federal court if the amount of money involved in that case exceeds $20 (most cases today involve a much larger sum); that right may be waived (relinquished, put aside) if both parties agree to a bench trial (a trial by a judge, without a jury).

8th Amendment

Excessive bail shall not be required, nor excessive fines imposed, nor cruel and unusual punishment inflicted.

8th Amendment. **Punishment for Crimes**

Bail is the sum of money that a person accused of crime may be required to post (deposit with the court) as a guarantee that he or she will appear in court at the proper time. The amount of bail required and/or a fine imposed as punishment must bear a reasonable relationship to the seriousness of the crime involved in the case. The prohibition of cruel and unusual punishment forbids any punishment judged to be too harsh, too severe for the crime for which it is imposed.

9th Amendment

The enumeration in the Constitution, of certain rights, shall not be construed to deny or disparage others retained by the people.

9th Amendment. **Unenumerated Rights**

The fact that the Constitution sets out many civil rights guarantees, expressly provides for many protections against government, does not mean that there are not other rights also held by the people.

10th Amendment

The powers not delegated to the United States by the Constitution, nor prohibited by it to the States, are reserved to the States respectively, or to the people.

10th Amendment. **Powers Reserved to the States**

This amendment identifies the area of power that may be exercised by the States. All of those powers the Constitution does not grant to the National Government, and at the same time does not forbid to the States, belong to each of the States, or to the people of each State.

11th Amendment. **Suits Against States**

Proposed by Congress March 4, 1794; ratified February 7, 1795, but official announcement of the ratification was delayed until January 8, 1798. This amendment repealed part of Article III, Section 2, Clause 1. No State may be sued in a federal court by a resident of another State or of a foreign country; the Supreme Court has long held that this provision also means that a State cannot be sued in a federal court by a foreign country or, more importantly, even by one of its own residents.

11th Amendment

The Judicial power of the United States shall not be construed to extend to any suit in law or equity, commenced or prosecuted against one of the United States by Citizens of another State, or by Citizens or Subjects of any Foreign State.

12th Amendment. **Election of President and Vice President**

Proposed by Congress December 9, 1803; ratified June 15, 1804. This amendment replaced Article II, Section 1, Clause 3. Originally, each elector cast two ballots, each for a different person for President. The person with the largest number of electoral votes, provided that number was a majority of the electors, was to become President; the person with the second highest number was to become Vice President. This arrangement produced an electoral vote tie between Thomas Jefferson and Aaron Burr in 1800; the House finally chose Jefferson as President in 1801. The 12th Amendment separated the balloting for President and Vice President; each elector now casts one ballot for someone as President and a second ballot for another person as Vice President. Note that the 20th Amendment changed the date set here (March 4) to January 20, and that the 23rd Amendment (1961) provides for electors from the District of Columbia. This amendment also provides that the Vice President must meet the same qualifications as those set out for the President in Article II, Section 1, Clause 5.

12th Amendment

The Electors shall meet in their respective States and vote by ballot for President and Vice President, one of whom, at least, shall not be an inhabitant of the same State with themselves; they shall name in their ballots the person voted for as President, and in distinct ballots the person voted for as Vice President, and they shall make distinct lists of all persons voted for as President, and of all persons voted for as Vice President, and of the number of votes for each, which lists they shall sign and certify, and transmit sealed to the seat of the government of the United States, directed to the President of the Senate;— The President of the Senate shall, in the presence of the Senate and the House of Representatives, open all the certificates and the votes shall then be counted;— the person having the greatest Number of votes for President shall be the President, if such number be a majority of the whole number of Electors appointed; and if no person have such a majority, then, from the persons having the highest numbers not exceeding three on the list of those voted for as President, the House of Representatives shall choose immediately, by ballot, the President. But in choosing the President, the votes shall be taken by States, the representation from each State having one vote; a quorum for this purpose shall consist of a member or members from two thirds of the States, and a majority of all the States shall be necessary to a choice. And if the House of Representatives shall not choose a President whenever the right of choice shall devolve upon them, before the fourth day of March next following, then the Vice President shall act as President, as in case of death or other constitutional disability of the President. The person having the greatest number of votes as Vice President, shall be the Vice President, if such number be a majority of the whole number of Electors appointed, and if no person have a majority, then from the two highest numbers on the list, the Senate shall choose the Vice President; a quorum for the purpose shall consist of two thirds of the whole number of Senators, a majority of the whole number shall be necessary to a choice. But no person constitutionally ineligible to the office of President shall be eligible to that of Vice-President of the United States.

13th Amendment. **Slavery and Involuntary Servitude**

Proposed by Congress January 31, 1865; ratified December 6, 1865. This amendment forbids slavery in the United States and in any area under its control. It also forbids other forms of forced labor, except punishments for crime; but some forms of compulsory service are not prohibited—for example, service on juries or in the armed forces. Section 2 gives to Congress the power to carry out the provisions of Section 1 of this amendment.

13th Amendment

Section 1. Neither slavery nor involuntary servitude, except as a punishment for crime whereof the party shall have been duly convicted, shall exist within the United States, or any place subject to their jurisdiction.

Section 2. Congress shall have power to enforce this article by appropriate legislation.

14th Amendment

Section 1. All persons born or naturalized in the United States and subject to the jurisdiction thereof, are citizens of the United States and of the State wherein they reside. No State shall make or enforce any law which shall abridge the privileges or immunities of citizens of the United States; nor shall any State deprive any person of life, liberty, or property, without due process of law; nor deny to any person within its jurisdiction the equal protection of the laws.

14th Amendment. **Rights of Citizens**

Proposed by Congress June 13, 1866; ratified July 9, 1868. Section 1 defines citizenship. It provides for the acquisition of United States citizenship by birth or by naturalization. Citizenship at birth is determined according to the principle of jus soli—"the law of the soil," where born; naturalization is the legal process by which one acquires a new citizenship at some time after birth. Under certain circumstances, citizenship can also be gained at birth abroad, according to the principle of jus sanguinis—"the law of the blood," to whom born. This section also contains two major civil rights provisions: the Due Process Clause forbids a State (and its local governments) to act in any unfair or arbitrary way; the Equal Protection Clause forbids a State (and its local governments) to discriminate against, draw unreasonable distinctions between, persons.

Most of the rights set out against the National Government in the first eight amendments have been extended against the States (and their local governments) through Supreme Court decisions involving the 14th Amendment's Due Process Clause.

Section 2. Representatives shall be apportioned among the several States according to their respective numbers, counting the whole number of persons in each State, excluding Indians not taxed. But when the right to vote at any election for the choice of electors for President and Vice President of the United States, Representatives in Congress, the Executive and Judicial officers of a State, or the members of the Legislature thereof, is denied to any of the male inhabitants of such State, being twenty-one years of age and citizens of the United States, or in any way abridged, except for participation in rebellion, or other crime, the basis of representation therein shall be reduced in the proportion which the number of such male citizens shall bear to the whole number of male citizens twenty-one years of age in such State.

The first sentence here replaced Article I, Section 2, Clause 3, the Three-Fifths Compromise provision. Essentially, all persons in the United States are counted in each decennial census, the basis for the distribution of House seats. The balance of this section has never been enforced and is generally thought to be obsolete.

Section 3. No person shall be a Senator or Representative in Congress, or elector of President and Vice President, or hold any office, civil or military, under the United States, or under any State, who, having previously taken an oath, as a member of Congress, or as an officer of the United States, or as a member of any State legislature, or as an executive or judicial officer of any State, to support the Constitution of the United States, shall have engaged in insurrection or rebellion against the same, or given aid or comfort to the enemies thereof. But Congress may, by a vote of two thirds of each House, remove such disability.

Section 3 limited the President's power to pardon those persons who had led the Confederacy during the Civil War. Congress finally removed this disability in 1898.

Section 4. The validity of the public debt of the United States, authorized by law, including debts incurred for payment of pensions and bounties for services in suppressing insurrection or rebellion, shall not be questioned. But neither the United States nor any State shall assume or pay any debt or obligation incurred in aid of insurrection or rebellion against the United States, or any claim for the loss or emancipation of any slave; but all such debts, obligations and claims shall be held illegal and void.

Section 4 also dealt with matters directly related to the Civil War. It reaffirmed the public debt of the United States; but it invalidated, prohibited payment of, any debt contracted by the Confederate States and also prohibited any compensation of former slave owners.

Section 5. The Congress shall have power to enforce, by appropriate legislation, the provisions of this article.

15th Amendment. **Right to Vote—Race, Color, Servitude**

Proposed by Congress February 26, 1869; ratified February 3, 1870. The phrase "previous condition of servitude" refers to slavery. Note that this amendment does not guarantee the right to vote to African Americans, or to anyone else. Instead, it forbids the States from discriminating against any person on the grounds of his "race, color, or previous condition of servitude" in the setting of suffrage qualifications.

15th Amendment

Section 1. The right of citizens of the United States to vote shall not be denied or abridged by the United States or by any State on account of race, color, or previous condition of servitude.

Section 2. The Congress shall have power to enforce this article by appropriate legislation.

16th Amendment. **Income Tax**

Proposed by Congress July 12, 1909; ratified February 3, 1913. This amendment modified two provisions in Article I, Section 2, Clause 3, and Section 9, Clause 4. It gives to Congress the power to levy an income tax, a direct tax, without regard to the populations of any of the States.

16th Amendment

The Congress shall have power to lay and collect taxes on incomes, from whatever source derived, without apportionment among the several States, and without regard to any census or enumeration.

17th Amendment. **Popular Election of Senators**

Proposed by Congress May 13, 1912; ratified April 8, 1913. This amendment repealed those portions of Article I, Section 3, Clauses 1 and 2 relating to the election of senators. Senators are now elected by the voters in each State. If a vacancy occurs, the governor of the State involved must call an election to fill the seat; the governor may appoint a senator to serve until the next election, if the State's legislature has authorized that step.

17th Amendment

The Senate of the United States shall be composed of two Senators from each State, elected by the people thereof, for six years; and each Senator shall have one vote. The electors in each State shall have the qualifications requisite for electors of the most numerous branch of the State legislatures.

When vacancies happen in the representation of any State in the Senate, the executive authority of such State shall issue writs of election to fill such vacancies: Provided, That the legislature of any State may empower the executive thereof to make temporary appointments until the people fill the vacancies by election as the legislature may direct.

This amendment shall not be so construed as to affect the election or term of any Senator chosen before it becomes valid as part of the Constitution.

18th Amendment. **Prohibition of Intoxicating Liquors**

Proposed by Congress December 18, 1917; ratified January 16, 1919. This amendment outlawed the making, selling, transporting, importing, or exporting of alcoholic beverages in the United States. It was repealed in its entirety by the 21st Amendment in 1933.

18th Amendment

Section 1. After one year from the ratification of this article the manufacture, sale, or transportation of intoxicating liquors within, the importation thereof into, or the exportation thereof from the United States and all territory subject to the jurisdiction thereof for beverage purposes is hereby prohibited.

Section 2. The Congress and the several States shall have concurrent power to enforce this article by appropriate legislation.

Section 3. This article shall be inoperative unless it shall have been ratified as an amendment to the Constitution by the legislatures of the several States, as provided in the Constitution, within seven years of the date of the submission hereof to the States by Congress.

19th Amendment. **Equal Suffrage—Sex**

Proposed by Congress June 4, 1919; ratified August 18, 1920. No person can be denied the right to vote in any election in the United States on account of his or her sex.

19th Amendment

The right of citizens of the United States to vote shall not be denied or abridged by the United States or by any State on account of sex.

Congress shall have power to enforce this article by appropriate legislation.

20th Amendment

Section 1. The terms of the President and Vice President shall end at noon on the 20th day of January, and the terms of Senators and Representatives at noon on the 3d day of January, of the years in which such terms would have ended if this article had not been ratified; and the terms of their successors shall then begin.

Section 2. The Congress shall assemble at least once in every year, and such meeting shall begin at noon on the 3d day of January, unless they shall by law appoint a different day.

20th Amendment. **Commencement of Terms; Sessions of Congress; Death or Disqualification of President-Elect**

Proposed by Congress March 2, 1932; ratified January 23, 1933. The provisions of Sections 1 and 2 relating to Congress modified Article I, Section 4, Clause 2, and those provisions relating to the President, the 12th Amendment. The date on which the President and Vice President now take office was moved from March 4 to January 20. Similarly, the members of Congress now begin their terms on January 3. The 20th Amendment is sometimes called the "Lame Duck Amendment" because it shortened the period of time a member of Congress who was defeated for reelection (a "lame duck") remains in office.

Section 3. If, at the time fixed for the beginning of the term of the President, the President elect shall have died, the Vice President elect shall become President. If a President shall not have been chosen before the time fixed for the beginning of his term, or if the President-elect shall have failed to qualify, then the Vice President elect shall act as President until a President shall have qualified; and the Congress may by law provide for the case wherein neither a President elect nor a Vice President elect shall have qualified, declaring who shall then act as President, or the manner in which one who is to act shall be selected, and such person shall act accordingly until a President or Vice President shall have qualified.

This section deals with certain possibilities that were not covered by the presidential selection provisions of either Article II or the 12th Amendment. To this point, none of these situations has occurred. Note that there is neither a President-elect nor a Vice President-elect until the electoral votes have been counted by Congress, or, if the electoral college cannot decide the matter, the House has chosen a President or the Senate has chosen a Vice President.

Section 4. The Congress may by law provide for the case of the death of any of the persons from whom the House of Representatives may choose a President whenever the right of choice shall have devolved upon them, and for the case of the death of any of the persons from whom the Senate may choose a Vice President whenever the right of choice shall have devolved upon them.

Congress has not in fact ever passed such a law. See Section 2 of the 25th Amendment, regarding a vacancy in the vice presidency; that provision could some day have an impact here.

Section 5. Sections 1 and 2 shall take effect on the 15th day of October following the ratification of this article.

Section 5 set the date on which this amendment came into force.

Section 6. This article shall be inoperative unless it shall have been ratified as an amendment to the Constitution by the legislatures of three fourths of the several States within seven years from the date of its submission.

Section 6 placed a time limit on the ratification process; note that a similar provision was written into the 18th, 21st, and 22nd amendments.

21st Amendment

Section 1. The eighteenth article of amendment to the Constitution of the United States is hereby repealed.

Section 2. The transportation or importation into any State, Territory, or possession of the United States for delivery or use therein of intoxicating liquors, in violation of the laws thereof, is hereby prohibited.

Section 3. This article shall be inoperative unless it shall have been ratified as an amendment to the Constitution by conventions in the several States, as provided in the Constitution, within seven years from the date of the submission hereof to the States by the Congress.

21st Amendment. **Repeal of 18th Amendment**

Proposed by Congress February 20, 1933; ratified December 5, 1933. This amendment repealed all of the 18th Amendment. Section 2 modifies the scope of the Federal Government's commerce power set out in Article I, Section 8, Clause 3; it gives to each State the power to regulate the transportation or importation and the distribution or use of intoxicating liquors in ways that would be unconstitutional in the case of any other commodity. The 21st Amendment is the only amendment Congress has thus far submitted to the States for ratification by conventions.

22nd Amendment. **Presidential Tenure**

Proposed by Congress March 21, 1947; ratified February 27, 1951. This amendment modified Article II, Section I, Clause 1. It stipulates that no President may serve more than two elected terms. But a President who has succeeded to the office beyond the midpoint in a term to which another President was originally elected may serve for more than eight years. In any case, however, a President may not serve more than 10 years. Prior to Franklin Roosevelt, who was elected to four terms, no President had served more than two full terms in office.

22nd Amendment

Section 1. No person shall be elected to the office of the President more than twice, and no person who has held the office of President, or acted as President, for more than two years of a term to which some other person was elected President shall be elected to the office of the President more than once. But this Article shall not apply to any person holding the office of President, when this Article was proposed by the Congress, and shall not prevent any person who may be holding the office of President, or acting as President, during the term within which this Article becomes operative from holding the office of President or acting as President during the remainder of such term.

Section 2. This article shall be inoperative unless it shall have been ratified as an amendment to the Constitution by the legislatures of three fourths of the several states within seven years from the date of its submission to the States by the Congress.

23rd Amendment. **Presidential Electors for the District of Columbia**

Proposed by Congress June 16, 1960; ratified March 29, 1961. This amendment modified Article II, Section I, Clause 2 and the 12th Amendment. It included the voters of the District of Columbia in the presidential electorate; and provides that the District is to have the same number of electors as the least populous State—three electors—but no more than that number.

23rd Amendment

Section 1. The District constituting the seat of Government of the United States shall appoint in such manner as the Congress may direct:

A number of electors of President and Vice President equal to the whole number of Senators and Representatives in Congress to which the District would be entitled if it were a State, but in no event more than the least populous State; they shall be in addition to those appointed by the States, they shall be considered, for the purposes of the election of President and Vice President, to be electors appointed by a State; and they shall meet in the District and perform such duties as provided by the twelfth article of amendment.

24th Amendment. **Right to Vote in Federal Elections—Tax Payment**

Proposed by Congress August 27, 1962; ratified January 23, 1964. This amendment outlawed the payment of any tax as a condition for taking part in the nomination or election of any federal officeholder.

24th Amendment

Section 1. The right of citizens of the United States to vote in any primary or other election for President or Vice President, for electors for President or Vice President, or for Senator or Representative in Congress, shall not be denied or abridged by the United States or any State by reason of failure to pay any poll tax or other tax.

Section 2. The Congress shall have power to enforce this article by appropriate legislation.

25th Amendment. **Presidential Succession, Vice Presidential Vacancy, Presidential Inability**

Proposed by Congress July 6, 1965; ratified February 10, 1967. Section 1 revised the imprecise provision on presidential succession in Article II, Section 1, Clause 6. It affirmed the precedent set by Vice President John Tyler, who became President on the death of William Henry Harrison in 1841.

Section 2 provides for the filling of a vacancy in the office of Vice President. The office had been vacant on 16 occasions and remained unfilled for the rest of each term involved. When Spiro Agnew resigned the office in 1973, President Nixon selected Gerald Ford per this provision; and, when President Nixon resigned in 1974, Gerald Ford became President and chose Nelson Rockefeller as Vice President.

25th Amendment

Section 1. In case of the removal of the President from office or of his death or resignation, the Vice President shall become President.

Section 2. Whenever there is a vacancy in the office of the Vice President, the President shall nominate a Vice President who shall take office upon confirmation by a majority vote of both Houses of Congress.

Section 3. Whenever the President transmits to the President pro tempore of the Senate and the Speaker of the House of Representatives his written declaration that he is unable to discharge the powers and duties of his office, and until he transmits to them a written declaration to the contrary, such powers and duties shall be discharged by the Vice President as Acting President.

This section created a procedure for determining if a President is so incapacitated that he cannot perform the powers and duties of his office.

Section 4. Whenever the Vice President and a majority of either the principal officers of the executive departments or of such other body as Congress may by law provide, transmit to the President pro tempore of the Senate and the Speaker of the House of Representatives their written declaration that the President is unable to discharge the powers and duties of his office, the Vice President shall immediately assume the powers and duties of the office as Acting President.

Thereafter, when the President transmits to the President pro tempore of the Senate and the Speaker of the House of Representatives his written declaration that no inability exists, he shall resume the powers and duties of his office unless the Vice President and a majority of either the principal officers of the executive department or of such other body as Congress may by law provide, transmit within four days to the President pro tempore of the Senate and the Speaker of the House of Representatives their written declaration that the President is unable to discharge the powers and duties of his office. Thereupon Congress shall decide the issue, assembling within forty-eight hours for that purpose if not in session. If the Congress, within twenty-one days after receipt of the latter written declaration, or, if Congress is not in session, within twenty-one days after Congress is required to assemble, determines by two-thirds vote of both Houses that the President is unable to discharge the powers and duties of his office, the Vice President shall continue to discharge the same as Acting President; otherwise, the President shall resume the powers and duties of his office.

Section 4 deals with the circumstance in which a President will not be able to determine the fact of incapacity. To this point, Congress has not established the "such other body" referred to here. This section contains the only typographical error in the Constitution; in its second paragraph, the word "department" should in fact read "departments."

26th Amendment

Section 1. The right of citizens of the United States, who are eighteen years of age or older, to vote shall not be denied or abridged by the United States or by any State on account of age.

Section 2. The Congress shall have the power to enforce this article by appropriate legislation.

26th Amendment. **Right to Vote—Age**

Proposed by Congress March 23, 1971; ratified July 1, 1971. This amendment provides that the minimum age for voting in any election in the United States cannot be more than 18 years. (A State may set a minimum voting age of less than 18, however.)

27th Amendment

No law varying the compensation for the services of the Senators and Representatives, shall take effect, until an election of Representatives shall have intervened.

27th Amendment. **Congressional Pay**

Proposed by Congress September 25, 1789; ratified May 7, 1992. This amendment modified Article I, Section 6, Clause 1. It limits Congress's power to fix the salaries of its members—by delaying the effectiveness of any increase in that pay until after the next regular congressional election.

Presidents of the United States

Name	Party	States[a]	Entered Office	Age On Taking Office	Vice President(s)
George Washington (1732–1799)	Federalist	Virginia	1789	57	John Adams
John Adams (1735–1826)	Federalist	Massachusetts	1797	61	Thomas Jefferson
Thomas Jefferson (1743–1826)	Dem-Rep[b]	Virginia	1801	57	Aaron Burr/George Clinton
James Madison (1751–1836)	Dem-Rep	Virginia	1809	57	George Clinton/Elbridge Gerry
James Monroe (1758–1831)	Dem-Rep	Virginia	1817	58	Daniel D. Tompkins
John Q. Adams (1767–1848)	Dem-Rep	Massachusetts	1825	57	John C. Calhoun
Andrew Jackson (1767–1845)	Democrat	Tennessee (SC)	1829	61	John C. Calhoun/ Martin Van Buren
Martin Van Buren (1782–1862)	Democrat	New York	1837	54	Richard M. Johnson
William H. Harrison (1773–1841)	Whig	Ohio (VA)	1841	68	John Tyler
John Tyler (1790–1862)	Democrat	Virginia	1841	51	none
James K. Polk (1795–1849)	Democrat	Tennessee (NC)	1845	49	George M. Dallas
Zachary Taylor (1784–1850)	Whig	Louisiana (VA)	1849	64	Millard Fillmore
Millard Fillmore (1800–1874)	Whig	New York	1850	50	none
Franklin Pierce (1804–1869)	Democrat	New Hampshire	1853	48	William R. King
James Buchanan (1791–1868)	Democrat	Pennsylvania	1857	65	John C. Breckinridge
Abraham Lincoln (1809–1865)	Republican	Illinois (KY)	1861	52	Hannibal Hamlin/Andrew Johnson[c]
Andrew Johnson (1808–1875)	Democrat	Tennessee (NC)	1865	56	none
Ulysses S. Grant (1822–1885)	Republican	Illinois (OH)	1869	46	Schuyler Colfax/Henry Wilson
Rutherford B. Hayes (1822–1893)	Republican	Ohio	1877	54	William A. Wheeler
James A. Garfield (1831–1881)	Republican	Ohio	1881	49	Chester A. Arthur
Chester A. Arthur (1829–1896)	Republican	New York (VT)	1881	51	none
Grover Cleveland (1837–1908)	Democrat	New York (NJ)	1885	47	Thomas A. Hendricks
Benjamin Harrison (1833–1901)	Republican	Indiana (OH)	1889	55	Levi P. Morton
Grover Cleveland (1837–1908)	Democrat	New York (NJ)	1893	55	Adlai E. Stevenson

Name	Party	States	Entered Office	Age On Taking Office	Vice President(s)
William McKinley (1843–1901)	Republican	Ohio	1897	54	Garret A. Hobart/ Theodore Roosevelt
Theodore Roosevelt (1858–1919)	Republican	New York	1901	42	Charles W. Fairbanks
William H. Taft (1857–1930)	Republican	Ohio	1909	51	James S. Sherman
Woodrow Wilson (1856–1924)	Democrat	New Jersey (VA)	1913	56	Thomas R. Marshall
Warren G. Harding (1865–1923)	Republican	Ohio	1921	55	Calvin Coolidge
Calvin Coolidge (1872–1933)	Republican	Massachusetts (VT)	1923	51	Charles G. Dawes
Herbert Hoover (1874–1964)	Republican	California (IA)	1929	54	Charles Curtis
Franklin Roosevelt (1882–1945)	Democrat	New York	1933	51	John N. Garner/ Henry A. Wallace/Harry S Truman
Harry S Truman (1884–1972)	Democrat	Missouri	1945	60	Alben W. Barkley
Dwight D. Eisenhower (1890–1969)	Republican	New York (TX)	1953	62	Richard M. Nixon
John F. Kennedy (1917–1963)	Democrat	Massachusetts	1961	43	Lyndon B. Johnson
Lyndon B. Johnson (1908–1973)	Democrat	Texas	1963	55	Hubert H. Humphrey
Richard M. Nixon (1913–1994)	Republican	New York (CA)	1969	56	Spiro T. Agnew[d]/Gerald R. Ford[e]
Gerald R. Ford (1913–2006)	Republican	Michigan (NE)	1974	61	Nelson A. Rockefeller[f]
James E. Carter (1924–)	Democrat	Georgia	1977	52	Walter F. Mondale
Ronald W. Reagan (1911–2004)	Republican	California (IL)	1981	69	George H. W. Bush
George H.W. Bush (1924–)	Republican	Texas (MA)	1989	64	J. Danforth Quayle
William J. Clinton (1946–)	Democrat	Arkansas	1993	46	Albert Gore, Jr.
George W. Bush (1946–)	Republican	Texas	2001	54	Richard B. Cheney
Barack Obama (1961–)	Democrat	Illinois (HI)	2009	47	Joseph R. Biden
Donald J. Trump (1946–)	Republican	New York	2017	70	Michael R. Pence

[a] State of residence when elected; if born in another State, that State in parentheses.
[b] Democratic-Republican
[c] Johnson, a War Democrat, was elected Vice President on the coalition Union Party ticket.
[d] Resigned October 10, 1973.
[e] Nominated by Nixon, confirmed by Congress on December 6, 1973.
[f] Nominated by Ford, confirmed by Congress on December 19, 1974.

US: Political

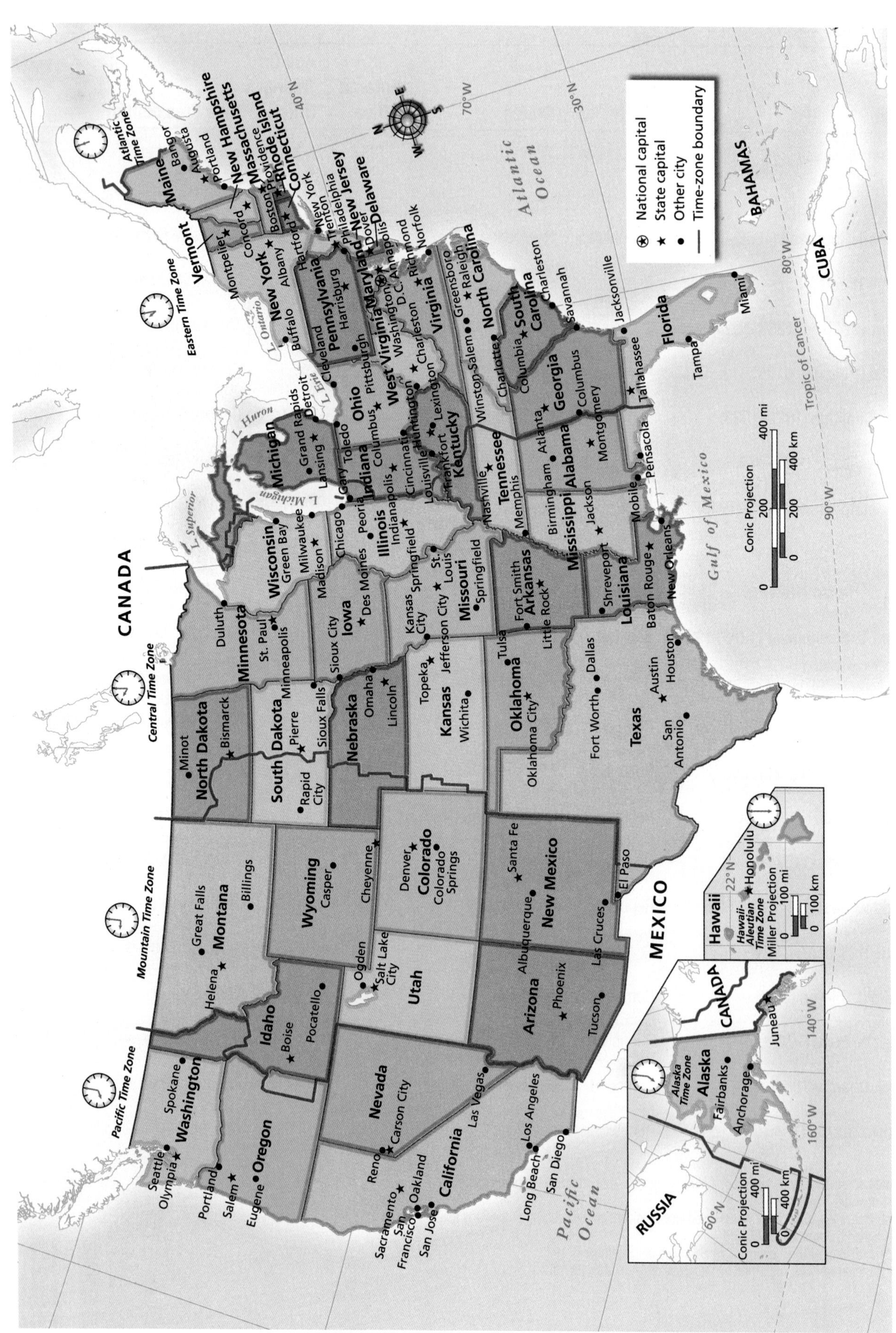

US: Physical

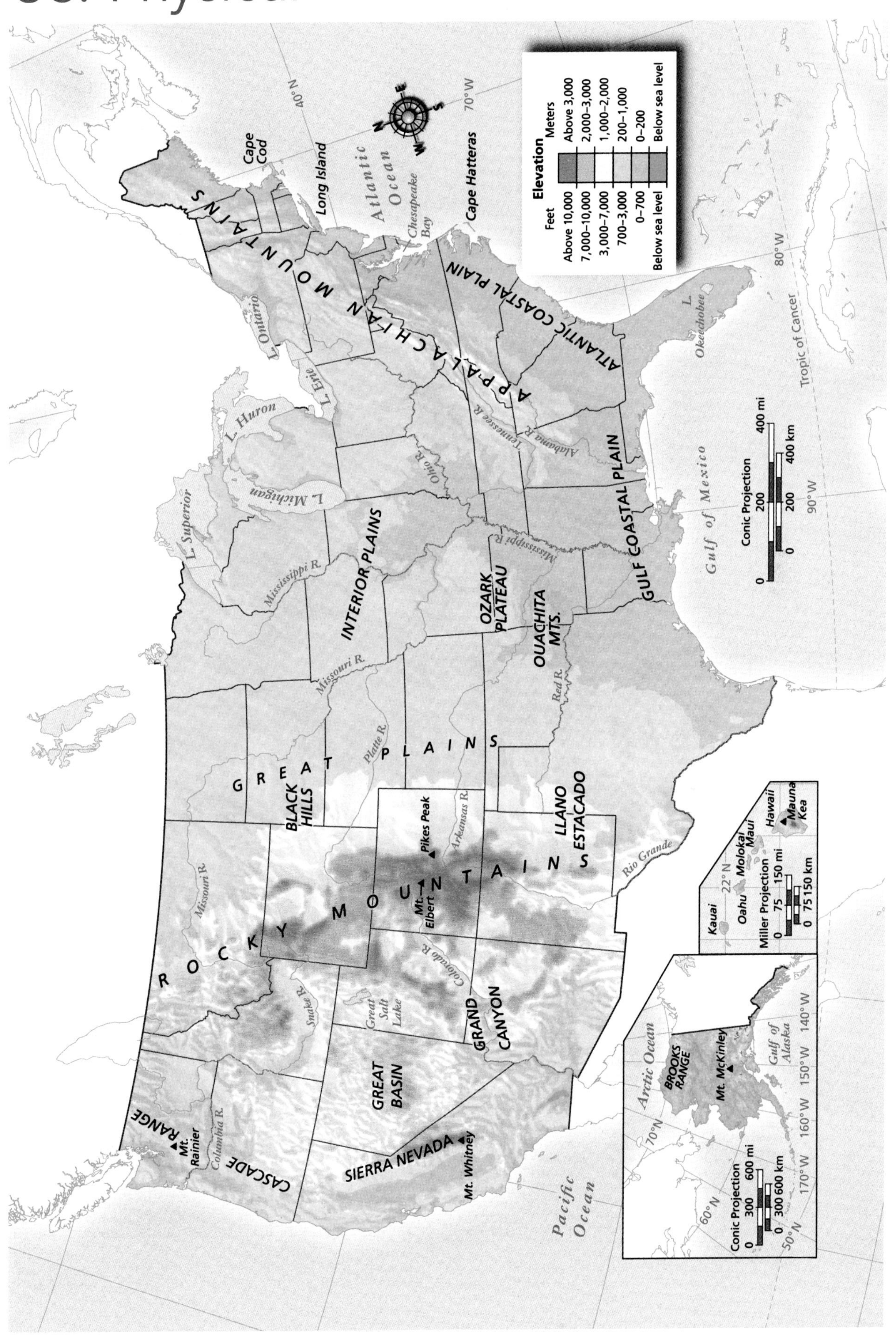

Cape Cod
Long Island
40° N
70° W
Atlantic Ocean
Chesapeake Bay
Cape Hatteras
Elevation
Feet | Meters
Above 10,000 | Above 3,000
7,000–10,000 | 2,000–3,000
3,000–7,000 | 1,000–2,000
700–3,000 | 200–1,000
0–700 | 0–200
Below sea level | Below sea level
APPALACHIAN MOUNTAINS
ATLANTIC COASTAL PLAIN
L. Okeechobee
80° W
Tropic of Cancer
L. Ontario
L. Erie
L. Huron
L. Michigan
L. Superior
Ohio R.
Tennessee R.
Alabama R.
GULF COASTAL PLAIN
Gulf of Mexico
Conic Projection
0 200 400 mi
0 200 400 km
90° W
Mississippi R.
INTERIOR PLAINS
OZARK PLATEAU
OUACHITA MTS.
Missouri R.
Red R.
Platte R.
GREAT PLAINS
BLACK HILLS
LLANO ESTACADO
Arkansas R.
Pikes Peak
Mt. Elbert
ROCKY MOUNTAINS
Rio Grande
Kauai
Oahu
Molokai
Maui
Hawaii
Mauna Kea
22° N
Miller Projection
0 75 150 mi
0 75 150 km
Colorado R.
Snake R.
Great Salt Lake
GRAND CANYON
GREAT BASIN
Columbia R.
CASCADE RANGE
Mt. Rainier
SIERRA NEVADA
Mt. Whitney
Pacific Ocean
Arctic Ocean
BROOKS RANGE
Mt. McKinley
Gulf of Alaska
70° N
60° N
50° N
170° W
160° W
150° W
140° W
Conic Projection
0 300 600 mi
0 300 600 km

The World: Political

Arctic Ocean
ICELAND
EUROPE
RUSSIA
ASIA
KAZAKHSTAN
MONGOLIA
CHINA
INDIA
JAPAN
NORTH KOREA
SOUTH KOREA
Pacific Ocean
Indian Ocean
Atlantic Ocean
AFRICA
AUSTRALIA
OCEANIA
INDONESIA
Southern Ocean
ANTARCTICA
Robinson Projection
MAURITANIA
MALI
NIGER
ALGERIA
Azimuthal Equidistant Projection
Gulf of Guinea
Conic Projection
Mediterranean Sea
Black Sea
North Sea
Baltic Sea

Africa: Political

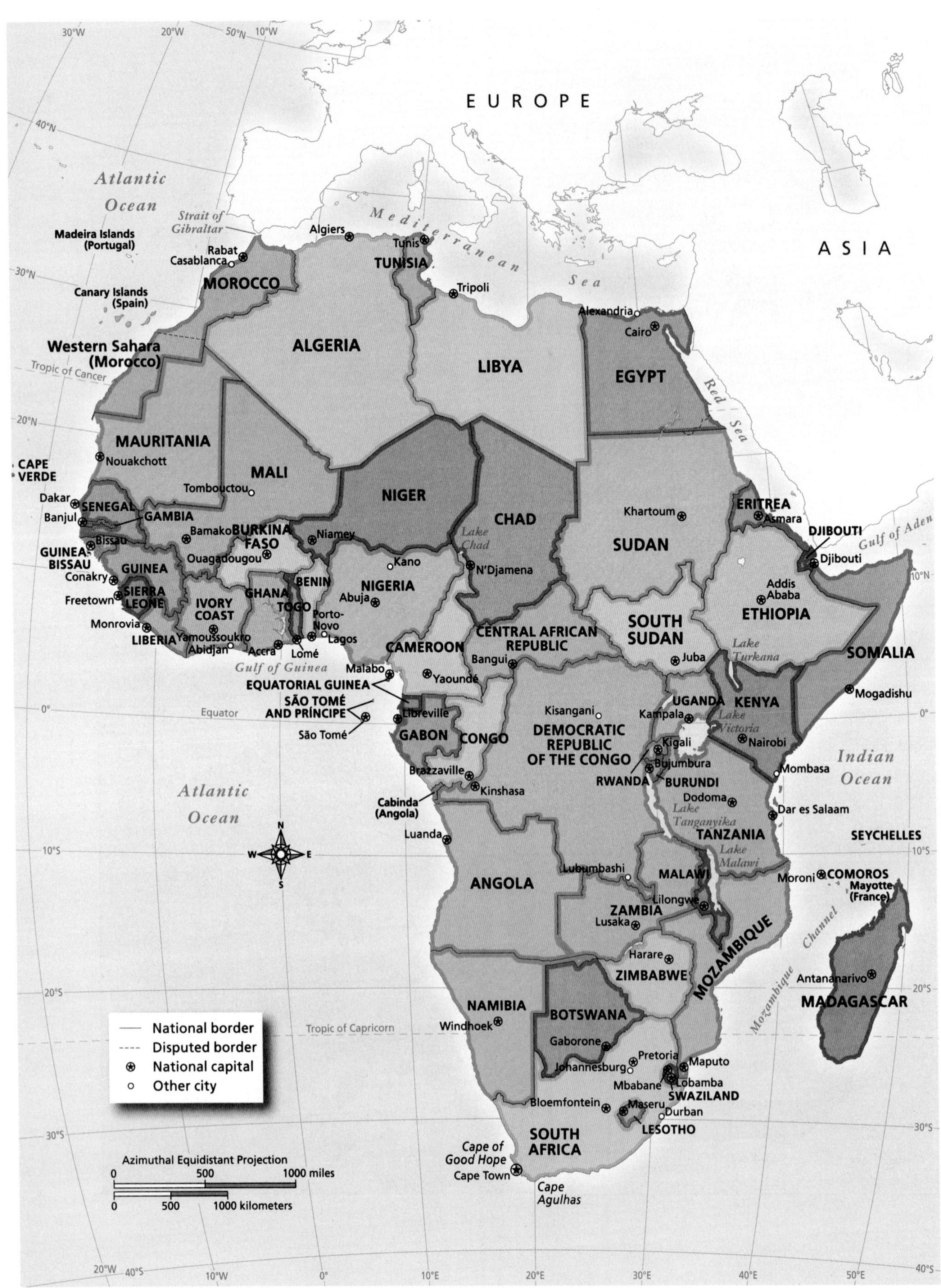

Africa: Physical

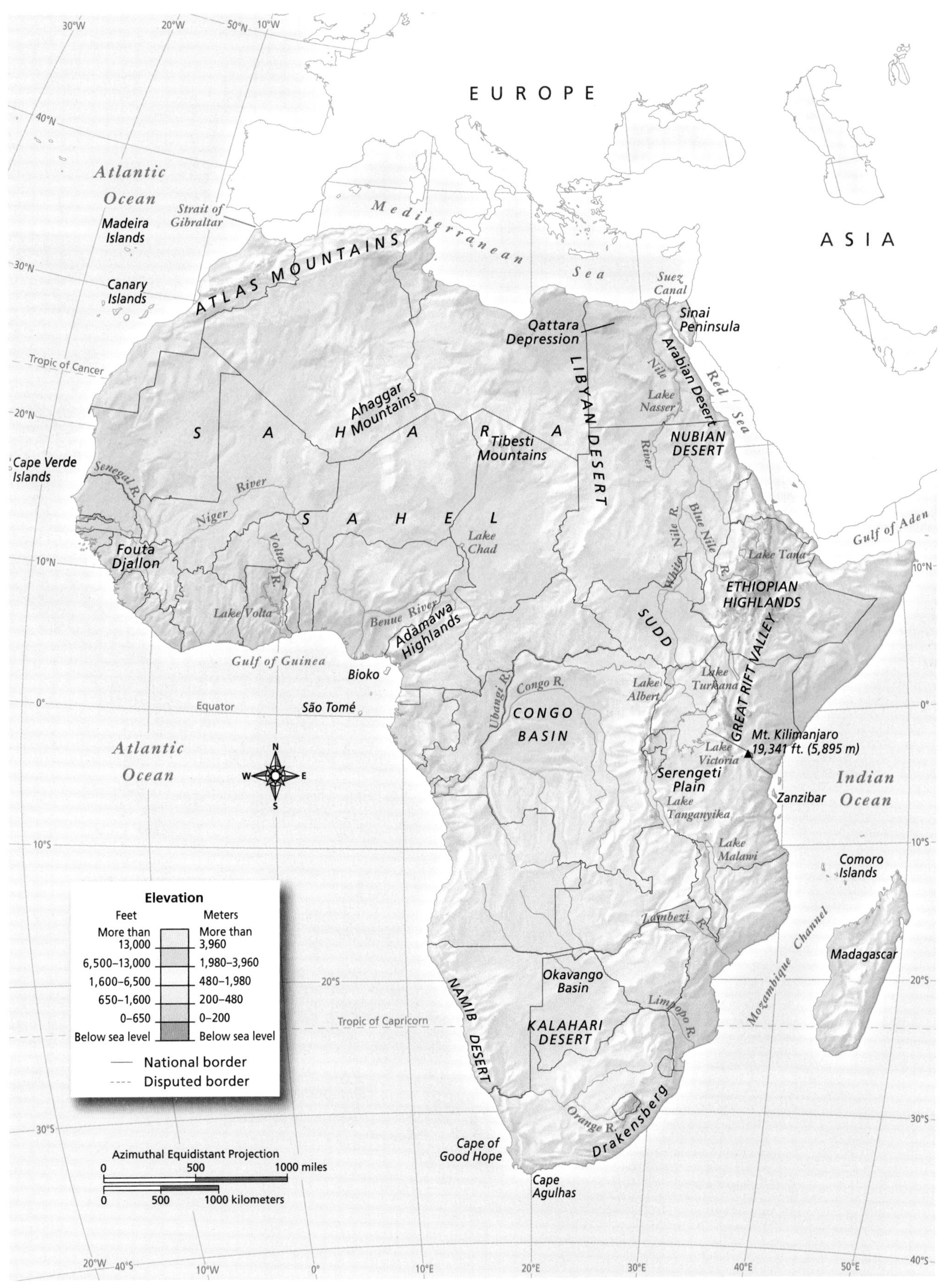

Asia: Political

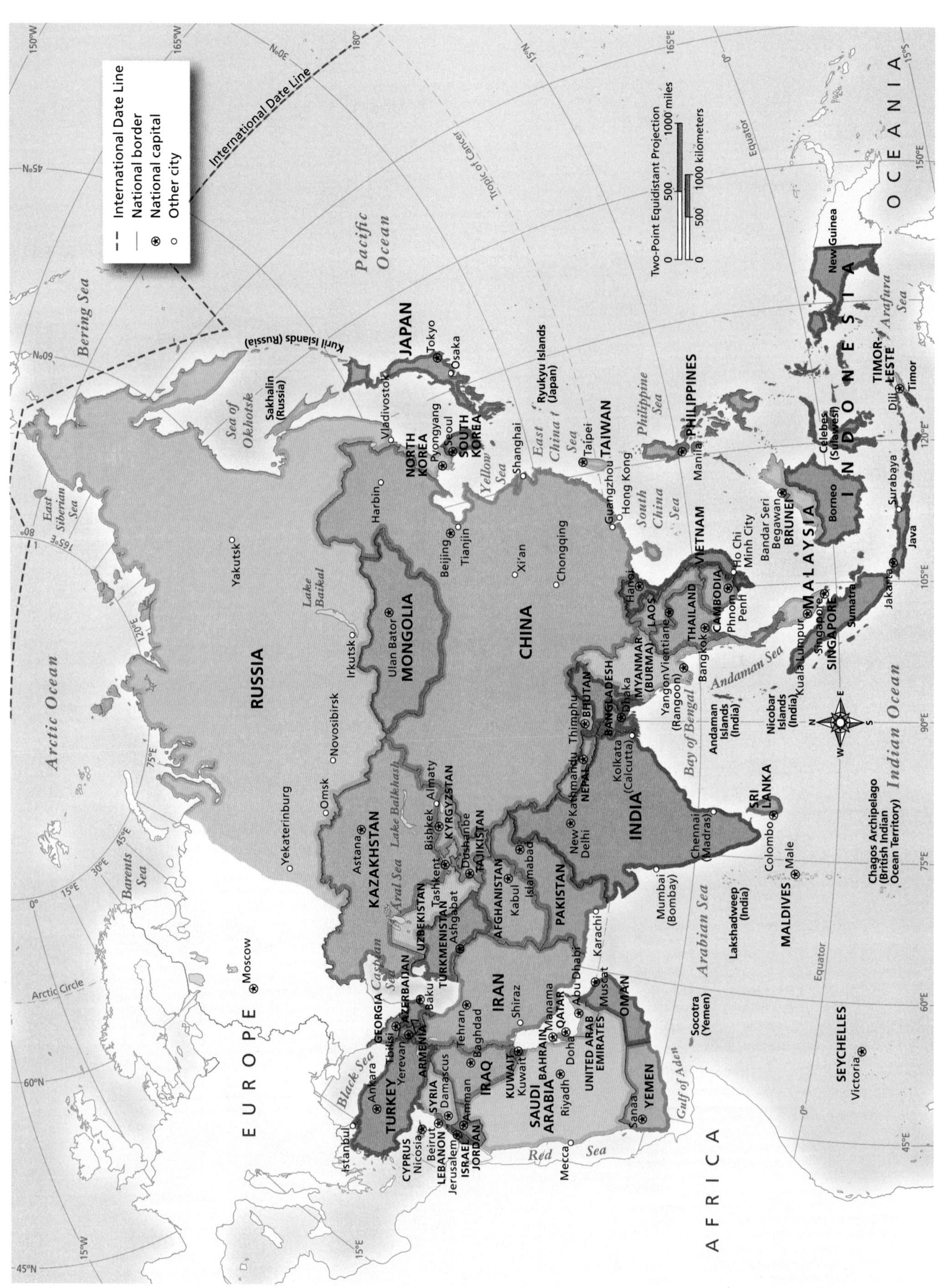

Asia: Physical

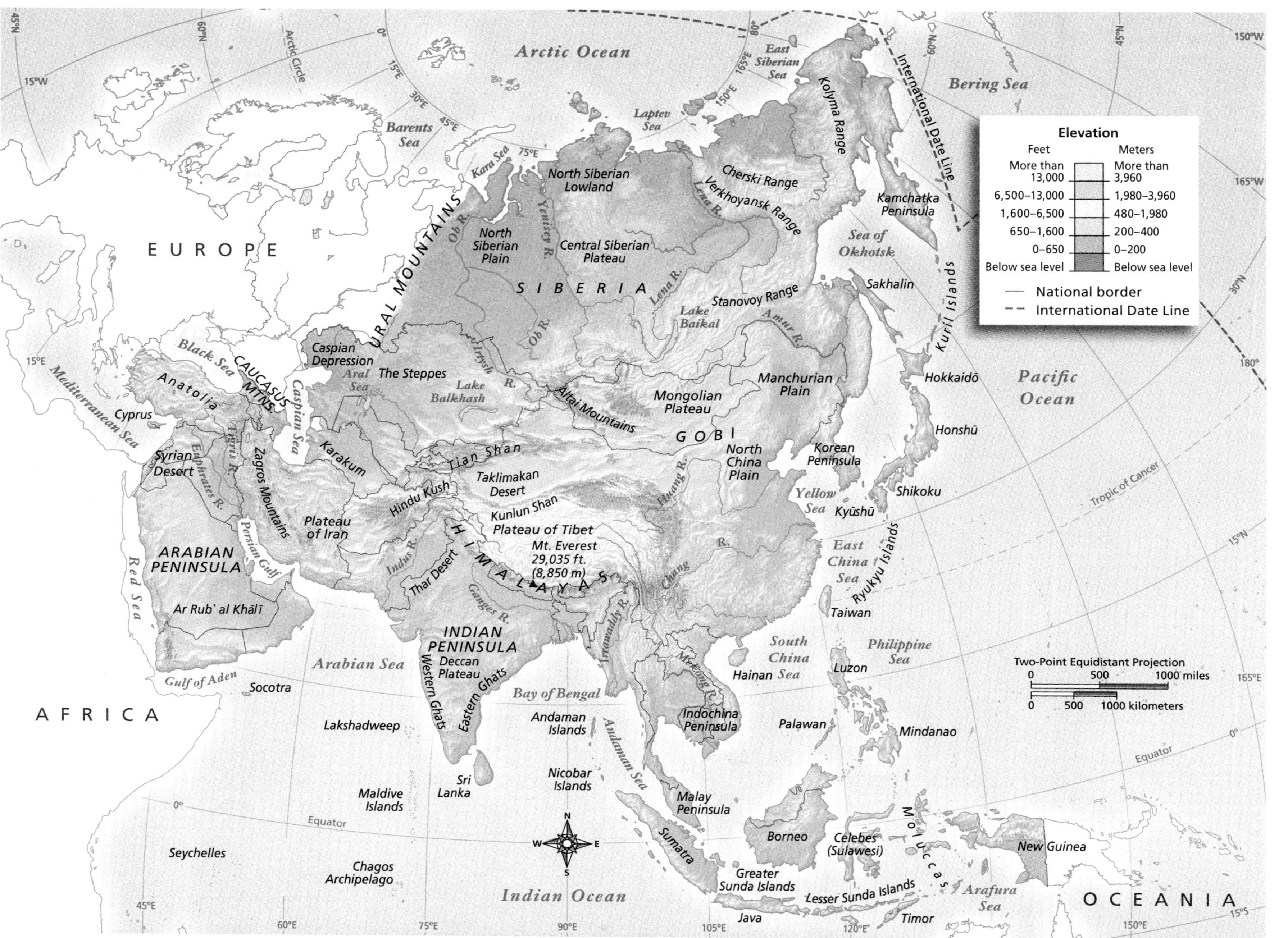

Europe: Political

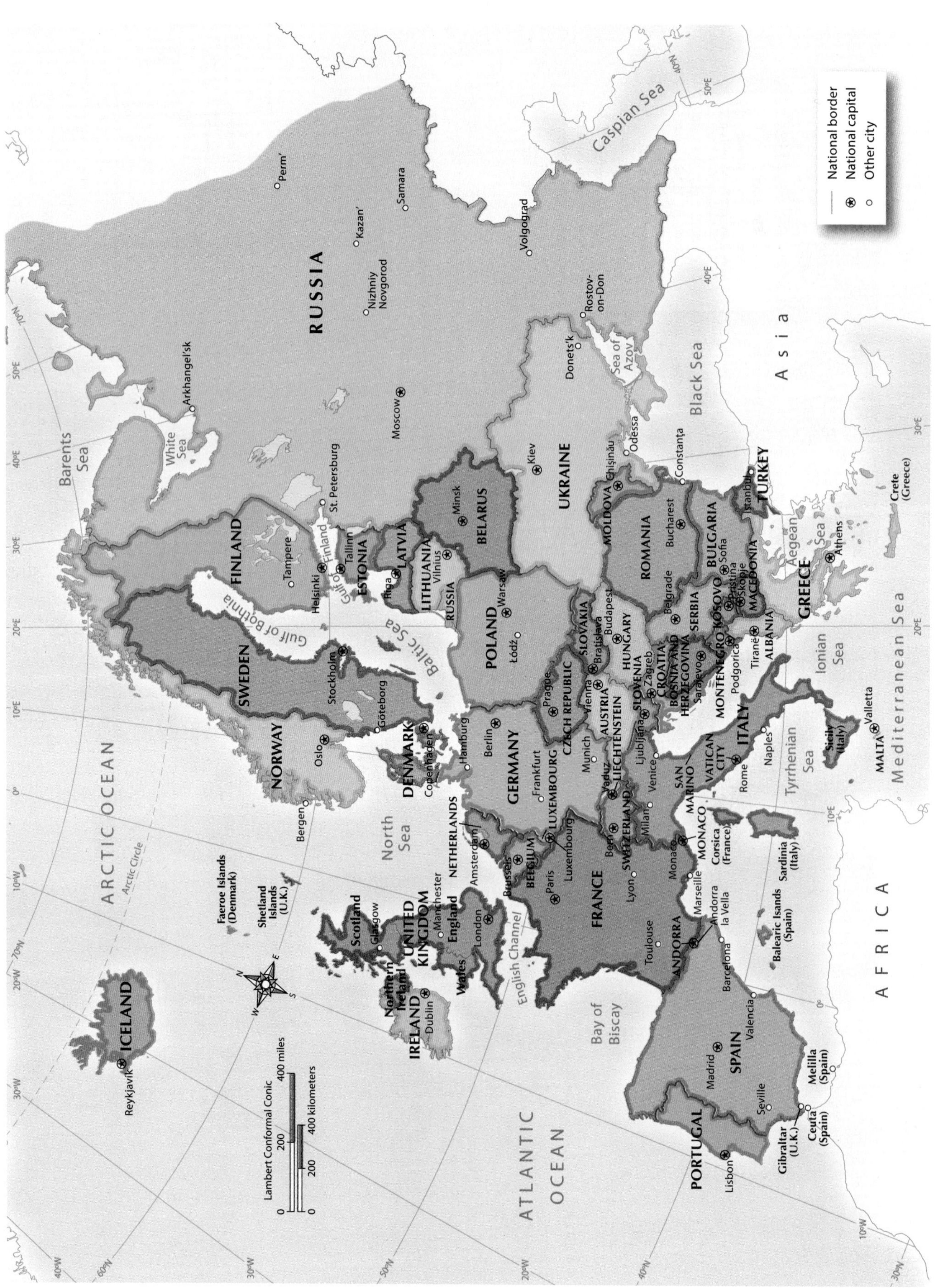

Europe: Physical

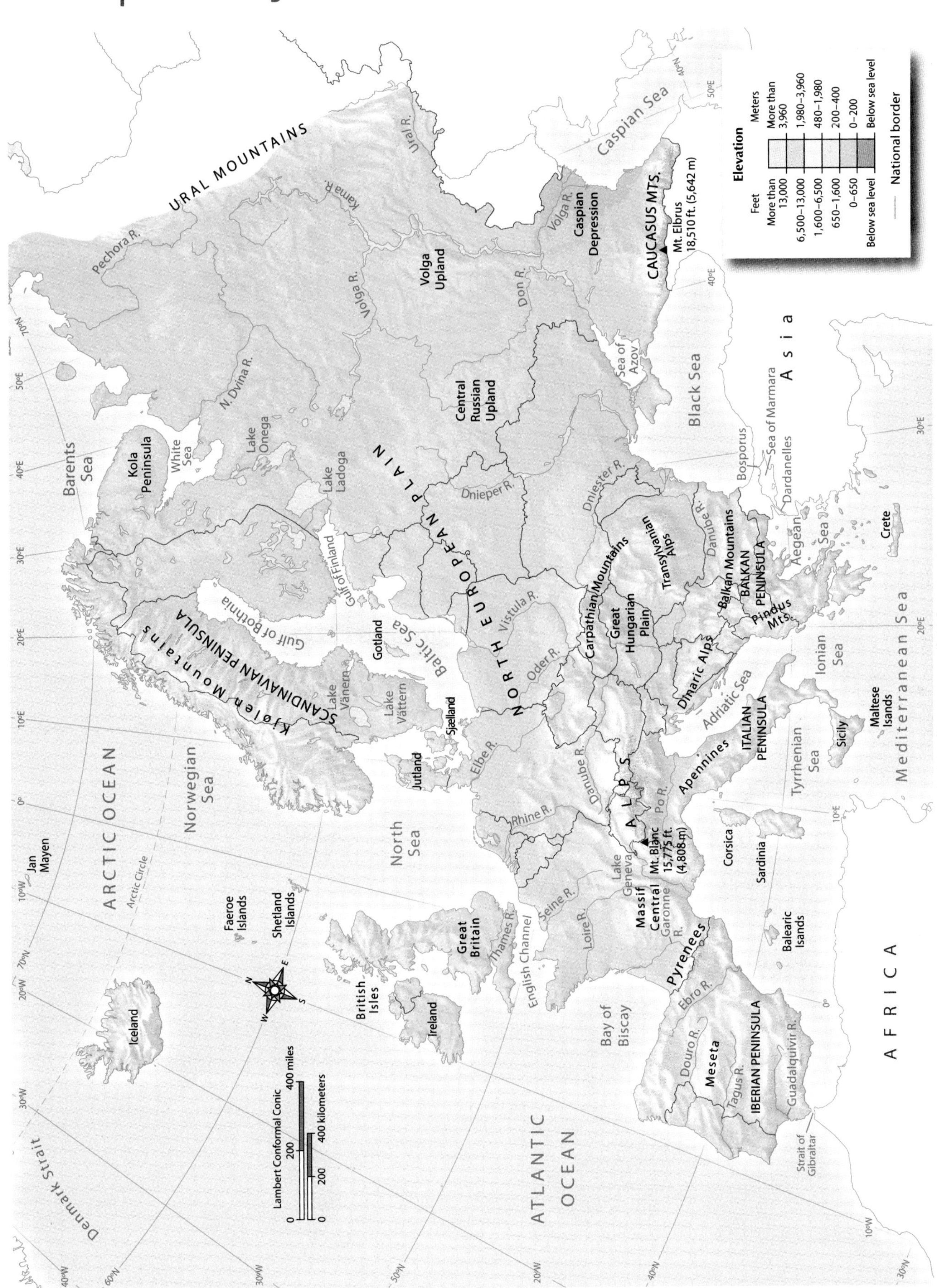

North & South America: Political

North & South America: Physical

Australia, New Zealand & Oceania: Political-Physical

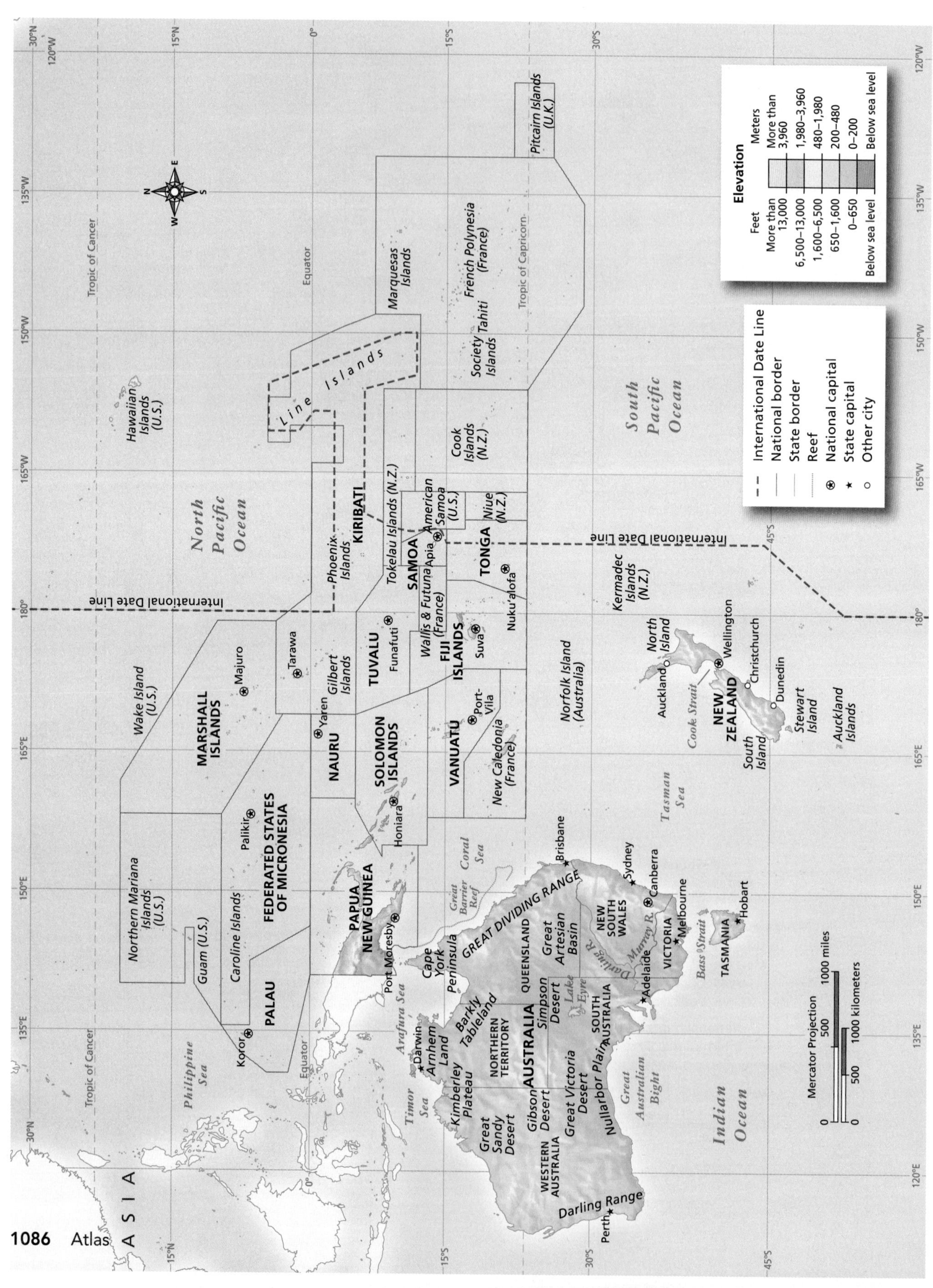

The Arctic: Physical

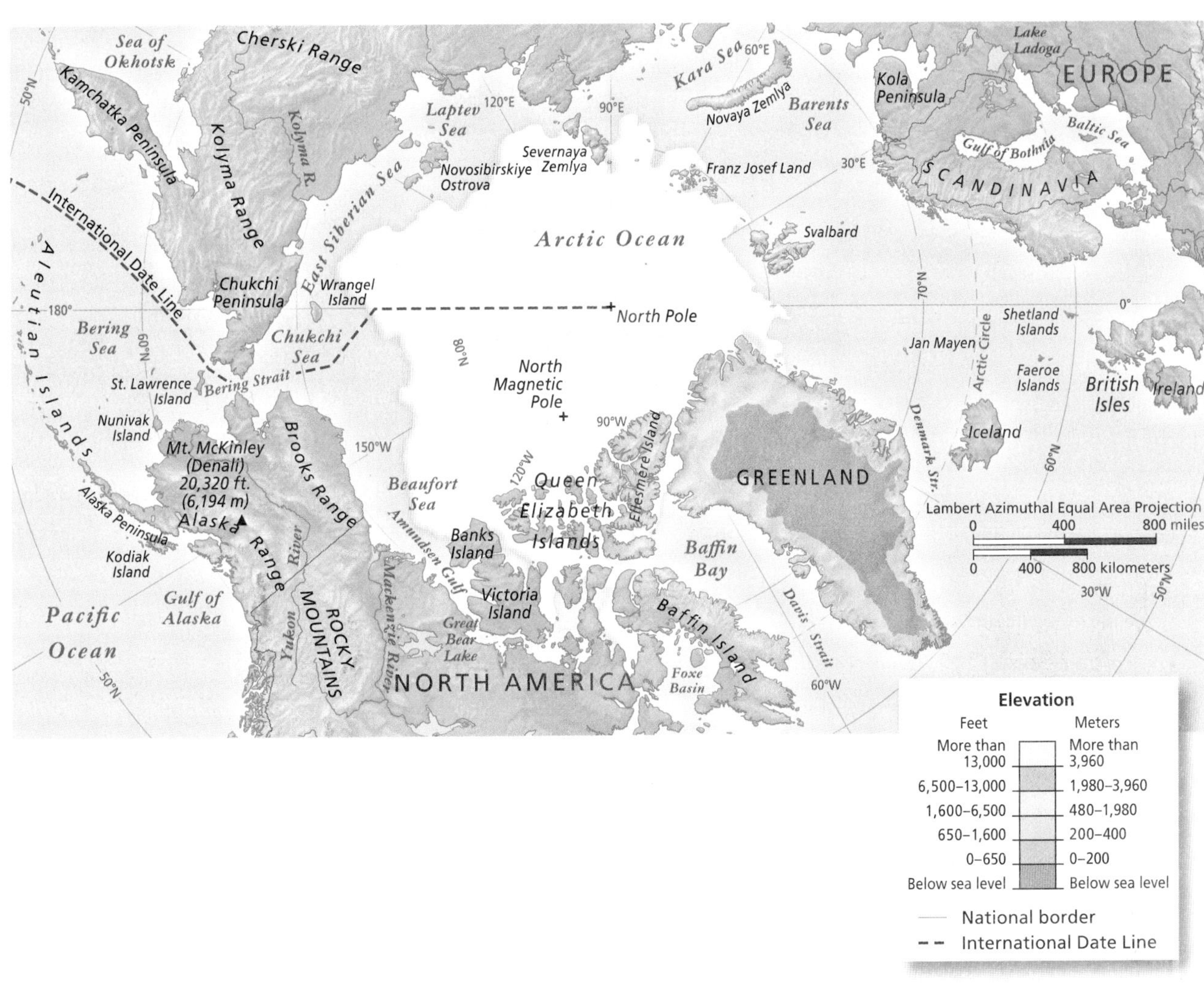

Antarctica: Physical

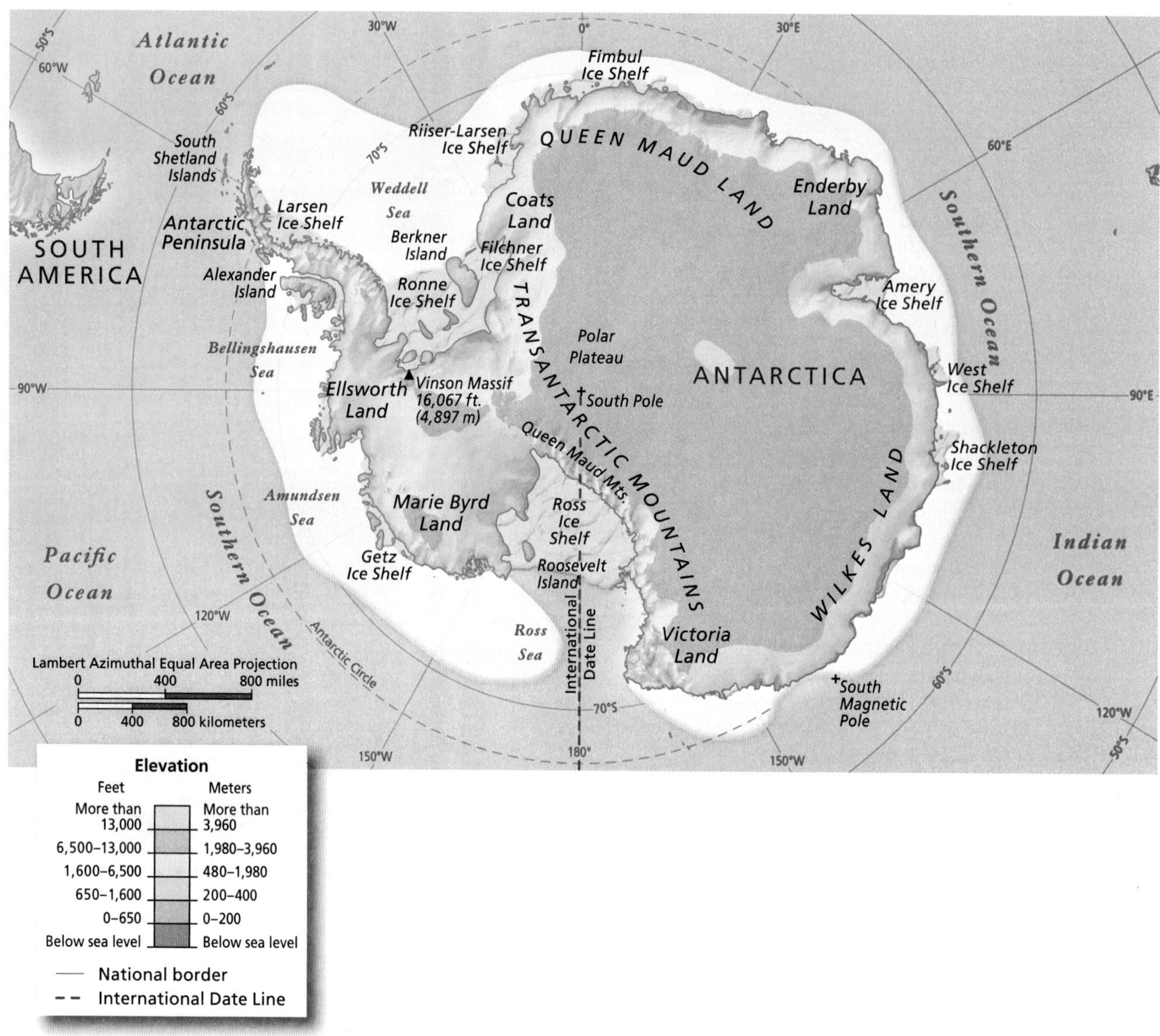

Glossary

38th parallel the dividing line between South and North Korea
54th Massachusetts Regiment an African American unit in the Union army

A

abolitionist a person who wanted to end slavery
according to *prep.*, as stated by
accordingly *adv.*, in a fitting or appropriate way
acculturation process of holding on to old traditions while adapting to a new culture
acquiescence agreeing or accepting something without arguing about it
acquire *v.*, to get (something)
Act of Toleration a 1649 Maryland law that provided religious freedom for all Christians
adobe sun-dried brick
advocate *n.*, a person who argues for or supports a cause or policy
affirmative action a program to provide more job and education opportunities for people who faced discrimination in the past
Affordable Care Act 2009 legislation that established comprehensive health insurance reform
aggression a warlike act by one country without just cause
AIDS acquired immunodeficiency syndrome, a disease that attacks the immune system and is often fatal
Alamo an old Spanish mission building in Texas where Mexican forces under Santa Anna besieged Texans in 1836
Albany Plan of Union a proposal by Benjamin Franklin to create a unified government for the British colonies
alliance an agreement between nations to aid and protect one another
Allied Powers the military alliance of France, Britain, Russia, Italy, and many other nations during World War I
Allies the World War II military alliance of Britain, France, the Soviet Union, the United States, China, and 45 other countries
allocate *v.*, to apportion, distribute
allocation *n.*, the dividing up of something for a special purpose
allotment an amount of something, such as land, distributed to a person
ally a nation that works with another nation for a common purpose
alternative *adj.*, offering a choice
amend to change
American Colonization Society an organization in the early 1800s that proposed to end slavery by helping African Americans to move to Africa
American Expeditionary Forces (AEF) American forces in Europe during World War I
American Recovery and Reinvestment Act a law signed by President Obama in 2009 to stimulate the economy and reduce unemployment by funding the creation of jobs, increasing unemployment benefits, and reducing taxes
American System a program for economic growth promoted by Henry Clay in the early 1800s that called for high tariffs on imports
amnesty a government pardon
anarchist person who opposes organized government
anticipate *v.*, expect or look ahead to
Antifederalist an opponent of a strong federal government
apartheid a strict separation of races practiced in South Africa
appeasement the practice of giving in to aggression in order to avoid war
Appomattox Court House a Virginia town that was the site of the Confederate surrender in 1865
apprentice a person who learns a trade or craft from a master
approach *v.*, to come near
Arab Spring 2010 protests against undemocratic Arab governments
armistice an agreement to stop fighting
arsenal a place where guns are stored
Articles of Confederation the first American constitution, passed in 1777, which created a loose alliance of 13 independent states
artisan a skilled worker
assumption *n.*, a belief held without proof
astrolabe a navigational instrument used to determine latitude, or location north or south of Earth's equator
Atlantic Charter a 1941 program developed by the United States and Britain that set goals for the postwar world
atrocity an act of cruelty and brutality
Axis the World War II military alliance of Germany, Italy, Japan, and six other nations

B

baby boom a large increase in birthrate from the late 1940s through the early 1960s
Bacon's Rebellion a 1676 revolt of Virginia colonists against the colony's government
balanced budget a condition that exists when the government spends only as much as it takes in
bank holiday one or more weekdays when banks are closed; during the Great Depression, a four-day period when the federal government ordered banks closed
bankrupt unable to pay debts
barrio a Mexican neighborhood in the United States
Battle of Antietam an 1862 Civil War battle in Maryland; also called the Battle of Sharpsburg
Battle of Belleau Wood a hard-fought American victory over the Germans in France in 1918
Battle of Britain Germany's failed attempt to subdue Britain in 1940 in preparation for invasion
Battle of Bull Run the first major battle of the Civil War; fought in Virginia in 1861; also called the Battle of Manassas

Battle of Chancellorsville an 1863 Civil War battle in Virginia; important victory for the Confederacy
Battle of Fredericksburg an 1862 Civil War battle in Virginia; one of the Union's worst defeats
Battle of Gettysburg an 1863 Civil War battle in Pennsylvania that ended in a Union victory and stopped the Confederate invasion of the North
Battle of Midway a 1942 battle in the Pacific during which American planes sank four Japanese aircraft carriers
Battle of Shiloh an 1862 Civil War battle in Tennessee that ended in a Union victory
Battle of the Argonne Forest the defeat of the Germans by French and American troops in France in October 1918
Battle of the Bulge a German counterattack in December 1944 that temporarily slowed the Allied invasion of Germany
Bay of Pigs invasion the failed invasion of Cuba in 1961 when a force of 1,400 Cuban exiles, backed by the United States, were captured after landing at the Bay of Pigs
Bear Flag Republic the nickname for California after it declared independence from Mexico in 1846
beatnik a 1950s person who criticized American culture for conformity and devotion to business
Berlin Airlift an American and British relief effort to airlift supplies to West Berliners from 1948 to 1949
Berlin Wall the wall built by the communist East German government in 1961 to seal off East Berlin from West Berlin
bilingual in two languages
bill a proposed law
Bill of Rights the first ten amendments to the United States Constitution
bill of rights a list of key individual rights and freedoms
biotechnology technology based on biology
Black Cabinet a group of Black leaders who unofficially advised President Franklin D. Roosevelt concerning the situation of African Americans
Black codes the southern laws that severely limited the rights of African Americans after the Civil War
blitzkrieg the swift and powerful German military attacks in World War II; "lightning war"
blockade the shutting of a port to keep people or supplies from moving in or out
boat people after the Vietnam War, refugees who escaped from Vietnam in small boats
bond a certificate that promises to repay money loaned, plus interest, on a certain date
bonus *n.*, an additional sum of money
Bonus Army a group of veterans who marched to Washington in 1932 to demand immediate payment of a World War I bonus
boom a period of rapid economic growth
bootlegger a person who smuggled liquor into the United States during Prohibition
Border Ruffians proslavery bands from Missouri who often battled antislavery forces in Kansas
border state a slave state that remained in the Union during the Civil War
boycott to refuse to buy or use certain goods or services
Bracero Program the recruitment of Mexican laborers to work in the United States during World War II
bribe *n.*, something valuable that is given in order to get someone to do something
bubble a situation that occurs when buyers drive prices higher than the actual worth of the product or stock in the hope that prices will rise higher still
building code a standard set by the government for building construction and safety
bull market a period of increased stock trading and rising stock prices
Bull Moose party a group of Progressive Republicans who supported Theodore Roosevelt during the 1912 election
bureaucracy a system of managing government through departments run by appointed officials
burgess a representative to the colonial Virginia government

C

Cabinet the group of officials who head government departments and advise the President
Camp David Accords a 1979 peace treaty between Israel and Egypt in which Israel agreed to return the Sinai Peninsula to Egypt and Egypt agreed to recognize Israel
capability *n.*, ability, capacity
capital money invested in a business venture
capitalism an economic system based on private ownership of property, a market economy, and the goal of making a profit, or income, from the use of one's property
capitalist a person who invests in a business to make a profit
caravan a group of people who travel together for safety
carpetbagger an uncomplimentary nickname for a northerner who went to the South after the Civil War
cash crop *n.*, a crop sold for money at market
cattle drive the herding and moving of cattle, usually to railroad lines
caucus a private meeting; often a political meeting
causeway a raised road made of packed earth
cavalry troops on horseback
cease *v.*, to stop; to end
cede to give up
censure to officially condemn
Central Powers the military alliance of Germany, Austria-Hungary, Bulgaria, and the Ottoman Empire during World War I
characteristic *n.*, a distinguishing trait, quality, or property
charter a legal document giving certain rights to a person or company
Chinese Exclusion Act 1882 law that barred Chinese laborers from entering the United States
circumnavigate to travel all the way around the Earth
citizen a person who owes loyalty to a particular nation and is entitled to all its rights and protections
city-state a political unit that controls a city and its surrounding land
civic *adj.*, having to do with being a citizen
civic virtue the willingness to work for the good of the nation or community even at great sacrifice

civil related to lawsuits involving the private rights of individuals
civil disobedience the refusal to obey unjust laws using non-violent means
civil rights the rights due to all citizens
Civil Rights Act 1964 law outlawing discrimination in hiring based on gender and on race
Civil Rights Movement the efforts of African Americans to win equal rights, particularly in the 1950s and 1960s
civil service all government jobs except elected offices and those in the military
civil war a war between people of the same country
civilian *adj.*, nonmilitary
civilization a society—or a people sharing a language, territory, and economy—that has certain basic features.
clan a group of two or more related families
Clermont the steamboat built in 1807 by Robert Fulton; first steamboat to be commercially successful in American waters
climate change any measurable long-term change in climate
collective bargaining a process by which a union representing a group of workers negotiates with management for a contract
colony an area settled and ruled by the government of a distant land
Columbian Exchange the global exchange of goods and ideas resulting from the encounter between the peoples of the Eastern and Western hemispheres
commence *v.*, to begin
committed *v.*, devoted
committee of correspondence a letter-writing campaign that became a major tool of protest in the colonies
commoner *n.*, a regular or average person
communism an economic system in which all wealth and property are owned by the state
company union a labor organization limited to a single company that is controlled by management
compel *v.*, force
complex *adj.*, composed of two or more parts
compose *v.*, to create or write
comprise *v.*, to be made up of
compromise a settlement or peaceful solution in which each side gives up some of its demands in order to reach an agreement or peaceful solution
Compromise of 1850 an agreement over slavery by which California joined the Union as a free state and a strict fugitive slave law was passed
Compromise of 1877 an agreement by Republican presidential candidate Rutherford B. Hayes to end Reconstruction in return for congressional Democrats accepting his inauguration as President after the disputed election of 1876
compulsory *v.*, required, as by law
concede to admit that you have been defeated
concentration camp a prison camp for civilians who are considered enemies of the state; camps used by the Nazis to imprison Jews and others in World War II
condemn *v.*, to state in a strong way that something is bad or wrong
conducive *adj.*, making it easy for something to happen
confederation an alliance of independent states or nations, usually with a shared military command
conquistador a Spanish explorer who claimed lands in America for Spain
consequently *adv.*, as a result
conservation *n.*, the protection of natural resources
consolidate to combine
constitute *v.*, to set up; to establish
constitution a document that sets out the laws, principles, organization, and processes of a government
Constitutional Convention the gathering of state representatives on May 25, 1787 to revise the Articles of Confederation
constitutional initiative the power of citizens to call for votes to change state constitutions
consumer goods *n.*, products bought for personal or home use
containment the policy of trying to prevent the spread of Soviet influence beyond where it already existed
continental divide a ridge that separates river systems flowing toward opposite sides of a continent
"Contract With America" the legislative package drawn up by House Republicans in 1994 that included trimming social welfare programs and slashing taxes
convey *v.*, to carry
cooperative a group of people who pool their money to buy or sell goods wholesale
Copperhead a northerner who opposed using force to keep the southern states in the Union
corporation business that is owned by investors whose risk of loss is limited
corral an enclosure for animals
cottonocracy a name for the wealthy planters who made their money from cotton in the mid-1800s
counterculture movement a protest movement in the 1960s that rejected traditional American values and culture
coureur de bois a French colonist who lived in the lands beyond French settlements as a fur trapper
cow town a settlement that grew up at the end of a cattle trail
credit *n.*, an agreement or contract in which a borrower receives money or goods now, with an agreement to repay a greater amount later
creole a person born in Spain's American colonies to Spanish parents
Crusades between 1100 and 1300, the series of wars fought by Christians to control Palestine, or the Holy Land
Cuban missile crisis a major Cold War confrontation in 1962 when Kennedy ordered Soviet ships carrying missiles to be blocked from entering Cuba
cultivate to prepare and work soil for planting and growing crops
culture an entire way of life developed by a people
culture region a region in which people share a similar way of life
currency money

D

dame school a school run by women, usually in their own homes
death camps the camps where people were systematically murdered
debt ceiling a limit placed by law on the amount of money that the U.S. government can borrow
debtor a person who cannot pay money he or she owes
decisive *adj.*, clearly settling a dispute or question
decline *v.*, to draw to a close
default a failure to repay a debt
deficit an amount of spending greater than the amount of income
deficit spending spending by government greater than its income
demilitarized zone (DMZ) an area in which military forces are prohibited
Democratic Party a U.S. political party dating from the 1820s to the present that at first spoke out for small farmers and workers against moneyed businessmen and whose policies have changed over the years
Democratic Republican a member of the political party founded by Thomas Jefferson
demonstrate *v.*, to prove something by being an example of it
denounce *v.*, to publicly state that some action or person is wrong or bad
deport to forcibly remove from a country
depression *n.*, a period when business activity slows, prices and wages fall, and unemployment rises
deprive *v.*, to take something away
deregulation a reduction of restrictions on businesses
despite *prep.*, in spite of; notwithstanding
determination *n.*, personal drive to continue trying to achieve one's goal
devise *v.*, to work out or create something
dictator a ruler with absolute power and authority over a country, usually through the use of violence
dictatorship a government in which one person or a small group holds complete authority
differentiate *v.*, to tell what makes one thing or person different from another
diffusion the process of spreading ideas from one culture to another
disarmament a reduction of armed forces and weapons of war
discrimination *n.*, a policy or practice that denies equal rights to certain groups of people
divest *v.*, to get rid of
dividends share of a corporation's profit
dollar diplomacy President Taft's policy of building strong economic ties to Latin America
domino theory the belief that if South Vietnam fell to communism, other countries in the region would follow like a row of falling dominoes
"Double V" campaign an African American civil rights campaign during World War II
downsizing reducing a workforce
draft a law that requires people of a certain age to enlist in the military
Dred Scott* v. *Sandford an 1857 Supreme Court case that brought into question the federal power over slavery in the territories
drought a shortage of water that hurts plants, animals, and energy production and increases the risk of wildfires
Dust Bowl the region in the central and southern Great Plains that was hit by severe drought, soil erosion, and dust storms in the 1930s
dynamic *adj.*, forceful and energetic
détente a policy that promotes the ending of strained or hostile tensions between countries

E

efficiency *n.*, a way of working that is most productive and least wasteful at the same time
eliminate *v.*, get rid of or do away with
elusive *adj.*, hard to find or achieve
Emancipation Proclamation an 1863 declaration by President Lincoln freeing enslaved African Americans in Confederate territory
embargo a ban on trade
embark *v.*, to make a start
embroil *v.*, to involve in conflict or difficulties
emission gas released into the air
employ *v.*, to make use of
enact to make something a law
encounter *v.*, to meet or come upon
endorse *v.*, to support publicly
English Bill of Rights a 1689 document that guaranteed the rights of English citizens
enhance *v.*, to increase or improve the quality of
Enlightenment the movement in Europe in the 1600s and 1700s that emphasized the use of reason
ensure *v.*, to make certain; to secure
Environmental Protection Agency a federal agency established in 1970 to protect human health and the environment
epidemic the rapid spread of contagious disease
Equal Pay Act a 1963 law requiring equal pay for equal work
Equal Rights Amendment a 1923 proposed constitutional amendment intended to prohibit all discrimination based on sex; the amendment was never ratified
Erie Canal the artificial waterway opened in 1825, linking Lake Erie to the Hudson River
essentially *adv.*, having to do with the most important part of an idea or of something
ethical *adj.*, following accepted standards for conduct or behavior
evident *adj.*, obvious; apparent
exceed *v.*, to go above or beyond
exceedingly *adv.*, to a very great degree; extremely
expatriate a person who leaves his or her own country and takes up residence in a foreign land
expedition a long voyage of exploration
expel *v.*, to push or force out

exploit *n.*, a heroic or daring act
export a trade product sent to markets outside a country
expose *v.*, to reveal or bring to light
exposure *n.*, the condition of experiencing something or being affected by something
extend *v.*, to expand or apply further
extended family a family group that includes grandparents, parents, children, aunts, uncles, and cousins
extensive *adj.*, having a large area or scope

F

faction a party, or an opposing group within a party
fad an activity or fashion that is taken up with great passion for a short time
Fair Deal President Truman's reforms that extended liberal policies and included a higher minimum wage, expanded Social Security, and loans for low-cost housing
famine a severe food shortage
fascism a political system that is rooted in militarism, extreme nationalism, and blind loyalty to the state
Federal Reserve Act a 1913 law that set up the Federal Reserve System to regulate the nation's financial sector
Federal Trade Commission (FTC) a government agency created in 1914 to ensure fair competition
Federalist a supporter of a strong federal government; a member of the party led by Alexander Hamilton that favored a strong federal government
Federalist Papers a series of essays by Federalists James Madison, Alexander Hamilton, and John Jay in support of ratifying the Constitution
feudalism a system of rule by lords who ruled their own lands but owed loyalty and military service to a monarch
Fifteenth Amendment an 1869 amendment to the United States Constitution that forbids any state to deny African Americans the right to vote because of race
fireside chat a radio speech given by President Franklin D. Roosevelt while in office
flapper a young woman in the 1920s who adopted unconventional fashions, including short hair and short skirts
flatboat a boat with a flat bottom used for transporting heavy loads on inland waterways
Foraker Act a law passed by Congress in 1900 under which the United States gave Puerto Ricans a limited say in government
Fort Wagner a fort in South Carolina that was the site of an attack by the African American 54th Massachusetts Regiment in 1863
forty-niner a term to describe one of more than 80,000 people who joined the California Gold Rush in 1849
forum *n.*, a setting where people exchange views, ideas, and opinions
fossil fuel a fuel formed in the distant past that has limited supplies and cannot be renewed, such as oil, coal, and natural gas
foster *v.*, to encourage something to develop
Fourteen Points President Wilson's goals for peace after World War I
Fourteenth Amendment an 1868 amendment to the United States Constitution that guarantees equal protection of the laws
fraud *n.*, deception that is meant to lead to personal or financial gain
free enterprise *n.*, an economic system in which businesses compete freely with little government control
Free-Soil Party the bipartisan antislavery party founded in the United States in 1848 to keep slavery out of the western territories
freedmen the men and women who had been enslaved
Freedmen's Bureau a government agency founded during Reconstruction to help former slaves
French and Indian War a war that took place from 1754 to 1763 that led to the end of French power in North America
frontier a border, especially the border of an area of settlement; a line past which land is not settled
fugitive a runaway
Fugitive Slave Act one of two acts passed in 1793 and 1850 that provided for the capture and return of fugitive slaves

G

gauge the width of a train track
General Court the elected representative assembly of the Massachusetts Bay Colony
generally *adv.*, in most cases
gentry the highest social class in the English colonies
Gettysburg Address the speech made by President Lincoln in 1863 after the Battle of Gettysburg
GI Bill of Rights a law that eased the return of World War II veterans by providing education, loans, and employment aid
glacier a thick sheet of ice
glasnost a policy in the Soviet Union in the late 1980s of speaking openly about problems
globalization the spread of links among the world's economies so that they form a global economy
Glorious Revolution in 1688, the movement that brought William and Mary to the throne of England and strengthened the rights of English citizens
Good Neighbor Policy President Franklin Roosevelt's policy intended to strengthen friendly relations with Latin America
grandfather clause in the post-Reconstruction South, a law that excused a voter from a literacy test if his grandfather had been eligible to vote on January 1, 1867
Great Awakening a religious movement in the English colonies in the mid-1700s, also known as the First Great Awakening
Great Compromise a plan at the Constitutional Convention that settled the differences between large and small states
Great Depression the most severe economic decline in United States history, beginning in 1929
Great Migration the movement of millions of African Americans from the South to the North during the early to mid-1900s
Great Society President Johnson's goal aimed at creating a decent living standard for every American

Great White Fleet the name for the steam-powered ships of the enlarged and modernized American navy of the early 1900s
guerrilla a fighter who uses hit-and-run attacks
guerrilla warfare a type of warfare in which small, informal military groups use surprise attacks and hit-and-run tactics
Gulf of Tonkin Resolution a Congressional resolution passed in 1964 that authorized military action in Vietnam
Gullah a combination of English and West African languages spoken by African Americans in South Carolina and Georgia

H

habeas corpus the right not to be held in prison without first being charged with a specific crime
haven *n.*, a place where people are protected from danger and trouble
hesitate *v.*, to stop briefly because of nervousness
Holocaust the slaughter of Europe's Jews by the Nazis before and during World War II
Hooverville a group of shacks in which the homeless lived during the Great Depression
hostility *n.*, an unfriendly feeling or action
Hudson River School a group of American artists based in New York who developed a unique style of landscape painting in the mid-1800s
Hull House settlement house founded by Progressive reformer Jane Addams in Chicago in 1889
Hundred Days the first hundred days of President Franklin D. Roosevelt's presidency, when much New Deal legislation was enacted

I

idealize *v.*, to see in the best possible light
illiterate unable to read or write
immigrant a person who enters another country in order to settle there
impeach to bring charges of serious wrongdoing against a public official
Imperialism a policy of powerful countries seeking to control the economic and political affairs of weaker countries or regions
implicit *adv.*, not expressed directly but able to be understood or inferred
imply *v.*, to suggest something without saying it directly or plainly
imports trade products brought into a country
imposition *n.*, something applied or created based on authority
impressment the practice of forcing people into military service
inauguration a ceremony in which the President publicly takes the oath of office
incline *v.*, to tend or to become drawn toward an opinion or action
income tax a tax on people's earnings
incriminate to give evidence against
incur *v.*, to become liable for
Indian New Deal a series of laws passed in the 1930s that gave American Indian nations greater control over their own affairs
Indian Removal Act a law passed by Congress in 1830 setting up territories west of the Mississippi River where American Indians living in existing states could be relocated
Indian Territory a region set aside for the relocation of American Indians, beginning with the Indian Removal Act, much of which later became part of the state of Oklahoma
indigo a plant used to make a valuable blue dye
individualism the belief in the uniqueness and importance of each individual
Industrial Revolution the change from manual production to machine-powered factory production that started in England in the late 18th century and spread to other places and brought a transformation in economy, society, and technology
inevitably *adv.*, universally, in a way that cannot be avoided
inflation a rise in prices and a decrease in the value of money
influential *adj.*, having great influence or power; effective
infrastructure a system of transit lines, highways, bridges, and tunnels
infringe *v.*, to restrict or put limits on
initiate *v.*, to begin
initiative a process by which voters can put a bill directly before the state legislature
innovation *n.*, a new method or idea
installment buying buying on credit, with regular payments to cover the full price plus interest
insurgency an armed rebellion
integration the mixing of different racial or ethnic groups
intense *adj.*, existing in an extreme degree
interchangeable parts identical, machine-made parts for a tool or an instrument
interest a fee charged for a loan, usually a percentage of the loan, to be paid monthly along with part of the original loan, until the loan is repaid
interest group *n.*, people who have a certain concern or belief in common
Internet an electronic communications network that connects computer networks and organizational computer facilities around the world
internment the temporary imprisonment of members of a specific group
interstate commerce business that crosses state lines
intervene *v.*, to interfere in order to stop or change something
intervention interference in the affairs of another
invoke *v.*, to call on; to appeal to
iron curtain a term coined by Winston Churchill to describe the border between the Soviet satellite nations and Western Europe
Iroquois League the alliance of the Iroquois nations
Islamic fundamentalist a Muslim who believes that Islamic religious texts should be taken literally
island-hopping during World War II, an Allied strategy of capturing Japanese-held islands to gain control of the Pacific
isolationism a policy of staying out of world affairs

isthmus a narrow strip of land that has water on each side with the strip of land connecting two larger bodies of land

J

jazz a music style developed by African Americans in the early 1900s that developed from blues, ragtime, and other earlier styles
jerky a type of dried meat
jihadism an Islamic fundamentalist movement that supports violence in the struggle against perceived enemies of Islam
Jim Crow laws laws that separated people of different races in public places in the South
judicial review the power of the Supreme Court to decide whether the acts of a President or laws passed by Congress are constitutional
jury duty the responsibility of every citizen to serve on a jury when called

K

Kansas-Nebraska Act an 1854 law that established the territories of Nebraska and Kansas, giving the settlers of each territory the right of popular sovereignty to decide on the issue of slavery
Khmer Rouge the communist party in Cambodia that imposed a reign of terror on Cambodian citizenship
kinship a relationship between people who share a common ancestor, or a system of classifying such relationships
Know-Nothing party a political party of the 1850s that was anti-Catholic and anti-immigrant
Ku Klux Klan a secret society organized in the South after the Civil War to reassert white supremacy by means of violence

L

laissez faire the idea that government should play as small a role as possible in economic affairs
League of Nations an association of nations formed after World War I under Wilson's Fourteen Points plan
legacy *n.*, something received by a predecessor or from the past
legislature a group of people, usually elected, who have the power to make laws
legitimate real or official
Lend-Lease Act the law that allowed the United States to sell arms and equipment to Britain during World War II
libel the act of publishing a statement that may unjustly damage a person's reputation
liberty *n.*, freedom
Liberty Bond a bond sold by the United States government to raise money for World War I
literacy test an examination to see if a person can read and write; used in the past to restrict voting rights
local color the speech and habits of a particular region
local government a government on the county, parish, city, town, village, or district level
lode a rich vein of gold, silver, or other valuable ore
Lowell girls young women who worked in the Lowell Mills in Massachusetts during the Industrial Revolution
Loyalist a colonist who remained loyal to Britain
lure *n.*, a thing that tempts or entices a person to go somewhere or do something
Lusitania a British passenger ship that was torpedoed by a German U-boat in 1915; 1,200 people died, including 128 Americans
lynch mob a mob that illegally seizes and kills someone

M

Magna Carta a British document signed in 1215 that contained two basic ideas: monarchs themselves have to obey the laws, and citizens have basic rights
maintain *v.*, to keep in an existing state
majority a group making up more than half of a larger group
mandate an authorization granted to a member of the League of Nations to govern a former German or Turkish colony
Manifest Destiny the 1800s belief that Americans had the right to spread across the continent
manor an area ruled by a lord, including the lord's castle and the lands around it
margin a strip along the edge; in stock trading, a fraction of the stock price given as a downpayment to gain ownership of stock
Marshall Plan an American plan to help European nations rebuild their economies after World War II
martial law rule by the army instead of the elected government
martyr a person who dies for his or her beliefs
mass culture a set of shared practices and beliefs that arise from widespread exposure to the same media
mass production process of making large quantities of a product quickly and cheaply
Mayflower Compact a 1620 agreement for ruling the Plymouth Colony
McCarthyism the use of reckless charges of disloyalty
mechanization *n.*, to change a process or action so it is performed with machines
mediator an agent who helps conflicting parties iron out their differences
mercantilism the theory that a nation's economic strength came from selling more than it bought from other nations
mercenary a soldier who fights for pay, often for a foreign country
merit *n.*, ability, achievement, or worthiness
mestizo in Spain's American colonies, a person of mixed Spanish and Indian background
Mexican Cession the Mexican territories of California and New Mexico given to the United States in 1848
middle class in the English colonies, a class that included skilled craft workers, farmers, and some tradespeople
migrant worker a person who moves from one region to another in search of work
militarism the policy of building up strong armed forces to prepare for war
militia an army of citizens who serve as soldiers during an emergency

minutemen colonial militia volunteers who were prepared to fight at a minute's notice
mission a religious settlement run by Catholic priests and friars; a settlement that aims to spread a religion into a new area
Missouri Compromise an agreement, proposed in 1819 by Henry Clay, to keep the number of slave and free states equal
modification *n.*, a change
monetary policy *n.*, actions taken by a country's central bank to regulate the money supply
Monitor an ironclad Union warship
monopoly a company or group having control of all or nearly all of the business of an industry
Monroe Doctrine President Monroe's foreign policy statement warning European nations not to interfere in Latin America
moral diplomacy President Wilson's policy of condemning imperialism, spreading democracy, and promoting peace
Moral Majority a religious organization that backed conservative political causes in the 1980s
Morrill Acts the acts passed in 1862 and 1890 that provided public land for agricultural colleges
mortgage a loan to purchase a piece of property that allows the lender to claim the property if the mortgage is not paid
mountain man a trapper who explored and hunted in the American West in the early 1800s
moving assembly line method of production in which workers stay in one place as products pass along a track or moving belt
muckraker a journalist who exposed corruption and bad business practices in the late 1800s and early 1900s
Munich Conference a 1938 meeting of the leaders of Britain, France, Italy, and Germany at which an agreement was signed giving part of Czechoslovakia to Hitler
mutualista a Mexican American mutual aid group

N

NAACP (National Association for the Advancement of Colored People) an organization founded in 1909 to work toward equal rights for African Americans
NAFTA The North American Free Trade Agreement, an agreement to remove barriers to trade between the United States, Canada, and Mexico, ratified by the U.S. Congress in 1993
national debt the total amount of money that the government of a country owes to companies, countries, etc.
National Road the first federally funded national road project, begun in 1811
nationalism a devotion to one's nation and its interests
nativist an American who sought to limit immigration and preserve the country for native-born, white Protestants
natural rights rights that belong to all people from birth
naturalize to grant citizenship to a person who has met official requirements for becoming a citizen
Navigation Acts a series of English laws beginning in the 1650s that regulated trade between England and its colonies
Nazi a member of the National Socialist German Workers' Party
Nazi-Soviet Pact an agreement signed between Hitler and Stalin in 1939 in which the two dictators agreed not to attack each other
negotiate *v.*, to confer with others in order to reach agreement
network a system of connected railroad lines
neutral not taking sides in a conflict
Neutrality Acts a series of laws passed by Congress in 1935 that banned arms sales or loans to countries at war
New Deal the program of President Franklin D. Roosevelt to end the Great Depression
New Freedom President Wilson's program to break up trusts and restore American economic competition
New Jersey Plan the plan at the Constitutional Convention, favored by smaller states, that called for three branches of government with a single-chamber legislature
"New South" a term used to describe the South in the late 1800s when efforts were being made to expand the economy by building up industry
nominating convention a meeting at which a political party chooses a candidate
North Atlantic Treaty Organization (NATO) a political and military alliance formed in 1949 by the United States, Canada, and European nations to fight Soviet aggression
Northwest Ordinance a 1787 law that set up a government for the Northwest Territory
northwest passage a waterway through or around North America
notorious *adj.*, well known for some bad quality or effect
Nuclear Non-Proliferation Treaty a treaty intended to prevent the spread of nuclear weapons, to promote cooperation in the peaceful uses of nuclear energy, and to further the goal of achieving disarmament
Nullification Act an act passed by South Carolina that declared that the Tariff of 1832 was unconstitutional
nullify to cancel
Nuremberg Trials the Nazi war crimes trials held in 1945 and 1946
nurture to give care and attention to

O

obtain *v.*, to get
OPEC (Organization of Petroleum Exporting Countries) a multinational organization of oil-producing countries that sets a common policy for the sale of petroleum
Open Door Policy a policy issued by Secretary of State John Hay in 1899 that allowed each foreign nation in China to trade freely in the other nations' spheres of influence
Operation Overlord the code name for the Allied invasion of Europe in 1944
Oregon Country a term used in the early 1800s for the region that includes present-day Oregon, Washington, and Idaho, as well as parts of Wyoming, Montana, and western Canada
Oregon Trail the route to the Oregon Country used by wagon trains in the 1800s
organic *adj.*, of, relating to, or obtained from living things

Organization of American States (OAS) an international organization that promotes peace and economic progress in the Americas
organize *v.*, to set up or establish a group, such as a labor union
organized crime criminal activity carried on by one or more organized groups as a business
override to overrule, as when Congress overrules a presidential veto

P

pacifist a person who objects to any war; believes war is evil
pact *n.*, a formal agreement or treaty
paralyze to make something unable to function
patent license for a new invention
Patriot a colonist who favored war against Britain
patriotism a feeling of love and devotion to one's country
patronage the practice of awarding government jobs to political supporters
Peace Corps a government organization that sends American volunteers to developing countries to teach or give technical advice
peninsular a person from Spain who held a position of power in a Spanish colony
Pennsylvania Dutch German-speaking Protestants who settled in Pennsylvania
pension a sum of money paid to people on a regular basis after they retire
perceive *v.*, notice or become aware of
perjury to lie under oath
persecution *n.*, the mistreatment or punishment of a group of people because of their beliefs
petition a formal written request to someone in authority that is signed by a group of people
Ph.D. *n.*, in the United States, the highest academic degree awarded in a discipline other than law or a medical field
Pickett's Charge the failed Confederate charge during the third day of the Battle of Gettysburg
Pilgrim an English settler who sought religious freedom in the Americas in the 1600s
pioneer someone who is one of the first people to move to and live in a new area
pioneer *v.*, to develop or to be the first to do something
Platt Amendment an amendment to the 1902 Cuban constitution that allowed the United States to intervene in Cuba
pledge *v.*, to promise
Plessy* v. *Ferguson an 1896 court case in which the Supreme Court ruled that segregation in public facilities was legal as long as the facilities were equal
PLO (Palestine Liberation Organization) a Palestinian Arab organization founded in 1964, originally committed to destroying Israel and later committed to promoting the interests of Palestinian Arabs through nonviolent means
pogrom in Eastern Europe, an organized attack on a Jewish community
poll tax a tax required before a person can vote
pollution harmful impurities added to the environment
pool a system in which several railroad companies agreed to divide up the business in an area and set prices
popular sovereignty government by consent of the governed
populist a person who claims to represent the common people
potlatch a ceremonial dinner held by some American Indians of the Northwest Coast to show off their wealth
preamble an introduction to a declaration, constitution, or other official document
precedent an act or decision that sets an example for others to follow
preliminary *adj.*, something that comes before or is introductory to something
prerequisite *n.*, something that is necessary for carrying out an act
presidio a fort where soldiers lived in the Spanish colonies
presume *v.*, to expect or suppose without proof
previous *v.*, earlier
primary an election in which voters choose their party's candidate for the general election
privatize *v.*, to put private individuals or companies in charge of something
productivity the average output per worker
profit *n.*, the difference between the cost of a good or service and its selling price
Progressive a reformer in the late 1800s and early 1900s who wanted to improve American life
prohibit *v.*, to refuse to allow; to forbid
prohibition in the late 1800s and early 1900s, the movement to ban alcohol production and sales in the United States, or, between 1920 and 1933, the constitutional ban on alcohol production and sales
Prohibition the legal ban on the manufacture, sale, and transportation of liquor anywhere in the United States from 1920 to 1933
prominent *adj.*, well-known
propaganda the spreading of ideas to help a cause or hurt an opposing cause
propose *v.*, to suggest something for people to consider
proprietary colony an English colony in which the king gave land to proprietors in exchange for a yearly payment
prosperous *adj.*, having success, usually by making a lot of money
protectorate a nation whose independence is limited by the control of a more powerful country
public opinion *n.*, the views held by people, in general
public works the construction of government-funded public buildings, roads, dams, and other public structures
pueblo a town in the Spanish colonies; a village or town of the Anasazi or other American Indian groups in the American Southwest
Puebloan One of a group of American Indians who live in the Southwest in flat-roofed houses in permanent towns
pull factor a condition that attracts people to move to a new area
Puritans a group of English Protestants who settled the Massachusetts Bay Colony

push factor a condition that drives people from their homeland

Q

Quakers Protestant reformers who believe in the equality of all people

quarters *n.*, living accommodations

quipu a device made of cord or string with knots that stood for quantities; used by the Inca to keep accounts and records

quota system a system that limits the number of certain kinds of people admitted to an institution or country; beginning in the 1920s, a system that allowed only a certain number of people from each country to immigrate to the United States

R

racism the belief that one race is superior to another

radical *adj.*, extreme

Radical Republican a member of Congress during Reconstruction who wanted to take power from the wealthy southern plantation owners and ensure that freedmen received the right to vote

ragtime a form of popular music of the late 1800s and early 1900s that had a lively, rhythmic sound

ratify to approve

rationing limiting the amount of certain goods that people can buy

reaffirm *v.*, to express again a strong belief in

Reaganomics President Reagan's economic program that cut taxes, cut federal spending on social programs, and cut regulations affecting business

realist a writer or artist who aims to show life as it really is

rebate a discount

recall a process by which voters can remove an elected official from office

recession an economic slump that is milder than a depression

Reconstruction the rebuilding of the South after the Civil War

Reconstruction Act an 1867 law that threw out the southern state governments that refused to ratify the Fourteenth Amendment

recount *v.*, to tell about something that happened

redeem *v.*, to buy back

referendum a process by which people vote directly on a bill

regulate *v.*, to make rules or laws that control something

relief *n.*, help for the needy, often in the form of money or food

religious tolerance the willingness to let others practice their own beliefs

reluctant *adj.*, not eager to do something

Renaissance the burst of learning in Europe from the late 1300s to about 1600

reparation a cash payment made by a defeated nation to a victorious nation to pay for losses suffered during a war

repeal to cancel, remove from law

representative government a political system in which voters elect representatives to make laws for them

republic a system of government in which citizens choose representatives to govern them

Republican Party a political party established in the United States in 1854 with the goal of keeping slavery out of the western territories

reservation a limited area of land set aside for American Indians

resident alien a person living in a country where he or she is not a citizen

resist *v.*, to fight against

resolve *v.*, to come to a firm decision or find an answer or solution to something

respect *n.*, understanding when something is serious and acting appropriately

responsibility *n.*, a duty or task one is expected to carry out

resume *v.*, to begin again after stopping

reunification *n.*, joining again to make a single thing

revenue money, especially money collected by a government for public use

Roosevelt Corollary a statement by Theodore Roosevelt that the United States had a right to intervene in Latin America to preserve law and order

Rosie the Riveter a fictional factory worker who became a symbol of American women's contribution to the war effort during World War II

royal colony a colony under direct control of the English crown

rugged individualist a person who follows his or her own independent course in life

S

sabotage the secret destruction of property or interference with production

SALT Agreement (Strategic Arms Limitation Talks) a treaty between the United States and the Soviet Union to limit the number of nuclear warheads and missiles

salvation *n.*, deliverance from sin

sanction trade restriction placed on a country to force it to obey international laws

Santa Fe Trail the route to Santa Fe, New Mexico, that was used by traders in the 1800s

scalawag a white southerner who supported the Republicans during Reconstruction

scapegoat a person or group who is made to bear the blame for others

scarcity a shortage, lack, or insufficient supply

secede to withdraw from membership in a group

Second Great Awakening a widespread religious movement in the United States in the early 1800s

sectionalism loyalty to a state or section rather than to the whole country

sedition the act of stirring up rebellion against a government

segregation the legal separation of people based on racial, ethnic, or other differences

Selective Service Act a law passed by Congress in 1917 that required all men from ages 21 to 30 to register for the military draft

self-determination the right of national groups to have their own territory and forms of government

self-sufficient able to produce enough for one's own needs

Seneca Falls Convention an 1848 meeting at which activists called for equal rights for women, often seen as the birthplace of the women's rights movement
separation of powers a principle by which the powers of government are divided among separate branches
setback *n.*, a defeat or a reversal of progress
settlement a place or region newly settled
settlement house a community center organized, beginning in the late 1800s, to offer services to the poor
sharecropper a person who rents a plot of land from another person and farms it in exchange for a share of the crop
Shays' Rebellion a 1786 revolt in Massachusetts led by farmers in reaction to high taxes
shrewd *adj.*, clever
siege to surround and blockade an enemy town or position with troops to force it to surrender
significant *adj.*, very important
signify *v.*, to indicate or be a sign of
silent majority Americans who were disturbed by unrest in the 1960s but did not protest publicly
Silk Road a network of overland trade routes linking China to the Middle East
sit-in a form of protest in which people sit and refuse to leave
skyscraper a tall building with many floors supported by a lightweight steel frame
slave codes laws that controlled the lives of enslaved Africans and African Americans and denied them basic rights
smart phone a phone with sophisticated computing capability and an ability to connect to the Internet via radio signals
smuggling the act of importing or exporting goods in violation of trade laws
Social Gospel movement within American Protestantism in the late 1800s that attempted to apply biblical teachings to society's problems
social reform an organized attempt to improve what is unjust or imperfect in society
socialism the belief in personal property for individuals and public ownership of the means of production, such as factories and natural resources
sodbuster a farmer on the Great Plains in the late 1800s
Solidarity an independent labor union that challenged Poland's communist government
soup kitchen a place where food is provided to the needy at little or no charge
Spanish-American War the war between Spain and the United States in 1898
specifically *adv.*, for a particular purpose
specify *v.*, name something exactly and in detail
speculation *n.*, risky buying in hope of a large profit
speculator someone who invests in a risky venture in the hope of making a large profit
spoils system the practice of giving supporters government jobs
Square Deal Theodore Roosevelt's campaign promise that all groups would have an equal opportunity to succeed
stabilize *v.*, to make steady or keep at a given level
stagflation an economic situation that arises from a combination of rising prices, high unemployment, and slow economic growth
standard of living a measurement that determines how well people live based on the amount of goods, services, and leisure time people have
Star Wars President Reagan's proposed weapons system to destroy Soviet missiles from space
states' rights the rights and powers independent of the federal government that are reserved for the states by the Constitution
statute *n.*, a law or rule
steerage on a ship, the cramped quarters for passengers paying the lowest fares
stimulate *v.*, to cause something to grow or to happen
stock a share of ownership in a corporation
Strategic Arms Reduction Treaty (START) a 1991 treaty signed by the United States and Soviet Union to reduce nuclear weapons
strike the refusal by workers to do their jobs until their demands are met
strikebreaker replacement for a striking worker
subprime mortgage a type of mortgage granted to individuals with poor credit histories
subsequently *adv.*, happening after something else
subsidize *v.*, to help pay for the costs of something
subsidy a land grant or other financial help from the government
suburb a residential area on the outskirts of a city
suffrage the right to vote
summit meeting a conference between the highest-ranking officials of different nations
Sunbelt the region stretching across the southern half of the country
superpower a nation with the military, political, and economic strength to influence events worldwide
supply the amount of goods or resources in stock, on hand, or available in the market to sell
suppress *v.*, to end or stop
surplus *n.*, an excess, or an extra amount
sustain *v.*, to undergo
sweatshop workplace where people labor long hours in poor conditions for low pay

T

tactic *n.*, method of achieving a goal
tariff a tax on foreign goods brought into a country
temperament the usual attitude, mood, or behavior of a person
temperance movement the campaign against alcohol consumption
tenement a small apartment in a city slum building
tepee a tent made by stretching buffalo skins on tall poles
terrace a wide shelf of land cut into a hillside
terrorism the use of violence and cruelty to achieve political goals

terrorist one who deliberately uses violence to spread fear and achieve political goals

Tet Offensive Vietcong surprise attacks on South Vietnamese cities on the Vietnamese New Year's holiday in 1968

The Liberator the most influential antislavery newspaper; begun by William Lloyd Garrison in 1831

Thirteenth Amendment an 1865 amendment to the United States Constitution that banned slavery throughout the nation

Three-Fifths Compromise an agreement at the Constitutional Convention that three-fifths of the enslaved residents in any state be counted in its population

tolerant *adj.*, willing to accept beliefs that are different from your own

totalitarian state a country where a single party controls the government and every aspect of people's lives

town meeting a meeting in colonial New England where settlers discussed and voted on local government matters

trade union association of workers in a specific trade, or line of work, formed to gain higher wages and better working conditions

Trail of Tears the forced migration by the Cherokee and other American Indian groups from their southeastern homelands to territories west of the Mississippi River

traitor a person who betrays his or her country

transatlantic crossing or spanning the Atlantic Ocean

transcendentalist one of a group of New England writers and thinkers who believed that the most important truths transcended, or went beyond, human reason

transcontinental railroad a railroad that stretches across a continent from coast to coast

travois a sled pulled by a dog or horse

treason a betrayal of or action against one's country

Treaty of Guadalupe-Hidalgo an 1848 treaty in which Mexico gave up California and New Mexico Territory to the United States for $15 million

Treaty of Kanagawa an 1854 treaty between Japan and the United States that opened up ports to American trade in Japan

Treaty of Paris a 1763 agreement between Britain and France that ended the French and Indian War and transferred much of North America from French to British control

Treaty of Versailles the treaty signed on June 28, 1919, by Germany and the Allies; formally placed the responsibility for World War I on Germany and its allies

trench warfare war combat in which soldiers are located in trenches dug into the ground

Triangle Fire fire in 1911 at the Triangle Shirtwaist Factory in New York City that killed nearly 150 workers

triangular trade the colonial trade route between New England, Africa, and the West Indies

tribe a community of people that share common customs, language, and rituals

tribute a payment by a weaker party to a stronger party in return for protection

trust group of corporations run by a single board of directors

trustbuster a person who wanted to destroy all trusts

turning point a moment in history that marks a decisive change

Tuskegee Airmen African American fighter pilots who trained in Tuskegee, Alabama, during World War II

U

U-boat a type of submarine used by Germany in World War I

ultimately *v.*, at the end of a period of time

unalienable rights rights that cannot be taken away

unamendable unable to be changed

unconstitutional not permitted by the Constitution

undergo *v.*, to experience something, especially something painful or unpleasant

Underground Railroad a network of abolitionists who secretly helped African Americans to escape to freedom

undermine *v.*, to make someone or something weaker or less effective

unify *v.*, to bring together as one; to unite

United Nations (UN) a world organization established in 1945 to provide peaceful resolutions to international conflicts

urbanization the movement of population from farms to cities

V

vaquero a Spanish or Mexican cowhand

varied *adj.*, having many forms or types

vary *v.*, to range or differ

vaudeville a type of variety show made popular in the late 1800s that included comedians, song-and-dance routines, and acrobats

verify *v.*, to confirm that something is true; to fact-check

veto to reject, as when the President rejects a law passed by Congress

victory garden during World War II, a vegetable garden planted to combat food shortages in the United States

vigilante a self-appointed enforcer of the law

Virginia an ironclad warship used by the Confederates in an attempt to break the Union blockade

Virginia Plan the plan at the Constitutional Convention that called for a strong national government with three branches and a two-chamber legislature

virtue *n.*, morally good behavior or character

vital *adj.*, extremely important

W

War Hawks the members of Congress from the South and the West who called for war with Britain prior to the War of 1812

War Production Board a government agency created during World War II to help factories shift from making consumer goods to making war materials

warmonger a person who tries to stir up war

Warsaw Pact a military alliance, established in 1955, of the Soviet Union and other communist states in Europe

Watergate a political scandal involving illegal activities that led to the resignation of President Richard Nixon in 1974

weapon of mass destruction (WMD) a chemical, biological, or nuclear weapon

Whig Party a political party organized by Henry Clay; they believed the federal government should help the economy and promote business

wholesale the buying or selling of something in large quantities at lower prices

women's rights movement an organized campaign to win legal, educational, employment, and other rights for women

Worcester* v. *Georgia an 1832 Supreme Court ruling that proclaimed state laws do not apply within American Indian territory

writ of assistance a legal document that allowed British customs officers to inspect a ship's cargo without giving a reason

Y

Yankees a nickname for New Englanders

yellow journalism a type of news reporting, often biased or untrue, that relies on sensational stories and headlines

Z

Zimmermann telegram a 1917 telegram sent from Germany's foreign secretary to the German minister in Mexico instructing the minister to urge Mexico to attack the United States if the United States declared war on Germany

Glosario

38th parallel > paralelo 38 línea divisoria entre Corea del Norte y Corea del Sur

54th Massachusetts Regiment > 54.o Regimiento de Massachusetts unidad del ejército de la Unión compuesta por afroamericanos

A

abolitionist > abolicionista persona que quería terminar con la esclavitud

according to > de acuerdo con según lo establecido por

accordingly > en consecuencia de una manera adecuada o apropiada

acculturation > aculturación proceso de adaptarse a una nueva cultura sin abandonar las viejas tradiciones

acquiescence > consentimiento acuerdo o aceptación de algo sin discutirlo

acquire > adquirir obtener algo

Act of Toleration > Ley de Tolerancia ley de Maryland de 1649 que garantizaba libertad religiosa para todos los cristianos

adobe > adobe ladrillo secado al sol

advocate > defensor persona que apoya o pelea a favor de una causa o política

affirmative action > acción afirmativa programa para proporcionar más oportunidades de empleo y educación a personas que sufrieron discriminación en el pasado

Affordable Care Act > Ley del Cuidado de Salud a Bajo Precio legislación de 2009 que estipula una extensa reforma en seguros médicos

aggression > agresión acto de guerra llevado a cabo por un país sin causa justa

AIDS > sida síndrome de inmunodeficiencia adquirida, una enfermedad generalmente mortal que ataca el sistema inmunológico

Alamo > El Álamo edificio de un vieja misión española donde las fuerzas mexicanas, al mando de Santa Anna, sitiaron a los texanos en 1836

Albany Plan of Union > Plan de Unión de Albany propuesta de Benjamin Franklin para crear un gobierno unificado para las colonias británicas

alliance > alianza acuerdo entre naciones para ayudarse y protegerse mutuamente

Allied Powers > Potencias aliadas la alianza militar entre Francia, Gran Bretaña, Rusia, Italia y muchas otras naciones durante la Primera Guerra Mundial

Allies > Aliados alianza militar de la Segunda Guerra Mundial entre Gran Bretaña, Francia, la Unión Soviética, los Estados Unidos, China y otros 45 países

allocate > asignar repartir, distribuir

allocation > asignación la división de algo con un propósito especial

allotment > asignación cantidad de algo, como por ejemplo tierra, que recibe una persona en un reparto

ally > aliado nación que colabora con otra para alcanzar un objetivo en común

alternative > alternativo que ofrece una opción

amend > enmendar modificar

American Colonization Society > Sociedad Estadounidense de Colonización organización de comienzos del siglo XIX que proponía ayudar a los afroamericanos a trasladarse a África para terminar con la esclavitud

American Expeditionary Forces (AEF) > Fuerzas Expedicionarias de los EE. UU. fuerzas estadounidenses destacadas en Europa durante la Primera Guerra Mundial

American Recovery and Reinvestment Act > Ley de Recuperación y Reinversión Estadounidense ley promulgada por el presidente Obama en 2009; su finalidad era estimular la economía y reducir el desempleo financiando la creación de empleos, aumentando los beneficios por desempleo y reduciendo los impuestos

American System > sistema estadounidense programa de crecimiento económico promovido por Henry Clay a principios del siglo XIX, que proponía aranceles elevados sobre las importaciones

amnesty > amnistía indulto concedido por el gobierno

anarchist > anarquista persona que se opone a un gobierno organizado

anticipate > anticipar esperar o prever algo

Antifederalist > antifederalista persona que se opone a un gobierno federal fuerte

apartheid > apartheid separación estricta de razas que se practicaba en Sudáfrica

appeasement > apaciguamiento práctica de aceptar las exigencias de un agresor para evitar la guerra

Appomattox Court House > Appomattox Court House pueblo de Virginia donde tuvo lugar la rendición de la Confederación en 1865

apprentice > aprendiz persona que aprende un oficio de un maestro

approach > aproximarse acercarse

Arab Spring > Primavera Árabe protestas realizadas en 2010 contra los gobiernos antidemocráticos árabes

armistice > armisticio acuerdo para terminar con la lucha

arsenal > arsenal lugar donde se guardan armas

Articles of Confederation > Artículos de la Confederación primera constitución estadounidense, aprobada en 1777, que creó un principio de alianza de 13 estados independientes

artisan > artesano trabajador calificado

assumption > presunción creencia sostenida como cierta sin pruebas

astrolabe > astrolabio instrumento de navegación usado para determinar la latitud, es decir, la ubicación al norte o al sur del ecuador de la Tierra

Atlantic Charter > Carta del Atlántico programa de 1941 desarrollado por los Estados Unidos y Gran Bretaña que establecía objetivos para el mundo de la posguerra

atrocity > atrocidad acto de crueldad y brutalidad

Axis > Eje alianza militar entre Alemania, Italia y Japón y otras seis naciones durante la Segunda Guerra Mundial

B

baby boom > baby boom significativo incremento en la tasa de natalidad que sucedió desde finales de la década de 1940 hasta principios de la década de 1960

Bacon's Rebellion > Rebelión de Bacon revuelta de los colonos de Virginia contra el gobierno de la colonia en 1676

balanced budget > presupuesto equilibrado situación que ocurre cuando el gobierno gasta solo la misma cantidad que ingresa

bank holiday > feriado bancario uno o más días entre lunes y viernes en que los bancos permanecen cerrados; durante la Gran Depresión, un periodo de cuatro días de cierre bancario ordenado por el gobierno federal

bankrupt > bancarrota situación de no poder pagar las deudas

barrio > barrio término que se usa en español en los Estados Unidos para referirse a un vecindario mexicano

Battle of Antietam > Batalla de Antietam batalla de la Guerra Civil que tuvo lugar en Maryland en 1862; también llamada Batalla de Sharpsburg

Battle of Belleau Wood > Batalla de Belleau Wood victoria que los estadounidenses obtuvieron sobre los alemanes tras un duro combate en Francia, en 1918

Battle of Britain > Batalla de Inglaterra intento fallido de Alemania de someter a Gran Bretaña en 1940, como preparación para invadirla

Battle of Bull Run > Batalla de Bull Run primera batalla importante de la Guerra Civil, que tuvo lugar en Virginia en 1861; también llamada Batalla de Manassas

Battle of Chancellorsville > Batalla de Chancellorsville batalla de la Guerra Civil que tuvo lugar en Virginia en 1863; importante victoria de la Confederación

Battle of Fredericksburg > Batalla de Fredericksburg batalla de la Guerra Civil que tuvo lugar en Virginia en 1862; una de las peores derrotas de la Unión

Battle of Gettysburg > Batalla de Gettysburg batalla de la Guerra Civil en Pennsylvania en 1863, que resultó en una victoria de la Unión y evitó que la Confederación invadiera el Norte

Battle of Midway > Batalla de Midway batalla ocurrida en el Pacífico en 1942 durante la cual los aviones estadounidenses hundieron cuatro portaviones japoneses

Battle of Shiloh > Batalla de Shiloh batalla de la Guerra Civil en Tennessee en 1862, que resultó en una victoria de la Unión

Battle of the Argonne Forest > Batalla del bosque de Argonne combate en el que las tropas francesas y estadounidenses derrotaron a los alemanes en Francia en octubre de 1918

Battle of the Bulge > Batalla de las Ardenas contraataque alemán ocurrido en diciembre de 1944, que demoró temporalmente la invasión aliada a Alemania

Bay of Pigs invasion > Invasión de Bahía de Cochinos fallida invasión de Cuba realizada en 1961, cuando una fuerza de 1,400 exiliados cubanos, respaldados por los Estados Unidos, fue capturada después de llegar a Bahía de Cochinos

Bear Flag Republic > República de la Bandera del Oso apodo de California tras declarar su independencia de México en 1846

beatnik > beatnik persona que, en la década de 1950, criticaba la cultura estadounidense por su conformismo y su devoción por los negocios

Berlin Airlift > puente aéreo de Berlín iniciativa de ayuda de emergencia estadounidense y británica para entregar provisiones por vía aérea a los berlineses del Oeste, de 1948 a 1949

Berlin Wall > Muro de Berlín muro construido en 1961 por el gobierno comunista de Alemania Oriental para aislar Berlín Oriental de Berlín Occidental

bilingual > bilingüe en dos idiomas

bill > proyecto de ley ley propuesta

Bill of Rights > Carta de Derechos las primeras diez enmiendas de la Constitución de los Estados Unidos

bill of rights > carta de derechos lista escrita de libertades que el gobierno promete proteger

biotechnology > biotecnología tecnología basada en la biología

Black Cabinet > Gabinete Negro grupo de líderes afroamericanos que, de manera extraoficial, asesoraron al presidente Franklin D. Roosevelt con respecto a la situación de los afroamericanos

Black codes > códigos negros leyes de los estados sureños que limitaban seriamente los derechos de los afroamericanos después de la Guerra Civil

blitzkrieg > blitzkrieg los repentinos y potentes ataques militares alemanes durante la Segunda Guerra Mundial; "guerra relámpago"

blockade > bloqueo cierre de un puerto con el fin de impedir la entrada y salida de personas y provisiones

boat people > balseros después de la guerra de Vietnam, refugiados que huyeron de Vietnam en pequeñas embarcaciones

bond > bono certificado que promete el pago de dinero que se ha prestado, más el interés, en una determinada fecha

bonus > bono cantidad adicional de dinero

Bonus Army > Ejército del Bono grupo de veteranos que marcharon a Washington en 1932 para exigir el pago inmediato de los bonos de la Primera Guerra Mundial

boom > auge período de crecimiento económico acelerado

bootlegger > contrabandista persona que introducía licor a los Estados Unidos durante la Prohibición

Border Ruffians > rufianes de la frontera bandas proesclavistas de Missouri que solían enfrentarse a las fuerzas antiesclavistas en Kansas

border state > estado fronterizo estado esclavista que permaneció en la Unión durante la Guerra Civil

boycott > boicot negarse a comprar o usar determinados bienes y servicios

Bracero Program > programa de braceros contratación de jornaleros mexicanos para trabajar en los Estados Unidos durante la Segunda Guerra Mundial

bribe > soborno algo valioso que se le da a alguien para que haga algo

bubble > burbuja situación que ocurre cuando los compradores provocan el alza de los precios por encima del valor real de un producto o una acción con la esperanza de que los precios suban incluso más

building code > reglamento de construcción estándar establecido por el gobierno para garantizar la seguridad de las edificaciones

bull market > mercado alcista período durante el cual el comercio de acciones aumenta y los precios se mantienen al alza

Bull Moose party > Partido del Alce Macho grupo de republicanos progresistas que apoyaron a Theodore Roosevelt durante la elección de 1912

bureaucracy > burocracia sistema de administración del gobierno mediante departamentos dirigidos por funcionarios nombrados

burgess > burgués representante del gobierno colonial de Virginia

C

Cabinet > gabinete grupo de funcionarios que dirigen departamentos gubernamentales y aconsejan al presidente

Camp David Accords > acuerdos de Camp David tratado de paz firmado en 1979 entre Israel y Egipto en el que Israel accedió a devolver a Egipto la península de Sinaí y Egipto accedió a reconocer a Israel

capability > capacidad habilidad, potencial

capital > capitalismo dinero con el que se inicia un negocio

capitalism > capitalismo sistema económico basado en la propiedad privada, la economía de mercado y la finalidad de obtener ganancias o ingresos mediante el uso de la propiedad privada

capitalist > capitalista persona que invierte en un negocio con el fin de obtener una ganancia

caravan > caravana grupo de personas que viajan juntas para protegerse entre sí

carpetbagger > carpetbagger apodo ofensivo usado para describir a los norteños que se mudaban al Sur después de la Guerra Civil

cash crop > cultivo comercial cultivo que se vende en el mercado para obtener dinero

cattle drive > arreo de ganado conducir y llevar ganado, por lo general hacia las vías del ferrocarril

caucus > asamblea partidaria reunión privada; por lo general, reunión política

causeway > calzada elevada camino elevado hecho con tierra comprimida

cavalry > caballería tropas a caballo

cease > cesar detenerse; parar

cede > ceder renunciar

censure > censurar condenar oficialmente

Central Powers > Potencias Centrales alianza militar de Alemania, Austria-Hungría, Bulgaria y el Imperio Otomano durante la Primera Guerra Mundial

characteristic > característica rasgo distintivo, cualidad o propiedad

charter > cédula documento legal que otorga ciertos derechos a una persona o una compañía

Chinese Exclusion Act > Ley de Exclusión China ley de 1882 que prohibía la entrada de trabajadores chinos a los Estados Unidos

circumnavigate > circunnavegar dar una vuelta completa a la Tierra en barco

citizen > ciudadano persona que debe lealtad a una nación en particular y a quien le corresponden todos sus derechos y protecciones

city-state > ciudad-estado unidad política que controla una ciudad y las tierras de sus alrededores

civic > cívico relacionado con ser un ciudadano

civic virtue > virtud cívica voluntad de trabajar por el bien de la nación o comunidad, incluso si eso implica un gran sacrificio

civil > civil relacionado con las demandas legales que involucran los derechos privados de los individuos

civil disobedience > desobediencia civil resistencia no violenta a acatar leyes que se consideran injustas

civil rights > derechos civiles derechos que deben tener todos los ciudadanos

Civil Rights Act > Ley de los Derechos Civiles ley de 1964 que prohibía la discriminación basada en género y raza al contratar empleados

Civil Rights Movement > Movimiento de los Derechos Civiles serie de esfuerzos por parte de los afroamericanos para obtener la igualdad de derechos civiles, particularmente durante las décadas de 1950 y 1960

civil service > servicio civil todos los empleos de gobierno, exceptuando los puestos de elección popular y los de las fuerzas armadas

civil war > guerra civil guerra entre personas del mismo país

civilian > civil no militar

civilization > civilización una sociedad, es decir, un pueblo que comparte un idioma, un territorio y una economía, que tiene ciertas características básicas

clan > clan grupo de dos o más familias relacionadas

Clermont* > *Clermont barco a vapor construido en 1807 por Robert Fulton; fue el primer barco a vapor que tuvo éxito comercial en aguas estadounidenses

climate change > cambio climático cualquier cambio medible y duradero del clima

collective bargaining > negociación colectiva proceso mediante el cual un sindicato en representación de un grupo de trabajadores negocia un contrato con los patrones

colony > colonia zona poblada y gobernada por el gobierno de un país distante

Columbian Exchange > intercambio colombino intercambio global de bienes e ideas que se dio como resultado del encuentro entre los pueblos de los hemisferios occidental y oriental

commence > comenzar empezar
committed > comprometido dedicado
committee of correspondence > Comité de Correspondencia campaña de intercambio de cartas que se convirtió en un importante instrumento de protesta en las colonias
commoner > plebeyo persona común
communism > comunismo sistema económico en el que el Estado es propietario de la riqueza y los medios de producción
company union > sindicato amarillo organización sindical que agrupa a los trabajadores de una sola compañía y que es controlada por los patrones
compel > forzar obligar
complex > complejo compuesto de dos o más partes
compose > componer crear o escribir
comprise > comprender estar formado por
compromise > acuerdo pacto en el que cada lado renuncia a parte de sus demandas con el fin de llegar a una solución pacífica
Compromise of 1850 > Acuerdo de 1850 acuerdo sobre la esclavitud por medio del cual California se sumaba a la Unión como estado libre y que incluía una estricta ley sobre esclavos fugitivos
Compromise of 1877 > Acuerdo de 1877 acuerdo del candidato presidencial republicano Rutherford B. Hayes en el que prometió dar fin a la Reconstrucción a cambio de que los congresistas demócratas aceptaran su toma de posesión del cargo de presidente tras la conflictiva elección de 1876
compulsory > obligatorio requerido, exigido por la ley
concede > reconocer admitir la derrota
concentration camp > campo de concentración campo de prisioneros para civiles que son considerados enemigos del Estado
condemn > condenar declarar con firmeza que algo es malo o equivocado
conducive > propicio que facilita que algo ocurra
confederation > confederación alianza de estados o naciones independientes que suele tener un mando militar compartido
conquistador > conquistador explorador español que tomaba posesión de tierras en las Américas en nombre de España
consequently > por consiguiente como resultado
conservation > conservación protección de los recursos naturales
consolidate > integrarse combinar
constitute > constituir fundar; establecer
constitution > constitución documento que establece las leyes, los principios, la organización y los procesos de un gobierno
Constitutional Convention > Convención Constitucional reunión de representantes de los estados el 25 de mayo de 1787 para revisar los Artículos de la Confederación
constitutional initiative > iniciativa popular poder de los ciudadanos de solicitar una votación para modificar las constituciones estatales
consumer goods > bienes de consumo productos que se compran para el uso personal o doméstico
containment > política de contención política que intentaba evitar la propagación de la influencia soviética más allá de donde ya existía
continental divide > línea divisoria continental cadena de montañas que separa sistemas fluviales que corren en direcciones opuestas en un continente
"Contract With America" > contrato con los Estados Unidos paquete legislativo aprobado en 1994 por los republicanos de la Cámara de Representantes que incluía el recorte de los programas de asistencia social y la reducción de impuestos
convey > transmitir transportar
cooperative > cooperativa grupo de personas que reúnen su dinero para comprar o vender bienes al por mayor
Copperhead > cabeza de cobre norteño que se oponía a hacer uso de la fuerza para que los estados sureños permanecieran en la Unión
corporation > corporación empresa propiedad de inversores cuyo riesgo de pérdida es limitado
corral > corral cercamiento para animales
cottonocracy > aristocracia del algodón nombre dado a los plantadores ricos que ganaban dinero gracias al algodón a mediados del siglo XIX
counterculture movement > movimiento contracultural movimiento de protesta, durante la década de 1960, que rechazaba los valores y la cultura estadounidenses tradicionales
coureur de bois > coureur de bois colono francés que vivía en las tierras más allá de los asentamientos franceses y era trampero de pieles
cow town > pueblo ganadero tipo de asentamiento que se desarrollaba donde terminaban los caminos de ganado
credit > crédito acuerdo o contrato en el que una persona recibe dinero o bienes ahora y se compromete a devolver más tarde una cantidad que es mayor a lo prestado
creole > criollo persona de padres españoles nacida en las colonias españolas de las Américas
Crusades > Cruzadas serie de guerras que libraron los cristianos para controlar Palestina, es decir, Tierra Santa, entre 1100 y 1300
Cuban missile crisis > crisis de los misiles de Cuba una de las principales confrontaciones de la Guerra Fría, sucedida en 1962, cuando Kennedy ordenó el bloqueo de navíos soviéticos que transportaban misiles hacia Cuba
cultivate > labrar preparar y trabajar el suelo para plantar y producir cultivos
culture > cultura forma de vida que lleva a cabo un pueblo
culture region > región cultural región donde las personas comparten una forma de vida similar
currency > moneda dinero

D

dame school > escuela de damas escuela dirigida por mujeres, habitualmente ubicada en sus propias casas

death camps > campos de muerte los campos donde la gente era asesinada de manera sistemática

debt ceiling > techo de endeudamiento límite legal sobre la cantidad de dinero que el gobierno de los Estados Unidos puede pedir prestado

debtor > deudor persona que debe dinero y no puede pagarlo

decisive > concluyente que decide claramente el resultado de una disputa o una cuestión

decline > declinar acercarse al final

default > cese de pagos no poder pagar una deuda

deficit > déficit cantidad de gasto que excede la cantidad de ingresos

deficit spending > gasto deficitario gasto gubernamental que es mayor al de los ingresos

demilitarized zone > zona desmilitarizada (ZDM) área en la que se prohíbe la presencia de fuerzas militares

Democratic Party > Partido Demócrata partido político de los EE. UU. que data de la década de 1820 y continúa en la actualidad; en un principio, representaba a los pequeños granjeros y trabajadores frente a los empresarios adinerados; sus políticas cambiaron durante los años

Democratic Republican > demócrata republicano miembro del partido político fundado por Thomas Jefferson

demonstrate > demostrar probar algo sirviendo como ejemplo

denounce > denunciar declarar públicamente que una acción o persona es incorrecta o mala

deport > deportar expulsar a alguien de un país por la fuerza

depression > depresión período en el que disminuye la actividad de negocios, caen los precios y salarios y aumenta el desempleo

deprive > privar quitar algo

deregulation > desregulación reducción de restricciones para los negocios

despite > a pesar aunque, no obstante

determination > determinación impulso personal para seguir intentando alcanzar los objetivos propios

devise > concebir desarrollar o crear algo

dictator > dictador gobernante que tiene poder y autoridad absolutos sobre un país, generalmente por medio de la violencia

dictatorship > dictadura sistema de gobierno en el que una persona o un grupo reducido tiene todo el poder

differentiate > diferenciar determinar lo que hace a una cosa o persona diferente de otra

diffusion > difusión proceso de transmitir ideas de una cultura a otra

disarmament > desarme reducción de fuerzas armadas y armamento bélico

discrimination > discriminación política o práctica que niega la igualdad de derechos a ciertos grupos de personas

divest > deshacerse librarse de algo

dividends > dividendos reparto de las ganancias de una corporación

dollar diplomacy > diplomacia del dólar política del presidente Taft que consistía en construir fuertes lazos económicos con América Latina

domino theory > teoría del dominó creencia de que si Vietnam del Sur se convertía al comunismo, otros países de la región lo seguirían, como fichas de dominó que caen una tras otra

"Double V" campaign > campaña "Doble V" campaña por los derechos civiles de los afroamericanos durante la Segunda Guerra Mundial

downsizing > reducción de plantilla reducción de la fuerza de trabajo

draft > conscripción ley que exige a las personas de determinada edad que realicen el servicio militar

***Dred Scott v. Sandford* > Dred Scott contra Sandford** caso de 1857 de la Corte Suprema que puso en duda el poder federal sobre la cuestión de la esclavitud en los territorios

drought > sequía escasez de agua que daña las plantas, los animales y la producción de energía, y que incrementa el riesgo de incendios

Dust Bowl > Dust Bowl región localizada en el centro y el sur de las Grandes Llanuras que fue asolada por la erosión y las tormentas de arena provocadas por la sequía, durante la década de 1930

dynamic > dinámico fuerte y enérgico

détente > distensión política que promueve el fin de las tensiones entre países

E

efficiency > eficiencia manera de trabajar que es más productiva y a la vez usa mejor los recursos

eliminate > eliminar librarse o deshacerse de algo

elusive > evasivo difícil de hallar o conseguir

Emancipation Proclamation > Proclamación de Emancipación declaración del presidente Lincoln presentada en 1863 en la que establecía la liberación de los afroamericanos esclavizados en el territorio confederado

embargo > embargo prohibición de comerciar

embark > embarcarse comenzar un viaje

embroil > enredar involucrar en un conflicto o en dificultades

emission > emisión liberación de gases en el aire

employ > emplear usar algo

enact > promulgar convertir a algo en ley

encounter > encontrar dar con alguien o algo

endorse > respaldar apoyar públicamente

English Bill of Rights > Declaración de Derechos inglesa documento de 1689 que garantizaba los derechos de los ciudadanos ingleses

enhance > acrecentar aumentar o mejorar la calidad de algo

Enlightenment > Ilustración movimiento europeo de los siglos XVII y XVIII que hizo hincapié en el uso de la razón

ensure > asegurar garantizar, afianzar

Environmental Protection Agency > Agencia de Protección Ambiental agencia federal establecida en 1970 para proteger la salud humana y el medio ambiente

epidemic > epidemia rápida diseminación de una enfermedad contagiosa

Equal Pay Act > Ley de Igualdad Salarial ley de 1963 que exigía dar igual pago por igual tarea

Equal Rights Amendment > Enmienda de Igualdad de Derechos enmienda constitucional propuesta en 1923 que intentaba prohibir toda discriminación basada en el sexo; nunca fue ratificada

Erie Canal > canal del Erie vía artificial de navegación fluvial inaugurada en 1825, que conecta el lago Erie con el río Hudson

essentially > esencialmente relacionado con la parte más importante de una idea o de algo

ethical > ético que sigue las normas aceptadas de conducta o comportamiento

evident > evidente obvio, aparente

exceed > sobrepasar ir más allá

exceedingly > sumamente en un grado muy alto; extremadamente

expatriate > expatriado(a) persona que deja su país y fija su residencia en otro

expedition > expedición largo viaje de exploración

expel > expulsar echar o sacar por la fuerza

exploit > hazaña acto heroico o que requiere coraje

export > exportación producto comercial que es enviado a los mercados de otros países

expose > exhibir revelar o sacar a la luz

exposure > exposición la condición de experimentar algo o ser afectado por algo

extend > extender expandir o aplicar más allá

extended family > familia extensa grupo familiar que incluye abuelos, padres, hijos, tíos y primos

extensive > extenso que tiene una gran área o alcance

F

faction > facción partido o grupo opositor dentro de un partido

fad > moda pasajera actividad o moda cuyo auge dura poco

Fair Deal > Trato Justo reformas del presidente Truman que extendían las políticas liberales e incluían un salario mínimo más alto, seguridad social extendida y préstamos de vivienda de bajo costo

famine > hambruna severa escasez de alimentos

fascism > fascismo sistema político basado en militarismo, nacionalismo extremo y lealtad ciega al estado

Federal Reserve Act > Ley de Reserva Federal ley de 1913 que establecía el Sistema de la Reserva Federal para regular el sector financiero nacional

Federal Trade Commission > Comisión Federal de Comercio (FTC) agencia gubernamental creada en 1914 para asegurar la competencia justa

Federalist > federalista persona que apoya un gobierno federal fuerte

Federalist > federalista miembro del partido liderado por Alexander Hamilton que apoyaba un gobierno federal fuerte

Federalist Papers > ensayos de The Federalist serie de ensayos de los federalistas James Madison, Alexander Hamilton y John Jay a favor de ratificar la Constitución

feudalism > feudalismo sistema de gobierno en el que los señores gobiernan sus tierras, pero le juran lealtad y prestan ayuda militar a un monarca

Fifteenth Amendment > Decimoquinta Enmienda enmienda de la Constitución de los Estados Unidos, de 1869, que prohíbe a los estados negar el derecho al voto a los afroamericanos por motivo de raza

fireside chat > charla junto al fuego discurso por radio del presidente Franklin D. Roosevelt durante su presidencia

flapper > chica flapper joven de la década de 1920 que adoptaba modas poco convencionales, incluyendo cabello corto y faldas cortas

flatboat > barcaza embarcación con base plana, usada para transportar cargas pesadas a través de vías fluviales

Foraker Act > Ley Foraker ley aprobada por el Congreso en 1900 por la cual los Estados Unidos daban a los puertorriqueños una participación limitada en su propio gobierno

Fort Wagner > fuerte Wagner fuerte de Carolina del Sur donde tuvo lugar un ataque liderado por el 54.° Regimiento de afroamericanos de Massachusetts

forty-niner > persona del 49 término que nombra a una de los más de 80,000 personas que en 1849 se unieron a la fiebre del oro

forum > foro lugar donde las personas intercambian puntos de vista, ideas y opiniones

fossil fuel > combustible fósil combustible formado en el pasado remoto que es limitado y no puede ser renovado, como el petróleo, el carbón y el gas natural

foster > promover estimular el desarrollo de algo

Fourteen Points > Los Catorce Puntos las metas del presidente Wilson para la paz que vendría después de la Primera Guerra Mundial

Fourteenth Amendment > Decimocuarta Enmienda enmienda de la Constitución de los Estados Unidos, de 1868, que garantiza igual protección de las leyes

fraud > fraude engaño con la intención de obtener ganancias personales o financieras

free enterprise > libre empresa sistema económico en el que las empresas compiten libremente con poco control del gobierno

Free-Soil Party > Partido del Suelo Libre partido antiesclavista bipartito fundado en 1848 en los Estados Unidos para evitar que la esclavitud entrara en los territorios del Oeste

freedmen > liberto hombre o mujer que había sido esclavizado

Freedmen's Bureau > Oficina de Libertos agencia gubernamental fundada durante la Reconstrucción para ayudar a quienes habían sido esclavos

French and Indian War > Guerra contra la Alianza Franco-Indígena guerra que tuvo lugar entre 1754 y 1763, y que puso fin al dominio francés en América del Norte

frontier > frontera límite, especialmente el límite de un asentamiento; línea tras la cual no hay asentamientos

fugitive > fugitivo que huye

Fugitive Slave Act > Ley de Esclavos Fugitivos cada una de las dos leyes aprobadas en 1793 y 1850 que se ocupaban de la captura y el regreso de los esclavos fugitivos

G

gauge > ancho de vía ancho de la vía de un ferrocarril

General Court > Corte General asamblea de representantes electos en la colonia de la bahía de Massachusetts

generally > generalmente en la mayoría de los casos

gentry > clase alta clase social que estaba en la cima de la sociedad en las colonias inglesas

Gettysburg Address > Discurso de Gettysburg discurso que dio el presidente Lincoln en 1863 después de la Batalla de Gettysburg

GI Bill of Rights > Declaración de Derechos del Soldado ley que facilitaba el regreso de los veteranos de la Segunda Guerra Mundial proporcionándoles educación, préstamos y empleo

glacier > glaciar capa gruesa de hielo

glasnost > glasnost política de la Unión Soviética de finales de la década de 1980, orientada a discutir abiertamente los problemas

globalization > globalización difusión de vínculos entre las economías del mundo, con la finalidad de formar una economía global

Glorious Revolution > Revolución Gloriosa movimiento de 1688 que llevó a Guillermo y María al trono de Inglaterra, y consolidó los derechos de los ciudadanos ingleses

Good Neighbor Policy > Política del Buen Vecino política del presidente Franklin Roosevelt orientada a fortalecer las relaciones de amistad con América Latina

grandfather clause > cláusula del abuelo en el Sur posterior a la Reconstrucción, ley que eximía a un votante de la prueba de alfabetización si su abuelo había calificado para votar el 1 de enero de 1867

Great Awakening > Gran Despertar movimiento religioso de las colonias inglesas a mediados del siglo XVIII, también conocido como Primer Gran Despertar

Great Compromise > Gran Concertación plan de la Convención Constitucional que resolvió las diferencias entre los estados grandes y pequeños

Great Depression > Gran Depresión la caída económica más grave en la historia de los Estados Unidos, que comenzó en 1929

Great Migration > Gran Migración movimiento de millones de afroamericanos desde el Sur hacia el Norte desde principios hasta mediados del siglo XX

Great Society > Gran Sociedad el propósito del presidente Johnson de crear un estándar de vida decente para todos los estadounidenses

Great White Fleet > Gran Flota Blanca nombre dado al conjunto de barcos de vapor que componían la aumentada y modernizada fuerza naval estadounidense a principios del siglo XX

guerrilla > guerrilla combatiente que usa tácticas de ataque y huida

guerrilla warfare > guerra de guerrillas tipo de guerra en la que grupos militares reducidos e informales usan ataques sorpresivos y tácticas de ataque y huida

Gulf of Tonkin Resolution > Resolución del Golfo de Tonkin resolución del Congreso aprobada en 1964 que autorizaba el uso de la fuerza militar en Vietnam

Gullah > gullah combinación del idioma inglés con idiomas de África occidental, hablado por los afroamericanos de Carolina del Sur y Georgia

H

habeas corpus > hábeas corpus el derecho a no ir a prisión sin antes ser acusado de un delito en particular

haven > refugio lugar donde las personas son protegidas del peligro y los problemas

hesitate > vacilar detenerse por un momento debido a los nervios

Holocaust > Holocausto la matanza de judíos en Europa efectuada por los nazis antes y durante la Segunda Guerra Mundial

Hooverville > Hooverville grupo de viviendas precarias donde vivían los indigentes durante la Gran Depresión

hostility > hostilidad sentimiento o acción agresiva

Hudson River School > Escuela de Hudson River grupo de artistas estadounidenses, con sede en Nueva York, que desarrollaron un estilo único de pintura de paisajes a mediados del siglo XIX

Hull House > Hull House asentamiento de viviendas fundado por la reformadora progresista Jane Addams en Chicago en 1889

Hundred Days > Cien días los primeros cien días de la presidencia de Franklin D. Roosevelt, cuando la legislación del Nuevo Trato fue promulgada

I

idealize > idealizar ver algo de la mejor manera posible

illiterate > analfabeto incapaz de leer o escribir

immigrant > inmigrante persona que ingresa a otro país con el objetivo de asentarse allí

impeach > enjuiciar políticamente presentar cargos contra un funcionario por ofensas graves

Imperialism > imperialismo política de los países poderosos con el fin de obtener el control de los asuntos económicos y políticos de países o regiones más débiles

implicit > implícito no expresado directamente, pero que se puede entender o inferir

imply > implicar sugerir algo sin decirlo directamente

imports > importaciones producto comercial que se trae de otro país

imposition > imposición algo aplicado o creado basándose en la autoridad

impressment > reclutamiento forzado práctica de obligar a las personas a realizar el servicio militar

inauguration > toma de posesión ceremonia en la cual el presidente realiza públicamente el juramento de su cargo

incline > inclinarse tender o tener preferencia por una opinión o acción

income tax > impuesto sobre la renta impuesto sobre los ingresos de una persona

incriminate > incriminar presentar pruebas en contra de alguien

incur > incurrir exponerse a tener la responsabilidad por algo

Indian New Deal > Nuevo Trato Indígena serie de leyes autorizadas en la década de 1930 que daban a las naciones de indígenas norteamericanos mayor control sobre sus propios asuntos

Indian Removal Act > Ley de Expulsión de Indígenas ley aprobada por el Congreso en 1830 que establecía tierras al oeste del río Mississippi para que los indígenas que vivían en los estados ya existentes se mudaran allí

Indian Territory > territorio indígena región establecida para la reubicación de los indígenas norteamericanos, que comenzó con la Ley de Expulsión de Indígenas; la mayor parte de esta región pasó a formar parte del estado de Oklahoma

indigo > añil planta usada para fabricar una valiosa tintura azul

individualism > individualismo creencia en la singularidad e importancia de cada individuo

Industrial Revolution > Revolución Industrial cambio de la producción manual a la producción hecha por máquinas en fábricas que comenzó en Inglaterra a fines del siglo XVIII y se expandió hacia otros lugares, y transformó la economía, la sociedad y la tecnología

inevitably > inevitablemente de una manera que no se puede evitar

inflation > inflación aumento de precios y disminución del valor del dinero

influential > influyente que tiene mucha influencia o poder; eficaz

infrastructure > infraestructura sistema de vías de tránsito, carreteras, puentes y túneles

infringe > infringir violar (leyes) o restringir (derechos)

initiate > iniciar empezar

initiative > iniciativa proceso mediante el cual los votantes pueden hacer llegar directamente un proyecto de ley a la legislatura estatal

innovation > innovación idea o método nuevo

installment buying > plan de pago a plazos comprar a crédito mediante pagos periódicos cuyo total es igual al precio más los intereses

insurgency > insurgencia rebelión armada

integration > integración la mezcla de grupos de distinta raza o diferente origen étnico

intense > intenso que existe en un grado extremo

interchangeable parts > piezas reemplazables piezas idénticas, hechas a máquina, de una herramienta o instrumento

interest > interés precio que se paga por tomar dinero prestado, generalmente un porcentaje del préstamo, y que debe ser pagado todos los meses junto con una parte del préstamo original, hasta que el préstamo sea devuelto

interest group > grupo de interés personas que tienen una preocupación o una creencia en común

Internet > Internet red de comunicaciones electrónicas que conecta redes de computadoras e instalaciones informáticas organizacionales alrededor del mundo

internment > internación aprisionamiento temporal de los integrantes de un grupo específico

interstate commerce > comercio interestatal comercio que atraviesa los límites estatales

intervene > intervenir interferir para detener o cambiar algo

intervention > intervención interferencia en los asuntos de otros

invoke > invocar recurrir o apelar a algo

iron curtain > Cortina de Hierro término acuñado por Winston Churchill para describir la frontera entre las naciones satélite soviéticas y Europa Occidental

Iroquois League > Liga Iroquesa alianza formada por las naciones iroquesas

Islamic fundamentalist > fundamentalista islámico musulmán convencido de que los textos religiosos del Islam deben tomarse de manera literal

island-hopping > salto entre islas durante la Segunda Guerra Mundial, estrategia de los Aliados para capturar islas dominadas por los japoneses con el fin de obtener el control del Pacífico

isolationism > aislacionismo política de mantenerse ajeno a los asuntos del mundo

isthmus > istmo franja estrecha de tierra con costas a ambos lados, que une dos extensiones de tierra más grandes

J

jazz > jazz género musical creado por afroamericanos a principios del siglo XX, desarrollado a partir del blues, el ragtime y otros estilos

jerky > carne seca carne cortada y secada sobre una rejilla

jihadism > yihadismo movimiento de fundamentalismo islámico que respalda el uso de la violencia contra los enemigos percibidos del islam

Jim Crow laws > Leyes de Jim Crow leyes que separaban a las personas según su raza en lugares públicos del Sur

judicial review > control de constitucionalidad poder de la Corte Suprema de decidir si los actos de un presidente o las leyes aprobadas por el Congreso son o no constitucionales

jury duty > servir como jurado responsabilidad de todos los ciudadanos de formar parte de un jurado cuando son convocados

K

Kansas-Nebraska Act > Ley Kansas-Nebraska ley de 1854 que estableció los territorios de Kansas y Nebraska y otorgó a los pobladores de cada territorio el derecho de soberanía popular para resolver el asunto de la esclavitud

Khmer Rouge > Jemer Rojo partido comunista de Camboya, que impuso un reino de terror entre los ciudadanos camboyanos

kinship > parentesco relación entre personas que comparten un ancestro en común o sistema de clasificación de tales relaciones

Know-Nothing party > partido Know-Nothing partido político de la década de 1850 que era anticatólico y antiinmigrante

Ku Klux Klan > Ku Klux Klan sociedad secreta organizada en el Sur después de la Guerra Civil con el fin de reafirmar la supremacía de los hombres blancos usando la violencia

L

laissez faire > laissez faire idea de que el gobierno debe tener la menor participación posible en los asuntos económicos

League of Nations > Liga de las Naciones asociación de naciones formada después de la Primera Guerra Mundial, a partir del plan de los Catorce Puntos de Wilson

legacy > legado algo recibido de un predecesor o del pasado

legislature > cuerpo legislativo grupo de personas, generalmente elegidos por medio del voto, que tienen la facultad de crear leyes

legitimate > legítimo real u oficial

Lend-Lease Act > Ley de Préstamo y Arriendo ley que permitía a los Estados Unidos vender armas y equipo a Inglaterra durante la Segunda Guerra Mundial

libel > difamación acto de publicar algo que puede dañar injustamente la reputación de otra persona

liberty > libertad condición de ser libre

Liberty Bond > Bono de la Libertad bono vendido por el gobierno de los Estados Unidos para recaudar fondos para el esfuerzo bélico de la Primera Guerra Mundial

literacy test > prueba de alfabetización prueba para comprobar si una persona puede leer y escribir; usada en el pasado para limitar el derecho al voto

local color > color local habla y hábitos de una región específica

local government > gobierno local gobierno a nivel del condado, feligresía, ciudad, pueblo, aldea o distrito

lode > filón rica veta de oro, plata u otro mineral valioso

Lowell girls > chicas Lowell mujeres jóvenes que trabajaban en las hilanderías de Lowell en Massachusetts durante la Revolución Industrial

Loyalist > leal al rey colono que se mantuvo leal a Gran Bretaña

lure > aliciente algo que tienta o estimula a una persona a ir a un lugar o hacer algo

Lusitania > Lusitania barco de pasajeros inglés torpedeado por un submarino alemán en 1915; 1,200 personas murieron, incluyendo 128 estadounidenses

lynch > linchamiento captura y asesinato de un sospechoso, llevado a cabo por una turba sin el debido proceso

M

Magna Carta > Carta Magna documento británico firmado en 1215 que contenía dos ideas básicas: los monarcas debían obedecer las leyes y los ciudadanos tenían derechos básicos

maintain > mantener conservar un estado existente

majority > mayoría grupo que representa más de la mitad de un grupo más grande

mandate > mandato autorización otorgada después de la Primera Guerra Mundial a un miembro de la Liga de las Naciones para gobernar una colonia que antes pertenecía a Alemania o Turquía

Manifest Destiny > Destino Manifiesto en el siglo XIX, la creencia de que los Estados Unidos tenían el derecho de expandirse a través de todo el continente

manor > feudo área gobernada por un señor, incluyendo su castillo y las tierras a su alrededor

margin > margen franja a lo largo del borde; en el comercio de acciones, fracción del precio de la acción dado como un pago inicial para obtener la propiedad de la acción

Marshall Plan > Plan Marshall plan estadounidense para ayudar a las naciones europeas a reconstruir sus economías después de la Segunda Guerra Mundial

martial law > ley marcial gobierno a manos de las fuerzas armadas en lugar de un gobierno electo

martyr > mártir persona que da la vida por sus ideales

mass culture > cultura de masas conjunto de prácticas y creencias derivadas de la amplia exposición a los mismos medios de comunicación

mass production > producción en masa proceso de fabricar grandes cantidades de un producto rápidamente y a bajo costo

Mayflower Compact > Pacto del Mayflower acuerdo de 1620 para gobernar la colonia de Plymouth

McCarthyism > macartismo uso de acusaciones de deslealtad injustificadas

mechanization > mecanización el cambio de un proceso o acción para que pueda ser realizado por máquinas

mediator > mediador agente que ayuda a las partes de un conflicto a resolver sus diferencias

mercantilism > mercantilismo teoría que plantea que la fortaleza económica de una nación proviene de vender más de lo que compra a otras naciones

mercenary > mercenario soldado que lucha a cambio de un salario, generalmente para un país extranjero

merit > mérito habilidad, logro o merecimiento

mestizo > mestizo en las colonias españolas de las Américas, persona de mezcla de sangre española e indígena

Mexican Cession > Cesión Mexicana los territorios mexicanos de California y Nuevo México otorgados a los Estados Unidos en 1848

middle class > clase media en las colonias inglesas, clase que incluía a artesanos calificados, agricultores y algunos comerciantes

migrant worker > trabajador migratorio persona que viaja de una región a otra en busca de trabajo

militarism > militarismo política de reforzar las fuerzas armadas como preparación para una guerra

militia > milicia ejército de ciudadanos que prestan servicios como soldados durante una emergencia

minutemen > milicianos voluntarios de las milicias coloniales, que estaban preparados para luchar en cualquier momento

mission > misión asentamiento de sacerdotes y frailes católicos; asentamiento cuyo objetivo es difundir la religión en una nueva área

Missouri Compromise > Acuerdo de Missouri acuerdo propuesto en 1819 por Henry Clay para mantener la misma cantidad de estados libres y de estados esclavistas

modification > modificación cambio

monetary policy > política monetaria acciones que toma el banco central de un país para regular la cantidad de dinero disponible

Monitor* > *Monitor barco de guerra acorazado de la Unión

monopoly > monopolio compañía o grupo de compañías que tiene el control de toda o casi toda la actividad de una industria

Monroe Doctrine > Doctrina Monroe declaración de la política exterior del presidente Monroe en la que advertía a las naciones europeas que no interfirieran en América Latina

moral diplomacy > diplomacia moral política del presidente Wilson que consistía en condenar el imperialismo, difundir la democracia y promover la paz

Moral Majority > Mayoría Moral organización religiosa que respaldaba causas políticas conservadoras en la década de 1980

Morrill Acts > Ley de Morrill leyes aprobadas en 1862 y 1890 que otorgaban tierras fiscales para la construcción de escuelas de agricultura

mortgage > hipoteca préstamo para comprar una propiedad que permite al prestamista reclamar la propiedad si el préstamo no es liquidado

mountain man > montañés trampero que exploraba y cazaba en el Oeste de los Estados Unidos a principios del siglo XIX

moving assembly line > línea de montaje móvil método de producción en el que los trabajadores permanecen en un lugar mientras que los productos pasan a lo largo de una cinta transportadora

muckraker > periodista de denuncia periodista que daba a conocer la corrupción y las malas prácticas comerciales a finales del siglo XIX y principios del XX

Munich Conference > Conferencia de Múnich reunión de los líderes de Inglaterra, Francia, Italia y Alemania, efectuada en 1939, en la que firmaron un acuerdo que cedía parte de Checoslovaquia a Hitler

mutualista > mutualista grupo de ayuda mutua mexicano-estadounidense

N

NAACP > NAACP (Asociación Nacional para el Avance de las Personas de Color) organización fundada en 1909 para trabajar en pos de la igualdad de derechos para los afroamericanos

NAFTA > TLCAN Tratado de Libre Comercio para América del Norte, un acuerdo para eliminar las barreras al comercio entre los Estados Unidos, Canadá y México; fue ratificado por el Congreso de los Estados Unidos en 1993

national debt > dueda nacional cantidad total de dinero que el gobierno de un país debe a compañías, países, etc.

National Road > Carretera Nacional primer proyecto de construcción de una carretera nacional financiado por el gobierno federal, comenzado en 1811

nationalism > nacionalismo devoción por el país propio así como por sus intereses

nativist > nativista estadounidense que quería limitar la inmigración y conservar el país para los protestantes blancos nativos

natural rights > derechos naturales derechos que todas las personas tienen desde su nacimiento

naturalize > naturalizar otorgar la ciudadanía a una persona que ha cumplido con los requisitos oficiales para convertirse en ciudadano

Navigation Acts > Leyes de Navegación serie de leyes inglesas que regulaban el comercio entre Inglaterra y sus colonias a partir de la década de 1650

Nazi > nazi miembro del Partido Obrero Nacionalsocialista Alemán

Nazi-Soviet Pact > Pacto nazi-soviético acuerdo firmado por Hitler y Stalin en 1939, en el que ambos dictadores acordaban no atacarse entre sí

negotiate > negociar tratar con otros para llegar a un acuerdo

network > red sistema de vías de ferrocarril conectadas

neutral > neutral que no toma partido en un conflicto

Neutrality Acts > Leyes de Neutralidad serie de leyes aprobadas por el Congreso en 1935 que prohibía la venta de armas o los préstamos a países en guerra

New Deal > Nuevo Trato programa del presidente Franklin D. Roosevelt para dar fin a la Gran Depresión

New Freedom > Nueva Libertad programa del presidente Wilson para desarticular los monopolios con la finalidad de restaurar la competencia económica en los Estados Unidos

New Jersey Plan > Plan de Nueva Jersey plan de la Convención Constitucional, respaldado por los estados pequeños, que proponía tres poderes de gobierno y un cuerpo legislativo de una sola cámara

"New South" > "Nuevo Sur" término usado para describir al Sur a fines del siglo XIX, cuando se intentó expandir la economía a través de la construcción de industrias

nominating convention > convención de nominación reunión en la que un partido político elige a un candidato

North Atlantic Treaty Organization > Organización del Tratado del Atlántico Norte (OTAN) alianza formada en 1949 por los Estados Unidos y naciones de Europa Occidental para hacer frente a las agresiones soviéticas

Northwest Ordinance > Decreto del Noroeste ley de 1787 que estableció un gobierno para el territorio del Noroeste

northwest passage > paso del Noroeste vía navegable que atraviesa o bordea América del Norte

notorious > de mala reputación conocido por una mala cualidad o efecto

Nuclear Non-Proliferation Treaty > Tratado sobre la no proliferación de las armas nucleares tratado que tenía como objetivo evitar la proliferación de armas nucleares, promover la cooperación para el uso pacífico de la energía nuclear y promover el desarme

Nullification Act > Ley de Anulación ley aprobada por Carolina del Sur en 1832 que declaraba que el Arancel de 1828 era inconstitucional

nullify > invalidar cancelar
Nuremberg Trials > Juicios de Núremberg juicios de los crímenes de guerra nazis que tuvieron lugar en 1945 y 1946
nurture > criar dar atención y cuidado

O

obtain > obtener recibir
OPEC > OPEP (Organización de Países Exportadores de Petróleo) organización multinacional de países productores de petróleo que establece una política común de precios para la venta del hidrocarburo
Open Door Policy > política de puertas abiertas política presentada por el secretario de estado John Hay en 1899 y que permitía a una nación comerciar en cualquier otra que perteneciera a la esfera de influencia de China
Operation Overlord > Operación Overlord nombre clave que se le dio a la invasión de Europa por parte de los aliados en 1944
Oregon Country > Territorio de Oregón término usado a comienzos del siglo XIX para la región que incluye los actuales Oregón, Washington, Idaho y partes de Wyoming, Montana y el oeste del Canadá
Oregon Trail > Camino de Oregón ruta que conducía al Territorio de Oregón, usada por las caravanas de carretas en el siglo XIX
organic > orgánico de los seres vivos o relacionado con ellos u obtenido de ellos
Organization of American States > Organización de los Estados Americanos (OEA) organización internacional que promueve la paz y el progreso económico en las Américas
organize > organizar crear o establecer un grupo, como un sindicato
organized crime > crimen organizado actividad criminal llevada a cabo por uno o más grupos organizados con fines lucrativos
override > invalidar anular, como cuando el Congreso anula un veto presidencial

P

pacifist > pacifista persona que objeta cualquier guerra porque está convencido de que la guerra es mala
pact > pacto acuerdo o tratado formal
paralyze > paralizar impedir que algo funcione
patent > patente licencia para un nuevo invento
Patriot > patriota colono que estaba a favor de la guerra contra Gran Bretaña
patriotism > patriotismo sentimiento de amor y devoción hacia el propio país
patronage > clientelismo práctica que consiste en otorgar empleos en el gobierno a los simpatizantes políticos
Peace Corps > Cuerpo de Paz organización gubernamental que envía voluntarios estadounidenses a los países en desarrollo para que enseñen o proporcionen asesoría técnica
peninsular > peninsular persona nacida en España que ocupaba una posición de poder en las colonias españoles
Pennsylvania Dutch > dutch de Pennsylvania protestante de habla alemana que se asentó en Pennsylvania
pension > pensión suma de dinero que se da regularmente a las personas después de que se retiran
perceive > percibir notar o advertir algo
perjury > perjurio mentir bajo juramento
persecution > persecución maltrato o castigo de un grupo de personas por sus creencias
petition > petición demanda escrita y formal, dirigida a una autoridad y firmada por un grupo de personas
Ph.D. > doctorado en los Estados Unidos, el grado académico más alto que se otorga en una disciplina que no sea el derecho ni la medicina
Pickett's Charge > Carga de Pickett ataque fallido de la Confederación en el tercer día de la Batalla de Gettysburg
Pilgrim > peregrino colono inglés que buscaba libertad religiosa en las Américas en el siglo XVII
pioneer > pionero persona que está entre los primeros en trasladarse a vivir a un área nueva
pioneer > promover iniciar o ser el primero en hacer algo
Platt Amendment > Enmienda Platt enmienda de 1902 a la constitución cubana que permitía a los Estados Unidos intervenir en ese país
pledge > jurar prometer
***Plessy* v. *Ferguson* > Plessy contra Ferguson** caso de 1896 en el que la Corte Suprema decretó que la segregación era legal en los lugares públicos siempre que las instalaciones fueran iguales
PLO > OLP (Organización para la Liberación de Palestina) organización árabe palestina fundada en 1964, comprometida originalmente con la destrucción de Israel y posteriormente con la promoción de los intereses de los árabes palestinos a través de medios no violentos
pogrom > pogromo en Europa Oriental, un ataque organizado contra una comunidad judía
poll tax > impuesto al voto impuesto que una persona debía pagar para poder votar
pollution > contaminación impurezas perjudiciales vertidas al medio ambiente
pool > asociación comercial sistema en el que las compañías de ferrocarril acuerdan dividir el negocio en un área y fijan los precios
popular sovereignty > soberanía popular gobierno cuyo poder deriva del consentimiento de los gobernados
populist > populista persona que dice representar a la gente común
potlatch > potlatch cena ceremonial realizada por algunos indígenas de la costa del Noroeste para mostrar su riqueza
preamble > preámbulo introducción de una declaración, constitución u otro documento oficial
precedent > precedente acto o decisión que funciona como un ejemplo para otros
preliminary > preliminar algo que viene antes o sirve como introducción a algo
prerequisite > prerrequisito algo que es necesario para llevar a cabo una acción
presidio > presidio fuerte donde vivían los soldados en las colonias españolas

presume > presumir suponer o considerar algo sin pruebas

previous > previo anterior

primary > elección primaria elección en la que los votantes eligen al candidato de su partido para la elección general

privatize > privatizar poner a individuos privados o empresas a cargo de algo

productivity > productividad producción promedio por trabajador

profit > ganancia la diferencia entre el costo de un bien y su precio de venta

Progressive > progresista reformador de finales del siglo XIX y principios del XX que quería mejorar las condiciones de vida en los Estados Unidos

prohibit > prohibir negarse a permitir; impedir

prohibition > prohibición a finales del siglo XIX y principios del XX, el movimiento para prohibir la venta y producción de alcohol en los Estados Unidos o, entre 1920 y 1933, la orden constitucional de ley seca que prohibía la producción y venta de alcohol

Prohibition > prohibición la orden legal que prohibía la producción, venta y transporte de alcohol en los Estados Unidos entre 1920 y 1933

prominent > prominente conocido

propaganda > propaganda la divulgación de ideas para promover cierta causa o perjudicar una causa opuesta

propose > proponer sugerir algo para que la gente lo considere

proprietary colony > colonia de propietarios colonia inglesa en la que el rey entregaba tierras a una o más personas a cambio de un pago anual

prosperous > próspero que tiene éxito, generalmente por ganar mucho dinero

protectorate > protectorado nación cuya independencia está restringida por el control de un país más poderoso

public opinion > opinión pública los puntos de vista de la gente, en general

public works > obras públicas construcción de edificios, caminos, presas y otras edificaciones públicas con fondos del gobierno

pueblo > pueblo asentamiento en las colonias españolas; aldea de los anasazis u otros grupos de indígenas norteamericanos del Suroeste de los Estados Unidos

Puebloan > indígenas pueblo uno de los grupos de indígenas que vive en el Suroeste en casas de techo plano en asentamientos permanentes

pull factor > factor de atracción condición que atrae a la gente a establecerse en una nueva zona

Puritans > puritanos grupo de protestantes ingleses que se asentaron en la colonia de la bahía de Massachusetts

push factor > factor de empuje condición que impulsa a la gente a dejar su sitio de origen

Q

Quakers > cuáqueros reformistas protestantes que creían en la igualdad de todas las personas

quarters > barracones alojamiento para trabajadores

quipu > quipu artefacto que consistía en una cuerda con nudos que representaban cantidades; era usado por los incas para llevar cuentas y registros

quota system > sistema de cuotas sistema que restringe la cantidad de ciertos tipos de personas que se admiten en una institución o un país; a partir de la década de 1920, sistema que permitía solo a cierto número de personas de cada país inmigrar a los Estados Unidos

R

racism > racismo creencia según la cual una raza es superior a otra

radical > radical extremo

Radical Republican > republicano radical durante la Reconstrucción, miembro del Congreso que quería someter a los adinerados dueños de plantaciones del Sur y garantizar que los libertos tuvieran derecho a votar

ragtime > ragtime forma de música popular de finales del siglo XIX y principios del XX con un sonido rítmico y vivaz

ratify > ratificar aprobar

rationing > racionamiento restricción de la cantidad de ciertos productos que la gente puede comprar

reaffirm > reafirmar expresar de nuevo una fuerte creencia en algo

Reaganomics > Reaganomía programa económico del presidente Reagan que reducía los impuestos, recortaba el gasto federal en programas sociales y disminuía la regulación que afectaba a las empresas

realist > realista escritor u otro artista que pretende mostrar la vida como es realmente

rebate > reducción de precio descuento

recall > referéndum revocatorio proceso mediante el cual los votantes pueden retirar del cargo a un funcionario elegido

recession > recesión reducción de la actividad económica de menor intensidad que una depresión

Reconstruction > La Reconstrucción la restauración del Sur después de la Guerra Civil

Reconstruction Act > Ley de Reconstrucción ley de 1867 que rechazaba a los gobiernos de los estados sureños que se negaban a ratificar la Decimocuarta Enmienda

recount > relatar contar algo que sucedió

redeem > recomprar volver a comprar

referendum > referendo proceso mediante el cual la gente vota directamente un proyecto de ley

regulate > regular crear reglas o leyes para controlar algo

relief > ayuda de emergencia ayuda para los necesitados, generalmente en forma de dinero o alimentos

religious tolerance > tolerancia religiosa actitud de permitir que cada uno practique sus propias creencias

reluctant > reacio que no tiene la voluntad de hacer algo

Renaissance > Renacimiento auge de conocimiento en Europa que tuvo lugar desde fines del siglo XIV hasta comienzos del siglo XVII

reparation > reparación pago en efectivo realizado por una nación derrotada a otra victoriosa para subsanar las pérdidas ocasionadas por la guerra

repeal > derogar cancelar o anular una ley

representative government > gobierno representativo sistema político en el que los votantes eligen a representantes para que creen las leyes en su nombre
republic > república sistema de gobierno en el que los ciudadanos eligen representantes para que los gobiernen
Republican Party > Partido Republicano partido político establecido en los Estados Unidos en 1854 cuyo objetivo principal era evitar que la esclavitud se estableciera en los territorios del Oeste
reservation > reserva área delimitada de tierra destinada a los indígenas norteamericanos
resident alien > extranjero residente persona que vive en un país del que no es ciudadana
resist > resistir luchar contra algo
resolve > resolver llegar a una decisión firme
resolve > resolver hallar una respuesta o solución para algo
respect > respeto comprender cuando algo es serio y actuar apropiadamente
responsibility > responsabilidad deber o tarea que se espera que uno haga
resume > retomar comenzar algo luego de haberse detenido
reunification > reunificación acción y efecto de volver a unir algo para hacer una sola entidad
revenue > ingresos dinero, especialmente el que recauda el gobierno para su uso público
Roosevelt Corollary > Corolario Roosevelt declaración de Theodore Roosevelt de que los Estados Unidos tenían el derecho de intervenir en América Latina para preservar la ley y el orden
Rosie the Riveter > Rosita la Remachadora obrera ficticia que se convirtió en el símbolo de la contribución de las mujeres estadounidenses al esfuerzo bélico durante la Segunda Guerra Mundial
royal colony > colonia de la corona colonia bajo control directo de la corona inglesa
rugged individualist > individualista extremo persona que sigue su propio camino independiente en la vida

S

sabotage > sabotaje destrucción de propiedad u obstaculización de la producción llevada a cabo de manera encubierta
SALT Agreement > Acuerdo SALT (Tratado de Limitación de Armas Estratégicas) acuerdo entre los Estados Unidos y la Unión Soviética para restringir el número de cabezas y misiles nucleares
salvation > salvación liberación del pecado
sanction > sanción restricción al comercio de un país para obligarlo a cumplir leyes internacionales
Santa Fe Trail > Camino de Santa Fe ruta que iba a Santa Fe, Nuevo México, usada por comerciantes en el siglo XIX
scalawag > sacalawag sureño blanco que apoyaba a los republicanos durante la Reconstrucción
scapegoat > chivo expiatorio persona o grupo a quien se culpa por las acciones de otros
scarcity > escasez falta de algo u oferta insuficiente
secede > separarse dejar de ser miembro de un grupo
Second Great Awakening > Segundo Gran Despertar amplio movimiento religioso en los Estados Unidos a principios del siglo XIX
sectionalism > seccionalismo lealtad a un estado o región antes que a todo el país
sedition > sedición acto de suscitar una rebelión en contra de un gobierno
segregation > segregación separación legal de las personas basada en diferencias raciales, étnicas u otras
Selective Service Act > Ley de Servicio Selectivo ley aprobada por el Congreso en 1917 que requería que todos los hombres de entre 21 y 30 años se alistaran para el servicio militar
self-determination > autodeterminación derecho de los grupos nacionales a tener sus propios territorios y formas de gobierno
self-sufficient > autosuficiente capaz de producir lo suficiente para satisfacer las propias necesidades
Seneca Falls Convention > Convención de Seneca Falls encuentro de 1848 en el que algunos activistas pidieron por la igualdad de derechos para las mujeres; considerado el origen del movimiento por los derechos de las mujeres
separation of powers > separación de poderes principio según el cual el gobierno se divide en poderes separados
setback > contratiempo derrota o suceso inoportuno que detiene el progreso de algo
settlement > asentamiento lugar o región recientemente poblado
settlement house > centro comunitario centro organizado, desde finales del siglo XIX, con la finalidad de ofrecer servicios a los pobres
sharecropper > aparcero persona que alquila una parcela de tierra a otra persona y la trabaja a cambio de una porción de los cultivos
Shays' Rebellion > Rebelión de Shays en 1786, levantamiento de granjeros en Massachusetts en contra de los altos impuestos
shrewd > astuto inteligente
siege > sitio situación en la que un ejército bloquea o rodea una ciudad o posición donde está un enemigo con el propósito de obligarlo a rendirse
significant > significativo muy importante
signify > significar indicar o ser el signo de algo
silent majority > mayoría silenciosa los estadounidenses molestos por la inconformidad de la década de 1960 pero que no protestaban públicamente
Silk Road > Ruta de la Seda red de rutas comerciales terrestres que unían China y Oriente Medio
sit-in > sentada forma de protesta en la que las personas se sientan y se rehúsan a irse
skyscraper > rascacielos edificio de gran altura y muchos pisos sostenido por una estructura ligera de acero
slave codes > códigos de esclavos leyes que reglamentaban la conducta de los africanos y afroamericanos esclavizados y en virtud de las cuales les quitaron sus derechos humanos básicos

smart phone > teléfono móvil inteligente teléfono con capacidades de computación y de conexión con Internet mediante señales de radio
smuggling > contrabando acto de importar o exportar mercancías que viola las leyes de comercio
Social Gospel > evangelio social movimiento dentro del protestantismo estadounidense surgido a finales del siglo XIX, que intentaba aplicar las enseñanzas bíblicas a los problemas de la sociedad
social reform > reforma social intento organizado de mejorar lo que es injusto o imperfecto en la sociedad
socialism > socialismo creencia en la propiedad personal para individuos y la propiedad pública de los medios de producción, como fábricas y recursos naturales
sodbuster > sodbuster granjero de las Grandes Llanuras a fines del siglo XIX
Solidarity > Solidaridad sindicato independiente que desafió al gobierno comunista polaco
soup kitchen > comedor comunitario lugar donde se proporciona comida a los necesitados gratis o a un precio muy bajo
Spanish-American War > Guerra Hispano-Estadounidense guerra entablada entre España y los Estados Unidos en 1898
specifically > específicamente con un propósito en particular
specify > especificar nombrar algo exactamente y en detalle
speculation > especulación compra riesgosa con la expectativa de una gran ganancia
speculator > especulador alguien que invierte dinero en un negocio arriesgado con la expectativa de obtener grandes ganancias
spoils system > sistema de botines práctica de dar empleos en el gobierno a los partidarios de ese gobierno
Square Deal > Trato Justo promesa de campaña de Theodore Roosevelt de que todos los grupos tendrían iguales oportunidades de éxito
stabilize > estabilizar mantener estable o en un nivel determinado
stagflation > estanflación situación económica caracterizada por una combinación de precios al alza, gran desempleo y crecimiento económico lento
standard of living > estándar de vida medida que determina el grado de bienestar de la gente según la cantidad de bienes, servicios y tiempo libre que tienen las personas
Star Wars > Iniciativa de Defensa Estratégica ("Guerra de las Galaxias") sistema de armamento propuesto por el presidente Reagan para destruir los misiles soviéticos desde el espacio
states' rights > derechos de los estados derechos y facultades independientes del gobierno federal que se reservan para los estados según la Constitución
statute > estatuto ley o regla
steerage > compartimiento de tercera clase en una embarcación, los atestados camarotes de pasajeros de más bajo precio
stimulate > estimular hacer que algo ocurra o crezca
stock > acciones fracción de propiedad de una compañía
Strategic Arms Reduction Treaty > Tratado de Limitación de Armas Estratégicas (TLAE) tratado de 1991 firmado por los Estados Unidos y la Unión Soviética para reducir los arsenales nucleares
strike > huelga negativa de los trabajadores a hacer su trabajo hasta que se satisfagan sus demandas
strikebreaker > rompehuelgas sustituto de un trabajador en huelga
subprime mortgage > hipotecas de alto riesgo tipo de hipoteca otorgado a los individuos con historiales crediticios deficientes
subsequently > posteriormente que ocurre después de otra cosa
subsidize > subsidiar ayudar a pagar el costo de algo
subsidy > subsidio concesión de tierras u otra ayuda financiera otorgada por el gobierno
suburb > suburbio zona residencial ubicada en las afueras de una ciudad
suffrage > sufragio derecho al voto
summit meeting > cumbre conferencia celebrada entre los funcionarios de mayor rango de distintas naciones
Sunbelt > Cinturón del Sol región que se extiende a lo largo del borde sur de los Estados Unidos
superpower > superpotencia nación que tiene la fuerza militar, política y económica como para influir en el resto del mundo
supply > oferta cantidad de bienes o recursos que están disponibles en el mercado para su venta
suppress > suprimir terminar o detener
surplus > superávit exceso o cantidad extra
sustain > padecer experimentar
sweatshop > talleres donde se explota al obrero lugar donde las personas trabajan largas jornadas en condiciones deficientes y con un salario insuficiente

T

tactic > táctica método para lograr un objetivo
tariff > arancel impuesto sobre los bienes extranjeros que ingresan a un país
temperament > temperamento actitud, estado de ánimo o conducta habituales de una persona
temperance movement > movimiento por la templanza campaña contra el consumo de alcohol
tenement > apartamento de vecindad pequeño apartamento en un edificio de un barrio marginal de la ciudad
tepee > tipi tienda hecha extendiendo pieles de búfalos en postes altos
terrace > terraza franja ancha de tierra escalonada en las laderas de las montañas
terrorism > terrorismo el uso de violencia y crueldad para alcanzar metas políticas
terrorist > terrorista alguien que usa la violencia deliberadamente para difundir el miedo y lograr metas políticas

Tet Offensive > ofensiva del Tet ataques sorpresa del Vietcong a ciudades de Vietnam del Sur el día de año nuevo vietnamita de 1968

The Liberator* > *The Liberator el periódico antiesclavista más influyente del país; fundado en 1831 por William Lloyd Garrison

Thirteenth Amendment > Decimotercera Enmienda enmienda de la Constitución de los Estados Unidos de 1865, que prohibía la esclavitud en toda la nación

Three-Fifths Compromise > Acuerdo de los Tres Quintos acuerdo de la Convención Constitucional según el cual tres quintos de los residentes esclavizados de cada estado serían contados como parte de la población

tolerant > tolerante dispuesto a aceptar creencias que son diferentes de las propias

totalitarian state > estado totalitario país donde un partido único controla el gobierno y todos los aspectos de las vidas de las personas

town meeting > reunión comunitaria en la Nueva Inglaterra colonial, reunión donde los colonos debatían y votaban sobre asuntos del gobierno local

trade union > sindicato asociación de trabajadores calificados formada con el fin de lograr salarios más altos y mejores condiciones laborales

Trail of Tears > Camino de Lágrimas migración forzada de los cheroquíes y otros grupos indígenas de sus hogares en el Sureste a los territorios al oeste del río Mississippi

traitor > traidor persona que traiciona a su país

transatlantic > transatlántico que cruza o abarca el océano Atlántico

transcendentalist > trascendentalista cada uno de los escritores y pensadores de Nueva Inglaterra que creían que las verdades más importantes de la vida trascienden la razón humana, es decir, la sobrepasan

transcontinental railroad > ferrocarril transcontinental ferrocarril que se extiende a través de un continente de una costa a la otra

travois > rastra trineo tirado por un perro o un caballo

treason > traición deslealtad o acciones contra el país propio

Treaty of Guadalupe-Hidalgo > Tratado de Guadalupe Hidalgo tratado de 1848 en el que México cedió California y el Territorio de Nuevo México a los Estados Unidos a cambio de 15 millones de dólares

Treaty of Kanagawa > Tratado de Kanagawa tratado de 1854 firmado entre Japón y los Estados Unidos para abrir los puertos al comercio estadounidense en Japón

Treaty of Paris > Tratado de París acuerdo de 1763 entre Gran Bretaña y Francia que puso fin a la Guerra contra la Alianza Franco-Indígena y estableció la transferencia de gran parte del territorio de América del Norte del control francés al británico

Treaty of Versailles > Tratado de Versalles tratado firmado el 28 de junio de 1919 entre Alemania y los Aliados; asignaba formalmente la responsabilidad por la Primera Guerra Mundial a Alemania y sus aliados

trench warfare > guerra de trincheras combate bélico en el que los soldados se resguardan en trincheras cavadas en el suelo

Triangle Fire > incendio de la fábrica Triangle Shirtwaist incendio ocurrido en 1911 en la fábrica Triangle Shirtwaist de Nueva York, cuyo saldo fue de 150 trabajadores muertos

triangular trade > comercio triangular ruta comercial colonial entre Nueva Inglaterra, África y las Indias Occidentales

tribe > tribu comunidad de personas que comparten costumbres, un idioma y rituales

tribute > tributo pago de una parte débil a una más fuerte a cambio de protección

trust > trust grupo de empresas dirigidas por un mismo consejo directivo

trustbuster > antimonopolio persona dispuesta a destruir todos los trusts

turning point > momento decisivo momento de la historia en el que se produce un cambio rotundo

Tuskegee Airmen > aviadores de Tuskegee pilotos de combate afroamericanos entrenados en Tuskegee, Alabama, durante la Segunda Guerra Mundial

U

U-boat > U-boot tipo de submarino empleado por Alemania durante la Primera Guerra Mundial

ultimately > finalmente al final de un período de tiempo

unalienable rights > derechos inalienables derechos que no pueden ser quitados

unamendable > no enmendable que no se puede modificar

unconstitutional > inconstitucional no permitido por la Constitución

undergo > padecer experimentar algo doloroso o desagradable

Underground Railroad > Tren Clandestino red de abolicionistas que ayudaban en secreto a los afroamericanos a escapar hacia la libertad

undermine > socavar debilitar algo o a alguien o hacerlo menos eficaz

unify > unificar reunir a varias partes para formar una unidad; unir

United Nations > Organización de las Naciones Unidas (ONU) organización mundial fundada en 1945 con la finalidad de proporcionar resoluciones pacíficas a los conflictos internacionales

urbanization > urbanización desplazamiento de la población de las granjas a las ciudades

V

vaquero > vaquero persona española o mexicana que se encargaba del ganado

varied > variado que tiene muchas formas o tipos

vary > variar cambiar o hacer diferente

vaudeville > vodevil tipo de espectáculo muy popular a finales del siglo XIX, que incluía comediantes, rutinas de baile y canto, así como acróbatas

verify > verificar confirmar que algo es cierto; comprobar información

veto > veto rechazo, como cuando el presidente rechaza una ley aprobada por el Congreso

victory garden > jardín para la victoria durante la Segunda Guerra Mundial, jardín de hortalizas sembrado con la finalidad de combatir la escasez de alimentos en los Estados Unidos

vigilante > justicia por mano propia cuando las personas toman la ley en sus propias manos

Virginia > Virginia acorazado que era un barco de guerra usado por la Confederación para atravesar el bloqueo de la Unión

Virginia Plan > Plan de Virginia plan de la Convención Constitucional que proponía un gobierno nacional fuerte con tres poderes y un cuerpo legislativo de dos cámaras

virtue > virtud buena conducta o carácter moral

vital > vital sumamente importante

W

War Hawks > Halcones miembros del Congreso provenientes del Sur y del Oeste que querían ir a la guerra con Gran Bretaña antes de la Guerra de 1812

War Production Board > Junta de Producción Bélica agencia gubernamental creada durante la Segunda Guerra Mundial con la finalidad de asistir a las fábricas para que pasaran de producir bienes de consumo a fabricar materiales bélicos

warmonger > belicista persona que promueve la guerra

Warsaw Pact > Pacto de Varsovia alianza militar, firmada en 1955, entre la Unión Soviética y otras naciones comunistas europeas

Watergate > Watergate escándalo político que incluyó actividades ilegales y que llevó a Nixon a renunciar a la presidencia en 1974

weapon of mass destruction > armas de destrucción masiva (ADM) armas químicas, biológicas o nucleares

Whig Party > Partido Whig partido político organizado por Henry Clay; estaba a favor de que el gobierno federal interviniera en la economía y estimulara los negocios

wholesale > venta al por mayor comprar o vender algo en grandes cantidades a un precio menor

women's rights movement > movimiento por los derechos de las mujeres campaña organizada llevada a cabo con el fin de obtener derechos legales, educativos, laborales y de otro tipo para las mujeres

***Worcester* v. *Georgia* > Worcester contra Georgia** fallo de 1832 de la Corte Suprema que estableció que las leyes estatales no regían en el territorio de los indígenas

writ of assistance > orden de asistencia documento legal que autorizaba a los soldados británicos a inspeccionar el cargamento de los barcos sin razón alguna

Y

Yankees > yankee apodo de los habitantes de Nueva Inglaterra

yellow journalism > periodismo amarillo tipo de periodismo, a menudo tendencioso o falso, basado en historias y encabezados sensacionalistas

Z

Zimmermann telegram > Telegrama de Zimmermann telegrama que el secretario del exterior de Alemania envió en 1917 al embajador alemán en México con la instrucción de urgir al gobierno mexicano a atacar a los Estados Unidos si este país invadía Alemania

Index

The letters after some page numbers refer to the following: *c* = chart; *g* = graph; *m* = map; *p* = picture; *q* = quotation.

B

D

G

H

I

N

Q

R

S

T

U

Acknowledgments

Photography

ELA 0 Hero Images Inc./Alamy Stock Photo; **ELA 1** Hero Images/ Getty Images; **ELA 9** Chassenet/BSIP SA/Alamy Stock Photo; **002–003** Dmitry Rukhlenko - Travel Photos/Alamy Stock Photo; **005T** Culture Club/Getty Images; **05CL** Mikael Utterström/Alamy Stock Photo; **005CR** Christopher Columbus (mosaic), Salviati, Antonio (1816-90)/Palazzo Tursi, Genoa, Italy/Peter Newark American Pictures/Bridgeman Art Library; **005B** Colport/Alamy Stock Photo; **006** Bjorn Landstrom/National Geographic/Getty Images; **007** Jan Wlodarczyk/Alamy Stock Photo; **009** Avalon/World Pictures/Alamy Stock Photo; **010** HIP/Art Resource, NY; **011** Felix Lipov/Alamy Stock Photo; **012** PhotoStock-Israel/Alamy Stock Photo; **013** Zoonar GmbH/ Alamy Stock Photo; **014** Tom Till/Alamy Stock Photo; **015** imageBROKER/Alamy Stock Photo; **018** Louise Murray/ Robertharding/Alamy Stock Photo; **019T** Bettmann/Getty Images; **019B** Buyenlarge/Getty Images; **020T** Male head, Natchez, 1200–1500 (stone), Mississippian culture (c.800–1500)/Private Collection/ Photo Dirk Bakker/Bridgeman Art Library; **020B** Franke Keating/ Science Source/Getty Images; **021** The Last of the Buffalo, c.1888 (oil on canvas), Bierstadt, Albert (1830–1902)/Corcoran Collection, National Gallery of Art, Washington D.C., USA/Gift of Mary (Mrs. Albert) Bierstadt/Bridgeman Art Library; **022** Sissie Brimberg/ National Geographic/Getty Images; **023** Nancy Carter/North Wind Picture Archives; **024** Philip Scalia/Alamy Stock Photo; **025** Fototeca Storica Nazionale/Hulton Archive/Getty Images; **027** World History Archive/Alamy Stock Photo; **029** Lebrecht Music and Arts Photo Library/Alamy Stock Photo; **031** Art Directors & TRIP/Alamy Stock Photo; **032** Mansa Kankan Musa I, 14th century king of the Mali empire (gouache on paper), McBride, Angus (1931–2007)/Private Collection/Look and Learn/Bridgeman Art Library; **033** Abraham Cresques/Getty Images; **034** African Village, published 1806 (lithograph), Alexander, W. (19th century) (after)/Private Collection/ Ken Welsh/Bridgeman Art Library; **035** Mariner's compass in an ivory case, probably Italian, c.1570/National Maritime Museum, London, UK/Bridgeman Art Library; **036** Ivy Close Images/Alamy Stock Photo; **037** Al Schaben/Los Angeles Times/Getty Images; **039** Mikael Utterström/Alamy Stock Photo; **040T** Christian Kober/ Robertharding/Alamy Stock Photo; **040B** Tupungato/Shutterstock; **041** Florilegius/SSPL/Getty Images; **043** Colport/Alamy Stock Photo; **044** Erich Lessing/Art Resource, NY; **045** Incamerastock/Alamy Stock Photo; **046** North Wind Picture Archives/Alamy Stock Photo; **047** Greg Balfour Evans/Alamy Stock Photo; **050–051** A View of Charleston, South Carolina (oil on canvas), Mellish, Thomas (18th century)/Ferens Art Gallery, Hull Museums, UK/Bridgeman Art Library; **053T** Portrait of Anne Hutchinson (1591–1643), American School, (20th century)/Schlesinger Library, Radcliffe Institute, Harvard University/Bridgeman Art library; **053CL** North Wind Picture Archives/Alamy Stock Photo; **053CR** Colport/Alamy Stock Photo; **053B** Dbimages/Alamy Stock Photo; **054** Timewatch Images/ Alamy Stock Photo; **055** Ipsumpix/Corbis Historical/Getty Images; **056** Library of Congress Prints and Photographs Division Washington [LC-USZC4-741]; **057** World History Archive/Alamy Stock Photo; **059** America/Alamy Stock Photo; **061** The Purebred Gentleman and his Spanish Wife Springs the Young Spaniard (oil on canvas), Spanish School, (18th century)/Museo de America, Madrid, Spain/Index/ Bridgeman Art Library; **062** V&A Images/Alamy Stock Photo; **064** World History Archive/Alamy Stock Photo; **065** North Wind Picture Archives/Alamy Stock Photo; **066** North Wind Picture Archives/Alamy Stock Photo; **067** Prisma Archivo/Alamy Stock Photo; **069** Bpk Bildagentur/Art Resource, NY; **071** North Wind Picture Archives/ Alamy Stock Photo; **072** Ira Block/National Geographic/Getty Images; **074** De Luan/Alamy Stock Photo; **076** Everett Collection Inc/ Alamy Stock Photo; **077** North Wind Picture Archives/Alamy Stock Photo; **078** North Wind Picture Archives/Alamy Stock Photo; **079** Brenda Kean/Alamy Stock Photo; **080** North Wind Picture Archives/ Alamy Stock Photo; **081** The Signing of the Mayflower Compact, c.1900 (oil on canvas), Moran, Edward Percy (1862–1935)/Pilgrim Hall Museum, Plymouth, Massachusetts/Bridgeman Art Library; **082** Marka/UIG/Getty Images; **083** Niday Picture Library/Alamy Stock Photo; **084** The NYC collection/Alamy Stock Photo; **086** Portrait of Anne Hutchinson (1591–1643), American School, (20th century)/ Schlesinger Library, Radcliffe Institute, Harvard University/ Bridgeman Art library; **089** Prisma Archivo/Alamy Stock Photo; **090** The Signing of the Mayflower Compact, c.1900 (oil on canvas), Moran, Edward Percy (1862–1935)/Pilgrim Hall Museum, Plymouth, Massachusetts/Bridgeman Art Library; **091** Anonymous Person/AKG Images; **093** Peter Mross/Alltravek/Alamy Stock Photo; **094** Andrew F. Kazmierski/Shutterstock; **095** Niday Picture Library/Alamy Stock Photo; **096** Ken Howard/Alamy Stock Photo; **097** Courthouse, Philadelphia (oil on canvas), Smith, Russell William Thompson (1812–98)/Philadelphia History Museum at the Atwater Kent,/ Courtesy of Historical Society of Pennsylvania Collection,/Bridgeman Art Library; **099** North Wind Picture Archives/Alamy Stock Photo; **100** North Wind Picture Archives/Alamy Stock Photo; **102T** Wildlife GmbH/Alamy Stock Photo; **102B** Everett Historical/Shutterstock; **103** Lanmas/Alamy Stock Photo; **104** North Wind Picture Archives/ Alamy Stock Photo; **105** North Wind Picture Archives/Alamy Stock Photo; **108** Pictorial Press Ltd/Alamy Stock Photo; **109** Everett Historical/Shutterstock; **110** North Wind Picture Archives; **111** MPI/ Getty Images; **112** Planetpix/Alamy Stock Photo; **113** Governor Peter Stuyvesant (1592–1672), c.1660 (oil on panel), Couturier, Hendrick (fl.1648–d.c.1684) (attr.)/Collection of the New-York Historical Society, USA/Bridgeman Art Library; **114** CSP_AlienCat/AGE Fotostock; **115** Lebrecht Music and Arts Photo Library/Alamy Photo Stock; **116** Gene Ahrens/Alamy Stock Photo; **117** North Wind Picture Archives/Alamy Stock Photo; **118** North Wind Picture Archives; **119** Dbimages/Alamy Stock Photo; **120** North Wind Picture Archives/ Alamy Stock Photo; **121** RMN-Grand Palais/Art Resource, NY; **123** Scala/Art Resource, NY; **125** North Wind Picture Archives; **128–129** Painting/Alamy Stock Photo; **131T** GL Archive/Alamy Stock Photo; **131CL** Photo Researchers, Inc/Alamy Stock Photo; **131CR** IanDagnall Computing/Alamy Stock Photo; **131B** Lebrecht Music and Arts Photo Library/Alamy Stock Photo; **132** Christian Delbert/Shutterstock; **133** Archive Images/Alamy Stock Photo; **135** Native American trading furs, 1777 (coloured engraving), American School, (18th century)/ Private Collection/Peter Newark American Pictures Bridgeman Images; **136** Pat & Chuck Blackley/Alamy Stock Photo; **138** 19th era/ Alamy Stock Photo; **139** Oronoz/Album/SuperStock; **142** North Wind Picture Archives; **143** North Wind Picture Archives/Alamy Stock Photo; **145** George Grenville (1712–70) (litho), Houston, Richard (1721–75)/Leeds Museums and Galleries (Leeds Art Gallery) U.K./ Bridgeman Art Library; **147** DeAgostini/SuperStock; **148** Historical/ Corbis/Getty Images; **149** North Wind Picture Archives; **150** North Wind Picture Archives/Alamy Stock Photo; **151T** Stock Montage/Getty Images; **151B** Archive Photos/Getty Images; **153L** North Wind Picture Archives/Alamy Stock Photo; **153R** North Wind Picture Archives/Alamy Stock Photo; **154** Photo Researchers, Inc/Alamy Stock Photo; **155** Debu55y/Shutterstock; **156** North Wind Picture Archives; **157** Revere, Paul (1735–1818) (after)/Private Collection/Bridgeman Images; **158** Roberts H. Armstrong/ClassicStock/Alamy Stock Photo; **159** Vlad G/Shutterstock; **161** Lebrecht Music and Arts Photo Library/ Alamy Stock Photo; **163** North Wind Picture Archives/Alamy Stock Photo; **165** North Wind Picture Archives/Alamy Stock Photo; **166** North Wind Picture Archives/Alamy Stock Photo; **167** Digital Image Library/Alamy Stock Photo; **168** GraphicaArtis/Getty Images; **169** Lawcain/Fotolia; **170** Loren File/Alamy Stock Photo; **171** Encyclopaedia Britannica, Inc./Library of Congress/Universal Images Group North America LLC/Alamy Stock Photo; **172** North Wind Picture Archives/Alamy Stock Photo; **173** DomonabikeUSA/Alamy Stock Photo; **174T** General John Stark at the Battle of Bennington, Vermont, 1902 (colour litho), Yohn, Frederick Coffay (1875–1933) (after)/Private Collection/Bridgeman Art Library; **174B** North Wind Picture Archives; **176** Heritage Image Partnership Ltd/Alamy Stock Photo; **177** Photo Researchers, Inc/Alamy Stock Photo; **178** George Washington at Valley Forge, preliminary sketch, 1854 (oil on canvas), Matteson, Tompkins Harrison (1813–84)/Private Collection/Photo Christie's Images/Bridgeman Images; **179** North Wind Picture Archives; **180** North Wind Picture Archives/Alamy Stock Photo; **181T** Kean Collection/Getty Images; **181B** Photo Researchers, Inc/Alamy Stock Photo; **182** The Massacre of Wyoming Valley in July 1778 (colour litho) (detail), Chappel, Alonzo (1828–87) (after)/Private Collection/Peter Newark American Pictures/Bridgeman Art Library; **183** North Wind Picture Archives/Alamy Stock Photo; **184** Visual Arts Library/The Art Gallery Collection/Alamy Stock Photo; **186** North Wind Picture Archives/Alamy Stock Photo; **188** The Museum of the City of New York/Art Resource, NY; **192–193** F11photo/Shutterstock; **195T** IanDagnall Computing/Alamy Stock Photo; **195C** North Wind Picture Archives/Alamy Stock Photo; **195B** Albert Knapp/Alamy Stock Photo; **196** The Metropolitan Museum of Art/Art Resource, NY; **197** Virginia Constitutional Convention of 1829–30 (oil on panel), Catlin, George (1796–1872)/Virginia Historical Society, Richmond, Virginia, USA/Bridgeman Art Library; **198** State of Massachusetts in Convention, State Constitution, 16th June 1780 (litho), American School, (18th century)/Gilder Lehrman Collection, New York, USA/ Bridgeman Images; **200** Lebrecht Music and Arts Photo Library/ Alamy Stock Photo; **202** North Wind Picture Archives/Alamy Stock Photo; **203** North Wind Picture Archives/Alamy Stock Photo; **204** North Wind Picture Archives/Alamy Stock Photo; **205** SuperStock; **206** World History Archive/Alamy Stock Photo; **209** North Wind Picture Archives/Alamy Stock Photo; **210** SuperStock/Getty Images; **211** Culture Club/Getty Images; **212** SuperStock/Alamy Stock Photo; **213** The Bill of Rights presented to William and Mary (engraving), English School, (19th century)/Private Collection/Look and Learn/Bridgeman Images; **214** World History Archive/Alamy Stock Photo; **215** Lebrecht Music and Arts Photo Library/Alamy Stock Photo; **216** GraphicaArtis/ Archive Photos/Getty Images; **217** The Metropolitan Museum of Art/ Art Resource, NY; **218** Albert Knapp/Alamy Stock Photo; **219** Courtesy of the New York Public Library; **220** National Archives and Records Administration; **221** North Wind Picture Archives; **222** Hulton Archive/MPI/Getty Images; **223** Courtesy of the New York Public Library; **225** Michael Ventura/Alamy Stock Photo; **226** Sean Rayford/ Images News/Getty Images; **227** Ken Cedeno/Corbis/Getty Images; **229** Orhan Cam/Shutterstock; **230** Tom Williams/CQ Roll Call/ Newscom; **231** Kim Warp The New Yorker Collection/The Cartoon Bank; **232** Bastiaan Slabbers/Alamy Stock Photo; **234** Roger L. Wollenberg/Pool/Corbis/Getty Images; **236** Artley Cartoons; **237** Jim West/Alamy Stock Photo; **239** SuperStock; **241** Ian G Dagnall/Alamy Stock Photo; **242** Andrew Cullen/Reuters/Alamy Stock Photo; **243** David Wall/Alamy Stock Photo; **244** Marmaduke St. John/Alamy Stock Photo; **245** National Geographic Creative/Alamy Stock Photo; **247** Kevin Shields/Alamy Stock Photo; **248** Roger Bacon/Reuters/ Alamy Stock Photo; **249** Spencer Grant/Alamy Stock Photo; **250** RosaIreneBetancourt 1/Alamy Stock Photo; **252** Kaisar Andreas/ Alamy Stock Photo; **253** Albert Knapp/Alamy Stock Photo; **256–257** Lewis & Clark on the Lower Columbia River, 1905 (oil on canvas), Russell, Charles Marion (1865–1926)/Private Collection/Peter Newark American Pictures/Bridgeman Art library; **259T** IanDagnall Computing/Alamy Stock Photo; **259CL** North Wind Picture Archives/ Alamy Stock Photo; **259CR** IanDagnall Computing/Alamy Stock Photo; **259B** North Wind Picture Archives/Alamy Stock Photo; **260** White House Photo/Alamy Stock Photo; **261** Science Source; **262** World History Archive/Alamy Stock Photo; **265** Everett Collection Inc/ Alamy Stock Photo; **266** Trekandshoot/Shutterstock; **267** Whiskey rebels escorting a tarred and feathered tax collector from his burning homestead (colour litho), American School, (18th century) (after)/ Private Collection/Peter Newark American Pictures/Bridgeman Art Library; **268** Lanmas/Alamy Stock Photo; **271** The Print Collector/ Glow Images; **272** Everett Collection Historical/Alamy Stock Photo; **273** Sipley/ClassicStock/Alamy Stock Photo; **274L** GL Archive/Alamy Stock Photo; **274R** IanDagnall Computing/Alamy Stock Photo; **275L** North Wind Picture Archives/Alamy Stock Photo; **275R** North Wind Picture Archives/Alamy Stock Photo; **276** Library of Congress Prints and Photographs Division Washington [LC-DIG-ppmsca-31832]; **278** Kean Collection/Getty Images; **279** IanDagnall Computing/Alamy Stock Photo; **281** North Wind Picture Archives/Alamy Stock Photo; **282** Satirising the XYZ Affair, 1797 (colour litho), American School, (18th century)/Archives du Ministere des Affaires Etrangeres, Paris, France/Archives Charmet/Bridgeman Images; **283** National Portrait Gallery, Smithsonian Institution/Art Resource, NY; **284** Jefferson, Thomas/Library of Congress Prints and Photographs Division Washington; **286** Bettmann/Getty Images; **287T** North Wind Picture Archives/Alamy Stock Photo; **287B** GL Archive/Alamy Stock Photo; **288** North Wind Picture Archives/Alamy Stock Photo; **289** Wiskerke/ Alamy Stock Photo; **290** Irene Abdou/Alamy Stock Photo; **292** Bettmann/Getty Images; **293** Bettmann/Getty Images; **294** View of New Orleans from the Plantation of Marigny, 1803 (oil on canvas), Woiseri, J. L. Bouquet de (fl.1797–1815)/Chicago History Museum, USA/Bridgeman Art Library; **297T** North Wind Picture Archives/ Alamy Stock Photo; **297B** Witold Skrypczak/Alamy Stock Photo; **299** The Hongs at Canton, before 1820 (oil on ivory), Chinnery, George (1774–1852) (follower of)/Ferens Art Gallery, Hull Museums, UK/ Bridgeman Images; **300** North Wind Picture Archives/Alamy Stock Photo; **302** Stevemart/Shutterstock; **303** North Wind Picture Archives/ Alamy Stock Photo; **304** North Wind Picture Archives/Alamy Stock Photo; **306** JT Vintage/Glasshouse Images/Alamy Stock Photo; **307** Kurz & Allison/Library of Congress Prints and Photographs Division Washington [LC-DIG-pga-01891]; **308** Cosmo Condina North America/Alamy Stock Photo; **309** Stock Montage/Getty Images; **310** Bettmann/Getty Images; **311** Everett Collection Historical/Alamy Stock Photo; **312** Our Flag was still there, War of 1812; The Defense of Fort McHenry. September 13–14, 1814, 2012 (oil on canvas), Troiani, Don (b.1949)/Private Collection/Bridgeman Art Library; **314** Carol M Highsmith/Library of Congress Prints and Photographs Division Washington [LC-DIG-highsm-09904]; **315** Ken Welsh/Design Pics/ Newscom; **316** Niday Picture Library/Alamy Stock Photo; **317** North Wind Picture Archives/Alamy Stock Photo; **318L** North Wind Picture Archives/Alamy Stock Photo; **318C** Classic Image/Alamy Stock Photo; **318R** Stock Montage/Getty Images; **319** CPC Collection/Alamy Stock Photo; **320** Mansell/The LIFE Picture Collection/Getty Images; **322** North Wind Picture Archives/Alamy Stock Photo; **323** Interfoto/Alamy Stock Photo; **325** Everett Collection Historical/Alamy Stock Photo; **326** Bettmann/Getty Images; **327** Bob Pardue - SC/Alamy Stock Photo; **328** Bank of Pennsylvania, c.1804 (oil on canvas), American School, (19th century)/Philadelphia History Museum at the Atwater Kent,/ Courtesy of Historical Society of Pennsylvania Collection/Bridgeman Art Library; **332–33** World History Archive/Alamy Stock Photo; **335T** Everett Collection Inc/Alamy Stock Photo; **335C** MPI/Getty Images; **335B** Newberry Library/SuperStock; **336** World History Archive/ Alamy Stock Photo; **337** Everett Collection Inc/Alamy Stock Photo; **338** Heritage Image Partnership Ltd/Alamy Stock Photo; **339** North Wind Picture Archives; **340L** Everett Collection Inc/Alamy Stock Photo; **340CL** SuperStock/Getty Images; **340CR** Kean Collection/ Staff/Getty Images; **340R** Stock Montage/Getty Images; **341** Library of Congress Print and Division[LC-DIG-pga-06984]; **342** Francis G. Mayer/Corbis Historical/Getty Images; **344** Library of Congress Prints and Photographs Division [LC-USZ62-2340]; **345** North Wind Picture Archives; **346** Danita Delimont/Alamy Stock Photo; **347** North Wind Picture Archives; **348** IanDagnall Computing/Alamy Stock Photo; **349** Everett Collection Historical/Alamy Stock Photo; **350L** North Wind Picture Archives/Alamy Stock Photo; **350C** North Wind Picture Archives/Alamy Stock Photo; **350R** The Print Collector/Alamy Stock Photo; **351** Niday Picture Library/Alamy Stock Photo; **352** ClassicStock/Alamy Stock Photo; **354** 'Jackson slaying the many headed monster', 1828 (colour litho), American School, (19th century)/Private Collection/Peter Newark American Pictures/ Bridgeman Images; **355** Herbert Orth/The LIFE Picture Collection/ Getty Images; **356** Bettmann/Getty Images; **357** Old Paper Studios/ Alamy Stock Photo; **358** Bygone Collection/Alamy Stock Photo; **360** North Wind Picture Archives/Alamy Stock Photo; **362** National Portrait Gallery, Smithsonian Institution/Art Resource, NY; **363** Nancy Carter/North Wind Picture Archives; **364** Newberry Library/ SuperStock; **366** Terry Smith Images/Alamy Stock Photo; **367** Willard R. Culver/National Geographic/Getty Images; **368** W H Jackson/MPI/ Getty Images; **372** Ian Dagnall/Alamy Stock Photo; **374** North Wind Picture Archives/Alamy Stock Photo; **375** Leon Werdinger/Alamy Stock Photo; **376** Everett Collection Inc/Alamy Stock Photo; **378** Jim Beckwourth (engraving) (b/w photo), Janet, Ange-Louis (Janet-Lange) (1815–72) (after)/Bibliotheque des Arts Decoratifs, Paris, France/ Archives Charmet/Bridgeman Art Library; **380** Witold Skrypczak/ Alamy Stock Photo; **381** North Wind Picture Archives/Alamy Stock Photo; **383** Interfoto/History/Alamy Stock Photo; **385** Ian Shaw/ Alamy Stock Photo; **386** North Wind Picture Archives/Alamy Stock Photo; **387** Carol M. Highsmith/Library of Congress Prints and Photographs Division [LC-DIG-highsm-27900]; **388** World History Archive/Alamy Stock Photo; **389** Bettmann/Getty Images; **392** Huntington Library/SuperStock; **393** Everett Collection Historical/

Alamy Stock Photo; **397** North Wind Picture Archives/Alamy Stock Photo; **398** Hulton Archive/Getty Images; **399** Robin Runck/Alamy Stock Photo; **400** Underwood Archives/Archive Photos/Getty Images; **401** Everett Collection Historical/Alamy Stock Photo; **404–405** Port of New Orleans, engraved by D.G. Thompson (coloured engraving), Waud, Alfred Rudolph (1828–91) (after)/Bibliotheque Nationale, Paris, France/Bridgeman Art Library; **407T** Stock Montage/Archive Photos/Getty Images; **407C** GL Archive/Alamy Stock Photo; **407B** VCG Wilson/Historical/Corbis/Getty Images; **408** GL Archive/Alamy Stock Photo; **409** Bettmann/Getty Images; **410** Chronicle/Alamy Stock Photo; **411** Frank Vetere/Alamy Stock Photo; **412** M841 Mississippi Contract Rifle by Eli Whitney/Private Collection/Photo Don Troiani/Bridgeman Art Library; **413** Historical/Contributor/Corbis Historical/Getty Images; **414** Library of Congress Prints and Photographs Division Washington; **415** Library of Congress Prints and Photographs Division Washington; **416** Weaving on Power Looms, Cotton factory floor, engraved by James Tingle (fl.1830–60) c.1830 (litho), Allom, Thomas (1804–72) (after)/Private Collection/Ken Welsh/Bridgeman Art Library; **417** Stock Montage/Archive Photos/Getty Images; **418L** Interfoto History/Alamy Stock Photo; **418R** Photo Researchers, Inc/Alamy Stock Photo; **419** De Agostini Picture Library/De Agostini Editore/AGE Fotostock; **420** Telegraphe de Hughes/Photo CCI/Bridgeman Art Library; **421L** Stock Montage/Archive Photos/Getty Images; **421R** Bettmann/Getty Images; **422** Everett Collection Inc/CSU Archives/Alamy Stock Photo; **424** Photo Researchers, Inc/Alamy Stock Photo; **425** UIG/Underwood Archives/Akg-images; **426** Frances/Everett Collection/Newscom; **427** Attack on a Potato Store in Ireland, c.1845 (engraving) (b&w photo), English School, (19th century)/Private Collection/Bridgeman Art Library; **428** Don Smetzer/Alamy Stock Photo; **429** Vespasian/Alamy Stock Photo; **430** Courtesy of the New York Public Library; **431** Ball Miwako/Alamy Stock Photo; **432** North Wind Picture Archives/Alamy Stock Photo; **433** North Wind Picture Archives/AP Images; **436** Franz Marc Frei/Look Die Bildagentur der Fotografen Gmbh/Alamy Stock Photo; **437** North Wind Picture Archives/Alamy Stock Photo; **438** Library of Congress Prints and Photographs Division Washington [LC-DIG-pga-04518]; **439** Hulton Archive/Staff/Getty Images; **440** North Wind Picture Archives/The Image Works; **441** Slave harness with bell (b/w photo), American School/Philadelphia History Museum at the Atwater Kent,/Courtesy of Historical Society of Pennsylvania Collection/Bridgeman Art Library; **442** Stock Montage/Getty Images; **443** Herbert Orth/The LIFE Picture Collection/Getty Images; **444** American Anti-Slavery Society/Library of Congress Rare Book and Special Collections Division Washington [LC-USZC4-5321]; **445** North Wind Picture Archives/Alamy Stock Photo; **446** Bailey-Cooper Photography/Alamy Stock Photo; **448** Niday Picture Library/Alamy Stock Photo; **449** North Wind Picture Archives; **451** Robert Martin/Alamy Stock Photo; **452** North Wind Picture Archives/Alamy Stock Photo; **454** MPI/Getty Images; **455** North Wind Picture Archives; **456** North Wind Picture Archives/Alamy Stock Photo; **457** Collection of the Orleans County Grammar Schools.; **458** Bettmann/Getty Images; **459** Akg-images/Newscom; **460** Bettmann/Getty Images; **461** VCG Wilson/Historical/Corbis/Getty Images; **463** Everett Collection Inc./AGE Fotostock; **464** North Wind Picture Archives/Alamy Stock Photo; **465** Niday Picture Library/Alamy Stock Photo; **466** Liszt Images/Artokoloro Quint Lox Limited/Alamy Stock Photo; **467** IanDagnall Computing/Alamy Stock Photo; **468** Moby Dick, English School, (20th century)/Private Collection/Look and Learn/Bridgeman Images; **469T** Travelib history/Alamy Stock Photo; **469B** Glasshouse Images/Newscom; **470** Zachary Frank/Alamy Stock Photo; **471** Photo Researchers, Inc/Alamy Stock Photo; **474–475** John Parrot/Stocktrek Images, Inc./Alamy Stock Photo; **477T** Hesler, Alexander/Library of Congress Prints and Photographs Division [LC-DIG-ppmsca-23723]; **477CL** Ames F. Gibson/Buyenlarge/Getty Images; **477C** Everett Collection Inc/Alamy Stock Photo; **477CR** World History Archive/Alamy Stock Photo; **477B** Photo Researchers, Inc/Alamy Stock Photo; **478** Abraham Lincoln with Allan Pinkerton and Major General John A. McClernand, 1862 (b/w photo), Gardner, Alexander (1821–82)/Collection of the New-York Historical Society, USA/Bridgeman Art Library; **479** Jerry Pinkney/National Geographic Creative/Alamy Stock Photo; **481** North Wind Picture Archives/Alamy Stock Photo; **483** Picture History/Newscom; **484** North Wind Picture Archives/Alamy Stock Photo; **486** Fotosearch/Stringer/Getty Images; **487** Bettmann/Getty Images; **488** North Wind Picture Archives/Alamy Stock Photo; **489** North Wind Picture Archives/Alamy Stock Photo; **491** North Wind Picture Archives/Alamy Stock Photo; **492** Photo Researchers, Inc./Alamy Stock Photo; **493** Pictorial Press Ltd/Alamy Stock Photo; **494** North Wind Picture Archives/Alamy Stock Photo; **495** Library of Congress Prints and Photographs Division Washington[LC-DIG-ds-00859]; **496** When They Were Young: Abraham Lincoln, Jackson, Peter (1922–2003)/Private Collection/Look and Learn/Bridgeman Art Library; **497** Abraham Lincoln (1809–65) in public debate with Stephen A. Douglas (1813–61) in Illinois, 1858 (colour litho), American School, (19th century)/Private Collection/Peter Newark American Pictures/Bridgeman Art Library; **499** Photo Researchers, Inc/Alamy Stock Photo; **501** North Wind Picture Archives; **503** The New York Historical Society/Contributor/Getty Images; **504** Pictorial Press Ltd/Alamy Stock Photo; **505L** Lincoln Lantern used for Presidential Campaign, 1864 (tin and glass with paint), American School, (19th century)/Collection of the New-York Historical Society, USA/Bridgeman Art Library; **505R** Nancy Carter/North Wind Picture Archives; **506** Popperfoto/Getty Images; **509** The Lexington of 1861, pub. by Currier & Ives, c.1861 (colour litho), American School, (19th century)/American Antiquarian Society, Worcester, Massachusetts, USA/Bridgeman Images; **510L** Hesler, Alexander/Library of Congress Prints and Photographs Division[LC-DIG-ppmsca-23723]; **510R** Photo Researchers, Inc/Alamy Stock Photo; **511** Glasshouse Images/JT Vintage/Alamy Stock Photo; **513** John Parrot/Stocktrek Images/Alamy Stock Photo; **514** Library of Congress Prints and Photographs Division [LC-DIG-ppmsca-35625]; **516T** GL Archive/Alamy Stock Photo; **516B** Mai/The LIFE Images Collection/Getty Images; **517** Niday Picture Library/Alamy Stock Photo; **518** Kean Collection/Archive Photos/Getty Images; **519** North Wind Picture Archives/Alamy Stock Photo; **520** 'Come and Join Us Brothers', Union recruitment poster aimed at Black volunteers (colour litho), American School, (19th century)/Private Collection/Peter Newark American Pictures/Bridgeman Art Library; **522** H. Armstrong Roberts/ClassicStock/Alamy Stock Photo; **523** Pete Cutter/Alamy Stock Photo; **524** Two Amputee Officers , 4th Vermont Vols. wounded at Petersburg, VA/Private Collection/Photo Don Troiani/Bridgeman Art Library; **525** The Protected Art Archive/Alamy Stock Photo; **526** Bettmann/Getty Images; **528** Glasshouse Images/Alamy Stock Photo; **529** Everett Collection Historical/Alamy Stock Photo; **530** Clara Barton tending wounded during the American Civil War (colour litho), American School, (19th century)/Private Collection/Peter Newark American Pictures/Bridgeman Art Library; **531** Fotosearch/Stringer/Getty Images; **533** Tom Lovell/National Geographic Creative/Alamy Stock Photo; **534** The Print Collector/Alamy Stock Photo; **535** Tim Sloan/APF/Getty Images; **536** Abraham Lincoln with Union Officers 1862/Universal History Archive/UIG/Bridgeman Art Library; **537** Niday Picture Library/Alamy Stock Photo; **538** Fototeca Gilardi/Hulton Archive/Getty Images; **539** Everett Collection Inc/Alamy Stock Photo; **540L** Courtesy U.S. National Archives; **540R** American Civil War (1861–1865): view of the ruins in Richmond, Virginia, after fall of the city april–june 1865, photo by Alexander Gardner/Photo PVDE/Bridgeman Art Library; **541** Timothy H. O'Sullivan/U.S. Library of Congress/Handout/Getty Images; **543** Ivy Close Images/Alamy Stock Photo; **546–547** BKGD George N. Barnard/George Eastman House/Getty Images; **547** Library of Congress Prints & Photographs Division Washington [LC-USF34-044277-D]; **549T** Prisma Archivo/Alamy Stock Photo; **549C** Pictorial Press Ltd/Alamy Stock Photo; **549B** Everett Collection/Newscom; **550** North Wind Picture Archives/Alamy Stock Photo; **551** LOC Photo/Alamy Stock Photo; **552** Hulton Archive/Getty Images; **553** Lightfoot/Getty Images; **554** Historical/Corbis/Getty Images; **555** Photo Researchers, Inc/Alamy Stock Photo; **556** Library of Congress Prints and Photographs Division Washington [LC-DIG-ppmsca-11312]; **557** Courtesy The New York Public Library; **558** Niday Picture Library/Alamy Stock Photo; **559** Charles Sumner (1811–74), US Senator; photo by George Warren, Boston (albumen print), American Photographer, (19th century)/American Antiquarian Society, Worcester, Massachusetts, USA/Bridgeman Art Library; **560** North Wind Picture Archives/Alamy Stock Photo; **563** MPI/Getty Images; **564** Universal Images Group North America LLC/Encyclopaedia Britannica, Inc./Library of Congress/Alamy Stock Photo; **566** Library of Congress [LC-USZ62-105555]; **567** Pictorial

Press Ltd/Alamy Stock Photo; **568** Everett Collection/Newscom; **569** GL Archive/Alamy Stock Photo; **570** Old Paper Studios/Alamy Stock Photo; **571** Bettmann/Getty Images; **572** Hulton Archive/Getty Images; **574** Hulton Archive/Getty Images; **576** North Wind Picture Archives/Alamy Stock Photo; **577** Courtesy of the New York Public Library; **579** Artokoloro Quint Lox Limited/Alamy Stock Photo; **582–583** Chris Hunter/Schenectady Museum; Hall of Electrical History Foundation/Corbis Historical/Getty Images; **585T** Pictorial Press Ltd/Alamy Stock Photo; **585CL** Photo Researchers, Inc/Alamy Stock Photo; **585CR** Classic Image/Alamy Stock Photo; **585B** Photo Researchers, Inc/Alamy Stock Photo; **586** Andrey Yurlov/Shutterstock; **587** AKG Images; **588** Bettmann/Getty Images; **589** Fotosearch/Getty Images; **590** World History Archive/Alamy Stock Photo; **591** Topham/The Image Works; **592** Everett Collection Inc/Alamy Stock Photo; **593** PF-(usna)/Alamy Stock Photo; **594** Fotosearch/Getty Images; **595** Kean Collection/Archive Photos/Getty Images; **597** Photo Researchers, Inc/Alamy Stock Photo; **598** Bettmann/Getty Images; **600** The Stampede, 1912 (oil on canvas), Leigh, William Robinson (1866–1955)/Private Collection/Peter Newark Western Americana/Bridgeman Art Library; **601** Bettmann/Getty Images; **602** MPI/Archive Photos/Getty Images; **603** Buyenlarge/Getty Images; **604** North Wind Picture Archives/Alamy Stock Photo; **605T** Deyan Georgiev - Premium RF/Alamy Stock Photo; **605B** Akg-images/Superstock; **606** Kean Collection/Archive Photos/Getty Images; **608** Library of Congress Prints and Photographs Division Washington [LC-DIG-ppmsca-28848]; **609** Niday Picture Library/Alamy Stock Photo; **610** World History Archive/Alamy Stock Photo; **611T** Stephen J. Krasemann/All Canada Photos/Alamy Stock Photo; **611B** The Buffalo Hunt, c.1832 (coloured engraving), Catlin, George (1796–1872)/Bibliotheque Nationale, Paris, France/Bridgeman Art Library; **612** MPI/Getty Images; **613** DeAgostini/Getty Images; **614** John N. Choate/MPI/Getty Images; **615** North Wind Picture Archives; **616** Archive Images/Alamy Stock Photo; **617L** Classic Image/Alamy Stock Photo; **617R** GL Archive/Alamy Stock Photo; **618** Education Images/UIG/Getty Images; **619** Furlong Photography/Alamy Stock Photo; **620** Classic Image/Alamy Stock Photo; **622** Everett Collection Inc/Alamy Stock Photo; **625** Glasshouse Images/Circa Images/Alamy Stock Photo; **626** Philip Scalia/Alamy Stock Photo; **627** Library of Congress Prints and Photographs Division Washington [LC-USZC4-494]; **629** Archive Pics/Alamy Stock Photo; **631** Everett Collection Historical/Alamy Stock Photo; **632** Vintage Images/Alamy Stock Photo; **633** North Wind Picture Archives/Alamy Stock Photo; **635** Franklin D. Roosevelt Library Photographs, 1870–2004/National Archives and Records Administration; **637** North Wind Picture Archives/Alamy Stock Photo; **638** Photo Researchers, Inc/Alamy Stock Photo; **639** Wm. J. Barker/Library of Congress Geography and Map Division Washington; **640** Pictorial Press Ltd/Alamy Stock Photo; **641** Mondadori Portfolio/Newscom; **642** SSPL/Getty Images; **643T** The Print Collector/Hulton Archive/Getty Images; **643B** CSU Archives/Everett Collection/Alamy Stock Photo; **644** Bettmann/Getty Images; **645** Mondadori Portfolio/Newscom; **648–649** Photo Researchers, Inc/Alamy Stock Photo; **650** Richard Broadwell/Alamy Stock Photo; **651T** Granamour Weems Collection/Alamy Stock Photo; **651CL** H.S. Photos/Alamy Stock Photo; **651CR** GL Archive/Alamy Stock Photo; **651B** North Wind Picture Archives/Alamy Stock Photo; **652** Glasshouse Images/JT Vintage/Alamy Stock Photo; **653** Photo Researchers, Inc/Alamy Stock Photo; **654** Keystone-France/Gamma-Keystone/Getty Images; **655** Josef Hanus/Shutterstock; **656** FPG/Getty Images; **657** Library of Congress Prints and Photographs Division Washington [LC-DIG-highsm-25215]; **660** North Wind Picture Archives/Alamy Stock Photo; **661** Everett Collection Historical/Alamy Stock Photo; **663** Library of Congress Prints and Photographs Division Washington [LC-DIG-det-4a25614]; **665** RoseOfSharon/Alamy Stock Photo; **666** Bettmann/Getty Images; **667** Library of Congress [LC-USZ62-107110]; **668** Bettmann/Getty Images; **670** Martin Thomas Photography/Alamy Stock Photo; **671** Bettmann/Getty Images; **672** Library of Congress Prints and Photographs Division Washington [LC-USZ62-7622]; **673** North Wind Picture Archives/Alamy Stock Photo; **674** Everett Collection Inc/Alamy Stock Photo; **675** Ivy Close Images/Alamy Stock Photo; **676** Sausage department at Armour and Company's meatpacking factory, Chicago, Illinois, USA. Men and boys stuffing sausage skins. Photograph c1893./Universal History Archive/UIG/Bridgeman Art Library; **677** Library of Congress [LC-USZ62-106669]; **680** George Rinhart/Corbis/Getty Images; **681** Akg-images/Newscom; **682** Library of Congress [LC-DIG-ppmsca-25680]; **684** Bettmann/Getty Images; **686** CSU Archives/Everett Collection/Newscom; **687** Everett Collection Historical/Alamy Stock Photo; **688** North Wind Picture Archives/Alamy Stock Photo; **690** GL Archive/Alamy Stock Photo; **691** Topical Press Agency/Hulton Archive/Getty Images; **692** GL Archive/Alamy Stock Photo; **693** PhotoEdit.Inc; **694** CH Collection/Alamy Stock Photo; **696** American Stock Archive/Getty Images; **698** Library of Congress [LC-USZ62-134202]; **699** National Baseball Hall of Fame Library/MLB Photos/Getty Images; **700** Bettmann/Getty Images; **701** Library of Congress Prints and Photographs Division Washington [LC-DIG-det-4a18131]; **702** Bettmann/Getty Images; **703** PhotoQuest/Getty Images; **704** Picture History/Newscom; **706T** Library of Congress [LC-USZ62-75620]; **706B** Cincinnati Museum Center/Getty Images; **707** Rischgitz/Getty Images; **708** Active Museum/Alamy Stock Photo; **709** Everett Collection Inc/Alamy Stock Photo; **712–713** Lebrecht Music and Arts Photo Library/Alamy Stock Photo; **715T** Photo Resource Hawaii/Alamy Stock Photo; **715CL** Everett Historical/Shutterstock; **715CR** Library of Congress Prints and Photographs Division Washington [LC-DIG-ppmsca-36082]; **715B** Library of Congress Prints and Photographs Division Washington [LC-DIG-det-4a26353]; **716** Image courtesy Jacques Descloitres, MODIS Land Rapid Response Team at NASA GSFC; **717** US Japan Fleet, Commodore Perry carrying 'The Gospel of God to the Heathen, 1853' (oil on canvas), Evans, James Guy (19th Century)/Chicago History Museum, USA/Bridgeman Art Library; **719** Bettmann/Getty Images; **722** Courtesy of U.S. Navy; **724** Rolf Richardson/Alamy Stock Photo; **725** Library of Congress Prints and Photographs Division Washington [LC-USZ62-108295]; **726** Bettmann/Getty Images; **727** Bettmann/Getty Images; **728** The Print Collector/Getty Images; **729** Chronicle/Alamy Stock Photo; **730** Bettmann/Getty Images; **731** North Wind Picture Archives/Alamy Stock Photo; **733** Everett Historical/Shutterstock; **734** Library of Congress Prints and Photographs Division Washington [LC-DIG-ppmsca-25667]; **735** North Wind Picture Archives/Alamy Stock Photo; **736** AP Images; **737** Everett Historical/Shutterstock; **739T** Library of Congress Prints and Photographs Division Washington [LC-DIG-ppmsca-36082]; **739B** Elena Fernandez Z/Shutterstock; **740** 'No Molly-Coddling Here', 1904 (litho), American School, (20th century)/Private Collection/J. T. Vintage/Bridgeman Art Library; **742** Library of Congress/Corbis/VCG/Getty Images; **743** Library of Congress Prints and Photographs Division Washington [LC-DIG-ggbain-10234]; **744** Buyenlarge/UIG/AGE Fotostock; **746L** Chronicle/Alamy Stock Photo; **746R** World History Archive/Alamy Stock Photo; **749** Library of Congress/Corbis/VCG/Getty Images; **750** Everett Collection Historical/Alamy Stock Photo; **751** Akg-images/Alamy Stock Photo; **752** Pictorial Press Ltd/Alamy Stock Photo; **754** Library of Congress; **756** The Keasbury-Gordon Photograph Archive/Alamy Stock Photo; **757** Library of Congress Prints and Photographs Division Washington [LC-USZC4-10232]; **758** Akg-images; **759** Akg-images; **760** Everett Historical/Shutterstock; **761** Photos 12/Alamy Stock Photo; **762** World History Archive/Alamy Stock Photo; **764** National Archives and Records Administrations; **765** Everett Collection Inc/Alamy Stock Photo; **766** PF-(usna)/Alamy Stock Photo; **768** American Photo Archive/Alamy Stock Photo; **769** Library of Congress Prints and Photographs Division Washington [LC-USZC2-6247]; **770** IanDagnall Computing/Alamy Stock Photo; **771** World History Archive/Alamy Stock Photo; **773** Mondadori Collection/UIG Universal Images Group/Newscom; **774** Library of Congress Prints and Photographs Division Washington [LC-USZ62-70331]; **775** Library of Congress Prints and Photographs Division Washington [LC-USZC2-6247]; **778–779** BKGD Lordprice Collection/Alamy Stock Photo; **779** Library of Congress Prints and Photographs Division [LC-USZ62-109777]; **781T** Elias Goldensky/Library of Congress Prints and Photographs Division Washington [LC-USZ62-117121]; **781CL** John Frost Newspapers/Alamy Stock Photo; **781CR** Folio/Alamy Stock Photo; **781B** Everett Collection Inc/Alamy Stock Photo; **782** Everett Collection Inc/Alamy Stock Photo; **783** Underwood Archives/Getty Images; **784** Library of Congress Prints and Photographs Division Washington [LC-DIG-ds-08077]; **787** Everett Collection Inc/Alamy Stock Photo; **788** Bettmann/Getty Images; **789** Library of Congress Prints and Photographs Division Washington [LC-USZ62-100382]; **791** Library of Congress Prints and Photographs Division Washington [LC-USZ62-76150]; **792** Library of Congress Prints and Photographs Division Washington [LC-USZ62-111335]; **794** Glasshouse Images/ Alamy Stock Photo; **795** Songquan Deng/Alamy Stock Photo; **796** AF Archive/Alamy Stock Photo; **797** Bettmann/Getty Images; **798** General Photographic Agency/Hulton Archive/Getty Images; **799T** Everett Collection Inc/Alamy Stock Photo; **799B** Hulton Archive/Getty Images; **800** Sueddeutsche Zeitung Photo/Alamy Stock Photo; **801** George Rinhart/Corbis/Getty Images; **803** Historic Florida/Alamy Stock Photo; **804** Everett Collection Inc/Alamy Stock Photo; **805** Photo Researchers, Inc/Alamy Stock Photo; **806** Heritage Image Partnership Ltd/Stapleton Historical Collection/Alamy Stock Photo; **807** Pictorial Press Ltd/Alamy Stock Photo; **808** Everett Collection Inc/Alamy Stock Photo; **809** Everett Collection Historical/Alamy Stock Photo; **811** AP Images; **813** Heritage Image Partnership Ltd/Stapleton Historical Collection/Alamy Stock Photo; **814** John Frost Newspapers/Alamy Stock Photo; **816** Interfoto/Alamy Stock Photo; **817** National Archives and Records Administration; **818** National Archives and Records Administration; **819** UbjsP/Shutterstock; **820** Underwood Archives/ Archive Photos/Getty Images; **821** Alexander Dux/Library of Congress Prints and Photographs Division Washington [LC-USZC4-4243]; **822** Keystone Pictures USA/Alamy Stock Photo; **823** Everett Collection/CSU Archives/Newscom; **825** Library of Congress Prints and Photographs Division Washington [LC-DIG-ppmsca-23061]; **826** Library of Congress Prints and Photographs Division Washington [LC-DIG-fsa-8b29516]; **828** Bettmann/Getty Images; **829** Fotosearch/Getty Images; **830** J.N. 'Ding' Darling/Bettman/Getty Images; **832** Library of Congress Prints and Photographs Division Washington [LC-DIG-ppmsca-07216]; **833** Elias Goldensky/Library of Congress Prints and Photographs Division Washington [LC-USZ62-117121]; **834** Pictorial Press Ltd/Alamy Stock Photo; **836T** Everett Collection Historical/Alamy Stock Photo; **836B** Library of Congress Prints and Photographs Division Washington [LC-USZ62-68542]; **837** Everett Collection/Newscom; **838** Afro American Newspapers/Gado/Getty Images; **839** Library of Congress Prints and Photographs Division Washington [LC-USZ62-119854]; **840** AF Archive/Alamy Stock Photo; **841** Art © Figge Art Museum, successors to the Estate of Nan Wood Graham/Licensed by VAGA, New York, NY/Danita Delimont/Alamy Stock Photo; **844–845** Patrol of 2nd US Marine Raider Battalion on Bourgainville Island, November 1943 (b/w photo), American Photographer, (20th century)/Private Collection/Peter Newark Pictures/Bridgeman Art Library; **847T** VintageCorner/Alamy Stock Photo; **847CL** U.S. Navy/ The LIFE Picture Collection/Getty Images; **847CR** Library of Congress Prints and Photographs Division Washington [LC-USZ62-64419]; **847B** Historical/Corbis/Getty Images; **848** Emily Russell/Alamy Stock Photo; **849** Dpa picture alliance/Alamy Stock Photo; **851** World History Archive/Alamy Stock Photo; **852T** Universal History Archive/ UIG/Getty Images; **852B** Universal Images Group/Sovfoto/AKG-Images; **854** Everett Collection Historical/Alamy Stock Photo; **855** Department of Defense. Department of the Navy. Naval Photographic Center/National Archives and Records Administration; **858** Lordprice Collection/Alamy Stock Photo; **860T** Fox Photos/Getty Images; **860B** Lebrecht Music and Arts Photo Library/Alamy Stock Photo; **861** W. Eugene Smith/The LIFE Picture Collection/Getty Images; **862** INTERFOTO/Alamy Stock Photo; **864** Department of Defense. American Forces Information Service. Defense Visual Information Center/National Archives and Records Administration; **865** Bettmann/Getty Images; **866** L.L. Yonally/AKG Images; **868** Library of Congress Prints and Photographs Division Washington [LC-USZC4-3357]; **869** Women Airforce Service Pilots Archives; **870** Library of Congress Prints and Photographs Division Washington [LC-DIG-ppmsca-13260]; **871** Everett Collection Historical/Alamy Stock Photo; **872** Library of Congress Prints and Photographs Division Washington [LC-DIG-fsa-8d29120]; **873** Randy Duchaine/Alamy Stock Photo; **874** Library of Congress Prints and Photographs Division Washington [LC-USZC4-4731]; **875** Everett Collection Inc/Alamy Stock Photo; **876** Everett Historical/Shutterstock; **877** PhotoQuest/ Getty Images; **879** Photo12/Archives Snark/Alamy Stock Photo; **880** Fred Ramage/Hulton Archive/Getty Images; **882** MPI/Archive Photos/ Getty Images; **883** Bettmann/Getty Images; **885** Keystone Pictures USA/Alamy Stock Photo; **888–889** Francis Miller/The LIFE Picture Collection/Getty Images; **891T** Arthur Schatz/The LIFE Picture Collection/Getty Images; **891CL** The LIFE Picture Collection/Getty Images; **891CR** Don Cravens/The LIFE Images Collection/Getty Images; **891B** World History Archive/Alamy Stock Photo; **892** Everett Collection/Newscom; **893** Universal Art Archive/Alamy Stock Photo; **894** Photo12/Archives Snark/Alamy Stock Photo; **895** Courtesy: CSU Archives/Everett Collection/Alamy Stock Photo; **899** PhotoQuest/ Archive Photos/Getty Images; **901** Sovfoto/UIG/Getty Images; **904** Paul Almasy/AKG Images; **905** Everett Collection/Alamy Stock Photo; **906** Bettmann/Getty Images; **907** R. Krubner/ClassicStock/Alamy Stock Photo; **908** MPI/Stringer/Archive Photos/Getty Images; **911** Shelly Grossman/FPG/Hulton Archive/Getty Images; **913** Michael Ochs Archives/Moviepix/Getty Images; **914** Joseph Scherschel/The LIFE Picture Collection/Getty Images; **916** Bettmann/Getty Images; **917** Everett Collection/SuperStock; **918** Everett Collection Historical/ Alamy Stock Photo; **919** Everett Collection Historical/Alamy Stock Photo; **921** Universal History Archive/UIG/Getty images; **922** Donald Uhrbrock/The LIFE Images Collection/Getty Images; **923** Bettmann/ Getty Images; **924** John D. Kisch/Separate Cinema Archive/Archive Photos/Getty Images; **925** Bettmann/Getty Images; **927** AP Images; **928** Bettmann/Getty Images; **929** Court Mast/AP Images; **930** Rightdx/iStock Editorial/Getty Images; **931** Ted Streshinsky Photographic Archive/Corbis Historical/Getty Images; **932** Bettmann/ Getty Images; **933** AP Images; **934** AP Images; **935** Fred W. McDarrah/Premium Archive/Getty Images; **936** Anonymous/AP Images; **937** Betyarlaca/iStock/Getty Images; **938** Salas Archive Photos/Alamy Stock Photo; **940** MR/AP Images; **942** Cartoon depicting Lyndon B. Johnson's vigorous domestic and cautious foreign policies (litho), American School, (20th century)/Private Collection/Peter Newark American Pictures/Bridgeman Art Library; **945** Bettmann/Getty Images; **946** CSU Archives/Everett Collection/ Alamy Stock Photo; **947** Blank Archives/Archive Photos/Getty Images; **948** The LIFE Picture Collection/Getty Images; **951** Jacques Pavlovsky/ Sygma/CORBIS/Getty Images; **952** NARA/Alamy Stock Photo; **954** Library of Congress/Corbis/VCG/Getty Images; **955** Bettmann/Getty Images; **958–959** Agencja Fotograficzna Caro/Kaiser/Alamy Stock Photo; **961T** WDC Photos/Alamy Stock Photo; **961CL** Peter De Jong/ AP Images; **961CR** J. Scott Applewhite/AP Images; **961B** AfriPics. com/Alamy Stock Photo; **962** Larry Downing/Sygma/Getty Images; **963** Robert R. McElroy/Archive Photos/Getty Images; **964** Wally McNamee/Corbis historical/Getty Images; **965** Tom McHugh/Science Source; **966** Fotosearch/Archive Photos/Getty Images; **969** J. Scott Applewhite/AP Images; **970** Allstar Picture Library/Alamy Stock Photo; **971** Mark reinstein/Alamy Stock Photo; **973** INTERFOTO/ Travel/Alamy Stock Photo; **974** Alain Dejean/Jacques Dejean/Sygma Premium/Getty Images; **975** Boris Yurchenko/AP Images; **976** Thomas Kienzle/AP Images; **977** Boris Yurchenko/AP Images; **979** Leif Skoogfors/Corbis historical/Getty Images; **980** Ira Schwartz/AP Images; **981** Roger Bacon/Reuters/Alamy Stock Photo; **982** US Air Force Photo/Alamy Stock Photo; **983** Jeff Widener/AP Images; **984** FILE PHOTO/KRT/Newscom; **986** Michael Stravato/AP Images; **987** Lana Harris/AP Images; **988** Reuters/Alamy Stock Photo; **990** ZUMA Press, Inc./Alamy Stock Photo; **991** Thomas Hartwell/The LIFE Images Collection/Getty Images; **992** Trinity Mirror/Mirrorpix/Alamy Stock Photo; **996–997** BKGD Jim West/Alamy Stock Photo; **997** Dpa picture alliance archive/Alamy Stock Photo; **999T** Eric Draper/United States Department of Defense; **999B** ZUMA Press, Inc./Alamy Stock Photo; **999C** World History Archive/Alamy Stock Photo; **1000** Charles O. Cecil/Alamy Stock Photo; **1001** Timur Abdullayev/News Team/TASS/ Alamy Stock Photo; **1002** Hubert Boesl/Picture-Alliance/DPA/AP Images; **1003T** Paul J. Richards/AFP/Getty Images; **1003B** Eric Draper/United States Department of Defense; **1006** Pete Souza/The White House/AP Images; **1007** Jamal Nasrallah/EPA/Newscom; **1009T** Kyodo/AP Images; **1009B** Kyodo/AP Images; **1011** Peter Macdiarmid/Getty Images; **1012** PO 2nd Class Hunter S. Harwell/ U.S. Navy/AP Images; **1013** 615 collection/Alamy Stock Photo; **1015** Cultura Creative (RF)/Alamy Stock Photo; **1017L** Susana Gonzalez/ Bloomberg/Getty Images; **1017C** Thomas Lee/Alamy Stock Photo; **1017R** Ken Gillespie Photography/Alamy Stock Photo; **1018** Andy Dean Photography/Shutterstock; **1021** Norma Jean Gargasz/Alamy Stock Photo; **1022** Nikolas Georgiou/Alamy Stock Photo; **1023** WDG Photo/Shutterstock; **1024** Triff/Shutterstock; **1025** Nyvlt-art/ Shutterstock; **1027** Hemis/Alamy Stock Photo; **1029** Bokehart/ Shutterstock; **1030** Everett Collection/Newscom; **1032** Paul Fell/

CartoonStock; **1033** John Moore/Getty Images; **1035** Jim Watson/AFP/Getty Images; **1036** Jewel Samad/AFP/Getty Images; **1037** Matt Wuerker/CartoonStock; **1039** JeffG/Alamy Stock Photo; **1040** Andrew Harnik/AP Images; **1041** ZUMA Press, Inc./Alamy Stock Photo; **1042** Chip Somodevilla/Getty Images; **1043** ZUMA Press, Inc./Alamy Stock Photo; **1048** Steve Gottlieb/Stock Connection Blue/Alamy Stock Photo.

Text

Academy of Achievement Interview with Rosa Parks. Copyright © by American Academy of Achievement. **Alfred A. Knopf** The Negro Speaks of Rivers, and My People from THE COLLECTED POEMS OF LANGSTON HUGHES by Langston Hughes, edited by Arnold Rampersad with David Roessel, Associate Editor, copyright © 1994 by the Estate of Langston Hughes. Used by permission of Alfred A. Knopf, an imprint of the Knopf Doubleday Publishing Group, a division of Random House LLC. All rights reserved. **Alfred A. Knopf, Inc.** Berlin Diary by William L. Shirer. Copyright © by Alfred a. Knopf. **Banks, Louis** Interview of Louis Banks, 1970. **CNN** America the Undemocratic by Fareed Zakaria. July 4, 2013. Courtesy of CNN. Reprinted with permission. **CNN** Riled about rail: Why all the anger over high speed trains? by Steven Harrod. April 21, 2011. Courtesy of CNN. Reprinted with permission. **Daily Press** A Dismal Refuge by Kimberly Lenz. Daily Press, February 08, 2004. Copyright © Daily Press. **Entrepreneur Magazine** William Levitt: The Sultan of Suburbia. Copyright © Entrepreneur Magazine. Reprinted by permission. **Environmental Law Policy Center** High Speed Rail Works by Environmental Law & Policy Center. elpc.org. **Ferrell, Melvin B** Men of D-Day by Melvin B. Ferrell. Copyright © Gail Ferrell. **George Washington University** The Secret History of the Great Asian War by Zenshiro Hoshina. Published by George Washington University. **Harold Ober Associates** The Collected Poems of Langston Hughes by Langston Hughes edited by Arnold Rampersad with David Roessel, Associate Editor. Copyright ©1994 by the Estate of Langston Hughes. Used by permission of Harold Ober Associates Incorporated. **Harper & Brothers** Giants in the Earth: A Saga of the Prairie by O E Rolvaag. Copyright © 1927 by Harper & Brothers. **Harper Collins Publishers** Little Town on the Prairie by Laura Ingalls Wilder. Published by Harper Collins Publishers. **Harper's Magazine** Race prejudice and the Negro artist by James Weldon Johnson. Copyright © Harper's Magazine 1928. **Houghton Mifflin** Silent Spring by Rachel Carson. Published by Houghton Mifflin Harcourt. **Jossey-Bass, Inc.an Imprint of Wiley** A Mouthful of Rivets (Wise) by Christy Wise and Nancy Baker Wise. Copyright Jossey-Bass, Inc., an imprint of Wiley. **Kent State University Press** Civil War History, Vol. 51, Issue: 4 by William Blair. Published by Kent State University Press, © 2005. **KERA** The Borderlands on the Eve of War by David J Weber. Copyright © KERA. www.kera.org. Reprinted with permission. **Langston Hughes** The Negro Speaks of Rivers by Langston Hughes. Copyright © Langston Hughes. Reprinted by permission. **McKay, Claude, Estate** If We Must Die by Claude McKay. Copyright © McKay Estate. **MISES INSTITUTE** Democracy's False Prophet by David Gordon. Copyright © MISES INSTITUTE. Reprinted with permission. **Mobley, Jack** A Case Against High-Speed Rail by Jack Mobley. Copyright © by Jack Mobley. Reprinted by Permission. **Modern Library** The Persian Wars by Herodotus. Translated by George Rawlinson. Copyright © Modern Library. **Navajivan Trus** Passive resistance is a method. Copyright © The Navajivan Trust. Reprinted by permission. **Nelson Mandela Foundation** Inaugural Speech, Pretoria, HOPE AND GLORY by Nelson Mandela. Copyright © by Nelson Mandela Foundation. Reprinted by permission. **Palgrave McMillan** THE HISTORY OF MEXICO © 2005 by Burton Kirkwood. Reprinted by permission of Palgrave Macmillan. All Rights Reserved. **Penguin Group** Freedom from Fear from FREEDOM FROM FEAR AND OTHER WRITINGS, REVISED EDITION by Aung San Suu Kyi, edited by Michael Aris, copyright ©1991, 1995 by Aung San Suu Kyi. Used by permission of Viking Penguin, a division of Penguin Group (USA) LLC. **Penguin Random House** Native American Testimony by Peter Nabokov. Copyright © 1999 by Penguin Random House. **Penguin Random House Canada** The Good Old Days—They Were Terrible! by Otto Bettmann. Copyright © Otto L. Bettmann. Published by Penguin Random House. **Penguin Random House.** Excerpts from Diary of a Young Girl: The Definitive Edition by Anne Frank, edited by Otto H. Frank and Mirjam Pressler, translated by Susan Massotty, translation copyright © 1995 by Doubleday, a division of Random House LLC. Used by permission of Doubleday, an imprint of the Knopf Doubleday Publishing Group, a division of Random House LLC. All rights reserved. **Random House, Inc.** The Collected Poems of Langston Hughes by Langston Hughes edited by Arnold Rampersad with David Roessel, Associate Editor. Copyright (c) 1994 by Random House, Inc. **Reason Foundation** The Pragmatic Case Against High-Speed Rail by Samuel Staley. Copyright © 2009 by Reason Foundation. Reprinted by permission. **Rookie** A Brief History of Forever by Tavi Gevinson. Published by Rookie, © 2013. **Simon and Schuster** A General's Life by Omar N. Bradley. Published by Simon and Schuster. **Southern Christian Leadership Conference** SCLC Statement. Copyright 1957 by Southern Christian Leadership Conference. **Tedx** Learning to Fail by Tara Suri and Niha Jain, 2011. **The American Prospect** Democracy-Proof by George Scialabba. Copyright © 2002. Used with permission of The American Prospect. www.prospect.org **The New York Times Magazine** Sandra Day O'Connor's Interview by Deborah Salomon, March 16, 2009. Copyright 2017 The New York Times Company. **Time Magazine** Royal Hawaii, Sunset Magazine, Volume: 190. Issue: 1. © 1993 Time Inc. All rights reserved. Reprinted/Translated from SUNSET and published with permission of Time Inc. Reproduction in any manner in any language in whole or in part without written permission is prohibited. **University of North Carolina Press** THE POEMS OF PHILLIS WHEATLEY edited and with an introduction by Julian D. Mason Jr. Copyright © 1966 by the University of North Carolina Press, renewed 1989. Used by permission of the publisher. www.uncpress.unc.edu **University of North Carolina Press** Dear Mrs. Roosevelt. LETTERS FROM THE CHILDREN OF THE GREAT DEPRESSION by Robert Cohen. Copyright © 2002 by University of North Carolina Press. Used by permission of the publisher. www.uncpress.unc.edu. **William Morrow & Company, Inc.** Over the Edge of the World by Laurence Bergreen. Published by William Morrow & Company, Inc. **Writers House** I Have a Dream, Speech by Martin Luther King, Jr. Reprinted by arrangement with The Heirs to the Estate of Martin Luther King Jr., c/o Writers House as agent for the proprietor New York, NY. Copyright Dr. Martin Luther King 1963; Copyright © renewed Coretta Scott King (1991) **Writers House** Speech by Martin Luther King, Jr. Reprinted by arrangement with The Heirs to the Estate of Martin Luther King Jr., c/o Writers House as agent for the proprietor New York, NY. Copyright Dr. Martin Luther King 1963; Copyright © renewed Coretta Scott King (1991) **Writers House LLC** Letters from a Birmingham Jail by Martin Luther King. Reprinted by arrangement with The Heirs to the Estate of Martin Luther King Jr., c/o Writers House as agent for the proprietor New York, NY. Copyright Dr. Martin Luther King 1963; Copyright © renewed Coretta Scott King (1991) **Youth Radio** Young Adults: Can you Picture Your Retirement by Asha Richardson, Ashley Williams and Sayre Quevedo, 2013. Copyright © Youth Radio.